Merry Christmas,
Dad
With love,
Bill & Angela

ALSO BY DAVID HERBERT DONALD

Look Homeward: A Life of Thomas Wolfe

Liberty and Union: The Crisis of Popular Government, 1830–1890

The Great Republic: A History of the American People
(with Bernard Bailyn, David Brion Davis, Robert Dallek,
John L. Thomas, Gordon S. Wood, and Robert H. Wiebe)

*Gone for a Soldier: The Civil War Memoirs
of Private Alfred Bellard* (editor)

Charles Sumner and the Rights of Man

The Nation in Crisis, 1861–1877

The Politics of Reconstruction, 1863–1867

Diary of Charles Francis Adam: Volume I, January 1820–June 1825,
and *Volume II, July 1825–September 1829*
(editor with Aïda DiPace Donald)

The Civil War and Reconstruction (with J. G. Randall)

Why the North Won the Civil War (editor)

Charles Sumner and the Coming of the Civil War

Lincoln Reconsidered: Essays on the Civil War Era

Divided We Fought: A Pictorial History of the War, 1861–1865
(with others)

Inside Lincoln's Cabinet: The Civil War Diaries of Salmon P. Chase

Lincoln's Herndon

LINCOLN

David Herbert Donald

Simon & Schuster

New York   London   Toronto   Sydney   Tokyo   Singapore

FOR AÏDA AND BRUCE,

WHO HAVE HAD TO LIVE WITH LINCOLN

FOR MOST OF THEIR LIVES

SIMON & SCHUSTER
ROCKEFELLER CENTER
1230 AVENUE OF THE AMERICAS
NEW YORK, NY 10020

DESIGNED BY LEVAVI & LEVAVI
MANUFACTURED IN THE UNITED STATES OF AMERICA

1   3   5   7   9   10   8   6   4   2

LIBRARY OF CONGRESS CATALOGING-IN-PUBLICATION DATA
DONALD, DAVID HERBERT, DATE.
LINCOLN / DAVID HERBERT DONALD.
P. CM.
INCLUDES BIBLIOGRAPHICAL REFERENCES (P.   ) AND INDEX.
1. LINCOLN, ABRAHAM, 1809–1865.
2. PRESIDENTS—UNITED STATES—BIOGRAPHY.   I. TITLE.
E457.D66   1995
973.7′092—DC20
[B]   95-4782   CIP
ISBN 0-684-80846-3

Frontispiece: Lincoln considered this photograph, made by
Alexander Hesler of Chicago in February 1857, "a very true one,"
but Mary Lincoln and others did not like it. "My impression,"
Lincoln said, "is that their objection arises from the disordered
condition of the hair." (Lloyd Ostendorf Collection)

I CLAIM NOT TO HAVE CONTROLLED EVENTS,

BUT CONFESS PLAINLY THAT EVENTS

HAVE CONTROLLED ME.

Abraham Lincoln to Albert G. Hodges,
April 4, 1864

Contents

---·■·---

MAPS

Preface

———

The only time I ever met President John F. Kennedy, in February 1962, he was unhappy with historians. A group of scholars had been in the Oval Office hoping to enlist him in a poll that ranked American presidents. I was not one of those visitors, but the next day when I gave a talk in the White House about Abraham Lincoln, the subject was much on his mind. He voiced his deep dissatisfaction with the glib way the historians had rated some of his predecessors as "Below Average" and marked a few as "Failures." Thinking, no doubt, of how his own administration would look in the backward glance of history, he resented the whole process. With real feeling he said, "No one has a right to grade a President—not even poor James Buchanan—who has not sat in his chair, examined the mail and information that came across his desk, and learned why he made his decisions."

This book was conceived in the spirit of President Kennedy's observations. In tracing the life of Abraham Lincoln, I have asked at every stage of his career what he knew when he had to take critical actions, how he evaluated the evidence before him, and why he reached his decisions. It is, then, a biography written from Lincoln's point of view, using the information and ideas that were available to him. It seeks to explain rather than to judge.

My biography is based largely on Lincoln's own words, whether in his letters and messages or in conversations recorded by reliable witnesses. I have tried as far as possible to write from the original sources—that is, from firsthand contemporary accounts by people who saw and talked with the President. Of course, I have consulted the voluminous secondary literature, but I have used it chiefly for letters and documents that I could not find elsewhere. My approach was made possible by the availability of the Abraham Lincoln Papers in the Library of Congress (now fortunately on micro-film). After use by Lincoln's authorized biographers, John G. Nicolay and John Hay, in 1890, these papers were sealed until 1947 and therefore could not be consulted for the major biographies by Albert J. Beveridge, William E. Barton, Carl Sandburg, and J. G. Randall.*

The results of my inquiries can most readily be defined in negative terms. This book is not a general history of the United States during the middle of the nineteenth century. I have stuck close to Lincoln, who was only indirectly connected with the economic and social transformations of the period. It is not even a history of the Civil War. There is, for example, almost nothing in the following pages about the internal affairs of the Confederacy, because these were matters that Lincoln could not know about. It is not a military history; I have not described campaigns and battles that Lincoln did not witness. I have not offered a broad philosophical discussion of the origins of the Civil War and I have not addressed the question of whether it was the first modern war. These are important subjects, but they did not present themselves to Abraham Lincoln in any practical way. I have not asked whether Lincoln freed the slaves or the slaves freed themselves, because Lincoln never considered these roads to emancipation as mutually exclusive. Certainly he knew that thousands of slaves, in individual heroic acts of rebellion, were leaving their masters to seek freedom behind the Union lines, but he also knew that ending the institution of slavery required official action on the part of the United States government.

In focusing closely on Lincoln himself—on what he knew, when he knew it, and why he made his decisions—I have, I think, produced a portrait rather different from that in other biographies. It is perhaps a bit more grainy than most, with more attention to his unquenchable ambition, to his brain-numbing labor in his law practice, to his tempestuous married life, and to his repeated defeats. It suggests how often chance, or accident, played a determining role in shaping his life. And it emphasizes his enormous capacity for growth, which enabled one of the least experienced and most poorly prepared men ever elected to high office to become the greatest American President.

More important, this biography highlights a basic trait of character evident throughout Lincoln's life: the essential passivity of his nature. Lincoln himself recognized it in a letter he wrote on April 4, 1864, to Albert G. Hodges, a fellow Kentuckian, who asked him to explain why he had shifted from his inaugural pledge not to interfere with slavery to a policy of emancipation. After relating how circumstances had obliged him to change his mind—

---

* This was true of the first two volumes of Randall's *Lincoln the President,* published in 1945. Professor Randall was able to make some use of the Lincoln Papers in the third volume of that work, subtitled *Midstream,* published in 1952. Richard N. Current drew heavily on the Lincoln Papers in completing the final volume, *Last Full Measure,* which appeared in 1955. But the basic structure and themes of Randall's magisterial work were selected before the Lincoln Papers became available.

ion and the use of African-American soldiers had become
ties—the President concluded: "In telling this tale I attempt
to my own sagacity. I claim not to have controlled events,
but confess plainly that events have controlled me."

From his earliest days Lincoln had a sense that his destiny was controlled by some larger force, some Higher Power. Turning away from orthodox Christianity because of the emotional excesses of frontier evangelicalism, he found it easier as a young man to accept what was called the Doctrine of Necessity, which he defined as the belief "that the human mind is impelled to action, or held in rest by some power, over which the mind itself has no control." Later he frequently quoted to his partner, William H. Herndon, the lines from *Hamlet:*

> There's a divinity that shapes our ends,
> Rough-hew them how we will.

From Lincoln's fatalism derived some of his most lovable traits: his compassion, his tolerance, his willingness to overlook mistakes. That belief did not, of course, lead him to lethargy or dissipation. Like thousands of Calvinists who believed in predestination, he worked indefatigably for a better world—for himself, for his family, and for his nation. But it helped to buffer the many reverses that he experienced and enabled him to continue a strenuous life of aspiration.

It also made for a pragmatic approach to problems, a recognition that if one solution was fated not to work another could be tried. "My policy is to have no policy" became a kind of motto for Lincoln—a motto that infuriated the sober, doctrinaire people around him who were inclined to think that the President had no principles either. He might have offended his critics less if he had more often used the analogy he gave James G. Blaine when explaining his course on Reconstruction: "The pilots on our Western rivers steer from *point to point* as they call it—setting the course of the boat no farther than they can see; and that is all I propose to myself in this great problem."

Both statements suggest Lincoln's reluctance to take the initiative and make bold plans; he preferred to respond to the actions of others. They also show why Lincoln in his own distinctively American way had the quality John Keats defined as forming "a Man of Achievement," that quality "which Shakespeare possessed so enormously . . . *Negative Capability,* that is when a man is capable of being in uncertainties, Mysteries, doubts, without any irritable reaching after fact and reason."

Much of the research for this biography was made possible through a generous grant from the Division of Research Programs of the National Endowment for the Humanities (Grant No. RO-2128-89). I am particularly indebted to Charles Ambler and George R. Lucas, Jr., in that division for their assistance.

I am also grateful to Dean Henry Rosovsky, Dean Michael Spence, and Dean Phyllis Keller, who were instrumental in arranging leaves of absence from my teaching duties at Harvard University.

Throughout the project I was fortunate to have the assistance of Laura Nakatsuka, who not merely performed expert secretarial services but proved a highly efficient research sleuth, uncovering Lincoln items in a dozen or more manuscript collections.

Several gifted Harvard undergraduate and graduate students have performed invaluable work as research assistants who scoured the newspapers and periodicals for material on Lincoln, and I am indebted to them all: Richard Bennett, Steven Chen, Martin Fitzpatrick, Elaine Goldenberg, Sally Hadden, Zachary Karabell, Timothy McCarthy, Matthew Pinsker, Gerald Prokopowicz, and Ronald Ryan.

The tedious work of verifying facts and checking quotations in my manuscript fell to Thomas J. Brown, Fred Dalzell, and Michael Vorenberg, and I thank all three for helping me to eliminate errors of fact and interpretation. Mr. Vorenberg, who is preparing the authoritative history of the Thirteenth Amendment, offered incisive criticisms that have greatly influenced my treatment of colonization and emancipation. On legal and constitutional issues I have profited much from Dr. Brown's unfailingly helpful suggestions.

To the blessed librarians everywhere my obligation is great. As always, Nathaniel Bunker, the Charles Warren Bibliographer at Harvard University, has been responsive to my needs for nineteenth-century American newspapers and manuscripts on microfilm. Thomas F. Schwartz, state historian of Illinois, graciously made available the immense resources of the Henry Horner Collection at the Illinois State Historical Library and patiently answered my frequent questions. Cheryl Schnirring did the same for the manuscript collections in that same great library, and Cheryl Pence assisted in my search for nineteenth-century Illinois newspapers. John Hoffmann was my gracious host at the Illinois Historical Survey in Urbana. At the Chicago Historical Society, Theresa A. McGill provided invaluable assistance, and Sherry Byrne of the University of Chicago Library helped me locate newspaper files. Dallas R. Lindgren served as my guide to the rich collections of the Minnesota Historical Society. At the Huntington Library, John H. Rhodehamel, Lita Garcia, and Karen E. Kearns were helpful in securing microfilm of important manuscript collections. Daniel Weinberg and Thomas Trescott of the Abraham Lincoln Book Shop in Chicago have energetically assisted me in dozens of bibliographical searches.

At the Lincoln Legal Papers, perhaps the most important archival investigation now under way in the United States, I was welcomed by the director, Cullom Davis, and by the assistant editor, William Beard, and was given full access to the enormous treasure-house of legal documents that they have built up.

Norman D. Hellmers, superintendent of the Lincoln National Home Site, guided me through the Lincoln home in Springfield and generously shared with me his enormously detailed knowledge of the history of the Lincoln family.

I have had the inestimable good fortune of receiving personally conducted tours of the White House, including the upstairs living quarters, from President and Mrs. John F. Kennedy and from President and Mrs. George Bush.

Numerous scholars and collectors have given me the benefit of their special information and insights, and I am especially grateful to Gabor S. Boritt, Michael A. Burlingame, Joan Cashin, Glen L. Carle, Stanley H. Cath, Eric T. Freyfogle, the late Arnold Gates, Robert Giroux, William F. Hanna, Harold Holzer, Ari A. Hoogenboom, Harold M. Hyman, Richard R. John, Jane Langton, Dick Levinson, John Niven, Matthew Pinsker, H. Douglas Price, Steven K. Rogstad, Scott Sandage, Rex Scouten, Louise Taper, Paul Verduin, and J. Harvey Young.

Through the generosity of Philip B. Kunhardt, Jr., Philip B. Kunhardt III, and Peter W. Kunhardt, I have been permitted to borrow extensively from the incomparable Meserve-Kunhardt Collection of photographs. Gerald J. Prokopowicz and Carolyn Texley have been equally gracious in sharing the rich photographic resources of the Lincoln Museum in Fort Wayne, Indiana. Rex W. Scouten, the curator of the White House, has made the Lincoln materials in that great collection available to me. Robert W. Remini helped me gain access to the Chicago Historical Society, where Diane Ryan made the collection of prints and photographs available. To Professor and Mrs. Gabor S. Boritt of Gettysburg College and to Mr. Jack Smith of South Bend, Indiana, I am indebted for permission to reproduce rare drawings and prints from their collections.

My interpretation of Lincoln's political philosophy and religious views has been much influenced by the ideas of John Rawls, who collaborated with me in teaching the first seminar ever offered on Abraham Lincoln at Harvard University. Thanks to an invitation from John C. Perry and the other trustees of the Bemis Fund, I was encouraged to explore some of these ideas before my fellow townsmen in Lincoln, Massachusetts, in a public lecture titled "Learning to Be President." I had a further occasion to test them when I delivered the Samuel Paley Lectures at the Hebrew University of Jerusalem, where Yehoshua Arieli, Menahem Blondheim, and Shlomo Slonim were my gracious hosts. In January 1990, I was afforded the opportunity of presenting a preliminary view of the Lincoln family in the White House when President George Bush invited me to give the inaugural lecture in his Presidential Lecture Series on the presidency.

I have learned most of all from the scholars who took time from their own important researches to read and criticize drafts of my chapters. Daniel Aaron of Harvard University went through every page of the manuscript, pointing out repetition and infelicitous language. My sections on Lincoln's assassination have been greatly strengthened by the expert review that Terry Alford of Northern Virginia Community College gave them. Cullom Davis and William Beard of the Lincoln Legal Papers closely examined my chapters that deal with Lincoln's legal practice, and they have saved me countless errors. Aida Donald, editor-in-chief of the Harvard University Press, gave the manuscript the benefit of her expert judgment of style and substance. Robert W. Johannsen of the University of Illinois reviewed the entire manuscript, offering especially valuable advice on Stephen A. Douglas and the Illinois Democratic party. A close reading by Mark E. Neely of St. Louis University caught dozens of errors, great and small, and provided much needed perspective on Lincoln's handling of civil liberties. Wayne C. Temple, deputy director of the Illinois State Archives, gave a detailed criticism of the entire manuscript and shared with me his incomparable expertise on Lincoln's early career.

To my editor, Alice E. Mayhew, and the other members of the editorial team at Simon & Schuster, including Sarah Baker, Eric Steel, and Roger Labrie, who have seen the book through the press, I am greatly indebted for encouragement and support. I also want to thank Victoria Meyer, who was in charge of publicity, and Frank and Eve Metz, at Simon & Schuster. Fred Wiemer did a superb job of copyediting my difficult manuscript. Saving me countless errors, Kathryn Blatt did the heroic work of proofreading the entire book.

With so much assistance I should have written a perfect book, but, of course, I haven't. I alone am responsible for all errors and misinterpretations.

CHAPTER ONE

Annals of the Poor

———◆———

Abraham Lincoln was not interested in his ancestry. In his mind he was a self-made man, who had no need to care about his family tree. In 1859, when friends asked him for autobiographical information to help promote his chances for a presidential nomination, he offered only the barest outline of his family history: "My parents were both born in Virginia, of undistinguished families—second families, perhaps I should say." The next year, when John Locke Scripps of the *Chicago Tribune* proposed to write his campaign biography, Lincoln told him: "Why Scripps, . . . it is a great piece of folly to attempt to make anything out of my early life. It can all be condensed into a single sentence, and that sentence you will find in Gray's Elegy,

The short and simple annals of the poor.

That's my life, and that's all you or any one else can make of it."

I

Lincoln knew almost nothing about his mother's family, the Hankses, who moved from Virginia to Kentucky about 1780. They were a prolific tribe, for the most part illiterate but respectable farmers of modest means. Their family tree is hard to trace because for generation after generation they tended to name all the males James or John, and the females Polly, Lucy, or Nancy. Abraham Lincoln's mother was one of at least eight Nancy Hankses born during the 1780s. Abraham Lincoln believed that his mother was illegitimate. It was a subject that he rarely discussed, but in the early 1850s, while driving his one-horse buggy from Springfield over to Petersburg, Illinois, he found himself talking about it. He and his law partner, William H. Herndon, were about to try a case in Menard County Court that involved a question of hereditary traits, and Lincoln observed that illegitimate children were "oftentimes sturdier and brighter than those born in lawful wedlock." To prove his point he mentioned his mother, who he said was "the illegitimate daughter of Lucy Hanks and a well-bred Virginia farmer or planter." From "this broad-minded, unknown Virginian" Lincoln believed he inherited the traits that distinguished him from the other members of his family: ambition, mental alertness, and the power of analysis.

Lincoln may well have been correct in reporting that his mother was born out of wedlock. A grand jury in Mercer County, Kentucky, presented a charge of fornication against his grandmother Lucy (or "Lucey," as it is spelled in the old records), and there were several recorded instances of bastardy among Hanks women of her generation. Since no wedding certificate was ever found for Lucy, there was room for endless speculation about Lincoln's maternal grandsire.

But Lincoln's remarks—if Herndon accurately reported them after a lapse of many years—were not based on any research into his Hanks ancestry. Instead they reflected his sense that he was different from the people with whom he grew up. Like other gifted young men, he wondered how he could be the offspring of his ordinary and limited parents. Some in Lincoln's generation fancied themselves the sons of the dauphin, who allegedly fled to America during the French Revolution. Lincoln imagined a noble Virginia ancestor.

Of his Lincoln ancestors he knew only a little more than he did about the Hankses. From his father he learned that his grandfather Abraham, for whom he was named, had moved from Virginia to Kentucky in the early 1780s. There was a vague family tradition that earlier Lincolns had lived in Pennsylvania, where they had been Quakers, but, as he recorded, the family had long since "fallen away from the peculiar habits of that people." Apart from that, William Dean Howells reported in his 1860 campaign biography, there was only "incertitude, and absolute darkness" about Abraham Lincoln's forebears.

Further research would have showed that the Lincolns did come from Virginia and that an earlier generation had indeed belonged to the Society of Friends in Pennsylvania. In turn, these could be traced to the original Samuel Lincoln, who emigrated from the County of Norfolk, England, and settled in Hingham, Massachusetts, in 1637. A weaver in England, Samuel became a prosperous trader and businessman in America, where he was a pillar of the church and begat eleven children who bore names like Daniel, Thomas, Mordecai, and Sarah, which became traditional in the family. Samuel's grandson Mordecai (1686–1736) was perhaps the most successful member of the family. An ironmaster and wealthy landowner in Pennsylvania, he was a member of the eighteenth-century economic and social elite; he married Hannah Slater, who was at once the daughter, the niece, and the granddaughter of members of the New Jersey assembly and the niece of the acting royal governor of that colony. It was their son, John Lincoln (1716–1788), who moved to the Shenandoah Valley of Virginia, where he established himself on a large farm in fertile Rockingham County. Mordecai was so successful that he could afford to give his son, Abraham Lincoln's grandfather, 210 acres of the best soil in Virginia. In sum, Abraham Lincoln, instead of being the unique blossom on an otherwise barren family tree, belonged to the seventh American generation of a family with competent means, a reputation for integrity, and a modest record of public service.

II

A closer study of the historical records would also have given Abraham Lincoln a different, and probably a kindlier, view of his father, Thomas. It was Thomas's father, the senior Abraham Lincoln, who sold his farm in Virginia and led his wife and five children over the mountains to seek their fortune. They had heard much of the rich lands in Kentucky from their distant relative, Daniel Boone, and they found in that vast, largely unsettled territory, which was still part of the Commonwealth of Virginia, all the opportunities Boone had promised. Within a few years the Lincolns owned at least 5,544 acres of land in the richest sections of Kentucky.

But the wilderness was dangerous. In 1786, while Abraham Lincoln and his three boys, Mordecai, Josiah, and Thomas, were planting a cornfield on their new property, Indians attacked them. Abraham was killed instantly. Mordecai, at fifteen the oldest son, sent Josiah running to the settlement half a mile away for help while he raced to a nearby cabin. Peering out of a crack between logs, he saw an Indian sneaking out of the forest toward his eight-year-old brother, Thomas, who was still sitting in the field beside their father's body. Mordecai picked up a rifle, aimed at a silver pendant on the Indian's chest, and killed him before he could reach the boy. This story in later years Thomas Lincoln repeated over and over again, so that it became, as Abraham said, "the legend more strongly than all others imprinted upon my mind and memory."

Both Thomas Lincoln and his son seem to have overlooked the economic consequences of the tragedy. According to Virginia law, which prevailed in the Kentucky region, the ancient rule of primogeniture was still in effect, and Mordecai Lincoln, the oldest son, inherited his father's entire estate when he came of age. In due course he became one of the leading citizens of Washington County, Kentucky, a man of considerable property, who was interested in breeding fine racehorses. The only Lincoln relative whom Abraham Lincoln ever knew, Mordecai was a man of considerable wit and great natural gifts, and his nephew once remarked that "Uncle Mord had run off with all the talents of the family." He had also, in effect, run off with all the money. Left without a patrimony, the other two Lincoln boys had to fend for themselves.

Thomas, the youngest, had a difficult time. The tragedy abruptly ended his prospects of being an heir of a well-to-do Kentucky planter; he had to earn his board and keep. Abraham Lincoln never fully understood how hard his father had to struggle during his early years. It required an immense effort for Thomas, who earned three shillings a day for manual labor or made a little more when he did carpentry or cabinetmaking, to accumulate enough money to buy his first farm, a 238-acre tract on Mill Creek, in Hardin County, Kentucky. He became a familiar figure in Elizabethtown and Hogdenville, a stocky, well-built man of no more than average height, with a shock of straight black hair and an unusually large nose. "He was an uneducated man, a plain unpretending plodding man," a neighbor remembered; one who "attended to his work, peaceable—quiet and good natured." "Honest" was the adjective most frequently used to describe Thomas Lincoln, and he was respected in his community, where he served in the militia and was called for jury duty. Never wealthy, Thomas owned a respectable amount of property, by 1814 ranking fifteenth (out of ninety-eight listed) in the county.

In 1806 he married Nancy Hanks, and the couple built a little house in Elizabethtown, where eight months later Sarah, their first daughter, was born. By 1809, Thomas Lincoln had bought another farm, this time one of three hundred acres, on the south fork of Nolin Creek (not far from Hogdenville). It was called the Sinking Spring Farm, because it had a magnificent spring that bubbled from the bottom of a deep cave. Here, on a little knoll near the spring, he built a one-room log cabin, measuring sixteen by eighteen feet. The sturdy building, which had only a dirt floor and no glass window, was as large as about 90 percent of the pioneer cabins of the region.

Here Abraham Lincoln was born on February 12, 1809. He had no recollection of the place of his birth, because his parents moved before he was two years old. The land on the Sinking Spring Farm proved very poor, "a barren waste, so to speak," as one contemporary described it, "save some little patches on the creek bottoms," and Thomas quickly learned that it would not support his family. He bought a smaller but more fertile farm, some ten miles to the northeast, on Knob Creek.

Here, once again, the family lived, as did most of their neighbors, in a one-room log cabin, but the setting was beautiful. The creek, which ran through the property, was so clear that you could see a pebble in ten feet of water; the bottomland, where Thomas planted corn, was rich and easy to cultivate; and on both sides rose small, steep hills, so clearly defined and separate as to be called "knobs"—after which the creek was named.

It was of this Knob Creek farm that Abraham Lincoln had his earliest memories, but few of them concerned his mother, who remains a shadowy image. It is not even clear what she looked like. No one ever bothered to draw a likeness of Nancy Hanks Lincoln, and the age of photography was far in the future. Many years later those who had known her described her variously as being tall or of average height, thin or stout, beautiful or plain. Most agreed that she was "brilliant" or "intellectual." According to tradition, she was able to read, but, like many other frontier women, she did not know how to write and had to sign legal documents with an X. Abraham must have remembered how his mother set up housekeeping, cooked the family meals, washed and mended the scanty clothing that her husband and children wore, and perhaps helped in the farming. But of her life on Knob Creek he recorded only that she gave birth to a third child, named Thomas, who died in infancy. On the rare occasions in later years when he mentioned her, he referred to his *"angel mother,"* partly in recognition of her loving affection, but partly to distinguish her from his stepmother, who was very much alive. If he ever said, as Herndon reported, "God bless my mother; all that I am or ever hope to be I owe to her," it was a tribute not so much to her maternal care as to the genes that she allegedly transmitted from his unnamed grandfather.

Lincoln's Knob Creek recollections were of working in what he called "the big field," of seven acres, where his father planted corn and the son followed, dropping two pumpkin seeds in every other hill on every other row. Once, as he remembered, there was a big rain in the hills, though not a drop fell in the valley, and "the water coming down through the gorges washed ground, corn, pumpkin seed and all clear off the field." He also remembered going for two brief periods to an "A.B.C. school," some two miles from the Lincolns' cabin, where he was sent, according to a relative, "more as company for his sister than with the expectation that he would learn much." It was first taught by one Zachariah Riney, about whom little is known except that he was a Catholic, and then by Caleb Hazel, who, according to a contemporary, "could perhaps teach spelling, reading and indifferent writing and perhaps could cipher to the rule of three, but had no other qualifications of a teacher, except large size and bodily strength to thrash any boy or youth that came to his school." Abraham probably mastered the alphabet, but he did not yet know how to write when the family left Kentucky.

In general, young Lincoln seems to have been an entirely average little boy, who enjoyed playing, hunting, and fishing. Perhaps he was quieter than his playmates and kept his clothes clean longer, but there was not much to distinguish him. As a relative declared, "Abe exhibited no special traits in K[entuck]y except a good kind—somewhat wild nature."

III

In 1816, when Abraham was only seven years old, the Lincolns moved across the Ohio River to Indiana. Many years later he stated, quite accurately, that his father left Kentucky "partly on account of slavery; but chiefly on account of the difficulty in land titles in Ky." In Thomas Lincoln's mind the two causes were interrelated. He had religious grounds for disliking slavery. He and his wife joined the Separate Baptist Church, whose members accepted traditional Baptist beliefs, like infant baptism and predestination, but refused to endorse any formal creed. Adhering to a very strict code of morality, which condemned profanity, intoxication, gossip, horse racing, and dancing, most of the Separate Baptists were opposed to slavery. Abraham shared his parents' views. He was "naturally anti-slavery," he remarked in 1864, adding, "I cannot remember when I did not so think, and feel."

Thomas Lincoln's hostility to slavery was based on economic as well as religious grounds. He did not want to compete with slave labor. Kentucky had been admitted to the Union in 1792 as a slave state, and in the central, bluegrass region of the state "nabobs" were accumulating vast holdings of the best lands, tilled by gangs of black slaves. Hardin County, just to the west of this region, was not so well suited to large-scale agriculture, but its inhabitants felt threatened. By 1811 the county had 1,007 slaves and only 1,627 white males over the age of sixteen.

Small farmers like Thomas Lincoln also worried about the titles to their land. Kentucky never had a United States land survey; it was settled in a random, chaotic fashion, with settlers fixing their own bounds to the property they claimed: a particular tree here, a rock there, and so on. Soon the map of the state presented a bewildering overlay of conflicting land claims, and nobody could be sure who owned what. So uncertain were land titles that Kentucky became one of the first states to do away with the freehold property qualification for voting—not so much out of devotion to democratic principles as because even the wealthy often had trouble proving they owned clear title to their acres. Naturally the courts were filled with litigation, and the lawyers in Kentucky were busy all the time. To a small farmer like Thomas Lincoln, who was unable to pay the attorneys' fees, it seemed that they were all working for the rich, slaveholding planters.

He had trouble gaining a clear title to any of the three farms that he purchased in Kentucky. The details were exceedingly complicated, and not particularly important: one had been improperly surveyed, so that it proved to be thirty-eight acres smaller than what he thought he had purchased; another had a lien on it because of a small debt by a previous owner; in the case of the Knob Creek farm, non-Kentucky residents brought suit against Thomas and other occupants of the rich valley, claiming prior title. Having neither the money nor the inclination to fight for his claims in court, he heard with great interest of the opening of Indiana, territory from which slavery had been excluded by the Northwest Ordinance. Here the United States government had surveyed the land and offered purchasers guaranteed titles to their farms.

In the fall of 1816 he made a trip across the Ohio to explore the region and stake out a claim. He found what he wanted in the heavily wooded, almost totally unoccupied wilderness on Pigeon Creek, in Perry (later Spencer) County, in southern Indiana. After selecting the site, he constructed what was called a "half-faced camp," a rough shelter, with no floor, about fourteen feet square, enclosed on three sides but open on the fourth. Then, blazing trees to mark the boundaries and heaping piles of brush on the corners of the tract he expected to occupy, he returned to Kentucky, gathered his small family and his few possessions, and set out for his new home. The Lincolns arrived in Indiana just as the territory was admitted to the Union as a state.

The land Thomas claimed was in an unbroken forest, so remote that for part of the distance from the Ohio there was no trail and he had to hack out a path so that his family could follow. It was a wild region, Abraham remembered, and the forests were filled with bears and other threatening animals. Many years later, when he revisited the region, his childhood fears surfaced in verse:

When first my father settled here,
 'Twas then the frontier line:
The panther's scream, filled night with fear
 And bears preyed on the swine.

The Lincolns stayed in the half-faced camp for a few days after they arrived, until Thomas, probably with the assistance of members of the seven other families in the general vicinity, built a proper log cabin. It offered more protection, but because of the freezing weather the men could not work up the usual mixture of clay and grass for chinking between the logs and the winds still swept through.

The family was able to get through the winter because they ate deer and bear meat. "We all hunted pretty much all the time," one of the party remembered. Young Abraham did his part, too. In February 1817, just before his eighth birthday, he spied a flock of wild turkeys outside the new log cabin. He seized a rifle and, taking advantage of one of the chinks, "shot through a crack, and killed one of them." But killing was not for him, and he did not try to repeat his exploit. Recalling the incident years later, he said that he had "never since pulled a trigger on any larger game."

The immediate task before the Lincolns was to clear away enough trees and undergrowth so that they could plant corn. Thomas could only do so much, and he had to enlist the services of his son. Though Abraham was only eight years old, he was, he recalled, "large of his age, and had an axe put into his hands at once; and from that till within his twentythird year, he was almost constantly handling that most useful instrument—less, of course, in plowing and harvesting seasons."

That first year in Indiana was a time of backbreaking toil and of desperate loneliness for all the family, but by fall they were fairly settled. Thomas was so satisfied with the site that he had chosen that he undertook the sixty-mile trip to Vincennes in order to make initial payments on two adjoining eighty-acre tracts he had claimed. Nancy also began to feel more at home, because Elizabeth (Hanks) and Thomas Sparrow, her aunt and uncle, who had lost their home in Kentucky through an ejectment suit, came to the Pigeon Creek neighborhood. They stayed for a while in the Lincolns' half-faced camp until they could build their own cabin on a nearby lot. Sarah and Abraham rejoiced because the Sparrows brought with them the eighteen-year-old Dennis Hanks, illegitimate nephew of Elizabeth Sparrow. They had known Dennis in Kentucky—indeed, he claimed to be the second person to touch Abraham after his birth—and they welcomed this young man of endless loquacity and irrepressible good spirits.

But shortly afterward everything began to go wrong. First, Abraham had a dangerous accident. One of his chores was to take corn over to Gordon's mill, some two miles distant, to be ground into meal. When he got there, he hitched his old mare to the arm of the gristmill. Because it was getting late and he was in a hurry to get home before dusk, he tried to speed up the mare by giving her a stroke of the whip with each revolution. She lashed out at him with a kick that landed on his forehead, and he fell bleeding and unconscious. At first it was thought that he was dead and his father was summoned. He could not speak for several hours, but he revived and suffered no permanent damage.

Then the Pigeon Creek community was devastated by an attack of what was called milk sickness (more properly, brucellosis). It was a mysterious ailment, which settlers realized was somehow connected with the milk of their cows, but it was not until many years later that scientists discovered that the cows, which ran wild in the forest, had been eating the luxuriant but poisonous white snakeroot plant. Dizziness, nausea, and stomach pains were the initial symptoms, followed by irregular respiration and pulse, prostration, and coma. Death usually occurred within seven days. Thomas and Elizabeth Sparrow were first afflicted, and Thomas Lincoln sawed rough boards to make coffins to bury them in. Then Nancy fell ill. She struggled on, day after day, for a week, but she knew she was failing. Calling her children to her bedside, she "told them to be good and kind to their father —to one an other and to the world." She died on October 5, and Thomas Lincoln buried another coffin on a wooded knoll a quarter of a mile from the cabin.

The next year may have been the hardest in Abraham Lincoln's life. With the help of Dennis Hanks, who moved in with the Lincolns after the Sparrows died, Thomas was able to put food on the table. "We still kept up hunting and farming," Dennis remembered. "We always hunted[;] it made no difference what came, for we more or less depended on it for a living— nay for life." Sarah, who had her twelfth birthday in February 1819, tried to cook and keep house, but at times she felt so lonesome that she would sit by the fire and cry. To cheer her up, Dennis recalled, "me 'n' Abe got 'er a baby coon an' a turtle, an' tried to get a fawn but we couldn't ketch any."

Abe—as Dennis and the other children insisted on calling the boy, even though he always disliked the nickname—left no words describing his sense of loss. His wound was too sensitive to touch. But many years later he wrote a letter of condolence to a bereaved child: "In this sad world of ours, sorrow comes to all; and, to the young, it comes with bitterest agony, because it takes them unawares. . . . I have had experience enough to know what I say."

Deeper consequences of the loss of his mother before he was eleven years old can only be a matter of speculation. It is tempting to trace his subsequent moodiness, his melancholy, and his occasional bouts of depression to this cause, but the connections are not clear and these patterns of behavior appear in persons who have never experienced such loss. Perhaps his mother's death had something to do with his growing aversion to cruelty and bloodshed. Now he began to reprove other children in the neighborhood for senseless cruelty to animals. He scolded them when they caught terrapins and heaped hot coals on their shells, to force the defenseless animals out of their shells, reminding them "that an ant's life was to it as sweet as ours to us." Certainly the death of his mother, coming so soon after the deaths of other friends and neighbors, gave a gloomy cast to his memories of his Indiana home. In the 1840s, revisiting his old neighborhood, he recorded his thoughts in verse:

> My childhood's home I see again,
>   And sadden with the view;
> And still, as mem'ries crowd my brain,
>   There's pleasure in it too.
>
>   . . .
>
> I range the fields with pensive tread,
>   And pace the hollow rooms,
> And feel (companion of the dead)
>   I'm living in the tombs.

IV

Within a year of Nancy's death, Thomas Lincoln recognized that he and his family could not go on alone, and he went back to Kentucky to seek a bride. In Elizabethtown he found Sarah Bush Johnston, whom he had perhaps unsuccessfully courted before he wed Nancy. She was the widow of the Hardin County jailer and mother of three small children. There was no time for a romantic engagement; he needed a wife and she needed a husband. They made a quick, businesslike arrangement for him to pay her debts and for her to pack up her belongings and move with him to Indiana.

The arrival of Sarah Lincoln marked a turning point in Abraham Lincoln's life. She brought with her, first, her collection of domestic possessions— comfortable bedding, a walnut bureau that had cost her forty-five dollars, a table and chairs, a spinning wheel, knives, forks, and spoons—so that the Lincoln children felt they were joining a world of unbelievable luxury. Her children—Elizabeth, John D., and Matilda, who ranged from nine to five years in age—brought life and excitement to the depressed Lincoln family. But most of all she brought with her the gift of love. Sarah Bush Lincoln must have been touched to see the dirty, ill-clad, hungry Lincoln children, and she set to work at once, as she said, to make them look "more human." "She soaped—rubbed and washed the children clean," Dennis Hanks remembered, "so that they look[ed] pretty neat—well and clean."

At her suggestion, the whole household was reorganized. Thomas Lincoln and Dennis Hanks had to give up hunting for a while to split logs and make a floor for the cabin, and they finished the roof, constructed a proper door, and cut a hole for a window, which they covered with greased paper. The cabin was high enough to install a loft, reached by climbing pegs driven into the wall, and here she installed beds for the three boys—Dennis Hanks, Abraham, and John D. Downstairs she had the whole cabin cleaned, a decent bedstead was built, and Thomas used his skill as a carpenter to make another table and stools. Remarkably, these reforms were brought about with a minimum of friction.

What was even more extraordinary, Sarah Bush Lincoln was able to blend the two families harmoniously and without jealousy. She treated her own children and the Lincoln children with absolute impartiality. She grew especially fond of Abraham. "Abe never gave me a cross word or look and never refused in fact, or even in appearance, to do anything I requested him," she remembered. "I never gave him a cross word in all my life. . . . His mind and mine—what little I had[—]seemed to move together—move in the same channel." Many years later, attempting to compare her son and her stepson, she told an interviewer: "Both were good boys, but I must say—both now being dead that Abe was the best boy I ever saw or ever expect to see."

Starved for affection, Abraham returned her love. He called her "Mama," and he never spoke of her except in the most affectionate terms. After he had been elected President, he recalled the sorry condition of Thomas Lincoln's household before Sarah Bush Johnston arrived and told of the encouragement she had given him as a boy. "She had been his best friend in this world," a relative reported him as saying, "and . . . no man could love a mother more than he loved her."

V

The years after Sarah Bush Lincoln came to Indiana were happy ones for young Abraham. Afterward, when he spoke of this time, it was as "a joyous, happy boyhood," which he described "with mirth and glee," and in his recollections "there was nothing sad nor pinched, and nothing of want." His parents enrolled him, along with the other four children in the household, in the school that Andrew Crawford had opened in a cabin about a mile from the Lincoln house. Though Sarah Bush Lincoln was illiterate, she had a sense that education was important, and Thomas wanted his son to learn how to read and cipher.

Possibly young Lincoln knew how to read a little before he entered Crawford's school, but Dennis Hanks, who was only marginally literate himself, claimed credit for giving Abraham "his first lesson in spelling—reading and writing." "I taught Abe to write with a buzzards quill which I killed with a rifle and having made a pen—put Abes hand in mind [sic] and moving his fingers by my hand to give him the idea of how to write." Abraham learned these basic skills slowly. John Hanks, another cousin who lived with the Lincolns for a time, thought he was "somewhat dull . . . not a brilliant boy—but *worked* his way by toil: to learn was hard for him, but he worked slowly, but surely." But Abraham's stepmother understood him better, recognized his need fully to master what he read or heard. "He must understand every thing—even to the smallest thing—minutely and exactly," she remembered; "he would then repeat it over to himself again and again—some times in one form and then in an other and when it was fixed in his mind to suit him he . . . never lost that fact or his understanding of it."

Abraham attended Crawford's school for one term, of perhaps three months. Crawford, a justice of the peace and man of some importance in the area, ran a subscription school, where parents paid their children's tuition in cash or in commodities. Ungraded, it was a "blab" school, where students recited their lessons aloud, and the schoolmaster listened through the din for errors. He was long remembered because, according to one student, "he tried to learn us manners" by having the pupils practice introducing each other, as though they were strangers. After one term Crawford gave up teaching, and the Lincoln children had no school for a year, until James Swaney opened one about four miles from the Lincoln house. The distance was so great that Abraham, who had farm chores to perform, could attend only sporadically. The next year, for about six months, he went to a school taught by Azel W. Dorsey in the same cabin that Crawford had used. With that term, at the age of fifteen, his formal education ended. All told, he summarized, "the agregate of all his schooling did not amount to one year."

In later years Lincoln was scornful of these "schools, so called," which he attended: "No qualification was ever required of a teacher, beyond 'readin, writin, and cipherin,' to the Rule of Three [i.e., ratio and proportions]. If a straggler supposed to understand latin, happened to sojourn in the neighborhood, he was looked upon as a wizzard."

Though his censure was largely deserved, a school system that produced Abraham Lincoln could not have been wholly without merit. Indeed, his teachers, transient and untrained as they were, helped him master the basic tools so that in the future he could educate himself. *Dilworth's Spelling-Book,* which he and Sarah had begun to use in Kentucky, provided his introduction to grammar and spelling. Beginning with the alphabet and Arabic and Roman numerals, it proceeded to words of two letters, then three letters, and finally four letters. From these the student began to construct sentences, like: "No man may put off the law of God." *Dilworth's* then went on to more advanced subjects, and the final sections included prose and verse selections, some accompanied by crude woodcuts—which may have been the first pictures that Abraham had ever seen. Other readers, like *The Columbian Class Book* and *The Kentucky Preceptor,* expanded and reinforced what he learned from *Dilworth's.*

Through constant repetition and drill the boy learned how to spell. Indeed, he became so proficient that it was hard to stump him in the school spelling bees. He was generous with his knowledge. Many years later a girl in his class told how he helped her when the teacher gave her a difficult word, "defied," which she was about to misspell "defyed." When she came to the fourth letter, she happened to look at Abraham, who pointed to his eye, and, taking the hint, she spelled the word correctly.

He also learned to write, in a clear, round hand. The handwriting of a bit of doggerel in his sum book is recognizably that of the future President:

Abraham Lincoln is my name
And with my pen I wrote the same
I wrote in both hast[e] and speed
and left it here for fools to read.

So adept did he become that unlettered neighbors in the Pigeon Creek community often asked him to write letters for them.

Even more important was the ability to read. Once he got the hang of it, he could never get enough. "Abe was getting hungry for book[s]," Dennis Hanks recalled, "reading every thing he could lay his hands on." He would carry a book with him when he went out to work, and read when he rested. John Hanks remembered that when Abraham returned to the house from work, "he would go to the cupboard, snatch a piece of corn bread, take down a book, sit down in a chair, cock his legs up as high as his head, and read."

His contemporaries attributed prodigies of reading to him, but books were scarce on the frontier and he had to read carefully rather than extensively. He memorized a great deal of what he read. "When he came across a passage that struck him," his stepmother remembered, "he would write it down on boards if he had no paper and keep it there till he did get paper —then he would re-write it—look at it [and] repeat it."

Other than classroom texts, his first books were the few that Sarah Bush Lincoln had brought with her from Kentucky. One was her family Bible. Abraham read it at times, she remembered, "though not as much as said: he sought more congenial books—suitable for his age." *The Pilgrim's Progress* was one of them, and the biblical cadences of Lincoln's later speeches owed much to John Bunyan. Another of Sarah Bush Lincoln's books was *Aesop's Fables,* which it was said Abraham read so many times that he could write it out from memory. The morals of some of the stories became deeply in-grained in his mind, like the lesson drawn from the fable of the lion and the four bulls: "A kingdom divided against itself cannot stand." In his step-mother's copy of *Lessons in Elocution,* by William Scott, he studied basic lessons on elocution, and the selections in this book were probably his introduction to Shakespeare. Among the set pieces it included was King Claudius's soliloquy on his murder of Hamlet's father, "O, my offence is rank, it smells to heaven." It remained one of Lincoln's favorite passages.

History also fascinated him. He probably read William Grimshaw's *History of the United States,* which began with the discovery of America and ended with the annexation of Florida. With a sharp denunciation of slavery as "a climax of human cupidity and turpitude," Grimshaw stressed the importance of the American Revolution and exhorted students: "Let us not only declare by words, but demonstrate by our actions, that 'all men are created equal.' " Even more than history, biography interested young Lincoln. He enjoyed the autobiography of Benjamin Franklin, but it was Parson Mason Weems's *Life of George Washington* that stirred his imagination. Many years later, when he was on his way to Washington and his first inaugural, he told the New Jersey Senate that Weems's account of Washington's heroic struggles at Trenton—"the crossing of the river; the contest with the Hessians; the great hardships endured at that time"—had made an indelible mark on his mind. "I recollect thinking then, boy even though I was," he said, "that there must have been something more than common that those men struggled for."

The pioneer schools of Indiana also gave Lincoln a good grounding in elementary mathematics. His teachers probably never used an arithmetic textbook but drew their problems from two handbooks, Thomas Dilworth's *Schoolmaster's Assistant* and Zachariah Jess's *American Tutor's Assistant.* Be-cause paper was scarce, he often had to cipher on boards, and, his step-mother recalled, "when the board would get too black he would shave it off with a drawing knife and go on again." Then from somewhere he found a few sheets of paper, which he sewed together to form a little notebook in which to write down the problems and his answers. In it he recorded complicated calculations involving multiplication (like 34,567,834 x 23,423) and division (such as 4,375,702 divided by 2,432), which he completed with exceptional accuracy, and he also solved problems concerning weights and measures, and figured discounts and simple interest. Apparently ratio and proportion taxed his instructors to their limits, but he was able to work out simple problems such as: "If 3 oz of silver cost 17s[hillings] what will 48 oz Cost." Neither the student nor the teachers seemed quite to get the idea of "casting out nines," a cumbersome and inaccurate method of verifying long division. Nevertheless, he liked the logic and the precision of mathematics, and years later, after serving a term in Congress, he went back to the subject and worked his way through most of a geometry textbook.

What Lincoln learned from school was not all in books. Here for the first time he had a chance to see children from other families and to pit his wits against theirs. Taller than most of the other students, he wore a coonskin cap and buckskin pants that were always too short, so that, a classmate remembered, "there was bare and naked six or more inches of Abe Lincoln's shin bone." Unconscious of his peculiar appearance, he would rapidly gather the other students around him, cracking jokes, telling stories, making plans. Almost from the beginning he took his place as a leader. His classmates admired his ability to tell stories and make rhymes, and they enjoyed his first efforts at public speaking. In their eyes he was clearly exceptional, and he carried away from his brief schooling the self-confidence of a man who has never met his intellectual equal.

VI

These happy years of Lincoln's boyhood were short, for his relationship with his father began to deteriorate. Thomas was perceptibly aging. After an exceptional burst of energy at the time of his second marriage, he began to slow down. He was probably not in good health, for one neighbor remembered that he became blind in one eye and lost sight in the other. He was not a lazy man, another settler reported, but "a tinker—a piddler—always doing but doing nothing great."

He was under considerable financial pressure after his marriage because he had to support a household of eight people. For a time he could rely on Dennis Hanks to help provide for his large family, but in 1826 Dennis married Elizabeth Johnston, Sarah Bush Lincoln's daughter, and moved to his own homestead a half mile or so away. As Abraham became an adolescent, his father grew more and more to depend on him for the "farming, grubbing, hoeing, making fences" necessary to keep the family afloat. He also regularly hired his son out to work for other farmers in the vicinity, and by law he was entitled to everything the boy earned until he came of age.

Generally an easygoing man, who, according to Dennis Hanks, "could beat his son telling a story—cracking a joke," Thomas Lincoln was not a harsh father or a brutal disciplinarian. He encouraged Abraham to go to school, though he had a somewhat limited idea of what an education consisted of, and he rarely interrupted his son's studies. "As a usual thing," Sarah Bush Lincoln remembered, "Mr Lincoln never made Abe quit reading to do any thing if he could avoid it. He would do it himself first." But Dennis Hanks said that Thomas thought his son spent too much time on his books, "having sometimes to slash him for neglecting his work by reading." The father would not tolerate impudence. When Abraham as a little boy thrust himself into adult conversations, Thomas sometimes struck him. Then, as Hanks recalled, young Abraham "never balked, but dropt a kind of silent unwelcome tear, as evidence of his sensations."

As Abraham became a teenager, he began to distance himself from his father. His sense of alienation may have originated at the time of his mother's death, when he needed more support and compassion than his stolid father was able to give. It increased as the boy got older. Perhaps he felt that his place in the household had been usurped by the second family Thomas Lincoln acquired when he remarried; contemporaries noted that Thomas seemed to favor the stepson, John D. Johnston, more than he did his own son. He disagreed with his father over religion. In 1823, Thomas Lincoln and his wife joined the Pigeon Baptist Church, as did his daughter Sarah soon afterward; but Abraham made no move toward membership. Indeed, as his stepmother said, "Abe had no particular religion—didn't think of these question[s] at that time, if he ever did." That difference appears to have led to the sharpest words he ever received from his father. Though Abraham did not belong to the church, he attended the sermons, and afterward, climbing on a tree stump, he would rally the other children around him and repeat—or sometimes parody—the minister's words. Offended, Thomas, as one of the children recalled, "would come and make him quit —send him to work."

The heavy chores he had to perform contributed to his dissatisfaction. The boy had limited energy because at about the age of twelve he began growing so rapidly. By the time he was sixteen he had shot up to six feet, two inches tall, though he weighed only about one hundred and sixty pounds. One contemporary remembered he was so skinny that he had a spidery look. He grew so fast that he was tired all the time, and he showed a notable lack of enthusiasm for physical labor. "Lincoln was lazy—a very lazy man," Dennis Hanks concluded. "He was always reading—scribbling— writing—ciphering—writing Poetry." The neighbors for whom he worked agreed that he was "awful lazy," and, as one remarked, "he was no hand to pitch in at work like killing snakes." Their dissatisfaction doubtless contributed to the friction between father and son.

But Abraham's pulling away from his father was something more significant than a teenage rebellion. Abraham had made a quiet reassessment of the life that Thomas lived. He kept his judgment to himself, but years later it crept into his scornful statements that his father "grew up, litterally without education," that he "never did more in the way of writing than to bunglingly sign his own name," and that he chose to settle in a region where "there was absolutely nothing to excite ambition for education." To Abraham Lincoln that was a damning verdict. In all of his published writings, and, indeed, even in reports of hundreds of stories and conversations, he had not one favorable word to say about his father.

VII

By the time Abraham Lincoln was in his late teens, he was itching to get away from Pigeon Creek. One after another, his ties to home and to the community were snapped. When he was seventeen, his sister, Sarah, married a neighbor, Aaron Grigsby, and the couple set up housekeeping several miles from the Lincoln cabin. Then Matilda, Sarah Bush Lincoln's youngest daughter, who had been very fond of Abraham, married Squire Hall and also moved away. A year and a half later Sarah Lincoln Grigsby died in childbirth. Abraham blamed the death of his sister on the negligence of the Grigsbys in sending for a doctor, and the ensuing quarrel further alienated him from his Pigeon Creek neighbors.

Increasingly he began to go farther afield from his father's cabin. A contemporary remembered that he went all over the county attending "house raisings, log rolling corn shucking and workings of all kinds." To be sure, he got bored easily and on many of these occasions, as Dennis Hanks remembered, "would Commence his pranks—tricks—jokes stories, and . . . all would stop—gather around Abe and listen." At the age of sixteen he, together with Dennis Hanks and Squire Hall, got the idea of making money by selling firewood to the steamers plying the Ohio River, and they set to work sawing logs at Posey's Landing, only to find that demand was slack and money was scarce. They were finally able to swap nine cords of firewood for nine yards of white domestic cloth, out of which, Hanks reported, "Abe had a shirt made, and it was positively the first white shirt which . . . he had ever owned or worn." Next he hired out to James Taylor, who ran a ferry across the Ohio River in the same vicinity; when he was not helping on the river, he plowed, killed hogs, and made fences, doing what he remembered as "the roughest work a young man could be made to do." He earned $6 a month, with 31¢ extra on days when he slaughtered hogs. In what spare time he had, he built a little flatboat, or rowboat. When two men asked him to row them out into the river so that they could take passage on a steamer that was coming downstream, he sculled them out, helped them aboard, and lifted their heavy trunks onto the deck. As they left, each of them tossed a silver half-dollar on the floor of his boat in payment. "I could scarcely believe my eyes as I picked up the money," Lincoln recalled nearly forty years later. "I could scarcely credit that I, a poor boy, had earned a dollar in less than a day. . . . The world seemed wider and fairer before me."

The lure of the river was irresistible, promising escape from the constricted world of Pigeon Creek. The next spring, when James Gentry, who owned the local store, decided to send a cargo of meat, corn, and flour down the rivers for sale in New Orleans, Lincoln accepted the offer to accompany his son, Allen, on the flatboat, at a wage of $8 a month. They made a leisurely trip, stopping frequently to trade at the sugar plantations along the river in Louisiana, until the dreamlike quality of their journey was rudely interrupted. "One night," as Lincoln remembered, "they were attacked by seven negroes with intent to kill and rob them. They were hurt some in the melee, but succeeded in driving the negroes from the boat, and then 'cut cable' 'weighed anchor' and left." New Orleans was by far the largest city the two country boys had ever seen, with imposing buildings, busy shops, and incessant traffic. Here they heard French spoken as readily as English. In New Orleans, Lincoln for the first time encountered large numbers of slaves. But neither boy made any record of their visit to the Crescent City; perhaps it was too overwhelming.

Returning to Indiana, Lincoln dutifully handed over his earnings to his father, but he began to spend more and more time away from home. He liked to go to the village of Gentryville, about a mile and a half away, where he occasionally helped out at James Gentry's store, and he worked sometimes with John Baldwin, the local blacksmith. As always, he was full of talk and plans and jokes and tricks, and he gathered about him all the young men who were about to come of age and were restless in the narrow society of southern Indiana.

In the spring of 1829, Lincoln and his little gang pulled off the most imaginative, and longest remembered, of their pranks when two sons of Reuben Grigsby—Reuben, Jr., and Charles—were married. The Lincolns had been carrying on something of a feud with the Grigsby family since Sarah's death, and when Abraham was not invited to the wedding celebration, he "felt miffed—insulted." Through a confederate he arranged that when the party was over and the bridegrooms were brought upstairs to their waiting brides, they would be led to the wrong beds. The mix-up was, of course, immediately discovered, but it became the cause of great gossip and much laughter in the Gentryville community. Its fame grew because Lincoln wrote out a scurrilous description of the affair, which he entitled "The Chronicles of Reuben." In language supposed to be reminiscent of the Scriptures, he recounted the story and then went on in verse to tell of another Grigsby brother, Billy, who was turned down by the girl he wooed:

You cursed baldhead,
My suitor you never can be;
Besides, your low crotch proclaims you a botch
And that never can answer for me.

Rejected, Billy turned to a male lover, Natty:

. . . he is married to Natty.
So Billy and Natty agreed very well;
And mamma's well pleased at the match.

Years afterward the doggerel was still remembered in southern Indiana. According to one settler, parts of it were known "better than the Bible—better than Watts hymns."

If the whole episode had any significance, it indicated that Lincoln needed to break away from home. He realized this as well as anyone. He longed to become a steamboat man and asked a neighbor, William Wood, to go with him to the Ohio River and give him a recommendation to a ship's captain. "Abe," Wood said, "your age is against you—you are not 21 yet." "I know that," the young man replied, "but I want a start." Unwilling to break the law or to offend his neighbor, Thomas Lincoln, Wood did make some discreet, though unsuccessful, inquiries in Abraham's behalf in Rockport.

But Abraham still legally owed Thomas Lincoln another year of labor, and he remained with his father out of obligation and with his stepmother out of affection. Early in 1830 he helped them move from Spencer County, Indiana, into Macon County, Illinois. John Hanks had already settled there and sent back glowing reports of the fertility of the Illinois lands, and Dennis Hanks was eager to move with his family. A rumor of a new outbreak of the milk sickness in southern Indiana triggered the Lincolns' decision to go with them. Selling his land, his hogs, and his corn, Thomas Lincoln gathered up his household, and in March started off in a wagon drawn by two yoke of oxen.

Abraham did his best to keep the company cheerful, making jokes as he goaded on the oxen. Such roads as there were proved almost impassable; the ground was still frozen from winter, and it melted a little each day only to freeze back at night. When the party crossed the Wabash River at Vincennes, the river was so high that the road was covered with water for half a mile at a stretch. Everywhere the streams were swollen, and usually there were no bridges. At one crossing Lincoln's favorite little fice dog jumped from the wagon, broke through the ice, and began struggling for his life. "I could not bear to lose my dog," Lincoln recalled many years later, "and I jumped out of the waggon and waded waist deep in the ice and water[,] got hold of him and helped out and saved him."

After passing through the village of Decatur, which consisted of fewer than a dozen log cabins, the Lincolns went on about ten miles to a tract of land on the north bank of the Sangamon River, which John Hanks had staked out for them. That summer they broke up fifteen acres of land, and Abraham and John Hanks split the rails to fence them in. Abraham already felt so much at home in Illinois that he signed a petition, along with forty-four other "qualified voters," asking for a change of polling place for elections— even though he had not lived in the state the six months required to qualify as an elector.

That summer, too, he made his first political speech, addressing a campaign meeting in front of Renshaw's store in Decatur. Two established politicians, candidates for the state legislature, made addresses, and when they failed to follow custom and offer the crowd something to drink, the boys about the store urged Lincoln to reply, expecting him to ridicule the candidates' stinginess. It was a small affair, but a notable step in Abraham's continuing effort to distance himself from his father. To put himself forward and make a public speech was something that Thomas Lincoln would never have dreamed of doing. But Abraham had for several years been reading anti-Jackson National Republican newspapers, like the *Louisville Journal,* and he ardently favored Henry Clay's "American System," which called for internal improvements, a protective tariff, and a national bank. He surprised his audience at Decatur, which had been expecting some rude political humor, with a plea for improving the Sangamon River for transportation. Showing no evidence of stage fright except for frequently shifting his position to ease his feet, he ended with an eloquent picture of the future of Illinois.

Abraham Lincoln was now a man, both physiologically and legally, and ready to leave the family nest forever. How he would support himself was not clear. He was willing to try anything—so long as it was not his father's occupations of farming and carpentry. So when Denton Offutt, a bustling, none too scrupulous businessman, asked him and John Hanks to take another flatboat loaded with provisions down to New Orleans, Lincoln, having nothing better to do, promptly accepted. When he went over to the river landing at Sangamo Town to help build the boat for Offutt, he left his father's house for good. He did not yet know who he was, or where he was heading, but he was sure he did not want to be another Thomas Lincoln.

CHAPTER TWO

A Piece of Floating Driftwood

The years after Abraham Lincoln left his father's household were of critical importance in shaping his future. In 1831 he was essentially unformed. It was not clear to him or to anybody else what career he might ultimately follow. His strong body and his ability to perform heavy manual labor equipped him only to be a farmer—his father's occupation, which he despised. In the next ten years he tried nearly every other kind of work the frontier offered: carpenter, riverboat man, store clerk, soldier, merchant, postmaster, blacksmith, surveyor, lawyer, politician. Experience eliminated all but the last two of these possibilities, and by the time he was thirty the direction of his career was firmly established.

I

Lincoln arrived at New Salem, which was to be his home for the next six years, by accident. He was, he used to tell fellow residents, "a piece of floating driftwood," accidentally lodged by the floodwaters of the Sangamon River. He first saw the village in April 1831, when the flatboat that he, John Hanks, and John D. Johnston had constructed for Offutt became lodged on the milldam that John Camron and James Rutledge had erected across the river. Loaded with barrels of bacon, wheat, and corn, the flatboat was too heavy to float over the dam, and it began taking on water at an ominous rate. The whole village turned out to watch as the crew frantically struggled to save the boat and the cargo. The young giant Lincoln attracted their special attention as he worked in the water, with his "boots off, hat, coat and vest off. Pants rolled up to his knees and shirt wet with sweat and combing his fuzzie hair with his fingers as he pounded away on the boat." Unable to budge the flatboat, he bored a hole in the bow and unloaded enough of the barrels in the rear so that the stern rose up. When the water poured out through the hole, the whole boat lifted and floated over the dam. Townsmen marveled at Lincoln's ingenuity, and Offutt, even more deeply impressed, vowed that, once the trip down the Mississippi was completed, he would set up a store in New Salem and make Lincoln the manager.

In late July, back from New Orleans, Lincoln returned to New Salem, to find that Offutt, characteristically, had not lived up to his great promises. There was as yet no store, though a stock of goods had been ordered from St. Louis. Now living—as he later expressed it—"for the first time, as it were, by himself," Lincoln had to take odd jobs to tide him over the summer, but, fortunately, laborers were always in demand on the frontier.

New Salem was a place for which young Abraham Lincoln was perfectly suited. Founded only two years earlier, on a high bluff above the Sangamon River, by the mill owners Camron and Rutledge, it was in 1831 not so much a frontier settlement as a commercial village that supplied the needs of the surrounding rural areas, like Clary's Grove and Concord. In addition to the sawmill and the gristmill, both powered by the river, New Salem counted a blacksmith's shop, a cooper's shop, an establishment for carding wool, a hatmaker, one or more general stores, and a tavern. With about one hundred residents, who occupied a dozen or so houses and stores, it was the largest community Lincoln had ever lived in.

Everyone grew very fond of this hardworking and accommodating young man, so able and so willing to do any kind of work. Quickly he established himself with the men of the town, who gathered daily at the store run by Samuel Hill and John McNeil, to exchange news and gossip. They welcomed Lincoln because, like his father, he had an inexhaustible store of anecdotes and stories. One concerned an Indiana Baptist preacher who, dressed in old-fashioned baggy pantaloons and a shirt fastened only at the collar, announced his text: "I am the Christ, whom I shall represent today." Then a little blue lizard ran up his leg, and the preacher, unable to slap him away and unwilling to stop his sermon, loosened his pants and kicked them off. But the lizard proceeded up the minister's back, and this time, without missing a word, he opened his collar button and swept off his shirt, too. The congregation looked dazed, but one old lady rose up and shouted: "If you represent Christ then I'm done with the Bible."

When no women were present, his stories sometimes took on a scatological tone. For instance, he recounted an anecdote he attributed to Colonel Ethan Allen, famed for his role in the American Revolution. Allegedly making a visit to England after the war, Allen found his hosts took great pleasure in ridiculing Americans, and George Washington in particular, and, to irritate their guest, hung a picture of the first President in the toilet. (In telling the story, Lincoln called it "the Back House.") Allen announced that they had found a very appropriate place for the picture, because "there is nothing that will Make an Englishman Shit so quick as the sight of Genl Washington."

Such stories had no special point. Unlike Lincoln's later anecdotes, they were not used to illustrate any argument or to ridicule any particular person. Lincoln repeated them because he thought they were funny and because he had grown up in a household where swapping stories was an accepted way of passing the time. Told at great length, with much mimicry and many gestures, his stories eased his acceptance by the predominantly masculine society of New Salem; it was the rare man who could fail to be amused when this shambling youth with the mournful visage began to spin out one of his tales. As he talked, one old-timer remembered, "his countenance would brighten up, the expression would light up not in a flash but rapidly, the muscles would begin to contract. Several wrinkles would diverge from the inner corners of his eyes, and extend down and diagonally across his nose, his eyes would sparkle, all terminating in an unrestrained laugh in which every one present willing or unwilling were compelled to take part."

In September, when Offutt's store finally opened, Lincoln had to gain acceptance from a different group. As a trading center, New Salem attracted farmers and laborers from the surrounding communities who came in to have their corn ground at the mill, to buy supplies, or to have a few drinks at the "groceries" (as stores that also sold liquor were known). These visitors came closer to being traditional frontiersmen than the relatively sedentary inhabitants of the village. None were wilder than the boys from Clary's Grove, a few miles to the west, whose leader was the stalwart Jack Armstrong. Uninhibited, ignorant, careless of rules and proprieties, these roughnecks were always ready for fun and a frolic. They could be generous and good-natured. For their friends, as Herndon remarked, they "could trench a pond, dig a bog, build a house," and they melted with sympathy for defenseless women and the invalid. But much of their time in New Salem was spent in devilment, like cockfighting and ganderpulling (a contest to see which rider could snap off the head of a live gander suspended from a tree limb). Above all, they valued physical strength.

When Offutt, enchanted with his new assistant, began boasting that Lincoln was not merely the smartest man in New Salem but also the strongest, the Clary's Grove boys called his bluff. They cared not at all about Lincoln's mental superiority, but they dared him to test his strength in a wrestling match with their champion, Jack Armstrong. Lincoln was reluctant, because he said he did not like all the "wooling and pulling" of a wrestling match, but the urging of his employer and the taunts of his rivals obliged him to fight. In the collective memory of New Salem residents, the contest was an epic one, and various versions survived: how Armstrong defeated Lincoln through a trick; how Lincoln threw Armstrong; how Armstrong's followers threatened collectively to lick the man who had defeated their champion until Lincoln volunteered to take them all on, but one at a time. The details were irrelevant. What mattered was that Lincoln proved that he had immense strength and courage, and that was enough to win the admiration of the Clary's Grove gang. Thereafter they became Lincoln's most loyal and enthusiastic admirers.

At the same time, the better-educated, more stable residents of New Salem came to think highly of this new arrival. Though the village was close to the frontier, a surprising number of the inhabitants were people of some culture and education. Dr. John Allen, for instance, was a graduate of Dartmouth College, and at least five residents had attended Illinois College, in nearby Jacksonville. Those without formal education often had intellectual interests. Fat, lazy Jack Kelso, for example, had a remarkable mastery of the writings of Burns and Shakespeare, which he could recite by the hour. Though self-educated, Mentor Graham conducted the town's only school. All were struck by Lincoln's unabashed eagerness to learn. They were also impressed by his participation in the New Salem debating club, which James Rutledge had started. When he first took the floor, with both hands thrust deeply into his pockets, Lincoln spoke diffidently, but as he proceeded, his voice grew more assured, he started using his hands for awkward gestures, and, one participant remembered, "he pursued the question with reason and argument so pithy and forcible that all were amazed."

Town worthies grew convinced that this was a young man with a future. They noted his painstaking attention to his duties at Offutt's store, which were presently extended to include management of the nearby gristmill and the sawmill. "He was among the best clerks I ever saw," schoolmaster Graham recalled; "he was attentive to his business—was kind and considerate to his customers and friends and always treated them with great tenderness—kindness and honesty." They took satisfaction in the great interest he showed in town affairs. For instance, he regularly attended the sessions of the local court, over which the corpulent Bowling Green, the justice of the peace, presided. Always looking for amusement, Green initially allowed the awkward young man to make informal comments on cases before the court because he told anecdotes that, as one contemporary recalled, produced "a spasmotic [sic] shaking of the fat sides of the old law functionary." But soon he came to recognize that Lincoln had not merely a sense of humor but a strong, logical mind. Presently neighbors began to rely on him for legal advice, and, following a book of forms, he was able to draft simple legal documents, like deeds and receipts.

In the spring of 1832, Green, James Rutledge, the president of the debating club, and several other residents suggested that Lincoln run for the state legislature. Their choice was not as extraordinary as it might initially appear. The future of New Salem was linked to the Sangamon River, which swirled under the bluff on which the town was located. Down the river went the surplus bacon, corn, and wheat of the area—just the commodities that Lincoln's flatboat had carried—and if the sluggish stream was improved, steamboats could bring up the river manufactured goods, salt, iron, and the dozens of other commodities that residents required. But the prospect that New Salem might become a commercial entrepôt for central Illinois was threatened by a plan to build a railroad from the readily navigable Illinois River to Jacksonville and Springfield, bypassing New Salem altogether. New Salem needed a man in the legislature to represent its interests, and nobody could do that better than Lincoln, with his practical experience as a river-boat man.

At his friends' urging, Lincoln in March 1832 announced himself a candidate for the state legislature. The move was another demonstration of the young man's supreme self-confidence, his belief that he was at least the equal, if not the superior, of any man he ever met. To be sure, the post he was seeking was not an elevated one. No special qualifications were required of state legislators, who dealt mostly with such issues as whether cattle had to be fenced in or could enjoy free range. Previous legislative experience was not a necessity and, indeed, might be considered a disadvantage. Nor did candidates have to have the backing of a strong political party or powerful patrons. As yet, Illinois politics was in a state of flux. While many residents strongly admired Andrew Jackson, who was seeking a second term as President, others, including Lincoln, almost worshiped Henry Clay, the rival candidate for that office. Differences between these two leaders over a national bank, the protective tariff, and federal support for "internal improvements"—meaning improvement of roads, canals, and rivers—would soon lead to the formation of Democratic and Whig parties, but in 1832 these national issues had not yet spilled over into Illinois local politics, which remained a matter of voters choosing their personal favorites for office.

Nevertheless, Lincoln's decision to announce himself a candidate for the state legislature in March 1832 was a revealing one. Less than a year earlier he had been, in his own words, a "friendless, uneducated, penniless boy, working on a flatboat—at ten dollars per month." He was now settled in New Salem, but, at the age of twenty-three, he was only a clerk in a small country store, a young man with less than a year of formal education and with no experience in the workings of government. As one contemporary remarked, "Lincoln *had nothing only plenty of friends.*" Hardly known outside of his little community, he would have to compete for votes in the entire county, contesting with men of far greater age and experience.

Other candidates had influential politicians present their names to the electorate, but Lincoln, lacking such support, appealed directly to the public in an announcement published in Springfield's *Sangamo Journal.* In drafting and revising it, he probably had some assistance from John McNeil, the storekeeper, and possibly from schoolmaster Mentor Graham, and they may have been responsible for its somewhat orotund quality. Lincoln began by challenging the proposed railroad project. "However high our imaginations may be heated at thoughts of it," he warned there was "a heart appalling shock accompanying the account of its cost." As an alternative he urged the improvement of the Sangamon River, which would be "vastly important and highly desirable to the people of this county," and he vouched for the practicability of this project by adducing his experience on the river, which was as extensive as that of "any other person in the country."

On other issues as well Lincoln spoke for the New Salem community. Chronically short of cash and needing credit, its businessmen were obliged to borrow at very high rates of interest, and Lincoln pledged to support a law against such usury, "this baneful and corroding system." But even as a very young man he recognized the limits of the possible. Usury legislation might have a useful symbolic effect, but, he noted wryly, it would not materially injure anyone because "in cases of extreme necessity there could always be means found to cheat the law." Like other New Salem residents, he favored improving education, "the most important subject which we as a people can be engaged in," though he offered no plan or program.

In a concluding paragraph Lincoln spoke for himself, rather than for his community, and here he employed his distinctive style, avoiding highfalutin language in favor of simplicity and directness. He declared that his only object was "that of being truly esteemed of my fellow men, by rendering myself worthy of their esteem." How well he would succeed "is yet to be developed." "I was born and have ever remained in the most humble walks of life," he reminded voters, in what was to become part of his standard appeal; on at least thirty-five other public occasions before 1860 he referred to himself as "humble" Abraham Lincoln. If elected, he would work hard for the people. But defeat would not be unbearable, because he was "too familiar with disappointments to be very much chagrined."

II

Lincoln's announcement was timely, because within days of its publication news spread that "the splendid, upper cabin steamer *Talisman*" had left Cincinnati on a voyage to demonstrate the navigability of the Sangamon River. After traveling down the Ohio and up the Mississippi and Illinois rivers to Beardstown, the vessel would push up the Sangamon to Portland Landing, about six miles from both New Salem and Springfield. The whole region was overjoyed.

Lincoln, along with several other residents of Springfield and New Salem, went to Beardstown and worked hard for several days cutting back the brush that overhung the river and removing obstructions where it flowed into the Illinois. When the *Talisman* arrived at Beardstown, he took charge, because, as he had said in his political announcement, he knew the Sangamon River better than anyone else, and he triumphantly piloted the steamer upstream to Portland Landing on March 24. Probably he joined in the celebration at the Springfield courthouse two days later.

News that the Sangamon was rapidly dropping put an end to the celebrations, and within a week the *Talisman,* with Lincoln again at the helm, beat a hasty retreat down the river. The water level was so low that a portion of the milldam at New Salem had to be destroyed to allow the vessel to pass through on its way back to Beardstown. The whole *Talisman* adventure impressively boosted Lincoln's reputation; it both demonstrated his skill as a river pilot and proved his political sagacity in urging that if the Sangamon was going to be navigable it would have to be improved with state support.

But Lincoln's promising political career was interrupted by the collapse of Offutt's business ventures. Offutt was, as one New Salem resident characterized him, "a gasy—windy—brain rattling man," full of visionary plans. On the verge of bankruptcy, he asked Lincoln to split enough rails to build a pen, at the base of the New Salem bluff, for a thousand hogs, which he was confident he would sell down the river. Even when his funds were exhausted, Offutt announced to the farmers of the Sangamon region that he was importing 3,000 or 4,000 bushels of seed corn, which he would sell for a dollar a bushel, along with cottonseed brought up from Tennessee. Undercapitalized and overextended, Offutt's enterprises faltered in the spring of 1832 and then, as Lincoln said later, "petered out."

Left without a job, Lincoln was saved by the outbreak of the Black Hawk War. The Sauk and Fox Indians, who had been tricked into moving west of the Mississippi River, ceding their vast tribal lands in northwestern Illinois, repudiated their treaty with the federal government, and in May one of their leaders, Black Hawk, returned to Illinois with about 450 warriors and 1,500 women and children, to reclaim their tribal homeland. Immediately the frontier was ablaze with alarm. When Governor John Reynolds called for volunteers to assist the federal troops in repelling the invasion, men rushed to offer their services, some out of patriotism, some out of long-cherished animosity toward Indians, and some who knew that military service would aid their political careers. In Lincoln's case all these motives were at work —with the added inducement that the pay of a militiaman would be very welcome to a man with no other means of support.

On April 21 he and other volunteers from the New Salem neighborhood met near Richland and were sworn in to service. As was customary, the men of the company elected their own officers. William Kirkpatrick, the owner of a sawmill, announced his candidacy, but some of the Clary's Grove boys proposed Lincoln. Both candidates stepped out in front, on the village green, and the men formed a line behind their favorite. To Lincoln's delight, two-thirds of the groups fell in line behind him, and most of the others presently deserted Kirkpatrick and joined them. The election was one of the proudest moments of his life. Many years later, after he had served four terms in the state legislature, had been elected to Congress, and had twice been nominated for the United States Senate, Lincoln said this election as militia captain was "a success which gave me more pleasure than any I have had since."

Lincoln tried with moderate success to secure some discipline in his company, and his task was made easier because Jack Armstrong was his first sergeant. He learned a little about close-order drill, but not enough to master the more complicated commands. Once when he found his company marching directly into a fence, he could not remember how to order them to pass through the narrow gate. With considerable presence of mind he called a halt, dismissed the company for two minutes, and ordered them to re-form on the other side of the fence. He did not hesitate to use physical strength to preserve order. When an old Indian, bearing a certificate of good character from American authorities, stumbled into camp, Lincoln's men talked of killing him, saying, "The Indian is a damned spy" and "We have come out to fight the Indian and by God we intend to do so." Drawing himself up to his full height, Lincoln stepped in front of the shivering Indian and offered to fight anyone who wanted to hurt the old man. Grumbling, the soldiers let the Indian slip away.

His service in the Black Hawk War was neither particularly dangerous nor heroic. Later, for political reasons, he used to poke fun at his military record. In 1848, when the Democrats nominated Lewis Cass, of Michigan, for President, emphasizing his alleged military record in the War of 1812, Lincoln reminded listeners that he, too, was a military hero. "Yes sir," he declared; "in the days of the Black Hawk war, I fought, bled, and came away." He invited comparison of his martial efforts with those of the Michigan governor. If Cass, as alleged, broke his sword in anger after Detroit was needlessly surrendered to the British, Lincoln joked, "It is quite certain I did not break my sword, for I had none to break; but I bent a musket pretty badly on one occasion." "If he saw any live, fighting indians, it was more than I did," Lincoln conceded; "but I had a good many bloody struggles with the musquetoes; and, although I never fainted from loss of blood, I can truly say I was often very hungry."

At the time, however, Lincoln was proud of his military service, and he enjoyed the hearty comradeship of men-at-arms. When his first month's enlistment expired, he, along with several other members of his company, signed up for another twenty days, this time serving as a private, and at the end of that period he reenlisted for another month. "I was out of work . . . and there being no danger of more fighting, I could do nothing better than enlist again," he explained afterward. He served until July 10, when he was honorably discharged.

His service in the Black Hawk War gave him some acquaintance with military life and his first experience as a leader of men. Meeting volunteers from different parts of the state was useful to him politically, for it extended his reputation. While he was in the army, he came into contact with a number of the rising young political leaders of the state, like Orville Hickman Browning, a cautious, conservative Quincy lawyer, who would become one of his most influential and critical friends. More important was his acquaintance with John Todd Stuart, a Springfield lawyer, who served as major in the same battalion as Lincoln. Handsome, polished, and well educated, Stuart was apparently the opposite of Lincoln in every way, but he saw great promise in his New Salem friend.

The most immediate benefit Lincoln derived from his brief military service was his compensation of about $110, plus the $14 bounty he received for enlisting. This was the total extent of his resources as he returned to New Salem, in time for a brief campaign before the election for the state legislature on August 6. The canvass was an informal one, and Lincoln, like the other twelve candidates, traveled about Sangamon County, introducing himself and soliciting votes. He was an odd-looking figure, his swarthy complexion now deeply sunburned, so that, as he told his listeners, he was "almost as red as those men I have been chasing through the prairies and forests on the Rivers of Illinois." On the campaign trail, as one observer remembered, "he wore a mixed jeans coat, clawhammer style, short in the sleeves and bob-tail—in fact it was so short in the tail he could not sit on it; flax and towlinen pantaloons, and a straw hat."

When he attended political rallies, members of the Clary's Grove gang, who had recently been his companions in arms, often accompanied him. At his maiden speech, in Pappsville, a village eleven miles west of Springfield, a fight broke out in the crowd, and Lincoln saw one of his supporters attacked. Quitting the platform, he strode into the audience, seized the assailant by the neck and the seat of his trousers, and, as one witness recalled, threw him twelve feet away. As usual, memory is elastic, but there is no doubt that Lincoln, who now stood six feet and four inches tall and weighed 214 pounds, was strong enough to intimidate any rival.

In his speeches the candidate made no attempt to conceal the fact that he was, as he said, "a stanch anti-Jackson, or Clay, man." But for the most part he discussed local issues, like the need to improve the Sangamon River, and avoided larger questions by announcing, "My politics are short and sweet, like the old woman's dance."

When the votes were counted, Lincoln ran eighth in a field of thirteen candidates, the top four of whom were elected. He was, of course, disappointed, and years later he made a point of noting that this election was the only time he "was ever beaten on a direct vote of the people." He could take comfort, however, from the returns from his own New Salem precinct, where he received 277 of 300 votes cast.

III

Consoling as that expression of neighborly support was, it did little to solve his acute financial problems. As he noted in an autobiographical statement: "He was now without means and out of business, but was anxious to remain with his friends who had treated him with so much generosity, especially as he had nothing elsewhere to go to." He began looking about for a job, and for a future. He considered becoming a blacksmith, but he wanted to avoid a life of physical labor. He thought of studying law. The profession had interested him even as a boy in Indiana, when, according to much later recollections, he attended sessions of local courts at Rockport and Boonville and supposedly read the copy of the *Revised Laws of Indiana* owned by the local constable, David Turnham. But on reflection he concluded that he needed a better education to succeed.

Opportunity came his way when James and J. Rowan Herndon decided to sell the general store they owned in New Salem. William F. Berry, who had been a corporal in Lincoln's company during the Black Hawk War, arranged to buy James Herndon's interest in the store, and J. Rowan Herndon offered the other half interest to Lincoln, who was boarding with him. No money passed hands; Lincoln signed a note for his share. "I believed he was thoroughly honest," Rowan Herndon explained, "and that impression was so strong in me I accepted his note in payment of the whole."

Lincoln and Berry now owned one of the three stores in New Salem, competing with the well-managed establishment of Samuel Hill and John McNeil and a newer business owned by Reuben Radford. In January 1833, Radford managed to offend the Clary's Grove boys, who retaliated by trashing his store—knocking out the windows, breaking the crockery, and turning the goods topsy-turvy. In despair, he decided to sell out. Canny young William Greene, Jr., bought his store and his damaged stock of goods for $400 and immediately sold both to Lincoln and Berry, making a profit of $250. Once again, the partners signed notes to cover most of their new purchase.

Moving their meager stock into Radford's building, Lincoln and Berry were ready for business. Like most other country stores, they supplied customers with tea and coffee, sugar and salt, and a few other commodities that could not be produced in the village. In addition, the store carried blue calico, brown muslin, men and women's hats, and a small selection of shoes.

There was rarely enough business to keep the partners occupied, and Lincoln was able to spend much of his time reading. Indeed, during his New Salem years he probably read more than at any other time in his life. Fiction did not interest him. He made one unsuccessful attempt at *Ivanhoe,* but he had no other acquaintance with the great British and American novelists. He did not care much for most history and biography, which he thought untrustworthy. Some poetry deeply moved him, and he memorized long passages from Shakespeare's plays. Jack Kelso probably introduced him to Robert Burns, whose "generous heart, and transcendent genius" he praised many years later, while President, and he was soon able to recite "Tam o'Shanter," "The Cotter's Saturday Night," and other long poems. He developed a liking for the melancholy, sentimental verse that was so popular during the era, and he thought Oliver Wendell Holmes's "The Last Leaf" "inexpressibly touching." When Dr. Jason Duncan showed him a poem called "Mortality," he was moved by its mournful message:

Oh! why should the spirit of mortal be proud?
Like a swift-fleeting meteor, a fast-flying cloud,
A flash of the lightning, a break of the wave,
He passeth from life to his rest in the grave.

Lincoln memorized all fifty-six lines, each more doleful than the last, and recited it so often that people began to think he was the author. Not until many years later did he learn that the poem was the work of William Knox, a Scotsman, who was a contemporary of Sir Walter Scott.

Lincoln's real interest was in the structure and use of language, and he decided that he needed to learn grammar. Samuel Kirkham's *English Grammar* was considered the best guide, and when Lincoln learned that a farmer named John C. Vance had a copy, he willingly walked six miles into the country to get it. He set himself systematically to master this detailed text, committing large segments to memory. Then he asked his friends to test his mastery, and when challenged to provide a definition of a verb, could recite, "A VERB is a word which signifies to BE, to DO, or to SUFFER; as I *am;* I *rule;* I *am ruled."* Some of those who participated in this drill—like Mentor Graham, the semiliterate schoolmaster, who did not himself own a grammar—later came to consider themselves Lincoln's instructors, but in fact he was, in grammar as in other subjects, essentially self-taught. He took pride in his mastery of Kirkham, and he thought it sufficiently important to mention in his 1860 autobiographical sketch that he had "studied English grammar, imperfectly of course, but so as to speak and write as well as he now does."

Lincoln's autobiography did not mention another kind of reading. Though New Salem had no churches, it was an intensely religious community. Baptists held services in the schoolhouse, and other denominations met regularly in private homes. In the summer the circuit-riding evangelist Peter Cartwright often conducted a revival meeting. There were no Catholic or Jewish residents, but Baptists, Methodists, and Presbyterians were constantly engaged in hairsplitting doctrinal controversies. A young Yale Divinity School graduate who came to teach in this central Illinois region found that he "was plunged without warning and preparation into a sea of sectarian rivalries, which was kept in constant agitation." Inevitably these religious wars attracted Lincoln's attention, though, like his father, he was reluctant to accept any creed. His parents' Baptist belief in predestination was deeply ingrained in his mind, though he felt more comfortable in thinking that events were foreordained by immutable natural laws than by a personal deity. To his cool, analytical mind the ideas of the evangelists were less persuasive than those of the few local freethinkers, who gathered about the store cracker barrel and, when there were no customers in sight, engaged in speculation about the literal accuracy of the Bible, the Virgin Birth, the divinity of Christ, and the possibility of miracles.

These conversations introduced Lincoln to Thomas Paine's *Age of Reason,* that classic rationalist attack on revealed religion, and he probably also read some of Constantin de Volney's *Ruins of Civilizations,* which argued that morality was the only essential, demonstrable part of religion. Discussion of such issues was heresy in this rigidly orthodox frontier community, and inevitably reports of Lincoln's participation in these conversations leaked out. So damaging was the allegation that he was "an open scoffer at Christianity" that in his race for Congress in 1846 he was obliged to issue a formal denial: "That I am not a member of any Christian Church, is true; but I have never denied the truth of the Scriptures; and I have never spoken with intentional disrespect of religion in general, or of any denomination of Christians in particular." He went on to explain with characteristic clarity his religious views: "It is true that in early life I was inclined to believe in what I understand is called the 'Doctrine of Necessity'—that is, that the human mind is impelled to action, or held in rest by some power, over which the mind itself has no control; and I have sometimes (with one, two or three, but never publicly) tried to maintain this opinion in argument."

There was time for endless abstract discussions in the Lincoln and Berry store, because it was clear from almost the beginning the enterprise was not going to be a success. It would be easy to blame the partners. Berry may well have been a heavy drinker, as tradition reports, and even the usually charitable Lincoln agreed that he was "a thriftless soul." Doubtless Lincoln was more interested in reading or in telling anecdotes than he was in selling his wares. But the basic reason for the failure was that by 1833 New Salem had ceased to grow. Forced to maintain what was essentially a barter economy because the Sangamon River was not adequate to carry their surplus produce to the market and there were no roads or railroads, its residents had no money to pay for even the meager goods offered by Lincoln and Berry.

The only branch of the business that showed any profit was the sale of whiskey, which Illinois law permitted the partners to sell, without license, in quantities of one quart or more for hard liquor or two gallons for beer and cider. On January 4, 1833, as business was clearly slipping, Berry first applied for a license to sell liquor by the drink—whiskey at 12½ cents, rum at 18¾ cents, and so on. The license was issued in the name of Berry & Lincoln, but Lincoln's signature was not in his own handwriting. Berry may have acted against his partner's will in converting the store, now nearly empty of other goods, into a "grocery." In later years memories would sharply differ over whether Lincoln himself ever sold liquor by the dram. Stephen A. Douglas called him "a flourishing grocery keeper in the town of New Salem," but the preponderance of the evidence supports Lincoln's own statement that he "never kept a grocery any where in the world." At any rate, the tavern license failed to save the Berry & Lincoln store, which, as Lincoln said, shortly afterward "winked out."

With the failure of the store, Lincoln was out of a job, and he had no money. Once more he did day labor, like splitting rails, and he said he worked the latter part of the winter "in a little still house at the head of a hollow." He picked up a few dollars serving on juries, clerking at elections, and carrying poll sheets to Springfield. But it grew obvious that without regular employment he would soon have to leave New Salem. Fortunately he had good friends, who wanted to make it possible for him to stay. Several of them rallied to procure for him the appointment as village postmaster. The incumbent, Samuel Hill, the storekeeper, apparently did not want the job very badly, because he neglected women standing in line for mail in favor of men desiring to purchase liquor. With a little pressure he was persuaded to resign, and on May 7 Lincoln received the place.

It was a very modest appointment—so modest that the Jackson administration overlooked his strong support of Henry Clay, considering, as Lincoln speculated, the office "too insignificant to make his politics an objection." But he was overjoyed by it. I "never saw a man better pleased," Dr. John Allen reported. As postmaster, he would "have access to all the News papers —never yet being able to get the half that he wanted before."

The duties of his new job were not onerous. Carried on horseback, the mails were supposed to arrive twice a week—when they were not delayed by snow, rain, floods, and other accidents. The recipient of a letter, rather than the sender, usually paid the postage, and it was the postmaster's job not merely to deliver the mail but to collect the fee. The charge varied with the weight of the letter and the distance it had traveled; for instance, it cost 6¢ to receive a letter consisting of a single sheet that had traveled thirty miles, and double that amount for a two-page letter. Newspapers paid a lower rate. The postmaster received a percentage of all receipts, but in New Salem the amount was small. In 1834–1835, the only full year of Lincoln's tenure for which records have been preserved, he received $55.70. The best estimate is that his compensation for the three years he served as postmaster was between $150 and $175.

Lincoln seems to have had the unusual notion that a public servant's first duty is to help people, rather than to follow bureaucratic regulations. If residents did not pick up their mail at the post office in Samuel Hill's store, he would often put the letters in his hat and deliver them in person, sometimes walking several miles to do so. He liberally interpreted the Post Office Department's rule that he could send and receive personal mail without charge but would be subject to a fine if he franked anyone else's letters. In a letter dated September 17, 1835, Mathew S. Marsh described the way Lincoln conducted the post office: "The Post Master (Mr. Lincoln) is very careless about leaving his office open and unlocked during the day— half the time I go in and get my papers, etc., without anyone being there as was the case yesterday. The letter was only marked twenty-five [cents] and even if he had been there and known it was double, he would not have charged me any more—luckily he is a clever fellow and a particular friend of mine. If he is there when I carry this to the office—I will get him to 'Frank' it." Risking a $10 fine, Lincoln wrote on the back: "Free, A. Lincoln, P.M., New Salem, Ill., Sept. 22."

At the same time, he was scrupulous in keeping financial records, and he fiercely resented any imputation of irregularity. When George C. Spears requested a receipt for the postage he had paid on his newspaper, Lincoln responded sharply: "I am some what surprised at your request. I will however comply with it. The law requires News paper postage to be paid in advance and now that I have waited a full year you choose to wound my feelings by insinuating that unless you get a receipt I will probably make you pay it again." More than a year after the New Salem office had been discontinued and after he moved to Springfield, he turned over to the Post Office Department the precise balance of his receipts, $248.63.

Though appointment as postmaster gave Lincoln a position in the community, an occasion to talk and visit with the residents of the town, and an opportunity to read all newspapers that came into the office, it did not provide a livelihood, and his friends looked for ways for him to supplement his income. One of them learned that John Calhoun, recently appointed county surveyor, was looking for an assistant and strongly recommended Lincoln. Before accepting, Lincoln hesitated because Calhoun was a very active Democratic politician, but he was assured that he would not be expected to compromise his principles. Knowing nothing of surveying, he secured copies of Abel Flint's *System of Geometry and Trigonometry with a Treatise on Surveying* and Robert Gibson's *Treatise on Practical Surveying*, scraped together enough money to procure a compass and chain, and, as he said, "went at it." Setting himself to learn the principles of trigonometry and their practical application to surveying, he studied very hard, and he was soon able to take to the field.

Surveying was difficult work. On a typical survey Lincoln, accompanied by two chainmen, had to push into briar patches, slog through swamps, and cut through wilderness undergrowth in order to set their markers and measure their angles. At the end of a day's work he would often come in with his clothes torn and his legs scratched up from the briars. When friends tried to commiserate with him, he would just laugh and say "that was a poore [sic] man's lot." But after one of his early surveys, for a farmer named Russell Godbey who lived six miles north of New Salem, he accepted as payment two buckskins, which Hannah Armstrong, Jack Armstrong's wife, used to "fox" his pants to protect him from briars. Ordinarily, however, he received payment in cash, according to a scale set up by the state, which allowed him $2.50 for each quarter section surveyed.

As Lincoln gained experience, he undertook increasingly complicated surveys. He was the principal surveyor in locating a road from the Sangamon

River, through New Salem, and on in the direction of Jacksonville. New Boston, Bath, Petersburg, and Huron were among the towns that he laid out. All his work was careful and meticulously accurate. As a resident of Athens, Illinois, recalled: "Mr Lincoln had the monopoly of finding the lines, and when any dispute arose among the Settlers Mr Lincolns Compass and chain always settled the matter satisfactorily."

When his surveying fees were added to his post office commission, he began to have enough to live on. Then the notes that he had so freely signed to finance the Berry & Lincoln store began to come due.

IV

This financial pressure gave special urgency to Lincoln's second race for the state legislature in 1834. Apart from all other reasons, he wanted to be elected because of the salary. Though party lines were by this time more sharply defined, with Democrats strongly backing their hero, Andrew Jackson, in his decision to kill the Bank of the United States, and their opponents, now known as Whigs, as fiercely loyal to Jackson's archenemy, Henry Clay, Lincoln made no mention of his support for Clay's American System. Indeed, he issued no statement of principles and published no speeches. Instead, he conducted a handshaking campaign, stopping to greet and talk with voters in every part of the county where his work as deputy surveyor brought him. Reaching Rowan Herndon's house near Island Grove, he went out into the field where some thirty men were at work harvesting grain. When some of them grumbled that they would never vote for a man who could not hold his own in the field, he responded, "Boys if that is all I am shure [sic] of your votes." Taking hold of the cradle with perfect ease, he led the harvesters on one full round of the field. "The Boys was satisfied," Herndon recalled, "and I don't think he Lost a vote in the Croud."

Behind Lincoln's silence on the issues lay political calculation. The village of New Salem was as strongly in favor of Whig policies as Lincoln himself; it needed the roads, commerce, and economic expansion that the Whig party promised. But the self-subsisting farmers in the countryside were Democrats, ardent supporters of President Jackson. Many of these, like the Clary's Grove boys, favored Lincoln on purely personal grounds and, according to Stephen T. Logan, his future law partner, "they told their democratic brethren in the other parts of the county that they must help elect Lincoln, or else they wouldn't support the other democratic candidates." As a result, Democratic leaders approached Lincoln with a deal. There were, again, thirteen candidates for the state legislature, only four of whom would be elected. Democrats especially feared John Todd Stuart, who was not only a leader of the Whig party but a likely candidate for the next United States Congress. They offered to drop their support of two Democratic candidates and to concentrate their votes on Lincoln, in the hope of electing him rather than Stuart.

Lincoln immediately put their proposition before Stuart, who was so confident of his own strength that he urged him to accept the Democrats' support. The election returns on August 4 justified Stuart's course. Lincoln received 1,376 votes—the second-highest number of any candidate—and was elected. So was Stuart, who narrowly edged out the strongest Democratic contender.

Elated, Lincoln began to prepare for his new job by beginning to study law. A year earlier he had thought about this possibility but had rejected it as being beyond his scope. But since that time he had had several opportunities to observe the proceedings in the Sangamon County Circuit Court in Springfield, where he was called as a witness in two cases and was impaneled as a juror in three small cases. Observing the highly informal procedures of the court and learning that most of the leading lawyers were self-educated doubtless led him to believe that this was a forum in which he could successfully compete. During the 1834 canvass Stuart encouraged him to reconsider his decision and offered to help him. After the election he often rode, or sometimes walked, into Springfield to borrow Stuart's law books. When he first showed up at the office, he was timid and quiet, and Henry E. Dummer, Stuart's law partner, thought him "the most uncouth looking young man I ever saw." On one of these trips to Springfield, he attended an auction, where he picked up a copy of Blackstone's *Commentaries* and then, as he wrote later, he "went at it in good earnest."

In other ways, too, Lincoln began readying himself for his first appearance at Vandalia, the state capital. Shortly after the election, he approached Coleman Smoot, one of the richest men in the New Salem area, asking to borrow some money to carry him over until he began to receive his legislator's salary. Of the $200 Smoot loaned him, Lincoln spent $60 on the first suit of clothes he ever owned. It was, for the time, a large amount—more than half a month's salary of the governor of the state—but Lincoln was determined, as he told Smoot, "to make a decent appearance in the legislature."

Lincoln's first session as an Illinois state legislator (December 1, 1834, to February 13, 1835) was not a memorable one. For the most part, he was a silent observer of the proceedings, exceptionally faithful in his attendance, and generally following the lead of more experienced legislators like Stuart, with whom he roomed. He found it easy enough to get around in Vandalia, which, though the state capital, was only a village of some 800 or 900 inhabitants. Like most of the eighty other legislators, he stayed at one of the boarding taverns, which bore names like the Vandalia Inn and the Sign of the Green Tree. Though he was the next-to-the-youngest member of the legislature, he quickly learned that he was no more inexperienced than most of his colleagues. All but nineteen of the fifty-five House members were, like himself, serving their first term.

The statehouse, where the legislators met, was a badly built, two-story brick building, hastily erected after fire had destroyed an earlier capitol. By 1834 it was already dilapidated, for the walls bulged ominously at points and falling chunks of plaster occasionally imperiled speakers. The House of Representatives met in a large, bare room on the ground floor, where members sat three to a table. Furnishings were spare: a pail and two or three tin cups for water; boxes containing sand for tobacco chewers; candles for night work; and a stove. Most of the business of the legislature, like that of any lawmaking assembly, was of a routine nature, like appropriating $2.50 to Marmaduke Vickery "for fixing the stoves for [the] State House," passing a bill to encourage the killing of wolves, and granting permission to Clayborn Bell to change his name to Clayborn Elder Bell.

As the session wore on, Lincoln grew more at home in the legislature. His skill in drawing up legislation, hesitant at first, steadily improved, and his colleagues, impressed by his mastery of the technical language of the law, began asking him to draft bills for them in his firm, legible handwriting. He participated more freely in the debates and apparently convulsed the house in brief remarks on the naming of a surveyor of Schuyler County. In the belief that the incumbent was dead, a new surveyor had been named, who discovered that his predecessor was very much alive. (He "persisted not to die," as Lincoln expressed it.) Legislators were in a quandary until Lincoln urged them to do nothing. If in the future "the old surveyor should hereafter conclude to die, there would be a new one ready made without troubling the legislature." Legislative wit is so rare that, however feeble, it elicits laughs.

V

At the end of the session Lincoln drew his salary warrant for $158—he had already received $100 in December—and returned to New Salem with more money than he had ever had before. He needed it all. Just before he left for Vandalia, the Sangamon County Circuit Court issued a judgment against him and Berry for overdue notes. When they were unable to pay, the sheriff attached their personal possessions, including Lincoln's horse, saddle, bridle, surveying compass, and other equipment. The action deprived Lincoln of his means of livelihood. Then, in January 1835, while Lincoln was still in Vandalia, Berry died, leaving practically no estate. Legally, Lincoln was responsible for only half their debts, but he insisted he would pay them all when he was able. That obligation, which Lincoln and his friends jokingly referred to as his "national debt," weighed heavily on him when he returned from the state capital. Indeed, it would be several years before he could pay it off.

With little else to do during the spring and summer of 1835 except deliver the mail twice a week, he could spend all his time on his law books. To judge from the advice that he later gave other law students, he read Blackstone through twice. As usual, he did not merely memorize the arguments but rephrased them two or three times in his own language until he had mastered them. R. B. Rutledge, whose father owned the inn at New Salem, recalled that "his practice was, when he wished to indelibly fix anything he was reading or studying on his mind, to write it down, [I] have known him to write whole pages of books he was reading." Soon he branched out to study the other standard texts of the era: Chitty's *Pleadings,* Greenleaf's *Evidence,* and Joseph Story's *Equity Jurisprudence.* In an 1860 autobiography one four-word sentence summarized how he mastered these difficult works: "He studied with nobody."

Much of the time as he read, he sat, barefoot, propped against a tree, and then, for variety, he would lie on his back and rest his long legs on the tree trunk. One friend noted with amusement that he moved as the sun moved, grinding around the trunk to keep in the shade. Even when he walked, he carried a book with him, and, though he pleasantly responded to interruptions, he promptly went back to reading. "He read so much—was so studious—too[k] so little physical exercise—was so laborious in his studies," Henry McHenry remembered, "that he became emaciated and his best friends were afraid that he would craze himself."

After a month or so, life began to get a little easier for him. In March, when the sheriff put up his belongings for auction, his horse was for some unexplained reason exempt. "Uncle" James Short, one of Lincoln's greatest admirers, bid in the surveying equipment for $120 and immediately returned it to him. By the end of the month he was again in the field, making surveys and earning fees. But, as he noted in an autobiographical statement, he only "mixed in the surveying to pay board and clothing bills."

Behind Lincoln's urgency to become a lawyer there was now a new force: he was romantically involved. From almost the day of his arrival in New Salem, the good women of the village had matrimonial plans for him. They found his awkward clumsiness touching, and they noted how tender he was with small children and how affectionate he was to kittens and other pets. He needed someone to cook for him and feed him, so as to fill out that hollow frame, someone to clean and repair his clothing, which—except for that expensive legislative suit—seemed never to fit and always to be in tatters. In short, he needed a wife.

But he was extremely awkward around women. With the wives of old friends, like Mrs. Hannah Armstrong, he could be courtly, even affectionate, but he froze in the presence of eligible girls. At his store he had been reluctant to wait on them, and at Rutledge Tavern he was unwilling to sit at the table when a well-dressed Virginia woman and her three daughters were guests. Efforts of New Salem matrons to match him with a Miss Short and a Miss Berry failed completely.

But one young woman in the village did interest him greatly. She was Ann Rutledge, the daughter of one of the founders of the village and the owner of the tavern, where he roomed and boarded some of the time. She was a very pretty girl, with fair skin, blue eyes, and auburn hair. Only five feet and three inches tall, she weighed between one hundred and twenty and one hundred and thirty pounds. "Heavy set," Mrs. Samuel Hill called her—but in Lincoln's eyes this was no disadvantage, for all of the women he loved were plump. In addition, a villager recalled, she was "good—kind, social—goodhearted." Another rhapsodized that she had "as pure and kind a heart as an angel, full of love—kindness—sympathy."

When Lincoln first came to New Salem, Ann was only a schoolgirl in Mentor Graham's school, and, as always, he found it easy to talk with someone younger than himself. Later he saw more of her when she took over the management of her father's tavern, the largest building in New Salem, a log house with two large rooms on the ground floor and two more upstairs for guests. Pretty, quick, and domestic, she naturally attracted the attention of eligible bachelors, like Samuel Hill, the ugly, crude, but well-to-do storekeeper, whose advances she did not encourage. Hill's partner, John McNeil, a New Yorker, who boarded at Rutledge Tavern, met a warmer reception. Presently it became known throughout the village that they were to be married. Then, toward the fall of 1833, McNeil made a confession to Ann. His real name was John McNamar. (Lincoln already knew this, because he had witnessed land transactions where the man signed his proper name.) His father had fallen on hard times in New York, and he had come West to redeem the family's fortune. He had changed his name because, as Herndon put it, he feared "that if the family in New York had known where he was they would have settled down on him, and before he could have accumulated any property would have sunk him beyond recovery." But now he had saved up, from his store and his farm, some $10,000 or $12,000, a sizable sum, and he was going to return to New York and bring his family back to New Salem with him. Then he and Ann would be married.

After McNamar left, Ann told his story to other members of her family, who received it with skepticism. There was, they thought, something wrong in McNamar's story about deserting his family in order to save them. A man who changed his name must have a lurid past. Probably he had jilted Ann and would never return to New Salem. Such fears, however, were kept very quiet, for in Victorian America, a spurned woman was suspected of having some moral blight.

Lincoln, of course, knew of the engagement and of McNamar's departure for the East. As postmaster, he was necessarily aware of the letters the engaged couple exchanged—fairly frequently at first, and then more and more rarely, until correspondence from McNamar ceased. But he, like everybody else, thought the couple was still betrothed, and, as Dr. Duncan, one of the two physicians in New Salem, said, he regarded Ann's engagement to McNamar as "an insurmountable bar[r]ier." These circumstances may have fostered rather than blighted his own interest in Ann. Had she remained free, he might well have remained distant and formal, as he was with other unmarried women, because he was always afraid of intimacy. But since Ann was committed to another, he was able to keep up a joking, affectionate relationship with her.

How that friendship developed into a romance cannot be reconstructed from the record. No letter from Ann Rutledge is known to exist, and in the thousands of pages of Lincoln's correspondence, there is not one mention of her name. Apart from one highly dubious anecdote about a quilting bee, there are no stories about the courtship, which, because of Ann's ambiguous relationship to McNamar, was intentionally kept very quiet. Lincoln's long, uninterrupted absence in Vandalia, from November through February, suggests an affectionate, rather than a passionate, affair.

Sometime in 1835, Lincoln and Ann came to an understanding. In later years old-time New Salem residents differed as to whether there was a formal engagement, and whether it was "conditional" or "unconditional." Both parties had good reason to hesitate. Lincoln, who had no profession and little money, doubted his ability to support a wife. Ann strongly felt "the propriety of seeing McNamar, [to] inform him of the change in her feelings and seek an honorable releas[e] before consum[m]ating the engagement with Mr. L. by Marriage." According to Ann's cousin, James McCrady Rutledge, they agreed "to wait a year for their marriage after their engagement until Abraham Lincoln was Admitted to the bar." Understandably, Ann hesitated before agreeing to such an indeterminate arrangement, telling her cousin "that engagements made too far a hed [sic], sometimes failed, that one had failed, (meaning her engagement with McNamar)."

That terrible summer of 1835, one of the hottest in Illinois history, when it rained every day, was desperately hard on these young people. When Lincoln was not slogging through the water that covered the whole country, completing his surveys, he worked so unceasingly on his law books that friends feared for his health. They had more reason to worry about Ann's, for in August she fell ill with "brain fever"—probably typhoid, caused when the flood contaminated the Rutledge well—and was put to bed. Though her doctor prescribed absolute quiet, she insisted on seeing Lincoln. A few days afterward she became unconscious, and on August 25 she died.

Lincoln was devastated. This terrible blow must have brought to his mind memories of earlier losses: his brother Thomas, his sister Sarah, and, above all, his mother. His nerves, already frayed by overwork and too much study, began to give way, and he fell into a profound depression. He managed to hold himself together for a time, but after the funeral it began to rain again and his melancholy deepened. He told Mrs. Bennett Abell, with whom he was staying, "that he could not bare [sic] the idea of its raining on her Grave." So distraught was he that his friends persuaded him to visit his old friend Bowling Green, who lived about a mile south of New Salem. There he found rest and comfort.

By September 24 he was back making surveys, but the memory of Ann Rutledge did not quickly fade. Many years later, after his first election as President, he began talking with an old friend, Isaac Cogdal, about early days in New Salem, asking the present whereabouts of many of the early settlers. When the name of Rutledge came up, Cogdal ventured to ask whether it was true that Lincoln had fallen in love with Ann. "It is true—true indeed I did,"

Lincoln replied, if Cogdal's memory can be trusted. "I loved the woman dearly and soundly: she was a handsome girl—would have made a good loving wife. . . . I did honestly and truly love the girl and think often—often of her now."

VI

The death of Ann Rutledge may have symbolized for Lincoln the approaching death of New Salem. After an auspicious beginning the village, lacking roads and river transportation for marketing its produce, began to decline. Property values dropped; the lot on which the Berry & Lincoln store stood, once valued at $100, now went at auction for $10. More and more residents moved away, mostly to nearby Petersburg, which Lincoln finished surveying in February 1836. It was clear that he, too, would soon have to leave.

The special session of the legislature, called for the winter of 1835–1836, did much to shape his future course, but Lincoln was not a leader in any of the three major changes it produced. At this session, for the first time, national politics intruded sharply into the proceedings of the legislature. A presidential election was approaching, and Democrats, aware of considerable hostility toward Andrew Jackson's choice of a successor, Martin Van Buren, sought to unite the party by convening a statewide political convention in Vandalia on the first day of the legislative session. In addition to endorsing Van Buren, the convention vigorously condemned all who were "striving by means of false representations, to create divisions and dissentions [*sic*] among the Democratic party." The action infuriated the Whigs, the minority party, who had hitherto been successful in statewide elections only by encouraging factionalism among the Democrats. Angrily Whig legislators, including Lincoln, condemned the convention system as a device of political manipulators to kill off candidates opposed to them, which "ought not to be tolerated in a republican government," because it was "dangerous to the liberties of the people." It took some years for the Whigs to learn that they, too, could benefit from just this same system, and in the future Lincoln's political career would be shaped in party conventions.

More immediately important was the reapportionment legislation of this session. The population of Illinois had been growing rapidly, mainly in the northern and central parts of the state, and the southern counties, which had been settled first, were heavily overrepresented. Lincoln was in favor of only a moderate reallocation of seats and consequently opposed the more drastic measure approved by the legislature, which gave Sangamon County the largest delegation in the House of Representatives—seven, rather than four, members. The change had major consequences for Lincoln's future political success.

In a third major initiative Lincoln was again a follower, not a leader. One of the main purposes for which Governor Joseph Duncan had called the special session was to enact legislation to support the building of a canal that, by connecting the Illinois and Chicago rivers, would link Lake Michigan to the Mississippi. This project held for Illinois an importance comparable with that of the Erie Canal for New York, but hitherto the state had been willing only to authorize and encourage the construction of the canal, rather than to assist the enterprise financially. Now, finally, it was clear that more was needed, and Duncan asked the state to give "the most liberal support" to the project. The legislature obliged by authorizing a loan of $500,000 to support the bonds of the Illinois and Michigan Canal. On a crucial vote (28 to 27) Lincoln supported the measure, which opened the way to subsequent state subsidies for the building of roads and canals.

The vote marked a shift in Lincoln's position on internal improvements. He had long been a supporter of improved river transportation, of canals, of better roads, and, eventually, of railroads, all of which were part of his vision of a prosperous society, linked together by a network of commerce and communication. For a time he hoped that the federal government would distribute "the proceeds of the sales of the public lands to the several states, to enable our state, in common with others, to dig canals and construct rail roads, without borrowing money and paying interest on it." But, failing that, he had felt that such improvements should be completed by private capital. Now, however, he was convinced that unless Illinois was to fall far behind other states, it must support internal improvements with the state's credit.

The impact these three changes had on Lincoln's course would not be evident until the 1836 session of the legislature, and before that he had to run for reelection. Announcing his candidacy in June, he explained his position on the suffrage issue, which was currently a subject of controversy. · Illinois extended the ballot to all white male citizens who had resided in the state for six months; foreign-born immigrants did not have the franchise until they were naturalized. Large numbers of these were Irish-born workers on the Illinois and Michigan Canal. Democrats favored giving them the vote, but most Whigs did not. Lincoln, who shared the standard Whig belief that property holding ought to be a prerequisite for voting, favored "all sharing the privileges of the government, who assist in bearing its burthens." That meant, he explained, "admitting all whites to the right of suffrage, who pay taxes or bear arms"—and then he obfuscated his message by adding "by no means excluding females." Far from being an early advocate of women's suffrage, Lincoln was apparently making a tongue-in-cheek joke, because everybody knew that under Illinois law women neither paid taxes (husbands or guardians paid them for women who owned property) nor served in the militia. Lincoln's announcement revealed incidentally that he, like virtually every other Illinois politician, did not think African-Americans were entitled to the ballot.

The campaign was a strenuous one. Lincoln, along with the sixteen other candidates, traveled by horseback from one village to another, addressing public meetings at hamlets like Salisbury, Allenton, and Cotton Hill. Speaking began in the morning and often continued until well into the afternoon, and, as party lines were coming to be more clearly defined, candidates gave their views not merely on local issues but on national ones as well. At times tempers flared. Ninian W. Edwards, the aristocratic and wealthy son of a former governor, was so offended by the remarks of one of his competitors that he drew a pistol on him. Even Lincoln, usually genial, lashed back angrily when "Truth Teller" falsely charged he had opposed paying a state loan, branding the author "a *liar* and a *scoundrel*" and promising "to give his proboscis a good wringing." Mostly, though, he managed criticism with more finesse. At a Springfield rally, when a rival named George Forquer, a well-to-do lawyer who had recently changed his allegiance to the Democratic party and had received a lucrative appointment in return, attacked Lincoln in a sarcastic speech, saying that it was time for this presumptuous young man to be taken down, Lincoln calmly waited his turn. Then, remembering that Forquer had recently installed a lightning rod on his house—the first Lincoln had ever seen, and an object of some curiosity—he lashed back: "The gentleman commenced . . . by saying that this young man will have to be taken down. . . . I am not so young in years as I am in the trick and trades of a politician; but . . . I would rather die now, than, like the gentleman, change my politics and simultaneous with the change receive an office worth $3,000 per year, and then have to erect a lightning-rod over my house to protect a guilty conscience from an offended God."

In the election on August 1, Lincoln received more votes than any other candidate. He continued to have the strong support of his neighbors in New Salem, who were Whigs like himself. But the more rural neighborhoods, like Clary's Grove, were Democratic, and even Jack Armstrong, who continued to be a warm personal friend, failed to vote for him. In the minds of some who had previously been his most loyal followers, Lincoln was distancing himself from his rural origins and was already less a part of New Salem than of Springfield.

VII

The Sangamon delegation to the 1836–1837 session of the legislature became known as the "Long Nine," because the two senators and the seven representatives were all unusually tall in an age when six-foot men were rare; some, like Lincoln, were veritable giants. Their collective height, it was said, totaled fifty-four feet. But they were distinguished even more by their enthusiastic support of two objectives: promotion of Springfield, and state support for internal improvements. The delegation looked to Lincoln, now an experienced legislator though the next-to-youngest member of the group, as their floor leader.

They came to Vandalia instructed by a recent county convention to promote internal improvements. At the capital a statewide convention further agitated the question, demanding a comprehensive program backed by $10,000,000 in state bonds. In the House of Representatives the initiative was taken by Stephen A. Douglas, the newly elected member from Morgan County (Jacksonville), who instantly assumed leadership of the Democrats. Only five feet four inches tall but with a massive head and a deep baritone voice, Douglas at the age of twenty-three had already mastered the arts of legislative politics, and he was eager to pass laws that would hasten the economic development of the state. Promptly he introduced a plan for the construction of a central railroad, running north and south through the state, connected with two major east-west lines, all underwritten by the state. Connected with this would be the speedy completion of the Illinois and Michigan Canal.

Whigs welcomed Douglas's initiative, for the internal improvements issue was neither sectional nor partisan. As the legislation moved through the House, more and more additions were made, in order to secure the support of those counties untouched by the main rail lines. Without making surveys or calling for expert advice, the legislature provided for loans up to $10,000,000 to construct a central railroad from Cairo to Galena; one major east-west line, the Northern Cross, connecting Jacksonville, Springfield, and Danville; and six spur lines connecting with the Cairo-Galena route. For the improvement of five rivers $400,000 was allotted, and those counties that benefited neither from railroads nor from river improvement were to receive $200,000. (The Illinois and Michigan Canal was funded under separate legislation.) The bill gave something to everybody.

Lincoln and the other members of the Long Nine strongly supported the measure. Though Lincoln was not a member of the committee that shaped the bill, he was frequently present during its deliberations, and on every roll call he and the rest of the Sangamon delegation voted for it and for all amendments expanding its scope. So did an overwhelming majority of all members of the state legislature. The law represented to them an ambitious but sensible program for the economic development of the state. Envying Massachusetts with its 140 miles of railroad in operation and Pennsylvania with its 218 miles of railroads and 914 miles of canals, nearly everyone agreed with the *Alton Telegraph* that the new legislation would be "the means of advancing the prosperity and future greatness of our state, as much as the birth of Washington did that of the United States."

The panic of 1837 put an end to these high hopes and effectively killed the internal improvements plan. Very little construction was ever completed, and the state was littered with unfinished roads and partially dug canals. The state's finances, pledged to support the grandiose plan, suffered, and Illinois bonds fell to 15¢ on the dollar, while annual interest charges were more than eight times the total state revenues. Inevitably there was a search for scapegoats, and questions were raised about Lincoln's role in promoting such a harebrained and disastrous scheme.

Such criticism was misplaced. It was not stupid or irresponsible to support the internal improvements plan. Had prosperity continued, it might have done as much for the prosperity of Illinois as the construction of the Erie Canal did for that of New York. Nor was it fair to blame Lincoln for the enactment of the legislation. Certainly he favored and supported it, but he was not a prime mover behind the bill. If any person could claim that role, it was Stephen A. Douglas.

Later some critics opposed to the internal improvements scheme suggested that Lincoln and the other members of the Long Nine supported it only as a means to secure the removal of the state capital to Springfield. In the next session of the legislature General W. L. D. Ewing charged "that the Springfield delegation had sold out to the internal improvement men, and had promised their support to every measure that would gain them a vote to the law removing the seat of government." But neither Lincoln's record nor that of the other members of the Long Nine showed a pattern of logrolling on the internal improvements legislation, and at the time there was no talk of a trade or a bribe.

It was certainly true that the primary objective of the Long Nine was the relocation of the capital to Springfield. The selection of Vandalia, most people felt, had been a mistake; it was too small, too inaccessible, and, most important, too far south in a state where the central and northern regions were growing most rapidly. But Springfield had rivals, for Alton, Jacksonville, Peoria, and other towns also recognized that relocation of the capital meant huge increases in land values, much new construction, and many jobs.

Those opposed to the choice of Springfield tried to whittle down the influence of the Sangamon delegation in the legislature. The leader in this maneuver was Usher F. Linder, the articulate and self-important representative from Coles County, who proposed splitting off the northwestern sections of Sangamon County, which was half the size of the state of Rhode Island, in order to create a new county, named after Martin Van Buren. The maneuver troubled Lincoln and the other members of the Long Nine, because a reduction in the number of Sangamon representatives at just this time would jeopardize Springfield's chances. They countered by proposing that the new county be carved out of Morgan County as well as Sangamon County, knowing that the representatives of Jacksonville, in Morgan County, would oppose it. Referred to a committee of which Lincoln was chairman, the bill passed the house despite his negative report, but it was killed in the senate. That was exactly what Lincoln had hoped.

More serious was Linder's threat to investigate the Illinois State Bank, located in Springfield, which would probably put that institution out of business and at the same time deliver a severe blow to Springfield's chance to become the capital. Linder shared the general Democratic hatred of all banks and also opposed moving the capital to Springfield. Quickly friends of the bank rushed down from Springfield and supplied Lincoln with facts and ideas to defeat Linder's proposal.

Thus armed, Lincoln on January 11, 1837, took the floor to make his first extended speech in the state legislature. A clumsy, poorly organized effort, it was in part an *ad hominem* attack on Linder's haughty airs and entangled rhetoric. Lincoln claimed that the demand for an investigation was "exclusively the work of politicians," whom he defined as "a set of men who have interests aside from the interests of the people, and who, to say the most of them, are, taken as a mass, at least one long step removed from honest men." Then he tried to remove the sting of his remarks by adding: "I say this with the greater freedom because, being a politician myself, none can regard it as personal."

Clearly not at home in discussing the economic issues involved in banking, Lincoln resorted to demagogy. An investigation of the bank, he claimed, would encourage "that lawless and mobocratic spirit, . . . which is already abroad in the land, and is spreading with rapid and fearful impetuosity, to the ultimate overthrow of every institution, or even moral principle, in which persons and property have hitherto found security."

Despite its imperfections, the speech helped Lincoln's standing, both in the legislature and in the public press. The *Vandalia Free Press* published it in full, and Springfield's *Sangamo Journal* reprinted it, with the editorial comment, "Our friend carries the true Kentucky rifle and when he fires he seldom fails of sending the shot home."

A third legislative initiative may have been only indirectly connected with plans to block the transfer of the capital to Springfield. Since the first publication of William Lloyd Garrison's *Liberator* in 1831, Southern states had been growing increasingly angry over the rise of antislavery in the North, and Southern legislatures began passing resolutions demanding the suppression of abolitionist societies, which they said were circulating incendiary pamphlets among the slaves. These complaints received a generally favorable hearing in most Northern states, and Illinois, with its population largely of Southern birth, was no exception. The legislature passed a set of resolutions condemning abolitionist societies and affirming that slavery was guaranteed by the Constitution. For the most part, support of the resolutions was nonpartisan, though Democrats were more vehement in favoring them than Whigs, and they were adopted by the rousing vote of 77 to 6. The only reason to suspect that the opponents of Springfield had a hand in shaping these resolutions was the major role that Linder played in sponsoring them —the same Linder who had tried to partition Sangamon County and to destroy the Illinois State Bank at Springfield. Doubtless he wanted to show that Springfield, on that line where Southern and Northern settlements in Illinois were beginning to touch, was far less sympathetic to the slave states, which absorbed so much of the produce of Illinois, than Alton or Vandalia.

If this was his plan, it succeeded, because two of the Sangamon delegation, Lincoln and Dan Stone, a Vermonter, voted against the resolutions. Because neither made any public statement at the time, the damage that their votes did to support for Springfield in southern Illinois was kept to a minimum. Only after the removal of the capital and an internal improvements bill were agreed on did Stone and Lincoln present a protest against the resolutions. It was a cautious, limited dissent. Instead of the resolution of the General Assembly declaring that "the right of property in slaves, is sacred to the slave-holding States by the Federal Constitution," Stone and Lincoln suggested, "The Congress of the United States has no power, under the constitution, to interfere with the institution of slavery in the different States." Where the General Assembly announced, "we highly disapprove of the formation of abolition societies, and of the doctrines promulgated by them," the two Sangamon legislators voiced their belief "that the institution of slavery is founded on both injustice and bad policy; but that the promulgation of abolition doctrines tends rather to increase than to abate its evils."

After defeating all efforts to undermine the influence of the Sangamon delegation, Lincoln and the other members of the Long Nine shepherded through the legislature the bill to move the capital. The maneuvering required a delicate touch, and Lincoln's political skills were repeatedly tested. Several times it seemed that the bill to relocate the capital would meet certain defeat. On one occasion, in order to eliminate the smaller and poorer towns from the competition to replace Vandalia, Lincoln drafted an amendment requiring that the city selected must donate $50,000 and two acres of land for new state buildings; then, to keep it from being known that this was a move in the interest of Springfield, which could afford such a gift, he allowed the amendment to be introduced by a member from Coles County. Twice the bill was tabled, and it was, as Robert L. Wilson, one of the Long Nine recalled, "to all appearance . . . beyond resussitation [sic]." But Lincoln, Wilson reported, "never for one moment despaired but called his Colleagues to his room for consultation," and gave each an assignment to lobby doubtful members. When debate was renewed, the outcome was still doubtful. To win further support Lincoln accepted two unimportant amendments and added one of his own: "The General Assembly reserves the right to repeal this act at any time hereafter." It was in reality meaningless, for of course the legislature always had a right to repeal laws; but the change gave a plausible excuse to vote for the bill, which passed, 46 to 37. After that came the balloting on the site, and from the initial tally it was clear that Springfield had a strong lead. On the fourth ballot the work of the Long Nine paid off, and on February 28, Springfield received a clear majority of all the votes.

That night the victorious Sangamon delegation had a victory celebration, at Capp's Tavern, to which all members of the legislature were invited. Cigars, oysters, almonds, and raisins disappeared rapidly, as did eighty-one bottles of champagne, for which the wealthy Ninian Edwards paid $223.50. Afterward there were further celebrations in Springfield and other parts of Sangamon County, which the Long Nine attended. At the Athens rally the toast was "Abraham Lincoln one of Natures Noblemen."

When the legislature adjourned, Lincoln returned to New Salem to say good-bye to his old friends. In September two justices of the Illinois Supreme Court had licensed him to practice law, and on March 1 his name was entered on the roll of attorneys in the office of the clerk of the Supreme Court. On April 15, 1837, he removed to Springfield, where Stuart took him into partnership, and the two opened an office at No. 4 Hoffman's Row.

Lincoln's Early Years in Kentucky, Indiana, & Illinois

IOWA
MICHIGAN
ILLINOIS
INDIANA
OHIO
KENTUCKY
Areas of Detail

Sangamon R.
Beardstown
Petersburg
Quincy
New Salem
Sangamo Town
Decatur
Springfield
Jacksonville

Illinois R.

Mississippi R.

MISSOURI

ILLINOIS

Miles
0   30
Kms.
0   30

Vandalia

Alton

© A. Karl / J. Kemp, 1995

Vincennes

ILLINOIS

INDIANA

Wabash R.

Pigeon R.

Ohio R.

PERRY CO.

Louisville

Boonville

Little Pigeon Cr.

Rockport

HARDIN CO.

Elizabethtown

Knob Creek Farm

KENTUCKY

Green R.

Hogdenville

Kms.
0   30

Sinking Spring Farm (Lincoln's Birthplace)

Nolin Cr.

Miles
0   30

CHAPTER THREE

Cold, Calculating, Unimpassioned Reason

———◆———

On April 15, 1837, Lincoln rode into Springfield on a borrowed horse, with all his worldly possessions crammed into the two saddlebags. At the general store of A. Y. Ellis & Company on the west side of the town square, he inquired how much a mattress for a single bed, plus sheets and pillow, would cost. Joshua F. Speed, one of the proprietors, reckoned up the figures and announced a total of $17. Lincoln replied that was doubtless fair enough but that he did not have so much money. Telling Speed that he had come to Springfield to try an "experiment as a lawyer," he asked for credit until Christmas, adding in a sad voice: "If I fail in this, I do not know that I can ever pay you."

Speed, who knew this young man by reputation and had heard him make a political speech, suggested a way he could avoid incurring a debt that clearly troubled him. "I have a large room with a double bed up-stairs, which you are very welcome to share with me," he offered.

"Where is your room?" asked Lincoln.

When Speed pointed to the winding stairs that led from the store to the second floor, Lincoln picked up his saddlebags and went up. Shortly afterward he returned beaming with pleasure and announced, "Well, Speed, I am moved!"

Such a quick alternation from deep despair to blithe confidence was characteristic of Lincoln's early years in the new state capital. He was trying to put together the fragmented pieces of his personality into a coherent pattern. Sometimes he felt he was the prisoner of his passions, but at other times he thought that he could master his world through reason. Often he was profoundly discouraged, and during these years he experienced his deepest bouts of depression. But these moods alternated with periods of exuberant self-confidence and almost annoying optimism. In short, he was still a very young man.

I

To Eastern observers, Springfield in the 1830s was a frontier town. Though there were a few brick edifices, many of the residences were still log houses. If the roads were wide, they were unpaved; in the winter wagons struggled through axle-deep mud, and in the summer the dust was suffocating. The town had no sidewalks, and at crossings pedestrians had to leap from one chunk of wood to another. Hogs freely roamed the streets, and there was a powerful stench from manure piled outside the stables. After visiting Springfield, William Cullen Bryant came away with an impression of "dirt and discomfort."

But this was the most cosmopolitan and sophisticated place Lincoln had ever lived. Though Springfield had been in existence only since 1821, it was now a thriving community with 1,500 residents. The Sangamon County Courthouse occupied the center of the town, which was laid out in a regular, rectangular grid. The north-south streets were numbered; those running east-west were named after American presidents. The courthouse—soon to be replaced by the new state capitol—was surrounded by nineteen dry goods stores, seven groceries, four drugstores, two clothing stores, and a bookstore. Four hotels cared for transients. In addition to schools and an "academy" (roughly equivalent to a high school), the town boasted six churches. The professions were represented by eighteen doctors and eleven lawyers. There was a Whig newspaper, the *Sangamo Journal,* edited by Simeon Francis, to whom Lincoln during the previous sessions of the legislature had frequently sent news from Vandalia; and it would shortly be joined by the Democratic organ, the *Illinois Republican,* later rechristened the *Illinois State Register.*

Lincoln had every intention of becoming a part of this bustling community, but, in addition to a lack of education and money, he had a handicap: he was in a sense engaged. After the death of Ann Rutledge, the older women of New Salem urged him to find a wife, as most of the other young men his age were doing. But there were not many eligible young women in the vicinity, and, anyway, he was always awkward in their presence. He had, however, taken a liking to a sister of Mrs. Bennett Abell who visited New Salem in 1833 or 1834. The daughter of a well-to-do Kentucky family, Mary Owens was a handsome young woman with black hair, dark eyes, fair skin, and magnificent white teeth. She impressed everyone with her gay and lively disposition, and the residents of the village considered her "a very intellectual woman—well educated." After she returned to Kentucky, Lincoln is said to have boasted to Mrs. Abell that "if ever that girl comes back to New Salem I am going to marry her."

On her second visit—about a year after the death of Ann Rutledge—Lincoln began courting Mary Owens, and at first she reciprocated his interest. Then both began to have second thoughts. Granting Lincoln's "goodness of heart," Mary felt that "his training had been different from mine; hence there was not that congeniality which would otherwise have existed." Small events pointed to future difficulties. When she and Lincoln went for a walk with Mrs. Bowling Green, who was struggling to carry a very fat baby, he made no attempt to help her. On another occasion, when several young people were riding horseback to the Greens', she observed that all the other young women were assisted by their escorts in crossing a deep stream, while Lincoln rode ahead, paying her no attention. When she mentioned the neglect to him, he replied oafishly that he reckoned she could take care of herself. Soon she concluded that "Mr. Lincoln was deficient in those little links which make up the chain of woman's happiness."

Lincoln's doubts were even more severe. Maybe Mary had been a little too eager to return to New Salem. He feared "that her coming so readily showed that she was a trifle too willing." He began finding defects in her appearance. From her first visit he remembered that she was pleasingly stout —weighing between 150 and 180 pounds, according to contemporaries— but now she appeared "a fair match for Falstaff." In a burlesque account of the affair, written a few months later, he declared: "Now, when I beheld her, I could not for my life avoid thinking of my mother; and this, not from withered features, for her skin was too full of fat, to permit its contracting in to wrinkles, but from her want of teeth, weather-beaten appearance in general, and from a kind of notion that ran in my head, that *nothing* could have commenced at the size of infancy, and reached her present bulk in less than thirtyfive or forty years." His reservations were rationalizations. Painfully aware of his humble origins, he was not sure he could make this well-bred young woman happy, and he was too poor to support a wife in comfort. On a deeper level, the problem was that his personality was as yet so incompletely formed that he had great difficulty in reaching out to achieve intimacy with anyone else.

When Lincoln went to Vandalia in December 1836, he and Mary had not reached "any positive understanding," but both felt their informal arrangement might lead to marriage. For the next six months he engaged in an undignified attempt to get out of the liaison without injuring the lady's feelings or violating his sense of honor. Betraying no passion whatever and never mentioning the word "love," his letters to her were, as he admitted, "so dry and stupid" that he was reluctant to send them. His main purpose in writing was to get Mary to take the initiative in breaking off the courtship.

After he moved to Springfield, he grew more than ever convinced that she did not fit in. She would be unhappy, he warned. "There is a great deal of flourishing about in carriages here, which it would be your doom to see without shareing in it," he cautioned. "You would have to be poor without the means of hiding your poverty." "You have not been accustomed to hardship," he reminded her, "and it may be more severe than you now immagine."

Apparently neither Lincoln's letters nor the arguments he made when he revisited New Salem in the summer of 1837 convinced Mary that they were incompatible. He began to take a different tack, suggesting that it was for her emotional as well as her physical well-being that she should break off their relationship. "I want in all cases to do right, and most particularly so, in all cases with women," he told her, and he was convinced that it would be best for Mary if he left her alone. "For the purpose of making the matter as plain as possible," he wrote her, "I now say, that you can now drop the subject [of marriage], dismiss your thoughts (if you ever had any) from me forever, and leave this letter unanswered, without calling forth one accusing murmer from me." Indeed, if so doing would add to her peace of mind, "it is my sincere wish that you should." Then, having done his best to persuade her to break their understanding, he manfully announced: "I am willing, and even anxious to bind you faster, if I can be convinced that it will, in any considerable degree, add to your happiness."

If Mary wrote a reply to this left-handed proposal, it has not been preserved, but Lincoln recorded that she firmly and repeatedly refused his tepid offer of marriage. To his surprise, instead of being relieved, he felt "mortified almost beyond endurance." "My vanity was deeply wounded . . . that she whom I had taught myself to believe no body else would have, had actually rejected me with all my fancied greatness," he reported some months later. Once it was certain that Mary did not return his affections, he even began to suspect that he was "really a little in love with her." Immensely relieved that the whole affair was over, he wrote a farcical account of his failed courtship —carefully not mentioning Mary Owens by name—to amuse Mrs. O. H. Browning, which ended: "I have now come to the conclusion never again to think of marrying; and for this reason; I can never be satisfied with any one who would be blockhead enough to have me."

II

"This thing of living in Springfield is rather a dull business after all, at least it is so to me," Lincoln lamented to Mary Owens a month after he had moved from New Salem. "I am quite as lonesome here as [I] ever was anywhere in my life." No doubt he did feel isolated during his first few weeks in town, but he was probably exaggerating his feelings to discourage Mary from further thinking about marriage. Indeed, he was presently surrounded by friends and welcomed in Springfield society.

From the beginning Speed was his close companion, and he became perhaps the only intimate friend that Lincoln ever had. Four years younger than Lincoln, Speed was also a Kentuckian. Unlike Lincoln, though, Speed came from a prominent family that owned a prosperous plantation, called Farmington, near Louisville, tilled by seventy slaves. Speed had attended private schools in Kentucky and had studied for two years at St. Joseph's College, in Bardstown. Seeking to make his fortune, he came to Springfield and became a part proprietor of Ellis's store. With flashing blue eyes and a mane of dark curly hair, he was a handsome young man, whose vaguely Byronic air of elegance made him especially attractive to Springfield ladies.

For nearly four years Lincoln and Speed shared a double bed, and their most private thoughts, in the room above Speed's store. No one thought that there was anything irregular or unusual about the arrangement. It was rare for a single man to have a private room, and it was customary for two or more to sleep in the same bed. Years later, when Lincoln was a well-known lawyer, he and the other attorneys traveling the judicial circuit regularly shared beds; only Judge David Davis was allowed to sleep alone, not because of his dignified position but because he weighed over three hundred pounds. Much of the time when Lincoln and Speed were sharing a bed, young William H. Herndon, who had recently been withdrawn from Illinois College in Jacksonville and was clerking in Speed's store, slept in the same room, as did Charles R. Hurst, a clerk in another dry-goods store.

Around Lincoln and Speed gathered other young unmarried men of Springfield, like James H. Matheny, who would become the best man at Lincoln's wedding; Milton Hay, then a law student and clerk in the Stuart & Lincoln office; and James C. Conkling, a Princeton graduate who began practicing law in Springfield in 1838. Before the great fireplace in the back room of Speed's store, they met night after night, to talk and swap stories, and Lincoln with his endless repertoire of anecdotes was always the center of the group. Acting as an informal literary and debating society, the young men read each other's poems and other writings, and, as Herndon recalled, they staged debates on politics, religion, and all other subjects.

Lincoln quickly made other friends in town. William Butler, clerk of the Sangamon County Court, greatly liked this unusual young man who had just moved in from the country and, knowing that he was hard up, generously gave him free board at his house. Simeon Francis welcomed Lincoln to Springfield and opened the columns of the *Sangamo Journal* for anything he might care to write. And John Todd Stuart introduced his new partner to the more exclusive social circles of Springfield.

III

Lincoln found easy acceptance in Springfield because he arrived not as an unknown but as the partner of Stuart, one of the most prominent and successful lawyers in town. Unlike most beginning lawyers, who had to hunt around for business or accept cases that no one else would take, Lincoln began with a very full practice, for Stuart was concentrating on winning a seat in the United States House of Representatives and turned over most of the business of the firm to his junior partner.

Their office was a single room on the second floor in a group of brick buildings on Fifth Street known as Hoffman's Row, just a block north of the courthouse square. As Herndon remembered, it was furnished only with "a small lounge or bed, a chair containing a buffalo robe, in which the junior member was wont to sit and study, a hard wooden bench, a feeble attempt at a book-case, and a table which answered for a desk." Here Lincoln and Stuart received clients, heard their complaints, and advised what, if any, action was appropriate. If there was a question of legal precedents, the partners could consult their library, which consisted of a couple of volumes of *Illinois Reports* and some miscellaneous congressional documents, legislative proceedings, and law books; it was a meager resource, but at this time probably no law library in Springfield contained as many as one hundred books.

Lincoln had no difficulty in performing the routine work of the office, like drafting wills or writing deeds; he had done a certain amount of this for his neighbors in New Salem even before he was admitted to the bar. Many of the Stuart & Lincoln cases involved only an appearance before a justice of the peace, few of whom were lawyers. Thus when Joel Johnson accused John Grey of forcible detainer, Stuart & Lincoln represented him at Justice Clemment's hearing. Lincoln was thoroughly acquainted with these procedures, since he had regularly attended Bowling Green's court in New Salem.

More complex cases went to trial before the circuit court, where, again, Lincoln had some experience as an observer and as a witness. Indeed, his familiarity with the process, as well as his expertise as a surveyor, had caused the circuit court in Morgan County (Jacksonville) to use him, even before he was admitted to the bar, as what might be called a paralegal in a disputed case over land and timber.

But now, as a licensed attorney, usually operating without his partner or other associates, he had a much greater responsibility fully to master the forms and procedures of litigation, for even a minor, technical error could cause his client to lose his case. In bringing a case before the circuit court, a lawyer had first to decide whether to plead it "in law" or "in chancery"; the first referred to a highly formal set of proceedings and precedents derived from the British common law, while the second, sometimes called "equity" proceedings, followed somewhat more flexible and discretionary rules. In either case the attorney (and for clarity it will be assumed that he was representing the plaintiff) must first draft a praecipe, a brief request to the clerk of the court to issue a summons to the defendant; the praecipe included a brief statement of the nature of the controversy and the amount of the damages alleged. The plaintiff's lawyer then drafted what was called a declaration, indicating the form of action under which the suit was brought and setting forth the facts of the case.

In common law there were eleven major forms of action—trespass, trespass on the case, replevin, assumpsit, ejectment, etc.—each of which applied to different kinds of suits. An action for trespass, for example, rose when a plaintiff alleged that his person had been interfered with by assault or battery or that his land or property had been damaged; but an action for trespass on the case involved indirect or accidental damage or damage to intangible property. Thus a man who claimed a neighbor had stolen his cow would bring an action for trespass, while one who asserted that he had been slandered by his neighbor would bring one for trespass on the case. The lawyer who incorrectly identified the action he was bringing might have his case thrown out of court.

The declaration also included a full account of the plaintiff's version of the facts in the case. This had to be prepared with the utmost care. If it alleged facts that could not be proved in a trial, the plaintiff could lose, even if those facts were not necessary to sustain his case. If it alleged facts that differed from those presented at a trial, his case could be thrown out. In one 1859 decision a case was dismissed because the amount of a promissory note stated in the declaration differed by half a cent from the amount of the note as proved in the trial.

In his early cases Lincoln paid close attention to one of the form books that suggested the proper language for declarations, and in his desire to avoid all technical errors his documents often grew excessively legalistic and wordy. For instance in a May 1838 case in Fulton County for the collection of an unpaid note, his declaration alleged: "For that whereas the said defendants by, and under the name, style, and firm of 'John W. Shinn & Co' heretofore, towit, on the twentythird day of March in the year of our Lord one thousand eight hundred and thirtysix at Philadelphia, towit, at the county and state aforesaid made their certain promissory note in writing bearing date the date and year aforesaid and thereby then and there promised to pay Twelve months after the date thereof the said plaintiffs in their partnership name of 'Atwood & Co' the sum of Seven hundred and sixtytwo dollars and thirtysix hundredths of a dollar, for value received, and there and then delivered the said promissory note to the said plaintiffs. . . ." As he became more experienced, he pared the legalisms and redundancies, and his declarations became models of simplicity and clarity.

After Lincoln filed his declaration with the clerk of the Sangamon County Circuit Court, the lawyer for the defendant would come back with a demurrer, alleging that the plaintiff's allegations were defective as a matter of law, or a traverse, stating his client's version of the disputed facts or events. Lincoln, for the plaintiff, might respond with a replication, taking exception to that counterstatement, and the opposing attorney could submit a rejoinder. All these papers, which might run to many pages, had to be written out in longhand; there were no secretaries and no copying machines.

Fortunately most of the early cases in which Lincoln was engaged required more common sense than mastery of precedents. They concerned such matters as a suit by Speed, on behalf of A. Y. Ellis & Company, for payment of a debt to the store by one Thomas P. Smith. In a slightly more complicated case Lincoln represented Elijah Houghton, who had been swapping some of his land with David Hart for twelve acres or so along Rock

Creek, near New Salem—land that Lincoln himself had surveyed. The death of Hart put their handshake deal into question, and Houghton now asked the court to require Hart's three children and heirs to live up to the terms of the agreement.

From the beginning Stuart & Lincoln carried a heavy load of such cases. As early as the July 1837 term of the Sangamon County Circuit Court, the partners had nineteen common-law cases and seven chancery cases on the docket—more than twice as many as their closest rivals, Logan & Baker, and far more than any other attorneys. In the following terms Logan & Baker once exceeded the case load of Stuart & Lincoln, and from time to time, especially as Stuart prepared to take his seat in Congress, Samuel H. Treat also surpassed them. But always Lincoln had as much business as he could handle.

Lincoln's legal practice was not confined to Sangamon County. No lawyer could make his living from the two two-week terms that the circuit court met in Springfield each year, and Lincoln, like most of the other attorneys, traveled on the huge circuit that the judges were obliged to make, going from one county seat to another and holding sessions that lasted from two days to a week. Lincoln appeared at Bloomington, in McLean County, as early as 1837, and the following year he began regularly to attend the courts of Tazewell, Macon, Morgan, and other central Illinois counties.

A full schedule did not mean full pockets. Springfield was a town full of lawyers, and all were obliged to charge modest fees. For most of the cases Stuart & Lincoln handled, the fee was $5.00, and the ordinary range was from $2.50 to $10.00. In one case the partners charged $50.00, a fee so high that the client apparently asked to pay some of it by making a coat for Stuart, worth $15.00. In another, where the partners represented a Springfield hotelkeeper, the client paid their fee by giving Lincoln board for $6.00. It was Lincoln's job, as junior partner, to record these fees, which he and Stuart split equally.

He was also supposed to keep a record of the firm's income in a fee book, where he listed cases, the disposition, and the fees charged. Here, too, he entered expenses, such as for several loads of wood, which he apparently cut up with the $2.25 "wood-saw" he purchased, and for an $8.50 stovepipe. For a time he was conscientious in keeping records, but presently the task became onerous and long gaps began to appear. Neither Stuart nor Lincoln was systematic, and the firm's papers were deposited in drawers, in pockets, and, especially, in Lincoln's stovepipe hat. From time to time the partners had to apologize to clients for loss of papers or neglect of business. On one occasion, after Stuart left for Washington, Lincoln had to ask his partner how to silence one client who "is teasing me continually about some *deeds* which he says he left with you, but which I can find nothing of" and how to answer "a d——d hawk billed yankee" who was besetting him about a claim that had not been settled.

Despite careless bookkeeping, the firm was a successful one, and it afforded Lincoln a remarkable opportunity to begin his career at the bar. He quickly discovered that his brief and unsystematic training made him the match for other self-taught lawyers and even for those who had studied, usually without much direction, in the office of some older attorney. After Stuart left to serve in Congress, Lincoln had no doubts about his ability to run the firm in his partner's absence, and he marked the new era in the fee book: "Commencement of Lincoln's administration 1839 Nov 2."

IV

Much of the time during these early years Lincoln seemed to think of his legal career as an adjunct to his political aspirations. He had hardly settled in Springfield before he took on a case that became the occasion of assailing his political opponents. In May 1837, Mrs. Mary Anderson, together with her son Richard, engaged Stuart & Lincoln on a contingent fee to recover ten acres of land lying just north of Springfield—later to become the site of the Oak Ridge Cemetery. The tract was held by James Adams, a prominent Democratic officeholder in Springfield, but Mrs. Anderson claimed it was part of the estate of her recently deceased husband. On looking into the records, Lincoln became convinced that Adams's deed to the land was fraudulent and that Mrs. Anderson's claim was valid. Enlisting Stephen T. Logan, one of the ablest and most experienced lawyers in Springfield, as fellow counsel, he brought suit in the Sangamon County Circuit Court.

Up to that point his conduct was entirely professional, but soon his bitter political animus against Adams began to show. Adams was in fact a man with a shady past, who had fled New York rather than face charges that he had forged a deed to six hundred acres. But what angered Lincoln was Adams's candidacy for the lucrative office of judge of the probate court, for which Dr. Anson G. Henry, a Whig and a special friend of Lincoln's, was also running. While the court case against Adams was pending, Lincoln and his fellow lawyers began to try it in the newspapers. In six letters, signed "Sampson's Ghost," which they published weekly in the *Sangamo Journal,* they attacked Adams as a Tory and a supporter of the Hartford Convention, called on him "to explain to the citizens of this county by what authority he holds possession of two ... lots of ground in Springfield, upon which he now resides," and hinted that Adams's title to the Anderson land was also fraudulent.

Throughout the summer and fall of 1837, Springfield papers were filled with these charges against Adams and with countercharges by Adams and his friends. Though Lincoln may not have written all the "Sampson's Ghost" letters, Adams correctly identified him as his primary enemy and struck back with public letters that challenged his facts and his logic. Seeking to take advantage of Lincoln's unconventional religious views, Adams labeled him *"a deist."* Lincoln responded in a handbill, followed by two public letters, which tried to discredit Adams's witnesses and ridiculed his efforts to "tear, rend, split, rive, blow up, confound, overwhelm, annihilate, extinguish, exterminate, burst asunder, and grind to powder all his slanderers."

The unedifying and unprofessional controversy lost much of its point when Sangamon County voters in the fall election showed how little credence they gave to Lincoln's allegations by defeating Henry and electing Adams probate judge. The suit over the Anderson property, together with other related actions, dragged on for several years, but Adams remained in possession of the land at his death in 1843.

Lincoln exhibited the same fierce partisanship in the state legislature, which continued to meet in Vandalia, pending the completion of the new state capitol in Springfield. Now one of the more experienced members, he was twice the unsuccessful candidate of the Whigs for speaker of the house of representatives. In the 1838–1839 session he served on no fewer than fourteen committees, including the influential finance committee, but much of his work was done behind the scenes in organizing and managing the Whig minority. On the floor of the house he participated in the debates more easily and freely, occasionally lightening the proceedings with a bit of levity. When a representative from Montgomery County expressed fear about the mounting debts and deficits caused by the internal improvements plan, Lincoln said he was reminded of an eccentric Hoosier bachelor, "very famous for seeing *big bugaboos* in every thing," who went hunting and fired his gun repeatedly at a squirrel which he claimed was at the top of a tree. Unable to see anything in the tree, his brother examined the hunter's person carefully and "found on one of his eye lashes a *big louse* crawling about." "It is so with the gentleman from Montgomery," Lincoln joked. "He imagined he could see squirrels every day, when they were nothing but *lice.*"

Lincoln's main objective in the legislature was to protect Springfield. He introduced legislation to incorporate Springfield as a town and to secure state funds for the completion of the new statehouse. Until the actual removal of the state government in 1839, supporters of Vandalia made repeated efforts to repeal the legislation making Springfield the capital. In the 1837 session, for example, General W. L. D. Ewing, who represented Vandalia in the legislature, denounced "the arrogance of Springfield—its presumption in claiming the seat of government" and charged the legislation removing the capital had been obtained "by chicanery and trickery." Chosen by the Sangamon delegation to respond, Lincoln struck back with such severity that observers expected Ewing to challenge him to a duel.

Closely related to Lincoln's defense of Springfield's interests was his position on the ambitious internal improvements plan, which had foundered after the panic of 1837. In view of falling revenues and the collapse of the market for Illinois bonds, most leaders of both parties favored curtailing or abandoning the scheme to crisscross the state with railroads and canals. But not Lincoln. Admitting "that Sangamon county have received great and important benefits . . . in return for giving support, thro' her delegation to the system of Internal Improvement," he announced that the county was "*morally* bound," though "not *legally* bound," to support that system. To those who wanted to modify the scheme, he said the legislature had "gone too far to recede, even if we were disposed to do so." "We are," he added, "now so far advanced in a general system of internal improvements that, if we would, we cannot retreat from it, without disgrace and great loss."

Something more than face-saving lay behind Lincoln's support of internal improvements. He continued to think of America as buoyant and prosperous, a land of opportunity where poor boys like himself could get ahead. He had no doubt of the rich resources of Illinois, which, he said, "surpasses every other spot of equal extent upon the face of the globe, in *fertility* of soil" and was therefore capable of "sustaining a greater amount of agricultural wealth and population than any other equal extent of territory in the world." Railroads and canals were desperately needed to bring the state's produce to the world's markets. It was a terrible misfortune that the panic had occurred when the internal improvements plan was getting under way, just at the time when the largest investment was required and the least return could be expected. Consequently the state found itself "at a point which may aptly be likened to the dead point in the steam-engine—a point extremely difficult of turning." But he was confident that, "once turned," it would "present no further difficulty, and all again will be well." Using a different metaphor, he argued that stopping support of these projects now would be "very much like stopping a skift in the middle of a river—if it was not going up, it *would* go down."

Acknowledging "his share of the responsibility devolving upon us in the present crisis," Lincoln looked for alternative ways to finance the building of roads and canals. For a time he placed much hope in a plan, similar to one he had advanced earlier, for Illinois to purchase from the federal government all publicly owned lands in the state for $5 million. Profits from the sale of these lands to actual settlers would more than pay the cost of internal improvements, he argued. The legislature agreed to make the offer to Washington, but nothing came of it. Reluctantly he turned to taxation and favored a graduated levy on land, which had hitherto been taxed at a flat rate. Believing the change to be "equitable within itself," he reminded legislators that the increased levy would fall on the *"wealthy few,"* who, "it is still to be remembered, . . . are not sufficiently numerous to carry the elections." As the economy continued to deteriorate, Lincoln sought to retrieve something "from the general wreck" of the internal improvements scheme by continuing to fund "at least one work calculated to yield something towards defraying its expense," but, as he anticipated, his colleagues allowed the internal improvements system to be "put down in a lump."

Lincoln's pertinacity in defending the internal improvements system was equaled only by the vigor of his support for the State Bank of Illinois. Like most Whigs, he preferred a strong national bank. After Andrew Jackson destroyed the power of the Bank of the United States, Lincoln gave his allegiance to the State Bank, and particularly to its central branch in Springfield, which had been created during his first term in the legislature. Again and again, he voted to defeat Democratic proposals for investigating the bank, and in 1839, when the Democratic majority succeeded in authorizing a committee to look into the bank's affairs, Lincoln made sure that he was one of the members. He attended the meetings of the committee with fair regularity, despite the heavy calls on his time for other legislative business, and he saw to it that the long report of the investigation attributed the bank's suspension of specie payments "not . . . to any organic defects of the institutions themselves but to the irresistable law of trade and exchange which cannot be controaled by country banks."

The fate of the bank remained in doubt, as Democrats, opposed to all banks on principle and especially hostile to this Whiggish bank in Springfield, mounted campaign after campaign for its destruction. At times even Lincoln gave up on saving it, lamenting that the legislature was allowing the bank to forfeit its charter and that there was "but verry little disposition to resuscitate it."

Nevertheless, he persisted, and in December 1840 he demonstrated the extent of his devotion to the bank in an episode that became celebrated as what he called "that jumping scrape." The bank had been authorized to continue its suspension of specie payments only until the end of the legislative session, which was scheduled for the first week in December. Knowing that the bank would immediately be bankrupt if forced to pay out specie, Lincoln and his fellow Whigs hoped to prevent the adjournment of the legislature, now holding its first session in the newly completed capitol at Springfield. Of course, Democrats, who wanted to kill the bank, favored adjournment. The only way the Whigs could keep the legislature in session was by absenting themselves, so that there was no quorum. They left Lincoln, together with one or two of his trusted lieutenants, to watch the proceedings and to demand roll calls when the Democrats tried to adjourn. The session dragged on into the evening, and candles had to be brought in. Several Democrats rose from their sickbeds to help form a quorum. Rattled, Lincoln and his aides lost their heads and voted on the next roll call. Then, still hoping to block adjournment, they unsuccessfully tried to get out of the locked door. When the sergeant at arms rebuffed them, they jumped out the second-story window. Their effort was in vain, because the speaker recorded them as present and voting, and, with the quorum assured, the house adjourned and the bank was killed. The whole affair became the subject of much amusement among the Democrats, who ridiculed "Mr. Lincoln and his flying brethren" and noted that his celebrated leap caused him no harm because "his legs reached nearly from the window to the ground!"

Disliking to appear ridiculous, Lincoln allowed his affection for the bank to cool, and when the subject was introduced again the next year, he was noticeably less active in its defense. After one particularly sharp debate with John A. McClernand and other Democrats, who were, he said, trying to "crush the Bank" while he was trying to save "both it and the state," he wearily announced that he was "tired of this business." "If there was to be this continual warfare against the Institutions of the State," he went on, "the sooner it was brought to an end the better."

V

In addition to serving as the leader of the Whigs in the state legislature, Lincoln labored indefatigably to organize his party, and he became one of the best-known Whig leaders not merely in Springfield but in central Illinois. In 1838, combining politics with his legal business at all the county court-houses where he practiced, he solicited votes for Stuart, who was running for a seat in the U.S. House of Representatives. Lincoln exhibited special enthusiasm in his partner's behalf because the Democratic opponent was Stephen A. Douglas, whom he had already begun to consider his main political rival. Repeatedly Lincoln urged his friends to be vigilant: "If we do our duty we shall succeed in the congressional election, but if we relax an *iota,* we shall be beaten." Elected by a plurality of only thirty-six votes, Stuart faced a likely challenge to his credentials from Douglas, but Lincoln, along with other Springfield Whigs, mounted a counteroffensive designed to show that Douglas had received votes from unnaturalized foreigners, minors, and persons who had not resided in the state for the required six months. Shortly afterward Lincoln was able to report to Stuart with some glee that the Democrats would probably drop the challenge, though, he added,"You know that if we had heard Douglass say that he had abandoned the contest, it would not be verry authentic."

Eager for victory, Lincoln readily acquiesced when the Whigs deserted Henry Clay, one of the founders of the party, and nominated William Henry Harrison, the hero of the battle of Tippecanoe, to run against Martin Van Buren in 1840. Thinking "the chance of carrying the state, verry good," he began systematically organizing the Whigs of central Illinois. When a Democratic editor sneeringly referred to Harrison as a simple old man who wanted nothing better than to live in a log cabin and drink hard cider, Whigs capitalized on his blunder. His charge proved their candidate, in contrast to the aristocratic Van Buren, was a man of the people. Lincoln was afraid his party's rollicking populist campaign might not translate into votes. By this time his earlier aversion to nominating conventions and the other ma-chinery of party organization, which he shared with most Whigs, had disappeared. He explained that the Democrats, by recruiting "their double-drilled-army" of supporters, had "set us the example of organization; and we, in self defence, are driven into it." He now drew up a semimilitary plan for getting out the Whig votes. In order to bring about "the overthrow of the corrupt powers that now control our beloved country," he urged the appointment of county, precinct, and section captains to make sure "that every Whig can be brought to the polls in the coming presidential contest."

Lincoln also did his part in bringing the issues before the people. An assiduous reader of the newspapers and a careful student of the *Congressional Globe,* which published in full the interminable debates in the national legislature, he was thoroughly prepared to defend Whig economic policies. In the almost nightly meetings around the fireplace at the back of Speed's store, where he and other young Springfield politicians argued these questions, he had sharpened his debating skills. His opportunity to use them came when the discussion became heated one night and Douglas, now chairman of the Democratic state committee, challenged his Whig opponents to a full-scale public discussion of the issues in the campaign. Lincoln willingly accepted.

The first round of debate, on November 19, 1839, attracted much attention. Douglas, John Calhoun, the county surveyor who had once employed Lincoln, and two other Democrats opposed four leading Whigs: Edward D. Baker (the attorney who had made a name for himself in his oration at the laying of the cornerstone of the new capitol), Logan, Browning, and Lincoln. Most observers thought the contest a draw, but Lincoln felt he had not come up to the expectations of his friends. "He was conscious of his failure," Joseph Gillespie reported, "and I never saw any man so much distressed." He begged for another chance and challenged the Democrats to a return engagement in December. By the time Lincoln had his turn, on the day after Christmas, attendance was so embarrassingly small as to cast a damp upon his spirits. Nevertheless, he proceeded to deliver a carefully written address that, Gillespie recalled, "transcended our highest expectations."

His basic theme was the merits of a national bank as contrasted to the Independent Treasury system of federal depositories, independent both of state banks and private business, which the Democrats favored. Inevitably it contained a certain amount of rodomontade, such as a jeer at Douglas's "stupid" belief that his "groundless and audacious assertions" could go unchallenged, and a sneer that hundreds of Democratic officeholders were "scampering away with the public money to Texas, to Europe, and to every spot of the earth where a villain may hope to find refuge from justice." But for the most part it was a sober, reasoned defense of the economic stability provided by a national bank and a prediction of the adverse effects of the Democrats' subtreasury plan. Lincoln took pains to keep his arguments down to earth. Not content with generalizing that the Independent Treasury would bring about "distress, ruin, bankruptcy and beggary," he brought the issue home by showing that if it was established the man who *"now* raises money sufficient to purchase 80 acres, will *then* raise but sufficient to purchase 40, or perhaps not that much."

This address, published in full in the *Sangamo Journal* and also as a pamphlet, contained little that was new, but it showed that Lincoln had now mastered the standard Whig arguments on economic issues. It served as his basic text throughout the 1840 presidential campaign. Wherever his law practice took him or wherever he was invited, he made political speeches —at Jacksonville, Carlinville, Alton, Belleville, Tremont, Waterloo, Mount

Vernon, Carmi, Shawneetown, and Equality. Sometimes he made solo appearances, but as often he engaged in debates with Democratic leaders, especially Douglas.

In these speeches Lincoln at times indulged in the usual political rhetoric, demagogically attacking Van Buren for supporting the right of free blacks in New York to vote and offering what Whig papers called "a successful vindication of the civil and military reputation of the Hero of Tippecanoe." Remarkably, though, at a time when many Whigs were carefully avoiding all discussion of issues in favor of a mindless log-cabin-and-hard-cider campaign, Lincoln spent most of his time on the stump soberly discussing Whig economic policies.

VI

That course should have come as no surprise to those who had carefully followed Lincoln's career since his arrival in Springfield. As early as January 1838, in an address to the Young Men's Lyceum entitled "The Perpetuation of Our Political Institutions," he had attacked hyperemotionalism in politics, warning that the nation's "proud fabric of freedom" was endangered by the passions of the people—"the jealousy, envy, and avarice, incident to our nature."

His central theme was the threat posed by social disorder. His topic was a conventional one for these lyceum meetings, where aspiring young men of the town tested their rhetorical skill and improved their elocution before their peers, but Lincoln developed it in a highly personal way. Like many of his contemporaries, Lincoln was troubled by what he perceived as the rapid rate of change in American life. Canals and railroads were bringing about a transportation revolution; the population was swiftly spreading across the continent; immigration was beginning to seem a threat to American social cohesion; sectionalism was becoming ever more divisive as the controversy over slavery mounted; the political battles of the Jackson era had destroyed the national political consensus.

Most disturbing of all were the outbreaks of mob violence, which "pervaded the country, from New England to Louisiana." Two particular incidents Lincoln called to the attention of his audience: a vigilante outbreak in Mississippi, which began with the execution of gamblers but continued until "dead men were seen literally dangling from the boughs of trees upon every road side; and in numbers almost sufficient, to rival the native Spanish moss"; and the burning to death in St. Louis of a mulatto man named McIntosh, accused of murdering a prominent citizen. If "persons and property, are held by no better tenure than the caprice of a mob," "if the laws be continually despised and disregarded," Lincoln warned, citizens' affection for their government must inevitably be alienated.

As a remedy, Lincoln urged what he called a simple solution: "Let every

American, every lover of liberty, every well wisher to his posterity, swear by the blood of the Revolution, never to violate in the least particular, the laws of the country; and never to tolerate their violation by others. . . . Let reverence for the laws, be breathed by every American mother, to the lisping babe, that prattles on her lap—let it be taught in schools, in seminaries, and in colleges;—let it be written in Primmers, spelling books, and in Almanacs; —let it be preached from the pulpit, proclaimed in legislative halls, and enforced in courts of justice." "In short," he urged, "let it become the *political religion* of the nation."

This was, for the most part, standard Whig rhetoric, of a piece with Lincoln's speech in the legislature the previous year defending the State Bank against the "lawless and mobocratic spirit . . . abroad in the land." But at this point in the lyceum lecture, when most listeners must have thought he had nearly finished, Lincoln, in effect, began again, asking why the danger to American political institutions was so much greater now than it had been for the past fifty years. In the first half of the lecture he had offered essentially a sociological interpretation of the danger; now he offered a psychological explanation.

In previous generations, he suggested, when the outcome of the American venture in self-government was still in doubt, "all that sought celebrity and fame, and distinction, expected to find them in the success of that experiment." Even now there were "many great and good men" who aspired "to nothing beyond a seat in Congress, a gubernatorial or a presidential chair." But, he added, in a rare moment of self-revelation, *"such belong not to the family of the lion, or the tribe of the eagle."* Such honors were not enough for "men of ambition and talents." These routine offices would not satisfy "an Alexander, a Caesar, or a Napoleon," from whom the greatest danger to popular government must be expected. "Towering genius disdains a beaten path," Lincoln reminded his audience. "It seeks regions hitherto unexplored. . . . It thirsts and burns for distinction; and, if possible, it will have it, whether at the expense of emancipating slaves, or enslaving freemen."

Probably most of Lincoln's listeners thought this nothing more than another rhetorical flourish at the end of a long speech. Few could have realized that he was unconsciously describing himself. His ambition was no secret. As Herndon said, it was "a little engine that knew no rest." But only Speed understood how avid was his thirst for distinction. To this one intimate friend Lincoln confessed his ambition "to link his name with something that would redound to the interest of his fellow man," and in his darker moods he lamented "that he had done nothing to make any human being remember that he had lived."

It was to guard against "men of ambition and talents"—like himself— that Lincoln urged a second, and fundamentally different, way to preserve American political institutions. In the first half of his speech he had used conventional conservative rhetoric to favor the slow, organic growth of national feeling. Now he proposed erecting a new "temple of liberty," not resting on emotion and custom but carved "from the solid quarry of sober reason."

That invocation of reason accounted for one otherwise inexplicable omission from his lyceum address: his failure to mention the one instance of mob violence closest to Springfield and most familiar to his listeners. In November 1837 a mob at Alton, Illinois, had killed Elijah P. Lovejoy, editor of the abolitionist paper the *Observer*. The Maine-born minister, who dedicated his paper to a war on slavery, intemperance, and "popery," had been driven out of Missouri by the proslavery elements and the enraged Catholics of St. Louis, and he renewed his campaign from Alton, twenty-five miles up the Mississippi River, on the Illinois side. Breaking his repeated pledges to edit his paper in the interests of the Presbyterian Church alone, Lovejoy became increasingly strident in his abolitionism. Irate residents of Alton, tied by kinship and trade to the South, twice threw his printing presses into the river. When he and sixty young armed abolitionists from towns nearby vowed to defend a third press, the mob burned the warehouse where the press was stored and shot Lovejoy. This brutal infringement of the freedom of the press sent a shock wave through the North and provoked protest meetings in all the major cities. But when Lincoln spoke out against mob violence, he did not mention Lovejoy or Alton by name and offered only a passing condemnation of persons who—among other outrages—"throw printing presses into rivers, [and] shoot editors." Though Lincoln deplored the Alton riot, he also implicitly censured Lovejoy's abolitionist agitation; both resulted from unbridled passions, which could lead to the overthrow of popular government.

Lincoln's reservations about abolitionism extended to other humanitarian reform movements. For instance, he never joined the prohibition movement, even though he himself did not use liquor and often spoke at temperance rallies. But he disliked the emotionalism of the prohibitionists, who, he said, addressed drunkards and dramshop-keepers "in thundering tones of anathema and denunciation," blaming them for "all the vice and misery and crime in the land" and condemning them as persons to be "shunned by all the good and virtuous, as moral pestilences." To the outrage of local clergymen and do-gooders, he announced in an 1842 lecture that "if we take habitual drunkards as a class, their heads and their hearts will bear an advantageous comparison with those of any other class." Consequently he refused to coerce them into temperance, but he enthusiastically backed the Washingtonian Society's program of converting alcoholics by *"persuasion,* kind, unassuming persuasion."

In all such matters what he feared was uncontrolled emotion. Passion, he remarked in the conclusion of his lyceum lecture, "will in future be our enemy." In its stead the nation must rely on "reason, cold, calculating, unimpassioned reason." Only then, he told the Washingtonians, would come the "happy day, when, all appetites controled, all passions subdued, . . . *mind,* all conquering *mind,* shall live and move the monarch of the world. Glorious consummation! Hail fall of Fury! Reign of Reason, all hail!"

VII

The earnestness of Lincoln's efforts to impose rationality on public life reflected his intense internal struggle to bring coherence to his own, still unshaped personality. He was not yet sure who he was or how he wished to be perceived. He liked to associate with the "aristocratic" element of Springfield, who gathered around the wealthy and snobbish Ninian W. Edwardses, but he also wanted, as he said, to be "one of the boys," the young and active workingmen and clerks who time after time supported his election to the state legislature. In his role of courteous gentleman he could write a gallant letter to Mrs. Browning, urging her to accompany her husband to the meeting of the legislature in Springfield, where he promised to "render unto your Honoress due attention and faithful obedience"; but he knew that many in the house of representatives joined Ewing in thinking him a "coarse and vulgar fellow." He wanted to be regarded as a generous opponent, unwilling to hurt the feelings of a colleague; yet, with his high temper still not under control, he was capable of flaring up in debate and truculently announcing that if his opponents wanted to settle a dispute "at another tribunal" he "was always ready, and never shrunk from responsibility." He thought of himself as a speaker who advanced strong, logical arguments, yet he learned from the Democratic *Illinois State Register* that many deplored his habit in his public appearances of putting on "a sort of assumed clownishness in his manner which does not become him, and which does not truly belong to him."

Even Lincoln's style betrayed his inner uncertainty. In most of his public speeches and legal papers, he kept to simple, pithy statements, notably devoid of ornamentation or rhetorical flourish. But on occasion, as in the lyceum address, he adopted the florid style so common in nineteenth-century oratory. America need have no fear of foreign invasion, he boasted: "All the armies of Europe, Asia and Africa combined, with all the treasure of the earth . . . in their military chest; with a Buonaparte for a commander, could not by force, take a drink from the Ohio, or make a track on the Blue Ridge, in a trial of a thousand years." Or, in the unlikely context of defending the national bank, he announced: "If ever I feel the soul within me elevate and expand to those dimensions not wholly unworthy of its Almighty Architect, it is when I contemplate the cause of my country, deserted by all the world beside, and I standing up boldly and lone and hurling defiance at her victorious oppressors. Here, without contemplating consequences, before High Heaven, and in the face of the world, I swear eternal fidelity to the just cause . . . of the land of my life, my liberty and my love."

Similarly conflicted and contradictory were his attitudes toward women.

Lincoln liked women and he wanted to know them. A month after he moved to Springfield in 1837, he lamented, "I have been spoken to by but one woman since I've been here, and should not have been by her, if she could have avoided it." But he was awkward and uncomfortable when he was around them. He did not know how to behave. Sometimes he turned up for evening affairs wearing his rough Conestoga boots, and he once disrupted a party by commenting, "Oh boys, how clean these girls look."

He met eligible young women primarily at the Sunday soirees that Ninian and Elizabeth Edwards held at their luxurious mansion. Edwards was a snob who found Lincoln "a mighty rough man," but this ambitious son of a former Illinois governor thought the young lawyer might be politically useful. Elizabeth Todd Edwards's ambitions were matrimonial; she seemed always to have as a guest an unmarried friend or relative who was looking for a husband. She had just married off one sister, Frances, to a local physician, William Wallace, and was ready to welcome others from her Kentucky home.

Around the Edwardses gathered the brightest and best of Springfield society. The handsome and soldierly John J. Hardin, a relative of Mrs. Edwards and likely candidate for Congress, attended most of their parties. So did Edward D. Baker, the enormously popular young Whig orator, who might one day have aspired to the presidency but for his British birth. O. H. Browning represented the conservative, better-educated element of the Whig party. Though the Edwardses were staunch Whigs, their soirees were nonpartisan, and they welcomed Stephen A. Douglas, now the leading Democrat in the state, already known as the "Little Giant" because his power belied his size. Democrat James Shields, the handsome Irish-born state auditor, was often a guest.

The Edwards entourage included the most attractive young women in Springfield. From time to time, Ninian Edwards welcomed a relative, such as his niece, the beautiful and pious Matilda Edwards. Julia Jayne, daughter of a Springfield doctor, nearly always attended the Edwards parties, as did Mercy Ann Levering when she was visiting from Baltimore. But nobody in the Edwards circle attracted more interest than Mrs. Edwards's younger sister, Mary Todd.

The daughter of Robert S. Todd, a prosperous merchant and banker of Lexington, Kentucky, Mary had grown up in luxury, attended by family slaves and educated in the best private schools. Unable to get along with her stepmother, she decided, after a preliminary jaunt in 1837, to pay her sister an extended visit in 1839. Immediately this small, pretty young woman of twenty-two years, with beautiful fair skin, light chestnut hair, and remarkably vivid blue eyes, enchanted the other members of the group. Even Herndon, who came to hate her, described Mary as "young, dashing, handsome— witty . . . cultured—graceful and dignified," though he also noted that she could be "sarcastic—haughty—aristocratic." "She was an excellent conversationalist," Herndon continued, "and she soon became the belle of the town, leading the young men of the town a merry dance."

Abraham Lincoln was one of those who danced in attendance—literally so, since he first met Mary Todd at one of the Edwards' parties and told her he wanted to dance with her "in the worst way." And, Mary laughed, he did. Lincoln was enchanted by this vivacious, intelligent young woman, and soon he was one of her regular attendants at parties, on horseback rides, on jaunts to neighboring towns. Mary was entirely different from anyone he had ever known. He did not even feel awkward when talking to her, for she made up for his deficiencies as a conversationalist. Mrs. Edwards recalled that when they were together "Mary led the conversation—Lincoln would listen and gaze on her as if drawn by some superior power, irresistably [sic] so; he listened—never scarcely said a word." Lincoln, she added, "could not hold a lengthy conversation with a lady—was not sufficiently educated and intelligent in the female line to do so. He was charmed with Mary's wit and fascinated with her quick sagacity—her will—her nature—and culture."

In receiving Lincoln's attentions, Mary had to think of him, as she did of the other young men who gathered around her, as a potential husband. Marriage was now very much on her mind. She was just short of becoming an old maid, and, except for schoolteaching, no other career was open to women of her class. There were not many eligible bachelors. She very much liked Douglas, with whom she flirted outrageously, to their mutual amusement, but both quickly recognized that his mind was on his career and he was not seriously interested in matrimony. She found Speed handsome and charming, but he seemed attracted to the devout Matilda Edwards. The widower Edwin B. Webb, another Springfield attorney, was an earnest suitor, but he suffered from the disadvantages of being considerably older than Mary and of having what she called "two *sweet little objections*," the children of his first marriage. She was realistic enough to recognize that, despite all the attentions she received, "my beaux have *always* been *hard bargains*."

By comparison, Lincoln looked increasingly attractive. He lacked social graces, but his honesty, his courtesy, and his considerateness compensated for the deficiency. They shared many interests. Both were Kentuckians. Both loved poetry and had memorized many of the same poems, especially those by Robert Burns. Like him, she was a Whig. At a time when women were not supposed to profess an interest in politics, she openly supported Harrison for President in 1840, though, like Lincoln, she would have preferred Henry Clay, a friend of her family and a neighbor in Lexington. She was pleased by Lincoln's ambition; in Kentucky she had often said jokingly that she intended to marry a man who would some day become President of the United States.

By the fall of 1840 she and Lincoln were edging toward a closer relationship, and that prospect may have contributed to his sometimes boisterous conduct toward his fellow legislators and even to his much publicized leap from the statehouse window. The Edwardses favored the match. Ninian Edwards said he desired it "for policy." He did not explain his meaning, but doubtless he had in mind linking to his already influential family a promising young lawyer and politician. Mrs. Edwards also encouraged it, recognizing that Lincoln was "a rising man." Sometime around Christmas, Abraham and Mary became engaged.

Once Lincoln had made a commitment, he began to have second thoughts —much as he had done in his engagement to Mary Owens. It was as if he was reluctant to marry anyone who was willing to accept him. He began to suspect that the Edwardses had planned the match and had maneuvered him into proposing. Belatedly, though with some reason, he worried about his ability to support a wife. He had now an income of more than $1,000 a year from his legal practice, plus his salary as a state legislator, but neither source was certain. His law partnership was about to be dissolved. Stuart, who had been in Washington for most of the past two years, had contributed little to the practice, and, now that his reelection to a second term in the House of Representatives was virtually conceded, it made no sense to continue his empty partnership with Lincoln. Lincoln was not even assured of his income from the state legislature. With the collapse of the internal improvements system and the resulting bankruptcy of the state, he and his associates had come under increasingly bitter, and sometimes personal, attack. His political popularity was declining; in the 1840 election he was no longer the candidate who received the most votes, and in the rural precincts there was a movement to reject him and the other members of what was termed "the Springfield junto." He resolved not to stand for reelection when his present term in the legislature expired. Thus in 1840 he was a man without reliable income, who had no savings and owned no house but probably still owed something on his "National Debt" from his New Salem days. He knew he could not give Mary the life of wealth and luxury to which she was accustomed.

These anxieties covered his deeper uncertainties about marriage. Like Speed, with whom he shared his most intimate thoughts, he was probably still sexually inexperienced. Both young men had grown up in a rough frontier society where, except in family arrangements, men and women kept largely to themselves and where, in all-male gatherings, there was much big talk and rough humor about sex—and usually much less experience. Both young men had highly romantic notions about women and marriage; as Lincoln wrote his friend later, "It is the peculiar misfortune of both you and me, to dream dreams of Elysium far exceeding all that any thing earthly can realize." At the same time, they shared *"forebodings"* about marriage, which evoked fears of "something indescribably horrible and alarming." Probably they were anxious about their own, as yet untested, sexual adequacy; in addition, they must have worried about how to go about transforming the adored object of chaste passion into a bed partner. Both Lincoln and Speed rationalized their fears as apprehension that they did not love their fiancées as they should.

In Lincoln's case all these anxieties were heightened by Speed's decision to sell his interest in his store on January 1, in preparation for a return to

Kentucky in the spring. Lincoln had to move out of the upstairs room they shared and find lodgings with William Butler. A very private person, Lincoln was about to lose his best and closest friend, at just the moment when he was being rushed into a new, potentially very dangerous kind of intimacy with Mary. The man who wanted to live in a universe governed by cold reason found himself awash on a sea of turbulent emotions.

His nerve snapped. He decided he had to break the engagement, and he wrote Mary a letter saying that he did not love her. Speed tried to persuade him to burn it. "If you think you have *will* and manhood enough to go and see her and speak to her what you say in that letter," he told him, "you may do that. Words are forgotten . . . but once put your words in writing and they stand as a living and eternal monument against you."

Reluctantly Lincoln accepted his friend's advice and went to the Edwards mansion. When he told Mary he did not love her, she burst into tears. At first she blamed herself; remembering a young man in Kentucky whose attentions she had deliberately encouraged only to spurn him, she exclaimed, "The deciever shall be decieved wo is me." Deeply moved, Lincoln "drew her down on his knee kissed her—and parted."

When he told Speed what had happened, his friend said, "The last thing is a bad lick, but it cannot now be helped," and he assumed the engagement still stood. But after Lincoln left, Mary brooded over "the reason of his change of mind—heart and soul" and concluded—without any real justification—that he was in love with Matilda Edwards. She wrote Lincoln a letter releasing him from his engagement, yet letting him know "that she would hold the question an open one—that is that she had not changed her mind, but felt as always."

Instead of feeling relieved, Lincoln was devastated. Just as Mary Owens's refusal had caused him to suspect that he really loved her, so Mary's letter made him realize what he had lost. He became deeply depressed. During the first week in January he was able to go about his business, in a more or less perfunctory way, and to answer roll calls in the house of representatives. But then the burden of guilt and unhappiness became too great, and he took to his bed for about a week, unwilling to see anybody except Speed and Dr. Henry.

During this period some of his friends feared he might commit suicide. Years later Speed said he had felt obliged "to remove razors from his room —take any all knives and other such dangerous things," but a fellow legislator, who boarded with Lincoln at Butler's house, recalled: "His most intimate friends had no fears of his injuring himself. He was very sad and melancholy, but being subject to these spells, nothing serious was apprehended." His mind was in turmoil as he reflected on what he had done and how he had acted. Bitterly he reproached himself for inconstancy. "My own ability to keep my resolves when they are made," he told Speed, was once the source of pride "as the only, or at least the chief, gem of my character." Now that was lost. He was haunted by "the never-absent idea" that he had made Mary unhappy. "That still kills my soul," he wrote his best friend. "I can not but reproach myself, for even wishing to be happy while she is otherwise."

By the end of January he was able to resume his routine work, but in a listless, sporadic fashion. "I have, within the last few days, been making a most discreditable exhibition of myself in the way of hypochondriaism," he told Stuart on January 20, but he could not control his emotions even long enough to offer an explanation. "I have not sufficient composure to write a long letter," he informed his partner. Three days later his condition had not improved. "I am now the most miserable man living," he informed Stuart. "If what I feel were equally distributed to the whole human family, there would not be one cheerful face on the earth."

Lincoln's collapse became the subject of public comment and gossip. Some of his acquaintances, not aware of the seriousness of his illness, were lighthearted about Lincoln's having had "two Cat fits, and a Duck fit." Better informed, James C. Conkling wrote Mercy Levering that after a week in the sickroom Lincoln "is reduced and emaciated in appearance and seems scarcely to possess strength enough to speak above a whisper. His case at present is truly deplorable." The Edwardses said flatly that he was crazy. Presently there were rumors about the causes of his depression. Springfield concluded that Lincoln was grieving because Mary Todd had broken their engagement. In this scenario Lincoln appeared, as Conkling wrote, a "poor hapless simple swain who loved most true but was not loved again."

VIII

During the following months Lincoln tried to bring his life back under control. Dropping out of the Edwards social circle, he no longer saw much of his friends, and, as Conkling rightly suspected, he tried "to drown his cares among the intricacies and perplexities of the law." In April he took a major step toward solving his financial uncertainties by entering into law partnership with Stephen T. Logan. From the outset Logan & Lincoln, with an office on the east side of North Fifth Street, had many clients, but Lincoln, who probably received a third, rather than one-half, of the fees, did not make a great deal of money.

He was still unhappy and far from well. In August he decided to visit Speed, who had returned to Kentucky, and for nearly a month he stayed at Farmington, the Speed home near Louisville. In that spacious mansion, built by skilled Philadelphia artisans around 1809, he experienced a life of leisure that he had never known before. Everything was arranged for his comfort. One of the house slaves was even assigned to be his personal servant. Lincoln took long walks in the fields with Joshua. He made friends with Mary, Joshua Speed's half sister, and on trips into Louisville he met his brother, James Speed, who lent him books from his law library. The devout Mrs. Speed, observing that he was still very melancholy, had long, motherly talks with him and presented him with a Bible, urging him "to read it—to adopt its precepts and pray for its promises." "I intend to read it regularly when I return home," he promised, adding equivocally, "I doubt not that it is really . . . the best cure for the 'Blues' could one but take it according to the truth."

All in all, it was a most successful vacation, and Lincoln was so charmed by his Kentucky experiences that he did not even wince when, on the steamboat returning home, he encountered twelve chained slaves, "strung together precisely like so many fish upon a trot-line." A "gentleman" was taking them from their Kentucky homes to the Deep South, where, Lincoln recognized, "the lash of the master is proverbially more ruthless and unrelenting than any other where." Years later he would remember the brutality of the scene, but now, absorbed in his own unhappiness, he noted only that the slaves were "the most cheerful and apparently happy creatures on board."

In Kentucky he came to realize that Speed was facing a psychological crisis much like his own. His friend was engaged to Fanny Henning, a vivacious girl with what Lincoln called "heavenly *black eyes*," but as the time for marriage neared, he began to have second thoughts. He worried that he did not love Fanny as he should. Back in Springfield, Lincoln watched the development of the affair with almost painful interest, and he sent a stream of letters designed to keep his friend's spirits up and to encourage him to marry. In effect, Lincoln and Speed were acting out a game of doctor and patient; in the winter of 1840–1841 Lincoln had been the sufferer and Speed had offered encouraging advice; now it was Speed who was at risk and Lincoln was trying to save his health and sanity.

In arguing with Speed, Lincoln was also arguing with himself. Did his friend fear he did not love his fiancée enough? "What nonsense!" Lincoln exclaimed. Speed had not courted Fanny for her wealth, because she had none, and he had not wooed her because she was "moral, aimiable, sensible, or even of good character." He had asked her to marry him because he had fallen head over heels in love with her. After Speed confessed to "excessively bad feeling" when Fanny became seriously ill, Lincoln took this as "indubitable evidence of your undying affection for her." "Why Speed," he reasoned, "if you did not love her, although you might not wish her death, you would most calmly be resigned to it." As the date for Speed's marriage approached, Lincoln warned that it was "probable, that your nerves will fail you occasionally for a while," but he predicted that all would be well if his friend avoided exposure to bad weather—which, he noted, "my experience clearly proves to be verry severe on defective nerves"—and did not allow himself to be idle. "In two or three months, to say the most," he predicted, you "will be the happiest of men."

Once the wedding took place, a different note entered Lincoln's letters. He awaited "with intense anxiety and trepidation" Speed's report on his marriage. When Speed reported that he was far happier than he ever expected to be, Lincoln was overjoyed. "I am not going beyond the truth, when

I tell you, that the short space it took me to read your last letter, gave me more pleasure, than the total sum of all I have enjoyed since that fatal first of Jany. '41." He might have left it at that, but he needed to make sure that Speed, after all his doubts and suffering, was happy. Eight months after the wedding he asked bluntly: "Are you now, in *feeling* as well as *judgment,* glad you are married as you are?" "From any body but me," he realized, "this would be an impudent question not to be tolerated; but I know you will pardon it in me."

IX

He had a reason for asking Speed to reply quickly, for he was once more approaching marriage with Mary Todd. After their rupture the two had tried to avoid each other, but in a small town like Springfield each was always conscious of what the other was doing. Then Mrs. Simeon Francis, wife of Lincoln's good friend, the editor of the *Sangamo Journal,* decided to intervene. Inviting both Lincoln and Mary to a social affair, she brought them face-to-face and enjoined, "Be friends again."

Presently they began meeting at the Francis house, keeping the secret from everyone except Dr. Henry, who was carefully monitoring Lincoln's physical and emotional health, and Julia Jayne, Mary's most intimate friend. They took special care not to let the Edwardses know, because after the engagement was broken, they had bluntly told Mary that she and Lincoln "had better not ever marry—that their natures, mind—education—raising etc. were so different they could not live happily as husband and wife."

In these private meetings the couple rediscovered that they had many interests in common, and their growing intimacy was given a special boost by a political contretemps. In February 1842 the State Bank of Illinois, which Lincoln had so often defended in the state legislature, had been forced to close, and its notes became worthless. As commerce virtually ceased throughout Illinois, state auditor Shields quite properly issued a directive that the bank's notes would not be accepted in payment of taxes. Immediately Whigs tried to take advantage of the crisis to attack the Democratic administration of the state and especially Shields, who, next to Douglas, was the most prominent young Democrat in Illinois, almost certainly slated for higher office.

No one took a more active part in this assault than Lincoln, who always had access to the columns of the *Sangamo Journal.* Picking up the pseudonym of someone who had written several amusing letters to the editor from "Lost Townships," he used the persona of "Rebecca," a rough, uneducated, but shrewd countrywoman, to attack Democratic policies and to make fun of Shields. Effectively imitating the rural idiom, he reported "Aunt Becca's" conversation with "neighbor S——," who claimed that the financial crisis was invented by the politicians and that Shields's proclamation was "a lie, and not a well told one at that. It grins out like a copper dollar. Shields is a fool as well as a liar. With him truth is out of the question."

Then, allowing his sense of humor free rein, Lincoln had "Aunt Becca" report her neighbor's description of Shields at a charitable fair the previous winter attended by all the eligible young women of Springfield: "He was paying his money to this one and that one, and tother one . . . ; and the sweet distress he seemed to be in,—his very features, in the exstatic agony of his soul, spoke audibly and distinctly—'Dear girls, *it is distressing,* but I cannot marry you all. Too well I know how much you suffer; but do, *do,* remember, it is not my fault that I am so handsome and *so* interesting.' "

Obviously Lincoln had fun writing his "Lost Townships" letter, and when he proudly showed his manuscript to Mary Todd and Julia Jayne, they helped him sharpen its barbs before it appeared in the *Sangamo Journal* on September 2. Carried away by the excitement, the two young women decided to write their own letter, a rather clumsy effort that capitalized on the rumor that Shields was going to demand personal satisfaction for the insults he had received; they had Aunt Rebecca offer: "Let him only come here, and he may squeeze my hand. . . . If that ain't personal satisfaction, I can only say that he is the fust man that was not satisfied with squeezin my hand." They followed this up with a doggerel, signed "Cathleen," announcing Shields's approaching marriage to "Rebecca, the widow."

In selecting Shields as the object of their ridicule, the three were playing a dangerous game. They had attacked the state auditor at his most vulnerable points, for, though a man of good sense and excellent character, he had ornate and affected manners and fancied himself irresistible to women. Moreover he had no sense of humor. Hot-tempered and excitable, Shields demanded that Simeon Francis reveal the name of his anonymous assailant. In order to protect the women, Lincoln authorized Francis to say he was responsible for all the "Lost Townships" letters. On September 17, 1842, Shields wrote Lincoln "requiring a full, positive and absolute retraction of all offensive allusions used by you in these communications." The consequences of a refusal he did not specify, but they did not need spelling out: Shields, an expert shot, was a military man, familiar with the protocol of the code duello.

Shields's letter, borne by his designated friend, General John D. Whiteside, the state fund commissioner, reached Lincoln in Tremont, where he was attending the Tazewell County Circuit Court, and his initial reaction was that he was "wholly opposed to duelling, and would do anything to avoid it that might not degrade him in the estimation of himself and friends." Left to himself, he probably would have made peace with Shields, denying any intention to reflect on his character. But Lincoln made the mistake of consulting a hot-blooded young Springfield physician, Dr. Elias H. Merryman, who clearly wanted a duel to take place. Under Merryman's coaching he refused to apologize, because Shields's letter had contained "so much assumption of facts, and so much of menace." He would, he told Merryman, fight before submitting to "such *degradation.*"

After that, Whiteside brought Shields's challenge to a duel, and Lincoln named Merryman his second. As the party challenged, Lincoln had the right to name the weapons, and he chose broadswords. He had had some experience with cavalry swords during the Black Hawk War, and, under instruction from another young Springfield lawyer, Albert Taylor Bledsoe, he had probably been exercising with them for some weeks. Anyway, he realized that, with his height and long arms, broadswords would give him a considerable advantage over Shields, who was only five feet nine inches tall. Lincoln took the proposed encounter with great seriousness. "I did not intend to hurt Shields unless I did so clearly in self-defense," he said later. "If it had been necessary I could have split him from the crown of his head to the end of his backbone."

Because dueling was outlawed by the Illinois state constitution, with a penitentiary sentence of one to five years for those convicted of the offense, any encounter between Shields and Lincoln had to take place out of the state, and the parties agreed on a spot in Missouri, across the Mississippi River from Alton. Haste was necessary, for news of the impending duel had spread through Springfield, and arrests for all the participants were threatened.

Accompanied by Merryman, Bledsoe, and William Butler, Lincoln arrived at Alton on September 22 and crossed the river to the dueling ground, where they met Shields's party. Just as the encounter was about to begin, John J. Hardin, Lincoln's political associate and a relative of Mary Todd, and Dr. R. W. English intervened to try to stop the fight. As friends of both parties, they persuaded Shields to withdraw his insulting note, so that Lincoln could disavow any intention of injuring the auditor's "personal or private character or standing . . . as a man or a gentleman" and claim that he wrote the "Lost Townships" correspondence "solely for political effect."

With that, the parties shook hands and returned to Illinois. The episode remained one of Lincoln's most painful memories. He was so ashamed of it that he and Mary "mutually agreed—never to speak, of it." Years later during the Civil War, when an impertinent army officer referred to the affair, Lincoln, with a flushed face, replied, "I do not deny it, but if you desire my friendship, you will never mention it again." Of course, he was humiliated to remember that he had acted foolishly, and he was embarrassed that, as a lawyer and officer of the court, he had deliberately violated the law. But what really hurt was the realization that he had allowed himself to be ruled by his turbulent emotions. With anguish he remembered how he had so recently urged his fellow citizens to be guided by "reason, cold, calculating, unimpassioned reason."

But the Shields affair also had some unanticipated benefits. For one thing, it taught Lincoln a lesson about publishing anonymous letters. This practice, which probably dated back to his days as a freshman legislator in Vandalia, had led to the acrimonious exchanges with Adams in the "Sampson's Ghost" correspondence and now to the dangerous encounter with Shields in the "Lost Townships" letters. Thereafter Lincoln wrote no more such letters. It also helped him understand how painful the unintended effects of his undisciplined sense of humor could be. Rarely in the future did he use comedy to castigate and destroy; he had learned that his wit was most effective when directed against himself.

But the greatest positive result of the Shields encounter was the renewal of his engagement to Mary Todd, who was touched by his chivalry in covering her contributions to the "Lost Townships" letters. Encouraged by Speed's assurances that he was very happy with Fanny, Lincoln renewed his offer of marriage and was accepted. At the last possible moment they informed the Edwardses, for, as she told her sister, "the world—woman, and man were uncertain and slippery and . . . it was best to keep the secret courtship from all eyes and ears." Elizabeth Edwards, who delighted in giving grand parties, had only a few hours to prepare for the wedding on November 4.

Lincoln was equally secretive, and he did not ask James H. Matheny, his close friend who worked in the circuit court office, to act as his best man until late afternoon of the wedding day. As he prepared for the ceremony, Lincoln, like many another bridegroom, began to get cold feet, and Matheny recalled that he "looked and acted as if he were going to the slaughter." While he was dressing and blacking his boots, Speed Butler, the son of his landlord, asked where he was going, and Lincoln replied, "To hell, I suppose."

Despite the haste and the forebodings, the wedding ceremony, presided over by Episcopal minister Charles Dresser, went off without incident, and Lincoln placed on his wife's finger a ring engraved "Love is eternal."

CHAPTER FOUR

Always a Whig

———◆———

"Nothing new here," Lincoln wrote a friend on November 11, 1842, "except my marrying, which to me, is matter of profound wonder." In the years ahead he was to have many occasions to wonder, for his marriage marked a change in the direction of his career. After 1842 his turbulent mood swings, which alternated between grandiosity and depression, were greatly moderated. He put himself on the steady course of a proper, aspiring member of the bourgeoisie. He became a parent and a householder. He assiduously cultivated his profession and business as a lawyer. And he became what he had belittled in his lyceum speech, one of those "great and good men sufficiently qualified for any task they should undertake . . . , whose ambition would aspire to nothing beyond a seat in Congress, a gubernatorial or a presidential chair."

I

The newlyweds took up residence in the Globe Tavern, a simple, two-story wooden structure on the north side of Adams Street, between Third and Fourth streets. It had about thirty rooms, mostly for transients, but in addition, according to its advertisement, it offered "eight pleasant and comfortable rooms for boarders." There, for $4 a week, the Lincolns occupied an eight-by-fourteen-foot room on the second floor and took their meals in the common dining room. This was not an unusual arrangement for a young married couple. John Todd Stuart had taken his wife to the Globe for a time after their marriage. Indeed, Mary Lincoln's sister Frances and her husband, Dr. William Wallace, had stayed for three years in the very room that the

Lincolns occupied. Though the Globe was a respectable hotel, its accommodations were inferior to those of its principal competitor, the American House, and it was often noisy.

Lincoln, who was away at his law office most of the days when he was not out traveling the judicial circuit, was happy enough with the Globe Tavern; indeed, it was probably the most comfortable place he had ever resided. For Mary, the hotel was a comedown after her father's spacious house in Lexington and the Edwards's luxurious mansion; for the first time in her life she had no personal servants or slaves, no place to store or display her possessions, no private room where she could receive callers. To add to her discomfort, the proprietor of the Globe was stingy, scanting his guests on food and begrudging them candles.

But she voiced no dissatisfaction with her lot. Nor did she complain when her sisters, who had warned her against an unsuitable marriage, largely dropped her from their social circle. She was so much in love with her husband that she was willing to live a very quiet, almost secluded life, and the name of this formerly lively, sociable young woman virtually disappeared from Springfield letters and gossip.

Pregnancy helped account for the remarkable transformation. The sexual fears Lincoln had voiced before marriage proved groundless, and very soon Mary knew she was expecting a baby. She may not have told her husband right away, for in March, Lincoln, in response to a jovial inquiry from Speed, wrote, "About the prospect of your having a namesake at our house cant say, exactly yet." But by May, Springfield was buzzing about "coming events" in the Lincoln family, and William Butler wrote Speed the news. When Speed made further inquiry, Lincoln responded jokingly: "I had not *heard* one word before I got your letter; but I have so much confidence in the judgement of a Butler on such a subject, that I incline to think there may be some reality in it. What *day* does Butler appoint?" On August 1, 1843, just three days short of nine months after the wedding, the Lincolns' first child was born. They named him Robert Todd Lincoln, after Mary's father.

In this trying period Lincoln did his best to be supportive, and after Robert's birth Mary awoke to see her "darling husband, . . . bending over me, with such love and tenderness." But such displays of affection were rare. As Mary said years later, Lincoln "was *not* a demonstrative man, when he felt most deeply, he expressed the least." The relationship between husband and wife was never an equal one. She always addressed him, in formal Victorian style, as "Mr. Lincoln." Before they were married, he sometimes called her "Molly," but now in his letters he referred to her as "Mary." In private, he called her "Puss" and, more significantly, "little woman" or "child-wife." After Robert's birth, he always addressed her as "Mother."

Realizing that they could not raise a family in a hotel room, the Lincolns began looking for a house of their own, but money was scarce. Lincoln no longer had his salary from the legislature, and his income from his law practice had diminished during the final months of his partnership with

Stuart. Joining with Logan opened the prospect of a brighter future, but it offered no immediate increase in Lincoln's income. He was probably still paying off some of the debts he had accumulated during his New Salem days, and he felt obliged to contribute to the support of his father and stepmother, who were now settled in Coles County, on an unprofitable homestead called Goosenest Prairie.

The best the Lincolns could do was to rent a small, three-room frame house on South Fourth Street, to which they moved in the fall of 1843. There Robert S. Todd, Mary's father, found them shortly before Christmas, when he came to visit his four daughters who lived in Springfield and to inspect his newest grandchild and namesake. Todd took a great liking to his son-in-law, who was already representing him in a highly technical case before the Sangamon County Circuit Court involving some Illinois lands Todd had purchased. Todd was obviously touched by the meagerness of Mary's sur-roundings and without comment dropped a gold piece in her hand. After-ward he arranged for her to receive $120 a year for the rest of his lifetime —a considerable sum, which would more than cover the cost of hiring a maid at $1.50 a week. Todd also deeded to the Lincolns—as he did to each of his other married Springfield daughters and their husbands—eighty acres of Illinois land.

By 1844 the Lincolns felt able to buy a home of their own, and they purchased a cottage on the corner of Eighth and Jackson streets owned by the Reverend Charles Dresser, the Episcopal minister who had married them. It was small, to be sure. On the ground floor there were three rooms —a parlor, a sitting room, and a kitchen; in the half loft above, there were two bedrooms, but the ceilings under the sloping roof slanted so that there was only a small area, about four feet wide, in which Lincoln could stand erect. Over the kitchen there was an attic used for storage or as a maid's room. The downstairs rooms were heated by fireplaces and there were wood-burning stoves in the upstairs bedrooms. Of course, there was no gas or electric light. Water came from a cistern and a well in the backyard. A latrine near the back fence offered the only sanitary facilities. Despite its limitations, it was a sturdy, well-built house, and the Lincolns thought it worth every penny of what it cost—$1,200, plus a town lot on Adams Street, which Lincoln owned, valued at $300.

II

Running a household required money, and Lincoln set about earning it with greater energy than he had ever before demonstrated. A few years later, in notes he prepared for a lecture on the legal profession, he began, "The leading rule for the lawyer, as for the man, of every calling, is *diligence.*" He was speaking from experience. He worked incessantly, handling virtually every kind of business that could come before a prairie lawyer.

In the early months of his partnership with Stephen T. Logan, he spent much of his time in appearances before the United States District Court under the Bankruptcy Act, which went into effect on February 1, 1842. Designed to allow businessmen to escape some of the losses brought about by the unrelenting depression, the act permitted federal judges to declare petitioners bankrupt if their debts were greater than their assets. Of the 1,742 applicants in Illinois, nearly all employed lawyers. Before the law was repealed in 1843, Logan & Lincoln handled 77 of these cases—a number exceeded by only three other firms in the entire state. In most of these cases, which generally were uncontested, they earned fees of $10.

Though bankruptcy cases provided a welcome source of income during the first year of Lincoln's marriage, most of his earnings came from office work, like drafting wills and petitions, from petty suits before the justices of the peace or county commissioners, and especially from actions before the Sangamon County Circuit Court. On a single day at fall term of that court in November 1842, for instance, Logan & Lincoln had seventeen cases. They represented Thomas W. Sparks in his suit against Henry and Thomas Bird, who, he claimed, unlawfully withheld the possession of 106 acres of land; they appeared in behalf of John R. Herndon, administrator of the estate of John Wilson, who complained that one Seth Cutter failed to pay $220 for goods he had purchased; they obtained a divorce for John Jackson from his wife, Maria; and so on and on.

Business was so good that the partners could afford to leave their crowded quarters on North Fifth Street and move to the premier business location in Springfield, the newly constructed Tinsley Building, on the southwest corner of Sixth and Adams streets. The post office occupied the ground floor, and the United States District Court, before which both Logan and Lincoln frequently appeared, was on the second floor. Their office was just above it, in a front room overlooking both the state capitol and the county courthouse.

Billy Herndon, who was studying law with Logan and Lincoln, described how Lincoln dealt with a prospective client. He would listen to the man's story "well—patiently, occasionally now and then breaking in as the story progressed by asking a question: the man would answer it, and then he would proceed and end his story." After the man had finished, Lincoln would often say: "I am not exactly satisfied about some point—Come into the office in an hour or so, and I will give you my opinion—a positive one." When the client returned, Lincoln might say, "You are in the right," and they would proceed to draw up the papers leading to a suit. But he might also tell the client: "You are in the wrong of the case and I would advise you to compromise, . . . do not bring a suit on the facts of your case, because you are in the wrong."

Lincoln learned much from Logan, unquestionably the leading figure in the Sangamon County bar. Nine years older than Lincoln, Logan had made a name for himself as commonwealth's attorney in his native Kentucky before moving to Illinois, where his merits were so promptly recognized that he was elected circuit court judge. In that position he had certified Lincoln's enrollment in the Sangamon County bar in 1837. Unhappy over the meager compensation given judges, he resigned and returned to private practice with Edward D. Baker, a spellbinding orator who could mesmerize juries. Logan's sharp analytical mind and his knowledge of legal precedents and technicalities made him a formidable opponent in the courtroom. But his harsh, cracked voice kept him from becoming an effective public speaker, and juries were often put off by his wizened figure and his wrinkled countenance, topped by a mass of frowzy hair.

It was to compensate for these deficiencies that, after the breakup of his partnership with Baker, Logan turned to Lincoln, thinking, as he said later, he would be "exceedingly useful to me in getting the good will of juries." Lincoln's years as a surveyor and his service in the state legislature had given him a wide range of acquaintances. It was hard to find anyone in Sangamon County who did not recognize his lanky figure, and his remarkable memory enabled him to identify by name, residence, and family connections nearly every person called to jury duty.

In the courtroom Lincoln maintained that personal connection, seeming to speak to each juror individually and in a conversational tone. He rarely used technical language, and he was a master of the homespun anecdote to illustrate his point. In a McLean County case where a physician claimed that a man charged with murder was insane, evidencing that he frequently picked at his head, Lincoln, appearing for the state, skillfully deflated the doctor's testimony. "Now," he remarked, "I sometimes pick my head, and those joking fellows at Springfield tell me that there may be a living, moving cause for it, and that the trouble isn't at all on the inside. It's only a case for fine-tooth combs."

He knew the importance of an effective summing-up statement. In a lecture prepared for young lawyers he advised: "Extemporaneous speaking should be practiced and cultivated. It is the lawyer's avenue to the public. However able and faithful he may be in other respects, people are slow to bring him business, if he cannot make a speech." But he also knew that lawyers could not make "a more fatal error . . . , than relying too much on speech-making," instead of looking up precedents and logically examining the evidence. In his concluding remarks to a jury he usually spoke from a short but carefully prepared outline, and he avoided the flowery pastures of rhetoric into which he had strayed in his lyceum and temperance lectures. As he warned Herndon: "Billy, don't shoot too high—aim lower and the common people will understand you. They are the ones you want to reach."

To Logan's surprise, Lincoln proved to be much more than a courtroom litigator. Up to this point his knowledge of the law was, as Logan recalled, "very small," for he had largely imitated Stuart, who "never went much upon the law." But now he "began to pick up a considerable ambition in the law." Observing the care and precision with which his senior partner drafted his pleadings, Lincoln sought to make his own equally succinct and correct. On occasion, he would seek Logan's advice on technical points. Very early in the partnership, representing the plaintiff in a slander case, Lincoln drew up a declaration charging that the defendant had called his client "a damned rogue." Reviewing the document, Logan recognized that the words, though offensive, were not legally significant and inserted the necessary formula: "And the plaintiff . . . says that the Defendant thereby meant and intended to charge the plaintiff with the crime of Larceny and that he was so understood by those who heard him."

Mostly, though, Lincoln learned by reading. Logan's example taught him that there was more to the law than common sense and simple equity, and he began studying procedures and precedents. The partners had no considerable law library of their own, but after the Illinois Supreme Court moved into its quarters in the statehouse in 1841, attorneys had access to an excellent collection of legal reports and standard reference works.

Lincoln never did become a devoted reader of general texts or theoretical books on the law. Years later Herndon claimed that Lincoln "never thoroughly read any elementary law book. In fact . . . I never knew him to read through and through any law book of any kind." The charge was largely true. "I cannot read generally. I never read text books for I have no particular motive to drive and whip me to it," Lincoln explained. "I don't, and can't remember such reading." But Herndon's remark was really beside the point, for Lincoln spent night after night in the Supreme Court Library, searching out precedents that applied to the cases he was working on. This was work he enjoyed. "When I have a particular case in hand," he explained, "I . . . love to dig up the question by the roots and hold it up and dry it before the fires of the mind." Logan's final judgment on Lincoln's legal accomplishments was more perceptive than Herndon's: "I don't think he studied very much. I think he learned his law more in the study of cases. . . . He got to be a pretty good lawyer though his general knowledge of law was never very formidable. But he would study out his case and make about as much of it as anybody."

Lincoln's growing mastery of the law became evident in his increasingly frequent appearances before the Illinois Supreme Court. In his earliest ventures before the high court he based his case on the hairsplitting technicalities of which young lawyers are so often fond. In 1841, for instance, he represented a man named Amos Worthing, who had won a verdict in the Tazewell County Circuit Court, which his opponent, Jacob Maus, appealed. The law required Maus to post an appeal bond—a document guaranteeing that he would pay the costs of the appeal if he lost. The bond was supposed to be "under seal." In earlier days signatures on such legal documents had been attested by the impression of a signet ring in sealing wax, but by the 1840s a signer merely made a vaguely circular scrawl, looking something like a child's drawing of a puffy cloud, under his name. Discovering that Maus's surety had carelessly failed to add such a scrawl below his signature, Lincoln asked the supreme court to dismiss the case. A majority of the judges agreed, to the dismay of Justice Sidney Breese, who dissented: "The rule . . . seems to me to be destitute of any good reason on which to base it, and altogether too technical for this age."

In subsequent years Lincoln had many more cases before the Illinois Supreme Court, but, perhaps through Logan's influence, they less and less frequently depended on such technicalities. He came to feel very much at home in this court, where, as Herndon said, an attorney had "ample time to read the record and gather up the facts of the case—the issues and the law arising thereon." The court required attorneys to prepare "abstracts of the case . . . stating the facts in a condensed form and the issues made thereby." The supreme court limited oral arguments and made its decisions largely on the basis of these written briefs, which were sometimes elaborate, with extensive citations of precedents. In preparing his presentations for the court, Lincoln took nothing for granted and frequently offered precedents that stretched back to the beginnings of English common law. When Herndon asked why he went to so much trouble, he responded: "I dare not trust this case on presumptions that this court knows all things. I argued the case on the presumption that the court did not know any thing." His care and thoroughness made him one of the most successful practitioners before the court, and by the time he left for Washington in 1861 he had appeared before the highest court in Illinois in at least three hundred cases.

III

In the fall of 1844, Logan and Lincoln decided to dissolve their highly successful partnership. The senior partner told Lincoln that he wanted to go into business with his son, David Logan, and Lincoln did not argue with his decision. Perhaps he was not satisfied to receive less than half the income from the partnership; perhaps he realized that his political aspirations must clash with those of Logan, since both wanted to go to Congress. But there were no hard words as the partners decided, as Logan said, to go their ways "amicably and in friendship." The severance was not an abrupt one. Logan and Lincoln continued to appear together in the December term of the Illinois Supreme Court, and their professional notice ran in the *Sangamo Journal* until March 1845. They continued to join forces on important cases throughout the remaining years of Lincoln's practice.

Lincoln took a new partner. One fall morning in 1844 he came dashing up the stairs to the third floor of the Tinsley Building, where he found William H. Herndon busily studying. "Billy," he asked breathlessly, "do you want to enter into partnership with me in the law business?" Herndon managed to stammer, "Mr. Lincoln this is something unexpected by me—it is an undeserved honor; and yet I say I will gladly and thankfully accept the kind and generous offer." Sensing that the young man was flustered with gratitude, Lincoln remarked easily, "Billy, I can trust you, if you can trust me," and the partnership came into being.

Many found the new partnership puzzling. Now an established, prominent lawyer, Lincoln could have had his pick of distinguished Illinois attorneys. Herndon heard that John Todd Stuart very much wanted to renew his association with Lincoln and was resentful when a beginner was chosen instead. Lincoln left no record of his reasons, but it is clear that he was tired of being a junior partner and wanted to head his own firm. He was already attracting all the business he could handle, so that he did not need a partner with a name to draw in clients. He thought Herndon had considerable promise as a lawyer. He had watched him read law for two or three years in the office of Logan & Lincoln and found him "a laborious, studious young man . . . far better informed on almost all subjects than I have been."

There were also political reasons behind his choice of Herndon. Lincoln aspired to go to Congress, but the Whig party in central Illinois was split into two distinct factions. In the past, leadership had come from the eminently respectable Stuarts and Edwardses, few in number but rich in family tradition, but the majority of the Whig voters were now "self made men—men who had power," scorned the older leadership, and wanted a hand in shaping party policy. Lincoln needed the support of both factions. Marriage to the elegant Mary Todd gave him a connection to the silk-stocking element of the party, but the "shrewd, wild boys about town" favored the enormously popular Edward D. Baker. Recognizing that Herndon was a leader of this populist element in the party, Lincoln chose him as partner in part to give a signal to the insurgent young Whigs that he had not deserted them.

More important than any of these calculations was an essential fact: Lincoln really liked Herndon. He respected Stuart and he admired Logan, but for neither of them did he have genuine affection. Toward Herndon, however, he had an almost paternal feeling, and Herndon, in turn, gave him absolute and unquestioning loyalty. During the long years of their partnership he always addressed Herndon, nine years his junior, as "Billy," while Herndon invariably called him "Mr. Lincoln."

There was much to like about this new partner. He bubbled over with ideas and enthusiasm. He longed to be part of the larger intellectual world, and, though he had been born in Kentucky, he wrote that he steadily "turned *New Englandwards* for my ideas—my sentiments—my education." He developed an unmanageable appetite for books. A credulous law student believed that "in addition to all his professional reading, Mr. Herndon read every year more new books in history, pedagogy, medicine, theology, and general literature, than all the teachers, doctors, and ministers in Springfield put together." On his shelves were authors almost unknown in the Mississippi Valley—Kant, Renan, Fichte, Buckle, Froude. Perhaps he did not always understand what he read, but he learned enough to become a kind of frontier evangelist for transcendentalism, that Emersonian faith that the questioning heart could, without mediation of religion or authority, discern truth. He prided himself on his "mud instinct," his "dog sagacity," which enabled him to see "to the gizzard" of questions. What he saw encouraged him to believe in illimitable progress, and he greeted the unseen with a cheer: "The Struggles of this age and succeeding ages for God and man— Religion—Humanity and *Liberty* . . . may they triumph and Conquer forever, is my ardent wish and most fervent soul-prayer."

He and Lincoln were in almost every way exact opposites. Lincoln was tall, slow-moving, and careless in dress; Herndon was short, quick, and something of a dandy, affecting patent-leather shoes and kid gloves. Lincoln was melancholy, his depressed moods interrupted by outbursts of antic humor; Herndon was always upbeat and optimistic, and he had no sense of humor at all. The senior partner disliked generalities, and his mind cautiously moved in logical progression from one fact to the next, while his junior leapt ahead, using intuition to arrive at his conclusions.

Once when Herndon urged his partner to talk faster and with more energy when addressing a jury, Lincoln replied by graphically illustrating the difference between his mind and his partner's. "Give me your woman's little knife with its short twin blades, and give me that old jack knife lieing [sic] over there," he told Herndon. Then he opened the short blades of the small knife and said: "See here it opens quickly and at the point travels through but a small portion of space—but see this long bladed jack knife: it opens slowly and its points travel through a greater distance of space than your little knife: it moves slower than your little knife, but it can do more execution." "Just so with these long convolutions of my brain," Lincoln added; "they have to act slowly—pass as it were through a greater space than shorter convolutions that snap off quickly. . . . I am compelled by nature to speak slowly. I commence way back like the boys do when they want to get a good start. My weight and speed get momentum to jump far."

The new partners occupied a room in the Tinsley Building, and Herndon took the lead in buying desks, a table, and some basic books, at a cost of $168.65, half of which was charged to his partner. It remained wretchedly bare. Gibson W. Harris, a student in the law office, described it: "The furniture, somewhat dilapidated, consisted of one small desk and a table, a sofa or lounge with a raised head at one end, and a half-dozen plain wooden chairs. The floor was never scrubbed. . . . Over the desk a few shelves had been enclosed; this was the office bookcase holding a set of Blackstone, Kent's Commentaries, Chitty's Pleadings, and a few other books."

At the outset it was not an equal partnership. Lincoln interviewed most of the clients, wrote the important legal papers, and pleaded the suits in court. Herndon, still the student and the learner, performed routine jobs; he answered inquiries as to Lincoln's whereabouts or " 'toated books' and 'hunted up authorities' " for the senior partner's use. It was also his responsibility to manage the office, preserve the records, and keep the files straight. As Lincoln later told Henry C. Whitney, a fellow lawyer in Urbana, he supposed that Herndon "had system and would keep things in order."

His hope was misplaced, for Herndon was not an orderly person. It is doubtful, though, that anyone could have kept Lincoln's papers in order.

The firm had no filing cabinets and no files. In one corner of the office was a bundle of papers with a note in Lincoln's handwriting: "When you can't find it anywhere else, look in this." Herndon sometimes took legal papers home, where they were lost. Lincoln frequently stuck documents and correspondence in his stovepipe hat, which Herndon said was "his desk and his memorandum-book." As a result the partners were constantly looking for misplaced letters and documents, and there were times when they had to confess frankly that papers sent them were "lost or destroyed and cannot be found after search among the papers of Lincoln & Herndon."

Lincon's name drew clients to the new firm, and soon the partners had as much business as they could well manage. They appeared in their first case in the Sangamon County Circuit Court in March 1845, and their first suit in neighboring Menard County was called in May of the same year. During the first twelve months of the partnership, the firm had fourteen cases in the circuit court at Springfield; the following year the partners handled more than twice as many. The Lincoln & Herndon fee book for 1847 listed over one hundred cases in which Lincoln participated before he left in October to serve in Congress.

Like most other attorneys, Lincoln and Herndon took on whatever clients came their way. They defended persons charged with murder, burglary, assault, embezzlement, and almost every other kind of crime. Sometimes their clients were innocent and sometimes they were guilty, but the partners felt that all were entitled to be represented. Nor was Lincoln squeamish about the social implications of the cases that he argued. In 1841 he appeared before the Illinois Supreme Court in the case of *Bailey* v. *Cromwell,* which concerned the attempted sale of a young black woman, Nance, in Tazewell County. The court followed his reasoning in ruling: "the presumption of law was, in this State, that every person was free, without regard to color. . . . The sale of a free person is illegal." But six years later he appeared for Robert Matson, who was trying to recover his runaway slaves in Coles County. Matson had brought his Kentucky slaves across the Ohio River to work on his farm in southern Illinois. When the slaves ran away and, with the backing of local abolitionists, brought suit for their freedom, on the ground that the Northwest Ordinance forbade the introduction of slavery into the state of Illinois, Matson employed Lincoln, along with Usher F. Linder, to defend him. Characteristically Lincoln admitted his opponents' main argument, that the slaves were free if Matson had brought them to Illinois for permanent settlement, but he invoked the right of transit, which the courts had guaranteed to slaveholders who were taking their slaves temporarily into free territory. He placed great stress on Matson's public declaration, at the time he brought the slaves into Illinois, that he did not intend the slaves to remain permanently in Illinois and insisted that "no counter statement had ever been made publicly or privately by him." The circuit court ruled against Lincoln and his client, who, it was reported, left immediately for Kentucky without paying his attorneys' fees. Neither the

Matson case nor the Cromwell case should be taken as an indication of Lincoln's views on slavery; his business was law, not morality.

The partners' fees remained small. An appearance before a justice of the peace cost $5, and the usual fee for representing a client in the circuit court ranged from $10 to $25. In a very few cases of special difficulty the firm charged $50, and on one occasion an appearance before the Illinois Supreme Court brought $100. Lincoln believed strongly in making explicit financial arrangements before entering into a case. "The matter of fees," he noted in his projected lecture to young lawyers, "is important far beyond the mere question of bread and butter involved." Occasionally he took on a case for a contingency fee. If the client was willing to risk the cost, he promised in one letter, "I will do my best for the 'biggest kind of a fee' . . . if we succeed, and nothing if we fail." But for the most part he worked for fixed and agreed-upon fees, and he advised young lawyers not to take more than a small retainer in advance, lest they lose incentive and interest. He did not hesitate to dun a client: "I would like to have the little fee in the case, if convenient." He disliked suing for fees, but on at least six occasions he felt obliged to do so.

Despite differences in age and experience, the partners divided all income equally; Lincoln imitated the generosity that Stuart had shown him rather than the niggardliness that Logan had practiced. After the first few months the partners kept no systematic accounts, simply dividing equally the fees they received. As Lincoln told Whitney: "Billy and I never had the scratch of a pen between us; we *jest* divide as we go along." But Herndon did keep a record of cases in which the fees due to the partners were not immediately collected, carefully marking them "Paid" as the money was received.

IV

No amount of industry or care could earn a lawyer a satisfactory income from practice in Sangamon County alone. Most Springfield attorneys who were not independently wealthy felt obliged to travel with the judge of the circuit court when he made, twice every year, his pilgrimage from one county seat to another in his district. The vast Eighth Circuit, which eventually encompassed 11,000 square miles, stretched across two-thirds of the width of the state and one-third of its length. Both Stuart and Logan regularly traveled at least part of the circuit; even Herndon, who disliked the migratory life and preferred to remain in Springfield, estimated that he was on the circuit about one-fourth of the time. Lincoln, who had only occasionally attended courts in neighboring counties during the first years of his practice, became one of the most regular riders of the circuit.

The judge and the more affluent lawyers traveled the circuit in buggies, but Lincoln in the early days rode his rather decrepit horse, "Old Tom," carrying a change of underclothing, any necessary legal papers, and perhaps a book or two in his capacious saddlebags. When he could afford it, he had a local blacksmith make him a nondescript buggy. The countryside through which the procession traveled was sparsely inhabited, and they could go for miles without seeing another human. The caravan could usually travel only about four miles an hour, because the roads were atrocious. Most were little more than trails, and when the heavy black loam of the Illinois prairie began to thaw in the spring, it became fathomless mud, dangerous not merely to carriages but to horseback riders as well. Many streams had no bridges, and the judge often asked Lincoln, who had the longest legs of any member of the bar, to explore for a ford; if Lincoln could get over, the others would follow.

At night they stopped wherever they could find lodgings. Sometimes, Herndon remembered, they slept "with 20 men in the same room—some on old ropes—some on quilts—some on sheets—a straw or two under them." When they arose the next morning, a pitcher of cold water outside and a single towel served for their ablutions; those who got up late often found the towel too wet to use. After a breakfast of greasy food and what Leonard Swett, the Bloomington lawyer who regularly traveled the Eighth Circuit, called "pretty tough coffee—pretty mean," the caravan moved on toward the next county seat. Arriving on a Saturday or a Sunday, the lawyers resorted to a favorite hotel or tavern near the courthouse, where, again, they slept two or three to a bed.

The next morning the lawyers would be approached by litigants, often with their local counsel, who were glad to have the help of more experienced attorneys from Springfield and Bloomington—the two largest towns on the circuit. Business had to be transacted speedily—declarations and traverses drafted, petitions written, lists of witnesses drawn up—so that the judge could hear cases on Monday afternoon. There was little time to study cases closely, much less to look up precedents; lawyers on the circuit had to rely mostly on general knowledge and common sense.

Clients and local counsel eagerly sought Lincoln's services. On the circuit his reputation for integrity and fairness was even more important than in more technically difficult cases appealed to the state supreme court. In about a third of the cases in which Lincoln appeared on the circuit, he acted alone; in the others he worked with local counsel. He had few criminal cases and not many cases in chancery. Herndon enumerated the kinds of cases that formed the bulk of his circuit practice: "assault and battery—suits on notes —small disputes among neighbors—slander—warranties on horse trades —larceny of a small kind." Lincoln nearly always had as much business as he could readily handle, but it was never as great as that of the most prominent local attorneys.

After the court adjourned each day the lawyers had leisure to prepare new cases or they could explore the meager resources of the little towns they visited, all of which, except Springfield, Bloomington, and Pekin, had fewer than one thousand inhabitants. Mostly the attorneys had to amuse themselves, and, according to Herndon, they engaged in "fights—foot and horse races—knock down—wrestling—gambling etc." "Whiskey," he noted, "was abundant and freely used." After supper the judge and the lawyers might attend some local amusement, like a circus or a lecture, but if there was no other diversion they would sit before the fire and swap tall tales and anecdotes. When that happened, Lincoln, of course, was a center of attention, and, as Herndon remembered, "Judges—Jurors—Witnesses—Lawyers—merchants—etc etc have laughed at these jokes . . . till every muscle—nerve and cell of the body in the morning was sore at the whooping and hurrahing exercise." By the end of the week the session was ended, and the judge and the attendant lawyers moved on to the next county seat.

It took at least ten weeks to complete the circuit—and then the whole process had to be repeated in the fall. Consequently Lincoln spent about three months of every year traveling the Eighth Judicial Circuit—and he sometimes made additional trips on legal business to other counties that were not on this circuit. Many of the other attorneys returned to their homes over the weekends, but Lincoln generally remained with the court. In the early years of his marriage friends reported that he was "desperately homesick and turning his head frequently towards the south," and he usually broke the long fall term with a visit to Springfield. But it made no sense for him to keep rushing home; he was on the circuit to earn money, and the longer he stayed in the small county towns, the better acquainted he became with the local lawyers who could throw cases his way. His investment of time and energy paid off; he probably earned more than $150 a week, beyond expenses, while he was on the circuit.

Staying in these small towns also gave him a political advantage, and in his future political contests his strongest supporters were attorneys and clients he met on the circuit. He got to know thousands of central Illinois voters by name. In 1847, when J. H. Buckingham, a reporter for the *Boston Courier,* made a stage-coach trip through central Illinois with Lincoln, he found that he "knew, or appeared to know, every body we met, the name of the tenant of every farm-house, and the owner of every plat of ground." "Such a shaking of hands—such a how-d'ye-do—such a greeting of different kinds, as we saw, was never seen before," the newspaperman continued; "it seemed as if . . . he had a kind word, a smile and a bow for every body on the road, even to the horses, and the cattle, and the swine."

In addition, Lincoln remained on the circuit because he enjoyed the life. What others considered hardships were matters of complete indifference to him. He did not care where he slept, and he ate whatever food was put in front of him. If there were drawbacks to life on the circuit, the hearty, masculine atmosphere more than compensated for them. Traveling the circuit gave him relief from a domesticity that he sometimes found smothering.

V

The Lincolns' domestic life was often troubled. Husband and wife were as different in temperament as they were in physique. He was slow, moody, given to bouts of melancholy and long periods of silence. He depended on his inner resources. She was lively, talkative, and sociable, constantly needing the attention and admiration of others. Indifferent to what other people thought, he was not troubled when visitors found him in his favorite position for reading, stretched out at full length on the floor. She, who had grown up in houses with liveried black servants, was embarrassed when he answered the doorbell in his shirtsleeves.

A shortage of money contributed to their problems. Because Lincoln's income was low during the early years of their marriage, they could afford only a tiny house. Overcrowded when they moved in, it became more so after 1846 with the birth of their second son, Edward—named after Lincoln's political associate and friendly rival, Edward D. Baker. A minor remodeling of the house to create a new downstairs bedroom did not do much to ease the situation. Yet Mary loyally never made any public complaint about their straitened circumstances nor spoke of financial stringency in her letters. Instead she let gossip blame her for failing to show hospitality, when her house was so small that it had no dining room and meals had to be served in the kitchen. Similarly, she gained a reputation for stinginess when, in fact, she was trying to run a household on a very limited budget.

Lincoln, immersed in his own work, probably had no idea how hard his wife had to labor. She had to cook, clean, and scrub. She had to pump the water in the backyard and haul it into the house for heating. She had to keep the wood fire going in the kitchen stove and, during much of the year, in the living-room fireplace. Though Lincoln had his suits made by Benjamin R. Biddle, the local tailor, she had to sew all her own clothes, as well as those of her children; her purchases at John Irwin & Company, the Springfield general store, included needles, buttons, thread, muslin, calico, cambric, whalebones, and corset lace. And, above all, she had to pay close attention to her babies, especially to little Eddie, who was a sickly child. Despite the money her father gave her, she only occasionally had assistance in any of these chores. For a short time Harriet Hanks, one of Lincoln's cousins, who was attending the Springfield Female Seminary, helped out in the house, but she and Mary did not get along. More often she had an Irish-born maid—one of the "wild Irish," as she called them—but she thought they were undependable and lazy, and she quarreled with them all.

Mary Lincoln's bad temper was famous in Springfield. Everybody heard stories about the tongue-lashings that she gave to maids, to workmen about the house, to street vendors—and to her husband. In part, these were the result of overwork and exhaustion on the part of a woman who up to the time of her marriage had never turned her hand. In part, they reflected the unsteady condition of her health. Every spring she was afflicted with excruciating headaches—possibly the result of an allergy—and she suffered much from menstrual cramps. Highly emotional, she was terrified of lightning storms, of dogs, of robbers, and when she was in a panic, she could not control her actions.

In considerable measure Mary Lincoln's outbursts were reactions to her husband's behavior; he was a very difficult man to live with. For three months out of every year he was off riding the circuit, and she was left alone in her tiny house with two squalling children and, at best, an incompetent maid. She understood, and did not protest, the financial needs that sent Lincoln traveling, but she sadly told a neighbor "if her husband had staid at home as he ought to that she could love him better."

Even when he was at home, he did not provide the comfort, the warmth, the affection that she craved. After a busy day at work, seeing clients and attending to cases in court, he wanted to sit quietly before the fire, reading, and he failed to realize that his wife, cooped up in the house all day with no one to talk to but infants, longed for adult conversation. Sometimes his inattention made her fly off the handle. On one occasion as he sat reading in his rocking chair in the living room while she cooked dinner, she warned him that the fire was about to go out. Absorbed in his reading, he did not respond, and she called out again, and then a third time. Furious at being ignored, she found a way of getting his attention: she struck him on the nose with a piece of firewood.

Such episodes were infrequent. The subject of much gossip in Springfield, they incorrectly represented the Lincolns' marriage. For all their quarrels, they were devoted to each other. In the long years of their marriage Abraham Lincoln was never suspected of being unfaithful to his wife. She, in turn, was immensely proud of him and was his most loyal supporter and admirer. When someone compared her husband unfavorably to Douglas, she responded stoutly: "Mr. Lincoln may not be as handsome a figure . . . but the people are perhaps not aware that his heart is as large as his arms are long."

Their children further cemented their marriage. Both the Lincolns had to learn that parenting is a difficult art, and inevitably they made mistakes, especially with their first son, a short, chubby fellow, who from birth seemed to resemble the Todds more than the Lincolns. High-strung and overprotective, Mary constantly worried over Bob, and when the little boy disappeared from her sight for a few minutes, she was likely to alert the whole neighborhood that he was lost. Lincoln, for his part, gave too little attention to his oldest son. He did not ignore the child deliberately, but nothing in his upbringing suggested that a father should be comforting and nurturing. Occasionally he took the boy for walks, and when he was chopping firewood in the backyard he let his son help by splitting kindling. There is a touching account of Bob as a four-year-old trying to walk in his father's gigantic boots.

But Robert's principal memory of his father during these years was of his loading his saddlebags in preparation for going out on the circuit.

Both parents made some attempt to discipline their firstborn, who seems to have been a perfectly normal little boy, no more given to mischief than other children his age. But the whippings Mary administered were ineffectual—the more so because her husband made fun of her efforts—and when he tried to correct the child, she gave him a tongue-lashing. After the birth of Eddie, both parents pretty well gave up disciplining their offspring. Years later Mary reported that her husband said: "It is my pleasure that my children are free, happy and unrestrained by parental tyranny. Love is the chain whereby to bind a child to its parents."

Pride in their children helped the Lincolns through even the worst of their domestic discord. When Robert was only three years old, Lincoln described him to Speed in a characteristic understatement that could not conceal his satisfaction with his firstborn: "He is quite smart enough. I some times fear he is one of the little rare-ripe sort, that are smarter at about five than ever after." A few years later Mary did her own boasting when she wrote a friend: "I have a boy studying latin and greek and will be ten years old in a few days."

VI

Politics was another bond that held the Lincoln marriage together. Mary Lincoln, like her husband, was an ardent Whig. In a sense, they inherited their politics, for Mary's father was an influential Whig spokesman in Kentucky and Thomas Lincoln hoped for the election of a Whig President who would make "Locofoco [i.e., Democratic] principals crmble to dust." Both the Lincolns admired Henry Clay, the founder of the Whig party—Mary, because he was a friend of the Todd family in Lexington, her husband because Clay was his "beau ideal of a statesman."

From the beginning of Lincoln's political career he supported the Whig party. As late as 1859 he characterized himself as "always a whig in politics." He was a strong defender of Whig economic policies against the proposals offered by the rival Democrats, and he usually stressed one principal issue in each campaign. In 1840, for instance, he repeatedly argued for a national bank, favored by most Whigs, and opposed the Independent Treasury system, endorsed by the Democrats. During the presidential election of 1844, Lincoln, like most other Northern Whigs, made the protective tariff his weapon to combat the Democrats, who favored low customs duties or free trade.

On all these issues Lincoln closely followed the national Whig party line, which he sometimes seemed to echo rather than to understand. In the 1840 campaign his frequently repeated address attacking the Democrats' subtreasury plan and advocating a new national bank was a respectable, though certainly not an original, piece of work. His speeches in 1843–1844 on the tariff were confused and demagogic. A protective tariff, he claimed, would have no effect at all on the common man; it would be collected only from "those whose pride, whose abundance of means, prompt them to spurn the manufactures of our own country, and to strut in British cloaks, and coats, and pantaloons." On the stump he tried to argue that a high tariff made everything the farmers bought cheaper, but, according to a hostile reporter, "said also he could not tell the reason, but that it was so."

Lincoln was apparently sufficiently dissatisfied with his own argument that he continued to examine the tariff question after the election, and he studied Herndon's copies of both Henry C. Carey's *Essay on the Rate of Wages* (1835) and Francis Wayland's *Elements of Political Economy* (1837). He learned much from Wayland's lucidly written text but rejected its free-trade doctrines; Carey's pro-tariff tract made a deeper impression. Over several months he jotted down on eleven foolscap half sheets his thoughts and conclusions about protection that showed that he was still wrestling to master the subject. On reflection, he now concluded that tariff duties would not bear only on the rich; they would be shared equally among the producer, the merchant, and the consumer of taxed goods. To end protective tariffs would actually increase costs, because so much would be wasted on the *"useless labour"* of carrying goods back and forth to foreign markets. Such useless labor helped to perpetuate a system where *"some* have laboured, and *others* have, without labour, enjoyed a large proportion of the fruits." "This is wrong, and should not continue," Lincoln concluded. "To [secure] to each labourer the whole product of his labour, or as nearly as possible, is a most worthy object of any good government." But that reflection took him far beyond Whig orthodoxy, and far beyond any possible campaign speech. He quietly filed his notes away.

Membership in the Whig party meant something more than issues to Lincoln. He thought the party was grounded on principles in which he passionately believed. To him it embodied the promise of American life. Economically it stood for growth, for development, for progress. Clay's American System sought to link the manufacturing of the Northeast with the grain production of the West and the cotton and tobacco crops of the South, so that the nation's economy would become one vast interdependent web. When economic interests worked together, so would political interests, and sectional rivalries would be forgotten in a powerful American nationalism. Class antagonisms would also be erased, because this "just and generous, and prosperous system . . . opens the way for all—gives hope to all, and energy, and progress, and improvement of condition to all." This was a vision that attracted many of the wealthiest and best-educated members of society to the Whig party, but it was also one that appealed to young men who aspired to get ahead. Henry Clay, Lincoln's political idol, coined the term "self-made man" to describe Kentucky businessmen—but he might more accurately have applied it to Lincoln himself.

· · ·

VII

In return for his loyalty to the Whig party, Lincoln expected recognition, but the possibilities were decidedly limited. After the expiration of his fourth term in the Illinois state legislature in 1841, he did not seek reelection; that assemblage offered no new worlds to conquer. Statewide office was out of the question, because the Democrats had a hefty majority in Illinois; the state never voted for a Whig candidate for President, and it never elected a Whig governor or United States senator. Only in the newly created Seventh Congressional District, which included Sangamon County (Springfield) and Morgan County (Jacksonville), along with several of the other counties in the judicial circuit that Lincoln traveled so regularly, did the Whigs consistently have a majority. This included the counties (then within the old Third Congressional District) that John Todd Stuart represented from 1839 to 1843.

When Stuart made it clear that, after two terms, he was going to retire to his law practice, an intense rivalry arose among central Illinois Whigs in the Seventh District to become his successor. In the western part of the district John J. Hardin, of Jacksonville, a handsome, experienced Kentuckian, educated at Transylvania University, was the principal contender. In Sangamon County, Whigs were divided between Lincoln, the party workhorse, and Baker, the flamboyant orator.

During 1843, Lincoln sought to build support for his nomination by taking an active role in Whig meetings and in drawing up an elaborate "Address to the People of Illinois," a campaign circular from the Whig state committee. At the same time, he began quietly wooing delegates to the district convention that would choose the congressional candidate. "If . . . there are any whigs in Tazewell [County] who would as soon I should represent them as any other person," he wrote a former colleague in the state legislature, "I would be glad they would not cast me aside until they see and hear further what turn things take." "Now if you should hear any one say that Lincoln don't want to go to Congress," he wrote another friend, "I wish you . . . would tell him . . . he is mistaken. The truth is, I would like to go very much."

He found his efforts frustrated by a whispering campaign. Citing Lincoln's marriage into the wealthy, exclusive Edwards-Stuart elite, Baker's supporters began characterizing him "as the candidate of pride, wealth, and arristocratic family distinction." Lincoln was baffled. Surely everybody remembered that he was a self-made man with humble origins. He sought to refute the slur by assuring Baker's law partner, James H. Matheny: "Jim—I am now and always shall be the same Abe Lincoln that I always was," but the charge stuck. At the same time, Baker gained support because voters knew that he and his wife were devout Campbellites, while Lincoln, it was said, "belonged to no church, was suspected of being a deist, and had talked about fighting a duel."

Generously Lincoln did not blame Baker for these charges. The two men were close friends, who shared adjacent offices in the Tinsley Building; the

Lincolns thought so much of Baker that they named their second son for him. But the combined effect of these accusations undermined Lincoln's strength at the Sangamon County convention, which endorsed Baker. Then it elected Lincoln, against his will, to serve as one of the delegates to the district convention, to assist in getting the nomination for Baker. Wryly Lincoln wrote Speed that he was " 'fixed' a good deal like a fellow who is made groomsman to the man what has cut him out, and is marrying his own dear 'gal.' "

As it turned out, Baker as well as Lincoln lost the nomination at the Whig district convention that met in Pekin in May 1843, for Hardin was the choice of the delegates. Though disappointed, Lincoln could point to two considerable gains. At his urging, the convention adopted a resolution endorsing Baker "as a suitable person to be voted for by the Whigs of this district" in the 1844 congressional election. Thus the delegates in effect stipulated that Hardin should serve only a single term and committed themselves to the principle of rotation in office. If maintained, this rule, which was widely followed in many states, would almost guarantee that Lincoln would succeed Baker.

Equally important, the Whig delegates at Pekin endorsed the practice of holding conventions to nominate candidates. This ran counter to a strong streak of antipartyism among Whigs, a feeling that open political organization and management were not gentlemanly and had better be left to the wire-pulling Democrats. Many, like Hardin, preferred a less formal way of choosing the party's nominees: let aspiring candidates, or their friends, present their names directly to the public; if they did not secure a majority of the votes in a primary, they were entirely free to run as independents, but still Whigs, in the election. Lincoln had for some years been arguing for more system and organization in the party; "union is strength" was his maxim. A proliferation of candidates resulted only in Whig defeats at the polls. Employing a phrase that he would later put to better use, he reminded the party that "he whose wisdom surpasses that of all philosophers, has declared that 'a house divided against itself cannot stand.' " Unless the Whigs stood together, they would once again see "the spoils chucklingly borne off by the common enemy," the Democrats. Reluctantly the Seventh District Whigs accepted his argument.

The next year, as he had arranged, the Whigs of central Illinois met again in convention, and this time by prearrangement they nominated Baker to succeed Hardin in Congress. Lincoln vigorously campaigned for his friend, and for Clay, the Whig presidential candidate, making frequent speeches to expose "the absurdities of loco focoism" and confirm the soundness of the Whig candidates' position on protection, demonstrating, at least to the satisfaction of those already converted, that "the English are now flooding this country with tracts and money to break down the present Whig tariff." Throughout the district he addressed Clay Clubs, where the party faithful met to sing songs praising "Gallant Harry" and hear their hero's merits extolled. He was so effective that David Davis called him "the best stump speaker in the state," adding, "He shows the want of early education but he has great powers as a speaker." Loyally, Herndon agreed: "If Baker or Lincoln is missing at our meetings, it seems that something is lost."

All this activity was in behalf of both the Whig cause and Lincoln's own career. There was little chance that Clay could carry Illinois, but Baker won in the Seventh District—and Lincoln was in line to succeed him. In the fall of 1845, a full year before the next congressional election, Lincoln began actively working to secure the nomination. Getting a pledge from Baker not to run for a second term, Lincoln went over to Jacksonville to talk to Hardin, who, he learned, had enjoyed his two years in the House of Representatives and gave the impression that he would like to serve another term.

For the next six months Lincoln and Hardin tried to outmaneuver each other. Hardin's friends suggested nominating Lincoln for governor—knowing that would get him off the track of a congressional nomination and knowing, too, that there was no chance that he, or any other Whig, could be elected to statewide office. In turn, Lincoln's supporters proposed Hardin for governor. To avoid the appearance of "attempting to juggle Hardin out of a nomination for congress by juggleing him into one for Governor," Lincoln discouraged his closest editorial friend, Simeon Francis of the *Sangamo Journal,* from endorsing the scheme, but let it be known that he would have no objection if editors outside of Springfield urged it.

Counting on the support of Sangamon and Menard counties, Lincoln expected that Morgan County, along with Scott County, the small, adjacent county, would go for Hardin. It was necessary, then, for him to win in the northern part of the district, and he paid especial attention to Tazewell County, where he had a strong supporter in Benjamin F. James, the editor of the *Tazewell Whig,* to whom he wrote frequently and frankly about his political prospects. To Dr. Robert Boal, the state senator from this area, he appealed tactfully: "My reliance for a fair shake (and I want nothing more) in your county is chiefly on you, because of your position and standing, and because I am acquainted with so few others." To all he insisted that nothing must be said against Hardin, whom he described as "talented, energetic, usually generous and magnanimous." He based his claim to the nomination not on any difference between his record and Hardin's but simply on the grounds that "Turn about is fair play."

Lincoln's tactics were strikingly effective. In traveling the judicial circuit, he had sought and secured the endorsement of leading men throughout the district before anyone had an idea that Hardin wanted to go back to Congress. By January friends reported to Hardin that Lincoln had the nomination locked up. According to one of Hardin's correspondents, the general opinion was: "Hardin is a good fellow and did us and himself great credit . . . in Congress, Lincoln is also a good fellow and has worked hard and faithfully for the Party, if he desires to go to Congress let him go this time, *turn about is fair play.*" A friend in Tremont agreed, warning Hardin, "Our people think that it is Abraham's turn now."

Realizing that he stood no chance of being endorsed at a regular party convention, Hardin wrote to Lincoln proposing new rules for selecting the congressional candidate. He sought to undo all Lincoln's careful early preparation by reverting to the former system of independent candidates. In addition, he wanted Lincoln to agree that each candidate should campaign only in his own county—a proposal that would work to his advantage because, as a former congressman, he was more widely known throughout the district than Lincoln.

Lincoln rejected Hardin's proposals, declaring that he was "entirely satisfied with the old system under which you and Baker were successively nominated and elected to congress." It was hard for him to keep his temper, because Hardin repeatedly charged him with distorting the history of the previous Whig nominations and of unfairly managing the convention system to procure his own selection in 1846, but he held his tongue. So far as possible he kept his differences with Hardin out of the newspapers, warning editor James "that it will be *just all we can do,* to keep out of a quarrel— and I am resolved to do my part to keep peace." It was less important to make a crushing retort to an opponent who was behaving ungenerously than it was to avoid alienating Hardin's numerous supporters.

His tactics worked. Anticipating defeat, Hardin withdrew from the race and saved face by joining the army for the fight against Mexico. The Whig district convention, which met on May 1 at Petersburg, fell entirely under Lincoln's control. Herndon became the permanent secretary of the convention; Lincoln's previous law partner Logan was chairman of the committee on resolutions, which celebrated Lincoln's "firm support of Whig principles, [and] his abilities and integrity."

Lincoln's Democratic opponent was Peter Cartwright, the celebrated Methodist circuit rider, famed alike for his muscular Christianity and for his devotion to Jacksonian principles. Though Cartwright was personally popular, he was not an effective political campaigner, and his contest with Lincoln stirred little enthusiasm among voters. Indeed, there was so little interest in the campaign that newspapers only occasionally reported public appearances by either candidate and gave no extended accounts of their speeches.

Toward the end of the campaign, growing desperate, Cartwright, in the words of one Whig, *"sneaked* through this part of the district after Lincoln, and grossly misrepresented him" by asserting that he was an infidel. Troubled that this accusation, which was similar to charges that had been raised in previous elections, might succeed "in deceiving some honest men," especially in the northern counties of the district where he was less well known, Lincoln published a little handbill answering Cartwright's charges. Admitting that in the past he had argued for the "Doctrine of Necessity," he noted this was a position "held by several of the Christian denominations." It was true that he was "not a member of any Christian Church," but he denied ever having spoken "with intentional disrespect of religion in general, or of any denomination of Christians in particular" and declared that he could never "support a man for office, whom I knew to be an open enemy of, and scoffer at, religion."

Cartwright's charge obviously had little effect. On August 3 the voters of the Seventh District elected Lincoln by an unprecedented majority.

VIII

After his election victory Lincoln could relax. Since the Thirtieth Congress, to which he had been chosen, did not assemble until December 1847, he had over a year to prepare for his move to Washington. His only notable public appearance during the intervening months was as a delegate to a gigantic River and Harbor Convention, which met in Chicago in July to protest President James K. Polk's veto of a bill that would have provided federal funding for internal improvements. As the sole Whig congressman-elect from Illinois, Lincoln attracted some attention, and his name first appeared in a nationally circulated newspaper when Horace Greeley in the *New York Tribune* mentioned that this "tall specimen of an Illinoisian . . . spoke briefly and happily" to the convention.

But for the most part Lincoln spent his time contentedly attending to his family and cultivating his law practice. A daguerreotype made about this time—his first photographic likeness—showed a young congressman well satisfied with himself. In his best suit he sat stiffly for the photographer, obviously proud of his tailor-made clothing, his carefully buttoned satin waistcoat, his stiff, starched shirt with gold studs, his intricately knotted black tie. Because of photographic distortion his hands appeared even more enormous than they actually were, but it was not the daguerreotypist's fault that his chest looked thin and his head too small for such a tall body.

"He was not a pretty man by any means—nor was he an ugly one," wrote Herndon, who left the most vivid description of his partner's appearance; "he was a homely looking man." At this time Lincoln weighed about 160 pounds, and he was so thin that he appeared even taller than his six feet, four inches. His height, as Herndon pointed out, was due to the abnormal length of his legs. "In sitting down on common chairs," Herndon observed, "he was no taller than ordinary men from the chair to the crown of his head. A marble placed on his knee thus sitting would roll hipward, down an inclined plane. . . . It was only when he stood up that he loomed above other men."

"Mr. Lincoln's head," Herndon noted minutely, "was long and tall. . . . The size of his hat, measured at the hatters block was 7⅛, his head being from ear to ear 6½ inches—and from the front to the back of brain 8 inches. Thus measured it was not below the medium size." "Mr. Lincoln's forehead was narrow but high," Herndon continued. "His hair was dark—almost black and lay floating where the fingers or the winds left it, piled up at random. His cheek bones were high—sharp and prominent. His eye brows heavy and jutting out. Mr. Lincolns jaws were long up curved and heavy. His nose was large—long and blunt, having the tip glowing in red, and a little awry toward the right eye. His chin was long—sharp and up curved. His eye brows cropped out like a huge rock on the brow of a hill. His face was long —sallow—cadaverous—shrunk—shrivelled—wrinkled and dry, having here and there a hair on the surface. His cheeks were leathery and flabby, falling in loose folds at places, looking sorrowful and sad. Mr. Lincoln's ears were extremely large—and ran out almost at right angles from his head—caused by heavy hats and partly by nature."

For all Herndon's detail, he failed quite to capture the feeling conveyed by that 1846 daguerreotype. Because a sitter had to hold a pose for several seconds without moving, it showed Lincoln's face as grave and unsmiling, but it managed to convey a sense of a man who had attained his goals. No longer was he attempting to impose the rule of reason upon impassioned emotions; no longer was he afflicted by swings of mood that went from Napoleonic ambition to deep melancholy. He was at peace with himself.

He now felt able to come to terms with the painful memories of his early years. During the 1844 presidential campaign he had accepted an invitation to speak to the Whigs of Rockport, in southern Indiana—an invitation that suggested his growing recognition as leader of his party in the West—and for the first time in fifteen years he returned to the area where he had spent his youth. He was making his usual speech advocating the protective tariff, a subject which, a partisan paper ungrammatically declared, he "handled . . . in a manner that done honor to himself and the whig cause," when he spotted his old schoolmate, Nathaniel Grigsby, and, interrupting himself, called out, "There is Nat." Walking out into the audience, he greeted his old chum most cordially and insisted that he must stay overnight. After he finished his address, the two men returned to the house where Lincoln was staying and, as Grigsby remembered, they spent most of the night "telling stories and talking over old times." The next day they went on to Gentryville, where Lincoln saw friends he had grown up with and revisited "the neighborhood . . . in which I was raised, where my mother and only sister were buried."

That visit broke an emotional barrier that for years had kept him from mentioning the death of his mother or the loss of his sister. He could now complete the unfinished process of grieving over his mother—a process interrupted by the suddenness of her death, her hasty burial, the absence of religious service at her grave, and his father's prompt remarriage. His emotions welled up, and, over the next several months, he sought to master them by expressing them in verse. "That part of the country is, within itself, as unpoetical as any spot of the earth," he wrote a friend to whom he sent what he wrote; "but still, seeing it and its objects and inhabitants aroused feelings in me which were certainly poetry."

Lincoln expressed those feelings in four-line, rhyming stanzas, which he planned to arrange into "four little divisions or cantos." The first recaptured a bittersweet mixture of sorrow and joy produced by the visit. It began:

My childhood's home I see again,
  And sadden with the view;
And still, as memory crowds my brain,
  There's pleasure in it too.

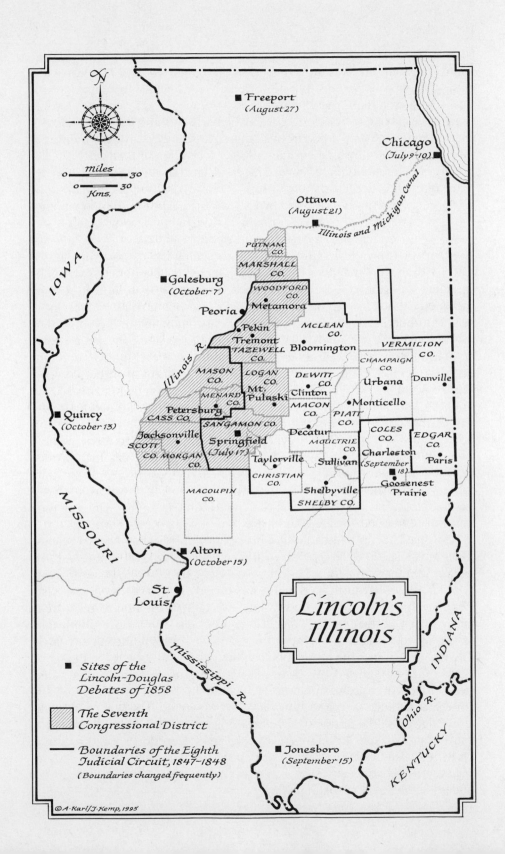

N

Freeport
(August 27)

Chicago
(July 9-10)

Miles
0 — 30
Kms.
0 — 30

Ottawa
(August 21)

Illinois and Michigan Canal

Galesburg
(October 7)

PUTNAM
CO.
MARSHALL
CO.
WOODFORD
CO.
Metamora
Peoria
Pekin
Tremont
TAZEWELL
CO.

McLEAN
CO.

Bloomington

VERMILION
CO.

CHAMPAIGN
CO.

MASON
CO.
LOGAN
CO.
Mt.
Pulaski
MENARD
CO.
Petersburg
CASS CO.

DEWITT
CO.
Clinton

Urbana

Danville

MACON
CO.

Monticello

PIATT
CO.

Quincy
(October 13)

Jacksonville
SCOTT
CO.
MORGAN
CO.

SANGAMON CO.
Springfield
(July 17)

Decatur
MOULTRIE
CO.

COLES
CO.

EDGAR
CO.

Taylorville

Sullivan

Charleston
(September
18)

Paris

IOWA

MISSOURI

CHRISTIAN
CO.

MACOUPIN
CO.

Shelbyville
SHELBY CO.

Goosenest
Prairie

Alton
(October 15)

St.
Louis

**Lincoln's
Illinois**

Mississippi R.

INDIANA

Ohio R.

KENTUCKY

■ Sites of the
Lincoln-Douglas
Debates of 1858

▨ The Seventh
Congressional District

── Boundaries of the Eighth
Judicial Circuit, 1847-1848
(Boundaries changed frequently)

Jonesboro
(September 15)

© A. Karl/J. Kemp, 1995

His verses mixed backwoods slang with archaic words from his favorite British poets, and he was quite correct in doubting "whether my expression of those feelings is poetry." But he accurately conveyed a fuguelike sense of almost forgotten memories, "Where things decayed, and loved ones lost / In dreamy shadows rise." No longer were the hardships and the sorrows of his youth important; now, "freed from all that's earthly vile," his early memories were "Like scenes in some enchanted isle, / All bathed in liquid light."

With his childhood experiences unlocked, Lincoln could explore another of his deepest concerns: the overthrow of reason. In his lyceum address he had urged the reign of reason to protect society against both mob violence and dictatorial ambition, and no doubt his deep, debilitating bouts of depression caused him also to realize the importance of reason as an internal gyroscope. His own fear of madness was too painful to explore, but he was able to deal with the case of Matthew Gentry, a schoolmate, whom he encountered again at Gentryville. Three years older than Lincoln, Gentry had been "rather a bright lad, and the son of *the* rich man of our very poor neighbourhood." "At the age of nineteen," Lincoln recalled, "he unaccountably became furiously mad, from which condition he gradually settled down into harmless insanity." After seeing his childhood friend in this sad plight, Lincoln felt impelled to describe in verse the condition of "A human form with reason fled, / While wretched life remains." The meter was lame, but Lincoln's lines managed to recapture the genuine terror he had felt at the acts of this "howling crazy man," who maimed himself, fought with his father, and sought to kill his mother. He could not erase from his memory the madman's maniac laughter and his mournful night screams; they seemed to him "the funeral dirge . . . / Of reason dead and gone." "O death!" Lincoln's poem concluded, in an apostrophe that linked the now harmless madman to the shadowy ghosts of Nancy and Sarah Lincoln, "Why dost thou tear more blest ones hence, / And leave him ling'ring here?"

With that Lincoln had exhausted his poetical inspiration. A third "canto" containing a spirited description of a frontier bear hunt was entirely different in tone, and at this point his muse deserted him, so that he never completed a proposed fourth section. He was proud enough of his effort to send a copy of his verses to a friend in Quincy, authorizing him to print them anonymously in the *Quincy Whig*. "Let names be suppressed by all means," he explained. "I have not sufficient hope of the verses attracting any favorable notice to tempt me to risk being ridiculed for having written them."

At home with himself, at peace with his past, Lincoln completed arrangements to depart for Washington. He leased his house in Springfield to Cornelius Ludlum, a brick contractor, for ninety dollars a year, carefully reserving one of the upstairs loft rooms for storing his furniture. With Herndon he agreed that the law firm of Lincoln & Herndon should continue while he was in Congress, with the expectation that the senior partner would resume his active practice after his term was over. On October 25 the Lincoln family left for Washington.

CHAPTER FIVE

Lone Star of Illinois

"Being elected to Congress, though I am very grateful to our friends, for having done it, has not pleased me as much as I expected," Lincoln wrote Speed several weeks after his victory over Peter Cartwright. As the only Whig representative from Illinois, he knew that he could have very little influence on the Democratic administration of President Polk. He hoped, however, to offer constructive leadership in his own party, which, despite its narrow majority in the House of Representatives, was foundering. Its most prominent national leaders, like Henry Clay and Daniel Webster, still yearned for another chance at the presidency, but they were clearly over the hill. Equally out of date were many of the traditional Whig issues, like a national bank, federal support of internal improvements, and a protective tariff. Lincoln saw his two years in Congress as an opportunity to help the Whig party to find fresh leadership and to adopt a program relevant to the times. He devoted himself to promoting the presidential prospects of General Zachary Taylor and to developing a new Whig ideology. In the first goal he was successful, but he failed in the second. At the end of his term he left Washington disappointed not so much with his own performance as with that of the political party to which he belonged.

I

The Lincolns arrived in Washington on December 2, 1847, just a few days before the Thirtieth Congress convened, and they went to Brown's Hotel. Presently they removed to the boardinghouse of Mrs. Ann G. Sprigg, where both Stuart and Baker had resided when they were in Congress. It was just east of the Capitol, in a row of houses on land now occupied by the Library of Congress. Eight other congressmen, all Whigs, boarded with Mrs. Sprigg, the most notable of whom was Joshua R. Giddings of Ohio, the stalwart and uncompromising enemy of slavery.

Lincoln immediately made himself at home in the boardinghouse, charming the other guests with his jokes and anecdotes. One of his fellow boarders, Dr. Samuel Busey, recalled that when there was a controversy over political issues, or especially over the subject of slavery, Lincoln would "interrupt it by interposing some anecdote, thus diverting it into a hearty and general laugh, and so completely disarrange the tenor of the discussion." For recreation Lincoln joined other members of the mess in bowling at the nearby alley owned by James Casparis. "He was a very awkward bowler," Dr. Busey remembered, "but played the game with great zest and spirit, solely for exercise and amusement." He punctuated his bowling by telling stories—"some of which were very broad"—and a crowd of listeners always gathered when he was playing.

Initially both the Lincolns found life in the national capital an exciting adventure. Washington, with its 40,000 inhabitants—including 2,000 slaves and 8,000 free blacks—was the largest and most cosmopolitan place either of them had ever known. The Capitol building, which they could see from Mrs. Sprigg's windows, was an imposing, though still unfinished, structure, its temporary, wooden dome suggesting the fragility of the federal Union. At the opposite end of Pennsylvania Avenue loomed the White House, certainly the grandest residence either of the Lincolns had seen. South of the Executive Mansion, preparations were under way for the laying of the cornerstone of the vast obelisk of the Washington Monument; as congressman, Lincoln took part in the dedication ceremonies. Most of the streets in the capital were still unpaved, but a cobblestoned stretch of Pennsylvania offered a tempting array of specialty shops with luxury goods.

As transients, the Lincolns, like other congressional families, were not admitted to the exclusive social life of long-term capital residents, but they could always find amusements. There were levees at the White House, though these were not heavily attended, since the Polks forbade dancing and offered guests neither food nor drink, and there were biweekly concerts by the Marine Band in the President's grounds. In the evenings there were sometimes lectures and concerts. On one notable occasion the Lincolns attended a performance by the Ethiopian Serenaders, minstrels in blackface who had recently sung for Queen Victoria and the royal family.

But Mary soon became dissatisfied. Her husband, busy with the work of Congress, had little time to spend with her; indeed, he wrote later, he thought she "hindered me some in attending to business." She lacked female companionship, because few of the congressmen were accompanied by their wives. The four Lincolns lived in a single large room, and she appeared downstairs only at meal times. Because the Lincoln children were noisy and undisciplined, there was inevitably friction with the other boarders. Robert, one of them remembered, was a bright boy, who "seemed to have his own way"; Eddie was sick much of the time. In the spring Mary Lincoln decided to take the children back to Lexington, Kentucky, where she stayed with her father. When Lincoln wrote her, he hinted at the sometimes tense relations at Mrs. Sprigg's: "All the house—or rather, all with whom you were on decided good terms—send their love to you. The others say nothing."

Lincoln was so absorbed in his congressional duties that at first he hardly missed her. Enthusiastically he threw himself into the work of the House, establishing a conspicuous record for faithful attendance. Of the 456 roll-call votes during his two years of service, he missed only 13. Appropriately, in view of his experience as a postmaster, he was assigned to the Committee on Post Offices and Post Roads, and he also served on the Committee on Expenditures in the War Department. In both committees he did his share of the work and effectively presented reports from the Post Office Committee to the House. He regularly and promptly submitted petitions from his constituents, most of which dealt with requests for land grants for constructing railroads. He did his best to help his friends who sought appointments from the federal government, even though he knew that there was little reason to think a Democratic administration would shower patronage on a freshman Whig congressman. Much of his time was spent in answering his correspondence, without, of course, the aid of a secretary or assistant. After he began making speeches in the House of Representatives, he took great pains to see that they reached his home audience, purchasing no fewer than 7,580 copies, which he painstakingly addressed and franked in his own hand—far more than most of the other members of the Congress.

The House of Representatives did not overawe him. If he was new to Washington, so were two hundred of the other representatives in this Thirtieth Congress, and his four terms in the Illinois state legislature had made him familiar with parliamentary procedures. Like any other freshman congressman, he had a little stage fright when he first gained the floor to make a few remarks, but he got over it quickly. "I find speaking here and elsewhere about the same thing," he reported to Herndon. "I was about as badly scared, and no worse, as I am when I speak in court."

Quickly he began to take the measure of his fellow representatives. Unlike the Senate, where his old rival Stephen A. Douglas now joined such august solons as Webster, John C. Calhoun, and Thomas Hart Benton, the House, for the most part, was composed of men of mediocre ability and only local reputation. The one great exception was John Quincy Adams, distinguished alike for his rocklike integrity and his implacable hatred of slavery, but the former President died early in the session, before Lincoln really got to know him. Apart from Giddings, whose presence Lincoln felt more as a moral than a political force, he was most taken by Georgia Whig Alexander H. Stephens, whom he described as "a little slim, pale-faced, consumptive man"; the young Southerner, like Lincoln, was looking for a way to rejuvenate and reunite the Whig party. Looking about the hall, Lincoln could readily identify a number of other industrious and competent representatives—men like David Wilmot of Pennsylvania, author of the celebrated proviso that would bar slavery from all territories gained in the Mexican War; Caleb B. Smith, the astute Indiana political manager, who would become Lincoln's first Secretary of the Interior; and Robert C. Schenck, of Ohio, whom Lincoln would one day appoint major general in the army. Not a modest man, Lincoln saw no reason to feel that these flickering lights outshined him.

He found his party in disarray. Though the Whigs had done very well in the off-year elections of 1846, party leaders were troubled by the outlook for the 1848 presidential election. The Democratic administration of James K. Polk had been extraordinarily successful: the President settled the festering boundary dispute with Great Britain over the Oregon Territory; by signing the Walker Tariff, which imposed very low duties, he set policy for the next decade; by firmly vetoing an internal improvements bill, he killed that question as a political issue; and he presided over a highly successful war that was about to add California and New Mexico to the Union. Whigs recognized that it would be very difficult to defeat the Democrat most often mentioned as Polk's probable successor, Senator Lewis Cass of Michigan, whose contradictory positions on the Wilmot Proviso allowed all factions to favor him.

The only issue on which the Democrats appeared to be vulnerable was the President's role in originating the Mexican War. This was not a subject to which Lincoln hitherto had given much attention. Like every other American, he knew about the Texas revolt from Mexico in 1836, and because he thought of the Mexicans as "greasers," he no doubt was pleased when Texas gained its independence. But in 1844 when President John Tyler urged the annexation of Texas to the United States, Lincoln, like Henry Clay, former President Van Buren, and Senator Thomas Hart Benton of Missouri, branded the move as "altogether inexpedient." He did not share Tyler's enthusiasm for territorial expansion because, as he later declared, he "did not believe in enlarging our field, but in keeping our fences where they are and cultivating our present possession, making it a garden, improving the morals and education of the people."

He had nothing to say when Texas was annexed or when President Polk sought aggressively to protect the new territory and also to settle long-standing claims and complaints against Mexico. In April 1846 fighting broke out between the Mexican army and American troops commanded by Zachary Taylor in territory between the Nueces River and the Rio Grande, a region claimed by both the United States and Mexico. The United States declared war. Unpopular in New England, the conflict stirred patriotic enthusiasm in other parts of the country, and in Illinois there was a rush to enlist in the volunteer army. Both Hardin and Baker, Lincoln's predecessors, became officers. But the Mexican War never surfaced as an issue in the congressional campaign that Lincoln and Peter Cartwright were waging. Lincoln's only utterance on the subject was a "warm, thrilling and effective" speech that he gave on May 30 at a public meeting to encourage volunteering. Even after he was elected to Congress, he made no comment on the war, believing, as he said later, "that all those who, because of knowing too *little,* or because of knowing too *much,* could not conscientiously approve the conduct of the President, in the beginning of it, should . . . as good citizens and patriots, remain silent . . . , at least till the war should be ended."

By the time Lincoln arrived in Washington, he felt free to speak out, because the fighting was substantially over. In hard-fought battles at Palo Alto, Resaca de la Palma, Monterey, and Buena Vista, General Taylor repeatedly routed the Mexican forces in the North, while General Winfield Scott led an expedition that captured Veracruz and, eventually, Mexico City itself. In his annual message of December 1847, President Polk asked Congress for additional funds to bring the war to a close, claiming the vast territories of New Mexico and California as partial indemnity. With a note of triumph he announced that he was about to conclude a war that Mexico had initiated by "invading the territory of the State of Texas, striking the first blow, and shedding the blood of our citizens on our own soil."

The message was the pretext for a sustained Whig attack upon the President, his administration, and, in general, the Democratic party. Lincoln led the assault on Polk. On December 22 he introduced a series of resolutions requiring the President to provide the House with "all the facts which go to establish whether the particular spot of soil on which the blood of our *citizens* was so shed, was, or was not, *our own soil.*" In the manner of a prosecuting attorney, he demanded that the President inform the Congress whether that spot had ever been part of Texas and whether its inhabitants had ever "submitted themselves to the government or laws of Texas, . . . by *consent,* or by *compulsion,* either by accepting office, or voting at elections, or paying taxes, or serving on juries, or . . . *in any other way.*" Lincoln clearly intended to show that the American army had begun the war by making an unprovoked attack on a Mexican settlement, despite the fact that "Genl. Taylor had, more than once, intimated to the War Department that . . . no such movement was necessary to the defence or protection of Texas."

The attack became more general on January 3, when Representative George Ashmun of Massachusetts introduced a resolution declaring that the war had been "unnecessarily and unconstitutionally begun by the President of the United States." It was adopted by the votes of eighty-five Whig representatives, including Lincoln's. A few days later Lincoln continued the campaign against Polk in a long speech, on which he had worked very hard. Subjecting Polk's version of the origins of the war to a close, lawyerly scrutiny, he chided the President for the gaps in his evidence and his logic. The mistakes could not be unintentional, because "Mr. Polk is too good a lawyer not to know that is wrong." After sifting "the whole of the President's evidence," he demanded that Polk respond to the interrogatories he had posed:

"Let him answer, fully, fairly, and candidly. Let him answer with *facts,* and not with arguments." Piously he professed that if the President could do so, "then I am with him for his justification." But if he failed to respond, that would show "that he is deeply conscious of being in the wrong—that he feels the blood of this war, like the blood of Abel, is crying to Heaven against him." The President, Lincoln speculated with a freedom that he would never have permitted himself in a courtroom, must have begun the war motivated by a desire for "military glory—that attractive rainbow, that rises in showers of blood—that serpent's eye, that charms to destroy." When that aim failed, his mind, "tasked beyond it's power," began "running hither and thither, like an ant on a hot stove," and this "bewildered, confounded, and miserably perplexed man" could now only speak in "the half insane mumbling of a fever-dream."

Proud of his effort, Lincoln hoped it would establish his place in the House of Representatives. Now feeling very much at home, he began to think of Washington as a very pleasant place, and he regretted his pledge that he—like Hardin and Baker before him—would serve only one term. When Herndon reported that some people thought he should be reelected, he replied that his word and honor forbade him to enter the race, but he added coyly, "If it should so happen that nobody else wishes to be elected, I could not refuse the people the right of sending me again."

II

His expectations were quickly dashed. In Washington nobody paid much attention to his resolutions, which the House neither debated nor adopted, or to his speech. The President made no response to Lincoln's interrogatories; he never mentioned Lincoln's name, even in his voluminous diaries. Congressmen were for the most part equally indifferent, regarding Lincoln's attack as part of the general Whig assault upon a Democratic administration. One obscure Indiana Democrat did chide Lincoln for having failed to tell his constituents during his election campaign that he was opposed to the war, and Representative John Jameson of Missouri professed to be astonished that the successor of John J. Hardin, killed at Buena Vista, and of E. D. Baker, a hero of the battle of Cerro Gordo, should make such an unpatriotic speech. There was little newspaper comment. The *Baltimore Patriot* carried a squib commending his "Spot" resolutions and commenting: "Evidently there is music in that very tall Mr. Lincoln," and the St. Louis *Missouri Republican* called his speech "one of great power, . . . replete with the strongest and most conclusive arguments." But none of the newspapers with national circulation paid attention to either Lincoln's resolutions or his address.

Very different were the responses from Illinois. As was to be expected, Democratic newspapers were uniformly critical. In Springfield, the *Illinois State Register* contrasted Lincoln's opposition to the war with the "gallantry and heroism" of Hardin, who had rushed to enlist in the army. Later the *Register* called Lincoln's speech "politically motivated," predicted that his ideas would be "repudiated by the great mass of people who voted for him," and warned that Lincoln would "have a fearful account to settle" with the veterans when they returned from Mexico. Other Democratic newspapers joined the attack. According to the Charleston *Illinois Globe,* Lincoln's resolutions showed "conclusively that the littleness of the pettifogging lawyer has not merged into the greatness of the statesman," and the *Peoria Press* denounced this "miserable man of 'spots' " for his "traitorous course in Congress." Throughout the Seventh District, public meetings—largely Democratic, though some were labeled nonpartisan—condemned Lincoln's course. The rally in Morgan County, where Hardin had lived, expressed "deep mortification" at Lincoln's "base, dastardly, and treasonable assault upon President Polk," and prophesied that "henceforth will this Benedict Arnold of our district be known here only as the Ranchero Spotty of one term."

Condemnation from Democrats was to be expected, and discounted, but Lincoln was troubled by the faintness of praise he received from fellow Whigs. Simeon Francis's *Illinois State Journal* (formerly the *Sangamo Journal*) loyally supported him, as did B. F. James's *Tazewell Whig.* Some Whig newspapers reported that his "crack speech" had placed him in the "front rank of the best speakers in the House." But most of the other editors imitated the *Quincy Whig,* which published Lincoln's resolutions with the mild comment that they were "based upon facts which cannot be successfully controverted."

More disturbing were the private messages he received from his political friends in Illinois. Dr. Henry strongly dissented from the prevailing Whig view of the war. If Illinois Whigs followed Henry Clay and opposed all territorial annexations as a result of the war, he warned, they would continue to be "the minority party for a long time." Soberly he wrote Lincoln, "It would be painful in the extreme to part company with you after having fought with you side by side so long." The Reverend John Mason Peck, a prominent Baptist of St. Clair County, sent a similar message, concluding "that the Government of the United States committed no aggression on Mexico."

Herndon, too, reported that "murmurs of dissatisfaction began to run through the Whig ranks." He deplored Lincoln's vote for the Ashmun resolution, took it for granted that Lincoln's opposition to the war meant that he would not vote to supply the armies in the field, and warned that his partner's course would not be well received by "the whig men who have participated in the war." Herndon argued that instead of condemning President Polk for invading Mexico and starting a war on Mexican soil, Lincoln ought to follow the law of nations and argue "that if it shall become *necessary, to repel invasion,* the President may, without violation of the Constitution, cross the line, and *invade* the territory of another country."

Because Herndon claimed to speak for a considerable Whig constituency in Illinois, Lincoln went to some pains to refute his arguments. As for the Ashmun resolution, he replied, he had no choice; if he had opposed it, he would have voted a lie. Though he censured the President's conduct in beginning the war, he had every intention of voting for supplies to the armies. As for the attitude of returning Whig soldiers, he pointed out that veterans in Washington, with hardly an exception, did "not hesitate to denounce, as unjust, the Presidents conduct in the beginning of the war." Lincoln dismissed Herndon's constitutional arguments: "Allow the President to invade a neighboring nation, whenever *he* shall deem it necessary to repel an invasion, . . . and you allow him to make war at pleasure." Thus Herndon would place "our President where kings have always stood."

The acerbity that crept into Lincoln's replies to Herndon reflected his discomfort that his partner, and whatever other Whigs he represented, had failed to understand the real intent of his attack on Polk. Now that the fighting was over and the peace treaty was expected in Washington momentarily, the only purpose that Lincoln and other Whigs had for assailing the President's course in beginning the war was political. Their object was to hurt the Democrats in the next presidential election.

They were aware that this course entailed a considerable risk; attacking the President's actions in beginning the war might easily be misunderstood as opposing the war itself. Whigs with a long memory knew how dangerous that position could be. When someone asked Justin Butterfield, a leading Chicago Whig, whether he would condemn the Mexican War as he had once denounced the War of 1812, he responded: "No, indeed! I opposed one war, and it ruined me. From now on I am for war, pestilence, and famine." But Lincoln, working closely with Alexander H. Stephens and the small group of other Whigs in the House who called themselves the Young Indians, thought he could resolve the difficulty. Whigs could assail the Democrats for having wrongly begun the war—and then demonstrate how loyally they supported their country's cause by nominating a general who was winning that war.

That general had to be Zachary Taylor, despite his total ignorance of public affairs and his lack of any political experience. Nobody knew where he stood on anything. That made him an available candidate, and Lincoln, eager to see new leadership in the Whig party, jumped on the Taylor bandwagon. "I am in favor of Gen: Taylor as the whig candidate for the Presidency," he announced, "because I am satisfied we can elect him, that he would give us a whig administration, and that we can not elect any other whig." "Our only chance is with Taylor," he explained. "I go for him, not because I think he would make a better president than Clay, but because I think he would make a better one than Polk, or Cass, or Buchanan, or any such creatures, one of whom is sure to be elected, if he is not."

Throughout the spring Lincoln worked earnestly to secure Taylor's nomination, and in early June he attended the Whig National Convention at Philadelphia, where he attracted a good deal of attention as the only Whig representative from Illinois. After the convention nominated Taylor on the fourth ballot, Lincoln, along with three other members of the House, addressed a ratification meeting in Wilmington, Delaware. Introduced as the "Lone Star of Illinois," he was received with three hearty cheers as he predicted a Whig victory in the fall. Taylor's nomination, he wrote Herndon, took the Democrats "on the blind side," by turning "the war thunder against them." Grimly jubilant, he told his partner, "The war is now to them, the gallows of Haman, which they built for us, and on which they are doomed to be hanged themselves."

Along with the other Young Indians, Lincoln hoped not just to elect a presidential candidate but to formulate a new set of beliefs for the Whig party in place of old doctrines that no longer aroused public interest. Without some vital, controlling principles, there was a danger that Whigs might follow local, sectional interests. In the South some Whigs were tempted to make a defense of slavery their central issue, so that they could demonstrate that they, rather than the Democrats, more truly represented their region's interests. In the Northeast many Whigs, troubled by the huge influx of immigrants, who tended to vote Democratic, flirted with the Native American party. Other party leaders thought that a strong antislavery platform could win back the Conscience Whigs, mostly in New England, who were so opposed to any extension of slavery that they were ready to join antislavery Democrats in nominating ex-President Martin Van Buren on the new Free-Soil ticket. All these approaches were tempting—and all would disastrously split the party. Even if Taylor was elected, he would find that he could not govern.

To avoid these dangers, Lincoln urged Taylor to put himself above all local and regional issues. The proper Whig policy ought to be one of "making Presidential elections, and the legislation of the country, distinct matters; so that the people can elect whom they please, and afterwards, legislate just as they please, without any hindrance [from the Chief Executive], save only so much as may guard against infractions of the constitution, undue haste, and want of consideration." He wanted Taylor to announce: "Were I president, I should desire the legislation of the country to rest with Congress, uninfluenced by the executive in it's origin or progress, and undisturbed by the veto unless in very special and clear cases." When Taylor made this pledge, Lincoln was jubilant, and he took the floor of the House of Representatives to explain what it meant: "In substance, it is this: The people say to Gen: Taylor 'If you are elected, shall we have a national bank?' He answers *Your* will, gentlemen, not *mine.*' 'What about the Tariff?' 'Say yourselves.' 'Shall our rivers and harbours be improved?' 'Just as you please.' "

Even on the most divisive issues relating to slavery, Lincoln believed Taylor's position should be the same. Though Taylor was a Southerner and the owner of more than two hundred slaves, he should declare that if Congress passed the Wilmot Proviso prohibiting the extension of slavery into the territories acquired from Mexico, he would not veto it. (Lincoln did not explain that this contingency was highly unlikely, since no version of the Wilmot Proviso could pass the Senate, which was dominated by Southerners.) This position, Lincoln maintained, was "the best sort of principle" for a party, "the principle of allowing the people to do as they please with their own business."

III

Lincoln's efforts to promote Taylor's election and to reformulate Whig ideology led him to advocate policies that would later come back to haunt him. His demand that President Polk prove that the United States owned the spot on which the first blood of the Mexican War was shed gave him the enduring sobriquet "Spotty Lincoln." Stephen A. Douglas repeatedly taunted him with it in their 1858 debates, and even during his presidency it was used to question his patriotism.

Equally embarrassing was Lincoln's argument that Polk acted unconstitutionally in ordering American troops into territory disputed with Mexico. He claimed that the Constitution gave the war-making power to Congress, not to the Chief Executive. The Founding Fathers, he told Herndon, had recognized that war was "the most oppressive of all Kingly oppressions" and they "resolved to so frame the Constitution that *no one man* should hold the power of bringing this oppression upon us." This was the very argument that Lincoln's enemies used during the Civil War to combat what they called his executive tyranny.

They also invoked Lincoln's statement about the right of revolution, which he included as a curious digression in his speech attacking Polk. Forgetting his own advice that "it is good policy to never *plead* what you *need* not, lest you oblige yourself to *prove* what you *can* not," Lincoln argued that the title to the disputed land between the Nueces and the Rio Grande depended on whether the inhabitants of that area had engaged in a revolution against Mexico. "Any people anywhere . . . have the *right* to rise up, and shake off the existing government, and form a new one that suits them better," he announced. "Any portion of such people that *can, may* revolutionize, and make their *own,* of so much of the territory as they inhabit." "This," he declared, "is a most valuable,—a most sacred right—a right, which we hope and believe, is to liberate the world." These were words he would have to eat in 1860–1861.

In another speech Lincoln went out of his way to challenge Polk's argument that federal funding of internal improvements required an amendment to the Constitution. Lincoln opposed any change in that document. "We would do much better to let it alone," he argued. "Better . . . habituate ourselves to think of it, as unalterable. It can scarcely be made better than it is." It was a peculiar position for a future President whose name would always be connected with the Thirteenth Amendment ending slavery.

The argument that Lincoln advanced during the 1848 campaign that would have the most pernicious effect on his own administration was for a weak Chief Executive who would not veto measures passed by the Congress or dictate policies to his cabinet members. These were not new ideas for Whigs. The party had been founded to oppose that "detestable, ignorant, reckless, vain and malignant tyrant," Andrew Jackson, who made the entire government subject to *"one responsibility, one discretion, one will."* But up to this time Whigs had opposed a strong President largely because they objected to the policies he advocated. Now, with the nomination of General Taylor, they favored a weak Chief Executive to conceal the fact that their candidate stood for nothing. But Lincoln was convinced by his own arguments, and his preference for a do-nothing President persisted into the Civil War years. Claiming that it was "better that congress should originate, as well as perfect its measures, without external bias," Lincoln as President exercised little influence over the legislative branch and used the veto power sparingly. On most issues he followed Whig doctrine by giving his cabinet members such a free hand that at times it seemed that his administration had no policy at all.

IV

After working out in his own mind a defense of Taylor and a reformulation of Whig principles, Lincoln was ready to go on the offensive against the Democrats. In July, after Taylor, Cass, and Van Buren were all in the field, the House of Representatives virtually abandoned all pretense of doing business and listened to what were essentially stump speeches for the three candidates. When Lincoln gained the floor on July 27, he was the eighth congressman to speak on the presidential question, but, fortunately for his hearers, he was able to leaven his arguments with humor. After paying a perfunctory tribute to Taylor, he turned to ridiculing the Democrats for always campaigning in the name of Andrew Jackson. "Like a horde of hungry ticks you have stuck to the tail of the Hermitage lion to the end of his life," he jeered; "and you are still sticking to it, and drawing a loathsome sustenance from it, after he is dead." He poked fun at Cass's military record, comparing the general's exploits in the War of 1812 with his own unheroic adventures in the Black Hawk War. Cass's changing positions on the Wilmot Proviso came in for a share of ridicule, and Lincoln gleefully described how the general, as territorial governor and Indian agent, had received pay in seven different capacities simultaneously. During one eight-month period, he asserted, Cass drew ten rations a day in Michigan, ten more in Washington, and five dollars' worth more on the road between the two places. The Democratic candidate, he joked, would never suffer the fate of Balaam's ass, starving to death because it was unable to choose between two stacks of hay. "The like of that would never happen to Gen: Cass; place the stacks a thousand miles apart, he would stand stock still midway between them, and eat them both at once; and the green grass along the line would be apt to suffer some too at the same time." "By all means, make him President, gentlemen," he urged the Democrats. "He will feed you bounteously,—if—if there is any left after he shall have helped himself."

It was a capital speech, the *Baltimore American* reported. Lincoln's manner "was so good natured, and his style so peculiar, that he kept the House in a continuous roar of merriment for the last half hour. . . . He would commence a point in his speech far up one of the aisles, and keep on talking, gesticulating, and walking until he would find himself, at the end of a paragraph, down in the center of the area in front of the clerk's desk. He would then go back and take another *head,* and work down again."

After Congress adjourned on August 14, Lincoln remained in Washington to work for Taylor's candidacy and the triumph of Whig principles. Helping with the Whig campaign newspaper, the *Battery,* he oversaw the distribution of thousands of campaign documents. He was not officially a member of the Whig Executive Committee of Congress, but he sent out circular letters in its name. Taking advantage of the acquaintances he had made while attending the Whig convention in Philadelphia, he kept close track of political developments in key states, for instance asking William Schouler, the editor of the *Boston Atlas,* for his "undisguised opinion as to what New England generally, and Massachusetts particularly will do" in the election. Similarly, he requested newly elected Representative Thaddeus Stevens, as an "experienced and sagacious Pennsylvania politician," to report "as to how the vote of that state, for governor, and president, is likely to go."

Very busy during the hot Washington summer, Lincoln was also very lonely. When Mary and the children were in Washington, he had found them in his way, but after they left, he began to miss them. "I hate to stay in this old room by myself," he complained to his wife, finding that "having nothing but business—no variety— . . . has grown exceedingly tasteless to me." Eagerly he read Mary's letters for news about the children, and when she asked him to find some stockings that would fit "Eddy's dear little feet," he searched the capital in vain, finding "not a single pair of the description you give, and only one plaid pair of any sort." He worried about the children, especially after he had what he called "that foolish dream about dear Bobby," and he wrote them little letters. "Dont let the blessed fellows forget father," he enjoined his wife.

But he missed Mary most of all. His letters to her, during this longest period of separation during their marriage, combined fatherly advice with mild sexual flirtatiousness. "Are you entirely free from head-ache?" he asked. "That is good—good—considering it is the first spring you have been free from it since we were acquainted." Then he went on to add: "I am afraid you will get so well, and fat, and young, as to be wanting to marry again." She responded in kind, with news of the boys and her family. "How much, I wish instead of writing, we were together this evening," she wrote. "I feel very sad away from you." Presently she began to think of returning to Washington. "Will you be a *good girl* in all things, if I consent?" Lincoln asked. "Then come along, and that as *soon* as possible. Having got the idea in my head, I shall be impatient till I see you."

By the time she was ready to travel, Lincoln was leaving on a campaign tour of New England, and Mary and the children joined him. Fond as she was of sightseeing, she probably got little pleasure out of the trip, because Eddie was sick. Certainly her husband was too busy to take much interest in historic landmarks. Appearing without much advance notice at Worcester, in central Massachusetts, on the day before the state Whig convention was to assemble, Lincoln accepted an invitation to speak at a city hall rally on September 12, and he gave an address that he repeated, with minor variations, in Boston, New Bedford, Lowell, Dedham, Taunton, and other places where he had appointments.

It was essentially the same speech he had given in Congress in July, defending Taylor and ridiculing Cass, but he now spent more time attacking Van Buren and the Free-Soilers, who threatened to cost the Whigs their normal majority in the state. Taking for granted the strong antislavery convictions of his listeners, he established his own credentials by reminding them "that the people of Illinois agreed entirely with the people of Massachusetts on this subject, except perhaps that they did not keep so constantly thinking about it." Both Whigs and Free-Soilers, he said, "agreed that slavery was an evil, but that we were not responsible for it and cannot affect it in the States of this Union where we do not live." Both were opposed to the extension of slavery to the new territories. The only question, then, was which party could most effectively curb the expansion of slavery. Since the Free-Soilers, by taking votes from Taylor, would contribute to the election of Cass, he concluded "that they were behind the Whigs in their advocacy of the freedom of the soil."

As was to be expected, Whig papers like the *Boston Daily Advertiser* praised Lincoln's speech as "showing a searching mind, and a cool judgement." "It was one of the best speeches ever heard in Worcester," reported the *Boston Atlas,* and the *Boston Herald* called Lincoln "a tremendous voice for Taylor and Fillmore." Democratic papers generally ignored Lincoln's appearances, and Free-Soil editors, when they troubled to notice them at all, sneered that his remarks were "rather witty, though truth and reason and argument were treated as out of the question, as unnecessary and not to be expected." The *Norfolk Democrat* found Lincoln's remarks "absolutely nauseous," and the *Roxbury Gazette* called his performance "a melancholy display."

Lincoln's manner attracted as much attention as the substance of his remarks. His enormous height startled his listeners, and they were puzzled that he began, "leaning himself up against the wall, . . . and talking in the plainest manner, and in the most indifferent tone, yet gradually fixing his footing, and getting command of his limbs, loosening his tongue, and firing up his thoughts, until he had got entire possession of himself and of his audience." Some were charmed by the rapid flow of "argument and anecdote, wit and wisdom, hymns and prophecies, platforms and syllogisms," while others deplored "his awkward gesticulations, the ludicrous management of his voice, and the comical expression of his countenance." With Yankee terseness one New Bedford man summed up his opinion: "It was a pretty sound, but not a tasteful speech."

Lincoln made no lasting impression on Massachusetts voters, but he left New England with indelible memories. Years later in the White House he could recall every detail of his visit, including "a grand dinner—a superb dinner"—that former Governor Levi Lincoln gave to Whig leaders in Worcester. It made such an impression that he could name every guest at the table and the order in which they were seated. "I went with hay seed in my hair," the President told a Massachusetts visitor, "to learn deportment in the most cultivated State in the Union."

He departed feeling that he had done his part to elect Taylor. The family went home by way of Albany, where Lincoln conferred with Thurlow Weed, the New York boss, who introduced him to Millard Fillmore, the Whig vice presidential candidate. Then they briefly visited Niagara Falls, which inspired Lincoln to momentary rhapsody: "Niagara is strong, and fresh to-day as ten thousand years ago. The Mammoth and Mastadon—now so long dead, that fragments of their monstrous bones, alone testify, that they ever lived, have gazed on Niagara. In that long—long time, never still for a single moment. Never dried, never froze, never slept, never rested"—and here his pen stopped as he recognized that he was not good at this sort of thing. Later, when Herndon asked him what reflections he had when he saw the falls, he remarked solemnly that he wondered where all that water came from.

V

In the excitement of helping to manage a national campaign, Lincoln became convinced that the Whigs would have "a most overwhelming, glorious, triumph" in the fall. He was chagrined to discover that Illinois Whigs did not share his enthusiasm. Many of them remained loyal to Henry Clay and resented Taylor's nomination. Others were troubled that the party was simultaneously opposing the Mexican War and backing a nominee who had helped win it. In the northern counties, recently settled by immigrants from New England, antislavery Whigs objected to the nomination of a slaveholder like Taylor; some of them had defected to the Liberty party in 1840 and 1844 and now a mass exodus was threatened. In the Galena district Whigs were bitterly divided when Baker, back from the war and recovered from his wounds, pushed aside local party leaders like Elihu B. Washburne and ran for Congress. Throughout the state Whigs were so divided that David Davis reported they were "in a more disorganized state than I have ever known them to be."

Nowhere was the disorganization more apparent than in Lincoln's own Seventh District, where Herndon reported Whig disaffections that Lincoln termed "heart-sickening." The Whig convention nominated Stephen T. Logan to succeed Lincoln in Congress, but voters thought him mean-spirited and avaricious. Thomas L. Harris, the Democratic candidate, questioned Logan's patriotism because he endorsed Lincoln's "Spot" resolutions, and the charge had greater force because it came from a veteran who had been wounded in the battle of Cerro Gordo. To help his former partner, Lincoln urged Herndon to "gather up all the shrewd wild boys about town"—and he named several—into Taylor clubs, where everyone should "play the part he can play best—some speak, some sing, and all hollow." "Dont fail to do this," he insisted. But Herndon responded with a long, melancholy letter, reflecting "severely on the stubbornness and bad judgment of the old fossils in the party, who were constantly holding the young men back." In the August congressional election, Illinois voters decisively defeated Logan; the district Lincoln had carried two years earlier by 1,511 votes gave a majority of 106 votes to the Democratic candidate.

On his return to Illinois in October, Lincoln tried to reverse this trend before the presidential election. In Chicago he made his usual speech, arguing that a vote for either of Taylor's opponents would be interpreted as a vote "against any restriction or restraint to the extension and perpetuation of slavery in newly acquired territory." As he neared Springfield, his effectiveness was repeatedly undercut by reminders of his unpopular stand against the Mexican War, which the *Illinois State Register* declared had caused the defeat of Logan in the recent congressional election. Lincoln made no campaign appearances in Springfield, but as assistant elector, appointed to stir up enthusiasm for the Whig ticket, he made nine addresses in the Seventh Congressional District. Most of the time he spoke in the northern counties of the district, where antislavery sentiment was strongest, reminding abolitionists that their defection to the Liberty party in 1844 had produced Polk's victory and warning that support of the Free-Soil ticket in 1848 would help elect Cass.

His warning was well taken, for Cass won Illinois with a vote less than that of the Whigs and Free-Soilers combined. In the Seventh Congressional District, Taylor's vote nearly equaled the record number Lincoln had received in 1846. Lincoln could take satisfaction in the fact that in all but one of the counties where he spoke, more voters supported Taylor than had turned out for Logan in the congressional contest. He had done his part to bring about the election of a Whig President.

VI

Next, he hoped, he could bring the party to adopt new principles. As soon as he returned to Washington in December—alone this time, for Mary and the children remained in Springfield—he saw that the central issues facing the new session of Congress were those relating to slavery and its expansion. These were not issues to which he had hitherto given much thought. He had little firsthand knowledge of slavery before he went to Washington. Except for whatever he had learned on his riverboat trips to New Orleans, he was acquainted with the South's "peculiar institution" only through his brief visits to Kentucky, where the patriarchal households of the Speeds and the Todds showed the institution in its least oppressive form. Yet he was, he said many times, "naturally anti-slavery," as his father had been. He expressed his views as early as 1837, in the protest he and Daniel Stone had presented to the Illinois state legislature, declaring "that the institution of slavery is founded on both injustice and bad policy." But he did not support any active measures to end slavery because, as the protest stated, "the Congress of the United States has no power, under the constitution, to interfere with the institution of slavery in the different States."

The extension of slavery was another matter. Like many of his contemporaries, Lincoln viewed slavery as an institution that would die out if it was confined to the areas where it already existed. Unless slavery could expand, he was convinced, it would become so unprofitable that it would be abandoned. From this point of view it was important not to arouse Southern defensiveness of slavery, and for this reason Lincoln believed "that the promulgation of abolition doctrines tends rather to increase than to abate its evils." But it was equally important not to permit slavery to go into free territory.

Even on this issue he tried not to be doctrinaire. He did not share the fears of abolitionists that the annexation of Texas would lead to the spread, and hence the perpetuation, of slavery. "Individually I never was much interested in the Texas question," he wrote one member of the Liberty party. "I never could see much good to come of annexation...; on the other hand, I never could very clearly see how the annexation would augment the evil of slavery. It always seemed to me that slaves would be taken there in about equal numbers, with or without annexation. And if more *were* taken because of annexation, still there would be just so many the fewer left, where they were taken from." This brought him to a restatement of his basic position: "I hold it to be a paramount duty of us in the free states, due to the Union of the states, and perhaps to liberty itself (paradox though it may seem) to let the slavery of the other states alone; while, on the other hand, I hold it to be equally clear, that we should never knowingly lend ourselves directly or indirectly, to prevent that slavery from dying a natural death." To this he added, significantly, that the duty of the free states included opposition to schemes "to find new places for it to live in, when it can no longer exist in the old."

Lincoln tried to maintain this balance after he took his seat in the House of Representatives. He took no part in the repeated and acrimonious debates over the Wilmot Proviso, which prohibited slavery in the territories acquired as a result of the Mexican War. During his first session in Congress his primary objective was the election of a Whig President, and, working closely with Southern Whigs like Stephens, he did not want to stir up sectional animosities. But he found it impossible to avoid the issue completely, and on at least five occasions, when the proviso was an issue, directly or indirectly, in a roll call, he voted for it.

He found it harder to stay aloof in his second congressional session. Antislavery congressmen, frustrated in their repeated attempts to pass the Wilmot Proviso, now turned their energies toward ending, or at least restricting, slavery in the District of Columbia. This was a question on which Lincoln and other members of Congress had mixed feelings. On the one hand, he wished to be conciliatory toward the South, and he deplored abolitionist agitation as counterproductive. On the other, he, like most other free-state men, found slavery in Washington a perpetual source of offense and of embarrassment. Every congressman had some contact with the two thousand slaves in the national capital. Joshua Giddings's experience was not unique. At Mrs. Sprigg's boardinghouse he, along with the other boarders—possibly including Lincoln—was present when three armed men forced their way in to arrest one of the black waiters. The man had been working to purchase his freedom and had paid off all but sixty dollars of the price, when his master changed his mind and ordered the police to take him into custody. Even more troubling was the slave trade in Washington. Only seven blocks from the Capitol stood the warehouse of Franklin & Armfield, the country's largest slave traders. Here, in what Lincoln called "a sort of Negro livery-stable," droves of slaves were collected, kept temporarily, and then sent on for sale to the Deep South. This notorious slave trade, which offended many Southerners as well as Northerners, was the source of repeated taunts from foreign observers who pointed out the irony of men and women being sold within sight of the Capitol of a nation supposedly dedicated to liberty.

Day after day, antislavery congressmen presented petitions from their constituents, calling for an end to slavery and the slave trade in the national capital. John Gorham Palfrey, one of the more aggressive Free-Soil representatives from Massachusetts, proposed to repeal all acts establishing or maintaining slavery in the federal district. Joshua Giddings favored holding a plebiscite in which residents of the District of Columbia could express their wishes as to the continuance of slavery. When pushed, Giddings announced that blacks as well as whites should vote in this election, saying that "when he looked abroad upon the family of man, he knew no distinctions" of race. The most successful of these efforts was that of Daniel Gott, a New York Whig representative, who managed, at a time when many Southerners were out of the chamber, to get the House to vote that the slave trade in the District of Columbia was "contrary to natural justice and the fundamental principles of our political system, . . . notoriously a reproach to our country throughout Christendom, and a serious hinderance [sic] to the progress of republican liberty among the nations of the earth."

In the angry discussion of these measures Lincoln rarely participated. He gave no explanation for his silence, but his position emerged from his votes.

Firmly believing in the First Amendment right of all citizens to petition the government for a redress of grievances, he consistently favored receiving all memorials and petitions, from whatever source, on the subject of slavery and the slave trade in the District of Columbia. But with equal consistency he voted against resolutions like Gott's that required the abolition of slavery or the ending of the slave trade without the consent of the inhabitants of Washington. His attitude was precisely what he had announced in 1837: he believed "that the Congress of the United States has the power, under the constitution, to abolish slavery in the District of Columbia; but that that power ought not to be exercised unless at the request of the people of said District."

Holding this view, Lincoln sought a compromise to end the debates that were beginning to tear his party apart just before a new Whig President was to be inaugurated. He prepared the way carefully. After drafting a proposal for compensated emancipation, he read it to Giddings and the other antislavery congressmen at Mrs. Sprigg's mess and secured their approval. In principle, Giddings was opposed to paying any compensation to slave owners, but, as he noted in his diary, "I believed it as good a bill as we could get at this time, and was willing to pay for slaves in order to save them from the southern market as I suppose nearly every man . . . would sell his slaves if he saw that slavery was to be abolished." Almost certainly Lincoln also got the blessing of Horace Mann, the Massachusetts anitslavery representative elected to succeed John Quincy Adams; years later he remembered how reasonable and kind Mann had been, adding, "It was *something* to me at that time to have him so—for he was a distinguished man in his way—and *I* was nobody." Then he consulted William W. Seaton, the conservative Whig mayor of Washington, who edited the influential *National Intelligencer,* and, as he stated, "about fifteen of the leading citizens of the District of Columbia." Hesitantly they endorsed his plan in principle—in Seaton's case because he was sure that Giddings and his associates would kill it in the House. Lincoln, as Giddings recorded, "did not undeceive him."

On January 10, 1849, Lincoln gained the floor of the House to introduce a proposed substitute for Gott's resolution, which was being reconsidered. He called for a referendum on slavery in the District of Columbia, in which "every free white male citizen" could participate. If a majority approved, slavery in the District would end, except for the personal servants of federal officials. Persons presently held in bondage would remain slaves, but the United States Treasury would pay "full cash value" to owners who agreed to free them. Children born of slave mothers after 1850 should be free. To sweeten this proposal for the slaveholding states, Lincoln required the municipal authorities in the District "to provide active and efficient means to arrest, and deliver up to their owners, all fugitive slaves escaping into said District."

Through quiet, patient negotiations, which would later be the hallmark of his presidential administration, Lincoln had worked out a compromise that both antislavery men and defenders of Southern rights could accept. He believed his reasonable, moderate approach was one that Whigs should adopt toward all major national problems.

Encouraged by the endorsements he received from the two extremes, Lincoln planned to submit a bill embodying his resolutions—only to find that support for his measure vanished once his plan was made public. On the Northern side, many antislavery men objected that paying slaveholders to emancipate their chattels would recognize the legitimacy of the "peculiar institution." They also could not endorse the fugitive-slave provision of Lincoln's proposal; in the mind of Wendell Phillips and other uncompromising abolitionists, it branded Lincoln permanently as "that slave hound from Illinois." Ardent Southerners also rallied against Lincoln's plan. Southern congressmen visited Mayor Seaton and persuaded him to withdraw his support of the plan because it was a covert first step toward abolishing slavery throughout the country. Not deigning to mention Lincoln by name, John C. Calhoun, the great Southern spokesman, used this proposal of "a member from Illinois" as one of the reasons why Southerners must band together to protect their rights; only thus could the North be "brought to a pause, and to a calculation of consequences."

Lincoln never introduced his bill. "Finding that I was abandoned by my former backers and having little personal influence," he explained much later, "I *dropped* the matter knowing that it was useless to prosecute the business at that time." He also began to feel that it was futile to hope that the Whig party could unite behind any constructive program.

VII

His discouragement was greater because the Taylor administration, which assumed office in March 1849, failed to use the patronage to cement the bonds of Whig party unity. Throughout the country Whigs assumed that Taylor's victory meant that Democratic officeholders would be removed and replaced by the party faithful, and Lincoln, like every other Whig congressman, was besieged by applications from hungry constituents. Everybody, it seemed, wanted an appointment—as register of the land office in Vandalia, United States attorney, secretary to the governor of the Territory of Minnesota, United States marshal for the District of Illinois, purser in the United States Navy, postmaster in Springfield, pension agent, and so on.

Conscious that every applicant who did not receive a job was potentially a political enemy, Lincoln took great pains to give encouragement without building false hopes. "I shall lay your letter by," he told an early applicant; "and if the disposition of these offices falls into my hands, in whole or in part, you shall have a fair hearing." To another he wrote frankly: "Two others, both good men, have applied for the same office before. I have made no pledge; but if the matter falls into my hands, I shall, when the time comes, try to do right, in view of all the lights then before me." Still another gained assurance that his application would receive "that consideration, which is due to impartiality, fairness, and friendship."

In making recommendations to the incoming administration, Lincoln made it clear that he thought the spoils of office ought to be used to strengthen the Whig party. Recognizing that President Taylor was disinclined to make wholesale removals of Democratic incumbents, Lincoln insisted that "when an office or a job is not already in democratic hands, that it should be given to a Whig"; otherwise, he warned, "I verily believe the administration can not be sustained." Whenever he learned that a Democratic appointee was strongly partisan, he favored replacing him with a Whig. For instance, in supporting the candidacy of Walter Davis to be receiver of the land office in Springfield, Lincoln wrote candidly to the Secretary of the Interior that the present incumbent had adequately discharged the duties of that office, but he added: "He is a very warm partizan; and openly and actively opposed the election of Gen: Taylor . . . the whigs here, almost universally desire his removal." Similarly, in asking that his old friend, A. Y. Ellis, be appointed postmaster of Springfield, he wrote: "J. R. Diller, the present incumbent, I can not say has failed in the proper discharge of any of the duties of the office. He, however, has been an active partizan in opposition to us . . . [and] he has been . . . a member of the Democratic State Central Committee."

Several of the applicants that Lincoln recommended for minor jobs did receive appointments, but he found the whole process frustrating and unsatisfactory. A lame-duck congressman, about to be succeeded by a Democrat, he did not have much influence with the Taylor administration. He was obliged to share control over the Illinois patronage with Baker, elected as a Whig representative in the next Congress, and inevitably there was a certain amount of friction. No one in Washington seemed to be listening to Lincoln's requests or to acknowledge that his exertions in behalf of the Taylor campaign entitled him to special consideration. By the beginning of May he lamented: "Not one man recommended by me has yet been appointed to any thing, little or big, except a few who had no opposition."

At the outset of Taylor's administration Lincoln himself was not an office-seeker but supported Baker's claim for a place in the cabinet or a foreign mission. At Lincoln's urging, Speed appealed to the influential John J. Crittenden on his friend's behalf, but the Kentucky governor had no favorable impression of Baker. "There is Lincoln," Crittenden said, "whom I regard as a rising man—if he were an applicant I would go for him." But the flattery did not turn Lincoln's head. "There is nothing about me which would authorize me to think of a first class office," he told Speed; "and a second class one would not compensate me for being snarled at by others who want it for themselves."

Shortly afterward he was ensnared in the very trap that he was trying to avoid. It became clear that the highest appointment to be given to any Illinois Whig would be that of commissioner of the General Land Office, a position that not merely paid the handsome salary of $3,000 a year but carried with it a great deal of power and some patronage. The commissioner was in general charge of all the public lands; his decisions determined how and when the lands were sold. He could do much to encourage the settlement of the West, and, since he controlled the sale of public lands to the state governments, he could promote the building of railroads and other internal improvements. Westerners thought it important to have the office filled by someone who knew Western laws and understood the needs of Western farmers and railroad developers; Illinois Whigs saw in the appointment a way of strengthening their party.

Some of Lincoln's friends urged him to apply for the post. It would be better than returning to his law practice, which, Judge David Davis warned, "at present promises you but poor remuneration for the labor." "Were I in your place," Davis suggested, "could I get it, I would take the Land Office." The judge might also have mentioned that this need not be a dead-end job, instancing that James Shields, Lincoln's old enemy, had held the office under President Polk, only to go on to election as senator from Illinois.

But Lincoln's interest was, at most, tepid. He was confident that "almost by common consent" the Whigs in Congress would support his candidacy, and he knew the job would pay him more than he could otherwise make; but he was reluctant to make "a final surrender of the law" as a career. Anyway, well before Taylor's inauguration he had promised to give his support to Cyrus Edwards, a former Whig legislator and unsuccessful Whig candidate for governor, who was a relative of his brother-in-law, Ninian W. Edwards.

But Edwards, it turned out, could not get the job because Baker disliked him and favored another candidate, James L. D. Morrison. As letters supporting both Edwards and Morrison piled up on the desk of Secretary of the Interior Thomas Ewing, there was a stalemate, and it seemed likely that Illinois might not receive the land commissioner's appointment after all.

At this point Lincoln's friends insisted that he must seek the position himself. He continued to hesitate, because he and Baker had agreed that if either Morrison or Edwards could be persuaded to withdraw they would support the other. "In relation to these pledges," Lincoln told his supporters, "I must not only be chaste but above suspicion." He could take the appointment only if both Edwards and Morrison declined it.

In April a new candidate appeared on the scene. Whigs in the rapidly growing northern section of Illinois felt that all appointments were going to the central and southern counties. "Mr. Lincoln," one of them grumbled, "can see nothing North of Springfield and Jacksonville in a favorable light." They were joined by E. B. Washburne and his Galena friends, eager to cut down Baker's influence. Jointly they came up with the name of Justin Butterfield, a distinguished Whig lawyer of Chicago who had served as United States attorney under Harrison and Tyler. Butterfield had the endorsement of both Henry Clay and Daniel Webster, and Secretary Ewing considered him "the most profound lawyer in the state, especially as a Land lawyer."

The news of Butterfield's candidacy aroused Lincoln. "He is my personal friend, and is qualified to do the duties of the office," he admitted; "but of the quite one hundred Illinoisians, equally well qualified, I do not know one with less claims to it." Butterfield had supported Clay, not Taylor, for the 1848 nomination and had hardly lifted a finger for the President's election. His appointment would be "an egregious political blunder," which would "gratify no single whig in the state, except it be Mr. B. himself." Lincoln resolved to enter the field himself, and he began soliciting letters of support from leading Illinois Whigs and from congressmen he had known in Washington. In order to blanket the country, he even enlisted Mary to write letters.

His campaign was strong enough to persuade the President to delay the appointment for three weeks, so that both Butterfield and Lincoln could rush to Washington and present their cases in person. Favoring Butterfield from the start, Secretary Ewing was impressed by the endorsements he gathered, including an anti-Lincoln petition signed by disgruntled Whigs from Springfield itself, who declared they were "dissatisfied with the course of Abraham Lincoln as a member of Congress from this Congressional District." One of them followed up with a letter declaring that Lincoln's stand on the Mexican War had rendered him "very unpopular, and inflicted a deep and mischievous wound upon the Whole Whig party of the State." In the end, Taylor followed his standard practice of allowing each cabinet member to make the appointments in his department and gave the office to Butterfield. Fuming, Lincoln declared that the President was getting "the unjust and ruinous character of being a mere man of straw."

Lincoln was disappointed, not so much for himself as for the Whig party. "I opposed the appointment of Mr. B. because I believed it would be a matter of discouragement to our active, working friends here, and I opposed it for no other reason," he wrote Ewing. "I never did, in any true sense, want the office myself." In his view Butterfield belonged to the "old fossil" wing of the party, content to live on occasional federal appointments without ever building a strong state organization. Lincoln saw the land commissioner's appointment as a means of building a viable Whig party in Illinois, which had never won in a presidential election or in a gubernatorial race. Properly used, that office could supplement the active local organizations that Lincoln had encouraged and the convention system that he had helped to establish.

At the end of his congressional career Lincoln returned to private life, discouraged about the prospects of his party. It did not relieve his gloom when Secretary of State John M. Clayton offered him, as a consolation prize, the office of secretary to the governor of the Oregon Territory, which he promptly declined. Then Interior Secretary Ewing, realizing the snub they had given to the most active Illinois Whig, tendered him the governorship of the Oregon Territory. Lincoln briefly toyed with the possibility but quickly concluded that it led nowhere. Oregon was strongly Democratic, and once it was admitted to the Union, it would hardly choose a Whig like Lincoln as governor or senator. Anyway, moving to the West Coast would be difficult and dangerous, especially because Eddie's health was uncertain. He declined the offer, putting the blame, as husbands so often do, on his wife, who, he said, put her foot down about moving.

With that his public career was apparently over. As he settled back in Springfield, he must have remembered a note he gave a few months earlier to an autograph collector who requested his "signature with a sentiment": "I am not a very sentimental man; and the best sentiment I can think of is, that if you collect the signatures of all persons who are no less distinguished than I, you will have a very undistinguishing mass of names."

CHAPTER SIX

At the Head of His Profession in This State

———

"From 1849 to 1854, both inclusive, [I] practiced law more assiduously than ever before," Lincoln wrote in an 1859 autobiographical sketch. This was a time for redirecting his career. He needed, first, to resettle his family after his sojourn in Washington, and the Lincolns moved back into their little house on Eighth and Jackson streets in Springfield. Next he had to resume his law career, his sole source of income now that he was no longer receiving a government salary. He turned down the tempting offer of Grant Goodrich to join his Chicago law firm, saying that if he moved to the city he "would have to sit down and study hard" and "it would kill him," because "he tended to consumption." Instead he and Herndon continued their partnership.

Political prospects played little part in these decisions. As he noted in an 1860 biography, "His profession had almost superseded the thought of politics in his mind." Illinois offered no future for an ambitious Whig politician. He recognized that his public career was at an end.

In these years of relative tranquillity Lincoln had time for self-examination. His years in Washington did nothing to undermine his supreme self-confidence, but he could not help observing that he had less education and professional training than most of his fellow congressmen. In a brief autobiography prepared for a congressional biographical directory, he commented tersely: "Education defective." He began, as Herndon said, "to realize a certain lack of discipline—a want of mental training and method." Believing, as did most of his contemporaries, that mental faculties, like muscles, could be strengthened by rigorous exercise, he secured a copy of Euclid's principles of geometry and with determination set himself to working out the theorems and problems. With quiet pride he reported in 1860 that he had "studied and nearly mastered the Six-books of Euclid."

I

Though some of his clients had drifted away during his term in Congress, it did not take long for Lincoln to reestablish his position at the bar. He retained some clients whose cases had begun before his election to Congress and were still pending. For instance, he continued to be involved in the never-ending litigation of Nancy Robinson Dorman to recover land in Gallatin County wrongfully diverted by her stepfather. After becoming Dorman's attorney in 1842, Lincoln kept an interest in her suit while in Congress and finally succeeded in winning a judgment in her favor in 1852. He had little difficulty in attracting new clients, because people remembered his enviable record of success in the courts before his election. Doubtless his reputation got a boost when he was admitted to practice before the United States Supreme Court in 1849, where he effectively argued a case.

After his return to Springfield he developed a sizable practice before the Illinois Supreme Court. Some of his early cases were trivial. For example, in 1851 he was asked to appear in the case of one Robert Nuckles, who was suing for damage Elijah Bacon's cattle did to his corn. Not satisfied with the $2.50 awarded him by the local justice of the peace, Nuckles employed a local attorney to sue Bacon in the Macon County Circuit Court. This time a jury awarded him damages in the amount of $3.33. Unhappy with the verdict, Bacon wanted his lawyer to engage Lincoln's services for an appeal to the Illinois Supreme Court. But soon Lincoln was involved in more important litigation, such as the suit of Oliver W. Browning, who fell and broke his leg on an unrepaired street in Springfield and sued the city for failing to maintain its roads. The common law provided no remedy for Browning, but Lincoln argued that the city charter required Springfield to keep its streets in repair. Adopting Lincoln's arguments, the supreme court ruled for Browning, establishing an often cited precedent in municipal law.

In these supreme court cases Lincoln and Herndon worked as a team. An omnivorous and rapid reader, Herndon made it his job in each case to go through all the relevant decisions he could locate in the well-stocked State Library and the Supreme Court Library, which had the reports of all the state supreme courts and the federal courts, as well as the usual legal reference works and dictionaries. Because so many of the subjects of litigation were repetitious, he compiled a kind of legal index in a large commonplace book, where he recorded the precedents he discovered on a wide variety of topics, from Streets and Improvements (a subject directly relevant to the Browning case) and Negligence in Building Bridges to larger subjects such as Corrupt Motives, Physical or Moral Nuisances, Trusts, and Specific Performances. As Lincoln & Herndon came more and more to deal with business firms, the junior partner prepared a separate, smaller notebook he entitled "Corporations," where he listed precedents on topics like Organization, Subscription, Forfeiture of Stock, and Forfeiture of Charter. In addition, he drew up briefs for many individual cases, outlining the principal issues and precedents.

For his part, Lincoln did virtually all the paperwork involved in these supreme court cases, preparing even the most formal and routine documents in his own hand. Because Herndon in 1848 began serving as deputy clerk of court, he was not free to make frequent appearances before that bench, and Lincoln usually appeared alone or with some other attorney. But both partners recognized the contribution that Herndon's research made to Lincoln's courtroom victories, and they continued to divide the fees from these cases equally.

Lincoln & Herndon also developed a thriving practice before the United States Circuit and District courts in Illinois, which handled suits between citizens of different states, suits brought by the United States government, and other miscellaneous types of cases. Admitted to practice before the United States courts in 1839, Lincoln had appeared in at least sixty-two cases before he left for Congress, and on his return he naturally sought to pick up additional business in the federal courts, where cases were likely to involve larger questions and greater fees than the purely local litigation of the state courts. Because the court system had changed somewhat during his absence, he found abundant opportunity. The growth of Chicago made it imperative to hold sessions of the federal courts there as well as in Springfield, and Congress in 1855 divided the state into two judicial districts, with Judge Thomas Drummond presiding in Chicago and Judge Samuel H. Treat in Springfield. This multiplication of jurisdictions was a boon to lawyers, and Lincoln was soon making fairly regular appearances in the United States courts in Chicago as well as in Springfield.

In the federal courts Lincoln handled almost every kind of proceeding, including, improbably enough, a case in admiralty, involving a salvage operation on a ferryboat in the Mississippi River. Much of his time was taken by suits for debt, brought against citizens of Illinois by plaintiffs residing in other states. In seventeen cases he represented Samuel C. Davis & Company, a wholesale firm in St. Louis, which sued to collect unpaid bills in Illinois. This was not work that Lincoln enjoyed, nor was it remunerative, because he had to hire a man to visit each of the localities where a debtor lived and appraise his property in order to determine whether a court decree could be executed. As other more interesting and rewarding cases came his way, he resolved to drop Davis & Company as a client, and he wrote the firm: "My mind is made up. I will have no more to do with this class of business. I can do business in Court, but I can not, and will not follow executions all over the world."

Other litigation in the federal courts he continued to find fascinating, especially when it involved mechanical devices and patents. His very first case in the Chicago federal court (*Z. Parker* v. *Charles Hoyt*) had to do with Hoyt's alleged infringement of Parker's patent for a waterwheel. Along with

Grant Goodrich, Lincoln represented Hoyt. Defending their client with great energy, Lincoln explained to the jury in clear, simple language that Hoyt's device was not a copy of Parker's patented waterwheel but was simply an application of an age-old principle of waterpower. He reinforced his point by describing his early experience as an operator of Offutt's sawmill at New Salem, which had been powered by the Sangamon River. When the jury came in with a verdict for the defendant, Lincoln said he "regarded this as one of the most gratifying triumphs of his professional life."

II

The heart of Lincoln's law practice continued to be in the circuit courts, and Lincoln & Herndon did its largest business in the Sangamon County Circuit Court. In August 1849, at the first session of that court held after Lincoln's return from Congress, the firm had three cases on the opening day, seventeen cases on the second day, and eight on the third day. Once again Lincoln & Herndon was back in business. In 1850 the partners were involved in 18 percent of all the cases brought before the Sangamon County Circuit Court, and by 1853 they participated in about one-third of all cases.

As business increased, the small back room in the Tinsley Building, to which Herndon had moved during Lincoln's absence, proved inadequate, and the partners rented a larger, second-floor office on the west side of the capitol square. It was a bare, unpretentious room, with two dirty windows looking out over sheds and an alley. There was no carpet. One long table occupied the center of the room, with a shorter one crossing it, to form a T, and both were covered with green baize. An old-fashioned secretary, with pigeonholes and a drawer to hold legal papers, a bookcase containing about two hundred law books, a couch, and some miscellaneous chairs completed the furnishings. The office was almost never cleaned.

In this office the partners worked until 1861. Unless they were on the circuit, both came in every morning, and they sat facing each other at opposite ends of the shorter table. From time to time, Lincoln would throw himself on the couch, resting his legs on two or three chairs or up against the wall, spilling himself out, as Herndon noted with irritable exaggeration, "easily over ¼ of the room." Often, to his partner's exasperation, Lincoln would read aloud from the daily newspapers or whatever book he was interested in. As he explained to Herndon: "When I read aloud my two senses catch the idea—1st I see what I am reading and 2dly I hear it read; and I can thus remember what I read the better."

On many cases the partners worked together, with Herndon doing the research and the bookwork while Lincoln dealt with clients and the courts. But both Lincoln and Herndon handled many cases independently, or with other attorneys. In a rough division of labor, Herndon managed the office —insofar as any management was performed—and supervised the one or two students who were reading law with the firm, while Lincoln more often appeared in court. Except when he handled cases in Menard County, Herndon usually stayed in Springfield, while Lincoln went out on the circuit.

Every spring, after the adjournment of the Sangamon County Circuit Court, Lincoln set out on the round of the other circuit courts in the Eighth Judicial District. He discovered that there had been some significant changes during his two-year absence. For one thing, Lincoln now found himself one of the senior lawyers traveling the circuit. Though he was only forty years old, he was more and more frequently called—though never to his face— "Old Abe," both because of his weather-beaten appearance and because of his many years in public life and at the bar. Some of the younger, ambitious lawyers thought of him as one of the "fossils," who wanted to keep down new talent, and Lincoln himself, while denying any desire to discriminate against younger attorneys, conceded, "I suppose I am now one of the old men."

Another change resulted from the election in 1848 of David Davis as judge of the Eighth Judicial District, to succeed Samuel H. Treat, who had presided over so many of Lincoln's earlier cases on the circuit. Davis, a native of Maryland educated at Kenyon College and the Yale Law School, had known Lincoln casually for a number of years, but the two men now became closely acquainted in traveling the interminable miles of the circuit and in sitting for endless hours in the county courts. In appearance they were a curiously mismatched pair. Davis, so portly that it was said he had to be surveyed for a pair of trousers, was a stickler for immaculate clothing and perfect grooming; Lincoln, thin to the point of emaciation, seemed always to be hastily dressed, usually in a bobtailed sack coat and jeans that did not come within inches of his feet. In the winter months he added to this ensemble a circular blue cape, or sometimes a gray shawl, which he wore over his shoulders, fastened with an immense safety pin; in the summer he traveled in a white linen duster, much stained and the worse for wear. But in many ways Lincoln and Davis were much alike. Both were devoted Whigs, dedicated to promoting the country's economic growth and national spirit. Border-state men, they detested slavery but deplored abolitionist efforts to end it. In legal matters Davis, despite his formal training, was neither particularly acute nor learned, and like Lincoln he took a commonsensical approach to the law, allowing principles to guide his decisions more often than precedents.

Davis and Lincoln did not become intimate friends. "Lincoln never confided to me anything," Davis remarked many years later, adding that "Mr. Lincoln was not a sociable man by any means" and that he had "no strong emotional feelings for any person—mankind or thing." That sour judgment derived from the essentially professional nature of their relationship, which was based on respect rather than affection. Each man developed a high opinion of the other's ability.

Davis, as he wrote to his wife, greatly admired "Mr. Lincoln's exceeding honesty and fairness." So great was the judge's confidence in Lincoln that on numerous occasions when called away from the bench by family illness or other emergencies he designated Lincoln to preside in his stead. The practice of asking a prominent attorney to substitute for the judge was a fairly common one on the frontier (until the Illinois Supreme Court put an end to it in 1877), but only when the substitute was an attorney like Lincoln, who had the respect of the other members of the bar, were his rulings accepted without protest. Most of the decisions that Lincoln made as judge were in routine or uncontested cases, but he also disposed of slander suits, divorces, and actions for debt.

For the next eleven years Davis and Lincoln, together with the other lawyers, traveled essentially the same circuit twice a year. In the spring, after concluding the session of the Sangamon County Circuit Court in Springfield, the judge and his entourage moved on to Tremont in Tazewell County; then to Metamora in Woodford County; thence south to Bloomington in McLean County, and to Mt. Pulaski in Logan County; next east to Clinton in DeWitt County, Monticello in Piatt County, Urbana in Champaign County, and Danville in Vermilion County; after that south to Paris in Edgar County; then, turning west, to Shelbyville in Shelby County, Sullivan in Moultrie County, Decatur in Macon County, and Taylorville in Christian County. After that the judge went back to his home in Bloomington and the lawyers dispersed. (The route varied slightly from year to year depending in part on the condition of the roads. Sometimes counties where there was little litigation could be skipped. From time to time, the legislature changed the boundaries of the Eighth Judicial District, adding or subtracting counties.) The area traveled, as Davis grumbled, was equal to the entire state of Connecticut.

Roads were slightly better than they had been in the earlier days. Lincoln never used the public stagecoaches that connected a few towns but traveled in his buggy, pulled by Old Buck, the successor to Old Tom. Accommodations remained miserable. Davis's letters to his wife recited a litany of complaints: there was mud in the winter and dust in the summer; taverns were overrun with mosquitoes, fleas, and bedbugs; the dining rooms were dirty and typically the "table [was] greasy—table cloth greasy—floor greasy and every thing else ditto"; the waitress was so filthy that he guessed "the dirt must be half an inch thick all over her." Worst of all was the food "hardly fit for the stomach of a horse." Lincoln, as always indifferent to his surroundings and careless of comfort, registered no complaints. Once when he arrived at a hard-luck hotel and found the landlord had run out of meat and bread, he cheerfully announced: "Well in the absence of anything to eat I will jump into this Cabbage."

Everywhere on the circuit Lincoln's services were much in demand, mostly by younger attorneys who needed his assistance in drafting legal papers and in presenting their cases to the court. With some of them he worked so frequently that they came to think of themselves as his partners, though they should more properly be termed his associates. With only one, Ward Hill Lamon, in Danville, was there anything like a formal arrangement; a local newspaper announced in 1852 the formation of the new firm of Lincoln & Lamon, Attorneys at Law. Possibly Lamon alone was responsible for inserting the advertisement, and perhaps Lincoln never knew of it. Anyway, he never rebuked Lamon because he was fond of this hard-drinking, two-fisted young giant with his endless repertory of off-color stories and Negro songs. The partnership, if it deserved that name, was limited to Vermilion County, where Lincoln and Lamon did frequently appear together, Lamon leaning heavily on the senior lawyer for guidance.

For the most part, Lincoln's cases in the circuit courts continued to be of no great interest or consequence to anyone except the parties involved in the litigation. For instance, at the 1850 session of the Tazewell County Circuit Court, where he always had a large practice, he represented three defendants who were being sued by the village of Tremont for establishing an "unwholesome business," a lard factory, that was polluting the neighborhood. Lincoln based his case on a highly technical point, involving a statute of limitations, and lost, and his clients were fined $10 each. The next year he and two local lawyers represented members of the Funk family, accused of cutting 1,200 trees on the property of John Shibley and hauling off the timber; he lost again, but the defeat was a technical one since the jury awarded the plaintiff only $104. In 1852 he defended Sheriff William Gaither and John Jones, accused of imprisoning and beating one Joseph F. Haines, on whom they were attempting to serve a writ. The jury acquitted Gaither but fined his assistant, Jones, $10; Lincoln could consider that half a victory. Later that same year he represented John P. Singleton, who was sued for nonpayment of a debt to Pearly Brown. In fact, Singleton had paid part of the debt and, at a time when cash was scarce in the West, had tried to pay the rest in corn, which Brown refused to accept. Lincoln negotiated a settlement. At the 1855 session he appeared for one Peter Duffy, accused of having repeatedly beaten, kicked, and thrown to the ground Benjamin Seaman, causing him to be "greatly hurt, bruised and wounded . . . sore, lame, and disordered." The grand jury found for Seaman but, under Lincoln's persuasion, reduced the damages awarded him from the $300 he claimed to only $3.

Lincoln's income from his circuit court practice depended on the volume of the cases he handled. His fees were generally modest, as were those charged by most other attorneys on the circuit. For most cases he received $10.00 or $20.00. Collecting a debt of $600.00, he retained as his fee only $3.50. He felt strongly that clients should not be overcharged. In 1856 when a man in Quincy sent him a check for $25.00 for drawing up some legal papers, Lincoln wrote: "You must think I am a high-priced man. You are too liberal with your money. Fifteen dollars is enough for the job." He returned the balance.

III

In handling hundreds of cases in the circuit courts, Lincoln firmly reestablished his reputation as a lawyer. It was a reputation that rested, first, on the universal belief in his absolute honesty. He became known as "Honest Abe" —or, often, "Honest Old Abe"—the lawyer who was never known to lie. He held himself to the highest standards of truthfulness. In notes for a lecture on the law, written about 1850, he referred to the "vague popular belief that lawyers are necessarily dishonest" and warned: "Let no young man, choosing the law for a calling, for a moment yield to this popular belief. Resolve to be honest at all events; and if, in your own judgment, you can not be an honest lawyer, resolve to be honest without being a lawyer. Choose some other occupation."

Clients and other attorneys also respected Lincoln's incredible capacity for hard work. Though most of the cases he argued on the circuit originated with local lawyers, he drafted nearly all the legal papers himself, from the purely formal praecipes to the most elaborate pleadings. Writing all these out in his own hand sometimes involved enormous labor. In the 1855 Macoupin County case of *Clark & Morrison* v. *Page & Bacon,* involving the claims of some St. Louis bankers and financiers, Lincoln for the defendants drafted a forty-three-page answer to the plaintiffs' bill of complaints; this was a task that required immense concentration, and Lincoln's handwriting suggested that he wrote the entire document at one sitting. Of course, few cases required so much labor, but Lincoln's clients rarely lost a suit because of carelessness or inattention on the part of their attorney.

Lincoln was also noted for his fairness to his opponents. Like any other lawyer, he resorted to technicalities in order to save his clients, but in these circuit court cases he preferred to base his arguments on justice rather than on legal precedents. His one standard move in the more serious of these cases was to apply for a change of venue, in the belief that the delay in hearing and the transfer of a case to another county would give his clients a fairer trial.

In court he rarely raised objections when opposing counsel introduced evidence. According to Leonard Swett, the young Bloomington lawyer who traveled the circuit with Lincoln, "he would say he 'reckoned' it would be fair to let this in, or that; and sometimes, when his adversary could not quite prove what Lincoln knew to be the truth, he 'reckoned' it would be fair to admit the truth to be so-and-so." But this, Swett noted, did not mean that he yielded essentials: "What he was so blandly giving away was simply what he couldn't get and keep." Many a rival lawyer was lulled into complacency as Lincoln conceded, say, six out of seven points in argument, only to discover that the whole case turned on the seventh point. "Any man who took Lincoln for a simple-minded man," Swett concluded, "would very soon wake up with his back in a ditch."

Rarely did Lincoln object to a judge's ruling on the admissibility of evidence, usually saying, when the argument went against him, "Well, I reckon I must be wrong." But when the point was essential to his case, he would vigorously controvert the court's ruling. In a celebrated 1859 case in the Sangamon County Circuit Court (which by this point was no longer part of David Davis's Eighth Judicial District), he, Logan, and Shelby M. Cullom represented Peachy Quinn Harrison, accused of stabbing Greek Crafton to death in the vicinity of Pleasant Plains. The stenographic transcript of the trial—the only such transcript for any case in which Lincoln was involved—showed that Lincoln and Logan did not attempt to deny that Harrison had killed Crafton but tried to prove that he did so because Crafton had repeatedly threatened to beat him up. The prosecuting attorney argued that evidence of these threats was inadmissible since it could not be proved that Harrison knew about them before the fatal stabbing. The judge, E. Y. Rice, a lifelong Democrat and political opponent of Lincoln, agreed and excluded the evidence. In a second line of defense, Lincoln and his associates attempted to introduce the testimony of Crafton's grandfather, Peter Cartwright. The venerable Methodist exhorter, who had once run against Lincoln for Congress, visited Crafton on his deathbed. Cartwright testified that his grandson had shown remorse for having threatened Harrison and said: *"I have brought it upon myself, and I forgive Quinn."* Again the prosecution objected, arguing that Crafton's dying statement was inadmissible and irrelevant, and Judge Rice agreed to exclude Cartwright's testimony.

Angrily Lincoln protested both decisions, saying in court that he "had never heard of such law." The trial transcript did not include his argument against Judge Rice's ruling, but Herndon, who was in the courtroom, vividly remembered that Lincoln denounced it as "absurd and without precedent in the broad world." He "spoke fiercely—strongly—contemptuously of the decision of the court," just managing to avoid anything that could be held as contempt. Under his withering attack Judge Rice retracted his ruling and allowed both Cartwright's testimony and the evidence concerning threats to go to the jury, which acquitted Lincoln's client.

"In his examination of witnesses," a newspaperman wrote of Lincoln in 1850, "he displays a masterly ingenuity and a legal tact that baffles concealment and defies deceit." His legendary skill as a cross-examiner was clearly demonstrated in his most celebrated criminal case, the 1858 trial of William "Duff" Armstrong for the murder of James Metzker. Attending a religious camp meeting at Virgin's Grove, near the now deserted site of New Salem, in August 1857, Armstrong, Metzker, and James Norris, all undoubtedly drunk, got into a fight, and Metzker was killed. Norris was accused of having hit Metzker on the back of his head with a piece of wood, and Armstrong was indicted for striking him in the eye with his metal slungshot. The two cases were separated, and Norris was convicted for manslaughter. Armstrong's mother, Hannah, asked Lincoln to defend her son. Remembering his long friendship for the young man's father, Jack Armstrong, and Hannah's many kindnesses during his years in New Salem, Lincoln readily agreed. He accepted no fee.

At the trial, which was moved to the Cass County courthouse in Beardstown, the state's principal witness was Charles Allen, who testified that Armstrong struck Metzker. Though it was eleven o'clock at night and Allen was standing 150 feet away, he claimed that he could see the attack clearly by the light of the nearly full moon shining directly overhead. On cross-examination, Lincoln slowly and with seeming casualness had Allen go through his story a dozen times, asking him to describe just what he had seen and how he was able to see it. Then, with the witness firmly committed to his story, Lincoln produced an 1857 almanac and read from it to show that at the time Allen claimed to have witnessed the attack the moon had already set. The roar of laughter that followed showed that Allen's credibility was demolished.

Lincoln's skill in making the closing argument in a case caused one Illinois journalist to place him "at the head of the profession in this state," adding, "though he may have his equal, it would be no easy task to find his superior." On rare occasions he ended with a powerful emotional address to the jury. In the Duff Armstrong case, after carefully reviewing the now discredited evidence advanced by the prosecution, he made an unabashedly sentimental appeal that, as the prosecuting attorney remembered, "took the jury by storm." He told the jurors "of his once being a poor, friendless boy; that Armstrong's father took him into his house, fed and clothed him, and gave him a home." There were tears in his eyes as he spoke, and the story he told with such pathos moved the jury to tears also. "His sympathies were fully enlisted in favor of the young man," the prosecutor recalled, "and his terrible sincerity could not help but arouse the same passion in the jury." Armstrong was acquitted. But that summation was unusual, for Lincoln ordinarily ended with a low-key, logical argument that jurors could readily understand. A reporter discovered "no false glitter, no sickly sentimentalism" in his arguments; instead, "bold, forcible and energetic, he forces conviction upon the mind."

IV

Davis and some of the attorneys were puzzled that Lincoln, up to 1854, generally remained with the court throughout the circuit without returning home, and sometimes they direly speculated that he must be having marital problems. They failed to realize that the law was Lincoln's only means of support. Unlike Davis, Logan, and a number of other Eighth District lawyers, he did not make a fortune from land speculation, nor did he own a farm or run a business. His law practice brought in a comfortable income of perhaps $2,000 a year, and by 1860 the census taker reported he owned real estate valued at $5,000 and a personal estate of $12,000. To maintain that level he had to be constantly at work. He stayed throughout the circuit because he could not afford to be absent.

It was fortunate that he could remain in Springfield for most of the summer months and during the winter, when the Illinois Supreme Court and the United States District Court met in the state capital, because he was much needed at home to help with a series of family crises. His father, Thomas Lincoln, was in failing health. Since 1840 the elder Lincolns had been living in a double log cabin on a 120-acre farm on Goosenest Prairie, in Coles County. Though Abraham Lincoln had developed an entirely different set of interests and values from those of his father and stepmother, he was concerned for their well-being and tried to help them live in modest comfort. In the 1840s when Thomas Lincoln got into financial difficulties, probably through partnership with his lazy and unreliable stepson, John D. Johnston, in a saw- and gristmill, Abraham Lincoln came to his rescue by paying him $200 for the east forty acres of his farm—a payment that was really a gift, since the agreement clearly specified that Thomas and Sarah Lincoln were to have "use and entire control" of the land during their lifetimes. From time to time, when his work on the circuit brought him near Coles County—where he had a certain amount of business, though it was not part of the Eighth Judicial District—he would visit his parents. While he was in Congress, Thomas begged him for a "Lone of, Twenty Dollars" to prevent his farm from being sold to settle a long-forgotten judgment against him. Lincoln promptly sent the money, though his letter made it clear that he thought it was "singular" that his father could not pay such a small debt and that such an obligation could have been forgotten for so long. In all probability he suspected Johnston of making up the whole story.

Toward his stepmother Lincoln always had the most affectionate feelings, and he closed his letter, "Give my love to Mother." Toward his father his attitude was more ambivalent. The two had never been close, and they had drifted apart even more since Abraham left home. Thomas Lincoln's unambitious, unsuccessful way of life came to represent the values his son wanted to repudiate. He had reason, too, to believe that his father, as he reached seventy, was becoming a little senile and was too much under the influence of the unreliable Johnston.

In May 1849, shortly after Lincoln returned from Washington, he heard from Johnston that Thomas Lincoln was dying. "He Craves to See you all the time," the stepbrother wrote, "and he wonts you to Come if you ar able to git hure, for you are his only Child that is of his own flush and blood and it is nothing more than natere for him to crave to see you." At Johnston's request, Augustus H. Chapman, Dennis Hanks's son-in-law, reinforced the plea with a letter describing Thomas Lincoln's "Seizure of the Heart" and his "truly Heart-Rendering" cries to see his only son. Though Lincoln at this point was actively campaigning to secure appointment as commissioner of the General Land Office, he rushed off to Coles County to see his father, probably missing a second letter from Chapman assuring him that Thomas Lincoln had no heart disease and would "doubtless be well in a Short time." Lincoln's visit to Goosenest Prairie delayed by nearly a week his trip to Washington, and it may have cost him the Land Office appointment.

The next winter, when John D. Johnston wrote him two more letters about Thomas Lincoln's declining health, Abraham Lincoln did not respond. He thought his stepbrother was again crying wolf. Only after he heard independently from Harriet Chapman did he take the news seriously. Repeating his "desire that neither Father or Mother shall be in want of any comfort either in health or sickness," he explained why he could not come to his father's sickbed. "My business is such that I could hardly leave home now," he wrote; besides, his wife was "sick-abed" with "baby-sickness." Both excuses had some plausibility. A trip by buggy to Coles County would take three days each way, at a time when Lincoln had cases before the United States Circuit and District courts and the Illinois Supreme Court almost every day. But had he truly wanted to go, he could have entrusted his cases to his partner or asked for postponements. It was also true that Mary had given birth to their third son on December 21. Though the delivery was perfectly normal, she doubtless would have been highly nervous if Lincoln left home while she had the entire responsibility of caring for a newborn baby. But, again, her illness was not serious, and there were friends and neighbors who could help her. Once again, the husband allowed his wife to take the blame for an uncomfortable decision.

The rest of Lincoln's letter, urging his father "to call upon, and confide in, our great, and good, and merciful Maker; who . . . notes the fall of a sparrow, and numbers the hairs of our heads," was in unconvincing and strained language, really addressed to his backwoods relatives who thought in the clichés of the Primitive Baptists. "Say to him," he enjoined Johnston, "that if we could meet now, it is doubtful whether it would not be more painful than pleasant; but that if it be his lot to go now, he will soon have a joyous meeting with many loved ones gone before; and where the rest of us, through the help of God, hope ere-long to join them." Unable to simulate a grief that he did not feel or an affection that he did not bear, Lincoln did not attend his father's funeral. He was not heartless, but Thomas Lincoln represented a world that his son had long ago left behind him.

During the years of his father's final illness, Lincoln had also to deal with family crises closer to home. In December 1849 his second son, Edward Baker, always a feeble child, became seriously sick. His disease was pulmonary tuberculosis, for which there was no known cure. After fifty-two days of acute illness, the little boy, who was not quite four years old, died on February 1, 1850. Both parents were devastated. Lincoln, as always, internalized his emotions, saying only, "We miss him very much." For his wife, Eddie's death, coming shortly after deaths both of her father and her beloved grandmother, was harder to bear, especially since she was exhausted from the long vigil of nursing the sick child. Like her husband, she lacked faith in conventional Christianity and consequently was denied the consolation of believing that her son's death was all for the best, as part of some divine plan. Restlessly she kicked against the pricks of fate, and more than two years after Eddie's death she wrote a Kentucky friend, "I grieve to say that even at this distant day, I do not feel sufficiently submissive to our loss."

A few weeks after Eddie's death she was expecting again. The Lincolns clearly intended to replace the lost boy. Her pregnancy was uneventful, but, once again, she was alone much of the time, since Lincoln was away on the circuit. The baby was named William Wallace Lincoln, after her physician brother-in-law who had been so helpful during Eddie's final days. Willie was the most intelligent and the best-looking of all the Lincoln children, and from the day he was born his father doted on him.

Then, because Willie needed a playmate, Mary in 1853 gave birth to a fourth child. The Lincolns had hoped this time for a girl, but they were soon reconciled to accepting another boy, whom they named Thomas after his recently deceased grandfather. The choice of the name suggested that Abraham Lincoln's memories of his father were not all unpleasant—and perhaps it hinted at guilt for not having attended his funeral. The infant was born with an unusually large head, as compared to his tiny body, and Lincoln playfully called him a little tadpole. The nickname "Tad" stuck to him for the rest of his life.

The careful two-and-a-half-year intervals between the births of the Lincoln children suggested that the parents were using some form of birth control. Doubtless they relied in part on the widespread belief that conception could not take place so long as the mother was nursing, for Mary Lincoln did not wean her babies until after they were eighteen months old. After the birth of Tad, it may have been impossible for her to have additional children. The delivery had been difficult, perhaps because of the size of the infant's head, and it left Mary for the rest of her life as "more or less a sufferer" from what she called, with Victorian propriety, troubles "of a womanly nature."

V

By the mid-1850s the nature of Lincoln's law practice was gradually changing. He continued to have numerous cases with small fees and less consequence, but increasingly his time was taken up with suits relating to the railroad network that began to spread across the state. Wherever railroads ran, there were legal problems—problems concerning charters and franchises; problems relating to right-of-way; problems concerning evaluation and taxation; problems relating to the duties of common carriers and the rights of passengers; problems concerning merger, consolidation, and receivership—and Lincoln, like other lawyers, found the ensuing litigation a major source of income.

Long an advocate of improved transportation as the key to economic development, Lincoln took on his first significant railroad case in 1851 for the Alton & Sangamon Railroad, which he considered "a link in the great chain of railroad communication which shall unite Boston and New York with the Mississippi." The suit arose when one of the original subscribers to the stock of the railroad, James A. Barret, who owned land in western Sangamon County, refused to pay the balance due on his pledge in order to protest a change in the planned route of the road. When he had subscribed for his thirty shares, it was to go by his 4,215 acres, which consequently would greatly increase in value, but a shift in the route, designed to cut off twelve miles in the length of the road, meant that he would derive no direct benefit from the construction. Employing Lincoln, the railroad sued for payment of Barret's pledge. Everyone realized the case was important because, as Lincoln said, if Barret won, it "might encourage others to stop payments" on their subscriptions. Lincoln took extraordinary pains to construct an airtight case for his client, designed to prove that Barret was indeed a stockholder and that the Alton & Sangamon Railroad had the right to sue for his delinquent payment. In frequent correspondence with officials of the railroad both in New York and in Alton, Lincoln insisted that they provide full documentation to support his brief, noting, "I have labored hard to find the law" that applied to cases like this. The Illinois Supreme Court accepted his argument, and Chief Justice Samuel Treat agreed that a "few obstinate stockholders should not be permitted to deprive the public and the company of the advantages that will result from a superior and less expensive route." The decision, subsequently cited in twenty-five other cases throughout the United States, helped establish the principle that corporation charters could be amended in the public interest, and it established Lincoln as one of the most prominent and successful Illinois practitioners of railroad law.

The following year he made his first appearances for the powerful Illinois Central Railroad, which was designed to connect Chicago with Mobile and the Gulf of Mexico. Participation in two minor cases whetted his desire to participate in larger litigation involving the railroad. When the state chartered the Illinois Central, it had granted an exemption from all taxation, provided the company paid the state treasury an annual "charter tax." Dissatisfied with this arrangement, the officials of McLean County argued that the state had no right to exempt the railroad from county taxes, and they levied a tax on its real estate within that county. The Illinois Central resisted, because paying county taxes in addition to the state charter tax would practically have forced it out of business. The resulting suit, Lincoln recognized, was "the largest law question that now can be got up in the State," and he wanted to be a party to it on one side or the other. He first approached the officials of Champaign County, who were contemplating a suit like the one in McLean, and when they did not respond, he wrote the solicitor for the Illinois Central: "I am now free to make an engagement for the Road; and if you think fit you may 'count me in.'" He received a retainer of $250.

The Illinois Supreme Court heard the case of *Illinois Central Railroad* v. *The County of McLean* in its spring 1854 term, with Lincoln's two former partners, Logan and Stewart, representing the county. Lincoln and James F. Joy, the railroad's attorney, appeared for the Illinois Central. Lincoln and Herndon prepared for the case very carefully. Drawing on Herndon's research, Lincoln developed a brief maintaining that the legislature had been constitutionally competent when it exempted the railroad property from local taxation, and he cited in support of his argument previous court decisions in New Jersey, Illinois, Maryland, Alabama, Indiana, Mississippi, and South Carolina.

Neither the plaintiff nor the defendant convinced the Illinois Supreme Court, which required a further hearing on the constitutionality of the legislative exemption, and the case was reargued at the December 1855 term. The court's decision, delivered in January 1856, completely accepted Lincoln's argument, citing, for the most part, precedents that Herndon had supplied.

The case was a major one, and, according to Herndon, Lincoln initially asked the Illinois Central for a fee of $2,000. "This is as much as Daniel Webster himself would have charged," railroad officials huffed. "We cannot allow such a claim." After consulting with six other prominent Illinois attorneys, Lincoln submitted a revised bill for $5,000, and when the railroad, short of funds, failed to pay, he brought suit. At the hearing before David Davis in McLean County, Lincoln argued his own case, pointing out that his fee was not unreasonable. Had the decision gone the other way, the railroad company would have had to pay out half a million dollars a year in local taxes. The court promptly returned a verdict in his favor, and he divided $5,000—less the $250 already received as a retainer—equally with Herndon. The action did not interrupt his amicable relationship with the Illinois Central Railroad, which he continued to represent in numerous subsequent cases.

Lincoln was also involved in another type of suit involving railroads—the inevitable litigation that arose when the bridges built to carry the trains interfered with navigation on the streams they crossed. Personally Lincoln saw merit on both sides of the dispute. As an old riverboat man, he had always favored water transportation, and as recently as 1848, on his return trip from Congress, he grew so interested in the problems encountered by vessels on the Great Lakes that he invented and patented a device using "adjustable buoyant chambers" to lift steamers over shoals. But he also had been, from his earliest days in the state legislature, a supporter of railroads as the key agent for economic growth.

When suits arose between railroad and steamboat interests, Lincoln represented the side that engaged his services. In 1851 he appeared in the United States Circuit Court on behalf of the plaintiff in the important Peoria bridge case (technically *Columbus Insurance Co.* v. *Curtenius et al.*), which arose after a canal boat struck a railroad bridge across the Illinois River and sank. The boat was insured by the Columbus Insurance Company, which sued the bridge builders for damages. The defendants countered that construction had been authorized by the state legislature. In his argument Lincoln challenged "the power of a state to authorize a total obstruction of a navigable stream running within its territorial limits," and Judge Thomas Drummond agreed that navigation of the Illinois River must "ever remain free, clear and uninterrupted." The trial, to determine whether the bridge in fact constituted an obstruction to navigation, resulted in a hung jury, and the case was finally settled out of court.

In 1857, Lincoln appeared on the opposite side of a quite similar case. In the *Effie Afton* case (as *Hurd* v. *Rock Island Bridge Co.* was generally known) he represented the railroad interests. The Rock Island Bridge Company had built the first bridge across the Mississippi River, to carry the tracks of the Chicago, Rock Island & Pacific Railroad. When the steamboat *Effie Afton* ran into one of its piers, was set on fire, and burned up, its owner, John S. Hurd, sued the bridge company. This landmark case pitted St. Louis and the river interests, which supported Hurd and free navigation on the inland waterways, against Chicago and its railroad interests, which required bridges to complete the rail network. Consequently the case attracted some of the best legal talent in the West. In preparation for the trial, which was held in the United States District Court in Chicago, Lincoln made a visit to Rock Island, where he carefully inspected the rebuilt bridge, measured the currents in the river, and interviewed riverboat men. In the trial he was able to argue, on the basis of his firsthand observation as well as his own experience as a pilot, that the *Effie Afton* crashed into the bridge pier not because it was an obstruction to traffic but because the steamer's starboard paddle wheel failed. Not content with technical arguments, he also put the case in a broader context of national economic development. Paying tribute to the importance of river transportation, he stressed that there was "a travel from East to West, whose demands are not less important than that of the river." To this East-West railroad connection he attributed "the astonishing growth of Illinois, having grown within his memory to a population of a million and a half, . . . [of] Iowa and the other young and rising communities of the Northwest." In the end, the jury in the case was deadlocked, and the court dismissed the case, in what amounted to a victory for the railroad.

In these railroad cases Lincoln acted on behalf of his clients. Unlike some of his great contemporaries at the bar, such as Rufus Choate of Massachusetts and David Dudley Field of New York, he had no consistent legal philosophy that he sought to push, nor did he leave behind him a record of cases that made a major contribution to the development of American legal thought. He sometimes argued for the railroads and sometimes represented their opponents, just as, in a different context, he had appeared both to secure the freedom of the African-American girl Nance and to return the Matson slaves into bondage. He was, as Herndon said accurately but with undeserved censure, "purely and entirely a case lawyer."

VI

In addition to greatly increasing Lincoln's income, the coming of the rail-roads made a great difference in his family life. Up through 1853 his semi-annual trips around the Eighth Judicial Circuit kept him away from home for weeks at a time. In 1851, for instance, he was absent from Springfield from April 2 until June 4. But with the spread of the rail network, it became possible for him to come home weekends, while keeping his full load of cases in the circuit courts. In April 1855, for example, he began the circuit as usual, in Logan and McLean counties, but he returned to Springfield on April 21; then he attended court at Metamora for three days but came back to Springfield for the weekend.

He could now devote more time to the needs of his family. After the death of one child and the birth of two others, Mary was not in good physical or emotional shape, and she needed frequent reassurance and support from her husband. When he was away, she often felt threatened—once she pan-icked when an old bearded umbrella-mender knocked at her door—and was at times on the edge of hysteria. After she learned that the maid was allowing a man to sneak into her bedroom at night, she was in an agony of fear and pitifully begged a neighbor, James Gourley, to protect her. "Mr Gourley—come—do come and stay with me all night—You can sleep in the bed with Bob and I." The invitation did not necessarily have sexual implications; the Lincolns still had only one bed for grownups.

Even when Lincoln was at home, his wife's behavior was unpredictable. Weeks of quiet family life could go by, with pleasant meals and long eve-nings of reading together by the fire. Naturally cheerful and lively, Mary would entertain her husband with accounts of the latest novel she was reading—he did not read fiction—with neighborhood gossip, and with speculation about politics, in which she retained a lively, if unladylike, inter-est. She was capable of great generosity and kindness toward her neighbors. Shortly after Tad's birth, when young Mrs. Charles Dallman was sick and unable to nurse her newborn infant, Mary breast-fed that baby along with her own. When she was feeling well, there would be parties and games for the Lincoln children. She could rarely entertain guests for dinner, because even after she created a dining room by partitioning off part of the kitchen, no more than six people could comfortably sit at her table; but she delighted in having sociables and strawberry parties. Then something would trigger her temper. Perhaps she was simply bored by being cooped up in a tiny house much too small for her growing family. Perhaps she was affected by the mental instability that was evident in several other members of her family. At any rate, she sometimes unpredictably flew off the handle at her husband. On one occasion, as Springfield gossip remembered years later, she chased him out of the house and down the street with a butcher knife —or maybe it was a broomstick—in her hand.

Lincoln tried to ignore these tantrums. When "Mrs. L. got the devil in her," James Gourley remembered, "Lincoln paid no attention—would pick up one of the children and walk off—would laugh at her." Often he went to the office until his wife's temper was spent. Her outbursts were usually short-lived, and afterward she felt ashamed and ill. Lincoln did not scold her but tried to remain more often at home so that he could offer her the constant support and reassurance she needed.

Now that he spent most weekends in Springfield, Lincoln also could see more of his children. He had been away so much while Robert was growing up that he never developed a close bond with his oldest son, but he was devoted to Willie and Tad. A sweet-tempered little boy, Willie was bright, articulate, and exceptionally sensitive toward the feelings of others. Lincoln believed the child's mind was much like his own. Watching Willie solve a difficult problem, he told a visitor, "I know every step of the process by which that boy arrived at his satisfactory solution of the question before him, as it is by just such slow methods I attain results." Affectionate and impulsive, Tad had a temperament more like his mother's. He was especially dear to his father because he was handicapped by a speech impediment and a bad lisp, made worse when his teeth grew in crooked.

Both the Lincolns were convinced that they had remarkable children, and whenever they had guests, they would dress the boys up and, as Herndon wrote, "get them to monkey around—talk—dance—speak—quote poetry etc." Mary would exhaust the English language in her rhapsodies over the boys, and Lincoln would try to conceal his pride by saying: "These children may be something sometimes, if they are not merely rareripes—rotten ripes —hot house plants."

When Lincoln could, he helped with the baby-sitting for the two little boys—a practice so unusual that Springfield gossips called him *"hen pecked."* Perhaps he felt an obligation to take over because Mary was over-worked and often not well; possibly the recent death of his father caused him to reflect on how much he had needed a nurturing parent when he was a boy. When Willie and Tad were very small, he would haul them around in a little wagon, pulling it up and down the street in front of his house, often reading from a book that he held in his hand. Sometimes he became so lost in thought that he forgot about his charges, and neighbors remembered the time he took the two children for a ride in their wagon and did not notice when one of them fell out. When the boys were a little older, they used to walk with him downtown, each holding onto a gigantic hand or perhaps his coattail. Inevitably one would complain that he was tired, and he would be hoisted on Lincoln's shoulders for a ride home. Once Frances Wallace, Lincoln's sister-in-law, saw him carrying Tad in this fashion and scolded: "Why, Mr. Lincoln, put down that great big boy. He's big enough to walk." But Lincoln replied: "Oh, don't you think his little feet get too tired?"

On Sundays, while Mary was at church, Lincoln often brought the boys with him to the law office, where Herndon found them a nuisance. "These children," Herndon remembered, "would take down the books—empty ash buckets—coal ashes—inkstands—papers—gold pens—letters, etc. etc in a pile and then dance on the pile. Lincoln would say nothing, so abstracted was he and so blinded to his children's faults. Had they s--t in Lincoln's hat and rubbed it on his boots, he would have laughed and thought it smart." "I have felt many and many a time," he recalled years later, "that I wanted to wring their little necks and yet out of respect for Lincoln I kept my mouth shut."

Herndon's animus toward the Lincoln children reflected his dislike, verging on hatred, of their mother. He had never got along with Mary Todd Lincoln. He met her first in 1837, when, as visiting belle from Kentucky, she attended a ball given by Colonel Robert Allen. Herndon asked her to dance and, intending to compliment her, observed that she "seemed to glide through the waltz with the ease of a serpent." Miss Todd, never distinguished by a sense of humor, flashed back: "Mr. Herndon, comparison to a serpent is rather severe irony, especially to a newcomer"—and she left him on the dance floor. Neither ever forgot that episode. Herndon strongly opposed Lincoln's courtship of Mary as a betrayal of his democratic origins in favor of the wealth and aristocracy of Springfield; he was not invited to their wedding. "This woman was to me a terror," Herndon remarked many years later; he thought she was "imperious, proud, aristocratic, insolent witty and bitter."

Doubtless Mary disliked her husband's choice of Herndon as a law partner. She might have preferred someone more socially respectable, like John Todd Stuart or James C. Conkling. In her judgment Herndon ran with a rowdy set in Springfield, and she knew that from time to time he was known to take too much to drink. She was not impressed by his active support of the local library association, of the temperance movement, or of women's rights, nor did Herndon's election as mayor of Springfield in 1854 change her opinion of him. But she recognized that the law practice was in her husband's sphere of activities, not in her domestic sphere, and she managed to maintain formal, if distant, relations with his partner. She came to the law office only infrequently, and he was never invited to a meal in the Lincoln house. Years later she summarized: "Mr. Herndon had always been an utter stranger to me, he was not considered an habitué, at our house. The office was more, in his line."

The antagonism between his wife and his law partner, which might have driven another man to distraction, troubled Lincoln not at all. Indeed, he rather thrived on the creative tension between Billy and Mary, both of whom were devoted to his interests but wanted his undivided attention. The knowledge that Mary was jealously watching helped spur Herndon to greater exertions and more care in the conduct of the law office, and the awareness that Herndon was a critical observer doubtless did something to curb Mary's demonstrations of temper.

The years following Lincoln's return from Congress were, then, relatively peaceful and prosperous. According to William Dean Howells's 1860 campaign biography, Lincoln, after turning away from politics to the law, was "successful in his profession, happy in his home, secure in the affection of his neighbors, with books, competence, and leisure—ambition could not tempt him." When a friend asked Lincoln to read Howells's book and mark any inaccuracies, he allowed this passage to stand unchanged.

CHAPTER SEVEN

There Are No Whigs

———◆———

Howells's description of Lincoln in retirement was accurate enough—but it did not capture the whole picture. During the years after his service in Congress he never truly lost interest in politics, nor did he completely withdraw from public life. He continued to worry about the nation's problems, and he constantly thought about how he could help solve them. As always, he yearned for distinction, but opportunities were few. Even though he was a highly successful lawyer, he often felt melancholy about his future. "How hard," he remarked to Herndon, "oh how hard it is to die and leave one's Country no better than if one had never lived for it."

I

A former congressman and a man of influence, Lincoln was repeatedly asked to endorse applications for jobs or candidates for office. Though he firmly declined to run for another term in Congress in 1850, he remained active in party management.

Privately he advised Richard Yates, the ambitious young Whig seeking election to the congressional seat Lincoln had occupied, how to deal with campaign issues. As Congress continued to wrangle over the issue of slavery in the territories acquired from Mexico, Lincoln urged Yates to be cautiously noncommittal. On the one hand, he should announce his opposition to the extension of slavery and his support for the Wilmot Proviso; on the other, he should make it clear that if adherence to the proviso would endanger the Union he "would at once abandon it," because "of all political objects the preservation of the Union stands number one." Yates ought to downplay

Southern threats to secede, and he should endorse the Compromise of 1850, which, among other things, admitted California as a free state, permitted the inhabitants of the New Mexico and Utah territories to make their own choice about allowing slavery, and gave the South a stringent new fugitive-slave law.

In the 1852 presidential campaign Lincoln played an active, though not a highly visible, role, and he was named Whig national committeeman for Illinois. When the party nominated Winfield Scott, Lincoln gave a long campaign address before the Springfield Scott Club in which he offered perfunctory praise for his party's candidate and made a rollicking attack on Franklin Pierce, the Democratic nominee, whose qualifications appeared to be that, at the age of seventeen, he was able to spell the word "but" for his father. But Scott's prospects were so dismal that, in the words of Howells's campaign biography, Lincoln "did less in this Presidential struggle than any in which he had ever engaged."

II

From time to time, Lincoln's behavior suggested that he was not entirely happy in his role of elder statesman. His lackluster speeches during the 1852 presidential campaign came alive only when he referred to Stephen A. Douglas, who was campaigning vigorously for Pierce. He sneered at Douglas's claim to be the true father of the Compromise of 1850 and accused the senator of stealing the ideas of Henry Clay and Daniel Webster. When Douglas correctly charged that the 1852 Whig platform was ambiguous, Lincoln sarcastically exclaimed: "What wonderful acumen the Judge displays on the construction of language!!!" The edge to Lincoln's remarks went beyond campaign banter and suggested his disappointment that his old rival Douglas, now the most powerful member of the United States Senate, was "a giant," while Lincoln remained one of the "common mortals."

There were other hints of Lincoln's unhappiness. Some days he would arrive at the office in a cheerful mood, but then, as Herndon recorded, he might fall into "a sad terribly gloomy state—pick up a pen—sit down by the table and write a moment or two and then become abstracted." Resting his chin on the palm of his left hand, he would sit for hours in silence, staring vacantly at the windows. Other days he was so depressed that he did not even speak to Herndon when he entered the office, and his partner, sensing his mood, would pull the curtain across the glass panel in the door and leave for an hour or so, locking the door behind him to protect the privacy of "this unfortunate and miserable man."

Lincoln's companions on the circuit also noticed his unpredictable moodiness. Henry Clay Whitney, who began traveling Judge Davis's circuit after 1854, reported that Lincoln was afflicted by nightmares. One night, when they were sharing a room, Whitney woke to see his companion "sitting up in bed, his figure dimly visible by the ghostly firelight, and talking the wildest and most incoherent nonsense all to himself." "A stranger to Lincoln would have supposed he had suddenly gone insane," Whitney added. Awaking suddenly, Lincoln jumped out of bed, "put some wood on the fire, and then sat in front of it, moodily, dejectedly, in a most sombre and gloomy spell, till the breakfast bell rang."

Herndon attributed Lincoln's melancholy to his domestic unhappiness; others, with about as much evidence, found the cause in his chronic constipation or in the blue-mass pills that he took to overcome it. Perhaps there was truth in all these theories, but they missed the essential point that Lincoln was frustrated and unhappy with a political career that seemed to be going nowhere.

Though he was out of office, he had no intention of being out of the public eye. This was the golden age of the lyceum movement, when men and women thronged the lecture halls and listened for hours to speakers who might edify, enlighten or, at least, amuse them. By the 1850s, with the completion of the railroad network, Springfield was on the regular circuit for Eastern lecturers, and residents raptly listened to Ralph Waldo Emerson, Henry Ward Beecher, Horace Greeley, and Bayard Taylor, as well as to numerous local speakers. Lincoln thought he might as well join the parade.

His efforts to become a popular lecturer were uniformly unhappy. His dithyramb on Niagara Falls was probably intended to be part of a lecture before he wisely decided to abandon it. He also aborted a proposed lecture on the law, which he began on a negative note: "I am not an accomplished lawyer. I find quite as much material for a lecture, in those points wherein I have failed, as in those wherein I have been moderately successful."

His most ambitious and curious effort was what he called "a sort of lecture" entitled "Discoveries and Inventions," which he first read to the Young Men's Association in Bloomington on April 6, 1858. The first half was Lincoln's version of the history of discoveries, ranging from Adam's invention of the fig-leaf apron in the Garden of Eden to the steam engine. The second half dealt with the invention of writing and printing—together with the discovery of America, the introduction of patent laws, and what Lincoln called, oddly enough, "the invention of negroes, or, of the present mode of using them." It was a commonplace production, resting on a few articles in the *Encyclopedia Americana* and on Old Testament references to such subjects as spinning and weaving. Over the next twelve months Lincoln delivered this lecture in several Illinois towns, but, though by this time he was a possible presidential candidate, it attracted only small and unenthusiastic audiences. It was, as Herndon said, "a lifeless thing—a dull dead thing, 'died a bornin [sic].' "

Lincoln was scarcely more successful in two eulogies he pronounced. Attending court in Chicago when Zachary Taylor died in July 1850, Lincoln was invited by members of the Common Council to memorialize the late President. "The want of time for preparation will make the task, for me, a very difficult one to perform, in any degree satisfactory to others or to myself," he replied, but he felt obliged to accept the assignment as a duty, which would incidentally keep his name before the growing population of northern Illinois. His address was largely a pedestrian recital of the facts of Taylor's life, interrupted by an occasional rhetorical flourish: "And now the din of battle nears the fort and sweeps obliquely by; . . . they fly to the wall; every eye is strained—it is—it is—the stars and stripes are still aloft!"

Only slightly more successful was the eulogy Lincoln delivered in Springfield on Henry Clay. He genuinely admired the Kentucky statesman, and he was beginning to think of himself as Clay's successor in leading a revitalized Whig party. But his analytical cast of mind kept him from indulging in effusive praise of anyone. Instead, he confined himself largely to a factual review of Clay's career, which unintentionally revealed more about the speaker than his subject. Clay's lack of formal education, Lincoln suggested in a clearly autobiographical passage, "teaches that in this country, one can scarcely be so poor, but that, if he *will,* he *can* acquire sufficient education to get through the world respectably." Clay's eloquence, he observed, did not consist "of types and figures—of antithesis, and elegant arrangement of words and sentences"; it derived its strength "from great sincerity and a thorough conviction, in the speaker of the justice and importance of his cause." Precisely the same could be said of the best of Lincoln's own productions.

III

Largely perfunctory, Lincoln's eulogy on Henry Clay came alive only in its final paragraphs. Of the hundreds of funeral addresses on the Kentucky statesman, Lincoln's was one of the very few that explicitly dealt with Clay's views on slavery. Clay "did not perceive, that on a question of human right, the negroes were to be excepted from the human race," Lincoln announced; consequently, "he ever was, on principle and in feeling, opposed to slavery." Because Clay recognized that it could not be "at *once* eradicated, without producing a greater evil," he supported the efforts of the American Colonization Society to transport African-Americans back to Africa and served for many years as president of that organization.

Endorsing Clay's views on colonization, Lincoln revealed a change in his own attitude toward slavery. He had all along been against the peculiar institution, but it had not hitherto seemed a particularly important or divisive issue, partly because he had so little personal knowledge of slavery. But in Washington his strongly antislavery friends in Congress, like Joshua F. Giddings and Horace Mann, helped him see that the atrocities that occurred every day in the national capital were the inevitable results of the slave system. As Lincoln's sensitivity to the cruelty of slavery changed, so did his memories. In 1841, returning from the Speed plantation, he had been amused by the cheerful docility of a gang of African-Americans who were being sold down the Mississippi. Now, reflecting on that scene, he recalled it as "a continual torment," which crucified his feelings.

He also began to understand the effect that slavery had on white Southerners. He took great interest in affairs in Kentucky, where his father-in-law, Robert S. Todd, along with Henry Clay, was working for gradual emancipation, which they hoped the Kentucky constitutional convention of 1849 would endorse. But the convention overwhelmingly rejected all plans to end slavery or even to ameliorate it. Todd, a candidate for the senate, died during the campaign; had he lived, he could have been disastrously defeated. These developments gave Lincoln a new insight into Southern society. Even nonslaveholders, who constituted an overwhelming majority of the Kentucky voters, were opposed to any form of emancipation. The prospect of owning slaves, he learned, was "highly seductive to the thoughtless and giddy headed young men," because slaves were "the most glittering ostentatious and displaying property in the world." As a young Kentuckian told him, "You might have any amount of land; money in your pocket or bank stock and while travelling around no body would be any wiser, but if you had a darkey trudging at your heels every body would see him and know that you owned slaves."

Lincoln looked for a rational way to deal with the problems caused by the existence of slavery in a free American society, and he believed he had found it in colonization. Like Clay and Chief Justice John Marshall, who belonged to the American Colonization Society, he became convinced that transporting African-Americans to Liberia would defuse several social problems. By relocating free Negroes from the United States—and, at least initially, all those transported were to be freedmen—colonization would remove what many white Southerners considered the most disruptive elements in their society. Consequently, Southern whites would more willingly manumit their slaves if they were going to be shipped off to Africa. At the same time, Northerners would give more support for emancipation if freedmen were sent out of the country; they could not migrate to the free states where they would compete with white laborers. Moreover, colonization could elevate the status of the Negro race by proving that blacks, in a separate, self-governing community of their own, were capable of making orderly progress in civilization. Thus, Lincoln thought, voluntary emigration of the blacks—and, unlike some other colonizationists, he never favored forcible deportation—would succeed both "in freeing our land from the dangerous presence of slavery" and "in restoring a captive people to their long-lost father-land, with bright prospects for the future."

The plan was entirely rational—and wholly impracticable. American blacks, nearly all of whom were born and raised in the United States, had not the slightest desire to go to Africa; Southern planters had no intention of freeing their slaves; and there was no possibility that the Northern states would pay the enormous amount of money required to deport and resettle millions of African-Americans. From time to time, even Lincoln doubted the colonization scheme would work. He would like "to free all the slaves, and send them to Liberia—to their own native land," he announced in 1854. "But," he added, "a moment's reflection would convince me, that whatever of high hope, (as I think there is) there may be in this, in the long run, its sudden execution is impossible. If they were all landed there in a day, they would all perish in the next ten days; and there are not surplus shipping and surplus money enough in the world to carry them there in many times ten days."

Though reality sometimes broke in, Lincoln persisted in his colonization fantasy until well into his presidency. For a man who prided himself on his rationality, his adherence to such an unworkable scheme was puzzling, though not inexplicable. His failure to take into account the overwhelming opposition of blacks to colonization stemmed from his lack of acquaintance among African-Americans. Of nearly 5,000 inhabitants of Springfield in 1850, only 171 were blacks, most of whom labored in menial or domestic occupations. Mariah Vance, who worked two days a week as a laundress in the Lincoln home and sometimes helped out with the cooking, was one of these; another was the Haitian, William de Fleurville, better known as "Billy the Barber," whom Lincoln advised on several small legal problems. These were not people who could speak out boldly to say that they were as American as any whites, that they had no African roots, and that they did not want to leave the United States.

Lincoln's persistent advocacy of colonization served an unconscious purpose of preventing him from thinking too much about a problem that he found insoluble. He confessed that he did not know how slavery could be abolished: "If all earthly power were given me, I should not know what to do, as to the existing institution." Even if he had a plan, there was no way of putting it into effect. After the Compromise of 1850 both the Whig and the Democratic parties had agreed that, in Lincoln's words, questions relating to slavery were "settled forever." For a man with a growing sense of urgency about abolishing, or at least limiting, slavery, who had no solution to the problem and no political outlet for making his feelings known, colonization offered a very useful escape.

IV

In 1854 reality replaced fantasy. On January 4, Stephen A. Douglas, the chairman of the Senate Committee on Territories, introduced a bill to establish a government for the Nebraska Territory (which constituted the northern part of the Louisiana Purchase, including the present states of Kansas and Nebraska). The measure was much needed. Immigrants from Missouri and Iowa were already pushing across the border into the unorganized region, and a favored route for the proposed transcontinental railroad ran through Nebraska. Slavery had been prohibited in this area by the Missouri

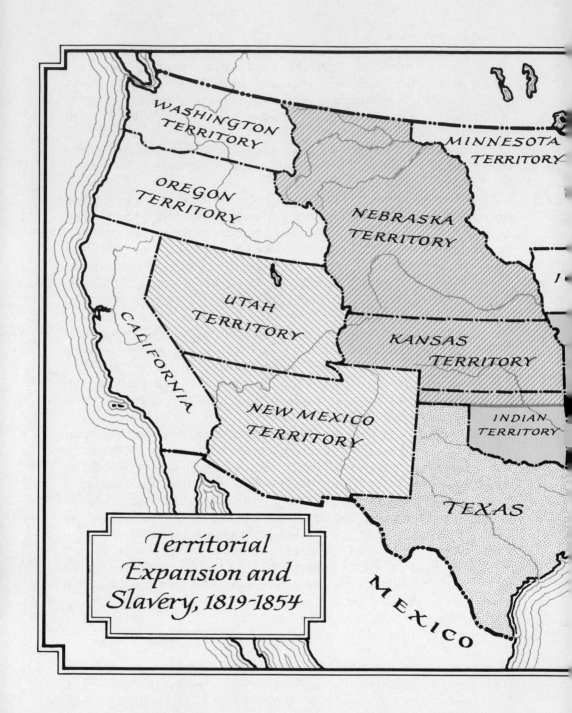

WASHINGTON
TERRITORY

MINNESOTA
TERRITORY

OREGON
TERRITORY

NEBRASKA
TERRITORY

UTAH
TERRITORY

CALIFORNIA

KANSAS
TERRITORY

NEW MEXICO
TERRITORY

INDIAN
TERRITORY

TEXAS

MEXICO

Territorial
Expansion and
Slavery, 1819-1854

CANADA

WISCONSIN

MICH.

MAINE

VT.

N.H.

NEW
YORK

MASS.

R.I.
CONN.

PA.

IA

OHIO

N.J.

ILLINOIS IND.

MD.

DEL.

VIRGINIA

MO.

KENTUCKY

NORTH
CAROLINA

ARK.

TENNESSEE

S.C.

GEORGIA

ALA.

MISS.

FLORIDA

LA.

*Atlantic
Ocean*

Slave States
and Territories, 1820

Admitted as
Slave State, 1845

Open to Slavery by the
Compromise of 1850

Open to Slavery by
the Kansas-Nebraska
Act of 1854

(Boundaries as of 1854)

Kms.

0 ▬▬ 300

0 ▬▬ 300

Miles

©A. Karl/J. Kemp, 1995

Compromise of 1820, but Southerners, fearful of the growing population and wealth of the North, had killed previous efforts to organize Nebraska as a free territory. Douglas sought to avoid a similar fate for his new bill by providing that the territory, "when admitted as a State or States, . . . shall be received into the Union, with or without slavery, as their constitution may prescribe." Taking these words from the 1850 acts organizing New Mexico and Utah, Douglas thus extended the doctrine of "popular sovereignty" to the Nebraska Territory. But because his measure said nothing about slavery in Nebraska during its territorial stage or about the Missouri Compromise restriction, proslavery senators pressed him to include an explicit repeal of the Missouri Compromise. Reluctantly he agreed, though he knew it would "raise a hell of a storm," and at the same time he assented to the division of the region into two territories, Kansas and Nebraska. Endorsed by the Pierce administration, the Kansas-Nebraska Act was passed by the Congress after a bitter struggle and became law on May 30.

This act, Lincoln said a few months later, "took us by surprise—astounded us. . . . We were thunderstruck and stunned." His immediate actions suggested that he was more stunned than astounded. He made no comment, public or private, on the Kansas-Nebraska measure while Douglas, with brilliant parliamentary management and unrelenting ferocity toward his opponents, forced it through both houses of Congress. He said nothing about the "Appeal of the Independent Democrats," drawn up by free-soil senators Charles Sumner of Massachusetts and Salmon P. Chase of Ohio, with assistance from other antislavery congressmen, which assailed the repeal of the Missouri Compromise "as a gross violation of a sacred pledge; as a criminal betrayal of previous rights; as part and parcel of an atrocious plot to exclude from a vast unoccupied region immigrants from the Old World and free laborers from our own States, and convert it into a dreary region of despotism, inhabited by masters and slaves." Certainly he read the congressional debates studiously, and he followed the crescendo of attacks on Douglas and his bill both in the *New York Tribune* and the *Chicago Tribune,* to which Lincoln & Herndon subscribed, and in the abolitionist papers, such as the *National Anti-Slavery Standard, Emancipator,* and *National Era,* which Herndon received. Herndon sent away for the speeches of antislavery spokesmen such as Sumner, Chase, and Senator William H. Seward of New York, and he regularly received those of Theodore Parker, the great Boston preacher, and Wendell Phillips, the abolitionist orator; and he made sure that his partner knew about them all. But Lincoln said and wrote nothing.

He was silent partly because he was extraordinarily busy at just the time the Kansas-Nebraska bill was working its way through the Congress. In addition to the demands of his regular legal practice, the suit of the *Illinois Central Railroad* v. *McLean County* was to be heard in the Illinois Supreme Court on February 28, and in the weeks before the hearing Lincoln spent all the time he could spare preparing his brief and his oral argument in a case that was probably the most important and certainly was the most remunerative in his entire legal career.

As a private citizen, holding and seeking no public office, he did not feel called upon to make a public statement about the Kansas-Nebraska bill. Neither Douglas nor his measure would come directly before the Illinois electorate in 1854. The only general election that year was for state treasurer, whose selection would not depend on his support of or opposition to Kansas-Nebraska. In the fall there would, of course, be elections for representatives in Congress and for the members of the state legislature, but the political situation was so confused that it was not clear how Lincoln could make any meaningful intervention.

In Illinois, as throughout the North, there was a firestorm of opposition to the Kansas-Nebraska Act, but Douglas's enemies were badly divided. In Chicago much of the hostility to Douglas was personal, led by his rival, the erratic but popular John Wentworth, who controlled the influential *Chicago Democrat*. The *Chicago Tribune* and the *Chicago Democratic Press* also kept up a drumbeat of criticism. Elsewhere in northern Illinois, where the Liberty party had shown strength in 1840 and 1844 and the Free-Soil party had won a considerable following in 1848, opposition to Douglas was more ideological, and New England–bred abolitionists like Owen Lovejoy found in the Kansas-Nebraska Act the occasion to launch a new antislavery party, which they christened "Republican." Southern Illinois, staunchly Democratic, was equally angered at the Kansas-Nebraska Act, because residents feared that opening Kansas to slaveholders would prevent the settlement of small farmers like themselves. Violently negrophobic, voters in this section wanted to have nothing to do with abolitionism; they fought under the banner of Anti-Nebraska Democrats. In central Illinois, hostility to Kansas-Nebraska was also strong, but the dominant conservatives had no desire to see that opposition translated into a general antislavery movement; they remained firm in their allegiance to the Whig party. Despite frequent calls for a fusion ticket, these disparate elements continued to march under different banners. In an October speech Lincoln graphically recaptured the "utter confusion" of Douglas's opponents, who were united only in their hostility toward the Kansas-Nebraska Act: "We rose each fighting, grasping whatever he could first reach—a scythe—a pitchfork—a chopping axe, or a butcher's cleaver." It was no wonder, he remarked, "that our drill, our dress, and our weapons, are not entirely perfect and uniform."

These divisions were enough to cause a politician to hesitate, but there were other cross-cutting fractures that made it even more difficult to take a stand. A rising tide of immigration fed the endemic American nativist sentiment. In Illinois the large number of foreign-born who came to build the railroad network aroused fear of foreign tongues and behavior and of the Catholic Church, to which many immigrants belonged. Fear became resentment when the sharp recession of 1854–1855 put a temporary halt to railroad construction and threw immigrant laborers into competition with local blue-collar workers. Native-born Protestants began to join secret societies, like the Order of the Star-Spangled Banner, which advocated lengthening the term for naturalization and restricting the rights of the Catholic Church. Just how large the Order was, nobody could tell, because members were sworn to reply to questions from outsiders about the movement, "I know nothing." When the Order, styling itself the Native American party, entered politics and secretly endorsed candidates, it seemed to pose more of a threat to normal political alignments than even the agitation over Kansas-Nebraska.

Lincoln had no sympathy for nativism, but he had to recognize that Know Nothings were a powerful political force when some of his strongest backers, including Simeon Francis, the editor of the *Illinois State Journal,* which had always been Lincoln's newspaper voice in the state capital, joined the movement. Later charges that Lincoln himself was a Know Nothing and that he had been seen at a Native American lodge in Quincy were roorbacks, but he did not go out of his way to alienate his old political friends who had become nativists. When a local committee solicited his support, he tried to avoid a commitment by deliberately misunderstanding their meaning. "Do [the Native Americans] not wear breech-clout and carry tomahawk?" he asked. "We pushed them from their homes and now turn upon others not fortunate enough to come over as early as we or our forefathers."

In public his position on nativism was circumspect. Initially he professed to know nothing—and perhaps the words themselves were significant—about the secret party. "If there was an order styled the Know-Nothings, and there was any thing bad in it, he was unqualifiedly against it," he said; "and if there was anything good in it, why, he said God speed it!"

With the political situation so volatile, Lincoln held back all summer, even though it was becoming clear that Illinois would be a major battleground for Douglas and the popular-sovereignty issue. Prominent antislavery men like Salmon P. Chase and Joshua R. Giddings spoke, and Lincoln carefully studied reports of their addresses. In July, Cassius M. Clay, the fiery Kentucky abolitionist, appeared in Springfield to denounce the Kansas and Nebraska outrage and call for "an organization of men of whatever politics, of Free Soilers, Whigs and Democrats, who should bury past animosities, and . . . unite in hurling down the gigantic evil which threatened even their own liberty." While Clay spoke, Lincoln lounged on the grass whittling and listening. It took him time to assimilate all these arguments and to make them his own.

He did not act until the end of August, when he spoke at the Scott County Whig convention in Winchester, attacking "the great wrong and injustice of the repeal of the Missouri Compromise, and the extension of slavery into free territory." His purpose in entering the campaign was a limited one; as he wrote later, "he took the stump with no broader practical aim or object than to secure, if possible, the reelection of Hon Richard Yates to congress." That purpose defined the role that Lincoln was prepared to play in repudiating Douglas and the Kansas-Nebraska Act: he campaigned as a Whig—not as an abolitionist, or an anti-Nebraska man, or even a fusionist—who was seeking the reelection of a fellow Whig to the House of Representatives.

V

Once Lincoln decided to take part in the campaign, he showed no further hesitation. Feeling again the joy of political combat, he devoted all his time to the anti-Nebraska cause, except for his necessary commitments to court cases. He became, in effect, Yates's campaign manager, spending hours conferring with the Whig candidate and advising him on tactics. Learning that English settlers in Morgan County were disturbed by reports that Yates was a Know Nothing, he drafted a letter denying the charge, which could be distributed "at each precinct where any considerable number of the foreign citizens, german as well as english—vote." When he heard that Democrats were whispering that Yates, though professing to be a temperate man, was a secret drinker, he recognized that the rumor might cost the Whigs the large prohibitionist vote and sought to kill the allegation. "I have never seen him drink liquor, nor act, or speak, as if he had been drinking, nor smelled it on his breath," he wrote. But then—almost as if he realized that the future would show that Yates did indulge in liquor, to the point of being intoxicated when he was inaugurated as governor of Illinois in 1861—Lincoln carefully explained his own position to a friend: "Other things being equal, I would much prefer a temperate man, to an intemperate one; still I do not make my vote depend absolutely upon the question of whether a candidate does or does not *taste* liquor."

Though Lincoln wanted to bolster Yates's candidacy, he resisted a plan to strengthen the Whig cause in Sangamon County by allowing himself to be nominated for the state legislature. This was not a position he wanted. Election to the state legislature, after a term in the United States House of Representatives, looked like a backward movement in his career. But several local antislavery leaders promised if he ran they would vote for him—and, implicitly, for Yates as well. At about the same time, a committee of Springfield Know Nothings informed Lincoln that their party was secretly nominating him for the legislature. Lincoln told his visitors frankly that "he was not in sentiment with this new party," but in the end he agreed that "they might vote for him if they wanted to; so might the Democrats." Even then he did not promise to run.

On September 3, while Lincoln was in Jacksonville campaigning for Yates, Dr. William Jayne, a prominent Springfield Whig who was also a Know Nothing, published an announcement of Lincoln's candidacy for the state legislature in the *Illinois State Journal*. Mary Lincoln, who was obviously well informed of her husband's wishes, rushed to the *Journal* office and demanded that Lincoln's name be withdrawn. When Lincoln returned, Jayne called on him at his house and insisted that he must run. He found Lincoln "the saddest man I ever saw—the gloomiest." As Jayne remembered many years later, he walked up and down the room, almost crying, as he resisted the appeal. "No—I can't," he insisted. "You don't know all. I say you don't begin to know one-half and that's enough."

Neither then nor later did Lincoln explain his misgivings, but in all probability he had his own political future in mind. He knew, of course, that the legislature to be elected in the fall of 1854 would choose a United States senator to succeed James Shields, the incumbent Democrat. Aware of the growing strength of the opposition to Douglas and the Kansas-Nebraska Act, he could foresee that the next senator would probably come from the anti-Nebraska coalition, and, not being a modest man, he realized that he would be a strong candidate for that office. But as a lawyer, he knew that the Illinois state constitution prohibited the election of a state legislator to the United States Congress. He did not know what to do. If he ran, he might be putting an end to his cherished hope for higher office; if he refused to run, he might well cause the defeat of the Whig ticket in Sangamon County (and also the defeat of Yates in the congressional district) and consequently would have no claim for support in the senatorial election. Unhappily he allowed Jayne to overcome his objections, and the *Journal* made his candidacy official.

Once he had committed himself, Lincoln wholeheartedly worked to build a coalition of all who were opposed to the Kansas-Nebraska Act. Feeling "anxious . . . that this Nebraska measure shall be rebuked and condemned every where," he tried to enlist Democrats known to be critical of Douglas. Learning that John M. Palmer, a state senator from Macoupin County, had "determined *not* to swallow the *wrong*," Lincoln begged him to make a few public speeches explaining his course. "Of course . . . I do not expect you to do any thing which may be wrong in your own judgment," Lincoln wrote, "nor would I have you do anything personally injurious to yourself."

Lincoln himself vigorously campaigned for Yates and against the Kansas-Nebraska Act. In the month after his first appearance he spoke at Whig rallies at Carrollton, at Jacksonville, and twice at Bloomington, being very careful not to alienate either the Know Nothings or the temperance advocates, since support from these two groups was essential to Whig success in central Illinois. At his second appearance in Bloomington he had an opportunity to make a tacit appeal to the prohibitionists. Douglas had spoken there in the afternoon, in defense of his Kansas policy, and Lincoln replied in an evening speech. Calling on Douglas, Lincoln found him surrounded by fellow Democrats, with whom the senator offered to share a decanter of red liquor. When Lincoln got ready to leave, Douglas asked: "Mr. Lincoln, won't you take something?"

"No, I think not," Lincoln replied.

"What! are you a member of the Temperance Society?" Douglas quizzed him.

"No," said Lincoln, "I am not a member of any temperance society; but I am temperate, *in this,* that I don't drink anything."

Lincoln's friends widely circulated reports of the encounter among prohibitionists.

VI

Alarmed when the elections in Iowa and Maine, both Democratic strongholds, went against his party, Douglas undertook a nonstop campaign to explain and defend the Kansas-Nebraska Act to Illinois voters. Everywhere his message was the same: he argued that it was his duty, as chairman of the Senate Committee on Territories, to provide for a government in the Nebraska region, which was rapidly being settled. The Missouri Compromise, prohibiting the introduction of slavery into that region, had been "superseded" by the Compromise of 1850, which wrote into law the Democratic principle of popular sovereignty. That principle derived from the fundamental right of self-government. By extending popular sovereignty to the territories, the Congress was merely granting the citizens of those regions the same right enjoyed by free men throughout the nation, the right to choose their own social institutions, including slavery. Under popular sovereignty the inhabitants of the territories would speedily organize governments and these would readily be admitted to the Union, without the rancorous controversies that had hitherto held up national expansion. Since the climate and soil of Kansas and Nebraska made it highly unlikely that anyone would bring slaves into those territories, they were destined to become free states. Opposition to the Kansas-Nebraska Act came from abolitionists, who sought to stir up sectional hatreds, and from Know Nothings, who were fomenting ethnic and religious strife. It was a powerful case, and Douglas presented it with passion and sincerity.

Lincoln was eager for an opportunity to challenge it. Thoroughly familiar with all of the senator's arguments, he carefully prepared to attack them, reading over the voluminous pamphlet literature, reviewing the laws and the speeches in Congress, and studying the census reports. The hostile *Illinois State Register* said that Lincoln "had been nosing for weeks in the State Library, pumping his brain and his imagination for points and arguments." He looked for a chance to debate Douglas, but the senator, who was attacked by the abolitionist Owen Lovejoy when he spoke in the northern part of the state, by Lyman Trumbull, the anti-Nebraska Democrat, when he appeared in the south, and by Chase and Giddings wherever they could find him, was unwilling to share his audiences with yet another opponent.

On October 3, when Douglas appeared in Springfield for the opening of the Illinois State Fair, he again declined to permit Lincoln to appear on the same platform. After a rainstorm forced the cancellation of a huge open-air rally, Douglas spoke in the hall of the House of Representatives in the state capitol. To mounting applause he delivered his defense of the Kansas-Nebraska Act, ending with a powerful attack on the Know Nothings. While he spoke, Lincoln paced back and forth in the lobby, listening carefully to every word. As the crowd dispersed, he appeared on the stairway to announce, in a shout, that he or Trumbull would answer Douglas the next day. He invited Douglas to be present and offered him a chance to respond.

The next afternoon when Lincoln appeared before a large crowd in the House of Representatives hall, he was fully prepared to meet all the arguments Douglas had advanced the previous day. The senator occupied a chair directly in front of the speaker and tried not to show any reaction until it came his chance to respond. But as Lincoln warmed the audience up with wry allusions to recent political events and compliments to "his distinguished friend, Judge Douglas," the senator felt he could not remain silent and from time to time engaged in banter with the speaker. When Lincoln cited Douglas's 1849 praise of the Missouri Compromise as "a sacred thing," the senator interjected, "A first-rate speech!" As Lincoln proved that Douglas had once attempted to extend the Missouri Compromise line to the Pacific, the senator snorted, "And you voted against it!" But Lincoln got in the last word: "Precisely so. . . . I was in favor of running the line a *great deal further south.*" The exchanges in themselves were of no consequence, but they helped establish the equality of the challenger and the challenged—something that Douglas hitherto had been unwilling to admit.

Before an audience described as "very large, intelligent, and attentive," Lincoln spoke for more than three hours. The afternoon was hot and sticky, and Lincoln, as though prepared for heavy physical labor, appeared in his shirtsleeves, without collar or tie. Unlike many other speakers, he did not pace back and forth on the platform or lean on the lectern; instead, as Herndon said, "he stood square on his feet, with both of his legs straight up and down, toe even with toe." As always, he was a little awkward at the outset, and initially his voice was "sharp—shrill piping and squeaky." Once he was under way, the pitch of his voice lowered and "became harmonious —melodious—musical." He nearly always held his hands behind his back when he began a speech, the left hand grasped in the palm of the right, but as he proceeded, would bring his hands forward, often holding the left lapel of his coat with his left hand while leaving the right hand free to emphasize his points. He did not gesture much with his hands, however, and mostly emphasized his points with a jerk and snap of his head. But occasionally he would stretch out his long right arm and his bony forefinger to drive an idea home, and at moments of great inspiration he would "raise both hands toward heaven at an angle of about 50 degrees, generally the palms up."

Lincoln began this address with several demurrers. He now concealed the sharp envy he had long felt toward Douglas and announced that he did "not propose to question the patriotism or to assail the motives of any man, or class of men." He sought to make the important distinction between slavery in the existing states, which was guaranteed under the Constitution, and the extension of slavery, for which there was no such authority. He made it clear that, unlike many in the anti-Nebraska coalition, he did not consider the repeal of the Missouri Compromise the result of a Southern plot, and he willingly recognized that the Southern people were "no more responsible for the origin of slavery, than we." Finally, he acknowledged that he thought it was impossible to free the slaves and make them "politically and socially, our equals." "My own feelings will not admit of this," he declared; nor would those of the majority of whites. "Whether this feeling accords with justice and sound judgment, is not the sole question," he added pragmatically. "A universal feeling, whether well or ill-founded, can not be safely disregarded."

With these matters, which he considered irrelevant in the present contest, pushed aside, Lincoln could concentrate on the Kansas-Nebraska Act and the defenses that Douglas had made for it. He began with a long, careful review of the history of national legislation concerning the extension of slavery, from the Northwest Ordinance to the Missouri Compromise to the Compromise of 1850, ending with the bill Douglas had introduced in 1853 for the territorial organization of Nebraska, noting that they all had recognized the right of Congress to exclude slavery from the national territories. Then Douglas made his astonishing about-face in the Kansas-Nebraska Act of 1854.

Lincoln next attacked Douglas's arguments in favor of that measure. Claiming that repeal of the Missouri Compromise was not necessary in order to set up a territorial government in Nebraska, he showed that in recent years both Iowa and Minnesota had been organized with the Missouri restriction; indeed, Douglas's 1853 bill, which "was within an ace of passing," proved that Nebraska could be similarly organized. Vehemently Lincoln denied that pressure of public opinion had forced Douglas to introduce the Kansas-Nebraska bill. He dismissed as "a *palliation—a lullaby*" Douglas's argument that slavery would not go into the new territories. The climate of Kansas would not exclude slavery; it was just like that in northwestern Missouri, where slavery was flourishing. Nor would the disposition of the early settlers, because Kansas was nearer slaveholding Missouri than it was to the free states of the North and West.

Up to this point Lincoln's appeal had been chiefly to reason and everyday experience, but his address took on a new tone when he turned to the next argument, that "the sacred right of self government" required restrictions on slavery be removed so the residents of the territories could decide for themselves whether to admit or exclude it. Of course the inhabitants of the territories should make their own laws, Lincoln conceded, and these should not be interfered with any more than "the oyster laws of Virginia, or the cranberry laws of Indiana." But whether they could permit or exclude slavery depended upon "whether a negro is *not* or *is* a man."

Here Lincoln reached the crux of his disagreement with Douglas. He and the senator might both regret that slavery had ever been introduced to the American continent and they might both believe that African-Americans could never be the moral or intellectual equals of whites. But their views of African-Americans were fundamentally different. Douglas, Lincoln said, "has no very vivid impression that the negro is a human; and consequently has no idea that there can be any moral question in legislating about him." But to Lincoln the African-American was very much a man. The Declaration of Independence taught him that all men—even men of limited abilities and prospects—are created equal. Because the Negro was a man, there could be no moral right to slavery, which was "founded in the selfishness of man's nature." "No man," Lincoln announced, "is good enough to govern another man, *without that other's consent.* I say this is the leading principle—the sheet anchor of American republicanism."

Though Lincoln's argument was terse and powerful, his audience found little in its substance that was new. After all, the Kansas-Nebraska issue had been before the American people for nine months, and the act had been repeatedly attacked from almost every conceivable direction. Indeed, a little later in the 1854 campaign Lincoln himself admitted that the flaws of Douglas's "iniquity" had been so often exposed, that "he could not help feeling foolish in answering arguments which were no arguments at all."

What listeners did find different and significant in Lincoln's speech was his tone of moral outrage when he discussed "the monstrous injustice of slavery." "There can be no moral right in connection with one man's making a slave of another," he thundered. It followed, then, that the extension of slavery into the territories and, prospectively, "to every other part of the wide world, where men can be found inclined to take it," was equally wrong. So was Douglas's *"declared* indifference, but as I must think, covert *real* zeal for the spread of slavery."

With this Lincoln reached the bedrock of his political faith, with its assurance that all men are created equal. (Frequently in his 1854 addresses he made a significant misquotation of the Declaration, to the effect that all men are created "free and equal.") "Our revolutionary fathers" understood that slavery was wrong. For practical reasons they could not eradicate it at the time they set up the new national government, but they "hedged and hemmed it in to the narrowest limits of necessity." They did not allow the word "slavery" in the Constitution but permitted only indirect references to it, "just as an afflicted man hides away a wen or a cancer, which he dares not cut out at once, lest he bleed to death; with the promise, nevertheless, that the cutting may begin at the end of a given time."

Sharply in contrast was the Kansas-Nebraska Act, with its open tolerance of this monstrous evil, and Lincoln reached a new oratorical height in denouncing Douglas's claim that he was merely acting in the spirit of the Founding Fathers in permitting self-government in the territories. In denouncing this heresy, Lincoln, as Herndon wrote a few days later in the *Illinois State Journal,* "quivered with feeling and emotion" and "his feelings once or twice swelled within and came near stifling utterance."

Equally powerful was Lincoln's insistence that the American struggle over slavery must be viewed in world perspective. He had always shown sympathy for liberal movements abroad, for instance, expressing sympathy with the efforts of the Hungarian revolutionary Louis Kossuth in his struggles against the Hapsburg monarchy, but only in recent years had he come to see the importance of America as an example to lovers of freedom everywhere. In his eulogy on Clay he echoed that statesman's feeling "that the world's best hope depended on the continued Union of these States." Now he saw that by permitting the expansion of slavery the United States was undermining its influence on "the liberal party throughout the world." "We were proclaiming ourselves political hypocrites before the world," he warned, "by thus fostering Human Slavery and proclaiming ourselves, at the same time, the sole friends of Human Freedom."

It was a remarkable address, more elevated in sentiment and rhetoric than any speech Lincoln had previously made, and when he finished, the women in the audience waved their white handkerchiefs in support and the men gave loud and continuous hurrahs. Douglas took the floor immediately and offered a rebuttal that lasted nearly two hours. According to Democratic partisans, the senator demolished Lincoln, but in Herndon's report, Douglas "was completely cut down by Lincoln, and . . . Douglas felt himself overthrown."

That was the way that party newspapers always reported such encounters, but in the next few days there was considerable evidence that Lincoln had made an immense impression. Immediately after Lincoln spoke, Ichabod Codding and Lovejoy, two of the most radical antislavery men, gave notice of a meeting that evening to organize a Republican party in the state, in order to oppose the further extension of the slave power. That the turnout was small—twenty-six men and a boy, according to the hostile *Register*— was hardly surprising; after three hours of oratory by Lincoln and two more by Douglas, nobody wanted to attend another political rally. But the next day there was a meeting of respectable size, and the delegates, mostly from the northern counties, adopted a party platform. The real excitement at the convention, however, was over Lincoln's speech. "Ichabod [Codding] raved, and Lovejoy swelled," the *Register* reported, and all pronounced it "a glorious abolition speech, worthy of Ichabod himself, . . . [which] ought to be reiterated all over the country." Although disappointed that Lincoln failed to attend, the Republicans, without asking his consent, named him to their state central committee.

The reaction of the *Register* suggested the impact of Lincoln's speech. Ordinarily the editors of this Democratic newspaper refrained from abusing Lincoln, a fellow townsman whom they liked and admired. But as it became clear that his arguments had weakened Douglas's position, the *Register* tried to counter with a mock eulogy on "the late Hon. Abe Lincoln." "Left to himself," it mourned with crocodile tears, "he might have been an honor to his kind," with his "talent to hoodwink the blind, and with a facility of speech well calculated to deceive the ignorant," but, "flattered and cajoled by his pretended friends," he had allowed himself to believe that he was a great man, capable of challenging Douglas. "Annihilation—utter annihilation"—had inevitably been his fate, and there was no hope "to resuscitate his lifeless remains."

Whig reactions also attested to the effectiveness of Lincoln's assault on Douglas. The day after the speech, B. F. Irwin and several other Springfield Whigs requested Lincoln to pursue Douglas for the remainder of the campaign, constantly challenging him and attacking his arguments "untill he runs him into his hole or makes him holler Enough."

Lincoln did just that. He asked to debate Douglas at Peoria on October 16, but the senator, exhausted from constant campaigning and so hoarse that he could hardly be heard, was reluctant. Privately he told a friend that he did not want to share the platform with "the most difficult and dangerous opponent that I have ever met"; but he recognized the political risk of refusing to meet his challenger. He resolved his dilemma by speaking for more than three hours in the afternoon, until well after five o'clock, so that Lincoln would have to face a tired and restive crowd, eager to go home. Recognizing the problem, Lincoln urged listeners to have their supper and reassemble at seven in the evening. Then, to keep the audience from scattering, he offered Douglas a final hour for rebuttal, saying candidly to the Democrats: "I felt confident you would stay for the fun of hearing him skin me."

At Peoria, Lincoln gave essentially the same speech that he had delivered in Springfield; this time he wrote it out for publication in full over a week's issues of the *Illinois State Journal,* so that it would be widely read throughout the state. He went on from Peoria to Urbana, where he delivered his speech so effectively that years later Henry C. Whitney declared it had never been equaled before or since. After Lincoln spoke in Chicago, a journalist reported that he created the impression "on all men, of all parties, . . . first, that he was an honest man, and second, that he was a powerful speaker."

VII

In the fall elections voters across the North repudiated Douglas and the Kansas-Nebraska Act. Twenty-nine of the thirty-one New York congressmen elected were anti-Nebraska men, and so were twenty-one out of the twenty-five Pennsylvania representatives. Every congressman in Ohio was an opponent of Kansas-Nebraska, as were all but two in Indiana. Illinois joined the movement. Though the anti-Nebraska coalition failed to reelect Yates to Congress, choosing instead Douglas's loyal lieutenant, Thomas L. Harris, the Democrats could boast of few other victories. Anti-Nebraska candidates won five of the state's nine seats in the House of Representatives, and anti-

Nebraska forces, by a small majority, would control the next General Assembly, whose principal duty would be to elect the next United States senator from Illinois.

Even before the makeup of the new legislature was clear, Lincoln began to campaign for that office. He had been thinking about the prospect for some time. His address at Chicago, for instance, was probably intended to consolidate his following in the northern part of the state. Once the election turned out so favorably for the anti-Nebraska coalition, he sprang into action. Three days after the election he wrote candidly to Charles Hoyt, a client whom he had represented in an important patent suit: "You used to express a good deal of partiality for me; and if you are still so, now is the time. Some friends here are really for me, for the U.S. Senate." He asked Hoyt and his other correspondents to "make a mark for me" with members of the new legislature and solicited "the names, post-offices, and *political position*" of the incoming senators and representatives. His appeal went mainly to members of the Whig party. "It has come round that a whig may, by possibility, be elected to the U. S. Senate," he wrote one new legislator; "and I want the chance of being the man. You are a member of the Legislature, and have a vote to give. Think it over, and see whether you can do better than to go for me." So assiduous was he in soliciting votes that, as Herndon wrote, during the weeks after the November election "he slept, like Napoleon, with one eye open."

Lincoln recognized that his candidacy was problematical. The new legislature was certain to be fragmented and disorganized; only four of the seventy-five representatives in the previous legislature retained their seats. The anti-Nebraska majority was slim and far from united on any one man. There were, he discovered, "ten or a dozen, on our side, who are willing to be known as candidates," plus "fifty secretly watching for a chance." The Democrats could be counted on to offer "a terrible struggle," and many vowed that, rather than elect an anti-Nebraska senator, they would prevent the state senate, where they were in the majority, from joining the house of representatives in a joint session and thus stave off any choice.

Lincoln understood, too, that there were particular problems blocking his own candidacy. For one thing, in November, Sangamon County voters had elected him again to the state legislature, with the largest number of votes given to any candidate. This was, at best, bittersweet news, because the Illinois constitutional provision prohibiting the legislature from electing one of its own members to higher office might give unenthusiastic legislators an excuse not to vote for him. Apart from that, the new legislature was going to be so closely divided that, if Lincoln accepted the office, he might have the deciding vote in the election of senator. Propriety dictated that a man should not vote for himself but must abstain or cast his ballot for his opponent. There was, then, a real possibility that if Lincoln served in the legislature he might be obliged to assist in the reelection of the Democratic candidate,

James Shields, his old political foe and Douglas's right-hand man. He thought about the problem for two weeks and then declined to accept election to the House of Representatives. "I only allowed myself to be elected," he explained, "because it was supposed my doing so would help Yates."

According to Charles H. Ray, of the *Chicago Tribune,* Lincoln's declination "did more than any thing else to damage him with the Abolitionists" throughout the state, for they thought he was putting his personal fortunes above those of the anti-Nebraska movement. The Know Nothings, who had supported Lincoln, were also resentful at what they considered betrayal; Dr. William Jayne reported that they were "down on Lincoln—hated him." Taken by surprise by Lincoln's refusal to serve, the anti-Nebraska forces in Sangamon County were unable to field a strong candidate in the special election held just before Christmas, and a Democrat won the Sangamon seat in the legislature. Opponents chuckled that the voters had slapped Lincoln's face, and Shields called the outcome "the best Christmas joke of the season."

Lincoln had also to steer his way out of his entanglement with the radical antislavery wing of the anti-Nebraska movement, which constituted the new Republican party. Whether from prudence or pressure of business, he had been absent from Springfield in October 1854, when their convention adopted a platform urging an end to slavery in all national territories and a repeal of the Fugitive Slave Act of 1850, and made him a member of the state central committee. Lincoln neither accepted nor declined membership and, indeed, made no response until after the election, when Codding requested him to attend a meeting of the committee. As delicately as possible, he tried to disengage himself from a group whose votes he wanted but with whom he could not afford to be publicly affiliated. "I have been perplexed some to understand why my name was placed on that committee," he wrote Codding. "I was not consulted on the subject; nor was I apprized of the appointment, until I discovered it by accident two or three weeks afterwards." He could easily have resigned, but he was not willing to repudiate voters whose support he needed for the senate election. "I suppose my opposition to the principle of slavery is as strong as that of any member of the Republican party," he continued; "but I had also supposed that the *extent* to which I feel authorized to carry that opposition, practically; was not at all satisfactory to that party." Did the Republicans misunderstand his position, he asked diplomatically, or did he misunderstand theirs?

Once again, Lincoln was making it clear that he opposed the Kansas-Nebraska Act as a Whig, not as a Republican, much less as an abolitionist. Despite the soaring eloquence of his Springfield speech, his message was a moderate one, which appealed to the conservatism of Whigs in central Illinois. Unlike the antislavery radicals, he did not favor prohibiting the admission of additional slave states to the Union; indeed, he stated explicitly that, much as he hated slavery, he "would consent to the extension of it rather than see the Union dissolved." Unlike Republicans, he did not call for the elimination of slavery in all national territories; he stood pledged to the Compromise of 1850, which allowed New Mexico and Utah to tolerate or to forbid slavery. He accepted the Fugitive Slave Act, though he suggested it should be modified so that it would "not, in its stringency, be more likely to carry a free man into slavery, than our ordinary criminal laws are to hang an innocent one." Rather than condemning Southerners for the immorality of slaveholding, he expressed sympathy for the South, where he and so many other Whigs in central Illinois had been born.

In thus distancing himself from the Republican wing of the anti-Nebraska coalition, Lincoln knew that he risked alienating the earnest antislavery element. In the northern part of the state many felt that no man closely identified with either of the old parties ought to be elected senator. From repeated betrayals they distrusted the professions of all "mere politicians." Many were suspicious of Lincoln because of his background. "I must confess I am afraid of 'Abe,'" Ray wrote. "He is Southern by birth, Southern in his associations and southern, if I mistake not, in his sympathies. . . . His wife, you know, is a Todd, of a pro-slavery family, and so are all his kin."

Through intermediaries Lincoln worked to assuage these doubts. The previous summer Herndon had tried to reach Zebina Eastman, the fiercely abolitionist editor of the Chicago *Free West*. Known to be more radical on the slavery issue than his partner, Herndon had a long talk with the editor about Lincoln and offered him "a sight of his heart." "Although he does not say much," he pledged, "you may depend upon it; Mr. Lincoln is all right." Eastman was impressed, but not convinced, and the *Free West* continued to lament Lincoln's shortcomings. For more effective assistance, Lincoln turned to Elihu B. Washburne, who had just been elected to Congress from the Galena district as a Republican but who as a former Whig had great admiration for Lincoln. Washburne earnestly recommended Lincoln to Eastman and the northern Illinois Republicans as "a man of splendid talents, of great probity of character," who at Springfield had "made the greatest speech in reply to Douglas ever heard in the State." Most influential of all with Illinois abolitionists was the veteran Ohio antislavery leader Joshua F. Giddings, who announced unconditional support for his old congressional messmate and declared that he "would walk clear to Illinois" to help elect Lincoln.

It was harder to know how to deal with the Know Nothings in the incoming legislature—in part because nobody was sure just who belonged to the secret order. Leonard Swett, who was rounding up support for Lincoln in northern Illinois, passed along the prediction of a local newspaper editor, himself a member of one of the lodges, that the Know Nothings would control the new General Assembly. There was a general belief that they favored Lincoln. The *Free West* announced bluntly, "Mr. Lincoln is a Know Nothing and expects the full vote . . . of the Know Nothings." That was not true, but even the rumor of nativism lost him support. Publicly to repudiate the Know Nothings would be even more costly. Lincoln held his peace and did nothing to alienate voters who belonged to the secret organization.

Many of the responses to Lincoln's letter-writing campaign were all that he could have hoped for. "It will give me pleasure to do what I can for your appointment to the Sennet," Charles Hoyt wrote him. "So far as any effort of mine, can aid in securing such a result," replied editor Robert Boal of Lacon, "it will not be spared, and in any way in which I can assist you, my services are at your disposal." A correspondent in Lewistown wrote that the most prominent Whigs of his vicinity were earnestly for Lincoln on the somewhat equivocal ground that "we want some one that can stand right up to the little Giant *(excuse me)* it takes a great Blackguard (you know) to do that— *and thou art* (excuse again) *the Man."*

But other responses were less encouraging. After talking with a new member of the legislature, Abraham Jonas, Lincoln's firm friend in Quincy, had to report, "I can get nothing out of him, except that he will act altogether with the Whig party in regard to Senator and will make no pledges." A representative from Coles County was said to think well of Lincoln, "tho he seems to make it a matter of pride not to commit himself." And Thomas J. Turner of Freeport, who was to become the speaker of the new House of Representatives, loftily replied: "I am not committed to any one for the office of U. S. Senator, nor do I intend to be untill I know where I can exert my influence the most successfully against those who are seeking to extend the era of Slavery."

Even so, when the legislature assembled on January 1, 1855, Lincoln believed that he had 26 members committed to his election—more than twice as many as pledged to any other candidate. He needed 25 more votes. By his estimate, 43 of the 100 members of the General Assembly were Douglas Democrats, none of whom would vote for Lincoln. Douglas had made the senatorial election a referendum on popular sovereignty, and he insisted that all true Democrats in the legislature must endorse the Kansas-Nebraska Act. They should also support Shields, who had been Douglas's loyal ally in the Senate. "Our friends in the Legislature should nominate Shields by acclamation, and nail his flag to the mast," the senator directed, "and never haul it down under any circumstances nor for any body." Even if that course resulted in a stalemate, with no candidate receiving a majority of the votes, that would be preferable to "the election of Lincoln or any other man spoken of." If Shields was defeated, the Democrats could "throw the responsibility on the Whigs of beating him *because he was born in Ireland."* "The Nebraska fight is over," Douglas counseled, "and Know Nothingism has taken its place as the chief issue in the future."

In order to win, therefore, Lincoln had to have the backing of nearly every anti-Nebraska legislator. Throughout January, as the rival elements in the anti-Nebraska coalition jockeyed for position, he constantly lobbied for election. He tried not to be too obvious in his efforts, but again and again, as he chatted with legislators, the senate election would come up and he would say, "That is a rather delicate subject for me to talk upon, but I must confess that I would be glad of your support for the office, if you shall conclude that I am the proper person for it." To assist his supporters in the legislature he prepared several small notebooks in which he carefully listed the members of the state senate and house of representatives, the counties they represented, and their political affiliations. David Davis temporarily threw aside his judicial robes to help plan Lincoln's legislative strategy. Logan, who had just been elected to the house of representatives, became his floor manager, entrusted with making necessary deals to secure the support of the northern antislavery members. Herndon did all he could to influence the abolitionist element, while Leonard Swett and Ward Hill Lamon buttonholed uncommitted legislators.

As a result of these efforts, Lincoln steadily gained strength during the early weeks of the legislative session. By careful negotiation his aides were able to win over all of what he called "the extreme Anti-Slavery men," conceding to them the speakership and all of the lesser offices in the house of representatives. But during the same time he lost the support of at least three Whig members, including an old friend, J. L. D. Morrison, of St. Clair County, who was married to a Catholic and distrusted Lincoln's reported connections with the Know Nothings. He could not afford to lose others. As January 31, the scheduled day for the election, approached, he still was about three votes short of a majority, and he did not see where they could come from.

A small group of Independent Democrats held the balance of power in the legislature—men like Norman B. Judd of Chicago, and John M. Palmer of Carlinville, who had been loyal Democrats all their lives but had broken with Douglas over the Kansas-Nebraska Act. They had little in common with the other elements in the anti-Douglas coalition: they detested the radical antislavery men who styled themselves Republicans; they rejected even the tacit support of the Know Nothings; and they strongly suspected the motives of the Whigs, against whom they had fought in election after election. These anti-Nebraska Democrats had no personal objection to Lincoln, but they announced that "having been elected as Democrats they could not vote for any one but a Democrat for US senator." Their candidate was Lyman Trumbull, the lifelong Democrat from Alton, in southern Illinois, whose hatred for slavery compelled him to give up his safe place on the Illinois Supreme Court to run a bitter, and successful, anti-Douglas campaign for a seat in the United States House of Representatives. As Lincoln summarized the situation, these four or five anti-Nebraska legislators were "men who *never could* vote for a whig; and without the votes of two of whom I *never could* reach the requisite number to make an election."

Voting was delayed by a fierce snowstorm, the worst since 1831, which isolated Springfield for twelve days and prevented the assembling of a quorum in the state legislature, but in the initial ballot on February 8 the results were pretty much what Lincoln had anticipated. He led with 45 votes, to Shields's 41, and Trumbull had 5.

Most significant, however, was the one vote cast for Governor Joel A. Matteson, for it suggested the Democrats' strategy. Aware that they probably could not elect Shields, local Democrats rejected Douglas's advice and quietly began rallying around the governor, a wealthy contractor for public works. Matteson had said just enough in favor of the Kansas-Nebraska Act not to offend Douglas but in private had expressed enough opposition to convince many of Douglas's enemies. His strength in the legislature came from members in the districts along the Illinois and Michigan Canal, whom he had repeatedly assisted with favors, both legal and otherwise, in connection with his construction work.

The Democrats stuck with Shields for six ballots, and then, by prearrangement, they switched to Matteson on the seventh. Lincoln's vote was dwindling, while Trumbull's was gradually increasing. On the ninth ballot Lincoln was down to 15 hard-core loyalists, while Trumbull had 35 votes and Matteson, with 47, lacked only three of election. The danger at this point was that Matteson might use his wealth and his patronage to bribe a few of Trumbull's supporters, and, according to one story, Lincoln learned of a "contract" that the governor had arranged with one of these men—Frederick S. Day, of La Salle County.

Once Lincoln was aware of the danger, he promptly directed that his fifteen remaining supporters go for Trumbull on the tenth ballot. Bitterly disappointed, Logan urged him to hold on to his support and try one or two ballots more, but Lincoln was firm. "I am for Trumbull," he told his followers, and they loyally cast their votes as he directed. On the tenth ballot Lyman Trumbull was elected to the United States Senate.

Privately, according to friends, Lincoln was "disappointed and mortified" by the outcome and found it hard to accept that his 45 supporters had to yield to Trumbull's five. "A less good humored man than I, perhaps would not have consented to it," he grumbled. Immediately after his defeat he was so dejected that he told Joseph Gillespie, an old friend, that "he would never strive for office again," because "he could bear defeat inflicted by his enemies with a pretty good grace—but it was hard to be wounded in the house of his friends." Logan was furious over Lincoln's defeat, as was David Davis, who distrusted Trumbull as "a Democrat all his life—dyed in the wool—as ultra as he could be." Mary Lincoln was bitterly disappointed with the outcome; after Trumbull's victory, she refused to speak to Mrs. Trumbull, the former Julia Jayne, who had been one of her oldest and most intimate friends.

But in public Lincoln gave no expression to his natural disappointment. "I regret my defeat moderately," he wrote Washburne, "but I am not nervous about it," adding, with an uncharacteristic lack of generosity, that Matteson's "defeat now gives me more pleasure than my own gives me pain." He expressed no animosity toward the four anti-Nebraska Democrats who had blocked his election, two of whom—Norman B. Judd and John M. Palmer—became wheel horses in his later political campaigns. He went to considerable pains to make it clear that Trumbull had engaged in no underhand dealings or maneuvers, and on the night after the election he made a point of appearing at a reception that the Ninian Edwardses gave for the victor—a reception that had originally been planned to honor Lincoln himself. There he was at his smiling best, and when his hostess said she knew how disappointed he must be, he moved forward to shake the hand of the newly elected senator, saying, "Not *too* disappointed to congratulate my friend Trumbull."

On reflection, Lincoln did not consider his defeat a disaster. After all, he had entered the contest dubious of success. He could take satisfaction in knowing that the outcome was a blistering rebuke to Douglas and his popular-sovereignty ideas, and he knew that Trumbull, who had endless persistence and a sharp tongue, would make life miserable for the senior senator from Illinois. In addition, this election cleared the way for Lincoln to run against Douglas himself in 1858. On the night after Trumbull's victory, the anti-Nebraska Democrats of the legislature, gratified by Lincoln's conduct, pledged to support him in the next Senate race. Later Trumbull confirmed that pledge when he wrote Lincoln: "I shall continue to labor for the success of the Republican cause and the advancement at the next election to the place now occupied by Douglas of that *Friend,* who was instrumental in promoting my own."

VIII

In March, Lincoln had to explain to a client why he had neglected some legal business directed to him back in December. "I was dabbling in politics; and, of course, neglecting business," he wrote, adding, "Having since been beaten out, I have gone to work again." For a full twelve months after his defeat, he made no speeches or public statements on political affairs but devoted himself to his law business trying, as he said, "to pick up my lost crumbs of last year."

Much of the summer and fall of 1855 he spent in preparing to participate in the patent infringement suit that Cyrus Hall McCormick, the inventor of the reaper, had brought against John H. Manny, who was building closely similar machines. The suit was an important one, for it was already apparent that the mechanical reaper was transforming wheat cultivation, and there was a huge market for these machines, which could replace thousands of farm laborers. In the hope of breaking McCormick's patent, a number of other Eastern and Western manufacturers helped finance Manny's defense, and he employed a team of the leading patent lawyers in the country, headed by George Harding of Philadelphia. Because it seemed likely that Judge Thomas Drummond, of the United States Court for the Northern District of Illinois, would hear the case, Harding thought the team should include a local Illinois attorney who knew the judge and had his confidence—though, he said in his superior Eastern way, "we were not likely to find a lawyer there who would be of real assistance in arguing such a case."

After failing to secure the services of the Chicago lawyer Isaac N. Arnold, Harding in June sent his associate, Peter Watson, a patent lawyer in Washington, to Springfield to see if Lincoln might do. Calling without notice at the house at Eighth and Jackson streets, Watson encountered "a very tall man having on neither coat nor vest, who said he was Lincoln and was just putting up a bed." Impressed neither by Lincoln's dress nor by his small, plainly furnished house, Watson concluded this was not the associate Harding wanted but thought it would be impolitic to risk his anger by turning him down after consulting him. Consequently he paid Lincoln a $400 retainer, arranged for a fee—reputedly $1,000—and left him with the impression that he was to make an argument at the hearing.

Lincoln began studying the case and went out to Rockford, where Manny's factory was located, so that he could examine the machines closely. Puzzled that Watson failed to send him copies of the depositions and other legal papers, he went to the United States District Court in Chicago and had his own copies made. From the newspapers he learned that the case would be heard not in Chicago but in Cincinnati, where Supreme Court Justice John McLean would preside, but neither Watson nor anybody else on Harding's team told him when the hearing was to be held or invited him to be present.

Nevertheless, he took the train to Cincinnati, where he called on Harding at the Burnet House. The Philadelphia lawyer was not impressed; he described Lincoln as "a tall rawly boned, ungainly back woodsman, with coarse, ill-fitting clothing, his trousers hardly reaching his ankles, holding in his hands a blue cotton umbrella with a ball on the end of the handle." This fellow clearly would not do, especially now that Edwin McMasters Stanton, the brilliant Pittsburgh lawyer, had joined the defense team. "Why did you bring that d——d long armed Ape here," Stanton asked Harding; "he does not know any thing and can do you no good." They made it clear to Lincoln that he could not participate in the trial. Lincoln remained in Cincinnati for the week of the hearing, closely observing the proceedings, but the other lawyers ignored him. "We were all at the same hotel," Harding recalled; but neither he nor Stanton "ever conferred with him, ever had him at our table or sat with him, or asked him to our room, or walked to or from the court with him, or, in fact, had any intercourse with him."

At the end of the week Lincoln left for home, feeling insulted and indignant. When he received a check for the remainder of his fee, he sent it back, saying that he had made no argument and therefore was not entitled to anything beyond the original retainer. But when Watson returned the check to him, with a note explaining that he had earned it, he cashed it. Lincoln said little to his Springfield associates about the trial, though he did tell

Herndon that he had been "roughly handled by that man Stanton." But the snub was a painful one, and it added to his dejection over the loss of the Senate election.

IX

Even though Lincoln's law practice occupied most of his time during 1855, he kept up a silent but active interest in public affairs. Following events closely, he anxiously observed the consolidation of Southern opinion in favor of slavery. Where earlier Southern statesmen like Thomas Jefferson had hoped for the gradual extinction of the peculiar institution, a new breed of fire-eaters favored its perpetuation and, indeed, its extension. Lincoln & Herndon subscribed to the *Charleston Mercury* and the *Richmond Enquirer,* both rabidly proslavery, and sadly noted that an institution once lamented as a necessary evil was now promoted as a positive good. Herndon bought a copy of *Sociology for the South,* by George Fitzhugh, the able and extreme Virginia polemicist, who argued that slave labor was preferable to free labor, because under slavery workers had security and greater real freedom.

The specious logic of Fitzhugh's ideas troubled Lincoln, and in memoranda to himself he pointed out the flaws in the Virginian's arguments. "Although volume upon volume is written to prove slavery a very good thing," he noted, "we never hear of the man who wishes to take the good of it, *by being a slave himself."* The contention that slavery offered labor the greatest real freedom ran into the inescapable fact "that the most dumb and stupid slave that ever toiled for a master, does constantly *know* that he is wronged." Defenses of slavery were, in fact, reversible arguments: "If A. can prove, however conclusively, that he may, of right, enslave B.—why may not B. snatch the same argument, and prove equally, that he may enslave A?" If slavery was justified on the ground that masters were white while slaves were black, Lincoln warned, "By this rule, you are to be slave to the first man you meet, with a fairer skin than your own." If it was defended on the ground that masters were intellectually the superiors of blacks, the same logic applied: "By this rule, you are to be slave to the first man you meet, with an intellect superior to your own."

The more Lincoln thought about these questions, the more pessimistic he became. In the summer of 1855 he wrote a Kentucky friend that decades of experience had demonstrated "that there is no peaceful extinction of slavery in prospect for us." "The condition of the negro slave in America . . . is now as fixed, and hopeless of change for the better, as that of the lost souls of the finally impenitent," he lamented, predicting, "The Autocrat of all the Russias will resign his crown, and proclaim his subjects free republicans sooner than will our American masters voluntarily give up their slaves." With voluntary emancipation nowhere in sight, the United States had to face up to reality: "Can we, as a nation, continue together *permanently—forever* half slave, and half free?" To this question he would return in the future, but now he evaded an answer: "The problem is too mighty for me. May God, in his mercy, superintend the solution."

Events in Kansas made the future of slavery an immediately pressing issue. As Lincoln had predicted, there could not have been "a more apt invention to bring about collision and violence, on the slavery question" than the Kansas-Nebraska Act. "It was," he said, "conceived in violence, passed in violence, is maintained in violence, and is being executed in violence." While the settlement of Nebraska went on in a peaceful fashion, Kansas was in turmoil. Settlers who rushed in to claim the best land and the most advantageously situated town sites discovered that there were no government land offices. The area was still technically an Indian reserve, and no effort had yet been made to settle the Indian claims. Land claims could only be defended by the six-shooter and the bowie knife. Inevitably there was friction among the settlers. By opening the territory to slavery, the Kansas-Nebraska Act served as a challenge to the antislavery forces, and organizations like Eli Thayer's New England Emigrant Aid Company began funneling in free-state immigrants, equipped with rifles and ammunition. Proslavery forces in Missouri countered by pouring over the border, ready to fight in order to keep Kansas a slave state. As Missourians swamped the polls, the election of a territorial legislature proved a farce, and the delegates chosen made it a felony to question the right to hold slaves in Kansas and a capital offense to give aid to a fugitive slave. Lincoln learned of these developments not merely from the national newspapers, like the *New York Tribune,* which gave incessant coverage to proslavery "outrages" in Kansas, but from the frequent letters he received from Mark W. Delahay, an old friend and distant relative, who was editing a free-state paper at Leavenworth.

Reports of proslavery aggression made Herndon and other antislavery men in Springfield almost frantic, and they urged "the employment of any means, however desperate, to promote and defend the cause of freedom" in the territory. Lincoln, as usual, intervened to calm his excitable partner, reminding the little group of radicals that "physical rebellions and bloody resistances" were wrong and unconstitutional. Nevertheless, he made a contribution to the Kansas cause, with the restriction that his money should be sent only when Judge Logan decided it was necessary for the defense of the people of that territory. But he ended by urging the abolitionist group to think of "other more effective channels" of action—namely, politics.

The problem was to know how political action could be effective. Reluctantly Lincoln was obliged to recognize that the Whig party, with which he had acted all his adult life, was dying. For some years Whig economic policies calling for federal promotion of economic growth had been sounding less and less realistic, and the prosperity that followed the discovery of gold in California in 1848 made the party's program obsolete. Nor did the

Whigs have more to offer in the way of political policies after they joined with the Democrats in endorsing the Compromise of 1850 as a finality. With the differences between the major parties blurred, party loyalties waned. Opponents of slavery, discouraged by the repeated waffling of the Whigs, began to look to a third party. So did the large number of Whigs who were hostile to foreigners, suspicious of the Catholic Church, and opposed to the sale of alcoholic beverages. After 1852, when Winfield Scott's managers made an inept and unsuccessful effort to attract foreign-born and Catholic voters, who had always supported the Democratic party, large numbers of native-born Whigs flocked to the Know Nothing banner.

Lincoln had trouble defining his own position. A practical man, he knew —as he had remarked in his eulogy of Henry Clay—that in America "the man who is of neither party, is not—cannot be, of any consequence." But it was not clear what party he should choose. When his old friend Joshua F. Speed, with whom he now differed politically, inquired where he now stood, he replied: "That is a disputed point. I think I am a whig; but others say there are no whigs, and that I am an abolitionist." But, he went on to explain, he resented efforts to "unwhig" him, since he was doing no more than oppose "the *extension* of slavery," which had long been the position of most Northern Whigs. Certainly, he explained to Speed, he was not a Know Nothing. "How could I be? How can any one who abhors the oppression of negroes, be in favor of degrading classes of white people?" The United States began with the declaration that all men are created equal; it now was practically read as "all men are created equal, *except negroes,*" and if the Know Nothings gained control it would read "all men are created equal, except negroes, *and foreigners, and catholics.*" When things came to this pass, he told Speed, "I should prefer emigrating to some country where they make no pretence of loving liberty—to Russia, for instance, where despotism can be taken pure, and without the base alloy of hypocracy."

By the end of 1855 he found it easier to choose his political course. The Whig party was no longer a viable political organization. The abolitionist Republican party of Codding and Lovejoy was too extreme to attract a wide following. The nativist movement had crested, as the defeat of a statewide prohibition referendum, sponsored by the Know Nothings and the temperance organizations, demonstrated. What was now needed in Illinois was what had already taken place in many other Northern states—a fusion of all the opponents to the extension of slavery in a new political party.

Lincoln was ready to take the lead. In January 1856, when Paul Selby of the Jacksonville *Morgan Journal* proposed a conference of anti-Nebraska editors to plan for the next presidential election, Lincoln endorsed his idea, and when the editors met at Decatur on February 22, he was the sole nonjournalist in attendance. With his guidance the group drafted a conservative declaration that called for restoration of the Missouri Compromise, upheld the constitutionality of the Fugitive Slave Act, and pledged noninterference with slavery in the states where it already existed. To appease the more radical antislavery element, the resolutions also affirmed the basic free-soil doctrine, which Salmon P. Chase and Charles Sumner had most forcibly enunciated, that the United States was founded on the principle that freedom was national, and slavery exceptional. To win foreign-born voters, the platform advocated religious toleration and opposed any changes in the naturalization laws, and to attract the Know Nothings it denounced "attacks" on the common school system—meaning Catholic efforts to secure aid for parochial schools. Still avoiding the name "Republican," the conference called for a state fusion convention to be held at Bloomington on May 29.

On the night the conference adjourned, the editors attended a banquet, where Lincoln played a conspicuous role. When one speaker suggested that he ought to be the candidate of the new party for governor, he emphatically refused, stating that an anti-Nebraska Democrat would be more available for that post. But in response to a toast praising him "as the warm and consistent friend of Illinois, and our next candidate for the U.S. Senate," he rose, after prolonged applause, and said "the latter part of that sentiment I am in favor of." Pointing out that he felt a little out of place at this gathering, where he was the only noneditor, he capitalized on his odd appearance by saying that he felt like the ugly man riding through a wood who met a woman, also on horseback, who stopped and said: "Well, for land sake, you are the homeliest man I ever saw."

"Yes, madam, but I can't help it," he replied.

"No, I suppose not," she remarked, "but you might stay at home."

Having thus disarmed criticism, he went on to announce "his hearty concurrence in the resolutions adopted by the Convention" and "his willingness to buckle on his armor" for the coming fight with the Democrats.

Despite Lincoln's very active role at the Decatur gathering, some of his more conservative friends were unaware he was so fully committed to the new political movement. On May 10, Herndon, who had been named a member of the anti-Nebraska state committee at the editors' meeting, published a call for a meeting of Sangamon County citizens opposed to the Kansas-Nebraska Act to select delegates to the Bloomington convention. Though Lincoln was out of the office, attending court in Pekin, Herndon signed both his name and Lincoln's. Dismayed at this evidence of radicalism, John Todd Stuart rushed into the Lincoln & Herndon office to ask whether Lincoln had actually signed the call. Herndon admitted his responsibility. "Then you have ruined him," muttered Stuart. But Herndon knew he was doing just what his partner wanted—just what the Decatur convention had expected him to do. To placate Stuart, he wired Lincoln that the announcement was causing a stir among conservative Whigs, and his partner promptly responded: "All right; go ahead. Will meet you—radicals and all."

Elected a delegate to the Bloomington convention, Lincoln was committed to the new anti-Nebraska party but was nevertheless nervous about the outlook. In view of the failure of several previous attempts to organize a statewide antislavery party, he had reason to worry that leading politicians might not attend and that southern Illinois, where Douglas was so strong, might send no representatives. Arriving in Bloomington early, he had time on his hands and, restless, left David Davis's mansion, where he was staying, to prowl the streets of the little city. To help pass the minutes, he stopped in a small jewelry store, where he bought his first pair of spectacles for 37½ cents. He "kinder" needed them, he told Henry C. Whitney, who accompanied him, because he was now forty-seven years old. Not until he met the late train from Chicago and found it filled with delegates to the convention was he satisfied that the political decision he had made was a wise one.

On May 29 about 270 delegates assembled in Major's Hall to organize the Illinois Republican party. All shades of opinion were represented: conservative Whigs like Lincoln, anti-Nebraska Democrats like Norman Judd, Know Nothings like newly elected Representative Jesse O. Norton, Germans like Adolph Mayer, and abolitionists like Lovejoy. After conferring with about twenty influential politicians representing all shades of opinion, Orville Browning, the conservative Quincy lawyer, constructed a platform on which all could stand. To placate an estimated 20,000 German voters, it included a pledge to proscribe no one "on account of religious opinions, or in consequence of place of birth"—a promise so vague that it did not alienate the Know Nothings. On slavery questions the platform ignored abolitionist demands and offered a mild declaration that Congress had the power and the duty to exclude slavery from the national territories. The slate of officers nominated was carefully balanced: William H. Bissell, an anti-Nebraska Democrat who was also a hero of the Mexican War, was the candidate for governor; the German leader Francis A. Hoffmann was nominated for lieutenant governor; and three other offices went to Know Nothings who were former Whigs.

The delegates recognized Lincoln's role in creating the new party by calling him to the platform to make the last major speech before adjournment. Obviously delighted that the proceedings had gone so smoothly, and undoubtedly relieved that at last his break with the Whig party was public and irrevocable, he gave what was universally acclaimed as the best speech of his life. Because he spoke extemporaneously, there was no reliable record of what he said. Even Herndon, who usually took notes when his partner spoke, gave up after about fifteen minutes and, as he said, "threw pen and paper away and lived only in the inspiration of the hour."

Only the *Alton Weekly Courier,* in a brief report, gave the highlights of this major address. After enumerating "the pressing reasons of the present movement," Lincoln identified slavery as the cause of the nation's problems. Mistaking the idiosyncratic George Fitzhugh as a representative thinker, he claimed that Southerners were more and more arguing not merely that slavery was a positive good for blacks but that it should be extended to white laborers as well. Quite erroneously he claimed that because of Southern pressure, Northern Democrats like Douglas, who had once advocated "the individual rights of man," were beginning to accept this argument. "Such was the progress of the National Democracy." To oppose this heresy, Lincoln urged a union of all who opposed the expansion of slavery, and again he pledged that he was "ready to fuse with anyone who would unite with him to oppose slave power." If the united opposition of the North caused Southerners to raise "the bugbear [of] disunion," they should be told bluntly, "the *Union must be preserved in the purity of its principles as well as in the integrity of its territorial parts.*" Firmly he made Daniel Webster's thundering reply to the South Carolina nullifiers the motto of the Republican party: "Liberty and Union, now and forever, one and inseparable."

"His speech was full of fire and energy and force," Herndon recalled; "it was logic; it was pathos; it was enthusiasm; it was justice, equity, truth, and right set ablaze by the divine fires of a soul maddened by the wrong; it was hard, heavy, knotty, gnarly, backed with wrath." To his partner Lincoln seemed seven feet tall that day.

X

Lincoln recognized that the Republican party faced formidable problems in the 1856 presidential contest. Not only was it a new and imperfectly articulated organization, but it had powerful competition. Shrewdly the Democrats passed over the controversial Douglas and nominated James Buchanan, the former Secretary of State, who had a distinguished career of public service—and the inestimable blessing of having been out of the country, as minister to Great Britain, during the controversy over the Kansas-Nebraska Act. The nativists, now calling themselves the American party, nominated ex-President Millard Fillmore, whose highly respectable Whig antecedents made him attractive to conservatives of all persuasions. Even Mary Lincoln, usually wholly committed to her husband's political views, confessed that her "weak woman's heart" compelled her to favor Fillmore, who understood "the *necessity* of keeping foreigners, within bounds."

To counter the appeal of these two conservative candidates, Lincoln thought it important for the Republican party, holding its first national convention in Philadelphia on June 17–19, to recognize that nine-tenths of the anti-Nebraska voters had formerly been Whigs. He wrote Trumbull, who attended the convention at his urging, that the nomination of Supreme Court Justice John McLean of Ohio "would save every whig, except such as have already gone over hook and line" to the Democrats, but he carefully explained that he was not inflexible in his choice. "I am *in,*" he pledged, "and shall go for any one nominated unless he be *'platformed'* expressly, or impliedly, on some ground which I may think wrong."

The Philadelphia convention did not follow his advice, nor did it nominate either of the most conspicuous leaders in the Republican movement,

William H. Seward of New York, or Salmon P. Chase of Ohio. Instead, it chose the flamboyant, highly popular John C. Frémont, widely known as the "Pathmarker of the West" because of his explorations of the Rocky Mountains.

But when it came to selecting a vice presidential nominee, the delegates did look to former Whigs. The most popular candidate was William L. Dayton, a former senator from New Jersey. Unhappy that the new party was failing to recognize the importance of the Northwest, Illinois delegates caucused, and Nathaniel G. Wilcox proposed that they present Lincoln's name to the convention. Trumbull, who was not a delegate but attended the caucus, agreed that Lincoln was a *"very good man,"* and all the other members backed Lincoln's candidacy. All through the evening they worked to secure support in other delegations, convincing the Indiana members that the nomination of Dayton would do great injustice to the Western states.

On June 19 the Illinois delegation arranged to have John Allison of Pennsylvania put Lincoln's name in nomination as "the prince of good fellows, and an Old-Line Whig." Then Illinois delegate William B. Archer seconded the nomination, saying that he had known Lincoln for thirty years and had always found him "as pure a patriot as ever lived." Anti-Nebraska Democrat John M. Palmer, who had been instrumental in preventing Lincoln's election to the senate in 1855, added his endorsement, announcing, "We [in Illinois] can lick Buchanan any way, but I think we can do it a little easier if we have Lincoln on the ticket with John C. Frémont."

But the Illinois movement got under way too late, after most of the delegates were already committed to other candidates. In an informal ballot for vice presidential nominee, Dayton received 253 votes to Lincoln's 110. Lincoln was, of course, flattered by the support he received, which was evidence that he was becoming nationally known as a leader of the new party, but he pretended indifference. On the circuit in Urbana when Davis and Whitney brought him the news, he said with charming false modesty, "I reckon that ain't me; there's another great man in Massachusetts named Lincoln, and I reckon it's him."

The nomination of Frémont did not discourage Lincoln. As he wrote Trumbull, in a carefully chosen double negative, he was "not without high hopes for the state," though Illinois Republicans would have had an easier time had McLean been nominated. From the start of the campaign he made it his mission to win over Fillmore's supporters to the Republican cause. Most of these were, as a man in Clinton wrote him, "still tender, old time whigs, . . . partly with and partly not with us," and they looked to Lincoln for leadership. "In you they *do* place more confidence than in any other man," his correspondent continued. "Others may make fine speeches, *but* it would not be *'Lincoln said so* in *his speech.' "*

Responding to the need, Lincoln entered the campaign wholeheartedly and, as he remembered, made more than fifty speeches in behalf of the

Republican ticket. Most of them were delivered in the central and southern parts of the state, where Fillmore was strong, and there Republican editors, attempting to appeal to the Southern-born voters, stressed that Lincoln was a Kentuckian, "a Southerner, with eloquence that would bear a comparison with Henry Clay's."

Few of Lincoln's 1856 campaign speeches were preserved—or were worth preserving. In them he only occasionally praised Frémont, as "our young, gallant and world-renowned commander," or attacked "Buchanan, and his gang." He made few attempts to excite his audiences with tales of recent atrocities against free-state men in Kansas; he did not mention the quasi-war raging between the proslavery Lecompton regime and the free-state Topeka government in the territory and said nothing about the sack of Lawrence by pro-Southern ruffians on May 21. Nor did he refer to the attack that South Carolina Representative Preston S. Brooks made the following day upon Charles Sumner in the Senate chamber because of his antislavery speeches. Instead, Lincoln offered low-key, reasonable arguments to persuade American voters opposed to the expansion of slavery not to waste their votes on Fillmore, who had no chance of winning.

In private letters to old Whig friends, Lincoln made the same argument, stressing that a vote for Fillmore was really a vote for Buchanan. "This," he told them, "is as plain as the adding up of the weights of three small hogs." Because he had no secretarial assistance and wanted to reach a larger number of his former political associates, Lincoln had lithographed a form letter, marked "Confidential," expressing these views. Filling in the date and salutation by hand, he sent out several dozen of these until one fell into the hands of a Democratic editor, who exposed them as form letters.

What effect Lincoln had on the outcome of the 1856 election in Illinois was hard for him or anybody else to determine. In Republican newspapers his speeches were invariably praised as "unanswerable," showing "great eloquence and power." Democratic papers described his speeches as "prosy and dull in the extreme." He himself was under no illusions about the impact of his campaigning, though he was pleased when local Republican leaders said they were "tolerably well satisfied" with his work.

In the end, the canvass verified the prediction Lincoln had made at the start: "With the Frémont and Fillmore men united, here in Illinois, we have Mr. Buchanan in the hollow of our hand; but with us divided, . . . he has us." The antislavery vote was split, and in November, Buchanan carried Illinois and won the election.

When Lincoln looked back on the events of the past two years, he had to recognize that he had received some severe rebuffs. He had been defeated in his quest for a Senate seat, he had been snubbed by Eastern lawyers in the McCormick reaper case, and he had been passed over for the first Republican vice presidential nomination. On the other side of the ledger he could enter the solid distinction he had earned in the campaign against the Kansas-Nebraska Act, the respect that was due him as the principal architect of the Republican party in Illinois, and the admiration he received as a powerful orator for the free-soil cause. After 1856 he found no further occasion to lament to Herndon about his future or to grieve that he had done nothing to make his country better.

CHAPTER EIGHT

A House Divided

After the 1856 elections Lincoln tried to maintain a low political profile. He declined most invitations to speak with the explanation, "Having devoted the most of last year to politics, it is a *necessity* with me to devote this, to my private affairs." He turned to his law practice with great assiduity, and 1857 became the busiest and most profitable year of his professional life. But he had no idea of giving up politics, and he worked, mostly behind the scenes, to maintain and perfect the Republican organization so that it could mount an effective challenge to the reelection of Stephen A. Douglas in 1858.

I

Two weeks after the 1856 presidential election the fall term of the Sangamon County Circuit Court opened, and Lincoln & Herndon had five cases on the first day, ten on the second. Thereafter the partners appeared in court day after day, mostly in suits of a routine sort. In addition to his usual work in the circuit courts, Lincoln in 1857 argued cases more and more frequently in the United States courts, both in Springfield and in Chicago. Often these suits involved greater issues—and brought larger fees—than trials in the local courts. For example, the trial of the *Effie Afton* case, which involved the rights of steamship companies as against those of the railroads, kept him in Chicago for most of September.

Lincoln devoted a good deal of time during the summer to collecting from the Illinois Central Railroad for his services in the McLean County tax case. He was obliged to sue for his fee, and when the local railroad officials failed to pay it, he went to New York, probably in the hope of collecting it at the company headquarters. Mary accompanied him on what became more of a vacation than a business trip, for the Illinois Central officials were not forthcoming, and the Lincolns spent some time, as Mary said, "most pleasantly in travelling east," visiting Niagara and Canada. On their return, Lincoln decided not to wait longer and secured a court order against the railroad's property. With that, the Illinois Central paid up—and just in time, for a month later the panic of 1857 struck and the road went into bankruptcy.

This was perhaps the happiest time of Mary Lincoln's life. Her marriage to one of the leading public figures in Illinois satisfied her need for status, and her husband's more than respectable income from his law practice soothed her chronic anxiety over financial insecurity. He was now well enough off to take his half of the Illinois Central fee (Herndon received the other half) out of the bank and lend it to Chicago attorney N. B. Judd, who was speculating in Iowa lands. Not needing the income immediately, Lincoln allowed the interest to accumulate, so that Judd's note was worth $5,400 when it was redeemed.

Because the Lincolns were now moderately well-to-do, Mary Lincoln could turn to expanding and renovating the mean little cottage in which she had lived uncomplainingly for thirteen years. By the mid-1850s it was bursting at the seams, housing husband, wife, three sons, and at times a live-in maid; anyway, it was not a residence becoming a prominent public man. Mary probably took the lead in the renovation, and she may have been able to pay for it with her own money, since in the fall of 1854 she received $1,200 for the eighty acres of Sangamon County farmland that her father had given to her ten years earlier. By April 1856 the contractors, Hannon & Ragsdale, were at work, and Springfield was buzzing about the changes that the Lincolns were making. "Mr Lincoln has commenced raising his back building two stories high," Mrs. John Todd Stuart reported to her daughter. "I think they will have room enough before they are done." And she added, a bit maliciously, "particularly as Mary seldom ever uses what she has."

The construction was completed while Lincoln was away on the circuit, and he returned to find the cottage transformed into a handsome two-story Greek Revival house, tastefully painted chocolate brown, with dark green shutters. Pretending bewilderment, he sauntered up to a neighbor. "Stranger, do you know where Lincoln lives?" he asked. "He used to live here." As so often happened, his humor miscarried, and it was seriously reported that Mary Lincoln had remodeled the house without her husband's knowledge or consent. Of course, he had known about the remodeling, but he did complain to his wife about the cost of the project. Thereafter she developed the bad habit of concealing her expenditures from her husband.

Adding a full second story to the house at least doubled the Lincolns' living space. The entrance to the house remained the same, but to the right of the front corridor there now was a large sitting room, a comfortable place where the parents could read and the children could play. A front parlor to the left of the corridor served as a formal room for receiving guests. It was connected by double sliding doors with a back parlor that was Lincoln's library and study. In a more pretentious household the two rooms would have been identically furnished, as a double parlor, but the Lincolns kept them as two separate rooms, which could be opened into one on the rare occasions of a large party.

On the second floor Mr. and Mrs. Lincoln now had separate, but connecting, bedrooms, which were large and comfortable. This was not a signal that intimacy, or sexual relations, between husband and wife had ended; it was the arrangement highly recommended for well-to-do couples by fashionable interior decorators. Separate bedrooms also meant that Mary was less frequently disturbed by her husband's insomnia and nightmares. Robert now had his own room on this floor, and Willie and Tad shared one adjacent to it. There was a handsome guest room and, at the rear, a small room for a maid. The remodeled Lincoln house was not a mansion like the Edwardses,' nor did it rival the very expensive home that Governor Matteson had just built, but it was one of the best in Springfield.

In furnishing the house, Mary Lincoln chose wall-to-wall carpets for the parlors and the sitting room, selecting a dark, floral pattern that had recently come in style. The parlors had light, patterned wallpaper, but for the sitting room and the bedrooms she picked dark, boldly figured paper, which was then popular. The heavy, swagged draperies, which hung from ceiling to floor, she economically had made of cotton damask rather than silk. The rooms were furnished comfortably and unpretentiously, in a variety of styles, and the house was remarkably uncluttered. "An air of quiet refinement pervaded the place," a visitor reported. "You would have known instantly that she who presided over that modest household was a true type of American lady."

That was precisely the impression that Mary Lincoln wanted it to convey, for the house on Eighth and Jackson Streets was the center of her world. Finally she felt comfortable. Her children were now old enough not to require constant supervision. Though the younger boys were still much in evidence and, as Mary complained, were *disposed* to be noisy," Robert after 1854 was away most days attending what was grandly called the Illinois State University—really a local preparatory school, so inadequate that in 1859 he failed all the entrance examinations when he tried to enter Harvard College and had to spend a year at the Phillips Exeter Academy in New Hampshire. Mary for the first time since her marriage had time to read and to write long, gossipy letters to her friends and relatives.

She also now felt able to entertain properly. Though her dining room was still small, she could give dinner parties for six or eight, and guests like Isaac N. Arnold of Chicago long remembered her excellent cooking and her table "loaded with venison, wild turkeys, prairie chickens, quails, and other game." But she preferred to give larger buffet suppers, like the "very handsome and agreable [sic] entertainment" she offered in February 1857—just possibly an unannounced party for her husband's forty-eighth birthday. No fewer than five hundred guests were invited, and it was not clear how she expected to squeeze all those people in. Fortunately a heavy rainstorm and a conflicting engagement kept many of them away. Even so, about three hundred had a chance to see her newly expanded and redecorated home. Weary but proud when the affair was over, she wrote her favorite sister in Kentucky, "You will think, we have enlarged *our borders,* since you were here."

II

In part, the Lincolns' hospitality was designed to maintain his network of political friends and acquaintances, because public office was never far from his mind. He was not dispirited by the outcome of the 1856 elections. After all, the Republicans had succeeded in electing William H. Bissell as governor. On the national scene, James Buchanan was chosen President only because the opposition vote was split between Frémont and Fillmore, who together had a majority of 400,000. If, he told a gathering of Chicago Republicans in December 1856, these factions could "let past differences, as nothing be" and could agree that the equality of men was " 'the central idea' in our political public opinion," they would surely carry the next election.

A decision handed down by the United States Supreme Court on March 6, 1857, two days after Buchanan's inauguration, made the need for a Republican victory both more necessary and more likely. The ruling concerned the fate of Dred Scott, a Missouri slave, who had been taken by his owner, an army surgeon, first to Rock Island, Illinois, a state where slavery was prohibited by the Northwest Ordinance and by its own constitution, and subsequently to Fort Snelling, in Minnesota Territory, from which slavery had been excluded by the Missouri Compromise. After returning with Scott to Missouri, his master died. Scott sued for his freedom on the ground that he had been resident first of a free state and then of a free territory. The case finally reached the Supreme Court. Speaking for a majority of the justices, Chief Justice Roger B. Taney ruled that Scott was not entitled to sue, because, as a Negro, he was not a citizen of the United States. At the time the nation was created, Taney pronounced, blacks were considered "so far inferior, that they had no rights which the white man was bound to respect," and the Founding Fathers had not included them in either the Declaration of Independence or the Constitution. The Chief Justice held further that residence in free territory did not entitle Scott to freedom, since all congressional enactments that excluded slavery from the national territories, including specifically the Missouri Compromise, were "not warranted by the constitution" and were "therefore void."

Antislavery spokesmen, like Horace Greeley of the *New York Tribune,* exploded in anger, denouncing the Court's decision as deserving no more respect than if made by "a majority of those congregated in any Washington bar-room," The *Chicago Tribune* predicted that it would force slavery upon the free states, so that Chicago might become a slave market, where men, women, and children would be sold on the block. Throughout the North antislavery clergymen erupted in denunciations of Taney and the majority of the Court, and opposition was so fierce that the *New York Herald* predicted that "the whole North will evidently be preached into rebellion against the highest constituted Court in the country."

But Lincoln, like most Illinois Republican politicians, was slow to react to the Dred Scott decision. Not until late May did he even refer to the case, when, without mentioning it by name, he said the federal courts no longer exercised jurisdiction over litigation that "might redound to the benefit of a 'nigger' in some way." This seeming indifference stemmed in part from the complexity of the Court's decision. The justices offered nine separate opinions, none of which addressed exactly the same issues; two of them were strong dissenting opinions by antislavery Justices John McLean and Benjamin R. Curtis. An initial examination of the opinions failed to give Lincoln much cause for alarm. As he explained later, he "never . . . complained *especially* of the Dred Scott decision because it held a negro could not be a citizen"; he agreed with Taney on this subject. Nor was he exercised because the Court invalidated the Missouri Compromise; the Kansas-Nebraska Act had already expressly repealed that compromise.

Lincoln was reluctant to challenge the Court's ruling. He had enormous respect for the law and for the judicial process. He felt these offered a standard of rationality badly needed in a society threatened, on the one side, by the unreasoning populism of the Democrats, who believed that the majority was always right, and the equally unreasonable moral absolutism of reformers like the abolitionists, who appealed to a higher law than even the Constitution. As recently as the 1856 campaign he had invoked the judiciary as the ultimate arbiter of disputes over slavery. "The Supreme Court of the United States is the tribunal to decide such questions," he announced, and, speaking for the Republicans, he pledged, "We will submit to its decisions; and if you [the Democrats] do also, there will be an end of the matter."

But the Dred Scott decision required him to rethink his position. If the Court had decided simply that Dred Scott was a slave, he "presumed, no one would controvert it's correctness." "If this important decision had been made by the unanimous concurrence of the judges, and without any apparent partisan bias, and in accordance with legal public expectation, and with the steady practice of the departments throughout our history," he continued, it would be "factious, nay, even revolutionary," not to accept it. But when a majority of the justices, overruling numerous previous judicial rulings and ignoring the extensive historical evidence that throughout American history many states had recognized blacks as citizens, which Justice Curtis adduced in his dissent, extended their ruling to the entire African-American race, their decision was simply wrong.

What troubled Lincoln most about the Dred Scott decision was the Chief Justice's gratuitous assertion that neither the Declaration of Independence nor the Constitution was ever intended to include blacks. Lincoln declared bluntly that Taney was doing "obvious violence to the plain unmistakable language of the Declaration," which had once been held sacred by all Americans and thought to include all Americans. Now, in order to make Negro slavery eternal and universal, the Declaration "is assailed, and sneered at, and construed, and hawked at, and torn, till, if its framers could rise from their graves, they could not at all recognize it." So blatant was the Chief Justice's misreading of the law, so gross was his distortion of the documents fundamental to American liberty, that Lincoln's faith in an impartial, rational judiciary was shaken; never again did he give deference to the rulings of the Supreme Court.

Lincoln kept these views to himself until June, when Douglas returned to Illinois and made a major address at Springfield defending the "honest and conscientious" judges who had handed down the Dred Scott decision and denouncing criticism of the highest tribunal as "a deadly blow at our whole republican system of government." Recognizing that the Supreme Court's ruling was unpopular, Douglas seized on Taney's dictum that the Negro was not included in the Declaration of Independence as an excuse to appeal to Illinois negrophobia. Blacks, he announced, belonged to "an inferior race, who in all ages, and in every part of the globe, . . . had shown themselves incapable of self-government," and he warned that Republicans favored the "amalgamation between superior and inferior races."

Two weeks later Lincoln offered the Republican reply to the senator. Part of his speech was a slashing attack on Douglas's popular-sovereignty doctrine as "a mere deceitful pretense for the benefit of slavery." He spent much time explaining the Republican position on Dred Scott. "We think the Dred Scott decision is erroneous," he declared unequivocally. "We know the court that made it, has often over-ruled its own decisions, and we shall do what we can to have it to over-rule this. We offer no *resistance* to it."

Not until Lincoln turned to the interpretation Taney and Douglas offered of the Declaration of Independence did his words take wings. He charged that the Chief Justice and the senator were working, together with other Democrats, to extend and to perpetuate slavery. To do so they joined in further oppression of the already oppressed Negro: "All the powers of earth seem rapidly combining against him. . . . They have him in his prison house; they have searched his person, and left no prying instrument with him. One after another they have closed the heavy iron doors upon him, and now they have him, as it were, bolted in with a lock of a hundred keys, which can never be unlocked without the concurrence of every key; the keys in the hands of a hundred different men, and they scattered to a hundred different and distant places; and they stand musing as to what invention, in all the dominions of mind and matter, can be produced to make the impossibility of his escape more complete than it is."

And Douglas, in order to make this oppression tolerable, lugged in the absurd charge that Republicans wanted "to vote, and eat, and sleep, and marry with negroes!" He was simply trying to capitalize on that "natural disgust in the minds of nearly all white people, to the idea of an indiscriminate amalgamation of the white and black races." Bluntly Lincoln rejected "that counterfeit logic which concludes that, because I do not want a black woman for a *slave* I must necessarily want her for a *wife.*" The authors of the Declaration of Independence never intended "to say all were equal in color, size, intellect, moral developments, or social capacity," but they "did consider all men created equal—equal in 'certain inalienable rights, among which are life, liberty, and the pursuit of happiness.'"

It was a powerful speech, but not a radical one. Indeed, Gustave Koerner, the German-American leader of the Republicans in Belleville, complained that it was "too much on the old conservative order" and concluded that Lincoln was "an excellent man, but no match to such impudent Jesuits and sophists as Douglas." What Lincoln omitted from his argument was as significant as what he said. Though many observers recognized that the Dred Scott decision had gutted Douglas's favorite doctrine of popular sovereignty by invalidating all congressional legislation concerning slavery in the national territories, Lincoln made no effort to point out the contradiction between the ideas of the Chief Justice and those of the senior senator from Illinois; nor did he discuss Douglas's theory that territorial governments, despite the Court's ruling in Dred Scott, could effectively exclude slavery by refusing to protect it. Lincoln's object was not to show differences between the two Democratic spokesmen but to picture them as united in oppressing the African-American and in extending the institution of slavery.

III

That was his basic strategy for the upcoming 1858 elections, which would choose members of the state legislature that would name the next United States senator. Lincoln believed that Douglas was vulnerable, and this time he had no intention of waiting for the outcome of the elections before announcing his campaign for the Senate. As early as August 1857 he began encouraging fellow Republicans to do something *"now,* to secure the Legislature,"* recommending that they draw up careful lists of voters by precincts. "Let all be so quiet that the adve[r]sary shall not be notified," he warned.

In planning for the next Senate election, Lincoln gathered around him a group of dedicated and hardworking advisers. Some of them were familiar faces from his earlier campaigns. Herndon was, as ever, loyal if indiscreet, valuable because of his contacts among abolitionists. Both Jesse K. Dubois, the state auditor, and Ozias M. Hatch, the secretary of state, were close political friends as well as neighbors in Springfield. Lamon and Whitney kept an eye on the north central part of the state. In the Bloomington area Lincoln counted on Leonard Swett and Judge Davis. In Chicago, Lincoln's strongest supporter was Norman B. Judd, who had refused to vote for him in 1855 but had since worked closely with him in business and legal matters. Charles H. Ray, of the *Chicago Press and Tribune,* had overcome his earlier misgivings and was now one of Lincoln's most loyal backers. In southern Illinois, Joseph Gillespie, with whom he had served in the state legislature, was his most effective supporter. It was Lincoln's special gift not merely to attract such able and dedicated advisers—and other names could readily be added to the list—but to let each of them think that he was Lincoln's closest friend and most trusted counselor.

By fall, events in Kansas and in Washington made it necessary for Lincoln and his advisers to be especially alert. In the hope of ending the turmoil and bloodshed in the Kansas Territory, President Buchanan, along with many other Democrats, favored the speedy admission of Kansas as a state, and in February the territorial government ordered an election for a constitutional convention. It was, as Lincoln remarked, "the most exquisite farce ever enacted." Free-soil voters, certain that the election was rigged to favor the proslavery faction, stayed at home, and only about 2,200 out of 9,000 registered voters participated. Nevertheless, the delegates assembled in Lecompton in September and October, drew up a constitution, and submitted it for the approval of the President and Congress. A proslavery document, it guaranteed not merely that the two hundred or so slaves already in Kansas would remain in bondage but that their offspring should also be slaves. The constitution could not be amended for seven years. Against the advice of both President Buchanan and Robert J. Walker, whom he had appointed territorial governor, the convention provided for a referendum not on the constitution itself but only on the question of whether more slaves could be introduced into the state. Eager to have the Kansas crisis finally settled, Buchanan, ignoring his previous pledges, approved this Lecompton Constitution and recommended it to the Congress.

Douglas decided to oppose it. He knew he was facing a strenuous reelection campaign in Illinois, where Lincoln almost certainly would be his opponent. He had lost much strength by his advocacy of the Kansas-Nebraska Act, and his endorsement of the Dred Scott decision, even though tepid, had cost him more. Support of the patently proslavery Lecompton Constitution would weaken him even further. As one of Trumbull's correspondents wrote: "if Kansas is admited under the Lecompton Constitution, there would not be a grease spot left of Douglas in Illinois." Aside from political considerations, Douglas felt that the document subverted his cardinal principle, popular sovereignty, because it denied the inhabitants of the Kansas territory the right to choose their own form of government. He vowed to "make the greatest effort of his life in opposition to this juggle." Breaking with President Buchanan, Douglas led the fight in the Senate against the Lecompton Constitution, denouncing it as a "flagrant violation of popular rights in Kansas," and an outrage on the "fundamental principles of liberty upon which our institutions rest." He made it clear that his objection was to the process by which the constitution was adopted rather than to particular provisions of that document. On the slavery referendum he professed neutrality. "It is none of my business which way the slavery clause is decided," he told the Senate, adding a statement that Lincoln would repeatedly quote out of context: "I care not whether it is voted down or voted up."

Douglas's opposition to Lecompton, and to the President, delighted Republicans. Horace Greeley, the influential editor of the *New York Tribune*, which was thought to have between 5,000 and 10,000 readers in Illinois, announced that Douglas's course was not merely right but "conspicuously, courageously, eminently so." Greeley began conferring with the senator on ways to defeat the measure, as did former Speaker of the House of Representatives, Massachusetts Republican Nathaniel P. Banks, and Benjamin F. Wade, the abolitionist senator from Ohio. Senator Henry Wilson of Massachusetts believed that Douglas was about to move into the Republican party, where he would be "of more weight to our cause than any other ten men in the country."

Lincoln's initial reaction to what he called the *"rumpus"* among the Democrats over Lecompton was to urge Republicans to stand clear of the quarrel, because both Buchanan and Douglas were in the wrong. He was convinced that Douglas's opposition to Lecompton was only a trick to deceive unwary Republicans. Douglas and his friends were "like boys who have set a birdtrap" and were now "watching to see if the birds are picking at the bait and likely to go under."

But by late December he began to fear that Greeley and other Eastern Republicans were walking into the trap. "What does the New-York Tribune mean by it's constant eulogising, and admiring, and magnifying [of] Douglas?" he angrily asked Senator Trumbull. "Does it, in this, speak the sentiments of the republicans at Washington? Have they concluded that the republican cause, generally, can be best promoted by sacraficing us here in Illinois?" During the spring Lincoln's suspicions increased as Eastern Republicans continued to praise Douglas's heroic, and ultimately successful, opposition to Lecompton. Further reinforcement came when Herndon, making a long-planned pleasure trip to Washington and the Northeast, reported that prominent Eastern Republicans favored Douglas's reelection and that Horace Greeley thought Illinois Republicans were fools to oppose him.

Resentful of outside interference, Illinois Republicans spurned the suggestion that they ought to drop Lincoln and back Douglas for reelection. "God forbid," exploded Jesse K. Dubois, *"Are our friends crazy?"* Such a shift was impossible, Herndon angrily wrote Greeley. "Douglas' abuse of us as Whigs—as Republicans—as men in society, and as individuals, has been so slanderous—dirty—low—long, and *continuous,* that we cannot soon forgive and *can never forget.*"

Lincoln and his friends were also troubled by the possibility that former Democrats might defect, as they had in 1855, and back another candidate for the Senate. The most likely possibility was "Long John" Wentworth of Chicago, the erratic but enormously popular former Democratic congress-man who had broken with Douglas over Kansas-Nebraska and had recently been elected Republican mayor of Chicago by the largest majority ever given in that city. Wentworth probably did have vague ambitions for the senatorship, but he wisely recognized that Lincoln was the choice of most Republicans and took no steps to make himself available. But Democratic newspapers, hoping to divide their opponents, touted his candidacy, claim-ing that he said Lincoln could never be elected and that he intended to pack the state convention with delegates "pledged to vote for him through thick and thin." Some of Lincoln's backers—notably Judd, who had repeatedly battled Wentworth in Chicago—took the threat seriously, as did Lincoln himself.

To prevent any erosion of Republican solidarity, Lincoln's friends began carefully planning for the fall elections, which would choose eighty-seven members of the next legislature. (There were thirteen holdover members of the state senate.) Though Lincoln himself remained curiously passive, his supporters in county convention after county convention passed resolutions declaring that he was their first, last, and only choice for senator. Then they arranged, for only the second time in American history, to have a party's state convention nominate a senatorial candidate. The procedure was so unprecedented that it attracted much attention, and a Philadelphia editor called this "dangerous innovation" a "revolutionary effort to destroy the true intent and spirit of the constitution." Its purpose, however, was much less grand. The nomination was designed, as Lincoln said, "more for the object of closing down upon this everlasting croaking about Wentworth, than anything else." Equally important, it was intended to give a clear signal to Eastern Republicans like Greeley that Illinois Republicans would never unite behind Douglas.

When the Republican state convention assembled in the statehouse at Springfield on June 16, the outcome was prearranged. Without dissent, the delegates adopted a noncontroversial platform Browning had drafted and nominated candidates for state treasurer and superintendent of education. Then they turned to the real business of the meeting. When Judd and the Chicago delegation brought in a banner inscribed COOK COUNTY IS FOR ABRA-HAM LINCOLN, the delegates exploded in applause. A member from Peoria moved to change the motto to "Illinois is for Abraham Lincoln," and the convention went wild. Unanimously the delegates voted that Abraham Lin-coln was "the first and only choice of the Republicans of Illinois for the United States Senate, as the successor of Stephen A. Douglas." It was, Hern-

don reported, "a grand affair," and the Republicans "all felt like exploding
—not with gass [sic], but with electric bolts, shivering what we struck."

IV

That evening, at eight o'clock, Lincoln gave his acceptance speech. He had
been thinking about it for several weeks, drafting sentences and paragraphs
on stray pieces of paper and the backs of envelopes, storing them in his tall
hat. Eventually he wrote out the entire speech with great care, closely revising every sentence. As long as possible, he kept the contents to himself,
and when Dubois asked what he was writing, Lincoln replied gruffly: "It's
something you may see or hear some time, but I'll not let you see it now."
After he had finished the final draft, he read it aloud, first to Herndon and
then to a dozen or so of his other close advisers. By the evening of the
convention every word was fixed in his tenacious memory, and he had no
need to refer to his manuscript when he delivered it.

In conscious imitation of the opening of Daniel Webster's celebrated
reply to Robert Hayne, he began:

> If we could first know *where* we are, and *whither* we are tending, we could
> then better judge *what* to do, and *how* to do it.
>
> We are now far into the *fifth* year, since a policy was initiated, with the
> *avowed* object, and *confident* promise, of putting an end to slavery agitation.
>
> Under the operation of that policy, that agitation has not only, *not ceased,*
> but has *constantly augmented.*
>
> In *my* opinion, it *will* not cease, until a *crisis* shall have been reached, and
> passed.
>
> "A house divided against itself cannot stand."
>
> I believe this government cannot endure, permanently half *slave* and half
> *free.*
>
> I do not expect the Union to be *dissolved*—I do not expect the house to
> *fall*—but I *do* expect it will cease to be divided.
>
> It will become *all* one thing, or *all* the other.
>
> Either the *opponents* of slavery, will . . . place it where the public mind
> shall rest in the belief that it is in the course of ultimate extinction; or its
> *advocates* will put it forward, till it shall become alike lawful in *all* the States,
> *old* as well as *new*—*North* as well as *South.*

The "house divided" quotation was one familiar to virtually everybody in
a Bible-reading, churchgoing state like Illinois; it appeared in three of the
Gospels. Lincoln himself had used the image as early as 1843 in urging party
solidarity among the Whigs. The idea behind the metaphor as he now used
it, that slavery and freedom were incompatible, had been a standard part of
the abolitionists' argument for decades, and in an 1852 speech Edmund
Quincy, the Massachusetts abolitionist, had used the house-divided quota-

tion to predict the death of slavery. More recently Southern apologists, such as George Fitzhugh, also argued that the United States must become all slave or all free.

Lincoln had been thinking about this house-divided theme for several years. As early as 1855, after his first defeat for the Senate, he raised the question with a Kentucky correspondent: "Can we, as a nation, continue together *permanently—forever*—half slave, and half free?" The next year during the Frémont campaign he several times announced "his opinion that our government could not last—part slave and part free." In December 1857 he drafted a speech arguing that the controversy over the Lecompton Constitution simply diverted attention from "the true magnitude of the slavery element in this nation," which was dividing political parties and even churches along sectional lines. *"A house divided against itself cannot stand,"* he concluded then. "I believe the government cannot endure permanently half slave and half free. . . . whether this shall be an entire slave nation, *is* the issue before us."

In using almost identical words now, Lincoln was setting the stage for the longer second section of his address, designed to show that Douglas was part of a dangerous plot to nationalize slavery. As proof of that conspiracy Lincoln evidenced first Douglas's Kansas-Nebraska bill opening all the national territory to slavery, which had upset a long-standing national consensus. Then he noted how President Franklin Pierce had pushed the bill to make it law. Next President James Buchanan, in his inaugural address, fervently urged citizens to accept the still unannounced opinion of the Supreme Court on the extension of slavery, and Chief Justice Roger B. Taney immediately afterward ruled that all congressional legislation restricting slavery in the territories was invalid. Unlike most other Republican leaders, Lincoln did not blame these measures extending slavery on the "Slave Power"—a phrase that he carefully avoided throughout the campaign—but attributed them to the Northern Democrats. He admitted that "we cannot absolutely *know*" that these Democratic leaders were in a conspiracy. "But," he said, using an image familiar to every Illinois farmer who had ever raised a barn, "when we see a lot of framed timbers, different portions of which we know have been gotten out at different times and places and by different workmen—Stephen, Franklin, Roger and James [i.e., Douglas, Pierce, Taney, and Buchanan], for instance—and when we see these timbers joined together, and see they exactly make the frame of a house or a mill, all these tenons and mortices exactly fitting, and . . . not a piece too many or too few," it was impossible not to believe that the four workmen had worked from a common plan or blueprint.

In the proslavery edifice so carefully constructed there was "another nice little niche," to be filled by a future Supreme Court decision declaring that the Constitution does not permit a state to exclude slavery from its limits. That was all that was needed to make slavery universal, and, Lincoln predicted, it was "probably coming, . . . unless the power of the present political dynasty shall be met and overthrown." "We shall *lie down* pleasantly dreaming that the people of *Missouri* are on the verge of making their State *free,*" he warned; "and we shall *awake* to the *reality,* instead, that the *Supreme* Court has made *Illinois* a *slave* State."

Lincoln probably genuinely believed in this alleged proslavery conspiracy among Northern Democratic leaders because he so totally distrusted Douglas. He thought the senator utterly unprincipled. He was quite ready to believe a wholly undocumented rumor that Douglas was sending "certain unknown personages" to Illinois in order to arouse the hitherto quiescent temperance movement, in the hope that that issue might divide Republicans; "it would be perfectly natural in him," he judged, "just like him." Lincoln's suspicion of Douglas was fueled by his rankling envy of his rival. In a fragmentary manuscript discussing his twenty-two years of acquaintance with Douglas, Lincoln could not help making a painful comparison of their careers: "With *me,* the race of ambition has been a failure—a flat failure; with *him* it has been one of splendid success." He complained to Joseph Gillespie that Douglas had "arrogated a superiority over him on account of his national reputation," adding, a bit wistfully, that "if our positions were changed I would not do that."

But his charge of conspiracy was not based on fact. Certainly Douglas and Pierce had cooperated to secure the adoption of the Kansas-Nebraska Act, but Buchanan had been out of the country and Taney had nothing to do with it. Taney's Dred Scott decision ran directly counter to Douglas's popular-sovereignty idea. Lincoln knew as well as anybody else that Douglas and Buchanan were now feuding, but in order to make his case he had to dismiss the fierce controversy over Lecompton as a "squabble," a kind of lovers' quarrel.

More defensible, though also highly speculative, was Lincoln's prediction of a second Dred Scott decision, which would protect slavery in all the states as well as the national territories. He could not have known that Chief Justice Taney, angered by criticism, was eager to issue what he called a "supplement" to the Dred Scott decision, but as a well-informed lawyer he realized there were bound to be cases in the near future where the justices would issue further rulings on slavery. It was no secret that the case of *Lemmon* v. *The People,* involving the right of a Virginia slaveholder to bring his slaves into the state of New York, while in transit to Texas, was working its way up to the Supreme Court, and it required no great feat of the imagination to guess how the present justices would rule.

But the specifics of Lincoln's conspiracy charge in his house-divided speech were less important than its general import. Its purpose was clear: to show Republicans, both in Illinois and in the East, that Douglas could not be trusted and must be defeated.

In the brief final section of his speech Lincoln asked who could best check this headlong rush to nationalize slavery. Surely not Douglas, even though his admirers "remind us that *he* is a very *great man,* and that the largest of *us* are very small ones." But Douglas's past record of supporting slavery aggressions made him now a caged and toothless lion, and—in an unfortunate phrase—Lincoln reminded his listeners "a *living dog* is better than a *dead lion.*" No, the cause of putting slavery on the road to ultimate extinction "must be intrusted to, and conducted by its own undoubted friends," the Republicans. "The result is not doubtful," he concluded. "We shall not fail—if we stand firm, we shall not fail."

Thus the three sections of Lincoln's house-divided speech had the inevitability of a syllogism: The tendency to nationalize slavery had to be defeated. Stephen A. Douglas powerfully contributed to that tendency. Therefore, Stephen A. Douglas had to be defeated.

Attracting national attention, Lincoln's house-divided speech sounded very radical. Advanced five months before William H. Seward offered his prediction of an "irrepressible conflict" between slavery and freedom, it was the most extreme statement made by any responsible leader of the Republican party. Even Herndon, to whom Lincoln first read it, told his partner: "It is true, but is it wise or politic to say so?" Lincoln's other advisers condemned it, especially deploring the house-divided image and saying "the whole Spirit was too far in advance of the times." As the editor John Locke Scripps explained, many who heard and read Lincoln's speech understood it as "an implied pledge on behalf of the Republican party to make war upon the institution in the States where it now exists."

Aware that his house-divided prediction was controversial, Lincoln in the months ahead tried to blunt its impact, telling Scripps "that whether the clause used by me, will bear such construction or not, I never so intended it." In this passage, he insisted, "I did not say I was in favor of anything. . . . I made a prediction only—it may have been a foolish one perhaps." But he never disavowed it; he knew it was the necessary first premise in his syllogism proving that Douglas should be defeated.

V

When Douglas learned that the Republicans were nominating Lincoln, he recognized that he would be up against a formidable opponent. "I shall have my hands full," he told a newspaperman. "He is as honest as he is shrewd; and if I beat him, my victory will be hardly won." He felt obliged to remain in Washington until he finally succeeded in defeating the Lecompton Constitution, and he stayed on in a vain attempt to prevent the passage of Representative William H. English's face-saving measure, endorsed by the Buchanan administration, providing for a referendum on that constitution, which everyone now recognized would be rejected. In July, Douglas returned home to Chicago and, before a huge outdoor audience, offered an extended reply to Lincoln's charges.

Announcing themes that he would repeat and develop in the coming campaign, Douglas claimed credit for the defeat of Lecompton, which, he said, was a vindication of popular sovereignty. That policy of allowing the people of the states and the territories to choose their own institutions, including slavery, was "dearer to every true American than any other," and any limitation on it would destroy "the fundamental principle of self-government." Referring to Lincoln, who sat on the balcony behind him, as "a kind, amiable, and intelligent gentleman, a good citizen and an honorable opponent," Douglas insisted that he had "totally misapprehended the great principles upon which our government rests" and was advocating "boldly and clearly a war of sections, a war of the North against the South." Continuing with a defense of the Supreme Court, Douglas insisted that Republicans who attacked the Dred Scott decision ignored the fact that "this government of ours is founded on the white basis. It was made by the white man, for the benefit of the white man, to be administered by white men." In advocating equal rights for the Negro, Republicans failed to understand that "any mixture or amalgamation with inferior races" could only lead to "degeneration, demoralization, and degradation." He ended with a fling at the Buchanan administration and the federal officeholders whom it had appointed for entering into "an unholy, unnatural alliance" with the Republicans.

The next night, from the same balcony of the same Chicago hotel, Lincoln replied to Douglas, denouncing his opponent for "quibbling about this . . . race and that race and the other race being inferior" and urging a return to the spirit of the Declaration of Independence, "the electric cord . . . that links the hearts of patriotic and liberty-loving men together . . . as long as the love of freedom exists in the minds of men throughout the world."

The exchange in Chicago set a pattern for the next six weeks of the campaign. When Douglas set out on an extended election tour of the state, Lincoln followed him at most places, often rising at the end of Douglas's speech to announce that he would make a reply, sometimes later in the evening but more often the next day. It was, the *New York Herald* observed, "somewhat of an anomaly for a Senator of the United States to be stumping the State, and another who wishes to be Senator following in his wake."

Lincoln thought that "speaking at the same place the next day after D. is the very thing," but his advisers doubted the wisdom of trailing around after the senator. Judd, Lincoln's unofficial campaign manager for northern Illinois, pointed out that it allowed Douglas constantly to put him on the defensive. A Decatur supporter explained that Douglas's ostentatious arrival attracted crowds from both parties but that only confirmed Republicans remained after the senator left. "In other words," he wrote, "Douglas takes the crowd and Lincoln the leavings." Douglas and his supporters were furious at Lincoln for poaching on the audiences that had assembled to hear him. The *Illinois State Register* claimed that Lincoln did so because he could not attract his own crowds. "Poor, desperate creature," sneered the Democratic *Chicago Times,* "he wants an audience, . . . [and] the people won't turn out to hear him." Perhaps he should join one of the "two very good circuses and menageries traveling through the State," for they always brought out a considerable audience.

Lincoln changed his battle plan after Douglas began devoting more and more time on the stump to attacking Lyman Trumbull, who had accused him of a corrupt bargain in the repeal of the Missouri Compromise. Seeing that this personal quarrel would divert public attention from his own campaign, he proposed a series of debates with Douglas. The senator was reluctant to agree. He had nothing to gain and much to lose by giving public exposure to his lesser-known rival. Lincoln's challenge came too late, he complained; he already had a heavy schedule of speaking appointments and he might also be asked to divide time with a potential third candidate, nominated by Democrats loyal to Buchanan. At the same time, Douglas knew he could not refuse, lest he seem afraid of Lincoln. Grudgingly he consented to participate in seven debates—one in each of the Illinois congressional districts, except the second and sixth (Chicago and Springfield), where the two candidates had already appeared.

The first of the debates would take place at Ottawa, in the north central part of the state, on August 21; the last, at Alton, in the south, along the Mississippi River, on October 15. In between there were to be debates at Freeport, in the extreme north (August 27); at Jonesboro, in the far south (September 15); at Charleston, in the east central region (September 18); at Galesburg, in the northwestern section (October 7); and at Quincy, in the west (October 13). Even though he fussed over details of the arrangements, Lincoln accepted them. His letter gave a rare glimpse of a hard ego that he usually concealed under a guise of humility: he had not challenged Douglas earlier, he explained, because "I did not know but that such proposal would come from you."

VI

Debating with Douglas was not Lincoln's only occupation during the 1858 campaign. With no secretarial staff, no full-time assistants, no designated campaign manager, he had to decide most of the details of the canvass himself. He raised money, reminding friends who had expressed an interest in his prospects that now was the time when help was needed. He tried to plant pro-Republican articles in even such minor newspapers as the *Paris* (Illinois) *Prairie Beacon,* and he supervised the printing and distribution of his campaign speeches, in both German and English. Recognizing how weak the Republicans were in southern Illinois, he joined with Trumbull and five other associates in promising to pay the young German-American newspaperman John G. Nicolay $500 to promote the circulation of the St. Louis *Missouri Democrat*—which, despite its name, was a staunchly Republican organ—in that part of the state.

Much of his time was taken in planning Republican strategy. From the returns in the 1856 election it was fairly clear that the two Republican candidates for general state offices—those of state treasurer and superinten- dent of education—would win. But the success of his own race for the Senate depended on the outcome of nearly a hundred local elections for the state legislature, over which he could exert little direct influence. The Republicans' task was, therefore, formidable, and at times, as Herndon re- ported, Lincoln grew "gloomy—rather uncertain, about his own success."

Rather than lamenting his luck, Lincoln prepared to make the best of the situation. He drew up a careful, detailed list of how the representative and senatorial districts had voted in the previous election and, assuming that the 1856 Fillmore voters would now support Republican candidates, tried to predict how each district would go in 1858. Some, mostly in southern Illi- nois, he wrote off as "desparate," meaning that there was no use wasting Republican resources there; others, chiefly in the north, he marked, "we take to ourselves, without question," so that no campaigning in these coun- ties was needed. He allocated his public appearances accordingly, making only four speeches in the north and only four in the south. The rest of his time he devoted to districts "we must struggle for," mainly in the central part of the state, where the Whig (and more recently the Know Nothing) party had been strongest.

Lincoln found his efforts to woo this old Whig vote frustrating. It was a warning of their disaffection that very few former Whigs participated in the Republican county conventions of 1858. Lincoln attempted to check this defection by stressing his long service to the Whig party and throughout the campaign claimed to wear the mantle of Henry Clay, but Douglas, too, campaigned as the great Kentuckian's successor in advocating sectional com- promise. Lincoln's effort to win over the old-line Whigs was severely dam- aged when Judge T. Lyle Dickey, one of the most prominent Whigs and hitherto a close friend, announced that he would support Douglas; Lincoln, he said, was "too closely allied to the abolitionists." Then Dickey let it leak out that he had a private letter from John J. Crittenden of Kentucky, Clay's political heir in the United States Senate, favoring Douglas. Much troubled, Lincoln wrote Crittenden that though he did not believe this story it made him uneasy. To his dismay, Crittenden responded that he did indeed think that Douglas's reelection was "necessary as a rebuke to the Administration, and a vindication of the great cause of popular rights and public justice."

Along with efforts to keep his own fragile coalition together, Lincoln tried to capitalize on divisions among the Democrats. Despite several attempts at compromise, the break between Douglas and Buchanan persisted, and the President and his Southern advisers resolved to help defeat the Illinois senator, partly out of vindictiveness, partly to demonstrate that Democrats must not rebel against their party leadership. Buchanan began removing Illinois postmasters and other federal officials appointed because of Doug- las's recommendation, replacing them with men known to be inveterate enemies of the senator. He also fostered the creation of a separate National Democratic party in Illinois. Some of these "Danites," as they were derisively called, after an alleged secret order of Mormons who acted as spies to suppress disaffection, openly endorsed Lincoln's election to the Senate; others favored a separate ticket in order to divide the Democratic vote.

Douglas charged that there was a corrupt bargain between these National Democrats and the Republicans, who had nothing in common except a desire to bring about his defeat. In reply to an urgent inquiry from Trumbull, Lincoln replied that, at least as far as he was concerned, there was no alliance with the Buchanan men. To be sure, he was "rather pleased to see a division in the ranks of the democracy" and certainly did nothing to prevent it; but he had made no agreement with them "by which there is to be any concession of principle on either side, or furnishing of the sinews, or partition of offices, or swopping of votes, to any extent." He chose his words carefully, as did Herndon, who also gave assurance that there was not "any contract . . . either express or implied, directly or indirectly," with the Danites.

Though that was literally the truth, it was not the whole truth. Only a few days after Lincoln wrote Trumbull, he met privately with Colonel John Dougherty, the National Democratic candidate for state treasurer, to discuss the election. When Dougherty promised that the National Democrats would field a candidate in every legislative district, Lincoln replied: "If you do this the thing is settled—the battle is fought." In most of his dealing with the Danites, however, Lincoln preferred to keep his hands clean by working through an intermediary. Herndon was one of the best, because his brother, Elliott Herndon, was editor of the *Illinois State Democrat,* the National Democratic newspaper in Springfield, and his father was also a strong supporter of Buchanan. "They make 'no bones' in telling me what they are going to do," Herndon boasted. He understood the importance of keeping Lincoln in the dark about these conversations. As he told Trumbull, "Lincoln . . . does not know the details of how we get along. I do, but he does not."

As the campaign progressed, ties between the Republicans and the National Democrats became even closer. In September so few Danites turned out for their party convention that Republicans had to pack the hall to keep it from becoming a joke. At this meeting, as Jesse Dubois reported to Lincoln, Republicans worked through "your man" to learn the National Democrats' campaign strategy. The underfinanced publisher of the *Illinois State Democrat* told one of his unpaid employees that "he expected $500 of Mr. Lincoln in a day or two"—which may, or may not, have been true.

VII

Lincoln could not stay in his office to manage the campaign because he was constantly in demand as a speaker. Day after day, both Democrats and Republicans held rallies all across the state. Republican foot soldiers were deployed to the smaller gatherings, in schoolhouses and village churches. At larger rallies Republicans often produced out-of-state dignitaries, like Governor Salmon P. Chase of Ohio, Representative Schuyler Colfax from nearby Indiana, and Francis P. (Frank) Blair, Jr., of the prominent border-state political family, who was editor of the influential *St. Louis Democrat.* Democrats felt less need to import speakers, though Representative Clement L. Vallandigham of Ohio made several speeches for Douglas in Illinois.

But Illinois voters wanted to hear the principals, not their surrogates, and both Lincoln and Douglas were almost constantly on the stump. Douglas gave 130 speeches during the campaign, and Lincoln 63, not including short responses to serenaders, remarks to small groups that assembled along the highways, and compliments paid to the standard Republican floats, featuring thirty-two ladies (one for each state, plus Kansas), which almost every village seemed able to produce. In the hundred days before the election Douglas traveled 5,227 miles; and Lincoln, between July and November, covered 4,350 miles—350 by boat, 600 by carriage, and 3,400 by train.

The seven formal debates between Lincoln and Douglas were, therefore, only a small part of the 1858 campaign, though they naturally attracted the greatest interest. All of them followed the same format. The speakers alternated in opening the debate. The opening speaker was allowed an hour for his presentation; his opponent had an hour and a half for reply; and the initial speaker then had a final half hour for rebuttal. Lincoln grumbled that the arrangement allowed Douglas to make four of the opening and closing statements, while he was allowed only three.

As the Republican *New York Times* observed, Illinois in 1858 was "the most interesting political battle-ground in the Union," and newspapers throughout the country offered extensive coverage of the canvass. Local papers, of course, gave it great attention. For the first time reporters were assigned to cover candidates throughout the long campaign season. The *Chicago Press and Tribune,* the most influential Republican paper in the state, sent the skilled shorthand expert Robert R. Hitt to report every word of the debates, and James B. Sheridan and Henry Binmore performed the same service for Douglas's organ, the *Chicago Times.* Though each side accused the other of garbling, mutilating, or revising the speeches, the verbatim reports, which were widely copied and circulated in other newspapers as well, were largely accurate, both in substance and in expression.

Reporters noted how sharply the candidates contrasted in appearance. Douglas, so short that he came up only to Lincoln's shoulder, was a ruddy, stout man, with regular features marred only by a curious horizontal ridge that stretched across the top of his nose, while Lincoln was exceptionally tall and painfully thin, with a melancholy physiognomy and sallow skin. Douglas had a booming, authoritative voice, while Lincoln spoke in a piercing tenor, which at times became shrill and sharp. Douglas used graceful gestures and bowed charmingly when applauded, in contrast to Lincoln, who moved his arms and hands awkwardly and looked like a jackknife folding up when he tried to bow.

There was also a marked contrast in the way the candidates presented themselves to the public. Douglas wished to appear a commanding figure, a statesman of national reputation. Accompanied by his beautiful, regal second wife, Adèle Cutts, he usually traveled by special train, splendidly fitted out for comfort and for entertaining. When he stood on the platform in his handsome new blue suit with silver buttons and in his immaculate linen, he was unquestionably a great United States senator reporting to his loyal constituents. Lincoln deliberately cultivated a different image. When he went by train, he traveled in the regular passenger cars—a practice that afforded him endless opportunities for meeting the voters and talking about their concerns. Except at the final debate in Alton, Mary Lincoln did not accompany him; it was not part of the persona he was projecting to display his elegantly dressed wife with her aristocratic bearing. Lincoln took pains to wear his everyday clothes during the debates, appearing usually in what Carl Schurz, the German-American leader, who campaigned for the Republican ticket, described as "a rusty black frock-coat with sleeves that should have been longer" and black trousers that "permitted a very full view of his large feet."

From time to time, Lincoln tried to capitalize on the differences between Douglas's appearance and his own. The senator's followers, he said, anticipated that their leader at no distant day would become President and saw in his "round, jolly, fruitful face" promises of "postoffices, landoffices, marshalships, and cabinet appointments, chargeships and foreign missions, bursting and sprouting out in wonderful exuberance," while in Lincoln's "poor, lean, lank, face" nobody ever saw "that any cabbages were sprouting out," because "nobody has ever expected me to be President." There was nothing false about all this; Lincoln was in fact a homely man with simple tastes, indifferent to personal comfort. It was important in this contest to present himself to the voters not as a man of considerable means and one of the most prominent lawyers in the state but as a countryman, shrewd and incorruptible.

VIII

The opening debate at Ottawa, a town of about 9,000 inhabitants some eighty miles southwest of Chicago, attracted 10,000 people, who came in on foot, by horseback or carriage, and even on Illinois River canal boats. A special train of seventeen cars brought visitors from Chicago, and another of eleven cars came from Peru and La Salle. Lincoln arrived about noon on the special train from Chicago and was greeted by Ottawa mayor Joseph O. Glover. Seated in a carriage that, according to the *Chicago Press and Tribune,* was "beautifully decorated with evergreens and mottoes by the young ladies of

Ottawa," he was escorted by a procession of military companies and brass bands, which stretched out for half a mile, to the public square and then to Mayor Glover's house. At about the same time a rival crowd went out to meet Douglas, who rode in from Peru in a handsome carriage drawn by four spirited horses.

By one o'clock people began moving into Lafayette Square, where the speaking was to take place, and there was considerable jostling for the best positions. There were no seats, and the audience had to remain standing for the entire three hours. Some "clowns" climbed upon the roof of the hastily built speakers' stand, the newspapers reported, and their weight broke through the boards, which fell on the unsuspecting heads of members of the reception committee. Fortunately order was restored in time for Douglas to begin speaking at two-thirty.

The ferocity of Douglas's opening statement apparently startled Lincoln. The senator intended to demonstrate that he was, as Lincoln had said, a lion —and very much a living lion, with sharp teeth. Announcing his major theme, which he would pursue throughout the campaign, the senator bluntly charged that Lincoln and Trumbull had since 1854 been conspiring to subvert both the Democratic and the Whig parties in order to create "an Abolition party, under the name and disguise of a Republican party." As evidence of this intent, he adduced a radical antislavery platform, which he said had been adopted in 1854 at the first state convention of the Republican party in Springfield and which Lincoln had presumably endorsed. Like a prosecuting attorney pinning down a reluctant witness, he demanded to know whether Lincoln still stood on this platform. Did Lincoln now, as in 1854, favor the unconditional repeal of the Fugitive Slave Act? Did he oppose the admission of more slave states to the Union? Was he opposed to the admission of a new state "with such a Constitution as the people of that State may see fit to make"? Did he support the abolition of slavery in the District of Columbia? Was he pledged to end the interstate slave trade? Did he wish to prohibit slavery in all the national territories? Did he oppose the acquisition of additional territory unless slavery was prohibited in it? Lincoln, he charged, was in favor of suppressing self-government and imposing uniformity on the different states, a policy "never dreamed of by Washington, Madison, or the framers of this Government."

How to reply bewildered Lincoln. At his best when he had time carefully to think through his ideas and revise his phrasing, he was clearly uncomfortable in debate format, which required extemporaneous speaking and swift rearrangement of arguments to meet the opponent's charges. Rather stumblingly he declared that he had had nothing to do with the 1854 resolutions Douglas had read and that his name had been used in connection with them without his authority. To establish that his true position on slavery was a very moderate one, he read at great length from his 1854 Peoria speech, in which he had announced that, given all earthly power, he would not know what to do about ending slavery.

Lincoln rushed through his speech, failing to use much of the time allotted to him. He had difficulty striking exactly the right tone. At times he
resorted to worn clichés of humor, calling Douglas's misrepresentations of
his views on race an example of that "specious and fantastic arrangement of
words, by which a man can prove a horse-chestnut to be a chestnut horse."
He lapsed into legal language that must have been all but incomprehensible
to his audience. Because Douglas had not denied the charge that he was
part of a proslavery conspiracy, Lincoln said, "in the language of the lawyers,
. . . I took a default on him." Then when Douglas did produce a belated
denial, Lincoln continued: "I demur to that plea. I waive all objections that
it was not filed till after default was taken, and demur to it upon the merits."
He declined to give immediate answers to Douglas's questions, even though
his position on all these issues had been firmly established for years; his
native caution was so great that he delayed his response until the next
debate, declaring: "I do not mean to allow him to catechise me unless he
pays back for it in kind."

After Douglas's rebuttal most in the audience hunted up any missing
members of the family and made a break for home, where the horses had
to be watered and the cattle fed. More dedicated partisans gathered around
to congratulate the rival candidates. As Douglas left the stand, according to
the partisan *Illinois State Register,* "nearly the entire crowd pressed around
him, and the living mass, with shouts and hurras bore him, in their midst, to
the hotel, the cheering and shouting being kept up incessantly." Lincoln's
partisans were equally enthusiastic, and, in what proved to be an unfortunate
effort to show approval, a dozen or so sturdy Republicans put him on their
shoulders and, preceded by a band, carried him to the mayor's house. He
was clearly uncomfortable, and the hostile reporter Henry Villard thought it
was a ludicrous sight to see Lincoln's "grotesque figure holding frantically
on to the heads of his supporters," while his legs were "dangling from their
shoulders, and his pantaloons pulled up so as to expose his underwear
almost to his knees."

Some of Lincoln's friends feared that he had exposed more than that at
the Ottawa debate. A few, like Richard Yates, reported that they were *"well
satisfied"* with his performance, and Lincoln himself was reasonably content
with the outcome, reporting the next day, "The fire flew some, and I am
glad to know I am yet alive." But most of his advisers thought he had not
been sufficiently forceful or aggressive. Ray, about to leave on a business
trip to New York, enjoined Congressman Washburne: "When you see Abe at
Freeport, for God's sake tell him to 'Charge Chester! Charge!' Do not let him
keep on the defensive." Joseph Medill, of the same newspaper, also urged
Lincoln to change his tactics. "Dont act on the *defensive* at all," he urged.
"Dont refer to your past speeches or positions, . . . but hold Dug up as a
traitor and conspirator a proslavery bamboozelling demogogue."

On reflection, Lincoln himself was sufficiently worried about his performance at Ottawa to call a kind of summit meeting of his advisers to discuss

how he should respond to Douglas's interrogatories. Gathering in Chicago on August 26, they called for a reconsideration of Lincoln's campaign strategy, and Medill, reporting for his colleagues, told Lincoln that he should "put a few ugly questions" of his own to Douglas the next day, at Freeport.

IX

At Freeport, Lincoln was clearly more in charge than he had been at Ottawa, only a week earlier. Before this sympathetic "vast audience as strongly tending to Abolitionism as any audience in the State of Illinois," he turned first to answering the interrogatories Douglas had posed at Ottawa. His answers contained no surprises: He was not in favor of repeal of the Fugitive Slave Act. He did not "stand pledged" against the admission of additional slave states to the Union (though he would be "exceedingly sorry" to have to pass on that question) nor against the admission of a new state with whatever constitution its inhabitants might see fit to make. He did not "stand to-day pledged" to the abolition of slavery in the District of Columbia (but he would be very glad to see it accomplished) or the prohibition of the interstate slave trade (though he admitted that he had not thought much about this subject). He was, on the other hand, "impliedly, if not expressly, pledged" to prohibit slavery in all federal territories. As to acquiring additional territory, he "would or would not oppose such acquisition," depending on whether it "would nor would not aggravate the slavery question among ourselves."

Then, finally taking the offensive, he posed to Douglas four questions of his own—four questions that were much like those that his Chicago advisers had recommended. First, would Douglas favor the admission of Kansas before it had the requisite number of inhabitants, as specified in the English bill? Second, could "the people of a United States Territory, in any lawful way, . . . exclude slavery from its limits prior to the formation of a State Constitution?" Third, would Douglas acquiesce in and follow a decision of the Supreme Court declaring that states could not exclude slavery from their limits? Finally, did he favor acquisition of additional territory "in disregard of how such acquisition may affect the nation on the slavery question?"

The second was the key question. Though advisers like Medill urged him to raise it, Lincoln had hesitated before asking it. He was in no doubt about how Douglas would answer; and, just as he expected, Douglas promptly replied that the passage of "unfriendly legislation" could keep slavery out of any territory because "slavery cannot exist a day or an hour anywhere, unless it is supported by local police regulations." Consequently—as "Mr. Lincoln has heard me answer a hundred times from every stump in Illinois" —"the people of a Territory can, by lawful means, exclude slavery from their limits prior to the formation of a State Constitution." Though Lincoln predicted this reply, which became known as the Freeport Doctrine, he thought it important to have Douglas state it explicitly; otherwise, as he wrote a friend, it would be "hard work to get him directly to the point." As long as Douglas could fudge the issue, he could pretend that he was loyal to the national party and even to the national administration. But when he was forced to make his position clear, he would further outrage President Buchanan and his advisers, who believed that the Dred Scott decision had killed popular sovereignty, and his stand would widen the division between Douglas Democrats and the Danites in Illinois. But by showing how greatly at odds Douglas was with the National Democracy, Lincoln risked undermining his basic argument that Douglas was part of a broad conspiracy to extend and perpetuate slavery. Nevertheless, pressed to take the offensive and realizing that this question might rattle his opponent, Lincoln decided to include the question.

Then, taking advantage of the research that Herndon and others had done for him in the Springfield newspapers, Lincoln dropped his bombshell. The abolition resolutions that Douglas had so elaborately read at Ottawa, which Lincoln allegedly endorsed, were not, as it turned out, ever adopted by any group in Springfield, much less at any meeting that Lincoln attended; they were passed by a convention or public meeting in Kane County. Indignantly Lincoln announced that it was *"most extraordinary"* that Douglas "should so far forget all the suggestions of justice to an adversary, or of prudence to himself, as to venture upon the assertion [concerning these resolutions] . . . which the slightest investigation would have shown him to be wholly false."

The revelation momentarily disconcerted Douglas, but he was such a skilled debater that he quickly recovered. Using diversionary tactics, he charged that Lincoln was avoiding either endorsing or repudiating these abolitionist resolutions by claiming that the platform had not been adopted "on the right 'spot,' " and that gave him an opportunity to attack Lincoln's "spot" resolutions criticizing the Mexican War. Sensing that this tactic was failing, he provoked the audience by repeatedly calling them "Black Republicans." When they began chanting "White, white" every time he used the phrase, he denounced them, announcing proudly, "I have seen your mobs before, and defy your wrath."

Nearly everyone agreed that Lincoln made a stronger showing at Freeport than in the first debate, and his devoted supporters, like Herndon, were convinced that "so far Lincoln has the decided advantage" in the contest. One distant admirer, a writer in the *Lowell* (Massachusetts) *Journal and Courier* even announced that Lincoln's speeches were so telling that people were "now calculating his fitness and chances for a more elevated position." But Washburne, a more objective reporter, found after the Freeport debate that "neither party was fully satisfied with the speeches, and the meeting broke up without any display of enthusiasm." In a confidential letter Medill confessed that Lincoln was not Douglas's equal on the stump and predicted the senator would be reelected. Nearly all the Republicans felt relieved that

Lyman Trumbull, who was considered a better speaker and had a wider reputation than Lincoln, had returned from Washington to assist the Republican cause.

X

Lincoln knew he was at a disadvantage in the third debate, at Jonesboro, an isolated town of 842 inhabitants in Union County, in the extreme southern part of the state. Settled by Southerners who had migrated chiefly from Kentucky and Tennessee, "Egypt" was solidly Democratic and overwhelmingly negrophobic. Rural, mostly poor, and relatively untouched by commercial ambition, voters in Union County had little use for the Republican party and its candidate. Fewer than 2,000 listeners attended the debate.

Lincoln and Douglas rehashed the issues they had raised in the previous debates, developing few ideas and adding little new information. Furious that Trumbull, that "excrescence from the rotten bowels of the Democracy," was now taking such a prominent part in the campaign, Douglas renewed his charge that Lincoln and Trumbull had conspired to abolitionize both parties in Illinois, and he now added, in the hope of dividing his opponents, the accusation that Trumbull in the 1855 election had "played a Yankee trick" on Lincoln, in order to secure his own, rather than Lincoln's, election to the Senate that year. Then, in an effort to goad Lincoln into responding, he elaborated on some of the racist charges he had made earlier in the campaign, announcing that "the signers of the Declaration [of Independence] had no reference to the negro whatever, when they declared all men to be created equal."

Shrewdly Lincoln refused to be baited. He knew there was no possibility of persuading this audience ("very few of whom are my political friends," he noted), and he avoided the issue of equal rights for Negroes. Much of his time he devoted to attacking Douglas's Freeport Doctrine, which threatened the credibility of Lincoln's charge that the senator was engaged in a conspiracy to expand slavery. Lincoln insisted that Douglas's claim that slavery could not enter a new territory without police protection was "historically false," for there was "vigor enough in slavery to plant itself in a new country even against unfriendly legislation."

At Charleston, three days later, he was on more hospitable ground. Many in Coles County had known Thomas Lincoln and his family, and some enthusiasts spread a gigantic painting, eighty feet long, across the main street, showing OLD ABE THIRTY YEARS AGO, on a Kentucky wagon pulled by three yoke of oxen. Democrats countered with a banner, captioned "Negro Equality," which depicted a white man standing with a Negro woman, and a mulatto boy in the background. Republicans found this so offensive that they tore it down before allowing the debate to begin.

Lincoln picked up on that theme in his opening remarks. He had, he said, recently been approached by an elderly man who wanted to know whether he was in favor of perfect equality between blacks and whites. This probably hypothetical inquiry gave him the opportunity to make his views explicit in a community where conservative old Whigs were strong. "I am not, nor ever have been, in favor of bringing about in any way the social and political equality of the white and black races," he announced. "I am not nor ever have been in favor of making voters or jurors of negroes, nor of qualifying them to hold office, nor to intermarry with white people." "There is a physical difference between the white and black races which I believe will forever forbid the two races living together on terms of social and political equality," he went on to add.

This was a politically expedient thing to say in a state where the majority of the inhabitants were of Southern origin; perhaps it was a necessary thing to say in a state where only ten years earlier 70 percent of the voters had favored a constitutional amendment to exclude all blacks from Illinois. It also represented Lincoln's deeply held personal views, which he had repeatedly expressed before. Opposed to slavery throughout his life, he had given little thought to the status of free African-Americans. Unlike many of his contemporaries, he was not personally hostile to blacks; indeed, Frederick Douglass remarked on "his entire freedom from popular prejudice against the colored race." But he did not know whether they could ever fit into a free society, and, rather vaguely, he continued to think of colonization as the best solution to the American race problem.

Turning from this subject abruptly, Lincoln inexplicably devoted most of his Charleston opening speech to endorsing a charge, originally made by Trumbull, that Douglas, despite his protestations of opposition to the Lecompton Constitution, had really been part of a plot to impose slavery on Kansas. The story was intricate and confusing, involving secret proceedings in Senate committees and parliamentary maneuvering in the Senate itself, and Douglas had flatly announced that Trumbull's evidence for the alleged plot "was forged from beginning to end." Unwilling to see Trumbull calumniated, Lincoln now leapt to his defense with a tedious and unconvincing review of the charge.

Douglas expressed amazement that Lincoln had spent nearly his entire time on this discredited issue. Rather petulantly he asked: "Why, I ask, does not Mr. Lincoln make a speech of his own instead of taking up his time reading Trumbull's speech?" Scornfully he declared, "I thought I was running against Abraham Lincoln, that he claimed to be my opponent." It was, he concluded, "unbecoming the dignity of a canvass" to spend time on "these petty personal matters."

XI

After Charleston, the lowest point in his campaign, Lincoln made a splendid recovery in the final three engagements with Douglas. The debate at Galesburg, which took place on the campus of Knox College, attracted one of the largest crowds, and in this antislavery area, heavily settled by Scandinavians, the audience was enthusiastic for the Republican candidate. Douglas, who was clearly tiring in the protracted campaign and was beginning to lose his voice, gave his standard speech, defending his unfailing fidelity in support-ing the right of self-government and bitterly attacking the "unholy and unnat-ural combination" of Republicans and National Democrats against him. Lincoln, he claimed, was a political chameleon, advocating "bold and radical Abolitionism" in the extreme northern part of Illinois but professing in the central and southern counties to be "an old line Whig, a disciple of Henry Clay"; at Chicago, Lincoln announced his belief in Negro equality, but at Charleston, he declared that there must be a superior and an inferior race. By contrast, Douglas asserted, his own views were clear and fixed. He knew that the authors of the Declaration of Independence never intended to include the Negro and that "this Government was made by our fathers on the white basis . . . made by white men for the benefit of white men and their posterity forever."

In his reply Lincoln was in good voice and in high spirits; he seemed to thrive on campaigning rather than being exhausted from it. Sensing that his audience was on his side, he appeared almost joyful as he rebutted Douglas's charges, most of which, he noted, had "previously been delivered and put in print." Douglas had been guilty of slandering the Founding Fathers, for "the entire records of the world, from the date of the Declaration of Inde-pendence up to within three years ago, may be searched in vain for one single affirmation, from one single man, that the negro was not included in the Declaration of Independence." Similarly he had misrepresented Lin-coln's views on race, because there was no conflict whatever between his view that it was impossible to produce perfect social and political equality between black and white races and his insistence that "the inferior races" were equal in their right to life, liberty, and the pursuit of happiness. He taunted Douglas on his repeated failure to repudiate the alleged Republican resolutions of 1854, which he had tried ever since the Ottawa debate to attach to Lincoln. In constantly reusing this "stale fraud" he was like "the fisherman's wife, whose drowned husband was brought home with his body full of eels." Said she "when she was asked, 'What was to be done with him?' *'Take the eels out and set him again.'* "

Then, becoming serious, he again charged ("without questioning motives at all") that Douglas was part of a plan to make slavery national. To do this Douglas was willing to distort history and to rewrite the story of the Ameri-can Revolution; he was "going back to the era of our liberty and indepen-dence, and, so far as in him lies, muzzling the cannon that thunders its annual joyous return." "He is blowing out the moral lights around us," Lincoln continued, borrowing a phrase from Henry Clay; "he is . . . eradicat-ing the light of reason and the love of liberty" in order to perpetuate slavery. Soon he would even extend it by making "a grab for the territory of poor

Mexico, an invasion of the rich lands of South America, then the adjoining islands."

At Quincy, a week later, each candidate went over the familiar arguments, and neither introduced many new ideas. Not until nearly the end of Lincoln's opening speech did he again state what he believed was the fundamental issue of the campaign: "the difference between the men who think slavery a wrong and those who do not think it wrong." Republicans believed that it was "a moral, a social and a political wrong," and wanted to limit its spread. The Democratic party, on the other hand, did not think slavery was a wrong, and Douglas, its "leading man," had "the high distinction, so far as I know, of never having said slavery is either right or wrong."

Douglas, in reply, defended his record and once again charged that Lincoln held "one set of principles in the Abolition counties, and a different and contradictory set in the other counties." He called the Dred Scott decision one from which "there is no appeal this side of Heaven," and charged that Lincoln was stirring up opposition to the Supreme Court and "stimulating the passions of men to resort to violence and to mobs instead of to the law." In the only new gambit in the debate, he suggested that Lincoln's plan to contain slavery was really genocidal, because it meant confining slaves to land where they could not support themselves; thus by putting slavery on the course of ultimate extinction he really meant "extinguishing the negro race." "This," he gibed, "is the humane and Christian remedy that he proposes for the great crime of slavery." Earnestly Douglas besought his listeners to return to the basic principle of self-government. If they recognized, as the fathers of the nation had always recognized, that "this Republic can exist forever divided into free and slave States," Americans could get on with their "great mission" of "filling up our prairies, clearing our wildernesses and building cities, towns, railroads and other internal improvements, and thus make this the asylum of the oppressed of the whole earth."

Lincoln in his rebuttal seized upon Douglas's admission that his "system of policy in regard to the institution of slavery *contemplates that it shall last forever.*" That, he said, proved what he had been arguing all along about the Democratic candidate.

XII

On the day after the Quincy debate, both Lincoln and Douglas got aboard the *City of Louisiana* and sailed down the Mississippi River to Alton, for the final encounter of the campaign. Looking haggard with fatigue, Douglas opened the debate on October 15 in a voice so hoarse that in the early part of his speech he could scarcely be heard. After briefly reviewing the standard arguments over which he and Lincoln had differed since the beginning of the campaign, he made the peculiar decision to devote most of his speech to a detailed defense of his course on Lecompton. He concluded with a rabble-rousing attack on the racial views he attributed to Republicans and an announcement "that the signers of the Declaration of Independence . . . did not mean negro, nor the savage Indians, nor the Fejee Islanders, nor any other barbarous race," when they issued that document.

In his reply Lincoln said he was happy to ignore Douglas's long account of his feud with the Buchanan administration; he felt like the put-upon wife in an old jestbook, who stood by as her husband struggled with a bear, saying, "Go it, husband!—Go it bear!" Once again he went through his standard answers to Douglas's charges against him and the Republican party. Recognizing that at Alton he was addressing "an audience, having strong sympathies southward by relationship, place of birth, and so on," he tried to explain why it was so important to keep slavery out of Kansas and other national territories. This was land needed "for an outlet for our surplus population"; this was land where "white men may find a home"; this was "an outlet for *free white people every where,* the world over—in which Hans and Baptiste and Patrick, and all other men from all the world, may find new homes and better their conditions in life."

And that brought him again to what he perceived as "the real issue in this controversy," which once more he defined as a conflict "on the part of one class that looks upon the institution of slavery *as a wrong,* and of another class that *does not* look upon it as a wrong." Rising to the oratorical high point in the entire series of debates, he told the Alton audience: "That is the issue that will continue in this country when these poor tongues of Judge Douglas and myself shall be silent. It is the eternal struggle between these two principles—right and wrong—throughout the world. They are the two principles that have stood face to face from the beginning of time; and will ever continue to struggle. The one is the common right of humanity and the other the divine right of kings."

With a brief rejoinder by Douglas, the debates were ended. After that both candidates made a few more speeches to local rallies, but everybody realized that the campaign was over, and the decision now lay with the voters.

XIII

It was hard to predict what that decision would be. Even an extremely conscientious citizen who made a point of attending all seven debates—or, more probably, a voter who attended one of the debates and read the detailed accounts the newspaper carried of the other six—might find it hard to make up his mind. In terms of debating skills he would have to judge the two speakers as about equal, Douglas giving a much more impressive performance at the start but Lincoln gaining in fluency and flexibility as the campaign progressed. Neither speaker exhibited the purest debating technique, enunciating a position, logically developing its implications, and systematically refuting the arguments of his opponent.

"THE RAILSPLITTER"

This 1860 life-sized oil painting, by an unknown artist, suggests the mythic qualities that helped elect Lincoln President. Forgotten here are Lincoln's highly successful law practice and his career in politics in order to stress, in a frontier setting, the homely virtues of physical strength and hard manual labor.

Sarah Bush (Johnston) Lincoln (1788–1869). Lincoln's stepmother was one of the most powerful influences in his life. In her old age, when this photograph was taken, she recalled: "Abe was a good boy. . . . His mind and mine, what little I had, seemed to run together . . . in the same channel."

Meserve-Kunhardt Collection

Mary Lincoln, around 1846. This is the earliest daguerreotype of Mrs. Lincoln, made, as she said, "when we were young and so desperately in love."

The Library of Congress

Abraham Lincoln, around 1846. Made at the same time as the portrait of Mary Lincoln, this daguerreotype was probably the work of N. H. Shepherd, one of the first photographers in Springfield, Illinois.

John Todd Stuart

Stephen T. Logan

The Lincoln & Herndon Law Office. This unusually tidy view was sketched after the senior partner had been elected President.

LINCOLN'S LAW PARTNERS

L. C. Handy Studios

William H. Herndon

Courtesy of the Illinois State Historical Library, Springfield

Lincoln at the age of forty-five. Taken in Chicago in 1854, this daguerreotype by Polycarp von Schneidau shows Lincoln as he reappeared on the political stage to fight the Kansas-Nebraska Act.

Chicago Historical Society

The Lincoln Museum, Fort Wayne, Indiana (#2149)

An 1860 photograph of the Lincoln House at Eighth and Jackson Streets in Springfield, Illinois, which was almost doubled in size after renovation in the 1850s. Lincoln and Tad stand just inside the fence.

ILLINOIS POLITICAL ADVISERS

Orville Hickman Browning

David Davis

Lyman Trumbull

Stephen A. Douglas

RIVALS IN THE GREAT DEBATES OF 1858

Abraham Lincoln

The President-elect
grows a beard.
In response to sugges-
tions by Grace Bedell and
others, Lincoln decided to
let his whiskers grow. By
the time he posed
for this photograph
in Chicago on
November 25, 1860,
he had a half beard.

Lincoln's disguise on his
night trip from Harrisburg
to Washington. To avoid a
threatened assassination
plot, Lincoln made a secret
night trip through Baltimore
on February 23, 1861, on
his way to the national
capital for his inauguration.
Cartoonists had a field day
with his supposed
disguise in a Scottish kilt
and tam.

"THE MacLINCOLN HARRISBURG
HIGHLAND FLING"

TWO CABINET RIVALS

William H. Seward,
Secretary of State

Salmon P. Chase,
Secretary of the Treasury

FOUR GENERALS
WHO CAUSED
LINCOLN
PROBLEMS

General Winfield Scott

General John C. Frémont

General Irvin McDowell

General Henry W. Halleck

Courtesy of the Illinois State Historical Library, Springfield

William Wallace ("Willie") Lincoln
(1850–1862)

Meserve-Kunhardt Collection

Thomas ("Tad") Lincoln
(1853–1871) and his father

Chicago Historical Society

Robert Todd Lincoln (1843–1926)

Mary Lincoln dressed for a ball. The only profile photograph of Mrs. Lincoln, probably taken in 1861, shows her love for beautiful clothing and her fondness for floral headdresses.

The Lincolns' White House reception, February 5, 1862. This was the most elaborate entertainment ever offered by the Lincolns. Upstairs, Willie Lincoln was desperately ill.

LINCOLN RECEIVES A
DELEGATION OF PLAINS INDIANS

On March 27, 1863, Lincoln received chiefs of the Cheyenne, Arapaho, Comanche, Apache, and other Western tribes in the East Room and promised to maintain peace "with all our red brethren."

If the Indian chiefs were not entirely reassured by Lincoln's promise, it was perhaps because they remembered that in the previous year General John Pope had ruthlessly put down an insurrection among the Sioux in Minnesota.

LINCOLN'S OFFICE IN
THE WHITE HOUSE

Lincoln's office was on the second floor of the White House, in the East Wing. The painting over the fireplace is of Andrew Jackson. This sketch was drawn by C. K. Stellwagen in October 1864.

Lincoln and his secretaries. John G. Nicolay is seated to Lincoln's right, while John Hay is standing.

General George B. McClellan

Meserve-Kunhardt Collection

Lincoln visits McClellan's headquarters after Antietam. Baffled by McClellan's inexplicable reluctance to advance after defeating Lee's army at Antietam, Lincoln visited the headquarters of the Army of the Potomac.

"A PRACTICAL REMINDER"
Colonel David H. Strother's
cartoon captured the impatience
felt by Lincoln and many other
Northerners at McClellan's
slowness in advancing on the
Confederate capital of Richmond.

Charles Sumner

THREE REPUBLICAN RADICALS WHO PUSHED LINCOLN TOWARD EMANCIPATION

Horace Greeley

Frederick Douglass

"FIRST READING OF THE EMANCIPATION PROCLAMATION OF PRESIDENT LINCOLN"

This engraving, made from Francis B. Carpenter's huge oil painting completed in 1864, shows the President reading the draft of his Emancipation Proclamation to members of the cabinet. On the left are Edward M. Stanton (seated) and Salmon P. Chase; William H. Seward is seated in front of the table, and Gideon Welles, Caleb B. Smith, Montgomery Blair, and Edward Bates are behind it. A parchment copy of the Constitution lies on the cabinet table, and a painting of Andrew Jackson is faintly visible through the chandelier.

"ABRAHAM LINCOLN WRITING THE EMANCIPATION PROCLAMATION"

This chromolithograph, made from an oil painting by David Gilmour Blythe in 1863, depicts a homespun Lincoln (his rail-splitter's maul is in the foreground) who has pushed aside the state-rights theories of John C. Calhoun and John Randolph and has carelessly allowed a bust of James Buchanan to hang from the bookcase, while he rests his hand on the Holy Bible and heeds the injunction of Andrew Jackson: "The Union Must & Shall be Preserved."

The Lincoln Museum, Fort Wayne, Indiana (#3252)

TWO VIEWS OF THE EMANCIPATION PROCLAMATION

"WRITING THE EMANCIPATION PROCLAMATION"
Adalbert Johann Volck's 1864 etching gives the Copperhead
version of the same event, showing Lincoln, with his foot on
the Constitution, writing with a pen dipped in the devil's
inkstand. On the wall one painting depicts John Brown as a
saint and another shows the atrocities that followed a slave
insurrection in Santo Domingo.

Because he was so tall, Lincoln did not like standing for a portrait, but this full-length photograph, made by one of Mathew Brady's assistants in April 1863, shows a poised and surprisingly youthful President.

THE PRESIDENTIAL CAMPAIGN OF 1864

Meserve-Kunhardt Collection

"THIS REMINDS ME OF A LITTLE JOKE"
This cartoon, from *Harper's Weekly* of
September 17, 1864, suggests how insignificant
McClellan's candidacy seemed in the weeks
before the presidential election.

Chicago Historical Society

Lincoln's 1864 running mate,
Andrew Johnson

The Lincoln Museum, Fort Wayne, Indiana (#1942)

**"LONG ABRAHAM LINCOLN
A LITTLE LONGER"**
Harper's Weekly of November 26,
1864, indicates how the presidential
election enhanced Lincoln's stature.

General Ulysses S. Grant

"THE PEACE MAKERS"

As the war drew to a close, Lincoln visited Grant's army in Virginia, and there, aboard the *River Queen,* he conferred with Grant, W. T. Sherman, who came up from North Carolina, and Admiral David D. Porter about the terms for ending the fighting. This painting by George P. A. Healy, which hangs in the White House, was one of President George Bush's favorites.

Taken by Alexander Gardner in Washington on November 8, 1863, this profile view shows how Lincoln had matured as President into a benign, self-assured leader who (despite the admonitions of the photographer to make absolutely no movement) dared venture a small smile.

LINCOLN ENTERS THE CITY OF RICHMOND, APRIL 4, 1865

This engraving, published in 1866, shows Lincoln, accompanied by Tad, as he ventured into the capital of the Confederacy escorted by only a handful of Marines. He received a boisterous welcome from the former slaves, but most white Virginians remained behind closed windows.

Abraham Lincoln, February 5, 1865. The weariness in this portrait by Alexander Gardner reveals how much the overwork and anxiety of four years of war had cost Lincoln.

John Wilkes Booth

"THE LAST OFFER OF RECONCILIATION" This 1865 lithograph, by Kimmel & Forster, imagines a scene in which Lincoln, backed by Seward, Stanton, Grant, and other Union officers, stretches out the hand of friendship to Jefferson Davis and Robert E. Lee. The goddess of Liberty looks on approvingly, while an African-American rejoices in his new freedom. Though the scene is entirely fictitious, it captures the generous spirit that animated Lincoln's Reconstruction policies.

The voter would have to give both Lincoln and Douglas passing marks for observing the amenities of debate, though there was a certain amount of horseplay. Douglas claimed that in his New Salem days Lincoln "could ruin more liquor than all the boys of the town together"—a charge that was not merely inaccurate but singularly inappropriate from a senator known to have a fondness for drink—and Lincoln jeered that Douglas's popular-sovereignty doctrine was "as thin as the homeopathic soup that was made by boiling the shadow of a pigeon that had starved to death." But on the whole both men behaved with propriety. In the early debates Douglas made a point of complimenting Lincoln's intelligence and ability, even while strongly disagreeing with his policies. Lincoln professed to be rather taken by the flattery, "especially coming from so great a man as Douglas," and said he was not used to it. "I was rather like the Hoosier, with the gingerbread, when he said he reckoned he loved it better than any other man, and got less of it." But he notably did not reciprocate by complimenting Douglas; he found it hard to tell even a white lie.

The informed Illinois voter would note, of course, that there was an enormous amount of repetition from one debate to another. Douglas used the same basic speech, with minor modifications, throughout the campaign; as Lincoln remarked, the senator's "successive speeches are substantially one and the same." Though more varied, Lincoln's speeches frequently included long quoted passages from his previous addresses, and in several of the debates he employed almost identical paragraphs or passages.

There was no evidence that any considerable number of voters were concerned that the Lincoln-Douglas debates concentrated almost exclusively on questions relating to slavery. The speakers could have discussed other serious issues of great importance to a country just emerging from the panic of 1857: regulation of banks, revision of tariffs, control of immigration, provision of homesteads for farmers, improvement of the lot of factory workers, and so on and on. But the debaters focused on none of these because they, and the Illinois voters, felt that the major concern of the country was the present condition and future prospects of the institution of slavery.

By concentrating on slavery, Lincoln and Douglas naturally exaggerated their differences. In a less combative arena they would have found much on which they could agree. For instance, both men disliked slavery; Lincoln openly deplored it and Douglas privately regretted its existence. Both denounced the Lecompton Constitution as a fraud and wanted Kansas to become a free state; indeed, that question had effectively been settled just before the debates began when Kansas voters on August 2 by a vote of 11,300 to 1,788 rejected the Lecompton Constitution, even with the incentives of a large land grant and the promise of early admission offered by the English bill. Neither man favored a slave code to protect slavery in the national territories, and neither would contemplate the extension of slavery into the free states. So numerous were their points of agreement, Lincoln candidly admitted at Jonesboro, that there was "very much in the principles that Judge Douglas has here enunciated that I most cordially approve, and over which I shall have no controversy with him."

But, of course, these were debates, not love feasts, and both men felt a need to stress the differences, real and imaginary, that divided them. Many of these were entirely immaterial to the 1858 senate race. For instance, Douglas's repeated accusation that Lincoln had failed to support his country during the Mexican War had no conceivable bearing on the present contest, nor did his elaborate attempts to show that Trumbull had been guilty of "the most infamous treachery" in helping to defeat Lincoln's election to the Senate in 1855. It was hard to understand why Lincoln's tedious account of Trumbull's charges against Douglas or Douglas's wearisome report of his differences with Buchanan had any place in this canvass.

Even the larger issues, over which the candidates did profoundly disagree, often had little practical relevance to this election. For example, the controversy over whether the framers of the Declaration of Independence intended to include blacks in announcing that all men are created equal dealt with an interesting, if ultimately unresolvable, historiographical problem, but it was not easy to see just what it had to do with the choice of a senator for Illinois in 1858. And the heated arguments over the capacity and the future of the Negro race, with related controversies over social and political equality of the races, while showing fundamental philosophical differences between the two candidates, did not deal with any issue or legislation that was, or was likely to be, under consideration by the Congress of the United States. Many Illinois voters must have understood Douglas's exasperated query at the Charleston debate: "What question of public policy, relating to the welfare of this State or the Union, has Mr. Lincoln discussed before you?" But many must also have understood that the same objection could be raised, with equal force, against Douglas himself.

Lincoln's friends thought he took a clear lead in the final three debates when he stressed the moral issue of slavery, and it was hard to resist the force of his argument. Douglas could only counter by showing that Lincoln's position was entirely negative: Lincoln was against slavery, but he offered no suggestion as to how it was to be placed "in a course of ultimate extinction."

For Douglas the fundamental issue in the debates was self-government. In his mind, the right of Americans, whether in the individual states or in the territories, to determine their own form of government and their own social institutions—including slavery, if they so desired—was a moral question, more basic than even the one Lincoln raised. In his final rebuttal in the last debate he once more made his view explicit. "I care more for the great principle of self-government, the right of the people to rule," he told listeners at Alton, "than I do for all the negroes in Christendom."

With the basic differences so formulated, well-informed Illinois voters understood that what was at stake was not just the choice between two candidates or political parties; it was a choice between two fundamentally opposed views of the meaning of the American experience. One way to formulate that difference was to see Douglas as the advocate of majority rule and Lincoln as the defender of minority rights. In Douglas's view there were virtually no limits on what the majority of the people of a state or a territory could do—including, if they so chose, holding black-skinned inhabitants in slavery. While Lincoln also valued self-government and would make no attempt to end diversity on, say, cranberry laws in Indiana and Illinois, he felt passionately that no majority should have the power to limit the most fundamental rights of a minority to life, liberty, and the pursuit of happiness.

XIV

How much the Lincoln-Douglas debates affected the voters remained problematical even after the ballots were tallied. Though November 2 was cold, wet, and raw, voters turned out in large numbers—more than in the 1856 presidential election. The Republican candidate for state treasurer received 125,430 votes, the Douglas Democratic candidate 121,609, and the National Democratic (Danite) candidate 5,071. Ballots for candidates for the state legislature were distributed in about the same proportion. As was expected, the Democrats carried all but three of the counties in southern Illinois and also those along the Illinois River, while Republicans won all of the northern counties, many by heavy majorities. In general, counties that had substantial towns tended to vote Republican, while poorer, slower-growing counties voted Democratic. The forty-nine central counties, where both Lincoln and Douglas had done most of their campaigning, were closely divided.

Since the name of neither Lincoln nor Douglas appeared on any ballot, there was no accurate way of measuring the personal popularity of either man or the impact of their campaigning, and analysts could adduce evidence to support opposite conclusions. On the one hand, it could be noted that in the state as a whole Democratic votes significantly increased in 24 counties where both Douglas and Lincoln spoke, while Republicans gained votes in only five of the counties where both men appeared. On the other, the returns showed that the Republicans fared slightly better in the seven counties where Lincoln and Douglas debated face-to-face than in the state as a whole. These contradictory statistics were less significant than the remarkable pattern of continuity demonstrated in the 1858 voting; the returns were closely similar to those in 1854 and 1856. The most immediate and obvious lesson of the election was that voting patterns in Illinois had become very stable, with the northern counties firmly Republican and the southern half of the state stalwartly Democratic. It was Douglas's split with the Buchanan administration and Lincoln's courtship of the Danites that gave Republicans a plurality and kept Douglas and his party from winning a clear majority in the state.

Though Republicans won in the popular vote (and elected their candidates for state treasurer and superintendent of education), they did not gain control of the state legislature, which would choose the next senator. In the state senate, thirteen members were holdovers (the terms of senators were staggered), and eight of these were Democrats. That meant that, in order to have a majority in a joint session of the two houses, the Republicans needed to have more than half the members in the new house of representatives. But seats in the house were apportioned according to the population in the 1850 census. In the years since 1850 the northern section of the state, where the Republicans were strongest, had grown much more rapidly than the southern counties, which the Democrats controlled. Because of the apportionment law, Republicans, who received about 50 percent of the popular vote, won only 47 percent of the seats in the house, while the Democrats with 48 percent of the popular vote gained 53 percent of the seats. That seemed unfair, but even if representation had been apportioned exactly on the basis of population, the Republicans would still have won only 44 seats —not enough, even when their five holdover senators were added, to elect Lincoln. In the balloting on January 5, 1859, Douglas received 54 votes to Lincoln's 46 and was thus reelected for another six years to the United States Senate.

After their defeat, many Republicans conducted postmortems on the election. The *Rockford Register,* along with many others, blamed "the unjust apportionment of the State, which deprives the people of a representation according to their numbers." Others pointed to illegal voters allegedly brought in by the Illinois Central Railroad to help the Democrats carry key counties, and Herndon claimed that "thousands of roving—robbing— bloated pock-marked Catholic Irish were imported upon us from Phila[del-phia]—St Louis and other cities." Many condemned Horace Greeley and other Eastern Republicans for their lukewarm support of Lincoln. "D——n Greeley etc," exclaimed a voter from Paris, Illinois; "they have done Lincoln more harm than all others." Some thought that Crittenden's endorsement of Douglas influenced thousands of former Whigs and Americans (Know Nothings), especially in the central part of the state, to go helter-skelter over to the Democrats.

Though Lincoln was not surprised by the outcome of the election, he was bitterly disappointed. Once again, he saw victory escape his grasp. With one more defeat added to his record, he had received yet another lesson in how little his fate was determined by his personal exertions. At times he felt very blue, and on the day the legislature elected Douglas, he was sure that his political career was ended. Confident only of the unquestioning loyalty of his partner, he remarked with some bitterness: "I expect everyone to desert me except Billy."

But as a leader he recognized his duty to cheer up his associates, who were also suffering from his defeat. "I am glad I made the late race," he wrote his old friend Dr. Henry. "It gave me a hearing on the great and durable question of the age, which I could have had in no other way; and though I now sink out of view, and shall be forgotten, I believe I have made some marks which will tell for the cause of civil liberty long after I am gone." "The fight must go on," he assured another friend. "The cause of civil liberty must not be surrendered at the end of *one,* or even, one *hundred* defeats."

CHAPTER NINE

The Taste *Is* in My Mouth

—————◆—————

"This year I must devote to my private business," Lincoln vowed in 1859, declining invitations to speak. "I have been on expences so long without earning any thing that I am absolutely without money now for even household purposes," Lincoln explained to Norman Judd. Accordingly, four days after the 1858 elections, Lincoln & Herndon appeared before the Sangamon County Circuit Court in a case where their client had to pay a judgment of $23 and costs. Other more remunerative cases followed during the next twelve months, but, except for the celebrated Peachy Harrison murder trial, none was of any special importance. As always, Lincoln was careful in his preparation and dependable in his court presentation, but the law had lost some of its excitement for him. At times his letters to clients sounded almost testy. To one, who was dissatisfied with the way Lincoln was handling his suit, he wrote bluntly: "I would now very gladly surrender . . . the case to anyone you would designate, without charging anything for the much trouble I have already had."

It was politics that really interested him now. As the leading Republican in Illinois, he felt a great responsibility in planning for his party's victory in the upcoming presidential election of 1860. To win, it was necessary to keep the fragile Illinois Republican coalition together, to block extreme or diversionary moves by Republicans in other states, and to select a presidential nominee who could combine the votes received by Frémont and Fillmore in 1856.

I

After the defeat in the senatorial election, the Illinois Republican coalition threatened to disintegrate. The party was in debt. Judd, the chairman of the state central committee, had incurred obligations of about $2,500, in addition to some $1,300 he had paid out of his own pocket. Republicans who had pledged contributions were reluctant to pay up, and Judd unhappily asked Lincoln to help him collect. Protesting that he was "the poorest hand living to get others to pay," Lincoln promised $250 himself, and then, along with O. M. Hatch and Jesse Dubois, asked Newton Bateman, the state superintendent of education, for assistance. Phrased as a request, their letter was in fact an assessment on the newly elected official who owed his position to the Republican party.

Republicans in central Illinois were slow to contribute because many felt that in the recent campaign the state central committee had slighted their section in favor of the Chicago area. Former Whigs like Judge David Davis resented the prominent role that former Democrats played in the campaign and correctly suspected that Judd was using his position as chairman of the central committee to promote his own gubernatorial prospects. Herndon was so vocal in charging Judd with misapplying party funds that the Chicago attorney had to ask Lincoln to curb his partner. Herndon gave a solemn promise to hold his tongue, but after this outburst Lincoln no longer shared political confidences with his partner.

A disruptive feud that continued to rage in Chicago between Judd and Wentworth was partly a personal vendetta and partly a bitter struggle for supremacy between Wentworth's *Chicago Democrat* and the *Chicago Press and Tribune,* which consistently supported Judd. In addition to assailing Judd's financial integrity, Wentworth accused him of conniving against Lincoln: Judd had helped defeat Lincoln's Senate bid in 1855; his mismanagement had brought about Republican defeat in 1858; and now he was plotting to promote Trumbull, rather than Lincoln, for the presidency. Judd, who desperately wanted to become governor, brought suit for libel, asking $100,000 in damages. Both men appealed to Lincoln for help. Wentworth tried to co-opt him by retaining him as his lawyer in the libel suit, while Judd insisted that he write a public letter vouching for his integrity. Lincoln attempted to remain neutral.

He also tried to keep Republicans in other states from shattering the party harmony. When Republicans in Massachusetts, where nativism was strong, endorsed a constitutional provision requiring naturalized citizens to wait two years before they could vote, Lincoln expressed forthright opposition. "I have some little notoriety for commiserating the oppressed condition of the negro," he explained; "and I should be strangely inconsistent if I could favor any project for curtailing the existing rights of *white men,* even though born in different lands, and speaking different languages from myself." Similarly, when Ohio Republicans adopted a platform calling for the repeal of the Fugitive Slave law, he bluntly warned Governor Salmon P. Chase that "the cause of Republicanism is hopeless in Illinois, if it be in any way made responsible for that plank." "In every locality," he urged, "we should look beyond our noses; and at least say *nothing* on points where it is probable we shall disagree."

He continued to worry about the fatal attraction that Stephen A. Douglas had for many Republicans. Though reelected to the Senate, Douglas had lost much Southern support because of his Freeport Doctrine. The almost unprecedented action of the Democratic Senate caucus in removing him from his cherished chairmanship of the Committee on Territories in December 1858 indicated just how few his Southern followers were. Shrewd and realistic, Douglas began making moves to attract backing from Republicans, just as he had done in the Lecompton controversy. He reminded them that he had consistently opposed enacting a slave code that would protect slavery in all the national territories and had fought the reopening of the African slave trade—both measures dear to Southern extremists.

Always suspicious of his great rival, Lincoln thought that Douglas was playing a double game. Douglas was presenting himself as a strong candidate for the Democratic presidential nomination in 1860 but at the same time was so positioning himself that if the Democrats rejected him he would "bolt at once, turn upon us, as in the case of Lecompton, and claim that all Northern men shall make common cause in electing him President as the best means of breaking down the Slave power." Lincoln knew that some Republicans, like Horace Greeley, had never recovered from their earlier infatuation with Douglas, and he was even more troubled when Kansas Republicans, after rejecting the Lecompton Constitution and thus ensuring that their state would be free, began speaking of their victory as a triumph of popular sovereignty. In Lincoln's first political appearance after the 1858 campaign, he warned Chicago Republicans of the dangers of "Douglasism": "Let the Republican party of Illinois dally with Judge Douglas; let them fall in behind him and make him their candidate, and they do not absorb him; he absorbs them."

Lincoln's anxiety became greater when he read the long article "The Dividing Line Between Federal and Local Authority: Popular Sovereignty in the Territories," which Douglas published in the September 1859 issue of *Harper's Magazine.* Taking as his texts Lincoln's house-divided speech and Seward's even more radical "irrepressible conflict" address, Douglas developed at great length his argument that popular sovereignty had consistently been the American policy from the days of the Revolution; that "great principle" meant "that the people of every separate political community (dependent Colonies, Provinces, and Territories as well as sovereign States) have an inalienable right to govern themselves in respect to their internal polity." By fairly tortuous reasoning he discovered that even the Dred Scott decision had recognized that right. He claimed that popular sovereignty, correctly construed, would block both the Republican efforts to exclude slavery from the territories by congressional act and Southern attempts to enact a national slave code.

Widely discussed, if not widely read, Douglas's article was a bold attempt to create a new party of the center—one that would unite moderate Democrats and conservative former Whigs and reject both Southern and Northern radicals. To bring this message to a larger audience, Douglas welcomed the opportunity to participate in the 1859 Ohio campaign, where he supported the local Democratic candidates but urged "all conservative men—all lovers of peace and of the law—all friends of the Union"—to rally in support of the great principle of popular sovereignty.

Lincoln found Douglas's activities decidedly threatening. Considering the Little Giant "the most dangerous enemy of liberty, because the most insidious one," he readily accepted an invitation from the Ohio Republican state central committee to participate in the campaign and thus "to head off the little gentleman."

He did not appear on the same platform with Douglas in Ohio, but his speeches at Columbus, Dayton, Hamilton, and Cincinnati (September 16–17), as well as one he delivered in Indianapolis two days later, were, in effect, continuations of the 1858 senatorial debates. For the most part, Lincoln presented arguments that he had advanced during those debates, but he was now freer in his criticisms of Douglas, apparently taking to heart Joseph Medill's advice: "As you are not a candidate you can talk out as boldly as you please. . . . Do not fail to get off some of your 'anecdotes and bits'. . . hit *below* the belt as well as above, and kick like thunder." He took obvious delight in mocking what he called Douglas's "gur-reat pur-rinciple" of popular sovereignty. As explained in "nineteen mortal pages of Harper," it amounted to saying "that, if one man chooses to make a slave of another man, neither that other man nor anybody else has a right to object."

Lincoln now developed some elements of his argument more fully than he had done in the Lincoln-Douglas debates. The real danger posed by Douglas, he explained, came from his "gradual and steady debauching of public opinion." Douglas's attempts to prove that the Declaration of Independence did not include African-Americans had already changed the way most whites viewed blacks. His recent remark "that he was for the negro against the crocodile, but for the white man against the negro" helped spread the opinion "that the negro is no longer a man but a brute; . . . that he ranks with the crocodile and the reptile." "Public opinion in this country is everything," Lincoln observed, and Douglas and his friends were serving as "the miners and sappers" to undermine resistance to the spread of slavery, so that state laws excluding slavery would soon be overruled, a national slave code enacted, and the African slave trade revived.

In these 1859 addresses Lincoln also elaborated on a subject that he had slighted during debates with Douglas: how "the mass of white men are really injured by the effect of slave labor in the vicinity of the fields of their own labor." The argument required him to lay out his view of American economic development. Like Francis Wayland and the other political economists whose books he had read years earlier, he firmly adhered to the labor theory of value: *"labor* is the source from which human wants are mainly supplied." Labor was thus "prior to, and independent of, capital"; indeed "capital is the fruit of labor, and could never have existed if labor had not *first* existed." But capital, though derivative, performed a valuable service in a free society, because those who had it could offer employment to "the prudent, penniless beginner in the world" who owned "nothing save two strong hands that God has given him, [and] a heart willing to labor." If this novice worked industriously and behaved soberly, he could in a year or two save enough to buy land for himself, to settle, marry, and beget sons and daughters, and presently he, too, would begin employing other laborers. Reminding his Ohio audiences that "at an early age, I was myself a hired laborer, at twelve dollars per month," he insisted that in a free society there was "no such thing as a man who is a hired laborer, of a necessity, always remaining in his early condition."

Lincoln's version of the American dream was in some ways a curiously limited one. Confident that advancement was open to all who worked hard, he was untroubled by the growing disparity of wealth between the poor and the rich. Viewing himself as a man of the people, he did not find it incongruous that some of his most loyal supporters were large-scale farmers like Isaac Funk, of McLean County, who owned 25,000 acres of prairie land, and William Scully, of Logan County, who owned 30,000 acres. Nor did he find it remarkable that his strongest political backer was David Davis, who was becoming one of the wealthiest landlords and land speculators in the state. Though Lincoln regularly represented railroads, the largest corporations in the country, he thought of economic opportunity primarily in terms of individual enterprise. In his analysis he gave scant attention to the growing number of factory workers, who had little prospect of upward social mobility.

To the free economy that Lincoln idealized, he juxtaposed the slave society of the South. There it was assumed that labor must always remain subordinate; there, as James Henry Hammond, of South Carolina, proclaimed, labor was the mudsill on which the social edifice was erected. In a slave society, Lincoln observed, "a blind horse upon a tread-mill, is a perfect illustration of what a laborer should be—all the better for being blind, that he could not tread out of place, or kick understandingly."

The free economy and the slave society had coexisted, more or less peacefully, since the founding of the republic, but now they were increasingly in competition and conflict. Like most Republicans, Lincoln believed that slavery had to expand or die; the exhaustion of the soil and the natural increase of the slave population meant that slaveholders were forced to move into new lands. But free society had also the imperative to expand. The basic impulse to improve one's condition, an "inherent right given to mankind directly by the Maker," required room. The national territories were "God-given for that purpose," and he had long believed that their best use was "for the homes of free white people." But if Douglas and the Southern Democrats had their way, free laborers who moved to the territories would be in competition with the unpaid slaves. Consequently, Lincoln exhorted his audiences, "it is due to yourselves as voters, as owners of the new territories, that you shall keep those territories free, in the best condition for all such of your gallant sons as may choose to go there."

II

The warm reception that Lincoln's speeches received in Iowa, Ohio, Indiana, Wisconsin, and Kansas during the last half of 1859 gave plausibility to suggestions that he ought to be nominated for high office. The idea had emerged right after the 1858 election, when some of his followers, bitter over his defeat and convinced "he is one of the best men God ever made," began to ask: "Cant we make him President or *vice.*"

Perhaps the obscure Lacon *Illinois Gazette* was the first newspaper seriously to propose Lincoln's name for the presidency, but a November 6 story in the *Sandusky* (Ohio) *Commercial Register* calling on Republicans to nominate Lincoln received more attention. Presently the *Olney* (Illinois) *Times* began running "Abram [sic] Lincoln for President for 1860" below its masthead, and favorable mention of his possible candidacy appeared in papers as diverse as the *New York Herald,* the *Rockford* (Illinois) *Republican,* and the *Reading* (Pennsylvania) *Journal.*

Neither Lincoln nor anybody else took these suggestions very seriously. He did not think himself presidential timber. During the 1858 campaign against Douglas he confided to the journalist Henry Villard that he doubted his ability to be a senator, though his wife was confident that he would one day become President. "Just think," he exclaimed, wrapping his long arms around his knees and giving a roar of laughter, "of such a sucker as me as President." Most of the newspaper stories were intended only to suggest that Lincoln was a prominent Republican, who deserved recognition as a favorite son of Illinois on the first ballot. Some of them were designed to promote his candidacy for the second place on the Republican ticket; the *Hennepin* (Illinois) *Tribune* endorsed him while frankly acknowledging that it favored William H. Seward for President, with Lincoln for Vice President. Wentworth's organ, the *Chicago Democrat,* seemed to be endorsing Lincoln, "the Great Man of Illinois," when it urged Republicans to nominate him for either President or Vice President; but it gave the editor's game away by also recommending Lincoln for governor, rather than Wentworth's archrival, Judd.

To all such suggestions Lincoln gave essentially the same answer. "I must, in candor, say I do not think myself fit for the Presidency," he wrote the admiring editor of the *Rock Island Register,* who wanted to promote the simultaneous announcement of Lincoln's candidacy in Republican newspapers across the state. He gave an identical answer to Samuel Galloway, who was trying to organize a Lincoln-for-President movement in Ohio.

In issuing these disclaimers Lincoln was not being coy, but realistic. To all outward appearances he was less prepared to be President of the United States than any other man who had run for that high office. Without family tradition or wealth, he had received only the briefest of formal schooling. Now fifty years old, he had no administrative experience of any sort; he had never been governor of his state or even mayor of Springfield. A profound student of the Constitution and of the writings of the Founding Fathers, he had limited acquaintance with the government they had established. He had served only a single, less than successful term in the House of Representatives and for the past ten years had held no public office. Though he was one of the founders of the Republican party, he had no close friends and only a few acquaintances in the populous Eastern states, whose vote would be crucial in the election. To be sure, his debates with Douglas had brought him national attention, but he had lost the senatorial election both in 1855 and in 1859. Dismissing his chances for the presidency, one of Hatch's Boston correspondents remarked scornfully: "As for Lincoln I am afraid he will kick the beam again as he is in the habit of doing."

Despite these handicaps, of which no one was more conscious than Lincoln himself, he did think about the presidency. Indeed, any public man with intelligence and ambition, looking over the sorry run of recent chief executives, was forced to consider whether he could not occupy the White House as satisfactorily as, say, Franklin Pierce or James Buchanan.

When Lincoln allowed himself to consider the possibility of running for President, his chances for securing the Republican nomination seemed better than average. The party had several strong candidates, but all had flaws. The leading name was William H. Seward, the senator and former governor of New York, an unquestionably able, experienced, and adroit politician of Whig antecedents, who was handicapped by an undeserved reputation for extremism because of his speeches proclaiming a higher law than the Constitution and predicting an irrepressible conflict between slavery and freedom; in addition, his emphatic opposition to nativism would alienate former Know Nothing voters. Pennsylvania Republicans, irate because the low tariff of 1857 had removed protection from their iron industry, mostly favored Simon Cameron, but he had few followers outside that state and was widely suspected of financial improprieties or even gross corruption. Salmon P. Chase, the Republican governor of Ohio, earnestly sought the nomination, and many of the more dedicated antislavery members of the party backed him; but he lacked personal magnetism as well as political adroitness. Another possibility was Edward Bates of Missouri, a conservative, free-soil Whig now sixty-six years old, who was not even a member of the Republican party; he was the improbable favorite of the erratic Horace Greeley, who was willing to back anybody who could defeat his former friend and now bitter rival, Seward. In addition to these front-runners, there were secondary candidates who might become winners if the convention was deadlocked: John C. Frémont, the defeated Republican candidate in 1856; William L. Dayton of New Jersey, who had been Frémont's running mate; Cassius M. Clay, the fiery, unstable Kentucky abolitionist; and Benjamin F. Wade, the blunt antislavery senator and Chase's principal rival in Ohio.

Shrewdly Lincoln recognized that his own chances against these better-known rivals could best be advanced not by an open announcement of his candidacy but by small, private moves to consolidate his strength and expand his influence. To ensure wider circulation of his ideas, he took an active role in compiling and preserving his 1858 debates with Douglas. With the assistance of Henry C. Whitney he collected the reports of his speeches that appeared in the *Chicago Press and Tribune* and those of Douglas in the *Chicago Times*. These he carefully pasted in a large scrapbook, which he hoped to have published. After plans for having a book printed in Springfield failed, he turned over the project to Follett, Foster & Company of Columbus, Ohio, which shortly before the national nominating conventions of 1860 issued a 268-page book titled *Political Debates Between Hon. Abraham Lincoln and Hon. Stephen A. Douglas, in the Celebrated Campaign of 1858, in Illinois*. It immediately became a best-seller.

In December 1859, Lincoln made another quiet move to gain broader recognition by preparing an autobiography for campaign purposes. Jesse W. Fell, a Bloomington politician, forwarded a request from Joseph J. Lewis, of the *Chester County* (Pennsylvania) *Times*, for biographical information he could use in preparing an article on Lincoln. Lincoln complied with a terse sketch that reviewed his homespun beginnings, summarized his public career, and ended: "If any personal description of me is thought desirable, it may be said, I am, in height, six feet, four inches, nearly; lean in flesh, weighing, on an average, one hundred and eighty pounds; dark complexion, with coarse black hair, and grey eyes—no other marks or brands recollected." This he sent to Fell, noting, "There is not much of it, for the reason, I suppose, that there is not much of me." Lewis evidently found the sketch meager, for he embroidered it with remarks on Lincoln's oratorical gifts and on his long record of support for a protective tariff, so dear to Pennsylvanians. His article, widely copied in other Republican newspapers, was the first published biography of Lincoln.

An even stronger indication of Lincoln's growing interest in a presidential race was the alacrity with which he accepted an invitation from New York to lecture at Henry Ward Beecher's Plymouth Church in Brooklyn in February 1860. Knowing that he would appear before a sophisticated Eastern audience, he promptly began more careful research and preparation than for any other speech of his life. He also ordered a brand-new black suit for the occasion, for which he paid the local tailors, Woods & Henckle, $100.

By the time he arrived in the East, sponsorship of the address had been taken over by the Young Men's Central Republican Union, a body that included sixty-five-year-old William Cullen Bryant, forty-nine-year-old Horace

Greeley, and other such youths, who were organizing a stop-Seward movement. Lincoln's was the third in a series of lectures—following addresses by
Frank Blair, the Missouri antislavery leader, and Cassius M. Clay, the Kentucky abolitionist—designed, according to the sponsors, "to call out our
better, but busier citizens, who never attend political meetings." Without
informing Lincoln, the Young Republicans also shifted the lecture from
Brooklyn to the Cooper Union in Manhattan. Learning of the change after
he arrived and registered at the Astor House, Lincoln spent his first day in
New York revising his address, so as to make it more suitable for a general
political audience than for a religious congregation.

On Monday, February 27, escorted by several of the Young Republicans,
he caught a glimpse of Broadway and had his photograph, which he called
his "shaddow," taken at Mathew B. Brady's studio, where he exchanged
pleasantries with George Bancroft. "I am on my way to Massachusetts,"
Lincoln told the historian, "where I have a son at school, who, if report be
true, already knows much more than his father." The portrait Brady produced after this sitting was a work of art; he retouched the negative in order
to correct Lincoln's left eye that seemed to be roving upward and eliminated
harsh lines from his face to show an almost handsome, statesmanlike image.

That night, after a warm introduction by Bryant, Lincoln appeared before
a capacity audience at the Cooper Union. Many of his listeners expected
"something weird, rough, and uncultivated," George Haven Putnam remembered, and Lincoln's appearance did nothing to undeceive them. "The long,
ungainly figure, upon which hung clothes that, while new for the trip, were
evidently the work of an unskilled tailor; the large feet; the clumsy hands, of
which . . . the orator seemed to be unduly conscious; the long, gaunt head
capped by a shock of hair that seemed not to have been thoroughly brushed
out," Putnam continued, "made a picture which did not fit in with New
York's conception of a finished statesman." Equally disconcerting was Lincoln's voice, for it was high and piercing in tone at the outset.

But the speech that he delivered, reading carefully and soberly from
sheets of blue foolscap, quickly erased the impression of a crude frontiersman. It was a masterful exploration of the political paths open to the nation.
In the first third of the address Lincoln closely examined Douglas's contention that popular sovereignty was simply a continuation of a policy initiated by the Founding Fathers. After digging through the records of the
Constitutional Convention and the debates in the earliest Congresses, he
was able to show that of the thirty-nine signers of the Constitution, at least
twenty-one demonstrated by their votes that the federal government had the
power to control slavery in the national territories; other noted antislavery
men, like Benjamin Franklin, Alexander Hamilton, and Gouverneur Morris,
should probably be added to that list, though they were not called to vote
on this specific question. This minutely detailed record confirmed a position
that Lincoln had been arguing for years: that prior to Douglas's introduction
of the Kansas-Nebraska Act it was impossible "to show that any living man

in the whole world ever did . . . declare that . . . the Constitution forbade the Federal Government to control as to slavery in the federal territories."

Next Lincoln examined the Southern position, though he had little hope that his arguments would be heard, much less heeded, in that section. Nevertheless, he seized the opportunity to argue that the Republicans were the true conservatives on questions relating to slavery; they adhered "to the old and tried, against the new and untried," while Southern fire-eaters "with one accord reject, and scout, and spit upon that old policy." This gave him a welcome opening to explain the Republican attitude toward the raid that John Brown and a handful of zealous followers had staged in October 1859 on Harpers Ferry, Virginia. At that time Lincoln denounced Brown's attempt to stir up an insurrection among the slaves as "wrong for two reasons. It was a violation of law and it was, as all such attacks must be, futile as far as any effect it might have on the extinction of a great evil." Though he had paid tribute to Brown's "great courage, rare unselfishness" and sympathized with his hatred of slavery, he concluded that the old abolitionist was "insane." Now he took the offensive, pointing out that Brown's raid was not a slave insurrection but "an attempt by white men to get up a revolt among slaves, in which the slaves refused to participate"; further, he pointed out, Southerners after an elaborate congressional investigation had failed to implicate a single Republican in it. Southern efforts to capitalize on John Brown's raid were simply additional evidence of their determination to "rule or ruin in all events." More recently Southerners had gone so far as to announce that if a Republican was elected President in 1860 the Union would be dissolved and the fault would be the North's. "That is cool," Lincoln exclaimed. "A highwayman holds a pistol to my ear, and mutters through his teeth, 'Stand and deliver, or I shall kill you, and then you will be a murderer!' "

What should Northerners do? Avoiding both the moral indifference with which Douglas approached the slavery issue and the proslavery zeal of the Southern radicals, Republicans should fearlessly and effectively persist in excluding slavery from the national territories, confining it to the states where it already existed. "Neither let us be slandered from our duty by false accusations against us, nor frightened from it by menaces of destruction to the Government nor of dungeons to ourselves," Lincoln announced in his spine-tingling peroration. "Let us have faith that right makes might, and in that faith, let us, to the end, dare to do our duty as we understand it."

As a speech, it was a superb performance. The audience frequently applauded during the delivery of the address, and when Lincoln closed, the crowd cheered and stood, waving handkerchiefs and hats. Noah Brooks, then working for the *New York Tribune,* exclaimed: "He's the greatest man since St. Paul," and a student at the Harvard Law School, trained to master his emotions, told his father, "It was the best speech I ever heard." The next day four New York papers printed the address in full. Bryant in the *New York Evening Post* called it forcible and "most logically and convincingly stated." Greeley, less restrained, announced: "Mr. Lincoln is one of Nature's orators, using his rare powers solely and effectively to elucidate and to convince, though their inevitable effect is to delight and electrify as well." Immediately published in pamphlet form, the Cooper Union address was issued and reissued as a Republican tract by the *New York Tribune,* the *Chicago Press and Tribune,* the *Detroit Tribune,* and the *Albany Evening Journal.*

It was also a superb political move for an unannounced presidential aspirant. Appearing in Seward's home state, sponsored by a group largely loyal to Chase, Lincoln shrewdly made no reference to either of these Republican rivals for the nomination. Recognizing that if the Republicans were going to win in 1860 they needed the support of men who had voted for Fillmore in the previous election, Lincoln in his Cooper Union address stressed his conservatism. He did not mention his house-divided thesis or Seward's irrepressible-conflict prediction; Republicans were presented as a party of moderates who were simply trying to preserve the legacy of the Founding Fathers against the radical assaults of the proslavery element. Even Lincoln's language contributed to the effect he sought; the careful structure of the speech, the absence of incendiary rhetoric, even the laborious recital of the voting records of the Founding Fathers, all suggested reasonableness and stability, not wide-eyed fanaticism. In short, it was, as one of the sponsors wrote, an enormous success. Sending Lincoln the agreed-upon fee of $200, he added, "I would that it were $200,000 for you are worthy of it."

The next day Lincoln moved on to New England, ostensibly to visit Robert, who had enrolled in the Phillips Exeter Academy the previous September. Of course, he was glad to see his son and to chat with his schoolmates. When one of them produced a banjo and gave an informal concert for the visitor, Lincoln was genuinely pleased and said to his stiff, unmusical son, "Robert, you ought to have one." But it quickly became clear that the real object of his visit was to cement connections with influential Republicans who would be attending the forthcoming national convention. After the success of the Cooper Union address, Lincoln was something of a lion, much in demand at Republican rallies, and during his four days with Robert he made campaign addresses at Concord, Manchester, Dover, and Exeter. On the last of these occasions many of the boys from the academy turned out, and he had an audience of about five hundred people. The students, who knew Bob as "a gentleman in every sense of the word; quiet in manner, with a certain dignity of his own," were astonished when Lincoln came into the hall, "tall, lank, awkward; dressed in a loose, ill-fitting black frock coat, with black trousers, ill-fitting and somewhat baggy at the knees." They observed his rumpled hair, his necktie turned awry, and his long legs that seemed to fit neither under or around his chair. "Isn't it too bad Bob's father is so homely?" they whispered to each other. "Don't you feel sorry for him?" But after Lincoln disentangled his legs, rose slowly from his chair, and began speaking, they forgot his appearance; they no longer pitied Bob but felt proud to know his father.

During his two weeks in New England, Lincoln spoke nearly every day, avoiding Massachusetts, which was a Seward stronghold, but attempting to help the Republican candidates in Rhode Island, New Hampshire, and Connecticut. He found it hard work. So many in his audiences had read the Cooper Union address that he could not simply repeat that speech, and he had to try to think of new ways of presenting his ideas. Perhaps his most telling innovation was his explanation of why Republicans firmly opposed to the extension of slavery were not pledged to eradicate it in the Southern states. If "out in the street, or in the field, or on the prairie I find a rattle-snake," Lincoln explained, "I take a stake and kill him. Everybody would applaud the act and say I did right." "But suppose the snake was in a bed where children were sleeping. Would I do right to strike him there? I might hurt the children; or I might not kill, but only arouse and exasperate the snake, and he might bite the children." The best way to end slavery, he insisted, was firmly to oppose its spread into the national territories. On this issue there could be no compromise. "Let us stand by our duty, fearlessly and effectively," he urged over and over again, often ending with the perora-tion of his Cooper Union address: "Let us have faith that right makes might; and in that faith, let us, to the end, dare to do our duty, as we under-stand it."

The success of Lincoln's Eastern trip edged him a step closer to becoming an avowed candidate for the Republican presidential nomination. As recently as January he had been hesitant about making a race. Conferring with Judd, Hatch, Jackson Grimshaw, and a few other prominent Illinois Republicans who pressed him to run, he expressed doubt whether he could get the nomination if he wished it. Only after a night of reflection—and doubtless of conferences with Mary Lincoln, who was even more ambitious than he was—did he authorize the little group to work quietly for his nomination. Even then he did not consider himself a serious candidate but hoped that endorsement as a favorite son would help unite the Illinois Republicans and confirm his party leadership. He explained that he was "not in a position where it would hurt much for me to not be nominated on the national ticket" but that "it would hurt some for me to not get the Illinois delegates" at the Republican convention. But after his return from New York and New England he made no attempt to conceal his desire for the nomination. By April he wrote to Trumbull, who inquired about his intentions: "I will be entirely frank. The taste *is* in my mouth a little."

III

Lincoln could not openly campaign for the nomination because tradition dictated that the office should seek the man, and he necessarily worked through aides and intermediaries, many of them veterans from his 1858 senatorial race. In Springfield he continued to rely on Hatch, the Illinois secretary of state, and Dubois, the state auditor, whose offices made them privy to detailed, confidential political information about every part of the state. In the Chicago area Wentworth offered to be Lincoln's Warwick, but he turned instead to Judd. He did not entirely trust Judd but recognized his power as chairman of the Illinois Republican state central committee and as the Illinois member of the Republican National Committee. Both Leonard Swett and Richard Yates, who were competing with Judd for the Republican gubernatorial nomination, served as Lincoln's agents in central Illinois. Gustave Koerner, the Belleville lawyer, was his principal connection to the German-American constituency, which he also tried to reach through Dr. Theodore Canisius, whose newspaper, the Springfield *Illinois Staats-Anzeiger,* he secretly owned. His most trusted adviser, however, was Judge David Davis, who emerged as his informal campaign manager."I keep no secrets from him," Lincoln declared.

These Lincoln managers were not an organized or unified group. Throughout Lincoln's career, his advisers felt connected only to him, not to each other or to some larger cause. Indeed, their loyalty to Lincoln was matched, in many cases, by the distrust they exhibited toward each other. Davis never forgave Judd's role in defeating Lincoln's election to the Senate in 1855; Judd hated Wentworth; Wentworth attacked not merely Judd but Hatch and Dubois; Swett and Yates were rivals united only by their dislike of Judd. Of course, Lincoln was aware of this dissonance, but he tolerated it; perhaps he believed that advisers in competition with each other would work all the harder.

One result of this decentralized command structure was that each member of the group came to think that he, and he alone, truly understood Lincoln and gave him useful advice. Curiously enough, many of Lincoln's advisers viewed him as a man who needed to be encouraged and protected. Even those who played only minor roles in the Republican party often shared this attitude. For instance, Nathan M. Knapp, chairman of the Scott County, Illinois, Republican party, believed that Lincoln was a greater man than he himself realized: "He has not known his own power—uneducated in Youth, he has always been doubtful whether he was not pushing himself into positions to which he was unequal." David Davis put it another way: "Lincoln has few of the qualities of a politician and . . . cannot do much personally to advance his interests," because he was such "a guileless man." Had Lincoln known of this pronouncement, he might have been amused.

While his managers were hard at work, Lincoln had to appear above the fray. To requests for his views on the political scene, he replied that he was not the fittest person to answer such questions because "when not a very great man begins to be mentioned for a very great position, his head is very likely to be a little turned." Nevertheless, he managed to offer opinions that, without being barbed or invidious, cast doubts on the availability of the other prominently mentioned candidates. Seward, he declared, "is the very best candidate we could have for the North of Illinois, and the very *worst* for the South of it." The same held for Chase, "except that he is a newer man." Bates "would be the best man for the South of our State, and the worst for the North of it." The strongest candidate, he asserted with apparent lack of guile, was Justice John McLean, aged seventy-five—if only he were fifteen, or even ten, years younger.

Even with avowed supporters Lincoln was cagey. When James F. Babcock, editor of the *New Haven Palladium,* who had been much impressed by the speeches Lincoln made in the recent Connecticut campaign, offered to promote his candidacy, he replied, in unusually opaque language: "As to the Presidential nomination, claiming no greater exemption from selfishness than is common, I still feel that my whole aspiration should be, and therefore must be, to be placed anywhere, or nowhere, as may appear most likely to advance our cause." Nevertheless, he passed along to Babcock a list of eleven "confidential friends" who were working for his nomination.

When one enterprising Illinois Republican suggested that he ought to have a campaign chest of $10,000, Lincoln replied that the proposal was an impossibility: "I could not raise ten thousand dollars if it would save me from the fate of John Brown. Nor have my friends, so far as I know, yet reached the point of staking any money on my chances of success." To a request for money from Mark W. Delahay, an old and somewhat disreputable Illinois friend who hoped to be a delegate to the Republican National Convention in order to promote his chance of being elected senator from Kansas, Lincoln responded, "I can not enter the ring on the money basis— first, because, in the main, it is wrong; and secondly, I have not, and can not get, the money." Yet, admitting that "in a political contest, the use of some [money], is both right, and indispensable," he offered to furnish Delahay $100 for his expenses in attending the convention. (As it turned out, Delahay was not chosen as a Kansas delegate but went to Chicago anyhow to root for Lincoln, who paid him the money he had promised.)

Central to Lincoln's planning was Douglas's expected role in the coming campaign. If the Democratic National Convention, scheduled to meet in Charleston, South Carolina, on April 23, nominated the Little Giant, the Republicans would be obliged to choose a candidate from the West, where Douglas was enormously popular. On the other hand, if the Democrats nominated a Southern-rights champion, like Vice President John C. Breckinridge of Kentucky, or if the party split, Republicans would feel free to nominate Seward, Chase, or any other antislavery leader. Thus, as had so often been the case, Lincoln's prospects varied directly with Douglas's.

Given this political reality, Lincoln adopted a very simple campaign strategy. He hoped to go into the Republican National Convention with the unanimous support of the Illinois delegation and perhaps with the backing of a few individuals in other delegations. If Seward failed to secure the nomination on the first ballot—a decision that would be determined in no small part by what happened to Douglas—Lincoln and other candidates would have their chance on a second ballot. Recognizing that most members of the convention would favor someone else, Lincoln thought that his great strength lay in the fact that no one made "any positive objection" to him. "My name is new in the field; and I suppose I am not the *first* choice of a very great many," he explained to Samuel Galloway. "Our policy, then, is to give no offence to others—leave them in a mood to come to us, if they shall be compelled to give up their first love."

The first step was to secure the unanimous support of the Illinois delegation. This was not an easy task, because both the Sewardites in northern Illinois and the Bates men in the south favored selecting delegates by districts, thus, as Judd said, "hoping to steal in a few men." Alerted that the votes of Yates and the other members of the central committee from central Illinois would determine this question, Lincoln promised: "I shall attend to it as well as I know how, which, G——d knows, will not be very well." In fact, he attended to it well enough, for the central committee voted for the statewide election of delegates.

It was equally important to have the Republican National Convention meet in Chicago, where the newspapers, the crowds, and the publicity would be heavily tilted in Lincoln's favor. The rival site was St. Louis, where the Bates influence would be strong. When Judd, as a member of the Republican National Committee, seemed slow to grasp the importance of this choice, Lincoln wrote him that "some of our friends here" thought the location of the convention of great consequence. With this prodding, Judd carried the case for Chicago to the meeting of the national committee, which chose the Windy City by a margin of one vote—his own.

Even more important was the action of the Illinois Republican state convention, which met at Decatur on May 9–10, a week before the national convention. To house the gathering the citizens of the town had followed a practice adopted by Republicans throughout the West and constructed what they called a Wigwam, a barnlike wooden structure capable of holding the hundreds of delegates and spectators. For many who attended, the principal business of this convention was the choice of a candidate for governor; eventually the supporters of Swett and Yates combined to defeat Judd and to give the nomination to Yates. As to presidential candidates, Illinois Republicans were divided, but it was generally recognized that the convention would give a complimentary endorsement of Lincoln as a favorite son. Even David Davis thought it was a foregone conclusion that the national convention would choose either Bates or Seward; a first-ballot vote for Lincoln would simply be a compliment.

But a few of Lincoln's warmest supporters were determined to make the Decatur convention a launching pad for a serious presidential campaign. They felt that what had been lacking so far was a catchy slogan, like "Log Cabin and Hard Cider," which had done so much to elect President Harrison in 1840. Of course, Lincoln was already widely known as "Old Abe" or "Honest Abe," but these sobriquets seemed so colorless as to be almost negative. Richard J. Oglesby, a vigorous young Decatur politician, felt Lincoln needed a more dynamic image. Consulting with the elderly John Hanks, a first cousin of Lincoln's mother, he located a rail fence that Hanks and Lincoln had put up in 1830 and carried two of the rails home with him. On the first day of the convention, during an interruption in the voting for governor, Oglesby introduced Hanks, who, with an assistant, marched down the aisle carrying into the Wigwam the two rails labeled:

ABRAHAM LINCOLN
The Rail Candidate
FOR PRESIDENT IN 1860.
Two rails from a lot of 3,000 made in 1830 by Thos. Hanks and
Abe Lincoln—whose father was the first pioneer of Macon County.

The label was not entirely accurate, for Lincoln's father had not been the first pioneer in the county and it was John, rather than Thomas, Hanks who had helped split the rails, but nobody cared. As the rails, decorated with flags and streamers, were carried to the front of the Wigwam, the crowd burst into deafening applause. Lincoln, called to the stand, blushed and told the delegates that he had indeed built a cabin and split rails thirty years ago near Decatur. Whether these particular rails were taken from that fence, he could not vouch, but, he said in his disarming way, "he had mauled many and many better ones since he had grown to manhood."

The cheers that greeted Lincoln's remarks suggested that even his managers had underestimated his popularity. Now labeled "the Rail Splitter"—just as Andrew Jackson had been "Old Hickory" and Harrison "Tippecanoe"— he acquired an image with enormous popular appeal: he could be packaged not merely as a powerful advocate of the free-soil ideology or as a folksy, unpretentious, storytelling campaigner, but also as the embodiment of the self-made man, the representative of free labor, and the spokesman of the great West. It mattered very little that this myth—like most myths—was only partially true: Lincoln, in fact, had little love for his pioneer origins; he disliked physical labor and left it as soon as he could; he owed his early advancement as much to the efforts of interested friends like John Todd Stuart, Stephen T. Logan, and David Davis as to his own exertions. Rather than a simple backwoodsman, he was a prominent and successful attorney representing the most powerful interests in emerging corporate America. The delegates at Decatur understood that myth was more important than reality. They cheered now not just for a favorite son but for a viable Illinois presidential candidate.

After the convention adjourned for the day, Lincoln met with Judd, Davis, and a few other friends in a grove near the Wigwam, where, lying on the grass, they carefully studied the list of delegates to be sent to Chicago. Lincoln personally selected the four at-large delegates. Judd, as a member of the Republican National Committee and as a representative of Chicago interests, was one, of course. Recognizing the importance of the German vote, Lincoln named Koerner for the second slot. For the third he picked

Browning, who had great influence among conservative old-line Whigs and, especially, among the former Know Nothings. Knowing that Browning preferred Bates, Lincoln relied on his old friend's personal loyalty and his devotion to Illinois interests. The final member of the team was David Davis.

Lincoln and his friends had no control over the selection of the eighteen other delegates who represented the individual congressional districts, but they suspected that about eight of them were Seward supporters. To prevent them from defecting, Lincoln's advisers agreed to ram through the convention the next day a resolution that John M. Palmer would introduce: "That Abraham Lincoln is the choice of the Republican party of Illinois for the Presidency, and the delegates from this State are instructed to use all honorable means to secure his nomination by the Chicago Convention, and to vote as a unit for him." At Chicago, Illinois would be unanimous for Lincoln.

IV

Lincoln was tempted to attend the Chicago convention. After he returned from Decatur, he told Leonard Swett that "he was almost too much of a candidate to go, and not quite enough to stay at home." On reflection, he decided to remain in Springfield while the delegates began to assemble. He cordially greeted the occasional member who passed through Springfield, assuring several of them that he was a candidate only for the presidency and did not wish to be considered for the second place on the Republican ticket. Recognizing that Seward would have the votes of the more extreme antislavery men, Lincoln sought to ensure that he would be presented in Chicago as a moderate candidate. To Edward L. Baker, editor of the *Illinois State Journal,* who was going to the convention, he entrusted a brief note: "I agree with Seward in his 'Irrepressible Conflict,' but I do not endorse his 'Higher Law' doctrine." The former he viewed as little more than a restatement of his own house-divided thesis, while he recognized that Seward's invocation of a law higher than the Constitution frightened moderate and conservative Republicans.

Lincoln was not directly involved in the tumultuous proceedings of the second Republican National Convention that assembled on May 16–18 in the huge Wigwam just completed in Chicago. The Illinois delegation took no prominent part in the first day's debates on the credentials of members. Nor did it attempt to shape the party platform, which somewhat moderated the tone, though not the meaning, of the 1856 denunciation of the slave power. Illinois Republicans went along with the party's attempt to broaden its appeal by endorsing a homestead act to please western farmers; federal appropriations for improving rivers and harbors to satisfy Detroit, Chicago, and other cities on the Great Lakes; and, in opaque language, a moderately protective tariff to appease the iron interests of Pennsylvania and New Jersey. With much difficulty they agreed on a compromise resolution that on the one hand carefully refrained from mentioning, much less condemning, the

Know Nothings and, on the other, cautiously opposed the Massachusetts plan of extending the period before naturalized citizens could vote; it ended with a balanced call for "giving a full and efficient protection to the rights of all classes of citizens, whether native or naturalized, both at home and abroad."

The focus of Lincoln's representatives in Chicago was not on the platform but on the presidency. They found Seward's position stronger than they had anticipated because the Democratic National Convention, deadlocked between Douglas's backers and the Southern states-rights advocates, had adjourned without making a nomination. Already assured of the support of what might be called Greater New England—the states of the upper North, ranging from Massachusetts through New York to Michigan, Wisconsin, Iowa, and Minnesota—Seward might win if the Democrats continued to deny the nomination to Douglas, their strongest candidate in the North. But realistic Republicans anticipated that when the Democratic National Convention reconvened in June, Douglas would be the nominee, with formidable strength in the Ohio Valley region—including Ohio, Indiana, Illinois, and Kentucky. Seward's rivals were further encouraged when the new National Union party, more or less a reincarnation of the Whig and American parties, on May 10 nominated John Bell of Tennessee and Edward Everett of Massachusetts; Seward could not compete with this ticket for votes in the upper South. Unless Seward came into the convention with great strength on the first ballot, Republican managers were bound to pause and look for a more available nominee.

The shrewdest Republicans at Chicago were looking for a candidate who, in addition to carrying all the Northern states that had gone for Frémont in 1856, could win in Pennsylvania, Indiana, and Illinois. Seward, for all his strength elsewhere, was weak in these three states. Chase had the support of only a part of his own Ohio delegation. Cameron had no following outside of Pennsylvania. Despite the vigorous backing of Greeley and the powerful Francis Preston Blair family in Maryland and Missouri, Bates probably could not carry even his own home state.

That left Lincoln. He was not a dark horse—i.e., a nominee unexpectedly chosen after a deadlock of the leading candidates—but from the first day of the convention a serious contender backed by the unanimous delegation from the critical state of Illinois. Though he was not widely known except in the West, he appeared to be exactly what the Republican party needed: he was unequivocally opposed to the expansion of slavery; he had for years favored economic development, including internal improvements and the protective tariff so dear to Pennsylvanians; he had strong emotional appeal to former Whigs who still considered themselves followers of Henry Clay; and he had managed to oppose the Know Nothing party without indulging in moral condemnation of the nativists. If the Republican delegates at Chicago followed the dictates of political reason, he would be their choice.

But, of course, Lincoln knew that emotion plays as large a role in politics as reason, and that is why he wanted his team of managers in place at Chicago, ready to provide information, squelch rumors, listen to complaints, give moral support, soothe ruffled egos, and flatter doubting delegates. From his rooms at the Tremont Hotel, David Davis took charge of the operation. His primary objective was to secure at least one hundred votes for Lincoln on the first ballot—more than any other candidate except Seward— with other votes in reserve so that Lincoln would appear to gain strength on a second ballot. For this purpose he sent out members of his team to talk with delegations where they might have influence; Swett, for instance, visited the delegation from Maine, the state of his birth, and S. C. Parks canvassed those from his native state of Vermont. Browning proved invaluable in talking with delegations that teetered between supporting Bates and Lincoln; known as a former Bates man, he was the better able to show the weaknesses of the Missouri candidate. Logan kept an eye on the Kentucky delegates; he carried a private letter from Lincoln authorizing him to withdraw his name if he thought it prudent to do so. Medill was in charge of newspaper publicity for Lincoln, and, aided by C. H. Ray, he kept up a barrage of pro-Lincoln editorials in the influential *Chicago Press and Tribune,* beginning with a three-foot editorial headed "The Winning Man, Abraham Lincoln" on the day before the convention came to order. Judd, in charge of seating arrangements in the Wigwam, took pains to put the New York delegation at one end of the hall and the Pennsylvania delegation at the other; separated by pro-Lincoln supporters, they could not confer or influence each other during the balloting. Aware that Thurlow Weed, commandant of the Seward forces, had come to Chicago on a special thirteen-car train filled with the New York senator's supporters, Judd also arranged for Illinois railroads to offer special rates so that thousands of Lincoln men could attend the convention. After the first day, when it seemed likely that Seward men would pack the Wigwam, Jesse W. Fell and Ward Hill Lamon oversaw the printing of duplicate tickets and made sure they went to Lincoln men who would come early and occupy the seats before the Seward backers arrived.

Inevitably there was talk at this convention—as at all political conventions —of horse trading between candidates and of promising undecided or unscrupulous delegates future patronage, or sometimes immediate cash, for their votes. Weed was prepared to make deals in Chicago just as he had long done in Albany. He dangled before the Illinois delegates a promise of the vice presidential nomination for Lincoln if they supported Seward on the first ballot and also offered to contribute $100,000 to the campaign chests of the Illinois and Indiana Republican parties.

Some of Lincoln's supporters wanted to play the same game. "You need a few trusty friends here to say words for you that may be necessary to be said," Ray warned Lincoln as the convention was assembling. "A pledge or two may be necessary when the pinch comes." Delahay, the Kansas Republican, whose expenses in Chicago Lincoln was paying, had a similar idea. He wrote the candidate that Davis, Dubois, and the other members of his team were "too honest to advance your Prospects as surely as I would like to see" and too innocent to compete with New York politicians, who were *"desperate gamblers."* Lincoln ought to pick one representative from Pennsylvania, Ohio, Massachusetts, and Iowa and promise each full control over all patronage in his state if he delivered the vote of his delegation. "I know that you have no relish for such a Game," Delahay continued, "but it is an old maxim that you must fight the *devil with fire."*

In response to such suggestions Lincoln sent a terse message to Chicago: *"Make no contracts that will bind me."* For the most part, his directive was unnecessary. Though Davis's team had been working incessantly to woo uncommitted delegates, they did not find it necessary to resort to bribery or corruption. Subsequent stories about the numerous bargains Davis and his aides made in Chicago were mostly based on speculation by ill-informed politicians who had been surprised by the showing Lincoln made at the convention. For instance, the charge that Davis promised a cabinet post to Caleb B. Smith in order to secure the vote of the Indiana delegation on the first ballot had no foundation. Before the convention met, a delegate from Vincennes, Indiana, alerted Lincoln "that the whole of Indiana might not be difficult to get," and at his instruction Davis and Dubois paid special attention to the Indiana delegation in Chicago. Indiana Republicans were looking for an alternative to Seward because Henry S. Lane, their candidate for governor, felt that he had no chance for success if the New Yorker headed the ticket. Some favored Bates, who appealed to the old Whigs, but others supported Lincoln. At a caucus of the delegation Bates's managers tried to woo the Hoosiers, but they were routed when Koerner reminded the delegates that German Republicans from nearly every Northern state, meeting at the Deutsches Haus in Chicago on May 14, had agreed to bolt the party before supporting any candidate, like Bates, who had a nativist record. The Indiana delegation then agreed to vote unanimously for Lincoln on the first ballot. No special pledge was needed to gain Smith's support; after serving with Lincoln in Congress and working with him to elect Zachary Taylor, he was proud to be chosen to second Lincoln's nomination in Chicago.

There was more credibility to the report that Davis made a bargain with the Pennsylvania delegation, offering a cabinet post to Simon Cameron if his supporters went for Lincoln after the initial ballot. Judge Joseph Casey, Cameron's representative in Chicago, demanded that Davis and Swett pledge that Cameron would become Secretary of the Treasury in Lincoln's cabinet, with control of all federal patronage in Pennsylvania, in return for the votes of that state on the second ballot. Davis responded vaguely that Pennsylvania would surely have a place in the cabinet and that he would personally recommend Cameron for it. Assuming Davis was authorized to speak for Lincoln, Casey thought he had received a pledge and shortly after the convention wrote Cameron that the switch of Pennsylvania votes to Lincoln "was arranged carefully and unconditionally in reference to Yourself—to our satisfaction." But Swett, who was present at the conference between Davis and the Pennsylvanian, came away with a different understanding and told a friend in a private letter written only nine days after the convention, "No pledges have been made, no mortgages executed." Davis himself, believing he had made only a personal, conditional promise, flatly denied any bargain: "Mr. Lincoln is committed to no one on earth in relation to office—He promised nothing to gain his nomination, and has promised nothing." That also was Lincoln's understanding when, three days after his nomination, he assured Joshua R. Giddings, "The responsible position assigned me, comes without conditions, save only such honorable ones as are fairly implied."

V

While the Republican National Convention was in session, Lincoln went quietly about his business in Springfield, but he eagerly sought to learn what was going on in Chicago. Up early on Friday, May 18, the day when nominations were to be made, he passed some time playing "fives"—a variety of handball—with some other men in a vacant lot next to the *Illinois State Journal* office. Learning that James C. Conkling had unexpectedly returned from Chicago, he went over to his law office to hear the latest news from the convention. Stretched out on an old settee, so short that his feet stuck out over the end, he listened to Conkling's prediction that Seward could not be nominated and that the convention would choose Lincoln. Lincoln demurred, unwilling to tempt fate by being overoptimistic, and said that either Bates or Chase would probably be the choice. Getting up, he announced: "Well, Conkling, I believe I will go back to my office and practice law."

At the Lincoln & Herndon office Baker, of the *Illinois State Journal,* came in with telegrams announcing that the names of the candidates had been placed in nomination and that Lincoln's was received with great enthusiasm. Shortly afterward, a new telegram announced the result of the first ballot: Seward 173½; Lincoln 102; Bates 48; Cameron 50½; Chase 49. The other votes were widely scattered; 233 were needed for a choice. Giving no indication of his feelings, Lincoln went over to the telegraph office, where a report on the second ballot was just coming in: Seward now had 184½ votes; Lincoln, largely as a result of a switch in the Pennsylvania vote, rose to 181 votes; and all the other candidates lost strength. Lincoln then awaited the results of the third ballot in the *Journal* office. As he had anticipated, this was the last ballot. Seward retained most of his strength, but nearly all the other delegates flocked to Lincoln, with a total of 231½ votes—one and a half votes short of a majority. At this point David K. Cartter rose to switch four Ohio votes from Chase to Lincoln, and other delegations promptly followed, giving him a total of 364, out of a possible 466, votes. The Seward men then moved to make the nomination unanimous.

"I knew this would come when I saw the second ballot," Lincoln remarked as he accepted the congratulations of his fellow townsmen. Emerging from the *Journal* office, he said jokingly to the ball players who broke off their game to congratulate him: "Gentlemen, you had better come up and shake my hand while you can—honors elevate some men." Then he headed for home, explaining: "Well Gentlemen there is a little woman at our house who is probably more interested in this dispatch than I am."

When the news of his nomination became official, along with a report that the convention had balanced the ticket by naming a former Democrat, Hannibal Hamlin of Maine, for Vice President, Lincoln felt under some pressure to go to Chicago, where he could bask in his triumph, allow the Republican delegates a chance to meet their candidate, and soothe the disgruntled Seward element in the party, but his advisers unanimously urged him to stay in Springfield. "Dont come here for God's sake," Davis wired succinctly, adding, "Write no letters and make no promises till you see me."

That was the policy that Lincoln followed. On May 19 a delegation from the convention, headed by George Ashmun of Massachusetts, came to his house in Springfield to notify him of his nomination. Initially the interview was very stiff. Only a few of the delegates had ever seen their candidate before, and they were startled by his appearance. Lincoln was tense because he and Mary had just had a quarrel over whether liquor should be served to the visitors—as it certainly would have been at her father's mansion in Kentucky. But Lincoln knew the strength of the temperance movement and insisted on offering only ice water. As he explained a little later, "Having kept house sixteen years, and having never held the 'cup' to the lips of my friends then, my judgment was that I should not, in my new position, change my habit in this respect." After Ashmun read the notice of his nomination, he responded cautiously that he needed more time fully to consider the platform—and in fact did not formally accept until four days later. To keep the meeting from being a fiasco, Lincoln resorted to a gambit he was frequently to employ in the White House. Singling out the lanky Pennsylvania delegate, William D. Kelley, he asked how tall he was.

"Six feet three," was the answer.

"I beat you," chuckled Lincoln. "I am six feet four without my high-heeled boots."

"Pennsylvania bows to Illinois," Kelley responded in a courtly fashion. "I am glad that we have found a candidate for the Presidency whom we can look up to."

As the visitors began to relax, they moved into the adjoining parlor to meet Mrs. Lincoln. She was such a charming conversationalist, in the Southern style, that Ashmun reported, "I shall be proud, as an American citizen, when the day brings her to grace the White House."

Most of Lincoln's encounters in the months between his nomination and the election were equally content-free. Now that he was a celebrity, everybody wanted to see him, and the number of visitors became too great to be handled at the house on Eighth and Jackson Streets, especially after Willie fell ill with scarlet fever. Gladly Lincoln accepted the invitation of Governor John Wood to use his office in the state capitol. He worked there daily during the summer. Nicolay, who was paid $75 a month from a fund contributed by ten of Lincoln's wealthy Springfield friends, served as his secretary and assistant.

Most of Lincoln's correspondence was of the usual but necessary inconsequential sort expected of public men. He had to make gracious acknowledgment of the hundreds of letters of congratulations he received. There were so many applications for autographs that he prepared a standard reply: "You request an autograph, and here it is. Yours truly A. Lincoln." He had politely to acknowledge election as honorary member of the Washington Agricultural Literary Society of the Farm School in Pennsylvania (later Pennsylvania State College) and to accept a "Chair of State," made of thirty-four different kinds of wood, each representing a state of the Union. Knox College, which had been the home of one of the Lincoln-Douglas debates, conferred on him the LL.D. degree, with the implication, as Browning joked, that he should thereafter "consider yourself a 'scholar,' as well as a 'gentleman,' and deport yourself accordingly."

Much of Lincoln's time was occupied in attempting to satisfy the enormous public curiosity about a candidate whose career was not widely known outside his own state. There was uncertainty about his first name, and he had to assure even Ashmun that he was "Abraham," rather than "Abram." Photographers flocked to Springfield to take his picture. The most successful was Alexander Hesler of Chicago, whose sharply defined prints gave, as Lincoln said, "a very fair representation of my homely face"; they showed Lincoln at the height of his powers and captured, as no other photographs ever did, the peculiar curve of his lower lip, the mole on his right cheek, and the distinctive way he held his head. But most photographers found it hard to take a good picture of the candidate whose face in repose showed such harsh lines that it looked like a mask, and their cameras could not catch the light that flashed in his eyes and the smile that animated his face when he was conversing or telling a story. Several artists also came to Springfield to paint his portrait, and Lincoln uncomplainingly sat for them. To combat the general impression in the East that Lincoln was a very ugly man, Judge John M. Read of Pennsylvania commissioned John Henry Brown to paint a miniature that would be "good-looking whether the original would justify it or not." The distinguished artist Thomas Hicks completed a romantic portrait, which Lincoln said would "give the people of the East . . . a correct idea of how I look at home. . . . I think the picture has a somewhat pleasanter expression than I usually have, but that, perhaps, is not an objection."

Along with Lincoln's portrait, people clamored for facts about his life. Requests for biographical information became so numerous that Lincoln drafted a form reply for Nicolay to send out: "Applications of this class are so numerous that it is simply impossible for him to attend to them." Hardly was the Chicago convention over before campaign biographies of Lincoln and Hamlin were announced. Probably the earliest to be published was the anonymous *Life, Speeches and Public Services of Abram [sic] Lincoln, Together with a Sketch of the Life of Hannibal Hamlin,* issued, in "The Wigwam Edition," by Rudd & Carleton in New York by June 2. Others quickly followed. The most significant, because of its authorship, was by William Dean Howells, which relied in considerable part on interviews that his research assistant, James Quay Howard, conducted in Springfield. Howard himself published another biography. Of greater lasting merit was a *Life of Lincoln,* by John Locke Scripps, an editor of the *Chicago Press and Tribune,* which was based on an extensive autobiographical sketch that Lincoln gave him. In all perhaps 100,000 to 200,000 of such campaign biographies were distributed.

Part of Lincoln's time was spent in attempting damage control of rumors about his record. Opponents whispered that he was a deist and a duelist. Stories of his stand on the Mexican War were resurrected, with charges that he failed to vote for supplies to the American army in the field. He was charged with slandering the memory of Thomas Jefferson by accusing him of "puling about liberty, equality, and the degrading curse of slavery" while selling off his own children into slavery. A report surfaced that Lincoln had attended a Know Nothing lodge in Quincy. All these Lincoln painstakingly refuted in private letters, cautioning his correspondents not to get him involved in controversy. "Our adversaries think they can gain a point, if they could force me to openly deny this charge," he explained to one. "For this reason, it must not publicly appear that I am paying any attention to the charge."

Forbidden by the unanimous advice of his friends from taking any public role in the canvass, Lincoln followed the campaign closely. After June, when the Democratic party split, with the Northern wing of the party nominating Douglas and the Southerners nominating John C. Breckinridge, he had little doubt that the Republicans would win the presidential election if the discordant and rival elements that composed the party could work together. He spent much time attempting to conciliate the rival factions in Pennsylvania, headed by Senator Cameron and Andrew G. Curtin, the Republican candidate for governor. Because that state was so crucial, he tried to impress on both the soundness of his record on the tariff, going so far as to send a collection of snippets from his addresses during the 1840s showing that he favored protection. Aware that Seward's followers were disgruntled because of his defeat in Chicago, Lincoln sent word to New Yorkers through David Davis that he "neither is nor will be . . . committed to any man, clique, or faction; and that . . . it will be his pleasure . . . to deal fairly with all." Again and again, he pledged that if elected his slogan would be *"Justice and fairness to all."* In welcoming visitors to Springfield and in writing letters, he firmly refused to make any distinction between Republicans who had supported his candidacy before Chicago and those who had favored other candidates. "I go not back of the convention," he explained to Carl Schurz, who had backed Seward, "to make distinctions among its' members." "You distinguish between yourself and my *original* friends," he told Schuyler Colfax, the glib young Indiana politician who had supported Bates; that was "a distinction which, by your leave, I propose to forget."

Despite all the visitors and all the correspondence, Lincoln found life as a presidential candidate confining. He rarely went to the law office these days, and when Herndon dropped in on his partner in the state capitol, he found his partner "bored—*bored badly,*" and exclaimed to Trumbull, "Good gracious, I would not have his place and be bored as he is."

Lincoln's one public appearance during the campaign was at a giant rally in Springfield in August, where he expected simply to see the people and to allow himself to be seen. Entreated to address the crowd, he reiterated his policy: "It has been my purpose, since I have been placed in my present position, to make no speeches." So enthusiastic was his reception that, when he got ready to leave, the crowd at the fairgrounds surrounded his carriage, broke through the top, and came near to smothering him. He escaped only when a friend backed his horse next to the carriage, pulled Lincoln out, "slipped him over the horses tail on to the saddle [and] led the horse to town."

Occasionally Lincoln thought of taking a more active role in the campaign, imitating Douglas, who was flouting precedent and making stump speeches in behalf of his candidacy. When Seward, who recovered from his momentary pique, went on a barnstorming tour of the West for the Republican ticket, Lincoln momentarily thought of going to Chicago to meet him, but friends persuaded him that he must not appear to be following the chariot wheels of the senator's triumphant procession. He remained at home, but when Seward passed through Springfield, the two men had a brief chat. Restive, Lincoln even considered, improbably enough, accepting an invitation to speak at a horse show in Springfield, Massachusetts, perhaps because the trip would allow him to visit Robert, who had just been admitted to Harvard College. But his friends convinced him that such a trip would be viewed as "evidence of Republican alarm," and he dropped the idea.

Necessarily, then, Lincoln was largely isolated from the hurly-burly of the campaign. He had little to do with the gigantic rallies Republicans held in most Northern cities, with the innumerable processions of young Republican "Wide-Awakes" clad in black oilcloth capes and caps, bearing rails surmounted by torches. He could only watch the exhibitions put on by Republican paramilitary groups, like the Zouave company recruited and drilled by his young friend Elmer Ellsworth, who was supposed to be reading law in the Lincoln & Herndon office. Such "parades, and shows, and monster meetings," Lincoln confessed, were not much to his liking anyway; it was the "dry, and irksome labor" of organizing precincts and getting out the voters that determined elections.

Impatiently Lincoln awaited the returns from the October state elections, especially in Pennsylvania, Ohio, and Indiana. The news of Republican victories in all three states confirmed the brilliance of the party campaign strategy. The returns—which would be closely paralleled in the general election a month later—showed that the Republicans by disavowing immigration restrictions had succeeded in holding on to a fair share of the foreign-born vote, especially among younger, Protestant voters. More important, they demonstrated that in nominating Lincoln, who had taken pains not to attack the Know Nothings publicly, the party was able to win most of the voters who had supported Fillmore in 1856. And, finally, they proved that, despite Lincoln's personal lack of interest, the Wide-Awake clubs, with their frequent meetings, organized drills, and processions, stimulated immense enthusiasm on the part of younger voters, many of whom cast their first ballots in this election. It was appropriate for the victory to be celebrated by a parade of the Springfield Wide-Awakes to Lincoln's house, where, standing on the doorstep surrounded by friends, he bowed silent acknowledgment of their applause. The next day he wrote Seward: "It now really looks as if the Government is about to fall into our hands. Pennsylvania, Ohio, and Indiana have surpassed all expectation."

Now all that was needed was to avoid any missteps during the remaining weeks before the general election on November 6. Silence was his best policy, because any new statement, or restatement, of his views would lead to "new misrepresentations" by opponents. To one worried adviser he gave assurance: "Allow me to beg that you will not live in much apprehension of my precipitating a letter upon the public."

On election day Herndon went to Lincoln's office in the state capitol and urged his partner to vote. Initially reluctant, Lincoln was persuaded that his ballot might be important in the state elections, and he cut off the top of the sheet, listing the presidential electors, so that he would not be voting for himself. Then, accompanied by Herndon and escorted on one side by Lamon and on the other by Ellsworth, he went to the polls. Republicans yelled and shouted as he approached and again after he cast his ballot. Even Democrats, who were proud of their local celebrity, respectfully raised their hats.

That evening Lincoln joined fellow Republicans who crowded the capitol to hear the returns, relayed from the telegraph office. Illinois went Republican, then Indiana, and the ticket did well in the other Western states. But there was still no news from the critical Eastern states, and Lincoln, Dubois, Hatch, and one or two others walked over to the telegraph office. Not until after ten o'clock did reports come in of Republican victories in Pennsylvania. While they were awaiting the news from New York, the party was invited to Watson's Saloon, where the Republican ladies who had taken it over for the night were serving supper. When Lincoln entered the room, the women greeted him: "How do you do, Mr. President!" After eating, Lincoln stayed on at the telegraph office until about two o'clock, when the news that his party had carried New York made his election certain. "I went home, but not to get much sleep," he remembered, "for I then felt as I never had before, the responsibility that was upon me."

It was days before the exact measure of his victory could be determined. When the final tally was made, the Republican ticket received 1,866,452 votes to 1,376,957 for Douglas, 849,781 for Breckinridge, and 588,879 for Bell. With less than 40 percent of the popular vote, the Lincoln and Hamlin ticket won 180 votes in the electoral college to 72 for Breckinridge, 39 for Bell, and 12 for Douglas. The Republican ticket carried all but one of the free states and divided that one—New Jersey—with Douglas. Douglas, despite his large popular vote, won only the Missouri and part of the New Jersey electoral vote. Bell's strength was in the states of the upper South—Virginia, Tennessee, and Kentucky. Breckinridge won in all the other slave states. It was ominous that Lincoln and Hamlin received not a single vote in ten of the Southern states.

In the days before the election, as Republican victory seemed increasingly likely, Lincoln's basic pessimism reemerged as he began fully to realize that a campaign initially undertaken primarily for local political reasons was going to place him in the White House. Just a few days before the election he remarked to a New York caller: "I declare to you this morning, General, that for personal considerations I would rather have a full term in the Senate —a place in which I would feel more consciously able to discharge the duties required, and where there is more chance to make a reputation, and less danger of losing it—than four years of the presidency."

CHAPTER TEN

An Accidental Instrument

———•———

Formidable problems faced the President-elect. At the news of his election, disunion erupted in the South. On November 10 the South Carolina legislature unanimously authorized the election of a state convention on December 6, to consider future relations between the state and the Union. Eight days later Georgia followed suit. Within a month every state of the lower South had taken initial steps toward secession. Northerners were divided over how to deal with the crisis. Some few thought the dissatisfied states should be allowed—even encouraged—to go in peace. A much larger number favored a new agreement in the spirit of the Missouri Compromise and the Compromise of 1850 that would keep the Southern states in the Union. At least as many others opposed any concessions to the South.

The United States government had no policy to deal with this crisis. President James Buchanan was torn between his belief that secession was unconstitutional and his conviction that nothing could be done to prevent it. The lame-duck Congress was controlled by the recently formed Republican party, a still imperfect fusion of former Whigs, former Democrats, and former members of the American party. With experience only as an opposition party, Republicans had never before been called on to offer constructive leadership.

All eyes now turned to Springfield, where an inexperienced leader with a limited personal acquaintance among members of his own party groped his way, on the basis of inadequate information, to formulate a policy for his new administration.

I

In the months after the election the President-elect went steadily about his business in Springfield. Working with Nicolay, his efficient, unflappable private secretary, he dealt with several baskets of mail that arrived each day. Presently the burden of correspondence was so great that Nicolay recruited young John Hay, a recent graduate of Brown University who was studying law in his uncle's office in Springfield, to help. Letters requesting Lincoln's autograph were the easiest to answer. Dozens of letters of congratulation and many more requesting jobs went promptly into the waste basket. Still, much correspondence required the attention of the President-elect himself.

At ten o'clock Lincoln opened his office in the state capitol to visitors, and they flocked in until he closed at noon, only to return for his afternoon hours from three to five-thirty. His callers were of every sort: politicians offering advice on policy and cabinet assignments; journalists looking for exclusive stories or at least local color; artists who wanted to paint his picture; women who simply asked to shake his hand; country bumpkins who came to gawk; old friends from his New Salem days. The room was always crowded. It could comfortably accommodate only about a dozen people, but Lincoln wanted to see everybody. Spying a delegation waiting in the hall, he would reach out to shake the leader's hand and insist, "Get in, all of you." Asking for their names, he would start a conversation and seemed never at a loss for words.

Visitors did not know what to make of this President-elect. He surprised even his old friends by growing a beard. During the campaign some New York "True Republicans," worried that Lincoln's unflattering photographs would cost the party votes, suggested that he "would be much improved in appearance, provided you would cultivate whiskers, and wear standing collars." A letter from an eleven-year-old girl in Westfield, New York, named Grace Bedell promised to get her brothers to vote for Lincoln if he let his beard grow. "You would look a great deal better for your face is so thin," she suggested. "All the ladies like whiskers and they would tease their husband's to vote for you and then you would be President." Amused, Lincoln replied, "As to the whiskers, having never worn any, do you not think people would call it a piece of silly affec[ta]tion if I were to begin it now?" He answered his own question and by the end of November was sporting a half beard, which he initially kept closely cropped. No one knew just what to make of the change. Perhaps it suggested that he was hiding his face because he knew he was not ready to be President. Or maybe it demonstrated the supreme self-confidence of a man who was willing to risk the inevitable ridicule and unavoidable puns like "Old Abe is . . . puttin' on (h)airs." Or possibly it hinted that the President-elect wanted to present a new face to the public, a more authoritative and elderly bearded visage. Or maybe the beard signified nothing more than that the President-elect was bored during the long months of inaction between his nomination and his inauguration.

Lincoln's manner as well as his appearance startled visitors. Though he was often called "Old Abe," he was, up to this point, one of the youngest presidents of the United States. Only fifty-one years old, he was a generation younger than his predecessor, James Buchanan. Vigorous and athletic, he loped along in his countryman's gait at a pace that tired out companions twenty years younger, and he bounded up stairways two or three steps at a time. His energy seemed inexhaustible.

So did his conversation. Visitors to his office often felt stunned by the sheer volume of his words. He showered upon them opinions, ideas, and anecdotes concerning almost every subject in the world—except secession, on which he closely kept his own counsel. What puzzled them most was his highly unpresidential habit of regaling guests with jokes and anecdotes. When telling these tales, his face lit up, and at the punch line his high-pitched laughter rang through the capitol. He might punctuate a story with a hearty slap on his thigh, and after a particularly good one he would rock with mirth, sometimes reaching out with his long arms to draw his knees up almost to his face. Lincoln liked puns, the more outrageous the better. He enjoyed Irish bulls, like the story of Patrick and his new boots: "I shall niver git em on," said the Irishman, "till I wear em a day or two, and stre[t]ch em a little." He delighted in tall tales, especially those with a frontier setting in Kentucky or Indiana.

Most stories he recounted simply because he thought they were funny. Laughing along with his visitors helped break the ice. But he also knew how to use storytelling to deflect criticism, to avoid giving an answer to a difficult question, and to get rid of a persistent interviewer. When former Governor Charles S. Morehead of Kentucky urged him to make concessions to the secessionists, Lincoln was reminded of Aesop's fable about the lion in love with a beautiful woman, whose parents were opposed to her marrying the beast but were afraid of his long claws and sharp teeth. Claiming that their daughter was frail and delicate, they asked the lion to have his claws cut off and his tusks drawn lest he do serious injury to her. Desperately in love, the lion consented, and as soon as his claws were clipped and his tusks removed, the parents took clubs and knocked him on the head. Disgruntled, Morehead remarked "that it was an exceedingly interesting anecdote, and very *apropos,* but not altogether a satisfactory answer." Lincoln used this technique throughout his presidency, to the bafflement of those who had no sense of humor and the rage of those who failed to get a straight answer from him.

II

In the three months after his election Lincoln issued no public statements and made no formal addresses. At most, he could be cajoled only into offering bland observations: "Let us at all times remember that all American citizens are brothers of a common country, and should dwell together in the bonds of fraternal feeling." He resisted the growing pressure to reassure the South or even to restate and clarify his views. "I could say nothing which I have not already said, and which is in print and accessible to the public," he explained in letters marked "Private and confidential."

Behind his silence lay a recognition of the weakness of his position. Though the Republicans had carried the election in November, not one vote had been cast for him personally. The presidential electors chosen in that election did not meet until December 5, and their ballots would not be officially counted until February 13, which Lincoln regarded as "the most dangerous point" in the whole election process. Until that time he had no legal standing as a public official.

He was also following the advice of most leaders of his party. Immediately after the election Thurlow Weed, who often spoke for Seward, urged him to preserve "the self-respect, courage and dignity maintained throughout the canvass" by refusing to make any public statement. Joseph Medill warned that Lincoln must ignore the pleas of the "d——d fools or knaves who want him to make a 'union saving speech'" to conciliate the South: "He must keep his feet out of all such wolfe [sic] traps." In part, Lincoln was reluctant to restate his views on the sectional conflict lest he inadvertently cause demoralization and panic in the North. Any indication that he was frightened by Southern bluster would only throw his supporters in the North into disarray. Consequently when Donn Piatt, a brilliant but erratic Cincinnati journalist, warned that the Southerners meant war and that within ninety days the land would be whitened with army tents, Lincoln dismissed his fears. "Well, we won't jump that ditch until we come to it," he said almost flippantly. "I must run the machine as I find it."

But Lincoln's stand also reflected his deeply held conviction that Unionists were in a large majority throughout the South and that, given time for tempers to cool, they would be able to defeat the secessionist conspirators. He put much faith in the old Whig element—men with whom he had worked closely in the 1848 movement to elect Zachary Taylor—and did not believe that any sizable number of rational citizens could contemplate disrupting the best government the world had ever seen. They must be bluffing. In the past Southerners had threatened to dissolve the Union—in the debates over the admission of Missouri in 1819–1820, in the controversy over the tariff and nullification in Jackson's time, in the protracted crisis over territories acquired in the Mexican War—in order to extract concessions from the North. That must be what was happening now. Appeals for him to modify his positions were just "the trick by which the South breaks down every Northern man." If he agreed to do it, he "would be as powerless as a block of buckeye wood."

But public pressure for him to redefine his position grew so great that he drafted two paragraphs for Senator Trumbull to insert in an address to a Republican victory celebration in Springfield on November 20. The passage pledged that under Lincoln's administration "each and all of the States will be left in as complete control of their own affairs respectively, and at as perfect liberty to choose, and employ, their own means of protecting property, and preserving peace and order . . . as they have ever been under any administration." Widely recognized as an official statement emanating from the President-elect himself, Trumbull's speech had almost no effect in quieting public anxiety. The *Boston Courier* thought it foreshadowed an abandonment of Republican principles, while the *Washington Constitution* called it an open declaration of war upon the South. This was just what Lincoln had expected. "These political fiends are not half sick enough yet. 'Party malice' and not 'public good' possesses them entirely." With biblical wrath he promised: " 'They seek a sign, and no sign shall be given them.' "

A passage in the paragraphs Lincoln gave Trumbull showed how poorly he understood the nature and extent of secessionist sentiment. Disunionists, he wanted Trumbull to say, were "now in hot haste to get out of the Union, precisely because they perceive they can not, much longer, maintain apprehension among the Southern people that their homes, and firesides, and lives, are to be endangered by the action of the Federal Government." Then Lincoln went on to add an astonishing paragraph: "I am rather glad of this military preparation in the South. It will enable the people the more easily to suppress any uprisings there, which their misrepresentation of purposes may have encouraged."

Wisely Trumbull suppressed this passage—but he then went on to undermine Lincoln's pacific purpose by denouncing secession as terrorism and vowing swift action against the "traitors" in the South.

III

On the night after the election Lincoln was too exhausted to sleep and, oppressed by the responsibility that would soon be his, he began casting about in his mind for advisers who could best help him. He jotted down eight names on the back of a blank card:

Lincoln	Judd
Seward	Chase
Bates	M. Blair
Dayton	Welles.

The list suggested the direction of his thinking. He was the nominal head of the Republican party, but he recognized that he had been chosen because of his availability rather than because of a demonstrated record of leadership. If his administration was to be successful, he needed the support of Seward,

Chase, and Bates, his principal rivals for the nomination. As he frankly told Thurlow Weed, "their long experience in public affairs, and their eminent fitness" gave them "higher claims than his own for the place he was to occupy."

That preliminary list also indicated Lincoln's understanding that the Republican party was not a unified, coherent organization but a collection of rival interest groups. The most important of these were the antislavery former Whigs and the free-soil Democrats, divided by party battles waged over more than a generation. If peace was to be maintained between these factions, neither must dominate the cabinet. The four names in the right-hand column had Democratic antecedents; the three cabinet members in the left column were former Whigs. Later when Weed observed that such an arrangement gave a preponderance to the Democrats, Lincoln replied: "You seem to forget that *I* expect to be there; and counting me as one, you see how nicely the cabinet would be balanced and ballasted."

Lincoln's initial list was balanced in other ways, too. Geographically it gave one cabinet member (Gideon Welles of Connecticut) to New England, two (William H. Seward and William L. Dayton) to the Northeastern states of New York and New Jersey, two (Salmon P. Chase and Norman B. Judd) to the Northwest, and two (Edward Bates and Montgomery Blair) to the border slave states. In thinking of Dayton, the unsuccessful Republican candidate for Vice President in 1856, Lincoln was not merely rewarding party service but recognizing the powerful protectionist interests of New Jersey and Pennsylvania. Naming Bates gave tacit recognition to the Know Nothing element that had supported the Republican ticket in 1860. Montgomery Blair represented both the incipient Republican party in Maryland and the Blair family, powerful in the border states since Jackson's day. Finally, in choosing Judd, Lincoln recognized the importance of Illinois and at the same time added a close friend to a cabinet otherwise made up of strangers.

Keeping this list in mind, Lincoln proceeded with his customary caution. Two days after the election he asked Hannibal Hamlin, whom he had never met face-to-face, to meet him in Chicago. There on November 21 the future President and the future Vice President began a three-day conference, which reporters described as "cordial in the highest degree." Much of the time they were joined by Trumbull, whom the newspapers called "the President's mouthpiece in the Senate," and from time to time other Republican leaders, like Carl Schurz of Wisconsin, were brought in for advice.

The main item on the agenda was the selection of the cabinet. There was ready agreement that the office of Secretary of State must be offered to Seward, in recognition of his services to the Republican party and his position in the Senate. But it was not certain that Seward would accept. Hurt because the Chicago convention passed him over, he might not be willing to serve as a subordinate to Lincoln. Hence the invitation must be so phrased that if he refused it would not seem a rebuff to the new administration.

Lincoln entrusted the handling of this delicate negotiation to Hamlin, who was experienced in the intricacies of Washington politics.

Lincoln's natural caution and his inexperience in national politics almost derailed Seward's appointment. The delay in publicly naming the New Yorker encouraged an anti-Seward faction in the New York Republican party, which included William Cullen Bryant, the editor of the *New York Evening Post,* and important New York City businessmen like Hiram Barney, George Opdyke, and W. C. Noyes. They put their opposition to Seward principally on the ground that Weed, his ally who at times seemed to be his alter ego, had been involved in corrupting the state legislature; they wanted "honest men with clean hands" in the cabinet. Lincoln's slowness to select Seward suggested that he was listening to these critics. Soon the rumor spread that he did not really want the New Yorker in his cabinet, that the appointment would be offered to him as a compliment with the expectation that he would decline it. So damaging was this report that Lincoln felt obliged to offer Seward an embarrassed explanation that he had all along intended to tender the State Department to him but had delayed "in deference to what appeared to me to be a proper caution in the case." Gratified but not entirely mollified, Seward agreed to take the offer under consideration. He did not, however, accept until Weed went out to Springfield for a heart-to-heart talk with the President-elect. After Lincoln assured Weed that in the distribution of patronage he really meant to honor his pledge, "Justice to all," Seward on December 28, "after due reflection and with much self distrust," agreed to serve.

Even before Seward accepted, he and Weed had begun to press Lincoln to deviate from his original list and name one or more cabinet members from the South. This move would assure the slave states that Lincoln was going to head a truly national administration—and at the same time it could block the appointment of Salmon P. Chase or other rivals of Seward. Lincoln was attracted by the idea but was not sure it was practical. To test its feasibility he wrote a short editorial for anonymous publication in the *Illinois State Journal,* inquiring whether any Southern "gentleman of character" would accept a place in his cabinet and on what terms: "Does he surrender to Mr. Lincoln, or Mr. Lincoln to him, on the political difference between them?"

The strongest of the Southern Unionists that Weed proposed—Lincoln called them "white crows"—was Representative John A. Gilmer of North Carolina, a conservative Whig opponent of secession. Impressed by Gilmer's sincere Unionism, Lincoln invited him to Springfield, but the North Carolinian failed to understand the signal and declined. In January, Weed and Seward approached Gilmer with a positive offer of a cabinet post, but he insisted that Republicans must offer federal protection to slavery in the territories in order to appease his "maddened brethren of the South." With that Gilmer's candidacy died.

The elimination of Gilmer made room for the selection of Montgomery Blair, who was on Lincoln's initial list. He was not from the Deep South, but he did live in the slave state of Maryland, where he had campaigned vigorously for the Republican presidential ticket. Though unprepossessing in appearance, with a mean, hatchet face, Blair had considerable support among former Democrats like Trumbull and Hamlin, and John A. Andrew, the abolitionist governor of Massachusetts, was one of his backers. Despite Weed's strong objections, Blair was picked as Postmaster General.

Lincoln did not approach Salmon P. Chase until after he received Seward's acceptance. The two men were such bitter rivals that an invitation to Chase might have caused Seward to decline. But now Lincoln felt free to invite him to Springfield. He had never seen the Ohioan, who had just ended his second term as governor and was about to take a place in the Senate, and wanted to talk with him before offering him an appointment. When they met on January 4 and 5, Lincoln was greatly impressed. He said later that Chase "is about one hundred and fifty to any other man's hundred." Tall and broad-shouldered, with a massive dome of a head that hinted at vast intellectual powers, Chase, Carl Schurz remarked, "looked as you would wish a statesman to look."

Even this first encounter hinted that their future relationship might not be easy. After explaining why he had offered the first place in the cabinet to Seward, Lincoln spoke to Chase about the Treasury Department. He said that Pennsylvanians had raised some objections to Chase because he was known as a free-trade advocate, but he believed these could be overcome. So he asked his visitor to "accept the appointment of Secretary of the Treasury, without, however, [my] being exactly prepared to offer it to you." Chase recorded he cagily responded to this nonoffer: "I did not wish and was not prepared to say that I would accept the place if offered." Despite considerable pressure from Chase's friends in Ohio and from anti-Seward Republicans in New York, Lincoln decided not to make the appointment until after he reached Washington.

At Chicago, Lincoln had promised that his Vice President could name the cabinet member from New England. It was a generous gesture, but Lincoln was pretty sure that Hamlin's choice would be his own: Gideon Welles, a former Democrat and editor of the influential *Hartford Evening Press,* who had headed the Connecticut delegation to Chicago and helped defeat Seward there. Lincoln and Hamlin settled on him for Secretary of the Navy because in the 1840s he had served as chief of the Bureau of Provisions and Clothing for the navy.

Meanwhile Lincoln approached another man on his original list for the cabinet. On December 15, Edward Bates came to see the President-elect in Springfield. In their very free discussion, as Bates recorded in his diary, Lincoln told Bates that his participation in the administration was "necessary to its complete success." Finding it convenient to forget that he had written to Seward a week earlier, he assured Bates that he was "the only man that he desired in the Cabinet, to whom he [had] yet spoken . . . [or] written a word, about their own appointments." Recognizing that the vast ego of the sixty-seven-year-old Missouri lawyer might lead him to expect the first place in the cabinet, Lincoln explained why it was politically necessary to offer Seward the State Department, but he made the news more palatable by giving Bates the impression that he hoped Seward would decline. In that case Bates would get the job. Until then he could offer the post of Attorney General. Suitably massaged, Bates accepted.

Lincoln's other cabinet selections were more difficult. Judd, who was on his original list, had the backing of the former Democrats in the Illinois Republican party but was strongly opposed by David Davis, Leonard Swett, and other former Whigs. Mary Lincoln also violently disliked him. Further to complicate matters, Lincoln had to weigh the interests of Illinois in a cabinet position against the rival claims of Indiana, which had done so much to make his nomination in Chicago possible. There Caleb B. Smith earnestly sought a cabinet seat, and David Davis reminded the President-elect: "No one rendered more efficient service from Indiana. . . . without his active aid and co-operation, the Indiana delegation could not have been got as a unit to go for you." But Lincoln also had to consider the claim of Smith's Indiana rival Schuyler Colfax, who had supported Bates for the presidential nomination but who had fought hard for Lincoln's victory in the election. It was no wonder that Lincoln, as he told Thurlow Weed, found that "the making of a cabinet . . . was by no means as easy as he had supposed."

Eventually he decided to eliminate Judd on the grounds that Illinois had already received so much recognition as the home of the President-elect. With Judd out, he had to choose between Smith and Colfax, and he eventually settled on Smith. "Colfax is a young man, is already in position, is running a brilliant career and is sure of a bright future in any event," he reasoned; "with Smith, it is now or never."

Indiana problems were simple compared to those of Pennsylvania. Lincoln did not initially plan to offer the state representation in his cabinet because Pennsylvania Republicans were so bitterly divided. One faction was loyal to Senator Cameron; another followed Governor-elect Andrew G. Curtin and A. K. McClure, chairman of the Pennsylvania Republican state committee. Certain that the rivals could never agree on a candidate for the cabinet, he thought that naming Dayton of New Jersey would adequately represent Pennsylvania's high-tariff interests.

That plan infuriated Cameron's supporters, who believed that Lincoln had not been "made *fully acquainted* with the conversations and understandings" that David Davis and Leonard Swett had had with the Pennsylvania delegation at the Tremont House the night before the nomination. Only two days after the election Cameron's representatives, escorted by both Davis and Swett, descended on Springfield for an interview with the President-elect. They found Lincoln hospitable, affable—and baffling. They learned nothing about cabinet prospects but heard story after story of frontier days.

At Davis's advice they went home and organized a letter-writing campaign in Cameron's behalf. Soon Lincoln's desk was covered with testimonials for the senator, and he could not help being impressed. Shortly afterward Swett gave him another nudge by reminding him that "the Cameron influence, as much as any thing nominated you."

But a chorus of opposition swelled when it became known that Cameron was under consideration for a cabinet post. Free-traders fought against appointing a man committed to a high protective tariff. Opponents of Seward and Weed feared the appointment because it would, in effect, give Seward a second vote in the cabinet. But most of the hostility stemmed from Cameron's checkered record. During Van Buren's administration he had served as commissioner to settle the claims of the Winnebago Indians and had allegedly defrauded his charges of $66,000; thereafter he was derisively known in Pennsylvania politics as the "Great Winnebago Chief." Using bribery and political intimidation, much as Thurlow Weed did in New York, Cameron became the boss of the Pennsylvania Republican machine. Principled Republicans thought Cameron's appointment to the cabinet would be disgraceful. "His general reputation is *shockingly bad,*" Horace White, of the *Chicago Press and Tribune,* wrote Trumbull. Even mild-mannered Hamlin protested that naming Cameron to the cabinet had an "odor about it that will damn us as a party."

Lincoln worried over the problem for much of December. Drawing up a memorandum of the charges against Cameron and a list of the numerous letters recommending him, he tentatively concluded that, on balance, the evidence favored the senator. He invited Cameron to Springfield, and they met in the senator's hotel room on December 28. Apparently Lincoln liked what he saw. Despite Cameron's malodorous reputation, he appeared to be an amiable, if somewhat reserved, gentleman, tall and thin, with a sharp face and thin lips. A self-made man like Lincoln, he had overcome the handicap of poverty by learning to be a printer and a newspaper editor before amassing a fortune in the iron and railroad business. That his reputation was not spotless was not altogether a negative; Lincoln always had a fondness for slightly damaged characters, like Mark Delahay, Lamon, and Herndon. The two very practical politicians hit it off at once and the next day, as Cameron was preparing to go home, Lincoln sent him a brief note promising that he would nominate him for either Secretary of the Treasury or Secretary of War.

Exultant, Cameron showed the letter to several friends on the way back to Washington. His rejoicing, however, was premature, for his train must have passed another bearing his old enemy, A. K. McClure, bringing documents to Springfield to prove Cameron's moral unfitness for high office. Lincoln recognized his blunder and promptly wrote Cameron that "things have developed which make it impossible for me to take you into the cabinet." He suggested that Cameron, to save face, should decline the appointment. In order to ease the blow, he asked Trumbull to promise that Cameron's friends should "be, with entire fairness, cared for in Pennsylvania, and elsewhere." Restlessly he waited for the desired telegram from Cameron but none came. Hearing that the Pennsylvanian's feelings were wounded by the abrupt phrasing of his letter, Lincoln apologized that it had been written "under great anxiety" and he drafted another, somewhat more tactfully phrased: "You will relieve me from great embarrassment by allowing me to recall the offer. This springs from an unexpected complication; and not from any change of my view as to the ability or faithfulness with which you would discharge the duties of the place." While newspapers and politicians buzzed and hundreds of pro- and anti-Cameron letters reached Lincoln every day, the Winnebago Chief maintained total silence.

To end the stalemate Lincoln let it be known that he would appoint no Pennsylvanian to the cabinet until he reached Washington. Then, on his trip East, he mentioned in passing that it might be good for the new administration to retain one or two members of Buchanan's cabinet, including perhaps the Secretary of the Treasury. At this point powerful business interests in Pennsylvania faced the prospect of having no voice in the Lincoln administration, and rival political factions, all of which represented the coal and iron industries, concluded it would be better to have Cameron with all his faults than to have no representation in the cabinet at all.

In this disorderly way Lincoln picked his closest official advisers. The selection process ensured that the cabinet would never be harmonious or loyal to the President.

IV

During the winter of 1860–1861 while Lincoln was constructing his cabinet, the country was falling to pieces. On December 3 the Congress reassembled to hear the plaintive message of retiring President Buchanan, who deplored secession but said nothing could be done to stop it. Three days later South Carolinians elected an overwhelmingly secessionist state convention, which on December 20 declared that the state was no longer a part of the Union. By the end of January, Florida, Mississippi, Alabama, Georgia, and Louisiana all followed, and secession was under way in Texas. In February representatives of six states of the Deep South met at Montgomery, Alabama, and drew up a constitution for the new Confederate States of America. As the Southern states seceded, they seized federal arsenals and forts within their borders. Apart from two minor installations in Florida, only Fort Pickens at Pensacola and the fortifications at Charleston, South Carolina, remained in the control of the United States government. Late in December, Major Robert Anderson, in command at Fort Moultrie on the shoreline at Charleston, transferred his small garrison to the more defensible Fort Sumter, erected on a rock shoal in the harbor. On January 9, when the *Star of the West,* bearing supplies and

200 additional troops, tried to reinforce the Sumter garrison, the South Carolinians fired on it and forced it to retreat.

In Washington government officials could not agree on how to deal with the increasingly serious crisis. The President, along with many other conservatives, favored calling a national convention to amend the Constitution so as to redress Southern grievances. The House of Representatives created the Committee of Thirty-three, with one congressman from each state, to deal with the crisis. After much debate the committee proposed admission of New Mexico as a state, more stringent enforcement of the Fugitive Slave Act, repeal of the personal liberty laws enacted by Northern states to prevent the reclamation of fugitives, and adoption of a constitutional amendment prohibiting future interference with slavery. The Senate set up a similar Committee of Thirteen, which was unable to agree on a program, but John J. Crittenden, one of its members, came up with a broad compromise proposal to extend the Missouri Compromise line through the national territories, prohibiting slavery north of that line but establishing and maintaining it with federal protection south of that line. Crittenden's plan also called for vigorous enforcement of the Fugitive Slave Act and for repeal of the personal liberty laws. In a parallel effort the Peace Conference, summoned to Washington by the Virginia legislature, proposed to Congress a multisectioned constitutional amendment that closely resembled Crittenden's compromise.

The chances for a compromise in 1860–1861 were never great. The Crittenden Compromise, the most promising of the suggested agreements, was opposed by influential Southerners and Northerners alike. Only intervention by the President-elect might have changed the attitude of Republicans in Congress and, in so doing, could conceivably have induced the Southerners to reconsider their position. But Lincoln considered these compromise schemes bribes to the secessionists. Grimly he told a visitor, "I will suffer death before I will consent or will advise my friend to consent to any concession or compromise which looks like buying the privilege to take possession of this government to which we have a constitutional right."

Lincoln believed the real object of the secessionists was to change the nature of the American government. In his view there were only two ways that could be done. One was through amending the Constitution, a right that everyone recognized. He himself did not desire any changes in that document, but if the people wanted a constitutional amendment, even the one forbidding interference with the domestic institutions of states—meaning slavery—he would not oppose it.

The other way of changing a government was through revolution. Since the Mexican War, Lincoln had been on record as a defender of the right of revolution, of that "most sacred right" of a people "to rise up, and shake off the existing government, and form a new one that suits them better." In theory, then, he might have approved when the Southern states declared their independence. But he had always carefully qualified his support of the right of revolution by insisting that it was a moral, rather than a legal, right that must be "exercised for a morally justifiable cause." "Without such a cause," he thought "revolution is no right, but simply a wicked exercise of physical power."

That was "the essence of anarchy," which he would not tolerate. "The right of a State to secede is not an open or debatable question," he told Nicolay; it had been settled in Andrew Jackson's time, during the nullification crisis. "It is the duty of a President to execute the laws and maintain the existing Government. He cannot entertain any proposition for dissolution or dismemberment." Consequently, as he wrote Weed, "No state can, in any way lawfully, get out of the Union, without the consent of the others; and . . . it is the duty of the President, and other government functionaries to run the machine as it is."

Lincoln's commitment to maintaining the Union was absolute. As a young man, he had looked to reason for guidance, both in his turbulent emotional life and in the disorderly society in which he grew up. When that proved inadequate, he found stability in the law and in the Constitution, but after the Dred Scott decision he could no longer have unqualified faith in either. The concept of the Union, older than the Constitution, deriving from the Declaration of Independence with its promise of liberty for all, had become the premise on which all his other political beliefs rested.

In objecting to all compromise measures, Lincoln was out of step with the members of his party in Congress who were better informed about affairs in the South and more alarmed as threats of secession became reality. Weed, speaking for Seward, floated the possibility of extending the Missouri Compromise line; Representative Charles Francis Adams proposed admitting New Mexico as a state without any prohibition on slavery; even Trumbull, hitherto adamantly opposed to compromise, urged that a soothing statement from Lincoln would be "the means of strengthening our friends South."

They pressed him to accept minor concessions that would yield nothing of substance but might give some support to Southern Unionists, and reluctantly he agreed. He had always accepted the constitutionality of the Fugitive Slave Law and now, to please the Southerners, he said he was willing to see it more efficiently enforced, provided that it contained "the usual safeguards to liberty, securing free men against being surrendered as slaves." The personal liberty laws were enacted by the state legislatures, not the Congress, but if such laws were "really, or apparantly, in conflict with such law of Congress," they should be repealed. As for Southern concern over the abolition of slavery in the District of Columbia or interference with the interstate slave trade, he wrote Seward, "I care but little, so that what is done be comely, and not altogether outrageous." He was even willing for New Mexico to be admitted without prohibition of slavery, "if further extension were hedged against."

But on one point he was immovable: the extension of slavery into the national territories. He continued to fear that Republicans might abandon the Chicago platform in favor of Douglas's popular-sovereignty doctrine. "Have none of it," he wrote Trumbull. "Let there be no compromise on the question of *extending* slavery." Over and over, he repeated the message to Republican congressmen: "Stand firm. The tug has to come, and better now, than any time hereafter."

Lincoln knew that any compromise permitting the spread of slavery into the national territories would disrupt the party that had elected him. Opposition to the extension of slavery, perhaps the only issue on which all Republicans agreed, was the central plank of the 1860 Republican platform, which Lincoln had pledged to uphold. He vowed, "By no act or complicity of mine, shall the Republican party become a mere sucked egg, all shell and no principle in it." What is more, he had a visceral objection to rethinking a conclusion that he had reached by laborious reasoning. As Mary Lincoln observed in a different context, "He was a terribly firm man when he set his foot down . . . no man nor woman could rule him after he had made up his mind." His Springfield friends were familiar with that inflexibility. Some thought it showed that he had backbone, but, as William Jayne said, "some of our folks think he is stubborn."

V

In January when the Illinois state legislature met, Lincoln had to vacate the governor's office in the state capitol, and he rented a room in the Johnson Building. Nicolay continued to handle his correspondence, but he himself did not spend much time in the new office. Constantly badgered by office-seekers, he often took refuge in an improvised studio in the St. Nicholas Hotel, where the sculptor Thomas D. Jones was preparing a bust of the President-elect.

Increasingly he felt the need for quiet in order to reflect on his inaugural address. He asked Herndon to lend him a copy of the Constitution, of President Jackson's proclamation against nullification, and of Henry Clay's great speech in behalf of the Compromise of 1850. He had no need to borrow another source he intended to use, Webster's celebrated Second Reply to Hayne, because he already knew it almost by heart; that oration extolling "Liberty *and* Union," he told Herndon, was "the very best speech that was ever delivered." When he had a draft that satisfied him, he asked William H. Bailhache, one of the owners of the *Illinois State Journal,* to have twenty copies secretly printed, so that he could get the advice and criticism of friends.

Like her husband, Mary Lincoln was also preparing to leave Springfield. She had found the presidential campaign tremendously exciting and the outcome highly gratifying. She was, as an Ohio cousin remarked, "an ambitious little woman," and her husband's triumph satisfied her heart's desire.

To those who knew her best, she seemed little changed by victory, and Mrs. Bailhache found her "just as agreeable as ever" and "as pleasant and talkative and entertaining as she can be." But others were troubled by her growing sense of self-importance and her extreme sensitivity to suspected social slights. A Springfield minister unkindly remarked that her ego was now so inflated "that she ought to be sent to the cooper's and well secured against bursting by iron hoops."

Looking forward to her new role in the White House, Mary Lincoln went to New York in January, accompanied by her brother-in-law, C. M. Smith, and Robert joined her there. Aware that in March her husband would begin drawing a salary of $25,000—at least five times as much as his average annual income in Springfield—she set about ordering a wardrobe that would show the Southern dowagers who dominated Washington society that she was no frontier woman. Eagerly merchants extended credit, and she began running up debts that she concealed from her husband. She saw nothing wrong about accepting presents from office-seekers and others who sought favors from the Lincoln administration. She was, after all, now a very important person who deserved special treatment.

Lincoln missed his wife. He was trying to keep house alone, and, the *New York Herald* reported, "Whatever his other qualifications may be, it is well known that in the management of the kitchen and in other domestic concerns he is sadly destitute of both talent and experience." On three consecutive nights he went in the snow and cold to meet the train from the East until Mary returned on January 25.

Five days later the President-elect set out on a journey of his own to see his stepmother in Coles County. He had to use a passenger train, a freight train, and a buggy to complete the difficult trip, but, away from journalists and job-hunters, he was in fine spirits. At dinner in Charleston, when an enthusiastic admirer vowed to shed the last drop of his blood to prevent any interference with his inauguration, Lincoln said he was reminded of the young man about to go to war whose loving sisters were making him a belt handsomely embroidered with the motto "Victory or death." "No, no," said the youth, "don't put it quite that strong. Put it 'Victory or get hurt pretty bad.'"

He found the seventy-three-year-old Sarah Bush Johnston Lincoln living with her daughter in Farmington, near Goosenest Prairie, and had a long and emotional visit with her. Afterward he visited his father's grave and said he intended to have a suitable tombstone erected, but he never did so. When he said good-bye, his stepmother was in tears. "I did not want Abe to run for Presdt.," she recalled years later, "did not want him, elected—was afraid somehow or other . . . that Something would happen [to] him . . . and that I should see him no more." "No No Mama," he comforted her. "Trust in the Lord and all will be well. We will See each other again."

On February 6 the Lincolns said good-bye to their friends in Springfield at a reception described in the New York papers as "the most brilliant affair of the kind witnessed here in many years." Standing side by side in their first-floor parlor from 7 P.M. until midnight, they welcomed seven hundred guests who, according to the *Baltimore Sun,* composed "the political élite of Illinois and the beauty and fashion of the area." The house was jammed, and it took twenty minutes to get in the hall door, but everybody reported the affair was a great success. "Mrs. Lincoln's splendid toilette," it was remarked, "gave satisfactory evidence of extensive purchases during her late visit to New York."

Dozens of practical details had to be arranged before leaving Springfield. The house at Eighth and Jackson streets was rented to Lucian Tilton, a retired railroad executive, for $350 a year. For $24 a year Lincoln took out an insurance policy on the house, valued at $3,000, and outbuildings. Surplus furnishings, like an extra mattress, a wardrobe, and six chairs, were sold and the rest put in storage. Designating Robert Irwin of the Springfield Marine & Fire Insurance Company as his fiscal agent, Lincoln drew up a list of the notes, mortgages, and bonds that he owned, which totaled $10,004.57, and authorized Irwin to collect interest on them and also to pay any bills that might come in after he left for Washington. Working day and night to make sure that everything was packed perfectly, Mary burned stacks of old letters and papers in the back alley.

All the Lincolns made affectionate farewell visits to their Springfield friends. One of Lincoln's last calls was on Herndon, whom Lincoln had not seen frequently during the months after the election. The partners discussed legal matters and talked about the state of the country and the pressure Lincoln was under from job-seekers. Exhausted, the President-elect told Herndon, "I am sick of office-holding already." After a time he asked, "Billy . . . how long have we been together?"

"Over sixteen years," was Herndon's answer.

"We've never had a cross word during all that time, have we?"

Promptly Herndon replied, "No, indeed we have not."

There was an awkward pause, and Lincoln said hesitantly: "Billy . . . there's one thing I have, for some time, wanted you to tell me. . . . I want you to tell me . . . how many times you have been drunk."

Herndon, flustered, had no quick reply. Lincoln changed the subject to tell of several attempts to have him take another partner. Having made his point, he gathered up some books and papers and talked for a moment or two more before going downstairs. Looking back, Lincoln glanced at the law shingle of Lincoln & Herndon. "Let it hang there undisturbed," he said, lowering his voice. "Give our clients to understand that the election of a President makes no change in the firm of Lincoln and Herndon. If I live I'm coming back some time, and then we'll go right on practising law as if nothing had ever happened."

VI

February 11 was cold and rainy, but a crowd of Springfield residents gathered at the Great Western Railroad depot to see Lincoln off. (Mary Lincoln had gone to St. Louis for additional shopping and would join her husband in Indianapolis.) The President-elect himself had roped the family trunks and labeled them A. LINCOLN, THE WHITE HOUSE, WASHINGTON, D.C. A special train had been chartered for the trip, at this point consisting of the Hinckley engine, the *L. M. Wiley,* a baggage car, and a "saloon" for the President and his party. At 7:55 A.M. the President-elect climbed the steps to his private car and paused to say a final farewell to his neighbors, one of whom reported that his "breast heaved with emotion and he could scarcely command his feelings sufficiently to commence."

My friends [he began]—No one, not in my situation, can appreciate my feeling of sadness at this parting. To this place, and the kindness of these people, I owe every thing. Here I have lived a quarter of a century, and have passed from a young to an old man. Here my children have been born, and one is buried. I now leave, not knowing when, or whether ever, I may return, with a task before me greater than that which rested upon Washington. Without the assistance of that Divine Being, who ever attended him, I cannot succeed. With that assistance I cannot fail.... let us confidently hope that all will yet be well. To His care commending you, as I hope in your prayers you will commend me, I bid you an affectionate farewell.

For the next twelve days the presidential train slowly moved across the country, in a journey of 1,904 miles over eighteen railroads. In addition to the President and his immediate family, the party included Nicolay, John Hay, Dr. William S. Wallace, Lincoln's brother-in-law and personal physician, and Elmer Ellsworth, arrayed in his Zouave uniform. Both Judd and David Davis, political enemies and rivals for Lincoln's affection, were aboard, and Hatch, Dubois, Yates, and Browning went part or all the way to Washington. No military officer was detailed to accompany the President-elect, but Colonel E. V. Sumner of the First United States Cavalry and Major David Hunter, the paymaster at Fort Leavenworth, volunteered to serve as escorts, as did Captain John Pope, who joined the party at Indianapolis. Ward Hill Lamon, resplendent in his personally designed uniform as an aide to the Illinois governor, remained close to the President-elect as his burly bodyguard. The presidential train moved from Springfield to Indianapolis to Cincinnati to Columbus; then, after a diversion to Pittsburgh, it proceeded to Cleveland, Buffalo, Albany, and New York City. On the final leg of the journey the President-elect visited Philadelphia and Harrisburg before going on to Washington. Special precautions were taken to prevent sabotage or accident along the route, and flagmen were stationed at every road crossing and at half-mile intervals along the tracks. For most of the journey the presidential train consisted of three cars—a fourth was sometimes added—with the first assigned to journalists, who covered the journey in great detail, the second to local dignitaries who gained prestige from traveling part of the way with the President-elect, and the third for the Lincoln family.

The procession combined all the elements of a traveling circus, a political campaign, and a national holiday. Along the route people gathered to cheer the train and, perhaps, to catch a glimpse of Lincoln. At little Ohio towns like Milford, Loveland, Morrow, and Xenia, where the train stopped only long enough for the President-elect to appear on the rear platform and bow, large crowds assembled, often with bands playing and artillery booming. At Columbus, which a New York reporter dismissed as "only a second class city," perhaps 60,000 citizens joined in the celebration. In the larger cities the throngs were immense, and police could not keep them from pressing close around the incoming President. At Buffalo there was such wild confusion that Major Hunter dislocated his shoulder in his efforts to protect the President-elect from his overenthusiastic admirers.

The stated object of this roundabout journey was to give the people an opportunity to become acquainted with their new Chief Executive, the first American President to be born west of the Appalachian Mountains. To satisfy this natural curiosity Lincoln made very frequent appearances at the rear of the train, where, as he said, he could offer people the opportunity "of observing my very interesting countenance." Presently he developed a formula that he used repeatedly: he came before the public, he announced, so "that I may see you and that you may see me, and in the arrangement I have the best of the bargain." He could afford to joke, because he generally made a favorable impression. From Columbus the *New York Herald* reported that "his personal appearance was pronounced by all much better than had been inferred from his portraits." Future President Rutherford B. Hayes, who met the President-elect in Indianapolis, could not help being amused by Lincoln's awkward attempt to bow to the crowds: "His chin rises—his body breaks in two at the hips—there is bend of the knees at a queer angle." But, "homely as L. is," Hayes concluded, "if you can get a good view of him by *day light* when he is talking he is by no means ill looking."

The journey offered superb opportunities for a politician, and Lincoln played the crowds with consummate skill. He complimented everybody and everything. At Cincinnati he said that the greeting he had received "could not have occurred in any other country on the face of the globe, without the influence of the free institutions which we have increasingly enjoyed for three-quarters of a century." Repeatedly he expressed admiration for the many "good-looking ladies" in his audiences. At Westfield, New York, he called up Grace Bedell, who had urged him to let his whiskers grow, and gave her a big kiss. He praised the bands, and, to avoid making a speech at London, Ohio, urged them to "discourse in their more eloquent music than I am capable of" while "the iron horse stops to water himself."

Recognizing that the crowds were interested in his family as well as himself, Lincoln from time to time urged Mary to join him at whistle stops, but, as he told the ladies at Ashtabula, "he should hardly hope to induce her to appear, as he had always found it very difficult to make her do what she did not want to." By the end of the journey her reserve had sufficiently broken down that she consented to appear on the platform of the train at the side of her tall husband, who told the audience that now they could see "the long and the short of it!"

Curiosity extended to the other members of the Lincoln family. The two little boys were largely shielded from the public, though they immensely enjoyed the long train ride. To relieve boredom, when visitors came aboard, Tad or Willie would ask, "Do you want to see Old Abe?" and then point out someone else. Robert was much in the public eye. Labeled the "Prince of Rails"—a pun that combined reference to his father's manual prowess and to the enthusiastic reception the Prince of Wales had received on his recent visit to the United States—he abandoned for once his natural taciturnity, flirted with the girls, drank too much Catawba wine, and even took a turn at driving the locomotive. The excitement apparently went to his head, and he forgot the one duty his father had asked him to perform: to guard the satchel containing copies of the inaugural address. Robert carelessly entrusted it to a hotel porter, who threw it on an unguarded pile of luggage behind the hotel desk. Expressing anger at one of his children for perhaps the only time in his life, the President-elect had to burrow through unclaimed baggage to identify his case, but fortunately it had not been tampered with and no harm was done.

The journey had the larger purpose of encouraging support for the Union and fostering loyalty among the Northern people. For this reason Lincoln insisted that all reception committees and demonstrations along the route be nonpartisan. He set the tone early in the journey in his remarks at Lafayette, Indiana: "While some of us may differ in political opinions, still we are all united in one feeling for the Union. We all believe in the main-tainance of the Union, of every star and every stripe of the glorious flag." Repeatedly he emphasized that the tumultuous welcome he received was not a personal tribute. He had been elected President, he said, with what was surely excessive modesty, "by a mere accident, and not through any merit of mine"; he was "a mere instrument, an accidental instrument, per-haps I should say," of the great cause of Union. He called himself "the humblest of all individuals that have ever been elected to the Presidency," a man "without a name, perhaps without a reason why I should have a name."

The journey was punctuated by constant calls on Lincoln to speak—to welcoming committees, at receptions, to state legislatures in Indiana, Ohio, New York, New Jersey, and Pennsylvania. The demands were so numerous that he became hoarse, and at times he lost his voice. For some of the major occasions he had prepared little addresses while he was sitting for his bust in Thomas Jones's studio, but mostly he had to improvise. Inevitably there was a good deal of repetition, and some of the speeches he made along the route seemed aimless and inconsequential. Supercilious young Charles Francis Adams, Jr., was appalled to learn that the "absolutely unknown" President-elect was "perambulating the country, kissing little girls and growing whiskers." But a more sober observer, the New York diarist George Templeton Strong, who carefully followed the presidential progress, reached a sounder judgment: "Lincoln is making little speeches as he wends his way toward Washington, and has said some things that are sound and creditable and raise him in my esteem."

Strong and others who followed Lincoln's speeches closely understood that he was laying the groundwork for the policies that his administration would pursue. One of his major themes was that the impending crisis was something "gotten up . . . by designing politicians." "Why all this excitement?" he asked in Cleveland. "Why all these complaints? . . . the crisis is all artificial." Many feared he failed to understand the gravity of the situation, but his intent was to challenge Southerners to "point us to anything in which they are being injured, or about to be injured." Because nobody could identify any specific grievances he felt "justified in concluding that the crisis, the panic, the anxiety of the country at this time is artificial."

At the same time, the President-elect repeatedly asked Northerners to stand firm in the crisis. Not once in the dozens of speeches he made along the journey did he suggest willingness to agree to secession, to acquiesce in Southern seizure of federal forts and arsenals, or to recognize the Confederacy. Over and over, he stressed that he had been elected to uphold the Constitution and enforce the laws. To those who argued this would mean "coercion" and "invasion" of the South, he responded in his Indianapolis speech with a rhetorical question: would it be coercion if the government "simply insists upon holding its own forts, or retaking those forts which belong to it, . . . or . . . the collection of duties upon foreign importations, . . . or even the withdrawal of the mails from those portions of the country where the mails themselves are habitually violated." But, unwilling to precipitate a crisis, he quickly added, "Now, I ask the question—I am not deciding anything."

As the presidential party moved toward the East, news from the South became more ominous. Jefferson Davis was inaugurated Provisional President of the Confederate States of America on February 18, while Lincoln was traveling to Washington; Alexander H. Stephens, Lincoln's old friend from whom he had expected a strong support of the Union, became Provisional Vice President. On that same day, General David E. Twiggs surrendered all the United States military outposts in Texas to the secessionists.

Lincoln responded to these developments by making it clearer than ever that he intended to preserve the Union. At a brief stop in Dunkirk, New York, he stepped from the train to grasp an American flag and asked his audience "to stand by me so long as I stand by it." In New York City he told the audience: "Nothing...can ever bring me willingly to consent to the destruction of this Union." In Trenton he promised the New Jersey legislature he would seek a peaceful settlement of the crisis, but he warned, "It may be necessary to put the foot down firmly."

VII

In the final days of the journey an unexpected development threatened the image of dignified courage that he was building. Allan Pinkerton, the head of the Pinkerton National Detective Agency, informed Judd of a plot to assassinate Lincoln as he passed through Baltimore. This was not the first warning of danger to the President-elect, but it seemed entitled to more credence than earlier alarms. Working for S. M. Felton, the president of the Philadelphia, Wilmington & Baltimore Railroad, who feared that secessionists might sabotage bridges along his route, Pinkerton found anti-Lincoln sentiment rampant in Baltimore, a strongly pro-Southern city with a long reputation for street violence, and his operatives reported details of a plot to kill the President-elect. When Lincoln's train from Philadelphia arrived at the Calvert Street Station, the President-elect and his party would have to get out and go across town to the Camden Street Station in order to board the Baltimore & Ohio train for Washington. Just as Lincoln emerged from the narrow vestibule of the Calvert Street Station, Cypriano Ferrandini, a Baltimore barber, and a few associates planned to assassinate him. Pinkerton urged the President-elect to leave Philadelphia immediately, passing through Baltimore on a night train before the conspirators could learn of his change of plans.

Lincoln refused to alter his schedule. "I can't go to-night," he insisted. He was committed to raising the flag at Independence Hall the next morning and he had promised to address the Pennsylvania legislature at Harrisburg later in the day. He vowed he would fulfill those engagements "under any and all circumstances, even if he met with death in doing so."

The threat was clearly on his mind as he spoke at Independence Hall on February 22. The country must be saved on the basis of the Declaration of Independence, which promised liberty for all and offered "hope to the world for all future time." "If it can't be saved upon that principle, it will be truly awful," he warned. "I was about to say I would rather be assassinated on this spot than to surrender it."

As he was leaving for Harrisburg, young Frederick W. Seward brought confidential news from Washington that both his father, the senator, and General Winfield Scott believed the Baltimore conspiracy was genuine. After Lincoln made the promised address to the Pennsylvania legislature, he and his most trusted advisers met to discuss the danger. Pinkerton proposed that Lincoln, traveling alone so as to avoid suspicion, should take a special train

from Harrisburg to Philadelphia; there, incognito, he would board the 11
P.M. train to Baltimore, passing unrecognized through that city at about 3:30
A.M. and arriving unannounced in Washington two and a half hours later.
Judd endorsed the plan. Colonel Sumner denounced it as "a d——d piece
of cowardice" and said it would be better to get a squad of cavalry to cut a
way to Washington, but Captain Pope favored Pinkerton's recommendation.
After considerable discussion, David Davis, who had expressed no opinion,
asked the President-elect: "What is your judgement on the matter?"

Lincoln said he was not entirely convinced that there was a conspiracy,
and he recognized that he might appear ridiculous in fleeing from a nonexistent danger. On the other hand, he respected Pinkerton's professional
judgment and was impressed that Frederick Seward's warnings confirmed
those of the detective. He concluded, "Unless there are some other reasons
besides fear of ridicule, I am disposed to carry out Judd's plan."

That left only the details to be arranged. Pinkerton wanted no one else in
the presidential party to be told of the change of plans, but Lincoln insisted
that his wife must know, "as otherwise she would be very much excited at
his absence." Against Colonel Sumner's protest, Lamon was chosen as his
only companion and bodyguard during the trip. Lamon may indeed have
been, as Pinkerton said, "a brainless egotistical fool," but he was big, brave,
and—most important of all—willing to lay down his life to save Lincoln's.

That evening the President-elect quietly slipped out of the hotel in Harrisburg. He was unrecognized because, instead of the usual stovepipe hat that
had become his trademark, he wore for the first time in his life a soft felt
"Kossuth" hat someone in New York had given him. To help conceal his tall
figure his long overcoat was thrown loosely over his shoulders without his
arms being in the sleeves. He boarded a special train in Harrisburg, where
all telegraphic communication had been interrupted to prevent possible
leaks to the conspirators. At Philadelphia, accompanied only by Pinkerton
and Lamon, he entered a sleeping car of the train to Baltimore and occupied
a berth Pinkerton had reserved for an "invalid passenger." He was so tall
that he could not stretch out on the bed. The train proceeded undisturbed to
Baltimore, and without being observed, Lincoln transferred to the Camden
Station and went on to Washington. Emerging from the car, he attracted no
attention until a loud voice hailed him: "Abe you can't play that on me."
Pinkerton and Lamon turned to attack the stranger when Lincoln interposed,
recognizing his old friend Congressman E. B. Washburne, who had learned
of the plan and come to meet him. He quickly drove with Lincoln to Willard's
Hotel at Fourteenth Street and Pennsylvania Avenue.

Inevitably Lincoln's secret night ride attracted unfavorable comment. It
took on elements of farce after an enterprising newspaperman, Joseph Howard, needing to flesh out his story for the *New York Times,* wrote that Lincoln
had not merely fled from Harrisburg but had disguised himself by wearing
a Scotch plaid cap and a long military coat. Cartoonists presently portrayed

the disguise as a tam and kilts. Even serious observers were troubled by the episode. "We take it for granted that Mr. Lincoln is not wanting in personal courage," the *New York Tribune* editorialized—but it wanted some proof that "imminent and great" danger had required him to take such a remarkable course. Soberly George Templeton Strong recorded his hope that Lincoln could prove beyond cavil the existence of a Baltimore plot; otherwise "this surreptitious nocturnal dodging or sneaking of the President-elect into his capital city ... will be used to damage his moral position and throw ridicule on his Administration."

Eventually the furor died down, but Lincoln came to regret that he had allowed himself to be persuaded to undertake the night trip. As he told the Illinois congressman Isaac N. Arnold, "I did not then, nor do I now believe I should have been assassinated had I gone through Baltimore as first contemplated, but I thought it wise to run no risk where no risk was necessary." That was a sound and reasonable decision—but it did nothing to sustain the reputation for firmness that he had been so carefully building on his long journey from Springfield.

VIII

The ten days between Lincoln's arrival in Washington and his inauguration were among the busiest in his life. On the first day, after he reached Willard's Hotel, he telegraphed Mary in Harrisburg of his safe arrival. He and Seward had breakfast together and then went to the White House, where he met President Buchanan and was introduced to the members of the cabinet. After calling on General Scott, who was not at home, he rode about Washington for an hour with Seward, who found him "very cordial and kind ... simple, natural, and agreeable." In the afternoon he received visitors, including Montgomery Blair, soon to be his Postmaster General, and his father, Francis P. Blair, Sr. In midafternoon Mary Lincoln and the boys arrived after an uneventful trip through Baltimore, and the family was reunited in the best suite at the hotel. Senator Douglas and other members of the Illinois delegation called later in the day, and the encounter between the two old rivals, both ardent supporters of the Union, was reported to be "peculiarly pleasant." At 7 P.M. he took a carriage to Seward's residence and dined privately with his Secretary of State–designate and Vice President–elect Hamlin. Returning to Willard's, he found the long hall lined with people and became so absorbed in greeting them that he forgot to remove his hat. Delegates from the Peace Conference, which was just ending its unprofitable deliberations, called at 9 P.M. and found the President-elect standing unattended in the public drawing room of the hotel. Senator Chase and Lucius E. Chittenden, who represented Vermont at the conference, took it upon themselves to introduce the delegates. Afterward Lincoln held an informal reception for members of Congress and other guests who had crowded into the hotel. Among them was the wealthy New York merchant William E. Dodge, who warned the President-elect that only concessions to the South could prevent national bankruptcy; it was up to Lincoln to say "whether the grass shall grow in the streets of our commercial cities." Looking quizzical, Lincoln responded that he preferred to see the grass grow in fields and in meadows but that he would defend the Constitution "let the grass grow where it may." At 10 P.M. the members of Buchanan's cabinet called to pay their respects. Not until they left could the weary President-elect go to bed.

The days that followed were similarly filled with endless calls and receptions. Both Vice President John C. Breckinridge and John Bell—like Douglas, defeated candidates in the 1860 election—paid their respects. Lincoln welcomed a call from the aged and infirm General Scott dressed in his full military regalia and wearing all his medals. The President-elect visited the Capitol and held an informal reception for members of Congress. He greeted the justices of the Supreme Court. Mayor James G. Berret and the Common Council of Washington tendered an official welcome to the city and, understanding that they had opposed his election, Lincoln expressed hope that "when we shall become better acquainted—and I say it with great confidence—we shall like each other the more."

On most evenings he and Mary received visitors in the hotel parlors. Some came out of a sense of duty, some in the hope of securing public office, and some out of idle curiosity. One Virginian described the President-elect as "a cross between a sandhill crane and an Andalusian jackass, . . . vain, weak, puerile, hypocritical, without manners, without moral grace," but most visitors thought him awkwardly charming. At parties he was relaxed and sociable. When he attended the dinner that Rudolph Schleiden, the minister from Bremen and the dean of the diplomatic corps in Washington, gave in his honor, he favorably impressed Lord Lyons, the British minister, and most of the other diplomats, though the ambassador from Holland complained: "His conversation consists of vulgar anecdotes at which he himself laughs uproariously."

All this socializing allowed the President-elect to sound Washington sentiment about the crisis. No words were more welcome than those of Douglas, who strongly favored conciliating the South and urged Lincoln to persuade Republicans to compromise. At the same time, he pledged that he and his Democratic followers would not try to gain political advantage from the crisis. "Our Union must be preserved," he told Lincoln solemnly. "Partisan feeling must yield to patriotism. I am with you, Mr. President, and God bless you." Touched and greatly cheered, Lincoln responded: "With all my heart I thank you. The people with us and God helping us all will yet be well." When the senator left, Lincoln exclaimed to another visitor, "What a noble man Douglas is!"

Lincoln's numerous conferences in the week before his inauguration also helped him make a final selection of his cabinet members. Until he arrived in Washington, only Seward and Bates had been formally offered posts. After the McClure-Curtin faction withdrew their objection, Cameron was assured of a place and Pennsylvanians insisted that he must head the Treasury Department. But there was a mounting cry for Chase to have that appointment. To settle the controversy Lincoln sought the advice of the Republican senators. Sending for them in alphabetical order, he asked their preferences for Secretary of the Treasury. Of the nineteen who responded, five wasted their votes on Dayton and James F. Simmons, a justly forgotten senator from Rhode Island; three cast votes for Cameron; and eleven favored Chase. With that, Lincoln had a mandate, and he offered the Treasury Department to Chase. Cameron was given a choice of the War Department or the Interior Department and rather grumpily chose the former. The appointment suggested how far Lincoln was from thinking about a war.

The selection of Chase was a bitter dose for Seward, who had increasingly come to think of himself as the premier of the incoming Lincoln administration. In his mind the brilliant policy he had pursued in the Senate had saved the country during the months since the election. By conciliating the South, he believed that he had stopped the hemorrhage of secession after the withdrawal of the seven states of the lower South. Though the legislatures of Virginia, North Carolina, Tennessee, and Arkansas authorized conventions to consider secession, Unionists were in control in all these states. He was convinced that they would remain loyal so long as peace was preserved.

Seward did not take seriously Lincoln's remarks made on the way to Washington and was confident he could persuade the President-elect to agree that the fever of secession should be allowed to run its course in the Deep South while Unionism should be fostered in the upper South by avoiding all provocations. He did not count on impressing Lincoln by his appearance. Slight in build, stooped and thin, with sallow complexion, a beaklike nose, and shaggy eyebrows, he was, unlike Chase, not an imposing figure. But he counted on his enormous intelligence and undeniable charm to win over the President-elect and was constantly with him at breakfasts, meetings, receptions, and dinners. Delighted with Seward's ebullience and lack of pomposity and sharing his fondness for jokes, Lincoln appeared docilely to follow the lead of his premier. "Old Abe is honest as the sun, and means to be true and faithful," growled Greeley, who distrusted Seward; "but he is in the web of very cunning spiders and cannot work out if he would."

In naming Chase, Lincoln broke out of the web. Seward was furious, but he could not have been surprised. He already knew from reading the draft of the inaugural address at the request of the President-elect that his policies were not Lincoln's. Selecting Chase, who bluntly denounced secession and made his motto "Inauguration first—adjustment afterwards," was a further signal that Lincoln was not going to follow Seward's cautious and conciliatory approach toward the South.

Frustrated and despondent, Seward remonstrated with Lincoln. He told the President-elect that he and Chase had irreconcilable differences. Out of "his conviction of duty and what was due to himself" he "must insist on excluding Mr. Chase if he, Seward, remained." Failing to convince Lincoln, Seward on March 2 dashed off a curt note: "Circumstances which have occurred since I expressed . . . my willingness to accept the office of Secretary of State seem to me to render it my duty to ask leave to withdraw that consent."

Lincoln faced a dilemma. He needed the New Yorker in his cabinet, but as he told Nicolay, "I can't afford to let Seward take the first trick." He signaled that Seward was not irreplaceable. When a deputation of New York merchants friendly to Seward descended on the President-elect to protest the appointment of Chase, he listened to their arguments that Chase's commitment to free trade and his hostility toward compromise with the South would further injure business prospects. Beyond that, they insisted, Seward could never work with Chase. Agreeing that he needed a harmonious administration, Lincoln brought out two lists—one his preferred choice of cabinet members, which included both Seward and Chase, and the other, he said, a poorer one naming Dayton as Secretary of State with Seward as minister to England. With that the stunned delegation shuffled out. He gave the same message to Judd, who was vastly excited about possible last-minute changes in the cabinet list. Knowing that Judd was an intimate of Weed and that anything said to him would be immediately reported to Seward, the President-elect vowed, "When that slate breaks again, it will break at the top."

But Lincoln said nothing directly to Seward, and he did not even acknowledge Seward's letter of withdrawal. On Sunday, the day before the inauguration, just as though nothing had happened, the President-elect gave a dinner party for all the prospective members of his cabinet, including both Seward and Chase. The next morning, while the inauguration procession was forming, he sent Seward a brief note, asking him to reconsider his decision. Lincoln's tactful handling of a difficult situation gave Seward time to reflect. Genuinely worried about the fate of the nation, the New Yorker felt that he did "not dare to go home, or to England, and leave the country to chance" —i.e., to Abraham Lincoln. He continued to doubt Lincoln's plan for what he termed "a compound Cabinet," but he told his wife, "I believe I can endure as much as any one; and may be that I can endure enough to make the experiment successful." He agreed to serve.

IX

At noon on March 4, James Buchanan and Abraham Lincoln entered an open barouche at Willard's Hotel to begin the drive down Pennsylvania Avenue to the Capitol. Determined to prevent any attempt on Lincoln's life, General Scott had stationed sharpshooters on the roofs of buildings along the avenue, and companies of soldiers blocked off the cross streets. He stationed himself with one battery of light artillery on Capitol Hill; General John E. Wool, commander of the army's Department of the East, was with another. The presidential procession was short and businesslike, more like a military operation than a political parade.

Entering the Capitol from the north through a passageway boarded so as to prevent any possible assassination attempt, Buchanan and Lincoln attended the swearing in of Vice President Hannibal Hamlin and then emerged to a smattering of applause on the platform erected at the east portico. Introduced by his old friend, the silver-tongued E. D. Baker, Lincoln rose but was obviously troubled by what to do with his tall stovepipe hat. Noting his perplexity, Douglas said, "Permit me, sir," took the hat, and held it during the ceremony. Lincoln read his inaugural, an eyewitness recalled, in a voice "though not very strong or full-toned" that "rang out over the acres of people before him with surprising distinctness, and was heard in the remotest parts of his audience." When he finished, the cadaverous Chief Justice Roger B. Taney, now nearly eighty-four years old, tottered forth to administer the oath of office to the sixteenth President of the United States.

The audience could not be quite sure what the new President's policy toward secession would be because his inaugural address, like his cabinet, was an imperfectly blended mixture of opposites. The draft that he completed before leaving Springfield was a no-nonsense document; it declared that the Union was indestructible, that secession was illegal, and that he intended to enforce the laws. "All the power at my disposal will be used to reclaim the public property and places which have fallen," he pledged, "to hold, occupy and possess these, and all other property and places belonging to the government, and to collect the duties on imports." Promising that "there needs to be no bloodshed or violence; and there shall be none unless forced upon the national authority," Lincoln urged secessionists to pause for reflection: "In *your* hands, my dissatisfied fellow countrymen, and not in *mine,* is the momentous issue of civil war. . . . With *you,* and not with *me,* is the solemn question of 'Shall it be peace, or a sword?' "

Lincoln showed this warlike draft to several of his associates. David Davis's comments were not recorded. Francis P. Blair, Sr., remembering his glory days when Andrew Jackson stared down the South Carolina nullifiers, approved it and urged that no change be made. Browning found it "able, well considered, and appropriate" but strongly advised Lincoln to delete the pledge to reclaim federal forts that had fallen into Confederate hands because this would be "construed into a threat or menace" in the Deep South and would be "irritating" in the border states. Lincoln accepted the suggestion.

More significant were the changes that Seward advised. Granting that Lincoln's basic argument was "strong and conclusive, and ought not to be in any way abridged or modified," Seward thought the speech much too provocative. If Lincoln delivered it without alterations, he warned, Virginia and Maryland would secede and within sixty days the Union would be obliged to fight the Confederacy for possession of the capital at Washington. Dozens of verbal changes should be made, deleting words and phrases that could appear to threaten "the defeated, irritated, angered, frenzied" people of the South. Something more than argument was needed "to meet and remove *prejudice* and *passion* in the South, and *despondency* and *fear* in the East." Entreating Lincoln to include "some words of affection," some "of calm and cheerful confidence," he proposed a less martial concluding paragraph: "I close. We are not we must not be aliens or enemies but fellow countrymen and brethren. . . . The mystic chords which proceeding from so many battle fields and so many patriot graves pass through all the hearts and all the hearths in this broad continent of ours will yet again harmonize in their ancient music when breathed upon by the guardian angel of the nation." Lincoln made many of the changes Seward proposed. Seward's suggested final paragraph was too ornate for his taste, but he incorporated its ideas in language distinctively his own:

> I am loth to close. We are not enemies, but friends. We must not be enemies. . . . The mystic chords of memory, stretching from every battlefield, and patriot grave, to every living heart and hearthstone, all over this broad land, will yet swell the chorus of the Union, when again touched, as surely they will be, by the better angels of our nature.

Reaction to the address was largely predictable. In the Confederacy it was generally taken to mean that war was inevitable. A correspondent of the *Charleston Mercury* viewed this pronouncement from "the Ourang-Outang at the White House" as "the tocsin of battle" that was also "the signal of our freedom." In the upper South the *Richmond Dispatch* said the message "inaugurates civil war," and the *Richmond Enquirer* said it meant that Virginia must choose between invasion by Lincoln's army or Jefferson Davis's. In the North, Republican papers generally praised the address. The *Indianapolis Daily Journal* called it "strong, straightforward and manly," and the *Detroit Daily Tribune* found it "able, firm, conciliatory, true to principle and of transparent honesty." But the *Albany Atlas and Argus,* a Douglas paper, dismissed this "rambling, discursive, questioning, loose-jointed stump speech," and the pro-Breckinridge *Columbus Daily Capital City Fact* predicted that Lincoln's policy meant that "blood will stain the soil and color the waters of the entire continent—brother will be arrayed in hostile front against brother."

The most thoughtful verdict was offered by the *Providence Daily Post,* a Democratic paper, which seemed to sense the differences between Lincoln's original draft and the address that he actually delivered: "If the President selected his words with the view of making clear his views, he was, partially at least, unsuccessful. There is some plain talk in the address; but . . . it is immediately followed by obscurely stated qualifications."

X

On the morning after the inauguration Lincoln found on his desk a report from Major Robert Anderson that the provisions for his garrison at Fort Sumter would be exhausted in about six weeks. Unless he was resupplied within that time, he would have to surrender. He warned that it would take a force of 20,000 well-disciplined men to make the fort secure.

Lincoln was not prepared for this emergency. As yet there was no executive branch of the government. The Senate had yet to confirm even his private secretary, John G. Nicolay. None of his cabinet officers had been approved. His Secretary of State–designate had not yet agreed to serve, and Salmon P. Chase had not even been informed of his nomination.

Lincoln needed all the help he could get because, as he freely admitted later, when he became President "he was entirely ignorant not only of the duties, but of the manner of doing the business" in the executive office. He tried to do everything himself. There was no one to teach him rules and procedures, and he made egregious mistakes. For example, he thought he could issue orders directly to officers in the navy, without even informing Secretary Welles, and he attempted, without congressional authorization, to create a new Bureau of Militia in the War Department headed by his young friend Elmer Ellsworth. "The difficulty with Mr Lincoln is that he has no conception of his situation," Senator Charles Sumner concluded. "And having no system in his composition he has undertaken to manage the whole thing as if he knew all about it."

The new President allowed office-seekers to take up most of his time. From nine o'clock in the morning until late at night, his White House office was open to all comers, and sometimes the petitioners were so numerous that it was impossible to climb the stairs. As Maine Senator William Pitt Fessenden said, they made up an "ill-bred, ravenous crowd," and Lincoln lamented that he was considered "fair game for everybody of that hungry lot." The pressure was so great, Nicolay wrote, that "we have scarcely had time to eat sleep or even breathe." Browning scolded the President: "You should not permit your time to be consumed, and your energies exhausted by personal applications for office." But Lincoln was incorrigible. With a sad smile he explained to Henry Wilson, the Massachusetts senator, that these people "dont want much and dont get but little, and I must see them."

The news from Fort Sumter forced this inexperienced and overworked administrator to make a hard choice: he must either reinforce Anderson's garrison or evacuate it. Lincoln's options were sharply limited by two principles firmly enunciated in his inaugural address. One promised to avoid "bloodshed or violence . . . unless it be forced upon the national authority." The other pledged to "hold, occupy, and possess the property, and places belonging to the government." That included Fort Sumter.

In the days after receiving the news from Anderson, Lincoln wrestled with his problem. He did not come to conclusions quickly, and he was temperamentally averse to making bold moves. It was his style to react to decisions made by others rather than to take the initiative himself. In these troubled hours he made no public pronouncements and did not even discuss the Sumter crisis at the first formal meeting of the cabinet on March 6, which Attorney General Bates characterized as "introductory" and "uninteresting." In subsequent informal conversations the President told Gideon Welles that he wanted to avoid hasty action so as to gain "time for the Administration to get in working order and its policy to be understood." Before taking any action, Lincoln, with his usual caution, tried to verify the facts. He asked General Scott to answer a set of interrogatories similar to ones that he used in the courtroom: How long could Anderson maintain his position? Was Scott now able to reinforce Fort Sumter? If not, what additional resources did he need? He received the disheartening response that it would require a naval expedition, 5,000 regular army troops, and 20,000 volunteer soldiers to reinforce the fort. Since these could not be produced, surrender was "merely a question of time."

The Sumter crisis was the principal topic of discussion at a cabinet meeting on March 9, when the secretaries learned for the first time how grave the situation was. If relieving Anderson required an expeditionary force of at least 25,000 men—at a time when the entire United States army numbered only 16,000, mostly scattered in outposts along the Indian frontier—the inescapable conclusion was that the fort must be surrendered.

Lincoln was not yet willing to accept that conclusion. Perhaps his reluctance was increased when Francis P. Blair, Sr., forced his way into the President's office and warned that evacuation of the fort was "virtually a surrender of the union" amounting to treason. The next day the old gentleman apologized for having said "things that were impertinent," but Lincoln got the message.

He also learned that all military experts were not as pessimistic as General Scott. Former Navy Lieutenant Gustavus Vasa Fox, Mrs. Montgomery Blair's brother-in-law, who was knowledgeable about coastal defenses, had for some time been advocating a plan to reinforce or resupply Sumter from the sea. He would use powerful light-draft New York tugboats under the cover of night to run men and supplies from an offshore naval expedition to the fort. His plan got nowhere under the Buchanan administration, and Scott, with the traditional scorn that army men showed for navy planners, thought it was impracticable. Now Montgomery Blair, who was a West Point graduate, endorsed it and Lincoln began to give it serious consideration.

On March 15 he asked each member of his cabinet to respond in writing to the question: "Assuming it to be possible to now provision Fort-Sumpter, under all the circumstances, is it wise to attempt it?" Seward took the lead in opposing any such attempt. An expedition to relieve Sumter would "provoke combat, and probably initiate a civil war." Cameron, Welles, and Smith echoed Seward's views. Chase took the opposite side of the question. He admitted having some doubts, and he did not advise reinforcing Sumter if it would precipitate a war, with the necessity of enlisting large armies and spending millions of dollars that the Treasury did not have. But on the whole he thought this unlikely and therefore voted in favor of resupplying Major Anderson. Montgomery Blair strongly urged an expedition. Southerners had been led to believe *"that the Northern men are deficient in the courage necessary to maintain the Government."* Only prompt reinforcement of Anderson and his garrison could "vindicate the hardy courage of the North and the determination of the people and their President to maintain the authority of the Government."

With his advisers divided, Lincoln was unable to reach a decision. As he saw it, his duty from a purely military point of view was clear: it was "the mere matter of getting the garrison safely out of the Fort." But evacuation "would be utterly ruinous" politically. "By many," he explained to Congress a few months later, "it would be construed as a part of a *voluntary* policy— that, at home, . . . would discourage the friends of the Union, embolden its adversaries, and go far to insure to the latter, a recognition abroad— . . . in fact, it would be our national destruction consummated."

"This could not be allowed," he concluded—but he did not know how to avoid it. Like any other administrator facing impossible choices, he postponed action by calling for more information. After several conversations with Fox, to whom he took a great liking, he sent the lieutenant to Charleston ostensibly to bring Anderson messages about possible evacuation but in reality to get a firsthand look at the fort and the Confederate fortifications that threatened it. In an entirely separate move, the President put Seward's views about Southern Unionism to the test by asking Stephen A. Hurlbut, an old friend from Illinois who had been born in Charleston, to go to South Carolina and ascertain the state of public opinion. Along with Hurlbut went Ward Hill Lamon, whose bibulous habits and open hostility to abolitionism might gain him access to a different class of South Carolinians.

By this time knowledge of the Sumter crisis had become general. From all sides the President heard imperative voices. Neal Dow, the Republican leader from Maine, wrote that evacuation of the fort would be "approved by the entire body of Republicans in this State" because it was "undoubtedly a Military *necessity."* Greeley's powerful *New York Tribune* spoke of allowing the Southern states to go in peace and opposed the use of any force. In the Senate, which was still in session to confirm presidential appointments, Douglas said that South Carolina was entitled to Fort Sumter and that "Anderson and his gallant band should be instantly withdrawn." From faraway San Francisco the *Daily Alta California* predicted that "if Mr. Lincoln does withdraw the troops from Fort Sumter, secession is dead, and every leader in the movement ruined."

On the other extreme some Republicans had long felt that the time had come for a test of strength with the South. Senator Zachariah Chandler, a blunt, hard-drinking Michigan businessman, held that "without a little blood-letting this Union will not, in my estimation, be worth a rush." William Butler, Lincoln's old Springfield friend, grew so angry at the prospect of giving up Fort Sumter without a fight that he lost control of grammar and orthography in a letter to Trumbull: "Is it passiable that Mr Lincoln is getting scared. I know the responsiability is grate; But for god sake tell Mr L to live by it; Or have the credit (If credit it may be termed) Of sinking in a richous cause." A caucus of Republican congressmen warned the President that failure to reinforce Sumter would bring disaster to the party. Trumbull introduced a resolution in the Senate that "it is the duty of the President to use all the means in his power to hold and protect the public property of the United States."

Amid these dissonant voices Lincoln heard from his emissaries to South Carolina. Fox returned to Washington more confident than ever that it was possible to resupply Fort Sumter by sea at night. On March 27, Hurlbut offered a bleak picture of public opinion in South Carolina. "Separate Nationality is a fixed fact," he reported; "there is no attachment to the Union. . . . positively nothing to appeal to." He judged that any attempt to reinforce Sumter would be received as an act of war; even "a ship known to contain *only provisions* for Sumpter [sic] would be stopped and refused admittance."

The next day Lincoln received shocking advice from Scott. The general asserted that evacuation of Fort Sumter would not be enough to retain the loyalty of the upper South, including Virginia, Scott's native state; it was necessary also to surrender Fort Pickens, on the Florida coast, even though that fort was securely in Union hands and could be reinforced at will. Only such liberality would "soothe and give confidence to the eight remaining slave-holding States, and render their cordial adherence to this Union perpetual."

Appalled, Lincoln managed to get through the first state dinner that he and Mary gave for members of his official family and distinguished guests that evening, but he asked the cabinet to remain after the others took their leave. Then, in a voice choked with emotion, he told them of Scott's recommendations. Blair erupted that the general was not offering military advice but "playing politician." Except for Seward, whose views Scott was echoing, the others agreed. Lincoln gave notice that he would hold a formal council the next day. That night he slept not at all, aware that the time had come for decision.

The next morning he was, he said, "in the dumps." He got up deeply depressed, conscious that he would have to ask the cabinet, which met at noon, for a final judgment on whether attempts should be made to relieve Fort Sumter and Fort Pickens. Each member—except Cameron, who was absent—gave a written opinion. Seward remained obdurately opposed to sending an expedition to provision or reinforce Sumter because it would precipitate a civil war, but sensing that the President was determined to take some action, he favored holding Fort Pickens "at every cost." Caleb Smith agreed. Bates also thought Fort Pickens must be held "at all hazards" and on Fort Sumter offered the unhelpful opinion that "the time is come either to evacuate or relieve it." But now Chase and Welles came out unequivocally for reinforcing Sumter, and Blair threatened to resign if the President followed the advice of General Scott.

The advice of the majority of the cabinet reinforced Lincoln's own view. He had already asked Fox for a memorandum of the ships, men, and supplies he would need to relieve Sumter, and he now directed Welles and Cameron to have an expedition ready to sail from New York by April 6. To organize the fleet Fox was sent to New York with verbal instructions to prepare for the voyage "but to make no binding engagements." The strain under which Lincoln labored in arriving at this decision was immense. All the troubles and anxieties of his life, he told Browning, did not equal those he felt in these tense days. The pressure was so great that Mary Lincoln reported that he "keeled over" and had to be put to bed with one of his rare migraine headaches.

A decision had been reached, but Seward was not willing to concede defeat. In the week between the crucial cabinet meeting and the date for the sailing of the fleet, he tried, with a growing sense of desperation, to reverse Lincoln's course. In the hope of avoiding hostilities, he had, through intermediaries, been in touch with the official commissioners the Confederate government sent to Washington in order to negotiate terms of separation, and he had given his word that the troops would be withdrawn from Fort Sumter. He was still confident he could negotiate a settlement of the crisis if Anderson's garrison was evacuated. Now he was trapped between his pledge and Lincoln's determination to proceed with a relief expedition.

Seward first sought to escape his dilemma by bluster. On April 1 he handed Lincoln a memorandum headed "Some thoughts for the President's consideration." It began with the pronouncement, "We are at the end of a month's administration and yet without a policy either domestic or foreign." From there the Secretary went on to urge that the question before the public be changed from slavery, which was a party issue, to *"Union or Disunion."* In order to bring about this shift Fort Sumter should be evacuated but Fort Pickens and the other minor forts in the Gulf of Mexico should be reinforced. Public interest should be diverted from domestic quarrels to foreign policy. In order "to rouse a vigorous continental *spirit of independence,"* he would demand explanations from Spain, which had sent troops to assist rebels in Santo Domingo, and France, which was showing too great an interest in Mexican affairs; he even added Great Britain and Russia to his list. If the French and Spanish governments did not give satisfactory answers, he would convene Congress and declare war against them. "Whatever policy we adopt," the memorandum concluded, "there must be an energetic prosecution of it. . . . Either the President must do it himself . . . or Devolve it on some member of his Cabinet. . . . It is not in my especial province. But I neither seek to evade nor assume responsibility."

Lincoln left no record of how he felt about this extraordinary document, which he must have been tempted to dismiss as an April Fool's Day joke. Certainly he recognized it as another of Seward's attempts to play the role of premier in the administration. What hit a nerve was the Secretary's assertion that the administration had no policy. Others shared this opinion. Senators Sumner and Fessenden were convinced that Lincoln had "no fixed policy except to keep mum and see what end those seceding states will come to." Carl Schurz warned of general discontent throughout the North because Lincoln lacked leadership. Everybody, Schurz told the President, felt that "any distinct line of policy, be it war or a recognition of the Southern Confederacy, would be better than this uncertain state of things."

Touchy on this subject, Lincoln stiffly pointed out to Seward that he did have a policy, announced in his inaugural address, of holding, occupying, and possessing the forts and other property belonging to the government. (Rightly interpreted, that meant a policy of not evacuating Fort Sumter.) This policy, he reminded the Secretary, had Seward's "distinct approval at the time." Ignoring Seward's warlike threats against European powers, Lincoln turned to his concluding observation that either the President must energetically prosecute whatever policy he adopted or delegate it to some member of the cabinet. Lincoln's answer was unequivocal: "I remark that if this must be done, *I* must do it." Then, recognizing how sharp his reply was, he probably did not send it. He kept the only known copy in his files and most likely discussed the memorandum with Seward, managing to combat its arguments without hurting the Secretary's feelings.

Certainly Seward was not at all disheartened by the rejection of his memorandum, and he continued to urge the President to explore face-saving solutions to the Sumter crisis. Anxious to avoid war, Lincoln willingly joined in these efforts. One possibility was an agreement to surrender Fort Sumter in return for a pledge of unconditional loyalty on the part of Virginia. There was nothing inherently implausible about such a deal. Though many Virginians sympathized with the states of the lower South, most were loyal to the Union, and Unionists had a clear majority in the state convention, which was still in session. The President hoped to confer with George W. Summers, the leading Unionist in that convention, but Summers declined to come to Washington. Instead, he sent John B. Baldwin, another Unionist, who had a long secret conference with Lincoln on April 4. What the two men said became a matter of dispute, but according to the most reliable account the President promised: "If you will guarantee to me the State of Virginia I shall remove the troops. A State for a fort is no bad business." Whether intentionally or inadvertently, Baldwin misunderstood the President, and nothing came of this offer.

Another of Seward's schemes was to deflect the Sumter expedition by the successful reinforcement of Fort Pickens. That, it appeared, could be done without provoking hostilities with the Confederates. In his March 29 cabinet memorandum Seward proposed—in lieu of reinforcing Sumter—to call on Captain Montgomery C. Meigs, the army engineer in charge of construction at the Capitol, to organize an expedition to relieve Pickens. That same day he brought Meigs to the White House. Fort Pickens, the President reminded the captain, had been virtually under siege since the secession of Florida. President Buchanan had sent two hundred additional soldiers to the fort on the warship *Brooklyn,* but they had not been permitted to land. Under an informal truce the Confederates promised not to attack the fort if it was not reinforced. On the day after his inauguration, Lincoln gave a verbal order to land the troops aboard the *Brooklyn,* only to discover, like many another President, that it was one thing to give an order and quite another to have it obeyed. On March 11 he renewed the order in writing, and Scott dispatched a vessel to direct that the troops be landed. Lincoln still did not know what had happened, but, he told Meigs, he guessed his order "had fizzled out." Now he asked Meigs, who was already familiar with the Florida forts, to organize a relief expedition.

Thus two projects got under way at the same time. The Sumter mission, pressed chiefly by Welles and Blair, was largely a naval expedition commanded by Fox; the Pickens expedition, sponsored by Seward, was an army affair led by Meigs. The task forces preparing these fleets worked in secrecy and, partly because of interservice rivalries, partly because of antagonisms among cabinet members, each was kept largely in the dark about what its rival was doing. Inevitably there were contests for the limited resources available for these projects. Welles intended the navy's most powerful steamer, the *Powhatan,* to be part of Fox's fleet, but Seward wanted it for Meigs's expedition. Placing an order assigning the ship to the Pickens fleet before the President in a pile of other documents, he got Lincoln's signature. On learning what had happened, Welles dragged Seward to the White House, where, though it was nearly midnight, Lincoln had not yet gone to bed. Confronted with the problem, "he looked first at one and then the other, and declared there was some mistake." Assured that there was no error, the President, as Welles remembered, "took upon himself the whole blame, said it was carelessness, heedlessness on his part" and that "he ought to have been more careful and attentive." He directed that the *Powhatan* be restored to Fox's expedition.

Even then there was further evidence of the total confusion that characterized the administration. Seward reluctantly telegraphed the President's message to New York, but the directive reassigning the ship was signed "Seward." Lieutenant David D. Porter, in command of the *Powhatan,* received the new order just as he was leaving the New York harbor but declined to follow it; a directive from the Secretary of State could not supersede his original orders signed by the President of the United States. Consequently the *Powhatan* sailed off to assist in the Pickens expedition, where it was not needed, and Fox's Sumter fleet was weakened through what Fox's wife called "this cruel treachery."

On April 4, Lincoln decided to send Fox's expedition to Fort Sumter, and he notified Anderson that the fleet would attempt to provision the garrison and, in case it met resistance, to reinforce it. He had taken a decisive step, but not yet an irrevocable one. Since the fleet did not actually leave New York until four or five days later, he had a little more time for maneuver. That was cut drastically short on April 6, when he learned, as he feared, that his order to reinforce Fort Pickens had not been carried out. Meigs's expedition could not possibly reach Fort Pickens before Fort Sumter must be reinforced or surrendered.

By this time Seward was almost reconciled to the inevitable, but he made one more attempt to avert hostilities. Because he had given his word to the Confederate commissioners that Sumter would not be reinforced without notice, he wrung from the President a promise to warn South Carolina officials before sending a relief expedition. On April 6, Lincoln sent Robert S. Chew, a clerk in the State Department, to Charleston with orders to inform Governor Francis Pickens that "an attempt will be made to supply Fort-Sumter with provisions only; and that, if such attempt be not resisted, no effort to throw in men, arms, or ammunition, will be made, without further notice." Intended to avoid provoking South Carolina authorities, this message destroyed the slight possibility that Anderson could be secretly reinforced.

The President had little hope of results from Chew's mission; he knew from Hurlbut's report that the South Carolinians would attack any Union ship, even one known to contain only provisions. But, in addition to giving Seward's schemes a last chance, he was building a historical record to prove his peaceable intent throughout the crisis. By this point he was fairly sure that the Sumter expedition would lead to bloodshed. When the governors of Indiana, Ohio, Maine, and Pennsylvania suggested the desirability of putting their state militias in fighting shape, he replied, "I think the necessity of being *ready* increases. Look to it."

On April 12, while the Union fleet lay helpless offshore, the Confederates began bombarding Fort Sumter, and after thirty-four hours Anderson and his garrison were forced to surrender. The war had begun.

XI

Afterward Lincoln gave several explanations of his course during the Sumter crisis. In his July 4 message to Congress he spoke of his decision to supply Fort Sumter as contingent on the reinforcement of Fort Pickens. The Sumter expedition was "intended to be ultimately used, or not, according to circumstances." He implied, though he never quite stated, that he would have canceled this expedition had he been able to reinforce Fort Pickens. Success at Fort Pickens "would be a clear indication of *policy,*" which "would better enable the country to accept the evacuation of Fort Sumter, as a military *necessity.*" But this interpretation was not supported by contemporaneous evidence. In none of Lincoln's letters or messages between his inauguration and the firing on Fort Sumter was the relief of the two forts linked. In all probability his memory failed him, and the policy he described to Congress in his July 4 message more accurately represented Seward's tactics rather than his own.

While Lincoln was preparing this message, Browning visited the White House, and the two old friends naturally talked about how the war began. According to Browning's rather arid diary, Lincoln did not denounce the Confederates, who after all fired the first shots, nor did he express any feeling of regret, much less of guilt, over his own role in bringing on the war. He mentioned the terrible stress of the weeks between his inauguration and the attack on Fort Sumter and spoke of his physical exhaustion, but he did not acknowledge that his ineffectual leadership contributed to the crisis and made no mention of divided counsels in the administration, inadequate preparation of the relief expeditions, and bureaucratic snarls and interservice rivalries. He probably remembered an instructive letter that Browning wrote him before his inauguration: "In any conflict . . . between the government and the seceding States, it is very important that the traitors shall be the aggressors, and that they be kept constantly and palpably in the wrong. The first attempt . . . to furnish supplies or reinforcements to Sumter will induce aggression by South Carolina, and then the government will stand justified, before the entire country, in repelling that aggression, and retaking the forts."

That was the scenario Lincoln had followed in sending the Sumter expedition. "The plan succeeded," he told Browning. "They attacked Sumter—it fell, and thus, did more service than it otherwise could." These were not idle words. When Gustavus Fox, bitter over the failure of his expedition to relieve Fort Sumter, asked for endorsement from his commander-in-chief, Lincoln responded, "You and I both anticipated that the cause of the country would be advanced by making the attempt to provision Fort Sumpter, even if it should fail; and it is no small consolation now to feel that our anticipation is justified by the result."

These cryptic utterances did not mean that Lincoln sought to provoke war. His repeated efforts to avoid collision in the months between his inauguration and the firing on Fort Sumter showed that he adhered to his vow not to be the first to shed fraternal blood. But he had also vowed not to surrender the forts. That, he was convinced, would lead to the "actual, and immediate dissolution" of the Union. The only resolution of these contradictory positions was for the Confederates to fire the first shot. The attempt to relieve Fort Sumter provoked them to do just that. Had the expedition been successful, the fort, which had no military value to the United States, would eventually have been abandoned because it could not be defended against a determined Confederate assault. In that sense, as he told Browning, by falling, the fort "did more service than it otherwise could." And, to use a phrase from his letter to Fox, "the cause of the country would be advanced" because everybody had to recognize that he did not start the war but had war forced on him. After the attack, he told the Congress, "no choice was left but to call out the war power of the Government; and so to resist force, employed for its destruction, by force, for its preservation."

CHAPTER ELEVEN

A People's Contest

◆

The attack on Fort Sumter cleared the air. The news revived the Lincoln administration, which had appeared indecisive and almost comatose, and gave it a clear objective: preserving the Union by putting down the rebellion.

Many Northerners were euphoric at the outbreak of war, confident that the Union with its vast natural resources, its enormous superiority in manufactures, its 300 percent advantage in railroad mileage was bound to prevail. Surely its 20,000,000 inhabitants could easily defeat the 5,000,000 in the Confederacy (which grew to 9,000,000 after the states of the upper South seceded). Seward thought the war would be over in ninety days. The *Chicago Tribune* anticipated success "within two or three months at the furthest," because "Illinois can whip the South by herself." The *New York Times* predicted victory in thirty days, and the *New York Tribune* assured its readers "that Jeff. Davis & Co. will be swinging from the battlements at Washington . . . by the 4th of July."

The President was not so optimistic. Overhearing boastful contrasts of Northern enterprise and endurance with Southern laziness and fickleness, Lincoln warned against overconfidence. Northerners and Southerners came from the same stock and had "essentially the same characteristics and powers." "Man for man," he predicted, "the soldier from the South will be a match for the soldier from the North and *vice versa.*"

I

On April 15, 1861, the day after Fort Sumter surrendered, Lincoln issued a proclamation announcing that the execution of the laws in the seven states of the Deep South was obstructed "by combinations too powerful to be suppressed by the ordinary course of judicial proceedings," and he called for the states to supply 75,000 militiamen "in order to suppress said combinations, and to cause the laws to be duly executed." At the same time, he summoned a special session of Congress, to meet on July 4.

A tidal wave of approval greeted his proclamation. "Cincinnati sustains proclamation great and universal enthusiasm," wired William M. Dickson. "Nothing can exceed the enthusiasm," two New York City merchants reported. Large Union demonstrations assembled in nearly every Northern city. Typical was a public meeting in Pittsburgh where thousands of citizens, disregarding all partisan feeling, vowed undying fealty to the nation and pledged their lives, fortunes, and sacred honor to defend their country.

Democrats as well as Republicans rallied behind the President. On April 14 during a private two-hour conversation, Lincoln showed Douglas the draft of the proclamation he intended to issue the next day. The senator forgot their past differences. In a statement released to the press he announced that while he "was unalterably opposed to the administration on all its political issues, he was prepared to sustain the President in the exercise of all his constitutional functions to preserve the Union, and maintain the government, and defend the Federal Capital." Returning to Illinois a few days later, Douglas worked heroically to persuade Democrats in the West to support the President because "the shortest way to peace is the most stupendous and unanimous preparation for war."

The only criticism of the President's proclamation was that it called for too few men. Douglas told Lincoln that he should have asked for 200,000 men, and Browning thought he needed 300,000. But in calling for only 75,000 men on April 15, Lincoln was acting on General Scott's advice. In addition, the President had to keep in mind the states of the upper South, still teetering between Union and secession. They would certainly regard the summoning of a vast army as proof that he intended to invade the South. And, most important of all, he recognized that the government was unprepared to arm, feed, transport, and train hundreds of thousands of new recruits.

Lincoln called for troops to serve only ninety days not because he believed that the war would be over quickly but because a 1795 law limited a call-up of militia to not more than thirty days after the assembling of Congress. With Congress called into session on July 4, the volunteer force would have to be disbanded by August 4. He could have convened Congress earlier, but that would have meant an even shorter term of service for the volunteers.

Promptly the Northern states began to fill their quotas of soldiers. Massachusetts Governor John A. Andrew, who had anticipated the outbreak of hostilities, instantly replied to Lincoln's call: "Dispatch received. By what route shall I send?" Other governors used more words to convey the same message. From the far north Israel Washburn assured the President that "the people of Maine of all parties will rally with alacrity to the maintenance of the Government." From the West, Governor O. P. Morton of Indiana pledged 10,000 men "for the defense of the Nation and to uphold the authority of the Government."

They had no trouble filling their quotas with eager volunteers. There were thousands of men like Renewick Dickerson of Nashua, New Hampshire, who wrote to the President: "I have but one son of seventeen Summers, he our only child, a man in stature—We are ready to volunteer, to fight for the integrity of the Union—These rugged hills of New Hampshire overlook strong arms and brave hearts." These volunteers, vowing "woe to the rebel hordes that meets them in battle array," were, as one youthful soldier reported to his mother, "wound up to the very pinnacle of patriotic ardor." "There are," this lad continued, "but two contingencies both equally glorious, either to die, and be numbered among the martyrs to freedom, or live to pass victoriously through this strug[g]le for the right and be crowned with an aureole of glory."

But the states of the upper South, still in the Union, gave a very different response. "I can be no party to this wicked violation of the laws of the country, and to this war upon the liberties of a free people. You can get no troops from North Carolina," Governor John Ellis responded to Lincoln's call, and the governors of Virginia, Tennessee, and Arkansas echoed his words. All four states promptly seceded from the Union. Within weeks all joined the Confederacy, which moved its capital to Richmond.

In the border slave states initial reactions to Lincoln's proclamation were also unfavorable. "Kentucky will furnish no troops for the wicked purpose of subduing her sister Southern States," Governor Beriah Magoffin responded, and Governor Claiborne Jackson of Missouri denounced the call for troops as "illegal, unconstitutional, and revolutionary in its object, inhuman and diabolical." In Delaware, where slavery was a minor factor, the governor refused to comply with Lincoln's requisition but permitted volunteer companies to offer their services for the support of the Constitution and laws of the country.

More important was Maryland, a state that nearly surrounded the national capital and controlled the only railroad access to the District of Columbia. "The excitement is fearful," Governor Thomas Hicks and Baltimore Mayor George W. Brown telegraphed the President on April 18. "Send no troops here." The next day the Sixth Massachusetts Regiment, on its way to defend Washington, was attacked by a secessionist mob as it attempted to cross Baltimore, and four soldiers, along with some civilians, were killed. Lincoln wanted to shore up the governor, a wavering Unionist who tended to collapse under secessionist pressure, and he agreed for the time that reinforcements would be marched around, rather than through, Baltimore.

Doubting that this arrangement would last, he said to the Marylanders half playfully: "If I grant you this concession, that no troops shall pass through the city, you will be back here to-morrow demanding that none shall be marched around it." He was right. Shortly afterward Governor Hicks asked him to stop sending any troops through Maryland and suggested asking Lord Lyons, the British minister, to mediate the sectional conflict. That was too much for Lincoln. When a Baltimore committee descended on his office on April 22 and demanded that he bring no more troops across Maryland and make peace with the Confederacy on any terms, he had had enough. "You would have me break my oath and surrender the Government without a blow," he exploded. "There is no Washington in that—no Jackson in that— no manhood nor honor in that." He had to have troops to defend the capital, and they could only come across Maryland. "Our men are not moles, and can't dig under the earth; they are not birds, and can't fly through the air," he reminded the committee. "Go home and tell your people that if they will not attack us, we will not attack them; but if they do attack us, we will return it, and that severely."

The threat was an empty one, because Lincoln did not have enough troops to defend Washington, much less to reduce Baltimore. After the firing on Fort Sumter the capital seemed almost deserted because of a steady exodus of pro-Confederate officials, including high-ranking army and navy officers. The most notable of these was Robert E. Lee, who declined an offer to head the Union armies because he felt he must go with his state, Virginia. To preserve some semblance of order in the national capital, Cassius M. Clay, wearing three pistols and an "Arkansas toothpick" (a sharp dagger), organized the Clay Guards, and Senator-elect James H. Lane of Kansas recruited the Frontier Guards from fellow Kansans who were in Washington looking for jobs. Lane's group was quartered in the East Room of the White House.

For nearly a week Washington was virtually under siege. Marylanders destroyed the railroad bridges linking Baltimore with the North and cut the telegraph lines. A Confederate assault from Virginia was expected daily, and everyone predicted that it would be aided by the thousands of secessionist sympathizers in the city. In the lonely hours, Lincoln paced the floor of the White House, gazing wistfully down the Potomac for the sight of ships bringing reinforcements and breaking out eventually in anguish: "Why don't they come! Why don't they come!" Every day there were rumors that additional troops, including the Seventh New York and a Rhode Island regiment, were coming soon, but none arrived. Chatting with the wounded soldiers of the Massachusetts Sixth Regiment, the President said with bitter irony: "I don't believe there is any North. The Seventh Regiment is a myth. R. Island is not known in our geography any longer. *You* are the only Northern realities."

On April 25 the arrival of the Seventh New York Regiment changed the picture. General Benjamin F. Butler had discovered an ingenious way of circumventing Baltimore by ferrying men down the Chesapeake Bay to Annapolis, where they could be entrained for Washington. Within days thousands of troops began pouring into Washington. There was still a danger that when the Maryland legislature met in Frederick on April 26 it would vote to secede. General Scott was ready to arrest secessionist politicians in advance of this meeting, but the President directed him to hold off, observe the proceedings, and, if it became necessary, then resort "to the bombardment of their cities—and of course the suspension of the writ of habeas corpus." Neither of these extreme measures proved necessary, but to make certain that Maryland remained loyal, General Butler occupied Federal Hill, overlooking Baltimore harbor, on May 13.

Meanwhile, on April 27, Lincoln did authorize the suspension of the privilege of the writ of habeas corpus along the route between Washington and Philadelphia. This meant that the military authorities could make summary arrests of persons thought to be aiding the Confederacy or attempting to overthrow the government. Such persons could be detained indefinitely without judicial hearing and without indictment, and the arresting officer was not obliged to release them when a judge issued a writ of habeas corpus. The President's action at this time was of limited scope and did not attract great attention until the arrest of one John Merryman, lieutenant of a secessionist drill company, at Cockeysville, Maryland. Imprisoned at Fort McHenry in Baltimore harbor, Merryman secured a writ of habeas corpus from Chief Justice Taney, which ordered that he be tried before a regular court or released. When the arresting officer, under Lincoln's orders, refused to accept the writ, Taney felt he had no alternative but to rule that the Chief Executive had acted unlawfully. He reminded Lincoln of his oath to "take care that the laws be faithfully executed" and warned that if such usurpation continued "the people of the United States are no longer living under a government of laws." Unprepared at this time to make a general argument for broad presidential war powers, Lincoln ignored Taney's ruling.

The situation in Kentucky was as critical as that in Maryland. Lincoln could not let his native state, which controlled the south bank of the vital Ohio River, fall under Confederate control. Ties of kinship and commerce, along with the institution of slavery, linked Kentucky to the South, but a long tradition, personified by Henry Clay and John J. Crittenden, bound the state to the Union. Lincoln's call for troops aroused the pro-Southern elements in the state to bitter opposition. Fortunately he had sober and responsible friends in Kentucky, like Joshua Speed and his brother James, a prominent attorney in Louisville, on whose advice he could implicitly rely. When Kentucky adopted a policy of neutrality, "taking sides not with the Administration nor with the seceding States, but with the Union against them both," the President shrewdly avoided a confrontation. He had "the unquestioned right at all times to march the United States troops into and over any and every State," Lincoln told former Kentucky Congressman Garrett Davis, but promised that "if Kentucky made no demonstration of force against the United States, he would not molest her."

Ostensibly respecting Kentucky's neutrality, both Union and Confederate authorities worked surreptitiously to strengthen their supporters in the state. Lincoln named Robert Anderson, the hero of Fort Sumter and a native of Kentucky, commander of the newly created Military Department of Kentucky, which embraced all of the state within one hundred miles of the Ohio River, and he authorized William Nelson, another Kentucky native, secretly to distribute 5,000 stand of arms to the Unionists in the state. But he avoided hostilities during the uneasy neutrality, recognizing that Unionism was growing faster in Kentucky than secessionist sentiment.

Less successful was Lincoln's handling of Missouri, a border slave state of enormous strategic importance because it controlled traffic on the Ohio, Mississippi, and Missouri river network so vital to the Northwest. Not familiar with the politics of the state, Lincoln had to rely on the Blairs, whose primary interest was in promoting the political fortunes of Frank Blair. The pro-Southern faction in eastern Missouri rallied at Camp Jackson (named after the prosecession governor) just outside St. Louis, while pro-Union forces organized inside that city under the command of the aggressive Nathaniel Lyon. When Lyon forced the men at Camp Jackson to surrender, fighting broke out in the streets of the city, and twenty-eight deaths resulted. Governor Jackson then formed a military force and put it under the control of ex-Governor Sterling Price. General William A. Harney, who commanded the Military Department of the West, worked out a truce with Price roughly comparable to the neutrality established in Kentucky. But Lyon, backed by the Blairs, undermined Harney's support in Washington, and Lincoln failed to support the truce. Internecine war resulted.

Lincoln was less involved in attempts to hold Virginia in the Union. Delegates from the strongly Unionist western counties, outraged when the state convention voted to secede, returned to their homes resolved to secede from secession. A Unionist convention held at Wheeling in effect set up a rival government to the Confederate government of Virginia in Richmond and elected Francis H. Pierpont governor. The convention also called for the creation of a new state out of the western counties of Virginia. Since the Constitution provides that no state shall be divided without its own permission, the Pierpont regime was set up as a kind of puppet government that would consent to this proposed partition. Pierpont fulfilled his function. Ostensibly speaking for the entire state of Virginia, he approved the secession of the western counties, which then applied for admission to the Union as the state of West Virginia. The Pierpont administration left Wheeling and spent the rest of the war under the shelter of federal guns at Alexandria. The whole process of partitioning Virginia was extraordinarily complicated and largely extralegal; and, at a time of great unrest when thieves, bandits, and desperate men roamed the countryside, neither the Pierpont regime nor the new government of West Virginia had the backing of more than a minority of the citizens. Lincoln could do little to shape the course of events. He extended formal recognition of Pierpont's regime as the legitimate government of all of Virginia (though it controlled only a few counties behind the Union lines), and he looked with considerable skepticism on the movement for statehood for West Virginia.

While maintaining a tenuous hold on the border states, Lincoln took steps to increase Northern preparedness. On May 3 he called up additional volunteers, this time for three years. Without waiting for congressional authorization, he also expanded the regular United States Army by adding eight regiments of infantry, one of cavalry, and one of artillery and ordered the enlistment of 18,000 seamen in the navy. Earlier, on April 19, he had proclaimed a blockade of the ports of the seven Confederate states, subsequently extended to include those of North Carolina and Virginia. Two days later, with the unanimous concurrence of his cabinet, he dispatched an armed revenue cutter to protect ships from California bearing gold so necessary for Union finances. At the same time, again without congressional authorization, he directed the commandants of the navy yards at Boston, New York, and Philadelphia each to purchase and arm five steamships in order to preserve water communication to Washington. In case that communication was temporarily cut off, he empowered Governor E. D. Morgan of New York and an associate, Alexander Cummings, who was recommended by Secretary Cameron, to act for the government in forwarding troops and supplies. He also authorized the Treasury Department, without requiring security, to advance $2,000,000 to a New York committee headed by John A. Dix, to pay "such requisitions as should be directly consequent upon the military and naval measures necessary for the defence and support of the government."

In the weeks after the firing on Fort Sumter, the demands on the President's time were incessant and exhausting, but now that he could clearly see what had to be done, he bore up well under the strain. When the writer Bayard Taylor visited Washington, he was delighted to discover, contrary to rumor, that Lincoln was not exhausted or sick but instead appeared "very fresh and vigorous . . . thoroughly calm and collected." Even Seward was impressed. "Executive skill and vigor are rare qualities," he wrote his wife in June. "The President is the best of us; but he needs constant and assiduous coöperation."

II

Lincoln's July 4, 1861, message to the special session of Congress offered a full explanation of the course he had pursued in the Sumter crisis, blamed the Southerners for beginning the conflict, and defended the subsequent actions he had taken to sustain the Union. Valuable as history, the message was more significant as prediction. Taken together with his proclamation of April 15, it clearly defined Lincoln's view of the war and explained how he intended to prosecute it.

The conflict, he consistently maintained, was not a war between the government of the United States and that of the Confederate States of America. So to define it would acknowledge that the Union was not a perpetual one and that secession was constitutional. This Lincoln could not even tacitly admit. Throughout the next four years he sustained the legal fiction that the war was an "insurrection" of individuals in the Southern states who joined in "combinations too powerful to be suppressed by the ordinary course of judicial proceedings." Though he sometimes referred to the conflict as a civil war, he usually called it a "rebellion"—a term he employed more than four hundred times in his messages and letters. He never recognized that any of the Southern states was, or could be, out of the Union, and he did not identify the enemy as the Confederate States of America. On the very rare occasions he was forced to refer to that government, it was always as "the so-called Confederate States of America."

In the years ahead Lincoln was not always able to keep to the purest formulation of his interpretation of the war. Had he done so, captured Confederate soldiers would have been treated as criminals and captured Southern seamen as pirates. This, as Jefferson Davis bluntly warned him, could only lead to retaliation. Without any public announcement, the Lincoln administration modified its position. Throughout the war captured Confederate soldiers and sailors were confined in prison camps—camps that were, in both the Union and the Confederacy, overcrowded and squalid beyond belief but were nevertheless preferable to the common jails where these prisoners might have been sent.

Lincoln's view of the war as simply a domestic insurrection was also contradicted by the naval blockade he imposed on Southern ports. As both Secretary Welles and Charles Sumner advised, under international law his proper course was to close all Southern ports. A blockade was an instrument of war between two belligerent powers; by imposing it, the President was tacitly recognizing the Confederacy as a belligerent. But Lincoln was convinced that an order closing the ports would be repeatedly tested by foreign vessels and that conflict with the European naval powers would result, and he ordered the blockade. Thaddeus Stevens, leader of the Pennsylvania Republicans, ridiculed this as "a great blunder and absurdity" because in legal terms it meant "we were blockading ourselves." When he angrily confronted the President over this issue, Lincoln put on his best simple-countryman air and said, "I don't know anything about the law of nations, and I thought it was all right."

"As a lawyer, Mr. Lincoln," Stevens remarked, "I should have supposed you would have seen the difficulty at once."

"Oh, well," the President replied, "I'm a good enough lawyer in a Western law court, I suppose, but we don't practice the law of nations up there, and I supposed Seward knew all about it, and I left it to him." "But it's done now and can't be helped," he added to Stevens's fury, "so we must get along as well as we can."

With these exceptions Lincoln adhered to his definition of the war, and throughout the next four years the implications of his decision were far-reaching. Because, in his eyes, the Confederacy did not exist, there could never be any negotiations leading to recognition or a peace treaty. Because the insurrection was the work of individuals, not of any organized government, the states of the South remained in the Union throughout the war, fully entitled to all the protections guaranteed by the Constitution. Those guarantees covered the right of private property—including slaves. Punishment for participating in the rebellion could be inflicted on traitorous individuals, not on the states in which they resided, and when victory came to the Union cause, the Southern states would be, as they always had been, equal to all others in the United States.

Lincoln's July 1861 message, together with his proclamations, also made it clear that he considered the prosecution of the war primarily a function of the Chief Executive, to be carried out with minimal interference from the other branches of the government and without excessive respect to constitutional niceties protecting individual rights. To carry out his duties as commander-in-chief, he believed that he could exercise powers normally reserved to the legislative branch of government. Proclaiming a blockade, extending the period for volunteer enlistment to three years, increasing the size of the regular army and navy, and entrusting public funds to private persons for the purchase of arms and supplies would ordinarily require the prior approval of Congress, but the emergency required the President to act before such authorization was granted. "It was with the deepest regret," he explained, "that the Executive found the duty of employing the war-power, in defence of the government, forced upon him." "These measures, whether strictly legal or not," he informed Congress in July, "were ventured upon, under what appeared to be a popular demand, and a public necessity; trusting, then, as now, that Congress would readily ratify them." "It is believed," he added, "that nothing has been done beyond the constitutional competency of Congress."

Even touchier was his decision to suspend the privilege of the writ of habeas corpus, an action that touched on the power both of the legislative and the judicial branches of the government. In neither law nor precedent was it clear where the authority for such suspension lay. The constitutional provision concerning suspension appeared in Article I, detailing the powers of Congress, but whether the Philadelphia convention had placed it there to identify it as a purely legislative function or for stylistic reasons because it did not fit elsewhere was unclear and subsequently became a matter of great controversy in the Congress and among legal experts.

Belief that only Congress had the right to suspend the writ was the basis for Chief Justice Taney's fulminations against the President in his *Merryman* ruling. Lincoln made no reply at the time, but in his message to Congress the President pointed out that the Constitution was silent as to who was to exercise the power of suspending the writ and claimed that in a dangerous emergency when the Congress was not in session the Chief Executive was obliged to act. "It was not believed that any law was violated," he added. Then he went on to suggest that "such extreme tenderness of the citizen's liberty" as Taney had shown could lead to the danger of allowing "all the laws, *but one,* to go unexecuted, and the government itself go to pieces, lest that one be violated."

The next years would see greater infringements on individual liberties than in any other period in American history. Repeatedly the writ of habeas corpus was suspended in localities where secession seemed dangerous, and on September 24, 1862, and again on September 15, 1863, Lincoln suspended the privilege of the writ throughout the country. Initially control of the arbitrary arrests of civilians was given to the Secretary of State, and by the best count, 864 persons were imprisoned and held without trial in the first nine months of the war. After February 1862, when such arrests became the province of the Secretary of War, the number of cases greatly increased. Most of the persons so arrested were spies, smugglers, blockade-runners, carriers of contraband goods, and foreign nationals; only a few were truly political prisoners, jailed for expressing their beliefs. It was nevertheless clear from Lincoln's first message to Congress that devotion to civil liberties was not the primary concern of his administration.

In his July 1861 message Lincoln palliated such transgressions of constitutional niceties because of the importance of the struggle in which the country was engaged. At issue in the contest was more than the fate of the United States. Anticipating a phrase he would use two years later in the Gettysburg Address, he suggested, "It presents to the whole family of man, the question, whether a constitutional republic, or a democracy—a government of the people, by the same people—can, or cannot, maintain its territorial integrity, against its own domestic foes." More, even, than that, it was a struggle for the rights of man. "This," he told the Congress, "is essentially a People's contest. On the side of the Union, it is a struggle for maintaining in the world, that form, and substance of government, whose leading object is, to elevate the condition of men—to lift artificial weights from all shoulders—to clear the paths of laudable pursuit for all—to afford all, an unfettered start, and a fair chance, in the race of life."

III

The Congress that heard Lincoln's message on July 5, when a clerk read it in a dull monotone, was controlled by members of his own party. After the withdrawal of Southern senators and representatives, Republicans held large majorities in both chambers—32 out of 48 members of the Senate, 106 out of 176 members of the House of Representatives. Congressmen from the border slave states who called themselves Unionists generally cooperated with the Republicans during this session. Only about one out of four members of either chamber belonged to the Democratic party, decimated by secession and demoralized by the unexpected death, on June 3 of Stephen A. Douglas, who might have led a loyal opposition to the Lincoln administration.

The reception of the President's message indicated that party lines were, for the moment, unimportant. Few had the heart to engage in partisan bickering, and "irrepressible applause" greeted Lincoln's recommendation that Congress appropriate $400,000,000 to sustain an army of 400,000 men. Converting itself, as one member said, into "a giant committee of ways and means," the Congress promptly went beyond the President's requests and appropriated $500,000,000 to field an army of 500,000 men.

In the country, too, the message was greeted with enthusiasm. Most commended the President's seemingly straightforward account of the events leading up to the attack on Fort Sumter. Several editors noted with pleasure that Lincoln made no mention of slavery or the extension of slavery in the national territories but put the issue before the country simply as one of Union versus Disunion. It was no surprise that a Republican paper like Greeley's *New York Tribune* praised the message for avoiding "episodes and circumlocutions" and going "straight to the hearts of the patriotic millions," but it was a sign of the times when the Democratic *New York World* commended "this excellent and manly Message," which contained "more unborrowed and vigorous thought" than any presidential utterance since the days of Andrew Jackson.

Promptly Congress moved to pass bills retroactively approving most of Lincoln's extraconstitutional actions. There was dissent only on the suspension of the writ of habeas corpus, which made many Republicans, as well as nearly all the Democrats, unhappy. Senator John Sherman of Ohio best captured the feeling of many congressmen: "I approve of the action of the President. . . . He did precisely what I would have done if I had been in his place—no more, no less; but I cannot here, in my place, as a Senator, under oath, declare that what he did do was . . . strictly legal, and in consonance with the provisions of the Constitution."

Such discord was muted because the Union army was preparing to advance while Congress debated. Pressure for an offensive had been building ever since Lincoln's initial call for troops, though nobody had a clear idea of what strategy should be followed. Initially Lincoln, who made no pretense of having military knowledge, thought the troops should be used to repossess Fort Sumter and other captured federal installations along the Southern coast, but this thoroughly impracticable scheme would have required large amphibious operations far beyond the competence of either the army or the navy in 1861. General Scott, the most revered military expert in the country, offered what was described as an "Anaconda Plan," which called for cordoning off the Confederacy with a tight naval blockade while advancing with an army of perhaps 85,000 down the Mississippi River from southern Illinois. The plan had some merit—but it rested on the remarkable assumption that the Confederate army in Virginia, which even Scott granted might total more than 100,000 men, would remain idle while the Union forces were advancing in the West. Montgomery Blair believed that "a very inconsiderable part" of the Union army could put down the rebellion by distributing arms to the Union men of the South, who were at present "overawed by the armed marauders that Jeff Davis has sent throughout the country." George B. McClellan, the hero of small engagements in western Virginia, proposed to gain victory by marching an army of 80,000 up the Great Kanawha Valley, across the Appalachian Mountains, to seize Richmond from the west. His scheme showed the ignorance of topography that was to characterize his subsequent campaigns.

Despite the absence of clear strategic plans, the demand for a Union advance became explosive after federal troops suffered several minor setbacks during the early months of the war. The most conspicuous of these occurred on May 24, the day after Virginia formally ratified its ordinance of secession, when Lincoln directed federal troops to cross the Potomac and occupy Alexandria. Moving stealthily, Union forces, including the Zouave regiment that Elmer Ellsworth had recruited in New York, compelled the Virginia troops to withdraw. Flushed with victory, Ellsworth spotted a secession flag flying above the Marshall House—a flag the President could see with his spyglass from the White House—and dashed up the stairs to tear it down. On his way down the hotelkeeper shot and killed him. Ellsworth's death deeply grieved Lincoln, who thought of this young officer as almost another son. The funeral ceremonies were held in the White House, and afterward the President wrote the young man's parents of their shared affliction: "So much of promised usefulness to one's country, and of bright hopes for one's self and friends, have rarely been so suddenly dashed, as in his fall."

The tragedy—one that would have gone almost unnoticed in later years, when deaths were reported by the thousands—reinforced the drumbeat of politicians and newspapers calling for action. Up to this point Lincoln had favored delay, but he now ordered an advance against the Confederate army near Manassas, Virginia, where it was a constant threat to Washington.

Since Scott was too old and infirm to take the field, Lincoln put General Irvin McDowell, a forty-two-year-old West Point graduate who had served with distinction in the Mexican War, in charge of the advance. On June 29, Lincoln met with his cabinet and military advisers in the White House to discuss McDowell's plans, which were simple and direct. Believing that General P. G. T. Beauregard had about 35,000 men at Manassas, he proposed to attack the Confederates before they could be reinforced. Scott demurred because he believed in "a war of large bodies," not "a little war by piecemeal," but the President and the cabinet overruled him, and McDowell was authorized to begin his campaign on July 9.

It was not until a week later that McDowell was ready to move—a very costly week's delay that gave the Confederacy a chance to reinforce Beauregard's army with Joseph E. Johnston's troops from the Shenandoah Valley. Slowly McDowell's army began to march out to meet the Confederate army at Manassas. (That is what the Southerners called the place; Yankees found that one undistinguished Southern crossroads looked much like another, and they called the field of engagement Bull Run, after the creek that meandered near it.) McDowell's plans were widely known in Washington, and his invading army was accompanied by six United States senators, at least ten representatives, scores of newspapermen, and many of what a reporter called "the fairer, if not gentler sex," who often brought picnic baskets in their buggies.

Assured by Scott that McDowell would be successful, Lincoln quietly went to church on July 21. In midafternoon he went to Scott's office, only to find the general-in-chief taking his afternoon nap. When the President woke him up, the general said that early reports from the battlefield signified nothing and before dropping off to sleep again predicted McDowell's victory. But by six o'clock that evening Seward came to the White House with the news that McDowell's army was in full retreat. At the War Department the President read the dispatch of an army captain of engineers: "The day is lost. Save Washington and the remnants of this army.... The routed troops will not re-form." All evening the President and the cabinet members clustered in Scott's office, hearing more and more alarming news. That night, stretched out on a couch in the cabinet room of the White House, the President listened to firsthand reports from terrified eyewitnesses of the defeat. He did not go to bed that night.

The next day Lincoln began to assess the damage. He learned that many of McDowell's troops had fought bravely and well. The Union army would have won the battle except for the unanticipated arrival of Johnston's forces from the Valley. Even then, facing overwhelming odds, most of the volunteer Union regiments had retreated in good order, and the demoralized mob described by so many witnesses was largely composed of teamsters, onlookers, and ninety-day troops whose terms of enlistment were about to expire. The army was defeated but not crushed, and McDowell's troops were fed into the substantial fortifications on the south side of the Potomac. By nightfall Cameron wired to worried New Yorkers, "The capital is safe."

The immediate political reaction to the defeat was to rally behind the President. In order to make that support clear, both houses of Congress voted almost unanimously for John J. Crittenden's resolution declaring "that this war is not waged ... for any purpose of conquest or subjugation, nor purpose of overthrowing ... established institutions [meaning slavery] ... but to defend ... the Constitution and to preserve the Union." That resolution echoed the pledge in Lincoln's inaugural address not to interfere with slavery within the states.

But such unity was only a façade. Bull Run was a severe Union defeat, and finger-pointing and recriminations inevitably followed. McDowell unfairly received a good share of the blame. Scott, too, was condemned for allowing such an ill-prepared campaign to get under way. Restive under criticism, the old general made an apology that was more like a defense when he talked with several Illinois congressmen in Lincoln's presence two days after the battle. "I am the greatest coward in America," he announced. "I will prove it; I have fought this battle, sir, against my judgment; I think the President of the United States ought to remove me to-day for doing it; as God is my judge, after my superiors had determined to fight it, I did all in my power to make the Army efficient. I deserve removal because I did not stand up, when my army was not in condition for fighting, and resist it to the last."

The President interjected, "Your conversation seems to imply that I forced you to fight this battle."

Scott avoided a direct response by saying, "I have never served a President who has been kinder to me than you have been."

Unlike the general, Lincoln was willing to assume the blame for the defeat. Coolly reviewing the evidence, he concluded that the Manassas campaign, though unsuccessful, had not been ill advised. He knew that Union soldiers were raw recruits, but so were their Confederate opponents. On neither side did commanding officers have experience in conducting large-scale engagements. A crushing defeat of the Confederate army at Bull Run could have ended the war.

The President moved immediately to remedy the causes of the Union defeat. To boost morale he visited the fortifications around Washington and assured the troops that as commander-in-chief he would make sure they had all needful supplies. But he also recognized the need for better discipline. When he inspected the troops at Fort Corcoran, a disgruntled officer complained that Colonel William T. Sherman had threatened to shoot him like a dog for planning to go to New York without a leave. In a stage whisper that the other soldiers could easily hear, the President said, "Well, if I were you, and he threatened to shoot, I would not trust him, for I believe he would do it."

Clearly a new commanding general was needed, and on the day after the battle Lincoln summoned George B. McClellan from western Virginia to take charge of the forces around Washington and to build a new army out of the three-year volunteer regiments that were just beginning to arrive in the capital.

IV

During the next months while McClellan was organizing and training the new soldiers, Lincoln had a breathing spell from political pressure, because everybody recognized that it would take time to build a real army. During these weeks the President and his family could for the first time enjoy living in the White House. Initially they had been overwhelmed by the size of the Executive Mansion with its thirty-one rooms, not including the conservatory, various outbuildings, and stables. The East Room alone was about as large as their entire Springfield house. Except for the family dining room, the first floor was open to all visitors. An aged Irish doorkeeper, Edward McManus, was supposed to screen visitors, but in practice anybody who wanted to could stroll in at any hour of the day and often late at night. On the second floor nearly half the rooms were also public, so that the Lincolns' private quarters, which at first seemed so palatial, proved to be remarkably constricted. The upstairs oval room became the family sitting room. The two adjoining rooms on the south side were those of the President and Mrs. Lincoln; as in Springfield, they had separate but connecting bedrooms. Across the wide corridor were the state guest room, called the Prince of Wales Room, and the infrequently used room of Robert, who was in the White House only during Harvard vacations. Tad and Willie had smaller rooms on the north side.

The younger boys found endless opportunities for mischief and adventure in the Executive Mansion. To adults the soldiers stationed on the south grounds of the White House were an ominous reminder of danger, but to Willie and Tad the members of the "Bucktail" Pennsylvania regiment were playmates who could always be counted on for stories and races. Catching the martial spirit, Willie and Tad took great pleasure in drilling all the neighborhood boys they could round up. With two special friends who just matched them in age—Bud and Holly Taft, sons of a federal judge who lived nearby—they commandeered the roof of the mansion for their fort, and there, with small logs painted to look like cannon, they resolutely fired away at unseen Confederates across the Potomac.

Children in the White House were something new for Americans, and citizens began showering the boys with presents. The most valued, and the most lasting, were the pets. Someone gave Willie a beautiful little pony, to which he was devoted; he rode the animal nearly every day and, being a generous boy, often allowed Tad to ride, even though the younger boy was so small that his legs stuck straight out on the sides. Especially cherished were two small goats, Nanko and Nanny, which frisked on the White House grounds and, when they had an opportunity, tore up the White House garden. At times the animals, like the general public, seemed to have the run of the White House. On one occasion Tad harnessed Nanko up to a chair, which served him as a sled, and drove triumphantly through the East Room, where a reception was in progress. As dignified matrons held up their hoop skirts, Nanko pulled the yelling boy around the room and out through the door again.

When Lincoln could find time, he played with his boys. One day Julia Taft, the teenage sister of Bud and Holly, heard a great commotion in the upstairs oval room and entered to find the President of the United States lying on his back on the floor, Willie and Bud holding down his arms, Tad and Holly, his legs. "Julie, come quick and sit on his stomach!" cried Tad, as the President grinned at her grandly. There were also quiet times when Lincoln told stories or read to the boys; he would balance Willie and Bud on each knee while Tad mounted the back of his big chair and Holly climbed on the arm.

But such relaxed times were rare because Lincoln worked harder than almost any other American President. After a meager breakfast he went immediately to his office, where he signed as many papers and commissions as he could before the day's regular schedule began. A solid black walnut table occupied the center of the office; here the cabinet members gathered for their biweekly sessions. Along one wall of the office were a sofa and two upholstered chairs, above which hung maps of the theaters of military operations. A large upright mahogany desk, so battered that one of Lincoln's secretaries thought it must have come "from some old furniture auction," was in one corner. The pigeonholes above it served as a filing cabinet. Lincoln's smaller working desk stood between the two windows.

Adjoining the President's office were rooms occupied by his small staff, equipped with nondescript furnishings. Most of the floor of this wing of the White House was covered with oilcloth, which made it easier to clean up after overflowing or missed spittoons. Lincoln's private secretary was the self-effacing, methodical Nicolay, and the effervescent John Hay served as Nicolay's assistant. As the burden of correspondence grew, William O. Stoddard, technically a clerk in the Interior Department, was brought in to help with the initial screening of the 200 to 300 letters that came in each day. One of his jobs was to throw away the letters from cranks and lunatics. Much later, when Stoddard became ill, Edward D. Neill of Minnesota, another clerk in the Interior Department, took his place. Hay spelled out the duties of these assistants when he instructed Neill to take charge in his temporary absence: "There will probably be little to do. Refer as little to the President as possible, Keep visitors out of the house when you can. Inhospitable, but prudent. I have a few franked envelopes. Let matters of ordinary reference go without formality of signature."

Absolutely devoted to Lincoln, Nicolay and Hay were convinced that he would be remembered as a great President, and they early agreed that they would someday write a history of his administration. Lincoln promised to help them. Behind Lincoln's back Nicolay and Hay affectionately referred to him as "the Ancient" (possibly derived from "Old Abe") or "the Tycoon," in reference to the all-powerful Emperor of Japan. Lincoln always addressed Nicolay by his last name and treated him with great respect, but he called Hay "John" and treated him like a son.

In the first days of his administration Lincoln tried to be orderly and businesslike. He attempted to scan and digest all the morning papers that reached the White House. Finding that too time-consuming, he instructed his secretaries to prepare a digest of the news for his perusal, but presently he discontinued even that. Though he occasionally glanced at the telegraphic news dispatches in one or two papers, he read none of the newspapers consistently and almost never looked at their editorials. There was, he believed, nothing that newspapermen could tell him that he did not already know.

From early morning until dusk visitors thronged these business rooms of the White House. In the early months of the administration the line was so long that it extended down the stairs to the front entrance, with a candidate for a job or a military appointment perched on each step. Most of these applicants could be handled expeditiously. Lincoln quickly scanned letters of recommendation, referred petitioners to the proper department heads, and listened intently to complaints and made proper sympathetic noises. Whenever possible he avoided flatly rejecting an application, preferring to tell one of his celebrated "leetle stories" to suggest how impossible the request was. When an officer accused of embezzling forty dollars of government money appealed for leniency on the ground that he had really stolen only thirty dollars, the President was reminded of an Indiana man who charged his neighbor's daughter with unseemly behavior in having three illegitimate children. " 'Now that's a lie,' said the man whose family was so outrageously scandalized, 'and I can prove it, for she only has two.' "

Remarkably, the President's systematic lack of system seemed to work. Stories of his accessibility to even the humblest petitioner, his patience, and his humanity spread throughout the North. For the first time in American history citizens began to feel that the occupant of the White House was *their* representative. They referred to him as Father Abraham, and they showered him with homely gifts: a firkin of butter, a crate of Bartlett pears, New England salmon. With special appropriateness a man from Johnsburgh, New York, sent the President "a live American Eagle[,] the bird of our land," which had lost one foot in a trap. "But," the New Yorker continued, "he is yet an Eagle and perhaps no more cripled [sic] than the Nation whose banner he represented, his wings are sound and will extend seven feet."

V

At the same time, Mary Lincoln was achieving some successes of her own, and she became the most conspicuous female occupant of the Executive Mansion since Dolley Madison. Brought up with an active interest in public affairs, deeply involved in her husband's political career, she had no intention of fading quietly into the Washington background. She intended to become the First Lady of the land—a term that was coined to describe her.

She enjoyed her role as hostess, and she made a favorable impression on most visitors. The cynical William Howard Russell, the American correspondent of the *Times* of London, found much to criticize about her appearance and manner, but he praised her simple jewelry and her "very gorgeous and highly colored" dress and could not fail to observe that she fluttered her fan a great deal to display her rounded, well-proportioned shoulders. Noting that Mrs. Lincoln was "of the middle age and height, of a plumpness degenerating to the *embonpoint* natural to her years," with plain features and a homely appearance "stiffened, however, by the consciousness that her position requires her to be something more than plain Mrs. Lincoln, the wife of the Illinois lawyer," Russell judged that she was "desirous of making herself agreeable," and rather grudgingly added, "I own I was agreeably disappointed."

She made refurbishing the White House her main project as First Lady. She found it in bad shape. The furniture was broken down, the wallpaper peeling, the carpeting worn, and the draperies torn. The eleven basement rooms were filthy and rat-infested. The whole place had the air of a run-down, unsuccessful third-rate hotel. Congress had appropriated $20,000 to be expended over the four years of her husband's term of office for rehabilitating the Executive Mansion, and she intended to put it to good use.

In the summer of 1861 she went to Philadelphia and New York to buy furnishings suitable for the mansion of the President of the United States and his First Lady. Merchants showed her the best and most expensive carpeting, material for upholstery and drapes, splendid furniture, and exquisite china. Mary was not entirely rational when it came to money and spending, and, having no head for figures, she bought everything: chairs, sofas and hassocks, fabrics of damask, brocade, pink tarlatan, plush, and "French Satin DeLaine"; wallpaper imported from France; and a full set of Haviland china in "Solferino and gold," with the American coat of arms in the center of each plate. For the Red Room she ordered 117 yards of crimson Wilton carpet, and for the East Room an imported Brussels velvet carpet, pale green in color, ingeniously woven as a single piece, which, one admirer gushed, "in effect looked as if the ocean, in gleaming and transparent waves, were tossing roses at your feet."

On her return to Washington she personally oversaw the scrubbing, painting, and plastering of the White House, so that for the first time in years the entire mansion was sparklingly clean. When her new furniture arrived, the whole place took on an air of elegant opulence.

But by fall, when the bills began to come in, she discovered that she had greatly overspent the congressional allowance not just for the year but for Lincoln's full term. Desperately she tried to keep her husband from learning what she had done. In her panic she exploded in rage at anyone who dared cross her. Nicolay and Hay, who had to deal with her temperamental outbursts, began to refer to her as "the Hell-cat." She authorized a sale of secondhand White House furniture, but it brought in almost as little money as did the sale of manure from the White House stables at ten cents a wagonload. Then John Watt, the White House gardener, showed her easier ways of covering her deficit, by padding bills for household expenditures and presenting vouchers for nonexistent purchases. Discharging the White

House steward, she secured that appointment for Mrs. Watt—and performed the duties and kept the salary herself.

None of this, however, could cover her enormous overrun of expenditures, and she had to ask Benjamin B. French, the commissioner of Public Buildings, who kept the White House accounts, to explain the situation to the President and to ask him to sponsor a supplemental congressional appropriation. Lincoln was furious. Never, he said, would he ask Congress for an appropriation "for *flub dubs for that damned old house!*" "It would stink in the land to have it said that an appropriation of $20,000 for furnishing the house had been overrun by the President when the poor freezing soldiers could not have blankets," he went on. The White House "was furnished well enough—better than any house *they* had ever lived in." Rather than ask Congress for more money he vowed he would pay for Mary's purchases out of his own pocket. Eventually, though, he was obliged to back down, and Congress quietly passed two deficiency appropriations to cover rehabilitating the White House.

VI

Support for the President, which appeared so overwhelming immediately after Bull Run, rapidly eroded. For many Democrats the defeat brought realization that the nation faced a long and costly war. Those who were styled "War Democrats" rallied behind the President. A larger group of Democrats reluctantly accepted the war as long as it was fought to preserve "the constitution as it is and the Union as it was," but they were nervous lest a prolonged conflict prove "the Trojan horse of tyranny." A few, like James A. Bayard of Delaware and Clement L. Vallandigham of Ohio, willingly acknowledged that they were Peace Democrats. Bayard took as his motto "Anything is better than a fruitless, hopeless, unnatural civil war."

These divisions deeply troubled Lincoln. He recognized what he called "the plain facts" of his situation. The Republicans, as he said, "came into power, very largely in a minority of the popular vote." His administration could not possibly put down the rebellion without assistance from the Democrats. It was, he observed, "mere nonsense to suppose a minority could put down a majority in rebellion." Consequently he carefully cultivated War Democrats in Congress like Andrew Johnson of Tennessee, the only Southern senator who refused to follow his state when it seceded, and Reverdy Johnson of Maryland, who sustained the President's use of war powers and refuted the arguments of Chief Justice Taney. He rewarded Joseph Holt, the staunch Kentucky Unionist who had been Secretary of War under Buchanan, by naming him judge advocate general. In making military appointments he tried to select commanders on the basis of military expertise rather than on what he called "political affinity," and a sizable number of the generals he selected were Democrats: George B. McClellan, Benjamin F. Butler, W. S.

Rosecrans, John A. McClernand, and many others. In policy, too, he tried to build a broad base of support by presenting the issue before the country as one of Union versus Disunion.

In attempting to build a consensus, the President ran the risk of dividing his own party. Many Republicans felt that he was neglecting the moral and political arguments against slavery that had been the foundation of their party's ideology. Two days after the defeat at Bull Run, Senator Zachariah Chandler of Michigan and Senator Sumner, accompanied by Vice President Hamlin, came to the White House and urged the President to make the war a contest between Freedom and Slavery. Sumner argued that emancipation was a military necessity, and Chandler asked Lincoln to free the slaves in order to create such chaos in the South that the Confederacy would collapse. The President listened politely but said such measures were too far in advance of public opinion.

Among disgruntled Republicans the feeling spread that Lincoln, though well meaning, was slow and incompetent. In his diary Count Adam Gurowski, the eccentric Polish nobleman who worked as a translator for the State Department, accurately captured the mood of Republicans in Congress: "Mr. Lincoln in some way has a slender historical resemblance to Louis XVI— similar goodness, honesty, good intentions; but the size of events seems to be too much for him." According to Gurowski, Senator Wade was so "disgusted with the slowness and inanity of the administration" that he remarked, "I do not wonder that people desert to Jeff. Davis, as he shows brains; I may desert myself." To express that dissatisfaction and to give some direction to the Union war effort, the Congress just before adjournment passed the Confiscation Act, which provided that a master would lose ownership of any slave employed to assist the Confederate armies. Lincoln signed the measure reluctantly, and it had little effect except as an expression of opinion.

In late August the diffuse feeling of unhappiness with the Lincoln administration found a focus. General John C. Frémont, named commander of the Department of the West, with headquarters in St. Louis, took drastic steps to defeat a Confederate invasion in southwestern Missouri and end widespread guerrilla warfare elsewhere. Proclaiming martial law in the entire state of Missouri, Frémont announced that civilians bearing arms would be tried by court-martial and shot if convicted and that slaves of persons who aided the rebellion would be emancipated.

Fremont's proclamation, issued without consultation with Washington, clearly ran counter to the policy Lincoln had announced in his inaugural address of not interfering with slavery and against the recently adopted Crittenden resolution pledging that restoration of the Union was the only aim of the war. It also violated the provisions of the Confiscation Act, which established judicial proceedings to seize slaves used to help the rebel army. Lincoln saw at once that Frémont's order must be modified. He directed the general to withdraw his threat to shoot captured civilians bearing arms.

"Should you shoot a man, according to the proclamation, the Confederates would very certainly shoot our best man in their hands in retaliation," he admonished Frémont; "and so, man for man, indefinitely." The President viewed Frémont's order to liberate slaves of traitorous owners as even more dangerous. Such action, he reminded the general, "will alarm our Southern Union friends, and turn them against us—perhaps ruin our rather fair prospect for Kentucky." He asked Frémont to modify his proclamation.

Though Lincoln said he was writing "in a spirit of caution and not of censure," Frémont took his letter as an undeserved rebuke. He, after all, was on the scene; he had to deal with the vindictiveness of Confederate sympathizers in Missouri; he had to defend the state when Washington conspicuously neglected to provide the men, the equipment, and even the food he needed to sustain his army. Very angry, he permitted his redoubtable wife, Jessie, the daughter of the celebrated Missouri Senator Thomas Hart Benton, to go to Washington and present his case in person to the President.

Mrs. Frémont arrived on September 10 and immediately asked the President to set a time for an interview. He replied tersely, "Now, at once." Though it was nine o'clock in the evening and she was tired and dusty from traveling all day, she went immediately to the White House. She did not find Lincoln hospitable. He received her in the Red Room, standing, and he did not offer her a seat. When she presented a letter from her husband explaining his position, Lincoln, as she remembered it, "smiled with an expression that was not agreeable" and read it without comment. Attempting to make Frémont's views clearer, she went on to talk about the need to strike a blow against slavery that would enlist British sentiment on the Union side. The President cut her off with "You are quite a female politician." Then, in a voice that she found both hard and "repelling," he told her, "It was a war for a great national idea, the Union, and . . . General Frémont should not have dragged the Negro into it."

The next day the President, taking note of Frémont's unwillingness to modify his proclamation on his own, "very cheerfully" ordered him to change it so as "to conform to, and not to transcend," the provisions of the Confiscation Act. Some of Lincoln's advisers feared that Frémont would disobey the President's order and "set up on his own." But Lincoln would not permit civilian authority to be overruled by the military, and he would not allow sensitive questions concerning slavery and emancipation to be decided by anyone but the President himself.

That was not the end of the Frémont problem. The general, who had made his reputation as a pathmarker of the Western trails to California, was never able to find his way across the Missouri political terrain. He quarreled with everybody. He scorned the duly elected, if ineffectual, governor of Missouri, Hamilton R. Gamble, who promptly went to Washington with complaints about military incompetence in St. Louis. He quarreled with his subordinates. He made the serious mistake of quarreling with the Blair family, which had originally sponsored his appointment as commander of the Department of the West, and eventually he even ordered the arrest of Frank Blair. "He is losing the confidence of men near him, whose support any man in his position must have to be successful," Lincoln observed. "His cardinal mistake is that he isolates himself, and allows nobody to see him; and by which he does not know what is going on in the very matter he is dealing with."

To ineptness, charges of fraud and corruption in the Department of the West were added, though nobody accused Frémont of using his command for personal gain. The Blairs exerted incessant pressure on the President to remove the general, but Lincoln was always reluctant to dismiss subordinates, however incompetent, and told Montgomery Blair that it was not "quite fair to squander Frémont until he has another chance." The very negative report that Adjutant General Lorenzo Thomas submitted in October decided the issue. Frémont was relieved from command on November 2.

The Frémont imbroglio caused an immense turmoil throughout the Union. In the border slave states, just as Lincoln predicted, Frémont's proclamation dealt a heavy blow to Unionist sentiment. "That foolish proclamation," Joshua Speed promptly warned the President from Kentucky, "will crush out any vestage [sic] of a union party in the state." "I am now fully satisfied," he wrote a few days later, "that we could stand several defeats like that at Bulls run [sic], better than we can this . . . foolish act of a military popinjay." Robert Anderson, now in command of the Department of Kentucky, warned that if the proclamation "is not immediately disavowed, and annulled, Kentucky will be lost to the Union." Frémont's decree came at the worst possible time, when the legislature was about to abandon the policy of neutrality for Kentucky. The legislature would not budge until the proclamation was modified, and there was danger that Union volunteers in Kentucky would desert to the Confederacy. By overruling the most offensive parts of Frémont's edict, Lincoln saved the state for the Union. As one Kentucky Unionist wrote, "The President handled that matter with an honesty of purpose, and a good sense that I have never seen surpassed."

In the North the reaction was exactly the opposite. Frémont's order aroused a public that was already tired of war and demanded decisive steps to end it. All the major newspapers approved it—not merely the staunchly Republican journals like the *New York Tribune,* the *New York Times,* and the *Chicago Tribune,* but also independent conservative papers like Washington's *National Intelligencer* and the Democratic *Boston Post* and *Chicago Times.* Even a cautious conservative like Browning wrote the President: "Fremont's proclamation was necessary and will do good. It has the full approval of all loyal citizens of the West and the North West."

From Iowa came a report that failure to sustain Frémont was causing *"extreme* dissatisfaction" and would end volunteering in the Northwest. "It would have been difficult to have devised a plan to more effectually dispirit the People of this section than your order," a Wisconsin voter wrote the

President. "My own indignation is too deep for words," raged Horace White of the *Chicago Tribune*. "Our President has broken his own neck if he has not destroyed his country." Benjamin Wade sneered that Lincoln's conduct was all that could be expected "of one, born of 'poor white trash' and educated in a slave State." Ironically Wade added, "I shall expect to find in his annual message, a recommendation to Congress, to give each rebel, who shall serve during the war, a hundred and sixty acres of land." Even Herndon, Lincoln's own law partner, thought the President had behaved shamefully. "Does he suppose he can crush—squelch out this huge rebellion by pop guns filled with rose water," he gibed. "He ought to hang somebody and get up a name for will or decision—for character. Let him hang some Child or woman, if he has not Courage to hang a *man*."

Sorely beset, Lincoln laid out his reasons for overruling Frémont's proclamation in a long, careful letter to Browning. If the general's order had been allowed to stand, he explained, Kentucky would probably have seceded. "I think to lose Kentucky is nearly the same as to lose the whole game," he went on. "Kentucky gone, we can not hold Missouri, nor, as I think Maryland. These all against us, and the job on our hands is too large for us. We would as well consent to separation at once, including the surrender of this capitol." He also offered an even more cogent reason, which he knew would appeal to men like Browning who loved the Constitution and respected the rule of law. "Genl. Fremont's proclamation, as to confiscation of property, and the liberation of slaves, is *purely political*," he wrote, "and not within the range of *military* law, or necessity." It was, in fact, simply dictatorship, because it assumed "that the general may do *anything* he pleases." Far from saving the government, such reckless action meant the surrender of the government. "Can it be pretended that it is any longer the government of the U.S.—any government of Constitution and laws—wherein a General, or a President, may make permanent rules of property by proclamation?"

VII

As indisputable evidence of Frémont's military incompetence and fiscal extravagance surfaced, support for the general waned, and criticism of the slow pace of the war effort focused on General McClellan, who only in July had been hailed as the defender of Washington and the savior of his country. At first everybody admired the thirty-four-year-old general. Handsome, with blue eyes and reddish brown hair, he gave an impression of strength and vigor. "He has brains," Browning thought, "looks as if he ought to have courage, and I think, is altogether more than an ordinary man." Everybody else thought so, too. "By some strange operation of magic," the young general wrote his wife, "I seem to have become the power of the land." When he visited the Senate, the members vied to shake his hand. "They give me my way in everything, full swing and unbounded confidence."

There was only admiration for the way McClellan reorganized the forces around Washington. A skilled engineer, he developed a ring of fortifications to protect the city from surprise attacks. Replacing the useless ninety-day soldiers who had formed McDowell's force (most of their terms were about to expire) with three-year volunteers, he began rigorously training his men and kept a close eye on them as they performed close-order drills, did target practice, and engaged in practice maneuvers. Dashing about on a magnificent horse, he seemed omnipresent, and no detail of his soldiers' life was too small to escape his notice. The men under his command—after August 15 called "the Army of the Potomac"—loved him as they loved no other commander throughout the war.

Along with his other talents, McClellan had an excellent sense of public relations, and he made a practice of inviting the President, the Secretary of War, other members of the cabinet, and senators to be present when he staged a review of the troops. The contrast between the general and his commander-in-chief as they rode down the lines struck some observers as ludicrous. McClellan was superb in full-dress uniform, while Lincoln, wearing his customary stovepipe hat, looked, according to one observer, "like a scare-crow on horseback." Though amused, the soldiers were in good spirits and they gave resounding cheers to a President who had not received much applause in recent months.

But by fall McClellan's honeymoon ended. Critics began to complain that he was not taking advantage of the fine weather to launch an offensive against the Confederates, still lodged at Manassas. Horace Greeley again demanded that the army march onward to Richmond. Senator Chandler, originally one of McClellan's strongest backers, lost faith in the general; he lamented that "Fremont[']s operations were bad enough in all conscience, but as compared with McLellan[']s they were splendid," and he blamed the general's failure on a *'timid* vacil[l]ating and inefficient" administration. Wade was even more intemperate, simultaneously denouncing "Old Abe" and General McClellan. He raged that the general was stripping the West of men and putting them in the Army of the Potomac so "that Mr Lincoln and his Cabinet may breathe freely and eat their dinners in peace, and that Mrs Lincoln may without interruption, pursue her French and dancing."

Abetted by Senator Trumbull, Wade and Chandler began worrying Lincoln into forcing McClellan to fight. Wade went so far as to say that he preferred an unsuccessful battle to further delay, because "a defeat could be easily repaired, by the swarming recruits." These critics were so persistent and vehement in their campaign against McClellan that John Hay labeled them "Jacobins," after the most extreme radicals of the French Revolution, and the name stuck. Lincoln told the general not to fight until he was ready, but he felt obliged to warn him that Wade voiced a widely held feeling of impatience, which he said was a reality that had to be taken into account. McClellan listened, but evidently he did not hear.

On October 21, McClellan's critics were infuriated when, after long inaction, an element of his army ventured across the Potomac at Ball's Bluff (or

Leesburg), ran into fierce Confederate opposition, and was thrown back with heavy losses. Colonel Edward D. Baker, Lincoln's longtime friend and a senator from Oregon, was killed. The Lincolns were devastated by the news and received no White House visitors the next day. In Congress grief over the fallen senator exploded into wrath at McClellan for having allowed such an ill-planned, poorly supported expedition. Lawmakers began to harbor a growing suspicion that not merely Baker's superior officer, Charles P. Stone, but McClellan himself might be disloyal to the Union.

McClellan defended himself by telling his congressional critics that he was hamstrung by the aged and nearly senile General Scott. They then descended on the White House to nag Lincoln into removing General Scott, and on November 1, with a heavy heart, the President accepted Scott's offer to retire, which had often been tendered. In a statement praising Scott's long and brilliant career, Lincoln expressed the country's gratitude for "his faithful devotion to the Constitution, the Union, and the Flag, when assailed by parricidal rebellion."

That left McClellan in charge, and Lincoln designated him to command the whole army of the United States. He was now in charge not merely of the Army of the Potomac but of Don Carlos Buell's Army of the Ohio, which was preparing for a push into Tennessee, and of Henry W. Halleck's Army of the Missouri, which was to move down the Mississippi River. In giving these increased responsibilities to McClellan, Lincoln said: "Draw on me for all the sense I have, and all the information. In addition to your present command, the supreme command of the Army will entail a vast labor upon you." Quietly McClellan responded, "I can do it all."

But the general still failed to launch a campaign, and his relations with both the President and the Congress rapidly deteriorated. After his first few weeks in Washington he concluded that "the Presdt is an idiot," but he rarely expressed his opinion until after he was placed in command of all the armies. Now he began consorting with Democratic politicians, and he wrote freely to his wife that Lincoln was "nothing more than a well meaning baboon," while Seward was "a meddling, officious, incompetent little puppy," Welles was a "garrulous old woman," Bates "an old fool," and Cameron a rascal. He grew weary of the President's constant visits to his headquarters to read the latest military dispatches and discuss projected campaigns. General Samuel P. Heintzelman was present on one such occasion when Lincoln poured over the map of Virginia making strategic suggestions which McClellan obviously thought absurd but which he pretended to listen to deferentially. After the President left, McClellan turned to his subordinate and laughed: "Isn't he a rare bird?"

Even more taxing were Lincoln's late-night visits to McClellan's house to discuss strategy, and the general decided to put an end to them. On the evening of November 13, when Lincoln and Seward, accompanied by John Hay, called on McClellan, he was out, and they decided to stay until he returned. After about an hour he came in and, paying no attention to the porter who told him the President was waiting, went straight upstairs. After another half hour the guests sent up a message that they were still waiting, only to receive the cool message that the general had gone to bed. Hay thought the President should feel greatly offended, but Lincoln said "it was better at this time not to be making points of etiquette and personal dignity." He paid no more visits to McClellan's house.

Though Lincoln said that he was willing to hold McClellan's horse if he would win a victory, he was growing disenchanted with his general-in-chief. In his December message to Congress, after expressing a hope that the country would support McClellan's exertions, he added a backhanded compliment: "It has been said that one bad general is better than two good ones; and the saying is true, if taken to mean . . . that an army is better directed by a single mind, though inferior, than by two superior ones, at variance."

Congressmen could afford to be less guarded in their language. Senator Chandler bluntly told Lincoln that if McClellan allowed his huge army to go into winter quarters without fighting a battle he "was in favor of sending for Jeff Davis *at once.*"

VIII

Lincoln's first State of the Union message, which a clerk read to Congress on December 3, 1861, was a perfunctory document. Cobbling together reports from the various heads of departments, the President made a few interesting recommendations, such as creating a Department of Agriculture (which Congress established the next year). He also urged the recognition of the two black republics of Haiti and Liberia—something inconceivable under previous pro-Southern administrations. It closed with an oddly incongruous disquisition on the relationship between capital and labor in a free society and with the assurance that the struggle in which the Union was engaged was "not altogether for today—it is for a vast future also."

One reason the message was so uncommunicative was that the United States was nearing a diplomatic crisis with Great Britain over the *Trent* affair, which could not be discussed publicly. The President could have summarized the facts succinctly. In October, James M. Mason of Virginia and John Slidell of Louisiana, named ministers plenipotentiary to represent the Confederacy in Great Britain and France, escaped through the blockade to Cuba. There they boarded the British mail packet *Trent.* Without orders from Washington, Captain Charles Wilkes, who commanded the USS *San Jacinto,* stopped and searched the vessel and removed the Confederate envoys, who were eventually imprisoned in Fort Warren in Boston harbor. Overwhelming jubilation greeted Wilkes's act in the North, but abroad it was viewed as a blatant violation of international law and an insult to the British flag. Lincoln had no advance knowledge of Wilkes's act.

In general, the President had little to do with foreign affairs. With no knowledge of diplomacy and no personal acquaintances or correspondents abroad, he willingly entrusted foreign policy to his Secretary of State. The only interest he showed in selecting American diplomatic representatives was to make sure that various claims for patronage were honored. He rewarded Judd's services by making him minister to Prussia and showed his gratitude to Carl Schurz by naming him to the court at Madrid, where the German-born former revolutionary met with a chilly reception. Cassius M. Clay was appointed minister to Russia, less perhaps as a reward than as a means for getting a troublemaker out of the country. But generally Lincoln accepted Seward's recommendations without question. When Charles Francis Adams, Seward's choice for minister to the Court of St. James's, came to the White House, Lincoln received his thanks for the appointment coolly: "Very kind of you to say so Mr Adams but you are not my choice. You are Seward's man." Then, turning to the Secretary of State, the President said in almost the same breath: "Well Seward, I have settled the Chicago Post Office."

Seward's bellicose memorandum of April 1, 1861, forced the President to take a more active interest in foreign policy, which increased when he read a warlike dispatch Seward proposed to send to Adams in May. Angered by the decision of the European powers to recognize the Confederates as belligerents—an entirely proper step and one in conformity with the actions of the Lincoln administration in blockading, rather than closing, Southern ports—Seward blustered that British intervention in the American conflict would mean that "we, from that hour, shall cease to be friends and become once more, as we have twice before been forced to be, enemies of Great Britain." Troubled, the President called on Charles Sumner, the chairman of the Senate Foreign Relations Committee, for advice. With Sumner's enthusiastic approval he excised the more offensive statements in Seward's dispatch and then directed that the revised document was for Adams's information only, not to be read or presented at the British Foreign Office.

From that time Lincoln consulted Sumner on all major questions relating to foreign policy. The two men formed an odd couple. Good-looking, Harvard-trained, and world-traveled, Sumner was the exact opposite of the homely self-educated President. With a decade's experience in the Senate, Sumner regarded the untried Lincoln as "honest but inexperienced." A compulsive worker, proud of his prompt and efficient attention to his official duties, the senator thought Lincoln's "habits of business ... irregular" and felt that the President "did not see at once the just proportions of things, and allowed himself to be too much occupied by details." Sumner was proud of the purity of his diction, and he was pained when the President called secession "rebellion sugar-coated" or said that the Confederates "turned tail and ran." Lacking a sense of humor, he found conversation with Lincoln "a constant puzzle," even though the President tried to be solemn and took his feet down from the desk when Sumner entered his office. But these two radically different men came to respect and ultimately to like each other. Lincoln knew the senator was incorruptible, if often irritating; Sumner found that the President wanted "to do right and to save the country." Lincoln turned so frequently to the senator for advice on foreign policy that Seward grumbled that there were now too many secretaries of state in Washington.

In the *Trent* affair Lincoln needed all the advice he could get. His initial reaction to the capture of Mason and Slidell was one of pleasure. At a time when Union victories were few, here at last was a success. Every member of the cabinet shared this view except Montgomery Blair, who immediately warned that the captives must be released. After the initial applause for Wilkes's bold act died down, thoughtful public opinion came around to Blair's assessment. To remove the Confederate diplomats from a neutral vessel was a clear violation of international law, and it contradicted the long-established American opposition to search and seizure on the high seas. Apart from legalities, Wilkes's boarding and search of the British mail packet had to be disavowed because it was an insult that no government in London could tolerate.

Greatly preoccupied with other matters, Lincoln did not recognize the seriousness of the *Trent* crisis until Sumner returned to Washington in late November. A regular correspondent of John Bright and Richard Cobden, the great British Liberal leaders, Sumner brought news of the immense anti-American excitement in Great Britain because of Mason and Slidell, and he had a letter from the Duchess of Argyll, whose husband was in Lord Palmerston's cabinet, calling the seizure of the two envoys "the maddest act that ever was done, and, unless the [United States] government intend to force us to war, utterly inconceivable." Moved and astonished by these reports, Lincoln began to meet almost daily with the senator to assess the latest news and consider the danger that this disagreement with the British might drift into conflict.

"There will be no war unless England is bent upon having one," the President assured the senator. Vexed that European governments misunderstood the pacific temper of his foreign policy, he offered to ignore bureaucratic protocol and talk face-to-face with Lord Lyons, the British minister. "If I could see Lord Lyons," he told Sumner rather wistfully, "I could show him in five minutes that I am heartily for peace." Sumner warned of the impropriety of such a step but, encouraged by John Bright, asked the President to think of submitting the issue with Great Britain to arbitration, either by the King of Prussia or by a group of learned publicists. Seizing upon Sumner's idea, Lincoln began drafting such a proposal. He was convinced, he told Browning, "that the question was easily susceptible of a peaceful solution if England was at all disposed to act justly with us."

But from all sides the President received warnings that there was no time for arbitration. Thurlow Weed, who was working in behalf of the Union cause abroad, told of steps the British government was taking toward war. Eight thousand soldiers were being sent to protect Canada, and an embargo on the shipment of saltpeter and other war materials to the United States was in place. From France, Minister Dayton reported that the government of Napoleon III would stand by the British in this crisis. When Lord Lyons on December 23 presented the formal British demands for the release of Mason and Slidell and for an apology from the United States government, they were hardly a surprise. Informally the British minister also let Seward know that unless a satisfactory answer was received within seven days he had instructions to close the embassy and leave Washington.

With that deadline in mind Lincoln summoned a cabinet meeting on Christmas Day, to which Sumner was invited in order to read the most recent letters he had received from Bright and Cobden urging the release of the Confederate diplomats. All realized that the decision they made on this historic occasion would determine "probably the existance [sic], of the nation." It was essential, everybody agreed, to avoid war with Great Britain, and the President said he had to avoid the folly of having "two wars on his hands at a time." Seward, who had finally awakened to the gravity of the crisis, read a paper he was preparing that would explain how Captain Wilkes had violated international law and why therefore Mason and Slidell must be released. The argument was hard for the other cabinet members, except Blair, to swallow. Chase said that it was "gall and wormwood" to him. Even the President resisted giving up the envoys, though he realized that they had become white elephants. The meeting ended without agreement on anything more than that they must meet again the next day.

After the others left, the President said: "Governor Seward, you will go on, of course, preparing your answer, which . . . will state the reasons why they ought to be given up. Now I have a mind to try my hand at stating the reasons why they ought *not* to be given up. We will compare the points on each side."

By evening the President gave up on his self-appointed task, and he told Browning that there would be no war with England. The next day when the cabinet reassembled, Seward read his final version of the reply he intended to give to Lord Lyons and it was endorsed with some expressions of regret but without dissent. After the meeting adjourned, the Secretary reminded the President, "You thought you might frame an argument for the other side?"

"I found I could not make an argument that would satisfy my own mind," Lincoln replied with a smile, "and that proved to me your ground was the right one."

With that decision the gravest threat that the American Civil War would become an international conflict was removed.

IX

Lincoln's domestic crises in the winter of 1861–1862 were almost as severe. Frustrated over the failure of Union armies to advance and angry over mounting expenses, Congress moved rapidly to take charge. On the day the session opened, even before the President's message was heard, Trumbull gave notice that he would introduce a bill for the confiscation of the land and slaves of all persons who were in arms against the United States or who aided or abetted the rebellion. The Illinois senator, once Lincoln's close political ally, was convinced that the President lacked "the *will* necessary in this great emergency" and believed that Congress must take steps to bring the war to a quick end.

Other congressmen tried to move the stalled war effort along through investigating committees, a device that had proved very effective to Republicans in undermining the Buchanan administration. A House committee headed by John F. Potter of Wisconsin had been working all summer to ferret out rebel sympathizers still holding jobs in the government departments, and it performed a needed service in bringing about dismissals and resignations.

The House Judiciary Committee, in its eagerness to investigate alleged "telegraphic censorship of the press," came perilously close to investigating the White House itself. Despite precautions for security, the *New York Herald* received an advance copy of the President's State of the Union message and published excerpts before members of Congress heard it. The *Herald's* source proved to be Henry Wikoff, an unsavory adventurer whom the paper had planted in Washington as its secret reporter. Cosmopolitan and flashy, Wikoff had made a great impression on Mary Lincoln, and he became an intimate in the White House. When the rival *New York Tribune* charged that Mrs. Lincoln had given Wikoff access to her husband's message, the House Judiciary Committee decided to investigate.

The decision was an easy one because almost nobody in the capital liked Mary Lincoln. Thinking her a renegade to the Southern cause, the dowagers who dominated Washington society condemned everything that she did. The smaller contingent of Northern women in the national capital, knowing that Mary Lincoln came from a Southern state and that some of her brothers had joined the Confederate army, suspected her loyalty to the Union. Murat Halstead of the *Cincinnati Commercial* sneered that she was "a fool—the laughing stock of the town, her vulgarity only the more conspicuous in consequence of her fine carriage and horses and servants in livery and fine dresses, and her damnable airs." The New York sophisticate John Bigelow ridiculed her pretensions to speak French and claimed that when asked if she could use the language she replied "Tres poo." Consequently there was much lip-smacking in Washington over the titillating possibilities of this gossip about Mrs. Lincoln and "Chevalier" Wikoff.

There was, it proved, less to the story than met the eye. Wikoff, subpoenaed by the committee, refused to disclose his source and was incarcerated overnight. The next day he agreed to testify, and as the committee members listened avidly, he revealed that he had received a copy of the President's message not from Mrs. Lincoln but from John Watt, the head White House gardener. The committee chewed over this information for several days before it decided to drop the investigation.

More significant were the activities of a special committee named in July to look into allegations of fraud and mismanagement in government contracts. Headed by Charles H. Van Wyck of New York, this committee was instrumental in exposing some of the scandals of the Frémont regime in Missouri. Much of its work justifiably centered on the War Department, a model of maladministration and waste. There was, of course, no question of the President's being involved in any of the shady deals that were making fortunes for manufacturers of shoddy goods. Lincoln was so punctilious that he refused to permit the army butcher to supply the White House with the choicest cuts of steak when he slaughtered cattle on the grounds of the Washington Monument. Told that this was a matter of little importance, he replied, "My observation is that frequently the most insignificant matter is the foundation for the worst scandal." Nor was Simon Cameron believed to be personally venal, but he was the head of a corrupt department and was responsible for its actions.

Lincoln did not need a congressional investigation to tell him that the War Department was badly run. Cameron, he remarked confidentially to Nicolay, was "utterly ignorant . . . Selfish and openly discourteous to the President[,] Obnoxious to the country [and] Incapable of either organizing details or conceiving and advising general plans." If he had any doubts, his mail offered a chorus of objections to the Secretary of War. "Cameron ought to resign," Gustave Koerner had warned Senator Trumbull as early as July 24. "The People have no confidence in him at all. . . . He is suspected of every sort of peculation. Lincoln *must* . . . have an *honest* man as war minister." "It is universally believed that Cameron is a thief," a New Yorker wrote the President, detailing how the War Department sold to the soldiers half-cotton blankets weighing less than five pounds for the same price as regulation all-wool blankets weighing ten or eleven pounds. The cautious Browning alerted Lincoln that his Secretary of War, "whether justly or not, has lost, or rather failed to secure the confidence of the country" and should be removed. A New York banker, James A. Hamilton, told the President that if he replaced Cameron the hard-pressed Treasury Department could immediately raise the $100,000,000 it needed to borrow.

Even though Lincoln had not wanted Cameron in his cabinet initially, he hesitated to fire him and tried to get rid of the Secretary by dropping hints. It might be unfair to replace Cameron now, he whispered to Schuyler Colfax, a friend of the Secretary—but he added "if it were an open question and to be settled de novo" he could see many advantages in having another person in the War Department. He let it be known that he had a great desire to turn the War Department over to Joseph Holt, who had capably served as Secretary of War in the last days of the Buchanan administration. But Cameron was impervious to suggestion and stayed on.

As pressure for his resignation grew, the Secretary took a daring gamble. Asked, as were the other members of the cabinet, to prepare a report on the activities of his department to be submitted to Congress along with the President's annual State of the Union message, he remembered how enthusiastically antislavery men had greeted Frémont's edict of emancipation in Missouri and decided to include in his report an announcement that "it is . . . clearly a right of the Government to arm slaves . . . and employ their service against the rebels." He then sent the document out to newspapers in the principal cities without informing the President. Lincoln immediately ordered the report recalled and Cameron's remarks concerning slaves expurgated. After that it was simply a matter of time before Cameron left the cabinet. The President could put up with incapacity and sloth in his administration, but he would not allow Frémont or Cameron to set government policy on slavery.

On January 11, 1862, Lincoln curtly notified Cameron that he could now gratify his "desire for a change of position" by nominating him as minister to Russia. Cameron had no such desire, and he broke into tears when Secretary Chase gave him Lincoln's letter, which he said was a personal affront which "meant personal as well as political destruction." To save Cameron's feelings the President withdrew his letter so that Cameron could submit his resignation. Lincoln then wrote another letter, this time expressing his "affectionate esteem" and praising Cameron's "ability, patriotism, and fidelity to public trust."

Lincoln's troubles with Cameron did not end with his resignation. To the considerable discomfort of the President, the House committee on contracts continued to investigate malfeasance in the War Department with such vigor that Lincoln accused one of the most prominent members, Representative Henry L. Dawes, of having "done more to break down the administration than any other man in the country." Acting on the committee's recommendation, the full House in April voted to censure the former Secretary for actions "highly injurious to the public service." At this point Lincoln had to intervene. Assuring the Congress that letting contracts without bids, disbursing public moneys without authorization, and other irregularities were actions taken of necessity in the early days of the war, he explained that Cameron, "although he fully approved the proceedings," was not primarily to blame for them; "not only the President but all the other heads of departments were at least equally responsible." Not wishing to bring down the entire government, the investigators let the subject die.

Investigations of military affairs fell to the Joint Committee on the Conduct of the War, set up at the beginning of this session of Congress, and they continued throughout the conflict. The original purpose of the committee was to look into the disaster at Ball's Bluff, but its scope was soon expanded to cover military operations throughout the country. It concentrated mainly on the activities—or the lack of activities—of the Army of the Potomac. Benjamin F. Wade, a severe critic of both Lincoln and McClellan, was chairman, and he had the enthusiastic collaboration of Zachariah Chandler. The three House Republicans on the committee, George W. Julian of Indiana, John Covode of Pennsylvania, and Daniel Gooch of Massachusetts, also sought to prod the general and the President into prosecuting the war more vigorously. The two Democratic members—Andrew Johnson, the sole senator from the Southern states who remained in Congress, and Moses Odell, a New Yorker—played lesser roles.

Lincoln viewed the creation of the Committee on the Conduct of the War with some anxiety, fearing that it might turn into an engine of agitation against the administration. When Wade and Chandler learned of his objections, they rushed to the White House to assure the President that their purpose was to aid, not to embarrass, the Chief Executive. Probably neither party believed the promise, but a surface harmony was maintained. Lincoln had his first meeting with the committee on December 31 and was relieved to find the congressmen "in a perfectly good mood."

Both the committee and the President were eager to learn McClellan's plans. The general was reticent even with Lincoln. He declined to outline the campaign he proposed but dropped a cryptic hint that he no longer thought of advancing against the Confederate army at Manassas and had his "mind actively turned towards another plan of campaign . . . not . . . at all anticipated by the enemy nor by many of our own people." The committee did not get even this much from him. He was called to testify, but shortly before Christmas he fell ill with typhoid fever. For three weeks he was unable to do any serious work, much less to appear before the committee. He had no second in command, no council of officers to whom he had entrusted his plan for the coming campaign. As frustrated as the President, the committee began taking testimony from anti-McClellan witnesses, and it became a powerful engine of criticism not merely of the general but of his commander-in-chief.

CHAPTER TWELVE

The Bottom Is Out of the Tub

———•———

"The Prest. is an excellent man, and, in the main wise," Attorney General Bates recorded in his final diary entry of 1861; "but he lacks *will* and *purpose,* and, I greatly fear he, has not *the power to command.*" That judgment by one of the most cautious and conservative members of the Lincoln administration represented a widely held opinion. Nearly everybody thought the President was honest and well meaning, and almost everyone who met him liked him. Ralph Waldo Emerson, for instance, who visited the White House with Senator Sumner in January 1862, was not put off by Lincoln's homely appearance and his awkward movements and gestures; he found the President a "frank, sincere, well-meaning man, with a lawyer's habit of mind, . . . correct enough, not vulgar, as described, but with a sort of boyish cheerfulness." But few thought he was up to his job.

He seemed unable to make things go right. With the surrender of Mason and Slidell the United States suffered a humiliating, if necessary, reverse in foreign affairs. Huge armies, raised at immense expense, lay idle in winter quarters. As the costs of the war mounted, the Treasury lived on credit, and banks throughout the country had to suspend specie payments. In the Northwest farmers were suffering as laborers went off to the army, and there was no market for farm produce because the Mississippi River was closed. "The people are being bled and as they believe to no purpose and will not long submit to it," warned one Illinois Cassandra.

So desperate did things look in early January that Lincoln for the first time thought that the Confederates might be successful, and he spoke "of the bare possibility of our being two nations."

I

At the heart of the problems was the failure of the armies to advance and win victories. Lincoln's general-in-chief was still recovering from typhoid fever and unable to work. When the Committee on the Conduct of the War met with the President on January 6, its members were appalled to learn that neither he nor anybody else knew McClellan's plans. Lincoln told the congressmen that he "did not think he had any *right* to know, but that, as he was not a military man, it was his duty to defer to General McClellan."

As pressure grew for action and McClellan was still incapacitated, the President tried to exercise the functions of the general-in-chief himself. He knew that McClellan had talked of a joint movement on the part of the armies west of the Appalachians, to be coordinated with an advance by the Army of the Potomac, and he wired Buell and Halleck to go ahead—only to learn that they knew nothing about the plan. Directing the two generals to get "in communication and concert at once," he urged Halleck to make a real or feigned attack on Columbus, in western Kentucky, while Buell advanced on Bowling Green, in the south central part of that state. Lincoln hoped that Buell would eventually push into eastern Tennessee, where the Union army could cut the major east-west rail line of the Confederacy, the "great artery of the enemies' communication." More important, it could liberate the thousands of strongly Unionist inhabitants of eastern Tennessee, whom the President considered "the most valuable stake we have in the South."

Both generals failed him. Lincoln was still too insecure to play the role of military commander. He offered "views" he hoped would be "respectfully considered" rather than orders, and the generals felt free to dispute or ignore them. Since the roads into eastern Tennessee were very bad in winter, Buell told the President he would prefer to go to Nashville—which, as Lincoln had pointed out, had no strategic value. Halleck responded that Buell's plans did not make much military sense; anyway, he could not spare troops from his widely scattered command for an attack on Columbus. Sadly the President sent the correspondence over to the War Department with the endorsement: "It is exceedingly discouraging. As everywhere else, nothing can be done."

With a growing sense of desperation Lincoln began to think of leading one of the armies into battle himself. After all, the Constitution made him commander-in-chief. He borrowed from the Library of Congress Henry W. Halleck's *Elements of Military Art and Science,* a standard text, and several other books on military strategy and began studying them. He conferred frequently with military commanders in the vicinity of Washington, and he assiduously read the reports from others who were in the field. At times he convinced himself that he could do a better job.

But he knew he was no military man and that this was all fantasy that helped him escape his real problems. On January 10, visiting Quartermaster General Montgomery C. Meigs, he summed up the difficulties he faced: "The people are impatient; Chase has no money and he tells me he can raise no more; the General of the Army has typhoid fever. The bottom is out of the tub." "What shall I do?" he asked.

Meigs advised him to call on some of the senior division commanders of the Army of the Potomac for advice. That evening Lincoln invited General McDowell and General William B. Franklin to the White House, where they met with him, Seward, Chase, and Assistant Secretary of War Peter Watson. To this informal council of war the President poured out his problems. He must talk to somebody, he said, because something had to be done. If General McClellan was not going to use the Army of the Potomac, the President continued, "he would like to *borrow* it, provided he could see how it could be made to do something." The generals gave different advice. McDowell urged another forward movement against Manassas, the scene of his defeat, while Franklin, who knew something of McClellan's wishes, talked of moving the army down the Potomac to the York River, so as to advance on Richmond from the east. The President asked the two generals to learn more about the actual state of the army and to come back the next day.

When the informal council of war reassembled, the commanders agreed that a move on Manassas was the best operation at this time, but Meigs and Montgomery Blair, who had joined the group, vigorously opposed this strategy because it would certainly lead to another Bull Run. Unsure how to resolve the conflict, Lincoln again adjourned the meeting.

On January 13, McClellan rose from his sickbed to join in the discussion. Clearly regarding these meetings as a conspiracy against him, the general-in-chief was sullen and uncommunicative. When Lincoln again rehearsed the urgent reasons for actions and asked what could be done, McClellan replied scornfully that "the case was so clear a blind man could see it"— and then diverted the conversation to his perpetual fear that the Confederate forces outnumbered his own. Eventually Chase asked him directly what he intended to do with his army and when he intended to move. The general sat silent. When Meigs whispered to him that the President had a right to know his intentions, McClellan responded in a voice inaudible to the rest of the group: "If I tell him my plans they will be in the New York Herald tomorrow morning. He can't keep a secret." After further urging he said that "he was very unwilling to develop his plans," because he believed that in military matters the fewer persons who knew them the better, but "that he would tell them if he was *ordered* to do so." All that Lincoln could get from him was a pledge that he did have a specific time in mind for an advance, though he was unwilling to divulge it. With that the President declared he was satisfied.

He was not, in fact, at all satisfied. His unhappiness grew when he discovered, a few days after these meetings, that a planned expedition to seize the mouth of the Mississippi River would be indefinitely delayed because army authorities had failed to prepare the necessary beds (or racks) for the mortars the ships were to carry. Exasperated, he told Gustavus Fox that he now believed "he must take these army matters into his own hands."

II

Persistent sniping from members of his own party in Congress made the President's burdens all the harder to bear. There was a growing lack of harmony among Republicans in Congress. On economic issues Republican legislators divided along sectional lines, with Easterners opposing Westerners on such issues as a land-grant college system, the chartering of a Pacific railroad, a proposed increase in the tariff, and the creation of an internal revenue system that would, for the first time since 1817, levy taxes on domestic producers and consumers. Lincoln was personally involved in few of these questions. What he called his "political education" as a Whig made him averse to trying to lead the Congress in such matters and reluctant to veto measures with which he disagreed.

But he was deeply involved in questions relating to the prosecution of the war, the future of the rebellious states, and the status of slavery, on which Republican congressmen also differed. Factional lines were not yet clear. At one end of the spectrum were the self-styled Radicals, who believed that vigorous prosecution of the war required confiscation of Southern property and the emancipation of slaves. At the other end, a less clearly defined group of Moderates (who sometimes referred to themselves as Conservatives) wanted the war to be conducted without destroying the property or social fabric of the South.

Neither group accepted Lincoln's view that the prosecution of the war was primarily a function of the Chief Executive, and neither was firmly committed to supporting the President and his policies. A Radical like Wade denounced Lincoln for incompetence and imbecility—but so did a Moderate like Senator William Pitt Fessenden of Maine, who lamented that "no man can be found who is equal to this crisis in any branch of the government" and added sarcastically, "If the President had his wife's *will* and would use it rightly, our affairs would look much better."

Republican congressmen were critical of the President partly because their party had never before been in power and they were not used to the responsibility of constructive leadership. The party's spokesmen had made their reputations by denouncing Presidents Pierce and Buchanan; the habit was hard to break. Many of the congressional leaders, especially in the Senate, were insiders with long experience in Washington, and they looked on Lincoln as an outsider. Responsible only to their local constituents, Republican senators and representatives had difficulty recognizing Lincoln's precarious position: as a minority President he had to receive support from Democrats as well as Republicans, border-state men as well as Northerners, Westerners as well as Easterners.

Consequently most Republican congressmen were indifferent to the President and his wishes. Now that the patronage had been distributed, they had little to expect from the Chief Executive. Lincoln did not make a practice of using the civilian and military appointments at his disposal to punish his enemies. Nor did he have the time or inclination to stroke inflated congressional egos. Legislators concluded that he was a well-meaning but incompetent President destined to serve only one term, who could be safely ignored.

A few of Lincoln's Republican critics were unwilling to maintain even a façade of good relations with the White House. These "Jacobins" were few in number, but because of their seniority they held some of the most important committee chairmanships. In the Senate, Wade, Chandler, and Trumbull were the most conspicuous of these anti-Lincoln Radicals, and James W. Grimes of Iowa and Morton S. Wilkinson of Minnesota often joined in attacking the administration. In public these Republican leaders generally maintained an attitude of unctuous deference to the President. In a compliment meant to kill, Wade referred to Lincoln in a Senate speech as "this mild, equitable, just man," so gentle that he exhibited "a toleration and mildness towards . . . traitors." But in private conversation Wade was ferociously hostile. When the Committee on the Conduct of the War met with Lincoln on December 31, Wade said bluntly, "Mr. President, you are murdering your country by inches in consequence of the inactivity of the military and the want of a distinct policy in regard to slavery." At times the Jacobins went out of their way to insult the President. Invited to attend a White House ball, Wade returned the card with the note: "Are the President and Mrs. Lincoln aware that there is a civil war? If they are not, Mr. and Mrs. Wade are, and for that reason decline to participate in feasting and dancing."

In part, the Jacobins' vindictive hostility to Lincoln stemmed from disappointment. Wade never got over his failure to receive the Republican nomination in 1860. Trumbull felt slighted in the distribution of patronage and angrily vowed never again to enter the White House while Lincoln was President. But personality conflicts were more important. Lincoln's flexibility and pragmatism fundamentally offended doctrinaires immovably committed to a fixed position. His gaily announced motto was "My policy is to have no policy." Even Chase, a member of his own cabinet, called this an "idiotic notion," while to Wade and Grimes it showed that the President had no principles. Humorless and literal-minded, Lincoln's Republican critics found his pragmatism either cowardly or frivolous, and they were unable to see that behind his adaptability as to means lay a firm commitment to ends, such as the preservation of the Union and the spread of liberty.

Hating no man himself, Lincoln found the ferocity of these Jacobins puzzling. It was not what he expected from men whose records as leaders of the antislavery cause he had studied and admired. He told John Hay that the

persistent opposition of Senator Grimes was one of his greatest disappointments as President. "Before I came here," Lincoln said, "I certainly expected
to rely upon Grimes more than any other one man in the Senate. I like him
very much. He is a great strong fellow. He is a valuable friend a dangerous
enemy. . . . But he got wrong against me, I do not clearly know how, and has
always been cool and almost hostile to me."

He failed to realize that there was a temperamental incompatibility between himself and these anti-Lincoln Radicals. The fault was not all theirs. If
the Jacobins were overbearing, Lincoln was often evasive and elusive. He
made few attempts to reveal his motives or explain his plans to these serious,
self-important men accustomed to deference. Lincoln was not a modest man
and, as John Hay astutely observed, he quite inadvertently exhibited toward
these critics an "intellectual arrogance and unconscious assumption of superiority" that mortally offended them.

III

Toward the end of January 1862 military affairs took a turn for the better.
When Lincoln finally got rid of Cameron, he moved quickly to replace him
with Edwin M. Stanton. The appointment was a surprising one. In view of
Lincoln's well-known unwillingness to cherish grudges, it was not important
that Stanton was the lawyer who had snubbed him in the McCormick reaper
case, but Stanton's lifelong record as a Democrat might have counted against
him. He had been Attorney General in the last days of the Buchanan regime
and had done something to give backbone to that feeble regime and to
make possible a peaceful transfer of power to the Lincoln administration.
Since the outbreak of the war, Stanton in his private correspondence had
unsparingly criticized "the imbecility of this administration," but he had
maintained a discreet silence in public and served as a confidential legal
adviser to Cameron. Always opposed to slavery, Stanton was secretly the
author of the passage in Cameron's report that called for freeing and arming
the slaves; he was thus responsible for the firing of the man whom he
succeeded.

That double role was not surprising to anyone who knew Stanton well.
Gideon Welles concluded that the new Secretary of War was "arrogant and
domineering toward those in subordinate positions" but "a sycophant and
intriguer in his conduct and language with those whom he fears." He managed to ingratiate himself with everybody whose support he needed. McClellan endorsed him, as did the Committee on the Conduct of the War. Fierce
Unionists like Joseph Holt praised him as "the soul of honor, of courage,
and of loyalty," and so did Fernando Wood, the New York mayor who
flirted with secession. Cameron recommended Stanton as his replacement.
Miraculously, so did both Seward and Chase, permanent antagonists in the
cabinet.

Stanton was neither amiable nor altogether stable, but Lincoln found him indispensable. A short, stocky figure, fifty-seven years old, the new Secretary of War was highly intelligent and fiercely honest. In the War Department he worked standing behind a long, high desk, which he moved into a room open to the public, where he excoriated shoddy contractors and blasted military officers angling for promotion. His extraordinary energy reminded Lincoln of an old Methodist preacher whose parishioners wanted to put bricks in his pockets to hold him down. "We may be obliged to serve Stanton the same way," Lincoln told Congressman Dawes, "but I guess we'll just let him jump a while first."

The President and his new War Secretary developed an excellent working relationship, which eventually became a warm friendship. The President knew that Stanton was imperious and hot-tempered and that he sometimes made decisions that appeared arbitrary. But he tried not to interfere. "Of course," he wrote to a friend who complained of Stanton's brusqueness, "I can over rule his decision if I will, but I cannot well administer the War Department independent of the Secretary of War." There developed a sort of tacit division of labor between the two men. Lincoln himself explained the system: "I want to oblige everybody when I can; and Stanton and I have an understanding that if I send an order to him which cannot be consistently granted, he is to refuse it. This he sometimes does." Occasionally the President pretended that the Secretary of War exerted a veto over his actions. Referring to the censorship of newspapers, a job he entrusted to Stanton, Lincoln once explained why he refused to make a public speech: "The Secretary of War, you know, holds a pretty tight rein on the Press, so that they shall not tell more than they ought to, and I'm afraid that if I blab too much he might draw a tight rein on me." But that, of course, was a joke. When Stanton turned down a request Lincoln thought important, the President overruled him with "Let it be done."

With Stanton in control at the War Department, the President could turn his attention back to the armies. His conferences with McClellan had disappointed him, and the general, whose health was now fully restored, was still reluctant to divulge his plans for an advance. On January 27, Lincoln forced the issue by publishing the "President's General War Order No. 1." It ordered all the land and naval forces of the United States to undertake a general advance on February 22 and threatened to hold all commanders to strict accountability for carrying out the order.

The order, which vented Lincoln's deep sense of frustration with the military, reflected his recent hasty reading of books on strategy. Since McClellan seemed to have no plan for operations against the Confederates, the President announced his own; as he told Browning, it was to "threaten all their positions at the same time with superior force, and if they weakened one to strengthen another seize and hold the one weakened." Both Lincoln's strategy and his order ignored such variables as the weather, readiness, roads, communications, and logistics—not to mention the location and strength of the Confederate armies—but he did not intend to announce a specific plan of battle. He wanted to give a jolt to the military, a warning that they must act.

In that sense it worked. February 22 passed without a general advance, but before that date Union armies in the West began to win victories. On January 19, a few days before Lincoln's order, Union troops under General George H. Thomas routed Confederate forces in the battle of Mill Springs and broke the Confederate line in eastern Kentucky. More significant was a campaign that General Ulysses S. Grant launched to open the Tennessee and Cumberland rivers. On February 6, Grant's forces, aided by navy gunboats under Flag Officer Andrew Foote, captured Fort Henry on the Tennessee River, and eleven days later they forced Fort Donelson to surrender. The Confederates had to abandon Kentucky and most of Tennessee, and on February 25, Buell's army occupied Nashville.

This was a heady time for an administration that up to now had had few successes. When Lincoln signed the papers promoting Grant to the rank of major general, he could hardly contain his satisfaction. He did not feel competent to speak about the fighting qualities of Eastern men, he observed, but the recent gallant behavior of Illinois troops showed that "if the Southerners think that man for man they are better than our ... western men generally, they will discover themselves in a grievous mistake." In the national capital there was a general sense of euphoria, a belief that with one big push by the Army of the Potomac the Confederacy could be defeated. Even Lincoln shared in this optimism. When Joshua Speed learned that the President, in order to make room for Cameron, was allowing Cassius M. Clay to resign as minister to Russia and take up a commission as major general, he rushed to the White House to protest the return of this loose cannon to Kentucky. The President assured his old friend that there was nothing to worry about because the war would be over before Clay could get back to the United States.

A large party the Lincolns gave on February 5—the very evening, as it happened, before Grant captured Fort Henry—was a sign of the changing times. Ignoring the advice of the protocol officers at the State Department that the President's entertainment should be confined to soirees open to the public at large and to small private dinners, Mary Lincoln decided to show off the newly refurbished White House to five hundred invited guests, who were required to present tickets of invitation at the door. Inevitably there was much grumbling among those who were not invited. Carriages began arriving about nine in the evening with besworded, overdecorated diplomats, generals in bright dress uniforms, members of the cabinet, Supreme Court justices, and selected senators and representatives. Ushered in by a staff dressed in new mulberry-colored uniforms to match the new Solferino china, guests were greeted in the East Room by the President, who was wearing a new black swallowtail coat, and the First Lady, whose white silk dress, decorated with hundreds of small black flowers, exposed a remarkably low décolletage. In the background the United States Marine Band played, its repertoire including a sprightly new piece, "The Mary Lincoln Polka." At midnight the doors to the dining room were opened to reveal a magnificent buffet concocted by Maillard's of New York, the most expensive caterer in the country. It displayed sugary models of the Ship of State, Fort Sumter, and Fort Pickens flanked by mounds of turkey, duck, ham, terrapin, and pheasant. Dinner was served until three, and many guests stayed till daybreak. Altogether, the *Washington Star* concluded, the party was "the most superb affair of its kind ever seen here."

IV

The Lincolns' celebrations were short-lived. Shortly before the party their son Willie had fallen ill with "bilious fever"—probably typhoid fever, caused by pollution in the White House water system. Deeply anxious, their parents considered canceling the grand reception, but the family doctor assured them that the boy was in no immediate danger. Even so, both the President and his wife quietly slipped upstairs during the party to be at their son's bedside. During the next two weeks Tad came down with the same illness while Willie grew worse and worse.

Sitting up with his sick children night after night, Lincoln was able to transact little business, and he seemed to stumble through his duties. There were fluctuations in Willie's illness, but during the two weeks after the grand party he grew weaker and weaker, and Lincoln began to despair of his recovery. On February 20 the end came. Stepping into his office, Lincoln said in a voice choked with emotion: "Well, Nicolay, my boy is gone—he is actually gone!" Then he burst into tears and left to give what comfort he could to Tad.

Both parents were devastated by grief. When Lincoln looked on the face of his dead son, he could only say brokenly, "He was too good for this earth ... but then we loved him so." It seemed appropriate that Willie's funeral, which was held in the White House, was accompanied by one of the heaviest wind and rain storms ever to visit Washington. Long after the burial the President repeatedly shut himself in a room so that he could weep alone. At nights he had happy dreams of being with Willie, only to wake to the sad recognition of death. On a trip to Fort Monroe, long after Willie was buried, Lincoln read passages from *Macbeth* and *King Lear* aloud to an aide, and then from *King John* he recited Constance's lament for her son:

And, father cardinal, I have heard you say
That we shall see and know our friends in heaven:
If that be true, I shall see my boy again.

His voice trembled, and he wept.

The President gained some respite from his suffering by caring for Tad, who was still very ill and was heartbroken over the loss of his brother. Often

Lincoln lay on the bed beside his sick son to soothe him and give him comfort.

During this time he increasingly turned to religion for solace. As Mary Lincoln said years later, "He first thought . . . about this subject . . . when Willie died—never before." That statement perhaps told more about the lack of intimacy in the Lincoln marriage than it did about the President's state of mind. Since his election he had come increasingly to speak and think in religious terms. Before 1860 he rarely invoked the deity in his letters or speeches, but after he began to feel the burdens of the presidency, he frequently asked for God's aid. In his farewell address in Springfield, for instance, he reminded his fellow townsmen, "Without the assistance of [the] Divine Being, . . . I cannot succeed." Again and again on his way to Washington, he praised "the Providence of God, who has never deserted us," and voiced confidence "that the Almighty, the Maker of the Universe" would save the nation. In his inaugural address he expressed the hope that impending war could be avoided by "intelligence, patriotism, Christianity, and a firm reliance on Him, who has never yet forsaken this favored land."

Though deeply felt, these were abstract invocations of a Higher Power to save a society; he now needed more personal reassurance to save himself. During the weeks after Willie's death Lincoln had several long talks with the Reverend Phineas D. Gurley, pastor of the New York Avenue Presbyterian Church in Washington, where the Lincolns rented a pew. Gently the clergyman comforted him with the assurance that Willie was not dead but still lived in heaven. Lincoln may not have believed him, but he wished to believe him. He did not experience a religious conversion, though when he looked back on the events of this tragic spring, he recognized that he underwent what he called "a process of crystallization" in his religious beliefs. Even so, he did not become a member of any Christian denomination, nor did he abandon his fundamental fatalism. He continued to quote *Hamlet:*

> There's a divinity that shapes our ends,
> Rough-hew them how we will.

Mary Lincoln's grief over Willie's death was even more devastating than her husband's. Having earlier lost Eddie in Springfield, she could not deal with this second death, and for three weeks she took to her bed, so desolated that she could not attend the funeral or look after Tad, who was slowly beginning to recover. For many months the mere mention of Willie's name sent her into paroxysms of weeping, and Lincoln had to employ a nurse to look after her. Never again did Mary Lincoln enter the bedroom where Willie died nor the downstairs Green Room, where his body had been embalmed. When she was finally able to emerge from her room, she went into such profound mourning dress that she was almost invisible under the layers of black veils and crepes.

For nearly a year all social activities at the White House were suspended.

Mary Lincoln's mourning was so absolute that she forbade the weekly concerts the Marine Band usually played on the grounds. "When we are in sorrow," she announced, "quiet is very necessary to us." A few people took mean satisfaction in the Lincolns' tragedy. "I suppose Mrs. Lincoln will be providentially deterred from giving any more parties which scandalized so many good persons who did not get invitations," a Washington merchant wrote. David Davis, who disliked Mary Lincoln as much as he admired her husband, speculated: "It may be that this affliction may save his wife from further gossip, and may change her notions of life."

V

At about the time of Willie's death Lincoln's optimism about military affairs also began to vanish. There were still some successes to celebrate. In the West the Union victory at Pea Ridge, Arkansas (March 6–8), ended the threat of a Confederate invasion of Missouri. In the East, Ambrose E. Burnside, after capturing Roanoke Island, moved inland to New Berne, North Carolina, which could serve as a base for future operations. But elsewhere there was no progress. After the victories at Forts Henry and Donelson the armies in the Mississippi Valley seemed unable to advance. Receiving no dispatches from Grant for two weeks, Halleck assumed that his subordinate was demoralized by victory and removed him from command. Reports spread that Grant had gone back to his old habits, and in Washington he was now considered "little better than a common gambler and drunkard." Eventually Halleck learned that Grant had been in Nashville conferring with Buell about a joint advance and that a telegraph operator failed to transmit his dispatches. The controversy was important only in that it entailed further delay before the army pushed south.

Even less encouraging were the activities of the Army of the Potomac. The President's General War Order No. 1 finally forced McClellan to discuss his broad strategy with his commander-in-chief. The general was now convinced that a frontal assault on the Confederate army at Manassas, whose size he consistently overrated, could only lead to another disaster like Bull Run. The proper object of the Union army, he argued, was the capture of Richmond, and he developed an elaborate strategy for attacking the Confederate capital from the east, where the navy could protect his line of supplies. In Lincoln's view the campaign ought to be directed not against the Southern capital but at the Confederate army, and he favored a direct advance on Manassas.

That essential difference shaped the relationship between Lincoln and McClellan. Over the next few months the general did everything in his power to promote acceptance of his strategy, while the President dragged his feet. Self-absorbed and insensitive, McClellan seemed totally unaware that in a democratic society military commanders are subordinate to civilian authorities, and he felt no need to keep the President informed, much less to seek his advice. For his part, Lincoln, reluctant directly to interfere with military matters when he had no expertise, failed to make McClellan understand that when he made a suggestion he expected the general to follow it. This mutual distrust destroyed any chance for a successful campaign.

Four days after his General War Order No. 1, Lincoln, whose patience was growing thin, issued another order specifically directing the Army of the Potomac to advance and seize Manassas on or before February 22. Upon receiving it, McClellan wrote a twenty-two-page letter to Stanton, detailing his objections to a proposed frontal attack on the Confederates at Manassas and spelling out, for the first time, his plan to attack Richmond from the east. Unimpressed, Lincoln posed a series of questions to the general: Would McClellan's plan take longer and be more costly than an advance against Manassas? Would it more certainly be successful? Would it offer a sure means of retreat in case of disaster? McClellan respectfully repeated his arguments against an attack on Manassas. Urging his own plan, he pledged, "I will stake my life, my reputation on the result—more than that, I will stake upon it the success of our cause." Lincoln was not convinced, but he acquiesced.

During the next month as McClellan prepared his expedition Lincoln watched his movements skeptically. Several minor developments increased his doubts. For some time Confederate batteries on the Virginia shore had closed the lower Potomac to navigation and their presence was both an embarrassment and a nuisance. The Army of the Potomac claimed it was unable to remove them. Then an enterprising young Union officer carried out an independent raid and discovered that there were hardly any fortifications on the Virginia side of the river. Even more embarrassing was McClellan's failure to force the Confederates out of Harpers Ferry, where they controlled the Baltimore & Ohio Railroad, a vital link between the national capital and the West. Planning to throw a force across the Potomac on a temporary bridge, McClellan had pontoon boats built and sent up the river. They proved to be six inches too wide for the locks on the Potomac and the whole project had to be abandoned. When General Randolph B. Marcy, McClellan's chief of staff and son-in-law, told Lincoln the news, he exploded: "Why in tarnation . . . couldn't the Gen[eral]. have known whether a boat would go through that lock, before he spent a million of dollars getting them there? I am no engineer; but it seems to me that if I wished to know whether a boat would go through a . . . lock, common sense would teach me to go and measure it. I am almost despairing at these results. . . . The general impression is daily gaining ground that the Gen[eral]. does not intend to do anything."

Lincoln's irritability on this occasion was undoubtedly related to the excitement he and everybody else in the cabinet felt about a conflict about to take place in Hampton Roads, near Norfolk and Fort Monroe. The former USS *Merrimack,* now heavily armored and rechristened the CSS *Virginia,* steamed out of Norfolk harbor and, virtually immune to shot and shell from the wooden ships of the Union navy, rammed and sank the *Cumberland,* burned the *Congress,* and damaged the *Minnesota* and other vessels. If unchecked, the Confederate ironclad could break the blockade. There was panic in Washington. Stanton, always excitable, broke out in recriminations against Gideon Welles and the navy and predicted that the *Merrimack* would soon send a cannon shot into the cabinet room. Lincoln, too, was clearly troubled, but he tried to conceal his agitation by eagerly reading the dispatches and interrogating the navy officers who brought news of the engagement. That evening the *Monitor,* a Union ironclad of such unusual design that it looked like a cheese box on a raft, appeared at Hampton Roads, ready to give battle the next day. In the engagement on March 9 the *Merrimack* was badly damaged and forced back to Norfolk.

During this period of great excitement Lincoln had a confrontation with McClellan. After complaining about the Harpers Ferry fiasco, he expressed fears that if McClellan moved his army down the Potomac to attack Richmond from the east he would leave Washington exposed. "It had been represented to him," he said, that McClellan's move "was conceived with the traitorous intent of . . . giving over to the enemy the capital and the government, thus left defenceless." The President did not identify his source, but he had been talking with the fiercely anti-McClellan members of the Committee on the Conduct of the War. Furious, McClellan sprang up and told Lincoln he would permit no man to call him a traitor. Much agitated, Lincoln backed down from his accusation and, according to McClellan, "said that he merely repeated what others had said, and that he did not believe a word of it."

At the end of the conversation McClellan agreed to consult the division commanders of the Army of the Potomac on his plan. Eight of them, all younger generals who owed their promotion to McClellan, favored it, but the four senior men opposed. They then trooped over to the White House, where the President and the Secretary of War questioned them closely. Both Lincoln and Stanton were clearly troubled about the safety of the national capital, but in the end the President accepted the decision of the majority and authorized McClellan to go ahead. "We can do nothing else than accept their plan and discard all others," he told Stanton afterward. "We can't reject it and adopt another without assuming all the responsibility in the case of the failure of the one we adopt."

The President, still unconvinced, made his dissatisfaction plain by ordering the reorganization of the twelve divisions of the Army of the Potomac into four corps. This action, which for some time the Committee on the Conduct of the War had been urging, was a sensible one. The Army of the Potomac was now so vast that no one commander could give sufficient attention to each of the twelve separate divisions. McClellan himself had favored such a reorganization—though he wanted to wait until after a battle and appoint as corps commanders generals who had distinguished themselves in the field. Lincoln overruled him and named as corps leaders Generals E. V. Sumner, Irvin McDowell, Samuel P. Heintzelman, and Erasmus D. Keyes—the first three of whom had opposed McClellan's plan of campaign.

Further evidence of the President's doubts about his commanding general's strategy appeared in a general war order forbidding the Army of the Potomac to change its base of operations until McClellan and the four corps commanders declared Washington entirely secure.

Three days later the President clipped McClellan's wings even closer in a broad reorganization of the army command. After Stanton made a full report to the cabinet blaming McClellan for the "great ignorance, negligence and lack of order and subordination—and reckless extravagance" evident in the management of the Army of the Potomac, Lincoln and his advisers agreed it was too much to expect any man to be both general-in-chief of all the armies and commander of the huge Army of the Potomac when it was about to take to the field. The President relieved McClellan from his duties as general-in-chief. Henceforth he was simply to be commander of the Department of the Potomac. Lincoln's order consolidated the several armies in the Mississippi Valley under the command of General Halleck, who claimed most of the credit for Forts Henry and Donelson. In order to pacify the abolitionists and the disgruntled German element in Missouri, Frémont was given command of the new Mountain Department, where it was assumed he would try to liberate the Unionists of eastern Tennessee. Perhaps the most significant change was that all three department commanders were to "report severally and directly to the Secretary of War," who now took full charge of bringing order and efficiency to army administration.

Most people welcomed the reorganization. McClellan himself, though disgruntled that he had to learn of the reshuffling of commanders from the newspapers, accepted his demotion in good spirits and wrote Lincoln: "I shall work just as cheerfully as ever before, and . . . no consideration of self will in any manner interfere with the discharge of my public duties."

Now at last the way was cleared for McClellan to begin his campaign, but one final episode further weakened the President's confidence in his commander. Hearing that the Confederates were pulling back from Manassas, the general led the entire Army of the Potomac, 112,000 strong, to see what was happening. The Confederates were indeed gone, and it was clear that they had numbered less than 50,000—about half of what McClellan had estimated. The Southern fortifications that had looked so formidable turned out to be mostly logs painted to resemble cannon. The whole country gave a giant horselaugh.

The Confederate withdrawal from the Manassas area forced McClellan to change his plan for transporting the Army of the Potomac down the Potomac and up the Rappahannock River to Urbanna, where it could make a quick dash of about fifty miles on Richmond. In their new position the Southern forces would be between him and the Confederate capital. Quickly revising his strategy, the general decided to go farther south to the peninsula between the York and James rivers, where Fort Monroe, guarding the entrance to the Chesapeake Bay, was still in Union hands. By April 1 part of the Army of the Potomac was on the peninsula. Lincoln continued to watch with anxiety and doubt. Months later he told Browning that he had always thought McClellan's strategy was a mistake and "that his opinion always had been that the great fight should have been at Manasses [*sic*]."

VI

Republicans who wanted Lincoln to remove McClellan also criticized the President for not attacking slavery, the cause of the war. In Congress these condemnations were usually indirect, as when Thaddeus Stevens, the powerful Pennsylvania Republican, without mentioning Lincoln by name, lamented that in this war there had been "no declaration of the great objects of Government, no glorious sound of universal liberty." But in private letters critics bluntly referred to the President's "imbecility" and to his folly in attempting to preserve slavery while engaged in a war against the slave power of the South. "A more ridiculous farce was never played," wrote one of Trumbull's correspondents. Francis W. Bird, one of the original organizers of the Republican party in Massachusetts, felt that Lincoln had "gone to the rescue of slavery, which had almost committed suicide." "The key of the slave's chain is now kept in the White House," he scolded. Some of Lincoln's close political friends were equally direct. "Our nation is on the brink of ruin," Joseph Medill lamented. "Mr. Lincoln, for God's sake and your Country's sake rise to the realization . . . that this is a Slave-holders rebellion." An Illinois man, enraged by Lincoln's course, predicted "that if a speedy change . . . did not soon occur, . . . some Brutus would arise and love his country more than he did the President."

Lincoln's views on slavery were not, in fact, so far from those of his critics. He made no attempt to disguise his antislavery feeling; as he told a group of border-state representatives, he "thought it was wrong and should continue to think so." He agreed that slavery was "somehow" the cause of the war, and he did not think it could long survive the present conflict. In areas where he felt he was constitutionally able to act, he took small but significant steps to dissociate himself from the proslavery stance of his predecessors. He willingly signed a law prohibiting slavery in all the national territories— even though the Supreme Court in the Dred Scott decision had declared such exclusion unconstitutional. He welcomed a new treaty with Great Britain for the more effective suppression of the Atlantic slave trade. At the urging of Charles Sumner, he refused to commute the death penalty for Nathaniel Gordon, the first American slave trader convicted and hanged for participating in the nefarious traffic.

But he was reluctant to adopt more sweeping policies. He was ready to use "all indispensable means" to preserve the Union, but he warned against hastily adopting "radical and extreme measures, which may reach the loyal as the disloyal." "In considering the policy to be adopted for suppressing the insurrection," he told Congress in December 1861, "I have been anxious and careful that the inevitable conflict for this purpose shall not degenerate into a violent and remorseless revolutionary struggle." Remembering his inaugural vow not to interfere with slavery in the states where it already existed and adhering to his theory that the seceded states were still part of the Union, he was not yet ready to strike at slavery in the Confederacy—especially since nothing he could do or say would have any practical effect there.

The constant barrage of criticism to which Lincoln was subjected had the wholesome result of forcing him to think through more systematically his position on slavery and emancipation. Up to this time he had not been called on to do much more than express his dislike for the peculiar institution, his hope that in time it would die out, and his vague wish that Negroes should be colonized elsewhere. As Stephen A. Douglas repeatedly pointed out in their 1858 debates, he never explained how he expected to bring slavery into a course of ultimate extinction. Now he was obliged to come up with a positive policy. There was all the more urgency for him to act because Congress was pushing ahead with consideration of Trumbull's second confiscation bill, which would, in effect, emancipate the slaves of all rebels.

Doubting both the constitutionality and the wisdom of proclaiming general emancipation, Lincoln felt obliged to deal with some immediate problems arising from slavery. One of these was what to do with the thousands of slaves who fled from their masters to seek freedom behind the lines of the Union armies. Since the Fugitive Slave Act was still in force, some Union commanders in the West, like Halleck, allowed slave masters to search their army camps and reclaim these fugitives. Unwilling to return the runaways, General Benjamin F. Butler, a Massachusetts antislavery man, called them contraband of war, on the ground that they were, or could be, used by their masters to help build Confederate fortifications, and refused to send them back to slavery. His decision was immensely popular in the North, and for the rest of the war slaves were often referred to as "contrabands." Lincoln made no official comment on Butler's action, or on the decision of other commanders to exclude slave hunters from their camps, but he told Browning as early as July 1861 "that the government neither should, nor would send back to bondage such as came to our armies."

What to do with these fugitives was a puzzle. They should not be returned to their masters; they could not live in idleness near Union army camps; and they must not be turned loose on the negrophobic border states. The Northern states did not want them. In his search for a solution, Lincoln turned back, as he so often did in a crisis, to the ideas of Henry Clay, and he proposed in his annual message to colonize these runaway slaves "at some place, or places, in a climate congenial to them."

The idea was not a new one for Lincoln. He had endorsed colonization as early as 1852 in his eulogy on Clay and subsequently made speeches before meetings of the Illinois Colonization Society. During the debates with

Douglas he more than once mentioned colonization, though he admitted it was an impractical solution of the race problem. More recently the Blair family, who for years had made colonization something of a hobby, had revived his interest in the subject. Frank Blair, as a representative from Missouri, had long favored emigration of the "sable race, bred in the pestilence of Africa," to Central America. With the outbreak of the war his father, Francis Preston Blair, Sr., alerted Lincoln that the time had come when "the deportation or extermination of the African race from among us" was inevitable. Montgomery Blair joined his father and brother in recommending colonization of freedmen as "absolutely indispensable to prevent unspeakable horrors," because blacks and whites could never live together in peace.

By the 1860s most colonizationists, who had earlier favored sending freedmen to Africa, endorsed setting up a colony of blacks under the protection of the United States somewhere in Central America or the Caribbean. Haiti, the Danish West Indies, Dutch Guiana, and British Honduras were among the sites considered possible, but a tract of land in New Granada (later Panama) on the Chiriqui Lagoon was the favorite of many. Here Ambrose W. Thompson, a Philadelphian who had made a fortune in shipbuilding, had acquired a claim to several hundred thousand acres of land located at what was likely to be the terminus of a projected railroad across the isthmus. The lagoon was supposed to be deep enough to serve as an American naval base; the land was especially suited for growing cotton; and it allegedly contained rich stores of coal, which Thompson promised to sell to the navy at half the usual price. It would, the Blairs urged, be the ideal location for a colony of American freedmen.

Lincoln thought the idea was worth looking into. He appointed Ninian W. Edwards, his wife's brother-in-law, to review the prospectus and other legal documents submitted by the Chiriqui Improvement Company and learned that the claims of Thompson and the other entrepreneurs were fully verified. Because the project would involve the navy, he asked Secretary Welles's opinion, but that resolute New Englander, opposed to colonization in principle, refused to have anything to do with the scheme. Because money would be needed for the project, the President also asked for Chase's advice. Responding more tactfully than Welles, the Secretary of the Treasury responded that he was generally "much impressed by the prospects" but that he was too busy to give it his close attention. Lincoln then turned the project over to Secretary of the Interior Smith, who he knew was in favor of colonization, and gave it his conditional blessing.

What began as a project for resettling runaway slaves escalated into a more ambitious plan for abolishing slavery in some, or perhaps all, of the border states, where it was a source of constant embarrassment to the Union government. Almost daily there was friction between local authorities sworn to uphold the state laws concerning slavery and military commanders reluctant to return fugitives to their masters. In addition, Lincoln knew that so long as these heavily populated and strategically located states maintained slavery there was a possibility that they might join the Confederacy. He was also aware the continued existence of slavery in the border states complicated foreign policy; so long as Delaware, Maryland, Kentucky, and Missouri remained slave states, European powers could not view the American conflict as one between freedom and slavery. Emancipation could thus strengthen the Union cause abroad, relieve friction between civil and military authorities in the upper South, and weaken the Confederacy.

During the winter of 1861–1862, despite all the other issues he had to deal with, Lincoln worked with exceptional finesse to disarm the likely critics of his plan. Aware that opposition both to compensated emancipation and to colonization was strongest in New England, he took great pains to keep Sumner, the most conspicuous spokesman of abolitionism in the Congress, on his side. Patiently he allowed Sumner to lecture him, sometimes two or three times a week, on his duty to act against slavery. In early December the President and the senator had a long conversation about the problems facing the new session of Congress and reviewed in great detail all issues relating to slavery. Sumner was delighted to discover that on all of them "we agreed, or agreed very nearly." As they parted, Lincoln said, "Well, Mr. Sumner, the only difference between you and me on this subject is a difference of a month or six weeks in time." "Mr. President," Sumner replied, "if that is the only difference between us, I will not say another word to you about it till the longest time you name has passed by."

A fortnight later Lincoln further involved Sumner in his plans. Since November the President had been working with George P. Fisher and Nathaniel B. Smithers to draft a bill for gradual emancipation in Delaware, where the number of slaves was inconsequential. Lincoln prepared two slightly different proposals, both of which promised federal funds to pay Delaware to emancipate its slaves. Under both plans emancipation would begin immediately. One looked to total emancipation by 1867, the other by 1893. Lincoln preferred the second version, which would require the nation to pay the state $23,200 per year for thirty-one years. The President's proposals were printed and distributed to members of the Delaware legislature but, as Fisher reported, "due to perceived opposition" they were never introduced as bills. Though the Delaware emancipation scheme proved abortive it was significant in that Sumner did not oppose it. Representing an abolitionist constituency that for three decades had insisted on immediate, uncompensated emancipation, Sumner was persuaded to go along with Lincoln's plan. "Never should any question of money be allowed to interfere with human freedom," he concluded.

With equal adroitness Lincoln enlisted Chase's backing for his plan. Like the President, Chase was a colonizationist. During the debates on the Compromise of 1850, he declared unequivocally that the black and white races could not live together "except under the constraint of force, such as that of slavery," and he looked forward "to the separation of the races" because the two were "adapted to different latitudes and countries." At the same time, he was a staunch advocate of equal rights for Negroes, and of all the members of the cabinet he was most clearly aligned with the antislavery element in the North. His voice, like Sumner's, would help still any clamor against gradual, compensated emancipation. Well aware of the Secretary's vanity, Lincoln consulted with him frequently when planning for emancipation, and he allowed Chase to draft a long, wordy message to Congress on the subject —which he quietly filed away unused.

The President did not turn to Chase simply as a matter of policy. The two men, complete strangers at the beginning of the administration, had developed an effective working relationship. Lincoln was impressed by the efficiency of Chase's Treasury Department and trusted the Secretary's judgment on financial questions. As he told John Hay a little later, he "generally delegated to Mr. C. exclusive control of those matters falling within the purview of his dept." In fact, the President knew a good deal about governmental finance and took an active role in helping Chase promote a national banking act, but he found it politic at times to claim total ignorance of such matters. "Money," he exclaimed to a group of New York financiers who wanted a change in banking legislation, "I don't know anything about 'money.' " For his part, Chase came to have a kind of grudging affection for the man who had appointed him, and, though he frequently differed with the President's policies and deplored his style of management, he kept reassuring himself in his diary that Lincoln was, after all, honest and well meaning.

To cement the loyalty of Chase and Sumner, Lincoln deliberately excluded Seward from all discussion of his emancipation project. The Secretary of State and Sumner were rivals for control of foreign relations, and Chase and Seward nearly always took opposing positions in the cabinet.

The *Trent* affair delayed Lincoln's introduction of his emancipation plan, and then Willie's death caused a further postponement, but by spring he was finally ready with a short message on the "abolishment" of slavery, the first such proposal ever submitted to Congress by an American President. Early in the morning on March 6, Sumner received an urgent summons to the White House. "I want to read you my message," Lincoln told him when he reached the White House. "I want to know how you like it. I am going to send it in today." First Lincoln read the manuscript aloud; then Sumner went over it himself. He had some reservations about some of the language— especially the word "abolishment"—but concluded that Lincoln's style was "so clearly . . . aboriginal, autochthonous" that it would not bear verbal emendation. Delighted with its contents, Sumner could hardly bear to part with the manuscript, and he read it over and over again until Lincoln was obliged to say: "There, now, you've read it enough, run away. I must send it in to-day."

In the message the President urged Congress to adopt a joint resolution declaring "that the United States ought to co-operate with any state which may adopt gradual abolishment of slavery, giving to such state pecuniary aid, to be used by such state in it's discretion, to compensate for the inconveniences public and private, produced by such change of system." Such a declaration, he held, was strictly constitutional because it made no claim of federal authority to interfere with slavery within state limits but allowed each state "perfectly free choice" to accept or reject the proposed offer. He argued for his resolution not on the basis of morality or justice but on the ground that it would remove any temptation for the border states to join the "proposed confederacy." To congressmen from those states he added the warning that as the war continued it would be "impossible to foresee all the incidents, which may attend and all the ruin which may follow it."

Lincoln's careful preparation led to an overwhelmingly positive reception of his proposal. How could anybody object to a proposal endorsed by the Blairs, by Sumner, and by Chase? The San Francisco *Daily Alta California* pretty well summarized press opinion by calling the message "just the right thing, at the right time, and in the right place." In New York the *Evening Bulletin,* the *Herald,* the *World,* and the *Evening Post* all endorsed Lincoln's plan. "This Message constitutes of itself an epoch in the history of our country," rejoiced the *New York Tribune,* often so critical of Lincoln. "It is the day-star of a new National dawn." The next day the *Tribune* added, "We thank God that Abraham Lincoln is President of the United States, and the whole country, we cannot doubt, will be thankful that we have at such a time so wise a ruler."

Lincoln followed press reactions to his proposal closely. When the *New York Times,* usually a faithful supporter of his administration, complained in an early edition about the cost of compensated emancipation, the President promptly straightened out the editor, Henry J. Raymond. Less than one-half of a day's cost of the war would pay for emancipating all the slaves in Delaware, he pointed out; and the cost of eighty-seven days of the conflict would free the slaves in all the border states plus the District of Columbia. Raymond, who had been out of the office, had already corrected his newspaper's slant and published several articles commending the message "as a master-piece of practical wisdom and sound policy."

But border-state congressmen said nothing. Lincoln sent for Montgomery Blair, who had made brave promises about the extent of emancipation sentiment in the upper South. Blair suggested that the congressmen were waiting for the army to win a victory. "That is just the reason why I do not wish to wait," Lincoln told him impatiently. "If we do have success, they may feel . . . it matters not whether we do anything about the matter."

The next day Blair brought the border-state representatives to receive the same message. Disclaiming "any intent to injure the interests or wound the sensibilities of the Slave States," Lincoln reminded them that failure to solve the problem of slaves who fled to Union lines "strengthened the hopes of the Confederates that at some day the Border States would unite with them" and thus prolonged the war. Stressing that his plan was voluntary and that it recognized "that Emancipation was a subject exclusively under the control of the States," he urged them to give it serious consideration. The congressmen haggled with him. Was his plan constitutional? Would Congress appropriate the money needed to put it in effect? Was this a first step toward a general emancipation? Would emancipation be followed by colonization of the freedmen? Lincoln tried to assuage their fears but salvaged nothing from the meeting except John J. Crittenden's assurance that all the congressmen believed the President was "solely moved by a high patriotism and sincere devotion to the happiness and glory of his Country."

Congressional debates on Lincoln's resolution were brief. Several representatives from the border states thought it was unconstitutional. At the other extreme John Hickman, an abolitionist representative from Pennsylvania, sneered that the message was an attempt on the part of the President to compensate for his failure "to meet the just expectation of the party which elected him to the office he holds." A few abolitionists outside of Congress saw in Lincoln's plan a design to save slavery. "Every concession made by the President to the enemies of slavery has only one aim," growled Gurowski; "it is to mollify their urgent demands by throwing to them small crumbs, as one tries to mollify a boisterous and hungry dog." But such dissents were few, and Congress adopted the resolution by overwhelming majorities.

Then, disappointingly, nothing happened. Because none of the border states agreed to accept the plan Congress had endorsed in general terms, there was no need for any further legislation. The only concrete result of the entire effort was a bill for compensated emancipation in the District of Columbia. It met some of Lincoln's specifications as a blueprint for freedom in that it provided for paying up to $300 to masters for every slave emancipated and appropriated $100,000 for colonizing "such of the slaves as desired to emigrate." But this was not the measure Lincoln really wanted. Emancipation imposed on the federal district was very different from abolition voluntarily adopted by the border slave states. "If some one or more of the border-states would move fast, I should greatly prefer it," he explained to Horace Greeley. But none did so, and he signed the District of Columbia bill on April 16.

VII

Lincoln's military plans bore equally meager results. After McClellan's demotion the President and the Secretary of War, neither of whom had any significant military experience, found themselves swamped by administrative detail as they tried to direct huge armies spread over half a continent. Yielding finally to suggestions from both Chase and Bates, Lincoln decided he needed his own military adviser, and he called on the sixty-four-year-old veteran Ethan Allen Hitchcock. The grandson of the Revolutionary hero Ethan Allen, Hitchcock had become a soldier mainly because family tradition demanded it, and, more interested in Swedenborg than in strategy, he retired from active duty in 1855 to devote his time to religious and philosophical investigations. Summoned to Washington in March, he learned from

Stanton that the President wanted his assistance. The next day Lincoln told him of the pressures to remove "the traitor McClellan"—as his enemies called him—and explained that as President he was "the depository of the power of the government and had no military knowledge." In his sickbed, recovering from two hemorrhages, the general thought he was asked to take McClellan's place as commander of the Army of the Potomac, but he did not perhaps get the message exactly right. The old general was reluctant. He wanted no post, and he recognized that neither Lincoln nor Stanton knew what they would like him to do. Unwillingly he accepted a staff appointment in the War Department, where his advice was of little use to either the President or the Secretary of War.

Left to manage on their own, Lincoln and Stanton received little encouraging news from any front. In the West at Pittsburg Landing on the Tennessee River the Confederates came close to routing Grant's army in the battle of Shiloh (April 6–7). The timely arrival of Buell's forces helped to save the day. In the end, Shiloh was a great Union victory, but the 13,000 Federal casualties marked this as the bloodiest engagement yet in the war. Halleck blamed Grant for the losses, and there was strong sentiment to have him removed. Lincoln overruled the objections with the quiet comment "I can't spare this man; he fights." But with Grant's reputation under a shadow, Halleck now took personal command of the heavily depleted Western army and began a slow and cumbersome march toward Corinth, Mississippi.

In the East progress was no more rapid. Frémont said that he could not move until his newly established Mountain Department received reinforcements and more supplies. The President had little to give him because McClellan was taking most of the Army of the Potomac down the Potomac to use in his Peninsula campaign, in which neither Lincoln nor Stanton had much faith. Stanton circulated reports of McClellan's disloyalty—only to declare sanctimoniously that of course he did not believe these imputations on the general. Lincoln said he had no reason to doubt McClellan's fidelity, yet he told Browning that he was "not fully satisfied with his conduct of the war—that he was not sufficiently energetic and aggressive." Offering a shrewd thumbnail character sketch, the President judged that McClellan "had the capacity to make arrangements properly for a great conflict, but as the hour for action approached he became nervous and oppressed with the responsibility and hesitated to meet the crisis."

Harboring such doubts, Lincoln had stipulated that McClellan must not embark on his campaign without leaving behind a sufficient force to make Washington "entirely secure." That requirement led to an unsolvable conflict between them. Lincoln was never able to make the general comprehend the political importance of the security of the national capital. McClellan, for his part, failed to convince the President that the best way to defend Washington was to attack Richmond.

Before leaving for the Peninsula, McClellan, as directed, held a council of war, and his corps commanders recommended that a force of 40,000 or 50,000 men was needed to protect the capital. McClellan believed he was carrying out this directive by stationing 22,000 men in and around Washington and by posting other troops nearby—at Manassas, at Warrenton, in the Shenandoah Valley, and on the lower Potomac—all in close proximity if the capital should be attacked. But he never explained his thinking to Lincoln and, except for quickly passing a paper under Hitchcock's nose, did not show anybody his troop disposition before he sailed for the Peninsula. Stanton, still new in his job and always highly nervous, feared for the safety of Washington and asked Hitchcock and General James Wadsworth, commandant of the forces in the capital, to verify that McClellan had followed the President's order to leave the capital secure. Both agreed that he had not. On April 3, Lincoln ordered McDowell's corps—approximately one-third of the army McClellan had hoped to muster on the Peninsula—held back for the defense of Washington.

After that there was endless bickering between McClellan and the civilian authorities in Washington. The general found the Confederates entrenched at Yorktown on the Peninsula and, as usual vastly overestimating the enemy's strength, demanded reinforcement. Without McDowell's men, he felt unable to carry the Confederate lines and settled down to besiege their fortifications. Impatiently Lincoln reminded him that, even after McDowell's corps was held back, he had 100,000 troops at his command and suggested: "I think you better break the enemies' line . . . at once." Furious, McClellan wrote his wife, "I was much tempted to reply that he had better come and do it himself."

Lincoln told Browning that he was "dissatisfied with McClellan's sluggishness of action," but he tried to soothe the general's feeling with a fuller explanation why McDowell's troops had been detained. For all his charity, he could not refrain from adding a word of self-justification: "You will do me the justice to remember I always insisted, that going down the Bay in search of a field, instead of fighting at or near Manassas, was only shifting, and not surmounting, a difficulty—that we would find the same enemy, and the same, or equal, intrenchments, at either place." The President assured the general that he would do his best to sustain the army, and he ended with a warning: *"But you must act."*

Relations between the general and his commander-in-chief were strained but not broken. After reevaluating the forces left to defend Washington, Lincoln detached Franklin's division from McDowell's corps and sent it to reinforce the army on the Peninsula. Grateful for this evidence of the President's "firm friendship and confidence," McClellan told Montgomery Blair that he was now convinced "that the Presdt had none but the best motives." He promised soon to report a success that would be "brilliant, although with but little loss of life."

On May 3, when the Confederates withdrew from Yorktown and McClellan began his long-planned advance up the Peninsula, Lincoln decided to move closer to the scene of operations. Accompanied by Chase and Stanton and escorted by General Egbert L. Viele, he boarded the Treasury Department's new revenue cutter, the *Miami,* sailed down the Potomac, and the next day arrived at Fort Monroe, where seventy-eight-year-old General John E. Wool commanded the garrison. After learning that McClellan would not join them because his army had just defeated the Confederates at Williamsburg and was pushing them back toward Richmond, the President and his associates decided that the time had come to liberate Norfolk, on the south side of the James estuary, where the hulking *Merrimack* was sheltered, still a threat to the Union navy.

Though the professional soldiers in General Wool's command advised that it was impossible to land troops anywhere near Norfolk because shoals would prevent boats from getting closer than a mile to the shore, Chase was determined to see for himself and, using the *Miami* and a tugboat, got very near to land. He reported his finding to Lincoln, who had been studying the maps and thought he had discovered another landing site nearby. Under a bright moon Lincoln and Stanton sailed in the tugboat right up to the shore, while Chase aimed the long-range guns of the *Miami* to protect them if they were attacked. The President insisted on climbing out on what Virginians called their "sacred soil" and, in bright moonlight, strolled up and down on the beach.

After showing that a landing was possible, Lincoln did not participate in the invasion the next day but remained at Fort Monroe attending to other business. That evening he heard how Chase had gone ashore, led the Union troops, and received the surrender of Norfolk. A huge explosion told the President's party that the *Merrimack,* abandoned by the Confederates, had been blown up. "So," Chase wrote to his daughter, "has ended a brilliant week's campaign of the President, for I think it quite certain that if he had not come down, [Norfolk] would still have been in possession of the enemy and the Merrimac as grim and defiant and as much a terror as ever."

The episode was of no particular importance except perhaps to confirm the distrust of professional military men that both Lincoln and Stanton shared. But the President would not allow his little adventure to be used to McClellan's discredit. Afterward, over dinner at General Wool's headquarters, when someone made a slurring reference to the commander of the Army of the Potomac, Lincoln rebuked him: "I will not hear anything said against Genl. McClellan, it hurts my feelings."

But McClellan, feeling victory almost within his grasp, was not so generous, and he insisted on reversing some of Lincoln's recent decisions. He had never liked the corps arrangement that the President had forced him to accept and now, claiming that it "very nearly resulted in a most disastrous defeat" at Williamsburg, planned to remove "incompetent commanders" of corps and divisions. Reluctantly Lincoln allowed McClellan to suspend the corps organization, though he reminded the general that it was based "on the unanimous opinion of every *military man* I could get an opinion from, and every modern military book, yourself only excepted." He warned McClellan that his actions would be perceived "as merely an effort to pamper one or two pets, and to persecute and degrade their supposed rivals" and asked whether he had considered the implications of reducing the rank of Generals Sumner, Heintzelman, and Keyes all at once.

McClellan continued to complain that he did not have enough men to confront the overwhelming Confederate force. He never ceased asking Lincoln for McDowell's army corps that had been held back to defend Washington (though he did not want McDowell himself, whom he regarded as an enemy who fed the Committee on the Conduct of the War material hostile to McClellan). Unwilling to leave Washington exposed, Lincoln thought he found a way to defend the capital while reinforcing McClellan: he would have McDowell's corps advance overland toward Richmond in such a way as to connect with the right wing of McClellan's forces on the Peninsula. But because he retained a residual distrust of McClellan's judgment, he instructed McDowell to operate not as a part of McClellan's force but as an independent cooperating army. As he expected, McClellan resisted the plan. He insisted that the reinforcements should be sent by water, and he announced that since he outranked McDowell that general would, under the sixty-second article of war, have to obey his orders.

To make sure McDowell understood his mission, the President went down to Aquia Creek, accompanied by Secretary Stanton and John A. Dahlgren, a naval officer to whom he had taken a great liking. When they reached the Potomac Creek, McDowell called their attention to a trestle bridge his men were erecting a hundred feet above the water in that deep and wide ravine. "Let us walk over," exclaimed the President boyishly, and though the pathway was only a single plank wide, he led the way. About halfway across Stanton became dizzy and Dahlgren, who was somewhat giddy himself, had to help the Secretary. But Lincoln, despite the grinding cares of his office, was in fine physical shape and never lost his balance.

His political equilibrium was not so steady. By the end of May 1862 his administration could point to few successes. In neither the East nor in the West had Union armies succeeded in crushing the Confederate forces. Only in faraway Louisiana, where David G. Farragut ran the fortifications on the lower Mississippi River and seized New Orleans, had there been a clear Union success. The Treasury was almost depleted. After exhausting the possibilities of borrowing, Secretary Chase had reluctantly been obliged to ask Congress to issue legal-tender paper money (usually called greenbacks). Like Chase, Lincoln doubted the constitutionality of the measure, but he had no choice but to approve it. In foreign affairs, European powers had nearly exhausted their patience and, as cotton shortages caused massive unemployment and suffering in the textile mills, were coming close to recognizing the Confederacy. In Congress the President had almost no defenders, and a few Jacobin members of his own party criticized almost every action he took. The prospects for Lincoln's presidency were not good. Edward Dicey, the perceptive American correspondent of the British journals the *Spectator* and *Macmillan's Magazine,* offered what he felt would be the verdict of history: "When the President leaves the White House, he will be no more regretted, though more respected, than Mr. Buchanan."

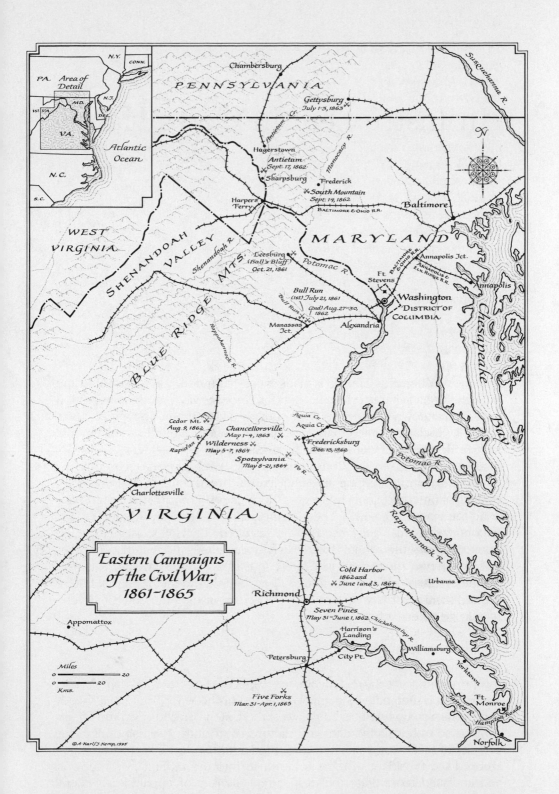

Eastern Campaigns of the Civil War, 1861–1865

Inset map (Area of Detail):
N.Y. CONN.
PA.
N.J.
MD. DEL.
W. VA.
VA.
N.C.
S.C.
Atlantic Ocean

Main map labels:

PENNSYLVANIA

Chambersburg

Gettysburg
July 1–3, 1863

Susquehanna R.

N

WEST VIRGINIA

Hagerstown

Antietam
Sept. 17, 1862

Sharpsburg

Frederick

South Mountain
Sept. 14, 1862

Baltimore

BALTIMORE & OHIO R.R.

Harpers Ferry

SHENANDOAH VALLEY

Shenandoah R.

MARYLAND

Leesburg
(Ball's Bluff)
Oct. 21, 1861

Potomac R.

Ft. Stevens

Annapolis Jct.

Annapolis

Washington
DISTRICT OF COLUMBIA

Bull Run
(1st) July 21, 1861
(2nd) Aug. 27–30, 1862

BLUE RIDGE MTS.

Rappahannock R.

Manassas Jct.

Alexandria

Chesapeake Bay

Cedar Mt.
Aug. 9, 1862

Chancellorsville
May 1–4, 1863

Aquia Cr.
Aquia Cr.

Rapidan

Wilderness
May 5–7, 1864

Spotsylvania
May 8–21, 1864

Po R.

Fredericksburg
Dec. 13, 1862

Potomac R.

Charlottesville

VIRGINIA

Rappahannock R.

Eastern Campaigns
of the Civil War,
1861–1865

Cold Harbor
1862 and
June 1 and 3, 1864

Urbanna

Appomattox

Richmond

Seven Pines
May 31–June 1, 1862

Chickahominy R.

Harrison's Landing

Williamsburg

York R.

Miles
0   20
0   20
Kms.

Petersburg

City Pt.

Yorktown

Five Forks
Mar. 31–Apr. 1, 1865

James R.

Ft. Monroe

Hampton Roads

Norfolk

© A. Karl / J. Kemp, 1995

CHAPTER THIRTEEN

An Instrument in God's Hands

Whenever Lincoln's plans were frustrated, he reverted to the fatalism that had characterized his outlook since he was a youth. A delegation of Quakers known as Progressive Friends who visited him on June 20, 1862, urging a proclamation to emancipate the slaves, found him in such a mood. At first he bandied words with them. Since he, as President, could not require obedience to the Constitution in the Southern states, could he be more effective in enforcing an emancipation proclamation? "If a decree of emancipation could abolish Slavery," he argued, "John Brown would have done the work effectually." Then, turning serious, he acknowledged to his visitors that he was "deeply sensible of his need of Divine assistance" in the troubles he and the country faced. He had sometimes thought that "perhaps he might be an instrument in God's hands of accomplishing a great work and he certainly was not unwilling to be," he told the memorialists. But he warned them: "Perhaps . . . God's way of accomplishing the end [of slavery] . . . may be different from theirs."

I

By the summer of 1862, Lincoln felt especially in need of divine help. Everything, it seemed, was going wrong, and his hope for bringing a speedy end to the war was dashed. In the West the Union drive to open the Mississippi River valley stalled after the capture of Corinth, Mississippi, and the key city of Vicksburg remained in Confederate hands. In Tennessee, Buell ignored the President's orders to advance into the mountainous regions, and so failed to liberate the desperate Unionists of Appalachia. Federal amphibious operations along the coasts and on the waterways, which had resulted in the seizure of New Orleans, the sea islands of South Carolina, and Cape Hatteras, seemed barren of results—except for endless bickering among factions of liberated Louisiana Unionists who demanded the President's attention. And—most important of all—the news from McClellan and the Army of the Potomac was discouraging.

The lack of military success blocked Lincoln's plan to unite all the moderate elements in the country in a just, harmonious restoration of the Union. If there were any loyal elements in the Confederacy, they gave no evidence of hearing his promises speedily to restore their states to their place in the Union. In the North the growing body of antislavery opinion chafed at the President's slowness to act against slavery and complained that he was under the control of the proslavery border states. At the same time, his plan for gradual, compensated emancipation in the border slave states went nowhere; representatives of those states could not see why as loyal supporters of the Union they should bear the burden of emancipation, while the peculiar institution was left intact in the Confederacy. Though Congress gave token support, in the amount of half a million dollars, for the President's scheme to colonize the freed African-Americans outside the United States, nobody, other than Lincoln himself, had much faith in this project.

Only McClellan's campaign on the Peninsula could break the stalemate, but Lincoln failed to reinforce the Army of the Potomac just as it came within sight of Richmond. He had promised to send McDowell's corps overland to assist McClellan's army, but when it was about to start, he diverted it to the Shenandoah Valley, where Thomas J. ("Stonewall") Jackson had begun a brilliant campaign designed to relieve the pressure on Richmond. Outmarching, outmaneuvering, and outfighting the Union forces in the valley commanded by Frémont, N. P. Banks, and James Shields (Lincoln's old Illinois rival), Jackson moved north toward Harpers Ferry, and there were reports that Union soldiers were "running and flinging away their arms, routed and demoralized," in "another Bull Run." Some feared that Jackson might cross the Potomac and threaten Washington itself. Even Lincoln at one point believed the Confederates were planning to take the national capital, and he wrote McClellan: "I think the time is near when you must either attack Richmond or give up the job and come to the defence of Washington."

That was, however, an uncharacteristic note. Most of the time Lincoln saw Jackson's campaign as an opportunity to cut off a Confederate army from its base and force it to surrender. He anticipated that Jackson, after pursuing Banks almost to Harpers Ferry, would have to turn south, and he hoped to trap him on the way back. It was for this reason, much more than for a fear for Washington's safety, that he rushed McDowell's force to the Shenandoah Valley, where it was supposed to cooperate with Frémont's army. Lacking a general-in-chief or a chief of staff, he and Stanton took over the day-by-day —and sometimes the hour-by-hour—management of the Union armies that were trying to trap Jackson. The President gave specific, even minutely detailed, orders to McDowell, to Banks, to Rufus Saxton the commander at Harpers Ferry, to Frémont.

But his plan failed. Jackson's men retreated faster than McDowell's men could come up. Catching the Confederates was "a question of legs," Lincoln saw, and he urged McDowell, "Put in all the speed you can." Frémont was of no help because he advanced by a route different from the one Lincoln had ordered him to take and spent eight days covering seventy miles—while Jackson's men marched fifty miles in two days. Lincoln's strategy was too ambitious. To trap the Confederates in the Valley would have required the close coordination of three separate armies approaching from different directions—Frémont from the west, Banks from the north, and McDowell from the east—and the timing needed to be perfect to catch the elusive Jackson. Lincoln did not have the experience or the technical knowledge to issue orders that were precise, unambiguous, and authoritative. It was deflating to realize, after his heady experience at Norfolk, that he was a political, not a military, leader.

Jackson's exploits in the Shenandoah served their intended purpose of distracting Lincoln's attention from the major fighting on the Peninsula. Slowly and methodically McClellan advanced toward Richmond at the rate of about two miles a day, constantly complaining that he was facing overwhelming odds, that he was handicapped by heavy rains and impassable roads, and, most of all, that he needed reinforcements. On May 31 the Confederate army, commanded by Joseph E. Johnston, launched an attack on the Army of the Potomac, while it was divided by the Chickahominy River. All Lincoln could do from Washington was to send encouragement to McClellan: "Stand well on your guard—hold all your ground, or yield any only, inch by inch and in good order." Though welcome, the advice was not needed, and the army fought fiercely in this battle of Seven Pines (or Fair Oaks) and on the second day forced the Confederates back on the defenses of Richmond. In the struggle Johnston was wounded, and Robert E. Lee became the new commander of the Southern army.

With 5,000 casualties, McClellan cried out for more men, and Lincoln did his best to supply his needs. He ordered McCall's division of McDowell's corps to go at once to the Peninsula, gave McClellan control over the forces at Fort Monroe (up to this point commanded by General Wool, who was replaced), and ordered Burnside to make available any troops from his North Carolina expedition that could be useful. But plans to send on the rest of McDowell's corps failed. Shields's division, as the President explained to McClellan, "got so terribly out of shape" chasing Jackson in the Valley that it was "out at elbows, and out at toes" and was not able to move.

With an army of 130,000 men McClellan prepared to advance on Richmond as soon as the rains ended and the roads permitted the passage of artillery. On June 18, when Lincoln gently asked when he planned to attack so that he "could better dispose of things," the general responded, "After tomorrow we shall fight the rebel Army as soon as Providence will permit."

In private, he resented what he considered prodding by the President, and he believed the report of Allan Pinkerton, his chief intelligence gatherer, that "Honest A has again fallen into the hands of my enemies and is no longer a cordial friend of mine!" To newspaper reporters at army headquarters he spoke of the overwhelming superiority of the Confederate army and complained publicly of the way he had been treated by the administration. General Fitz-John Porter, one of McClellan's favorite aides, helped spread the view that the administration was ignoring all calls to strengthen the Army of the Potomac. He urged the editor of the *New York World* to raise the question: "Does the President (controlled by an incompetent Secy) design to cause defeat here for the purpose of prolonging the war?"

On June 25, before McClellan could launch his proposed assault on Richmond, the Confederates ripped into his army. He had completely misjudged the character of the new Confederate commander, considering Lee *"too* cautious and weak under grave responsibility—personally brave and energetic . . . yet . . . wanting in moral firmness when pressed by heavy responsibility and . . . likely to be timid and irresolute in action." In a series of hard-fought engagements known as the Seven Days' battles (June 25–July 1), the Confederates forced the Army of the Potomac to retreat back across the Chickahominy and down the Peninsula to take refuge under the protection of federal gunboats on the James River.

While the Army of the Potomac was engaged in desperate fighting on the Peninsula, Lincoln slipped out of Washington and went to West Point, where General Scott was spending the summer. Old and infirm, the general was still thought to have a good head for military matters, and he was perhaps the only commander on whom Lincoln could rely for disinterested advice. The immediate problem the two men discussed was whether McDowell's corps, now stationed at Fredericksburg to protect the capital, should join McClellan's army on the Peninsula. No notes were made of his conversations with Scott, but afterward the general prepared a memorandum for the President that implicitly criticized his recent attempt to coordinate the forces in the Valley against Jackson and recommended that McDowell's corps be sent by water to reinforce McClellan. The old general reminded the President: "The defeat of the rebels, at Richmond, or their forced retreat, thence, . . . would be a virtual end of the rebellion."

Learning of the surprise visit, a small crowd greeted the President at Jersey City on his return the next day and trapped him into making a few remarks. His trip "did not have the importance which has been attached to it," Lincoln assured them. Indeed, so far as McClellan's campaign on the Peninsula was concerned, it had no consequences at all. Nothing that Scott told him changed his mind, and he returned to Washington with more doubts than ever about the value of military expertise. He did not send McDowell's corps to join McClellan. Instead, on the day he got back from West Point, he ordered the consolidation of all the federal forces in northern Virginia, including Frémont's and Banks's forces as well as McDowell's, into the new Army of Virginia, and he appointed John Pope to command it. In a huff, Frémont declined to serve under Pope, whom he outranked, and went on inactive duty.

Behind Lincoln's decision was his growing belief that McClellan, for all his undoubted gifts as an organizer, would never fight a decisive battle to take Richmond. With painful anxiety he continued to read the telegraphic dispatches from McClellan's headquarters, with their repeated excuses for not advancing and their constant complaints. The weather, wrote the general, was impossible; rains made mud bogs of the roads and repeatedly washed out all his bridges. Wryly Lincoln observed that the weather did little to restrict the movement of the Confederates, and he judged that McClellan believed, contrary to the Scriptures, that the rain fell more upon the just than the unjust. Still accepting the information supplied by the detective Allan Pinkerton, the general repeatedly lamented his great inferiority in numbers, claiming that he was facing 200,000 men in the Confederate armies; but Lincoln and Stanton had more realistic estimates of enemy strength, compiled by Generals Wool and Meigs, showing the Confederates much inferior to Union forces. Over and over, McClellan asked for—indeed, demanded—reinforcements, and Lincoln patiently explained that all the forces at his disposal were already committed. But occasionally McClellan's demands became too importunate, and the President's temper snapped. He rejected the general's demand for 50,000 additional troops as "simply absurd."

McClellan bitterly protested "that the Gov[ernmen]t has not sustained this Army," and both he and General Randolph B. Marcy, his chief of staff, spoke ominously about the possibility of capitulation. "If I save this Army now," McClellan concluded a message to Stanton on June 28, "I tell you plainly that I owe no thanks to you or any other persons in Washington—you have done your best to sacrifice this army." These final sentences were so mutinous that the supervisor of the telegraph deleted them from the copies shown to the President and the Secretary of War, and they were not published until months later.

II

During this anxious period Lincoln worried incessantly. Stanton reported that he was "very tired." He had lost weight because he felt under too much pressure to eat meals at normal hours. "Well, I cannot take my vittles regular," he explained to Dr. Henry W. Bellows of the Sanitary Commission. "I kind o' just browze round." Mary Lincoln reported that her husband was getting very little sleep at night. He looked so "weary, care-worn and troubled" that Browning feared his health was suffering. When he told the President of his anxiety, Lincoln held him by the hand, "pressed it, and said in a very tender and touching tone—'Browning I must die sometime.' "

But in public the President tried to present an air of calm. "Maintain your ground if you can," he instructed McClellan, "but save the Army at all events, even if you fall back to Fortress-Monroe. We still have strength enough in the country, and will bring it out." New troops were needed, but Lincoln felt that "a general panic and stampede" would follow a massive call for more men. Consequently he deputized Seward to go to meet with several Union governors in New York and urge them to supply more troops. "I expect to maintain this contest until successful," he pledged, "or till I die, or am conquered, or my term expires, or Congress or the country forsakes me." On reflection, Seward concluded that such a bleak message would be unsettling to the country and that it would be better to induce the governors to petition the President to enlist more men. Probably nobody was taken in by the ruse, but the governors' memorial gave Lincoln the occasion to call up 300,000 additional men "so as to bring this unnecessary and injurious civil war to a speedy and satisfactory conclusion."

By this time Lincoln had decided that the kind of warfare McClellan believed in would never defeat the Confederacy. He had arrived at this conclusion slowly, but for some time his dissatisfaction had been growing. Back in June, for example, he had overruled the general after a doctor protested that because of McClellan's orders Union soldiers were not allowed to use the White House estate owned by Mrs. Robert E. Lee, the healthiest and best hospital location on the Peninsula. The physician asked the President, "Are our brave soldiers to die off like rotten sheep there because General McClellan chooses to protect the grounds of a rebel?" "McClellan has made this promise," Lincoln told the doctor, "but I think it is wrong. . . . He does not want to break the promise he has made, and (with emphasis) *I will break it for him.*"

McClellan, who had never understood or fully trusted Lincoln, was aware of the President's dissatisfaction. It was easy to deduce Lincoln's growing impatience from his dispatches to the general. Many of them, though couched in friendly, reasonable language, were perhaps written less with the hope of influencing McClellan than with an eye to establishing a record to show that the President had done everything possible to assist an insatiably demanding commander.

At any rate, in early July Lincoln decided to visit McClellan's headquarters at Harrison's Landing and to inspect the Army of the Potomac himself. The evening he arrived, he reviewed the troops, and thousands of muskets flashed in the moonlight as the President rode along the lines. "Long and hearty was the applause and welcome which greeted him," one lieutenant recorded in his diary. "His presence after the late disaster . . . seemed to infuse new ardor into the dispirited army." The dispirited commander of that army did not share their enthusiasm. McClellan claimed that the soldiers did not welcome the President and that he *"had to order* the men to cheer and they did it very feebly." Lincoln, the general wrote his wife, is " 'an old stick'—and of pretty poor timber at that."

Shortly after Lincoln reached the army, McClellan handed him a confidential letter in which he outlined his "general views concerning the existing state of the rebellion," admitting that his ideas did "not strictly relate to the situation of this Army or strictly come within the scope of my official duties." His theme was that the war against the Confederates "should be conducted upon the highest principles known to Christian Civilization." That meant there must be no confiscation of rebel property, which was part of the stringent measure then being debated in Congress, and, especially, no "forcible abolition of slavery." To carry out this "constitutional and conservative" policy, the President needed to name a commander-in-chief of the army. "I do not ask that place for myself," McClellan concluded modestly. "I am willing to serve you in such position as you may assign me and I will do so as faithfully as ever subordinate served superior."

The letter was couched in respectful language, and there was nothing insubordinate about it. McClellan had earlier requested the President's permission to present his general ideas about the conflict and Lincoln said he would welcome his "views as to [the] present state of Military affairs throughout the whole country." Nor was the Harrison's Landing letter an unreasonable or extreme document, as some of McClellan's detractors later claimed. McClellan even argued that, while avoiding general emancipation of the slaves, the federal government had a right to order, with appropriate compensation for owners, the manumission of "all the slaves within a particular state," such as Missouri or Maryland. But what it did make clear was McClellan's view that the war should continue to be waged between professional armies, with minimal disruption of civilian life.

That policy had been pursued for over a year and Lincoln was convinced that it had failed. He was ready to move on. He read the letter but made no comment on it except to thank the general for his opinions. Later he remarked that McClellan's advice on how to carry on the affairs of the nation made him think of "the man whose horse kicked up and stuck his foot through the stirrup. He said to the horse, 'If you are going to get on I will get off.' "

The President did not visit Harrison's Landing to learn how the war should be conducted; he went looking for the best way to end a costly and fruitless campaign. McClellan was mortified that Lincoln asked him for no account of the recent battles and was not interested in explanations of the army's failure. Not confiding his views to the general, the President merely asked him and each of his corps commanders to estimate the strength of the Union forces and the location and condition of the Confederates. He then made the telling inquiry: "If you desired, could you remove the army safely?" McClellan saw pretty clearly the direction of Lincoln's thinking, and he reported to his wife that the President seemed like "a man about to do something of which he was much ashamed." "I do not know to what extent he has profited by his visit," he reflected; "not much I fear, for he really seems quite incapable of rising to the height of the merits of the question and the magnitude of the crisis."

On July 11, two days after the President returned to Washington, he showed just how much he had learned; he named Henry W. Halleck "to command the whole land forces of the United States, as General-in-Chief." That appointment signaled a repudiation of McClellan, and of McClellan's view of the war. It was a decision Lincoln had been working through for many weeks. Clearly he had had in mind both a change in command and a change in strategy when he visited General Scott in June. Though he told reporters who cornered him on the way back from West Point that his conference "had nothing whatever to do with making or unmaking any General in the country," this was a little less than the whole truth.

The appointment of Pope had been an early signal that Lincoln was changing his military strategy. The President had confidence in this handsome, black-bearded new general who was the son of an old Illinois associate and had been part of the presidential party on the inaugural trip to Washington. He liked his record. Pope had served well in the capture of Island No. 10 on the Mississippi River, and he had led a wing of Halleck's army in the campaign against Corinth. Doubtless he was pleased that Pope, unlike the generals closest to McClellan, was an ardent antislavery Republican. He was a protégé of Secretary Chase and the son-in-law of a stalwart Republican representative from Ohio. Even more, Lincoln liked Pope's idea of warfare. Boastful and indiscreet, Pope made no secret of his scorn of Eastern generals, like McClellan, who he thought grossly overestimated the strength of the Confederates, and he ridiculed those who believed that strategy was more important than fighting.

Finding Pope knowledgeable and articulate, Lincoln was reluctant to let him leave Washington, and during the desperate Seven Days' battles informally made him his chief military adviser and aide. Day after day, Pope worked alongside the President in the War Department telegraph office, helping Lincoln interpret McClellan's frequent dispatches and making no secret of his belief that the general's retreat to the James River was a blunder. But Pope grew restive in this advisory role and wanted to take to the field. It was at his repeated urging that the President brought in Halleck, who had also been warmly recommended by General Scott.

Freed from his desk job, Pope took up his command and immediately made it clear that, unlike McClellan, he would not fight a soft war. He published a series of tactless orders informing his exhausted and dispirited Eastern soldiers that he came from the West, "where we have always seen the backs of our enemies," and promising that he would pay more attention to his lines of advance than to his lines of retreat. Pope ordered his soldiers so far as possible to live on the country they were passing through, and he prescribed a stern loyalty oath for all "disloyal male citizens" behind Union lines, with heavy penalties for "evil-disposed persons." The words and the rhetoric were John Pope's—but before he issued his orders he submitted them to the President, who gave them his tacit approval.

As Pope took command, Lincoln's confidence began to return. Bustling and energetic, the new general rapidly whipped his troops into shape, and he projected a direct, overland advance against the Confederate capital—just the strategy that Lincoln had unsuccessfully urged McClellan to follow. Greatly encouraged, Lincoln by mid-August was so confident that he told Sumner the Union army would be in Richmond within two weeks.

III

Two days after Lincoln appointed Halleck general-in-chief, he made an equally significant shift in his policy toward slavery. Characteristically he made no public announcement of either change, and in neither case did he make a clean break with the past. Just as he continued to support McClellan's campaign on the Peninsula while he was creating a new army under Pope, so on the domestic scene he worked hard for his old policies of gradualism and compensation even while he was moving toward general emancipation.

Committed to his inaugural pledge that the federal government would not interfere with slavery in the states where it already existed, Lincoln continued to urge the individual states, with financial support from the federal government, to adopt a plan of gradual, compensated emancipation. On July 12, just before Congress adjourned, the President summoned the representatives and senators from the border states to the White House and again pleaded with them to endorse his plan. Slavery in their states, he pointed out, would soon be extinguished by the "mere friction and abrasion" of the war. Apart from that, he reminded them, his hand might soon be forced, because antislavery sentiment throughout the North "is still upon me, and is increasing." As patriots and statesmen they should recommend his plan to the people of their states as the way to bring speedy relief from the war. "As you would perpetuate popular government for the best people in the world," he urged, "I beseech you that you do in no wise omit this."

"Oh, how I wish the border States would accept my proposition!" Lincoln exclaimed to Illinois Representatives Isaac N. Arnold and Owen Lovejoy the day after this meeting. "Then you, Lovejoy, and you, Arnold, and all of us, would not have lived in vain!" But, as he doubtless anticipated, the border-state congressmen refused to follow his lead, and, with a few exceptions, joined in a long, legalistic rebuttal of Lincoln's appeal, questioning the logic of his arguments and the consistency of his policies. "Confine yourself to your constitutional authority" was the gist of their message.

Even before Lincoln received their predictable response he was moving toward a new course of action. On July 13, riding in a carriage with Secretaries Seward and Welles to the funeral of Stanton's infant son, he informed these two conservative members of his cabinet that he "had about come to the conclusion that we must free the slaves or be ourselves subdued." Both Seward and Welles were startled, because hitherto the President had been emphatic in rejecting any proposal to have the national government interfere with slavery. Both said they needed more time to consider the idea. But the President urged them seriously to think about it, because "something must be done."

The idea of emancipation by presidential decree was, of course, not a new one. On the day that the news of the firing on Fort Sumter reached Washington, Sumner had gone to the White House to remind the President that emancipation of the slaves of a military opponent fell within his war powers, and repeatedly he urged Lincoln to act. Frémont's proclamation in August 1861, freeing the slaves of Missouri rebels, was another reminder of what the executive power might accomplish. In December of that year, in his final report as Secretary of War, Cameron had also proposed emancipation by decree. As recently as May, General David Hunter, in command of the Military Department of the South, announced that "slavery and martial law in a free country are altogether incompatible" and proclaimed that therefore persons held as slaves in Florida, Georgia, and South Carolina were "forever free."

Though Secretary Chase insisted that it was "of the highest importance . . . that this order be not revoked," Lincoln promptly declared Hunter's proclamation "altogether void"—as he had all previous moves toward emancipation by executive decree. "No commanding general shall do such a thing, upon *my* responsibility, without consulting me," he told Chase. But in revoking Hunter's order, a new tone appeared in Lincoln's language. For the first time he made it clear that he had no doubt of his constitutional power to order emancipation. Whether he exercised that authority would depend on a decision that abolition had "become a necessity indispensable to the maintainance of the government." A little later he observed that he had no legal or constitutional reservations about issuing an emancipation proclamation because, "as commander-in-chief of the army and navy, in time of war, I suppose I have a right to take any measure which may best subdue the enemy."

After overruling Hunter's proclamation, Lincoln began to think of emancipation as a question to be decided on grounds of policy rather than of principle, and he started to formulate his ideas for a proclamation of freedom. He probably talked over the idea with Stanton in May, and he may have discussed a very preliminary draft of such a proclamation with Vice President Hamlin as early as June 18. Later that month, in the cipher room of the War Department telegraph office, which the President frequented while anxiously awaiting dispatches from the army, he asked Major Thomas T. Eckert for some foolscap, because, he said, "he wanted to write something special." At the telegraph office, he remarked, he was able to work "more quietly and command his thoughts better than at the White House, where he was frequently interrupted." He then sat down at Eckert's desk, which faced onto Pennsylvania Avenue, and began to write. "He would look out of the window a while and then put his pen to paper," Eckert remembered, "but he did not write much at once. He would study between times and when he had made up his mind he would put down a line or two, and then sit quiet for a few minutes." That first day he filled less than a page, and as he left he asked Eckert to take charge of what he had written and not allow anyone to see it. Almost every day during the following weeks he asked for his papers and revised what he had written, adding only a few sentences at a time. Not until he had finished did he tell Eckert that he had been drafting a proclamation "giving freedom to the slaves in the South."

During June and July when Lincoln was drafting an emancipation order, he often played a kind of game with the numerous visitors who descended on him to urge him to free the slaves. The measures they advocated were precisely those that he was attempting to formulate in his document at the War Department. If he challenged their arguments, he was, in effect, testing his own. No doubt he enjoyed his little game, relishing the use of his lawyer's skills to make the worst cause sound the best. No doubt, too, he was pleased to retain total flexibility, since these discussions committed him to nothing.

Thus to Sumner, who called at the White House twice on July 4 "to urge the reconsecration of the day by a decree of emancipation," the President said that a general order was "too big a lick," though Sumner believed he was "not disinclined" to issue a proclamation covering eastern Virginia. On reflection, though, Lincoln changed his mind about even that limited measure, because, as he told the senator, such a proclamation might cause Missouri, Kentucky, and Maryland to secede. Besides, it would probably be mere *brutum fulmen,* unless he could enforce it.

IV

But by mid-July he was ready to show his hand. "Things had gone on from bad to worse, until I felt that we had reached the end of our rope on the plan of operations we had been pursuing," he explained later, "that we had about played our last card, and must change our tactics, or lose the game!" McClellan's defeats on the Peninsula contributed to his decision, as did the demoralization of the soldiers in the Army of the Potomac and the near-mutinous state of some of their officers. So, too, did the growing chorus of antislavery opinion in the North and the dwindling trickle of volunteers for the army—a flow that Governor Andrew of Massachusetts bluntly told the President could not be increased so long as he persisted in fighting a war that would leave slavery intact.

Especially influential was the passage on July 17, 1862, by Congress, with virtually unanimous Republican support, of the Second Confiscation Act, a measure that defined the rebels as traitors and ordered the confiscation of their property, including the freeing of their slaves. Lincoln had serious doubts about many of the provisions of the Confiscation Act and drafted a message vetoing it, reminding Congress that "the severest justice may not always be the best policy." Only after Senator Fessenden, working closely with the President, secured modification of some of the more stringent provisions did Lincoln agree to sign the measure—and even then he took the unprecedented step of placing before Congress his statement of objections to the bill he had approved.

No part of the Second Confiscation Act troubled the President more than the section declaring that, after a period of sixty days, the slaves of rebels should be "forever free of their servitude, and not again held as slaves." "It is startling to say that congress can free a slave within a state," he remarked, for such a statement would directly contradict the Republican platform on which he and most of the congressmen of his party had been elected. "Congress has no power over slavery in the states," he told Browning, "and so much of it as remains after the war is over . . . must be left to the exclusive control of the states where it may exist." If power over slavery within the states existed anywhere in the federal government, it was to be found in the war powers, which he believed could only be exercised by the President as commander-in-chief. But rather than confront Congress over the abstract issue, Lincoln decided to accept the bill—and to undercut the congressional initiative for emancipation by acting first.

His preliminary conversation with Seward and Welles on July 13 had been intended to prepare the way for such action, and a week later the President was ready to discuss emancipation with the full cabinet. On July 22 his advisers did not immediately realize that they were present at a historic occasion. The secretaries seemed more interested in discussing Pope's orders to subsist his troops in hostile territory and schemes for colonizing African-Americans in Central America, and they had trouble focusing when the President read the first draft of his proposed proclamation. The curious structure and awkward phrasing of the document showed that Lincoln was still trying to blend his earlier policy of gradual, compensated emancipation with his new program for immediate abolition. It opened with an announcement that the Second Confiscation Act would go into effect in sixty days unless Southerners "cease participating in, aiding, countenancing, or abetting the existing rebellion." The President then pledged to support pecuniary aid to any state—including the rebel states—that "may voluntarily adopt, gradual abolishment of slavery." Only at the end did he, "as Commander-in-Chief of the Army and Navy of the United States," proclaim that "as a fit and necessary military measure"—not as a measure that was just or right—he would on January 1, 1863, declare "all persons held as slaves within any state . . . , wherein the constitutional authority of the United States shall not then be practically recognized, . . . forever . . . free."

At the outset of the meeting the President informed the cabinet that he had "resolved upon this step, and had not called them together to ask their advice, but to lay the subject-matter of a proclamation before them," and the discussion that followed was necessarily rather desultory. Stanton and Bates staunchly urged "immediate promulgation" of the proclamation. Rather surprisingly, Chase was cool. He feared an emancipation proclamation might be "a measure of great danger," since it would unsettle the government's financial position. "Emancipation could be much better and more quietly accomplished," he believed, "by allowing Generals to organize and arm the slaves (thus avoiding depredation and massacre on the one hand, and support to the insurrection on the other)." Despite his reservations, he promised to give Lincoln's proclamation his hearty support.

Postmaster General Blair, who came in late, deprecated the proposed policy "on the ground that it would cost the Administration the fall elections." Secretary of the Interior Smith said nothing but was strongly opposed to emancipation; he was already thinking of resigning from a cabinet where he felt increasingly out of sympathy with the President. Seward, who had been thinking over the consequences of emancipation since his carriage ride with Lincoln and Welles, argued strongly against immediate promulgation of the proclamation. He feared it would "break up our relations with foreign nations and the production of cotton for sixty years." Foreign nations might intervene in the American civil war in order to prevent the abolition of slavery for sake of the cotton their factories so badly needed. More persuasively he argued that issuing an emancipation proclamation at this particular moment, after the severe military reverses experienced by the Union armies, would "be viewed as the last measure of an exhausted government, a cry for help." "His idea," Lincoln recalled later, "was that it would be considered our last *shriek,* on the retreat."

With his advisers divided, Lincoln adjourned the cabinet meeting without reaching a decision on issuing the proclamation, though he later told one visitor that he expected to issue it the next day. But that night Seward's ally, Thurlow Weed, came to the White House and again strongly argued that an emancipation proclamation could not be enforced and that it would alienate the important border states. Reluctantly Lincoln put the document aside. Shortly afterward, when Sumner on five successive days pressed the President to issue his proclamation, Lincoln responded, "We *mustn't issue it* till after a victory."

V

In the following weeks Lincoln repeatedly argued the issue of emancipation in his own mind. To help clarify his thinking, he summoned his old Illinois friend Leonard Swett to the White House and carefully reviewed with him all the arguments for and against an emancipation proclamation, reading some of the correspondence he had received on both sides of the question. "His manner did not indicate that he wished to impress his views *upon* his hearer," Swett later recalled, "but rather to weigh and examine them for his own enlightenment *in the presence* of his hearer." So neutral was the President's presentation that Swett after the interview wrote confidently to his wife, "He will issue no proclamation emancipating negroes."

Lincoln's actions appeared to confirm Swett's prediction, for he stubbornly refused to commit his administration, even indirectly, to a policy of emancipation. On the vexed question of enlisting African-Americans in the Union armies, strongly advocated by abolitionists as a matter of principle and supported by many Northern governors as an expedient way of filling their military quotas, he remained resolutely negative. Though willing "in common humanity" to insist that African-Americans who fled to the lines of the Union armies must not "suffer for want of food, shelter, or other necessaries of life," he was not ready to enroll them in the army. He was not sure that the freedmen would fight, and he feared that guns placed in their hands would promptly fall into the hands of the Confederates. Besides, he told Browning, arming the blacks "would produce dangerous and fatal dissatisfactions in our army, and do more injury than good." Though Sumner repeatedly pressed him on this issue, arguing that by enlisting black soldiers "the rear-guard of the rebellion [would] be changed into the advance guard of the Union," Lincoln continued to resist, saying "that half the Army would lay down their arms and three other States would join the rebellion." So strongly did he feel on this matter that when a delegation of Western politicians insistently urged him to accept Negro regiments, Lincoln grew impatient and finally exclaimed: "Gentlemen, you have my decision. I have made my mind up deliberately and mean to adhere to it.... if the people are dissatisfied, I will resign and let Mr. Hamlin try it."

But at the same time, Lincoln began preparing public opinion for a proclamation of freedom if one was to be issued. Because one of the chief objections to emancipation was the widespread belief that whites and blacks could never live together harmoniously, he revived his long-cherished idea of colonizing free blacks outside the United States. On August 14 he summoned a delegation of African-American leaders to the White House in order to discuss future relations between blacks and whites. "You and we are different races," he reminded them. "We have between us a broader difference than exists between almost any other two races." Nowhere in America were blacks treated as equals of whites. "It is better for us both, therefore, to be separated," he concluded, and he urged these blacks to take the lead by accepting government aid and forming a colony in Central America. If he could find a hundred—or even fifty, or twenty-five—"able-bodied men, with a mixture of women and children," he could make a successful beginning of the colonization project. Earnestly he besought the leaders before him to consider his plan, not as "pertaining to yourselves merely, nor for your race, and ours, for the present time, but as one of the things, if successfully managed, for the good of mankind."

Lincoln's proposal was promptly and emphatically rejected by most black spokesmen. The words of the President, declared the editor of the *Pacific Appeal,* an influential black newspaper, made it "evident that he, his cabinet, and most of the people, care but little for justice to the negro. If necessary, *he* is to be crushed between the upper and nether millstone—the *pride* and *prejudice* of the North and South." Nor did it win support from white antislavery leaders. "How much better would be a manly protest against prejudice against color!—and a wise effort to give freemen homes in America!" Chase wrote in his diary. Abolitionist critics of the President's shortsighted racial views failed to note that this was the first occasion in American history when a President received a delegation of African-Americans in the White House. They also did not realize that some influential African-American leaders, like the Reverend Henry Highland Garnet, who understood that Lincoln's purpose was to save *"our emancipated brethren from being returned to their former condition of slavery,"* supported his initiative as "the most humane, and merciful movement which this or any other administration has proposed for the benefit of the enslaved."

Lincoln's critics, white or black, also did not understand that the President's plea for colonization—heartfelt and genuine as it was—was also a shrewd political move, a bit of careful preparation for an eventual emancipation proclamation. No doubt he expected his proposal to be rejected. But he knew that a plan for the voluntary removal of blacks from the country would make emancipation more palatable to the border states and also relieve Northerners of a fear that they would be inundated by a migration of free Negroes from the South.

Shortly afterward Lincoln took a further step to prepare public opinion by publishing a reply to an intemperate editorial by Horace Greeley in the *New York Tribune,* called "The Prayer of Twenty Millions." To Greeley's complaint that he was "strangely and disastrously remiss" in not proclaiming emancipation, as required by the Second Confiscation Act, and the editor's charge that it was "preposterous and futile" to try to put down the rebellion without eradicating slavery, Lincoln replied: "My paramount object in this struggle *is* to save the Union, and is *not* either to save or to destroy slavery. If I could save the Union without freeing *any* slave I would do it, and if I could save it by freeing *all* the slaves I would do it; and if I could save it by freeing some and leaving others alone I would also do that. What I do about slavery, and the colored race, I do because I believe it helps to save the Union; and what I forbear, I forbear because I do *not* believe it would help to save the Union."

Written at a time when the draft of the Emancipation Proclamation had already been completed, Lincoln's letter to Greeley later seemed puzzling, if not deceptive. But the President did not intend it to be so. He was giving assurance to the large majority of the Northern people who did not want to see the war transformed into a crusade for abolition—and at the same time he was alerting antislavery men that he was contemplating further moves against the peculiar institution. In Lincoln's mind there was no necessary disjunction between a war for the Union and a war to end slavery. Like most Republicans, he had long held the belief that if slavery could be contained it would inevitably die; a war that kept the slave states within the Union would, therefore, bring about the ultimate extinction of slavery. For this reason, saving the Union was his "paramount object." But readers aware that Lincoln always chose his words carefully should have recognized that "paramount" meant "foremost" or "principal"—not "sole."

Widely published in Northern newspapers, Lincoln's letter to Greeley received universal approval. "It [will] clear the atmosphere, and gives ground to stand on," Thurlow Weed judged. "The triumphant manner in which you have so modestly and so clearly set forth the justification of your fixed purposes," George Ashmun told the President, "dispels all doubts of the expediency and wisdom of your course." "It is the best enunciation of the best platform we have had since the Chicago Convention adjourned," wrote Senator Timothy O. Howe of Wisconsin. "Whatever is honest and earnest in the Nation will march to that music." Almost unnoted in the chorus of praise were the phrases in Lincoln's letter reaffirming his "oft-expressed *personal* wish that all men every where could be free" and promising that he would "adopt new views so fast as they shall appear to be true views."

But he could not announce new views, nor act on his personal convictions yet. The draft of his emancipation proclamation lay locked in a drawer. Every now and then he took it out, and, as he recalled later, "added or changed a line, touching it up here and there, anxiously watching the progress of events." But he needed a victory.

VI

Victory did not come. Throughout July, McClellan's huge army sweltered on the Peninsula, its commander unable to take the offensive and unwilling to withdraw. The general was furious that Halleck, and not he, had been named general-in-chief, and he spent much of his time brooding over the insult that Lincoln and Stanton had inflicted on him. He had learned of Halleck's appointment from the newspapers. He complained that Lincoln had "acted so as to make the matter as offensive as possible—he has not shown the slightest gentlemanly or friendly feeling and I cannot regard him as in any respect my friend." "I am confident that he would relieve me tomorrow if he dared do so," he told his wife. "His cowardice alone prevents it."

For his part, Lincoln had concluded that McClellan never would fight. "If by magic he could reinforce McClelland [*sic*] with 100,000 men to-day," he remarked to Browning, "he would be in an ecstacy over it, thank him for it, and tell him that he would go to Richmond tomorrow, but that when tomorrow came he would telegraph that he had certain information that the enemy had 400,000 men, and that he could not advance without reinforcements."

The President informed Halleck, now in command of all the armies, that he could keep McClellan at the head of the Army of the Potomac or remove him as he pleased. He promptly got an unwelcome insight into the character of his new general-in-chief. Halleck had arrived in Washington with a reputation as a broadly informed student of the art of war and an experienced commander of armies that had won victories from the Confederates in the West. But the general, who was called "Old Brains" because he had been a professor at West Point, had more experience with theories of warfare than with realities of military politics. When it dawned upon him that Lincoln, Stanton, and some other members of the cabinet sought to have him take the blame for removing McClellan, he shied away. "They want me to do what they are afraid to attempt," he wrote his wife. Even after Lincoln sent him down to the James to inspect the army himself, Halleck seemed incapable of exercising the authority the President had vested in him. Repeatedly Halleck urged, begged, cajoled, and ordered McClellan to move his army from the Peninsula back to the vicinity of Washington, where he would be in a position to reinforce Pope's advancing army. Always slow, McClellan had no interest in assisting his archrival and dragged his feet, while Halleck wrung his hands. "I am almost broken down," the general-in-chief complained; "I can't get General McClellan to do what I wish."

With McClellan apparently immovable on the Peninsula, the hope for Union victory rested with John Pope's Army of Virginia, now advancing south of Manassas. Lincoln closely watched Pope's progress. He was not discouraged when "Stonewall" Jackson checked his advance at Cedar Mountain on August 9, but he again urged McClellan to speed his departure from the James in order to be able to reinforce Pope. Even after Lee, rightly judging that McClellan's army no longer posed a threat to Richmond, dispatched General James Longstreet's corps to assist Jackson and threw the strength of the full Army of Northern Virginia on Pope's forces in the second battle of Bull Run, the President remained optimistic. During the first two days of the fighting (August 28–29) he spent most of his time in the telegraph office of the War Department and closely monitored the dispatches from the front. On August 30 he was relaxed enough to attend an informal supper at Stanton's house, presided over by the Secretary's "pretty wife as white and cold and motionless as marble, whose rare smiles seemed to pain her." Stanton assured the President "that nothing but foul play could lose us this battle," and after dinner at the War Department, Halleck also exuded quiet confidence. Lincoln retired, expecting to receive news of victory in the morning. His new plan for a hard, decisive war against the Confederacy was about to succeed.

But at about eight in the evening he came to Hay's room with the news he had just received: "Well, John, we are whipped again, I am afraid." Pope had been defeated and forced back to Centreville, where he reported he would "be able to hold his men." "I don't like that expression," Lincoln said, doubtless recalling dozens of similar messages he had received from McClellan. "I don't like to hear him admit that his men need 'holding.'" Though the news was all bad, Lincoln was not in despair and hoped to resume the offensive. "We must hurt this enemy before it gets away," he kept saying; "we must whip these people now."

By the next morning he had absorbed the full extent of Pope's defeat. Once again, Confederate troops threatened Washington. Once again, every hospital bed in the capital was filled with the wounded, and the streets of the city were crowded with stragglers and deserters. Though the Union soldiers, who had fought bravely, were less demoralized than after the first battle of Bull Run, their commanders were more so. Pope denounced McClellan for failing to reinforce him and urged courts-martial for Generals Fitz-John Porter and William B. Franklin. While the generals bickered, the army, in disarray, retreated to the outskirts of the capital.

Exhausted from long hours spent in the telegraph office attempting to learn the news and trying to speed reinforcements to Pope's army, Lincoln fell into a deep depression. Once again, his plans had all failed. The strenuous, aggressive war that, in theory, should have resulted in the defeat of Lee's army and the capture of the Confederate capital had aborted. With its failure disappeared Lincoln's opportunity to issue a proclamation abolishing slavery, the cause of the war. Nothing that Lincoln did, it seemed, could speed Union victory. Again, the President returned to his bleak, fatalistic philosophy. "I am almost ready to say . . . that God wills this contest, and wills that it shall not end yet," he wrote in an informal memorandum to himself. After all, God could "have either *saved* or *destroyed* the Union without a human contest," yet He allowed the war to begin. "And having begun He could give the final victory to either side any day. Yet the contest proceeds." "In the present civil war," Lincoln echoed his old doctrine of necessity, "it is quite possible that God's purpose is something different from the purpose of either party." Consequently, as he explained to an English Quaker a few weeks later, he had to believe "that He permits [the war] for some wise purpose of his own, mysterious and unknown to us."

With great reluctance the President abandoned the idea of waging an aggressive war against the Confederacy and returned to a defensive posture. With this reversal of policy he looked again to the indispensable man, McClellan. By this time Lincoln harbored no illusions about the general; he thought McClellan was the "chief alarmist and grand marplot of the Army," ridiculed his "weak, whiney, vague, and incorrect despatches," and considered his failure to reinforce Pope unpardonable. Yet he knew that McClellan was a superb organizer and an efficient engineer. And—what was equally important—he recognized that nothing but the reinstatement of McClellan would restore the shattered morale of the Army of the Potomac. "I must have McClellan to reorganize the army and bring it out of chaos," he concluded, adding, "McClellan has the army with him." Without consulting any of his advisers, and merely informing Halleck of his decision, the President asked McClellan to take command of the troops that were falling back into Washington and to defend the capital. "Mad as a March hare" over what he considered repeated snubs, McClellan accepted the assignment with reluctance and only after he had "a pretty plain talk" with Lincoln and Halleck about his new responsibilities. "I only consent to take it for my country's sake and with the humble hope that God has called me to it," he explained to his wife.

Lincoln moved without consulting his advisers because he was aware that nearly all the members of his cabinet shared his reservations about McClellan. Hearing rumors that McClellan might be recalled to command, Stanton in great excitement told Welles that he "could not and would not submit to a continuance of this state of things." When reminded that the President alone had the final say in selecting a general, he said "he knew of no particular obligations he was under to the President who had called him to a difficult position and imposed upon him labors and responsibilities which no man could carry, and which were greatly increased by fastening upon him a commander who was constantly striving to embarrass him in his administration of the [War] Department." Together with Chase, Stanton drew up a written protest, charging that McClellan was an incompetent and probably a traitor, and he tried to get other members of the cabinet to sign it. Smith agreed to do so. In the hope of getting as many cabinet signatures as possible, Stanton and Chase permitted Bates to tone down the protest to read that it was "not safe to entrust to Major General McClellan the command of any of the armies of the United States," and the Attorney General then signed. But Welles refused to join the others. He agreed that McClellan's "removal from command was demanded by public sentiment and the best interest of the country," but he thought the remonstrance "discourteous and disrespectful to the President."

Already "wrung by the bitterest anguish" over the recent defeat, Lincoln was distraught when he received the memorial, and he told the cabinet that at times "he felt almost ready to hang himself." He respected the "earnest sincerity" of his cabinet advisers who denounced the reinstatement of McClellan and in face of their unanimous opposition (Seward was absent and Blair was silent) declared he would "gladly resign his place; but he could not see who could do the work wanted as well as McClellan." "We must use what tools we have," he explained.

Lincoln expected McClellan's role to be a temporary, defensive one, but Lee, instead of resting after his victory at Second Bull Run, pushed across the Potomac and invaded Maryland. Initially the President saw the invasion as an opportunity. "We could end the war by allowing the enemy to go to Harrisburg and Philadelphia," he believed; far from his supplies and reinforcements, Lee could be readily defeated. But the approach of the Confederates had demoralized Pennsylvania state officials and the militia was almost on the point of mutiny. Halleck insisted that only McClellan could turn back the invasion. Lincoln agreed reluctantly to restoring McClellan to permanent command, placing full responsibility on Halleck. "I could not have done it," the President explained to Welles, "for I can never feel confident that he will do anything."

Despite his reservations, Lincoln during the next two weeks did all he could to strengthen McClellan's army. To prevent the Army of the Potomac from being dispersed, he fended off urgent requests for aid from local authorities in the path of the Confederate invasion. He had to turn aside a plea from the excitable governor of Pennsylvania for 80,000 troops, reminding Curtin: "We have not ... eighty thousand disciplined troops, properly so called, this side of the mountains." He had also to convince panic-stricken mayors from Harrisburg, Philadelphia, and Baltimore that the best way to protect their cities was to keep the Union troops together in pursuit of Lee's army.

The Confederate invasion of Maryland, coming so close after Lee's smashing victory at Second Bull Run, fanned criticism of the President and his conduct of the war. Recent events convinced George Templeton Strong that Lincoln, though an "honest old codger," was simply "unequal to his place." Old friends like Samuel Galloway of Ohio warned the President that "this changing from McClellan to Pope, and from Pope to McClellan, creates distrust and uncertainty." Other critics were blunter. From Chicago the Reverend Robert Laird Collier, a Methodist minister, issued a call for the moral heroism that the President obviously lacked: "Tale-telling and jesting illy suit the hour and become the man in whose hands the destiny of a great nation is trembling. . . . Earnestness, unmixed and terrible, is the demand alike of the crisis and the people."

Demands rose for a complete reorganization of the administration. Kentucky Senator Garrett Davis urged the President to fire both Stanton and Chase, "the most sinister of all the cabinet." Others demanded that Lincoln oust McClellan. Chase condemned the President's "humiliating submissiveness" to the general and lamented that Lincoln, for all his "true, unselfish patriotism," had "yielded so much to Border State and negrophobic counsels that he now finds it difficult to arrest his own descent towards the most fatal concessions." Massachusetts Governor Andrew began trying "if possible to save the Prest. from the infamy of ruining his country," and he summoned a conference of his fellow war governors at Altoona, Pennsylvania, in late September.

VII

Caught in a cross fire, Lincoln had to reconsider his emancipation policy as well as his military strategy. The logical parallel to reinstating McClellan to fight a limited, defensive war waged by professional armies was a return to his inaugural pledge not to interfere with slavery within the states. Many of his oldest and most loyal supporters urged exactly this policy, warning that a more radical policy would surely cost the Republicans support in the fall congressional elections. From Illinois, Browning, who was campaigning for the Republican candidates in that state, entreated him not to listen to the "few very radical and extreme men who can think, nor talk, nor dream of any thing but the negro." If Lincoln held to a moderate course, Browning continued, he would have behind him not merely the members of his own party but the Democrats, who "are for you almost to a man—quite as near a unit in your support as the Republicans."

More than once in the days after McClellan's return to command, Lincoln seemed to revert to this policy. On September 13 when a delegation of Chicago Christians representing all denominations urged him to issue an emancipation order, he reminded them of the practical difficulties in the way of any attempt to free the slaves. He noted that the recent Confiscation Act had not "caused a single slave to come over to us." "What *good* would a proclamation of emancipation from me do, especially as we are now situated?" he asked. "I do not want to issue a document that the whole world will see must necessarily be inoperative, like the Pope's bull against the comet!"

But Lincoln was under increasing pressure to act. His call for additional volunteers had met a slow response, and several of the Northern governors bluntly declared that they could not meet their quotas unless the President moved against slavery. The approaching conference of Northern war governors would almost certainly demand an emancipation proclamation. He also had to take seriously the insistent reports that European powers were close to recognizing the Confederacy and would surely act unless the United States government took a stand against slavery.

Always reluctant to be out in front of public opinion, always hesitant to assume positions from which there could be no retreat, Lincoln deliberated long before making a hard choice. Ultimately he chose to leave the decision to a Higher Power. To the Chicago Christians who urged him to issue a proclamation of emancipation, he pledged: "It is my earnest desire to know the will of Providence in this matter. *And if I can learn what it is I will do it!*" Seeking a sign, he closely monitored the news of Lee's invasion of Maryland and the reports from McClellan's pursuing army. As he told the cabinet later, he "made a vow, a covenant, that if God gave us the victory in the approaching battle, he would consider it an indication of Divine will, and that it was his duty to move forward in the cause of emancipation."

On September 17, McClellan's victory at Antietam, though not the overwhelming success Lincoln had hoped for, gave the President the omen he had sought. Turning back to his long-delayed proclamation of emancipation, Lincoln, as he said, "fixed it up a little" over the weekend, and called the cabinet together on September 22 to hear it. Now that the decision was made, he was more relaxed and at home with himself than he had been for weeks. Partly, no doubt, to break the ice in the cabinet meeting but chiefly because he wanted others to share his good humor, he began by reading a selection titled "High-Handed Outrage at Utica" from a new book the humorist Artemus Ward had sent him. This bit of clownery about "a big burly feller" from that "trooly grate sitty" who saw a display of wax figures of the apostles at the Last Supper and caved in the head of the false apostle to prove "that Judas Iscarrot can't show hisself in Utiky with impunerty by a darn site," the President found very funny, and, except for the irascible Stanton, the other heads of departments also enjoyed it—or pretended to.

The President then turned to business, reminding the cabinet of their earlier discussion of emancipation and of the reasons the proclamation had been delayed. "I think the time has come now," he told them. "I wish it were a better time. I wish that we were in a better condition." But now he could redeem the promise he had made to himself and, he said, hesitating a little, to his Maker. He did not seek their advice "about the main matter," for that, he explained, he had determined for himself, but he was willing to accept criticisms of any expressions used or "any other minor matter."

The document the President presented for cabinet consideration lacked the memorable rhetoric of his most notable utterances. The proclamation, in the words of the atrabilious Gurowski, was "written in the meanest and the most dry routine style; not a word to evoke a generous thrill, not a word reflecting the warm and lofty . . . feelings of . . . the people." Totally absent was any reference to the barbarism of slavery, nor was morality invoked as a reason for striking it down. Instead, Lincoln cited as his authority for acting against slavery his powers as "President of the United States of America, and Commander-in-chief of the Army and Navy thereof," and the provisions of both the First and Second Confiscation Acts. His sole announced purpose was "the object of practically restoring the constitutional relation between the United States, and each of the states, and the people thereof." The President remained reluctant, even at this late hour, to offer unqualified freedom to the slaves. He promised to continue to press for compensated emancipation and for the colonization of African-Americans outside the country. Yet, for all his hesitation, Lincoln announced at the end that on January 1, 1863, "all persons held as slaves" within any state or part of a state still in rebellion would be "then, thenceforward, and forever free."

In presenting the Emancipation Proclamation to the cabinet, Lincoln made it clear that he was as uncertain about its expediency as he was doubtful of its success. He was unsure how his new policy would be received. "I know very well that many others might, in this matter, as in others, do better than I can," he told the cabinet; "and if I were satisfied that the public confidence was more fully possessed by any one of them than by me, and knew of any Constitutional way in which he could be put in my place, he should have it. I would gladly yield it to him." But since that was not possible, he concluded, "I must do the best I can, and bear the responsibility of taking the course which I feel I ought to take."

In the discussion that followed, Seward proposed two minor verbal alterations in the document. Ponderously Chase offered: "The Proclamation does not, indeed, mark out exactly the course I should myself prefer. But I am ready to take it just as it is written, and to stand by it with all my heart." Only Blair expressed dissent, not because he opposed emancipation but because he feared the proclamation would have a bad influence on the border states and the army and that it might strengthen the Democrats in the fall congressional elections. Lincoln said that he had considered the first of these dangers and discounted it; as for the second, he said, it "had not much weight with him." Accordingly the document was handed to the Secretary of State to be copied and officially published.

Two days later, responding to serenaders who came to the White House in celebration of the Emancipation Proclamation, the President revealed that he still felt uncertain about his action. "I can only trust in God I have made no mistake," he told the crowd. "It is now for the country and the world to pass judgment on it. . . . I will say no more upon this subject." He concluded lamely, "In my position I am environed with difficulties."

CHAPTER FOURTEEN

A Pumpkin in Each End of My Bag

———◆———

In time, Lincoln came to think of the Emancipation Proclamation as the crowning achievement of his administration. It was, he told his old Kentucky friend Joshua F. Speed a measure that would ensure his fame by linking "his name with something that would resound to the interest of his fellow man." But in the months immediately following the preliminary proclamation, he was much less sanguine. The proclamation threatened to break up the tenuous coalition of Republicans, War Democrats, and border-state leaders that he had so carefully been building since the outbreak of the war. At the same time, it strengthened the peace element in the Democratic party, and it seemed likely to provoke a mutiny in the army. During the hundred days after he issued the preliminary proclamation, Lincoln's leadership was more seriously threatened than at any other time, and it was not clear that his administration could survive the repeated crises that it faced.

I

The initial Northern responses to the Emancipation Proclamation were predictable. Antislavery men were jubilant. "God bless Abraham Lincoln," exclaimed Horace Greeley's *New York Tribune.* The President, announced Joseph Medill's *Chicago Tribune,* had promulgated "the grandest proclamation ever issued by man." In every major city throughout the North there were huge rallies to celebrate the proclamation, marked by bonfires, parades with torches and transparencies, and, inevitably, fountains of oratory.

Scores of letters of commendation poured into the President's office.

"God bless you for the word you have spoken!" wrote three correspondents from Erie, Pennsylvania. "All good men upon the earth will glorify you, and all the angels in Heaven will hold jubilee." "The virtuous, the reflecting, the intelligently patriotic . . . as one man hail your edict with delight," the veteran Pennsylvania abolitionist J. M. McKim told the President, "and [they] bless and thank God that he put it in your heart to issue it." A Baltimorean took an odd way of showing his enthusiasm for the proclamation by sending the President half a dozen hams.

Nearly every notable man of letters, especially those from New England, voiced approval of the proclamation. John Greenleaf Whittier, William Cullen Bryant, and James Russell Lowell all wrote eloquently in its praise. Hitherto cool toward Lincoln, Ralph Waldo Emerson was now prepared to forget "all that we thought shortcomings, every mistake, every delay," because the President had "been permitted to do more for America than any other American man."

For the moment, Lincoln's critics within his own party were silenced. Thaddeus Stevens and Benjamin F. Wade, both of whom had scathingly attacked Lincoln for his incompetence and for his slowness to move against slavery, had nothing to say. Charles Sumner, locked in a close contest in Massachusetts for reelection to the Senate, saw that the proclamation would help erase the doubts that his abolitionist supporters continued to feel toward Lincoln and jubilantly announced that he stood "with the loyal multitudes of the North, firmly and sincerely by the side of the President." The governors of the Northern states who gathered at Altoona in the hope of pushing Lincoln to prosecute the war more vigorously, found that the President had preempted their ground, and somewhat lamely their leaders trooped down to Washington to congratulate the President on his proclamation "as a measure of justice and sound policy."

No doubt such tributes were gratifying to a President who had hitherto received little public praise, but Lincoln was too much of a realist to overestimate their importance. "Commendation in newspapers and by distinguished individuals is all that a vain man could wish," he reported to Hannibal Hamlin, but he noted that subscriptions to government securities had fallen off and volunteering had dropped. "The North responds to the proclamation sufficiently in breath," he told the Vice President, "but breath alone kills no rebels."

In the South, so far as the President could determine, the reaction to the Emancipation Proclamation was altogether negative. Jefferson Davis denounced it as an attempt to stir up servile insurrection and called it a further reason why the Confederacy must fight for its independence. On Southern Unionism the proclamation had a chilling effect. In Tennessee, Emerson Etheridge discovered in Lincoln's proclamation "treachery to the Union men of the South," and Thomas A. R. Nelson, one of the most vigorous opponents of secession in eastern Tennessee, attacked "the atrocity and barbarism of Mr. Lincoln's proclamation." Lincoln could learn little of its impact on

African-Americans in the South; not until the war was over did they dare admit that they had learned of impending emancipation through the grapevine and were preparing to escape to freedom at the first opportunity.

Even more disappointing was the initial foreign reaction to the proclamation, for one of Lincoln's purposes had been to forestall threatened moves by Great Britain and France toward the recognition of the Confederacy. Eventually, immense throngs in London, Birmingham, and other British cities would rally to celebrate Lincoln's declaration of freedom and an outraged public opinion would make it impossible for any British government to intervene on behalf of the slaveholding Confederacy, but the immediate foreign response was negative. Many were sure that the proclamation would be ineffective, since it applied only to slaves beyond the reach of Union arms while doing nothing to free those behind Union lines. Others anticipated that it would incite a servile war; Lord John Russell, the British foreign minister, predicted "acts of plunder, of incendiarism, and of revenge." As Seward had warned, many Europeans feared that emancipation might interfere with the cotton supply so necessary for British and French mills.

Even in the North, once the initial euphoria had abated, the Emancipation Proclamation came under skeptical scrutiny. Abolitionists noted that Lincoln had only made a promise of freedom and that, apart from being conditional, his promise could be withdrawn before January 1. A few even claimed that the proclamation postponed emancipation as required by the Second Confiscation Act. Recovering from his initial enthusiasm, Greeley lamented that Lincoln exempted from his decree most of Louisiana and Tennessee, two states which had "more than One Hundred Thousand of their citizens in arms to destroy the Union." Similarly, William Lloyd Garrison regretted that the proclamation left "slavery, as a system . . . , still to exist in all the so-called loyal Slave States."

More troubling to the President was the disaffection the proclamation caused his moderate supporters. Some border-state Unionists believed that his action would undermine the loyalty of Maryland, Kentucky, and Missouri. Conservative Republicans thought the proclamation unconstitutional and unwise. Orville H. Browning, one of Lincoln's oldest friends and one of the few in Washington in whom he had hitherto confided freely, was so offended by it that he avoided discussing public issues with the President. Even some of the President's cabinet advisers regretted his proclamation. Seward loyally supported the President once he had made his decision, but he continued to think that the emancipation decree was both unnecessary and ineffective. Montgomery Blair muffled his criticisms, but his sister accurately captured the feelings of the Blair clan when she called the proclamation "a mistake . . . a paper pronunciamento and of no practical result." Less significant was the muted opposition of Secretary of the Interior Caleb B. Smith, whose unhappiness with Lincoln's policies, together with ill health, caused him to resign in November.

From the start many Democrats were bitterly opposed to the proclamation. The *New York World* declared that Lincoln was now "adrift on a current of radical fanaticism." Terming the proclamation a violation of both the Constitution and the law of nations, the *New York Evening Express* called it "an act of Revolution," which would render "the restoration of the old Constitution and Union impossible," while the *New York Journal of Commerce* predicted that the proclamation would "lead to . . . a continuation of the war, in a dark future, in which the end is beyond our vision."

Much of the dissatisfaction with the Emancipation Proclamation was muted, because the President on September 24 issued another proclamation, which suspended the privilege of the writ of habeas corpus throughout the country and authorized the arbitrary arrest of any person "guilty of any disloyal practice, affording aid and comfort to Rebels against the authority of the United States." To the President this seemed such a routine matter that he did not even mention it to the cabinet. Stanton, as authorized by the Militia Act of July 17, 1862, had been issuing stringent orders to suppress criticism of the newly instituted draft; enforced by petty officials all across the country, these regulations had resulted in hundreds of cases of violation of civil liberties, when civilians were subjected to arbitrary, and often quite unreasonable, arrests. Lincoln's proclamation was simply designed to codify these War Department rules, but Democrats like Senator James A. Bayard of Delaware read it to mean that the President was "declaring himself a Dictator, (for that and nothing less it does)." Whatever Lincoln's intent, the new proclamation had a chilling effect on public dissent. Editors feared that they might be locked up in Fort Lafayette or in the Old Capitol Prison in Washington if they voiced their criticisms too freely, and even writers of private letters began to guard their language.

II

However muffled, the voice of the people found expression in the 1862 fall elections for governors and congressmen, in which the President's party suffered major reverses. The outcome was hardly surprising to Lincoln. After all, he had been elected by a minority of the voters in 1860, and many of the Republican members of Congress chosen that year owed their seats to divisions among their opponents. As the war dragged on, the strength of the Democrats increased. Under Lincoln's leadership, Union armies seemed on occasion to be successful but never victorious. The cost of the war in lives and suffering was appalling, and the President's call for 600,000 more men suggested that the endless drain was far from over. Meanwhile the country's finances were in perilous shape, and the decision to resort to paper currency appeared to be an act of desperation.

Throughout the early months of 1862 the President had received repeated warnings that his party was in trouble, and he anticipated losses in the fall elections, when, as he wryly predicted to Carl Schurz, Democrats would fail to support his administration because it was too radical and Republicans because it was not radical enough.

Alarmed by the prospect, influential Republicans urged him to use his influence to strengthen the party. "If only the President could be induced to employ his vast patronage to sustain his friends," John W. Forney, a Pennsylvania editor, lamented, "this calamity [of Democratic victory] might be averted." To the chagrin of party leaders, he did nothing. He even refused to endorse his old friend Owen Lovejoy, who was in a fierce battle for reelection in his Illinois district. During the summer of 1862 the President was, of course, preoccupied with directing a vast military operation—but at no other time in Lincoln's life was he too busy for political management, at which he was so skilled. He held aloof from the congressional contests because there was not much he could do to influence their outcome. As a number of other chief executives have discovered, presidential coattails are of little use in off-year congressional elections. In any case, Lincoln realized that he was not a popular President. Indeed, he told the cabinet members in September, "I believe that I have not so much of the confidence of the people as I had some time since."

The President also understood that intervention in a local or state race might involve him in bitter factional quarrels within his own party. In New York, for example, as able Governor E. D. Morgan was about to finish his term, Seward and Thurlow Weed sought to broaden the Republican party into a Union party and favored nominating the stalwart War Democrat General John A. Dix for governor. Constantly suspicious of Seward's conservatism and intent on pushing the antislavery agenda of the more radical wing of the Republican party, Horace Greeley successfully pressed for the nomination of the earnest abolitionist General James S. Wadsworth. The contest weakened both Republican factions, and Wadsworth entered the fall campaign crippled by disaffection among Republican voters. To oppose him, New York Democrats nominated their ablest and most thoughtful spokesman, Horatio Seymour.

In his home state of Illinois the President did interfere, though less by design than by inadvertence. Illinois Republicans, alarmed earlier in the year by the narrowness of their success in defeating a Democratic new state constitution, joined a Union fusion movement, in which, they said, "party lines and partisan feelings should be swallowed up in patriotism." As part of this strategy they redrew the boundaries of the state's congressional districts. Sangamon, Lincoln's home county, always staunchly Democratic, was now linked with three other counties thought to be predictably Republican. The new district was expected to elect David Davis. But before Davis was nominated, Lincoln let it be known that he intended to appoint his old friend to a vacancy on the United States Supreme Court, a post that Davis coveted. Illinois Republicans were obliged to fall back on Leonard Swett, who, like Davis, had worked for Lincoln's nomination. To oppose Swett the Democrats named John Todd Stuart, Lincoln's first law partner.

Most congressional and gubernatorial nominations were made before Lincoln issued the preliminary Emancipation Proclamation, but inevitably it became a key issue in all the Northern elections. In New England and in the states of the upper Northwest, the proclamation strengthened the Republican party, bringing back the support of disaffected abolitionists. "It is," wrote one Vermonter, "a document for an open sea and plain sailing." But elsewhere, as the President had anticipated, the result was decidedly negative. As a correspondent wrote Secretary Chase, Democrats throughout the North now howled, "I told you so[;] can't you see this is an Abolition war and nothing else."

Expecting to lose Republican votes because of the emancipation issue, Lincoln was evidently surprised by the Democrats' effective use of a second issue, the suspension of the writ of habeas corpus announced in his proclamation of September 24. Democrats seized on this proclamation as evidence that the President sought to make himself a dictator. The federal government, claimed the Democratic *Illinois State Register,* was "seeking to inaugurate a reign of terror in the loyal states by military arrests . . . of citizens, without a trial, to browbeat all opposition by villainous and false charges of disloyalty against whole classes of patriotic citizens, to destroy all constitutional guaranties [sic] of free speech, a free press, and the writ of 'habeas corpus.' " This became the main theme of the Democratic campaign in New York when Horatio Seymour pledged that if arbitrary arrests continued after his election he would resist "even if the streets be made to run red with blood." In Illinois, John Todd Stuart made effective use of the fear inspired by the proclamation to avoid debating his opponent, Swett. Stuart claimed that if either man in the course of a debate too freely expressed what he thought or felt, he might be arrested.

As the October and November elections approached, the President looked to the outcome with great anxiety. Visitors thought he seemed "literally bending under the weight of his burdens." "His introverted look and his half-staggering gait," a Chicago woman wrote, "were like those of a man walking in sleep," and his face "revealed the ravages which care, anxiety, and overwork had wrought." Ordinarily the master of his emotions, he let his self-control slip at times during these trying weeks. When Thomas H. Clay, Henry Clay's son, asked, "as a favor," that a particular army division be reassigned to Kentucky for rest and relaxation, Lincoln snapped back a refusal: "I sincerely wish war was an easier and pleasanter business than it is; but it does not admit of holy-days."

His anxieties were warranted. When the votes were tallied, the President learned that the voters had administered to him and his party a severe rebuff. In state after state that had gone Republican in 1860, Democrats made huge gains: New York, Pennsylvania, Ohio, Indiana, and Illinois. New Jersey, which divided its electoral vote in 1860, now went Democratic. The Wisconsin delegation, formerly solidly Republican, was split. Major Republican leaders in the House of Representatives, including Roscoe Conkling of New

York, John A. Bingham of Ohio, and even the Speaker, Galusha A. Grow of Pennsylvania, went down to defeat. The Democrats carried the President's home district in Illinois, electing Stuart over Swett. The Republican party retained control of the new House of Representatives in the Thirty-eighth Congress, which would not meet until December 1863, but its majority would be drastically reduced. In state elections New Jersey elected Joel Parker, an able Democrat, as governor. And, most serious of all from the point of view of the Lincoln administration, Seymour was chosen governor of New York. As the *New York Times* concluded, the elections, taken as a whole, amounted to a "vote of want of confidence" in the President.

Disgruntled Republicans deluged the President with analyses of their defeats. In Illinois, Republican losses were attributed to an ill-timed order of Secretary Stanton, issued just days before the Emancipation Proclamation, for the resettlement of "contrabands" temporarily housed in Cairo on farms throughout the state; Democrats charged the administration was attempting to "Africanize" Illinois. Many Republicans found it comforting to believe that the Democrats won because so many Republicans of voting age were in the armies, and Lincoln himself argued that "the democrats were left in a majority by our friends going to the war." But there was little evidence to support this conclusion, since volunteering in Democratic counties was as heavy as in Republican counties.

Others, like the astute New York lawyer David Dudley Field, attributed the outcome to the administration's policy of arbitrary arrests. "There was nobody to pronounce them legal," he told the President, "nobody to consider them expedient, even if they had been legal." Unless the administration abandoned the practice of arresting citizens without legal process, he warned, "there is every reason to fear that you will be unable, successfully, to carry on the Government." Lincoln did not publicly admit that violations of civil liberties were responsible for Republican defeats, but the President, who had given little personal attention to the issue of arbitrary arrests even during the worst excesses of 1862, kept a closer eye on them in the following months. Without abandoning or diminishing his claim to extraordinary authority under the war powers, he began to formulate more careful rationalizations for the use of that authority. He told a visitor who was in touch with influential New York Democrats that he would arrange "that by imperceptible (comparatively) degrees, perhaps, military law [which came into effect following the suspension of habeas corpus] might be made to relent." On November 22 the War Department ordered the release of most prisoners charged with discouraging enlistment or other disloyal conduct.

Most blamed Republican defeats on what Lincoln called "the ill-success of the war." That failure they attributed to the President. Carl Schurz scolded the Lincoln administration for admitting "its professed opponents to its counsels. It placed the Army, now a great power in this Republic, into the hands of its enemy's." Even more bluntly a New Yorker charged that Lincoln's "weakness, irresolution, and want of moral courage," which had kept traitors like McClellan and Buell in command, was responsible for the "disgraceful" outcome of the elections.

Many prominent Republican politicians agreed. Immediately after the elections several Pennsylvania congressmen came to the White House to report the outcome in their districts, and all blamed "the general tardiness in military movements," for which they held McClellan and Buell responsible. Since Lincoln insisted on retaining these generals in command, J. K. Moorhead, the representative from the Pittsburgh district, told him candidly, "It was not your fault that we were not all beaten." Some Pennsylvania Republican leaders, he continued, "would be glad to hear some morning that you had been found hanging from the post of a lamp at the door of the White House."

Deeply depressed, the President responded in a subdued voice: "You need not be surprised to find that that suggestion has been executed any morning. The violent preliminaries to such an event would not surprise me."

III

If Lincoln seriously feared violence, it was not from disappointed Republican politicians but from the army. Ordinary soldiers and noncommissioned officers of the Union armies were nearly all loyal supporters of the government, but among officers there was talk of a dictator to oust the marplots in the administration, like Stanton and Halleck, who allegedly failed to support the generals.

Lincoln received few reports of such a mutinous spirit in the Western armies. He knew he could count on General U. S. Grant, in command of the Army of the Mississippi. Though a former Democrat, Grant expressed no interest in politics and no reservations about the President's emancipation policies; instead, he concentrated his energies on defeating the Confederates. The battle of Corinth, Mississippi, on October 3–4, in which federal troops from his army, under the immediate command of General W. S. Rosecrans, repelled an attacking Confederate force, gave the President one of the few clear-cut Union victories in the last quarter of 1862.

Nor did Lincoln doubt the loyalty of General Buell, who commanded the Army of the Ohio in central Tennessee. But he was often exasperated with that general, who was nearly as slow as McClellan, and he fumed when Buell resolutely ignored directives to invade mountainous eastern Tennessee, where Union loyalists lived under a Confederate reign of terror, and insisted on remaining in the Nashville region. In the fall his unhappiness increased after two Confederate armies, under Braxton Bragg and Edmund Kirby-Smith, launched an invasion of Kentucky, timed to coincide with Lee's raid into Maryland, and forced Buell to retreat to Louisville. His patience exhausted, Lincoln gave General George H. Thomas the command of the army unless, at the time Thomas received his orders, Buell was actually preparing to fight. The indecisive battle of Perryville, Kentucky (October 8, 1862) temporarily saved Buell from removal.

But the officer corps of the Army of the Potomac was another matter. The principal generals and most of the headquarters staff were Democrats, and many felt no special loyalty to a Republican President who seemed bent on changing the nature and scope of the war. These high-ranking officers had developed an intense loyalty to their commander, and they generally shared McClellan's view that warfare was for professionals and that civilian property —including slaves—should not be touched by the armies. Most of them attributed McClellan's failure on the Peninsula to ill-advised and politically motivated meddling by civilian authorities. Pope's humiliating defeat at the second battle of Bull Run and Lincoln's vacillation over restoring McClellan to command strengthened their contempt for the President. Just before the battle of Antietam members of McClellan's staff were reported to have seriously discussed "a plan to countermarch to Washington and intimidate the President," so that he would abandon his attempt to interfere with slavery and the war could be ended. The President's Emancipation Proclamation, reported General Fitz-John Porter, "was ridiculed in the army—causing disgust, discontent, and expressions of disloyalty to the views of the administration, amounting . . . to insubordination." Among the "Potomac Army clique," General Pope reported, there was open talk "of Lincoln's weakness and the necessity of replacing him by some stronger man."

After the battle of Antietam, Lincoln moved with great delicacy to determine whether McClellan was involved in these schemes. The general, for his part, was equally curious whether he still held the President's confidence. Because Lincoln sent him only meager congratulations after the battle of Antietam, which McClellan considered "a masterpiece of [military] art," the general feared the President had fallen under the sway of his opponents. Consequently he sent Allan Pinkerton, his chief of intelligence, who was presumably an expert in ferreting out information, to the White House. In Pinkerton's long interview with the President on September 22—the day the Emancipation Proclamation was issued, though that document was never mentioned—McClellan was using his chief detective to spy on the President, and the President was using the detective to spy on his commanding general.

From Pinkerton, Lincoln learned a great deal more than the detective thought he was revealing. Employing the techniques for cross-examining a witness he had perfected during his years at the bar, he expressed himself, so Pinkerton wrote McClellan, as humbly "desirous of knowing some things which he supposed from the pressure on your mind, you had not advised him on or that you considered was of minor importance, not sufficiently worthy of notice for you to send to him." Then, using language so deferential that Pinkerton did not realize he was being grilled, the President asked a series of telling questions: Why had McClellan failed to come to the rescue of the Union garrison at Harpers Ferry, which had been forced to surrender to Stonewall Jackson just before Antietam? What was the relative strength of the Union and Confederate forces at Antietam? (He appeared to accept McClellan's and Pinkerton's preposterous estimate that the Confederates had 140,000 men, when in fact Lee's effective troops numbered about 52,000.) Why did the Union army not renew the attack the day after the battle? How were the Confederates able to slip back unhindered across the Potomac River?

Lincoln impressed the detective as entirely friendly toward McClellan. He was not at all suspicious when the President used uncharacteristically effusive language to express the nation's "deep debt of gratitude" to McClellan for his "great and decisive victories" at South Mountain and Antietam. Lincoln told him he had no doubt that McClellan had fought the battle of Antietam skillfully—"much more so than any General he knew of could have done"—and said that he was "highly pleased and gratified with all you had done." "I am rather prejudiced against him," Pinkerton concluded his report, "but I must confess that he impresses me more at this interview with his honesty towards you and his desire to do you justice than he has ever done before."

The information Lincoln wormed out of Pinkerton convinced the President that Antietam had not been a great victory but a lost opportunity, squandered by the high command of the Army of the Potomac. While he did not get any evidence from Pinkerton that McClellan was disloyal, his suspicions grew as the detective ingenuously poured out a story of wasted chances. He came to suspect that the leaders of the Army of the Potomac had only a halfhearted commitment to crushing the Confederacy.

There was little reliable evidence to justify this belief, but in these days after the battle of Antietam and the issuing of the Emancipation Proclamation, Lincoln was in a highly anxious state, and he magnified barroom boasting and military gossip about the need for a dictator into a real threat. He resolved to end it. Just a few days after his interview with Pinkerton, the President learned that Major John J. Key, of Halleck's staff, had been reported as saying that the Union army had not "bagged" the Confederates after Antietam because "that is not the game." "The object is that neither army shall get much advantage of the other," Key went on, "that both shall be kept in the field till they are exhausted, when we will make a compromise and save slavery."

Summoning Key to the White House on September 27, the President held an impromptu court-martial, heard the evidence against the major, ruled that it was "wholly inadmissible for any gentleman holding a military commission from the United States to utter such sentiments," and ordered him dismissed "forthwith" from the army. If there ever had been a "game" among Union men not to take advantage of victories over the Confederates, the President stated grimly, "it was his object to break up that game."

Lincoln terminated Key's promising military career with reluctance, but he thought it necessary to give "an example and a warning" to "a class of officers in the army, not very inconsiderable in numbers." He feared Key's silly, treasonable remarks were "staff talk and I wanted an example." In all probability he knew that John J. Key's brother was Thomas M. Key, acting judge advocate on McClellan's staff and one of the general's most trusted political advisers.

Lincoln's suspicion that McClellan was disloyal had no basis, but he was correct in thinking that the general did not approve of his policies. McClellan was opposed to both the Emancipation Proclamation, which he privately labeled "infamous," and the suspension of habeas corpus. He asked William H. Aspinwall, a political adviser in New York, what he ought to say about these measures, which meant "inaugurating servile war, emancipating the slaves, and at one stroke of the pen changing our free institutions into a despotism." Aspinwall replied that the general was under no obligation to make any public statement, since he was under oath to obey his commander-in-chief. When the Blair family reminded him of what had happened to John Key, McClellan gave up any plan of public opposition to the proclamations.

Determined to test the stories about disloyalty in McClellan's entourage, the President, with almost no notice, slipped out of Washington on October 1 to visit the sites of the recent battles and to inspect the army. He was late in arriving at the headquarters of McClellan's army, and some soldiers were disappointed to see the President of the United States driving up in "a common ambulance, with his long legs doubled up so that his knees almost struck his chin, and grinning out of the windows like a baboon." "Mr. Lincoln," concluded one, "not only is the ugliest man I ever saw, but the most uncouth and gawky in his manners and appearance." Taking the President out to the Antietam battlefield, McClellan tried to explain what had taken place on September 17, but Lincoln turned away abruptly and returned to camp. He spent the night in a tent adjacent to McClellan's.

At daybreak the next day the President woke up O. M. Hatch, a Springfield neighbor who accompanied him on this trip, and walked with him to a high point from which almost the entire army camp could be seen. Leaning toward his friend, Lincoln almost whispered: "Hatch—Hatch, what is all this?" "Why, Mr. Lincoln," replied Hatch, "this is the Army of the Potomac." After a moment's pause the President straightened up and said in a louder voice: "No, Hatch, no. This is *General McClellan's body-guard.*"

Later Lincoln, mounted on a spirited coal black horse, reviewed the troops, but they received from him none of the cordial greetings and salutes to which they were accustomed. Instead, he rode the lines at a quick trot, apparently taking little notice of the men and offering, one disgruntled officer related, "not a word of approval, not even a smile of approbation." After the review of Burnside's corps, ambulances took him and his party the two or three miles to Fitz-John Porter's corps, and along the way he asked Ward Hill Lamon to sing his favorite "little sad song," a ballad called "Twenty Years Ago." Afterward, to break the gloomy mood, Lamon also sang "two or three little comic things," including a piece called "Picayune Butler." The episode was one Lincoln came to regret, for opponents later charged that he had desecrated the battlefield by singing ribald songs over the graves of the Union dead.

During the visit Lincoln managed to conceal his negative view of McClellan, and the general hid his low opinion of the President. McClellan reported to his wife that the President was "very kind personally" and "very affable," and that he said "he was convinced I was the best general in the country." Shortly afterward McClellan attempted to reciprocate the compliment by issuing a general order to his troops, announcing, for the first time, that the President had issued an Emancipation Proclamation and that it was the duty of good soldiers to obey their country's laws. He took care to see that a copy of this document reached the President himself.

Lincoln returned to Washington generally pleased with his visit. "I am now stronger with the Army of the Potomac than McClellan," he told a friend. The troops that had been most resentful when he named Pope to command recognized that he had tried to rectify his mistake by restoring McClellan to command. During the recent campaign they saw that the President and the War Department gave McClellan everything that he asked for, but he had thrown away his chance to win a decisive battle and had lost the opportunity to push Lee's army into the Potomac. "The supremacy of the civil power has been restored," he rejoiced, "and the Executive is again master of the situation."

Now confident that he could remove McClellan without causing a mutiny, the President nevertheless delayed. While at Antietam he had warned the general against "over-cautiousness," and he thought he had McClellan's promise to pursue Lee's army into Virginia. He wanted to give the general one more chance. Lincoln, as Nicolay noted scornfully, habitually indulged McClellan "in his whims and complaints and shortcomings as a mother would indulge her baby."

But McClellan began giving arguments why he could not advance. He exhausted the President's patience with plaintive reports that his troops were worn out and his supplies depleted. Exasperated, Lincoln noted that McClellan delayed for nineteen days before putting a man across the Potomac and that it took nine more days to bring the whole army across. While his huge army lay quietly north of the Potomac, "Jeb" Stuart led a daring Confederate cavalry raid into Maryland and Pennsylvania, where he destroyed military stores, machine shops, and trains at Chambersburg, and returned almost unscathed. The raid had no special military importance, but because it occurred just a few days before the elections, it was especially vexatious and embarrassing. Lincoln, as Nicolay reported, "well-nigh lost his temper over it," but once again he restrained himself.

In the months after Antietam and Perryville the President exhibited a growing mastery of military affairs. Getting little help from Halleck, who responded to inquiries by scratching his elbows and taking all sides of every question, Lincoln had to apply his good common sense to the problems of the army. On his trip to Antietam he had been impressed by the number of stragglers from the Union army, and he began making notes on the enormous number of soldiers who were absent from their regiments. Some were deserters, but more had furloughs. "You won't find a city . . . , a town, or a village, where soldiers and officers on furlough are not plenty as blackberries," he complained to some visitors in early November. "To fill up the army is like undertaking to shovel fleas. You take up a shovelful"—and he made a comical gesture—"but before you can dump them anywhere they are gone."

The root of this problem, he began to realize, was that neither the generals nor the people had recognized that they were at war and that it would take hard, tough fighting to win it. "They have got the idea into their heads that we are going to get out of this fix, somehow, by strategy!" he exclaimed. "That's the word—strategy! General McClellan thinks he is going to whip the rebels by strategy; and the army has got the same notion." It was to this belief in strategy that he attributed both Buell's leisurely pursuit of Bragg into Tennessee after the battle of Perryville and McClellan's slowness to move against Lee after Antietam.

Leaving Halleck to urge Buell on, Lincoln devoted himself to getting McClellan to move, and he began sending the general pointed, short messages that amounted, as Nicolay said, to "poking sharp sticks under little Mac's ribs." Resenting "the mean and dirty character of the dispatches" he received from Washington, McClellan told his wife, "There never was a truer epithet applied to a certain individual than that of the 'Gorilla.'"

The breaking point came in late October. Facing a bitterly contested election, the Republican governors and representatives from Ohio, Indiana, and Illinois demanded that Lincoln remove Buell, whose Army of the Ohio was largely recruited from those states. When that general, oblivious to political reality and apparently indifferent to the wishes of his military superiors in Washington, announced that he was not going into eastern Tennessee, where Unionists were clamoring for protection, but was going to make his winter quarters in the comfortable city of Nashville, even the President could no longer defend him. On October 24, Buell was relieved, and a few days later Rosecrans took command of his troops, reorganized as the Army of the Cumberland.

At almost the same time, McClellan informed the President that the Army of the Potomac could not pursue Lee because his cavalry horses were "absolutely broken down from fatigue and want of flesh." Lincoln's temper snapped. "Will you pardon me for asking what the horses of your army have done since the battle of Antietam that fatigue anything?" he shot back. In a subsequent message he attempted to tone down his language and said he certainly intended "no injustice," but the fate of McClellan had been decided. He told Francis P. Blair, Sr., that "he had tried long enough to bore with an auger too dull to take hold."

Telling Secretary Chase that it was "inexpedient" to remove the general before the elections, the President bided his time, but on November 5 he directed Halleck to relieve McClellan and entrusted the command of the Army of the Potomac to Ambrose E. Burnside.

IV

Naming Rosecrans and Burnside was a shrewd move. Burnside, in particular, was a happy choice. In addition to having some military reputation from his expedition against Roanoke Island, he looked like a great commander. His sturdy figure, his commanding presence, and even his elaborate side-whiskers gave an impression of manly competence. Generally considered a protégé of McClellan, he would be less objectionable to that general's admirers than almost any other possible commander. Yet McClellan's ene-mies were aware that their friendship had recently cooled, since McClellan spoke slightingly of Burnside's slowness to advance at Antietam.

Known to be generally in favor of the President's policies, Rosecrans and Burnside were politically neutral. Unlike McClellan, they were not Demo-cratic partisans, nor were they aligned with either the Moderate or the Radical faction of the Republican party. In the past, Republican Moderates had supported commanders like McClellan and Buell, practitioners of lim-ited war, waged by professionals, with minimal impact on civilians. The Radicals—and more particularly the vocal ultra-Radical Jacobins—looked to military leaders like Joseph Hooker, who promised to bring the war to the people of the Confederacy and to revolutionize Southern society. Belonging to neither group, Lincoln tried to stake out the central ground for his own.

Whether the appointments of Burnside and Rosecrans were a shrewd military move was open to question. Burnside himself said that he was not capable of leading the Army of the Potomac, and Rosecrans had hitherto displayed no talent for a large command. But for the moment, most were willing to give the new commanders a fair trial, and the President gained a little time to attend to some of the numerous other duties of his office, necessarily neglected during the previous months of crisis.

He continued to work long hours, rising early, often after a sleepless night, to go to his White House office before his breakfast, which consisted of a cup of coffee and an egg. Returning to his desk after breakfast, he examined papers and signed commissions for another hour or so. There were always routine matters to be handled, like the required congratulations to Frederick Grand Duke of Baden, on the announcement of the marriage of Her Grand Ducal Highness the Princess Leopoldine of Baden to His Most Serene Highness the Prince Hermann of Hohenloe Langenburg. Of course, the State Department drafted these messages, but the President had to sign them. In the course of a morning he efficiently handled many requests by briefly endorsing the papers: "Submitted to Gen. Halleck, asking as favorable consideration as may be consistent," or, to Secretary Caleb B. Smith, "Let the appointment be made, as within recommend[ed]," or "Sec. of War, please make such response to this as may seem proper."

At ten o'clock his office hours for petitioners and visitors began. A visitor, C. Van Santvoord, made notes on those who called on the President in a single morning: One "dapper, smooth-faced, boyish-looking little person" whispered a request, apparently for a clerkship, until the President dismissed him with an emphatic "Yes, yes, I know all about it, and will give it proper attention." A lieutenant asked to be appointed to head a colored regiment, though the decision to employ blacks in the army had not yet been made, but Lincoln saw that he really was only asking to be promoted to colonel and cut him off. Then "a sturdy, honest-looking German soldier," who had lost a leg and hobbled in on crutches, asked the President for a job in Washington, but he had no papers or credentials to show how he had lost his leg. "How am I to know that you lost it in battle, or did not lose it by a trap after getting into somebody's orchard?" Lincoln asked with a droll smile. Then, relenting, he gave the young man a card to present to a local quartermaster.

The next visitor got a less kindly reception. Apparently he wanted to use the President's name in connection with a business project, pleading that he was too old and obscure to start up on his own. "No!" exclaimed Lincoln indignantly. "Do you take the President of the United States to be a commission broker? You have come to the wrong place, and for you and every one who comes for such purposes, there is the door!"

After that, a "white-haired, gentlemanly-looking person" and his "very pretty and prepossessing" daughter asked simply to pay their respects, and the President greeted them cordially in his "frank, bland, and familiar manner." Next a Scottish visitor reported that his countrymen hoped the President would stand firmly behind his Emancipation Proclamation, and Lincoln pledged: "God helping me, I trust to prove true to a principle which I feel to be right."

His final caller of the morning, a rough Western countryman, had come by "to see the President, and have the honor of shaking hands with him." Eyeing his tall visitor, Lincoln engaged in a little exercise that he always found amusing and challenged the man to compare heights with him. When the countryman proved a shade taller than six foot four inches, Lincoln congratulated him and could not resist the inevitable pun: "You actually *stand higher* to-day than your President."

On the day when Van Santvoord was an observer, the President ended his open office hours at noon, but on most days after a brief lunch—when he remembered to eat anything—he continued to receive petitioners in the afternoons. Though his secretaries fretted that he was wasting his time in these interviews, Lincoln felt he gained much from what he called his "public opinion baths." These visits—random, sporadic, and inconsequential as they often proved to be—offered the President an opportunity, in these days before scientific public opinion polling, to get some idea of how ordinary people felt about him and his administration.

Customarily the President's open office hours were suspended on two afternoons each week for cabinet meetings. Occasionally, when he could spare the time, he went for a horseback ride in the afternoon, and from time to time Mrs. Lincoln, concerned about her husband's health, insisted that he come on a carriage ride with her, usually to visit the army camps around Washington or the soldiers' hospitals. Then after dinner, when Lincoln absently ate whatever was put in front of him and drank no wine, he frequently returned to his White House office, sometimes working three or four more hours. When important military movements were under way, he would often wrap his long gray shawl about his shoulders and walk over to the telegraphic office in the War Department, usually without escort or guard. There he would read the latest dispatches from the armies and talk and banter with the telegraph operators. Often it was near midnight before he got back to the living quarters of the White House. "I consider myself fortunate," Mary Lincoln lamented, "if at eleven o'clock, I once more find myself, in my pleasant room and very especially, if my tired and weary Husband, is *there,* resting in the lounge to receive me—to chat over the occurrences of the day."

V

Even in the brief honeymoon period after Burnside and Rosecrans assumed command of their armies, there were few uneventful days like the one chronicled by Van Santvoord. Serious problems arose that only a President could decide. During October and November much of Lincoln's attention had to be given to an uprising among the Sioux Indians of Minnesota. Bureaucratic delays in paying these Indians the annuities promised to them at the time they gave up most of their land left the Sioux desperate and almost starving. During the summer their agent unsuccessfully tried to get food for them, but his supplier announced, "So far as I am concerned, if they are hungry let them eat grass or their own dung." In August some young Sioux men, raiding an Acton, Minnesota, farm for eggs, broke into the house and killed five white settlers. Quickly violence spread throughout southwestern Minnesota, and before the Indian uprising could be quelled, more than 350 whites had been killed. It was the largest massacre of whites by Indians in American history.

When news of the uprising reached Washington, Lincoln was almost wholly absorbed by Lee's invasion of Maryland, and he could devote little attention to Indian affairs. He did dispatch General Pope, fresh from his defeat at Second Bull Run, to take charge of military operations against the Sioux. The general accepted the assignment reluctantly. He felt that the President had been "feeble, cowardly, and shameful" in failing to defend him from his critics.

Once in Minnesota, Pope deflected his hostility from the President to the rebellious Indians. Finding "panic everywhere in Wisconsin and Minnesota" and predicting "a general Indian war all along the frontier, unless immediate steps are taken to put a stop to it," he announced: "It is my purpose utterly to exterminate the Sioux if I have the power to do so. . . . They are to be treated as maniacs or wild beasts." With the enthusiastic cooperation of Minnesota authorities, who saw an opportunity both to gain revenge and to secure additional Indian lands, Union troops by early October broke the back of the rebellion, and a military commission began to try more than 1,500 Indians, including women and children, who had been captured.

As soon as the news reached Washington, in mid-October, the President told Pope to stage no executions without his sanction. To gain further information and to help restore peace, he sent Assistant Secretary of the Interior John P. Usher (soon to replace Caleb B. Smith in the cabinet) to Minnesota, and he also sought the advice of Episcopal Bishop Henry B. Whipple, who advised "a new policy of *honesty* was needed" for dealing with this "wronged and neglected race."

Lincoln admitted that he was poorly informed on Indian affairs. In September, when Chief John Ross had urged him to offer military protection to the Cherokees, who had fallen under Confederate control, the President told him, "In the multitude of cares claiming my constant attention I have been unable to examine and determine the exact treaty relations between the United States and the Cherokee Nation." He had little acquaintance with Indians. In general, like most whites of his generation, he considered the Indians a barbarous people who were a barrier to progress. The ceremonial visits of Indian chiefs, dressed in their tribal regalia, he welcomed, both because they were exotic and because he rather enjoyed playing the role of their Great Father, addressing them in pidgin English and explaining that "this world is a great, round ball." Occasionally, as during the following year, he would offer them little homilies on how they could profit by learning "the arts of civilization." Pointing out the "great difference between this pale-faced people and their red brethren," he told a group in the White House that whites had become numerous and prosperous partly because they were farmers rather than hunters. Even though he admitted that "we are now engaged in a great war between one another," he also offered another reason for white success: "We are not, as a race, so much disposed to fight and kill one another as our red brethren." The irony was unintentional.

Nor did Lincoln know much about the operations of the Office of Indian Affairs in the Department of the Interior. When he had appointed Caleb B. Smith as Secretary of the Interior and William P. Dole as Indian Commissioner, he was rewarding them for political favors, not for interest in or concern for the Indians. In naming their subordinates, the President almost invariably followed the wishes of the Republican members of Congress. A typical note directed Smith: "Please make out and send blank appointments for all Indian places, to serve in Wisconsin, in favor of the persons unitedly recommended by the Wisconsin Congressional delegation." It was assumed that Indian agents and Indian traders would make profits from their positions, not merely for themselves but for their Republican sponsors.

But what was now going on in Minnesota far exceeded the usual fraud and embezzlement connected with the Indian service. Whites who had been terrified during the uprising were determined to secure vengeance. Republican Governor Alexander Ramsey, calling the Sioux "assassins" and "ravishers of . . . wives and sisters and daughters," insisted that whites in his state "will not tolerate their presence . . . in any number or in any condition." Many thought the defeat of the Sioux offered an opportunity to drive not merely that tribe but the peaceable Chippewas out of the state and to confiscate their lands.

On November 8, Lincoln received from Minnesota a list of 303 Sioux men the military commission had condemned to die. Promptly the President directed General Pope to send complete records of these convictions, indicating the more guilty and influential of the culprits. Pope responded that the people of Minnesota were so exasperated that if everyone on the list was not executed it would be "nearly impossible to prevent the indiscriminate massacre of all the Indians—old men, women, and children." Minnesota Senator Morton S. Wilkinson echoed the threat: "Either the Indians must be punished according to law, or they will be murdered without law." Governor Ramsey added that unless every condemned Sioux Indian was executed "private revenge would on all this border take the place of official judgment on these Indians."

But the President, greatly influenced by Bishop Whipple and Commissioner Dole, refused to be stampeded. He consulted Judge Advocate General Joseph Holt about a way of avoiding a decision, by allowing state authorities to determine which Indians should die. When Holt told him firmly, "The power cannot be delegated," the President deliberately went through the record of each convicted man, seeking to identify those who had been guilty of the most atrocious crimes, especially murder of innocent farmers and rape. He came up with a list of thirty-nine names, which he carefully wrote out in his own hand: "Te-he-hdo-ne-cha," "Tazoo" alias "Plan-doo-ta," and so on. Wiring the list to the military authorities, he warned the telegraph operator to be particularly careful, since even a slight error might send the wrong man to his death.

On December 26 the thirty-eight men (one more man was pardoned at the last minute) were executed—the largest public execution in American history. Few praised Lincoln for reducing the list of condemned men. On the contrary, his clemency lighted a brief firestorm of protest in Minnesota, which did not die down until the Secretary of the Interior promised the white settlers "reasonable compensation for the depredations committed." Even so, considerable resentment remained against Lincoln and his administration, so that in 1864, Republicans lost strength in Minnesota. Senator (formerly Governor) Ramsey told the President that if he had hanged more Indians he would have had a larger majority. "I could not afford to hang men for votes," Lincoln replied.

VI

The Indian uprising in Minnesota was but one of the many subjects that the President had to address in his annual message to Congress on the state of the Union. Indeed, preparing that message, which was due on December 1, took up so much of his time that he felt obliged to limit his public receptions to two hours each day during November.

The message offered Lincoln an opportunity to reformulate the basic goals of his administration. He knew that it would be addressed to a highly critical audience. Congressional Democrats, cheered by the outcome of the recent elections, which would increase their membership in the next House of Representatives from forty-four to seventy-two, could be counted upon to be more partisan than usual, less inclined to follow the lead of a Republican President. Republicans in both houses would likely be more restive, too. Many of the more conservative Republican representatives, especially those from New York, Pennsylvania, and Ohio, were now lame ducks, and their influence was diminished. The Radical members had a growing sense of desperation. Many feared that Lincoln, after studying the election returns, would fall under conservative influences. Signs of a retreat were discovered in his appointment of Burnside, instead of a Radical general like Joseph Hooker, and they worried that he might renege on his promise to issue a final emancipation decree on January 1. Thaddeus Stevens thought it was urgent to commit the President to a Radical program "before the Locos [i.e., the Democrats] came in." All expected the message to define the President's position.

Lincoln did not deliver his message in person to the Congress. Instead, as was customary, his secretary, Nicolay, took the document to Capitol Hill, where a clerk read it aloud. Much of the message was entirely routine in nature, summarizing the work of the departments, usually in words supplied to the President by members of the cabinet. It began with a long account of foreign relations that concluded with a balanced sentence written by Seward: "If the condition of our relations with other nations is less gratifying than it has usually been at former periods, it is certainly more satisfactory than a nation so unhappily distracted as we are, might reasonably have apprehended." The President then claimed the congressmen's "most diligent consideration" of financial affairs, and, in passages supplied by Secretary Chase, called for "a return to specie payments . . . at the earliest period compatible with due regard to all interests concerned" and urged the creation of a national banking system. The message went on to discuss the condition of the Post Office Department, which reported "much improved" efficiency; of the Department of the Interior, including a summary of the Sioux uprising; and of the newly created Department of Agriculture (which was headed by a commissioner and was not represented in the cabinet).

Lincoln then turned, rather surprisingly, to a restatement of the physical impossibility of separating the United States into two republics and quoted a long extract from his inaugural address on this point. Rather puzzlingly he next paid tribute to the upper Mississippi and Ohio Valley region, which he said was "the great body of the republic." Having no seacoast, this region could never consent to a partition of the Union that would deprive it of either its Eastern or its Western outlets.

As the clerk droned on, congressmen must have felt that they were listening to a fairly conventional, if not especially well-organized, presidential message, but it came alive when Lincoln reached the topic that really interested him: compensated emancipation. The subject came as a surprise to many, who thought the Emancipation Proclamation had settled that question. But by referring to the Emancipation Proclamation only in passing, Lincoln was expressing his continuing doubts about the efficacy of his decree. In private conversations, even more than in his public message, he was pessimistic, predicting that the Proclamation "would not make a single negro free beyond our military reach." About this time he entertained a group of clergymen who visited the White House with an anecdote about a case in a Western court where a lawyer tried to establish that a calf had five legs by calling the tail a leg. "But," said the President, "the decision of the judge was that *calling* the tail a leg, did not make it a leg, and the calf had but four legs after all." So, he reminded his guests, "proclaiming slaves free did not make them free." The President was aware that neither the preliminary proclamation nor the final decree promised on January 1 affected slavery in the border states and in the states of the upper South. Moreover, he recognized that the Emancipation Proclamation had a legal basis only as an act of war. Once peace came, the courts might declare it unconstitutional, or a new administration might retract it.

Consequently his State of the Union address suggested a way of permanently getting rid of slavery throughout the land. In an unusual attempt at executive leadership, the President proposed three amendments to the Constitution. The first authorized the payment of United States bonds to any state that abolished slavery by January 1, 1900; the second guaranteed the freedom of all slaves who "enjoyed actual freedom by the chances of the war" but authorized payment to their masters if they were not disloyal; and the third authorized congressional appropriations for "colonizing free colored persons, with their own consent, at any place or places without the United States."

The package was new, but the proposals were similar to those the President had put forward in his March message to Congress, and the whole plan was much like the one he had vainly entreated the border-state congressmen to accept in June. Most who were allowed to preview the President's mes-

sage judged the plan impracticable. Though touched by the "noble sentiments and admirable language" of the message, Chase advised against
including the specifics of the plan, since "there is no probability that a vote
of two thirds can be commanded for *any* amendment of the constitution
touching slavery or that any such amendment can obtain the sanction of two
thirds of the States." Browning judged that the President was suffering from
a "hallucination" in proposing a scheme which, even if unopposed, would
require at least four years to be adopted.

Aware of the difficulties, Lincoln argued for his plan with a passion and
eloquence not shown in his public addresses since the Lincoln-Douglas
debates. "Mr Lincoln's whole soul is absorbed in his plan of remunerative
emancipation," David Davis reported, "and he thinks if Congress dont fail
him that the problem is solved." Feeding his uncharacteristic optimism
were rumors that Maryland and Kentucky might now be ready to accept
compensated emancipation. Moreover, the President thought there was a
good possibility—though he was careful not to mention this to Congress—
that some of the Southern slave states, or parts of them, would be back in
the Union before the end of the year.

Throughout the fall Lincoln had been actively encouraging both Southern
Unionists and army officers stationed in the South to bring about what was,
in effect, a secession from the Confederacy through the election of loyal
representatives and senators, who would ask for their rightful seats in the
United States Congress. He had some hope that these elections would take
place in the occupied areas of Tennessee, Arkansas, and the Norfolk region
of Virginia, but he pinned his hopes on Louisiana, where, he hoped, "gentlemen of character, willing to swear support of the constitution, as of old, and
known to be above reasonable suspicion of duplicity," would take the lead
in restoring their state to the Union so as "to have peace again upon the old
terms under the constitution of the United States." "All see how such action
will connect with, and affect the proclamation of September 22," he added
significantly. In other words, if the Southern states, or parts of them, set up
loyal governments and sent representatives to Congress, they would be
exempt from the final proclamation of emancipation.

Elated that he might be able to bring some of the rebellious states back
into the Union, and confident that if Burnside or Rosecrans or Grant could
inflict a crippling blow on the enemy others would follow, Lincoln foresaw
the possibility that by January the war might be nearly over and the Union
might be restored—but the United States would still be a slaveholding
nation.

This was not a prospect that troubled him for the long run, because he
was convinced that slavery was doomed. "He thinks the foundations of
slavery have been cracked by the war, by the Rebels," a visitor reported in
November. Consequently the main task now was to plan for a transition
from slavery to freedom. Such a plan had to be acceptable to the whites of
the border states, whose support Lincoln now needed even more because

of Republican defeats in the recent elections, and it had to be attractive to whites in the Deep South, if their newly restored loyalty was to prove genuine. But what concerned him most, the interviewer recorded, was "to provide for the blacks—he thinks still that many of them will colonize, and that the South will be compelled to resort to the Apprentice System." He was confident his plan would meet all these goals.

But if the plan was to work, it would have to be adopted immediately. Time was short because he was firmly committed to issuing his final Emancipation Proclamation on January 1. "From the expiration of the 'days of grace,'" he told a visitor, "the character of the war will be changed. It will be one of subjugation and extermination." The prospects for voluntary emancipation in the border states would be diminished. Lost, too, would be the President's most powerful hold on whites in the Confederacy: the possibility that they could retrieve something from their "peculiar institution" if they returned to the Union.

Behind Lincoln's urgency was another, less clearly articulated purpose. There had been grave erosion of support in the coalition on which he depended. During the past six months necessity and—as Lincoln thought—Providence had pushed his administration, though in uncertain spurts and starts, in a more radical direction. The Emancipation Proclamation and the removal of McClellan were the most obvious examples. These moves had cost him much of his support from Moderates yet did little to win the support of Radical Republicans. If the President was to survive politically, he had to assert his leadership by moving back toward the center.

That need gave to the State of the Union message what Lincoln himself admitted might seem a tone of "undue earnestness." Ardently he urged the Congress to unite behind his plan, which "would restore the national authority and national prosperity, and perpetuate both indefinitely." "The dogmas of the quiet past, are inadequate to the stormy present," he reminded the legislators. "The occasion is piled high with difficulty, and we must rise with the occasion. As our case is new, so we must think anew, and act anew. We must disenthrall our selves, and then we shall save our country."

"Fellow-citizens," he began his concluding paragraph, "*we* cannot escape history. We of this Congress and this administration, will be remembered in spite of ourselves. . . . We know how to save the Union. The world knows we do know how to save it." Now the time had come to act, and, in phrases that had a Shakespearean cadence, the President reminded the legislators: "In *giving* freedom to the *slave,* we *assure* freedom to the *free*—honorable alike in what we give, and what we preserve." Now was the time for decision. "We shall nobly save, or meanly lose, the last best, hope of earth."

VII

Any chance for Lincoln's plan for a speedy restoration of the Union was lost on December 13. General Burnside, against the advice and warnings of the

President, threw the Army of the Potomac across the Rappahannock into Fredericksburg. Then he ordered his soldiers to advance directly uphill toward Marye's Heights, where the Confederates lay waiting for them. By the end of the day one in ten of Burnside's soldiers was a casualty—dead, wounded, or missing; the Confederate losses were less than half as great. It was the worst defeat in the history of the American army.

News of Burnside's defeat was slow to reach the anxious President. Not until late at night did he learn of the outcome from Henry Villard. Lincoln grilled the journalist, who had come straight from the battlefield, about the extent of Union losses, the morale of the troops, and the chances for success if another attack was made. Fearing that the President did not fully understand the extent of the catastrophe, Villard stressed that every general officer he had encountered thought that success was impossible and that the army might suffer a worse disaster unless it was immediately withdrawn to the north side of the river. "I hope it is not so bad as all that," Lincoln said with a melancholy smile.

It was. As the news of Fredericksburg trickled out, a wave of anger swept the North. Little of it was directed at Burnside, who frankly admitted his incompetence and expressed willingness to assume all the responsibility. Halleck was the object of much of the abuse, as was Stanton, for they were charged with failing to support the army. But most of the blame was heaped on the Lincoln administration, for the bloody defeat at Fredericksburg seemed only a part of a larger pattern of failure and incompetence. As Joseph Medill of the *Chicago Tribune* declared, "Failure of the army, weight of taxes, depreciation of money, want of cotton . . . increasing national debt, deaths in the army, no prospect of success, the continued closure of the Mississippi [River] . . . all combine to produce the existing state of despondency and desperation." Everybody, he concluded, felt that "the war is drawing toward a disastrous and disgraceful termination."

The notes of complaint and disillusionment with the Lincoln administration, clearly audible since the failure of the Peninsula campaign, now became deafening. A few critics blamed the President personally. One angry Wisconsin resident demanded that both Lincoln and "the traitoress Mrs. Lincoln" resign, and Senator Wilkinson of Minnesota, outraged at the leniency Lincoln showed toward the Sioux Indians, asserted there was no hope for the country "except in the death of the President and a new administration."

But most critics were willing to admit Lincoln's good intentions even though they doubted his will. Recognizing that they could not replace a President who still had nearly half his term to serve, they looked for ways to give the administration backbone. Lincoln, said Senator Grimes, was only a " 'tow string' of a President," who had to be bound up "with strong, sturdy rods in the shape of cabinet ministers."

Discontent with the administration, then, centered on the cabinet. Throughout the last half of 1862 newspapers frequently carried stories of impending cabinet reorganization. Most of the reports stressed the want of harmony in the cabinet, and in many cases they were true. Except for Seward, nearly every cabinet member complained of Lincoln's lack of system in consulting his ministers. There were, in theory, two cabinet meetings a week, but in actuality, as Gideon Welles reported, these sessions were "infrequent, irregular and without system." Seward often failed to attend, though there was general reluctance to discuss major issues in the absence of the Secretary of State; he preferred, as Welles said censoriously, to spend "a considerable portion of every day with the President, patronizing and instructing him, hearing and telling anecdotes, relating interesting details of occurrences in the Senate, and inculcating his political party notions." When Stanton attended, said Welles, it was only "to whisper to the President, or take the dispatches or the papers from his pocket and go into a corner with the President." The meetings were highly informal. Charles Sumner reported that at some of the cabinet sessions he was invited to attend, the President put his feet up on the table, his heels higher than his head, and the other members appropriated extra chairs to rest their legs on. Chase complained that the meetings followed no agenda and allowed no real exchange of views among the secretaries. Secretary of the Interior Smith added that, unlike other presidents, Lincoln decided the most important questions without consulting his cabinet, seeking their advice—as he did when he was about to issue the Emancipation Proclamation—"as critics only."

Members of the cabinet did not get along with each other. Welles and Chase distrusted Seward because they suspected his bland amiability and his perpetual optimism and believed that he failed to understand the seriousness of the nation's crisis. Stanton's irascible, secretive manner prevented other cabinet members from becoming his friends, though he generally managed to work amicably with Chase. Welles, wearing his massive wig, was something of a figure of fun to his colleagues. Even Lincoln made gentle jokes about "Father Neptune," who was thought to be such an old fogy that he was "examining a model of Noah's ark, with a view to its introduction into the United States Navy." Nearly everybody agreed that Smith was a cabinet member of no consequence, and, as David Davis reported, a man with "neither heart nor sincerity about him." His resignation was eagerly awaited. And Montgomery Blair, the Postmaster General, was bitterly opposed to anyone who might stand in the way of his, or his family's, advancement; Chase and Stanton were the particular objects of his hatred.

Lincoln was not only aware of this dissonance; he was prepared to tolerate, and perhaps even to encourage, creative friction among his advisers. He understood that the conflicts among his cabinet members were not so fundamental as they seemed. The irritable clashes among the cabinet officers reflected differences in personality, not ideology; unconsciously they were rivals for the esteem and affection of the President. It was a problem that Lincoln, like other men of enormous personal magnetism, had to live with throughout his life; and he understood that the rivalry between Seward and Chase, or between Stanton and Welles, was much like that between Herndon and Mary Lincoln back in Springfield, or between Mrs. Lincoln and Nicolay and Hay during the White House years.

During the months when the President seemed to be on a radical course, it was the Conservative Republicans who demanded that he reorganize his cabinet. For instance, in early September, Samuel Galloway warned that the cabinet members' "selfish purposes [had] over-borne their patriotism" and tried to persuade Lincoln to drop Chase, whom he considered too radical on the slavery question. Even within the cabinet itself, Montgomery Blair, after consulting with Seward, went to the President with a report that the nation was "going to ruin for the want of a proper Head to the War Dept." and begged him to oust Stanton.

But after early November most of the demands for cabinet changes came from the Radical, antislavery wing of Lincoln's party. In calling for a reorganization of the cabinet, Radicals often hoped to oust Smith, who was "nothing but a doughface," and Bates, who was "a fossil of the Silurian era." But the chief focus of their attention was Seward, who had come to represent everything that was wrong with the Lincoln administration. The Secretary of State, they alleged, had never had his heart in the war: he had tried to negotiate with the Confederate envoys during the secession crisis; he had opposed making a stand at Fort Sumter; he had been McClellan's principal defender; he had opposed, and then delayed, the issuance of the Emancipation Proclamation; he and Thurlow Weed had undermined the candidacy of Radical General Wadsworth for governor of New York. The publication in December of Seward's diplomatic dispatches to Charles Francis Adams, the American minister in London, gave further evidence that the Secretary failed to understand the meaning of the American conflict; as late as July 5, Seward denounced both "the extreme advocates of African slavery and its most vehement opponents," the abolitionists, as being equally responsible for the Civil War. "Seward must be got out of the Cabinet," Joseph Medill of the *Chicago Tribune* announced. "He is Lincoln's evil genius. He has been President *de facto,* and has kept a sponge saturated with chloroform to Uncle Abe's nose."

Lincoln became aware of the full extent of the hostility to the Secretary of State on December 16, three days after the battle of Fredericksburg, when a messenger brought him a note from Seward: "I hereby resign the office of Secretary of State of the United States, and have the honor to request that this resignation may be immediately accepted." In identical language Frederick W. Seward, his son, resigned as assistant secretary of state. With a face full of pain and surprise the President turned to Senator Preston King of New York, who accompanied the messenger, and asked: "What does this mean?"

King reported that because of the immense popular excitement over the defeat at Fredericksburg there had been an extraordinary caucus of

Republican senators that afternoon in order "to ascertain whether any steps could be taken to quiet the public mind and to produce a better condition of affairs." The real purpose of the caucus became clear when Senator Wilkinson accused Seward of exercising "a controlling influence upon the mind of the President" and predicted that "so long as he remained in the Cabinet nothing but defeat and disaster could be expected." Senator Grimes offered a resolution declaring a want of confidence in the Secretary of State and calling for his removal from office. The highly respected Jacob Collamer argued that "the President had no Cabinet in the true sense of the word," and sharp-spoken William Pitt Fessenden said that "there was a back-stairs influence which often controlled the apparent conclusions of the Cabinet itself." He refused to name Seward but declared that "senators might draw their own conclusions." Taken by surprise, the friends of the Secretary of State were nevertheless able to prevent unanimous adoption of Grimes's resolution of censure. Frustrated, Seward's opponents pressed for adjournment until the next day and, by a vote of 16 to 13, got their way.

King had not stayed for the final vote but went immediately to Seward's house, where he reported the proceedings to the Secretary. "They may do as they please about me," Seward declared, "but they shall not put the President in a false position on my account." He wrote out a letter of resignation.

That evening the President called at Seward's house but found the Secretary resolute in his determination to resign. He wired his family, who had been planning to join him in the capital, not to come, and he and his son began packing up their books and papers in preparation for a return to his home in Auburn, New York.

Keeping Seward's resignation secret during the next two days, the President anxiously awaited the outcome of the Republican caucus. For months the Radicals in this group had been in frequent contact with Secretary Chase, who fed them stories of Lincoln's failure to consult with his cabinet advisers. For instance, he told Zachariah Chandler that there was "at the present time no cabinet except in name"; though the heads of departments met now and then, "no reports are made; no regular discussions held; no ascertained conclusions reached." Chase was also the source of Fessenden's statement about Seward's "back-stairs" influence at the White House. Believing Chase's rumors, the caucus agreed on a resolution calling for "a change in and a partial reconstruction of the Cabinet." The senators then voted unanimously —with only two Republican senators absent, and Senator King not voting— to name a committee to present their views to the President.

Lincoln, who had a good idea of what went on in the caucus, was in anguish because of this new assault, coming so close after the devastating news from Fredericksburg. When he met Browning in the afternoon of December 18, he asked, "What do these men want?" And he answered himself: "They wish to get rid of me, and I am sometimes half disposed to gratify them." "We are now on the brink of destruction," he told Browning.

"It appears to me the Almighty is against us, and I can hardly see a ray of hope."

But when the committee representing the Senate caucus called at the White House at seven o'clock that evening, he had regained his composure, and he greeted his visitors with what Fessenden called "his usual urbanity." Patiently he listened as Collamer, the chairman of the committee, read resolutions that the senators had agreed on, which, in very general terms and without mentioning any names, called for changes in the composition of the cabinet so that its members would agree with the President "in political principles and general policy" and urged that no important military command should go to anyone who was not "a cordial believer and supporter of the same principles."

Wade then bluntly censured Lincoln for entrusting the conduct of the war to "men who had no sympathy with it or the cause," and blamed Republican defeats in the recent elections on "the fact that the President had placed the direction of our military affairs in the hands of bitter and malignant Democrats."

After professing confidence in the integrity and patriotism of the President, Fessenden alleged "that the Cabinet were not consulted as a council—in fact, that many important measures were decided upon not only without consultation, but without the knowledge of its members." Seward, he claimed, exerted an injurious influence upon the conduct of the war. Branching out in his indictment, he went on to say that the commanders of the armies were "largely pro-slavery men and sympathized strongly with the Southern feeling," and some of them, like McClellan, had used their position to blame the administration for failing to support them and their men.

At this point Lincoln interrupted. From his long experience in the courtroom he knew the value of a well-timed digression as a way of defusing hostility. If the occasion had not been so serious, he might have told the senators an anecdote. Instead, producing a large bundle of papers, he spent nearly half an hour in reading aloud his letters to McClellan, showing that the government had consistently sustained him to the best of its powers.

By the time the senators got back to their main subject, their tempers had cooled, and nobody got very excited about Sumner's charge that Seward had written offensive diplomatic dispatches, "which the President could not have seen or assented to."

After three hours the meeting broke up without taking any action. By the end of the session the President was, as Fessenden thought, "apparently in cheerful spirits," and he promised to give careful consideration to the resolutions submitted by the committee. As they left the White House, Radical Republicans were exultant "at the prospect of getting rid of the *whole Cabinet*" and Chandler rejoiced with "our best and truest men" that they were going to oust Seward, "the millstone around the Administration."

The President had other plans. The next morning at a cabinet meeting where all members except Seward were present, he reported on the resig-

nation of the Secretary of State and on his visit from the committee representing the Republican caucus. He observed that they considered Seward
"the real cause of our failures." "While they believed in the President's
honesty," he said in his quaint language, "they seemed to think that when
he had in him any good purposes Mr. S[eward]. contrived to *suck them out
of him unperceived.*" He then asked the cabinet members to meet with him
again, "to have a free talk," that evening at seven-thirty.

The committee was invited for the same hour, and as senators and cabinet
members met in the anteroom, they exchanged looks of wild surmise. The
President began the meeting with a long statement, commenting "with some
mild severity" on the resolutions presented by the senators the previous
evening, admitting that he had not been very regular in consulting the
cabinet as a whole, but arguing "that most questions of importance had
received a reasonable consideration" and that he "was not aware of any
divisions or want of unity." He then called on the members of the cabinet
to state "whether there had been any want of unity or of sufficient consultation."

Most of the cabinet members unhesitatingly agreed that they had indeed
been consulted on important matters, but Chase was in a very embarrassing
position. If he now repeated his frequent complaints to the senators, his
disloyalty to the President would be apparent. If he supported Lincoln's
statement, it would be evident that he had deceived the senators. Chase
tried to get out of the trap by blustering "that he should not have come here
had he known that he was to be arraigned before a committee of the Senate." But finding no escape, he swallowed both truth and consistency and
averred "that questions of importance had generally been considered by the
Cabinet, though perhaps not so fully as might have been desired" and that
there was no want of unity in the cabinet.

The meeting went on for some time after that, as senators repeated all
the familiar charges against Seward, but it was evident that Chase's forced
admission had undercut the case against the Secretary of State. At one
o'clock, when the senators and the cabinet officers left the White House, no
conclusion had been reached, but there was a general feeling that there
would be no changes in the cabinet.

Chase began to realize that his position was untenable and wrote out his
resignation as Secretary of the Treasury. The next morning when Lincoln
summoned him to the White House, he brought the letter with him. He,
along with Stanton and Welles, was already in the executive office when the
President arrived. Turning at once to the Treasury Secretary, Lincoln said: "I
sent for you, for this matter is giving me great trouble." Chase stammered
that he, too, had been painfully affected by the meeting the previous night
and that he had prepared his resignation.

"Where is it?" asked Lincoln quickly. "I brought it with me," said Chase,
taking a paper from his pocket. "I wrote it this morning."

"Let me have it," said Lincoln, his long arm and fingers reaching out for the document, which Chase was apparently reluctant to release. Evidently the Secretary intended to say more, but Lincoln took the letter and opened it. "This . . . cuts the Gordian knot," he said with a triumphant laugh. "I can dispose of this subject now."

Then Stanton offered his resignation, but Lincoln brushed him aside. "You may go to your Department," he told the Secretary of War. "I don't want yours." Then he ended the interview abruptly: "I will detain neither of you longer."

Having both Seward's resignation and Chase's in his hand, the President declined to accept either and insisted that both men remain in his cabinet. They balanced each other, he told Senator Ira Harris of New York. Remembering how as a boy in Indiana he had worked out a way to carry pumpkins while he was on horseback, he told the senator: "I can ride on now. I've got a pumpkin in each end of my bag!"

By the end of the week the cabinet crisis was over. In one sense not much had been solved. Yet there were lessons from the crisis. Radicals learned that, no matter how carefully they planned and intrigued, they lacked the power to take control of the government from the President. Lincoln told Browning firmly that "he was master, and they should not do that." Chase's reputation had suffered a serious blow. When the crisis was over, senators asked Collamer how Chase, after alleging that the President had no system and failed to consult his advisers, could have told the group that the cabinet was harmonious. The blunt Vermont senator replied, "He lied." Fessenden accurately assessed the results: "He will never be forgiven by many for deliberately sacrificing his friends to the fear of offending his and their enemies." Seward's place was secure, and to some, like Nicolay, it seemed that the Secretary had "achieved a triumph over those who attempted to drive him out, in this renewed assurance of the President's confidence and esteem." But reflection suggested that Seward now, more than ever, owed his place to the goodwill of the President, and in the months ahead the Secretary became more discreet in his utterances and meddled less in the affairs of other departments.

Lincoln, too, learned from the experience. He now realized that he had not been either very businesslike or even courteous about consulting his cabinet colleagues. For a time, he meticulously invited their opinions on controversial issues. For instance, at the very end of the year he requested all of them to submit to him in writing their opinions as to whether he should veto or approve the bill that carved the new state of West Virginia out of the territory of Virginia. At a cabinet meeting on December 30 he made a point of distributing copies of his draft of the edict of emancipation to be issued on January 1, asking each member to offer suggestions. Ignoring most of the substantive changes that cabinet members proposed, he accepted several stylistic improvements, and he added to his final Emancipation Proclamation a concluding paragraph, embodying an idea Chase proposed at the instigation of Charles Sumner: "And upon this act, sincerely believed to be an act of justice, warranted by the Constitution, upon military necessity, I invoke the considerate judgment of mankind, and the gracious favor of Almighty God."

But more than anything else, the crisis taught Lincoln his own strength. Looking back on his handling of the affair nearly a year later, he told John Hay: "I do not now see how it could have been done better. I am sure it was right. If I had yielded to that storm and dismissed Seward the thing would all have slumped over one way and we should have been left with a scanty handful of supporters. When Chase sent in his resignation I saw that the game was in my own hands and I put it through." Proud that he was able to keep together an administration dominated neither by Radicals nor by Conservatives, he confided his final assessment of the crisis to Leonard Swett: "I may not have made as great a President as some other men, but I believe I have kept these discordant elements together as well as anyone could."

CHAPTER FIFTEEN

What Will the Country Say!

———◆———

Throngs attended the White House reception on New Year's Day of 1863. First came the members of the diplomatic corps, in full court dress, who were presented to the President by the Secretary of State. Lincoln shook hands with everyone in a cordial but businesslike manner, which reminded some observers of a farmer sawing wood. Then he passed the guests along to Mrs. Lincoln, who wore a rich dress of velvet, with lozenge trimming at the waist; it was black since she was still in mourning for Willie. Members of the cabinet followed the diplomats, and then came officers of the army and navy. In their wake what young Fanny Seward, daughter of the Secretary of State, called "people generally" passed through the reception line. Not until after noon could Lincoln escape upstairs to his office, where Seward and his son Frederick, the assistant secretary of state, presently brought him the duly engrossed copy of the final proclamation of emancipation. Excepting Tennessee and portions of other Southern states that were already under the control of Union armies, it declared that all slaves in the states or portions of states still in rebellion "are, and henceforward shall be free." For this "act of justice, warranted by the Constitution, upon military necessity," the President invoked "the considerate judgment of mankind, and the gracious favor of Almighty God." "I never, in my life, felt more certain that I was doing right, than I do in signing this paper," Lincoln remarked, but he added ruefully that his arm was so stiff and numb from so many handshakes that he was not sure he could control a pen. "Now, this signature is one that will be closely examined," he said, "and if they find my hand trembled, they will say 'he had some compunctions.' But, any way, it is going to be done!"

Then, grasping the pen firmly, he slowly and carefully wrote his name at the end of the proclamation.

In the months ahead he would frequently need to exhibit the same care and firmness, for his administration was beset from all sides. Union armies were defeated or immobilized. Union naval expeditions were spectacular failures. The border states were in turmoil, and Missouri was the scene of a guerrilla war. Foreign powers offered to mediate the conflict between the Union and the Confederacy. Discontent was on the rise in the North, and confidential sources told the President that secret pro-Confederate societies were plotting to overthrow the administration. Within the Republican party factional lines sharpened, and both Conservatives and Radicals agreed that Lincoln was a failure as President. Whatever self-assurance Lincoln had gained from the cabinet crisis of December 1862 was sorely tested during the first six months of 1863, for he found that the shrewdness, tact, and forbearance that had served him so well in face-to-face disagreements were not easily applied to large groups in conflict. In short, Lincoln still had much to learn about how to be President.

I

The year began with little good news from the armies. To be sure, in eastern Tennessee Rosecrans's army more than held its own against Bragg's in the protracted and costly battle of Stones River (December 30–January 2), and Lincoln praised the general's "skill, endurance, and da[u]ntless courage." But when the Confederates withdrew from the field, Union forces did not follow. For the rest of the winter Rosecrans remained immobile at Murfrees-boro, ignoring the President's prompting to advance against Chattanooga. Like Buell, Rosecrans found the roads impassable, supplies too hard to collect, and his lines of communication with Nashville and Louisville too tenuous. When Lincoln gently pointed out that the Confederates faced similar difficulties but still were able to do much damage with small raids, "harrassing, and discouraging loyal residents, supplying themselves with provisions, clothing, horses, and the like," and proposed mounting *"counter-raids,"* Rosecrans ignored his letter, doubtless resenting civilian interference in military decisions. Instead of acting against the enemy, he brooded over perceived slights. He complained bitterly that he was out-ranked because Grant was issued a commission as major general that ante-dated his own. The President was finally obliged to tell him bluntly: "Truth to speak, I do not appreciate this matter of rank on paper, as you officers do. The world will not forget that you fought the battle of 'Stone River' and it will never care a fig whether you rank Gen. Grant on paper, or he so, ranks you." Still, Rosecrans would not move.

Farther west, the outlook for the Union forces was even bleaker. On January 1 the federal garrison at Galveston, Texas, surrendered to attacking

Confederates. In Louisiana, General Benjamin F. Butler proved so rapacious that the President had to replace him, and the new commander, N. P. Banks, had yet to demonstrate his ability. Most serious of all was Grant's failure to capture Vicksburg. After an unsuccessful attempt to proceed overland through central Mississippi, Grant entrusted the offensive to W. T. Sherman, who led his troops on December 29 in a disastrous assault on the Chickasaw Bluffs defending Vicksburg that was reminiscent, on a smaller scale, of Burnside's fiasco at Fredericksburg. Recognizing how vital Vicksburg was, the President watched these operations closely, but in the months after Sherman's defeat he heard mostly complaints about Grant. The general, reported Murat Halstead of the *Cincinnati Commercial,* "is a jackass in the original package. He is a poor drunken imbecile. He is a poor stick sober, and he is most of the time more than half drunk, and much of the time idiotically drunk." Further controversy rose over Grant's ill-conceived order banning "Jew peddlers" from his lines. The President promptly revoked it "as it . . . proscribed an entire religious class, some of whom are fighting in our ranks."

Most troubling of all was the situation of the Army of the Potomac, demoralized after Fredericksburg. Burnside gained some credibility from his manly acknowledgment that he alone, and not the President nor the War Department, was responsible for the defeat. Greatly pleased at this statement, because he was used to being blamed for his subordinates' failures, Lincoln told Burnside "he was the first man he had found who was willing to relieve him of a particle of responsibility." But the general had lost the confidence of his subordinate officers and his troops. Learning that Burnside was preparing another assault on the impregnable Confederate defenses at Fredericksburg, two of his major generals, William B. Franklin and William F. Smith, violated military protocol by writing directly to the President, warning that "the plan of campaign already commenced will not be successful." But when Halleck complained of the "very disheartening" inactivity of the Army of the Potomac, Burnside pushed ahead and began organizing a wide flanking movement to cross the Rappahannock River below Fredericksburg.

At this point discontent in the Army of the Potomac bubbled over. Many of the officers, convinced of Burnside's incompetence, were despondent almost to the point of mutiny. Anticipating another disaster, Generals John Newton and John Cochrane on December 30 made a quick trip to Washington to alert the President of the danger. Though Lincoln distrusted the reports of all these subordinates, because he was convinced their real purpose was to restore McClellan to command, he ordered a halt to Burnside's advance: "I have good reason for saying you must not make a general movement of the army without letting me know."

On New Year's Day, before the public reception, Burnside came to the White House to explain and defend his plans. With an army of 120,000 men immediately confronting the enemy in Virginia, he thought it imperative to begin an advance, whether below or above Fredericksburg, but since not one of his division commanders supported his plan he was willing to give it up, and with it the command of the Army of the Potomac and even his commission in the United States Army. In announcing that he would "most cheerfully give place to any other officer," Burnside suggested that Lincoln ought to look not just at the ability of the commanding general but at the honesty and loyalty of both Secretary of War Stanton and General-in-Chief Halleck. He warned that they had not given the President the "positive and unswerving support in [his] public policy" or assumed "their full share of the responsibility for that policy."

Lincoln was in a quandary. Not knowing what else to do, he asked Halleck's opinion of Burnside's planned operation. The general declined to give one, making it clear, as he had on a previous occasion, "that a General in command of an army in the field is the best judge of existing conditions." Impatiently the President then directed Halleck to go to Burnside's headquarters, examine the ground, talk with the officers, and, after forming his own opinion, tell Burnside either that he approved or disapproved of his planned advance. "If in such a difficulty as this you do not help, you fail me precisely in the point for which I sought your assistance," he wrote sharply. "Your military skill is useless to me, if you will not do this."

Halleck's response was to offer his resignation as general-in-chief, on the ground that "a very important difference of opinion in regard to my relations toward generals commanding armies in the field" made it impossible to perform the duties of his office "satisfactorily at the same time to the President and to myself."

Lincoln felt he had no alternative but to rescind his order, endorsing it "Withdrawn, because considered harsh by Gen. Halleck." Heading an administration which he had barely saved from collapse, after the two principal members had offered their resignations and others had been prepared to follow, and facing the likelihood of a change of command in the almost mutinous Army of the Potomac, the President could not permit further evidence of dissension among his advisers. But it was not a decision that he made readily, and in the future he spoke of Halleck as little more than "a first-rate clerk."

It was harder to know what to do with Burnside. Lincoln was always reluctant to dismiss a faithful subordinate, however unsuccessful; perhaps the President remembered that at times he himself had seemed to most people a failure. He genuinely liked Burnside's modesty and loyalty. While recognizing the general's limitations, he admired his fighting spirit, and he respected the "consummate skill and success with which [he] crossed and re-crossed the river, in face of the enemy." He tended to distrust the generals critical of Burnside, suspecting they were McClellan partisans. Anyway, there was no obvious successor to Burnside, and Lincoln wrote him candidly: "I do not yet see how I could profit by changing the command of the A[rmy of the] P[otomac]."

The general was given one more chance. With Halleck's blessing he planned to cross the Rappahannock west of Fredericksburg, hoping to flank Lee's army. Lincoln approved the advance but instructed the general, "Be cautious, and do not understand that the government, or country, is driving you." On January 19 the Army of the Potomac lumbered out of camp on a mission that most of Burnside's division commanders felt was doomed to failure. The weather reinforced their objections. As heavy rain turned to sleet, the army bogged down, and after three days Burnside called off what reporters scornfully called the "Mud March."

Back in camp Burnside boiled over. Blaming the failure on the disloyalty of his subordinates, he drafted an order dismissing four of his major generals from the army and relieving four other generals from their commands. Taking the order to Washington, he told Lincoln he could not continue in command unless the order was approved. "I think you are right," Lincoln said, but he reserved a decision until he could talk with Stanton and Halleck. The next morning, when Burnside returned to the White House, Lincoln told him he was to be replaced as commander of the Army of the Potomac.

The President had difficulty in choosing a successor. Despite considerable public pressure, he gave no thought to restoring McClellan to command. He could have brought in either Rosecrans or Grant, though neither had yet been notably successful, but to impose a Western commander would have been insulting to the Army of the Potomac. Of Burnside's subordinates, E. V. Sumner was too old, Franklin and Smith were thought to be McClellan partisans, and others had yet to prove they could command a huge army.

Rather uncertainly Lincoln turned to Joseph Hooker. The general had some decided negatives. He was known to be a hard drinker. He had been outspoken almost to the point of insubordination in his criticisms of Burnside's incompetence, and he let it be known that he viewed the President and the government at Washington as "imbecile and 'played out.'" "Nothing would go right," he told a newspaper reporter, "until we had a dictator, and the sooner the better." But the handsome, florid-faced general had performed valiantly in nearly all the major engagements of the Peninsula campaign and at Antietam, where he had been wounded, and his aggressive spirit earned him the sobriquet "Fighting Joe." Lincoln decided to take a chance on him.

Calling Hooker to the White House, he gave the general a carefully composed private letter, which commended his bravery, his military skill, and his confidence in himself. At the same time, he told Hooker, "there are some things in regard to which, I am not quite satisfied with you." He lamented Hooker's efforts to undermine confidence in Burnside and mentioned his "recently saying that both the Army and the Government needed a Dictator." "Of course," he continued, "it was not *for* this, but in spite of it, that I have given you the command." "Only those generals who gain successes, can set up dictators," he reminded the new commander. "What I now ask of you is military success, and I will risk the dictatorship." Promising the full support of the government, he warned, "Beware of rashness."

The appointment of Hooker, which was generally well received in the North, relieved some of the immediate pressure on the President. Everybody understood that the new commander would require some time to reorganize the Army of the Potomac and to raise the spirits of the demoralized soldiers. The President could, for the moment, turn his attention to other problems.

II

Foreign relations did not occupy a great deal of Lincoln's time. For the most part, he was content to allow the Secretary of State to manage diplomatic affairs—just as he permitted the other cabinet members to conduct the business of their departments with minimal interference. He trusted Seward, and he respected the Secretary's knowledge of diplomatic protocol.

With most nations the relations of the United States were entirely amicable, and there were few occasions that called for special exertions by either the Secretary of State or the President. No doubt Lincoln derived some amusement from his correspondence with the King of Siam, who, as a token of his goodwill and friendship for the American people in their present struggle, sent gifts of a photograph of himself, a sword and a scabbard, and a pair of elephant tusks, and offered to supply to the government a stock of breeding elephants. "Our political jurisdiction," the President replied, in words probably drafted by Seward, "does not reach a latitude so low as to favor the multiplication of the elephant, and steam on land, as well as on water, has been our best and most efficient agent of transportation in internal commerce."

From time to time, the eccentric or unauthorized behavior of American diplomats caused minor ripples, as when Theodore Canisius, once Lincoln's partner in the *Illinois Staats-Anzeiger* and now American consul to Vienna, initiated, quite on his own, negotiations to offer a command in the Union armies to the great Italian general Garibaldi. Somewhat more serious was the game of musical chairs played with the American ministry to St. Petersburg. The post went first to Cassius M. Clay, the Kentucky abolitionist, as a reward for his strong support for Lincoln in the Chicago nominating convention of 1860. Despite several street brawls, in which Clay demonstrated to startled Russian challengers the merits of the bowie knife, the minister grew bored and sought a more active life in the Union army. Lincoln replaced him with Simon Cameron, thinking St. Petersburg an excellent place to remove his first Secretary of War from the hands of his congressional investigators, hot on the scent of fraud and scandal. Cameron lasted only long enough to present his credentials to the Czar and then asked for a furlough so that he could come back to Pennsylvania and run for the Senate. Meanwhile Clay proved noisy, importunate, and time-consuming with his constant advice to the President on how to conduct all aspects of the war, and Lincoln decided the Union cause would benefit by sending him back to Russia. The Czar was graciously understanding, for his government throughout the war was staunchly pro-Union, and it repeatedly discouraged all suggestions of European intervention in the American conflict.

Much more sensitive were relations with Great Britain and France, the two powers with major interests at stake in the American conflict. In neither was the government particularly favorable to the Union cause, and in both the upper levels of society looked with scorn combined with fear at the democracy of the North and fancied a kinship to the slaveholding oligarchy of the South. The Union blockade, which cut off the export of Southern cotton, produced real suffering in the textile-manufacturing regions of both Britain and France. Shipbuilders in France and especially in Britain saw the possibility of huge profits in outfitting vessels for the Confederate navy. With so much at stake, the two great powers had early moved to issue proclamations of neutrality, which recognized the Confederacy as a belligerent (though not as an independent nation); these had doubtless been proper, even necessary, under international law, but the actions had struck the Lincoln government as precipitate. British willingness to go to the brink of war over the *Trent* affair had offered further evidence that the American Civil War could be easily transformed into an international conflict. And the decision of the Emperor Napoleon III to send French troops to Mexico, in order to bolster the shaky regime of his puppet-king Maximilian, was a direct challenge to the Monroe Doctrine and to the Union government.

Holding firmly to his axiom "One war at a time," Lincoln allowed Seward to manage the day-to-day relations with the two great powers but when there was a crisis used his personal authority to preserve peace. For instance, early in 1863 when Union blockaders captured the *Peterhoff,* a British-owned merchant ship carrying goods to Matamoros, Mexico, just across the Rio Grande from Brownsville, Texas, the British protested this violation of international law, while Secretary Welles defended the navy, claiming the *Peterhoff* was carrying contraband intended for the Confederacy. The mails aboard the *Peterhoff* posed a specially touchy issue, because they might prove the vessel was really a blockade-runner. The British, whose position was strongly backed by Seward, insisted that under international law mails were inviolate, while Welles, whose views were endorsed by Sumner, of the Senate Foreign Relations Committee, argued that only the courts could decide whether they had been lawfully seized. This controversy, which was in reality a minor affair though it had the potential for becoming an explosive issue, occupied much of the time of the Secretary of State and the Secretary of the Navy until the middle of May, and Lincoln gave respectful hearing to both sides. In the end, the President sided with Seward and released the mails, reminding his cabinet members that "we were in no condition to plunge into a foreign war on a subject of so little importance in comparison with the terrible consequences which must follow our act."

Lincoln demonstrated the same caution in dealing with the larger issues of international relations. It was perhaps well that neither he nor Seward realized how close Great Britain and France came to intervening in the American conflict in the summer and fall of 1862, when a long succession of Confederate victories seemed to prove W. E. Gladstone's assertion that Jefferson Davis had made a nation of the Confederacy. Economic hardship, disruption in the patterns of trade, and unwillingness to see a debilitating conflict further protracted moved Napoleon to suggest joint intervention to the British government, and both Lord Palmerston, the Prime Minister, and Earl Russell, the Foreign Secretary, looked favorably on the French plan. Only after an angry debate in the British cabinet, in which defenders of the Union were strengthened by the news of McClellan's success at Antietam and of Lincoln's Emancipation Proclamation, was intervention rejected.

Washington knew of these ominous developments only through rumor, and Lincoln was not, of course, obliged to take any official notice of them. But in early 1863 he could not ignore another scheme for foreign intervention in the war. Horace Greeley, the unpredictable editor of the *New York Tribune,* concluding that the war was hopeless, announced in his influential editorials that the North was ready to restore "the Union as it was." That was tantamount to saying that the Emancipation Proclamation, which the editor had so vigorously urged on the President, should be dropped and that mediation by England, France, or even Switzerland, if offered "in a conciliatory spirit," would be welcomed. Greeley had come under the influence of an unstable mining speculator, William Cornell ("Colorado") Jewett, just back from France with a mediation proposal from Napoleon III, and, flushed with enthusiasm, the editor dashed off to Washington to enlist the French minister, Henri Mercier, in his cause. He found the President noncommittal, and Charles Sumner, the chairman of the Senate Committee on Foreign Relations, said that the Union armies needed another chance for victory. But Greeley was not discouraged, and he told his fellow editor, Henry J. Raymond, of the *New York Times,* that he intended to bring the war to a close by mediation. When Raymond asked what the President had to say about his scheme, he replied: "You'll see . . . that I'll drive Lincoln into it."

Greeley's attempt at peacemaking was so heavy-handed that Seward threatened to prosecute him under the Logan Act, which prohibited American citizens from negotiating with foreign representatives. Lincoln joked that the editor had probably done more "to aid in the successful prosecution of the war than he could have done in any other way," because his overearnest advocacy of peace had, "on the principles of antagonism, made the opposition urge on the war." Certainly Greeley's activities did much to blunt the impact of the formal proposal made by Napoleon's government suggesting that the Union and the Confederacy appoint delegates to meet at some neutral place to explore the possibilities of reunion or permanent division of the United States. With Lincoln's entire approval, Seward promptly rejected the proposal. Virtually all American newspapers commended the government's course, and the often critical *New York Herald* praised not merely "the masterly diplomacy of our sagacious Secretary of State" but also Lincoln's "sagacity, consistency and steadiness of purpose" in sustaining him.

The mediation crisis alerted the President to the importance of influencing public opinion abroad in favor of the Union cause. Charles Francis Adams, the American minister to the Court of St. James's, and William L. Dayton, the minister to France, were both doing excellent work, but their scope was necessarily restricted by their official positions and duties. To reach a wider public in Great Britain and France, Lincoln's administration encouraged informal missions by American businessmen like the shipping magnate John Murray Forbes and the railroad tycoon William H. Aspinwall, by clergymen like Catholic Archbishop John J. Hughes and Episcopal Bishop Charles P. McIlvaine, and by worldly-wise politicians like Thurlow Weed, who could explain and defend their government's actions.

At the same time, Lincoln himself began a campaign to win popular support in Great Britain, where, with some hidden subvention from American funds, numerous public meetings were held to voice support for the Union cause and especially for the emancipation of the slaves. With the help of Charles Sumner, the American who had perhaps the widest circle of acquaintances abroad, the President drafted shrewdly crafted messages to the workingmen of Manchester and London voicing sympathy for their suffering in unemployment and skillfully blaming the cotton shortage not on the Union blockade of the South but on "the actions of our disloyal citizens." Lavishly he praised the ardent Unionism of British workingmen, whose self-interest would have dictated support of the Confederacy. They offered, the President said, "an instance of sublime Christian heroism which has not been surpassed in any age or in any country."

In these messages to British workingmen Lincoln oversimplified the complex American struggle. Ignoring the fact that his government had for nearly two years firmly refused to make emancipation a Union war aim, he now claimed that the conflict was a test "whether a government, established on the principles of human freedom, can be maintained against an effort to build one upon the exclusive foundation of human bondage." Once the American Civil War was so understood, he was convinced that there could be no doubt where British sympathies would lie. In the hope of putting the issue even more forcefully, he drafted a statement that he asked Sumner to present to British friends of the Union, pointing out that the fundamental objective of the rebellion was "to maintain, enlarge, and perpetuate human slavery," and resolving that "no such embryo State [such as the Confederacy] should ever be recognized by, or admitted into, the family of christian and civilized nations."

The effectiveness of the President's personal propaganda warfare could not be measured, for it was not so much public statements or popular rallies as the internal dynamics of British and French politics, plus fears of ultimate American reprisal, that determined a course of neutrality for the two major European powers. But for Lincoln the opportunity to use the White House as a pulpit, to speak out over the dissonant voices of foreign leaders to the common people, daringly broadened the powers of the Presidency. It was a practice he could in the future use to good effect at home.

III

Greeley was not alone in advocating mediation by foreign powers. Heartened by their successes in the recent fall elections, Democrats made mediation by the French Emperor part of the broad assault they launched upon the Lincoln administration. In December, on the first day of the session, Representative S. S. ("Sunset") Cox of Ohio began the attack with a resolution demanding the immediate release of all political prisoners and charging that arbitrary arrests were "unwarranted by the Constitution and laws of the United States, and . . . a usurpation of power never given up by the people to their rulers." In January, as the military situation deteriorated, Senator Willard Saulsbury of Delaware, whose dark, scowling face made him look like a chained mastiff, lamented that the President treated the abridgment of civil liberties "with jocular and criminal indifference," and he warned that the recently issued final Emancipation Proclamation "would light their author to dishonor through all future generations." More important was the full-scale address Representative Clement L. Vallandigham made on January 14 in the House of Representatives. Handsome, plausible, and articulate, the Ohio congressman denounced Lincoln's effort to restore the Union by war as an "utter, disastrous, and most bloody failure." Claiming that the President by "repeated and persistent arbitrary arrests, the suspension of *habeas corpus*, the violation of freedom of the mails, of the private house, of the press and of speech, and all the other multiplied wrongs and outrages upon public liberty and private right" had converted the United States into "one of the worst despotisms on earth," Vallandigham sought the intervention of a friendly foreign power to bring about "an informal, practical recognition" of the Confederacy.

Vallandigham did not speak for the entire Democratic party. War Democrats, who consistently supported Lincoln's efforts to subdue the Confederacy, sustained his administration in all measures they considered constitutional. But many other Democrats throughout the country, weary of the bloodshed, were ready to end the war through negotiation and compromise. At a mass meeting in New York City, for instance, the former mayor, the unsavory and duplicitous Fernando Wood, spoke for these Peace Democrats when he urged the President to cease hostilities, call a conference with the Confederates, and "restore the Union without further loss of blood." Extreme opponents of the administration favored peace at any price; some favored subverting the Lincoln administration and a few of these were in contact with Southern authorities. Republicans called them "Copperheads," probably after the poisonous snake that attacks without notice.

Discontent was strongest and most dangerous in the Middle West. When the war broke out, Westerners had quickly rallied to the colors, and these recruits made up the powerful Union armies that operated in the Mississippi Valley. They had suffered uncounted losses during the first two years of the war, and many were growing angry and disillusioned. After volunteering almost stopped during the winter of 1862–1863, the Lincoln administration put its weight behind a new conscription act, signed by the President on March 3. It promised further hardship for Western farms and families.

Western dissatisfaction was the greater because that region had only imperfectly shared in the general prosperity that the war brought to the North. As long as the Confederacy controlled the Mississippi River, the main Western trade outlet was blocked, and Westerners were forced to pay prohibitively high freight rates to send their produce east by canal and rail. At the same time, Republican tariff legislation protected Northeastern manufacturers at the expense of Western consumers.

But the greatest cause of disaffection in the West was Lincoln's emancipation policy. Few Westerners were abolitionists. Those who had joined the Republican party in the 1850s were, like Lincoln himself, more concerned with the expansion of slavery into the national territories than with its eradication. A considerable majority of Westerners, especially those in the lower parts of Ohio, Indiana, and Illinois, where ties of family and commerce to the South were strong, were Democrats of the Stephen A. Douglas stripe, devoted to the preservation of the Union but indifferent to the future of slavery. For these, the Emancipation Proclamation changed the character of the war. Democratic leaders in the Western states now told their followers: "We told you so. The war is solely an abolition war. We are for putting down Rebellion, but not for making it an anti-slavery crusade!"

Fear that emancipation would lead to a heavy immigration of freedmen from the South strengthened Western hostility toward the administration. "Ohio," it was predicted, "will be overrun with negroes, they will compete with you and bring down your wages, *you* will have to work with them, eat with them, your *wives* and *children* must associate with theirs and you and your families will be degraded to their level." This fear was not wholly irrational; Stanton in September had ordered the "contrabands" assembled at Cairo, Illinois, sent north to replace farm laborers who had joined the army. Anxiety on this subject was pervasive enough that Lincoln felt obliged to devote several pages of his December 1862 message to Congress to refuting this "largely imaginary, if not sometimes malicious" objection to emancipation. Cleverly he tried to turn it into an argument for the colonization of the freedmen "in congenial climes, and with people of their own blood and race." But Westerners were not convinced and many believed that the effect of the President's emancipation policy would be to establish Negro equality.

In the West discontent manifested itself in sporadic outbreaks of violence. In several counties there was resistance to the arrest of deserters from the Union armies; on occasion Union men or soldiers at home on furlough were murdered; there were demonstrations and armed parades against continuing the war. Ugly racism was often evident in these outbreaks. In a Detroit race riot many blacks were beaten and some thirty-five houses were burned.

Numerous mass meetings and county conventions announced "that the Union can never be restored by force of arms," protested the conversion of the war into an abolition crusade, challenged the impending conscription legislation as unconstitutional, and called for a cease-fire. Many of these meetings favored summoning a national convention, to be held at Louisville on the first Tuesday in April, in order "to obtain an armistice and cessation of hostilities." So strong was antiwar sentiment that the *Times* of London believed that Lincoln's Emancipation Proclamation had "proved a solvent which has loosened the federal bond in the North itself" and predicted the imminent secession of the Western states from what remained of the Union.

Many Western Unionists shared that foreboding, and they passed along their fears to the President. John A. McClernand, a sturdy Illinois Democrat, warned the President of "the rising storm in the Middle and Northwestern States," and predicted "not only a separation from the New England States but reunion of the Middle and Northwestern States with the revolted States." Republicans were even more alarmed, finding "Treason . . . everywhere bold, defiant—and active, *with impunity!*" In Illinois the Democratic majority in the state legislature insisted that the Union could not be restored unless Lincoln withdrew the Emancipation Proclamation and urged him to declare an armistice; they also tried to appoint delegates to the Louisville peace convention, to block arbitrary arrests, and to prohibit the immigration of blacks into the state. Republican Governor Richard Yates felt obliged to prorogue the legislature, for the first time in history, and to rule without legislative authorization. Similarly in Indiana the Democrats who controlled the legislature threatened to take over control of the state's military efforts; they were blocked only when the Republican members, bolting the chamber to prevent a quorum, brought about adjournment before any appropriations bills could be passed. For the next two years Republican Governor Oliver P. Morton governed the state without legislative authorization. Both governors attributed Democratic obduracy to secret, pro-Confederate organizations, especially the Knights of the Golden Circle, which were allegedly fomenting disloyalty throughout the West.

Lincoln credited these reports of discontents and conspiracies. Governor

Yates, whom he had known for many years, had his entire confidence, but he was not quite so ready to believe Morton, who, he said, was "at times . . . the skeeredest man I know of." When the governor urged him to meet him in Harrisburg, Pennsylvania, to confer on the crisis, Lincoln refused, because the absence of both the President of the United States and the Governor of Indiana from their respective capitals would be "misconstrued a thousand ways." Nevertheless, he read attentively Morton's long report, drafted by the reformer Robert Dale Owen, detailing the activities of secret peace societies in the West and revealing the Democratic plan to end the war, recognize the Confederacy, and organize a new nation with the New England states left out. All such news the President found exceedingly troubling. He never realized that most of the supposedly disloyal agitation in the West was less an expression of hostility to the Union or the war than to the Republican party. Deeply worried, he confided to Charles Sumner that he now feared " 'the fire in the rear'—meaning the Democracy especially at the North West —more than our military chances."

Promptly his administration moved to support the loyal Republican regimes in the West and to stamp out disaffection and discontent. In January, Yates informed him that it was imperative to have four well-armed regiments stationed in Illinois in order to keep an eye on the legislature and disperse it if necessary, and the President promptly endorsed the proposal. When Morton, who was trying to govern in the absence of the state legislature, ran out of money, Stanton was able to find $250,000 for him in the budget of the Union War Department.

The administration employed the new conscription law not merely to raise troops but to suppress dissent. Lincoln named Colonel James B. Fry provost marshal, and assistant provost marshals were assigned to each state, where they worked closely with the governors. Their primary duty was to enroll soldiers, but if they encountered opposition, as they did in many parts of the West, they promptly jailed the disaffected, invoking Lincoln's suspension of the writ of habeas corpus to deny them trial. Newspapers that attacked the government too vigorously or tried to discourage enlistments were suppressed, sometimes for a single issue, sometimes for a longer period.

Lincoln had the bad judgment to put Ambrose E. Burnside in charge of his effort to keep the West loyal to the Union. Fresh from his defeat at Fredericksburg, Burnside, as commander of the Department of the Ohio, was determined that no carelessness or oversight on his part should lead to further disaster, and he energetically fought what he considered "treason, expressed or implied." On April 13 he issued General Order No. 38 announcing that anyone who committed "acts for the benefit of the enemies of our country" would be arrested and tried as a spy or traitor. The order specifically prohibited "the habit of declaring sympathies for the enemy."

Vallandigham, the leading Peace Democrat in the West, resolved to test this order, which clearly violated the constitutional guarantee of freedom of speech, and on May 1 he made a bitter, rousing address at Mount Vernon, Ohio, denouncing Burnside's order as a base usurpation of tyrannical power. He attacked the President as "King Lincoln," who was waging war for the liberation of the blacks and the enslavement of the whites. Four days later Burnside had him arrested, and a military commission promptly found him guilty of "declaring disloyal sentiments and opinions with the object and purpose of weakening the power of the Government in its efforts to suppress an unlawful rebellion." The former congressman was sentenced to close confinement in a United States fortress for the duration of the war.

Vallandigham's arrest and trial posed a dangerous problem for Lincoln. His instinctive judgment was to sustain the action of his subordinate in the field. Burnside had sent a copy of his Order No. 38 to Washington, and neither Halleck nor the President disapproved of it. After all, the general was acting under the authority of the President's own proclamation of September 24, 1862, suspending the writ of habeas corpus. That authority was further strengthened by a recent act of Congress, which—depending on the legislator's interpretation—either granted the President authority to suspend the great writ or affirmed that he already had the authority. Accordingly, on May 8, Lincoln telegraphed Burnside his "kind assurance of support" in the Vallandigham arrest.

On reflection, he came to view the arrest in another light. All the cabinet regretted the necessity of arresting Vallandigham, and some doubted that there really was a necessity. Gideon Welles judged bluntly: "It was an error on the part of Burnside." Within the administration there was unhappiness that the ex-congressman had been tried before a military tribunal, even though the civil courts in Ohio were available. David Davis, now a justice of the Supreme Court, repeatedly hammered on the theme that military trials in these circumstances were unconstitutional and wrong, and he capitalized on the President's own known opposition to such military tribunals. As Halleck wrote Burnside, "in the loyal States like Ohio it is best to interfere with the ordinary civil tribunals as little as possible." Others regretted that Vallandigham had been sentenced to imprisonment, rather than to banishment to the Confederate lines.

The dismay over Burnside's actions within the administration was nothing when compared to the furor of anger the arrest of Vallandigham roused in the country. The rabidly Democratic *New York Atlas* set the tone by declaring that "the tyranny of military despotism" exhibited in the arrest of Vallandigham demonstrated "the weakness, folly, oppression, mismanagement and general wickedness of the administration at Washington." At a huge rally in New York City one speaker asserted that if Vallandigham's arrest went unrebuked, "free speech dies, and with it our liberty, the constitution and our country." Another pointedly reminded the President that Vallandigham's speech was not nearly so strong as Lincoln's own denunciation of President Polk in the Mexican War. Still another shouted that "the man who occupied the Presidential chair at Washington was tenfold a greater traitor to the country than was any Southern rebel." Across the country newspapers, many of unquestioned loyalty, assailed the arrest of Vallandigham and joined the *New York Herald* in fearing that it was only the first of "a series of fatal steps which must terminate at last in bloody anarchy."

Bowing to pressure, Lincoln on May 19, against the advice of General Burnside, commuted Vallandigham's sentence and ordered that the ex-congressman be exiled to the Confederacy.

The Vallandigham affair had a chastening effect on Lincoln. On June 1, when Burnside ordered the strongly antiwar *Chicago Times* suspended, the President immediately overruled him. Though the paper, edited by Wilbur F. Storey, had strongly condemned the administration's emancipation policy as "a monstrous usurpation, a criminal wrong, and an act of national suicide" and said the President was sacrificing soldiers' lives without cause, Lincoln said the irritation produced by suppressing the newspaper would do more harm than its publication.

But the damage resulting from the Vallandigham case was too extensive to be erased. Ohio Democrats showed what they thought of the President by nominating Vallandigham for governor though he was still in exile. More important, the episode had a profound effect on the War Democrats. Their most prominent spokesman, Governor Horatio Seymour of New York, de-nounced the arrest as an offense "against our most sacred rights" and warned that the administration was moving toward revolution and military despotism.

IV

Seymour's speech killed hopes of a political realignment that would have created a centrist party consisting of most Republicans and War Democrats. Talk of such a realignment had been in the air for months. Indeed, in the fall elections of 1862 in several states Republicans, aware that they had been a minority party in 1860, and Democrats, self-conscious because they had in the past been aligned with the South, joined in putting forward "Union" tickets. The fusion was incomplete and unsuccessful, but the idea of a reor-dering of the parties persisted.

One version of realignment was promoted by the Francis Preston Blair family, which was powerful in the border states. Pushed primarily by Post-master General Montgomery Blair, this scheme called for the President to reorganize his cabinet, eliminating both Seward and Stanton, and to restore McClellan to command of the armies. Francis Preston Blair, Sr., was to become "the private counsellor—not to say dictator—of the President" because, Montgomery Blair said, his father was "beyond all question, the ablest and best informed politician in America." The plan went nowhere; as Attorney General Bates sourly noted, the Blairs believed "fully in trick and contrivance" and mistook cunning for wisdom.

The schemes of conservative New York Republicans like Thurlow Weed made more sense. Continuing to blame their defeat in the 1862 election on Horace Greeley and the abolitionists, one of Weed's associates developed plans for "a speedy sloughing off of the secession sympathizers from the Dem[ocratic] party, of the ultras from the Rep[ublicans] and a *new* organization for 1864." Many thought the best scenario was for Seward to step forward as the voice of moderation, the spokesman of Conservative Republicans and loyal Democrats, making himself available as a candidate in the next presidential election. But Seward would have no part in the plan. To be sure, he had differences with the President, for he had not favored emancipation and regarded Lincoln's proclamations as "unfortunate" and "pernicious," but he was loyal. When approached, he eulogized Lincoln "without limitation" and let it be known that he thought the President "the best and wisest man he has ever known."

Another way of bringing about a realignment would be to have the conservative Republicans and border-state men who supported Lincoln join forces with the Democrats who backed Horatio Seymour. After all, Seymour, though a vigorous critic of the administration, was no Copperhead. So attractive was this idea that, in January, Thurlow Weed, much to Lincoln's surprise, gave up the editorship of the influential *Albany Evening Journal* in order to promote it. Free from obligations to his party, he could resist what he called the "Fanaticism" of Greeley and the abolitionists, which, if unchecked, was bound to "end our Union and Government." Weed's alienation was so public that Vice President Hamlin predicted that he was joining the Democrats.

Lincoln himself was not above giving a slight nudge to this plan to build a party of the center. In January he attempted to enlist Governor Seymour's support for the measures of the administration. Reminding the governor's brother, John, that he and Seymour had the same stake in the preservation of the Union, he observed that if the Union was broken, there would be no "next President" of the United States, whether Republican or Democratic. He listened sympathetically to John Seymour's complaints against "some of the Republican party who claimed to have a patent right for all the patriotism." Because Lincoln understood Seymour's importance as "the head of the greatest State" in the nation, he also initiated a direct correspondence with the governor, "chiefly," as he said, "that we may become better acquainted." Cleverly assuming that he and the governor agreed on the importance of "maintaining the nation's life, and integrity," he sought to minimize differences and to eliminate "unjust suspicions on one side or the other." Though Seymour, fearing a trap, cagily delayed a reply for more than three weeks, he eventually responded, in his ponderous way, that he intended "to show to those charged with the administration of public affairs a due deference and respect and to yield them a just and generous support in all measures . . . within the scope of their constitutional powers." Lincoln refused to be put off, and in the following months took great care to see that even the governor's minor requests for patronage were promptly and courteously attended to.

Out of this stately mating dance emerged the story that the President, using Weed as intermediary, promised to support the governor for the Union nomination as his successor in 1864 if Seymour backed the administration's efforts to suppress the rebellion. As is usually the case with such rumors, the story was greatly exaggerated. After all, it was not within Lincoln's power to give Seymour the succession even in the unlikely event that he decided not to run for a second term. Neither Lincoln nor Seymour made any record of this offer, if one was ever extended, and Weed's own words did not substantiate the usual story. "Governor Seymour . . . can wheel the Democratic party into line, put down rebellion, and preserve the government," was what the editor later remembered the President as saying. "Tell him for me, that if he will render this service to his country, I shall cheerfully make way for him as my successor." This was not an offer on Lincoln's part to withdraw from the presidential race in Seymour's favor. It was, instead, simply a prediction, as Lincoln told Weed, that if the governor used his power "against the Rebellion and for his Country, he would be our next President."

But all hope of enlisting Seymour as an ally, or as a confederate in a realignment of parties, was shattered by the Vallandigham case. War Democrats fell into disarray, and leadership in the party fell into the hands of leaders who were strongly opposed to Lincoln.

V

Simultaneously opposition to the President was mounting within his own party. Notwithstanding Lincoln's success in handling the cabinet crisis of December 1862, some Republicans continued to believe that the administration needed thorough reorganization and new leadership.

Congress, which had assembled in December 1862, was a center of anti-Lincoln agitation. It was a lame-duck session, and many of the Republican representatives, serving their final terms, felt embittered toward an administration they considered responsible for their defeat in the fall elections. Conservative Congressmen from the border states and from the southern parts of the Northwest blamed Republican losses on the President's emancipation policy; Radicals from New England, parts of the mid-Atlantic states, and the northern districts of the Old Northwest attributed defeat to Lincoln's slowness to move against slavery. Neither faction trusted the President. Visiting Washington in January, former Supreme Court Justice Benjamin R. Curtis reported general agreement on "the utter incompetence of the Pres-[iden]t," adding: "He is shattered, dazed and utterly foolish. It would not surprise me if he were to destroy himself." Conservative Republicans thought that he had unnecessarily converted a war for the Union into a crusade against slavery, and they objected to the suppression of free speech, the censorship of the press, and the arbitrary arrest of political dissidents. Radicals, on the other hand, blamed Lincoln for moving too slowly against slavery and his failure to understand that the entire social system of the South must be reorganized before the disloyal states could be readmitted to the Union. In the heated debates of this session of Congress, Republicans, when not attacking each other, now openly turned their guns on the White House. Thaddeus Stevens, the unquestioned leader of the Radical Republicans in the House of Representatives, dismissed all Lincoln's actions since the beginning of the war as "flagrant usurpations, deserving the condemnation of the community" and insisted that the President adopt his theory that the South should be treated like a conquered province.

Despite these bitter intraparty quarrels, Republicans in the Thirty-seventh Congress managed to enact an impressive body of legislation. In this third session (1862–1863) they passed a conscription law—one with teeth. Unlike the 1862 act allocating military quotas to the states, it took the recruiting of soldiers out of the hands of state officials and made able-bodied males between the ages of twenty and forty-five subject to call into the national service. They also enacted, at Chase's strong urging and with Lincoln's quiet pressure, the National Banking Act, which for the first time established a national currency and permitted the creation of a network of national banks. In previous sessions this Congress had passed the Homestead Act, enacted an internal revenue law that permanently altered the tax structure of the nation, adopted tariff legislation that offered genuine protection to American industry, chartered a transcontinental railroad, established a system of land-grant colleges, and created the Department of Agriculture—all at the same time it dealt with weighty issues concerning the raising of armies and fighting a great civil war. To some this record of substantial achievement, brought about by the cooperation of all factions of the Republicans acting with the President, was surprising, but Joseph Medill, the editor of the *Chicago Tribune,* succinctly explained Republican thinking: "An awful responsibility rests upon our party. If it carries the war to a successful close, the people will continue it in power. If it fails, all is lost, Union, party, cause, freedom, and abolition of slavery. Hence we sustain Chase and his National Bank scheme, Stanton and his impulsiveness, Welles and his senility, and Lincoln and his slowness. Let us first get the ship out of the breakers; then court-martial the officers if they deserve it."

That many Republicans of all factions were ready to court-martial the President at the first safe opportunity was evident in the early months of 1863. When Richard Henry Dana, Jr., the Massachusetts author and lawyer, went to Washington in March, he found "the most striking thing is the absence of personal loyalty to the President. It does not exist." Conservatives like Murat Halstead, editor of the influential *Cincinnati Commercial,* thought the President "an awful, woeful ass," and protested, "If Lincoln was not a damn fool, we could get along yet." Radicals were equally censorious. One Michigan resident thought the President "so vacillating, so week [sic] . . . so fearful . . . and so ignorant . . . that I can now see scarcely a ray of hope left." Another predicted that "the administration of Abraham Lincoln will stand even worse . . . with posterity than that of James Buchanan."

While Moderate Republicans sought to make Seward or the Blairs the dominant force in Lincoln's cabinet, Radical Republicans pressed for the elimination of Conservatives from the administration. The chief object of their attack continued to be Secretary of State Seward, whose "perverse, unfaithful and insidious policy" Radicals blamed for the failures of the Union armies. Zachariah Chandler, the outraged Radical senator from Michigan, was almost convinced that Seward was "a traitor *out* and *out.*" James W. White, a zealous anti-Seward judge in New York, launched a petition drive for the removal of the Secretary, and it received the endorsement of Radicals like Trumbull and Thaddeus Stevens, though Sumner, who hoped to suc- ceed Seward in the State Department, declined to sign it. At one point in January, Stevens contemplated introducing a resolution expressing a lack of confidence in the Lincoln administration, and the Republican congressional caucus considered sending another delegation to the White House de- manding the removal of Seward.

When the Radicals found they could not revolutionize the administration, they tried to reform it. One of their targets was military leadership. They charged that the principal officers in the army were, or had been, Demo- crats, who were suspected of lacking enthusiasm for the Union cause and, more particularly, of sabotaging emancipation. Just as Moderates kept press- ing the President to reinstate McClellan, so Radicals insisted that he give another command to General Benjamin F. Butler. This paunchy, cross-eyed Massachusetts politician, a staunch Democrat before the war, was a recent ardent convert to Radicalism. During his command of captured New Orleans he had vigorously suppressed pro-Confederate sentiment in that rebellious city, helped to emancipate the slaves, and enlisted freedmen in the Union army. But he had also tolerated—and perhaps participated in—fraud and peculation, and Lincoln had felt compelled to replace him. Now, pressed by Sumner, whom he needed to appease, Lincoln considered sending Butler back to the lower Mississippi Valley to help recruit black troops, but the appointment was not prestigious enough for the ambitious general, who preferred to be near the center of power in Washington. Butler had to be content with an invitation to an informal dinner at the White House.

Radicals did not fare much better in promoting the elevation of Frémont, who was dear to them because of his early attempts to emancipate the slaves in Missouri. But Frémont carried much baggage with him. His administration of the Department of the West was scandal-ridden, and he had there made mortal enemies of the powerful Blair family. Subsequently he had served without distinction in the Shenandoah Valley but had resigned in a huff.

Under Radical pressure Lincoln conferred with the general during the winter of 1862–1863 and planned to authorize him to recruit a great Negro army, which he hoped would soon be 10,000 strong, but, probably because of the opposition of Halleck, who favored West Pointers, the appointment was never made. Disgruntled, Frémont retreated to New York.

Increasingly, Radical Republicans came to feel that it was the President, and not just his cabinet members or his generals, who ought to be replaced. Early in the year a group of Radicals met with Vice President Hamlin to offer their support if he declared himself a presidential candidate for 1864. Privately believing that Lincoln was "a good man if there ever was one—But God did not make him of such stuff as these times demand," Hamlin rebuffed the offer, saying, "I am loyal to Lincoln, and it is our duty now to lay aside our personal feelings and stand by the President."

Though some Radicals hoped to bring General Butler, *"who is always equal to the emergency* (which Mr. Lincoln and the Cabinet *never* is)," into the administration and give him "almost dictatorial powers," most came to think that the logical successor to the unsuccessful President was his Secretary of the Treasury. Chase had lost credibility with some senators during the cabinet crisis, but he still had a reputation for being a dynamic leader, a strong administrator, and, above all, an ardent antislavery man. He would be, the veteran abolitionist Joshua R. Giddings predicted, "the only Republican Candidate" in the next election, and there could "be no serious opposition" to him. Chase did nothing to discourage such speculation. Even before the December cabinet crisis he had been writing sympathizers about the need for "a new organization of parties," which should be "really democratic and really republican," whose leader would be a former Democrat who was now an earnest Republican. The description exactly fit Chase himself.

VI

Battered from all sides, Lincoln grew deeply despondent. In February a close observer, noting that "his hand trembled . . . and he looked worn and haggard," felt that the President was "growing feeble." Admiral John A. Dahlgren, a frequent visitor to the White House, recorded in his diary on February 6, "I observe that the President never tells a joke now." When the Massachusetts abolitionist Wendell Phillips spoke of Lincoln's chances for a second term, the President replied, "Oh, Mr. Phillips, I have ceased to have any personal feeling or expectation in that matter,—I do not say I never had any,—so abused and borne upon as I have been."

Constantly surrounded by bureaucrats, civilian and military job applicants, and sightseers, he was the loneliest man in Washington. After Browning was defeated for reelection to the Senate, Lincoln had no personal friends in the Congress. Of the cabinet members he most enjoyed Seward, with whom he liked to exchange stories, but these two men, who first met when they were both adults and prominent politicians, never confided their deepest feelings to each other.

From Mary he no longer received much emotional support. Still dressed in mourning, she grieved for Willie, and on the anniversary of his death in February, she again felt brokenhearted. "Only those, who have passed through such bereavements, can realise, how the heart bleeds at the return, of these anniversaries," she wrote Mrs. Gideon Welles. Refusing to let Willie's memory go, she consorted with spiritualists, notably one Nettie Colburn, who she thought put her in communication with her son's spirit. Perhaps as many as eight séances were held in the White House itself. Lincoln attended one, but he was not convinced. Presently Mary began to feel that she herself, without the intercession of a medium, could lift the veil that separates the living and the dead and conjure up the spirits of both her dead sons. "Willie lives," she told her half sister. "He comes to me every night and stands at the foot of the bed with the same sweet adorable smile he always has had. . . . Little Eddie is sometimes with him."

With Mary moving like a cloud of doom, the White House was a depressing place these days. She no longer took much interest in the expensive furnishings and elaborate ornamentation with which she had redecorated the Executive Mansion. The formal receptions, once a source of great pleasure, she now considered a trial, especially when vandals snipped off pieces of the lace curtains or damask draperies as souvenirs or even, as the newspaper correspondent Noah Brooks reported, cut out "small bits of the gorgeous carpet, leaving scars on the floor as large as a man's hand." Mary managed to bring herself to attend the huge New Year's Day reception, but her heart was clearly not in it, and she greeted her guests mechanically.

There were few entertainments or diversions at the White House now. An exception was a hastily arranged reception for "General Tom Thumb" (Charles Sherwood Stratton) and his bride, who had just been married on February 10 in New York. Mary apparently staged the affair out of a sense of duty, but the President thoroughly enjoyed it, bending down from his six-foot-four-inch height to talk gravely with his three-foot-four-inch guest.

In her distraught state Mary seemed unaware that her husband needed relief from the ordeal he was undergoing, and Lincoln, protective of his wife's fragile mental health, did not burden her with his problems. In any event, it was doubtful that she could have been much help. Her sensitive political antennae, which had served them both so well in Springfield, functioned badly in the nation's capital. Classifying politicians as friends or foes, Mary hated anyone who might be considered a rival to her husband. From the beginning she distrusted Seward and wanted him to resign. She became aware of Chase's presidential aspirations perhaps earlier than Lincoln himself. From her point of view her husband mishandled the cabinet crisis, because he ought to have used it as an excuse to purge every member except Montgomery Blair, whom she thought loyal to Lincoln. Her eccentric judgment troubled Lincoln less than her habit of making her views public in conversation or in letters. She never understood that every action of a President's wife is judged in political terms. Thus she did not see that she was making a political statement when she chose Rhoda White as one of her closest friends; Mrs. White was an unexceptionable lady, but her husband, Judge James W. White, was leading the petition drive to oust Seward from the cabinet. In the circumstances, Lincoln found it best not to confide much in his wife.

Lincoln drew much comfort from Tad, to whom he became even more attached after the death of Willie. He spent much time playing with the boy, and he helped him raise his kitten and train his dog, "a very cunning little fellow," according to Leonard Swett, who "runs about the house, . . . Barks and stands straight up on his hind feet—holds his fore feet up." Bright and affectionate, Tad was also wholly undisciplined. The nine-year-old boy could still not dress himself, and, despite the efforts of a series of tutors, he could neither read nor write. Lincoln refused to worry over his slowness in such matters. "Let him run," said his father; "there's time enough yet for him to learn his letters and get pokey." Because of his speech defect most people could not understand Tad, but his father always could—and he knew how frustrated the child became when he could not express himself. Consequently even when Tad burst in on cabinet meetings, jabbering something to "Papa-day," as he called his father (perhaps he meant to say something like "Papa dear"), the President interrupted everything to give the lad his full attention. In turn, Tad adored his father, and he would often hang around the President's office until late at night, sometimes falling asleep on one of the couches or chairs. When Lincoln got ready to retire, he would pick the boy up and carry him off to his big bed, where Tad now mostly slept.

For more mature companionship Lincoln did not look to his oldest son, Robert, who was off studying at Harvard College most of the year. In his own way he was proud of Robert and he bragged to visitors that his son was getting "the best of educations," even if "it was hard for him to afford it." But in an obscure way he viewed his eldest as a competitor. "Bob was brighter than himself, he had never had but one year of education," he remarked, "but he guessed Bob would not do better than he had." When Robert spent his holidays in the White House, Washingtonians thought him a good-looking young man with excellent manners and, in private conversation, a good sense of humor. But he felt stiff and awkward around his father, and the two never seemed to find anything to say to each other. It was rather a relief to everybody when Robert had to go back to Cambridge.

In his two secretaries Lincoln found the sons that Robert could never be. Working side by side for long hours with John G. Nicolay and John Hay, Lincoln came to know these young men extremely well and to enjoy their company. Because they lived right in the White House, he got in the habit of dropping in on them at night to chat and review the day's news. Once at midnight he came in, laughing, to read them an amusing poem by Thomas Hood, "seemingly utterly unconscious," Hay noted in his diary, "that he with his short shirt hanging above his long legs and setting out behind like the tail feathers of an enormous ostrich was infinitely funnier than anything in the book he was laughing at."

He valued their absolute loyalty. They, in turn, watched him grow into the presidency, and admired the skill with which he operated the levers of power. They revered him as "a backwoods Jupiter" who wielded "the bolts of war and the machinery of government with a hand equally steady and equally firm." His secretaries were among the first to recognize Lincoln's mastery of the English language. As a graduate of Brown University, Hay felt he had to deplore "some hideously bad rhetoric—some indecorums that are infamous" in Lincoln's public papers, yet he recognized these documents would take their "solid place in history, as a great utterance of a great man." Bonding to the President, they resented anyone else who tried to get close to him. A fierce rivalry developed between the two secretaries and Mrs. Lincoln. Ostensibly their clashes had to do with the management and refurbishing of the White House, but at base they stemmed from jealousy over the President's affections.

VII

Aware of his unpopularity during these early months of 1863, Lincoln thought he understood the cause. When a group of New England abolitionists descended on the White House to complain that the Northern people believed the Emancipation Proclamation was not being honestly carried out by the generals and soldiers in the field, the President replied: "My own impression . . . is that the masses of the country generally are only dissatisfied at our lack of military successes. Defeat and failure in the field make everything seem wrong."

During this time, when his generals and admirals were concerting plans for a new assault upon the Confederacy, he did what he could to ensure success. It was his job to see that the commanders had everything they required in the way of men and weapons. Manpower now posed a real problem. There had been severe losses in a contest that had now lasted nearly two years. The terms for which many regiments had enlisted were about to expire, and soldiers wanted to go home. Thousands were absent without leave, and Lincoln's offer of amnesty to those who returned to their regiments had only limited success. There were almost no new volunteers. It would be months before the new conscription act could bring in recruits.

Reluctantly, and after great hesitation, Lincoln turned to the one source of manpower he had vowed he could never use: African-Americans. It was a move that many abolitionists and black leaders had been urging since the beginning of the war. Frederick Douglass demanded, "Let the slaves and free colored people be called into service, and formed into a liberating army, to march into the South and raise the banner of emancipation among the slaves." But powerful conservative voices opposed the idea. Some maintained that Negroes would never fight, so that arms given to them would simply be seized by the Confederates; others predicted that armed blacks would rise against their masters and make of the South another Santo Domingo. Though the Confiscation Act of July 1862 specifically authorized Negro enlistments, the President was averse to pursuing so revolutionary a policy. When General David Hunter, in the Department of the South, attempted to raise black regiments in South Carolina, the President overruled him, stating that he "would employ all colored men as laborers, but would not promise to make soldiers of them."

Lincoln's resistance to using Negro troops persisted even after he issued his preliminary Emancipation Proclamation. That proclamation was designed to persuade Confederates to return to the Union within one hundred days or else lose their slaves; it would have been illogical and counterproductive at the same time to announce that those slaves who were successful in escaping from their masters would be organized into regiments of the Union army. From Lincoln's point of view it made more sense to talk of colonizing the blacks out of the country than to plan on making them soldiers. But the movement to enlist black troops had become irresistible. Even before the Emancipation Proclamation was issued, Stanton, without Lincoln's knowledge, but also without his disapproval, authorized General Rufus Saxton to enlist blacks in South Carolina; General Benjamin F. Butler began mustering in free men of color in Louisiana; and in Kansas, James H. Lane's Jayhawkers welcomed recruits of any race.

Under continuous pressure, especially from Sumner, whose support, or at least neutrality, was needed during the cabinet crisis, Lincoln began to shift his position on Negro troops. Perhaps he was influenced by several talks with Vice President Hamlin, who brought to the White House a delegation of young army officers, including one of his sons, to volunteer for command of colored troops. Surprised and moved that these promising young men were willing to risk their careers in a cause that aroused strong racial prejudice, Lincoln told them, "I suppose the time has come." Recognizing that the Emancipation Proclamation had "in certain quarters" worked against recruitment for the Union armies, he concluded he ought to "take some benefit from it, if practicable" by enrolling black soldiers.

In his final Emancipation Proclamation he announced that former slaves would be received into the armed forces—though as yet he limited their role "to garrison and defend forts, positions, stations, and other places, and to man vessels of all sorts." An unstated corollary of the President's new position was that plans to colonize blacks outside the United States were abandoned. Henceforth Lincoln recognized that blacks were to make their future as citizens of the United States.

Once converted, Lincoln began actively urging his commanders to employ black troops. For instance, he asked General John A. Dix, in command of Yorktown and Fort Monroe in Virginia, whether these posts "could not, in whole or in part, be garrisoned by colored troops, leaving the white forces now necessary at those places, to be employed elsewhere."

By spring the President was urging a massive recruitment of Negro troops. When neither General Butler nor General Frémont accepted his offer to go South and raise a black army, Lincoln turned directly to men already in the field. "The colored population is the great *available* and yet *unavailed* of, force for restoring the Union," he reminded Andrew Johnson, whom he had appointed military governor of Tennessee, and he urged Johnson to take the lead in raising a force of black troops. "The bare sight of fifty thousand armed, and drilled black soldiers on the banks of the Mississippi," he predicted, "would end the rebellion at once."

Eventually he found it necessary to be more aggressive. As the spring campaigns were about to get under way, he authorized General Daniel Ullmann of New York to raise a brigade of volunteers from the freedmen in Louisiana. In a more ambitious undertaking he and Stanton sent Adjutant General Lorenzo Thomas into the Mississippi Valley to recruit blacks; by the end of 1863 Thomas had enrolled twenty regiments of African-Americans.

Along with supplying troops, Lincoln made it his responsibility to see that the armies had the best, and most up-to-date, arms. In this effort he was constantly hampered by the army bureaucracy, slow-moving and hidebound. James W. Ripley, his chief of ordnance, who had been born in 1794, was a traditionalist, who objected to every new idea and referred every innovation to a board of inquiry, where most were killed. Ripley was opposed to the breech-loading rifle, to the repeating rifle, to the "coffee-mill gun" (a precursor of the machine gun), and to virtually all other military novelties. The President found the navy more willing to experiment, as the enormous risk that Secretary Welles took in supporting the *Monitor* proved, but here, too, the bureaucratic machinery often worked creakingly.

Lincoln, on the other hand, was interested in any new ideas that promised to shorten the war—including a number that were wholly impractical. He spent a good deal of time with one Francis L. Capen, who claimed that he could save thousands of lives and millions of dollars through his expert prediction of the weather. After a trial of the scheme, Lincoln recorded on April 28: "It seems to me Mr. Capen knows nothing about the weather, in advance. He told me three days ago that it would not rain again till the 30th of April or 1st. of May. It is raining now and has been for ten hours. I can not spare any more time to Mr. Capen."

Always interested in machinery and gadgets, Lincoln accumulated models of proposed new weapons—a cuirass of polished blue steel far too heavy for a soldier to carry into battle, a grenade that served as a presidential paperweight, a brass cannon, which he used to hold down land patents.

Himself an inventor, he wanted to give those who came up with fresh ideas a fair chance. Sometimes he tried out their inventions on the back lawn of the White House. More often he went to the Washington Navy Yard, where Dahlgren was always ready to test new weapons and explosives. Secretary Welles thought Dahlgren was a courtier who was trying to ingratiate himself with the President, and no doubt he hoped to advance his own career. But Lincoln found the lean fifty-two-year-old Philadelphian a man of broad-ranging intellectual curiosity and of sound judgment. Hardly a week passed that he did not visit the Navy Yard, sometimes to escape the pressure from job hunters and other visitors at the White House, more often to witness the trials of some new weapon or explosive.

He took great interest, for instance, in a repeating rifle of a French inventor named Rafael (or perhaps "Raphael") and referred this "new patern of gun" to Dahlgren for testing. Dahlgren got good results and invited the President to a demonstration at the Navy Yard. Accompanied by Seward, Stanton, and a correspondent of the *New York Tribune,* the President spent more than two hours watching the machine gun shoot at targets on the Potomac. Afterward there was talk about how the mechanism of the gun prevented the escape of gas at the breech, and the President said, with a mischievous glance at the *Tribune* correspondent, "Now have any of you heard of any machine, or invention, for preventing the escape of 'gas' from newspaper establishments?"

The chief benefit from the President's exertions was perhaps that he got out of doors and improved his health. Few of the new weapons he examined proved practicable or ever got into the hands of the soldiers. What Gideon Welles called Lincoln's "well-intentioned but irregular proceedings" in the testing of new weapons made him "liable to be constantly imposed upon by sharpers and adventurers."

VIII

After Congress adjourned in March, Lincoln found himself, unexpectedly, with time on his hands. There were no senators to be soothed, no representatives to be placated, no bills to be signed. Talk of foreign mediation had died down, and rumors of Copperhead uprisings in the West had abated. One day in April, after a long visit with Dahlgren at the Navy Yard, the President remarked good-humoredly that it was time for him to leave. "Well I will go home," he said; "I had no business here; but, as the lawyer said, I had none anywhere else."

That moment of tranquillity signified that the plans for a great spring assault on the Confederacy were finally in place. A huge armada, including both ironclad monitors and conventional warships, was being prepared to attack Charleston, the heart of the Confederacy. Generals Grant and Sherman were readying a new campaign to capture Vicksburg, the last major link between the eastern states of the Confederacy and the trans-Mississippi region. From New Orleans, General Banks was supposed to push north to join forces with Grant. In eastern Tennessee, Rosecrans was poised for a drive that would capture Chattanooga, break the most important rail connection between the seaboard and Mississippi Valley states of the Confederacy, and, most important of all from Lincoln's point of view, liberate the long-suffering Unionists of the mountain regions. And in the East, Hooker's vast Army of the Potomac was eager to advance against Robert E. Lee's Army of Northern Virginia.

Anxiously Lincoln watched all these elements in his grand strategy that could bring about the collapse of the Confederacy. He frequently consulted Secretary Welles about the naval expedition off South Carolina, and he went almost daily to the War Department to learn of preparations and progress for the military campaigns. He kept the Army of the Potomac under closest scrutiny, partly because it was so near at hand, partly because he had residual doubts about Hooker. But that general in the months since he assumed command had proved, for all his bluster and bragging, an expert at army organization, and the Army of the Potomac was in better physical shape and had higher morale than at any time in its history.

In early April, Lincoln, perhaps at the suggestion of Mary, who thought her husband needed respite from the cares of office, decided to visit Hooker's headquarters in northern Virginia. The general's welcoming telegram set the tone for the visit: "I . . . only regret that your party is not as large as our hospitality."

Accompanied by Mrs. Lincoln and Tad, together with Attorney General Bates, Dr. Anson G. Henry, an old friend from Springfield, Noah Brooks, the Washington correspondent of the *Sacramento Union,* and a few others, Lincoln sailed down the Potomac on the unarmed *Carrie Martin* and, after being delayed by a snowstorm, was taken by train to Hooker's headquarters. On April 6 he reviewed the entire cavalry of the Army of the Potomac, which Hooker had recently reorganized into a single corps, and the soldiers, though they found him "an ungainly looking man," gave him a hearty welcome because, as one lieutenant wrote in his diary, they "respect him for his integrity, and good management of the war." Mrs. Lincoln received a less favorable rating as "a pleasant, but not an intelligent looking woman." But Tad was the star of the occasion. Booted and spurred, he galloped along on a pony, clinging tenaciously to the saddle with his gray cloak billowing behind him.

During the next three days, in addition to visiting soldiers in the army hospital, the President reviewed more than 60,000 of the troops under Hooker's command. Most of the time he rode a large bay horse, and if, as one soldier remarked, his appearance was "not very graceful, and . . . hardly calculated to inspire much admiration," he was nevertheless roundly cheered by the soldiers as he rode past them. Mary Lincoln, accompanied by Attorney General Bates, watched the reviews from a carriage drawn by four spanking bays. Though the reviews were exhausting, they were impressive, and Lincoln did not fail to notice the high state of readiness: "Uniforms were clean, arms bright as new, equipments in sp[l]endid condition." As the presidential party left the army headquarters, Lincoln could afford a feeling of satisfaction that he had done everything possible to make the forthcoming campaign a success, and the salute he received at Aquia Creek from all the vessels in port and locomotives on shore, with whistles blown, bells rung, and flags displayed, should have given him a sense of confidence.

But with his native caution, the President was not ready to predict victory. When asked about the chances for Union success in the operations that were already under way, he remarked, "I expect the best, but I am prepared for the worst." Even during the euphoria of his visit to army headquarters, some nagging doubts arose. While he was still in Hooker's camp, discouraging information trickled in from Confederate newspapers and rebel pickets about the assault on Charleston.

Lincoln was also troubled by some things he saw and heard at Hooker's camp. In describing his plans to the President, the general frequently prefaced remarks with "When I get to Richmond" or "After we have taken Richmond." Taking Noah Brooks aside, Lincoln remarked in a whisper: "That is the most depressing thing about Hooker. It seems to me that he is over-confident." He was also troubled that Hooker and his generals were debating whether the best road to Richmond was by going around Lee's left flank or moving around his right flank, and he jotted down for their guidance a memorandum that combined common sense and a superior military insight: "Our prime object is the enemies' army in front of us, and is not with, or about, Richmond—at all, unless it be incidental to the main object." Finally, as he heard plans of battle discussed, he feared his new commander of the Army of the Potomac might follow his predecessors in throwing in his forces a few at a time. Not wishing to assume personal responsibility for planning a battle, the President just before leaving told Hooker and General Darius N. Couch: "I want to impress upon you two gentlemen in your next fight . . . put in all of your men."

Over the next few weeks all of Lincoln's forebodings seemed to be justified. On April 7, while he was with the Army of the Potomac, Samuel F. Du Pont's fleet of nine ironclads steamed into Charleston harbor and attacked Fort Sumter. By the end of the day five of Du Pont's ironclads had been badly damaged, and he was forced to withdraw. Lincoln, who, as Gideon Welles observed, had "often a sort of intuitive sagacity," never had high hopes for this largest naval operation of the Civil War; Du Pont's dispatches and movements reminded him of McClellan's. All he could do now was to put the best face possible on this major defeat. To someone who remarked that Du Pont had suffered a repulse at Charleston, he replied sharply: "A check, sir, not a repulse." He ordered the fleet to hold its position inside the bar near Charleston, in order to prevent the Confederates from erecting new defenses or batteries.

Equally disappointing were the operations on the Mississippi River. After Grant's army spent much of the spring digging a canal on the Louisiana side of the Mississippi River in the hope of bypassing Vicksburg, the banks caved in, and the whole enterprise was abandoned. An attempt by Union warships to run the batteries of Vicksburg was successful but costly. Then Grant, taking no one into his confidence, marched his troops down the west side of the river, crossed into Mississippi, and disappeared, with no one in Washington knowing where he was or what he planned to do. Banks, after a delay so long that his movement was of no assistance to Grant, moved up the Mississippi and staged an ill-timed and bloody assault on Port Hudson, Louisiana.

By way of contrast, in Tennessee, Rosecrans offered only inaction. He seemed to operate under the curious idea that the art of war permitted only one campaign to be fought at a time. While Grant was moving against Vicksburg, the rules required him to remain stationary in eastern Tennessee. Nothing Lincoln could do or say could disabuse Rosecrans of this notion. Instead of staging an offensive against Bragg, or, at the least, sending reinforcements to Grant, he spent his time in worrying about alleged slights and indignities. Lincoln was finally obliged to assure him, "I really *can not* say that I have heard any complaints of you." But Rosecrans was unconvinced and remained inactive.

Lincoln watched most closely the Army of the Potomac, where, on April 28, Hooker began moving 70,000 of his men across the Rappahannock River and threatened to crush Lee's flank. The President had asked to be informed of Hooker's strategy before the battle, and he wanted frequent dispatches once the fighting began. When he did not receive sufficiently detailed information, he wired General Daniel Butterfield, Hooker's chief of staff: "Where is Gen. Hooker? Where is Sedgwick? where is Stoneman?" His concern was, once more, that all the Union forces be thrown into the engagement.

The concern was warranted. Hooker, after a most promising start, paused at Chancellorsville and failed to push his offensive. Lee took advantage of his hesitation, boldly divided his much smaller army, and sent "Stonewall" Jackson by a circuitous route to fall on Hooker's right. The Confederates gained another major victory, and Hooker was forced to retreat to the north side of the Rappahannock.

News of the battle of Chancellorsville was slow in reaching Washington. Highly optimistic predictions after the first day's fighting withered as more and more bad news came in. Lincoln spent most of the time at the War Department, showing "a feverish anxiety to get facts." He feared that Hooker had been licked, although he still held on to a shred of hope. But in mid-afternoon of May 6, holding a telegram in his hand, he came into the room in the White House where Dr. Henry and Noah Brooks were talking. His face was ashen, and his voice trembled as he said to his guests, "Read it—news from the Army." At no other time, Brooks thought, did the President appear "so broken, so dispirited, and so ghostlike." As Brooks and Dr. Henry read of Hooker's defeat and his retreat back across the river, Lincoln paced up and down the room, exclaiming: "My God! my God! What will the country say! What will the country say!"

CHAPTER SIXTEEN

A New Birth of Freedom

T he weeks after the battle of Chancellorsville were among the most depressing of Lincoln's presidency. Everything went wrong—at Charleston, at Vicksburg, in eastern Tennessee, and, especially, in northern Virginia. Failure of Union arms led to renewed protests against the war and to demands for peace negotiations. Controversy over the arrest of Vallandigham and the suppression of civil liberties mounted. So did complaints about the incompetence of Lincoln's administration. At one end of the political spectrum a Democratic politician addressing a huge peace rally in New York City characterized the President as a donkey in a china shop and urged, "You must get him out or he will smash the crockery." At the other end Missouri Radical Republicans attacked Lincoln for his compromising, indecisive course and for refusing to put abolitionist generals like Frémont and Butler in command of the armies. Even more disturbing were reports that some army officers, like Major Charles J. Whiting of the Second United States Cavalry, were denouncing this "damned abolition nigger war," claiming that "the President had exceeded his authority in proclaiming the niggers free, and in suspending the writ of Habeas Corpus, and that Republicans would not have the war cease, if they could. . . . They were all making money out of it, and consequently it was for their interest to prolong the war."

Grimly Lincoln informed his critics that it might be "a misfortune for the nation that he was elected President. But having been elected by the people, he meant to be President, and to perform his duty according to *his* best understanding, if he had to die for it." But the downward spiral of events during the past six months finally convinced the reluctant President that he had to exert more active leadership, both in the conduct of military operations and in the shaping of public opinion. Firmly taking the lead, he recovered much of the ground he had lost during the previous months of indecision and inaction.

I

The immediate issue after Chancellorsville was what to do about the Army of the Potomac. In public the President tried to be of good cheer, but in private he predicted that effects of the defeat at Chancellorsville "would be more serious and injurious than any previous act of the war."

Immediately he set about determining responsibility for the disaster, and on May 6, accompanied by Halleck, he went to the headquarters of the Army of the Potomac at Falmouth, Virginia. Pleased to discover that the "troops are none the worse for the campaign," he let it be known that he was "agreeably surprised with the situation." Less encouraging was the mental state of their commander. Hooker, as always, was "cool, clear and satisfied," unwilling to recognize his mistakes and unable to learn from his defeat.

In deciding on the general's future, Lincoln was torn. He genuinely liked Hooker, who had shown himself candid and brave. He also learned that the general had skillfully planned the battle and had been on the verge of victory until he was stunned by a falling beam when a Confederate cannonball hit his headquarters at the Chancellor house. Sardonically the President mused that if the ball had been aimed lower—so as to hit Hooker—the battle would have been a great Union success. On leaving Falmouth he announced to a newspaper correspondent that "his confidence in Gen. Hooker and his army [was] unshaken." When another reporter asked whether he intended to replace the general, he replied with some displeasure that since he had tried McClellan "a number of times, he saw no reason why he should not try General Hooker twice."

He was determined, though, to keep a closer personal control of the general's future operations. "What next?" he asked Hooker. Did the general have in mind a new movement against the enemy that would "help to supersede the bad moral effect of the recent one"? Hooker remarked that less than one-third of his army had been engaged at Chancellorsville and promised that in the next action "the operations of all the Corps" would be under his personal supervision. Lincoln did not remind him that was exactly what he had instructed the general to do before the battle.

Hooker had a plan—a hopelessly wrongheaded one. Learning that Lee was moving north of the Rappahannock, he proposed to cross that river and attack the Confederate rear guard at Fredericksburg. Promptly Lincoln warned, "I would not take any risk of being entangled upon the river, like an ox jumped half over a fence, and liable to be torn by dogs, front and rear, without a fair chance to gore one way or kick the other." But Hooker seemed not to learn. Within a week he suggested that if Lee invaded the North the Army of the Potomac should march south and attack Richmond.

Quietly Lincoln reminded him of the dangers of this harebrained scheme and pointed out a basic truth so many of his commanders seemed unable to grasp: *"Lee's* Army, and not *Richmond,* is your true objective point."

Certainly Hooker was obtuse, but the President himself was in part responsible for the general's failure. Though Lincoln had excellent strategic sense, which improved as the war progressed, he was not a professional military man and knew that he was not competent to draft proper orders for a military campaign. He also knew how much military men objected to what they regarded as meddling by a civilian. Consequently he deprecated the advice he offered as "my poor mite" and advanced ideas hesitantly, "incompetent as I may be." Expressing his wishes as suggestions, rather than commands, he relied on Halleck, his general-in-chief, to translate his ideas into military orders that the armies could follow.

Besides being cumbersome, the system could not work because of Halleck. That general, as Lincoln knew very well, was unwilling to take the initiative or assume responsibility. Like McClellan, Halleck was a master of procrastination when he did not agree with the President's ideas. He could always find technical reasons why Lincoln's suggestions could not be carried out, and the President usually yielded to his objections, saying, "It being strictly a military question, it is proper I should defer to Halleck whom I have called here to counsel, advise and direct, in these matters, where he is an expert." Gideon Welles accurately described the resulting stalemate: "No one more fully realizes the magnitude of the occasion, and the vast consequences involved than the President—he wishes all to be done that can be done, but yet [in army operations] will not move or do except by the consent of the dull, stolid, inefficient and incompetent General-in-Chief."

In dealing with Hooker, Lincoln faced the further problem that Halleck disliked the commander of the Army of the Potomac, who had once borrowed money from him in California and failed to pay it back; indeed, Halleck had opposed Hooker's appointment. For his part, Hooker despised the general-in-chief and would have as little as possible to do with him. When he took command of the Army of the Potomac, he had insisted on communicating directly with the President, bypassing the War Department, yet, now, with Lee on the march, he complained that he had "not enjoyed the confidence of the Major General Commanding the Army."

As the Confederates swept through western Maryland, many in Washington panicked. Rumor had it that a steamer was anchored in the Potomac, ready to take the President and his cabinet to safety when the rebels arrived. But Lincoln was in excellent spirits, spending much of his time in the telegraph office of the War Department, joking and reading the latest dispatches. He improved the occasion to instruct the sober quartermaster general, Montgomery C. Meigs, about the writings of Orpheus C. Kerr. "Any one who has not read them must be a heathen," he exclaimed. The humorist's papers delighted him, he said, except when their wit was turned on him; then he found them unsuccessful and rather disgusting. "Now the hits that are given to you, Mr. Welles I can enjoy," he laughingly told the Secretary of the Navy, "but I dare say they may have disgusted you while I was laughing at them. So *vice versa* as regards myself."

Lincoln's good cheer stemmed from his conviction that Lee's invasion offered a chance to bag the entire Confederate army. The Army of the Potomac, facing the rebels on Union soil, could not "help beating them, if we have the man," Lincoln told Welles, but he worried that "Hooker may commit the same fault as McClellan and lose his chance."

That remark revealed his doubts about Hooker. Like everybody else, he heard reports that the general was drinking too much. He knew, too, that there had been much grumbling against Hooker since the defeat at Chancellorsville. Both General Darius N. Couch and General Henry W. Slocum asked the President to remove Hooker. In a long interview at the White House, General John F. Reynolds, disavowing any desire to command the Army of the Potomac himself, urged Lincoln to replace Hooker with his fellow Pennsylvanian George Gordon Meade. Lincoln demurred, saying that he was not inclined to throw away a gun because it had once missed fire but "would pick the lock and try it again," but he thought the complaints sufficiently serious to warn Hooker that he did not have the full confidence of some of his division commanders.

What eventually turned the President against his commanding general was Hooker's obdurate failure to follow directions. The general refused to recognize that Lincoln's homespun suggestions were, in fact, commands. At the same time, he also ignored Halleck's more specific orders, not realizing that they came from the President. Eventually Lincoln was forced to put Hooker in his place in a dispatch of two terse sentences: "To remove all misunderstanding, I now place you in the strict military relation to Gen. Halleck, of a commander of one of the armies, to the General-in-Chief of all the armies. I have not intended differently; but as it seems to be differently understood, I shall direct him to give you orders, and you to obey them."

II

While Lincoln was trying to establish his control over the Army of the Potomac, he also sought to give a new direction to public opinion. Up to this point he had largely accepted the traditional view that the President, once elected, had no direct dealings with the public. His job was to administer the government and to report his actions and wishes to the Congress. Presidents rarely left the capital city, except for brief vacations; they almost never made public addresses; and they maintained, in theory, a sublime indifference to public opinion and political pressures.

Like many other self-made men, Lincoln was very conventional and hesitated to break this tradition. It never occurred to him to go in person before Congress and read his eloquent messages, for that was something that had not been done since Jefferson's day. Though occasionally he would say a few words at a Union rally in Washington, he knew that he was not good at extemporaneous speaking and rarely made any public appearances outside the White House. His one innovation had been to maintain an open house at the Executive Mansion, during which as many of the curious and the complainers, the office-seekers and the favor-hunters, as wanted to wait in line had an opportunity to speak with the President.

Though that kind of openness certainly did not injure him in public esteem, it did little to get his message across to the people, and by mid-summer of 1863 it was desperately important that the administration's policies should be understood. On no issue was this need so great as on the abrogation of civil liberties. Curtailment of the freedom of speech and of the press, arrests of dissenters and the disloyal—always called "arbitrary arrests" by his opponents—and, above all, suspension of the privilege of the writ of habeas corpus deeply troubled many Americans. Of course, the Peace Democrats vigorously protested against these measures, and, after the arrest and trial of Vallandigham, many of the War Democrats joined them. But they were not alone. Within the President's own party a Conservative like his friend Browning believed that the arrests ordered by the Lincoln administration "were illegal and arbitrary, and did more harm than good, weakening instead of strengthening the government." The Radical Lyman Trumbull agreed that "all arbitrary arrests of citizens by military authority . . . are unwarrantable, and are doing much injury, and that if they continue unchecked the civil tribunals will be completely subordinated to the military, and the government overthrown." Even in the President's own cabinet, Gideon Welles lamented "that our military officers should, without absolute necessity, disregard those great principles on which our government and institutions rest." Most dangerous of all was the growing sentiment in the army that, as one Massachusetts soldier wrote his family, the President, "without the people having any legal means to prevent it, is only prevented from exercising a Russian despotism by the fear he may have of shocking too much the sense of decency of the whole world."

Aware of the widespread public unhappiness, Lincoln grew restive at remaining a prisoner of the White House. For a time he considered attending a huge July 4 celebration planned for Philadelphia, where he could for the first time since his inauguration have a chance to speak directly to the public, but Lee's impending invasion of Pennsylvania put an end to that idea. The favorable reception of his public letters to friends of the Union cause in Manchester and London suggested another way he could explain to the people why he had found it necessary to suspend the writ of habeas corpus. As ideas came to him that "seemed to have force and make perfect answer to some of the things that were said and written" about his actions, he jotted them down on scraps of paper and put them in a drawer. When the appropriate time came, he could put together these disconnected thoughts in a public letter.

The protest of a group of New York Democrats against the arrest of

Vallandigham gave him the opportunity for which he had been waiting. Headed by Erastus Corning, president of the New York Central Railroad, the meeting adopted resolutions strongly condemning the arrest and trial of Vallandigham as a "blow . . . against the spirit of our laws and Constitution" and an abrogation of "the liberty of speech and of the press, the right of trial by jury, the law of evidence, and the privilege of habeas corpus." If sustained by the President, the arrest and banishment would strike "a fatal blow at the supremacy of law, and the authority of the State and Federal Constitutions."

When a copy of the resolutions reached Lincoln, he realized that his enemies had been delivered into his hands. The signers of the Albany protest were not, apart from Corning himself, persons of much political influence, nor were they supporters of the Union cause whose loyalty was being tested by the Vallandigham case. Instead, they were obscure local Democratic politicians, who made their partisanship clear by including a gratuitous complimentary reference to Governor Horatio Seymour in the resolutions. The whole affair, as one White House intimate judged, had "the stinking aroma of party politics," and the protesters, with "no defined idea of moulding the present state of things into a sane unity," wanted either "to run the machine independently of the President, or to bully him into their notions."

Drawing on the notes he had collected in his drawer, Lincoln took exceptional care in preparing his response, although he said he "put that paper together in less time than any other of like importance ever prepared by me" because he had already given too much thought to the subject. On June 5 he took the unusual precaution of reading his proposed response to the members of the cabinet, and Gideon Welles noted, "It has vigor and ability and with some corrections will be a strong paper." By June 12 he had revised and polished his letter, and he sent it off to Corning that day—with a copy to the influential *New York Tribune*.

Lincoln's public letter began disarmingly with praise for the Albany protesters' "eminently patriotic" statement that they favored sustaining the Union and would uphold the administration in all constitutional measures. That left the question whether the military arrests and subsequent trials, for which the President was "ultimately responsible," were constitutional. Willingly Lincoln conceded that in normal times these would be violations of constitutionally guaranteed rights, but he pointed out that the Constitution itself provided for the suspension of these liberties "in cases of Rebellion or Invasion, [when] the public Safety may require it." Clearly the United States now faced a rebellion, "clear, flagrant, and gigantic," so that public safety did require suspension of the writ of habeas corpus. "Thoroughly imbued with a reverence for the guarranteed rights of individuals," Lincoln explained that he had been "slow to adopt the strong measures" of his administration, and he predicted that "the time [was] not unlikely to come when I shall be blamed for having made too few arrests rather than too many."

Turning directly to the protesters' objection that Vallandigham had been arrested far from any insurrection and outside any military lines, Lincoln bluntly replied that the suspension of civil liberties was "constitutional *wherever* the public safety does require them." Vallandigham, he pointed out, was not jailed because he was a political opponent of the administration or of the commanding general, Burnside, but "because he was damaging the army, upon the existence, and vigor of which, the life of the nation depends."

Then, in his most effective paragraph, the President noted that even his Albany petitioners had to recognize his right and duty to sustain the armies by punishing desertion, even with the death penalty. "Must I shoot a simple-minded soldier boy who deserts," he asked, "while I must not touch a hair of a wiley agitator who induces him to desert?"

Finally, Lincoln rejected the argument that the precedent set by military arrests during the rebellion would be followed in the peaceful postwar future. This argument, he suggested, was like saying "that a man could contract so strong an appetite for emetics during temporary illness, as to persist in feeding upon them through the remainder of his healthful life."

Lincoln considered his letter to Corning the best state paper he had written up to that time, and public response confirmed his feeling. If it did nothing to convince the disloyal or the more extreme among the Peace Democrats, it reassured Unionists genuinely troubled by an assumption of despotic power on the part of the President. Lincoln's low-key announcement that he regretted the arrest of Vallandigham—or, as he carefully phrased it, that he was "pained that there should have seemed to be a necessity for arresting him"—and his promise to discharge the congressman "so soon as . . . the public safety will not suffer by it" undercut charges of presidential tyranny and gave credence to his statement to a White House visitor that he was more of a "Chief Clerk" than a "Despot." If Lincoln's letter was—perhaps by intention—not an overwhelming, technical defense of the constitutionality of his actions, it was a clear demonstration of their necessity. Its lasting impact could be measured by the fact that henceforth Clement L. Vallandigham would always be stigmatized as "a wiley agitator."

Proud of his letter, Lincoln had copies printed and sent out under Nicolay's frank to leading Republicans. Their response was enthusiastic. "The right word has at last been spoken by the right man, at the right time, and from the right place," rejoiced John W. Forney of the *Washington Chronicle.* "It will thrill the whole land." It was "one of your best state Papers," judged former Governor E. D. Morgan, and another New Yorker considered it "of more value to the cause we all have at heart than a victory." Praising the letter as "felicitous and timely," Roscoe Conkling, defeated in the recent congressional contest, recognized the value of the document in the upcoming New York elections, where he thought it made "the best campaign document we can have in this state." Published in the *New York Tribune,* reissued as a pamphlet, and given further distribution as a publication of the Loyal Publication Society, at least 500,000 copies of the Corning letter were read by 10,000,000 people.

So successful was Lincoln's first attempt to reach out directly to the people that he lost no time in following it with a second public letter, this time addressed to Matthew Birchard and other delegates to the Ohio state Democratic convention who came to the White House in order to protest Vallandigham's arrest, trial, and banishment. Ohio Governor David Tod wanted Lincoln to treat these visitors "with the contempt they richly merit." Secretary Chase, who understood the intricacies of Ohio politics, urged him to respond to the delegation in writing. Aware that the Ohio Democrats had just chosen Vallandigham as their gubernatorial candidate, even though he was a convicted lawbreaker now in exile, Lincoln issued a hard-hitting statement. Vallandigham, he bluntly asserted, was responsible "personally, in a greater degree than . . . any other one man," for the desertions from the army, the resistance to the draft, and even the assassination of Unionists. By endorsing him the Ohio delegation was itself encouraging "desertion, resistance to the draft and the like." He concluded by promising to allow Vallandigham to return to the country providing that each member of the delegation would sign a pledge to "do all he can to have the officers, soldiers, and seamen of the army and navy . . . paid, fed, clad, and otherwise well provided and supported."

The refusal of the Ohio Democrats to accept his offer, considering it a "sacrifice of their dignity and self respect," simply confirmed Lincoln's message to the people that his administration was exercising exceptional powers only in the interest of self-preservation.

III

Self-preservation also dictated a change in the command of the Army of the Potomac. As Lee moved across the Potomac, Hooker closely followed, offering an effective screen for Washington and Baltimore and keeping his troops in readiness for a major combat on Northern soil. But as usual, he resisted accepting suggestions or orders. Lincoln, who saw in the Confederate invasion "the best opportunity we have had since the war began," wanted to maintain a sizable garrison at Harpers Ferry, where, to the left and the rear of the Confederate advance, it might compel Lee to divide his forces—as he had been obliged to do in the Antietam campaign. Then Hooker could deliver the devastating defeat to the Army of Northern Virginia that McClellan had failed to inflict in September 1862. But Hooker believed in the military doctrine of concentration of force and insisted that Harpers Ferry be abandoned. When Halleck ordered him to sustain that garrison, Hooker resigned—assuming, no doubt, that on the eve of a major battle his resignation would be rejected.

It was not. Ignoring the widespread outcry for the recall of McClellan, Lincoln on June 28 replaced Hooker with George Gordon Meade, one of the most experienced corps commanders of the Army of the Potomac, who had been in every major engagement since the first battle of Bull Run. Tall, thin, and bespectacled, Meade was not a charismatic leader; he looked, a Massachusetts soldier reported, like "a good sort of a family doctor." But he was well organized and highly professional, and he had the respect, if not necessarily the affection, of his men.

As Meade took command and followed Lee into Pennsylvania, Lincoln showed how much he had learned from his dealings with Hooker. To this new commander went no fatherly notes of admonition, no folksy advice about strategy. Indeed, he wrote to Meade not at all but made his wishes known only through Halleck. The President devoted his energies to raising new troops to reinforce Meade's army, in order to protect the crossings of the Susquehanna River and other routes that led to Philadelphia, and to calming the excited officials of Pennsylvania and New Jersey who feared their states were in the way of the Confederate advance.

Lincoln's attention was not focused solely on the Army of the Potomac, for he kept a close eye on Grant's campaign against Vicksburg. The President had never tried to direct Grant's strategy; the distances were too great for the army on the Mississippi to be managed from Washington. But he thought that Grant should bypass Vicksburg, go south and join forces with N. P. Banks, who was advancing up the Mississippi River from Louisiana. Instead, Grant plunged into the interior of Mississippi, defeated Confederate forces in a series of engagements, and pushed John C. Pemberton's army back into Vicksburg. During much of this campaign Grant told no one of his plans and seemed simply to have disappeared. Failing to reach him by letter or telegram, Lincoln desperately sought for news of his army from reports in the Confederate newspapers. "Do the Richmond papers have anything about . . . Vicksburg?" he wired General John A. Dix at Fort Monroe. "Have you any thing from Grant?" he telegraphed to General Rosecrans at Murfreesboro.

As news slowly filtered in, he began to get a better idea of Grant's campaign, and by the time the Union army put the Confederates under siege in Vicksburg, he could understand both the boldness and the skill of his general. "Whether Gen. Grant shall or shall not consummate the capture of Vicksburg," he wrote a complainer on May 26, "his campaign from the beginning of this month up to the twenty second day of it, is one of the most brilliant in the world."

Even so, as the siege of Vicksburg stretched on through June, he worried constantly about Grant and his army. Carefully he scrutinized Confederate newspapers, which carried reports—all erroneous—that Sherman had been seriously wounded during the siege, that Banks had lost an arm in his campaign for Port Hudson, that Confederate General Edmund Kirby-Smith

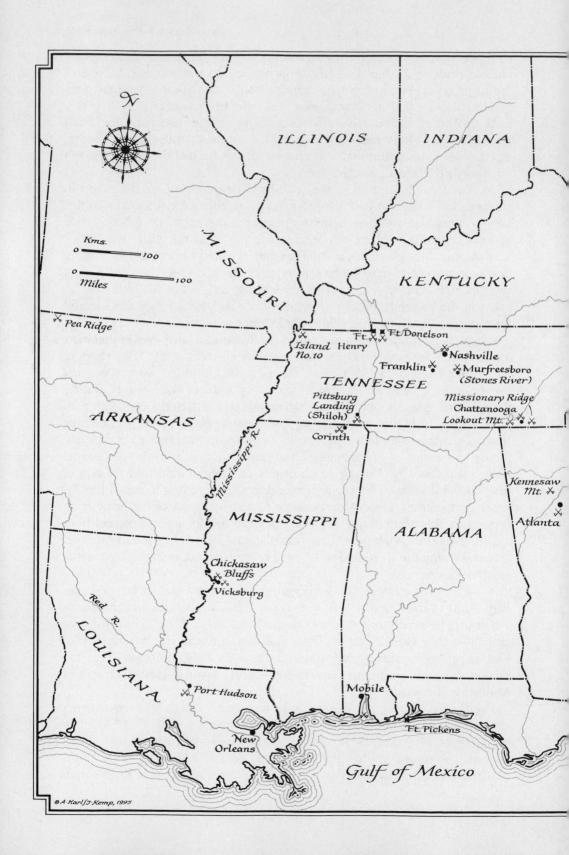

ILLINOIS

INDIANA

MISSOURI

KENTUCKY

Kms.
0 — 100

Miles
0 — 100

⚔ Pea Ridge

⚔ Ft. Donelson

⚔ Ft.
Henry

Island
No.10

● Nashville

Franklin ⚔

⚔ Murfreesboro
(Stones River)

TENNESSEE

ARKANSAS

Pittsburg
Landing
(Shiloh) ⚔

Missionary Ridge
Chattanooga
Lookout Mt. ⚔

⚔
Corinth

Kennesaw
Mt. ⚔

Mississippi R.

MISSISSIPPI

ALABAMA

● Atlanta

Chickasaw
Bluffs ⚔
Vicksburg

Red R.

LOUISIANA

⚔ Port Hudson

● Mobile

⚔ Ft. Pickens

New
Orleans

Gulf of Mexico

© A·Karl/J·Kemp, 1995

OHIO

PENNSYLVANIA

NEW JERSEY

⚔ Gettysburg

⚔ Antietam

WEST VIRGINIA

1st and 2nd Bull Run ⚔

Washington D.C. ⊙

DELAWARE

Bristoe ⚔

Falmouth ⚔

MARYLAND

Kelly's Ford ⚔

SHENANDOAH VALLEY

Mine Run ⚔

Chancellorsville ⚔

Fredericksburg ⚔

Kanawha R.

Kanawha Valley ⚔

Richmond ⊙

Area of Detail

James R.

Ft. Monroe

Hampton Roads ⚔

Atlantic

Appomattox ·

VIRGINIA

Norfolk

Ocean

NORTH CAROLINA

⚔ ROANOKE ISLAND

New Bern ⚔

Wilmington

Ft. Fisher ⚔

SOUTH CAROLINA

GEORGIA

Ft. Sumter ⚔

Major Engagements of the Civil War, 1861~1865

Savannah ⚔

VIRGINIA

Mechanicsville · ✕

Richmond ⊙ ⚔

✕

Rappahannock R.

Chickahominy R.

✕

Seven Pines (Fair Oaks) ⚔

✕

York R.

James R.

Williamsburg ·

Olustee ⚔

FLORIDA

✕ Seven Days' Battle Sites

Yorktown ·

Kms. 0 —— 15

0 —— 15

Miles

was bringing reinforcements from the trans-Mississippi region to relieve Vicksburg. Because there was always the danger that the Confederates might draw troops from another arena to assist Pemberton, Lincoln vainly urged Rosecrans, in Tennessee, to do his "utmost, short of rashness, to keep Bragg from getting off to help [Joseph E.] Johnston against Grant."

Under the enormous strain of worry about two armies poised for decisive battle, the President's health began to suffer. He had a nightmare about Tad, who had accompanied his mother on a shopping trip to Philadelphia. His "ugly dream" featured the pistol he had permitted the boy to have—"big enough to snap caps—but no cartridges or powder"—and he wired Mary: "Think you better put 'Tad's' pistol away." A visitor found the President's face told a story of anxiety and weariness, noting "the drooping eyelids, looking almost swollen; the dark bags beneath the eyes; the deep marks about the large and expressive mouth."

Then, on July 4, finally came the news that Lincoln had so long awaited. Staying close to the telegraph office in the War Department, he learned of a great and bloody battle that had been fought during the three previous days at Gettysburg, Pennsylvania. Though details were lacking, it appeared that Lee had been defeated and was retreating. Jubilantly the President issued a press release from the War Department announcing this "great success to the cause of the Union" and urging "that on this day, He whose will, not ours, should ever be done, be everywhere remembered and reverenced with profoundest gratitude." Three days later Secretary Welles received a dispatch from Admiral David Dixon Porter announcing the fall of Vicksburg and rushed to the White House with the news. His face beaming with joy, Lincoln caught Welles's hand and, throwing his arm around him, exclaimed: "What can we do for the Secretary of the Navy for this glorious intelligence? . . . I cannot, in words, tell you my joy over this result. It is great, Mr. Welles, it is great!"

For a few days in early July it seemed that the end of the war was at hand. With the fall of Vicksburg, where Pemberton surrendered his army of 30,000, and Port Hudson (July 8), the Mississippi, from Cairo to New Orleans, was once more in Union hands. The fleet, now under Admiral Dahlgren, who succeeded Admiral Du Pont on July 6, was slowly battering Charleston to rubble. And in the East, Meade had to fight just one more battle to destroy Lee's army, which was trapped between the advancing Army of the Potomac and the Potomac River, swollen with summer rains.

But Meade did not advance swiftly and, after a council of war with his senior generals, postponed an attack. Lee escaped into Virginia. Never was Lincoln so disappointed and so furious. "If I had gone up there, I could have whipped them myself," he exclaimed. "Our army held the war in the hollow of their hand and they would not close it," he fumed. He took special offense at a dispatch of Meade's praising his army for "driving the invader from our soil." "The whole country is our soil," he insisted, and he feared that Meade's purpose was not to defeat Lee but "to get the enemy across the river again without a further collision." His anger did not fade quickly. Weeks later he expressed deep mortification that Lee's army had not been destroyed. "Meade and his army had expended their skill and toil and blood up to the ripe harvest," he grieved, "and then allowed it to go to waste."

From the depths of his unhappiness he wrote a bitter letter to Meade, expressing gratitude for his "magnificent success" at Gettysburg but lamenting: "My dear general, I do not believe you appreciate the magnitude of the misfortune involved in Lee's escape. He was within your easy grasp, and to have closed upon him would, in connection with our other late successes, have ended the war. As it is, the war will be prolonged indefinitely. . . . Your golden opportunity is gone, and I am distressed immeasureably because of it."

Then, characteristically, he did not sign or send the letter. As he cooled down, he came to recognize that he was expecting too much of Meade. At the time the battle of Gettysburg began, Meade had been in command of the Army of the Potomac for only four days, and he was working with new and untried subordinates. His army had suffered enormous losses during the three days of battle, and some of its ablest and most aggressive generals were dead or wounded. Meade himself was exhausted. As he wrote his wife on July 8, "Now over ten days, I have not changed my clothes, have not had a regular night's rest, and many nights not a wink of sleep, and for several days did not even wash my face and hands, no regular food, and all the time in a great state of mental anxiety." It was asking too much of him to attack Robert E. Lee.

Lincoln withheld his letter—though he permitted Halleck to wire that the escape of Lee's army had "created great dissatisfaction in the mind of the President." Meade promptly submitted his resignation, and Halleck was forced to backtrack, saying that his telegram "was not intended as a censure, but as a stimulus to an active pursuit."

By this time Lincoln had recovered his equanimity and could speak of Meade "as a brave and skillful officer, and a true man," who was responsible for the success at Gettysburg. Indeed the President's spirits were so high that he composed a doggerel, "Gen. Lees invasion of the North written by himself," which he gave to John Hay:

In eighteen sixty three, with pomp,
    and mighty swell,
Me and Jeff's Confederacy, went
    forth to sack Phil-del,
The Yankees they got arter us, and
    giv us particular hell,
And we skedaddled back again,
    and didn't sack Phil-del.

IV

In the next few weeks Lincoln had need of his good humor. On July 2, Mary Lincoln, who had come back from Philadelphia, had a carriage accident while returning alone to the White House from the presidential cottage at the Soldiers' Home, an elevated spot three miles from the capital, where the Lincolns sought relief from the oppressive Washington heat. Someone, probably in the hope of injuring the President, had unscrewed the bolts to the driver's seat in her carriage, and when it became detached, the horses grew frightened and ran away. Mary was thrown out and hit her head on a sharp rock. Initially it seemed that she had only received severe bruises, and the President telegraphed Robert: "Dont be uneasy. Your mother very slightly hurt by her fall." But the wound became infected, and for three weeks she required round-the-clock nursing. After this accident Mary's headaches, of which she had long complained, became more frequent, and Robert thought she never fully recovered from her fall.

Lincoln could not spend much time at his wife's bedside because on July 13 draft riots erupted in New York City. Attempts to enforce the conscription act led to resistance in many parts of the country—in Holmes County, Ohio, Rush and Sullivan counties in Indiana, in Milwaukee, in the mining districts of Pennsylvania, and elsewhere—but only in New York was there a full-scale insurrection. For three days working-class mobs, consisting mostly of Irish-Americans, roamed the streets, looting and burning. More than 100 people were killed before Union troops, fresh from the battle of Gettysburg, arrived to preserve order.

Briefed by reports filtered to him by Sydney Howard Gay, the managing editor of the *New York Tribune,* the President anxiously followed these events. The news from New York, which coincided with reports that Lee's army had escaped unscathed across the Potomac, deeply depressed him. At one cabinet meeting he told his colleagues that "he did not believe we could take up anything in Cabinet to-day. Probably none of us were in a right frame of mind for deliberation—he was not." But it was not clear what he could do to help quell the rioting, especially since Governor Seymour did not ask for federal assistance.

When the violence in New York died down, there was pressure on the President to appoint a special commissioner to investigate the causes of the riots, but Lincoln, after toying with the notion, turned it down. If the commissioner made a thorough investigation, he said, his report would "have simply touched a match to a barrel of gunpowder." It was best to shy away from the issue. "One rebellion at a time is about as much as we can conveniently handle."

The rest of the summer was a relatively tranquil time for the President. Military affairs were under control, with capable professionals like Meade and Grant in command of the armies. The Congress had adjourned, and the President was not constantly badgered by demands from Capitol Hill. During the exceptionally hot weather Lincoln stayed mostly at the Soldiers' Home. He was often alone, because Mary, after recovering from her accident, went with Robert and Tad to the White Mountains of New Hampshire. Some of the time the President was lonely, but he kept in touch with his traveling family by letters and telegrams. One carried sad news for Tad about the fate of his little goat, Nanny, who caused such destruction in the gardens at the Soldiers' Home that she had to be brought back to the White House. There she was presently discovered "resting herself, and chewing her little cud, on the middle of Tad's bed." Then she disappeared, and, the President wrote his family, "This is the last we know of poor 'Nanny.'"

During this quiet period Lincoln had time to assess his administration, and on the whole he was pleased with what he had been able to accomplish. Now that he had roused himself from the torpor into which repeated military and political reverses had cast him, he once more felt himself a leader with a loyal constituency. Increasingly self-confident, he relied less and less on the advice of his cabinet officers. In their separate spheres he recognized their expertise and let them have their own way. When Secretary Chase came to him with a set of complicated regulations for trading with the South, the President promptly signed them, saying, "You understand these things: I do not." But the cabinet as a whole he consulted only sporadically and unsystematically. Nearly every cabinet member complained. "There is, in fact, *no Cabinet,*" grumbled Bates, "and the show of Cabinet-councils is getting more and more, a mere show—Little matters or isolated propositions are sometimes talked over, but the great business of the country— questions of leading policy—are not mentioned." Even the loyal Gideon Welles had to confess that there was no consultation about major issues like slavery and the restoration of the Southern states to the Union. "Of the policy of the administration, if there be one," he told a correspondent, "I am not advised beyond what is published and known to all."

Lincoln was not being intentionally rude to his advisers. Sharing "the general impression that we near the end of the war," he simply did not think that they could offer any useful ideas on how to eradicate slavery and bring the Southern states back into the Union. These problems the President alone could solve. He did not shrink from the responsibility, and now that he had asserted himself as a popular leader, he rather enjoyed his role as leader of opinion. "The Tycoon is in fine whack," John Hay reported in August. "I have rarely seen him more serene and busy. He is managing this war, the draft, foreign relations, and planning a reconstruction of the Union, all at once. I never knew with what tyrannous authority he rules the Cabinet, till now. The most important things he decides and there is no cavil."

He brought this sense of serenity and power to a controversy that Governor Seymour opened after the New York City draft riots. Seymour, whom critics had accused of coddling the rioters, tried to persuade the President to suspend the draft in New York, on the grounds, first, that conscription was unconstitutional, and, second, that the quotas allotted to his state were "glaringly unjust." In a series of letters the governor detailed his objections and his protests against the draft quotas.

In what Hay called "a sockdolager" of a reply, which was widely published in the newspapers, Lincoln showed none of the hesitancy that had paralyzed him for the past six months. If discrimination against New York could be shown, he wrote Seymour, he was willing to make concessions "so far as consistent, with practical convenience," but he was not prepared to hold up the draft until Seymour could procure a United States Supreme Court ruling on its constitutionality. The Confederacy, he pointed out, was forcing every able-bodied man into their army, "very much as a butcher drives bullocks into a slaughter-pen," and the Union could not spare the time either for another experiment with the failed volunteer system or for a test in the courts.

The correspondence between the New York governor and the President sputtered on for several weeks, Seymour insisting "that there is no theory which can explain or justify the enrollments [i.e., the draft quotas] in this State" and Lincoln persisting: "My purpose is to be just and fair; and yet to not lose time." Eventually the President felt forced to prepare an order calling the New York State militia into federal service for the purpose of enforcing the draft, but Seymour yielded just in time, and the draft began without much incident on August 19. In the showdown, the governor, not the President, blinked.

At about the time of this controversy, Lincoln, remembering the success of his letters to Corning and to Birchard about the Vallandigham affair, began drafting another public paper that would explain the draft and defend its constitutionality. "I . . . address you without searching for a precedent upon which to do so," he began, noting that it was especially important to avoid "misunderstanding between the public and the public servant." To opponents who claimed the draft was unconstitutional, he pointed out that the Constitution explicitly gives Congress the power "to raise and support armies." The conscription act was thus "a law made in litteral pursuance of this part of the United States Constitution." Nor was there doubt about the expediency of the draft. Only by raising additional armies could the "republican institutions, and territorial integrity of our country . . . be maintained," he continued. "There can be no army without men." Since voluntary recruiting had ceased, the draft was necessary.

But when it came to defending specific provisions of the conscription act, which exempted a man from the draft if he provided a substitute or paid a commutation fee of $300, Lincoln's language became murky and his reasoning tortured. Confusingly, he termed the commutation clause a boon to poor men because without it the price of substitutes might skyrocket, "thus leaving the man who could raise only three hundred dollars, no escape from personal service." He also had trouble defending the draft quotas allocated to states and districts, arguing that absolute equality was unattainable and adding, somewhat feebly, that "errors will occur in spite of the utmost fidelity."

It was not a satisfactory document and, probably because he realized he was trying to defend the indefensible, Lincoln shelved it. If he was going to reach out directly to the people, he needed a stronger case.

V

No letter, public or private, could help Lincoln resolve the tangle of problems in Missouri. Still close to the frontier stage of development, with a heritage of violence from the antebellum struggles over Kansas, Missouri was a constant source of difficulty to the Lincoln administration. After General Samuel R. Curtis's major victory at Pea Ridge, Arkansas, on March 7–8, 1862, organized Confederate military operations in the state ceased, but Southern troops continued to lurk along the border in Arkansas, encouraging and assisting numerous bands of bushwhackers and guerrillas, the most notable of which was the murderous band of William C. Quantrill. The depredations of these pro-Confederate groups were matched by the raids staged by "Jayhawkers" from Kansas, who sought revenge for the destruction wrought by the Missouri "Border Ruffians" during the Kansas imbroglio. As a result, civilian life and property was at risk throughout the state. The sparsely settled western counties became a war zone, and throughout the state there was security only in sight of federal troops or state militia.

After Governor Claiborne F. Jackson fled Missouri in 1861, a state convention named Hamilton R. Gamble, a conservative former Whig, provisional governor, and he continued to hold this office until 1864. Gamble and General John M. Schofield, whom Lincoln appointed to succeed Halleck in Missouri, got along well enough, but after September 1862, when Curtis replaced Schofield, relations between the governor and the military deteriorated. Curtis began to listen to Missouri antislavery men, who complained that Gamble was motivated only by "hunkerism, and a wish for political influence." Presently the governor and the general were locked in controversy, and both appealed to the President for help.

When the rival factions in Missouri presented clear-cut issues to the President, he had no hesitation in choosing his course—though he sometimes had difficulty in getting his subordinates to follow his orders. In December 1862 when federal troops arrested the Reverend Samuel B. McPheeters, pastor of the Pine Street Presbyterian Church in St. Louis, for "unmistakeable evidence of sympathy with the rebellion," Lincoln warned General Curtis "that the U. S. government must not . . . undertake to run the churches" and ordered him to "let the churches, as such take care of themselves." After an interview with the minister the President was convinced that McPheeters was, at heart, a rebel sympathizer, but so long as he committed no overt act, Lincoln did not want him punished "upon the suspicion of his secret sympathies." Then, having taken the high ground, he made the mistake of leaving the final decision to General Curtis. Hearing no further complaint, Lincoln supposed that his wishes had been carried out—only to learn, nearly a year later, that Curtis had prohibited McPheeters from preaching in his own church. Exasperated, the President repudiated the military order, making his position explicit: "I have never interfered, nor thought of interfering as to who shall or shall not preach in any church; nor have I knowingly, or believingly, tolerated any one else to so interfere by my authority."

More complicated Missouri issues the President tried to decide on a case-by-case basis, giving a free hand neither to civilian authorities nor to the military. Pressed by Gamble to rule whether the new militia companies he was raising were going to be under the authority of the governor or the federal commander, Lincoln declined to give an opinion on the abstract merits of the question and demanded to know the consequences of whatever action he might take. "I . . . think it is safer," he wrote Attorney General Bates, with characteristic pragmatism, "when a practical question arises, to decide that question directly, and not indirectly, by deciding a general abstraction supposed to include it, and also including a great deal more."

As the war progressed, Unionists in Missouri divided into bitterly hostile factions called the "Charcoals" (so called because of their concern for blacks and abolition) and the "Claybanks" (named because their principles were thought to be a pallid gray), and both groups demanded presidential support. Lincoln found it hard to choose between them. Temperamentally he felt closer to the Claybanks (or Conservatives), many of whom were, like himself, former Whigs who had been moderate on the slavery question. Gamble and his fellow Conservatives had loyally stood by the Union in the secession crisis. The President said later that they had "done their whole duty in the war faithfully and promptly" and when they disagreed with the President's actions had "been silent and kept about the good work." At the same time, he realized that when it came time to cast about for votes the Conservatives were "tempted to affiliate with those whose record is not clear." The Charcoals (or Radicals), on the other hand, were ideologues, whose dogmatic support of abolition and assumption of moral superiority Lincoln found hard to endure. But he recognized that the Radicals were "absolutely uncorrosive by the virus of secession." Personally hostile to the President, they were "the unhandiest devils in the world to deal with," though he admitted that "after all their faces are set Zionwards."

He refused to back either faction. When the Radicals charged him with favoring their opponents in a controversy over patronage in St. Louis, Lincoln replied firmly, "I have stoutly tried to keep out of the quarrel, and so mean to do." But it grew harder and harder to maintain his balance. By May 1863 he was writing with a real note of exasperation: "It is very painful to me that you in Missouri can not, or will not, settle your factional quarrel among yourselves. I have been tormented with it beyond endurance for months, by both sides. Neither side pays the least respect to my appeals to your reason."

By the end of the month he decided to end this "pestilential factional quarrel" by removing Curtis, who had been charged with being too friendly with the Radicals, and reinstating Schofield, who was thought to be more broadly acceptable. He offered the new commander a simple test for success: "If both factions, or neither, shall abuse you, you will probably be about right. Beware of being assailed by one, and praised by the other."

By that test Lincoln himself was an enormous success. The Conservatives considered him a prisoner of the Charcoals. The Radicals were convinced that the President was supporting Governor Gamble's plot to restore the slave power with the aid of Schofield, whose odor in the public nostrils they said was "less fragrant than that of a polecat."

Both factions began to attack Lincoln. The awkwardness of the President's position became clear in the summer of 1863, when Missourians were debating plans for the gradual emancipation of the slaves, a topic that had long been dear to Lincoln's heart. "You and I must die," he told a congressman, "but it will be enough for us to have done in our lives if we make Missouri free." Aware that emancipation sentiment in a slave state had to be carefully nurtured, he repeatedly warned against those who urged radical steps. A state like Missouri that tolerated slavery, he suggested, was like a man who had "an excrescence on the back of his neck, the removal of which, in one operation, would result in the death of the patient, while 'tinkering it off by degrees' would preserve life." He let it be known that "the Union men in Missouri who are in favor of gradual emancipation represented his views better than those who are in favor of immediate emancipation." But he refused to endorse the Conservatives' plan, which would not end slavery in Missouri until 1870 and provided for peonage ranging from eleven years to life. This scheme Lincoln found "faulty in *postponing* the benefits of freedom to the slave, instead of giving him an immediate vested interest therein."

Angered by the President's neutrality, Governor Gamble came to Washington in a vain effort to win his support for the Conservative plan, but he got nowhere. Leaving, he attacked Lincoln as "a mere intriguing, pettifogging, piddling politician."

Lincoln's position equally infuriated the Radicals. In September they organized a delegation, headed by Charles D. Drake, to go to Washington and demand the removal of Schofield. They intended to present their demands to the President in the strongest possible terms, giving him, as one said, the choice "whether he would ride in their wagon or not."

Exasperated by a problem that was taking up too much of his time and attention and angered by Radical attacks on General Schofield, against whom no charge of dishonesty or incompetence had ever been raised, Lincoln gave the Missourians a frosty reception when they came to the White House on September 30. He rejected their demands that he remove Schofield, put the entire state back under martial law, decree immediate emancipation, and authorize the recruitment of Missouri blacks into the army. Informing the Radicals that he understood the causes of the chaos in Missouri as well as they did, he observed that in time of war "blood grows hot, and blood is spilled.... Confidence dies, and universal suspicion reigns. Each man feels an impulse to kill his neighbor, lest he be first killed by him. Revenge and retaliation follow.... But this is not all. Every foul bird comes abroad, and every dirty reptile rises up. These add crime to confusion." The circumstances required harsh measures to preserve order, and General Schofield had effectively carried those measures out. Bristling, he bluntly declined to remove Schofield and stoutly announced: "I ... shall do what seems to be my duty.... It is my duty to hear all; but at last, I must ... judge what to do, and what to forbear." The Radicals went home his permanent enemies.

Lincoln no longer believed that he could solve the Missouri question to anyone's satisfaction, including his own. He had, he told Attorney General Bates, "no *friends in Missouri.*" The whole issue reminded him of a lesson he had learned as a boy when he was plowing. "When he came across stumps too deep and too tough to be torn up, and too wet to burn," he said, "he plowed round them."

VI

Never at his best when dealing with factions within his own party, Lincoln welcomed opportunities to rally behind him all of the Republicans, as well as those Democrats who endorsed his war policies. The approach of the fall elections gave him the opportunity to show that he was still a master politician.

The 1863 elections were crucial for Lincoln and his party. At stake were important local offices throughout the North and, especially, governorships in Maine, Massachusetts, Pennsylvania, Ohio, Wisconsin, Minnesota, Kentucky, and Iowa. If the strong Democratic resurgence manifest in the fall elections of 1862 continued, Republican chances of winning the next presidential election would be in peril. "All the instant questions will be settled by the coming elections," reported a White House intimate. "If they go for the Democracy, then Mr. Lincoln will not wind up the war [and] a new feeling and spirit will inspire the South."

Lincoln watched all these races closely, monitoring frequent reports from Republican workers in the field. Convention prohibited him from taking an active part in most of the canvasses, but, with or without the President's explicit approval, his aides did whatever was necessary to ensure the defeat of the Democrats. In Kentucky, General Burnside proclaimed martial law, and the imprisonment of Democratic candidates and voters helped secure the election of Governor Thomas E. Bramlette, a "Union Democrat" favored by the Lincoln administration. In Pennsylvania, Republican Governor Curtin was in a close battle for reelection against Pennsylvania Chief Justice George W. Woodward, whose court held preliminary hearings on the constitutionality of the conscription act in September. Secretary Chase rallied banker Jay Cooke and all the others who had benefited from the financial policies of the administration by warning, "Gov. Curtin's reelection or defeat is now the success or defeat of the administration of President Lincoln." To strengthen the Republican vote, the President acceded to Curtin's request and authorized a fifteen-day leave so that government clerks from Pennsylvania could go home to vote, and Secretary of War Stanton permitted commanders to furlough Pennsylvania troops, who could be counted on to vote Republican.

Ohio was a source of special worry to Lincoln, for the Democrats had nominated Vallandigham for governor. The President found it hard to believe that "one genuine American would, or could be induced to, vote for such a man as Vallandigham," yet he recognized that his opponents saw this election as a means to repudiate his administration. Consequently he watched the Ohio election, he told Gideon Welles, with "more anxiety . . . than he had in 1860 when he was chosen," and he encouraged his friends and the members of his administration to work for the election of the Republican candidate, John Brough. In Ohio, as in Pennsylvania, government clerks and soldiers were furloughed so that they could go home to vote. Secretary Chase stumped his home state for Brough, and Governor Yates of Illinois and Governor Morton of Indiana also campaigned for him.

Illinois was also critical, and, as Lincoln's home state, it offered the one contest in which propriety permitted the President to participate. Republicans thought his presence was badly needed, because Union victories at Gettysburg and Vicksburg had the paradoxical effect of strengthening peace sentiment. Many voters believed that, with the Confederacy on its last legs, it was time to end the fighting and negotiate peace. On June 17, even before those victories, the antiwar forces held a huge rally in Springfield, presided over by Senator William A. Richardson, the Democrat elected to succeed Browning. After listening to angry antiadministration oratory, the mass meeting demanded "the restoration of the Union as it was" and voted against "further offensive prosecution of this war."

Lincoln believed such resolutions, which were echoed by other antiadministration gatherings all over the North, rested on fundamentally wrongheaded assumptions. A call for the restoration of the Union as it was meant abandonment of the Emancipation Proclamation and all other measures against slavery. It also meant an end to the recruitment of blacks into the Union armies, just at the time when Negro soldiers were proving their valor at Port Hudson on the Mississippi and in Charleston harbor, where black troops of the Fifty-fourth Massachusetts Colored Infantry, under Robert Gould Shaw, made a heroic but unsuccessful assault on Battery Wagner.

Equally misguided, in the President's judgment, was talk of negotiated peace. Gettysburg and Vicksburg indicated that Confederate power was at last beginning to disintegrate, and, as he told John Hay, he anticipated "that they will break to pieces if we only stand firm now." He was convinced that the Confederate army controlled the South. It was Jefferson Davis's "only hope, not only against us, but against his own people"; without that military control, the Southern people "would be ready to swing back to their old bearings." Until the Confederate army was ready to sue for peace, there could be no meaningful negotiation. For this reason Lincoln refused to receive Confederate Vice President Alexander H. Stephens, who asked permission to come to Washington under a flag of truce, ostensibly in order to facilitate exchange of prisoners. Curbing his personal wish to go to Fort Monroe for an informal chat with Stephens, the President allowed his cabinet to persuade him not to have any official communication with the Davis government. Even the appearance of peace negotiations would strengthen the enemy.

Eager to put his views before the public, Lincoln welcomed an invitation from James C. Conkling to attend a huge rally "in favor of law and order and constitutional government" at Springfield on September 3. Doubtless he was tempted by Conkling's promise "that not only would the thousands who will be here be prepared to receive you with the warmest enthusiasm but the whole country would be eager to extend to you its congratulations on the way." Conkling reminded him that party activity in Illinois was already spirited and noted, "The Presidential campaign for your successor *(if any)* has already commenced in Illinois."

The President really wanted to go back to Springfield, but he was not able to get away from his duties in Washington because Rosecrans had finally begun his long-awaited campaign to maneuver the Confederates out of Chattanooga. Tied to his desk, Lincoln sent Conkling a carefully composed letter to be read to the assembly. "Read it very slowly," he urged. He wanted his views to be heard and understood.

The letter was a hard-hitting defense of his administration's policies. Though it began with a tribute to "all those who maintain unconditional devotion to the Union," it was a frankly partisan message. He dismissed as "deceptive and groundless" charges that he was preventing peace through compromise. Suppressing any notice of Alexander Stephens's aborted mission, he assured his listeners that he had "no word or intimation . . . in relation to any peace compromise" from the rebels. He then turned to a defense of his Emancipation Proclamation, which his opponents condemned as unconstitutional. "I think differently," he stoutly replied. "I think the constitution invests its commander-in-chief, with the law of war, in time of war." And, according to the laws of war, property, including slaves, could be taken when needed. As a military measure, he had offered the slaves freedom, and he firmly insisted, "The promise being made, must be kept." To opponents who said that they would not fight to free Negroes, he replied, "Fight you, then, exclusively to save the Union." But when peace did come, he predicted, "there will be some black men who can remember that, with silent tongue, and clenched teeth, and steady eye, and well-poised bayonet, they have helped mankind on to this great consummation; while, I fear, there will be some white ones, unable to forget that, with malignant heart, and deceitful speech, they have strove to hinder it."

"The signs look better," he wrote. Because Western armies had captured Vicksburg, "The Father of Waters again goes unvexed to the sea. Thanks to the great North-West for it." Thanks, too, went to the sons of New England, New York, Pennsylvania, and New Jersey, "hewing their way right and left." And he did not forget the Union soldiers from "the Sunny South . . . , in more colors than one." Nor did he ignore what he called, in an inappropriate attempt at cuteness, "Uncle Sam's Web-feet," which had made their tracks on the bays, rivers, bayous, and "wherever the ground was a little damp." "Thanks to all," he cheered. "For the great republic—for the principle it lives by, and keeps alive—for man's vast future,—thanks to all."

Received "with the greatest enthusiasm" by the 50,000 to 75,000 cheering Unionists who attended the Springfield rally, Lincoln's letter to Conkling was published in full in nearly every major newspaper throughout the country. The Democratic *New York World* criticized it as Lincoln's first stump speech in his reelection campaign, but it won strong praise from the President's supporters. It was a "noble, patriotic, and Christian letter," wrote Senator Henry Wilson of Massachusetts, and his colleague, Charles Sumner, echoed praise for this "true and noble letter, which is an historic document." Read to a mass meeting in New York City, it "was received with shouts, cheers, thanksgiving, and tears." The force and wisdom of the letter caused the *New York Times* to express gratitude that the nation was led by "a ruler who is so peculiarly adapted to the needs of the time as clear-headed, dispassionate, discreet, steadfast, honest Abraham Lincoln." Praising the letter as "one of those remarkably clear and forcible documents that come only from Mr. Lincoln's pen," the *Chicago Tribune* editorial ended, "God bless Old Abe!"

That euphoria was only slightly diminished by news of Union military reverses at the end of September. On the morning of September 21, coming into John Hay's bedroom before the secretary was up, Lincoln sat down on his bed and said: "Well, Rosecrans has been whipped, as I feared. I have feared it for several days. I believe I feel trouble in the air before it comes." Rosecrans had pushed on beyond Chattanooga, and Confederates routed the Union troops in the costly battle of Chickamauga, where only the rock-like firmness of George H. Thomas saved the Army of the Cumberland from disaster. Afterward, while the Union army huddled in the city of Chattanooga, under siege and virtually cut off from supplies, Rosecrans behaved, Lincoln said, "like a duck hit on the head."

So grave was the situation that Stanton called a hurried midnight council on September 23–24, asking the President to come back to the city from the Soldiers' Home. Rosecrans, Stanton announced, could hold out for ten days but badly needed reinforcements. Since Meade had no significant operations under way, Stanton proposed to detach 30,000 men from the Army of the

Potomac, transporting them by rail from Virginia, across the Appalachian Mountains, and south through Kentucky and Tennessee; he promised they would come to Rosecrans's rescue in five days. Lincoln, who had seen so many brilliant military stratagems fail, was pessimistic and remarked, "I will bet that if the order is given tonight, the troops could not be got to Washington in five days." Stiffly Stanton replied that he was not inclined to bet on so grave a subject, and he persuaded the group to authorize the immediate sending of the Eleventh and Twelfth corps, under Joseph Hooker, with more troops to follow. To the President's surprise and delight Stanton's plan worked. Making an innovative and carefully coordinated use of railroads for military purposes, the War Department transported about 20,000 men and 3,000 horses and mules from Virginia to eastern Tennessee, traveling 1,159 miles in seven to nine days.

Shortly afterward, Lincoln put Grant in charge of the new Division of the Mississippi, which combined the former departments of the Ohio, the Cumberland, and the Tennessee, and replaced Rosecrans with Thomas. By the end of October, Grant relieved Chattanooga, and the Union armies began preparing to drive Bragg's troops back into Georgia.

Politically the news of the rescue could not have come at a better time for Republicans. Buoyed by this military success, Iowa Republicans reported that they had "swept the state overwhelmingly." From Curtin's campaign for reelection, the President received welcome news: "Pennsylvania stands by you, keeping step with Maine and California to the music of the Union." And —most critical in Lincoln's eyes—Chase telegraphed from Cincinnati that Vallandigham's defeat in Ohio was "complete, beyond all hopes." The next month Republicans also carried the New York elections. It was evident, a Democratic observer sourly remarked, that the Republicans had "effectively . . . inoculated the general mind with ideas which involve, sooner or later, the acquiescence of the community in any measures that may be adopted against the Democracy."

For these successes Republicans gave much credit to Lincoln's public letters—to the Conkling letter in particular, but also to those addressed to Corning and Birchard concerning Vallandigham and to Seymour concerning the draft. These letters were considered so effective that they were collected and republished for wide circulation as *The Letters of President Lincoln on Questions of National Policy* in a twenty-two-page pamphlet, which sold for 8 cents a copy. No one could measure their impact on the voters, but Governor Israel Washburn, reporting "the square and unqualified support" of the administration in the Maine election, wrote the President that his letter to Conkling "aided not a little in swelling our wonderful majority."

As news of further Republican victories became known, Lincoln enjoyed a burst of unaccustomed popularity. The *Chicago Tribune,* so often critical of the President and his administration, now called him "the most popular man in the United States" and flatly predicted: "Were an election for President to be held tomorrow, Old Abe would, without the special aid of any of his friends, walk over the course, without a competitor to dispute with him the great prize which his masterly ability, no less than his undoubted patriotism and unimpeachable honesty, have won."

VII

During the fall of 1863 there was, apart from the campaigns around Chattanooga, a lull in the war. The federal fleet, under Admiral Dahlgren, continued to bombard the fortifications of Charleston harbor but without decisive results. In northern Virginia, Meade followed a strategy of maneuver and minor engagement with Lee, with no major battle in prospect. The President, for once, had time on his hands, and he busied himself with such matters as an interview with a Mrs. Hutter, who had invented some earmuffs she wanted to introduce into the service, and a recommendation for "one of Mrs. L's numerous cousins" for a job in the Treasury Department.

When Mary returned refreshed from her vacation in the mountains, a normal social life began again at the White House. The Lincolns began going to the theater again, seeing Maggie Mitchell's performance of *Fanchon, the Cricket* at Ford's Theatre. But, pleading a diplomatic indisposition, Mary did not accompany her husband when he attended the wedding of Kate Chase, daughter of the Secretary of the Treasury, to Senator William Sprague, the millionaire Rhode Island manufacturer, on November 12. She regarded Kate, who was younger, prettier, and slimmer, as a rival for the social leadership of the capital and rightly suspected that she was promoting her father's presidential prospects. To compensate for his wife's absence, Lincoln stayed for an unusually long time at the wedding.

In this period of relative quiet the President allowed his thoughts to turn to making another public statement—this time something less defensive than his extraordinarily successful letters to Corning, Birchard, Seymour, and Conkling, something that would explain to the American people the significance of the huge war into which they had stumbled. Lincoln had been brooding over this idea for some time. Shortly after the news of Gettysburg and Vicksburg reached Washington, he responded to a group of serenaders by pointing out how appropriate it was that the Union victory occurred on the nation's birthday. What better way was there to celebrate that day when—"How long ago is it?—eighty odd years—since on the Fourth of July for the first time in the history of the world a nation by its representatives, assembled and declared as a self-evident truth that 'all men are created equal.' " The root of the rebellion was "an effort to overthrow the principle that all men were created equal," and now it had suffered major defeats on the anniversary of the Declaration of Independence. But the President's thoughts were not yet sufficiently matured for full expression, and he concluded, "Gentlemen, this is a glorious theme, and the occasion for a speech, but I am not prepared to make one worthy of the occasion."

During the following months the larger significance of the war was never far from Lincoln's mind. The need for a broad statement on the subject began to seem more and more pressing as Northerners, convinced by the victories at Vicksburg and Gettysburg that the end of the war was in sight, began debating the terms on which the Southern states should be restored to the Union. Many urged the President to address the people directly on these issues, describing the significance of the conflict and explaining why the enormous sacrifices required by the war were worthwhile. Even before the news from Gettysburg and Vicksburg, Horace Greeley, impressed by Lincoln's letter to the Albany Democrats, begged the President to write such a "greatly needed" letter "on *the causes of the War and the necessary conditions of Peace.*" From Boston, the wealthy merchant and railroad man John Murray Forbes suggested that the President should address "the public mind of the North and of such part of the South as you can reach" on the basic issue of the war, which he saw as not just a contest of "North against South but *the People against the Aristocrats.*" If Lincoln would seize every opportunity to hammer home the simple idea "that we are fighting for Democracy or (to get rid of the technical name) for liberal institutions," Forbes predicted, "the Rebellion will be crushed."

In November, after the elections, the opportunity came to do just what Forbes had urged. The President was invited to attend the dedication of the cemetery at Gettysburg, where the thousands of men killed in that battle, imperfectly identified and hastily buried, were being reinterred. The orator for the occasion, Edward Everett, the former president of Harvard College, former United States senator, and former Secretary of State, could be counted on to give an extended speech. The President was asked, "as Chief Executive of the nation, formally [to] set apart these grounds to their sacred use by a few appropriate remarks." The invitation to the President was not an afterthought on the part of David Wills and the other members of the Gettysburg Cemetery Commission; to make sure that their letter would be favorably received, they doubtless preceded it by informal contacts through Ward Hill Lamon, who was known to be an intimate of the President, and they probably chose Lamon to be grand marshal of the procession at Gettysburg just for this reason.

Lincoln accepted, and during the following weeks he gave much thought to the brief remarks that he would make on November 19. He took the assignment very seriously and in the course of his preparation called to the White House William Saunders, the landscape architect in charge of planning the Gettysburg cemetery, in order to learn the topography of a place he had never visited but knew well from his commanders' reports of the great battle. Using White House stationery, Lincoln began writing out an address expressing the ideas he had voiced in his brief response to the serenade after Gettysburg and Vicksburg. By this time the President had his facts straight. No longer did he refer to the Declaration of Independence as having been written "about eighty years ago"; now he wrote without hesitation, "Four score and seven years ago." For the most part, the writing went smoothly and without interruptions—a sure sign that he had carefully reflected on his words—but toward the end of the first page of the short address Lincoln faltered after writing "It is rather for us, the living, to stand here . . . ," crossed out the last three words, and substituted "we here be dedicated." He had trouble with the ending, and shortly before he went to Gettysburg he told James Speed that he had found time to write only about half of his address.

But he had the rest of it in his mind before he left the White House on November 18 and needed only a few quiet minutes to write it all out. He chose his words deliberately, preferring, as he always did, short words to long, words of Anglo-Saxon origin to those of Latin derivation. From the first two rhyming words—"Four score"—the cadences were somberly musical, and his gravely repetitive phrases—"we can not dedicate—we can not consecrate—we can not hallow"—had a solemnity worthy of the occasion. Antithesis was his basic rhetorical strategy, contrasting the living with the dead, "what we say here" with "what they [the soldiers] did here." He did not strive for novelty in language but drew, consciously or unconsciously, on the stores of his memory. Many of his phrases had echoes of the King James version of the Bible. His closing promise of survival for "government of the people, by the people, for the people" may have had its origin in Daniel Webster's 1830 speech calling the American government "made for the people, made by the people, and answerable to the people," but more probably he derived it from a sermon of Theodore Parker, to which Herndon had called his attention, defining democracy as "a government of all the people, by all the people, for all the people." Lincoln had made earlier use of the idea in his July 1861 message to Congress when he referred to the United States as "a democracy—a government of the people, by the same people."

Moving from past to present to future, Lincoln's address assumed an hourglass form: an opening account of the events of the past that had led up to the battle of Gettysburg; three brief sentences on the present occasion; and a final, more expansive view of the nation's future. His tone was deliberately abstract; he made no specific reference to either the battle of Gettysburg or of the cemetery that he was dedicating, he did not mention the South or the Confederacy, and he did not speak of the Army of the Potomac or of its commanders. He was deliberately moving away from the particular occasion to make a general argument.

Lincoln read his draft to no one before he reached Gettysburg, and he explained to no one why he had accepted the invitation to attend the dedication ceremonies or what he hoped to accomplish in his address. Yet his text suggested his purpose. When he drafted his Gettysburg speech, he did not know for certain what Edward Everett would say, but he could safely predict that this conservative former Whig would stress the ties of common origin, language, belief, and law shared by Southerners and Northerners and appeal for a speedy restoration of the Union under the Constitution. Everett's oration could give another push to the movement for a negotiated peace and strengthen the conservative call for a return to "the Union as it was," with all the constitutional guarantees of state sovereignty, state rights, and even state control over domestic institutions, such as slavery.

Lincoln thought it important to anticipate this appeal by building on and extending the argument he had advanced in his letter to Conkling against the possibility of a negotiated peace with the Confederates. In the Gettysburg address he drove home his belief that the United States was not just a political union, but a nation—a word he used five times. Its origins antedated the 1789 Constitution, with its restrictions on the powers of the national government; it stemmed from 1776. It was with the Declaration of Independence that "our fathers brought forth, upon this continent, a new nation, conceived in Liberty, and dedicated to the proposition that all men are created equal." This was, of course, not a new idea for Lincoln; his first inaugural address carefully developed the thesis that the Union was older than the Constitution. Nor was it an original contribution to American political discourse. It had been an essential part of the ideology of the Whig party, which had been elaborated by Daniel Webster; indeed, almost any advocate of a broad construction of the powers of the federal government was forced to appeal from the constraints of the Constitution to the liberties of the Declaration.

In invoking the Declaration now, Lincoln was reminding his listeners— and, beyond them, the thousands who would read his words—that theirs was a nation pledged not merely to constitutional liberty but to human equality. He did not have to mention slavery in his brief address to make the point that the Confederacy did not share these values. Instead, in language that evoked images of generation and birth—using what the Democratic *New York World* caustically called "obstetric analogies"—he stressed the role of the Declaration in the origins of the nation, which had been "conceived in Liberty" and "brought forth" by the attending Founding Fathers. Now the sacrifices of "the brave men, living and dead, who struggled here" on the battlefield at Gettysburg had renewed the power of the Declaration. "The last full measure of devotion" which they gave made it possible to "highly resolve that these dead shall not have died in vain" and to pledge "that this nation, under God, shall have a new birth of freedom."

Compressed into 272 words, Lincoln's message was at once a defense of his administration, an explanation why the war with its attendant horrors had to continue, and a pledge that because of these exertions "government of the people, by the people, for the people, shall not perish from the earth."

For all Lincoln's careful preparation, it seemed for a while that he might not be able to attend the dedication ceremonies. On the day he was scheduled to go to Gettysburg, Tad was ill, too sick to eat his breakfast, and Mary Lincoln, recalling the deaths of her other boys, became hysterical at the thought that her husband would leave her at such a critical time. But so important was the occasion and so weighty was the message he intended to deliver that he brushed aside his wife's pleas and about noon left Washington on a special train of four cars. All the members of the cabinet had been invited to attend the ceremonies, but only Seward, Blair, and Secretary of the Interior John P. Usher were able to accompany the President. The presence of only the more conservative members of the administration in the President's entourage caused derisive comment in Washington, where United States Treasurer Francis E. Spinner guffawed, *"Let the dead bury the dead."* The party also included Nicolay and Hay, the President's secretaries; William Johnson, Lincoln's black manservant; Benjamin B. French, who had written a hymn to be performed at the ceremonies; the ubiquitous Lamon; members of the diplomatic corps; and some foreign visitors, along with the Marine Band and a military escort from the Invalid Corps. The President was in good spirits, laughing and joking with his companions on the train. At one stop a beautiful little girl lifted a bouquet of rosebuds to the open window in the President's car, saying with her childish lisp, "Flowrth for the President!" Stepping to the window, Lincoln bent down and kissed the child, saying: "You're a sweet little rose-bud yourself. I hope your life will open into perpetual beauty and goodness."

Arriving about five o'clock at Gettysburg, where David Wills and Edward Everett met his train, Lincoln was relieved to receive a telegram from Stanton: "Mrs. Lincoln informed me that your son is better this evening." After dinner at Wills's impressive mansion, Lincoln was called out to respond to a serenade by the Fifth New York Artillery Band. Never happy at extemporaneous speaking, the President apologized that he had "several substantial reasons" for not making a speech, the chief of which was that he had no speech to make. "In my position," he observed, "it is somewhat important that I should not say any foolish things." A voice from the crowd said, "If you can help it." "It very often happens," Lincoln responded, "that the only way to help it is to say nothing at all."

Disappointed at hearing only what the Dutch ambassador scornfully called one of Lincoln's "pasquinades," the crowd moved on to serenade Seward, who gave them the kind of speech they wanted, praising the United States as "the richest, the broadest, the most beautiful, the most magnificent, and capable of a great destiny, that has ever been given to any part of the human race." But Seward's tone of reconciliation with the rebellious Southerners as friends and brothers and his insistence that the sole objective of the war was to establish "the principle of democratic government" were not exactly in tune with the message that the President proposed to deliver the next day. Perhaps partly for this reason Lincoln, after working for a while in his room at Wills's house to prepare a clean copy of his remarks, took it over to Seward's room, where he presumably read it to the Secretary.

On the morning of the nineteenth Lincoln, after giving the final touches to his address, made a clear copy and appeared at the door of the Wills house at about ten o'clock, dressed in a new black suit, with which the white gauntlets he was wearing sharply contrasted. His stovepipe hat bore a black band, to indicate that he was still mourning the death of his son Willie. After he mounted his horse, which some observers thought too small for so tall a man, there was a considerable delay before the procession got under way, and the President spent the time shaking hands with the well-wishers who crowded about him. Finally the procession began, with four military bands providing music, and the President, along with his three cabinet officers, representatives of the military, and members of the Cemetery Commission representing the various states, made a slow march of about three-quarters of a mile to the burial ground. Recognizing the solemnity of the occasion, the President appeared somber and absorbed in thought.

At the speakers' platform, where he was joined by several governors of Northern states, Lincoln had to wait again until Edward Everett appeared. The Massachusetts orator, who was suffering from bladder trouble, knew that the occasion was going to be physically taxing, and he had arranged for a small tent to be erected at one end of the platform so that he might relieve himself before beginning his oration. After an interminable invocation by the chaplain of the House of Representatives, which the irreverent John Hay called "a prayer which thought it was an oration," Everett began his two-hour address. Contrary to expectations, it was not full of purple passages or rhetorical ornamentation. For the most part, it was a clear exposition, based on information provided by General Meade and others, of just what had happened during those fiercely hot three days in July, when the nation's life hung in the balance. Everett had committed his long oration to memory, and most in the audience thought he recited it perfectly, though he himself noted that "parts of the address were poorly memorized, several long paragraphs condensed, [and] several thoughts occurred at the moment as happens generally." Even though many in the audience had been standing for four hours, they listened with absorbed interest, and only toward the end did some break away from the crowd and begin informal exploration of the battlefield. It was a moving address and, according to Benjamin B. French, left "his audience in tears many times during his masterly effort." When Everett concluded, the President pressed his hand with great fervor and said, "I am more than gratified, I am grateful to you."

Then, after French's unmemorable hymn, hastily composed for the occasion, Lamon introduced the President of the United States. With his high, penetrating voice, in which some listeners detected a strong Kentucky accent, Lincoln began. A little restive after Everett's long oration, many in the crowd focused on the unsuccessful efforts of a photographer to get his equipment in place to take a picture of the President. Expecting another long speech, most thought that Lincoln was only getting under way when he pledged "that this government of the people, by the people, for the people, shall not perish from the earth" and sat down. So brief were his remarks that those in the audience came away with very different recollections of the occasion—whether Lincoln read his manuscript or relied on his memory, whether he made gestures, whether he inserted the phrase "under God" in his promise of a new birth of freedom, whether he was interrupted by applause.

Immediately afterward, Lincoln may have felt that his Gettysburg address was not successful. "Lamon, that speech won't *scour!*" he is supposed to have said, referring to the plows used on the western prairies that failed to turn back the heavy soil and allowed it to collect on the blade. If he felt disappointment, it may have been because during so short an address there was no time to build up the sort of rapport that a speaker needs with his audience, and its abrupt ending left listeners with a sense of being let down. No doubt his judgment was also affected by his fatigue and by illness, which would prostrate him by the time he returned to the White House.

But responses to his address quickly made it clear that, however his words affected his immediate audience, they reached the general public. Most newspapers reporting the Gettysburg ceremonies properly devoted most of their attention to Everett's oration, but praise for the President's address mounted. "The dedicatory remarks by President Lincoln will live among the annals of man," announced the *Chicago Tribune,* in one of the earliest expressions of appreciation. In the *Washington Chronicle,* John W. Forney wrote that Lincoln's address, "though short, glittered with gems, evincing the gentleness and goodness of heart peculiar to him." The *Springfield* (Massachusetts) *Republican* carried a more extensive evaluation, probably written by Josiah G. Holland, who called Lincoln's "little speech . . . deep in feeling, compact in thought and expression, and tasteful and elegant in every word and comma." "We know not where to look for a more admirable speech than the brief one which the President made," declared the Providence *Journal,* asking whether "the most elaborate and splendid oration [could] be more beautiful, more touching, more inspiring, than those thrilling words of the President." "The few words of the President were from the heart to the heart," wrote George William Curtis, the editor of *Harper's Weekly,* who called the address "as simple and felicitous and earnest a word as was ever spoken."

The impact of the speech could be measured in the number of times that the President was asked to provide autograph copies of his Gettysburg address. There are at least five copies in Lincoln's own handwriting—more than for any other document Lincoln wrote—and doubtless others have been lost.

Another measure of its significance was the criticism that opponents leveled against it. The earliest attacks simply condemned "the silly remarks of the President," but abler critics recognized the importance of Lincoln's argument. Accusing the President of "gross ignorance or willful misstatement," the *New York World* sharply reminded him that *"This* United States" was not the product of the Declaration of Independence but "the result of the ratification of a compact known as the Constitution," a compact that said nothing whatever about equality. Similarly Wilbur F. Storey of the ultra-Democratic *Chicago Times* recognized that in invoking the Declaration of Independence Lincoln was announcing a new objective in the war. Calling the Gettysburg address "a perversion of history so flagrant that the most extended charity cannot regard it as otherwise than willful," Storey insisted that the officers and men who gave their lives at Gettysburg died "to uphold this constitution, and the Union created by it," not to "dedicate the nation to 'the proposition that all men are created equal.' " The bitterness of these protests was evidence that Lincoln had succeeded in broadening the aims of the war from Union to Equality and Union.

CHAPTER SEVENTEEN

The Greatest Question Ever Presented to Practical Statesmanship

———

Lincoln returned from Gettysburg with a fever, and his doctor put him to bed, diagnosing varioloid, a mild variant of smallpox. For the next three weeks he remained under quarantine in the White House, seeing few visitors and transacting little public business. But he remained in good spirits, and newspapers reported that he was able to joke that his illness gave him an answer to the incessant demands of office-seekers. "Now," he is supposed to have said, "I have something I can give everybody."

His convalescence gave him an opportunity to reflect on the tasks that still lay ahead of him. The most immediate of these was the drafting of his annual message to Congress, which assumed great importance because it would deal with the thorny question of the terms on which the rebellious Southern states could be restored to the Union. This, the President believed, was "the greatest question ever presented to practical statesmanship." Intertwined with this issue was rivalry over the next Republican presidential nomination. And affecting all were the operations of the Union armies. If the armies continued to be victorious and if the President could secure the united backing of his party, the prospects for his reelection and for his program of reconstruction were good.

I

In the fall of 1863, Lincoln occupied a commanding political position. His recent public letters had done much to rally public opinion behind his administration. The fall elections demonstrated the strength of his popular following and the resilience of his party. In military affairs, too, things were looking up. In November decisive Union victories of Grant, Sherman, and George H. Thomas at Lookout Mountain and Missionary Ridge pushed the rebels out of most of Tennessee and opened the way for a drive into Georgia, the heartland of the Confederacy. In foreign affairs as well the administration scored victories. In September the decision of the British government to seize the formidable rams being built for the Confederacy in the Laird shipyards ended the last major threat to the Union blockade and vindicated Lincoln's and Seward's diplomacy. That same month the arrival of Russian fleets at Atlantic and Pacific ports, sent in reality to keep them from being bottled up in the Baltic in the event of a likely war with Great Britain, suggested to most Americans that the Czar's sympathy for the Union cause would lead him to block any British or French intervention in the American Civil War. To celebrate this unlikely liaison between the most autocratic and the most democratic rulers in the world, the Lincolns gave a reception for the Russian visitors, who, as John Hay commented, were "fiendishly ugly," and demonstrated "vast absorbent powers."

To be sure, the President would have to work with reduced majorities in the Thirty-eighth Congress, scheduled to assemble in December, whose membership reflected Republican defeats in the 1862 elections, but it was possible that a smaller group of Republicans might give him more consistent support than the unwieldy majorities of the previous Congress. Throughout the fall Lincoln closely monitored the preliminary steps toward the organization of the new Congress. Warned that Emerson Etheridge, the clerk of the House of Representatives, was planning to take advantage of a technicality and refuse to accept the credentials of Republican congressmen, thus throwing the organization of the House into the hands of the Democratic minority, the President urgently wrote Republican leaders in all the Northern states to make sure that representatives arrived in Washington with impeccably correct credentials. He insisted that all Republican members should be present on the day the House was organized. If Etheridge persisted in his scheme, the President remarked grimly, he would "be carried out on a chip," and he promised to have a troop of soldiers ready to assist.

With that danger, real or imaginary, averted, the President turned his attention to the election of a new Speaker of the House. The leading candidate was Schuyler Colfax of Indiana, whom Lincoln considered "a little intriguer,—plausible but not trustworthy." In addition, the President remembered that Colfax had been the special protégé of Secretary Chase, Horace Greeley, and other Radical Republicans. For a time he put his hopes on Frank Blair—the brother of Postmaster General Montgomery Blair— who had recently been reelected to Congress from Missouri as a Conservative Republican but had strong ties to War Democrats throughout the North. The selection of Blair would give Lincoln a Congress controlled by a centrist coalition. It would, in effect, ratify the transformation of the Republican party into a National Union party, a change that the President's strongest supporters had for some time been advocating.

The problem was that Blair was also a major general in Sherman's army in Tennessee. Lincoln urged him to "come here, put his military commission in my hands, take his seat, go into caucus with our friends, abide the nominations, help elect the nominees, and thus aid to organize a House of Representatives which will really support the government in the war." If elected Speaker, Blair would preside over a House majority that would strongly back the President's policies; if defeated, he could resume his commission and rejoin the army. But when Blair, who was in hot pursuit of the Confederates in eastern Tennessee, did not arrive in Washington in time for the organization of Congress, Lincoln quietly began to campaign for the selection of his old friend Illinois Representative E. B. Washburne as Speaker. After Washburne's candidacy failed to take off, the President invited Colfax to the White House and secured from the slippery Indiana congressman what was not exactly a pledge of support but a promise of neutrality in the upcoming fights in Congress between Radicals and Conservatives.

Those contests, it was clear, would center on how to restore the Southern states to the Union. This was not a new problem for Lincoln. In a sense he had been dealing with it since the outbreak of the war. Early in the conflict his use of federal troops to hold Maryland, Kentucky, and Missouri in the Union had brought about a reorganization of the governments of those states and a change in the relationship between local and national authorities. In 1862 he had taken a further step toward reconstruction by appointing military governors for Tennessee, Louisiana, Arkansas, and North Carolina. But these had been essentially military measures, designed primarily to end the war. Now, after the decisive Union victories at Gettysburg, Vicksburg, and Chattanooga, when the collapse of the Confederacy seemed imminent, pressure grew for a clear statement of the terms of reconstruction.

Lincoln was aware of three possible plans. The first was advocated by Democrats ranging from the pro-Confederate Fernando Wood of New York to the staunchly Unionist Reverdy Johnson of Maryland; it called for the President to withdraw the Emancipation Proclamation and to offer a general amnesty to the rebels. The Southern states, which had never legally been out of the Union, would simply send new congressmen to Washington, and the war would be over.

Conservative Republicans made Liberty as well as Union their war aim. Apart from insisting on the Emancipation Proclamation, they favored generous terms for the conquered South. Seward let it be known that he hoped that no conditions, beyond the emancipation of the slaves, would be imposed on the returning rebels, and his powerful friend Thurlow Weed believed that Southern planters, mostly former Whigs like himself, would recognize the impending defeat of the Confederacy and lead their states back into the Union. Montgomery Blair wanted the President to appeal to the small farmers of the South to overthrow their slaveholding leadership and return to the Union. The Postmaster General also favored the compulsory deportation and colonization of the freed blacks.

Radical Republicans sought to add Equality as a third war aim. Most called for a drastic reorganization of Southern social and economic life before the rebellious states could be readmitted. Thaddeus Stevens, the powerful head of the House Ways and Means Committee, favored treating the South as a conquered province, wholly subject to the legislative will of the Congress. In a more elaborate argument, Charles Sumner maintained that the rebellion had vacated all government in the South and the region now fell under the exclusive jurisdiction of Congress, like any other national territory. It followed that slavery, which could not exist without the protection of positive law, was abolished in the entire region—not merely in the more limited areas designated in Lincoln's Emancipation Proclamation. It was the duty of the Congress to ensure that all citizens in the South, regardless of race, were guaranteed the equal protection of the law. Moreover, Sumner argued, "as a restraint upon the lawless vindictiveness and inhumanity of the Rebel States," Southern lands should be "divided among patriot soldiers, poor whites, and freedmen."

These differences over reconstruction had been simmering for months, but the division among Republicans became public in October, when Sumner articulated his plan in an unsigned article, "Our Domestic Relations," published in the influential *Atlantic Monthly*. Blair, irritated by Sumner's arguments and further angered because the Radical congressional candidate, Henry Winter Davis, was threatening the Blair family's hegemony in Maryland, countered in a public address at Rockville, Maryland, on October 3. "The revolutionary schemes of the ultra abolitionists," he charged, led to the eradication of the constitutional rights of the states and promoted the "amalgamation" of the black and white races. The best policy of reconstruction was to entrust government in the rebellious states to loyal men and then restore each Southern state to "its place in the councils of the nation with all its attributes and rights." To Sumner's claim that Congress alone had power to manage reconstruction, Blair replied that the "safe and healing policy of the President" was the proper way to restore the Union.

In the fierce controversy that erupted after Blair's speech, Lincoln stayed carefully neutral. No doubt he was aware of the speculation, reported by a Washington insider, that Blair's address had been made "by the authority of the President as a faithful exposition of his views; or . . . [was] instigated by him with a view to feel the public pulse," but he neither avowed nor repudiated the ideas of his Postmaster General. He did not join Connecticut Senator James Dixon in praise of Blair's "words of truth and wisdom" in exposing "Sumner's heresies," but he did not endorse Thaddeus Stevens's denunciation of Blair as "this apostate," whose address was "much more infamous than any speech yet made by a Copperhead orator."

The whole argument, Lincoln felt, was "one of mere form and little else." He was certain that Blair, for all his insistence that the people of the Southern states must control their own destinies, would not agree to admit Jefferson Davis to a seat in Congress as a representative of Mississippi, and he was equally confident that Sumner, once the loyal people of Southern states gained direction of their own affairs, would not exclude their representatives from Congress. Avoiding a theoretical argument over whether control of reconstruction belonged to the President or to Congress, he was confident that there could be "little difference among loyal men" over the practical issue of keeping "the rebellious populations from overwhelming and outvoting the loyal minority."

In his sickroom the President began working on an annual message to Congress that would avoid both extreme Republican positions. In preparing it he sought the advice of his cabinet, securing statistics on the army from Stanton and suggestions from Chase about details of his reconstruction program. The first half of the message was simply a pasting together of paragraphs submitted by the several heads of departments, summarizing their work during the past twelve months and referring to their longer official reports, which were published separately.

The message showed that it had been composed under difficulty; it was, several newspapers remarked, less "Lincolnian" than his earlier messages, and certainly it missed several opportunities. The President did follow up one of the themes of his Gettysburg address in announcing that "under the sharp discipline of civil war, the nation is beginning a new life," but he did not develop the idea of a new birth of freedom. Nor did he point to the significance of the first national day of Thanksgiving, which, at the urging of Sarah Josepha Hale, editor of *Godey's Lady's Book,* he had proclaimed for the last Thursday in November. And he failed to note the symbolic significance of the completion of the Capitol building, despite all the strains of war, and to make mention of the placing of Thomas Crawford's nineteen-foot statue of Armed Liberty atop the lantern of the dome on December 2.

The President also failed to use the occasion to stress the growing importance of blacks in the Union war effort. He did point out that more than 100,000 blacks were now serving in the Union armies, but he did not praise their heroism in battle, as he had earlier done in his letter to Conkling. He did not discuss the exceptionally successful efforts of General Lorenzo Thomas, whom he and Stanton had sent into the Mississippi Valley to raise black troops. Nor did he refer to his growing friendship with the great black leader Frederick Douglass, who was very active in raising Negro troops in the North. In August, Lincoln had welcomed Douglass into the White House and, in response to Douglass's fears that he was vacillating about the value of Negro troops, assured him, "I think it cannot be shown that when I have once taken a position, I have ever retreated from it."

Only at the end of the message did Lincoln's distinctive voice emerge. Announcing a proclamation of amnesty and reconstruction, the President offered "full pardon . . . with restoration of all rights of property, except as to slaves," to all rebels, excepting high-ranking Confederate officials, who would have to take an oath of future loyalty to the Constitution and pledge to obey acts of Congress and presidential proclamations relating to slavery.

In order to encourage the political reorganization of the Southern states, he promised to extend recognition when they reestablished governments supported by as few as one-tenth of their 1860 voters who took the oath of allegiance.

Lincoln defended his proclamation as one in which, "as is believed, . . . nothing is attempted beyond what is amply justified by the Constitution." An oath, he explained, was necessary to separate the loyal from the disloyal elements in the South, and he preferred a liberal oath, "which accepts as sound whoever will make a sworn recantation of his former unsoundness." The requirement that rebels must swear to uphold the legislation and proclamations ending slavery was necessary to prevent any attempt at reenslavement of the newly freed blacks, which would be "a cruel and an astounding breach of faith," and he went on to pledge, "While I remain in my present position I shall not attempt to retract or modify the emancipation proclamation; nor shall I return to slavery any person who is free by the terms of that proclamation." Recognizing that loyal Union men might disagree on the mechanisms of reconstruction, the President allowed for approaches other than his own: "Saying that reconstruction will be accepted if presented in a specified way, it is not said it will never be accepted in any other way."

This program for reconstruction outlined in Lincoln's December 1863 message marked a decided change in his thinking about the future of the Southern states. At the outbreak of the war, believing that secession was the work of a small, conspiratorial minority, he hoped that the Unionist majority in the South would reassert itself, throw out the traitors, and send loyal representatives and senators to Washington. The military governors he had appointed were intended simply to facilitate this process. But as the war wore on, he increasingly came to question whether loyal whites were in the majority in the seceded states. His early hope of preventing the war from degenerating "into a violent and remorseless revolutionary struggle" faded, and he had felt obliged to strike at the basic social and economic structure of the South by announcing the emancipation of the slaves. Now, late in 1863, he was afraid that the South might follow the very course that he had favored in the first months of the conflict. There was a real possibility that the Confederates, admitting defeat, might claim that they had never been out of the Union—a legal fiction he and his advisers had always stoutly maintained—and send back to Washington the same congressmen who had denounced the Union in 1861. Lincoln dreaded "to see . . . 'the disturbing element' so brought back into the government, as to make probable a renewal of the terrible scenes through which we are now passing." In order to prevent this possibility, his proclamation of amnesty required much sterner tests of loyalty and an acceptance of emancipation.

Lincoln's message to Congress may have lacked his usual literary elegance, but it was certainly not wanting in political adroitness. It contained something for everybody. The President seemed to agree with the Conservative Republican position that the war was a rebellion of individual Southerners—not of Southern states—against their government, and he carefully refrained from discussing whether the rebellious states continued to be states in the Union or reverted to territorial status. (He dropped a passage discussing this issue from the draft of the message.) To Conservatives the message offered the assurance that reconstructed governments in the South would maintain "the name of the State, the boundary, the subdivisions, the constitution, and the general code of laws" as before the war. And, most important, Lincoln gave some hope to extreme Conservatives and War Democrats who doubted the legality of the Emancipation Proclamation by pledging to uphold it only "so long and so far as not modified or declared void by decision of the Supreme Court."

But there was more in the message for Radical Republicans. They were cheered by Lincoln's assurance that Southerners must accept emancipation as an essential condition for reconstruction and by his promise that slaves freed by the Emancipation Proclamation would never be restored to owners. The requirement that all citizens in the rebellious states must take the loyalty oath before participating in the government erased a distinction between loyal and disloyal Southerners that Radicals had long questioned; all white Southerners, at least for a time, would occupy a legal status lower than that of the citizens of the loyal states. In addition, by saying that the governments in the rebellious states had been "subverted," Lincoln implied that they had ceased to be fully equal states in a constitutional sense. With its careful balancing of Radical and Conservative proposals, the message was, as the Democratic *New York World* sourly remarked, "a creditable specimen of political dexterity," which "trims with marvelous adroitness between the two factions of the Republican party."

So dexterous was it that when it was read to Congress on December 9 reactions were, as John Hay reported, "something wonderful." Among the Radicals, Sumner was beaming, Zachariah Chandler, who had recently warned the President that he must take a bold stand, was delighted, and Henry Wilson of Massachusetts said the President had "struck another great blow" for freedom. At the other extreme, Conservative Senator Dixon and War Democrat Reverdy Johnson pronounced the message "highly satisfactory." With the lions lying down with the lambs, it really seemed to Hay "as if the millennium had come."

In the country at large, reactions were equally favorable. Of course, a few antiwar Democratic newspapers condemned it. It was, declared the *New York Journal of Commerce,* a "ukase from the chambers of an autocrat"; the *Chicago Times* suggested that the severity of the terms for Lincoln's proposed amnesty demonstrated that the President was either "insane with fanaticism, or a traitor who glories in his country's shame." But most other public voices enthusiastically endorsed the President's plan. Greeley's Radical *New York Tribune* declared that no presidential message since George Washington's had "given such general satisfaction," while the anti-Radical *New York Herald* praised the President for repudiating "the abolition plan of Senator Sumner." Sumner himself spoke of Lincoln's message "with great gratification," because it satisfied "his idea of proper reconstruction without insisting on the adoption of his peculiar theories." On the other hand, the Blairs praised it because it supported the Conservative position and annihilated "Sumners and Chase's territorial project." From all over the country the President received letters of praise. Friends were "in jubilee over the Message," reported a New Yorker; it was *"Magnificent,"* wrote a Washington resident; "Posterity will regard you as . . . the restorer of *honor,* peace and prosperity to our land," promised another correspondent; while from Ohio came the report that everybody agreed that Lincoln had "said the right word at the right time."

Perhaps the strongest words of praise came from the *Chicago Tribune,* whose editor, Joseph Medill, had often been critical of Lincoln. After the President's message, Medill felt, "the political future begins to look clear." To finish off the war and bring about a restoration of the Union required "a clear head, an honest mind, and clean hands." "Who [is] so fit to carry on what is begun," asked the *Tribune,* "as he who has so well conducted us . . . thus far?" Looking ahead to the next presidential election, the *Tribune* editors saw "many worthy men discharging important national trusts" but found only one "in whom the nation more and more confides—Abraham Lincoln." In his private correspondence Medill was positive that "Old Abe has the inside track so completely that he will be nominated by acclamation when the [Republican] convention meets."

II

That kind of talk, of course, made the problem of reconstruction a part of the contest for the next presidential race. From time to time during the previous year, there had been talk of reelecting Lincoln in 1864, but for the most part it had been desultory and not particularly fervent. Republican newspaper editors, when the question of a second term was raised, usually combined praise for Lincoln with commendation of other conceivable Republican presidential candidates—Seward, Chase, Banks, Butler, Frémont, and so on. Lincoln tried to think as little as possible about the 1864 election. Nowhere in his letters or his public papers during the first two and a half years of the war did he mention renomination or reelection. When newspapers began to agitate the issue, he remarked testily: "I wish they would stop thrusting that subject of the Presidency into my face. I don't want to hear anything about it."

But, for all the burdens of his office, he did desire reelection. As he remarked later, he viewed a second term not as just a personal compliment but as an expression of the people's belief that he could "better finish a difficult work . . . than could any one less severely schooled to the task." By the fall of 1863, when E. B. Washburne asked Lincoln to let some of his confidential friends know his intentions with regard to the next presidential election, he answered with only a minimum of tentativeness: "A second term would be a great honor and a great labor, which together, perhaps I would not decline, if tendered." By November he was more open, and an Illinois visitor who talked with him in the White House reported, "He will be a candidate again—if his friends so desire—of course."

There was little that Lincoln could do openly to promote his renomination and reelection. Custom prohibited him from soliciting support, making public statements, or appearing to campaign for office. But as the nominating season approached, he made a point of hosting numerous social activities at the White House. Both the Lincolns were resolved to make the winter of 1863–1864 a brilliant social season, which could only boost the President's hopes for a second term.

Mary Lincoln willingly cooperated in promoting her husband's reelection. Her mental and physical health had improved, and she gained greater control over her emotions when she was obliged to contrast her own problems with those of her youngest half sister, Emilie Todd Helm, whose husband, Confederate General Benjamin Hardin Helm, was killed at Chickamauga. Seeking to return from the Deep South to her home in Kentucky, Emilie was passed through the Union lines in December and sought refuge in the White House. The Lincolns tried to keep her visit a secret, because the presence of the widow of a high-ranking Confederate officer in the White House was a potential source of embarrassment, especially since Emilie remained outspoken in her loyalty to the South. Inevitably the news leaked out, and General Daniel Sickles, who had lost a leg in the battle of Gettysburg, told the President, "You should not have that rebel in your house." Firmly Lincoln responded: "General Sickles, my wife and I are in the habit of choosing our own guests. We do not need from our friends either advice or assistance in the matter." After a week, with a pass from the President allowing her to cross the army lines, Emilie left for Kentucky.

Inspirited by Emilie's visit, Mary shed her depressing mourning clothing and appeared at the White House New Year's Day reception in a purple dress trimmed with black velvet. The President wore a long black coat, which, an English observer noted, "seemed to hang on him." With more enthusiasm than they had displayed for many months, both the President and his wife greeted the visitors who thronged the White House. At this reception, for the first time in American history, the guests presented to the President included what one newspaper described as "four colored men of genteel exterior, and with the manners of gentlemen." As each visitor was introduced, the President shook hands and bowed, usually saying only "Good morning, Mr. Jones" or "Mr. Smith, how do you do?" Occasionally he paused to exchange a few words with an old friend. Once when a woman asked whether these receptions were not hard work, he replied, "Oh, no—no.... Of course this is tiresome physically; but I am pretty strong, and it rests me, after all, for here nobody is cross or exacting, and no man asks me for what I can't give him!"

In addition to receptions, the Lincolns gave a number of dinner parties, to which political friends and possible supporters were invited. Fiercely loyal, Mary wanted to exclude her husband's rivals, and when Nicolay came up with a guest list for the annual cabinet dinner on January 14, she struck off Chase, his daughter, Kate, and his son-in-law, William Sprague. Nicolay appealed to the President, who ordered the names restored. "There soon arose such a rampage as the [White] House hasn't seen for a year," Nicolay reported, and Mary, whom the secretary referred to as "her Satanic Majesty," announced that she was going to take charge of all the arrangements for the dinner. Finding that she was unable to manage, she summoned Nicolay on the very afternoon of the dinner, apologized to him, and asked his help. "I think," reported the young secretary smugly, "she has felt happier since she cast out that devil of stubbornness."

Both Lincolns gave particular attention to Charles Sumner, who had shown a disturbing tendency during the previous summer to oppose the administration's policies. Lincoln respected Sumner for his knowledge, his sacrifices in the antislavery cause, and his seriousness of purpose, and, as they became better acquainted, found the man behind the cold and haughty senatorial mask. Sumner and Lincoln, Mary said, used to talk and "laugh together like *two* school boys." Mary found the handsome bachelor senator equally attractive, and they became fast friends. They wrote each other notes in French, they went for carriage drives, and they lent each other books; he let her read his correspondence from European notables, and she sent him bouquets from the White House conservatory. The senator, Mary recalled later, "was a constant visitor at the W[hite] H[ouse]. both in office and drawing room—he appreciated my noble husband and I learned to converse with him, with more freedom and *confidence* than any of my other friends." No doubt a good deal of calculation lay behind the attentions that Sumner received from the White House, for the President realized that the senator was a powerful force in the extreme abolitionist wing of his party.

But Lincoln knew that it was going to take more than White House receptions or bouquets for Charles Sumner to assure his reelection. No President since Andrew Jackson had served a second term, and within the Republican party there was considerable sentiment in favor of rotation in office—especially among those opposed to Lincoln. He could readily identify several groups of such opponents. The most vocal were abolitionists, mostly in New England but also powerful in the West, who feared he might negotiate a peace that did not completely eradicate slavery. Typical was an Iowa caucus of abolitionists that condemned the President as "an insignificant man," who had "clogged and impeded the wheels and movements of the revolution"; moreover, because he was "a Kentuckian by birth, and his brothers-in-law being in the rebel army," he had "always shielded the rebels." German-Americans were also disaffected. Many thought that Lincoln, together with Stanton and especially Halleck, was at heart a nativist who discriminated against German-born generals like Franz Sigel and Carl Schurz. As the prominent *Indiana Freie Presse* said, "We cannot and dare not vote for Lincoln, unless we are willing to participate in the betrayal of the republic, unless we are willing to remain for all future the most despicable step-children of the nation." The Charcoal, or Radical, faction of Missouri Republicans was especially hostile, believing that the President had shabbily rejected their overtures of friendship.

In nearly every Northern state Lincoln's reelection was opposed by one or more factions within the Republican party. Sometimes these factions continued the rivalry between former Whigs and former Democrats; in other states they reflected nothing more than intense personal rivalries. Thus in New York one faction consisted of the supporters of Seward and Thurlow Weed, who seemed to be the principal beneficiaries of the appointments and contracts given by the Lincoln administration; the other, which clustered around Greeley and David Dudley Field, was usually critical of the President. In Maryland an intense struggle between the Blairs and Henry Winter Davis continued; when Lincoln sustained his Postmaster General, Davis became one of the President's most articulate and vituperative enemies.

In most cases dissatisfaction with the President did not derive from fundamental ideological differences. Virtually all Republicans agreed that the war must be fought until victory, that slavery had to be abolished, and that some conditions had to be imposed on the Southern states before they could be readmitted to the Union. But there was disagreement over Lincoln's ability to attain these goals. Many considered him an ineffectual administrator who tolerated looseness and inefficiency throughout the government. The best evidence was that, after two and a half years of costly, bloody warfare, the 20,000,000 loyal citizens of the North were unable to overcome 5,000,000 rebellious white Southerners.

Republican members of Congress, who were in the best position to observe the workings of the administration, gave little support for Lincoln's renomination. The chairmen of the most important Senate committees— such as Henry Wilson of Massachusetts, chairman of the Military Affairs Committee; Benjamin F. Wade of Ohio, chairman of the Committee on Territories; Zachariah Chandler of Michigan, chairman of the Commerce Committee; and James W. Grimes of Iowa, chairman of the Committee on the District of Columbia—were openly opposed to a second term, and only careful management kept Sumner, who headed the Foreign Relations Committee, from joining the opposition. Republican leaders in the House of Representatives were also mostly hostile to Lincoln. Early in 1864 when a visiting editor asked Thaddeus Stevens to introduce him to some congressmen who favored Lincoln's renomination, the Pennsylvania congressman brought him to Representative Isaac N. Arnold of Illinois, explaining: "Here is a man who wants to find a Lincoln member of Congress. You are the only one I know and I have come over to introduce my friend to you."

Aware of this congressional dissatisfaction, Lincoln and his friends took solace in the belief that it was shared by only a few disgruntled politicians.

Surely the mass of the people thought differently, and his supporters convinced themselves that there was "a widespread and constantly increasing concurrence of sentiment in favor of the reelection of Mr. Lincoln." "Mr. Lincoln has the inside track," announced the *Chicago Tribune;* "he has the confidence of the people, and even the respect and affections of the masses." Lincoln's mail was filled with repeated assurances of the support of the voters. "Acting upon *your* own convictions—irrespective of those who threaten, as well as of those who fawn and flatter," wrote a Bostonian, "you have touched and *taken* the popular heart—and secured your re-election beyond a peradventure—should you desire it." Especially heartening were the expressions of support from the army. "The soldier will trust no one but Abraham Lincoln," announced one veteran in the Army of the Potomac. "I believe it is God's purpose . . . to call Abraham Lincoln again to the Presidential chair."

Such letters encouraged Lincoln's managers to present him in the role of an outsider, who had the support of the people if not the politicians. In several states, Union meetings begged the President to become "the People's candidate for re-election," accepting "the nomination so generously tendered without awaiting a nomination from a [Republican] National Convention." Nowhere was this movement stronger than in New York City, where a National Conference Committee of the Union Lincoln Association, headed by the wealthy Simeon Draper, urged the people throughout the nation to meet on February 22 and express their support for Lincoln's reelection. The Democratic *New York World* thought it reasonably certain that Lincoln would "nominate himself and leave the Republican Convention, if there should be one, nothing to do but hold a ratification meeting."

That prospect helped to mobilize Lincoln's opponents within the Republican party, but to have any chance of success they needed a rival candidate. Some looked to General Grant. Others thought of Benjamin F. Butler, famous for his severity during the occupation of New Orleans, but Lincoln largely neutralized him by giving him a dead-end job as commander at Fort Monroe. John C. Frémont had backers as well, both because he was known to hate Lincoln and because he had substantial support among the Germans and the Radicals, especially in Missouri. But in the winter of 1863–1864 most rested their hopes on Salmon P. Chase.

Chase's disaffection with the administration of which he was part had steadily increased since his embarrassing role in the cabinet crisis of December 1862. Though he and Lincoln had developed an effective working relationship, they were not personally congenial. Chase was stiff, reserved, and ponderous. In the course of a general conversation he was given to uttering profundities like: "It is singularly instructive to meet so often as we do in life and in history, instances of vaulting ambition, meanness and treachery failing after enormous exertions and integrity and honesty march straight in triumph to its purpose." He resented the easygoing relationship Lincoln had established with Seward; the President often made impromptu evening visits to Seward's home to pass along the latest news and gossip or to share his most recent joke, but he never thought of dropping in on Chase. But there was more to it than that. Chase's discontent stemmed fundamentally from his conviction that he was superior to Lincoln both as a statesman and as an administrator.

Chase also felt that his labors in the Treasury Department were unappreciated. His exhausting efforts to borrow money and raise taxes in order to finance the war seemed to go unnoticed. Chase especially resented the President's decentralized administrative policy of allowing each cabinet officer to run his own department without interference or even consultation with his colleagues. What was at stake here was not just Chase's power drive; it was his sense that he was the only one responsible for keeping the government's financial tub filled, while the War, Navy, and other departments controlled the spigots that drained it.

He was willing to admit that the President had always treated him with kindness, and he did not doubt Lincoln's fairness or integrity of purpose. But he believed Lincoln's policies toward the South and slavery were too slow and too cautious. The Secretary was determined that the end of the war must bring about "unconditional and immediate emancipation in all the Rebel States, no retrograde from the Proclamation of Emancipation, no recognition of a Rebel State as a part of the Union, or [any] terms with it except on the extinction, wholly, at once and forever of slavery." Repeatedly he prodded the President to extend his Emancipation Proclamation to areas in the South under Union military control, which Lincoln had excepted. Increasingly he came to share Sumner's belief that the only true Unionists in the South were the blacks, and he favored the participation of "colored loyalists" in the reconstruction of the rebellious states.

Lincoln was aware of these dissatisfactions of his Secretary of the Treasury. For the most part, Chase openly and honorably expressed his dissents, and the President made no complaint about them. Nor did he object when Chase sought to make the army of Treasury Department employees, a force greatly enlarged after the passage of the Internal Revenue Act of 1862, loyal to him personally, rather than to the administration. He did not even protest when the Secretary made heavy-handed efforts to woo the support of key senators, as when he allowed John Conness of California to nominate the customs collector at San Francisco. But Lincoln could not help noticing that whenever he made a decision that offended some influential person, the Secretary promptly ranged himself in opposition and tried to persuade the victim that he had been unjustly dealt with and that things would have been different had Chase been in control. Thus he leapt to ingratiate himself with Frémont after Lincoln required him to withdraw his hasty proclamation against slavery in Missouri, with General Hunter after his emancipation order was overruled, with General Butler after he was recalled from New Orleans, with General Rosecrans when he was replaced by Grant, and with the Missouri Radicals after they failed to get the President's endorsement. "I am entirely indifferent as to his success or failure in these schemes," Lincoln told John Hay, "so long as he does his duty as the head of the Treasury Department."

For the most part Lincoln regarded Chase's rather clumsy efforts to promote himself with detached amusement. Generally he was willing to appoint the Secretary's partisans to positions in the Treasury Department, preferring, as he said, to let "Chase have his own way in these sneaking tricks than getting into a snarl with him by refusing him what he asks." When he learned that Chase was trying to make political capital out of the removal of Rosecrans, he laughed and said, "I suppose he will, like the bluebottle fly, lay his eggs in every rotten spot he can find." Behind Lincoln's easy tolerance was his recognition that his Secretary of the Treasury would probably make a very good President—and his confidence that he would never have a chance to do so.

The President could afford to be confident because throughout the North his partisans were quietly working to secure his renomination. It was not considered proper for a presidential candidate himself to seem to have anything to do with these maneuvers, and Lincoln kept a strict public silence about them. But whenever Republican party leaders came to Washington, they gained easy access to the White House and were often closeted with the President for hours. Out of these conferences arose the strategy of opening the offensive against Chase in New Hampshire, the state of his birth. When Republicans of the Granite State met in Concord on January 7, their only stated business was to renominate Governor Joseph A. Gilmore, but young William E. Chandler seized the occasion to rush through a resolution praising Lincoln's "unequaled sagacity and statesmanship" and declaring him "the people's choice for re-election to the Presidency in 1864." Chase's supporters had to be content with the backhanded compliment of a resolution that expressed confidence in the financial abilities of the Secretary of the Treasury—but urged him "promptly to detect, expose and punish all corruption and fraud upon the Government."

Spurred by the action of New Hampshire, Simon Cameron sprang into action in Pennsylvania. Loyal to a President who had generously accepted part of the blame for his mismanagement of the War Department, Cameron also recognized that Lincoln's renomination would be a blow to the rival Republican faction in Pennsylvania headed by Thaddeus Stevens. Back in December, finding the President pessimistic about his chances for renomination, Cameron reminded him that when Andrew Jackson sought a second term his managers outflanked any possible rivals by procuring a petition from the members of the Pennsylvania legislature asking him to run again. "Cameron," asked Lincoln, "could you get me a letter like that?" "Yes I think I might," replied the wily Pennsylvanian, and he went to work. By January 9 he had secured the signatures of all the Republican members of the Pennsylvania house and senate to a request that the President would allow himself to be reelected. "I have kept my promise," he told John Hay.

Promptly other Republican organizations began to swing into line. Throughout the North chapters of the Union League, originally formed in 1862 to restore Northern morale shaken by political and military reverses, came out in support of Lincoln's reelection. The Philadelphia Union League, for example, praised the President for "showing himself the leader of a people and not a party." The Trenton Union League declared that he had shown "his pre-eminent fitness" for the presidency. The New England Loyal Publication Society, which issued patriotic broadsides distributed to nearly nine hundred newspapers, broke its rule against taking a position on political contests and published a powerful editorial urging Lincoln's reelection. The Union members of the legislatures of New Jersey, Kansas, California, and the Territory of Colorado all came out in favor of a second term.

With Lincoln's supporters on the move, Chase's backers were forced into the open. They had begun to organize as early as December 9, the day after Lincoln issued his amnesty proclamation, when an advisory committee met in Washington to consider plans to make Chase the next President. The core membership included two Ohio congressmen, an Ohio army paymaster who was in the employ of the Treasury Department, and Whitelaw Reid, the consistently pro-Chase Washington correspondent of the *Cincinnati Gazette.* Subsequently it was expanded by the addition of Senator John Sherman and Representative James A. Garfield, both of Ohio, and Senator Samuel C. Pomeroy of Kansas, who felt aggrieved because Lincoln had favored his rival fellow senator, James H. Lane, in the distribution of Kansas patronage.

Early in February the Chase campaign tested the waters by issuing a pamphlet, *The Next Presidential Election,* which deplored efforts to procure "the formal nomination of Mr. Lincoln in State Legislatures and other public bodies." "The people have lost all confidence in his ability to suppress the rebellion and restore the Union," the pamphlet continued. The "vascillation [sic] and indecision of the President," "the feebleness of his will," and his "want of intellectual grasp" were responsible for the failure of Union armies to crush the rebellion. "Mr. Lincoln cannot be re-elected to the Presidency," the argument ran. The next Republican candidate must be "an advanced thinker; a statesman profoundly versed in political and economic science, one who fully comprehends the spirit of the age." Salmon P. Chase's name was not mentioned; it did not have to be.

This secret, anonymous attack on Lincoln backfired on its authors. As early as February 6, Ward Hill Lamon learned of this "most scurrilous and abusive pamphlet" and warned the President of its existence. When it was circulated in Ohio under the franks of Senator Sherman and Representative James M. Ashley, Lincoln's supporters were already on the alert. The document was "so mean and dastardly in its character," one correspondent wrote Sherman, "that it will brand with infamy your character as a statesman and your honor as a gentleman." Another protested this attempt on the part of "a few politicians at Washington" to turn the people against "Old Honest Abe" and instructed the senator: "You cant do it and Mr. Sherman you need not try it. If you were to resign tomorrow you could not get 10 votes in the Legislature. . . . If you cant do anything better you had better quit."

Undeterred, Chase's backers continued to organize and in late February, under the signature of Senator Pomeroy, distributed a second circular, again marked "Private," declaring that the reelection of Lincoln was "practically impossible." This time they frankly announced that Chase, with his "record, clear and unimpeachable, showing him to be a statesman of rare ability, and an administrator of the very highest order," possessed "more of the qualities needed in a President during the next four years, than are combined in any other available candidate." Sent to hundreds of Republicans throughout the North, this Pomeroy Circular promptly became a matter of public knowledge. The *Washington Constitutional Union* published it on February 20, and two days later the *National Intelligencer* gave it broad circulation.

Once again, Chase found himself in the embarrassing position of appearing disloyal to the President to whose favor he owed his office, and he quickly disclaimed responsibility for the Pomeroy Circular. He was, he wrote Lincoln, only a reluctant candidate, and he had not been consulted by the friends who were organizing in his behalf. Choosing his words very carefully, he denied knowledge of the existence of the Pomeroy Circular before it was published—a statement that may have been literally true, though the author of the document, James M. Winchell, remembered that the Secretary was informed in advance of the plan to send it out and fully approved it. Chase offered his resignation, declaring, "I do not wish to administer the Treasury Department one day without your entire confidence."

Coolly Lincoln acknowledged the Secretary's letter, promising to answer fully when he could find time to do so, and he left Chase dangling in the wind. Lincoln's aides were furious over the "unscrupulous and malicious" activities of the "treasury rats" who were out to injure the President, but Lincoln held his peace for a week. Then, in a rare attempt to discuss political questions with Robert, who was home from Harvard for the holidays, he strolled into his son's room one evening and showed him Chase's letter.

Calling for pen and paper, the President drafted a reply to the Secretary, stating that he did "not perceive occasion for a change" in the Treasury Department. He had not read the Pomeroy Circular and did not think he would read it. He was, however, "not shocked, or surprised" by its appearance, for he had been aware of Pomeroy's pro-Chase organization for several weeks. "I have known just as little of these things as my own friends have allowed me to know," he assured Chase. "They bring the documents to me, but I do not read them—they tell me what they think fit to tell me, but I do not inquire for more."

When Robert asked in surprise if he really had not seen the circular, his father replied almost sternly that, though "a good many people had tried to tell him something he did not wish to hear," his answer to Chase was literally true.

Before his low-key letter reached Chase, Lincoln had already delivered a different sort of reply. On February 22 the National Committee of the Republican party (which in the forthcoming election was to call itself the National Union party) met in Washington, and four-fifths of its members, who were mostly federal officeholders appointed by Lincoln, expressed support for his reelection. The committee also followed the President's wishes in appointing an early date, June 7, for the national convention, to be held in Baltimore. The next day in Indianapolis, where John D. Defrees, the superintendent of the Government Printing Office, had been working with the President's knowledge and approval to check the Chase forces, the Indiana Republican convention endorsed Lincoln's reelection. Two days later the President's supporters in the Ohio state Republican convention rammed through a resolution urging his renomination. Then, on February 27 in the House of Representatives, Frank Blair, on leave from his army command by permission of the President, launched a savage attack on corruption in the Treasury Department and placed the blame squarely on Chase. Referring directly to the Pomeroy Circular, Blair remarked, "It is a matter of surprise that a man having the instincts of a gentleman should remain in the Cabinet after the disclosure of such an intrigue against the one to whom he owes his portfolio," and he speculated, "I presume the President is well content that he should stay; for every hour that he remains sinks him deeper in the contempt of every honorable mind."

Sore and unhappy, Chase withdrew from the presidential contest on March 5, on the grounds that his home state of Ohio had expressed a preference for another candidate. He sent a copy of his letter of withdrawal to the President. Few took Chase's declination at face value. Playing on the first name of the Secretary of the Treasury, the *New York Herald* reminded its readers: "The salmon is a queer fish, very shy and very wary. Often it appears to avoid the bait just before gulping it down; and even after it is hooked it has to be allowed plenty of line and must be 'played' carefully before it can be safely landed." So Chase, it suggested, was still playing with the bait of a presidential nomination, and he would probably leap at it again. David Davis, now an associate justice of the Supreme Court but still a political adviser to the President, was more blunt: "Mr. Chase's declination is a mere sham, and very *ungracefully* done. The plan is to get up a great opposition to Lincoln through Fremont and others and . . . , when the convention meets, . . . present Chase again."

III

Inevitably these political maneuvers affected Lincoln's program for reconstructing the Southern states. Always alert to what they perceived as a threat of Caesarism, Democrats immediately saw political implications in the 10 percent plan. "By setting up . . . state governments, representing one-tenth of the voters, in Arkansas, Louisiana, Tennessee, and North Carolina," the *New York World* noted, Lincoln could "control as many electoral votes as may be needed to turn the scale" in the next presidential election, and it reminded its readers that if the President was successful "one voter in Arkansas will exert as much political power as ten citizens of New York." Governor Horatio Seymour pointed out that under Lincoln's plan 70,000 men in the reconstructed Southern states could cast as many electoral votes as the 16,000,000 residents of New York, Pennsylvania, Illinois, Indiana, Massachusetts, Missouri, Kentucky, and Wisconsin.

But Republicans, in the general applause that immediately followed Lincoln's proclamation of amnesty, initially paid little attention to the political implications of his message. The House of Representatives promptly created a special committee on reconstruction to devise legislation to carry out the President's plan. Though it was chaired by Henry Winter Davis, a critic of the administration, the committee throughout January and February concentrated on a bill introduced by James M. Ashley that largely followed the President's ideas but also provided for Negro suffrage.

But then Republican congressmen began receiving reports on the political activities of the President's agents in the Southern states that were under the control of the Union army. In Tennessee, Andrew Johnson, who had been serving as military governor since 1862, seemed less interested in building broad-based Unionist sentiment than in constructing his own political faction pledged to the reelection of Lincoln. In Arkansas the President entrusted reconstruction to General Frederick Steele, whom he advised to cooperate with an irregularly convened constitutional convention in which it was doubtful whether a single delegate had authority to represent a county. Lincoln was aware that there were doubts about the legitimacy of this Arkansas regime, but he instructed Steele not to worry over legal niceties; if the provisional government abolished slavery, the general could "fix the rest." In Florida, learning that "some worthy gentlemen" wanted to restore a loyal government, the President sent his private secretary, John Hay, with blank books to record the oaths of those who swore allegiance. The effort was not successful, for the military force supporting the scheme was defeated at Olustee on February 20, and Hay was unable to gather the 1,400 signatures required to make up 10 percent of the state's 1860 voters. To Lincoln's critics these moves suggested that the Chief Executive was trying to use the military to set up governments that would support his own reelection.

Louisiana provided the real test both of presidential intentions and of congressional perceptions. It was more important, both strategically and diplomatically, than any other Southern state yet conquered by the Union armies. Situated at the mouth of the Mississippi River, it offered the best launching pad for Union military expeditions against Texas and other regions under the control of Confederate General Edmund Kirby-Smith, and it could also be a base for operations against Mobile. With its French and Spanish traditions, Louisiana was better known to Europeans than any other Southern state, and New Orleans, the largest city in the seceded states, was a major port. If Louisiana could be made a showcase of reconstruction, Europeans would receive an inescapable signal of the inevitable collapse of the Confederacy.

Ever since Farragut captured New Orleans in April 1862, Lincoln had been hoping for the reorganization of Louisiana as a loyal state and its readmission to the Union. Initially he hoped that Louisiana Unionists, who claimed to be in a majority, would reassert themselves, disavow the ordinance of secession, and return to the Union, but he found them reluctant to take the initiative. They wanted, he said, "to touch neither a sail nor a pump, but to be merely passengers,—dead-heads at that—to be carried snug and dry, throughout the storm, and safely landed right side up." Consequently neither Benjamin F. Butler, the Union military commander, nor George F. Shepley, whom the President named military governor of the state, was able to make much progress in persuading Louisianians to return to their old allegiance. But the President continued to push for the organization of a loyal government. Pressing Butler and Shepley to register voters and hold local elections, he insisted on prompt action. "Do not waste a day about it," he directed. "Follow forms of law as far as convenient, but at all events get the expression of the largest number of the people possible." He cautioned that these elections must represent the real residents of Louisiana, not the Union soldiers nor the Northern carpetbaggers in the state. "To send a parcel of Northern men here, as representatives, elected as would be understood, (and perhaps really so,) at the point of the bayonet," he informed Shepley, "would be disgusting and outrageous." But the results were meager. In December 1862, Butler staged elections in the two congressional districts under federal military control, and Benjamin F. Flanders and Michael Hahn, both of New Orleans, were sent to Washington. Neither represented any sizable constituency. After long debates over their credentials, they were given seats in the House of Representatives just as the term expired.

The President hoped for better things from Nathaniel P. Banks, who replaced Butler at the end of 1862, but he gave the general a larger task. Since his Emancipation Proclamation had applied only to the areas still in rebel hands, it had left slavery intact in the most prosperous and populous region of the state around New Orleans. Now, convinced that the war was soon coming to an end, Lincoln was troubled that Louisiana might apply for readmission as a slave state. To prevent that course, he desired Banks to sponsor the creation of a free-state government that would end slavery throughout Louisiana. To sugarcoat the pill, he declared that he was willing to accept "some practical system by which the two races could gradually live themselves out of their old relation to each other, and both come out better prepared for the new." But Lincoln did not think he had authority to require the elimination of slavery throughout the state. "While I very well know what I would be glad for Louisiana to do," he wrote Banks, "it is quite a different thing for me to assume direction of the matter."

During the first half of 1863 little progress was made in setting up a loyal government in Louisiana, because Banks was preoccupied first with his campaign against Port Hudson on the Mississippi River and then with a planned expedition against Confederate Texas. In August, Lincoln gave him a strong nudge, urging him to confer with "intelligent and trusty citizens of the State" like Hahn and Flanders and endorsing a plan for Louisiana Attorney General Thomas J. Durant to register eligible voters in preparation for a state constitutional convention.

Four months later the President found to his dismay that nothing had been done. Bitterly disappointed, he told Banks to get on with the job—only to learn that the general claimed that he did not know he was responsible for reorganizing a state government in Louisiana and that, besides, whatever moves he had made in that direction had been frustrated by Shepley and Durant. Firmly Lincoln reminded Banks that he was the supreme authority in his military district. "I now tell you that in every dispute, with whomsoever, you are master," he wrote, and, to make the point emphatic, he repeated the word "master" three more times in the same letter.

Before he received the President's letter, Banks had already begun work to establish a free-state government in Louisiana. "It can be effected now in sixty days,—let me say even in *thirty* days, if necessary—with less public excitement than would attend the ennactment [sic] of a 'dog Law' in one of the eastern States," he promised Lincoln, with his usual overoptimism. In his newfound zeal, Banks decided to take a shortcut. Instead of calling a convention to draw up a new constitution for the state, he decided that "the *only speedy and certain* method" of accomplishing the President's objective was to hold elections under the antebellum Louisiana constitution, merely declaring that all provisions in that document relating to slavery were *"inoperative and void."*

This was not the procedure Lincoln had suggested, nor was it the process favored by Thomas J. Durant and other members of the Free-State General Committee. In their view the entire state constitution needed revision, not merely to eradicate slavery but also to eliminate inequities in representation that had favored the planter class. They pointed out that, under Banks's proposal, voters would only be required to swear to accept the Emancipation Proclamation, which left the institution of slavery intact in much of Louisiana. In that event, they warned, "There is nothing to prevent the continuance of this as a Slave State if the pro-slavery party get control." But Banks justified his course to the President as one "far more acceptable to the Citizens of Louisiana" than submitting the question of slavery to an election, since "their self respect, their *Amour propre* will be appeased if they are not required to vote for or against it."

Lincoln approved Banks's decision and urged him to go right ahead with the election of seven state officers planned for February 22. Durant, Flanders, and others in the Free-State General Committee were unhappy with Banks's action, but their objections carried little weight with him since

Durant, their principal spokesmen, had originally been a very conservative Unionist, who once complained that the presence of Union troops in Louisiana disrupted the relationship between masters and slaves. The President failed to see an enormous difference between Banks's program of holding state elections before holding a constitutional convention and the Free-State Committee's plan for choosing a constitutional convention before holding state elections. Besides, Lincoln was always loyal to his subordinates when they were attempting, however awkwardly, to carry out his wishes, and he could hardly disavow Banks's actions after having repeatedly urged him to move.

Lincoln watched with some satisfaction as the election came off smoothly enough on February 22, with the participation of about 11,000 voters who had sworn to support the Union and the presidential proclamations concerning slavery. Hahn, Banks's candidate, was chosen governor over both Flanders, the candidate of the Free-State Union men, and J. Q. A. Fellows, a Conservative. Jubilantly the general reported to the President: "The change that has occurred in this state since Jan: 1863 is without paralell [sic], in history," and he promised that Louisiana would now become "one of the most loyal and prosperous states, that the world has ever seen."

Lincoln probably discounted Banks's enthusiasm, but he was encouraged by these developments. He thought the setting up of a free-state government in Louisiana, to be followed shortly by a constitutional convention, marked an important step in the restoration of that state to the Union—but only an initial step. He was not entirely happy about the victory of the more conservative wing of the free-state movement, and he was sensitive both to the demands of justice for the newly freed blacks and to the pressures from their abolitionist allies in the North. Even while congratulating Michael Hahn "as the first-free-state Governor of Louisiana," he asked "whether some of the colored people . . . —as, for instance, the very intelligent, and especially those who have fought gallantly in our ranks" should be permitted to vote. That would help "to keep the jewel of liberty within the family of freedom." But, hesitating to overstep his constitutional powers, he offered this advice "only [as] a suggestion."

Many Republican congressmen looked on developments in Louisiana with suspicion. Antislavery men already distrusted Banks because he had set up a labor system in Louisiana that allowed plantation owners to employ former slaves as sharecroppers who would receive one-fourteenth of the crops produced. With restrictions on the movement of freedmen, the system seemed to many Northern observers only a slight improvement over slavery. Republican congressmen heard regularly from disaffected Free-State Union leaders about Banks's plans for reorganizing the state government, and Durant warned them that the general adhered to "the absurd and despotic doctrine that 'the fundamental law of the State is martial law,' i.e. the caprice of a military officer." Sensitive to the interests of the more Radical Republicans in Congress, Free-State General Committee leaders raised the issue of

Negro suffrage as a weapon in their war against Banks. Unaware of Lincoln's private interest in this matter, they publicly proposed enfranchising the "free men of color" of Louisiana—i.e., those blacks and mulattoes who had been free before the war, but not the general population of freedmen—while Banks believed this question could wait until other, more pressing issues were resolved.

Inescapably, Northern Republicans came to recognize the political implications of the reconstruction efforts Lincoln was promoting in the South. Once these states were reorganized and recognized, they would be eligible to send delegates to the Republican National Convention and to cast their electoral votes in the next presidential election. The factional lines among Unionists in the Southern states were not always clear, but in general those who favored a reorganization under the presidential plan were likely to be Lincoln supporters. In Louisiana, for instance, one conservative rejoiced in the election of Michael Hahn as "a triumph over Mr. Chase and all his faction," which would send "our worthy President" the message that the people of Louisiana were "willing that the State should be free, but *they cannot stand Radicalism.*"

Consequently those Republicans in Congress opposed to Lincoln's renomination took the lead in attacking the governments set up under the President's plan of reconstruction as a way of blocking the renomination of Lincoln. Angered by the President's failure to support him in his fierce battle against the Blair faction in Maryland politics, Henry Winter Davis by late January concluded that "Lincoln is thoroughly Blairized" and publicly showed his animosity by proposing a resolution in the House: "There is no legal authority to hold any election in the State of Louisiana; . . . [and] any attempt to hold an election . . . is a usurpation of sovereign authority against the authority of the United States." On February 15 he introduced a measure in the House designed to replace Ashley's bill, which had generally followed the President's plan of reconstruction; Davis proposed giving a major role in the process of reconstruction to the Congress, not the President. A little later he denounced the President's efforts to organize a "hermaphrodite government, half military, half republican, representing the alligators and the frogs of Louisiana." The timing of Davis's outburst was significant; it occurred just four days before the publication of the Pomeroy Circular, urging Chase's candidacy for the presidency. Accurately concluding that the Maryland representative "was now an active friend of the Secretary of the Treasury," Lincoln saw clearly that the fate of his reconstruction plan depended on the outcome of the race for the presidential nomination.

IV

In turn, that contest would depend on the success of the Union armies, and in the winter of 1863–1864 the outlook for the Lincoln administration was bad. In the East, ever since Gettysburg the Army of the Potomac and the

Army of Northern Virginia seemed to be doing a slow dance. In the West, after the brilliant victories at Lookout Mountain and Missionary Ridge, the Union armies remained largely idle for the next six months. At the same time, the strength of the armies was dwindling through death and desertions, and there were virtually no new volunteers. On February 1, Lincoln felt obliged to order a draft of 500,000 more men, and on March 14 he directed the conscription of 200,000 more.

In these grim months a streak of ruthless determination, not hitherto noticeable, began to appear in Lincoln's character. It was not manifested toward the private soldiers in the army, for he was even more considerate than usual of what he called his "leg cases"—men who, he said, could not help running away because God had given them a cowardly pair of legs. But in other actions he betrayed his sense that the war had gone on too long, with too much loss of blood and treasure, and that it was time to force it to a close. His impatience was in evidence as early as September, when he threatened to jail and exile judges who used the writ of habeas corpus to interfere with the draft. Only with difficulty did Chase and other cabinet members persuade him simply to announce the suspension of the writ throughout the country.

Outraged when the Confederacy threatened to shoot captured Negro soldiers, Lincoln issued an order of retaliation. "For every soldier of the United States killed in violation of the laws of war," it read, "a rebel soldier shall be executed; and for every one enslaved by the enemy . . . , a rebel soldier shall be placed at hard labor on the public works." It was an order that pleased many Northerners, horrified by reports of Confederate brutalities toward Union prisoners. For instance, the widow of Horace Mann urged the government to "cull out from our prisoners of war the most valuable officers . . . and shoot or hang them," and she reported that Ralph Waldo Emerson shared her views. But Lincoln's order remained an empty threat, even as he continued to fume over mistreatment of Northern prisoners. In time, he came to reject retaliation because, he wrote Stanton, "blood can not restore blood, and government should not act for revenge."

Out of this frustration, and out of his growing sense that something had to be done to break the military stalemate, arose the plan for a daring raid against Richmond. It originated with the son of Admiral Dahlgren, Colonel Ulric Dahlgren, a longtime favorite of the President. Though this young man had lost a leg in battle, he was vigorous and ambitious, and he convinced Lincoln that a two-pronged cavalry raid, with the larger force led by General Hugh Judson Kilpatrick and a smaller troop under his own command, could swoop behind the Confederate lines, attack Richmond simultaneously from the east and the west, break through its defenses, and reach the infamous Belle Isle Prison, where many Union captives were held. The ill-fated expedition got under way on February 28. Both forces were repulsed on the outskirts of Richmond, and Dahlgren was killed. On his body Confederates claimed they discovered papers that showed Dahlgren planned, after releasing the prisoners, to destroy and burn the Virginia capital, pledging not to allow "the rebel leader Davis and his hateful crew" to escape. High-ranking Union officers immediately, but not altogether convincingly, denied the authenticity of these documents, and they could not be linked to Lincoln. But Dahlgren's raid did reflect the President's determination to take whatever steps were necessary to end the rebellion.

The President saw little evidence that the commanders of the Army of the Potomac shared his sense of urgency. Throughout the fall and into the winter Meade engaged Lee in an elaborate campaign of feints and maneuvers, but nothing came of the sharp clashes at Bristoe, Kelly's Ford, and Mine Run. Unimpressed by Meade's strategy, the President told him bluntly on the eve of one of these engagements, "Only be sure to fight; the people demand it of the Army of the Potomac." But Meade was not about to seek a head-on collision with the Army of Northern Virginia. With growing exasperation Lincoln kept prodding him, and he even made him a kind of no-lose offer, promising that if Meade would attack the enemy "with all the skill and courage, which he, his officers and men possess, the honor will be his if he succeeds, and the blame may be mine if he fails."

But the general did not rise to the bait. Aware that the President and Halleck still felt that he had permitted Lee to escape after Gettysburg, he now sought to avoid further mistakes. Instead of taking the initiative, he allowed his campaigns to be micromanaged from Washington. If he suggested taking the offensive, he was informed that the President was "unwilling he should now get into a general engagement on the impression that we here are pressing him." If he proposed a defensive strategy, he learned that the President thought he was throwing away his advantage in numbers over the Army of Northern Virginia. His plan to push Lee's army back into its entrenchments at Richmond drew the President's blunt comment which none of his commanders seemed able to understand: "Lee's army, and not Richmond, [was] it's objective point."

Inevitably Lincoln began to contrast the lethargy of the Army of the Potomac with the extraordinary energy demonstrated by the Western armies under Grant and Sherman—failing to recognize that no small part of the success of these generals stemmed from the inability of the President, the Secretary of War, or the chief of staff to interfere with the execution of their plans. When Lincoln learned that Meade had allowed Longstreet's army, which had been fighting in eastern Tennessee, to retreat into western Virginia without molestation by Union forces, he exploded in anger. "If this Army of the Potomac was good for anything—if the officers had anything in them—if the army had any legs, they could move thirty thousand men down to Lynchburg and catch Longstreet," he exclaimed. "Can anybody doubt if Grant were here in command that he would catch him?"

Still he was not yet ready to bring Grant in from the West. One reason was that the general was beginning to be talked about as a possible presidential candidate in 1864. He was a favorite of the influential *New York Herald,* and, since his political views were unknown, he was wooed by both Democrats and Republicans. With General McClellan conspicuously courting the Democrats, Lincoln was not about to appoint another general-in-chief who had political aspirations, and he asked E. B. Washburne, the representative from Grant's district, to report on the general's political ambitions. Washburne referred him to J. Russell Jones, a close friend of Grant and his investment adviser, who brought to the White House Grant's letter pledging that nothing could persuade him to be a candidate for President, particularly since there was the possibility of reelecting Lincoln. "You will never know how gratifying that is to me," the President said after reading the letter. "No man knows, when that presidential grub gets to gnawing at him, just how deep it will get until he has tried it; and I didn't know but what there was one gnawing at Grant."

With that obstacle removed, Lincoln enthusiastically backed a measure in Congress to create the rank of lieutenant general, unused since the days of George Washington, and he promptly appointed Grant to that rank. Summoned east, Grant arrived in Washington on March 8, just in time for the weekly White House reception. He had lost the key to his trunk and had only his rough traveling uniform, which was a good deal the worse for wear, but he decided to go anyway since it had been reported that he might put in an appearance. Arriving at the White House, the general made his way through the throng of buzzing visitors toward the tall figure of the President. When Lincoln spotted this medium-sized, unobtrusive, inconspicuously dressed man, he greeted him warmly, saying, "Why, here is General Grant! Well, this is a great pleasure, I assure you!" Lincoln introduced the visitor to Secretary Seward, who in turn presented him to Mrs. Lincoln. A few minutes later Grant was led into the crowded East Room, and so many people pressed to greet him that he was obliged to stand on a sofa to prevent being trampled while he was shaking hands. It was at least an hour before Grant, flushed and perspiring, was able to return to the President.

Lincoln reminded him of a brief ceremony the next day, when he would receive his commission as lieutenant general. Aware that Grant was not used to public speaking, he gave the general a copy of the remarks he intended to make and considerately suggested that Grant might want to write out his response, which could include a statement to put him on as good terms as possible with the Army of the Potomac and obviate the jealousy of other commanders.

Determined to get good publicity from the occasion, Lincoln summoned all his cabinet officers for the brief ceremony at the White House. At one o'clock Stanton and Halleck escorted Grant into the President's office, where Lincoln presented the general with his commission and made a brief speech. "With this high honor devolves upon you also, a corresponding responsibility," he reminded the warrior, but he promised, "As the country herein trusts you, so, under God, it will sustain you." Grant then took a paper from his vest pocket and began reading, but his voice failed. Straightening up, he threw his shoulders back, took the paper in both hands, and started again at the beginning and read it through. Accepting "the full weight of the responsibilities now devolving" on him, he did not directly address either of the concerns the President had suggested the night before, though he did praise "the noble armies that have fought on so many fields for our common country." After that, members of the cabinet were introduced to Grant.

Nearly everybody applauded Lincoln's appointment of Grant as general-in-chief of the armies, with Halleck as his chief of staff. Militarily the new arrangement made a great deal of sense, but it was also politically wise. The *New York Herald* grumbled that Lincoln had only elevated Grant in order to remove a possible rival for the presidency, though that was unfair since Grant had made it abundantly clear that he was not, and would not be, a candidate. Still, with Grant now definitely out of the picture and Chase at least ostensibly out of the race, Lincoln's prospects improved. "The canvass for the nomination, is practically closed," ex-Governor Dennison of Ohio wrote the President. "No person but yourself is seriously thought of for the succession."

CHAPTER EIGHTEEN

It Was Not Best to Swap Horses

—◆—

Naming Grant to head the Union armies won Lincoln a brief respite from pressure to produce a military victory, since everybody recognized that it would take a while for the new commander to take control and to develop a strategy. But there was no armistice in the political warfare as Radical and Conservative Republicans maneuvered for position. During the weeks before the Republican National Convention, Lincoln tried to maintain a cautious neutrality between the rival wings of his party and to build bridges to the War Democrats. His tactics easily secured his renomination, but as reports poured in of the ghastly losses in Grant's Virginia campaign, his reelection remained in doubt. At times even he despaired, and increasingly he came to feel that the outcome of the war, and of his administration, was in the hands of a Higher Power.

I

"It seems clear to me that the people desire the re-election of Mr. Lincoln," Representative James A. Garfield remarked in late February. His opinion was the more significant because he had recently been one of the leaders in the aborted Chase boom. After the appointment of Grant nearly all Republican leaders came to the same conclusion. From Maine came the report, "The feeling for Lincoln is very strong here, and his renomination seems now to be a foregone conclusion." It was echoed from California: Lincoln "was the choice of the people overwhelmingly."

But many politicians were sure that the unanimity was superficial. "The feeling for Mr. Lincoln's re-election *seems* to be very general," Lyman Trumbull wrote, "but much of it I discover is only on the surface." Some who conceded that the President would be renominated claimed to discover "a want of confidence in Lincoln with the people." One alienated Ohio Republican wrote that voters were supporting the President simply because "everybody thinks that everybody else goes for Lincoln."

Among the disaffected there was still no agreement on who could best replace Lincoln at the head of the Republican ticket. Lacking consensus, Lincoln's critics proposed to delay the national convention scheduled to meet in Baltimore on June 7. William Cullen Bryant, editor of the *New York Evening Post,* Horace Greeley, editor of the *New York Tribune,* and other influential New York Republicans demanded that the convention be postponed until at least September 1. "The country is not now in a position to enter into a Presidential contest," they announced in a widely circulated broadside. Upon the ability of the Lincoln administration "to finish the war during the present Spring and Summer, will depend the wish of the people to continue in power their present leaders, or to change them." Approaching Republican leaders in other states, the New Yorkers gained support in Illinois from Medill of the *Chicago Tribune,* who declared, "I don't care a pinch if the convention is put off till Aug[ust]," because Lincoln was exhibiting "some very weak and foolish traits of character." But Simon Cameron in Pennsylvania opposed the delay.

The movement faded when it became clear that it was not possible to beat the President with nobody, and Lincoln's opponents began touting several rival candidates. The *New York Herald* continued to beat the drum for General Grant, who showed no interest. Frémont's support was largely confined to the Radical Germans of Missouri. Benjamin F. Butler let it be known that he would not enter into a combination with other rivals of the President—but did "not decline the use of his name for the office." There was always the possibility that Chase might reenter the race. His supporters, detecting "a strong undercurrent—not yet noisy, nor visible to the masses —in favor of *pressing* Mr. C's claim," were convinced that the Secretary of the Treasury could take advantage of a likely division of Republican delegates between Lincoln and Frémont, since "both sides will prefer Chase to the Other."

Lincoln was confident that Grant would not become a candidate, but he took as serious rivals the others mentioned for the presidency. He knew he could do nothing with Frémont; that general hated the President for ousting him from command first in Missouri and later in western Virginia and then for shelving his alleged military talents for the rest of the war. Frémont made it clear that if he could not break Lincoln's hold on the Republican delegates he would run as an independent, and his backers called a convention to be held in Cleveland on May 31, just a week before the regular Republican meeting in Baltimore.

Butler the President handled with kid gloves, especially after learning that Chase's backers had approached him with the offer of a vice presidential nomination. He had scant respect for the general's ability, but he recognized that Butler could cause trouble, and he attended to his wishes and complaints with considerable deference and protected the notoriously inept general when Grant wanted to remove him from command at Fort Monroe. Claiming to speak for the President, Cameron explored with the general the possibility of a Lincoln-Butler ticket, only to be told, laughingly, that Butler would accept the vice presidency only if Lincoln gave him "bond with sureties, in the full sum of his four years' salary, that he will die or resign within three months after his inauguration." No doubt the President was relieved as well as amused to hear Cameron's report of the conversation.

Chase had to be handled differently. After the fiasco of the Pomeroy Circular and Chase's forced withdrawal from the presidential race, Lincoln's supporters wondered why he let the Secretary of the Treasury remain in the cabinet, and even Butler advised the President that "tipping him out" was the only remedy for the Chase problem. But Lincoln knew that Chase was less dangerous as a disgruntled member of the cabinet than he would be if he left the administration.

During these months, facing mounting government deficits, a Congress reluctant to enact a realistic tax program, and the constantly mounting price of gold as compared to greenbacks, Chase often thought of resigning, and it seemed that he had found a pretext when Lincoln began planning changes in the New York Customs House, which offered the most remunerative patronage positions at the disposal of the federal government. Conservative Republicans in New York felt that Hiram Barney, whom Chase had selected as the collector back in 1861, favored the Radical wing of the party, and they demanded his removal. Lincoln liked Barney and had confidence in his honor and integrity but, suspecting that the collector had "ceased to be master of his position," proposed sending him as minister to Portugal. Barney refused to resign under fire, and Chase dug in his heels. Angrily he warned that if the collector left the New York Customs House he would resign. Reluctantly Lincoln backed down.

In so doing, he grievously offended New York Conservatives led by Thurlow Weed. "Distinctly and emphatically" Weed asked David Davis to tell the President "that if this Custom House is left in custody of those who have for two years sent 'aid and comfort' to the enemy, *his* fitness for President will be questioned." Disaffection among Conservatives became greater when Lincoln, without notice, followed the recommendation of the Secretary of the Treasury and named John T. Hogeboom as appraiser in the New York Customs House. "The President [had] rather appoint Chase's friends *than to say no,*" Senator Edwin D. Morgan grieved. Weed was enraged. "After *this* outrage and insult," he fumed, he would cease to annoy the President with the letters and advice he had constantly showered on him since his election; he could no longer be subjected "to the mortifications of knowing that the President has no respect for my opinions." Deeply troubled, Lincoln sent his private secretary to New York to make peace with the aging boss, but Nicolay found him "quite disheartened and disappointed." Privately Weed began expressing his belief that the people had "not had the worth of their Blood and Treasure" from the Lincoln administration and his doubts about the advisability of renominating the President were so public that rumor had it that "old Weed was undoubtedly opposed to Lincoln."

If the President seemed to support the Radicals in New York, in Washington he appeared to back the Conservatives. In late April, Representative Francis P. Blair, Jr., outraged by charges, made with the apparent connivance of Treasury Department officials, that he had profited from illegal trade along the Mississippi River, took the floor to denounce Secretary Chase for fostering fraud and corruption in order to boost his chances for the presidency. In a blistering attack Blair charged that Chase had not really withdrawn from the race after the "disgraceful and disgusting" Pomeroy Circular; he simply "wanted to get down under the ground and work there in the dark as he is now doing, and running the Pomeroy machine on the public money as vigorously as ever." Chase, he continued, was using "that poor creature" Frémont as a cat's-paw, believing that the threat of an independent third party would frighten the Republicans into dropping Lincoln. Then "Chase, who has *so magnanimously* declined to be a candidate, will then be taken up as a compromise candidate."

What made Blair's vituperative speech the more infuriating to Radicals was his announcement immediately afterward that he was giving up his seat in Congress to resume his commission as major general commanding a corps in Sherman's army. Blair, it became known, had a "distinct verbal understanding" with Lincoln that he might resign his commission in order to serve in Congress but that he could, "at any time during the session, at his own pleasure, withdraw said resignation, and return to the field." Lincoln's enemies raged that this arrangement was both illegal and unconstitutional; it proved that the President had been behind Blair's assault on the Secretary of the Treasury. Indignant, Chase planned to resign, but he allowed his friends to persuade him to delay until they could see the President.

When former Congressman Albert G. Riddle of Ohio, accompanied by Rufus P. Spalding, "the personal and confidential friend nearest the Secretary," met with Lincoln on April 25, they received a frosty reception. He melted, however, after Riddle explained that he had come not to confront the President but to hear his assurance that he was "in no way a party to or responsible for a word uttered by Mr. Blair." Lincoln explained that he had not known in advance of Blair's speech; indeed, he did not learn of it until three hours after he had reinstated the general in command. Realizing *"that another beehive was kicked over,"* he initially thought of canceling the order restoring Blair's commission but on reflection decided to let it stand. "If I was wrong in this," he told his visitors, "the injury to the service can be set right."

As the time for the Baltimore convention approached, the stress of mediating between the two Republican factions was beginning to tell on the

President. Riddle, who had not seen him for five months, was shocked by the change in his appearance. Now, he reported, the President "looked like a man worn and harassed with petty faultfinding and criticisms, until he had turned at bay, like an old stag pursued and hunted by a cowardly rabble of men and dogs."

II

These days Lincoln found it easier to get along with his generals than with the politicians. In Grant he had a commander whom he liked and trusted. Everything about the unpretentious, businesslike general pleased the President. It was an advantage that Grant was from Illinois. His lack of flamboyance, his seeming inattentiveness to rank and protocol endeared him to the President. Lincoln was struck by the simplicity and directness of the language Grant used in his reports. He was even more impressed by their infrequency and brevity. "Gen. Grant," he had noted back in July 1863, "is a copious worker, and fighter, but a very meagre writer, or telegrapher." He was pleased that Grant, unlike McClellan, Buell, and some other generals, unquestioningly accepted his policies on emancipation and the recruitment of Negro troops. Most of all, he told another officer, he liked Grant because "he doesn't worry and bother me. He isn't shrieking for reinforcements all the time. He takes what troops we can safely give him . . . and does the best he can with what he has got."

The President wanted to give the new general-in-chief everything that he reasonably could. He approved the general's decision to reorganize and consolidate the cavalry of the Army of the Potomac into a separate corps, and he agreed to the appointment of Grant's young favorite, Philip Sheridan, to command it. He backed Grant's decision to make sharp reductions in the numbers of soldiers stationed far behind the lines maintaining civil order in the border states and guarding lines of transportation, and he accepted the general's decision to terminate profitless expeditions like the months-long siege of Charleston harbor. When Grant demanded that the quartermaster, ordnance, and commissary departments be brought under his control, Lincoln replied that, though he could not legally give him the command of these departments, "there is no one but myself that can interfere with your orders, and you can rest assured that I will not." Once Grant offended Stanton by withdrawing too many men from the fortifications of Washington, and both men took their cases to the White House. After hearing them out, Lincoln told his Secretary of War: "You and I, Mr. Stanton, have been trying to boss this job, and we have not succeeded very well with it. We have sent across the mountains for Mr. Grant, as Mrs. Grant calls him, to relieve us, and I think we had better leave him alone to do as he pleases."

In his first private interview with the general, the President assured him "that he had never professed to be a military man or to know how campaigns should be conducted, and never wanted to interfere in them." In the past, "procrastination on the part of commanders, and the pressure from the people at the North and Congress, *which was always with him,"* had forced him to play a more active role. But "all he wanted or had ever wanted was some one who would take the responsibility and act, and call on him for all the assistance needed, pledging himself to use all the power of the government in rendering such assistance." "The particulars of your plans I neither know, or seek to know," he wrote Grant later. "You are vigilant and self-reliant; and, pleased with this, I wish not to obtrude any constraints or restraints upon you."

It was a tribute to Lincoln's skill in managing men that, even while giving the general these assurances of independence, he succeeded in reshaping Grant's strategy—and that his tact and diplomacy permitted the general to think that he was conducting the war with a free hand. It was probably the President's quiet influence that caused Grant to give up his plan, ardently urged on him by Sherman, to avoid the political atmosphere in Washington by having his headquarters in the West; instead, he set up his command near the Army of the Potomac, over which he exercised strategic control while Meade remained in tactical command. It was not Grant's wish, but the President's, that Halleck became chief of staff, a position in which he performed well, acting as intermediary between the commander-in-chief, the Secretary of War, and the general-in-chief. For political reasons Lincoln picked officers for several subordinate commands who were not favored by Grant. For instance, Benjamin F. Butler, despite his well-known incompetence, remained at the head of the Army of the James because he had a powerful following among Radical Republicans, and Franz Sigel, who had minimal military skills but was a favorite of German-Americans, was chosen to head the Union forces in the Shenandoah Valley.

Much more important were the shifts that Lincoln, often with Halleck's assistance, brought about in Grant's strategic thinking. Grant was painfully aware that the Army of the Potomac and the Army of Northern Virginia for three long years had "fought more desperate battles than it probably ever before fell to the lot of two armies to fight, without materially changing the vantage ground of either." He was convinced that success would never come through more such inconclusive engagements, and he proposed "an abandonment of all previously attempted lines to Richmond." Instead he favored a series of massive raids against the Confederacy—not just by the cavalry, which was unable to inflict permanent damage, but by small armies of 60,000 men—designed to destroy the essential railway lines. One such raid, using Banks's command at New Orleans, should move against Mobile and then proceed northward to cut the railroads in Alabama and Georgia. A second, under Sherman, should sweep through Georgia and destroy the main east-west transportation line of the Confederacy. A third, moving inland from Suffolk, Virginia, should demolish the rail lines between Weldon and Raleigh, North Carolina, on which Lee depended for supplies to his army.

This, Grant concluded, "would virtually force an evacuation of Virginia and indirectly of East Tennessee."

Under the influence of Lincoln and Halleck, Grant abandoned nearly all of this plan. The President would not consent to weakening the force between Lee's army and the national capital; he feared that while Grant was involved in a raid through North Carolina, Lee would seize Washington and again invade the North. Apart from that, Lincoln had developed a contempt for what he scornfully called "strategy." What he thought was needed was not more maneuvering but assault after assault on the Confederate army. For months that was what he had been urging on Meade, without much success; now he expected Grant to fight.

Without even being aware that he was abandoning his original strategy, Grant developed a new plan for simultaneous massive attacks on the Confederate heartland by all the Union armies. Banks was to advance toward Mobile, Sherman was to move toward Atlanta, Sigel was to cut the Confederate rail line in the Shenandoah, Butler was to advance up the James River against Petersburg and, ultimately, Richmond, while Meade pushed the Army of Northern Virginia back to the Confederate capital. The concerted movement was to begin on the fifth of May.

When Lincoln learned of Grant's new plan, he was, as Hay recorded, "powerfully reminded" of his "old suggestion so constantly made and as constantly neglected, to Buell and Halleck, et al., to move at once upon the enemy's whole line so as to bring into action to our advantage our great superiority in numbers." But he pretended to be surprised when Grant told him about it and, Grant recalled, "seemed to think it a new feature in war." When Grant explained how all the armies could contribute to victory simply by advancing even if they won no battles, the President remarked, in all apparent innocence: "Oh, yes! I see that. As we say out West, if a man can't skin he must hold a leg while somebody else does."

Even with this greatly revised strategy Grant did not succeed in having things his own way. His plan to use Banks's force for a raid on Mobile and central Alabama had to be scratched. Before Grant became general-in-chief, the War Department, at the President's urging, had dispatched Banks on a campaign up the Red River, designed in part to liberate more of Louisiana from Confederate rule—and incidentally to liberate 50,000 to 150,000 bales of cotton thought to be stored in central and western Louisiana. Equally important in the President's mind was the lesson that Banks's success would send to the French in Mexico, where the Archduke Ferdinand Maximilian of Austria on April 10 accepted the throne of a puppet government protected by the troops of Napoleon III. The Red River expedition was a total disaster. Its only result was to prevent Banks's army of 40,000 men from helping in Grant's campaign.

But the other parts of Grant's plan fell into place. In the early hours of Wednesday, May 4, the Army of the Potomac moved across the Rapidan River to begin a new campaign against the Army of Northern Virginia. The next day Butler landed 30,000 troops on the south side of the James River, threatening Petersburg. On May 7, Sherman launched his campaign for the capture of Atlanta.

Lincoln watched the campaign with painful interest. For the first two days as Grant's army plunged into the Wilderness, that trackless tangle of trees and undergrowth which had been the scene of Hooker's defeat, he received no news because his general-in-chief had forbidden newspaper correspondents to use the telegraph. During this time the President haunted the War Department offices; an observer thought he was "waiting for despatches and, no doubt, sickening with anxiety." Not until Friday morning did he receive even an indirect report from Grant: "Everything pushing along favorably." At two o'clock the next morning he interviewed a correspondent from the *New York Tribune,* who had just left the army. Grant told him: "If you do see the President, . . . tell him that General Grant says there will be no turning back." With that much reassurance Lincoln felt able to tell a Pennsylvania woman that he was "considerably cheered, just now, by favorable news" from the army, and in response to a serenade by a large crowd that assembled on the White House lawn he gave thanks to "the brave men," their "noble commanders," and "especially to our Maker" for victory.

Then the shattering real news began to come in. Grant had thrown his army of 100,000 men against Lee's much smaller force in the Wilderness, attempting to flank it, and in two days of ferocious fighting had suffered more than 14,000 casualties. Unsuccessful in turning Lee's army, Grant then moved east, only to encounter Lee again at Spotsylvania, where between May 10 and 19 more than 17,500 Union soldiers were killed or wounded. Over a period of two weeks the Army of the Potomac lost nearly 32,000 men, and thousands more were missing.

During these terrible days Lincoln tried to keep up a pretense of regular business, though his impatience and bitterness occasionally overcame him. Speaker Colfax found him pacing up and down his office, "his long arms behind his back, his dark features contracted still more with gloom," as he exclaimed: "Why do we suffer reverses after reverses! Could we have avoided this terrible, bloody war! . . . Is it ever to end!" He hardly slept at all these nights. One morning Francis B. Carpenter, the young artist who was painting a picture he called *First Reading of the Emancipation Proclamation of President Lincoln,* caught sight of him in the hallway of the Executive Mansion, "clad in a long morning wrapper, pacing back and forth a narrow passage leading to one of the windows, his hands behind him, great black rings under his eyes, his head bent forward upon his breast—altogether . . . a picture of the effects of sorrow, care, and anxiety."

Despite the hideous losses, the President did not despair, because Grant, unlike all the previous commanders of the Army of the Potomac, did not withdraw after his engagements with the enemy but continued to push against Lee's army. Lincoln took great comfort from the message that Grant sent Stanton on the seventh day of the fighting: "I propose to fight it out on this line if it takes all summer." "It is the dogged pertinacity of Grant that wins," the President said hopefully to John Hay.

During the weeks after the unsuccessful assault at Spotsylvania, Lincoln continued strongly to support the general. There was no alternative to Grant. Except for Sherman, whose capacity for independent command had yet to be fully tested, and George H. Thomas, who was considered too slow, there were no other generals who could be put in charge. Besides, Grant was carrying out the President's own favored plan of operations. Lincoln did his best to keep his spirits up, and he was encouraged that Grant after each engagement went on to launch a new offensive. "The great thing about Grant," Lincoln said during the battle of the Wilderness, "is his perfect coolness and persistency of purpose.... he is not easily excited ... and he has the *grit* of a bull-dog! Once let him get his 'teeth' *in,* and nothing can shake him off."

III

With a general-in-chief who shared his determination to destroy the Confederate armies, Lincoln directed his own efforts to seeing that the Union forces were adequately supplied and constantly reinforced. Manpower was a constant problem. Many of the Union soldiers had enlisted for three-year terms, which would expire in 1864. Though Congress offered special inducements in the way of bounties and furloughs to those who would reenlist, at least 100,000 decided not to. When the casualties from the Wilderness campaign were added to this number, it was obvious that more recruits were needed. Since volunteering had virtually ceased, Lincoln on May 17 felt forced to draft an order for the conscription of 300,000 additional men.

The order was never issued because on May 18 the *New York World* and the *Journal of Commerce* published a proclamation, purportedly originating in the White House, in which Lincoln announced that, "with a heavy heart, but an undiminished confidence in our cause," he was ordering an additional draft of 400,000 men. This depressing news caused a flurry of speculation on Wall Street, and the price of gold, as measured in greenbacks, rose 10 percent. That was the object of the authors of the bogus proclamation, Joseph Howard, an editor of the *Brooklyn Daily Eagle,* and Francis A. Mallison, a reporter for that paper, who managed a fairly skillful imitation of Lincoln's style. Doubtless Howard, who had worked for the *New York Times* and the *New York Tribune,* heard rumors of an impending draft call, and he took advantage of inside information in the hope of making a fortune in the gold market.

The Lincoln administration came down heavily on the two newspapers. In an order drafted by Stanton, Lincoln directed the army to "take possession by military force" of the premises of the two offending papers and ordered the arrest of their editors and proprietors. Shortly afterward authorities discovered that Howard and Mallison were responsible, and the two men were imprisoned in Fort Lafayette.

Though the editors and owners of the papers were promptly released and the *World* and the *Journal of Commerce* resumed publication after two days, the episode further illustrated the determination, amounting almost to ferocity, with which Lincoln was prosecuting the war. Offered an opportunity to disavow responsibility for the order suppressing the newspapers by blaming subordinates, he refused to do so. He was already angry at the speculators and profiteers who were making money from the war, often by betting against the success of the government. Gold speculators—and Howard planned to be one—were a special object of his wrath. Banging his clenched fist on the table for emphasis, he told Governor Curtin: "I wish every one of them had his *devilish* head shot off!"

Fortunately for Lincoln neither the bogus proclamation nor the news of Grant's losses in Virginia had much immediate effect on the slow political processes that were inevitably moving toward the Republican nominating convention. State after state continued to wheel into line behind the President. Support for Lincoln was strongest in the Western states, like California, Iowa, and Wisconsin, where National Union (Republican) conventions chose delegates unanimously pledged to vote for his renomination. In Illinois, one Republican wrote, the people "think that God tried his best when he made Mr Lincoln and they are all for his re election."

In the East, Cameron, as he had promised, persuaded the Pennsylvania Republican convention to reinforce the endorsement already given by the state legislators, and the Keystone State sent a delegation, loaded with federal employees appointed by the President, to cast fifty-two votes for Lincoln. In Massachusetts, despite foot-dragging by Governor John A. Andrew and angry opposition from the abolitionist Wendell Phillips, the Republican convention instructed its twenty-four delegates to support the renomination of the President. The Ohio convention, composed as a critic said of "aspirants for Congress, who expect Administration favor," echoed the earlier vote of Republicans in the legislature and strongly endorsed Lincoln, while rejecting a resolution that praised Chase's services in the Treasury Department. In New York, an even larger prize with sixty-six convention votes, Thurlow Weed momentarily forgot his disenchantment with Lincoln and procured a delegation unanimous for the President.

The only remaining obstacle to Lincoln's renomination was the convention of disaffected Republicans that assembled in Cleveland on May 31. Called to protest the "imbecile and vacillating policy of the present Administration in the conduct of the war," it initially seemed a real threat to Lincoln, who had agents on the ground to observe and report on the proceedings. But the gathering was poorly attended, with only 350 to 400 persons present, only 158 of whom were actual delegates. Most of these represented the German-American element, especially in Missouri, where hatred of Lincoln burned bright and loyalty to Frémont was fierce. To these was added a small contingent of ultra-Radical abolitionists from the Northeast, men who broke with William Lloyd Garrison, now a Lincoln supporter, and followed Wendell Phillips, who denounced the administration as "a civil and military failure" and attacked the President for supporting a reconstruction policy "more disastrous to liberty than even disunion." Most of the delegates were political unknowns. Prominent anti-Lincoln Eastern Republicans, who hoped that the convention would nominate Grant and thus provide a real challenger to Lincoln in the National Union Convention, stayed away after learning that the assembly was heavily packed in favor of Frémont. Horace Greeley, who had earlier touted the Cleveland meeting, quietly withdrew the support of the *New York Tribune.*

With little debate the delegates in Cleveland adopted a radical platform demanding a constitutional amendment abolishing slavery and guaranteeing "to all men absolute equality before the law." It also called for direct election of the President, who should serve only one term, preservation of the rights of free speech, a free press, and habeas corpus, and the confiscation of the lands of rebels. The convention, styling itself the Radical Democracy, then proceeded unanimously to nominate John C. Frémont for President.

One of Lincoln's agents on the spot reported that the convention was a "most magnificent fizzle," and administration organs like the *New York Times* agreed that it was "a congregation of malcontents . . . representing no constituencies, and controlling no votes." It was, as John Hay remarked, "rather a small affair every way." Lincoln was amused by the proceedings. When a friend gave him a detailed report on the convention and the small number of delegates, he quietly picked up the Bible, which customarily lay on his desk, and read a passage from I Samuel: "And every one that was in distress, and every one that was in debt, and every one that was discontented, gathered themselves unto him; and he became a captain over them: and there were with him about four hundred men."

During the week before the National Union Convention in Baltimore many of the delegates came first to Washington, some to confer with their congressmen, but most, as Hay remarked, "to pay their respects and engrave on the expectant mind of the Tycoon, their images, in view of future contingencies." Most of the delegations were legitimate, but some were bogus and irregular. Lincoln cordially welcomed them all. Warned that the delegation from South Carolina was a swindle, consisting of a few sutlers, cotton dealers, and Negroes, the President grandly remarked, "They won't swindle me."

With Lincoln's renomination already assured, many of the delegates tried to learn the President's wishes about the vice presidential nominee. He took pains to be noncommittal, remarking that he did not want to take sides since all the men mentioned for that office—the incumbent, Hannibal Hamlin, Benjamin F. Butler, Andrew Johnson, and others—were all personal and professional friends of his. One of his private secretaries was convinced that he favored renominating Hamlin; the other, that he wanted Johnson. When anyone interrogated him on the subject, he would say something vague, like

"Mr. Hamlin is a very good man." As a result of Lincoln's evasiveness, more than one self-important delegate went on to Baltimore confident that he, and he alone, was the repository of the President's secret preference for a running mate.

The Baltimore convention, which met on June 7–8, was a fairly tame affair. Count Gurowski, who witnessed the proceedings in the Front Street Theater, found the convention "a crowd of sharp-faced, keen, greedy politicians," and he saw "everywhere shoddy, contractors, schemers, pap-journalists, expectants." Nicolay, whom Lincoln permitted to attend, thought it "almost too passive to be interesting—certainly . . . not at all exciting as it was at Chicago" in 1860. With the presidential nomination already decided, there was little suspense, and what little enthusiasm the delegates had was quieted by the news that 7,000 men in the Army of the Potomac had just been killed or wounded in Grant's ill-conceived charge on the Confederate lines at Cold Harbor. "This Convention hasn't the enthusiasm of a decent town meeting," one Illinois delegate grumbled.

The retiring chairman of the National Union Executive Committee, Senator E. D. Morgan of New York, opened the proceedings by urging, at Lincoln's suggestion, that the convention "declare for such an amendment of the Constitution as will positively prohibit African slavery in the United States." The prolonged applause that greeted this recommendation indicated that from the very outset the Republicans were prepared to seize a central plank of the platform of the Radical Democracy and claim it for their own.

Speeches frequently emphasized that this was not just the third national convention of the Republican party but the first convention of the National Union party. In his opening address, Dr. Robert J. Breckinridge of Kentucky, the temporary president of the convention, sounded the key note: "As a Union party I will follow you to the ends of the earth. . . . But as an Abolition party—as a Republican party—as a Whig party—as a Democratic party—as an American party, I will not follow you one foot." The permanent president of the convention, former Governor William Dennison of Ohio, echoed this sentiment. The delegates, he said, were not "representatives of either of the old political parties"; the only test of membership in the Union party—"if party it can be called"—was "an unreserved, unconditional loyalty to the Government and the Union." Clearly the strategy was to avoid divisive factional issues among Republicans and to woo the support of the War Democrats. Naming Lincoln for a second term was the best way of doing that.

Lincoln's supporters completely dominated the convention. Their control was so assured that Justice David Davis, again one of Lincoln's principal managers, did not even bother to attend. "The opposition is so utterly beaten," he wrote the President, "that the fight is not even interesting." There were few issues, and all were decided as the President wished. Despite the growling of Radicals like Thaddeus Stevens against representation from "damned secessionist provinces," the convention admitted delegations from Tennessee, Louisiana, and Arkansas, states that were undergoing reconstruction under Lincoln's 10 percent plan. A contest arose over the representation of Missouri, because both the Claybanks (Conservatives) and the Charcoals (Radicals) sent delegations, but a fight was averted when Lincoln's men agreed to seat the Radicals and they, in turn, promised not to bolt but to abide by the action of the convention.

The platform endorsed Lincoln for "the practical wisdom, the unselfish patriotism and unswerving fidelity to the Constitution" he had exhibited. Masterminded by Henry J. Raymond, editor of the *New York Times,* it was throughout a strongly proadministration document. It insisted on the integrity of the United States, demanded an unconditional surrender of the Confederates, and endorsed a constitutional amendment abolishing slavery. An effort on the part of "all the malignants and malcontents" to include a plank censuring Seward, Blair, and other Conservative members in the cabinet was watered down to an ambiguous resolution deeming it "essential to the general welfare that harmony should prevail in the National Councils" and that "those only who cordially endorse the principles proclaimed in these resolutions" were worthy of public trust.

The only real excitement at the convention came from an unseemly squabble over who should have the privilege of placing the President's name in nomination. Once the roll call began, state after state unanimously cast its votes for Lincoln, but Missouri, acting on instructions from its state convention, gave 22 votes for Grant. After the chair announced that Lincoln had received 484 of the 506 votes, the chairman of the Missouri delegation moved to change the vote of his state and Lincoln was unanimously renominated.

When the convention next turned to selecting a running mate, the President's advisers gave no guidance. Initially it was generally assumed that Hamlin would be renominated, though there had been some talk about selecting a War Democrat, like Johnson, Butler, or Daniel S. Dickinson, a former United States senator from New York, whose loyal support of the Lincoln administration had led to his election as attorney general of that state in 1861. Delegates pressed Nicolay so hard to learn the President's preference that he wrote John Hay at the White House for instruction. Lincoln endorsed his letter: "Wish not to interfere about V.P. Can not interfere about platform. Convention must judge for itself." Hay passed the message on to Baltimore.

Left to make their own selection, the delegates floundered in a sea of politics. Quite early Whitelaw Reid, correspondent of the *Cincinnati Gazette,* judged that "Hamlin had lost his hold. Men seemed to consider it their duty to support him; but there was no enthusiasm about it." The New England delegations failed to give him unanimous support and cast many votes for Johnson and Dickinson. New Yorkers realized that Seward would probably have to resign as Secretary of State if Dickinson was nominated, because one state could not claim two of the highest offices in the administration, and they threw their weight behind Johnson, who was already strong in the Southern and Western states. After much last-minute shifting of ballots, Johnson was nominated.

Lincoln never explained his stand on the vice presidential nomination. Years later Alexander K. McClure, a prominent Pennsylvania Republican, claimed that just before the Baltimore convention the President had urged him to work for the selection of Johnson, and he rounded up a number of other contemporaries who claimed they had received the same instructions. These charges outraged both Nicolay, who believed the President incapable of deceit, and Charles E. Hamlin, who thought his grandfather's defeat resulted from machinations of Charles Sumner, and they collected a large number of statements to prove that the President had really preferred Hamlin. The evidence was evenly balanced and inconclusive.

All that could be stated positively was that if Lincoln had really wanted Hamlin renominated the convention would have followed his wish. His failure to name Hamlin may have reflected his awareness that Hamlin was very radical on questions relating to slavery and the South. Lincoln jokingly remarked that he did not fear the Confederates would assassinate him, because they knew Hamlin would take his place. Lincoln also thought that there was something to be said for choosing a War Democrat to symbolize the broad coalition on which the National Union party hoped to rest and for picking a Southerner to stress that all the states still remained in the Union. He admired Johnson for his courage in sticking to the Union after his state seceded, and he was gratified that, as military governor of Tennessee, Johnson heartily endorsed his reconstruction program. But at bottom he simply did not think much about the office of the Vice President. Like most American presidents, he saw little of his second-in-command and never thought of giving the Vice President duties that would make him a kind of coexecutive. Consequently it did not make a great deal of difference whom the convention selected. And, finally, Lincoln recognized that the delegates to the Baltimore convention, held under strict control by his managers, needed a chance to blow off steam, to assert their independence, and to prove that they were not presidential puppets by choosing their own vice presidential nominee.

At any rate, Lincoln was pleased by the outcome of the convention. When a committee of delegates came to the White House on June 9 to give him official notification of his renomination, he replied: "I will neither conceal my gratification, nor restrain the expression of my gratitude, that the Union people, through their convention . . . have deemed me not unworthy to remain in my present position." Voicing strong approval of the call for a constitutional amendment ending slavery, he nevertheless cautiously declared that he should not definitely accept the nomination "before reading and considering what is called the Platform." The same day he met with a delegation from the national Union League, which had endorsed the Baltimore nominations, and he expressed satisfaction that the group found him "not entirely unworthy" of a second term. In this connection he was reminded of "a story of an old Dutch farmer, who remarked to a companion once that 'it was not best to swap horses when crossing streams.' "

IV

Lincoln's renomination put him in a better position to assert his leadership both in his administration and in his party. Chase was the first to feel the President's new strength. His department faced formidable problems in meeting the vast expenditures caused by the war. Despite his urging, the Congress failed to levy taxes adequate to meet minimal needs of the Treasury. He had great difficulty in disposing of a new bond issue after he was not allowed to reappoint Jay Cooke, the banker who had been so successful in promoting earlier bonds. The currency was depreciating, and the premium on gold skyrocketed. At Chase's demand, Congress passed a law designed to outlaw speculation in gold, but it only hampered honest businessmen while gamblers continued to profit by the constantly climbing premium.

Worn ragged by these pressures, Chase became more prickly in his relations with the President. The two men felt uncomfortable when they were in the same room, and Chase only occasionally attended cabinet meetings. Lincoln no longer needed to keep Chase in his cabinet. He tried to pass along a message to the Secretary through Representative Samuel Hooper of Massachusetts, that he continued to hold Chase in high esteem and intended to appoint him Chief Justice when a vacancy occurred—and with the subtext that his departure from the cabinet would relieve strain. Not fully understanding what he was told, Hooper failed to give the word to Chase.

But toward the end of June, the Secretary precipitated a crisis. The respected John J. Cisco resigned as assistant treasurer of the United States in New York City—a post that was next only to the Secretary of the Treasury in importance. Unaware that anything had changed in his relationship to the President, Chase proposed to replace Cisco with one of his cronies, Maunsell B. Field. It was a politically disastrous move, because Senator E. D. Morgan, former governor of New York and retiring chairman of the National Union Executive Committee, favored other candidates for the job, as did Senator Ira Harris. Lincoln refused to nominate Field and asked the Secretary to reconsider.

When Chase replied by asking for a personal conference with the President, Lincoln declined. "The difficulty does not . . . lie within the range of a conversation between you and me," he told the Secretary. "As the proverb goes, no man knows so well where the shoe pinches as he who wears it." The whole question of the New York patronage was a source of "much embarrassment" to him; he reminded Chase that retaining Barney in the

New York Customs House had been "a great burden" and that the appointment of Judge Hogeboom had brought New York Republicans—he did not
mention Thurlow Weed by name—to "the verge of open revolt."

Rather than defy the President, Chase successfully entreated Cisco to
withdraw his nomination, and he forwarded that news to Lincoln, adding
self-righteously that in suggesting appointments he took no consideration of
politics and simply tried "to get the best men for the places." Cisco's decision ended the present difficulty, he thought, but the stiff tone of Lincoln's
letter made him think that his continued service in the cabinet was "not
altogether agreeable" to the President. Once again he submitted his resignation.

Lincoln read Chase's letter as saying: "You have been acting very badly.
Unless you say you are sorry, and ask me to stay and agree that I shall be
absolute and that you shall have nothing, no matter how you beg for it, I
will go." In the circumstances he felt he had no choice but to accept Chase's
resignation. "Of all I have said in commendation of your ability and fidelity,"
he wrote the Secretary, "I have nothing to unsay; and yet you and I have
reached a point of mutual embarrassment in our official relation which it
seems can not be overcome, or longer sustained, consistently with the public service."

Chase was dumbfounded by the failure of tactics that repeatedly worked
in the past. It never occurred to him that the Baltimore convention had
changed the political landscape. He professed to be unable to understand
Lincoln's letter. "I had found a good deal of embarrassment from him," he
confided to his journal, "but what he had found from me I could not imag-
ine, unless it has been created by my unwillingness to have offices distributed as spoils ... with more regard to the claims of divisions, factions,
cliques and individuals, than to fitness of selection."

Chase's friends rallied to his defense, but Lincoln refused to reconsider
his decision. When Governor John Brough of Ohio, who happened to be in
Washington, offered to mediate the dispute, Lincoln told him: "This is the
third time he [Chase] has thrown this [resignation] at me, and I do not think
I am called on to continue to beg him to take it back, especially when the
country would not go to destruction in consequence.... On the whole,
Brough, I reckon you had better let it alone this time."

In order to avoid political and financial damage, Lincoln moved swiftly to
name a replacement. Without consulting anyone else, he nominated another
Ohioan, former Governor David Tod. It was an unfortunate choice, for Tod,
as the *New York Herald* unkindly put it, knew "no more of finances than a
post." He was a hard-money man, opposed to the paper money with which
the administration had been conducting the war. Vastly upset, the Senate
Finance Committee, headed by William Pitt Fessenden of Maine, came to the
White House to urge that Tod's name be withdrawn, but the President
refused. A crisis was avoided when Tod telegraphed his declination, on the
grounds of poor health.

The next morning Lincoln nominated Fessenden, who was confirmed in an executive session lasting not more than two minutes. The President had not consulted the senator, who was horrified when he heard the news. Fessenden did not want to leave the Senate, did not want an executive office, and felt physically unable to perform the duties of the job, and he wrote Lincoln a letter declining the appointment. The President refused to receive it. Appealing to Fessenden's sense of duty, reminding him that "the crisis was such as demanded any sacrifice, even life itself," he persuaded the senator to reconsider. When Fessenden turned to Stanton for advice, saying that he thought the job would kill him, the Secretary of War responded bluntly, "Very well, you cannot die better than in trying to save your country." Then telegrams and letters began to pour in, from boards of trade, chambers of commerce, bankers, and public officials, warning Fessenden that he must serve to prevent a financial crisis.

Unhappily he accepted, but not without taking to heart the advice of his close friend, Senator Grimes of Iowa, that he must "make such terms as would prevent you from being slandered and backbitten out of the Cabinet in a few weeks by your associates." On July 4, Fessenden and the President came to an agreement, which Lincoln put in writing, that the Secretary was to have "complete control of the [Treasury] department." "I will keep no person in office in his department, against his express will," the President promised; and Fessenden agreed that in appointing subordinates he would "strive to give his willing consent to my wishes in cases when I may let him know that I have such wishes."

With his cabinet reconstituted, Lincoln turned to asserting his leadership of the Republican party in the Congress. By the end of June 1864 the first session of the Thirty-eighth Congress was drawing to an end, a session marked more by rancorous squabbling than by constructive legislation. Congressional Republicans were now more sharply divided into Radical and Conservative factions, both of which were critical of the President. Congressmen found many grounds of complaint, and most shared a sense that the executive branch had aggrandized itself during the war at the expense of the legislative branch. On no issue was there more hostility to the President than on reconstruction. Support of Lincoln's 10 percent plan dropped sharply after Banks permitted the reconstructed government of Louisiana to preserve that state's antebellum constitution, which failed to protect the rights of blacks. To show their disapproval, majorities in both houses of Congress refused to seat persons claiming to represent Louisiana and Arkansas. United in opposing the President's wishes, the Republican majority in Congress was slow to agree on alternative positive actions. They failed to establish a much needed Freedmen's Bureau, intended to oversee the transition of African-Americans from slavery to freedom, and they could not muster a sufficient majority to adopt the Thirteenth Amendment abolishing slavery, which the President and the National Union Convention had strongly urged.

In the final days of the session, when many members were absent, Republican leaders suddenly realized that they were about to adjourn without having passed any significant legislation concerning slavery, the freedmen, or reconstruction. Hastily they turned to a bill that Henry Winter Davis called "the *only* practical measure of emancipation *proposed* in this Congress." Called the Wade-Davis bill, after the chairmen of the House and Senate committees that sponsored it, the measure asserted congressional, rather than executive control over the reconstruction process. It required, as a first step in the reorganization of any Southern state, the complete abolition of slavery. The bill specified that 50 percent, rather than 10 percent, of the 1860 voters must participate in elections to reconstitute these governments. Further, it imposed on electors of constitutional conventions in the seceded states what was called an "iron-clad" oath of loyalty, requiring them to swear that they had never voluntarily borne arms against the United States or aided the rebellion, rather than the oath of prospective loyalty in Lincoln's plan of amnesty.

Passed by Congress on July 2, the bill reflected Davis's personal hostility toward Lincoln for siding with the Blairs, the leaders of the rival Republican faction in Maryland. It also demonstrated the continuing opposition on the part of some Radical Republicans to Lincoln's reelection, despite his renomination by the Baltimore convention. Looking toward an alternative or third-party candidacy for the presidency, they feared that Lincoln might win re-election through the electoral votes of states under military control, like Louisiana, Arkansas, and Tennessee, which were in effect pocket boroughs.

Faced with a revolt on the part of Republican congressional leadership, Lincoln decided to reassert his authority. Indeed, he had to do so if he hoped to keep together the tenuous coalition of War Democrats and Republicans on which his reelection campaign rested. Rumors spread that he was not going to sign the bill. Two days before adjournment, Representatives Thaddeus Stevens, E. B. Washburne, and John L. Dawson of Pennsylvania descended on the White House officially to ask if the Chief Executive had any further messages to transmit to the Congress but actually to urge Lincoln to approve the Wade-Davis bill. After greeting his visitors, Lincoln sat down at his desk, turned his back on them, and resumed his work, merely tilting his head a little as Stevens read the official message. Dawson thought the President looked "as if he was ashamed of himself, out of place," and the representatives returned to Capitol Hill suspecting that Lincoln would veto the reconstruction bill. Hearing their news, Representative Jesse O. Norton, a Radical from Illinois and an old friend of the President, rushed to the White House, and he too got the impression that Lincoln would not sign. Lincoln was about to make a great mistake, Norton reported, but there was "no use trying to prevent it."

As Congress tried to complete its business by noon on July 4, the President was in his room at the Capitol examining and signing numerous measures that had been passed during the final hours of the session. Intensely anxious about the fate of the Wade-Davis bill, Republican senators and representatives gathered about him and watched him push that measure aside. When Zachariah Chandler, the Radical senator from Michigan, came in, he asked the President whether he was going to sign, and Lincoln replied with some impatience, "Mr Chandler, this bill was placed before me a few minutes before Congress adjourns. It is a matter of too much importance to be swallowed in that way."

Warned by Chandler that the veto "will damage us fearfully in the Northwest," Lincoln defended his action on the ground that Congress had no authority to abolish slavery in the reconstructed states. When Chandler reminded him that this was no more than what he himself had done, the President testily replied, "I conceive that I may in an emergency do things on military grounds which cannot be done constitutionally by Congress." He further objected to the bill because he believed incorrectly that it implied that the rebellious states were no longer in the Union. "Now we cannot survive that admission, I am convinced," he told the little group around him, and he reminded them that the whole war was fought on the assumption that it was not possible for a state to secede. "If that be true, I am not President, these gentlemen are not Congress."

As he left the Capitol, he was warned that offending the Radicals might hurt his chances in the November election, and he responded with controlled anger: "If they choose to make a point upon this I do not doubt that they can do harm. They have never been friendly to me and I don't know that this will make any special difference as to that. At all events, I must keep some consciousness of being somewhere near right: I must keep some standard of principle fixed within myself."

After he had cooled off a little, Lincoln decided to pocket-veto the Wade-Davis bill—that is, to decline to sign it, so that, with the adjournment of Congress, it would fail to become law. He took his case to the people by issuing a proclamation explaining his decision. He was not prepared "to be inflexibly committed to any single plan of restoration," he wrote; nor was he prepared "to declare, that the free-state constitutions and governments, already adopted and installed in Arkansas and Louisiana, shall be set aside and held for nought, thereby repelling and discouraging the loyal citizens who have set up the same, as to further effort." He was unwilling to acknowledge "a constitutional competency in Congress to abolish slavery in States." Then, attempting to paper over differences with the Congress, he declared that he was "fully satisfied with the system for restoration contained in the Bill, as one very proper plan for the loyal people of any State choosing to adopt it," and he offered assistance to any state that decided to do so. The assurance was virtually meaningless, however, since the terms imposed by Congress were so much harsher than those required under the presidential plan of reconstruction.

Radicals reacted angrily to the defeat of the Wade-Davis bill. The President seemed to be toying with them: first he used a pocket veto, a rare procedure up to this time; then he issued what was in effect a veto message, which was not required for a pocket veto; and finally he suggested that some Southern states might want to accept the conditions laid down in the bill he had just killed. According to a newspaperman, Davis, "pale with wrath, his bushy hair tousled, and wildly brandishing his arms, denounced the President in good set terms." "I am inconsolable," Charles Sumner grieved. But other congressmen, who perhaps had not paid careful attention to the debates on the measure, "began to wish that it had never gone to the President." Resentment continued to smolder against Lincoln, but he remained in control of the field, clearly in charge both of his cabinet and of the reconstruction process.

V

How long he would remain in charge depended on the outcome of military operations, and the prospects were gloomy. By July it seemed that Grant's campaign—which followed Lincoln's grand strategy—was a failure. In the West, Banks's army was demoralized after the failed Red River expedition, and it was months before General Edward R. S. Canby, who superseded Banks, was able to take to the field in a drive against Mobile. In Georgia, Sherman pushed the Confederates under Joseph E. Johnston back toward Atlanta, but the Southerners repeatedly escaped the traps he set for them. Eventually Sherman grew so exasperated that he ordered a direct attack on the entrenched Confederates at Kenesaw Mountain, where on June 27 he met a bloody defeat.

In the East, Butler allowed his Army of the James to be hemmed in on a peninsula between the James and the Appomattox rivers, and there, as Grant remarked acidly, his army was as useless "as if it had been in a bottle strongly corked." In the Shenandoah Valley, Franz Sigel suffered a serious defeat at New Market on May 15 and had to be removed from command. His successor, David Hunter, began a campaign of devastation in the Valley, but when Lee sent in troops under Jubal A. Early, Hunter retreated into the Kanawha Valley, leaving the Shenandoah an open corridor for the Confederates.

Most serious of all were the reverses of the Army of the Potomac, over which Grant personally presided. Failing to overwhelm Lee's army either in the Wilderness or at Spotsylvania, Grant ordered the senseless and doomed charge at Cold Harbor. After this defeat he no longer talked about fighting it out on this line, because he had learned a lesson: "Without a greater sacrifice of human life than I am willing to make, all cannot be accomplished that I had designed."

In a shift of strategy, on June 14 he began moving the Army of the Potomac through the swamps of the Chickahominy River, where McClellan's troops had fought in 1862, to the south side of the James River. There the Army of the Potomac, joining with Butler's army, could be supplied by sea, and there

—in a return to Grant's original strategic plan—it could cut the rail lines that connected Richmond to the South. Grant's change of base was brilliantly executed, so that Lee had no certain idea of his whereabouts. Once his army had crossed the James, Grant launched an immediate assault on the heavily fortified city of Petersburg, through which three of the key railroads ran. Repulsed, he settled down for a siege. Now, for the first time, he contemplated a campaign of attrition; he would pin Lee's army down so that no reinforcements could be sent to fight against Sherman.

In six weeks of incessant fighting the Union armies lost in killed and wounded nearly 100,000 men—more than the total number in Lee's army at the beginning of the campaign. The people of the North, who had been overly optimistic when Grant assumed command of the armies, were slow to realize what was happening. Their newspapers, controlled by War Department censorship, told them that Grant had "won a great victory," that the Army of the Potomac "again is victorious," that the troops had been "skillfully, and bravely handled," and that Grant had "succeeded, if not in defeating Lee, certainly in turning his strong position and forcing him to retreat step by step to the very confines of Richmond." But then the daily black-bordered newspaper columns listing the dead brought home the enormity of war. So did the stories from newspaper correspondents and the letters from soldiers describing the suffering of the maimed and wounded. As thousands of the injured poured into the hospitals around Washington, it was no longer possible to conceal the costs of the campaign. The country shuddered with a sickening revulsion at the slaughter. Grieving for "our bleeding, bankrupt, almost dying country," Horace Greeley wrote the President of the widespread dread of "the prospect of fresh conscriptions, of further wholesale devastations, and of new rivers of human blood."

Lincoln himself was sensitive to the suffering. His friend Isaac N. Arnold recorded that during these days he was "grave and anxious, and he looked like one who had lost the dearest member of his own family." One evening, after riding past a long line of ambulances carrying the wounded to the hospital, he turned to Arnold in deep sadness and said: "Look yonder at those poor fellows. I cannot bear it. This suffering, this loss of life is dreadful."

The Lincolns did what they could to mitigate the hardships. Mary Lincoln regularly visited army hospitals, bringing the wounded flowers from the White House conservatory and comforting words. For his part the President set aside a morning of nearly every week to review the court-martial sentences of soldiers who had found the stress of battle more than they could bear. One week he examined the records in sixty-seven cases; in another, seventy-two cases; in yet another, thirty-six cases. Whenever possible he found excuses to release the prisoners and allowed them to return to duty. He was, he explained, "trying to evade the butchering business lately." But all his exertions could not erase the knowledge that in the final analysis he was responsible for all this suffering.

Increasingly he brooded over the war and his role in it. "Doesn't it seem strange to you that I should be here?" he once asked Representative Daniel Voorhees of Indiana. "Doesn't it strike you as queer that I, who couldn't cut the head off of a chicken, and who was sick at the sight of blood, should be cast into the middle of a great war, with blood flowing all about me?" Often, when he could spare the time from his duties, he sought an answer to his questions in the well-thumbed pages of his Bible, reading most often the Old Testament prophets and the Psalms.

He found comfort and reassurance in the Bible. He was not a member of any Christian church, for he was put off by their forms and dogmas, and consequently he remained, as Mary Lincoln later said, "not a technical Christian." But he drew from the Scriptures such solace that he was prepared to forget his earlier religious doubts. One evening during this dreadful summer of 1864, his old friend Joshua Speed found him intently reading the Bible. "I am glad to see you so profitably engaged," said Speed.

"Yes," replied the President, "I am profitably engaged."

"Well," commented the visitor, "if you have recovered from your skepticism, I am sorry to say that I have not."

Looking his old comrade in the face, Lincoln said, "You are wrong, Speed, take all of this book upon reason that you can, and the balance on faith, and you will live and die a happier and better man." He had come to feel, as he told a delegation of Baltimore African-Americans who presented him a magnificently bound Bible in appreciation of his work for the Negro, that "this Great Book . . . is the best gift God has given to man."

Reading the Bible reinforced Lincoln's long-held belief in the doctrine of necessity, a belief that admirably fitted the needs of his essentially passive personality. The idea that the actions of any individual were predetermined and shaped by the unknowable wishes of some Higher Power was not a new one for him, but with the burden of a never-ending war weighing ever more heavily on his shoulders, he reverted to it more and more frequently. In April he wrote a long letter to Albert G. Hodges, editor of the *Frankfort* (Kentucky) *Commonwealth,* explaining why he had felt compelled to shift from his inaugural pledge not to interfere with slavery to the policy of emancipation. It contained his most explicit view of individual responsibility: "I claim not to have controlled events, but confess plainly that events have controlled me." "Now," he continued, "at the end of three years struggle the nation's condition is not what either party, or any man devised, or expected. God alone can claim it."

Again and again he reverted to the idea that behind all the struggles and losses of the war a Divine purpose was at work. Never did he express this view more eloquently than in a letter he wrote in September to Mrs. Eliza P. Gurney, who extended the sympathy and prayers of the Society of Friends: "The purposes of the Almighty are perfect, and must prevail, though we erring mortals may fail to accurately perceive them in advance. We hoped for a happy termination of this terrible war long before this; but God knows best, and has ruled otherwise. . . . we must work earnestly in the best light He gives us, trusting that so working still conduces to the great ends He ordains. Surely He intends some great good to follow this mighty convulsion, which no mortal could make, and no mortal could stay." This comforting doctrine allowed the President to live with himself by shifting some of the responsibility for all the suffering.

VI

As Grant and Sherman grappled with the enemy, Lincoln did what he could to sustain the army and to boost civilian morale. On every possible occasion —even on such an unlikely one as the resumption of White House concerts by the Marine Band—he asked his listeners to give three cheers for "Grant and all the armies under his command." Again and again, he expressed gratitude to the soldiers, to the officers, and especially to "that brave and loyal man," the "modest General at the head of our armies." After his renomination, when the Ohio delegation serenaded him with a brass band, he responded: "What we want, still more than Baltimore conventions or presidential elections, is success under Gen. Grant," and he urged his hearers to bend all their energies to support "the brave officers and soldiers in the field."

He continued to have great faith in Grant, but he was conscious of the swelling chorus of criticism of the general. Many doubted Grant's strategic ability and pointed out that in shifting his base to the James River he was simply repeating what McClellan had done—with far fewer casualties. "Why did he not take his army south of the James at once, and thus save seventy-five thousand men?" asked Senator Grimes, who pronounced Grant's campaign a failure. Even in the President's own household there was distrust of the general. "He is a butcher," Mary Lincoln often said, "and is not fit to be at the head of an army."

The outcry against Grant made the President want to see for himself what was happening with the Army of the Potomac, and on June 20, accompanied by Tad, he made an unheralded visit to Grant's headquarters at City Point. Looking, as Horace Porter, one of Grant's aides, wrote, "very much like a boss undertaker" in his black suit, the President announced as he landed: "I just thought I would jump aboard a boat and come down and see you. I don't expect I can do any good, and in fact I'm afraid I may do harm, but I'll put myself under your orders and if you find me doing anything wrong just send me [off] right away."

For the next two days he visited with Grant, Meade, Butler, and the troops. Much of the time he rode Grant's large bay horse, Cincinnati. Though he managed the horse well, he was, as Porter remembered, "not a very dashing rider," and as his trousers gradually worked up above his ankles, he gave "the appearance of a country farmer riding into town wearing his Sunday clothes." As news of the President's arrival reached the troops, they gave cheers and enthusiastic shouts. When he rode out to see the African-American troops of the Eighteenth Corps, the soldiers "cheered, laughed, cried, sang hymns of praise, and shouted . . . 'God bless Master Lincoln!' 'The Lord save Father Abraham!' 'The day of jubilee is come, sure.' " Telling frequent anecdotes and showing interest in every detail of army life, the President appeared to have no object in his visit, but his purpose emerged when there was talk of anticipated military maneuvers. Quietly he interposed, "I cannot pretend to advise, but I do sincerely hope that all may be accomplished with as little bloodshed as possible."

Tired and sunburned, Lincoln returned to the White House on June 23, and Gideon Welles remarked that the trip had "done him good, physically, and strengthened him mentally." He took satisfaction in repeating what Grant had told him: "You will never hear of me farther from Richmond than now, till I have taken it. . . . It may take a long summer day, but I will go in." But Attorney General Bates found the President "perceptably [sic], disappointed at the small measure of our success, in that region." More than ever Lincoln realized that the war would be long and costly.

CHAPTER NINETEEN

I Am Pretty Sure-Footed

———◆———

In early July 1864 a visitor found Lincoln deeply depressed, "indeed quite paralyzed and wilted down." He had reason to feel blue. War weariness was spreading, and demands for negotiations to end the killing were becoming strident. In the Middle West the Copperhead movement was strong, and there were rumors of an insurrection intended to bring about an independent Northwest Confederation. The Democrats were organizing for their national convention to be held in Chicago at the end of August, and they were likely to adopt a peace platform. The Republicans were badly divided, and Lincoln was whipsawed between those who thought he was too lenient toward the South and those who thought him too severe. Worst of all, the Union armies appeared stalemated. Sherman, at the head of the Western armies, was approaching Atlanta but was not, apparently, nearer victory over Joseph E. Johnston. In the East, the Army of the Potomac was bogged down in a siege of Petersburg.

I

To make matters worse, Washington itself was once more threatened. In an attempt to relieve Grant's pressure on Richmond, Jubal A. Early, heading the Second Corps of the Army of Northern Virginia, marched down the Shenandoah Valley almost without opposition and on July 5 crossed the Potomac. His force was small—only about 15,000 men—but as it spread out over the Maryland countryside, it was strong enough to levy tribute from Hagerstown and Frederick before turning east toward Washington. On July 9 at the Monocacy River the invaders pushed aside the ill-assorted Union defending force of green hundred-day volunteers commanded by General Lew Wallace and moved close to the national capital.

It seemed that nobody was in charge of the defenses of Washington—or perhaps everybody was. Off in Virginia, Grant doubted that the Confederates were making any significant northward movement and was reluctant to divert troops from the siege of Petersburg. Stanton questioned the seriousness of Early's raid. Halleck did what he could by giving rifles to the clerks in the government offices and arming the ambulatory soldiers in the hospitals, but it was far from clear that this makeshift force could hold off the Confederate invaders.

Alarmed, General Ethan Allen Hitchcock tried to alert the President that the capital was in great danger, but Lincoln wearily replied, "We are doing all we can." Early's army might not be strong enough to hold Washington, Hitchcock warned, but if they occupied it for only a few days the nation would be dishonored and the Confederacy would be recognized abroad. He insisted that Grant ought to be directed to send reinforcements. Seeming "almost crushed" and speaking very faintly, Lincoln responded that he would confer with the Secretary of War.

Unlike many in the capital, the President was not worried about his own safety. He only reluctantly obeyed Stanton's directive to move back into the city from the exposed Soldiers' Home where he, Mary, and Tad were spending the summer, and he was furious when he learned that Gustavus V. Fox had ordered a naval vessel to be ready in the Potomac in case the Lincolns needed to escape.

As during previous invasions of the North, he was less concerned about the security of Washington than with the capture of the Confederate force, but he was hamstrung by his pledge not to interfere with Grant's operations. Knowing how severely he had been criticized for meddling with military matters, especially in the case of McClellan, he was reluctant now to give direct orders to his general-in-chief. All he felt he could do was to keep a close watch over Early's progress and try to prevent panic in Washington and Baltimore. But when Grant grandly announced that there were already enough forces in the area to defeat the invaders and offered to come to the capital himself only if the President thought it necessary, Lincoln responded on July 10 that he should leave enough men to retain his hold on Petersburg and "bring the rest [of your army] with you personally, and make a vigorous effort to destroy the enemie's force in this vicinity." But the President ended his telegram: "This is what I think, upon your suggestion, and is not an order."

Still not understanding the seriousness of the threat, Grant chose to remain where he was, dispatching some veteran troops of the Sixth Corps, under General Horatio G. Wright, to assist in the defense of Washington. On July 11, before they could arrive, Early's men had already pushed down the Seventh Street Pike, marched through Silver Spring, where Francis Preston

Blair, Sr., and Postmaster General Montgomery Blair both had houses, and approached the sturdy but feebly manned defenses of Fort Stevens. The Confederates drove in the Union pickets and came within 150 yards of the fort before artillery fire forced them back.

Lincoln was in the fort when it was first attacked. Having driven out from Washington in his carriage, he mounted to the front parapet. He borrowed a field glass from signal officer Asa Townsend Abbott and looked out over the field where the Confederates were advancing. "He stood there with a long frock coat and plug hat on, making a very conspicuous figure," Abbott recalled. When the Confederates came within shooting distance, an officer twice cautioned Lincoln to get down, but he paid no attention. Then a man standing near him was shot in the leg, and a soldier roughly ordered the President to get down or he would have his head knocked off. He coolly descended, got into his carriage, and was driven back to the city, where he went to the wharf to greet troops of the Sixth Corps, "chatting familiarly with the veterans, and now and then, as if in compliment to them, biting at a piece of hard tack which he held in his hand."

The next day Early made one last effort to capture the capital. Once again the heaviest fighting was at Fort Stevens, and President and Mrs. Lincoln, along with many other prominent public officials and their wives, came out to witness the fighting. Thoughtlessly Wright invited the President to mount the parapet in order to get a clear view as Union soldiers charged the enemy line, and the general recorded that Lincoln "evinced remarkable coolness and disregard of danger." After a surgeon standing near him was shot, Wright ordered the parapet cleared and asked the President to step down. Lincoln insisted on remaining until the general said he would have him removed forcibly. "The absurdity of the idea of sending off the President under guard seemed to amuse him," Wright recalled, "but, in consideration of my earnestness in the matter, he agreed to compromise by sitting behind the parapet instead of standing upon it."

After the failure of his final assault, Early retreated from Washington. Wright made a halfhearted attempt to follow the Confederates, but he soon halted, as Lincoln said scornfully, "for fear he might come across the rebels and catch some of them." Browning found the President "in the dumps," lamenting "that the rebels who had besieged us were all escaped." Though half a dozen generals—Wright, Hunter, Sigel, Wallace, and others—were involved, nobody was in charge of pursuing the enemy. As Assistant Secretary of War Charles A. Dana wrote Grant: "There is no head to the whole and it seems indispensable that you should at once appoint one.... Gen Halleck will not give orders except as he receives them—The President will give none, and until you direct positively and explicitly what is to be done everything will go on in the deplorable and fatal way in which it has gone on for the past week."

Lincoln's patience, even with Grant, began to wear thin. Early continued to stage raids from the Shenandoah, and on July 30 his men rode into Chambersburg, Pennsylvania, demanded a ransom of $500,000 in currency or $100,000 in gold, and, when the townsmen were unable to pay it, burned the town. Northern newspapers decried the humiliation of the raids, which showed "there is folly or incompetence somewhere in our military administration," but Grant, still entrenched before Petersburg, seemed little concerned. Not even a personal visit from the President, who summoned him to Fort Monroe on July 31, stirred the general from the lethargy into which he had unaccountably lapsed. On hearing of Early's continuing activities, he telegraphed that all the Union forces in the Shenandoah Valley command should put themselves south of the enemy and follow him to the death. Lincoln replied that his strategy was just right, but he added tartly: "Please look over the despatches you may have rece[i]ved from here . . . and discover, if you can, that there is any idea in the head of any one here, of 'putting our army *South* of the enemy' or of [']following him to the *death*' in any direction." "I repeat to you," the President insisted, "it will neither be done nor attempted unless you watch it every day, and hour, and force it." Called to heel, Grant immediately started for Washington, and after consultation with the President named the brilliant young cavalry officer Philip Sheridan to command all the Union forces operating in the Valley.

II

It was not only Grant who tried Lincoln's patience during these unusually hot, depressing summer months of 1864. Usually he was ready to spend countless hours listening to visitors who brought him their complaints and petitions, sometimes over quite trivial matters, but now he had had enough. When two citizens of Maine asked him to intervene to settle a personal problem, the President sharply responded: "You want me to end your suspense? I'll do so. Dont let me hear another word about your case." A few days later his anger erupted again when Charles Gibson resigned as solicitor in the Court of Claims, protesting the radicalism of the Republican platform but expressing gratitude to the President for treating him with "personal kindness and consideration." With what Bates called "blind impetuosity" Lincoln lashed back that there were "two small draw-backs upon Mr. Gibson's right to still receive such treatment, one of which is that he never could learn of his giving much attention to the duties of his office, and the other is this studied attempt of Mr. Gibson's to stab him."

In calmer times Lincoln would have ignored a semiliterate communication from a Pennsylvania man who urged him to remember that "white men is in class number one and black men is in class number two and must be governed by white men forever." But now, in his irascible mood, he drafted a reply to be sent out over Nicolay's signature requesting the writer to inform him "whether you are either a white man or black one, because in either case, you can not be regarded as an entirely impartial judge." "It may be," the President continued, in an unusual tone of sarcasm, "that you belong to a third or fourth class of *yellow* or *red* men, in which case the impartiality of your judgment would be more apparant."

Lincoln's sharp temper extended at times even to his closest advisers. Montgomery Blair, furious because Early's men had burned his house in Silver Spring, denounced the "poltroons and cowards" responsible for the defenses of Washington. Halleck, always defensive of professional military men, demanded that the President either endorse "such wholesale denouncement and accusation" or dismiss Blair. Lincoln replied that he did not approve the Postmaster General's remarks but that his words, which "may have been hastily said in a moment of vexation at so severe a loss," were not sufficient grounds for removing him. "I propose continuing to be myself the judge as to when a member of the Cabinet shall be dismissed," he said sternly, and he took the unusual step of reading to the entire cabinet a carefully prepared memorandum: "I must myself be the judge, how long to retain in, and when to remove any of you from, his position. It would greatly pain me to discover any of you endeavoring to procure anothers removal, or, in any way to prejudice him before the public. Such endeavor would be a wrong to me; and much worse, a wrong to the country."

On the more important issue of possible peace negotiations with the Confederates, the President was obliged to control his anger. Indeed, he gained a certain sardonic pleasure from his skillful handling of the question. The prime mover was the erratic and excitable editor of the *New York Tribune*. Just as Early's men were approaching the capital, Greeley wrote Lincoln that his "irrepressible friend" William C. ("Colorado") Jewett was certain that representatives of the Confederate government were on the Canadian side of Niagara Falls with full authority to negotiate a peace. Greeley urged the President to explore the possibility, because the country was in such desperate shape. A full and generous announcement of Union conditions for ending the war, even if they were not accepted, would remove the "wide-spread conviction that the Government and its prominent supporters are not anxious for Peace" and help the Republican cause in the fall elections.

Correctly Lincoln suspected a trap. He could not know why the three Confederate emissaries—former Mississippi Congressman Jacob Thompson, former Alabama Senator Clement C. Clay, and Professor James P. Holcombe of the University of Virginia—were in Canada, but his instincts told him that their purpose was not to make peace but to meddle in Northern politics with a view to influencing the presidential election.

He could not reject the proposed negotiations outright, even though he thought Greeley unreliable and mendacious. But this chosen intermediary of the Confederates had the power to shape Northern opinion. The *New York Tribune,* widely distributed in the West as well as in the East, boasted the largest national circulation of any newspaper. The editor's letter, which reminded the President "how intently the people desire any peace consistent with the national integrity and honor" and that an offer of fair terms would "prove an immense and sorely needed advantage to the national cause," thinly masked a threat to go public in case Lincoln turned down this opportunity. If the *Tribune* portrayed the President as flatly rejecting a reasonable peace negotiation, it could do irreparable damage.

Shrewdly Lincoln solved his problem by naming Greeley himself as his emissary to the Confederates at Niagara and authorizing him to bring to Washington under safe conduct "any person anywhere professing to have any proposition of Jefferson Davis in writing, for peace, embracing the restoration of the Union and abandonment of slavery." Greeley objected. For all his countrified looks and his shuffling gait, the editor was no fool, and he was unwilling to become "a confidant, far less an agent in such negotiations." But the President refused to let him off the hook. "I not only intend a sincere effort for peace," he wrote Greeley, "but I intend that you shall be a personal witness that it is made." When Greeley continued to delay, the President expressed disappointment: "I was not expecting you to *send* me a letter, but to *bring* me a man, or men." He then ordered John Hay to accompany Greeley to Niagara Falls, bearing a letter that spelled out the terms on which he was willing to deal with the Confederate emissaries.

Lincoln himself drafted the letter, consulting only Seward. Addressed "To Whom It May Concern," it read: "Any proposition which embraces the restoration of peace, the integrity of the whole Union, and the abandonment of slavery . . . will be received and considered by the Executive government of the United States." It also offered safe-conduct to the Confederate negotiators and "liberal terms on other substantial and collateral points."

The letter reflected Lincoln's careful balancing of political considerations against military needs. He could best promote his chances in the fall election by requiring only minimal conditions for beginning negotiations with the Confederates. If he announced that reunification of the nation was the sole condition for peace, he would cement the alliance that he had been trying for months to build with the War Democrats, who loyally supported his efforts to restore the Union, even though many of them had reservations about his emancipation policy. If, as he anticipated, Jefferson Davis rejected this reasonable, lenient offer, these Democrats could more easily favor the reelection of a Republican President.

But there was an unacceptable military risk in this approach. Conceivably the Confederates might accept reunion as a condition for discussing peace. If they did, they could propose a cease-fire during the progress of any negotiations, and Lincoln knew that the people were so war-weary and exhausted that it would be almost impossible to resume hostilities once arms were laid down. "An armistice—a cessation of hostilities—is the end of the struggle," he concluded, "and the insurgents would be in peaceable possession of all that has been struggled for."

Consequently he had to appear open to peace negotiations while proposing terms that would make them impossible. The first of his conditions, the restoration of the Union, was easy to predict; that was what the war, from the outset, had been about. But the second, requiring "the abandonment of slavery" as a condition for peace talks, was a surprise. It went considerably beyond his own Emancipation Proclamation or any law of Congress. The Emancipation Proclamation had freed slaves only in specified areas and had not ended the institution of slavery itself, and Congress had just failed to adopt the Thirteenth Amendment outlawing slavery. This condition was one Lincoln knew the Confederates would never accept.

Lincoln expected that the Confederate emissaries would spurn his offer. When they rushed to print his "To Whom It May Concern" letter, in order to show that he had torpedoed meaningful peace talks, he countered by publicizing the report he had just received from James R. Gilmore and James F. Jaquess, who had recently conducted their own unofficial peace mission to Richmond. There Jefferson Davis told them: "The war . . . must go on till the last man of this generation falls in his tracks, . . . *unless you acknowledge our right to self-government*. We are not fighting for slavery. We are fighting for Independence,—and that, or extermination, we *will* have." Reasonable people could only conclude that neither President wanted serious peace negotiations.

III

The *New York Herald* announced that publication of the President's "To Whom It May Concern" letter "sealed Lincoln's fate in the coming Presidential campaign." By making abolition as much a war aim as Union, the President gave new strength to the Democratic party, preparing for its national convention in Chicago at the end of August. Opposition leaders declared the letter proved Lincoln did not really want to end the war "even if an honorable peace were within his grasp." "All he has a right to require of the South is submission to the Constitution," Democratic editors announced. They were sure that "the people of the loyal states will teach him, they will not supply men and treasure to prosecute a war in the interest of the black race."

The President's letter also undermined his support in his own party. At first, oddly enough, the erosion was most noticeable among the Radicals. Greeley's animus toward the President increased after his venture into amateur diplomacy became a subject of ridicule. He was not alone. Radicals, who should have been pleased by the President's firm insistence on abolition, felt they had Lincoln on the run, and they began to express all their pent-up grievances and frustrations at the President's slowness, his timidity, his indecisiveness, his fence-straddling, his incompetence, his leniency toward the rebels. Chase, though ostensibly out of politics, spent much of the summer in New England conferring with other anti-Lincoln Republicans and spreading the news that there was "great and almost universal dissatisfaction with Mr. Lincoln among all earnest men." In Boston he frequently conferred with Sumner, who grumbled that the country needed "a president with brains; one who can make a plan and carry it out." Pomeroy, the original head of the Chase movement, and Wade, coauthor of the reconstruction bill Lincoln had just vetoed, joined them for a conference, which, as a newspaper correspondent shrewdly surmised, "boded no good to Father Abraham." Radical disaffection was not confined to New England. In Iowa, Grimes concluded: "This entire administration has been a disgrace from the very beginning to every one who had any thing to do with bringing it into power. I take my full share of the . . . shame to myself. I can atone for what I have done no otherwise than in refusing to be instrumental in continuing it."

On August 5 this dissatisfaction with Lincoln exploded with the publication of a protest by Wade and Henry Winter Davis against Lincoln's "grave Executive usurpation" in pocket-vetoing their reconstruction bill. The congressmen found the President's public message explaining the reasons for his action even more offensive than the veto. "A more studied outrage on the legislative authority of the people has never been perpetrated," they fumed; it was "a blow at the friends of his Administration, at the rights of humanity, and at the principles of republican government." Lincoln must know that "the authority of Congress is paramount and must be respected . . . ; and if he wishes our support, he must confine himself to his executive duties—to obey and execute, not make the laws."

Publication of the Wade-Davis "Manifesto," as it was generally called, produced a short-lived political commotion. Democrats, of course, enjoyed the spectacle of prominent congressional leaders attacking the presidential nominee of their own party, and they congratulated "the country that two Republicans have been found willing at last to resent the encroachments of the executive on the authority of Congress." The manifesto, according to the *New York World,* was "a blow between the eyes which will daze the President." The *New York Herald,* always glad to jab at the administration, called it an acknowledgment that Lincoln was "an egregious failure" who ought "to retire from the position to which, in an evil hour, he was exalted." But the rhetoric of the proclamation was so excessive and the accusations against Lincoln so extreme that the charges backfired. Most Republican papers criticized Wade and Davis more severely than they did the President.

Lincoln did not read the manifesto. He had no desire to get involved in a controversy with its authors, he told Welles. The attack saddened him, and he admitted to Noah Brooks, "To be wounded in the house of one's friends is perhaps the most grievous affliction that can befall a man." But he refused to brood about it. "It is not worth fretting about," he joked; "it reminds me of an old acquaintance, who, having a son of a scientific turn, bought him a microscope. The boy went around, experimenting with his glass upon everything. . . . One day, at the dinner-table, his father took up a piece of cheese. 'Don't eat that, father,' said the boy; 'it is full of *wrigglers.*' 'My son,' replied the old gentleman, taking . . . a huge bite, 'let 'em *wriggle;* I can stand it if they can.' "

Less public, but more dangerous to the President, was a Radical plan to replace Lincoln, already the official nominee of his party, with another candidate who would be more positive and energetic, who would be more deeply committed to equal rights, and who would, presumably, have a greater chance of success. Little groups of Radicals in Boston, Cincinnati, and, especially, New York concocted plans for summoning a new Republican nominating convention. Some of the schemers favored Chase; others, Butler. Few looked to Frémont, whose candidacy was already failing, and they tried to get him to withdraw from the race on the condition that Lincoln did so. Most put their hopes on Grant.

In a preliminary meeting on August 18, about twenty-five Radicals gathered at the house of Mayor George Opdyke of New York. The editors of the major newspapers—Greeley of the *Tribune,* Parke Godwin of the *Evening Post,* Theodore Tilton of the *Independent,* and George Wilkes of the *Spirit of the Times*—were present, as were Wade, Davis, and Governor John A. Andrew of Massachusetts. Chase sent his regrets, hoping that the deliberations would be "fruitful, of benefit to our country, never more in need of wise words and fearless action by and among patriotic men." Sumner too stayed away. "I do not as yet see the Presidential horizon," he explained. "I wait for the blue lights of [the Democratic convention at] Chicago, which will present the true outlines." Those who did attend—the diarist George Templeton Strong termed them "our wire-pullers and secret, unofficial governors"—decided to send out a circular letter calling for a new convention, to be held at Cincinnati on September 28, which would "concentrate the union strength on some one candidate who commands the confidence of the country, even by a new nomination if necessary." Less politely Davis said that the convention was intended "to get rid of Mr Lincoln and name new candidates." To make final arrangements they promised to meet again on August 30.

Inevitably reports of these plans reached Lincoln's ears. He was neither surprised nor worried by most of the schemes to replace him as the nominee of the Republican party, but he was alarmed when he heard that the dissidents were thinking of running Grant. He did not think the general had political aspirations but, concluding that he ought to sound him out again, he asked Colonel John Eaton, who had worked closely with Grant in caring for the freedmen in the Mississippi Valley, to go to the Army of the Potomac and ascertain his views. At City Point, Eaton told Grant that many people thought he ought to run for President, not as a party man but as a citizens' candidate, in order to save the Union. Bringing his hand down on the arm of his chair, Grant replied: "They can't do it! They can't compel me to do it!" He went on to say that he considered it "as important for the cause that

[Lincoln] should be elected as that the army should be successful in the field." When Eaton reported the conversation to the President, his relief was obvious. "I told you," he said, "they could not get him to run until he had closed out the rebellion."

IV

Lincoln was more troubled by the effect that his "To Whom It May Concern" letter had on the conservative elements of his following. It hit the War Democrats hardest. Charles D. Robinson, Democratic editor of the *Green Bay* (Wisconsin) *Advocate,* best expressed their views. Up to now, despite sharp criticism from other Democrats, he had sustained the President's war policy as the only method of putting down the rebellion. He had even accepted the Emancipation Proclamation, because he believed that depriving the Confederacy of its laborers weakened the rebels. But now, he lamented in a letter to Lincoln, the requirement of the abandonment of slavery as a condition for peace talks "puts the whole war question on a new basis, and takes us War Democrats clear off our feet, leaving us no ground to stand upon."

Recognizing that Robinson spoke for large numbers of War Democrats, whose support for the National Union ticket was central to his reelection strategy, Lincoln felt compelled to draft a reply. Had he failed to insist on abolition as a condition for peace negotiations, he explained, he would be guilty of treachery to the hundreds of thousands of African-Americans who had "come bodily over from the rebel side to ours." Such a betrayal could not "escape the curses of Heaven, or of any good man." Apart from the moral issue, there was the practical consideration that without "the physical force which the colored people now give, and promise us, . . . neither the present, nor any coming administration, *can* save the Union."

But recognizing the genuineness of Robinson's concerns, the President also sought to soften his policy. "Saying re-union and abandonment of slavery would be considered, if offered, is not saying that nothing *else* or *less* would be considered, if offered," he suggested. "If Jefferson Davis wishes . . . to know what I would do if he were to offer peace and re-union, saying nothing about slavery, let him try me."

The President's apparent willingness to modify his peace terms in order to hold the allegiance of the War Democrats was echoed the next day in the *New York Times:* "Mr. Lincoln did say that he *would* receive and consider propositions for peace, . . . *if* they embraced the integrity of the Union and the abandonment of Slavery. But he did not say that he would not receive them unless they embraced both these conditions."

Lincoln decided to hold his letter to Robinson until he could discuss its contents with former Governor Alexander W. Randall and Judge Joseph T. Mills, both, like Robinson, from Wisconsin. As he talked to them, his impatience with the War Democrats became increasingly evident. If they really wanted to end the war without interfering with slavery, "the field was open to them to have enlisted and put down this rebellion by force of arms . . . long before the present policy was inaugurated." But now, if he followed their advice, he would have to do without the help of nearly 200,000 black men in the service of the Union. In that case "we would be compelled to abandon the war in 3 weeks." Practical considerations aside, there was the moral issue. How could anybody propose "to return to slavery the black warriors of Port Hudson and Olustee to their masters to conciliate the South"? "I should be damned in time and in eternity for so doing," he told his visitors. "The world shall know that I will keep my faith to friends and enemies, come what will."

That same afternoon Lincoln tried his letter out on Frederick Douglass, the great African-American spokesman whom he considered "one of the most meritorious men in America." When Douglass heard that the President would be willing to consider a peace plan that did not include abolition, his eyes flashed in anger and he strongly objected to the letter. "It would be given a broader meaning than you intend to convey," he warned. "It would be taken as a complete surrender of your antislavery policy, and do you serious damage."

Touched by Douglass's earnestness and, no doubt, affected by his own eloquence in the interview with Randall and Mills, Lincoln put aside the letter to Robinson and never sent it. In effect, he gave up on winning the support of the War Democrats, most of whom quietly returned to their allegiance to the Democratic party in the fall elections.

Even more serious was the erosion of the President's support among Conservative Republicans. These moderates did not form a cohesive group, either in the Congress or in the country, and their opinions on issues like emancipation and reconstruction covered a broad range. Most recognized that the end of slavery was inevitable but were distressed that Lincoln had now chosen to make abolition a necessary condition for peace negotiations. Claiming to speak for "the great body of the respectable part of the country," the New York merchant prince William E. Dodge wanted a peace that "would be honorable to the North and so liberal to the South as to give the lie to the assertion that the North hated them and wished to destroy them." Lincoln's peace terms suggested that he was "so fully committed to the entire abolition of slavery as a condition of peace that he will use all the power of the Government to continue the war till either the South is destroyed or they consent to give up the slaves." Many of the Moderates were sure that the President's policy would strengthen the Confederate will to resist; more were troubled because the President's policy opened them to attack as abolitionists, miscegenationists, and amalgamationists.

Had the war been moving toward a rapid conclusion, most of these fears could have been allayed, but in the late summer of 1864 disaster continued to follow disaster. On July 30, after weeks of inactivity, Grant tried to break the defenses of Petersburg by exploding a huge mine under the Confederate line; 15,000 Union troops rushed into the crater produced by the explosion, but they were poorly led by drunken or incompetent officers and within hours 4,000 men were killed or wounded and the rest had to be withdrawn. Even before this fiasco, as losses in both the Army of the Potomac and in Sherman's army continued to mount, Lincoln had felt obliged to call for 500,000 more soldiers; if by September there were not enough volunteers, he would resort to a draft. This time the draft was going to hit comfortable, middle-class families, because Congress had recently abolished the provision that had allowed a man to "commute" his military service by paying $300. Almost simultaneously, as the costs of the war grew steadily, Secretary of the Treasury Fessenden had to announce a new $200,000,000 loan, and the credit of the government was now so poor that he had difficulty finding purchasers.

Faced with all these problems, Moderate Republicans rarely broke with the President, but they gave his reelection campaign only tepid support. In the cabinet itself Attorney General Bates saw no alternative to Lincoln but felt that the country lacked direction and "that our great want was a competent man at the head of affairs, . . . a competent leader." Orville Browning felt even more alienated, and he wrote a fellow Moderate: "You know, strange as it may seem to you, that I am personally attached to the President, and have faithfully tried to uphold him, and make him respectable; tho' I never have been able to persuade myself that he was big enough for his position. Still, I thought he might get through, as many a boy through college, without disgrace, and without knowledge; and I fear he is a failure."

In New York disaffection among Moderates posed a special problem for Lincoln because their leader, Thurlow Weed, was more critical of the President than ever. The New York boss was convinced that Lincoln went too far in making abolition a condition for peace negotiations. "As things now stand Mr Lincoln's re-election is an impossibility," he concluded. "The People are wild for Peace," he explained to Seward. "They are told that the President will only listen to terms of Peace on condition [that] Slavery be abandoned."

"I am fearful our hold upon Mr Weed is slight," wrote Abram Wakeman, the New York postmaster, who was one of Lincoln's staunchest supporters. "He evidently has his eye upon some other probable candidate." Weed was indeed flirting with the Democrats. Though he said he would zealously support Lincoln if the Democrats nominated a Peace man, he publicly offered his voice and vote to any presidential nominee who took as his platform the Crittenden resolution of 1861, which declared that the sole object of the war was the preservation of the Union.

As usual, Weed's disenchantment with the administration stemmed not merely from Lincoln's policies but from his distribution of the patronage and public funds in New York. Chase's protégé, Hiram Barney, remained the collector in the all-important customs house, though a Moderate complained "that he is a perfect negative man, and possesses no knowledge of politics in any shape and makes no pretentions [sic] to such knowledge." Rufus F. Andrews, the surveyor, was "a political adventurer from the start," who failed to support the regular nominees of the Republican party. Other Moderates alerted the President that there must be "an *immediate change* in the offices of the Collector and Surveyor of the Port of New York."

"The tide is setting strongly against us," Henry J. Raymond, chairman of the National Union Executive Committee, warned the President on August 22. Raymond had heard from Washburne that Illinois would go Democratic, from Cameron that Pennsylvania would be against Lincoln, and from Governor Morton that "nothing but the most strenuous efforts can carry Indiana." He himself predicted that New York would give the Democratic candidate a majority of 50,000 votes. Some voters were complaining of the want of military successes; others voiced "fear and suspicion . . . that we are not, to have peace *in any event* under this Administration until Slavery is abandoned." "Nothing but the most resolute and decided action on the part of the Government and its friends," he told Lincoln, "can save the country from falling into hostile hands."

This message confirmed Lincoln's own pessimistic appraisal of the situation. "You think I don't know I am going to be beaten," he said to a friend, "*but I do* and unless some great change takes place *badly beaten.*" On August 23, with Raymond's letter before him, he drafted and signed a memorandum: "This morning, as for some days past, it seems exceedingly probable that this Administration will not be re-elected. Then it will be my duty to so co-operate with the President elect, as to save the Union between the election and the inauguration; as he will have secured his election on such ground that he can not possibly save it afterwards."

Lincoln's language revealed not merely his pessimism about his own fortunes but his realistic understanding of the forces that opposed his reelection. He did not say that if he was defeated the country would fall into the hands of Copperheads who would consent to the division of the Union and the recognition of the Confederacy. He did not think the Democrats were disloyal. There had been "much impugning of motives, and much heated controversy as to the proper means and best mode of advancing the Union cause," he conceded, but he derived great satisfaction in recording that "a great majority of the opposing party" was as firmly committed as the Republicans to maintaining the integrity of the Union, and he noted with pride that "no candidate for office whatever, high or low, has ventured to seek votes on the avowal that he was for giving up the Union." Nor did he have doubts about the loyalty of George B. McClellan, whose nomination by the Democrats he anticipated. But he did think that if the Democrats elected McClellan the party platform would force the new administration to seek an armistice, which virtually assured Confederate independence.

Folding and sealing his memorandum carefully, so that none of the text was visible, Lincoln put it aside until the next cabinet meeting, when he asked each member to sign his name on the back of the document. As he explained later, his purpose was to talk with McClellan, whose election he thought probable, saying: "General, the election has demonstrated that you are stronger, have more influence with the American people than I. Now let us together, you with your influence and I with all the executive power of the Government, try to save the country." He had little hope that McClellan would do anything, but, he added, "At least . . . I should have done my duty and have stood clear before my own conscience."

V

Then, in the last days of August, with the assembling of the Democratic National Convention at Chicago, the outlook for Lincoln's reelection suddenly brightened. When he asked the newspaperman Noah Brooks to be his informal observer at the convention, the President predicted the outcome: "They must nominate a Peace Democrat on a war platform, or a War Democrat on a peace platform; and I personally can't say that I care much which they do." The Democrats lived up to his expectations. Their platform announced that "after four years of failure to restore the Union by the experiment of war, . . . justice, humanity, liberty and the public welfare demand . . . a cessation of hostilities," with a view to ending the war "on the basis of the Federal Union of the States." It was not exactly a peace platform, for the Democrats, like the Republicans, were pledged to preserve the Union; but the condemnation of the war and the call for an end of fighting made it easy to brand the platform "the Chicago Surrender." Then the convention nominated General George B. McClellan, the leading War Democrat, for President. The two wings of the Democratic party had struck a bargain: the Peace Democrats, most conspicuously represented by Vallandigham, dictated the platform while their opponents named the presidential candidate. In effect, the Democrats chose to make party harmony their principal goal, even at the risk of defeat in the election.

From all quarters McClellan's friends warned that the platform was a "wet blanket"; "universally condemned," it had probably been "concocted to destroy their candidate." After some delay the general disavowed the peace plank. He could not look in the face of his "gallant comrades of the army and navy, who have survived so many bloody battles, and tell them that their labors and the sacrifice of so many of our slain and wounded brethren had been in vain." But the damage was done. As one of McClellan's admirers said, his letter accepting the nomination of a party on whose platform he could not run amounted to "twaddle and humbug."

On September 4, as if timed to make a mockery of the Democratic announcement that the war was a failure, came a message from Sherman: "Atlanta is ours, and fairly won." After Jefferson Davis named the impetuous

John Bell Hood as commander of the Confederate Army of Tennessee, replacing the capable Joseph E. Johnston, Sherman was able to put Atlanta under partial siege and force its evacuation. Almost simultaneously with Sherman's victory message the North received the news that Rear Admiral David G. Farragut had captured Mobile, the last major Gulf port in Confederate hands. Joyfully Lincoln proclaimed a day of thanksgiving and prayer for "the signal success that Divine Providence has recently vouchsafed to the operations of the United States fleet and army in the harbor of Mobile . . . and the glorious achievements of the Army under Major General Sherman . . . resulting in the capture . . . of Atlanta."

These Union victories, combined with the nomination of McClellan on a peace platform, had a devastating effect on the schemes of Radical Republicans to replace Lincoln as their party's nominee. On August 30, the day the Democrats chose McClellan, disaffected Republicans met, as scheduled, at David Dudley Field's house in New York City, but a number of major Radical leaders were not present. Chase was absent; he now doubted the possibility of the success of the movement and advised his followers to support the regular Republican ticket. Wade recommended further deliberations before taking any action. Sumner remained in Boston. Agreeing that Lincoln's nomination had been "ill-considered and unseasonable," he thought there could be no alternative candidate *"unless he withdraws patriotically and kindly, so as to leave no breach in the party."*

But the extreme Radicals, like Greeley, Henry Winter Davis, Field, Professor Francis Lieber of Columbia College, John Austin Stevens of the New York Union League, Parke Godwin, Theodore Tilton, and George Wilkes, were in attendance, and they agreed "that it was useless and inexpedient to attempt to run Mr. Lincoln." The group proposed that Lincoln should withdraw in favor of a new candidate. To prepare the ground for these moves, Greeley, Godwin, and Tilton agreed to send out letters to Northern governors, asking whether Lincoln's election was a probability, whether he could carry their respective states, and whether the interests of the country required the substitution of another candidate in Lincoln's place.

The answers they received showed how out of touch these Radicals were with reality, how little they had assimilated the consequences of McClellan's nomination, and how ill prepared they were to deal with Sherman's victory. Even Governor Andrew of Massachusetts declined to endorse their program. Lincoln was "essentially lacking in the quality of leadership" and his nomination had been a mistake, he granted; but now "correction is impossible" and "Massachusetts will vote for the Union Cause at all events and will support Mr. Lincoln so long as he remains the candidate." The other governors were blunter. Richard Yates of Illinois wrote that substitution of another candidate for Lincoln would be "disastrous in the highest degree." Governor James T. Lewis of Wisconsin told the editors, "In my judgment the interests of the Union party, the honor of the nation and the good of mankind, demand that Mr Lincoln should be sustained and re-elected."

"The conspiracy against Mr Lincoln collapsed on Monday last," Thurlow Weed jubilantly wrote Seward on September 10. Theodore Tilton suddenly discovered the Democrats' Chicago platform was "the most villainous political manifesto known to American history" and that Sherman's victory at Atlanta had produced "a sudden lighting up of the public mind." When he brought his *Independent* out for Lincoln, the *Evening Post* and even the *Tribune* followed suit. Presently Greeley began making campaign speeches for the Republican ticket—though he made a point of not mentioning Lincoln by name.

VI

Kept closely informed of these activities, Lincoln moved to reunite his party, offering concessions to both factions. He had first to address the concerns of the Conservatives, who continued to be alarmed by his insistence that abolition was a necessary condition for peace. Raymond, the chairman of the National Union Executive Committee, spoke for this group and claimed to represent the President's "staunchest friends in every state." He pressed Lincoln to make a distinct offer of peace to Jefferson Davis *"on the sole Condition of acknowledging the supremacy of the Constitution,"* with all other questions—including emancipation—to be settled by a subsequent convention. Raymond was confident that the Confederates would reject such an offer, but by making it Lincoln could "rouse and concentrate the loyalty of the country and . . . give us an easy and a fruitful victory."

Lincoln believed that such a scheme meant "utter ruination," but he could not afford to dismiss Raymond's scheme out of hand. In late August, when the Executive Committee met in Washington, he had a long conversation with the editor and went so far as to draft possible instructions for a mission to Richmond. The emissary would be told to ignore the President's consistent refusal to speak of Jefferson Davis as President of the Confederate States of America and to address him in any terms necessary to secure a conference. He should then propose that "the war shall cease at once, all remaining questions to be left for adjustment by peaceful modes." If this was rejected, he should then inquire what terms of peace the Confederates would be willing to accept. When Raymond went over the draft, he realized what Lincoln had known all along: that "his plan of sending a commission to Richmond would be worse than losing the Presidential contest—it would be ignominiously surrendering it in advance." Persuaded, Raymond gave up diplomacy and went back to managing the campaign, and in a few days the news from Chicago and Atlanta vindicated the President's position.

It took something more than persuasion to allay the unhappiness of Conservatives like Thurlow Weed. The President sent Nicolay to New York City to negotiate changes in the customs house that would placate the boss. It was, as the secretary said, a "very delicate, disagreeable and arduous duty," because the New York Conservatives were no longer willing to share the patronage with the Radicals. Yielding to necessity, Lincoln, with some reluctance, ousted Hiram Barney, the collector, on September 5 and replaced him with Simeon Draper, a respected New York merchant who was an intimate of Seward and Weed. Ten days later he removed Andrews, the surveyor of the port, another Chase supporter, and appointed in his stead Abram Wakeman, the New York City postmaster who had become an intimate friend of Mrs. Lincoln. Taking hold, Draper announced that he would "hold every body *responsible,* for Mr Lincoln's reelection, and I will countenance nothing else." By making a few dismissals, he brought the rest of the customs house gang in line. "It is remarkable to note," the *New York Herald* reported, "the change which has taken place in the political sentiments of some of these gentlemen within the last forty-eight hours—in fact, an anti-Lincoln man could not be found in any of the departments yesterday."

VII

Lincoln had also to enlist the support of the Radicals, most of whom had not favored his renomination and some of whom had been trying to replace him with another candidate. His task was made easier because many of the Radicals had an institutional loyalty to the party they had helped found. Others made a cold-eyed calculation that they stood to benefit more from the victory of a Republican candidate whom they distrusted than from the success of any Democrat.

He was fortunate that Zachariah Chandler, the blunt, self-educated Detroit businessman who represented Michigan in the Senate, took on himself the task of reconciling the Radicals and the President. Though the Michigan senator thought poorly of Lincoln's record and believed he was "perfectly infatuated with Seward and Blair," he was concerned for the victory of his party. "If it was only Abe Lincoln," he wrote his wife, "I would say, go to ___ in your own way." But now it was a choice between an inadequate Republican candidate and the "Traitor McLelland [sic]."

During the final weeks of August, Chandler began exploring ways to bring Wade and Davis, the two Radicals most openly critical of Lincoln, back into the regular Republican fold. Wade's resistance was the first to crack. He had been overwhelmed by the hostile reception of the Wade-Davis Manifesto, and his friends warned that "Lincoln has been more firmly seated in the saddle than at any time since the premature action of the Baltimore convention placed him there." Chandler persuaded him to swallow his pride and agree to endorse the Lincoln-Johnson ticket, provided that Davis did so, too. Davis was also ready to negotiate. Distrusting Lincoln, he virulently hated Blair, leader of the rival Republican faction in Maryland. He agreed to support Lincoln but only on condition that the President dismiss the Postmaster General from the cabinet. His purpose was not merely to kill off Blair but to show Lincoln up as a "mean and selfish old dog who sacrificed his *friend* to his prospects."

Skillfully Chandler presented Davis's demand not to Lincoln himself but to "his *particular* friends, those who drop in and chat with him of evenings and who have his confidence." Probably he referred to men like Leonard Swett, John W. Forney, and Noah Brooks. As Davis scornfully reported, Chandler imbued "the President's *familiar spirits* . . . with the darkest views of Lincoln's prospects, and sent [them] there night after night to regale him with some new tale of defection or threatened disaster." At the end of eight days—according to Davis, who was not present—Lincoln was "in the condition of a child frightened by ghost stories and ready to take refuge anywhere."

In fact, Lincoln did not panic, and he resisted dismissing Blair in order to secure party unity and his own reelection. He had genuine respect for all the members of the Blair family. Francis P. Blair, Sr., had been a loyal, conservative adviser throughout the war, and Frank Blair, after his intemperate attacks on the Radicals in Congress, had displayed ability as a commander in Sherman's army. For Montgomery Blair the President had real affection, and he was sure that Blair "had made the best Post master Genl that ever administered the Dept."

But the Postmaster General had become a controversial figure, more hated by the Radicals than even Seward. His blunt denunciations of abolitionists, his continuing advocacy of the colonization of African-Americans, his fierce opposition to Radical schemes for reconstruction, his zealous advocacy of Lincoln's renomination and reelection—all aroused hostility. So did his bitter, and often unwarranted, personal enmities. He carried on a bitter feud with Frémont, he hated Chase, he despised Halleck, and he could hardly bear to be in the same room as Stanton. Lincoln was distressed by the vindictiveness Blair demonstrated in his frequent quarrels, but as he told the senior Blair, he "could not believe there was any profit to be expected on the sacrifice of a good and true friend from first to last for false ones."

Chandler offered to sweeten the pot by suggesting that, in return for Blair's resignation, the President might secure not only the support of Wade and Davis but the withdrawal of Frémont from the race. Though Frémont's campaign had been slipping, he retained a fiercely loyal following, especially among German-Americans in the West, and the President feared he might siphon off enough votes to cost the Republicans Indiana, Illinois, and Missouri and thus the election. "The President," according to Chandler, "was most reluctant to come to terms *but came.*" The senator then hotfooted it to New York to see Frémont.

Establishing headquarters at the Astor House, Chandler met several times with Frémont, urging him, in the name of the President, the Union Congressional Committee, and the National Union Executive Committee, to consider withdrawing from a race in which his candidacy could only help elect McClellan. If Frémont agreed, Chandler promised that he would receive a new command as major general in the Union army and that his old enemy, Blair, would be dismissed from the cabinet.

Frémont took Chandler's offer under advisement and asked the opinion of his friends. He heard dissonant voices. Wendell Phillips urged him to continue his candidacy. A supporter in Pittsburgh begged him to come out "as soon as practicable in favor of Lincoln and Johnson" after receiving "assurance of Mr. Blair's immediate removal and also Mr. Stanton's and the assurance that Mr. Seward will not be reappointed." On September 17, Gustave Paul Cluseret, the editor of Frémont's campaign newspaper, the *New Nation,* published an editorial supporting Lincoln and warning readers that the general listened to "any man who causes imaginary popular enthusiasm to glitter before his eyes, spends his money, profits by his natural indolence to cradle him in an illusion from which he will only awaken ruined in pocket and in reputation." That same day Frémont decided to drop out of the race. Chandler wanted his withdrawal to be "a *conditional* one to get Blair out," but Frémont honorably refused. "I will make no conditions—my letter is written and will appear tomorrow," he said. In a public letter he announced that he was leaving the race not because he had changed his opinion of Lincoln, whose "administration has been politically, militarily, and financially a failure," but because McClellan would restore the Union with slavery.

When the news of Frémont's withdrawal reached Washington, Lincoln, according to Davis, grew "excited at the form of it, and showed symptoms of flying from the bargain." But Chandler reminded him that, "offensive as it was," Frémont's letter was "a substantial advice to support Lincoln." Reluctantly the President agreed to live up to the terms he had agreed on, and on September 23 asked for Blair's resignation. To take his place he named former Governor William Dennison of Ohio, who was, as David Davis said, "honorable, highminded, pure, and dignified." While Blair's resignation was pending, both Wade and Henry Winter Davis took the stump in Lincoln's behalf.

That left Salmon P. Chase and his followers as the final group of disgruntled Republicans who were still unwilling to endorse the reelection of the President. Nursing an ego bruised by his forced resignation from the cabinet, Chase had quietly encouraged moves to replace Lincoln on the Republican ticket, but in public he assumed an air of disinterested statesmanship. He advised those who wrote him to accept Lincoln's renomination "as decisive and to give him their support dutifully and manfully"—but he told his correspondents not to publish his views. With the collapse of the anti-Lincoln movement in September, he warmed a little and recognized Lincoln and Johnson as "nominees of the Party whose principles and measures . . . I fully accept." But he could not help adding wistfully, "We can't have everything as we would wish."

In late September, Chase began giving different political signals. Chief

Justice Roger B. Taney was ailing (he was, after all, eighty-seven years old), and his anticipated death raised a possibility that Chase had more than once considered. Returning to Washington to consult with Fessenden on Treasury problems, he made a point of calling on Lincoln and was quite cordially received. "But he is not at all demonstrative, either in speech or manner," Chase reported to his diary, adding the telling observation, "I feel that I do not know him." Shortly after this visit he began to say positive things about Lincoln: "The best interests of the country require his reelection and I shall give him my active support."

Taney's death on October 12 made the naming of the next Chief Justice a public question. Sumner immediately urged Lincoln to appoint Chase, reminding the President that he had several times spoken of his former Treasury Secretary for this position. Chase's friends sent a barrage of letters to the White House backing his appointment. But there were other candidates. Attorney General Bates asked Lincoln for the appointment "as the crowning, retiring honor of my life." Mrs. Stanton wanted her husband, exhausted by his demanding labors in the War Department, to be Chief Justice, and she enlisted Browning to urge his case with Lincoln. Dozens of letters recommended elevating Noah Swayne, the antislavery corporate lawyer whom Lincoln had named an associate justice in 1862. William M. Evarts, the careful New York lawyer, had his supporters. Francis P. Blair, Sr., earnestly implored Lincoln to appoint his son Montgomery, "to remove the cloud which his ostracism from your Cabinet" had caused.

Lincoln listened and read but took no action. He had probably decided to name Chase, but, as he told Nicolay, he was resolved to be "very 'shut pan' about this matter." Eager for the appointment, Chase wrote the President a friendly letter about Republican prospects in Ohio. Without reading it, Lincoln directed: "File it with his other recommendations." As the President failed to act, Sumner's urgency grew greater, and he persuaded Chase to write a letter that he could show Lincoln: "It is perhaps not exactly *en règle* to say what one will do in regard to an appointment not tendered to him; but it is certainly not wrong to say to you that I should accept." Chase went on to add words that must have choked him: "Happily it is now certain that the next Administration will be in the hands of Mr Lincoln from whom the world will expect great things." Still Lincoln did not name a Chief Justice. Finally getting the cue, Chase took to the stump, urging rallies at Louisville, Lexington, St. Louis, Cleveland, Detroit, and Chicago to vote for Lincoln's reelection.

It was all just as the *New York Herald* had wickedly anticipated in August. Now the "sorehead republicans"—as the paper called the dissident Radicals—were "all skedaddling for the Lincoln train and selling out at the best terms they can." The *Herald* had predicted that the "ultra radical, ultra shoddy, and ultra nigger soreheads ... will all make tracks for Old Abe's plantation, and will soon be found crowing, and blowing, and vowing, and writing, and swearing and stumping the States on his side, declaring that he, and he alone, is the hope of the nation."

As Chase canvassed the West, he reflected on a conversation he had had some weeks earlier with a New Yorker "who thought Lincoln very wise," observing that if he were "more radical he would have offended conservatives—if more conservative the radicals." Wonderingly, Chase asked himself: "Will this be [the] judgment of history?"

VIII

"I cannot run the political machine," Lincoln was quoted as saying during the campaign; "I have enough on my hands without *that.* It is the *people's* business." He did not take part in any of the hundreds of campaign marches and torchlight processions staged by the National Union (Republican) party throughout the North. He was not involved in the work of the Loyal Publication Societies, headed by Francis Lieber in New York and by John Murray Forbes in Boston, which distributed more than half a million Union pamphlets bearing titles like "No Party Now but All for Our Country." He did nothing to encourage partisan newspapers that attacked the Democrats as Copperheads or charged that they were engaged in a "Peace Party Plot!" (Indeed, he discounted tales of Copperhead conspiracies as puerile.)

Nor did Lincoln take public notice of the attacks Democrats made on him during the campaign. He did not comment on Democratic rallies where partisans carried banners reading TIME TO SWAP HORSES, NOVEMBER 8TH or NO MORE VULGAR JOKES. He probably never saw scurrilous Democratic pamphlets, like *The Lincoln Catechism, Wherein the Eccentricities & Beauties of Despotism Are Fully Set Forth,* which called him "Abraham Africanus the First" and quoted the first of the President's own Ten Commandments: "Thou shalt have no other God but the negro." The repeated Democratic charge that he and the Republicans favored intermarriage of blacks and whites Lincoln acknowledged only indirectly, joking that miscegenation was "a democratic mode of producing good Union men, and I dont propose to infringe on the patent." He did not respond to Democratic charges, raised in as respectable a journal as the *New York World,* that his administration was characterized by "ignorance, incompetency, and corruption." Though he was, as Mrs. Lincoln said, "almost a monomaniac on the subject of honesty," he did not refute the charge that he had helped a relative defraud the Quartermaster's Department in St. Louis.

Only once was he tempted to reply to a personal attack. Democratic newspapers now revived the canard that while touring the Antietam battlefield in September 1862 he had asked Ward Lamon to sing "a comic negro song"; they claimed that such behavior demonstrated that he was not "fit for any office of trust, or even for decent society." Belligerently Lamon attempted to refute the slander, but Lincoln, thinking it would be better simply to state the facts, wrote out his own account of how he had indeed—days after the battle and far from the soldiers' cemetery—asked Lamon to sing "a little sad song." Then he told Lamon not to publish his reply, saying, "I dislike to appear as an apologist for an act of my own which I know was right."

Lincoln's public appearances during the campaign were rare. In June he did attend the Great Central Sanitary Fair, held in Philadelphia to raise money for the Sanitary Commission and other groups providing for the needs of the soldiers, but he said little. "I do not really think it is proper in my position for me to make a political speech," he told a group at the Hotel Continental, "and . . . being more of a politician than anything else, . . . I am without anything to say." When volunteer regiments, on their way home as their terms of enlistment expired, came by the White House, he thanked them for their service and said nothing more partisan than that they should "rise up to the height of a generation of men worthy of a free Government."

But if Lincoln did not take a public role in the campaign, he was intimately involved in all the details of behind-the-scenes management. Indeed, as Fessenden remarked, "The President is too busy looking after the election to think of any thing else." Repeatedly he intervened to end party squabbling. In Pennsylvania, for example, antagonism between the Cameron and Curtin factions was so great that, as Lincoln was told, it produced "distraction and indifference, *which may, possibly, be fatal.*" Cameron seemed to be conducting the campaign primarily with a view to his own election to the Senate, while Governor Curtin was so disaffected that he predicted "the reelection of this admin[istration] is [going] to send us to hell." Lincoln summoned the Pennsylvania governor, with his aide, Alexander K. McClure, to the White House and used all his personal powers of persuasion to get his people to work with the Cameron forces until after the election.

The President intervened in congressional contests when local feuds among Republicans threatened to affect the outcome of the election. In New York, a group of Conservative Republicans was working to defeat the election of Roscoe Conkling, the party's nominee for Congress. When Conkling's friends asked Lincoln's assistance, he replied with a strong letter: "I am for the regular nominee in all cases; and . . . no one could be more satisfactory to me as the nominee in that District, than Mr. Conkling." Again, when he learned that the postmaster of Philadelphia was using his influence to defeat Representative William D. Kelley, he summoned the official to Washington and told him bluntly: "I am well satisfied with Judge Kelly as an M.C. and I do not know that the man who might supplant him would be as satisfactory." The postmaster could vote for whom he chose, but he must "not constrain any of [his] subordinates to do other than as he thinks fit."

Lincoln recognized the influence that newspapers had on public opinion, and he tried to enlist the support of prominent editors. He even went so far as to approach the notorious James Gordon Bennett, whose *New York Her-*

ald had yet to take a public position on the election. Because the circulation and influence of the *Herald* were so great, Lincoln's New York friends suggested that it might be worthwhile to woo the editor with flattery. They knew that Bennett, whose reputation for immorality was as well deserved as his paper's reputation for scandal, longed for respectability. When they approached him, the canny editor asked bluntly, "Will I be a welcome visitor at the White House if I support Mr. Lincoln?" The President may have shared John Hay's conviction that Bennett was "too pitchy to touch," and he initially offered only a vague promise that "whoever aids the right, will be appreciated and remembered" after the election. Bennett responded that the offer "did not amount to much." When intermediaries began to explore the possibility that Lincoln might offer Bennett an appointment as American minister to France, the tone of the *Herald* toward the administration became notably kinder. Bennett did not endorse Lincoln, telling a go-between to say to the President "that puffs did no good, and he could accomplish most for you by not mentioning your name." But the bitterness of his attacks on Lincoln diminished. Though he continued to call Lincoln a failure, he termed McClellan "no less a failure . . . though a failure perhaps in a less repulsive way," and in the end the *Herald* endorsed neither candidate. After the election Lincoln paid the price for Bennett's neutrality by offering the editor the French ministry, which he knew he would decline.

But there were limits to what Lincoln would do to secure a second term. He did not even consider canceling or postponing the election. Even had that been constitutionally possible, "the election was a necessity." "We can not have free government without elections," he explained; "and if the rebellion could force us to forego, or postpone a national election, it might fairly claim to have already conquered and ruined us." He did not postpone the September draft call, even though Republican politicians from all across the North entreated him to do so. Because Indiana failed to permit its soldiers to vote in the field, he was entirely willing to furlough Sherman's regiments so that they could go home and vote in the October state elections —but he made a point of telling Sherman, "They need not remain for the Presidential election, but may return to you at once."

Though it was clear that the election was going to be a very close one, Lincoln did not try to increase the Republican electoral vote by rushing the admission of new states like Colorado and Nebraska, both of which would surely have voted for his reelection. On October 31, in accordance with an act of Congress, he did proclaim Nevada a state, but he showed little interest in the legislation admitting the new state. Despite the suspicion of both Democrats and Radicals, he made no effort to force the readmission of Louisiana, Tennessee, and other Southern states, partially reconstructed but still under military control, so that they could cast their electoral votes for him. He reminded a delegation from Tennessee that it was the Congress, not the Chief Executive, that had the power to decide whether a state's electoral votes were to be counted and announced firmly, "Except it be to give protection against violence, I decline to interfere in any way with any presidential election."

IX

Both what Lincoln did in the campaign of 1864 and what he refrained from doing reflected his sense of the importance of this election. In part, as he admitted, he sought a second term out of "personal vanity, or ambition." "I confess that I desire to be re-elected," he said frankly. "God knows I do not want the labor and responsibility of the office for another four years. But I have the common pride of humanity to wish my past four years Administration endorsed." Honestly believing that he could "better serve the nation in its need and peril than any new man could possibly do," he wanted the opportunity "to finish this job of putting down the rebellion, and restoring peace and prosperity to the country."

His wife wanted a second term at least as much as he did. To Mary Lincoln, reelection meant not merely vindication of her husband but escape from her own personal difficulties. After Willie's death she had largely given up on refurbishing the White House and had turned to decorating and ornamenting herself. She went deeply into debt, purchasing clothing and jewelry from New York and Philadelphia merchants such as a white point lace shawl valued at $2,000, a pearl-and-diamond ring, an onyx breast pin with earrings, and two diamond-and-pearl bracelets. David Davis heard a rumor that she purchased three hundred pairs of kid gloves from a Washington merchant. "I must dress in costly materials," she explained to Elizabeth Keckley, her dressmaker. "The people scrutinize every article that I wear with critical curiosity. The very fact of having grown up in the West, subjects me to more searching observation." Convinced that her appearance was helping her husband's bid for reelection, she also saw victory in November as a means of postponing a reckoning of her debts, which Lincoln did not know about. "If he is re-elected," she told Mrs. Keckley, "I can keep him in ignorance of my affairs; but if he is defeated, then the bills will be sent in, and he will know all."

Lincoln believed that there was more than personal satisfaction at stake in the 1864 election. He saw it as a test of the feasibility of democratic government. The will of the people was "the ultimate law for all." If the people supported the Union cause, he said, they would act "for the best interests of their country and the world, not only for the present, but for all future ages." If, on the other hand, "they should deliberately resolve to have immediate peace even at the loss of their country, and their liberty, I know not the power or the right to resist them. It is their own business, and they must do as they please with their own." The decision they made would determine "the weal or woe of this great nation."

This view of the 1864 election was shared by many Americans, including some who had not hitherto been notably warm toward the Lincoln administration. Most African-Americans hoped and prayed for Lincoln's reelection, even though few of them were allowed to vote. A few black spokesmen were reluctant to support this "fickle-minded man" who had been reluctant to announce emancipation, slow to enroll Negro troops, unwilling to fight for equal pay for blacks who did enlist, and publicly silent on Negro voting, and some, like Frederick Douglass, initially favored Frémont. But when the election narrowed to a choice between Lincoln and McClellan, African-Americans saw their duty clearly. At the National Convention of Colored Men, held in Syracuse in October, the black Massachusetts lawyer John S. Rock put the choice concisely: "There are but two parties in the country today. The one headed by Lincoln is for Freedom and the Republic; and the other, by McClellan, is for Despotism and Slavery."

Impressive as were the endorsements of such black leaders, Lincoln may have gained more solace from individual African-Americans who spoke only for themselves. Early in 1864 his old acquaintance William de Fleurville (Billy the Barber) wrote from Springfield, hoping that Lincoln would be reelected because then "the oppressed will shout the name of their deliverer, and generations to come will rise up and call you blessed." Late in October the President had a visit from Sojourner Truth, the elderly black woman who, after having been sold three times on the auction block, escaped to freedom and afterward brought out other fugitives on the Underground Railroad. She declared that she "never was treated by any one with more kindness and cordiality," and she was proud that the President wrote in her autograph book "with the same hand that signed the death-warrant of slavery." "I felt that I was in the presence of a friend," the old woman said, "and I now thank God from the bottom of my heart that I always advocated his cause."

Though abolitionists had often been sharply critical of Lincoln, a majority of the reformers now favored his reelection. Earlier in the year the Massachusetts Anti-Slavery Society was shattered after a debate between its two most notable leaders—Wendell Phillips, who announced that Lincoln had no commitment to liberty and was "knowingly preparing for a peace in disregard for the negro," and William Lloyd Garrison, who countered that the President had shown great capacity for growth and had moved as fast as public opinion allowed. In the months that followed, Phillips became one of the most conspicuous supporters of Frémont's candidacy and vowed that he would "cut off both hands before doing anything to aid Abraham Lincoln's election," while Garrison insisted that if Lincoln had made mistakes "a thousand incidental errors and blunders are easily to be borne with on the part of him who, at one blow, severed the chains of three millions three hundred thousand slaves."

The quarrel splintered the abolitionist movement, but Garrison and his followers retained control of the two most important periodicals, the *Liberator* and the *Anti-Slavery Standard,* both of which gave consistent support to

Lincoln's campaign. Garrison himself attended the National Union Convention in Baltimore, and afterward he had two long interviews with the President. Much pleased "with his spirit, and the familiar and candid way in which he unbosomed himself," the veteran abolitionist was more confident than ever of Lincoln's desire "to uproot slavery, and give fair-play to the emancipated."

The support the President received from Protestant religious groups was overwhelming. He had made a point of consulting religious leaders and of praising their contribution to the war effort. In May when a delegation from the Methodist Episcopal Church pointed out the denomination's record for loyalty and support of the administration, he replied, "God bless the Methodist Church—bless all the churches—and blessed be God, Who, in this our great trial, giveth us the churches." The same month he offered thanks to the American Baptist Home Mission Society for "the effective and almost unanimous support which the Christian communities are so zealously giving to the country, and to liberty." Now they returned the compliment. Methodist Bishop Gilbert Haven announced the church's duty of the hour was to "march to the ballot-box, an army of Christ, with the banners of the Cross, and deposit, as she can, a million of votes for her true representative, and she will give the last blow to the reeling fiend." As the *Christian Advocate and Journal* observed, "There probably never was an election in all our history into which the religion element entered so largely, and nearly all on one side."

Northern men and women of letters also endorsed Lincoln's reelection with unprecedented unanimity. Mostly from the Northeast, these writers initially viewed Lincoln with skepticism, thinking him an uncouth, uneducated frontiersman who was certainly not a gentleman, and his hesitant course on slavery had reinforced their suspicions. But their appreciation of the difficulties the President faced and of the skill with which he handled them had grown, and now, faced with a choice between McClellan and Lincoln, virtually all supported the Union candidate. Ralph Waldo Emerson was not active in politics, but he shared Lincoln's view of the significance of the election. "Seldom in history," he said, "was so much staked on a popular vote.—I suppose never in history." "We breathe freer," Henry Wadsworth Longfellow wrote when he felt confident that the President would have a second term. "The country will be saved." Harriet Beecher Stowe was a firm supporter of Lincoln. She remembered how kindly the President had received her in the White House back in 1862, when, according to a family story, he exclaimed, "So this is the little lady who made this big war?" She defended Lincoln from irresponsible attacks, remarking, "Even the ass can kick safely and joyfully at a lion in a net." Though John Greenleaf Whittier preferred Frémont, he was happy enough to see "all loyal men rallying in favor of Lincoln" and exclaimed, "Between him and that traitor platform [of the Democrats] who could hesitate!" With great pleasure Edward Everett agreed to be one of the Massachusetts Republican electors, pledged to vote for Lincoln as an "entirely conscientious" and "eminently kind-hearted" man, who had "administered the Government with the deepest sense of responsibility to his country and his God."

None of Lincoln's literary supporters was more loyal or more influential than James Russell Lowell, one of the editors of the *North American Review.* The four long articles he published in 1864 amounted to an extended argument in favor of Lincoln's reelection. The final one, "The Next General Election," which appeared on the eve of the election, ridiculed Democratic talk of conciliating the Confederates and praised Lincoln as "a long-headed and long-purposed man," who had "shown from the first the considerate wisdom of a practical statesman."

X

Even with such a strong party organization and so many influential backers, Lincoln could not be sure of reelection. The October elections for state officials in Indiana, Ohio, and Pennsylvania suggested how close the race still was. Lincoln spent the evening of October 11 at the War Department, where he, Stanton, Assistant Secretary of War Dana, and Hay eagerly scrutinized the telegraphic returns as they trickled in. Between dispatches the President read aloud several chapters from the recently published *Nasby Papers* by David Ross Locke. Lincoln found these comic sketches about Petroleum V. Nasby, a dissolute, semiliterate Copperhead who lived at Confederate X Roads, vastly amusing, and he once told Charles Sumner, "For the genius to write these things I would gladly give up my office." Usually Stanton found Lincoln's humor irritating, but this time he was in a good mood and enjoyed Nasby's adventures almost as much as the President did.

From the beginning the news from Ohio and Indiana was good. But the Pennsylvania reports, as Hay remarked, began to be "streaked with lean." Lincoln grew anxious because, he said, Pennsylvania's "enormous weight and influence which, [if] cast definitely into the scale, w[oul]d close the campaign." The final totals were not in for several days, when it became evident that the continuing Cameron-Curtin feud had hurt the ticket and the anticipated huge Republican majority had been whittled down to about 400 home votes in the entire state. Only the soldiers' vote, overwhelmingly Republican, assured victory.

Two days after the October elections Lincoln tried to predict the national vote in November. Jotting down an estimate of the electoral vote, he calculated that McClellan would carry New York, Pennsylvania, New Jersey, and Delaware, all of the border states, and Illinois, with a total of 114 electoral votes, while he would get 117 from all the rest of the states. (Someone else added the three electoral votes of Nevada to his column.) It was too close for comfort.

But in the next few days he became more optimistic. Republican strength in Indiana and Ohio proved greater than anticipated. Maryland adopted a constitution outlawing slavery. The soldier vote was overwhelmingly Republican. And Republicans could take heart from the vigorous campaign that Sheridan was waging to clear Early's Confederates out of the Shenandoah Valley. Lincoln revised his thinking. "It does look as if the people wanted me to stay here a little longer," he told a visitor, "and I suppose I shall have to, if they do."

During the remaining weeks of the campaign he did his best to make the outcome certain. He continued to try to consolidate his party by sending his private secretary out to Missouri with a view to mediating between the Charcoal and Claybank factions. Nicolay found that the endless party feud in that state "hinged, not on either principle or policy, but upon personal spite and greed for spoils," and he tried to persuade both factions that it was in their best interests to support Lincoln's reelection. Lincoln encouraged soldier voting in the field so enthusiastically that E. B. Washburne said, "If it could be done in no other way, the president would take a carpet bag and go around and collect those votes himself." He even went so far as to permit Republican agents to use a government steamer on the Mississippi River to collect the ballots of sailors on the federal gunboats. On election day hundreds of federal employees in Washington were furloughed in order to return to their homes and vote. "Even the camps and hospitals are depleted," reported the banker Henry D. Cooke; "the streets wear a quiet Sunday air—in the Department building[s], the empty corridors respond with hollow echoes to the foot fall of the solitary visitor; the hotels are almost tenantless, and the street cars drone lazily along the half-filled seats."

The election went off smoothly. From the earliest returns it was clear that the Republicans had won a huge victory; they carried every state except New Jersey, Delaware, and Kentucky. The Democrats had waged a vigorous campaign with a united party, and Democratic candidates made a strong showing in the cities and in those counties where there were large numbers of Irish-American and German-American voters. The 45 percent of the popular vote that McClellan received was more than respectable, especially in view of the fact that all the Southern states were still out of the Union and, of course, not voting. Republican success was due largely to the same groups of voters who had supported the party in 1860—native-born farmers in the countryside, better-off skilled workers and professional men in the city, and voters of New England descent everywhere. As in 1860, younger voters were especially attracted to the Republican party, and the soldier vote went overwhelmingly for Lincoln.

Election night was rainy and foggy in Washington, and the President spent the evening at the War Department waiting for the returns. The first reports were encouraging, and he sent them over to Mrs. Lincoln, saying, "She is more anxious than I." Presently Thomas T. Eckert, head of the telegraph office, came in, wet and muddy because he had fallen while crossing the street. In a genial mood, the President was reminded of another rainy evening back in 1858 when he had been on the square at Springfield reading the returns on his contest with Douglas for the Senate. On his way home he nearly fell in the muddy street, but he recovered himself and thought, "It's a slip and not a fall." "For such an awkward fellow," he remarked to the group in the telegraph office, "I am pretty sure-footed."

CHAPTER TWENTY

With Charity for All

———◆———

"*Laus Deo!*" George Templeton Strong wrote in his diary on the day after the election. "The crisis has been past, and the most momentous popular election ever held since ballots were invented has decided against treason and disunion. . . . The American people can be trusted to take care of the national honor." "How glorious the result of the election," echoed one of Senator John Sherman's correspondents. "Language cannot describe nor imagination conceive its importance to our country and the world. It is the great political event in all history."

Lincoln himself rejoiced that the balloting "demonstrated that a people's government can sustain a national election, in the midst of a great civil war. Until now it has not been known to the world that this was a possibility." But he was careful not to seek personal advantage from his victory. On election night when Gustavus V. Fox pointed out to him that two of the most vehement Radical critics of the administration had been defeated and crowed that "retribution has come upon them both," Lincoln remarked: "You have more of that feeling of personal resentment than I. Perhaps I may have too little of it, but I never thought it paid." He had no intention of using his impressive mandate to settle old quarrels with his Republican critics. "I am in favor of short statutes of limitations in politics," he said. Nor did he gloat over the defeat of the Democrats. On November 10, when serenaders came to the north portico of the White House to celebrate his victory, he appeared in a second-floor window to make a brief response. Instead of celebrating the Republican triumph, he sought reconciliation with his political foes, asking, "Now that the election is over, may not all . . . re-unite in a common effort, to save our common country?" "For my own part," he continued, "I have striven, and shall strive to avoid placing any obstacle in the way. So long as I have been here I have not willingly planted a thorn in any man's bosom."

I

The President's address did not placate his bitterest enemies. Pro-Confederate sympathizers in the North viewed Lincoln's reelection as a disaster. Most leaders of the Confederacy shared that opinion. Jefferson Davis and his associates had cherished the hope that Lincoln would be defeated. To that end, in the months before the election Confederate emissaries in Canada had tried to influence Northern opinion through the aborted peace negotiations with Horace Greeley and through financial subvention for the Vallandigham Peace Democrats; they had planned an uprising at Chicago during the Democratic National Convention; they had sent agents to incite violence in Chicago and New York on election day; and they had staged raids on the Great Lakes and at St. Albans, Vermont. None of these tactics had persuaded the North to repudiate Lincoln. Sadly Confederate newspapers lamented that henceforth Southerners had to recognize that "the people who lately called us brethren" were "insatiable for our blood"—at least so long as they were led by "a vulgar buffoon" who exercised more autocratic powers than "King, Emperor, Czar, Kaiser, or even despotic Caesar himself."

Facing certain defeat unless some drastic measures could be taken, Confederates in the final months of 1864 began to explore their options. Some looked to further peace negotiations with the North. Others sought foreign intervention, and President Davis sent the wealthy Louisiana planter Duncan Kenner abroad to offer emancipation of the slaves in return for British and French recognition. Many Southerners were willing to take the desperate risk of enrolling blacks in the Confederate armies. And, inevitably, a few began to think that the only way to avert Confederate defeat was by removing the head of the Union government.

The idea of eliminating Abraham Lincoln was not a new one in 1864. Even before his first election in 1860 he began to receive threats against his life. Initially these threats caused him some concern—and they made Mary frantic with worry. As President-elect, he had felt obliged to make a secret night trip through Baltimore to avoid attack by secessionists. But once he was settled in the White House, he ceased to pay much attention to the danger and directed his secretaries to throw away most threatening letters without showing them to him. By 1864, Lincoln told Francis B. Carpenter such letters no longer caused him apprehension. When the artist expressed surprise, he replied, "Oh, there is nothing like getting *used* to things!"

Lincoln believed that in a democratic society the Chief Executive must not be screened from the public. "It would never do," he told a member of Halleck's staff, "for a President to have guards with drawn sabres at his door, as if he fancied he were, or were trying to be, or were assuming to be, an emperor." In addition, he recognized that it was impossible for him to be fully protected. If a group of conspirators plotted his death, he said, "no vigilance could keep them out. . . . A conspiracy to assassinate, if such there were, could easily obtain a pass to see me for any one or more of its instruments."

Consequently, like many other American presidents, Lincoln took few precautions to protect his security. During the first years of his presidency he often took long walks through the streets of Washington late at night or in the early morning hours, either alone or with a single companion. Nearly every night before going to bed Lincoln strolled through the densely shaded White House grounds to the War Department, often with no escort or guard. During the hot months when the Lincolns stayed at the Soldiers' Home, he often rode back and forth to the White House on horseback or in an unguarded carriage. He frequently attended the theater in Washington accompanied only by Mary, or sometimes Tad, and one or two civilian friends. His indifference to security on these occasions drove his old friend Ward Lamon, the marshal of the District of Columbia who felt responsible for his safety, nearly to distraction. Once Lamon angrily offered to resign when he heard that the President had gone to the theater attended only by Charles Sumner and the Baron Gerolt, the elderly Prussian minister, "neither of whom," Lamon sneered, "could defend himself against an assault from any able-bodied woman in this city."

At the outbreak of the war there was no military guard at the White House, and the two civilian attendants—one for the outer door, the other for the President's office on the second floor—were often absent from their posts. In 1862, General James S. Wadsworth, the military commander of the District of Columbia, improved security by detailing a body of cavalry to escort the President on his rides to and from the Soldiers' Home, but Lincoln objected that the soldiers made such a clatter with their sabers and spurs that he and Mary "couldn't hear themselves talk." The next summer these soldiers were replaced by the Union Light Guard, a company of one hundred carefully selected Ohioans mounted on handsome black steeds. Two of these guards were stationed at all times at each of the gateways to the Executive Mansion, and a noncommissioned officer was posted at the front portico. An infantry company of Pennsylvania Bucktails guarded the southern approaches to the White House. At Lamon's urging, the chief of the Washington Metropolitan Police detailed four officers for special duty at the Executive Mansion. Wearing civilian clothing and carrying concealed weapons, these men were supposed to accompany the President on his walks and to escort him to the theater. At night one of them remained on duty upstairs in the White House outside the Lincolns' private rooms.

These increased precautions reflected Stanton's growing anxiety that the President's life was in danger. In 1864, Lincoln began to receive an unusual number of letters about plots to kidnap or assassinate him. Most were anonymous and undocumented. For instance, in July, "Lizzie W.S." alerted the

President that there were "hordes of Secesh-sympathizers" around Washington who would not hesitate to shoot him on his rides to the Soldiers' Home. "If, you value your life! *do,* I entreat of you, *discontinue* your visits, out of the City," she begged. A laborer in West Virginia reported overhearing a conversation in which one man assured another "that the plan was all made that if old Abe was Re alected we are agoin to kill him and I am the man that is agoin to do it with your help."

Hostility toward the President sharply increased during the last months of 1864 because both disaffected Northerners and embittered Confederates began to realize that what they considered the abuses and excesses of the Lincoln administration were going to be continued for another four years. Evils that up to this point had seemed transient now felt intolerable. Since the ballot did not remove the despot, it was time to find other means. In August, direly anticipating Lincoln's success, the *La Crosse* (Wisconsin) *Democrat,* edited by the notorious Copperhead Marcus M. ("Brick") Pomeroy, observed: "And if he is elected . . . for another four years, we trust some bold hand will pierce his heart with dagger point for the public good."

In the Confederacy more thought was given to kidnapping Lincoln than to assassinating him. Abducting the President of the United States would present the South with several advantages. If Lincoln could be safely seized and spirited away to Richmond, perhaps he would finally agree to negotiate with the Confederate government; the person of the President might make a powerful argument for suspending Grant's merciless attacks; and—the most appealing argument of all—Lincoln could be used as a hostage to secure the release of some 200,000 captured Confederate soldiers languishing in Northern prisons. In the early years of the war Confederate authorities firmly discouraged all such schemes, and Secretary of War James A. Seddon announced, "The laws of war and morality, as well as Christian principles and sound policy forbid the use of such means." But after the Kilpatrick-Dahlgren raid in February and March of 1864, when the Confederates captured documents purporting to show that the invaders planned to burn Richmond and kill Jefferson Davis, more Southerners were willing to contemplate some form of retaliation against Lincoln.

In late September 1864, Thomas Nelson Conrad, a Confederate preacher and spy, led a team of three associates through the lines into Washington, where they hoped to seize the President as his carriage turned into the grounds of the Soldiers' Home. To their surprise they found Lincoln surrounded by a heavy guard. Possibly the War Department had been alerted by an anonymous letter the President received a few days earlier, warning him to "Keep watch and ward, with arms ready and at hand" against a likely attack on September 26. More likely Stanton ordered additional protection because of what seemed to be an attempt on Lincoln's life. While the President was returning to the Soldiers' Home one evening in August, someone fired a shot at him. Lincoln was unscathed because his frightened horse raced for safety, but the next day the soldiers in his guard found his "eight-dollar plug-hat" with a bullet hole through the crown. Unable to get near the President, Conrad remained in Washington until at least November 10, hoping for another opportunity, but he was obliged to report that his mission had been a "humiliating failure."

Lincoln never knew of Conrad's plan to kidnap him, but frequent threats and warnings reminded him of his vulnerability. Showing John W. Forney a pigeonhole in his office desk where he had filed more than eighty letters of this sort, he told the newspaperman, "I know I am in danger; but I am not going to worry over threats like these."

II

In the weeks after his reelection Lincoln felt he had more important matters to worry about. As he was about to begin a second term, party workers demanded rewards for their service in the campaign, and they harassed the President with applications for jobs. Once again, his office was filled with office-seekers, and sometimes, he said, it seemed that every visitor "darted at him, and with thumb and finger carried off a portion of his vitality." Overwhelmed, he asked Senator Daniel B. Clark of New Hampshire: "Can't you and others start a public sentiment in favor of making no changes in offices except for good and sufficient cause? It seems as though the bare thought of going through again what I did the first year here, would *crush* me." In the end, he concluded that he would change as few officeholders as possible, because, he observed, "To remove a man is very easy, but when I go to fill his place, there are *twenty* applicants, and of these I must make *nineteen* enemies."

But some changes were necessary in his own official family. Both Nicolay and Hay were exhausted after nearly four years of arduous service as his private secretaries, and Nicolay was in poor health. Lincoln decided to give Nicolay the lucrative appointment as United States consul at Paris and to make Hay the secretary of legation in France. He planned to offer the post of private secretary to Noah Brooks, the affable and politically astute correspondent of the *Sacramento Union*. Friends told him that Brooks "was capable of rendering him infinitely more substantial service" than Nicolay.

In the months between his election in November and his inauguration in March, the President had also to select four new members for his cabinet. He had already appointed William Dennison, who had presided over the National Union Convention at Baltimore, acting Postmaster General, and he now made that appointment permanent. Shortly after the election Edward Bates, now seventy-one years old, offered his resignation as Attorney General. To replace him Lincoln first turned to the highly efficient Joseph Holt, but the judge advocate general declined. At Holt's suggestion the President then gave the post to another loyal Kentuckian, James Speed, brother of Joshua F. Speed. Lincoln had never found John P. Usher a very satisfactory colleague, and when the Secretary of the Interior resigned on March 8, he welcomed an opportunity to replace him with Senator James Harlan of Iowa. Harlan had been one of the administration's strongest defenders in Congress, and the engagement of his daughter, Mary, to Robert Todd Lincoln strengthened his personal attachment to the President. In February, just before the beginning of the new term, Fessenden had also asked to be relieved of his duties as Secretary of the Treasury, so that he could return to the Senate. Lincoln wanted to replace him with Senator E. D. Morgan, the former governor of New York, who had been chairman of the Republican National Committee and had arranged for the Baltimore convention. When Morgan declined, the President selected the colorless but efficient comptroller of the currency, Hugh McCulloch.

Made over a period of months, these appointments, taken together, offered insight into the likely character of the second Lincoln administration. In contrast to the members of the original cabinet, none of these appointees was a major party leader and none had aspirations for the presidency. Lincoln now felt so strong that he did not have to surround himself with the heads of the warring Republican factions. He did not require ideological conformity of the men he chose; Dennison, Holt, and Speed became more or less affiliated with the Radical wing of the Republican party, but Morgan and McCulloch were strong Conservatives. The President did not want his cabinet members to be rubber stamps, and he was supremely confident of his ability to handle disagreement among his advisers. Unlike his original cabinet, his new appointees—like the holdovers, Seward, Stanton, and Welles—were warmly attached to Lincoln personally. He could now afford the luxury of a loyal cabinet.

No appointment at the President's disposal had potentially greater significance than that of Chief Justice of the United States to succeed Roger B. Taney. Lincoln was fully aware of the importance of his choice. Along with the associate justices he had already appointed—Noah Swayne, Samuel F. Miller, David Davis, and Stephen J. Field—the next Chief Justice would form a majority on the Court that would decide vital cases arising out of the Civil War. A lawyer himself, the President wanted to name a man deeply versed in the law, rather than an ideologue or a theorist; he hoped the new Chief Justice would recognize that "the function of courts is to decide *cases*—not *principles.*"

Lincoln had deliberately postponed announcing a choice until after the election. In the interval he went over in his mind the list of strongly recommended candidates and rejected one after another for what appeared good reasons: Bates was too old; Stanton could not be spared from the War Department; Evarts was not widely known; Blair could never be confirmed by the Senate.

In the end, as at the beginning, he was left with the name of Salmon P. Chase. The strongest argument against Chase was his unquenchable political ambition. "If he keeps on with the notion that he is destined to be President of the United States, and which in my judgment he will never be," Lincoln remarked to a senator, "he will never acquire that fame and influence as a Chief Justice which he would otherwise certainly attain." But the arguments for Chase were much stronger. During the next few years the most difficult cases likely to come before the Court were those involving the constitutionality of Lincoln's emancipation policies and the validity of the greenbacks with which the war was being financed. In selecting a judge, Lincoln explained to Representative George S. Boutwell of Massachusetts, "we cannot ask a man what he will do, and if we should, and he should answer us, we should despise him for it. Therefore we must take a man whose opinions are known." Chase's record, the President thought, put him unquestionably on the right side of these basic issues.

The President chose Chase to be Chief Justice because he thought him worthy—but he expected to receive political advantages from his choice. The appointment was part of his broader program of conciliating all the factions within the Republican party. He tried to make the selection of a Radical as painless as possible to Conservative Republicans. When Francis P. Blair, Sr., renewed his plea for the appointment of his son, the President agreed that Montgomery's qualifications were indeed estimable but said he had to consult his advisers before making a choice. "Although I may be stronger as an authority," he told the elder Blair, "yet if all the rest oppose, I must give way. . . . If the strongest horse in the team *would* go ahead, he *cannot,* if all *the rest hold back.*" Any insider would have recognized that Lincoln's statement was absurd; he did not consult the cabinet about the appointment and did not even tell them his choice until after he sent Chase's name to the Senate. But to the elder Blair his explanation made perfectly good sense. The President had learned how to make his hard decisions appear to be the work of a committee.

At the same time, he sought to secure the greatest possible advantage with the Radicals from the appointment. With Chase's partisans he gained credit for magnanimity in selecting a man who had been his sharp critic and a formidable political rival. Radicals credited rumors that the President had to force himself to make this choice, that, according to one report, rather than nominate Chase he would have swallowed the elk horn chair that the frontiersman Seth Kinman had given him. (Another had him say "he would sooner have eat flat irons than do it.") A few days after he sent Chase's name to the Senate, Lincoln candidly explained his purpose to Ward Lamon: "His *appointment* will satisfy the Radicals and after that they will not dare kick up against any appointment I may make." With unwonted optimism he added that it was hard to see how in the future they could "interpose a reasonable objection" to his policies.

III

His calculations proved exactly right, for the new session of Congress, which assembled on December 5, proved remarkably supportive of his policies.

Congressmen judged that it was not politically expedient to attack the policies of a President who had just been triumphantly reelected. Military victories further strengthened Lincoln's hand. The capture of Atlanta had probably determined the outcome of the 1864 election, and now, while Grant grimly pinned down Lee's army before Richmond, Sherman continued his march to the sea, cutting a swath of devastation through Georgia. Like Grant, Lincoln initially was *"anxious,* if not fearful" of Sherman's plan, and the draft of his annual message to Congress included a promise that "our cause could, if need be, survive the loss of the whole detached force." He deleted the phrase, doubtless because it sounded too pessimistic, but his doubts did not disappear until he received a telegram from Sherman on December 25: "I beg to present you as a Christmas gift the city of Savannah with 150 heavy guns and plenty of ammunition and also about 25000 bales of cotton." During the same time General Thomas's forces checked the Confederate invasion of Tennessee at Franklin (November 30) and on December 15–16 routed Hood's army in the decisive battle of Nashville. The double victory of Thomas and Sherman, Lincoln rejoiced, "brings those who sat in darkness, to see a great light."

The President probably did not intend to refer to members of Congress, but certainly their views underwent a remarkable transformation. Many who had hitherto strongly opposed Lincoln now muted their criticisms. When Henry Winter Davis, always implacable in his hatred of Lincoln and his administration, proposed to condemn the President for failing to adopt a more belligerent policy toward the French in Mexico, the President found an unlikely defender in Thaddeus Stevens, hitherto one of Lincoln's most vocal critics. Other Radicals chimed in to praise "an Executive who is doing his utmost in a patriotic spirit to preserve unimpaired all the institutions of our country" and to condemn those who, like Davis, wished to "impugn his integrity in any respect whatsoever." It did seem, as the *National Intelligencer* observed, that the country was entering on a new Era of Good Feeling.

In the spirit of conciliation Lincoln reached out for the support of Democrats as well as Republicans. His annual message contained an earnest plea to his political opponents to support the proposed constitutional amendment abolishing slavery throughout the United States. In the previous session of Congress the measure had failed to secure the required two-thirds vote in the House of Representatives, because all but four of the Democratic members voted against it. At Lincoln's urging, the National Union Convention had made the amendment a central plank in the platform on which he and a heavy Republican majority in the next Congress were elected. He now asked the lame-duck session of the Thirty-eighth Congress to reconsider the amendment. "Without questioning the wisdom or patriotism of those who stood in opposition," the President urged the Democrats to rethink their position. "Of course," he admitted, "the abstract question is not changed; but an intervening election shows, almost certainly, that the next Congress will pass the measure if this does not." Since adoption was simply a matter of time, he asked, "may we not agree that the sooner the better?" Arguing that "some deference shall be paid to the will of the majority, simply because it is the will of the majority," he appealed for support of the amendment now.

Not content with rhetorical exhortation, Lincoln used his personal authority and considerable charm to influence Democratic and border-state congressmen whose votes were in doubt. Not since 1862, when he tried hard to persuade border-state congressmen to support his gradual emancipation plan, had the President been so deeply involved in the legislative process. He worked closely with James M. Ashley of Ohio, the principal sponsor of the amendment in the House, to identify members who might be persuaded to support the amendment and invited them to the Executive Mansion. For instance, he had a long talk with Representative James S. Rollins of Missouri, who had voted against the amendment in June, and entreated him as an old Whig and follower of "that great statesman, Henry Clay," to join him now in supporting the measure. When Rollins said that he was ready to vote for the amendment, Lincoln pressed him to use his influence with the other congressmen from his state. "The passage of this amendment will clinch the whole subject," the President assured him; "it will bring the war, I have no doubt, rapidly to a close."

If Lincoln used other means of persuading congressmen to vote for the Thirteenth Amendment, his actions were not recorded. Conclusions about the President's role rested on gossip and later recollections like those of Thaddeus Stevens, who remarked, "The greatest measure of the nineteenth century was passed by corruption, aided and abetted by the purest man in America." Lincoln was told that he might win some support from New Jersey Democrats if he could persuade Charles Sumner to drop a bill to regulate the Camden & Amboy Railroad, but he declined to intervene, not on grounds of principle but because, he said, "I can do nothing with Mr. Sumner in these matters." One New Jersey Democrat, well known as a lobbyist for the Camden & Amboy, who had voted against the amendment in July, did abstain in the final vote, but it cannot be proved that Lincoln influenced his change.

Whatever the President's role, in the final balloting more than two-thirds of the House members voted for the Thirteenth Amendment and submitted it to the states for ratification. Celebrating, the House adjourned after inadvertently sending the resolution to the President, who happily signed it on February 1. He was untroubled when senators pointed out that, according to a Supreme Court decision of 1798, presidential approval was not required for constitutional amendments. He was convinced that, with or without his signature, the Thirteenth Amendment would root out "the original disturbing cause" of the rebellion and would fully settle all questions about the legal validity of the Emancipation Proclamation. Finally the country had "a King's cure for all the evils."

IV

One important bit of assistance Lincoln gave to the adoption of the Thir-teenth Amendment he was not prepared to make public at the time. During the last days of debate in the House of Representatives, rumors spread that Confederate commissioners were on their way to Washington to negotiate a settlement, that peace was at hand. Fearing defections among the reluctant supporters of the measure, Ashley anxiously asked the President whether there was any truth in the reports. Choosing his words with care, Lincoln replied: "So far as I know, there are no peace commissioners in the city, or likely to be in it." His note calmed the Democrats, who, as he said later, "would have gone off in a tangent at the last moment had they smelt Peace."

In fact, at that very moment a Confederate peace commission, consisting of Alexander H. Stephens, the Vice President of the Confederacy, John A. Campbell, the Confederate assistant secretary of war, and Robert M. T. Hunter, the prominent Virginia Confederate senator, was crossing into Union lines—but at City Point, not Washington.

Behind their visit lay some careful planning on Lincoln's part. Earlier he had strongly opposed any negotiation with the Confederates, refusing to meet with Stephens in 1863 and as recently as July insisting on terms he knew the Confederate emissaries at Niagara Falls could not accept. Talk of peace, he then thought, would lower army morale; worse, it might lead to an armistice that, in effect, gave the Confederacy its independence. But now things had changed. The overwhelming victories of Sherman and Thomas in the West, coupled with the unremitting devastation that Grant and Sheri-dan were wreaking in Virginia, had weakened the Southern will to fight, and there were strong indications that the Confederacy might be coming to pieces. Grant believed that half of Lee's army would desert if there was an armistice. The governors of Georgia and North Carolina were openly talking of making a separate peace; the Committee on Foreign Affairs of the Confed-erate House of Representatives debated a resolution creating a peace com-mission; Representative Henry S. Foote demanded a "cessation of hostilities and restoration of peace" and declared that only Jefferson Davis stood in the way of ending the war.

Lincoln's annual message to Congress in December 1864 sought to take advantage of this disarray among the Confederates. After what he had learned through the Jaquess-Gilmore mission, he was confident "that no attempt at negotiation with the insurgent leader"—whenever possible he avoided Jefferson Davis's name and never referred to him as President of the Confederate States—"could result in any good. He would accept nothing short of severance of the Union—precisely what we will not and cannot give." But, the President continued: "What is true . . . of him who heads the insurgent cause, is not necessarily true of those who follow. Although he cannot reaccept the Union, they can." To encourage these second-level Confederate leaders, the President promised generous terms: "They can, at any moment, have peace simply by laying down their arms and submitting to the national authority under the Constitution." But the generous program of amnesty and pardon, which he had offered in December 1863 and which was still "open to all," would not remain so indefinitely. "The time may come—probably will come," he said, "when . . . more rigorous measures . . . shall be adopted."

Several intermediaries attempted to follow the lead the President offered. James R. Gilmore wanted to try another peace mission, this time to North Carolina, where he was sure he could persuade Governor Zebulon B. Vance to bring the state back into the Union, but Lincoln did not think this approach expedient. The plan of a former Illinois legislator evoked a more favorable response from the White House. Backed by Browning, James W. Singleton, a leading Peace Democrat, secured Lincoln's permission to go to Richmond in order to sound Confederate opinion on ending the war. Singleton spent two pleasant weeks in the Confederate capital and had interviews with Jefferson Davis, Robert E. Lee, and others. He returned to tell the President that Southerners were eager for peace on generous terms but that they were unwilling to give up slavery except for "a fair compensation coupled with other liberal terms of reconstruction secured by Constitutional Amendments." Lincoln listened, but his faith in Singleton, always slight, dwindled when it became clear that he was less interested in peace than in buying up huge quantities of Southern cotton and tobacco.

The most conspicuous effort at peacemaking was that of Francis P. Blair, Sr., who reached Richmond on January 11. He had wanted to go earlier, but Lincoln had refused permission, saying, "Come to me when Savannah falls." When the President did allow the elder statesman to cross the lines, he declined to talk with him about his project or to offer any instructions; Blair was on his own. In a long interview with Jefferson Davis, who had been a close friend of his family before the war, Blair argued that slavery was no longer "an insurmountible [sic] obstruction to pacification," since the recent decision to enroll blacks in the Confederate army necessarily entailed giving them freedom. The reunion of the North and South was now inevitable. Only the machinations of European monarchs could prevent it, and the activities of France's puppet ruler of Mexico, Maximilian, showed how real was this danger. Davis could remove this threat by agreeing to an armistice with the Union and removing his armies to Texas, where—as dictator, if necessary—he could lead the fight to drive out the French invaders. Doubtless many Northern soldiers would volunteer to join his forces, and Blair offered the services of his son, General Frank Blair.

According to the elder Blair, Davis rose to the bait. He doubted—or perhaps it was Blair who doubted—the good faith of Seward in any negotiations, but he was willing to accept Blair's assurance that if Lincoln "plights his faith to any man . . . , he will maintain his word inviolably." He gave Blair a letter to take to Washington, promising to appoint a commission that

WITH CHARITY FOR ALL • 557

would enter into negotiations "with a view to secure peace to the two countries."

This was not at all what Lincoln had in mind. He wanted to undermine the authority of the Confederate government and to fragment the Confederate state, not to negotiate with its leader as an equal. Promptly he sent Blair back to Richmond with the message that he would be willing to receive a Confederate commission that looked toward "securing peace to the people of our one common country."

That should have been that. But on both sides of the battle lines sentiment for peace was now too strong to be derailed. Under pressure, Davis named three leading advocates of negotiation—Stephens, Campbell, and Hunter— as commissioners authorized not merely to secure peace between the two countries but to discuss "the issues involved in the existing war." Lincoln and Stanton were ready to refuse to receive the commissioners because they would not concede, even for purposes of discussion, that the Confederacy was a separate nation. At this point Grant, who was increasingly eager to finish off the war and who was not attuned to the niceties of diplomatic negotiations, intervened. He persuaded the commissioners to delete from their instructions the reference to two separate countries and wired to Washington that he hoped Lincoln could meet with them.

Agreeing with Grant that to send the three Confederates back to Richmond "without any expression from any one in authority" would be impolitic, Lincoln forthwith joined Seward at Fort Monroe for a conference from which he expected little. On the morning of February 3, Stephens, Hunter, and Campbell came aboard the President's steamer, the *River Queen,* at Hampton Roads for an interview of several hours. Lincoln had not seen Stephens for sixteen years, when they were both Whig members of the House of Representatives, and he greeted the Confederate Vice President with a smile and a handshake. Watching the ninety-pound Stephens take off his thick gray woolen overcoat, his long wool muffler, and several shawls, he laughed, "Never have I seen so small a nubbin come out of so much husk."

The five men agreed that the discussion was to be informal, that no papers or documents would be read, and that no notes would be taken. Stephens opened by asking, "Well, Mr. President, is there no way of putting an end to the present trouble, and bringing about a restoration of the general good feeling and harmony . . . between the different States and Sections of the country?" Thus at the outset he avoided making an issue of whether there was now one country or two.

Lincoln replied "that there was but one way that he knew of, and that was, for those who were resisting the laws of the Union to cease that resistance."

The Confederates then began to explore the path that Blair had apparently opened. Stephens asked whether, in order to give time for passions to cool, there was "no Continental question" that could temporarily engage the attention of both sides to the present conflict? In short, just as Blair had suggested, could there not be an armistice, during which Southern and Northern armies could join in driving the French out of Mexico? Lincoln replied bluntly that he had not authorized Blair's mission and that he could not consider any proposition of an armistice that was not based "upon a pledge first given, for the ultimate restoration of the Union."

Since Stephens was obviously unwilling to give up the possibility of a Mexican adventure, Seward suggested that he develop what he called a "philosophical basis" for that scheme, and the Confederate Vice President did so at considerable length, discoursing on the importance of maintaining the Monroe Doctrine. Seward raised objections to his arguments, and Hunter made it clear that he differed with Stephens and thought the Southern people "would be found unwilling to kindle a new war with the French on any such pretence." All three men realized that the discussion was pointless since, as Stephens said, "Lincoln had virtually closed all further conference on that subject."

Campbell then asked what terms of reconstruction would be offered if the Confederate states agreed to return to the Union. Lincoln replied that once resistance to the national authority ceased, "the States would be immediately restored to their practical relations to the Union"—a phrase that he used repeatedly. But he made it clear that he would not enter into negotiations while Southerners were in arms against the United States. When Hunter attempted to show that governments had often entered into agreements with rebels and pointed out that Charles I of England had frequently negotiated with those who were fighting against him, the President responded tartly: "I do not profess to be posted in history. On all such matters I will turn you over to Seward. All I distinctly recollect about the case of Charles I, is, that he lost his head in the end."

As to slavery, Seward reminded the Confederates of Lincoln's pledge, made most recently in his annual message to Congress: "I shall not attempt to retract or modify the Emancipation Proclamation, nor shall I return to slavery any person who is free by the terms of that Proclamation, or by any of the Acts of Congress." The Secretary then dropped a bombshell by telling the commissioners that Congress had just submitted the Thirteenth Amendment to the states for ratification. Seeing that the Confederates were rattled by the news, Lincoln turned to Stephens: "I'll tell you what I would do if I were in your place: I would go home and get the Governor of the State [of Georgia] to call the Legislature together, and get them to recall all the State troops from the war; elect Senators and Members to Congress, and ratify this Constitutional Amendment *prospectively,* so as to take effect—say in five years. Such a ratification would be valid in my opinion."

Hunter gagged at Lincoln's terms, which he saw as nothing but "an unconditional surrender on the part of the Confederate States and their people." Shortly afterward Stephens concluded that it was "entirely fruitless" to have further discussion of a peace settlement, and he turned to the vexed problem of the exchange of prisoners, which Lincoln said he had placed entirely in Grant's hands. On leaving the *River Queen,* the Confederate Vice President urged the President to think again about his plan for an armistice and a Mexican adventure, and Lincoln replied, "Well, Stephens, I will re-consider it, but I do not think my mind will change, but I will re-consider."

The Hampton Roads conference, as Lincoln reported to Congress, "ended without result." It was a failure, as he had expected it to be, because he would not negotiate with Jefferson Davis. But in the course of the conversations Lincoln made two remarkable suggestions that showed the direction of his thinking about ending the war. Discussing possible terms of reconstruction, Stephens asked what would be the status of the Southern slaves who had not been freed by the Emancipation Proclamation. He and Seward agreed that only about 200,000 slaves had up to that point gained their freedom. According to Campbell, Lincoln said that there were different opinions about the effects of his proclamation: "Some believed that it was not operative at all; others that it operated only within the circle which had been occupied by the army and others believed that it was operative everywhere in the States to which it applied." This was a question that only the courts could decide, but, if Stephens's later report can be credited, the President added: "His own opinion was, that as the Proclamation was a *war measure,* and would have effect only from its being an exercise of the war power, as soon as the war ceased, it would be inoperative for the future. It would be held to apply only to such slaves as had come under its operation while it was in active exercise."

Stephens's record would be highly suspect were it not confirmed by other, more contemporary evidence that Lincoln did not now insist upon the end of slavery as a precondition for peace. He told Representative Singleton that his "To Whom It May Concern" letter to the Confederate commissioners at Niagara Falls had "put him in a false position—that he did not mean to make the abolition of slavery a condition" of peace and that "he would be willing to grant peace with an amnesty, and restoration of the union, leaving slavery to abide the decisions of judicial tribunals." On the day before Christmas, Lincoln repeated these views to Browning, who was advising Singleton; he declared "that he had never entertained the purpose of making the abolition of slavery a condition precedent to the termination of the war, and the restoration of the Union."

If these conversations can be believed, the President of the United States who had demanded emancipation as a precondition for negotiations in July 1864, who had insisted that his party's platform include a call for abolition, who had pledged that he would never retract a word of his proclamations or send a man back into slavery, who had just been working closely with Congress to secure the adoption of the Thirteenth Amendment, had now changed his mind about eradicating slavery. Since Lincoln himself left no record of any of these interviews, it is possible that all the witnesses distorted his message. But it is more likely—though this can only be a speculation—

that Lincoln's remarks stemmed from his realization that slavery was already dead. His principal concern now was that the war might drag on for at least another year. His purpose was to undermine the Jefferson Davis administration by appealing to those "followers" mentioned in his annual message to Congress. He wanted to raise their hopes, if necessary through a campaign of misinformation. Clearly the three Confederate commissioners at Hampton Roads would have an easier task in persuading other Southerners to lay down their arms if they promised that at least the remnants of their "peculiar institution" could still be saved.

A second suggestion that Lincoln made to the Confederate commissioners at Hampton Roads reinforces this view of his intent. Pledging that he would be generous in restoring Southern property seized under the Confiscation Acts, he went on to say, according to Stephens and Hunter, "that he would be willing to be taxed to remunerate the Southern people for their slaves." He had all along favored compensated emancipation, and he believed that many Northerners were "in favor of an appropriation as high as Four Hundred Millions of Dollars for this purpose." Seward strongly dissented, showing his impatience by getting up and pacing the floor, exclaiming "that in his opinion the United States had done enough in expending so much money on the war for the abolition of slavery," but Lincoln said that both sections were responsible: "If it was wrong in the South to hold slaves, it was wrong in the North to carry on the slave trade and sell them to the South." He "could give no assurance—enter into no stipulation" on this subject, but he told the Confederates that he could mention persons, "whose names would astonish you, who are willing to do this, if the war shall now cease without further expense, and with the abolition of slavery as stated."

That this proposal was not a figment of the Confederates' imagination is attested by the proposal that Lincoln drew up when he returned to Washington, which asked Congress to appropriate $400,000,000 to be distributed to the Southern states in proportion to their slave population. Half would be paid by April 1, if all resistance to the national authority ceased, and the remaining half by July 1, provided that the Thirteenth Amendment was ratified. This astonishing document told much of Lincoln's generosity of spirit and of his understanding of the problems the South faced in making the transition from a slave society to a free society. But it revealed even more his almost desperate sense of urgency to bring the war to a speedy end.

The President laid his plan before the cabinet at an evening session on February 5, earnestly defending it "as a measure of strict and simple economy." "How long has this war lasted, and how long do you suppose it will still last?" he asked his advisers. Answering his own question, he told them: "We cannot hope that it will end in less than a hundred days. We are now spending three millions a day, and that will equal the full amount I propose to pay, to say nothing of the lives lost and property destroyed." But his colleagues were not convinced. Welles thought the President's wish to conciliate the South was commendable, "but there may be such a thing as so overdoing as to cause a distrust or adverse feeling." "The Rebels," he predicted, "would misconstrue it if [the offer was] made," doubtless taking it as evidence of Northern weakness or war-weariness. Anyway, as Fessenden noted, it was "not advisable" to submit the proposal to Congress now, "because there would probably be no chance of its being adopted before the adjournment." The cabinet members felt strongly "that the only way to effectually end the war was by force of arms, and that until the war was thus ended no proposition to pay money would come from us." "You are all against me," Lincoln said sadly, and he reluctantly gave up his proposal, noting, as he folded the papers away, that they "were drawn up and submitted to the Cabinet and unanimously disapproved by them."

V

All along Lincoln believed that the surest way to undermine the Confederacy was by setting up loyal governments in the Southern states as they fell under the control of the Union armies. His terms for reconstruction were both generous and vague, for he was thinking less of the status of the South after the war than of means to stop the fighting. For this reason he was not greatly troubled when his military commanders failed to follow the letter of the law in setting up new Unionist regimes in the Southern states, nor was he interested in the details of registration and voting requirements. What he wanted was a series of seemingly viable loyal governments in several Southern states that could present a believable alternative to the Confederacy.

That focus had led to fierce disputes with Radicals in his own party, who were worried about what would happen in the South after the war—about the continuing economic and political power of the Southern planter class, the protection of the civil rights of the freedmen, and the status of black labor in the postwar South. The President was not indifferent to any of these concerns, but he preferred to postpone discussion of such divisive issues until the defeat of the Confederacy. In July these differences between President and Congress had come to a head when the legislators refused to recognize the reconstruction governments he had set up in Louisiana and Arkansas and, instead, insisted on their own program in the Wade-Davis bill, which the President vetoed.

Now, during the winter of 1864–1865, the President and the Congress faced precisely the same issues—but the outcome was remarkably different. As the Congress assembled, Lincoln let it be known that he would veto any reconstruction bill that did not recognize the free-state government he had been carefully nurturing in Louisiana. Instead of leading to a crisis, his insistence produced a compromise. On December 15, Representative Ashley, who was also in charge of the Thirteenth Amendment, introduced a bill designed to please both Conservatives and Radicals, one that he hoped the Congress would approve and the President sign. It extended congressional recognition to Lincoln's 10 percent government in Louisiana but required the other Southern states to follow the procedures announced in the ill-fated Wade-Davis bill—namely, that voters must take the "iron-clad" oath that they had never supported the rebellion and that more than 50 percent of the eligible voters must favor any new, reconstructed government. In addition, Ashley's bill called for Negro suffrage, a provision that Radicals increasingly insisted was the only way to ensure the loyalty of the Southern states.

Over the next weeks Ashley's compromise measure underwent intense scrutiny from all parties. For the more extreme Radicals, Charles Sumner accepted the proposal, grumbling about the readmission of Louisiana—"which ought not to be done"—but rejoicing that giving suffrage to blacks in the other Southern states was "an immense political act." Montgomery Blair and N. P. Banks, both Conservatives, went over the measure with the President, who thought the provision for black jurors and voters "might be objectionable to some." Agreeing that this clause "would simply throw the Government into the hands of the blacks, as the white people under that arrangement would refuse to vote," Banks promised that the objectionable juror clause would be removed. Congressmen of various persuasions weighed in with suggestions for change, which ranged from simply admitting Louisiana and Arkansas to insisting that all new Southern state constitutions must guarantee "equality of civil rights before the law . . . to all persons."

Obligingly Ashley amended his bill again and again in the hope of attracting a majority. He even added one remarkable provision that would recognize the existing Confederate governments in the Southern states as legitimate if they submitted to the United States, repudiated the Confederate debt, and ratified the Thirteenth Amendment. But no combination worked, and on February 21, Ashley was obliged to give up, conceding that "no bill providing for the reorganization of loyal State government in the rebel States can pass this Congress."

The defeat of Ashley's bill was a major victory for Lincoln. Seven months earlier every Republican in the Senate and all but six Republicans in the House had voted for the Wade-Davis bill, to take the process of reconstruction out of the President's hands. Only Lincoln's pocket veto had kept the reconstruction process under the control of the executive branch. Now, in a remarkable turnabout, the Congress failed to adopt any reconstruction legislation. The approaching end of the congressional session left the reconstruction entirely in Lincoln's hands. Lamenting the change, Henry Winter Davis, the arch-Radical who was now a lame-duck congressman, mourned: "Sir, when I came into Congress ten years ago, this was a Government of law. I have lived to see it a Government of personal will. Congress has dwindled from a power to dictate law and the policy of the Government to a commission to audit accounts and appropriate moneys to enable the Executive to execute his will and not ours."

The November elections were principally responsible for the change. It was one thing for Republican congressmen to break with the head of their own party when he appeared to be a failure, whose bid for reelection was doomed to disgraceful defeat. It was quite another to defy a President recently reelected by a huge majority with a clear popular mandate.

Republicans also found it easier to go along with the President's wishes on reconstruction because circumstances had changed since the previous summer. While the Congress was debating the proposed Thirteenth Amendment and Ashley's reconstruction bill, it was also moving, with the President's blessing, to create the new Bureau of Refugees, Freedmen, and Abandoned Lands, intended to supervise the transition from slavery to freedom in the South. This Freedmen's Bureau Act, which gave the federal authorities guardianship over the recently emancipated slaves in order to protect them from exploitation by their former owners, made it easier for Republican congressmen to accept even imperfect reconstruction governments in the South, since they would be shorn of much of their power.

The adoption of the Thirteenth Amendment provided another incentive for Republicans to recognize the reconstruction regimes Lincoln had established. Before that amendment could go into effect, it had to be ratified by twenty-seven of the thirty-six states. Illinois, as Lincoln proudly reported, began the process on February 1, and the other Northern states were sure to follow promptly. The border states of Maryland, West Virginia, and Missouri had all now abolished slavery, and they were expected to ratify it. But slavery persisted in Delaware and Kentucky, and the outcome in those states was doubtful. Even if they both approved, the votes of two additional states were needed—and those votes could only come from states that had been in the Confederacy. The most likely possibilities were Louisiana, Arkansas, and Tennessee. By recognizing the regimes that Lincoln had created in those states, congressmen could ensure the speedy death of slavery throughout the nation.

Congressmen, then, were in a receptive mood toward presidential reconstruction, and Lincoln, who had had very little to do with earlier congressional deliberations on the subject, now presented his case with great skill and force. He addressed the concerns of Radicals, who were beginning to argue that the only way to protect the rights of African-Americans in the South was to give them the ballot. Lincoln assured William D. Kelley that he, too, now believed in Negro suffrage, at least for the better educated and those who had served in the Union armies, and he showed the Pennsylvania congressman a copy of his letter to Governor Hahn of Louisiana, suggesting limited enfranchisement of blacks. Radical Senator B. Gratz Brown also saw a copy of that letter and quoted from it in urging his Missouri constituents to accept enfranchisement of Negroes as an "imperative necessity admitted on all sides."

To present to Congress the more attractive side of the reconstruction government in Louisiana, Lincoln detained N. P. Banks in Washington for six months so that the general, who had once been Speaker of the House of Representatives and still kept up his political contacts in the capital, could lobby in behalf of the regime he had helped to create. The President was also prepared to use brass-knuckle tactics if necessary. When the Radical abolitionists Wendell Phillips and George Luther Stearns tried to organize a protest against recognition of the Louisiana regime, they got nowhere. Congressmen told them, "A.L. has just now all the great offices to give afresh and can[']t be successfully resisted. He is dictator."

This combination of forces was strong enough to enable Lincoln to keep control of the reconstruction process in his own hands—but it was not quite enough to secure congressional approval of his actions. After the failure of Ashley's reconstruction bill in mid-February, administration supporters moved to secure the admission of Louisiana. Lyman Trumbull, the chairman of the Senate Judiciary Committee, took the lead. In the past he had often been a severe, even waspish, critic of the President, but his attitude had remarkably softened since November. He seemed to have experienced what Ben Wade called "the most miraculous conversion that has taken place since St. Paul's time"; possibly he recalled that his next race for the Senate would occur while Lincoln was still in the White House. At any rate, Trumbull conferred with the President about recognizing the reconstructed government of Louisiana and seating its two recently elected senators. As usual, Lincoln cut through the legal verbiage that surrounded these issues and put the issue plainly: "Can Louisiana be brought into proper practical relations with the Union, sooner, by *admitting* or by *rejecting* the proposed Senators?"

A clear majority of the Republicans in the Senate joined Trumbull in following the President's wishes, but a small group of Radicals resolved to block the move. Joined by Wade, Grimes, and a few other Radicals, Sumner began a filibuster against recognizing Louisiana that often deteriorated into an angry shouting match with the President's supporters. He blasted "the pretended State government in Louisiana" as "a mere seven-months' abortion, begotten by the bayonet in criminal conjunction with the spirit of caste, and born before its time, rickety, unformed, unfinished—whose continued existence will be a burden, a reproach, and a wrong." The Radicals, who opposed the Louisiana regime because it did not give African-Americans the vote, worked in close cooperation with the Senate Democrats, who wanted to deny the suffrage to blacks; they shared only opposition to recognizing Lincoln's government in Louisiana. Because of pressing business that the Senate had to attend to before adjourning, Trumbull was forced to give way, and the admission of Louisiana was defeated.

Lincoln was angry with Sumner. "He hopes to succeed in beating the President so as to change this Government from its original form and make it a strong centralized power," he growled. According to Washington insiders, the cordial personal relations that had existed between the senator and Lincoln were at an end now that Sumner had "kicked the pet scheme of the

President down the marble steps of the Senate Chamber." But Lincoln did not permit a difference over policy to become a personal quarrel; he not only genuinely liked and admired Sumner, but he needed his support in the future. Only a few days after Sumner had talked the Louisiana bill to death, the President invited him to the inaugural ball, where the senator promenaded with Mrs. Lincoln, richly dressed in white moire ornamented with lace, on his arm. The President could afford to be generous because he, like nearly everyone else, was certain that the next Congress would admit Louisiana. As the *New York Herald* predicted, "This extraordinary railsplitter enters upon his second term the unquestioned master of the situation in reference to American affairs, at home and abroad."

VI

Inauguration Day, March 4, 1865, began wet and windy. It had been raining for several days in Washington, and the streets were a sea of mud at least ten inches deep. During the previous week delegations from all parts of the country had been arriving in the capital, and all the hotels were full, with Willard's accommodating overflow guests on cots in the hallways and parlors. Despite the abominable weather, a crowd began to gather at the east front of the Capitol before ten o'clock, and by the time the ceremonies began at noon, the spectators were sodden. Women, wearing their long, cumbersome dresses, were in a "most wretched, wretched plight," Noah Brooks observed; "crinoline was smashed, skirts bedaubed, and moire antique, velvet, laces, and such dry goods were streaked with mud from end to end."

First came the swearing in of the Vice President, which took place in the Senate chamber. Andrew Johnson had hoped to remain in Tennessee to witness the installation of a new, loyal state government under a constitution with "the foul blot of Slavery erased from her escutcheon," but Lincoln and his advisers felt that it was unsafe for him not to be in Washington on March 4. Exhausted from the long trip, unsteady from a recent bout of typhoid fever, Johnson asked for some whiskey to calm his nerves. He was especially sensitive to alcohol, and the drink went to his head. In a long, maudlin speech he boasted of his plebeian origins and reminded the embarrassed members of the Supreme Court, the cabinet, and even the diplomatic corps —"with all your fine feathers and gewgaws"—that they were but creatures of the people. Lincoln had to sit silently through Johnson's ramblings, and an observer noted that he "closed his eyes and seemed to retire into himself as though beset by melancholy reflections." When Johnson finally finished and took the oath, the President leaned over to the parade marshal and whispered, "Do not let Johnson speak outside."

Then the presidential party moved onto the platform at the east front of the Capitol. As Lincoln's tall figure appeared, "cheer upon cheer arose, bands blatted upon the air, and flags waved all over the scene." After the sergeant-at-arms of the Senate quieted the crowd, the President stepped forward holding a half sheet of foolscap on which his inaugural address was printed in two columns. At just that moment the sun burst through the clouds and flooded the scene with light; Chief Justice Chase saw it as "an auspicious omen of the dispersion of the clouds of war and the restoration of the clear sun light of prosperous peace."

In his clear, high-pitched voice that reached even the outer edges of the huge crowd, Lincoln read one of the shortest inaugural addresses in American history (703 words) and also the most memorable. He began by reminding his listeners that at this time there was "less occasion for an extended address" outlining policy than there had been at his first inauguration. During the past four years of war, he noted in a tone of weariness, "public declarations have been constantly called forth on every point and phase of the great contest." Consequently he could devote the larger part of his address to an explanation of the origins of the conflict and an examination of its significance.

It was a remarkably impersonal address. After the opening paragraph, Lincoln did not use the first-person-singular pronoun, nor did he refer to anything he had said or done during the previous four years. Notably lacking from his brief account of how the war began was any attribution of blame. "All dreaded it—all sought to avert it." But one of the parties to the conflict —throughout, he carefully avoided referring to the South or the Confederacy—"would *make* war rather than let the nation survive; and the other would *accept* war rather than let it perish." Interrupted by a burst of applause at this point, Lincoln continued, "And the war came." Slavery was, "somehow, the cause of the war." It was the one institution that divided the nation. The people of both sections had shared values; they "read the same Bible, and pray to the same God, and each invokes His aid against the other." In his one deviation from impartiality between the sections, Lincoln felt obliged to remark that "it may seem strange that any men should dare to ask a just God's assistance in wringing their bread from the sweat of other men's faces," but he promptly added, "Let us judge not that we be not judged."

Lincoln then sought, both for himself and for the American people, an explanation of why the war was so protracted. His answer showed no trace of any late-at-night anguish over his own responsibility for the conflict. If there was guilt, the burden had been shifted from his shoulders to those of a Higher Power. The war continued because "the Almighty has His own purposes," which are different from men's purposes. This, Lincoln said later, was "a truth which I thought needed to be told," because to deny it was "to deny that there is a God governing the world."

He might have put his argument in terms of the doctrine of necessity, in which he had long believed; but that was not a dogma accepted by most Americans. In an earlier private meditation he had concluded that it was "probably true—that God wills this contest, and wills that it shall not end," thinking it "quite possible that God's purpose is something different from the purpose of either party" to the conflict. But that was too gnostic a doctrine to gain general credence. Addressing a devout, Bible-reading public, Lincoln knew he would be understood when he invoked the familiar doctrine of exact retribution, the belief that the punishment for a violation of God's law would equal the offense itself. Quoting from Matthew, he announced, "Woe unto the world because of offences! for it must needs be that offences come; but woe to that man by whom the offence cometh!" That warning might seem to apply only to slaveholders, but Lincoln had consistently held Northerners as well as Southerners responsible for introducing slavery and for protecting it under the Constitution. Consequently, as God now willed to remove the offense of slavery, he gave "to both North and South, this terrible war, as the woe due to those by whom the offence came."

How long, then, would the war last, and when would retribution cease? In the summer of 1864, Lincoln had said that the war might go on for three more years. More recently he had spoken of another year, or at least another hundred days, of fighting. Now he offered no promises. Early in the address he said flatly, "With high hope for the future, no prediction in regard to it is ventured." Returning to the subject, he made no firmer pledge: "Fondly do we hope—fervently do we pray—that this mighty scourge of war may speedily pass away." Then he went on to add one of the most terrible statements ever made by an American public official: "Yet, if God wills that it continue, until all the wealth piled by the bond-man's two hundred and fifty years of unrequited toil shall be sunk, and until every drop of blood drawn with the lash, shall be paid by another drawn with the sword, as was said three thousand years ago, so still it must be said, 'the judgments of the Lord, are true and righteous altogether.' "

This was a harsh doctrine, but it was one that absolved both the South and the North of guilt for the never ending bloodshed. And, by leaving the execution of this sanguinary judgment to the Almighty, Lincoln could turn in his final paragraph to the more limited responsibilities of mortals. Here he had a chance to voice his deeply held sense of the nation's debt to those who had fought, suffered, and died in the army and navy. Recently he had expressed that feeling in a beautiful letter to Mrs. Lydia Bixby, a Boston widow who, he was told, was "the mother of five sons who have died gloriously on the field of battle." "I pray that our Heavenly Father may assuage the anguish of your bereavement," he wrote her, "and leave you only the cherished memory of the loved and lost, and the solemn pride that must be yours, to have laid so costly a sacrifice upon the altar of Freedom." Now he returned to that theme, promising "to care for him who shall have borne the battle, and for his widow, and his orphan."

With soaring eloquence Lincoln concluded his address: "With malice toward none; with charity for all; with firmness in the right, as God gives us to see the right, let us strive on to finish the work we are in; to bind up the nation's wounds; . . . to do all which may achieve and cherish a just, and a lasting peace, among ourselves, and with all nations."

After immense applause, Lincoln turned to Chief Justice Chase, and, laying his right hand on an open page of the Bible, repeated after him the oath of office, ending with an emphatic "So help me God!" He then kissed the Bible and, as a salvo of artillery boomed and the crowd cheered, he began his second term.

Except for Copperhead journals like the *Chicago Times,* which denounced the speech as "so slip shod, so loose-joined, so puerile" that "by the side of it, mediocrity is superb," most newspapers gave Lincoln's second inaugural address a respectful if somewhat puzzled reception. In general, English editors praised it more highly than did the Americans. But the Washington *National Intelligencer* felt the President's final words, "equally distinguished for patriotism, statesmanship, and benevolence," deserved "to be printed in gold."

Lincoln was not troubled that his address was not immediately popular. He recognized that "men are not flattered by being shown that there has been a difference of purpose between the Almighty and them." But he was pleased when it received praise. He positively beamed when Frederick Douglass, who was in the throng at the White House reception after the inauguration, pronounced it "a sacred effort." As Lincoln told Thurlow Weed, he expected it "to wear as well as—perhaps better than—any thing I have produced." "Lots of wisdom in that document, I suspect," he said as he filed away his manuscript.

VII

Lincoln was so exhausted after the inauguration ceremonies that he took to his bed for a few days. There was nothing organically wrong. Despite his sedentary work, he continued to be a physically powerful man, but he often felt terribly tired. For some time he had been losing weight, and strangers now noted his thinness rather than his height. Though he was only fifty-six, observers at the second inauguration thought he looked very old. His photographs showed a face heavily lined, with sunken cheeks. Joshua Speed, who had not seen the President for some time, was shocked to find him looking so "jaded and weary." "Speed," said Lincoln, "I am a little alarmed about myself; just feel my hand." It was, remembered Speed, "cold and clammy," and his feet were obviously cold, too, for he put them so near the fire that they steamed.

Mary worried about his health. "Poor Mr. Lincoln is looking so broken-hearted, so completely worn out," she told Elizabeth Keckley, her dressmaker, "I fear he will not get through the next four years." For months she had been urging her husband to keep a lighter schedule, and in order to get him away from his desk she encouraged him to go to the theater frequently. He attended both Grover's Theatre on E Street between Thirteenth and Fourteenth streets, and Ford's Theatre on Tenth Street, between E and F streets. Usually Mary accompanied him, but occasionally he went with Tad or with one or both of his secretaries, and occasionally the Lincolns made up a small party of friends to occupy the presidential box. He enjoyed all sorts of theatrical entertainment, including Barney Williams, the blackface minstrel and Irish comedian, and he attended numerous plays that were little noted nor long remembered, like *Leah,* starring Avonia Jones, and *The Marble Heart,* featuring the brilliant young actor John Wilkes Booth.

Shakespeare's plays appealed to him most. As a boy, he had memorized the soliloquies contained in William Scott's *Lessons in Elocution,* and in Springfield he owned and frequently read his own copy of Shakespeare's works, but he had never seen Shakespeare performed on the stage until he became President. After that he rarely missed an opportunity. In February and March 1864, at one of the most dangerous periods of the war, he took time off from his duties to see the great tragedian Edwin Booth perform in *Richard III, Julius Caesar, The Merchant of Venice,* and *Hamlet.*

He enjoyed them all. Shakespeare's wit delighted him, and he was enchanted by the magic of his language. The great tragedies, with their stories of linked ambition and guilt, especially appealed to him. As an often lonely leader, he found it easy to identify with Shakespeare's heroes; he could sympathize with their fears and understand their anxieties. "It matters not to me whether Shakespeare be well or ill acted," he remarked; "with him the thought suffices." Still, he had decided ideas about how the plays should be performed. He insisted, for instance, that the choicest part of *Hamlet* was not the familiar "To be or not to be" soliloquy but King Claudius's meditation "O my offence is rank, it smells to heaven."

Once his fondness for Shakespeare led to an embarrassment. In August 1863, after seeing James H. Hackett as Falstaff in *Henry IV,* he wrote the actor commending his performance and expressing the hope that he would have a chance to make his personal acquaintance when he next performed in Washington. The President went on to say that he had never read some of Shakespeare's plays but that he had gone over others—mentioning *King Lear, Richard III, Henry VIII, Hamlet,* and *Macbeth*—"perhaps as frequently as any unprofessional reader." "I think nothing equals Macbeth," he added. "It is wonderful." Though the letter was intended to be personal, Hackett printed and distributed it, and newspapers had a field day, criticizing the President as would-be dramatic critic. To Hackett's apology Lincoln replied that the hostile comments "constitute a fair specimen of what has occurred to me through life." He added, in one of his most perfectly balanced sentences: "I have endured a great deal of ridicule without much malice; and have received a great deal of kindness, not quite free from ridicule. I am used to it."

Mary Lincoln also tried to divert her husband by going with him to concerts and the opera. The President was so impressed by the singing of Felicita Vestvali—"Magnificent Vestvali," as the newspapers called her—that he attended her long-forgotten musical play called *Gamea, or the Jewish Mother* not once but twice, and within a week returned to hear her in two other musical dramas. After 1863, when New York opera companies began offering a special Washington season, the Lincolns were regular patrons. They attended performances of Gounod's *Faust,* Weber's *Der Freischütz,* and Flotow's *Martha,* among others. Few of the President's comments on the music were recorded, but in March when he heard *The Magic Flute,* he remarked to Colonel James Grant Wilson that the exceptionally large, flat feet of one of the leading female singers meant "the beetles wouldn't have much of a chance there!" During most of the opera, Wilson recalled, the President "sat in the rear of the box leaning his head against the partition, paying no attention to the play and looking . . . worn and weary." When Wilson asked if he was enjoying the opera, Lincoln replied: "Oh, no, Colonel; I have not come for the play, but for the rest. I am being hounded to death by office-seekers, who pursue me early and late, and it is simply to get two or three hours' relief that I am here." But when Mary asked if he would like to leave before the ending, he said: "Oh, no, I want to see it out. It's best when you undertake a job, to finish it."

When he was too tired to be diverted by either drama or opera, the President was able to forget his work and his worries only during the carriage rides Mary arranged to take with him several afternoons a week. These were times for quiet conversation, when Lincoln remembered the past and planned for the future. Though he was only into the first weeks of his second term, he looked forward to the end of his administration, when, he told Mary, he wanted to take the whole family to Europe. After that "he intended to return and go to California over the Rocky Mountains and see the prospects of the soldiers etc. etc. digging gold to pay the National debt." He was not sure where they would ultimately make their home. Earlier he had always talked of returning to Springfield and practicing law, but now he thought less about settling than of "roving and travelling."

Lincoln could afford to think in rosy terms of the future. Unaware of the very considerable debts Mary had accumulated, he was confident that he and his wife were comfortably provided for. His estate had been worth about $15,000 in 1861, but it had grown rapidly during the war years. Most of his expenses while living in the White House were covered by congressional appropriations, so that he was able to save the bulk of his $25,000 annual salary and invest it in Treasury notes or certificates of deposit. Interest and premiums on this paper, which amounted to nearly $10,000 over four years, he promptly reinvested. Because he did not have time properly to manage his funds—indeed, at the time of his death there were four uncashed salary warrants in his desk—he turned to Chase for advice, and in June 1864 brought over to the Secretary's desk "a confused mass of Treasury notes, Demand notes, Seven-thirty notes, and other representatives of value" and asked for help in reinvesting his funds in government bonds. By April 1865 he owned, in addition to his house in Springfield, two hundred acres of land in Iowa, a town lot in Lincoln, Illinois, and nearly $60,000 in government securities—not an inconsiderable sum, and one certain to double in the next four years.

During these few quiet weeks after the second inauguration, the Lincolns had a chance to talk about Robert, who was now in the army. After graduating from Harvard in 1864, the President's oldest son wanted to enlist. Indeed, he had been under considerable pressure to do so for some time, because critics did not hesitate to brand him a "shirker," who was "old enough and strong enough to serve his country." But his mother was afraid; she had already lost two sons, and she grew hysterical at the possibility of losing another. When her husband tried to intercede for the boy, she replied, "Of course, Mr. Lincoln, I know that Robert's plan to go into the Army is manly and noble and I want him to go, but oh! I am frightened he may never come back to us." Unwilling to do anything to upset his wife's precarious emotional balance, Lincoln encouraged Robert to go to Harvard Law School, but when he came home for the Christmas vacation in 1864, he was determined to "see something of the war before it ends." In January, finally overcoming Mary's resistance, Lincoln, writing "as though I was not President, but only a friend," asked whether Grant could give Robert "some nominal rank" and allow him to join his military family. Promptly Grant welcomed the young man and commissioned him a captain. Grant made sure that Robert was not exposed to danger, and his principal duty was to escort visitors to the Army of the Potomac from one place to another.

VIII

On March 20, at Mrs. Grant's prompting, General Grant invited the President to come down to army headquarters at City Point for a few days, suggesting that the rest would do him good. Lincoln accepted immediately, adding that Mrs. Lincoln "and a few others" would come with him. Despite a furious gale, the Lincolns, accompanied by Tad, Mary Lincoln's maid, White House guard William H. Crook, and Captain Charles Penrose, assigned by Stanton to protect the President, boarded the *River Queen* and sailed down the Potomac on March 23.

They were eager to get away from Washington, which Mary thought was a place filled with their enemies and which Lincoln knew was a city filled with office-seekers. They wanted to learn how Robert was faring in the army. And, most of all, they needed rest.

They did not get much of it at City Point, where they were welcomed with a round of lunches, dinners, receptions, parties, and dances. Tad probably had the best time. Aboard the *River Queen* his "investigating mind led him everywhere," and, Crook reported, he "studied every screw of the engine and knew and counted among his friends every man of the crew." Once on land, he was a special pet of the soldiers, and he was allowed to accompany his father everywhere.

Though Lincoln was unwell aboard the *River Queen,* he began to feel better once he was away from Washington and from the press of office-seekers. On his first day at City Point he rode out on a special train to General Meade's headquarters, where he saw evidence of recent fighting, heard a terrific Union bombardment of the Confederate lines at Petersburg, and witnessed an attack by the Sixth Corps on the enemy picket line. The next morning he had a chance to greet General Sheridan's troops, which had cleaned the Confederates out of the Shenandoah Valley and had come to assist Grant in the final campaign against Richmond. That afternoon he reviewed part of General Edward O. C. Ord's Army of the James at Malvern Hill. On another day Lincoln visited the army field hospital at City Point, where for more than five hours he moved from tent to tent, greeting each patient, pausing at the bedside of the seriously ill or wounded, and making a point of shaking hands with the hospitalized Confederates.

He had very little time for relaxation, and his "very care-worn and fatigued appearance" reappeared whenever he let his guard down. In particular, Mary reported, he found that the visit to the hospital, "although a labor of love, to him, fatigued him very much." But the cheers of the troops that he reviewed and the demonstrations of the sailors on the vessels he passed in the James River were exhilarating, and he gained strength from the scent of coming victory.

On the whole, the Union soldiers and their officers were pleased by their President. To be sure, the very superior young Boston aristocrat Colonel Theodore Lyman, attached to Meade's headquarters, found him "the ugliest man I ever put my eyes on," with an offensive "expression of plebeian vulgarity in his face"; but after some conversation with the President, Lyman concluded he was "a very honest and kindly man," who looked "much like a highly intellectual and benevolent Satyr." "I never wish to see him again," the colonel dismissed his commander-in-chief, "but, as humanity runs, I am well content to have him at the head of affairs."

Mary Lincoln had a bad time on the trip down the Potomac on the *River Queen.* Highly nervous, she was greatly upset when her husband made the mistake of telling her that he dreamed the White House was on fire, and she insisted on sending not one but two telegrams to Washington to be sure everything was all right. At army headquarters she felt out of place, and the few other women who were present, like Julia Grant and Mary Ord, seemed not to pay sufficient deference to the wife of the President of the United States. Lincoln, intent on fulfilling his many obligations, gave her too little attention and assumed that she could cope in his absence. She could not.

When Ord's troops were to be reviewed at Malvern Hill, the President and most of the men rode ahead on horseback, leaving Mrs. Lincoln and Mrs. Grant to proceed in an ambulance over roads calf-deep in mud. A sudden jolt bounced the ladies against the top of the carriage, crushing their bonnets and bumping their heads. Mary, who had never fully recovered from her 1863 carriage accident, probably had an attack of migraine. When she finally arrived at the site of the review, she discovered that it had begun without her. Her husband was riding down the lines accompanied by Mrs. Ord, a strikingly handsome young woman, whose appearance must have reminded Mary that she had now become corpulent and her face heavy, with permanent down-turned lines. When Mrs. Ord rode up to pay her respects, Mary, now hysterical, "positively insulted her, called her vile names . . . , and asked what she meant by following up the President."

That night before the guests at dinner aboard the *River Queen,* Mary repeatedly attacked her husband for flirting with Mrs. Ord and demanded that General Ord be removed from command. Deeply mortified, the President tried to ignore his wife's remarks, but she continued her tirade of abuse until late in the night. For the next several days, ill and embarrassed, she spent most of her time in her cabin, and on April 1, to her husband's undoubted relief, she went back to Washington, leaving Tad with his father.

Once his wife was out of the picture, Lincoln could reveal that recreation was not his only object in going to City Point. His greatest worry now was that Union generals might let victory slip through their hands. Grant, preparing to launch the final assault of the Army of the Potomac against Petersburg, felt that the President's anxiety was unwarranted. So did Sherman, who had now pushed into the Carolinas and was so sure of success that he felt able to leave his army and come up to City Point for a final conference on strategy. But Lincoln had had too many experiences with overconfident commanders, and he knew how wily and dangerous the Confederates still were. Again and again during his two weeks at the front, he expressed concern that Lee might break away from Grant, lead his forces into North Carolina, where they could join the remnants of the Confederate army again under Joseph E. Johnston, and either fight another great battle or escape south to continue the war. He feared that Johnston might slip out of Sherman's grasp and "be off South again with those hardy troops of his." "Yes," he told the general, "he will get away if he can, and you will never catch him until after miles of travel and many bloody battles."

Equally important was the President's determination to keep control of any peace negotiations generally thought to be in the offing. Old Francis P. Blair on his mission to Richmond had made the dangerous suggestion that Grant and Lee should get together to talk about peace terms, and the Confederate commissioners at Hampton Roads had worked through Grant to secure the conference they desired with the President. More recently, Lee had directly approached Grant asking "an interchange of views" on "the subjects of controversy between [the] belligerents," and the President had been obliged to tell his commanding general that he must "have no conference with General Lee unless it be for the capitulation of General Lee's army." "Such questions," Lincoln directed, "the President holds in his own hands, and will submit them to no military conferences or conventions."

Lincoln was not just ordering the generals to follow protocol; he wanted to make sure that any negotiations led not merely to a suspension of fighting but to a peace that would ensure his war aims of Union, Emancipation, and at least limited Equality. His worst fear, which he repeatedly expressed, was that once the Confederate armies were defeated Southern soldiers "would not return to their homes to accept citizenship under a hated rule; and with nothing but desolation and want through the South, the disbanded Confederate soldiers would be tempted to lawlessness and anarchy." Consequently his objective was to secure not merely peace but reconciliation. Bringing Grant, Sherman, and Admiral David D. Porter together for a conference aboard the *River Queen* on March 28, Lincoln discussed the approaching end of the war and talked of offering the most generous terms in order to "get the deluded men of the rebel armies disarmed and back to their homes." "Let them once surrender and reach their homes," he said, "[and] they won't take up arms again. Let them all go, officers and all, I want submission, and no more bloodshed. . . . I want no one punished; treat them liberally all round. We want those people to return to their allegiance to the Union and submit to the laws."

I Will Take Care of Myself

———◆———

The visit to City Point rejuvenated Lincoln. Once he was away from the nagging pressures of Washington, his health returned. Buoyed by the adulation of the soldiers and exhilarated by the sense that final victory over the Confederacy was at hand, he had a new sense of strength. After his visit to the army hospital, where he shook hands with patients for several hours, a surgeon expressed fear that his arm must ache from the exertion. The President smiled and, saying that he had "strong muscles," picked up a heavy ax that lay beside a log. He chopped away vigorously for a few minutes and then, taking the ax in his right hand, extended it horizontally, holding it steady without even a quiver. After he left, some strong soldiers attempted to duplicate his feat but failed.

Lincoln had every right to be pleased with himself. After four exhausting years he was now fully master of the almost impossible job to which he had been elected. The only Chief Executive elected for two terms since Andrew Jackson, he was unquestionably the choice of the American people, not a minority or accidental President. He headed an administration, and a bureaucracy, that followed his leadership. As party leader, he commanded overwhelming support in both houses of Congress. He was commander-in-chief of the largest military and naval forces the country had ever raised, and at last they were functioning with machinelike efficiency. The United States Navy controlled the ocean and, after the capture of Fort Fisher, off Wilmington, North Carolina, in January, was strangling the Confederacy with its blockade. As Sherman's tough Western army cornered Joseph E. Johnston's weakened forces in North Carolina, Grant was moving to the south of Petersburg and Richmond. On April 1 he launched an attack with Sheridan's dismounted cavalry and Gouverneur K. Warren's Fifth Corps that crumpled Lee's right flank in the battle of Five Forks and almost encircled Petersburg. Lee warned Jefferson Davis that he must be prepared to flee Richmond.

Lincoln wanted to be in on the finish. On April 3, learning that Petersburg had been evacuated, he closely followed the federal troops as they entered the city. The Secretary of War was horrified by the risk he was taking. "Allow me respectfully to ask you," Stanton scolded, "to consider whether you ought to expose the nation to the consequence of any disaster to yourself in the pursuit of a treacherous and dangerous enemy like the rebel army." But Lincoln, elated to learn that the Confederate government had fled and Richmond was in Union hands, brushed aside the warning. "I will take care of myself," he promised Stanton.

I

On April 4, as soon as the navy had removed most of the Confederate torpedoes in the James River, Lincoln set out with a small party to visit Richmond. When the *U.S.S. Malvern,* Admiral Farragut's flagship, could not pass a line of obstructions the Southerners had placed in the river, the President transferred to a shallow-draft barge, pulled by the tugboat *Glance.* After the strong river current forced the *Malvern* against a bridge, the tugboat was detached to rescue it, and twelve sailors rowed Lincoln's barge upstream. The President was amused. "Admiral," he said to David D. Porter, who was in his party, "this brings to my mind a fellow who once came to me to ask for an appointment as minister abroad. Finding he could not get that, he came down to some more modest position. Finally he asked to be made a tide-waiter. When he saw he could not get that, he asked me for an old pair of trousers." "But it is well to be humble," Lincoln concluded.

Landing without notice or fanfare, the President was first recognized by some black workmen. Their leader, a man about sixty, dropped his spade and rushed forward, exclaiming, "Bless the Lord, there is the great Messiah! ... Glory, Hallelujah!" He and the others fell on their knees, trying to kiss the President's feet. "Don't kneel to me," Lincoln told them, embarrassed. "That is not right. You must kneel to God only, and thank him for the liberty you will hereafter enjoy." Quickly word of the President's arrival spread, and he was soon surrounded by throngs of blacks, who shouted, "Bless the Lord, Father Abrahams Come."

As the small party walked up to Main Street, six of the sailors from the barge, armed with carbines, headed the procession, and six others brought up the rear, with Lincoln, leading Tad with his left hand, and Admiral Porter in the center. It was a beautiful, warm day, and the President soon shed his long overcoat, which reached below his knees, but continued to wear his tall stovepipe hat, though he frequently removed it to wipe away big drops of perspiration on his forehead. Encountering a squad of New York soldiers, the President asked for directions to the headquarters of General Godfrey

Weitzel, whom Grant had named to command the Union forces occupying Richmond.

The soldiers escorted him to the Confederate White House, where he sank into a comfortable chair in what had been Jefferson Davis's study. After a little rest he went on a tour of the building and then had a simple lunch with Weitzel and his staff. While they were eating, the general's three-seated army hack, drawn by four horses, was brought to the front of the building, and Tad, who had finished lunch early, climbed into the back seat and began to hold a reception, shaking hands with all the freedmen, and some whites as well, who crowded around.

When the President emerged, there was cheering, and some members of the crowd threw their hats and bonnets into the air. Driving past St. Paul's Church, the President made a stop at the Virginia statehouse, which had housed the Confederate Congress. As one of his party recalled, it gave "every evidence of hasty abandonment and subsequent looting"; members' desks and chairs were upset, official documents were scattered about, and Confederate $1,000 bonds littered the floors. Afterward, as the President drove through the more fashionable residential districts of the city "blinds or shades were drawn and no faces were to be seen," but in the working-class areas he was surrounded by enthusiastic crowds. Proceeding south, Lincoln went through part of the business section, devastated by the fires that had broken out as the Confederates evacuated the city, and stopped at the hated Libby Prison where so many Northern soldiers had been held during the war. In the late afternoon he went aboard the *Malvern,* which had finally made its way through the obstructions on the James River.

Even here he was not allowed to rest undisturbed. Throughout the day members of his entourage had been fearful of attempts on his life, for it was almost impossible to protect the President when so many people pushed close to inspect and admire him. There was a moment of panic when a man clad in a gray Confederate uniform stood in a second-story window and appeared to point a rifle directly at Lincoln; but no shot was fired, and the group moved on. In the evening two suspicious persons attempted to board the *Malvern,* claiming to bear dispatches for the President. Concerned for Lincoln's safety, Admiral Porter posted a guard outside his cabin door. The next morning General Edward H. Ripley, who commanded one of Weitzel's brigades, brought a report from a Confederate soldier that the President was in danger and ought to take greater care if he went ashore again. Lincoln ignored the threat, saying, "I cannot bring myself to believe that any human being lives who would do me any harm."

Lincoln's motive in going to Richmond was not just natural curiosity about the citadel of the Confederacy; it was a desire to help in the process of restoring peace. For this reason he took time while in the Confederate White House to meet with John A. Campbell, one of the Southern commissioners at Hampton Roads and the only high-ranking Confederate to remain in the capital. Urging the President to pursue a policy of "moderation, magnanimity and kindness" toward the South, Campbell secured his ready agreement "not to exact oaths, interfere with churches, etc." and, in general, to make "no requisitions on the inhabitants [of Richmond]... of any sort save as to police and preservation of order." But these promises did little to solve the larger issues involved in bringing Virginia back into the Union, and for that purpose Campbell suggested that Lincoln confer with the influential moderate leaders of the state, like R. M. T. Hunter, who "were satisfied that submission was a duty and a necessity."

The President invited Campbell to bring a delegation of such leaders aboard the *Malvern* the next morning. Campbell asked six or seven influential Virginians to accompany him, but only Gustavus A. Myers, a prominent Richmond attorney, agreed to do so. Lincoln had General Weitzel at his side. The President began by restating his indispensable terms for peace: "restoration of the national authority"; "no receding by the Executive of the United States on the slavery question"; and "no cessation of hostilities short of an end of the war, and the disbanding of all forces hostile to the government." If these were acceded to, he promised to consider other proposed conditions "in a spirit of sincere liberality." For instance, he promised to return property seized under the Confiscation Acts to any state that withdrew its troops from the Confederate army. At the same time, he warned that "if the war be now further persisted in," the costs would have to be paid from confiscated Confederate property.

Campbell responded by saying that slavery was now "defunct" and therefore no longer an issue between North and South. Virginia could be brought back into the Union if Lincoln offered a general amnesty. "To cover appearances," there should also be "a military convention" to end the fighting, but there was no Confederate authority willing or able to sign such an agreement dismantling the Southern government. Jefferson Davis had avoided the decision, saying that only a convention of the Southern states could end the Confederacy. The Confederate Congress had refused to overrule its President. General Lee, as usual, stuck to his military duties and declined to act on political questions, such as the terms of peace.

The situation was exactly what Lincoln had most feared. The war was not yet over, and further fighting and more bloodshed lay ahead. Even if there were no more pitched battles, thousands of Southern soldiers, turned loose on the countryside, would probably resort to guerrilla warfare. Society would be broken up, and anarchy was likely.

To prevent these disasters, the President told Campbell and Myers, he had been thinking of a plan for the speedy restoration of Virginia to the Union. If he gave safe-conduct assurances to members of the state's Confederate legislature, they could meet at Richmond and vote to withdraw the state from the Confederacy. It was not an idea that he had fully worked out, but it was not a completely novel one. Representative Ashley, a leading Radical, had advanced a similar proposal in the last session of Congress. To secure stable governments in the South, he argued, "the President may lawfully and rightfully treat with [rebel officials] and recognize them as the existing government." In his conversations with Grant and Sherman at City Point, Lincoln had probably discussed the possibility of dealing with Confederate state authorities, at least during a transitional period. But Lincoln recognized that this plan entailed risks. For one thing, it overturned the policy of nonrecognition of the Confederacy that he and his administration had resolutely adhered to for more than four years. For another, in the case of Virginia it raised problems about the legitimacy of the existing Unionist government, headed by Francis Pierpont. To be sure, this Pierpont regime had, as the President admitted, a "somewhat farcical" quality, since it governed only the areas of the state that were under Union guns, but both he and the Congress had repeatedly recognized it. These were weighty objections, to be balanced against the President's desire to see "the very Legislature which had been sitting 'up yonder'—pointing to the capitol—to come together and to vote to restore Virginia to the Union, and recall her soldiers from the Confederate army."

Eagerly his listeners seized on his idea. As Weitzel later reported, Campbell and Myers "assured Mr. Lincoln that if he would allow the Virginia Legislature to meet, it would at once repeal the ordinance of secession, and that then General Robert E. Lee and every other Virginian would submit; that this would amount to the virtual destruction of the Army of Northern Virginia, and eventually to the surrender of all the other rebel armies, and would insure perfect peace in the shortest possible time."

Possibly their enthusiasm made the President pause, for he announced that he would not make a decision until he returned to City Point. When he got back to army headquarters, he tried to make his plan more precise, directing Weitzel to allow "the gentlemen who have acted as the Legislature of Virginia, in support of the rebellion," to assemble at Richmond in order to "take measures to withdraw the Virginia troops, and other support from resistance to the General government." Reporting his decision to Grant, the President added, "I do not think it very probable that anything will come of this." The Union army, he observed sardonically, was "pretty effectually withdrawing the Virginia troops from opposition to the government" without the assistance of Campbell or other Confederate intermediaries.

At City Point the President received two pieces of news. Telegrams from Washington reported that Mary Lincoln, determined to show she had recovered from her bout of paranoia, was returning to army headquarters with a party that included Charles Sumner, the Marquis de Chambrun, a young French nobleman, Senator Harlan (whose appointment as Secretary of the Interior did not take effect until May 15) and his wife, and Attorney General Speed. At the same time, Stanton wired that Secretary Seward had been badly injured in a carriage accident and that the President ought to return to the capital. Subsequent dispatches from Stanton indicated that the Secretary of State, though seriously hurt, was in no immediate danger, and Lincoln was able to stay on at army headquarters for a few more days.

Hoping to remain until the final Confederate surrender, Lincoln carefully studied the dispatches that Grant, Sheridan, and Meade forwarded to him. He rejoiced to read Sheridan's report that he had routed the enemy at Burke's Station, which ended: "If the thing is pressed I think that Lee will surrender." Promptly the President wired Grant, "Let the *thing* be pressed."

But when surrender did not seem to be imminent, Lincoln and his party prepared to leave City Point on April 8. Before their departure he requested the military band on the *River Queen* to play the *Marseillaise* in honor of the Marquis de Chambrun, who, the President remarked, had to come all the way to America to hear the revolutionary song that was banned under the Second Empire. Then Lincoln asked the surprised band director to play *Dixie.* "That tune is now Federal property," he announced, and it's "good to show the rebels that, with us in power, they will be free to hear it again."

On the slow river trip back to Washington, Lincoln was silent much of the time, absorbed in thought. He deflected any possibility of a political discussion with Sumner, who was always eager to press a Radical reconstruction program on the President, and did not mention his tentative plan to reconvene the Virginia legislature. Instead, he turned to literary subjects and for several hours read to his guests on the *River Queen* passages from Shakespeare. From *Macbeth* he chose the reflections of the king, who has murdered his predecessor, Duncan, only to be overtaken by horrible torments of mind:

> . . . we will eat our meal in fear, and sleep
> In the affliction of these terrible dreams,
> That shake us nightly: better be with the dead . . .
> Than on the torture of the mind to lie
> In restless ecstasy. Duncan is in his grave:
> After life's fitful fever he sleeps well,
> Treason has done his worst; nor steel, nor poison,
> Malice domestic, foreign levy, nothing
> Can touch him further.

Then, struck by the weird beauty of the lines, Lincoln paused, as Chambrun recalled, and "began to explain to us how true a description of the murderer that one was; when, the dark deed achieved, its tortured perpetrator came to envy the sleep of his victim; and he read over again the same scene."

II

At about sundown on April 9, Lincoln returned to a capital still celebrating the capture of Richmond and eagerly anticipating the surrender of Robert E. Lee. His first visit was to his Secretary of State, who was confined to his bed by the accident in which he had broken both his arm and his jaw. To keep Seward from trying to move his head, the President stretched out at full length across the bed and, resting on his elbow, brought his face near that of the injured man. "I think we are near the end at last," he said, and he told of Grant's victories and of his visit to Richmond. He proposed to issue a proclamation for a day of thanksgiving, but the Secretary whispered that he should wait until Sherman captured Joseph E. Johnston. As Seward drifted off to sleep, the President quietly left the room.

That night he learned that Lee had surrendered to Grant at Appomattox, and he immediately told Mary. At daylight the next day the firing of five hundred cannon gave the news to the entire capital. "Guns are firing, bells ringing, flags flying, men laughing, children cheering," recorded Gideon Welles; "all, all jubilant." Throngs of people collected around the White House, filling the north portico, the carriageways, and the sidewalks. "The crowds around the house have been immense," Mary wrote; "in the midst of the bands playing, they break forth into singing." Repeatedly they called for the President, and when he failed to appear, the shouting grew even louder. A great cheer rose when Tad appeared at a second-story window, waving a Confederate flag. Finally Lincoln came out to say a few words. Anticipating that there would be a more formal demonstration the following night, he told the crowd, "I shall have nothing to say if you dribble it all out of me before." But again he asked the band to play *Dixie,* "one of the best tunes I have ever heard," and joked that he had a legal opinion from the Attorney General that the song was "a lawful prize," since "we fairly captured it."

It was a busy day for the President, because he had to catch up the accumulated work that had piled up during his two weeks with the army. A cabinet meeting dealt with only routine business, for Lincoln apparently did not tell his associates of his conversations with Campbell in Richmond or of his tentative agreement to allow the Virginia rebel legislature to reconvene. That subject was, however, much on his mind, and he summoned Governor Pierpont, the head of the Unionist government of Virginia, for a conference. Despite all distractions, he spent much of his time composing a speech for the next day.

On April 11 it seemed that the whole city turned out to celebrate. All the government buildings and many of the private houses were illuminated. Though the evening was misty, the illuminated dome of the Capitol could be seen for miles. Across the Potomac, Lee's home, Arlington, was brightly lit, and thousands of freedmen gathered on the lawn to sing "The Year of Jubilee." An immense throng of people, many carrying banners, poured into the semicircular driveway leading to the north portico of the White House. After repeated loud calls, the President appeared in a second-story window just under the portico, and "cheers upon cheers, wave after wave of applause, rolled up." Lincoln began to read from his carefully prepared manuscript in order to avoid any misunderstanding or misinterpretation of his ideas, but the light was bad. After unsuccessfully trying to hold a candle in one hand and the pages of his manuscript in the other, he beckoned to Noah Brooks, who took a place behind the draperies and held up the light while the President read. As he finished each page, he dropped it to the floor, where Tad scrambled about, collecting them and, growing restless, importuned his father for "another."

"We meet this evening, not in sorrow, but in gladness of heart," the President began, and he expressed hope that the recent victories "give hope of a righteous and speedy peace." Promising a day of national thanksgiving, he offered the nation's gratitude to "Gen. Grant, his skilful officers, and brave men." That much was to be expected—but the rest of the address was not at all what the crowd had anticipated. "The re-inauguration of the national authority" was his principal subject, and he warned that it was going to be "fraught with great difficulty," the more so since "we, the loyal people, differ among ourselves as to the mode, manner, and means of reconstruction."

The larger part of his address reviewed his relationship to the reconstructed government of Louisiana and offered a defense of that regime. It was not in every way satisfactory, he admitted, and it would be more credible if it was supported by twenty, thirty, or fifty thousand voters instead of the twelve thousand who participated in its election. But he raised the same question that he had asked Senator Trumbull during the recent session of Congress: "Can Louisiana be brought into proper practical relation with the Union *sooner* by *sustaining,* or by *discarding* her new State Government?" The answer, he thought, was obvious: "Concede that the new government of Louisiana is only to what it should be as the egg is to the fowl, we shall sooner have the fowl by hatching the egg than by smashing it." And he reminded his listeners that if Louisiana was not readmitted, "we also reject one vote in favor of the proposed amendment to the national constitution."

Lincoln never explained why he chose this forum, and this occasion, for a major statement on reconstruction, but the final sentences of his talk gave a hint of his purpose. "In the present *'situation'* as the phrase goes, it may be my duty to make some new announcement to the people of the South," he said in conclusion, after many of his listeners had grown bored and drifted off elsewhere in search of more conventional oratory. "I am considering, and shall not fail to act, when satisfied that action will be proper."

The meaning of that cryptic message puzzled his hearers, who guessed that he intended anything from an announcement of amnesty for all rebels to a proclamation putting the entire South under military rule to a decree imposing universal suffrage on the rebellious states.

None of these expectations was realistic. Certainly, Lincoln was not in favor of punishing the Confederates. As he said to the Marquis de Chambrun shortly after his talk, it was "his firm resolution to stand for clemency against all opposition." He had no wish to capture and try even the leaders of the Confederacy. "He hoped there would be no persecution, no bloody work, after the war was over," he told the cabinet. "None need expect he would take any part in hanging or killing those men, even the worst of them." "Frighten them out of the country, open the gates, let down the bars, scare them off," he said—making a gesture as if herding sheep. But he wished to avoid making a public pronouncement on this point. At City Point, when Sherman asked what was to be done with Jefferson Davis and the other Confederate leaders, Lincoln intimated that they ought to "escape the country," though he could not say so openly. To make his position clear he told Sherman one of his favorite stories, about the man who declined a drink because he had taken a total-abstinence pledge and asked for lemonade instead. When a friend suggested that it would taste better with a little brandy in it, the man said he would not object if it could be added " 'unbeknown' to him."

Nor was he about to issue a proclamation for the general reorganization of the Southern states. The sole item on his agenda was peace, and Lincoln did not in this speech—or elsewhere—offer a broad vision of the future, outlining how the conquered South should be governed. He stipulated only that loyal men must rule. His was not the view of the Conservatives, who simply wanted the rebellious states, without slavery, to return to their former position in the Union, nor was it the view of the Radicals, who wanted to take advantage of this molten moment of history to recast the entire social structure of the South. He did not share the Conservatives' desire to put the section back into the hands of the planters and businessmen who had dominated the South before the war, but he did not adopt the Radicals' belief that the only true Unionists in the South were African-Americans.

Equally improbable was any announcement that African-Americans must have full political and economic equality. Lincoln had not given much thought to the role that the freedmen would play in the reorganization of the South. The stalwart service rendered by nearly 200,000 African-Americans in the military had eroded his earlier doubts about their courage and intelligence. Perhaps he still questioned whether blacks could ever achieve equality with whites in the same society, but the failure of his colonization schemes had taught him that African-Americans were, and would remain, a permanent part of the American social fabric. He believed that the more intelligent blacks, especially those who served in the army, were entitled to the suffrage. Hence he encouraged the education of the freedmen, and he supported the Freedmen's Bureau to protect them from exploitation by their former masters. But beyond this he was not prepared to go. Unlike the Radicals, he gave no thought to dividing up the estates of the defeated Southern planters and giving each black family forty acres and a mule. He offered no opinions on school integration, interracial marriages, or social equality between blacks and whites. In April 1865 he thought these were all hypothetical questions, pernicious abstractions, which could have no other effect than to divide the friends of the Union at a time when they ought to be united in a search for peace.

The announcement he contemplated probably had to do with his plan to allow the members of the rebel legislature of Virginia to assemble in order to withdraw their state from the Confederacy. He was prepared to extend the same offer to other states. In his mind this move did not amount to recognition of the Confederate governments in these states, nor was he conceding that they had ever seceded from the Union, a point central to his thinking throughout the war. But he contemplated giving a limited recognition to interim governments for the specific purpose of withdrawing troops from the Confederate armies. He had returned from City Point with a new sense of urgency about reconstruction. He now had firsthand knowledge of the devastation wrought by the war and a fuller understanding of the suffering it had caused soldiers and civilians in the South. More strongly than ever he felt that immediate action must be taken to restore stability in the conquered region. "Civil government must be reëstablished . . . as soon as possible," he told Welles; "there must be courts, and law, and order, or society would be broken up, the disbanded armies would turn into robber bands and guerrillas, which we must strive to prevent."

Aware that his plan would arouse opposition, he intended his speech, as he told an old friend the next day, "to blaze a way through the swamp" of legal entanglements and political objections to his course. He had good reason to anticipate that Radicals would oppose his efforts in Virginia. Many of them had not accepted their defeat in the recent session of Congress. Some, like Sumner, were now implacable in their hostility to Lincoln's plans. Aware that the President was likely to make some pronouncement on reconstruction on April 11, the senator had declined Mrs. Lincoln's invitation to view the victory celebration from the White House. He felt that his presence at the inaugural ball had been interpreted as giving symbolic approval of the Lincoln administration, and he was not going to allow himself to be so used again. Other Radicals also continued to agitate for harsh terms toward the South. For instance, Benjamin F. Butler demanded that leaders of the rebellion should be disfranchised and disqualified from holding any public office and that "the masses, including the negroes, should have the rights of citizenship." Chief Justice Chase, who did not give up his political interests when he joined the Court, enjoined the President to remember that "the easiest and safest way" to reorganize the Southern states was through "the enrollment of the loyal citizens without regard to complexion."

Lincoln's April 11 speech was an attempt to defuse such criticisms by making significant concessions to his Radical critics. Though he defended the Unionist government of Louisiana, he explicitly disavowed any claim that reconstruction was exclusively a function of the executive branch; he reminded his audience that he had from the outset "distinctly stated that this was not the only plan which might possibly be acceptable" and "that the Executive claimed no right to say when, or whether members should be admitted to seats in Congress from such States." Admitting that he had promised General Banks to sustain the Louisiana regime, he was ready to retract it: "As bad promises are better broken than kept, I shall treat this as a bad promise, and break it, whenever I shall be convinced that keeping it is adverse to the public interest." "But," he cautioned, "I have not yet been so convinced." Recognizing that Radicals objected to the Louisiana constitution because it did not give African-Americans the ballot, he declared that he shared their discontent: "I would myself prefer that it were now conferred on the very intelligent, and on those who serve our cause as soldiers." This was an opinion Lincoln had previously expressed in private, but never before had any American President publicly announced that he was in favor of Negro suffrage.

III

At least one member of the crowd outside the White House that night recognized how much Lincoln was conceding to the Radicals. John Wilkes Booth fumed with hatred for the President. Born in Maryland in a slaveholding community, the twenty-six-year-old actor thought of himself as a Northerner who understood the South. He was a handsome, vain young man, the next-to-the-youngest son and his mother's darling in her brood of ten children. He grew up on the family farm near Bel Air, Maryland, to which his alcoholic and mentally unstable father repaired between bouts of acting, and in Baltimore. Erratic attendance at several private schools in the vicinity supplied him with a smattering of learning, some elements of military drill, and a conviction that he belonged to the Southern gentry.

He seemed destined for the theater. His father, Junius Brutus Booth, and his brother Edwin were great actors; his brother Junius Booth, Jr., was a major producer; and his brother-in-law was a noted comedian. From his debut at the age of seventeen Wilkes Booth was almost constantly on the stage. He had no training, and his early performances were crude and sometimes laughable. But he constantly improved as an actor, and he learned a formidable number of roles. He looked the part of the hero. Though he was only five feet eight inches tall, he held himself erect, and his broad chest contributed to the impression of greater height. Strikingly handsome, with curly black hair and a full mustache, he had a slightly exotic look, which women often found irresistible. "He had an ivory pallor that contrasted with his raven hair," one of them remembered, "and his eyes had heavy lids which gave him an Oriental touch of mystery."

It was in Southern theaters, notably in Richmond, that he first gained recognition. Southerners appreciated his flamboyant, athletic style of acting: the twelve-foot leaps he sometimes used to make his first appearance on stage, the duels that were so realistic that blood was shed, the impassioned love scenes. When he began playing Shakespearean roles, considered the real test of an actor in the 1850s, he reminded audiences of his father, perhaps the greatest Shakespearean performer of his generation, and of Edwin Forrest. Southern audiences preferred Wilkes Booth's portrayal of Hamlet as an unmistakably mad prince and of Richard III as a diabolical monster to the coolly intellectual characterizations offered by his older brother Edwin.

Offstage, Southerners found Wilkes Booth delightful, and they were charmed by his quick excitability, his love of fun, and his joyousness. "He was one of the best *raconteurs* to whom I ever listened," a fellow actor recalled. "As he talked he threw himself into his words, brilliant, ready, enthusiastic." Young Southern men were impressed by his ability to hold his liquor. His excellent manners won him access to social circles in the Deep South from which he had been excluded in Maryland, where people remembered that he was illegitimate. Deserting a first wife in England, his father had come to America with Mary Anne Holmes, who became the mother of John Wilkes Booth and his nine siblings.

Southerners also liked Wilkes Booth because he held conventional Southern views about slavery, which he considered "one of the greatest blessings (both for themselves and us) that God ever bestowed upon a favored nation." He firmly believed "the country was formed for the white, not for the black man." As sectional tensions mounted, he denounced what he called the treasonable activities of the abolitionist Republicans and called for retribution: "The South wants justice, has waited for it long, and she will wait no longer." Acting in a Richmond theater when he heard the news of John Brown's capture, he borrowed a uniform and went with the Richmond Grays to witness the execution of the old abolitionist.

When the war broke out, Booth made no attempt to conceal his sympathies for the Confederacy. "So help me holy God!" he swore to his sister, "my soul, life, and possessions are for the South." But he did not rush to enlist in the Confederate army, explaining to his brother Edwin, a loyal supporter of the North, that he had promised their mother to keep out of the quarrel. His contempt for President Lincoln was open. He was offended by "this man's appearance, his pedigree, his coarse low jokes and anecdotes, his vulgar similes, and his frivolity" as much as he was by Lincoln's efforts "to crush out slavery, by robbery, rapine, slaughter and bought armies."

Booth did little more than grumble about Lincoln until August or September 1864, when the reelection of the President seemed increasingly probable, but he then decided that something must be done to rid the country of this "false president," who clearly was "yearning for kingly succession." No doubt the chronic hoarseness that was clouding his career as a theatrical star and the failure of his investments in Pennsylvania oil schemes to pay off contributed to his general unhappiness, which was now directed against the President. Exactly how Booth got in touch with the Confederate secret service is not known, but he had many contacts in the South, and the private funds he had used to buy quinine and other needed medicines to be smuggled into the Confederacy gave evidence of his good faith. Presently, after conferring with Southern agents in Maryland, in Boston, and in Canada, he came up with the scheme of kidnapping Lincoln, taking him behind the

Confederate lines in Virginia, where he would be held hostage for the release of thousands of Southern soldiers languishing in Northern prisons. It cannot be proved that any Confederate authority—much less the heads of the Confederate government—knew about, authorized, or even approved Booth's plan, though it is clear that, at least at the lower levels of the Southern secret service, the abduction of the Union President was under consideration. Indeed, Booth's scheme was very much like the one that Confederate authorities permitted Thomas N. Conrad to attempt in the fall of 1864.

Booth recruited for his plot two of his boyhood friends from Baltimore, Samuel B. Arnold and Michael O'Laughlin. Expecting to take the President across the Potomac below Washington, he added the Prussian-born George A. Atzerodt from Port Tobacco, Maryland, because he had ferried Confederate spies across the river and knew all the creeks and inlets. John H. Surratt, who had repeatedly served as a courier between secessionist sympathizers in Baltimore and Southern authorities in Richmond, added firsthand knowledge of the Confederate underground that was active in southern Maryland, and his mother, Mary Surratt, who may or may not have known the plots that were being hatched, offered headquarters for the conspirators in the inn she owned at Surrattsville, Maryland, and in the boardinghouse she opened on H Street in Washington. For brute strength needed to overcome any resistance on the part of the President, Booth enrolled the burly, violent Lewis Paine (or "Payne," or "Powell," or "Wood," as he variously called himself), who had served in Mosby's Confederate Rangers before taking the oath of allegiance to the Union cause. And finally he allowed the young druggist's clerk, David E. Herold, to join the group; Herold was a trifler who gave the appearance of being not very bright but, as an avid bird hunter, he was supposed to know the poorly mapped roads below Washington. It was a loose, informally organized group, tied together only by devotion to the Confederate cause, personal attachment to Booth, and the considerable amounts of money that the actor paid to house and feed his team in Washington.

During the fall and winter of 1864, while Booth was recruiting his band of conspirators, he spent much time studying the maps and exploring the roads in Charles County, Maryland, in order to plan for carrying the kidnapped President across the Potomac. The whole venture, despite its deadly seriousness, had a theatrical quality about it, and at times Booth, who had trouble separating fantasy from reality, seemed to be playing one of his more melodramatic theatrical roles. To make sure that nobody misunderstood the script that he was following, he took time to write an impassioned letter explaining his actions in advance, which he sealed and entrusted to his brother-in-law. "There is no time for words," he asserted—only to run on for some thirteen hundred words attacking Lincoln, defending the South, and announcing that he intended "to make for her a prisoner of this man to whom she owes so much misery." He signed the document, "A Confederate at present doing duty on his own responsibility." Then he paused and struck through "at present."

How much of this was playacting is hard to determine. Certainly Booth's first plan, to capture Lincoln while he was attending Ford's Theatre on January 18, bind him and lower him from the box to the stage, and then carry him off to the Confederacy was pure theater, more akin to farce than to tragedy. Only an inferior playwright could conceive a scenario in which the powerful six-foot-four-inch Lincoln could be bound and gagged while a thousand spectators quietly watched the abduction. The plan was never tried, because the President stayed at home on this stormy night.

A more practicable plan for abducting the President, similar to that of Conrad, the Confederate agent, was to capture him while he was riding in his carriage on the outskirts of the city. Learning that Lincoln planned to attend a performance of *Still Waters Run Deep* at the Campbell Hospital, near the Soldiers' Home, on March 17, the conspirators decided to intercept the President, overpower him and his coachman, and rush him through southeastern Maryland and across the Potomac. At the last minute the attempt had to be aborted when Booth learned that Lincoln had remained in the city to review a returning regiment of Indiana volunteers rather than attend the play.

Instead of discouraging Booth, these failures led him to contemplate a new course of action. As early as March 4—even before the failure of the kidnapping scheme—he had begun to think of assassination rather than abduction. Standing in the rotunda of the Capitol as Lincoln passed through to the portico, where he gave his second inaugural address, Booth reflected on the excellent chance he had to kill the President if he wished.

The failure of the abduction scheme made that wish an obsession. Because the collapse of the Confederacy removed the source of any orders or suggestions for his conspiracy, Booth was now acting entirely on his own, and there was nothing to curb his fervid imagination. Drinking very heavily at this time, he increasingly came to think of himself as not just a self-appointed Confederate secret agent but as the reincarnation of one of the tragic theatrical heroes whose lines he mouthed so eloquently. Sometimes he fancied himself a present-day William Tell. More often he saw himself as Brutus, striking down the despotic Caesar. Always he brought death to the tyrant.

Lincoln's address on April 11 triggered Booth's shift from thought to action. In the crowd outside the White House that evening, he heard the President recommend suffrage for blacks who were educated or had served in the Union armies. "That means nigger citizenship," the actor muttered, and he vowed, "That is the last speech he will ever make." He urged Lewis Paine to shoot the President on the spot. When Paine refused, Booth turned in disgust to his other companion, David Herold, and exclaimed, "By God, I'll put him through."

IV

Lincoln, of course, knew nothing of these plots as he continued to plan for a speedy restoration of the Union under lenient terms of reconstruction. But he found few were ready to follow his lead. In Virginia, Campbell and his associates in the Virginia legislature seemed to be dragging their feet. On April 6 the President had authorized them to meet, but nothing much happened. During the next three days, while fighting continued, Campbell took time to constitute a committee of the legislators; the committee took time to compose an address; the military took time to approve the address and then it had to be published in the newspapers; it took more time to assure the members of the legislature that they would be given safe-conduct and provided with transportation to Richmond. Lacking any sense of urgency, Campbell took an increasingly enlarged view of his role in the negotiations, calling for an armistice—something that Lincoln had explicitly refused—and suggesting peace negotiations with the Confederate legislature of South Carolina as well as that of Virginia. It seems not to have occurred to him that Lee's surrender on April 9 made his activities largely irrelevant.

Along with foot-dragging from the Confederates, Lincoln had to deal with opposition in the North. Radicals overwhelmingly rejected the compromises he had offered in his April 11 speech. One of Sumner's abolitionist correspondents in Boston thought that it again demonstrated Lincoln's "backwardness" and argued that "it will be wicked and blasphemous for us as a nation to allow any distinction of color whatever in the reconstructed states." Sumner agreed. He rejected Lincoln's egg-and-fowl metaphor for the Louisiana government—an image the President was particularly pleased with—noting grimly that only crocodiles emerge from crocodile eggs. By failing to adopt "a just and safe system" of reconstruction—meaning one that enfranchised all the freedmen—the President was going to promote "confusion and uncertainty in the future—with hot controversy." "Alas! Alas!" he grieved.

The President's immediate advisers also objected to the proposed meeting of the Virginia legislators, which seemed much less urgent after Lee surrendered at Appomattox. He had deliberately not broached the subject in the cabinet meeting before he gave his speech, but some of the members knew about the plan because Charles A. Dana, who was with the President at City Point, sent Stanton detailed reports on Lincoln's meetings with Campbell. Stanton apparently leaked news of the Virginia peace negotiations to Speed and Dennison, and he possibly also informed Chief Justice Chase.

On April 12, when Lincoln brought the question of Virginia reconstruction before the cabinet, nobody favored his plan. Afterward both Stanton and Speed had private interviews with the President in order to express their marked dissatisfaction and irritation with the proposal. In a second conversation that afternoon at the War Department, Stanton vehemently argued against "allowing the rebel legislature to assemble, or the rebel organizations to have any participation whatever in the business of reorganization," and he warned that Lincoln's action "would put the Government in the hands of its enemies; that it would surely bring trouble with Congress; [and] that the people would not sustain him."

With Seward bedridden, Lincoln thought his strongest supporter would be Gideon Welles, but the Secretary of the Navy, to his surprise, also objected to "the policy of convening a Rebel legislature." The President explained that all he was trying to do was "to effect a reconciliation as soon as possible, and he should not stickle about forms, provided he could attain the desired result." But Welles was not convinced. "As we had never recognized any of [the Confederate] organizations as possessing validity during the war," he argued, "it would be impolitic, to say the least, to now recognize them and their governments as legal." Besides, he pointed out, there already was a Unionist government of Virginia, headed by Francis Pierpont.

Rather feebly the President countered that the Pierpont government "could be considered legal, but public sentiment or public prejudice must not be overlooked." But Welles's argument registered, and shortly afterward, when Pierpont came to the White House for a conference, Lincoln assured him, "I intended to recognize the restored government, of which you were head, as the rightful government of Virginia."

With all his advisers opposed to the reassembling of the Virginia legislature, the President concluded, as he told Welles, that "he had perhaps made a mistake, and was ready to correct it if he had." He decided to get out of the Virginia scheme with the best grace he could. If he had blundered, because of insufficient preparation and imprecise directives, he could blame the Southerners for dilatoriness and misinterpretation of his orders. On April 12 he wired General Weitzel that Campbell had exceeded his authority. Reminding the general that he had permitted the calling not of the legislature but of "the gentlemen who have *acted* as the Legislature of Virginia in support of the rebellion," Lincoln denied that he had ever intended to recognize them "as a *rightful* body"; they were only a group of influential individuals who had the power to withdraw Virginia support from resistance to the United States. Their action was not needed now, "particularly as Gen. Grant has since captured the Virginia troops, so that giving a consideration for their withdrawal is no longer applicable." "Do not now allow them to assemble," he directed Weitzel; "but if any have come, allow them safe-return to their homes." Consequently Lincoln never made the announcement to the people of the South, promised in his speech of April 11.

What he considered a temporary setback did not dishearten him, and he continued to plan a speedy restoration of the Confederate states to the Union on the most generous terms. This was the principal subject of discussion in the cabinet meeting on Friday, April 14, which General Grant attended. The President was in great form. Speed thought he had never seen him in better spirits, and Stanton remarked he was "grander, graver, more thoroughly up to the occasion than he had ever seen him." According to Frederick W. Seward, who attended in place of his injured father, all members expressed "kindly feeling toward the vanquished, and [a] hearty desire to restore peace and safety at the South, with as little harm as possible to the feelings or the property of the inhabitants." The cabinet quickly agreed on the importance of promptly restoring normal commercial relations with the former Confederate states and of abolishing, as soon as possible, all the military and Treasury regulations that had been necessary during the war to govern trade with the South. With obvious pleasure the President responded to a petitioner who asked for a pass to permit him to travel to Virginia: "No pass is necessary now to authorize any one to go to and return from Petersburg and Richmond. People go and return just as they did before the war."

How the Southern states were to be governed during the transition from disunion to loyalty remained to be settled. Lincoln had now given up the idea of temporarily working with the rebel legislatures, admitting to the cabinet that he "had perhaps been too fast in his desires for early reconstruction." But he felt strongly that the reorganization of these states could not be directed from Washington. "We can't undertake to run State governments in all these Southern States," he told the cabinet. "Their people must do that,—though I reckon that at first some of them may do it badly."

Stanton brought up a plan for the appointment of military governors, who would rule under martial law in the South until civilian rule could be reestablished. Under his proposal, which he had submitted to the President the previous day and had also discussed with Grant, the military authorities would preserve order and enforce the laws while the several executive departments resumed their normal functions in the South: the Treasury Department would proceed to collect the revenues; the Interior Department would set its Indian agents, surveyors, and land and pension agents to work; the Postmaster General would reestablish post offices and mail routes, and so on. This was, Lincoln noted approvingly, "substantially, in its general scope, the plan which we had sometimes talked over in Cabinet meetings," and it would bear further study. But Stanton also called for a single military governor for Virginia and North Carolina, and Welles strongly objected to the eradication of state boundaries and stressed the commitment that the administration had made to the Pierpont regime in Virginia.

Tactfully Lincoln handled the disagreement among his advisers by asking Stanton to revise his proposal, making separate plans for Virginia and North Carolina, which required different treatment. As to the former, the President said, "We must not . . . stultify ourselves as regards Virginia, but we must help her." Declaring that he had not yet had a chance to study the details of Stanton's proposal, he urged all the members to think carefully about the subject of reconstruction, because "no greater or more important one could come before us, or any future Cabinet."

It was providential, he observed, that the administration could settle on a plan for reconstruction without interference from "the disturbing elements" of Congress, which was in recess. "If we were wise and discreet," the President told his cabinet, "we should reanimate the States and get their governments in successful operation, with order prevailing and the Union reestablished, before Congress came together in December." "We could do better," he assured his advisers; "accomplish more without than with them." "There were men in Congress," he observed, "who, if their motives were good, were nevertheless impracticable, and who possessed feelings of hate and vindictiveness in which he did not sympathize and could not participate."

The discussion then drifted to the military situation, and everybody wanted to hear Grant's account of the surrender at Appomattox. Asking what terms had been extended to the common soldiers in the rebel army, Lincoln beamed when Grant said, "I told them to go back to their homes and families, and they would not be molested, if they did nothing more." Cabinet members wanted to know whether there was any news from Sherman in North Carolina. Grant replied that he was expecting word momentarily. Lincoln remarked that he was confident that there soon would be good news, since the previous night he had had the recurrence of a dream: he was on the water, and "he seemed to be in some singular, indescribable vessel, and . . . he was moving with great rapidity towards an indefinite shore." This dream, he said, had come to him before nearly every important Union victory—Antietam, Gettysburg, Stones River, Vicksburg, Fort Fisher, and so on.

Grant, who had no faith in superstitions and dreams, interjected that Stones River was certainly no Northern victory. Looking at the general curiously, Lincoln continued that, judging from the past, the dream meant that there would be good news soon. "I think it must be from Sherman," he said. "My thoughts are in that direction as are most of yours."

V

Absorbing as were the prospects for victory and peace, they did not occupy all the President's time even on so eventful a day. He had been up since seven o'clock, dealing with routine business, such as the appointment of one William T. Howell as Indian agent in Michigan. After breakfast, where he heard details of Lee's surrender at Appomattox from Robert, who was just back from Grant's army, the President went back to his office to face the endless line of visitors and petitioners who were waiting for him. In the next two hours he had a conversation with Speaker of the House Schuyler Colfax and Representative Cornelius Cole about California and the Western territories; a brief talk with William A. Howard, the postmaster of Detroit; a conference with Senator J. A. J. Creswell of Maryland, about patronage; an audience with John P. Hale, whom he had recently appointed minister to

Spain; and an interview with Charles M. Scott, a Mississippi riverboat pilot whose cotton had been confiscated by the Confederates. After slipping away for a brief visit to the War Department in the hope of receiving more news from the armies, Lincoln returned to the White House in time for the cabinet meeting at eleven. After the cabinet meeting, too busy to have lunch, the President ate an apple as he went back to his office. There he held more interviews, read more petitions, signed more papers.

This was proving to be the usual exhausting day of a busy Chief Executive, but Lincoln, now that the long ordeal of war was over, handled his duties expeditiously and efficiently. Indeed, since the news of Lee's surrender, his associates found he acted like a different man. "His whole appearance, poise, and bearing had marvelously changed," Senator Harlan recalled. "He seemed the very personification of supreme satisfaction. His conversation was, of course, correspondingly exhilarating."

At three o'clock he broke away from his desk to take a ride with Mary in an open carriage. As they started out, she asked whether he wanted any guests to accompany them, but he said, "No—I prefer to ride by ourselves to day." They drove about the city and went out to the Navy Yard, in southeastern Washington, where the President chatted with several of the sailors and went aboard the *Montauk,* a monitor that had been hit forty-seven times during the assault on Charleston harbor. Throughout the afternoon he was "cheerful—almost joyous," his wife recalled, and his spirits were so high that she said to him, laughing, "Dear Husband, you almost startle me by your great cheerfulness."

"And well I may feel so, Mary," he responded, "I consider *this day,* the war, has come to a close." He then added, in what was as close to a reprimand as he ever offered to his wife, "We must *both,* be more cheerful in the future—between the war and the loss of our darling Willie—we have both, been very miserable."

Back at the White House, Lincoln found still more visitors, and he had a long chat with Governor Richard J. Oglesby and General Isham Haynie, both of Illinois, to whom he read so many chapters of the *Nasby Letters* that he had to be summoned several times to dinner. The meal was served early, because the Lincolns had promised to attend a performance of the comedy *Our American Cousin* at Ford's Theatre. By this time Mary had developed a headache and was inclined to stay at home, but her husband said that he must attend. The evening newspapers had carried an announcement that he would be present and tickets had been sold on the basis of that expectation. Anyway, he added, if he remained at the White House, he would have to receive company all evening and would get no rest. Even as the Lincolns prepared to get in their carriage, he had to deal with yet more callers. Just as they were leaving, Congressman Isaac N. Arnold walked up. "Excuse me now," Lincoln said. "I am going to the theatre. Come and see me in the morning."

VI

Lincoln's advisers urged him not to go to the theater. Before leaving on a mission to Richmond, Lamon, who often served as a presidential bodyguard, begged him, "Promise me you will not go out at night while I am gone, particularly to the theater." But the President had so often heard the marshal on this subject that, as Lamon said later, he "thought me insane upon the subject of his safety," and he would only pledge, "Well, I promise to do the best I can toward it." Stanton, too, repeatedly warned Lincoln against mingling with promiscuous crowds at the theater. The occasion this evening was more dangerous than most, because it had been widely advertised that General Grant, fresh from his victories in Virginia, would join the President in the state box at Ford's Theatre.

The Lincolns had trouble making up a theater party on April 14, perhaps because it was Good Friday. They invited the Stantons, but the Secretary of War refused because, he said, "Mr. Lincoln ought not to go—it was too great an exposure." Anyway, Mrs. Stanton disliked Mrs. Lincoln. After initially accepting a verbal invitation, Grant also declined. Julia Grant, who remembered all too well Mary Lincoln's behavior during her visit to City Point, was unwilling to be confined for hours in a box at the theater with a woman of such uncertain temper: She decided to visit her children in Burlington, New Jersey, and the general, always glad of an excuse to escape the limelight, asked to be excused so that he could join her. Governor Oglesby and General Haynie were asked, but they had a meeting to attend. Lincoln invited Howard, the Detroit postmaster, but he was leaving Washington that evening. William H. Wallace, governor of Idaho Territory, and his wife also declined.

On one of his visits to the War Department, Lincoln asked Stanton if Major Thomas T. Eckert, chief of the telegraph bureau, could accompany him to the theater. Eckert was a man of exceptional strength, who once, in order to demonstrate the poor quality of the cast-iron pokers that were supplied for use at the War Department grates, broke five of them by striking them across his left arm. Here surely was a man who could defend the President against whatever danger Stanton feared. But the Secretary said that Eckert was needed for important work. Going over Stanton's head, the President approached Eckert directly. "Now, Major," he cajoled, "come along. You can do Stanton's work to-morrow, and Mrs. Lincoln and I want you with us." But Eckert, in deference to the Secretary's wishes, declined.

The Lincolns next turned to a young couple of whom they were fond: Clara Harris, the daughter of the senator from New York, and her stepbrother (who was also her fiancé) Major Henry R. Rathbone, who had served with distinction in the war and could presumably offer the President protection. After picking up their guests, the Lincolns drove to Ford's Theatre on Tenth Street through streets still illuminated in celebration of the recent victory.

By the time they arrived, at about eight-thirty, the performance had already begun, though the spectators kept glancing at the empty presidential box. There had been some grumbling because, in anticipation that both Lincoln and Grant would attend, scalpers bought up most of the tickets, which regularly cost $.75 or $1.00, and resold them for $2.50 each. But when the President and his party entered, the orchestra, led by William Withers, interrupted the actors and played "Hail to the Chief," and the audience rose and cheered. As he climbed the stairs to the dress circle, the President walked slowly, and his shoulders seemed noticeably stooped. Carrying his high silk hat in his left hand, he led the way along a narrow corridor to the presidential box. (Actually it was two boxes, but the management had removed the partition between them to give more room for the presidential party.) The audience continued wildly cheering, and, one witness remembered, "the President stepped to the box rail and acknowledged the applause with dignified bows and never-to-be-forgotten smiles." Knowing that the President preferred a rocking chair, Harry C. Ford, brother of the owner of the theater, had thoughtfully provided one from his private quarters, and there were also comfortable chairs and a small sofa for the other guests. The velvet balustrade in front of the box, eleven feet and six inches above the stage, had been decorated with patriotic colors, and the blue regimental flag of the Treasury Guard flew above a gilt-framed portrait of George Washington on the center pillar. The occupants of the box could not be seen by most of the audience.

The play, which starred Laura Keene, was a creaky farce about an American bumpkin, Asa Trenchard, who goes to England to claim a fortune he has inherited from a noble relative. He is pursued by a fortune-hunting Englishwoman, Mrs. Mountchessington, who wants to marry him to her daughter, Augusta. The play had been a hit for five years, and the lines were familiar enough to allow the actors a little improvisation for special occasions like this one. So when the frail heroine asked for a seat protected from the draft, Lord Dundreary, instead of saying "Well, you're not the only one that wants to escape the draft," replied: "You are mistaken. The draft has already been stopped by order of the President!"

Though the draperies concealed the President so that he could only be seen when he leaned forward, the Lincolns appeared to enjoy the play. When the actors scored hits, Mary applauded, but her husband simply laughed heartily. A man seated in the orchestra observed that Mrs. Lincoln often called the President's attention to actions on the stage and "seemed to take great pleasure in witnessing his enjoyment." Seated so close to her husband that she was nestled against him, she whispered: "What will Miss Harris think of my hanging on to you so?" With a smile he replied: "She wont think any thing about it."

One of the most predictable crowd-pleasers in the play came during the second scene of the third act, when Mrs. Mountchessington, learning that Asa Trenchard has given away his inheritance, denounces him for not knowing how to behave and makes a haughty exit. Asa's lines read: "Don't know the manners of good society, eh? Well, I guess I know enough to turn you inside out, old gal—you sockdologizing old man-trap." The laughter and burst of applause almost covered the sound of a shot in the presidential box.

VII

John Wilkes Booth had been busy since the night of April 11. "Our cause being almost lost," he concluded, "something decisive and great must be done." Remembering that Jefferson Davis was still at large and that Johnston's army in North Carolina was still under arms, he devised a plan to give the Confederacy one last chance by decapitating the Union government at Washington. Both Lincoln and Andrew Johnson would be killed. Seward would also be murdered, since, as Secretary of State, he would have the responsibility for holding new elections in the North. In the demoralization and disorder that would surely follow, the South might still gain its independence.

Booth had trouble getting his fellow conspirators to go along with his plan. John Surratt, the ablest of his associates, went off on a trip to Canada for his Confederate employers. Accusing Booth of mismanagement and fearing that "the G[overnmen]t suspicions something is going on," Arnold favored postponing action until someone could "go and see how it will be taken at R[ichmon]d." Later he decided to cut loose from Booth's scheme and took a job as a clerk at Old Point. O'Laughlin, too, was disillusioned; willing enough to take part in a kidnapping, he wanted no part of a murder. But Booth still had three devoted followers: Atzerodt, Herold, and Paine.

It was not until midday on April 14, when he learned that Lincoln would be attending Ford's Theatre, that Booth decided to implement his plan. At about eight o'clock he summoned Atzerodt to meet him and Paine at the Herndon House, where he gave them their marching orders. Atzerodt was told to murder Andrew Johnson, who was staying at the Kirkland House. "I won't do it!" the German said in terror. "I enlisted to abduct the President of the United States, not to kill." But under Booth's threats and curses he agreed to consider the assignment. Paine willingly accepted the order to kill Seward. Calling Booth "Captain," he thought of himself as a soldier obeying the commands of a superior officer. Because Paine was not familiar with the streets of Washington, Booth directed Herold to show him the way to the house of the Secretary of State. The assassination of the President was left for Booth himself, who expected to have some assistance in making his getaway from Edman Spangler and other stagehands at Ford's Theatre. All three assaults were to take place simultaneously, at 10:15 P.M.

In anticipation of the slaughter, Booth prepared a letter for publication in the *National Intelligencer,* explaining and defending his motives. The friend to whom he entrusted the letter destroyed it and remembered only its closing words: "The world may censure me for what I am about to do, but I am sure that posterity will justify me." The communication probably contained the same ideas that Booth later jotted down in his diary, where he recorded that the country owed all its troubles to Lincoln, "and God simply made me the instrument of his punishment." He was a modern Brutus or William Tell, though his action would be seen as purer than that of either. They had private motives, but "I struck for my country and that alone. A country groaned beneath this tyranny and prayed for this end."

As Atzerodt and Paine fanned out to seek their targets, Booth, a celebrated actor, familiar to everybody who worked at Ford's Theatre, had no trouble in slipping upstairs during the performance of *Our American Cousin.* Moving quietly down the aisle behind the dress circle, he stood for a few moments near the President's box. A member of the audience, seeing him there, thought him "the handsomest man I had ever seen." John Parker, the Metropolitan policeman assigned to protect the President, had left his post in the passageway, and the box was guarded only by Charles Forbes, a White House footman. When Booth showed Forbes his calling card, he was admitted to the presidential box. Barring the door behind him, so as not to be disturbed, he noiselessly moved behind Lincoln, who was leaning forward, with his chin in his right hand and his arm on the balustrade. At a distance of about two feet, the actor pointed his derringer at the back of the President's head on the left side and pulled the trigger. It was about 10:13 P.M.

When Major Rathbone tried to seize the intruder, Booth lunged at him with his razor-sharp hunting knife, which had a 7¼-inch blade. "The Knife," Clara Harris reported, "went from the elbow nearly to the shoulder, inside, —cutting an artery, nerves and veins—he bled so profusely as to make him very weak." Shoving his victim aside, Booth placed his hands on the balustrade and vaulted toward the stage. It was an easy leap for the gymnastic actor, but the spur on his heel caught in the flags decorating the box and he fell heavily on one foot, breaking the bone just above the ankle. Waving his dagger, he shouted in a loud, melodramatic voice: *"Sic semper tyrannis"* ("Thus always to tyrants"—the motto of the state of Virginia). Some in the audience thought he added, "The South is avenged." Quickly he limped across the stage, with what one witness called "a motion . . . like the hopping of a bull frog," and made his escape through the rear of the theater.

Up to this point the audience was not sure what had happened. Perhaps most thought the whole disturbance was part of the play. But as the blue-white smoke from the pistol drifted out of the presidential box, Mary Lincoln gave a heart-rending shriek and screamed, "They have shot the President! They have shot the President!"

The first doctor to reach the box, army surgeon Charles A. Leale, initially thought the President was dead. With his eyes closed and his head fallen forward on his breast, he was being held upright in his chair by Mrs. Lincoln, who was weeping bitterly. Detecting a slight pulse, the physician ordered the President to be stretched on the floor so that he could determine the extent of his injuries. Finding his major wound was at the back of his head, he removed the clot of blood that had accumulated there and relieved the pressure on his brain. Then, by giving artificial respiration, he was able to induce a feeble action of the heart, and irregular breathing followed.

As soon as it was clear that instant death would not occur, the President was moved from the crowded theater. Some wanted to take him to the White House, but Dr. Leale warned that he would die if jostled on the rough streets of Washington. They decided to carry him across Tenth Street to a house owned by William Petersen, a merchant-tailor. There he was taken to a small, narrow room at the rear of the first floor. Because Lincoln was so tall, his body could not fit on the bed unless his knees were elevated. Finding that the foot of the bedstead could not be removed or broken off, the doctors placed him diagonally across the mattress, resting his head and shoulders on extra pillows. Though he was covered by an army blanket and a colored wool coverlet, his extremities grew very cold, and the physicians ordered hot-water bottles.

Here Lincoln lay for the next nine hours. Dr. Leale and Dr. Charles S. Taft, who had also been in the audience for *Our American Cousin,* were constantly in attendance, and during the night, as Taft noted, "nearly all the leading men of the profession in the city tendered their services." When Dr. Robert King Stone, the Lincolns' family doctor, arrived at about eleven o'clock, he became the physician in charge, and he consulted with Dr. Joseph K. Barnes, the surgeon general of the United States. From the first, all of them agreed that there was no chance of recovery. The doctors agreed that the average man could not survive the injury Lincoln had received for more than two hours, but Dr. Stone noted that the President's "vital tenacity was very strong, and he would resist as long as any man could." He never regained consciousness.

Mary was with her husband through the long night. Frantic with grief, she sat at his bedside, calling on him to say one word to her, to take her with him. When Robert came in with Senator Sumner, he saw what desperate shape his mother was in and sent for Elizabeth Dixon—wife of Connecticut Senator James Dixon—who was perhaps Mary's closest friend in the capital. Mrs. Dixon persuaded her to retire to the front room of the Petersen house, where she rested as well as she could, returning every hour to her husband's side. On one of these visits she sobbed bitterly, "Oh, that my little Taddy might see his father before he died!" but the physicians wisely decided that this was not advisable. Once when Lincoln's breathing became very stertorous, Mary, who was approaching exhaustion, became frightened, leapt up with a piercing cry, and fell fainting on the floor. Coming in from the adjoining room, Stanton called out loudly, "Take that woman out and do not let her in again."

During the night, as crowds gathered in the street in front of the Petersen house, all the members of the cabinet except Seward came to see their fallen chief. Much of the night Secretary Welles sat by the head of the

President's bed, listening to the slow, full respiration of the dying man. Vice President Johnson was summoned, but Sumner urged him not to stay long, knowing that Mary Lincoln detested him and might cause a scene. The Reverend Phineas D. Gurley, pastor of the New York Avenue Presbyterian Church, which the Lincolns frequently attended, came to give spiritual comfort.

Stanton promptly took charge. Making an adjacent room in the Petersen house his headquarters, he summoned Assistant Secretary of War Dana to help him and began rapidly dictating one order after another designed to keep the government functioning during the crisis. Stanton immediately started an investigation of the assassination, taking testimony from witnesses, ordering all bridges and roads out of the capital closed, and directing the military to search for the murderers. By dawn he had a massive manhunt under way. He soon learned that there had been not one but two assaults. Though Atzerodt decided not to attack Andrew Johnson and spent the night wandering aimlessly about the city, Paine, following Booth's directions, had burst into Seward's house; he fiercely attacked the Secretary of State, who was still bedridden after his carriage accident, and left him bleeding copiously and barely alive. By morning Paine and Atzerodt were under arrest, and the other conspirators—including those who had only been involved in the kidnapping plot—were promptly seized. But Booth, who was accompanied by Herold, escaped. Not until April 26 did Stanton's men trace him to a farm in northern Virginia, where he was shot.

Long before that, Lincoln was dead. As the night of April 14–15 wore on, his pulse became irregular and feeble, and his respiration was accompanied by a guttural sound. Several times it seemed that he had ceased breathing. Mary was allowed to return to her husband's side, and, as Mrs. Dixon reported, "she again seated herself by the President, kissing him and calling him every endearing name." As his breath grew fainter and fainter, she was led back into the front room. At twenty-two minutes past seven, on the morning of April 15, the struggle ended, and the physicians came in to inform her: "It is all over! The President is no more!"

In the small, crowded back room there was silence until Stanton asked Dr. Gurley to offer a prayer. Robert gave way to overpowering grief and sobbed aloud, leaning on Sumner for comfort. Standing at the foot of the bed, his face covered with tears, Stanton paid tribute to his fallen chief: with a slow and measured movement, his right arm fully extended as if in a salute, he raised his hat and placed it for an instant on his head and then in the same deliberate manner removed it. "Now," he said, "he belongs to the ages."

Sources and Notes

———◆———

The basic source for any biography of Abraham Lincoln is his own writings. *The Collected Works of Abraham Lincoln,* edited by Roy P. Basler and others, is authoritative; eight volumes were published in 1953 by the Rutgers University Press, an Index volume followed in 1955, and two small supplements were issued in 1974 and 1990. I evaluated the technical merits of this edition in the *American Historical Review* 59 (October 1953): 142–149. Almost equally important are the largely unpublished Abraham Lincoln Papers in the Library of Congress, which contain Lincoln's incoming correspondence together with drafts and copies of many of his own letters and messages. Fortunately these are available on microfilm in ninety-seven reels. A rich sampling of these papers up to July 1861 appears in David C. Mearns, ed., *The Lincoln Papers* (2 vols.; Garden City, N.Y.: Doubleday & Co., 1948). Harold Holzer, ed., *Dear Mr. Lincoln: Letters to the President* (Reading, Mass.: Addison-Wesley Publishing Co., 1993), includes many other letters, mostly from the same collection. Rivaling the Lincoln Papers in importance is the Herndon-Weik Collection, also in the Library of Congress, which contains thousands of pages of legal documents, interviews, and letters collected by Herndon for his Lincoln biography. These papers are also available on microfilm, in fifteen reels. Selections from these papers, sometimes inaccurately edited, appeared in Emanuel Hertz, ed., *The Hidden Lincoln: From the Letters and Papers of William H. Herndon* (New York: Viking Press, 1938).

An enormous amount has been published about Lincoln. Jay Monaghan's *Lincoln Bibliography, 1839–1939* (2 vols.; Springfield: Illinois State Historical Library, 1943), lists 3,958 books and pamphlets, and thousands more have appeared since. Paul M. Angle, *A Shelf of Lincoln Books: A Critical Selective Bibliography of Lincolniana* (New Brunswick, N.J.: Rutgers University Press, 1946), is a judicious evaluation of this literature. Monaghan's bibliography does not include articles in magazines, some of which can be located through Richard Booker, *Abraham Lincoln in Periodical Literature, 1860–1940* (Chicago: Fawley-Brost Co., 1941).

The Lincoln Kinsman (54 numbers, 1938–1942) was devoted to Lincoln's genealogy and relatives. Beginning with April 15, 1929, *Lincoln Lore,* a publication of the Lincoln National Life Insurance Co., Fort Wayne, Indiana, has offered thousands of valuable short articles. The *Lincoln Herald,* published quarterly by Lincoln Memorial University, Harrogate, Tennessee, carries more extensive essays. The *Abraham Lincoln Quarterly,* published by the Abraham Lincoln Association in Springfield between 1940 and 1952, included some of the best scholarship, and since 1979 its tradition has been upheld in *Papers of the Abraham Lincoln Association* (after 1988 called *Journal of the Abraham Lincoln Association*).

Lincoln Day by Day: A Chronology, 1809–1865, edited by Earl S. Miers and others (3 vols.; Washington, D.C.: Lincoln Sesquicentennial Commission, 1960), is an indispensable guide. So is *The*

Abraham Lincoln Encyclopedia, by Mark E. Neely, Jr. (New York: McGraw-Hill, 1982). Archer H. Shaw, ed., *The Lincoln Encyclopedia* (New York: Macmillan Co., 1950), is also useful.

Of the many biographies *Abraham Lincoln: A History* (10 vols.; New York: Century Co., 1890), by John G. Nicolay and John Hay, is the most complete. *Herndon's Lincoln: The True Story of a Great Life* (3 vols.; Chicago: Belford, Clarke & Co., 1889), by William H. Herndon and Jesse W. Weik, is revealing on Lincoln's early years. Albert J. Beveridge's *Abraham Lincoln, 1809–1858* (2 vols.; Boston: Houghton Mifflin Co., 1928), offers the fullest account of Lincoln's career in Illinois politics. Carl Sandburg's *Abraham Lincoln: The Prairie Years* (2 vols.; New York: Harcourt, Brace & Co., 1926) and *Abraham Lincoln: The War Years* (4 vols.; New York: Harcourt, Brace & Co., 1939) together form the most imaginative and humanly flavorful of all the biographies. The most scholarly large-scale biography remains J. G. Randall, *Lincoln the President* (4 vols.; New York: Dodd, Mead & Co., 1945–1955), the last volume of which was ably completed by Richard N. Current.

Two important recent studies which—correctly, in my opinion—emphasize the war years are Mark E. Neely, Jr., *The Last Best Hope of Earth: Abraham Lincoln and the Promise of America* (Cambridge, Mass.: Harvard University Press, 1993), and Phillip S. Paludan, *The Presidency of Abraham Lincoln* (Lawrence: University Press of Kansas, 1994).

Of the many one-volume lives the best are Benjamin P. Thomas, *Abraham Lincoln: A Biography* (New York: Alfred A. Knopf, 1952); Reinhard H. Luthin, *The Real Abraham Lincoln* (Englewood Cliffs, N.J.: Prentice-Hall, 1960); and Stephen B. Oates, *With Malice Toward None: The Life of Abraham Lincoln* (New York: Harper & Row, 1977). Because I wanted, so far as possible, to write a biography from the original sources, I have not read or consulted these distinguished works in the preparation of the present volume. I cannot say, however, that I have not been influenced by them, for I used these books in my classes for many years and there are doubtless unconscious echoes of them in this biography.

Charles Hamilton and Lloyd Ostendorf, *Lincoln in Photographs: An Album of Every Known Pose* (Dayton, Ohio: Morningside, 1985), is authoritative. James Mellon, *The Face of Lincoln* (New York: Viking Press, 1979), offers superb reproductions of the best of these photographs. *Lincoln: An Illustrated Biography* (New York: Alfred A. Knopf, 1992), by Philip B. Kunhardt, Jr., et al., is a fascinating photographic history.

On Lincoln historiography readers should consult Benjamin P. Thomas, *Portrait for Posterity: Lincoln and His Biographers* (New Brunswick, N.J.: Rutgers University Press, 1947), and Merrill D. Peterson, *Lincoln in American Memory* (New York: Oxford University Press, 1994), which is especially valuable.

It has been difficult to know how to annotate this book. Almost every aspect of Lincoln's life has been the object of much study; most subjects are treated not merely in the biographies and the general histories of the period but in specialized monographs. If I were to cite all the books and articles consulted in the preparation of this biography, I would have a book at least twice as long as the present one. My solution of the problem has been to offer for each chapter a brief discussion of the principal sources I found most useful. I hope these paragraphs may serve as guides to further reading.

The actual notes are largely confined to giving sources for quotations and facts included in the text. I have not thought it my task to use these notes to correct errors that I think previous biographers have made or, except in a few absolutely necessary cases, to enter into historiographical discussions. This is a book about Lincoln—not a book about the literature about Lincoln.

I have tried to quote my sources as accurately as I could. In particular, I have given Lincoln's words exactly as he wrote them and have not thought it necessary to interject [*sic*] in order to point out his infrequent errors in spelling or grammar. In the interest of readability I have throughout transcribed "&" as "and." I have also taken the liberty of omitting initial and final ellipses. Thus, had I decided to use a phrase from Lincoln's July 20, 1860, letter to Cassius M. Clay, I would not give it as ". . . at Rockport you will be in the county within which I was brought up . . . ," but as "At Rockport you will be in the county within which I was brought up." I believe that this usage does not distort the meaning but makes it easier for a reader to follow the story. (Ellipses have been scrupulously employed to signify that words within a passage have been omitted.)

ABBREVIATIONS AND SHORT TITLES EMPLOYED IN NOTES

AL—Abraham Lincoln
ALQ—Abraham Lincoln Quarterly

Baker, *Mary Todd Lincoln*—Jean Harvey Baker, *Mary Todd Lincoln: A Biography* (New York: W. W. Norton & Co., 1987)

Bates, *Diary*—Howard K. Beale, ed., *Diary of Edward Bates, 1859–1866* (Washington, D.C.: Government Printing Office, 1933)

Beveridge—Albert J. Beveridge, *Abraham Lincoln, 1809–1858* (2 vols.; Boston: Houghton Mifflin Co., 1928)

Browning, *Diary*—Theodore C. Pease and James G. Randall, eds., *The Diary of Orville Hickman Browning* (2 vols.; Springfield: Illinois State Historical Library, 1925–1933)

Carpenter, *Six Months*—Francis B. Carpenter, *Six Months at the White House with Abraham Lincoln* (New York: Hurd & Houghton, 1866)

Chase, *Diary*—David Herbert Donald, ed., *Inside Lincoln's Cabinet: The Civil War Diaries of Salmon P. Chase* (New York: Longmans, Green & Co., 1954)

Chase MSS—All citations are to the microfilm edition issued by the Library of Congress, which includes Chase letters from the Historical Society of Pennsylvania, the Library of Congress, and other sources.

CW—*Collected Works of Abraham Lincoln,* ed. Roy P. Basler

Day by Day—Earl Schenk Miers, ed., *Lincoln Day by Day* (3 vols.; Washington, D.C.: Lincoln Sesquicentennial Commission, 1960)

Donald, *Lincoln's Herndon*—David Herbert Donald, *Lincoln's Herndon* (New York: Alfred A. Knopf, 1948)

Donald, *Sumner*—David Herbert Donald, *Charles Sumner and the Rights of Man* (New York: Alfred A. Knopf, 1970)

Duff, *A. Lincoln*—John J. Duff, *A. Lincoln: Prairie Lawyer* (New York: Rinehart & Co., Inc., 1960)

Hay, *Diary*—Tyler Dennett, ed., *Lincoln and the Civil War in the Diaries and Letters of John Hay* (New York: Dodd, Mead & Co., 1939)

HEH—Huntington Library, San Marino, California

Herndon's Lincoln—William H. Herndon and Jesse W. Weik, *Herndon's Lincoln: The True Story of a Great Life* (3 vols.; Chicago: Belford-Clarke, 1890). Throughout I have cited this edition, which appears to be identical to the first edition, published in 1889.

Hidden Lincoln—Emanuel Hertz, ed., *The Hidden Lincoln: From the Letters and Papers of William H. Herndon* (New York: Viking Press, 1928)

HWC—Herndon-Weik Collection, Library of Congress

ISHL—Illinois State Historical Library, Springfield

JISHS—*Journal of the Illinois State Historical Society*

Journal—Springfield *Illinois State Journal*

LC—Library of Congress

LH—*Lincoln Herald*

Lincoln MSS, LC—The Abraham Lincoln Papers, Library of Congress

LL—*Lincoln Lore*

McClellan, *Civil War Papers*—Stephen W. Sears, ed., *The Civil War Papers of George B. McClellan* (New York: Ticknor & Fields, 1989)

Nicolay and Hay—John G. Nicolay and John Hay, *Abraham Lincoln: A History* (10 vols.; New York: Century Co., 1890)

Pratt, *Personal Finances*—Harry E. Pratt, *The Personal Finances of Abraham Lincoln* (Springfield, Ill.: Abraham Lincoln Association, 1943)

Randall, *Lincoln the President*—J. G. Randall, *Lincoln the President* (4 vols.; New York: Dodd, Mead & Co., 1945–1955). The final volume, *Last Full Measure,* was completed by Richard N. Current.

Randall, *Mary Lincoln*—Ruth Painter Randall, *Mary Lincoln: Biography of a Marriage* (Boston: Little, Brown & Co., 1953)

Register—Springfield *Illinois State Register*

Sandburg—Carl Sandburg, *Abraham Lincoln: The War Years* (4 vols.; New York: Harcourt, Brace & Co., 1939)

Segal, *Conversations*—Charles M. Segal, ed., *Conversations with Lincoln* (New York: G. P. Putnam's Sons, 1961)

Strong, *Diary*—Allan Nevins and Milton Halsey Thomas, eds., *The Diary of George Templeton Strong: The Civil War, 1860–1865* (New York: Macmillan Co., 1952)

Turner, *Mary Todd Lincoln*—Justin G. Turner and Linda Levitt Turner, *Mary Todd Lincoln: Her Life and Letters* (New York: Alfred A. Knopf, 1972)

UR—University of Rochester

Welles, *Diary*—Howard K. Beale and Alan W. Brownsword, eds., *Diary of Gideon Welles, Secretary of the Navy Under Lincoln and Johnson* (3 vols.; New York: W. W. Norton & Co., 1960)

WHH—William H. Herndon

Zornow—William F. Zornow, *Lincoln and the Party Divided* (Norman: University of Oklahoma Press, 1954)

CHAPTER ONE: ANNALS OF THE POOR

The basic source for Abraham Lincoln's early years is the collection of letters and statements that his law partner, William H. Herndon, made shortly after the President's death. The originals of these documents are in the Herndon-Weik Collection in the Library of Congress, and there are copies in the Ward Hill Lamon MSS in the Huntington Library. Emanuel Hertz published an extensive sampling of these papers in *The Hidden Lincoln: From the Letters and Papers of William H. Herndon* (New York: Viking Press, 1938), but the transcriptions are not very reliable.

Drawing heavily on the Herndon materials, Albert J. Beveridge, *Abraham Lincoln, 1809–1858* (Boston: Houghton Mifflin Co., 1928), is the most richly detailed account of Lincoln's early years, but it is marred by the author's much too negative view of the Hanks family and his low opinion of Thomas Lincoln. Louis A. Warren offers a valuable corrective in *Lincoln's Parentage and Childhood* (New York: Century Co., 1926) and *Lincoln's Youth: Indiana Years, Seven to Twenty-One, 1816–1830* (New York: Appleton-Century-Crofts, 1959). Ida M. Tarbell, *In the Footsteps of the Lincolns* (New York: Harper & Brothers, 1924), presents much information in a charming fashion. Charles B. Strozier, *Lincoln's Quest for Union: Public and Private Meanings* (New York: Basic Books, 1982), is an intelligent and persuasive interpretation of Lincoln's early years from a psychoanalytical perspective.

19 *in his ancestry:* He did answer a number of inquiries about his Lincoln ancestors, saying that he knew only about members of his father's and his grandfather's generations. *CW,* 1:455–456, 459–460, 461–462; 2:217–218; 4:37, 117.

19 *"I should say":* CW, 3:511.

19 *"make of it":* John L. Scripps to WHH, June 24, 1865, HWC.

19 *during the 1780s:* Adin Baber, *Nancy Hanks of Undistinguished Families* (Kansas, Ill., privately published, 1960), p. 40.

20 *power of analysis: Herndon's Lincoln,* 1:3–4. Lincoln cautioned Herndon not to mention this conversation while he was alive. So far as I know, Herndon first revealed it in a letter to the bibliographer Charles Henry Hart, dated Dec. 28, 1866. Hart MSS, HEH. Thereafter, he told it many times, with a number of variations. For instance, in letters to Ward H. Lamon (Feb. 24, 1869, and Mar. 6, 1870, Lamon MSS, HEH), he declared that Lincoln said that "a Virginia nabob" or "nobleman" took advantage of his "poor and credulous" grandmother.

20 *out of wedlock:* There used to be much controversy about the legitimacy of Nancy Hanks. William E. Barton, *The Lineage of Lincoln* (Indianapolis: Bobbs-Merrill Co., 1929), accepted Herndon's story. Warren, *Lincoln's Parentage and Childhood,* vigorously rejected it. The argument has now died down, and most—but not all—scholars believe she was illegitimate.

20 *charge of fornication:* For an explanation of this charge, and a defense of Lincoln's grandmother, see James A. Peterson, *In re Lucey Hanks* (Yorkville, Ill., privately published, 1973), chap. 5.

20 *Lincoln's maternal grandsire:* See two careful explorations by Paul H. Verduin: "New Evidence Suggests Lincoln's Mother Born in Richmond County, Virginia, Giving Credibility to Planter-Grandfather Legend," *Northern Neck of Virginia Historical Magazine* 38 (Dec. 1988): 4354–4589, and "Lincoln's Tidewater Virginia Heritage: The Hidden Legacy of Nancy Hanks Lincoln" (unpublished address to the Lincoln Group of the District of Columbia, Oct. 17, 1989).

20 *"of that people":* CW, 4:60–61.

20 *"and absolute darkness":* W. D. Howells, *Life of Abraham Lincoln* (facsimile ed.; Springfield, Ill.: Abraham Lincoln Association, 1938), p. 18. Howells's biography carries unusual authority because Lincoln, at the request of a friend, read it and corrected what errors he found in the margins.

21 *of public service:* This account of the Lincoln family relies heavily on Thomas L. Purvis, "The Making of a Myth: Abraham Lincoln's Family Background in the Perspective of Jacksonian Politics," *JISHS* 75 (Summer 1982): 148–160, an important interpretation. Ida Tarbell, *In the*

Footsteps of the Lincolns, offers excellent sketches of these early Lincolns. Those interested in the more technical aspects of Lincoln genealogy should consult J. Henry Lea and J. R. Hutchinson, *The Ancestry of Abraham Lincoln* (Boston: Houghton Mifflin Co., 1909); Marion Dexter Learned, *Abraham Lincoln: An American Migration* (Philadelphia: William J. Campbell, 1909); and Waldo Lincoln, *History of the Lincoln Family* (reprint ed.; Boston: Goodspeed's Book Shop, 1981).

21 *"mind and memory": CW,* 2:217.

21 *"of the family":* Francis F. Browne, *The Every-Day Life of Abraham Lincoln* (Chicago: Browne & Howell Co., 1913), 1:4. See also "Uncle Mordecai Lincoln: Only Lincoln Relative with Whom the President Was Familiar," *Lincoln Kinsman,* no. 12 (June 1939).

22 *a difficult time:* My account of Thomas Lincoln and his property holding derives principally from Warren, *Lincoln's Parentage and Childhood.*

22 *"and good natured":* Samuel Haycraft to WHH, Aug. 1, 1865 [?], HWC.

22 *"the creek bottoms":* E. R. Barbee to William H. Herndon, May 25, 1866, Lamon MSS, HEH.

22 *a shadowy image:* Betty J. Atkinson, "Some Thoughts on Nancy Hanks," *LH* 73 (Fall 1971): 127–137, reviews the historiography. The only attempt at a biography is Harold E. Briggs and Ernestine B. Briggs, *Nancy Hanks Lincoln: A Frontier Portrait* (New York: Bookman Associates, 1952).

23 his *"angel mother":* Joshua F. Speed, *Reminiscences of Abraham Lincoln and Notes of a Visit to California: Two Lectures* (Louisville, Ky.: John P. Morton and Co., 1884), p. 19.

23 *"owe to her": Herndon's Lincoln,* 1:3.

23 *"off the field":* Warren, *Lincoln's Parentage and Childhood,* p. 143.

23 *"would learn much":* Dennis F. Hanks, statement written by A. H. Chapman, Sept. 8, 1865, HWC.

23 *was a Catholic:* Roger H. Futrell, "Zachariah Riney: Lincoln's First Schoolmaster," *LH* 74 (Fall 1972): 136–142.

23 *"to his school":* Samuel Haycraft to WHH, Hardin Co., Ky., [Aug. 1, 1865], Lamon MSS, HEH.

23 *"somewhat wild nature":* Dennis Hanks, statement written by A. H. Chapman, Sept. 8, 1865, HWC.

24 *"land titles in Ky.": CW,* 4:61–62.

24 *opposed to slavery:* Warren, *Lincoln's Parentage and Childhood,* chaps. 14 and 18, offers an excellent account of the Lincolns' religious views.

24 *"think, and feel": CW,* 7:281.

24 *age of sixteen:* Mark E. Neely, Jr., *The Abraham Lincoln Encyclopedia* (New York: McGraw-Hill Book Co., 1982), p. 188.

25 *on the swine: CW,* 1:386.

25 *proper log cabin:* Charles H. Coleman, "The Half-Faced Camp in Indiana—Fact or Myth?" *ALQ* 7 (Sept. 1952): 138–146, demolishes the myth that the Lincolns remained in the half-faced camp for the entire winter.

25 *"all the time":* Dennis F. Hanks to WHH, June 13, 1865, HWC.

25 *"any larger game": CW,* 4:62.

25 *"and harvesting seasons":* Ibid.

26 *no permanent damage: Herndon's Lincoln,* 1:51–52.

26 *called milk sickness:* Milton H. Shutes, *Lincoln and the Doctors* (New York: Pioneer Press, 1933), pp. 4–5; Philip D. Jordan, "The Death of Nancy Hanks Lincoln," *Indiana Magazine of History* 40 (June 1944): 103–110; Warren, *Lincoln's Youth,* pp. 51–53, 228–229.

26 *"to the world":* Dennis F. Hanks to WHH, June 13, 1865, HWC.

26 *"nay for life":* Ibid.

26 *"couldn't ketch any":* Warren, *Lincoln's Youth,* p. 58.

27 *"what I say": CW,* 6:16–17. For this quotation, and for a thoughtful discussion of Lincoln's attitude toward death, I am indebted to Robert V. Bruce, *Lincoln and the Riddle of Death* (Fort Wayne, Ind.: Louis A. Warren Lincoln Library and Museum, 1981).

27 *matter of speculation:* See the discussion of this issue in Charles B. Strozier, *Lincoln's Quest for Union,* pp. 24–30, with a masterful summary of the psychoanalytical literature on p. 239. Howard I. Kushner's analysis in *Self-Destruction in the Promised Land: A Psychocultural Biology of American Suicide* (New Brunswick, N.J.: Rutgers University Press, 1989), chap. 5, is suggestive. John Bowlby's three vols. entitled *Attachment and Loss* are very important, esp. vol. 3, *Loss: Sadness and Depression* (New York: Basic Books, 1980).

27 *"ours to us":* Matilda Johnston Moore, statement to WHH, Sept. 8, 1865, HWC.

27 *"in the tombs"*: *CW,* 1:378–379.

28 *look "more human"*: Mrs. Thomas Lincoln, statement to WHH, Sept. 8, 1865, HWC.

28 *"well and clean"*: Dennis F. Hanks to WHH, June 13, 1865, HWC.

28 *"expect to see"*: Mrs. Thomas Lincoln, statement to WHH, Sept. 8, 1865, HWC.

28 *"he loved her"*: Charles H. Coleman, *Abraham Lincoln and Coles County, Illinois* (New Brunswick, N. J.: Scarecrow Press, 1955), p. 199.

28 *"nothing of want"*: Allen Thorndike Rice, ed., *Reminiscences of Abraham Lincoln by Distinguished Men of His Time* (New York: North American Review, 1888), p. 468.

29 *"how to write"*: Dennis F. Hanks to WHH, June 13, 1865, HWC.

29 *"slowly, but surely"*: John Hanks, statement to WHH, undated, HWC.

29 *"understanding of it"*: Mrs. Thomas Lincoln, statement to WHH, Sept. 8, 1865, HWC.

29 *they were strangers:* Nathaniel Grigsby, statement to WHH, Sept. 12, 1865, HWC.

29 *"to one year"*: *CW,* 4:62.

29 *"as a wizzard"*: *CW,* 3:511.

29 *grammar and spelling:* On the books Lincoln studied and read I have closely followed the excellent accounts in Beveridge, 1:70, 73–77, and in Warren, *Lincoln's Youth,* pp. 28–30, 87–95, and 103–111. Douglas L. Wilson, "What Jefferson and Lincoln Read," *Atlantic Monthly* 267 (Jan. 1991): 51–62, is a thoughtful essay. There is much useful information in M. L. Houser, *Lincoln's Education and Other Essays* (New York: Bookman Associates, 1957).

30 *the word correctly: Herndon's Lincoln,* 1:35.

30 *"fools to read"*: Facsimile of page from Lincoln's Sum Book, at the beginning of vol. 1 of *The Collected Works.*

30 *"his hands on"*: Dennis F. Hanks to WHH, June 13, 1865, HWC.

30 *"head, and read"*: John Hanks, undated statement to WHH, HWC.

30 *"[and] repeat it"*: Mrs. Thomas Lincoln, statement to WHH, Sept. 8, 1865, HWC.

30 *"for his age"*: Ibid.

31 *"men struggled for"*: *CW,* 4:235–236.

31 *in elementary mathematics:* The following paragraph is based on an excellent article by Maurice Dorfman, "Lincoln's Arithmetic Education: Influence on His Life," *LH* 68 (Summer 1966): 61–80. Lloyd A. Dunlap, "Lincoln's Sum Book," *LH* 61 (Spring 1959): 6–10, is also valuable.

31 *"go on again"*: Mrs. Thomas Lincoln, statement to WHH, Sept. 8, 1865, HWC.

32 *"Lincoln's shin bone"*: Nathaniel Grigsby, statement to WHH, Sept. 12, 1865, HWC.

32 *began to deteriorate:* For a sensitive interpretation of Lincoln's difficult relations with his father, see Charles B. Strozier and Stanley H. Cath, "Lincoln and the Fathers: Reflections on Idealization," in Stanley H. Cath et al., eds., *Fathers and Their Families* (Hillsdale, N. J.: Analytic Press, 1989), chap. 14.

32 *sight in the other: Hidden Lincoln,* p. 367.

32 *"doing nothing great"*: Nathaniel Grigsby, statement to WHH, Sept. 12, 1865, HWC.

32 *"hoeing, making fences"*: Beveridge, 1:67.

32 *"it himself first"*: Mrs. Thomas Lincoln, statement to WHH, Sept. 8, 1865, HWC.

32 *"work by reading"*: Dennis Hanks to WHH, June 13, 1865, HWC.

32 *"of his sensations"*: Ibid.

33 *boy got older:* It is possible that Abraham Lincoln doubted that Thomas Lincoln really was his father. There was a strong undercurrent of gossip in Kentucky that mumps, or perhaps an accidental castration, rendered Thomas Lincoln impotent. That left the door open for speculation that Abraham's father was one Abraham Enlow, who bore more of a physical resemblance to the future President than Thomas Lincoln did. These legends have long ago been exploded, and the story of Lincoln's bastardy is utterly groundless. See William E. Barton, *The Paternity of Abraham Lincoln: Was He the Son of Thomas Lincoln?* (New York: George H. Doran Co., 1920), for a sober, but unintentionally funny, examination of allegations that Abraham Lincoln was fathered by Enlow, Chief Justice John Marshall, John C. Calhoun, and others. The point here, however, is that the story about Enlow (sometimes spelled "Inlow") was circulated at least by the time of the Civil War. For instance, John J. Joel wrote to William H. Seward on July 22, 1863 (Seward MSS, UR), that the President's "real name is Abraham Hanks.—He is the illegitimate son by a man named Inlow—from a Negress named Hanna Hanks." Such rumors may well have reached Abraham Lincoln's ears when he was a boy.

33 *John D. Johnston:* A. H. Chapman to WHH, Sept. 28, 1865, HWC.

33 *"he ever did"*: Mrs. Thomas Lincoln, statement to WHH, Sept. 8, 1865, HWC.

33 *"him to work"*: Matilda Johnston Moore, statement to WHH, Sept. 8, 1865, HWC.

33 *"ciphering—writing Poetry":* Dennis F. Hanks, statement to WHH, Sept. 8, 1865, HWC.
33 *"like killing snakes":* John Romine, statement to WHH, Sept. 14, 1865; Elizabeth Crawford to WHH, Sept. 7, 1865—both in HWC.
33 *"ambition for education":* CW, 3:511; 4:61.
33 *about his father:* Strozier, *Lincoln's Quest for Union,* p. 14, strongly makes this point.
34 *"of all kinds":* Beveridge, 1:79.
34 *"Abe and listen":* Dennis F. Hanks to WHH, June 13, 1865, HWC.
34 *"owned or worn":* Jesse W. Weik, *The Real Lincoln: A Portrait* (Boston: Houghton Mifflin Co., 1922), p. 25.
34 *"made to do":* Herndon's Lincoln, 1:52.
34 *he slaughtered hogs:* Green B. Taylor, statement to WHH, Sept. 16, 1865, HWC.
34 *"fairer before me":* Carpenter, *Six Months,* pp. 97–98.
34 *" 'weighed anchor' and left":* CW, 4: 62.
35 *"felt miffed—insulted":* William Wood, statement to WHH, Sept. 15, 1865, HWC.
35 *"The Chronicles of Reuben":* Herndon's Lincoln, 1:45–48, gives a detailed account. Howard M. Feinstein, "The Chronicles of Reuben: A Psychological Test of Authenticity," *American Quarterly* 18 (Winter 1966): 637–654, makes a striking case for Lincoln's authorship.
35 *at the match:* HL, pp. 286–287.
35 *"than Watts hymns":* William Wood, statement to WHH, Sept. 15, 1865, HWC.
35 *"want a start":* Ibid.
36 *"and saved him":* Peter Smith to J. Warren Keifer, July 17, 1860, MS in private hands (copy through the courtesy of Glenn L. Carle).
36 *as an elector:* CW, 1:2.
37 *future of Illinois:* Howells, *Life of Abraham Lincoln,* p. 28; Jane Martin Johns, *Personal Recollections of Early Decatur, Abraham Lincoln, Richard J. Oglesby and the Civil War,* ed. Howard C. Schaub (Decatur, Ill.: Decatur Chapter Daughters of the American Revolution, 1912), pp. 60–61.
37 *another Thomas Lincoln:* This interpretation is similar to that offered by Jean H. Baker, in *"Not Much of Me": Abraham Lincoln as a Typical American* (Fort Wayne, Ind.: Louis A. Warren Lincoln Library and Museum, 1988), from which I have learned much.

CHAPTER TWO: A PIECE OF FLOATING DRIFTWOOD

The basic source for Lincoln's New Salem years is William H. Herndon's collection of letters and statements by Lincoln's friends and associates, mostly written shortly after the President's death. The originals are in the Herndon-Weik Collection of the Library of Congress, and copies are in the Herndon-Lamon MSS at the Huntington Library. Ward Hill Lamon, *The Life of Abraham Lincoln* (Boston: James R. Osgood & Co., 1872), was the first biography to draw on this material, but the most frequently used secondary account is William H. Herndon and Jesse E. Weik, *Herndon's Lincoln: The True Story of a Great Life* (Chicago: Belford-Clarke Co., 1890). Because all subsequent accounts necessarily have drawn on Herndon and his sources, there is inevitably a considerable amount of repetition in the biographies, the best of which for this period is Albert J. Beveridge, *Abraham Lincoln, 1809–1858* (Boston: Houghton Mifflin Co., 1928).

In addition to the Herndon-Weik Collection, this chapter rests heavily on several excellent secondary works. Benjamin P. Thomas, *Lincoln's New Salem* (New York: Alfred A. Knopf, 1954), is an indispensable study, both charming and informative. It can be supplemented at points by John Mack Faragher, *Sugar Creek: Life on the Illinois Prairie* (New Haven, Conn.: Yale University Press, 1986), a model study of another community in the Sangamon valley, some forty miles from New Salem. William E. Baringer, *Lincoln's Vandalia: A Pioneer Portrait* (New Brunswick, N.J.: Rutgers University Press, 1949), offers a vigorous, entertaining account of life in the state capital. The authoritative work on Lincoln's years in the legislature is Paul Simon, *Lincoln's Preparation for Greatness: The Illinois Legislative Years* (Urbana: University of Illinois Press, 1971).

38 *"of floating driftwood":* Herndon's Lincoln, 1:79.
39 *"on the boat":* Day by Day, 1:14.
39 *"were, by himself":* CW, 4:64.
39 *was perfectly suited:* See, in addition to Benjamin P. Thomas's admirable *Lincoln's New Salem,* Thomas P. Reep, *Lincoln at New Salem* (Petersburg, Ill.: Old Salem Lincoln League, 1927).

39 *"done with the Bible": Herndon's Lincoln,* 1:79–80.

40 *"of Genl Washington":* A. Y. Ellis, undated statement to WHH, HWC.

40 *no special point:* See Benjamin P. Thomas, "Lincoln's Humor: An Analysis," *Abraham Lincoln Association Papers, 1935* (Springfield, Ill.: Abraham Lincoln Association, 1936), pp. 61–83.

40 *"to take part":* Robert L. Wilson to WHH, Feb. 10, 1866, HWC.

40 *and the invalid: Herndon's Lincoln,* 1:82.

40 *"wooling and pulling":* Henry McHenry, statement to WHH, Oct. 10, 1866, HWC.

41 *"all were amazed": HL,* p. 314.

41 *"kindness and honesty":* Mentor Graham to WHH, May 29, 1865, HWC.

41 *"old law functionary":* Jason Duncan to WHH, [1865], HWC.

42 *"dollars per month": CW,* 1:320.

42 "plenty of friends": Roy P. Basler, ed., "James Quay Howard's Notes on Lincoln," *ALQ* 4 (Dec. 1947): 391.

43 *"in the country":* All quotations in the following paragraphs are from this announcement. *CW,* 1:5–9.

43 *"cabin steamer* Talisman": For a detailed account, see Harry E. Pratt, "Lincoln Pilots the Talisman," *ALQ* 2 (Sept. 1943): 319–329.

44 *"brain rattling man":* Hardin Bale to WHH, May 29, 1865, HWC.

44 *down the river:* Mentor Graham to WHH, May 29, 1865, HWC.

44 *"petered out": Herndon's Lincoln,* 1:85.

44 *Black Hawk War:* For detailed accounts of Lincoln's military experiences, see Harry E. Pratt, "Lincoln in the Black Hawk War," *Bulletin of the Abraham Lincoln Association,* no. 54 (Dec. 1938): 3–13, and Pratt's article on the same subject in O. Fritiof Ander, ed., *The John H. Hauberg Historical Essays* (Rock Island, Ill.: Augustana Book Concern, 1954), pp. 18–28.

44 *sworn in to service:* Wayne C. Temple, *Lincoln's Arms, Dress and Military Duty During and After the Black Hawk War* (Springfield: State of Illinois Military and Naval Department, 1981), p. 12.

44 *and joined them:* Reep, *Lincoln at New Salem,* p. 40.

44 *"have had since": CW,* 3:512.

45 *"to do so":* W. G. Greene to WHH, May 30, 1865, HWC.

45 *"often very hungry": CW,* 1:509–510.

45 *"than enlist again": Herndon's Lincoln,* 1:100.

46 *"Rivers of Illinois":* Henry McHenry to WHH, May 29, 1865, HWC.

46 *"and a straw hat": Herndon's Lincoln,* 1:103.

46 *"or Clay, man":* Lincoln's corrections in W. D. Howells, *Life of Abraham Lincoln* (Springfield, Ill.: Abraham Lincoln Association, 1938), p. 40.

46 *"old woman's dance": Herndon's Lincoln,* 1:104.

46 *"of the people": CW,* 4:64.

46 *"to go to":* Ibid., pp. 64–65.

47 *"of the whole": Herndon's Lincoln,* 1:107.

47 *selection of shoes:* Beveridge, 1:127.

47 *and American novelists:* The story that Lincoln read the sentimental novels of Caroline Lee Hentz at this time is incorrect, since Mrs. Hentz's first novel was not published until 1846. Roy P. Basler, ed., *Abraham Lincoln: His Speeches and Writings* (Cleveland: World Publishing Co., 1946), p. 6.

47 *"and transcendent genius": CW,* 8:237.

48 *"inexpressibly touching":* Carpenter, *Six Months,* p. 59.

48 *Sir Walter Scott:* Ibid., pp. 60–61.

48 *"I am ruled":* M. L. Houser, *Lincoln's Education and Other Essays* (New York: Bookman Associates, 1957), pp. 117–118.

48 *"he now does": CW,* 4:62.

48 *"in constant agitation":* William J. Wolf, *The Almost Chosen People: A Study of the Religion of Abraham Lincoln* (Garden City, N.Y.: Doubleday & Co., 1959), p. 42.

49 *"opinion in argument": CW,* 1:382.

49 *"a thriftless soul":* Lincoln let this characterization go uncorrected in Howells, *Life of Abraham Lincoln,* p. 42.

50 *"in the world":* William H. Townsend, *Lincoln and Liquor* (New York: Press of the Pioneers, 1934), remains authoritative. See also Wayne C. Temple, "Lincoln's Tavern License," *LH* 82 (Fall 1980): 463–464.

50 *"winked out"*: CW, 4:65.

50 *"of a hollow"*: Townsend, *Lincoln and Liquor,* p. 37.

50 *to purchase liquor:* Jason Duncan to WHH, [1866], HWC.

50 *"politics an objection"*: CW, 4:65.

50 *"he wanted before"*: Basler, ed., "James Quay Howard's Notes on Lincoln," *ALQ* 4 (Dec. 1947): 388.

50 *were not onerous:* The following paragraphs rely heavily on Benjamin P. Thomas's excellent study, "Lincoln the Postmaster," *Bulletin of the Abraham Lincoln Association,* no. 31 (June 1933), pp. 1–9.

50 *$150 and $175:* For information on this point I am indebted to Dr. Richard John, who has closely examined the *Official Registers* of the period. See also Pratt, *Personal Finances,* pp. 16–17.

51 *"to 'Frank' it"*: Thomas, "Lincoln the Postmaster," p. 7. Marsh's letter was written a few weeks after Ann Rutledge's death, when Lincoln may have been more careless than usual in managing the post office.

51 *"pay it again"*: CW, 1:25.

51 *receipts, $248.63:* Thomas, *Lincoln's New Salem,* pp. 98–99.

51 *"went at it"*: CW, 4:65.

51 *to the field:* Adin Baber, *A. Lincoln with Compass and Chain* (Kansas, Ill., 1968), is the authoritative treatment of Lincoln as surveyor.

51 *"poore [sic] man's lot"*: Mrs. E. Abell to WHH, Feb. 15, 1867, HWC.

51 *quarter section surveyed:* Thomas, *Lincoln's New Salem,* p. 103.

52 *"the matter satisfactorily"*: Robert L. Wilson to WHH, Feb. 10, 1866, HWC.

52 *"in the Croud"*: J. R. Herndon to WHH, May 28, 1865, HWC.

52 *"other democratic candidates"*: John G. Nicolay, notes on a conversation with S. T. Logan, July 6, 1875, Lincoln MSS, LC.

53 *the Democrats' support:* Thomas, *Lincoln's New Salem,* pp. 113–114.

53 *"I ever saw"*: Herndon's Lincoln, 1:181n.

53 *"in good earnest"*: CW, 4:65.

53 *"in the legislature"*: Coleman Smoot to WHH, May 7, 1866, HWC.

53 *a memorable one:* My account of Lincoln's service in the legislature is drawn almost entirely from Paul Simon's authoritative *Lincoln's Preparation for Greatness,* but I have also used William E. Baringer's spirited *Lincoln's Vandalia.*

53 *their first term:* Simon, *Lincoln's Preparation for Greatness,* p. 20.

54 *Clayborn Elder Bell:* Ibid., pp. 22, 27.

54 *"troubling the legislature"*: CW, 1:31.

54 *his "national debt"*: Basler, ed., "James Quay Howard's Notes on Lincoln," *ALQ* 4 (Dec. 1947): 398. For an informed discussion of Lincoln's troubled finances, see Thomas F. Schwartz, "Lincoln's National Debt" (unpublished paper, 1992), to which I am much indebted.

55 *"he was reading"*: Hidden Lincoln, p. 321.

55 *"He studied with nobody"*: CW, 4:65.

55 *"would craze himself"*: Henry McHenry to WHH, May 29, 1865, HWC.

55 *returned it to him:* James Short to WHH, July 7, 1865, HWC.

55 *"and clothing bills"*: CW, 4:65.

55 *She was Ann Rutledge:* The Ann Rutledge story is highly controversial. It derives almost exclusively from letters and statements that Herndon collected after Lincoln's death. In a lecture delivered in November 1866, Herndon gave wide publicity to the Lincoln-Rutledge romance, going far beyond his evidence to argue that Ann Rutledge was the only woman Lincoln ever loved and that her death left Lincoln so desolated that "his mind wandered from its throne." Later Herndon went on to speculate that Lincoln's persisting infatuation for Ann explained the unhappiness in his marriage to Mary Todd Lincoln, whom he never loved. For an account of Herndon's lecture and the sources on which it was based, see David Herbert Donald, *Lincoln's Herndon* (New York: Alfred A. Knopf, 1948), chap. 15. Widely echoed by romantic biographers, Herndon's story came under close scrutiny from twentieth-century Lincoln scholars such as Paul M. Angle, and J. G. Randall made a devastating analysis of Herndon's sources in "Sifting the Ann Rutledge Evidence," in his *Lincoln the President: Springfield to Gettysburg* (New York: Dodd, Mead & Co., 1945), 2:321–342. Much of Randall's criticism was justified, for it is clear that Herndon's inferences and speculations about the Lincoln-Rutledge romance were unwarranted.

Moreover, Randall showed that the basic facts concerning the affair could not be proved in a court of law, where the firsthand testimony of two independent witnesses would be required. On the other hand, the court of history usually accepts a less rigorous standard of proof; indeed, if Randall's criteria were applied, almost nothing could be unquestionably proved about the first thirty years of Lincoln's life. With these problems in mind, scholars have recently undertaken a reexamination of the Ann Rutledge story. For their findings, from which I have learned a great deal, see John Y. Simon, "Abraham Lincoln and Ann Rutledge," *Journal of the Abraham Lincoln Association* 11 (1990): 13–33, and Douglas L. Wilson, "Abraham Lincoln, Ann Rutledge, and the Evidence of Herndon's Informants," *Civil War History* 36 (Dec. 1990): 301–324. For a more general attempt to restore faith in Herndon's credibility, see Douglas L. Wilson, "William H. Herndon and His Lincoln Informants," *Journal of the Abraham Lincoln Association* 14 (Winter 1993): 15–34. John Evangelist Walsh, *The Shadows Rise: Abraham Lincoln and the Ann Rutledge Legend* (Urbana: University of Illinois Press, 1993), is a retelling of the Ann Rutledge story, largely on the basis of a reexamination of Herndon's sources.

55 *"Heavy set"*: Mrs. Samuel Hill, statement to WHH, [1866], HWC.
56 *"kindness—sympathy"*: Henry McHenry, statement to WHH, undated, HWC; W. G. Greene to WHH, May 30, 1865, HWC.
56 *"him beyond recovery"*: Herndon's Lincoln, 1:133.
56 *to save them:* There was, in fact, something odd about McNamar's story, since his father died on Apr. 10, 1833. It is not clear why he was unable to return to New Salem until 1835. Simon, "Abraham Lincoln and Ann Rutledge," p. 23.
56 *"an insurmountable bar[r]ier"*: Jason Duncan to WHH, undated, HWC.
57 *"engagement with McNamar"*: R. B. Rutledge to WHH, Nov. 18, 1866, and Nov. 21, 1866, HWC; James M. Rutledge, statement to William H. Herndon, undated, HWC.
57 *"on her Grave"*: Mrs. E. Abell to WHH, Feb. 15, 1867, HWC.
58 *"of her now"*: Isaac Cogdal, statement to WHH, undated, HWC.
58 *"the Democratic party"*: Frank E. Stevens, "Life of Stephen Arnold Douglas," *JISHS* 16 (Oct. 1923–Jan. 1924): 295. For the effort to achieve party regularity through a convention system, see Theodore C. Pease, *The Frontier State, 1818–1848* (Chicago: A. C. McClurg & Co., 1918), chap. 13.
58 *"of the people"*: Simon, *Lincoln's Preparation for Greatness*, p. 34.
59 *"interest on it"*: CW, 1:48.
59 *"means excluding females"*: Ibid.
59 *in the militia:* Faragher, *Sugar Creek* (New Haven: Yale University Press, 1986), p. 106.
60 *"a good wringing"*: CW, 8:429.
60 *"an offended God"*: Joshua F. Speed, *Reminiscences of Abraham Lincoln and Notes of a Visit to California: Two Lectures* (Louisville, Ky.: John P. Morton & Co., 1884), pp. 17–18.
60 *to vote for him:* Mark E. Neely, Jr., "The Political Life of New Salem, Illinois," *LL*, no. 1715 (Jan. 1981).
60 *their floor leader:* Once again, my account of Lincoln in this session of the legislature is drawn from Simon, *Lincoln's Preparation for Greatness*, with additional information from Baringer, *Lincoln's Vandalia*.
61 *something to everybody:* For a full, disapproving account, see Pease, *The Frontier State*, chap. 10.
61 *"of the United States"*: Simon, *Lincoln's Preparation for Greatness*, pp. 84, 86.
61 *total state revenues:* Ibid., p. 52.
62 *"seat of government"*: Usher F. Linder, *Reminiscences of the Early Bench and Bar of Illinois* (Chicago: Chicago Legal News Co., 1879), pp. 62–63.
62 *or a bribe:* Simon, *Lincoln's Preparation for Greatness*, chap. 4, definitively explodes this myth. See also Gabor S. Boritt, *Lincoln and the Economics of the American Dream* (Memphis: Memphis State University Press, 1978), pp. 8–11.
63 *"hitherto found security"*: CW, 1:61–69.
63 *"the shot home"*: Baringer, *Lincoln's Vandalia*, p. 99.
64 *"abate its evils"*: CW, 1:75.
64 *lobby doubtful members:* Robert L. Wilson to WHH, Feb. 10, 1866, HWC.
64 *"Natures Noblemen"*: Ibid.
64 *the Supreme Court:* Paul M. Angle, "Where Lincoln Practiced Law," *Lincoln Centennial Association Papers, 1927* (Springfield, Ill.: Lincoln Centennial Association, 1927), p. 19.

CHAPTER THREE: COLD, CALCULATING, UNIMPASSIONED REASON

Paul M. Angle, *"Here I Have Lived": A History of Lincoln's Springfield, 1821–1865* (New Brunswick, N.J.: Rutgers University Press, 1950), is a superior social history. The three best books on Lincoln's law practice are Albert A. Woldman, *Lawyer Lincoln* (Boston: Houghton Mifflin Co., 1936); John J. Duff, *A. Lincoln: Prairie Lawyer* (New York: Rinehart & Co., 1960); and John P. Frank, *Lincoln as a Lawyer* (Urbana: University of Illinois Press, 1961), but a reappraisal of this topic is needed in light of the vast amount of documentary sources collected by the Lincoln Legal Papers in Springfield. Gabor S. Boritt, *Lincoln and the Economics of the American Dream* (Memphis: Memphis State University Press, 1978), is an important study of Lincoln's Whig philosophy and of his role in the campaign of 1840. The standard works on Lincoln's courtship and marriage are by Ruth Painter Randall: *Mary Lincoln: Biography of a Marriage* (Boston: Little, Brown & Co., l953), and *The Courtship of Mr. Lincoln* (Boston: Little, Brown & Co., 1957).

66 *"I am moved!":* Joshua F. Speed, *Reminiscences of Abraham Lincoln and Notes of a Visit to California: Two Lectures* (Louisville, Ky.: John P. Morton & Co., 1884), pp. 21–22.

67 *a frontier town:* The following sketch of Springfield is drawn from Paul M. Angle, *"Here I Have Lived,"* pp. 42–46, and Beveridge, 1:206–208.

67 *"to marry her":* WHH, interview with Mentor Graham, April 1, 1866, HWC; Beveridge, 1:155.

68 *"of woman's happiness":* Herndon's Lincoln, 1:148; WHH, interview with Johnson G. Green, [1866], Lamon MSS.

68 *"or forty years":* CW, 1:117–118. Lincoln was probably referring to his stepmother, Sarah Bush Johnston Lincoln, not to Nancy Hanks Lincoln, of whose appearance he could have had only a vague memory since she died when he was nine years old.

68 *"so dry and stupid":* CW, 1:55.

69 *"you now immagine":* CW, 1:78.

69 *"to your happiness":* CW, 1:94–95.

69 *"to have me":* CW, 1:118–119.

69 *"in my life":* CW, 1:78.

69 *his close companion:* The only biography, which includes the Lincoln-Speed correspondence, is Robert L. Kincaid, *Joshua Fry Speed: Lincoln's Most Intimate Friend* (Harrogate, Tenn.: Lincoln Memorial University, 1943).

70 *above Speed's store:* See the sensible comment on this point in Charles B. Strozier, *Lincoln's Quest for Union: Public and Private Meanings* (New York: Basic Books, 1982), p. 43.

70 *all other subjects: Herndon's Lincoln,* 1:187–189.

71 *"for a desk":* Ibid., p. 148.

71 *Justice Clemment's hearing:* Stuart & Lincoln Fee Book, ISHL.

71 *over land and timber: Robert Davidson* v. *Isham Reavis,* Morgan County Circuit Court, July 1836, photostat, Lincoln Legal Papers.

71 *procedures of litigation:* The following paragraphs lean heavily on an illuminating unpublished study, "The Common-Law Forms of Action and Rules of Pleading in Lincoln's Illinois," by Eric T. Freyfogle (1991). See also Abraham Caruthers, *History of a Lawsuit; or a Treatise on the Practice in Suits and Proceedings of Every Description* (Cincinnati: Robert Clarke & Co., 1866).

72 *"the said plaintiffs....": Atwood & Co.* v. *Shinn & Vittum,* Fulton County Circuit Court, May 1838, photostat, Lincoln Legal Papers.

73 *of the agreement:* Rufus R. Wilson, ed., *Uncollected Works of Abraham Lincoln* (Elmira, N.Y.: Primavera Press, 1947), 1:147–148, 150–152.

73 *also surpassed them:* Beveridge, 1:211–212n. For slightly different figures, see Duff, *A. Lincoln: Prairie Lawyer,* p. 46.

73 *central Illinois counties:* These and numerous other engagements are recorded in *Day by Day,* vol. I. See also Paul M. Angle, "Abraham Lincoln: Circuit Lawyer," *Lincoln Centennial Papers, 1928* (Springfield, Ill.: Lincoln Centennial Association, 1928), pp. 19–41.

73 *a fee book:* Stuart & Lincoln Fee Book, ISHL.

73 *"hawk billed yankee":* CW, 1:158–159.

74 *six hundred acres:* Kent L. Walgren, "James Adams: Early Springfield Mormon and Freemason," *JISHS* 75 (1982): 121–136, and Wayne C. Temple, "An Aftermath of 'Sampson's Ghost': A New Lincoln Document," *LH* 91 (Summer 1989): 42–48.

74 *"Sampson's Ghost"*: For these letters, see Wilson, *Uncollected Works,* 1:153–161. The editors of the *Collected Works* excluded these letters because "internal evidence . . . does not determine Lincoln's handiwork." *CW,* 1:89n.

75 *"all his slanderers"*: *CW,* 1:105–106.

75 *"nothing but* lice": *CW,* 1:244.

75 *to a duel:* Usher F. Linder, *Reminiscences of the Early Bench and Bar of Illinois* (Chicago: Chicago Legal News Co., 1879), pp. 62–63.

76 *"not* legally *bound"*: *CW,* 1:144. (The body of this quotation is italicized in the source.)

76 *"to do so"*: *CW,* 1:123.

76 *"and great loss"*: *CW,* 1:135.

76 *"will be well"*: *CW,* 1:135–136.

76 "would *go down"*: *CW,* 1:196.

76 *"the present crisis"*: *CW,* 1:216.

76 *"carry the elections"*: *CW,* 1:148.

76 *"defraying its expense"*: *CW,* 1:201.

76 *"in a lump"*: *CW,* 1:184.

77 *"by country banks"*: *CW,* 1:194.

77 *"to resuscitate it"*: *CW,* 1:159.

77 *"that jumping scrape"*: *CW,* 1:226.

77 *"to the ground!"*: The best account of this episode is in chap. 4 of *Illinois' Fifth Capitol: The House That Lincoln Built and Caused to Be Rebuilt (1837–1865)* (Springfield, Ill.: Phillips Brothers Printers, 1988), by Sunderine Wilson Temple and Wayne C. Temple. See also Paul Simon, *Lincoln's Preparation for Greatness: The Illinois Legislative Years* (Urbana: University of Illinois Press, 1971), pp. 227–230.

78 *"end the better"*: Ibid., p. 264.

78 *"shall be beaten"*: *CW,* 1:120.

78 *required six months: CW,* 1:151.

78 *"be verry authentic"*: *CW,* 1:154.

78 *"state, verry good"*: *CW,* 1:184.

78 *"driven into it"*: *CW,* 1:205.

78 *"coming presidential contest"*: *CW,* 1:180–181, 201.

79 *"our highest expectations"*: *Hidden Lincoln,* p. 289.

79 *"not that much"*: *CW,* 1:159–179. (Quotations are from pp. 177 and 163.) For a careful appraisal of this speech and its political significance, see Boritt, *Lincoln and the Economics of the American Dream,* chap. 6.

80 *"Hero of Tippecanoe"*: *CW,* 1:210.

80 *"Our Political Institutions"*: The text of the address is in *CW,* 1:108-115. For the circumstances in which it was delivered, see Thomas F. Schwartz, "The Springfield Lyceums and Lincoln's 1838 Speech," *Illinois Historical Journal* 83 (1990): 45–49. This address has attracted more scholarly attention than anything else Lincoln wrote before 1858. Edmund Wilson first suggested that Lincoln's fiery warning against a future Caesar "seemed to derive as much from admiration as apprehension" and argued that Lincoln "projected himself into the role against which he is warning." Wilson, *Patriotic Gore: Studies in the Literature of the American Civil War* (New York: Oxford University Press, 1962), pp. 99–130. George B. Forgie's *Patricide in the House Divided: A Psychological Interpretation of Lincoln and His Age* (New York: W. W. Norton & Co., 1979), chap. 2, essentially adopts the Wilson argument, noting, however, that Lincoln was unconsciously projecting himself as the towering genius who threatened republicanism. Dwight G. Anderson, in *Abraham Lincoln: The Quest for Immortality* (New York: Alfred A. Knopf, 1982), carried Wilson's argument even further, to depict Lincoln as a "demonic" man, who "acted from motives of revenge" to strike down the Founding Fathers. In *Crisis of the House Divided: An Interpretation of the Issues in the Lincoln-Douglas Debates* (Garden City, N.Y.: Doubleday & Co., 1959), chap. 9, Harry V. Jaffa argued that in this address Lincoln was looking to the future, when the nation could be saved "by one who has all Caesar's talent for domination, one who could, if he would, govern the people without their consent, but who prefers the people's freedom to their domination" (p. 225). Other scholars, like George M. Fredrickson, "Lincoln and His Legend" (*New York Review of Books,* July 15, 1982, pp. 13–16), have suggested that these interpretations are exaggerated, and Richard O. Curry, "Conscious or Subconscious Caesarism?" (*JISHS,* Apr. 1984, p. 71) stresses that Lincoln, "a devout Whig, was utilizing standard Whig rhetoric—which continually employed the imagery of Caesarism in

attacking 'King Andrew I.' " For a critical review of this literature, see Mark Neely, "Lincoln's Lyceum Speech and the Origins of a Modern Myth," *LL,* nos. 1776–1777 (1987). The imagery Lincoln used was conventional. See Major L. Wilson, "Lincoln and Van Buren in the Steps of the Fathers: Another Look at the Lyceum Address," *Civil War History* 29 (1983): 197–211.

80 *"to our nature":* CW, 1:114–115.

80 *"native Spanish moss":* CW, 1:109–110.

81 "religion *of the nation":* CW, 1:112.

81 *"in the land":* CW, 1:69.

81 *"or enslaving freemen":* CW, 1:113–114.

81 *"knew no rest":* Herndon's Lincoln, 2:375.

81 *"he had lived":* Joshua F. Speed to WHH, Feb. 1866, copy, Lamon MSS, HEH.

82 *"[and] shoot editors":* CW, 1:111.

82 *"as moral pestilences":* CW, 1:273.

82 *"any other class":* CW, 1:278.

83 *"Reason, all hail!":* CW, 1:279.

83 *"one of the boys":* WHH, monograph on "Lincoln & Mary Todd," [1887], HWC.

83 *"and faithful obedience":* CW, 1:156.

83 *"coarse and vulgar fellow":* Linder, *Reminiscences of the Early Bench and Bar,* pp. 62–63.

83 *"shrunk from responsibility":* CW, 1:124–125.

83 *"belong to him":* Simon, *Lincoln's Preparation for Greatness,* p. 171.

83 *"a thousand years":* CW, 1:109.

83 *"and my love":* CW, 1:178–179.

84 *"have avoided it":* CW, 1:78.

84 *"these girls look":* Baker, *Mary Todd Lincoln,* p. 89.

84 *sister, Mary Todd:* The standard, highly sympathetic life is Ruth P. Randall, *Mary Lincoln: Biography of a Marriage* (Boston: Little, Brown & Co., 1953). Jean H. Baker, *Mary Todd Lincoln,* is more balanced. For Mary Todd's family and Kentucky background, see William H. Townsend, *Lincoln and the Bluegrass: Slavery and Civil War in Kentucky* (Lexington: University of Kentucky Press, 1955).

84 *"a merry dance":* WHH, Jan. 16, 1886, HWC; WHH, monograph on "Lincoln & Mary Todd," [1887], HWC.

85 *"nature—and culture":* WHH, interview with Mrs. N. W. Edwards, [Jan. 10, 1866], HWC.

85 *"been* hard bargains": Turner, *Mary Todd Lincoln,* pp. 18, 26.

85 *"for policy":* WHH, interview with N. W. Edwards, Sept. 22, 1865, HWC.

86 *"a rising man":* WHH, interview with Mrs. N. W. Edwards, [Jan. 10, 1866], HWC.

86 *still sexually inexperienced:* For sensitive comment on this point, see Strozier, *Lincoln's Quest for Union,* pp. 47–48.

86 *"horrible and alarming":* CW, 1:280.

87 *His nerve snapped:* Herndon's elaborate story of how Lincoln failed to show up at the wedding ceremony planned for Jan. 1, 1841, has been thoroughly discredited. See Randall, *Mary Lincoln,* chap. 4.

87 *"her—and parted":* WHH, interview with Joshua F. Speed, undated, HWC. I have reversed the order of the first two quoted sentences. For the best reconstruction of this interview, which was recorded on two separate pieces of paper, see Douglas L. Wilson, "Abraham Lincoln and 'That Fatal First of January,' " *Civil War History* 38 (1992): 104–106.

87 *with Matilda Edwards:* Those who blamed Matilda Edwards for the rupture seem to have their information from Mary Todd, who was looking for a face-saving reason for Lincoln's actions. There is no credible evidence that Lincoln was in love with Matilda Edwards; to the contrary, Matilda told Elizabeth Edwards, "On my word he never mentioned such a subject to me: he never even stooped to pay me a compliment."

87 *"felt as always":* WHH, interview with Mrs. N. W. Edwards, [Jan. 10, 1866], HWC. As Douglas L. Wilson has pointed out ("Abraham Lincoln and 'That Fatal First of January' "), it is difficult to construct a correct chronology of these events. I judge that the breaking of the engagement occurred on what Lincoln referred to as "that fatal first of Jany. '41." My guess is that Mary did not write her letter immediately but delayed by as much as a week. That would explain why Lincoln was able to go about his business in the legislature during the first week in January but was prostrated with guilt and depression during the second week.

87 *might commit suicide:* WHH, interview with James Matheny, May 3, 1866, HWC.

87 *"such dangerous things":* WHH, interview with Joshua F. Speed, [1866], HWC.

87 *"serious was apprehended"*: Wilson, "Abraham Lincoln and 'That Fatal First of January,' " p. 123.
87 *"of my character"*: CW, 1:289.
88 *"she is otherwise"*: CW, 1:282.
88 *"on the earth"*: CW, 1:228–229.
88 *"a Duck fit"*: Wilson, "Abraham Lincoln and 'That Fatal First of January,' " p. 124 and note.
88 *"not loved again"*: Carl Sandburg and Paul M. Angle, *Mary Lincoln: Wife and Widow* (New York: Harcourt, Brace & Co., 1932), pp. 179–180.
88 *"of the law"*: Ibid., p. 180.
89 *"for its promises"*: J. F. Speed to WHH, Sept. 17, 1866, HWC.
89 *"to the truth"*: CW, 1:261.
89 *"creatures on board"*: CW, 1:260.
89 *"heavenly* black eyes": CW, 1:266.
89 *doctor and patient:* I borrow this image from Wilson, "Abraham Lincoln and 'That Fatal First of January,' " p. 127.
89 *"for a while"*: CW, 1:266–269.
89 *"on defective nerves"*: CW, 1:265.
89 *"happiest of men"*: CW, 1:270.
90 *"of Jany. '41"*: CW, 1:282.
90 *"pardon it in me"*: CW, 1:303.
90 *"Be friends again"*: Herndon's Lincoln, 2:227.
90 *except Dr. Henry:* See Harry E. Pratt, *Dr. Anson G. Henry: Lincoln's Physician and Friend* (Harrogate, Tenn.: Lincoln Memorial University, 1944), and Wayne C. Temple, *Dr. Anson G. Henry: Personal Physician to the Lincolns* (Milwaukee: Lincoln Fellowship of Wisconsin, 1988).
90 *"husband and wife"*: WHH, interview with Mrs. N. W. Edwards, [Jan. 10, 1866], HWC.
91 *"out of the question"*: CW, 1:294–295.
91 *"and* so *interesting"*: CW, 1:295–296.
91 *"Rebecca, the widow"*: Beveridge, 1:343–344.
91 *the code duello:* For a spirited account of the Lincoln-Shields affair, see James E. Myers, *The Astonishing Saber Duel of Abraham Lincoln* (Springfield, Ill.: Lincoln-Herndon Building Publishers, 1968). The letters exchanged by the principals and their seconds are included in *Herndon's Lincoln,* 2: 243–259.
92 *"much of menace"*: CW, 1:299.
92 *"such* degradation": Beveridge, 1:345.
92 *"of his backbone"*: Herndon's Lincoln, 2:260.
92 *"for political effect"*: Ibid., 2:256.
92 *"mention it again"*: Turner, *Mary Todd Lincoln,* pp. 296, 299.
93 *"eyes and ears"*: WHH, interview with Mrs. N. W. Edwards, [Jan. 10, 1866], HWC.
93 *"to the slaughter"*: WHH, interview with James Matheny, May 3, 1866, HWC.
93 *"hell, I suppose"*: Herndon's Lincoln, 2:229.

CHAPTER FOUR: ALWAYS A WHIG

The title of this chapter comes from Joel H. Silbey's excellent article, " 'Always a Whig in Politics': The Partisan Life of Abraham Lincoln," *Papers of the Abraham Lincoln Association* 8 (1986): 21–42, an interpretation that I have drawn on heavily. A thoughtful chapter in Daniel Walker Howe's *The Political Culture of the American Whigs* (Chicago: University of Chicago Press, 1979) places Lincoln in the Whig tradition. Gabor S. Boritt's magisterial *Lincoln and the Economics of the American Dream* (Memphis: Memphis State University Press, 1978) is especially valuable on Lincoln's economic ideas.

On Lincoln's legal career all the works cited in the previous chapter continue to be valuable, but I have drawn most heavily on John J. Duff, *A. Lincoln: Prairie Lawyer* (New York: Rinehart & Co., 1960). My account of the Lincoln & Herndon partnership repeats, often in the same words, material I included in *Lincoln's Herndon* (New York: Alfred A. Knopf, 1948).

Ruth P. Randall's *Mary Lincoln: Biography of a Marriage* (Boston: Little, Brown & Co., 1953) needs to be balanced with William H. Herndon and Jesse W. Weik, *Herndon's Lincoln: The True Story of a Great Life* (Chicago: Belford-Clarke Co., 1890). Jean H. Baker, *Mary Todd Lincoln: A Biography* (New York: W. W. Norton & Co., 1987), is shrewd and insightful. Michael Burlingame, *The Inner World of Abraham Lincoln* (Urbana: University of Illinois Press, 1994), which presents an exceedingly hostile account of Mary Lincoln, appeared too late for me to consider it in preparing the present biography.

Donald W. Riddle, *Lincoln Runs for Congress* (New Brunswick, N.J.: Rutgers University Press, 1948) is a thorough account of Lincoln's quest for office.

94 *"of profound wonder"*: *CW*, 1:305.

94 *"a presidential chair"*: *CW*, 1:114.

94 *"rooms for boarders"*: Baker, *Mary Todd Lincoln*, pp. 99–100; "The Lincolns' Globe Tavern," in *The Collected Writings of James T. Hickey* (Springfield: Illinois State Historical Society, 1990), pp. 49–73. It is not clear whether the Lincolns paid $4 a week each or for both.

95 *Globe was stingy:* Mrs. David Davis to Mrs. Daniel R. Williams, Feb. 23, 1846, photostat, David Davis MSS, Chicago Historical Society.

95 *"say, exactly yet"*: *CW*, 1:319.

95 *"does Butler appoint?"*: *CW*, 1:325.

95 *"love and tenderness"*: Randall, *Mary Lincoln*, p. 81.

95 *"expressed the least"*: Charles B. Strozier, *Lincoln's Quest for Union* (New York: Basic Books, 1982), p. 78.

96 *Todd had purchased:* The case was *Todd* v. *Ware* (1844). The very extensive file on this case in the Lincoln Legal Papers shows what careful attention Lincoln paid to the minute details of his father-in-law's case.

96 *in her hand:* Baker, *Mary Todd Lincoln*, p. 103.

96 *home of their own:* On Lincoln's house, see Wayne C. Temple's authoritative *By Square and Compasses: The Building of Lincoln's Home and Its Saga* (Bloomington, Ill.: Ashlar Press, 1984). Also valuable are several reports prepared for the National Park Service: Floyd Mansberger, "Archaeological Investigations at the Lincoln Home National Historic Site, Springfield, Illinois" (1987); Vergil E. Noble, "Further Archaeological Investigations at Lincoln National Historic Site, Springfield, Illinois" (1988); and Katherine B. Menz, "Furnishings Plan . . . : The Lincoln Home" (1983). I have profited enormously from a private conducted tour of the Lincoln Home National Historic Site that Mr. Norman D. Hellmers, the superintendent, gave me and have learned much from the careful drawings of the house and outbuildings that he kindly provided.

96 *"calling, is* diligence": *CW*, 10:19.

97 *fees of $10:* Harry E. Pratt, "Lincoln and Bankruptcy Laws," *Illinois Bar Journal* 31 (Jan. 1943): 201–206. The staff of the Lincoln Legal Papers has recently discovered complete transcripts of twelve bankruptcy cases in which Logan and Lincoln appeared. These will make possible a much fuller treatment of Lincoln's practice in bankruptcy proceedings. *Lincoln Legal Briefs* (October–December 1994), No. 32.

97 *seventeen cases: Day by Day,* 1:195. For pleadings in these cases, see Rufus Rockwell Wilson, ed., *Uncollected Works of Abraham Lincoln* (Elmira, N.Y.: Primavera Press, 1948), 2:252–254, 211.

97 *Tinsley Building:* Paul M. Angle, "Where Lincoln Practiced Law," *Lincoln Centennial Association Papers, 1927* (Springfield, Ill.: Lincoln Centennial Association, 1927), pp. 30–31.

97 *"in the wrong"*: WHH, "Lincoln as Lawyer Politician and Statesman," undated monograph, [1887], HWC.

98 *"will of juries"*: "Stephen T. Logan Talks About Lincoln," *Lincoln Centennial Association Bulletin* 12 (Sept. 1, 1928): 3.

98 *"fine-tooth combs"*: John J. Duff, "This Was a Lawyer," *JISHS* 52 (Spring 1959): 158.

98 *"make a speech"*: *CW*, 10:19.

98 *"want to reach"*: Herndon's *Lincoln*, 2:325.

98 *a courtroom litigator:* For thoughtful appraisals of Lincoln as a lawyer, see Charles W. Moores, "Abraham Lincoln: Lawyer," *Indiana Historical Society Publications* 7 (1922): 483–535; Benjamin P. Thomas, "Abe Lincoln, Country Lawyer," *Atlantic Monthly* 193 (Feb. 1954): 57–61; Cullom Davis, *Lincoln the Lawyer* (Springfield, Ill.: Lincoln Legal Papers, 1990); and Cullom Davis, "Abraham Lincoln, Esq.: The Symbiosis of Law and Politics," unpublished paper (Springfield, Ill., 1992).

98 *"ambition in the law"*: "Stephen T. Logan Talks About Lincoln," p. 3.

99 *"who heard him"*: Wilson, *Uncollected Works,* 2:256-258; John P. Frank, *Lincoln as a Lawyer* (Urbana: University of Illinois Press, 1961), p. 13.

99 *"it as anybody"*: Herndon's opinions are in his lecture "Analysis of the Character of Abraham Lincoln," *Abraham Lincoln Quarterly* 1 (Dec. 1941): 431, and in his monograph, "Lincoln as

Lawyer Politician and Statesman," HWC; Logan's are in "Stephen T. Logan Talks About Lincoln," p. 5.

100 *"for this age": Maus* v. *Worthing*, 4 Ill. 26 (1841). See the able summary in John Long, *The Law of Illinois*, vol. 1, *Lincoln's Cases Before the Illinois Supreme Court from His Entry into the Practice of Law Until His Entry into Congress* (Shiloh, Ill.: Illinois Co., 1993), pp. 3–10.

100 *"know any thing":* WHH, "Lincoln as Lawyer Politician and Statesman," HWC.

100 *three hundred cases:* All figures concerning the extent of Lincoln's law practice have to be provisional, pending the completion of the work of the indefatigable researchers connected with the Lincoln Legal Papers. Dan W. Bannister's thorough and informed *Lincoln and the Illinois Supreme Court* (Springfield, privately printed, 1995), appeared too late for me to consult it in preparing my account of Lincoln's appellate practice.

100 *"and in friendship":* "Stephen T. Logan Talks About Lincoln," p. 5.

100 *until March 1845:* Angle, "Where Lincoln Practiced Law," pp. 29–30.

100 *a new partner:* The following paragraphs are drawn from Donald, *Lincoln's Herndon,* pp. 18–21.

101 *this new partner:* Ibid., chap. 4.

102 *"to jump far":* WHH, "Lincoln as Lawyer Politician and Statesman," HWC.

102 *"a few other books":* Angle, "Where Lincoln Practiced Law," p. 32.

102 *"things in order":* Donald, *Lincoln's Herndon,* pp. 21–22.

103 *"his memorandum-book":* Duff, *A. Lincoln,* p. 117.

103 *"person is illegal": Bailey* v. *Cromwell,* 4 Ill. 71 (1841). See also the summary in Long, *The Law of Illinois,* pp. 11–12. See also W. H. Williamson, "Lincoln and Black Nance," typescript in the Lincoln Legal Papers, which points out that Lincoln never represented Nance and did not win freedom for her; he simply demonstrated that her alleged owner *"could not prove* that she was a slave." The Northwest Ordinance forbade the introduction of slavery into the territory that later became the state of Illinois, but it did not emancipate slaves who were already residing in the territory. Nor did the Constitution of Illinois. Moreover—as the Matson case, discussed just below, reveals—the law did not prevent slave owners from bringing their chattels temporarily into the state. The 1840 United States census showed 331 slaves still living in Illinois.

103 *"privately by him":* The file on *Matson* v. *Rutherford* in the Lincoln Legal Papers contains much valuable information. For the account of O. B. Ficklin, one of the attorneys who opposed Lincoln and Linder, see "A Pioneer Lawyer," *Tuscola Review,* Sept. 7, 1922 (in broadside collection, ISHL). See also Anton-Hermann Chroust, "Abraham Lincoln Argues a Pro-Slavery Case," *American Journal of Legal History* 5 (Oct. 1961): 299–308, and Jesse W. Weik, "Lincoln and the Matson Negroes," *Arena* 17 (Apr. 1897): 752–758.

104 *"and butter involved": CW,* 10:19.

104 *"if we fail": CW,* 1:305.

104 *"case, if convenient": CW,* 1:345.

104 *to do so:* For these cases, see William H. Townsend, *Lincoln the Litigant* (Boston: Houghton Mifflin Co., 1925), pp. 7–30.

104 *money was received:* Donald, *Lincoln's Herndon,* p. 33. The firm did have a partnership account at the Springfield Marine & Fire Insurance Co. (which performed the functions of a bank after the failure of the State Bank of Illinois), but it was used simply for the collection of drafts. Duff, *A. Lincoln,* pp. 114–115.

104 *riders of the circuit:* Paul M. Angle, "Abraham Lincoln: Circuit Lawyer," *Lincoln Centennial Association Papers, 1928* (Springfield, Ill.: Lincoln Centennial Association, 1928), pp. 19–41; Benjamin P. Thomas, "The Eighth Judicial Circuit," *Bulletin of the Abraham Lincoln Association,* no. 40 (September 1935): 1–9.

105 *a nondescript buggy:* Wayne C. Temple, "Lincoln Rides the Circuit," *LH* 62 (1960): 139–143.

105 *"two under them":* William H. Herndon, *A Letter . . . to Isaac N. Arnold* (1937).

105 *"coffee—pretty mean":* Duff, *A. Lincoln,* p. 198.

105 *"a small kind":* WHH to Mrs. Leonard Swett, Feb. 22, 1890, Leonard Swett MSS, ISHL.

105 *prominent local attorneys:* Angle, "Abraham Lincoln: Circuit Lawyer," remains the best evaluation.

106 *"and hurrahing exercise":* Herndon, *A Letter . . . to Isaac N. Arnold.*

106 *visit to Springfield: Day by Day,* 1:205. Charles Strozier (*Lincoln's Quest for Union,* pp. 116–117) has calculated that Lincoln was absent from home for ten to fourteen weeks a year during the 1840s.

106 *on the circuit:* Paul M. Angle reckoned that Lincoln in 1853 earned $325 in two weeks on the

circuit. "Abraham Lincoln: Circuit Lawyer," pp. 36–37. Harry E. Pratt, using anecdotal evidence, arrived at a different figure. Pratt, *Personal Finances,* pp. 37–38.

106 *"and the swine":* Harry E. Pratt, ed., *Illinois as Lincoln Knew It: A Boston Reporter's Record of a Trip in 1847* (Springfield, Ill.: 1938), pp. 33–34.

107 *ease the situation:* I am grateful to Mr. Norman Hellmers, superintendent of the Lincoln National Home Site, for a careful drawing of the Abraham Lincoln cottage, 1846–1854, showing the extent of these changes.

107 *had to labor:* Baker, *Mary Todd Lincoln,* is the only biography that recognizes how much, and how hard, Mary Lincoln had to work. See esp. pp. 109–112. The reference to the "wild Irish" is on p. 107.

107 *and corset lace:* Harry E. Pratt, ed., "The Lincolns Go Shopping," *JISHS* 48 (1955): 65–81.

108 *"love him better":* WHH, interview with James Gourley, copy, Lamon MSS, HEH.

108 *piece of firewood: Hidden Lincoln,* p. 141. For other, similar anecdotes, see *Herndon's Lincoln,* 3:425–431.

108 *"arms are long": Herndon's Lincoln,* 2:296.

109 *out on the circuit:* Gibson W. Harris to AL, Nov. 7, 1860, Lincoln MSS, LC; Frederick T. Hill, *Lincoln the Lawyer* (New York: Century Co., 1906), p. 164n. See also John S. Goff, *Robert Todd Lincoln: A Man in His Own Right* (Norman: University of Oklahoma Press, 1969), and Ruth P. Randall, *Lincoln's Sons* (Boston: Little, Brown & Co., 1955).

109 *"to its parents":* Randall, *Mary Lincoln,* p. 101.

109 *"than ever after": CW,* 1:391.

109 *"a few days":* Mary Lincoln to My Dear Friend, July 23, 1853, photostat, ISHL.

109 *"crmble to dust":* For Todd's political career, see William H. Townsend, *Lincoln and the Bluegrass* (Lexington: University of Kentucky Press, 1955); for Thomas Lincoln's political views, see Mark E. Neely, Jr., *The Abraham Lincoln Encyclopedia* (New York: McGraw-Hill Book Co., 1982), p. 188.

109 *"of a statesman": CW,* 3:29.

109 *"whig in politics": CW,* 3:512.

110 *"it was so": CW,* 1:313, 334.

110 *"any good government": CW,* 1:407–416 (quotations from pp. 408, 412, 415). For a more positive view of these ruminations on the tariff, together with a fine account of what Lincoln read on the subject, see Boritt, *Lincoln and the American Dream,* chap. 9.

110 *"condition to all": CW,* 3:478–479, 468. The quoted words are from an 1859 speech, but Lincoln's views did not change.

110 *"self-made man":* Irvin G. Wyllie, *The Self-Made Man in America* (New York: Free Press, 1954), pp. 9–10.

111 *"go very much": CW,* 1:306–307.

111 *"I always was":* WHH, interview with James H. Matheny, May 3, 1866, HWC.

111 *"fighting a duel": CW,* 1:320.

112 *"own dear 'gal' ": CW,* 1:319.

112 *would succeed Baker:* The following pages depend heavily on Donald W. Riddle, *Lincoln Runs for Congress* (New Brunswick, N.J.: Rutgers University Press, 1948).

112 *"the common enemy": CW,* 1:315.

112 *"present Whig tariff": CW,* 1:333; Anson G. Henry to John J. Hardin, Mar. 25, 1844, Hardin MSS, Chicago Historical Society.

113 *"as a speaker":* David Davis to Will P. Walker, May 4, 1844, photostat, Davis MSS, Chicago Historical Society.

113 *"something is lost":* WHH to John J. Hardin, Feb. 12, 1844, Hardin MSS, Chicago Historical Society.

113 *"one for Governor": CW,* 1:351.

113 *"is fair play": CW,* 1:350, 353.

113 *"is fair play":* P. U. Thompson to John J. Hardin, Jan. 17, 1846, Hardin MSS, Chicago Historical Society.

113 *"Abraham's turn now":* Riddle, *Lincoln Runs for Congress,* p. 102.

114 *"elected to congress": CW,* 1:356.

114 *"to keep peace": CW,* 1:366.

114 *"abilities and integrity":* Riddle, *Lincoln Runs for Congress,* p. 157.

114 *"grossly misrepresented him": CW,* 1:384.

114 *"some honest men"*: CW, 1:383.

114 *"scoffer at, religion"*: CW, 1:382.

115 *to the convention*: New York Tribune, July 14, 1847. The *Chicago Daily Journal* announced that this was Lincoln's "first visit to the Commercial emporium of the state." Wayne C. Temple, *Lincoln's Connections with the Illinois & Michigan Canal, His Return from Congress in '48, and His Invention* (Springfield: Illinois Bell, 1986), pp. 22–23, provides the best account of Lincoln's participation in the convention.

115 *"homely looking man"*: All quotations in the two following paragraphs are from WHH, "Analysis of the Character of Abraham Lincoln," *ALQ* 1 (Sept. 1941): 357–359. As Herndon indicated, Lincoln's hair was usually disheveled, but on this occasion, while posing for a daguerreotype, it was carefully slicked down.

116 *"the whig cause"*: CW, 1:341.

116 *"over old times"*: WHH Herndon, interview with Nathaniel Grigsby, Sept. 16, 1865, HWC.

116 *"sister were buried"*: CW, 1:378.

116 *loss of his sister*: For sensitive psychoanalytical comments on Lincoln's verse and the suggestion of "incomplete mourning," I am indebted to Strozier, *Lincoln's Quest for Union*, pp. 28–30.

116 *"were certainly poetry"*: CW, 1:378.

118 *"in liquid light"*: CW, 1:378–379.

118 *"into harmless insanity"*: CW, 1:384.

118 *"him ling'ring here?"*: CW, 1:385–386.

118 *frontier bear hunt*: CW, 1:386–389.

118 *"having written them"*: CW, 1:392.

CHAPTER FIVE: LONE STAR OF ILLINOIS

Two valuable monographs deal with Lincoln's years in Congress: Donald W. Riddle, *Congressman Abraham Lincoln* (Westport, Conn.: Greenwood Press, 1979), which is sharply critical; and Paul Findley, *A. Lincoln: The Crucible of Congress* (New York: Crown Publishers, 1979), which takes a more favorable view. Albert J. Beveridge, *Abraham Lincoln, 1809–1858* (Boston: Houghton Mifflin Co., 1928), offers many valuable details.

The best general account of the final year of Polk's administration is *The Impending Crisis, 1848–1861*, by David M. Potter (completed by Don E. Fehrenbacher) (New York: Harper & Row, 1976). There is also an excellent survey in Allan Nevins, *Ordeal of the Union: Fruits of Manifest Destiny, 1847–1852* (New York: Charles Scribner's Sons, 1947), chap. 1. Robert W. Johannsen, *To the Halls of the Montezumas: The Mexican War in the American Imagination* (New York: Oxford University Press, 1985), is a spirited account of public reactions to the conflict. The standard work on dissent and opposition to the war is John H. Schroeder, *Mr. Polk's War* (Madison: University of Wisconsin Press, 1973).

119 *"as I expected"*: CW, 1:391.

120 *he was playing*: Samuel C. Busey, *Personal Reminiscences and Recollections of Forty-Six Years' Membership in the Medical Society of the District of Columbia and Residence in This City* (Washington, D.C., privately printed, 1895), pp. 25–27.

120 *"attending to business"*: CW, 1:465.

121 *"his own way"*: Busey, *Personal Reminiscences*, p. 28.

121 *"others say nothing"*: CW, 1:465.

121 *missed only 13*: Paul Findley, *A. Lincoln: The Crucible of Congress* (New York: Crown Publishers, 1979), pp. 167–168.

121 *of the Congress*: Pratt, *Personal Finances*, p. 101.

121 *"speak in court"*: CW, 1:430.

121 *"pale-faced, consumptive man"*: CW, 1:448.

122 *Mexicans as "greasers"*: Mark E. Neely, Jr., "War and Partisanship: What Lincoln Learned from James K. Polk," *JISHS* 74 (Autumn 1981): 205.

122 *as "altogether inexpedient"*: CW, 1:337.

122 *"of the people"*: CW, 2:4.

123 *to encourage volunteering*: Day by Day, 1:273; Beveridge, 1:381.

123 *"should be ended"*: CW, 1:432.

123 *"our own soil":* James D. Richardson, ed., *A Compilation of the Messages and Papers of the President* (Washington, D.C.: Government Printing Office, 1897), 4:534.

123 *"protection of Texas":* CW, 1:421–422.

123 *"that is wrong":* This passage in Lincoln's manuscript (Lincoln MSS, LC) was deleted from the printed speech.

124 *"charms to destroy":* CW, 1:437, 439.

124 *"on a hot stove":* This passage in Lincoln's manuscript (Lincoln MSS, LC) was deleted from the printed speech.

124 *"of a fever-dream":* CW, 1:439–442.

124 *"sending me again":* CW, 1:431.

124 *an unpatriotic speech:* Riddle, *Congressman Abraham Lincoln,* pp. 50–51.

124 *"tall Mr. Lincoln":* Ibid., p. 35.

124 *"most conclusive arguments":* Herbert Mitgang, ed., *Abraham Lincoln: A Press Portrait* (Chicago: Quadrangle Books, 1971), p. 55.

125 *"of one term":* Riddle, *Congressman Abraham Lincoln,* pp. 35–39, gives an excellent sampling of editorial opinion.

125 *"in the House":* Gabor S. Boritt, "Lincoln's Opposition to the Mexican War," *JISHS* 67 (Feb. 1974): 91.

125 *"be successfully controverted":* Riddle, *Congressman Abraham Lincoln,* pp. 35–36.

125 *"side so long":* Anson G. Henry to AL, Dec. 29, 1847, Lincoln MSS, LC.

125 *"aggression on Mexico":* CW, 1:473.

125 *"the Whig ranks":* Herndon's Lincoln, 2:279.

125 *"of another country":* Herndon's letters have not been preserved, but it is possible to reconstruct their contents from Lincoln's replies in CW, 1:446–447, 451–452.

126 *"have always stood":* Ibid.

126 *"pestilence, and famine":* Riddle, *Congressman Abraham Lincoln,* p. 56.

126 *the Young Indians:* In addition to Lincoln and Stephens, the group included Truman Smith, the Connecticut political organizer, Robert Toombs of Georgia, and three first-term Virginia congressmen. Holman Hamilton, *Zachary Taylor: Soldier in the White House* (Indianapolis: Bobbs-Merrill Co., 1951), pp. 63–64.

126 *"if he is not":* CW, 1: 452, 463.

127 *in the fall:* CW, 1:475–476.

127 *"be hanged themselves":* CW, 1:477.

127 *"want of consideration":* CW, 1:506.

127 *"and clear cases":* CW, 1:454.

127 *" 'as you please' ":* CW, 1:503–504.

128 *"their own business":* CW, 1:505.

128 *"Spotty Lincoln":* E.g., in his August 27, 1858, speech at Freeport. CW, 3:56–57.

128 *"oppression upon us":* CW, 1:452.

128 *"you can not":* CW, 1:453.

128 *"liberate the world":* CW, 1:438. See Thomas J. Pressly, "Bullets and Ballots: Lincoln and the 'Right of Revolution,' " *American Historical Review* 67 (Apr. 1962): 647–662.

128 *"than it is":* CW, 1:488.

129 *policy at all:* I have developed this argument more fully in "Abraham Lincoln: Whig in the White House," in *Lincoln Reconsidered: Essays on the Civil War Era* (New York: Vintage Books, 1961), pp. 196–208.

130 *"have helped himself":* CW, 1:501–516. Quotations are from pages 508, 514.

130 *"work down again":* Riddle, *Congressman Abraham Lincoln,* p. 105.

130 *"likely to go":* CW, 1:516; 2:1.

130 *"fellows forget father":* CW, 1:465–466.

130 *"to marry again":* Ibid.

130 *"away from you":* Turner, *Mary Todd Lincoln,* p. 38.

131 *"I see you":* CW, 1:477.

131 *he had appointments:* The following paragraphs draw heavily on William F. Hanna's excellent monograph, *Abraham Among the Yankees: Abraham Lincoln's 1848 Visit to Massachusetts* (Taunton, Mass.: Old Colony Historical Society, 1983), and on Wayne C. Temple's authoritative *Lincoln's Connections with the Illinois & Michigan Canal, His Return from Congress in '48, and His Invention* (Springfield: Illinois Bell, 1986).

131 *"of the soil":* CW, 2:3–4.

131 *"a melancholy display"*: For these newspapers' verdicts, see Hanna, *Abraham Among the Yankees,* pp. 30, 34, 37, 64.

132 *"of his countenance"*: Ibid., pp. 72–73.

132 *"a tasteful speech"*: Sheldon H. Harris, "Abraham Lincoln Stumps a Yankee Audience," *New England Quarterly* 38 (June 1965), p. 228.

132 *"in the Union"*: E. L. Pierce to Jesse W. Weik, Feb. 12, 1890, HWC; Hanna, *Abraham Among the Yankees,* p. 40.

132 *visited Niagara Falls:* The date of this visit is problematic. By careful research in the shipping records Wayne C. Temple has shown that the Lincolns probably arrived in Buffalo on Sept. 25 and left the next morning for Chicago on the Great Lakes steamer *Globe.* He concludes that "it is most doubtful that they visited Niagara Falls for anything more than a brief glance, if at all." They did return and see the Falls in 1857. Temple, *Lincoln's Connections with the Illinois & Michigan Canal,* pp. 32–34.

132 *water came from:* Donald, *Lincoln's Herndon,* p. 128.

132 *"overwhelming, glorious triumph"*: CW, 1:477.

132 *"known them to be"*: David Davis to W. P. Walker, May 16, 1848, photostat, David Davis MSS, Chicago Historical Society.

133 *termed "heart-sickening"*: CW, 1:490.

133 *Lincoln's "Spot" resolutions:* Thomas L. Harris to Messrs. Lanphier and Walker, Apr. 5, 1848, in Charles C. Patton, comp., "Glory to God and the Sucker Democracy" (Springfield, Ill., 1973, photocopy), vol. 2.

133 *"to do this"*: CW, 1:491.

133 *"young men back"*: *Herndon's Lincoln,* 2:285.

133 *the Democratic candidate:* Herndon blamed Logan's defeat on Lincoln's Mexican War stand, which he said was the equivalent of committing "political suicide" (*Herndon's Lincoln,* 2:284), and a number of subsequent biographers echoed this view. It has recently been challenged by Gabor S. Boritt in "Lincoln's Opposition to the Mexican War" and by Mark E. Neely, Jr., in "War and Partisanship," and in "Lincoln and the Mexican War: An Argument by Analogy," *Civil War History* 24 (Mar. 1978): 5–24, who point out that Lincoln's antiwar views were shared by most Western Whigs and that criticism of his stand came mostly from partisan Democratic sources. Sangamon County poll books show that Mexican War veterans must not have been alienated by Lincoln's stand, since they split their vote almost evenly between Logan and Harris. Mark E. Neely, Jr., "Lincoln, the Mexican War, and Springfield's Veterans," *LL,* no. 1701 (Nov. 1979).

133 *"newly acquired territory"*: CW, 2:11.

133 *the congressional contest:* Mark E. Neely, Jr., "Did Lincoln Cause Logan's Defeat?" *LL,* no. 1660 (June 1976).

133 *and its expansion:* For Lincoln's limited commitment to antislavery up to 1854, see Robert W. Johannsen's incisive *Lincoln, the South, and Slavery: The Political Dimension* (Baton Rouge: Louisiana State University Press, 1991), chap. 1.

134 *"the different States"*: CW, 1:75.

134 *"abate its evils"*: Ibid.

134 *"in the old"*: CW, 1:347–348.

135 *voted for it:* Beveridge, 1:480. Beveridge correctly notes that Lincoln's 1854 statement that he had voted for the Wilmot Proviso forty times while in Congress was "a campaign exaggeration."

135 *him into custody:* Findley, *A. Lincoln: The Crucible of Congress,* p. 130.

135 *"Negro livery-stable"*: Ibid., p. 124.

135 *"of the earth"*: *Congressional Globe,* 30 Cong., 2 sess., pp. 31, 38, 55, 83.

136 *"of said District"*: CW, 1:75.

136 *"to be abolished"*: Findley, *A. Lincoln: The Crucible of Congress,* pp. 138, 139.

136 *"I was nobody"*: Arlin Turner, "Elizabeth Peabody Visits Lincoln, February, 1865," *New England Quarterly* 48 (March 1975): 119.

136 *"District of Columbia"*: CW, 2:22.

136 *"into said District"*: CW, 2:20–22.

137 *"bound from Illinois"*: Beveridge, 1:482.

137 *throughout the country:* W. D. Howells, *Life of Abraham Lincoln* (Springfield, Ill.: Abraham Lincoln Association, 1938), p. 64.

137 *"calculation of consequences"*: Riddle, *Congressman Abraham Lincoln,* p. 170; Beveridge, 1:485. Lincoln's proposal was not a moving cause for Calhoun's Address of the Southern Delegates in Congress, to their constituents, which had been prepared in a preliminary form

some weeks earlier. Charles M. Wiltse, *John C. Calhoun: Sectionalist, 1840–1850* (Indianapolis: Bobbs-Merrill Co., 1951), p. 541.

137 *"at that time"*: CW, 2:22.

138 *"fairness, and friendship"*: CW, 2:22–24.

138 *"not be sustained"*: CW, 2:43.

138 *"State Central Committee"*: CW, 2:39–40.

138 *"had no opposition"*: CW, 2:46.

138 *"go for him"*: J. F. Speed to WHH, Feb. 14, 1866, copy, Lamon MSS, HEH.

138 *"it for themselves"*: CW, 2:28–29.

139 *"the Land Office"*: David Davis to AL, Feb. 21, 1849, Lincoln MSS, LC.

139 *at most, tepid:* The most persuasive account of this episode, which I have closely followed, is Thomas F. Schwartz, " 'An Egregious Political Blunder': Justin Butterfield, Lincoln and Illinois Whiggery," *Papers of the Abraham Lincoln Association* 8 (1986): 9–19.

139 *"by common consent"*: CW, 2:29.

139 *"surrender of the law"*: CW, 10:14.

139 *Morrison declined it:* CW, 2:41.

139 *"in a favorable light"*: John H. Morrison to David Davis, Apr. 26, 1849, photostat, David Davis MSS, Chicago Historical Society.

140 *"a Land lawyer"*: Josiah M. Lucas to AL, May 9, 1849, Lincoln MSS, LC.

140 *Butterfield's candidacy:* For the story from Butterfield's perspective, see Thomas Ewing, "Lincoln and the General Land Office, 1849," *JISHS* 25 (Oct. 1932): 139–153.

140 *"Mr. B. himself"*: CW, 2:43, 51.

140 *to write letters:* CW, 2:52.

140 *"of the State"*: Riddle, *Congressman Abraham Lincoln,* pp. 210, 122. The author of the letter, Caleb Birchall, was angry because Lincoln had failed to recommend him to be postmaster at Springfield. Boritt, "Lincoln's Opposition to the Mexican War," p. 96.

140 *"man of straw"*: CW, 2:60.

140 *"the office myself"*: CW, 11:5–6.

141 *declined the offer:* CW, 11:5.

141 *"mass of names"*: CW, 2:19.

CHAPTER SIX: AT THE HEAD OF HIS PROFESSION IN THIS STATE

Much of the information in this chapter comes from the hundreds of unpublished documents in the files of the Lincoln Legal Papers in Springfield. John J. Duff, *A. Lincoln: Prairie Lawyer* (New York: Rinehart & Co., 1960), is the fullest account of Lincoln's law practice, and I have relied heavily on its accurate and informed accounts of Lincoln's major legal cases. David Herbert Donald, *Lincoln's Herndon* (New York: Alfred A. Knopf, 1948), discusses the Lincoln & Herndon partnership.

142 *"than ever before"*: CW, 3:512.

142 *"tended to consumption"*: WHH, interview with David Davis, Sept. 19, 1866, HWC.

142 *"in his mind"*: CW, 4:67.

142 *"Education defective"*: CW, 2:459.

142 *"training and method"*: Herndon's Lincoln, 2:307.

143 *"Six-books of Euclid"*: CW, 4:62.

143 *Nancy Robinson Dorman:* For a full account of this case, see William D. Beard, "Lincoln's 'Jarndyce v. Jarndyce': A Family Dispute on the Illinois Frontier," unpublished monograph, Lincoln Legal Papers.

143 *argued a case:* For details on this case, reported at 48 U.S. (7 Howard) 776, see James D. Maher, Clerk of the U.S. Supreme Court, to Willis Van Devanter, Feb. 15, 1918, and Willis Van Devanter to Jesse W. Weik, Feb. 16, 1918, both in the Herndon-Weik Collection, LC. Lincoln was also attorney of record in five other cases, but he did not argue them in person. *Lincoln Legal Briefs,* no. 31 (July–Sept. 1994). See also Duff, *A. Lincoln,* pp. 156–157.

143 *amount of $3.33:* Bacon v. Nuckles File, Lincoln Legal Papers.

143 *in municipal law:* Duff, *A. Lincoln,* pp. 261–262.

144 *issues and precedents:* Both these notebooks are in ISHL.

144 *left for Congress:* See the careful list of Lincoln's cases in the United States Circuit and District courts in the files of the Lincoln Legal Papers. For an informed discussion, see Benjamin P.

Thomas, "Lincoln's Earlier Practice in the Federal Courts, 1839–1854," *Bulletin of the Abraham Lincoln Association,* no. 39 (June 1935).

144 *found abundant opportunity:* The records of Lincoln's cases before the United States District and Circuit courts for the Southern District of Illinois after 1855 have been microfilmed by the National Archives. *Lincoln at the Bar: Selected Case Files from the United States District and Circuit Courts, Southern District of Illinois, 1855–1861* (Washington, D.C.: National Archives and Records Administration, 1989), is a useful guide.

144 *as in Springfield:* Duff, *A. Lincoln,* chap. 13, gives an excellent overview of Lincoln's federal practice.

144 *"over the world": CW,* 3:338.

145 *"his professional life":* Grant Goodrich to WHH, Dec. 9, 1866, HWC.

145 *the third day: Day by Day,* 2:18–19.

145 *of all cases:* Donald, *Lincoln's Herndon,* p. 44.

145 *completed the furnishings: Herndon's Lincoln,* 2:316–317.

145 *"of the room":* WHH to Jesse W. Weik, Oct. 21, 1885, HWC.

145 *"read the better":* WHH to Weik, Feb. 18, 1887, HWC.

146 *"Old Abe":* The first time E. B. Washburne heard Lincoln called "Old Abe" was at the 1847 River and Harbor Convention in Chicago. Washburne, "Abraham Lincoln in Illinois," *North American Review,* 141 (Oct. 1885): 313.

146 *"the old men": CW,* 1:497. Lincoln was here referring to the discontent of young Whig politicians, like Herndon, but his remark applied equally to young lawyers.

146 *David Davis:* The standard biography, on which I have drawn heavily in the following paragraphs, is Willard L. King, *Lincoln's Manager: David Davis* (Cambridge, Mass.: Harvard University Press, 1960).

146 *of his feet:* King, *Lincoln's Manager,* p. 74.

146 *immense safety pin:* Jane Martin Johns, *Personal Recollections of Early Decatur, Abraham Lincoln, Richard J. Oglesby and the Civil War,* ed. Howard C. Schaub (Decatur, Ill.: Decatur Chapter Daughters of the American Revolution, 1912), p. 62.

146 *"mankind or thing":* WHH, interview with David Davis, Sept. 19, 1866, HWC.

147 *"honesty and fairness":* King, *Lincoln's Manager,* p. 73.

147 *actions for debt:* Harry E. Pratt, " 'Judge' Abraham Lincoln," *JISHS* 48 (Spring 1955): 28–30; Duff, *A. Lincoln,* chap. 17.

147 *Old Tom:* Francis Orlando Krupka, "Historic Structure Report: Abraham Lincoln Home" (Springfield, Ill.: Lincoln Home National Historic Site, 1992), pp. 424–439, gives a detailed account of Lincoln's horses.

147 *"of a horse":* King, *Lincoln's Manager,* pp. 77, 83.

147 *"into this Cabbage":* WHH, interview with David Davis, Sept. 19, 1866, copy, Lamon MSS, HEH.

148 *lawyer for guidance:* Duff, *A. Lincoln,* pp. 212–214.

148 *to only $3:* These cases before the Tazewell County Circuit Court are: *People* v. *Nathaniel Wright et al.* (Apr. term, 1850); *John Shibley* v. *Adam Funk et al.* (Apr. term, 1851); *Joseph F. Haines* v. *John Jones and William Gaither* (Sept. term, 1852); *Pearly Brown* v. *John P. Singleton* (Spring term, 1852); *Benjamin Seaman* v. *Peter Duffy* (Oct. term, 1855)—all in the files of the Lincoln Legal Papers.

148 *"for the job": CW,* 2:332–333. See the excellent statement on Lincoln's fees in Duff, *A. Lincoln,* pp. 224–228.

149 *"some other occupation": CW,* 10:20.

149 *at one sitting:* A recent discovery, this elaborate document is in the files of the Lincoln Legal Papers.

149 *"in a ditch": Herndon's Lincoln,* 2:334.

150 *"must be wrong":* Ibid.

150 *the stenographic transcript:* The recently discovered manuscript trial transcript of *People of Illinois* v. *Peachy Quinn Harrison* (Sangamon County Circuit Court, 1859) is in the Illinois State Historical Library. I have used a typed transcription of this document through the courtesy of the Lincoln Legal Papers. For astute commentary on this trial, see an unpublished paper by Cullom Davis, "Crucible of Statesmanship: The Law Practice of Abraham Lincoln" (Springfield, Ill.: 1989).

150 "I forgive Quinn": *People* v. *Peachy Quinn Harrison* (Sangamon County Circuit Court, 1859), p. 72.

150 *"of such law":* Ibid., p. 68.

150 *held as contempt:* WHH to Jesse W. Weik, Nov. 20, 1885, HWC.

150 *"and defies deceit":* "Cog," in Danville *Illinois Citizen,* May 29, 1850, photostat, David Davis MSS, Chicago Historical Society.

151 *credibility was demolished:* The fullest account of this celebrated trial is Duff, *A. Lincoln,* pp. 350–359. So successful, and unexpected, was Lincoln's demolition of Allen's testimony that a story later gained circulation that Lincoln played a trick on the jury by reading from an 1856, rather than an 1857, almanac. The story was inherently improbable, because it was wholly out of character for Lincoln, who valued his reputation for integrity above all else, and it was vigorously denied by two members of the jury who examined the almanac during the trial—as did the judge and the prosecuting attorney. Astronomers have recently proved that there would have been no reason for Lincoln to substitute another almanac, since in 1857 at the time of the murder the moon was very low and near to setting. Donald W. Olson and Russell L. Doescher, "Lincoln and the Almanac Trial," *Sky and Telescope* 80 (Aug. 1990): 184–188.

151 *"find his superior":* "Cog," in Danville *Illinois Citizen,* May 29, 1850, photostat, David Davis MSS, Chicago Historical Society.

151 *Armstrong was acquitted:* J. Henry Shaw to WHH, Aug. 22, 1866, and Sept. 5, 1866, copies in Lamon MSS, HEH.

151 *"upon the mind":* "Cog," in Danville *Illinois Citizen,* May 29, 1850, photostat, David Davis MSS, Chicago Historical Society.

151 *remained with the court:* By one calculation Lincoln in 1850 spent 125 days on the circuit (not including Sangamon County), with 26 additional days, largely on legal business, in Chicago; he was in Springfield only 190 days. In 1852 he was away from home, attending to business or traveling from one court to another, 156 days and was in Springfield 210 days. Richard F. Lufkin, "Mr. Lincoln's Light from Under a Bushel—1850," *LH* 52 (Dec. 1950): 5, and Lufkin, "Mr. Lincoln's Light from Under a Bushel—1852," *LH* 54 (Winter 1952): 9.

152 *estate of $12,000:* Wayne C. Temple, "Lincoln in the Census," *LH* 68 (Fall 1966): 139.

152 *in failing health:* Charles H. Coleman, *Abraham Lincoln and Coles County, Illinois* (New Brunswick, N.J.: Scarecrow Press, 1955), offers the fullest account of Thomas Lincoln's later years and documents Lincoln's repeated financial assistance to his father.

152 *in modest comfort:* Too much has been made of the failure to invite Thomas and Sarah Bush Lincoln to their son's wedding. That ceremony was a hastily arranged, almost impromptu affair. Even the best man and the maid of honor were selected on the day of the wedding.

152 *John D. Johnston:* See Marilyn G. Ames, "Lincoln's Stepbrother: John D. Johnston," *LH* 82 (Spring 1980): 302–311.

152 *for so long:* This correspondence is most readily accessible in Coleman, *Abraham Lincoln in Coles County,* pp. 73–76. Thomas Lincoln's letter—his only extant letter—was written for him by John D. Johnston, who added an appeal of his own for an additional $80. Lincoln refused, on the ground that his stepbrother had the "habit of uselessly wasting time." "You are not *lazy,*" he wrote, "and still you *are* an *idler.*"

152 *"to see you":* John D. Johnston to AL, May 25, 1849, Lincoln MSS, LC.

152 *"truly Heart-Rendering" cries:* Augustus H. Chapman to AL, May 24, 1849, Lincoln MSS, LC.

153 *"in a Short time":* Augustus H. Chapman to AL, May 28, 1849, Lincoln MSS, LC.

153 *with "baby-sickness":* CW, 2:96–97.

153 *an uncomfortable decision:* For Lincoln's schedule during his father's final days, see *Lincoln Day by Day,* 2:46–47. Charles B. Strozier, *Lincoln's Quest for Union: Public and Private Meanings* (New York: Basic Books, 1982), pp. 53–55, shows that Lincoln's excuses were not insurmountable.

153 *"to join them":* CW, 2:96–97.

153 *became seriously sick:* Harry E. Pratt, "Little Eddie Lincoln—'We Miss Him Very Much,'" *JISHS* 47 (Autumn 1954): 300–305.

153 *no known cure:* Wayne C. Temple, "Government Records as Historical Sources," *Illinois Libraries* 52 (Feb. 1970): 169–170. For informed medical opinion, see Baker, *Mary Todd Lincoln,* pp. 125–126.

153 *"him very much":* CW, 2:77.

154 *"to our loss":* Mary Lincoln to "My Dear Friend," July 23, 1853, photostat, ISHL.

154 *"a womanly nature":* Randall, *Mary Lincoln,* p. 148.

154 *was gradually changing:* John W. Starr, Jr., *Lincoln & the Railroads* (New York: Arno Press, 1981), offers good general treatment of Lincoln's railroad cases.

154 *significant railroad case:* This account of the Barret case is drawn from the admirable mono-

graph by William D. Beard, " 'I Have Labored Hard to Find the Law': Abraham Lincoln for the Alton and Sangamon Railroad," *Illinois Historical Journal* 85 (Winter 1992): 209–222. A shorter commentary, together with pertinent documents, has been published as *Barret v. Alton and Sangamon Railroad Company, Illinois Supreme Court, December Term 1851* (Springfield, Ill.: Abraham Lincoln Association, 1989). This was not Lincoln's first railroad case. In 1849 he had appeared on behalf of the plaintiff in *John B. Watson* v. *Sangamon & Morgan Railroad* (HWC, LC).

155 *two minor cases:* The first was *Houser* v. *Illinois Central Railroad,* McLean County Circuit Court, Apr. 15, 1853 (Lincoln Legal Papers). The second is discussed in Duff, *A. Lincoln,* p. 210.

155 *"got up in the State": CW,* 2:202.

155 *" 'count me in' ": CW,* 2:205. In 1854, James F. Joy, agent of the Illinois Central Railroad, urged the company to employ a lobbyist at Springfield for a retainer or salary of $1,000 a year, and he recommended an unnamed man who would be "a valuable ally and a dangerous opponent in any matter before the Legislature." Pratt, *Personal Finances,* pp. 48–49. Some historians believe that Lincoln was the man retained. I think this is doubtful, because in correspondence subsequent to this date Lincoln repeatedly had to ask to be retained in cases involving the railroad.

156 *for the Illinois Central:* Albert A. Woldman, *Lawyer Lincoln* (Boston: Houghton Mifflin Co., 1936), pp. 165–169, offers a full account of this case.

156 *and South Carolina:* Lincoln's brief is in Emanuel Hertz, *Abraham Lincoln: A New Portrait* (New York: Horace Liveright, 1931), 2:675–677, where, however, beginning with the third paragraph on p. 677, it is confused with Lincoln's 1856 opinion on land titles in Beloit, Wisconsin. Cf. *CW,* 2:336–339.

156 *"such a claim": Herndon's Lincoln,* 2:352.

156 *steamers over shoals: CW,* 2:32–36. With the help of Walter Davis, a Springfield cabinetmaker, Lincoln built an elaborate model of this invention. Wayne C. Temple, *Lincoln's Connections with the Illinois & Michigan Canal, His Return from Congress in '48, and His Invention* (Springfield: Illinois Bell, 1986), pp. 35–36, 54–58.

157 *"its territorial limits": Register,* Dec. 20, 1851.

157 *"clear and uninterrupted": Journal,* Jan. 28, 1852.

157 *"of the Northwest": CW,* 2:415.

157 *for the railroad:* See the excellent account in Duff, *A. Lincoln,* chap. 20.

157 *American legal thought:* John P. Frank, *Lincoln as a Lawyer* (Urbana: University of Illinois Press, 1961), pp. 171–172.

157 *"a case lawyer":* WHH, monograph on "Lincoln as Lawyer Politician and Statesman," HWC.

158 *his family life:* Benjamin P. Thomas, "Lincoln and the Courts, 1854–1861," *Abraham Lincoln Association Papers, 1933* (Springfield, Ill.: Abraham Lincoln Association, 1934), pp. 59–62.

158 *edge of hysteria:* Randall, *Mary Lincoln,* pp. 118–120, offers a sympathetic account.

158 *"Bob and I":* WHH, interview with James Gourley, undated [1866], copy, Lamon MSS, HEH.

158 *with her own:* William Dodd Chenery, in *Register,* Feb. 27, 1938.

159 *"laugh at her":* WHH, interview with James Gourley, [1866], copy, Lamon MSS, HEH.

159 *grew in crooked:* Ruth Painter Randall, *Lincoln's Sons* (Boston: Little, Brown & Co., 1955), is an affectionate portrait of the Lincoln children.

159 *"hot house plants":* WHH to Jesse W. Weik, Jan. 6, 1886, HWC.

159 "hen pecked": Milton Hay to Mary Hay, Apr. 6, 1862, Stuart-Hay MSS, ISHL.

159 *them fell out:* WHH to J. W. Weik, Nov. 19, 1885, HWC.

159 *"get too tired?":* Randall, *Lincoln's Sons,* p. 41.

160 *"thought it smart":* WHH to J. W. Weik, Feb. 18, 1887, HWC.

160 *"my mouth shut":* WHH to J. W. Weik, Nov. 19, 1885, HWC.

160 *of their mother:* The following paragraphs follow Donald, *Lincoln's Herndon,* pp. 188–189.

160 *"insolent witty and bitter":* WHH to J. W. Weik, Jan. 9, 1886, HWC.

160 *"in his line":* Randall, *Mary Lincoln,* p. 117.

161 *"not tempt him":* W. D. Howells, *Life of Abraham Lincoln* (Springfield, Ill.: Abraham Lincoln Association, 1938), pp. 69–70.

CHAPTER SEVEN: THERE ARE NO WHIGS

For comprehensive overviews of the political events discussed in this chapter, see Allan Nevins, *Ordeal of the Union, vol. 2, A House Dividing, 1852–1857* (New York: Charles Scribner's Sons, 1947), and David M. Potter and Don E. Fehrenbacher, *The Impending Crisis, 1848–1861* (New York: Harper & Row, 1976). Albert J. Beveridge, *Abraham Lincoln, 1809–1858* (Boston: Houghton Mifflin Co., 1928), gives extensive coverage to Lincoln's life during the 1850s, and, though it is marred by excessive dependence on Herndon's belated recollections, I have drawn on it frequently.

My account of the political realignment of the 1850s rests heavily on two important books by Michael F. Holt: *The Political Crisis of the 1850s* (New York: John Wiley & Sons, 1978), and *Political Parties and American Political Development from the Age of Jackson to the Age of Lincoln* (Baton Rouge: Louisiana State University Press, 1992). William E. Gienapp, *The Origins of the Republican Party, 1852–1856* (New York: Oxford University Press, 1987), is definitive.

Don E. Fehrenbacher, *Prelude to Greatness: Lincoln in the 1850's* (Stanford, Calif.: Stanford University Press, 1962), is a brilliant interpretation of Lincoln's reemergence as a political leader. Robert W. Johannsen, *Lincoln, the South, and Slavery* (Baton Rouge: Louisiana State University Press, 1991), is an incisive account of Lincoln's growing concern with the slavery question.

The literature on Lincoln and colonization is extensive, but the best study, which offers full citation of previous works, is Michael Vorenberg, "Abraham Lincoln and the Politics of Black Colonization," *Journal of the Abraham Lincoln Association* 14 (Summer 1993): 23–45.

For Lincoln's unsuccessful bid for the Senate in 1855, see Matthew Pinsker's authoritative "Senator Abraham Lincoln," *Journal of the Abraham Lincoln Association* 14 (Summer 1993): 1–21. Pinsker's unpublished paper, "If You Know Nothing: Abraham Lincoln and Political Nativism," is by far the best account of Lincoln and the Know Nothings, but Tyler Anbinder, *Nativism & Slavery: The Northern Know Nothings & the Politics of the 1850s* (New York: Oxford University Press, 1992), is also useful.

162 *"lived for it":* WHH to W. H. Lamon, Mar. 6, 1870, Lamon MSS, HEH.
162 *Congress in 1850:* CW, 2:79.
162 *"stands number one":* Mark E. Neely, Jr., "Lincoln's Theory of Representation: A Significant New Lincoln Document," *LL,* no. 1683 (May 1978).
163 *for his father:* CW, 2:148.
163 *"had ever engaged":* W. D. Howells, *Life of Abraham Lincoln* (Springfield, Ill.: Abraham Lincoln Association, 1938), p. 69.
163 *"construction of language!!!":* CW, 2:140–141.
163 *the "common mortals":* CW, 2:144.
163 *at the windows:* WHH to Jesse W. Weik, July 10, 1886, HWC.
163 *"and miserable man":* WHH, "Lincoln's domestic Life," undated monograph, HWC.
164 *"breakfast bell rang":* Henry C. Whitney, *Life on the Circuit with Lincoln,* ed. Paul M. Angle (Caldwell, Idaho: Caxton Printers, 1940), p. 68.
164 *"been moderately successful":* CW, 10:18.
164 *"a sort of lecture":* CW, 3:374.
164 *"Discoveries and Inventions":* In Lincoln's *Collected Works* the editors showed two lectures on this subject (2:437–442 and 3:356–363), but through elegant detective work Wayne C. Temple has proved these were parts of a single lecture. For an illuminating account of that lecture and the circumstances in which it was delivered, see Wayne C. Temple, "Lincoln as a Lecturer on 'Discoveries, Inventions, and Improvements,' " *Jacksonville Journal Courier,* May 23, 1982.
164 *"of using them":* CW, 3:362.
164 *" 'died a bornin' ":* WHH to Jesse W. Weik, Feb. 21, 1891, HWC.
165 *"or to myself":* CW, 2:82.
165 *"are still aloft!":* CW, 2:85.
165 *"the world respectably":* CW, 2:124.
165 *"of his cause":* CW, 2:126.
165 *views on slavery:* Mark E. Neely, Jr., "American Nationalism in the Image of Henry Clay: Abraham Lincoln's Eulogy on Henry Clay in Context," *Register of the Kentucky Historical Society* 73 (Jan. 1975): 31–60.

165 *"a greater evil"*: CW, 2:130.

165 *knowledge of slavery*: On his two flatboat trips down the Mississippi, Lincoln was more concerned with river currents than with social institutions. But he did remember distinctly that on his first trip he was "attacked by seven negroes with intent to kill." CW, 4:62. William H. Townsend argued that on his visits to his father-in-law in Lexington, Kentucky, Lincoln "had an opportunity to study the institution of slavery at close range," and he detailed a number of horrors and atrocities that Lincoln might have witnessed. *Lincoln and the Bluegrass: Slavery and Civil War in Kentucky* (Lexington: University of Kentucky Press, 1955), pp. 126–132. Benjamin Quarles, *Lincoln and the Negro* (New York: Oxford University Press, 1962), also says Lincoln "could not have missed" the whipping post, the slave pens, and the slave auctions in Lexington. But neither author gives any evidence that Lincoln did witness these scenes, and he never made any reference to them.

166 *crucified his feelings*: Compare Lincoln's letter of Sept. 27, 1841, to Mary Speed with that of Aug. 24, 1855, to Joshua F. Speed. CW, 1:260, 2:320.

166 *"you owned slaves"*: Joseph Gillespie to WHH, Jan. 31, 1866, HWC.

166 *it in colonization*: The most perceptive account is Michael Vorenberg, "Abraham Lincoln and the Politics of Black Colonization," *Journal of the Abraham Lincoln Association* 14 (Summer 1993): 23–45. On the Colonization Society, see P. J. Staudenraus, *The African Colonization Movement, 1816–1865* (New York: Columbia University Press, 1961). For a thoughtful analysis, see George M. Fredrickson, *The Black Image in the White Mind: The Debate on Afro-American Character and Destiny, 1817–1914* (New York: Harper & Row, 1971), pp. 6–25.

166 *"for the future"*: CW, 2:132.

167 *"times ten days"*: CW, 2:255.

167 *171 were blacks: The Seventh Census of the United States, 1850* (Washington, D.C.: Robert Armstrong, 1853), p. 715.

167 *small legal problems*: Lloyd Ostendorf, "A Monument for One of the Lincoln Maids," *LH* 66 (Winter 1964): 184–186; John E. Washington, *They Knew Lincoln* (New York: E. P. Dutton & Co., 1942), pp. 183–202. See also Quarles, *Lincoln and the Negro,* pp. 25–28.

167 *"the existing institution"*: CW, 2:255.

167 *were "settled forever"*: CW, 2:232.

167 *very useful escape*: For this interpretation I am indebted to Gabor S. Boritt, "The Voyage to the Colony of Linconia: The Sixteenth President, Black Colonization, and the Defense Mechanism of Avoidance," *Historian* 37 (1975): 619–632.

167 *the Nebraska Territory*: Potter and Fehrenbacher, *The Impending Crisis,* chap. 7, offers the most satisfactory account of the Kansas-Nebraska Act. For Douglas's motives, see Robert W. Johannsen, *Stephen A. Douglas* (New York: Oxford University Press, 1973), chapters 16–18.

168 *"thunderstruck and stunned"*: CW, 2:282.

168 *"masters and slaves"*: David Herbert Donald, *Charles Sumner and the Coming of the Civil War* (New York: Alfred A. Knopf, 1960), p. 252.

168 *about them all*: WHH to James H. Wilson, Aug. 18, 1889, copy, HWC; Herndon to Zebina Eastman, Feb. 6, 1866, Eastman MSS, Chicago Historical Society.

169 *"perfect and uniform"*: CW, 2:282.

170 *"or our forefathers"*: Matthew Pinsker, "If You Know Nothing: Abraham Lincoln and Political Nativism," unpublished essay, p. 6.

170 *"God speed it!"*: CW, 2:229, 234.

170 *whittling and listening*: Townsend, *Lincoln and the Bluegrass,* p. 213.

170 *"into free territory"*: CW, 2:227.

170 *"Yates to congress"*: CW, 4:67.

171 *"as english—vote"*: CW, 2:284.

171 *"not taste liquor"*: CW, 10:24.

171 *Yates as well*: Franklin T. King to WHH, Sept. 12, 1890, HWC.

171 *"might the Democrats"*: Pinsker, "If You Know Nothing," p. 65.

172 *"and that's enough"*: WHH, interview with William Jayne, Aug. 15, 1866, HWC.

172 *"injurious to yourself"*: CW, 2:228.

173 *"don't drink anything"*: Paul M. Angle, ed., *Abraham Lincoln by Some Men Who Knew Him* (Chicago: Americana House, 1950), p. 43.

173 *"points and arguments"*: George Fort Milton, *The Eve of Conflict: Stephen A. Douglas and the Needless War* (Boston: Houghton Mifflin Co., 1934), p. 180.

174 *"intelligent, and attentive"*: *Journal*, Oct. 5, 1854.

174 *"the palms up"*: WHH, "Lincoln's Ways—Methods—Positions—Pose etc when Rising to Address . . . the People," undated monograph, HWC.

174 *"class of men"*: *CW*, 2:248. Because Lincoln's speech in Springfield was not fully reported, it is easier to follow his argument in the version of the same address that he delivered on Oct. 16 at Peoria. Quotations in the following paragraphs, unless otherwise identified, are from the Peoria speech.

175 *"slavery, than we"*: *CW*, 2:255.

175 *"be safely disregarded"*: *CW*, 2:256.

175 *"ace of passing"*: Ibid.

175 *"a* palliation—*a* lullaby": *CW*, 2:262.

175 "is *a man"*: *CW*, 2:265.

176 *"legislating about him"*: *CW*, 2:281.

176 *"of American republicanism"*: *CW*, 2:266.

176 *"arguments at all"*: *CW*, 2:283.

176 *"spread of slavery"*: *CW*, 2:255, 266.

176 *"a given time"*: *CW*, 2:274.

176 *"near stifling utterance"*: *Journal*, Oct. 10, 1854.

177 *"of these States"*: *CW*, 2:126.

177 *"throughout the world"*: *CW*, 2:276.

177 *"of Human Freedom"*: This quotation is from a newspaper report of Lincoln's speech in Springfield. *CW*, 2:242.

177 *"felt himself overthrown"*: *Journal*, Oct. 10, 1854.

177 *"all over the country"*: *Register*, Oct. 7, 1854.

178 *"his lifeless remains"*: Ibid., Oct. 9, 1854.

178 *"him holler Enough"*: B. F. Irwin to WHH, Feb. 8, 1866, HWC.

178 *"have ever met"*: Frank E. Stevens, "Life of Stephen Arnold Douglas," *JISHS* 16 (Oct. 1923–Jan. 1924):487.

178 *"him skin me"*: *CW*, 2:248.

178 *throughout the state*: Herndon's claim that, after the encounter at Peoria, Douglas asked Lincoln for a truce in debating and then promptly violated that agreement (*Herndon's Lincoln*, 2:373–374) has been rejected by nearly all Lincoln scholars.

178 *before or since*: Henry C. Whitney, undated reminiscence, David Davis MSS, Chicago Historical Society.

178 *"a powerful speaker"*: *Day by Day*, 2:130.

178 *two in Indiana*: Nevins, *Ordeal of the Union*, 2:341–344.

179 *for that office*: For an admirable account of Lincoln's unsuccessful effort to be elected senator in 1854–1855, on which I have relied heavily in the following pages, see Pinsker, "Senator Abraham Lincoln," 1–21.

179 *senators and representatives*: *CW*, 2:286.

179 *"go for me"*: *CW*, 2:288.

179 *"one eye open"*: *Herndon's Lincoln*, 2:375.

179 *"for a chance"*: *CW*, 2:303.

179 *"a terrible struggle"*: *CW*, 2:293.

179 *election of senator*: Beveridge, 2:275–276.

180 *"would help Yates"*: *CW*, 2:289.

180 *"with the Abolitionists"*: C. H. Ray to E. B. Washburne, Dec. 29, 1854, Washburne MSS, LC.

180 *"Lincoln—hated him"*: WHH, interview with William Jayne, Aug. 15, 1866, HWC.

180 *"of the season"*: Shields to Charles Lanphier, Dec. 30, 1854, in Charles C. Patton, comp., "Glory to God and the Sucker Democracy" (Springfield, Ill., 1973, photocopy), vol. 3.

180 *pressure of business*: For a skeptical view of Herndon's claim that he was responsible for Lincoln's leaving town in order to avoid connection with the odious abolitionist group, see Donald, *Lincoln's Herndon*, pp. 77–78.

180 *"to that party"*: *CW*, 2:288.

181 *"the Union dissolved"*: *CW*, 2:270.

181 *"an innocent one"*: *CW*, 2:256.

181 *all "mere politicians"*: Zebina Eastman to WHH, Jan. 2, 1866, HWC.

181 *"all his kin"*: C. H. Ray to E. B. Washburne, Dec. 24, 1855, Washburne MSS, LC.

181 *"is all right"*: Zebina Eastman, *History of the Anti-Slavery Agitation, and the Growth of the Liberty*

and Republican Parties in the State of Illinois (pamphlet in Eastman MSS, Chicago Historical Society), p. 671.

181 *"in the State":* E. B. Washburne to Zebina Eastman, Dec. 19, 1854, Eastman MSS, Chicago Historical Society.

181 *help elect Lincoln:* Pinsker, "Senator Abraham Lincoln," p. 12.

181 *new General Assembly:* Leonard Swett to AL, Dec. 22, 1854, Lincoln MSS, LC.

182 *lost him support:* Pinsker, "If You Know Nothing," p. 12.

182 *"to the Sennet":* Charles Hoyt to AL, Nov. 20, 1854, Lincoln MSS, LC.

182 *"at your disposal":* Robert Boal to AL, Dec. 7, 1854, Lincoln MSS, LC.

182 *"again)* the Man": Hugh Lamaster to AL, Dec. 11, 1854, Lincoln MSS, LC.

182 *"make no pledges":* Abraham Jonas to AL, Dec. 2, 1854, Lincoln MSS, LC.

182 *"to commit himself":* Thomas A. Marshall to AL, Dec. 8, 1854, Lincoln MSS, LC.

182 *"era of Slavery":* Thomas J. Turner to AL, Dec. 10, 1854, Lincoln MSS, LC.

182 *"in the future":* Robert W. Johannsen, ed., *The Letters of Stephen A. Douglas* (Urbana: University of Illinois Press, 1961), p. 331.

183 *"person for it":* Pinsker, "Senator Abraham Lincoln," p. 11.

183 *"Anti-Slavery men":* CW, 11:9.

183 *"for US senator":* Joseph Gillespie to WHH, Sept. 19, 1866, HWC.

183 *"make an election":* CW, 11:9.

184 *Trumbull had 5:* For a summary of the votes on the ten ballots, see Fehrenbacher, *Prelude to Greatness,* p. 175.

184 *La Salle County:* Pinsker, "Senator Abraham Lincoln," pp. 18–19.

184 *as he directed:* WHH, interview with Stephen T. Logan, undated, Lamon MSS, HEH. See also WHH, interview with S. C. Parks, undated, Lamon MSS, HEH.

184 *"disappointed and mortified":* Joseph Gillespie to WHH, Sept. 19, 1866, HWC.

184 *"consented to it":* CW, 2:307.

184 *"of his friends":* Joseph Gillespie, memorandum, Apr. 22, 1880, MS, Chicago Historical Society.

184 *"he could be":* Willard L. King, *Lincoln's Manager: David Davis* (Cambridge, Mass.: Harvard University Press, 1960), p. 108.

184 *"gives me pain":* CW, 2:306.

185 *"my friend Trumbull":* Horace White, *The Life of Lyman Trumbull* (Boston: Houghton Mifflin Co., 1913), p. 45.

185 *"promoting my own":* Pinsker, "Senator Abraham Lincoln," p. 20.

185 *"to work again":* CW, 2:308.

185 *"of last year":* CW, 2:317.

185 *closely similar machines:* For a succinct account, see Albert A. Woldman, *Lawyer Lincoln* (Boston: Houghton Mifflin Co., 1936), pp. 172–176.

186 *"such a case":* Robert H. Parkinson, "The Patent Case that Lifted Lincoln into a Presidential Candidate," *ALQ* 4 (Summer 1946): 105–122. For further details, see Pratt, *Personal Finances,* pp. 54–56.

186 *"you no good":* WHH to Jesse W. Weik, Jan. 6, 1887, HWC.

187 *"that man Stanton":* Herndon's *Lincoln,* 2:356.

187 *greater real freedom:* Harvey Wish, *George Fitzhugh: Propagandist of the Old South* (Baton Rouge: Louisiana State University Press, 1943), pp. 154–156.

187 *"he is wronged":* CW, 2:222. The editors of Lincoln's *Collected Works* tentatively attributed these reflections on slavery to July 1, 1854, but I believe it is more likely that they were written the following year.

187 *superior to your own:* CW, 2:222–223.

188 *"superintend the solution":* CW, 2:318.

188 *"executed in violence":* CW, 2:321.

188 *"more effective channels":* Donald, *Lincoln's Herndon,* pp. 81–82.

188 *life, was dying:* For a brilliant explanation of the death of the Whig party, see Michael F. Holt, "The Mysterious Disappearance of the American Whig Party," in his *Political Parties and American Political Development,* pp. 236–264.

189 *"of any consequence":* CW, 2:126.

189 *"alloy of hypocracy":* CW, 2:322–323.

189 *new political party:* The authoritative account of this fusion is Gienapp, *The Origins of the Republican Party.*

190 *free-soil doctrine:* For an incisive exposition, see Eric Foner, *Free Soil, Free Labor, Free Men:*

The Ideology of the Republican Party Before the Civil War (New York: Oxford University Press, 1970), chap. 3.

190 *on May 29:* Paul Selby, "The Editorial Convention of 1856," *JISHS* 5 (Oct. 1912): 343–349.

190 *"in favor of":* CW, 2:333.

190 *"stay at home":* Beveridge, 2:359.

190 *with the Democrats:* CW, 2:333.

190 *"radicals and all":* Herndon later claimed that he had "forged" Lincoln's name, without his consent. For an examination of the evidence, see Donald, *Lincoln's Herndon,* pp. 86–88.

191 *"kinder" needed them:* Whitney, *Life on the Circuit,* p. 92.

191 *were former Whigs:* Gienapp, *Origins of the Republican Party,* pp. 294–295. Hoffmann was found to be ineligible, and a substitute was named.

191 *what he said:* In the September 1896 issue of *McClure's Magazine,* Whitney published what purported to be the text of this speech. Nearly all Lincoln scholars question its authenticity. See Paul M. Angle's introduction to Whitney, *Life on the Circuit,* pp. 24–25.

191 *"of the hour":* Herndon's Lincoln, 2:384.

192 *"one and inseparable":* CW, 2:341.

192 *tall that day:* Herndon's Lincoln, 2:384. There are strong reasons for doubting Herndon's story that, shortly after the Bloomington convention, only three persons attended a Republican ratification meeting in Springfield. Donald, *Lincoln's Herndon,* pp. 90–91.

192 *"foreigners, within bounds":* Turner, *Mary Todd Lincoln,* p. 46.

192 *"may think wrong":* CW, 2:342–343.

193 *the Western states:* Nathaniel G. Wilcox to AL, June 6, 1864, Lincoln MSS, LC; Jesse W. Weik, "Lincoln's Vote for Vice-President in the Philadelphia Convention of 1856," *Century Magazine* 76 (June 1908): 186–189.

193 *"John C. Frémont":* Charles W. Johnson, *Proceedings of the First Three Republican National Conventions of 1856, 1860 and 1864* (Minneapolis: Charles W. Johnson, 1893), pp. 61–62.

193 *to Lincoln's 110:* Ibid., pp. 63–64. On the formal ballot, after Lincoln received 20 votes from Connecticut, New York, and Pennsylvania, Palmer withdrew his name in favor of Dayton. Ibid., pp. 65–66.

193 *"reckon it's him":* Whitney, *Life on the Circuit,* p. 96.

193 *"for the state":* CW, 11:11.

193 *"in his speech":* M. P. McKinley to AL, July 22, 1856, HWC.

194 *"with Henry Clay's":* CW, 2:380.

194 *"world-renowned commander":* CW, 2:379.

194 *"and his gang":* CW, 2:358.

194 *as form letters:* CW, 2:374–375.

194 *"eloquence and power":* CW, 2:349, 375.

194 *"in the extreme":* CW, 2:359.

194 *"tolerably well satisfied":* CW, 2:360.

194 *"he has us":* CW, 2:358.

CHAPTER EIGHT: A HOUSE DIVIDED

Don E. Fehrenbacher, *Prelude to Greatness: Lincoln in the 1850's* (Stanford, Calif.: Stanford University Press, 1962), is by far the best analysis of the Lincoln-Douglas debates. My indebtedness to this brilliant book, both for facts and interpretations, is evident throughout this chapter.

For the general background of the Lincoln-Douglas debates, David M. Potter, *The Impending Crisis, 1848–1861,* completed and edited by Don E. Fehrenbacher (New York: Harper & Row, 1976), is invaluable. For a fuller, more descriptive account, see Allan Nevins, *The Emergence of Lincoln: Douglas, Buchanan, and Party Chaos, 1857–1859* (New York: Charles Scribner's Sons, 1950). Kenneth M. Stampp, *America in 1857: A Nation on the Brink* (New York: Oxford University Press, 1990), is a rewarding analysis of the events that led up to the Lincoln-Douglas debates. Arthur C. Cole, *The Era of the Civil War, 1848–1870* (Springfield: Illinois Centennial Commission, 1919), remains the authoritative account of Illinois politics during this period. My discussion of the Dred Scott case has benefited immensely from Don E. Fehrenbacher's *Dred Scott Case: Its Significance in American Law and Politics* (New York: Oxford University Press, 1978), a masterful work.

On the debates themselves, Richard Allen Heckman, *Lincoln vs. Douglas: The Great Debates Campaign* (Washington, D.C.: Public Affairs Press, 1967), is the best general account. No student should neglect the concise and thoughtful articles on each of the debates in Mark E. Neely, Jr., *The Abraham Lincoln Encyclopedia* (New York: McGraw-Hill Book Co., 1982).

Some Lincoln biographers have taken a rather negative view of the debates. Albert J. Beveridge, *Abraham Lincoln, 1809–1858* (Boston: Houghton Mifflin Co., 1928), announced (2:635): "Solely on their merits, the debates themselves deserve little notice." J. G. Randall, in *Lincoln the President: Springfield to Gettysburg* (New York: Dodd, Mead & Co., 1945), 1:127, took much the same view. But beginning with Harry V. Jaffa's important *Crisis of the House Divided: An Interpretation of the Issues in the Lincoln-Douglas Debates* (Garden City, N.Y.: Doubleday & Co., 1959), scholars have treated them as significant and revealing of basic American beliefs. David F. Ericson's chapters on the debates in *The Shaping of American Liberalism: The Debates over Ratification, Nullification, and Slavery* (Chicago: University of Chicago Press, 1993), is one of the most original and persuasive statements of this view. David Zarefsky, *Lincoln, Douglas, and Slavery: In the Crucible of Public Debate* (Chicago: University of Chicago Press, 1990), is a masterful analysis of the arguments used by both participants, on which I have leaned heavily.

My account of Douglas's role in the debates draws primarily on Robert W. Johannsen's authoritative *Stephen A. Douglas* (New York: Oxford University Press, 1973), but I have also found useful George Fort Milton, *The Eve of Conflict: Stephen A. Douglas and the Needless War* (Boston: Houghton Mifflin Co., 1934). The best account of the Democratic party during these years is Roy F. Nichols, *The Disruption of American Democracy* (New York: Macmillan Co., 1948).

There is no wholly reliable text of the debates. Shortly after the debates Lincoln collected the verbatim reports of his speeches, as published in the Chicago *Press and Tribune,* and those of Douglas that appeared in the Chicago *Times,* and pasted them in a large scrapbook. It is now in the Library of Congress, and a facsimile edition, with a careful introduction by David C. Mearns, has been published with the title *The Illinois Political Campaign of 1858: A Facsimile of the Printer's Copy of His Debates with Senator Stephen Arnold Douglas as Edited and Prepared for Press by Abraham Lincoln* (Washington, D.C.: Government Printing Office, 1958). In preparing this notebook, Lincoln corrected a few typographical errors in reports of his own remarks but made no alterations in those of Douglas's, believing "it would be an unwarrantable liberty for us to change a word or a letter in his [speeches]" (*CW,* 3:510). He did delete numerous bracketed passages in the newspaper reports indicating laughter and applause from the audience. This scrapbook became the basis for the first publication of the debates in book form, *Political Debates Between Hon. Abraham Lincoln and Hon. Stephen A. Douglas, in the Celebrated Campaign of 1858, in Illinois* (Columbus, Ohio: Follett, Foster & Co., 1860), and that, in turn, provided the text from which most subsequent editions of the debates were drawn. Of these the most useful is Edwin Erle Sparks, ed., *The Lincoln-Douglas Debates of 1858* (Springfield: Illinois State Historical Library, 1908), which is especially valuable because it includes much journalistic description and commentary. Roy P. Basler and the other editors of *The Collected Works of Abraham Lincoln* (New Brunswick, N.J.: Rutgers University Press, 1953), volume 3, went back to Lincoln's scrapbook, and this version restored references to cheering and other interruptions, which Lincoln had deleted. In *Created Equal? The Complete Lincoln-Douglas Debates of 1858* (Chicago: University of Chicago Press, 1958), Paul M. Angle followed a similar practice, as did Don E. Fehrenbacher in *Abraham Lincoln: Speeches and Writings, 1832–1858* (New York: Library of America, 1989).

Recently Harold Holzer has produced a very different version of the texts in *The Lincoln-Douglas Debates: The First Complete, Unexpurgated Text* (New York: HarperCollins Publishers, 1993). Holzer exactly reversed the procedure followed by Lincoln and presented the Democratic *Chicago Times* version of what Lincoln said and the *Chicago Press and Tribune* version of what Douglas said. I am not persuaded that this tactic necessarily gives a more authentic version of what the two speakers said, in part because the reports of the two rival reporting teams may not have been composed entirely independently, chiefly because there is little reason to believe that a hostile reporter is more objective than a friendly one. On the biases and distortions introduced in the *Chicago Times* reports of Lincoln's remarks, see Michael Burlingame, "Mucilating Douglas and Mutilating Lincoln: How Shorthand Reporters Covered the Lincoln-Douglas Debates of 1858," *Lincoln Herald* 96 (Spring 1994): 18–23. For further thoughtful questions about Holzer's edition, see Douglas L. Wilson, "The Unfinished Text of the Lincoln-Douglas Debates," *Journal of the Abraham Lincoln Association* 15 (Winter 1994): 70–84. Nevertheless, Holzer's book, reporting all the digressions, interruptions, and asides, gives a better feel for the debates than any of the other sources; it shows that these encounters were not just a discussion of political philosophy but a restless, roaring, brawling exchange in which the audience was vigorously involved.

In the following pages all quotations from the debates are taken from the accessible and accurate edition edited by Robert W. Johannsen, *The Lincoln-Douglas Debates of 1858* (New York: Oxford University Press, 1965), but I have checked every quotation against Holzer's edition, noting variations if they are of any consequence.

196 *"my private affairs": CW,* 2:395.
197 *"in travelling east":* Turner, *Mary Todd Lincoln,* p. 50.
197 *it was redeemed:* Pratt, *Personal Finances,* pp. 54, 77–79.
197 *"what she has":* See the excellent account of the expansion of the Lincolns' house in Wayne C. Temple, *By Square and Compasses: The Building of Lincoln's Home and Its Saga* (Bloomington, Ill.: Ashlar Press, 1984), chap. 5.
197 *"used to live here":* WHH, interview with James Gourley, undated, Lamon MSS, HEH.
198 *large and comfortable:* Cf. Baker, *Mary Todd Lincoln,* pp. 116–117.
198 *best in Springfield:* I learned many of the details of this renovation during a personally conducted tour that Mr. Norman D. Hellmers, superintendent of the Lincoln Home National Site in Springfield, gave me. Richard S. Hagen, " 'What a Pleasant Home Abe Lincoln Has,' " *JISHS* 48 (Spring 1955): 5–27, is also valuable. See also the very interesting video documentary *The Lincolns of Springfield, Illinois* (Springfield, Ill.: Sangamon State University, 1989).
198 *"type of American lady":* Katherine B. Menz, "Furnishings Plan, . . . The Lincoln Home," unpublished report to the National Park Service, U.S. Department of the Interior, 1983.
198 *"to be noisy":* Turner, *Mary Todd Lincoln,* p. 61.
198 *Phillips Exeter Academy:* John S. Goff, *Robert Todd Lincoln: A Man in His Own Right* (Norman: University of Oklahoma Press, 1969), pp. 22–26.
198 *"and other game":* Isaac N. Arnold, *The Life of Abraham Lincoln* (Chicago: Jansen, McClurg, & Co., 1885), p. 83. Contrary to rumors that Mary was stingy in feeding her family, recent excavations of the privy and rubbish heap behind the Lincoln home suggest that she used the best cuts of meat, with much pork and chicken—both Southern delicacies. See the fascinating discussion of the Lincolns' diet in Floyd Mansberger, "Archaeological Investigations at the Lincoln Home National Historic Site, Springfield, Illinois," report prepared for the National Park Service, 1987, pp. 229–274.
199 *"you were here":* Turner, *Mary Todd Lincoln,* pp. 48–49.
199 *"political public opinion": CW,* 2:385.
199 *of Dred Scott:* The following paragraphs closely follow Fehrenbacher, *The Dred Scott Case,* the definitive account.
200 *"in the country":* Beveridge, 2:486–491.
200 *"in some way": CW,* 11:13.
200 *"be a citizen": CW,* 3:298–299.
200 *the judicial process:* George M. Fredrickson, "The Search for Order and Community," in Cullom Davis et al., eds., *The Public and the Private Lincoln: Contemporary Perspectives* (Carbondale: Southern Illinois University Press, 1979), pp. 86–98. See also Robert A. Ferguson's admirable essay, "Lincoln: An Epilogue," in his *Law and Letters in American Culture* (Cambridge, Mass.: Harvard University Press, 1984), pp. 305–317.
200 *even the Constitution:* In 1852, Lincoln voiced his "unqualified condemnation" of Seward's doctrine that there was a higher law than the Constitution. *CW,* 2:156.
200 *"of the matter": CW,* 2:355.
200 *"controvert it's correctness": CW,* 2:388.
200 *to accept it: CW,* 2:401.
201 *"all recognize it": CW,* 2:404.
201 *"and inferior races":* Johannsen, *Stephen A. Douglas,* pp. 569–571.
201 *"benefit of slavery": CW,* 2:399.
201 *"resistance to it": CW,* 2:401.
202 *"than it is": CW,* 2:404.
202 *"pursuit of happiness": CW,* 2:405–406.
202 *"sophists as Douglas":* Gustave Koerner to Lyman Trumbull, July 4, 1857, Trumbull MSS, LC.
202 *"not be notified": CW,* 2:412–413.
203 *the Kansas Territory:* For an informed account of these developments regarding Kansas, see Kenneth M. Stampp, *America in 1857: A Nation on the Brink* (New York: Oxford University Press, 1990).
203 *"farce ever enacted": CW,* 2:400.
203 *"Douglas in Illinois":* Jeff L. Duggan to Lyman Trumbull, Jan. 28, 1858, Trumbull MSS, LC.

204 *"to this juggle":* Johannsen, *Stephen A. Douglas,* p. 587. For an excellent analysis of Douglas's course, see Robert W. Johannsen, "The Lincoln-Douglas Campaign of 1858: Background and Perspective," *JISHS* 73 (Winter 1980): 242–262.

204 *"or voted up":* Johannsen, *Stephen A. Douglas,* pp. 590–591.

204 *"courageously, eminently so":* Johannsen, "The Lincoln-Douglas Campaign," p. 253.

204 *"in the country":* David M. Potter, *The Impending Crisis, 1848–1861,* edited and completed by Don E. Fehrenbacher (New York: Harper & Row, 1976), p. 321.

204 *in the wrong: CW,* 2:427.

204 *"to go under": CW,* 2:448.

204 *"here in Illinois?": CW,* 2:430.

204 *to oppose him:* For an account of this trip and what Herndon learned, see Donald, *Lincoln's Herndon,* pp. 112–116.

204 "Are our friends crazy?": Jesse K. Dubois to Lyman Trumbull, Apr. 8, 1858, Trumbull MSS, LC.

205 "can never forget": WHH to Horace Greeley, Apr. 8, 1858, Greeley MSS, New York Public Library.

205 *make himself available:* Beveridge (2:564–568) gave great credit to rumors of Wentworth's candidacy, but Don E. Fehrenbacher has shown these were largely the work of Democrats seeking to divide the Republicans. Fehrenbacher, *Chicago Giant: A Biography of "Long John" Wentworth* (Madison, Wis.: American History Research Center, 1957), pp. 155–157.

205 *"thick and thin":* Beveridge, 2:566.

205 *did Lincoln himself: CW,* 2:472.

205 *the second time:* Neely, *The Abraham Lincoln Encyclopedia,* p. 79.

205 *"of the constitution":* Fehrenbacher, *Prelude to Greatness,* p. 49.

205 *"than anything else": CW,* 2:472.

205 *"Stephen A. Douglas":* Beveridge, 2:571–572.

206 *"what we struck":* WHH to Lyman Trumbull, June 24, 1858, Trumbull MSS, LC.

206 *his acceptance speech:* It was not technically that. In the debates that followed, Lincoln told Douglas that if he examined the speech he would "find no acceptance in it." *CW,* 3:120.

206 *"see it now": Herndon's Lincoln,* 2:397. Herndon wrote several variants of this story, differing chiefly as to when Dubois interrupted Lincoln.

206 *to Robert Hayne:* Richard Nelson Current, *Speaking of Abraham Lincoln: The Man and His Meaning for Our Times* (Urbana: University of Illinois Press, 1983), pp. 11–12.

206 *"well as* South": *CW,* 2:461–462. After delivering this speech, Lincoln went to the *Illinois State Journal* office and carefully oversaw the printed version that appeared in that paper. The paragraphing is, therefore, exactly what he wanted, and the italics indicate the words he emphasized in delivering the speech. Even so, the account of the speech in the *Journal,* which is followed in most editions of Lincoln's writings, is not entirely correct. See Don E. Fehrenbacher, *Lincoln in Text and Context: Collected Essays* (Stanford, Calif.: Stanford University Press, 1987), esp. pp. 275–277, 279–280.

206 *of the Gospels:* Matthew 12:25, Mark 3:25, and Luke 11:17.

207 *or all free:* Zarefsky, *Lincoln, Douglas, and Slavery,* p. 44.

207 *"and half free?": CW,* 2:318.

207 *"and part free":* T. Lyle Dickey to WHH, Dec. 8, 1866, HWC.

207 *"issue before us": CW,* 2:453–454. For the dating of this fragment, see Robert W. Johannsen, *Lincoln, the South and Slavery: The Political Dimension* (Baton Rouge: Louisiana State University Press, 1991), p. 59n.

207 *plan or blueprint: CW,* 2:465–466.

208 *"a slave State": CW,* 2:467.

208 *"just like him":* AL to "Dear Sir," incomplete draft of a letter, [early 1858], MS auctioned by Frank H. Boos Gallery, Detroit, 1994.

208 *"of splendid success": CW,* 2:383.

208 *"not do that":* Joseph Gillespie, statement, Apr. 22, 1880, John J. Hardin MSS, Chicago Historical Society.

208 *as a "squabble": CW,* 2:463.

208 *justices would rule:* Fehrenbacher, *The Dred Scott Case,* pp. 444–447.

209 *"shall not fail": CW,* 2:467–468.

209 *"to say so?": Herndon's Lincoln,* 2:398. Perhaps Herndon did say this, though very shortly afterward he was writing to Theodore Parker that Lincoln's speech was a little too conservative. Herndon to Theodore Parker, July 8, 1858, Herndon-Parker MSS, University of Iowa Library.

209 *"of the times"*: WHH, interview with John Armstrong, undated, HWC. By this point Herndon had reconsidered his objections and was the only member of this little group to urge Lincoln to make the, speech, predicting—if belated memories can be trusted—"Lincoln, deliver that speech as read and it will make you President." *Herndon's Lincoln*, 2:400. Cf. WHH to Jesse W. Weik, Oct. 29, 1885, HWC.

209 *"it now exists"*: John Locke Scripps to AL, June 22, 1858, Lincoln MSS, LC.

209 *"so intended it"*: CW, 2:471.

209 *"foolish one perhaps"*: CW, 2:491.

209 *"be hardly won"*: John W. Forney, *Anecdotes of Public Men* (New York: Harper & Brothers, 1873), 2:179.

210 *"an unholy, unnatural alliance"*: Johannsen, *Lincoln-Douglas Debates*, pp. 22–36.

210 *"throughout the world"*: CW, 2:500–501.

210 *"in his wake"*: Edwin Erle Sparks, ed., *The Lincoln-Douglas Debates of 1858* (Springfield: Illinois State Historical Library, 1908), p. 46.

210 *"the very thing"*: CW, 3:84.

210 *on the defensive:* N. B. Judd to Lyman Trumbull, July 16, 1858, Trumbull MSS, LC.

210 *"Lincoln the leavings"*: W. J. Usrey to AL, July 19, 1858, Lincoln MSS, LC.

211 *a considerable audience:* Sparks, *Lincoln-Douglas Debates,* pp. 56–57.

211 *"come from you"*: CW, 2:529.

212 *"his own success"*: WHH to Lyman Trumbull, July 8, 1858, Trumbull MSS, LC.

212 *counties was needed:* Harry E. Pratt, *The Great Debates of 1858* (Springfield: Illinois State Historical Library, 1956), pp. 8–9.

212 *had been strongest:* For these careful calculations, see CW, 2:476–481, 503.

212 *"to the abolitionists"*: Beveridge, 2:555.

212 *"and public justice"*: J. J. Crittenden to AL, July 29, 1858, Lincoln MSS, LC.

213 *"to any extent"*: CW, 2:471–472.

213 *with the Danites:* WHH to Lyman Trumbull, June 24, 1858, Trumbull MSS, LC.

213 *"going to do"*: WHH to Lyman Trumbull, July 8, 1858, Trumbull MSS, LC.

213 *"he does not"*: WHH to Lyman Trumbull, June 24, 1858, Trumbull MSS, LC.

213 *Democrats' campaign strategy:* Jesse K. Dubois to AL, Sept. 7, 1858, Lincoln MSS, LC.

213 *have been true:* A. Sherman to O. M. Hatch, Sept. 27, 1858, Hatch MSS, ISHL.

214 *3,400 by train:* Pratt, *The Great Debates,* p. 5.

214 *and in expression:* For an excellent account of the reporting of the debates, which stresses the distortion caused by partisan reporting, see Harold Holzer's introduction to *The Lincoln-Douglas Debates: The First Complete, Unexpurgated Text* (New York: HarperCollins Publishers, 1993). Also valuable are Tom Reilly, "Lincoln-Douglas Debates of 1858 Forced New Role on the Press," *Journalism Quarterly* 56 (Winter 1979): 734–743, 752; Robert S. Harper, *Lincoln and the Press* (New York: McGraw-Hill Book Co., 1951), pp. 21–30; and Sparks, *The Lincoln-Douglas Debates,* pp. 75–84.

215 *"his large feet"*: Carl Schurz, "Reminiscences of a Long Life," *McClure's Magazine* 28 (Jan. 1907): 253.

215 *"to be President"*: CW, 2:506.

216 *By one o'clock:* For details on Ottawa and the arrangements for the debate, see the newspaper reports in Sparks, *The Lincoln-Douglas Debates,* pp. 124–145.

216 *apparently startled Lincoln:* In the following pages my account of the debates generally follows, and usually paraphrases, the texts as given in Johannsen, *Lincoln-Douglas Debates.* I have given specific citations only for quoted passages.

216 *"a Republican party"*: Johannsen, *Lincoln-Douglas Debates,* p. 39.

216 *"of this Government"*: Ibid., p. 48.

217 *"a chestnut horse"*: Ibid., p. 52.

217 *"upon the merits"*: Ibid., p. 58.

217 *"it in kind"*: Ibid., p. 52.

217 *"to his knees"*: Sparks, *Lincoln-Douglas Debates,* pp. 140–141; Henry Villard, *Memoirs of Henry Villard, Journalist and Financier, 1835–1900* (Boston: Houghton, Mifflin & Co., 1904), 1:93. There was a good deal of chaffering about this episode in subsequent debates, Douglas claiming that Lincoln had been so demolished that his supporters actually had to carry him from the platform, Lincoln responding that Douglas must be "actually crazy" to tell such a story. Johannsen, *Lincoln-Douglas Debates,* p. 151.

217 *"am yet alive"*: Richard Yates to AL, Aug. 26, 1858, Lincoln MSS, LC; CW, 3:37.

217 *"on the defensive"*: Jay Monaghan, *The Man Who Elected Lincoln* (Indianapolis: Bobbs-Merrill Co., 1956), p. 115.

217 *"proslavery bamboozelling demogogue"*: Joseph Medill to AL, [Aug. 27, 1858], Lincoln MSS, LC.

218 *day, at Freeport*: Fehrenbacher, *Prelude to Greatness*, pp. 124–126.

218 *"State of Illinois"*: Johannsen, *Lincoln-Douglas Debates*, p. 79.

218 *"question among ourselves"*: Ibid., pp. 76–79.

218 *"the slavery question?"*: Ibid., p. 79.

218 *Douglas would answer*: CW, 2:530.

218 *"a State Constitution"*: Johannsen, *Lincoln-Douglas Debates*, p. 88.

219 *"to the point"*: CW, 2:530.

219 *include the question*: Explaining the true intent of the Freeport question, Fehrenbacher (*Prelude to Greatness*, pp. 122–128) demolishes the legend that Lincoln, against the warnings of his advisers, asked the question in order to deprive Douglas of Southern support in the 1860 presidential election. But the impact of the Freeport Doctrine on Douglas's support in the South was heavy, for it appeared to rob Southerners of their victory in Dred Scott. For this reason in the next session of Congress the Democratic senatorial caucus, dominated by Southerners, virtually read Douglas out of the party and stripped him of his chairmanship of the Committee on Territories.

219 *"be wholly false"*: Johannsen, *Lincoln-Douglas Debates*, p. 81.

219 *"defy your wrath"*: Ibid., pp. 97, 100.

219 *"the decided advantage"*: WHH to Theodore Parker, Aug. 31, 1858, Herndon-Parker MSS, University of Iowa Library.

219 *"more elevated position"*: Lowell (Mass.) *Journal and Courier,* Aug. 30, 1858.

219 *would be reelected*: Zarefsky, *Lincoln, Douglas, and Slavery,* p. 58.

220 *the Republican cause*: On Trumbull's role, see Mark M. Krug, "Lyman Trumbull and the Real Issues in the Lincoln-Douglas Debates," *JISHS* 57 (Winter 1964): 380–396.

220 *debate, at Jonesboro*: For an excellent account of this debate, which gives much insight into the social, economic, and political life of "Egypt," see John Y. Simon, "Union County in 1858 and the Lincoln-Douglas Debate," *JISHS* 62 (Autumn 1969): 267–292.

220 *Senate that year*: Johannsen, *Lincoln-Douglas Debates*, pp. 122–123.

220 *"be created equal"*: Ibid., p. 128.

220 *"my political friends"*: Ibid., p. 136.

220 *"against unfriendly legislation"*: Ibid., pp. 146–147. The *Chicago Times* gave what is probably a better version: "vigor enough in the tendency to force slavery into a territory without positive police regulations." Holzer, *Lincoln-Douglas Debates*, p. 170.

220 *debate to begin*: Sparks, *Lincoln-Douglas Debates*, pp. 314, 324. The best account is Charles H. Coleman, *The Lincoln-Douglas Debate at Charleston, Illinois (Eastern Illinois University Bulletin,* no. 220 [Oct. 1, 1957]).

221 *"and political equality"*: Johannsen, *Lincoln-Douglas Debates*, p. 162.

221 *American race problem*: Two excellent analyses of Lincoln's racial views are George M. Fredrickson, "A Man but Not a Brother: Abraham Lincoln and Racial Equality," *Journal of Southern History* 41 (Feb. 1975): 39–58, and Don E. Fehrenbacher, "Only His Stepchildren," in *Lincoln in Text and Context,* pp. 95–112. The chapter on Lincoln in George Sinkler's *The Racial Attitudes of American Presidents: From Abraham Lincoln to Theodore Roosevelt* (Garden City, N.Y.: Doubleday & Co., 1971) is also important. It would, I think, be a mistake to attempt to palliate Lincoln's racial views by saying that he grew up in a racist society or that his ideas were shared by many of his contemporaries. After all, there were numerous Americans of his generation—notably, many of the abolitionists—who were committed to racial equality. At the same time, it ought to be noted that Lincoln fortunately escaped the more virulent strains of racism. Unlike many of his fellow Republicans, he never spoke of African-Americans as hideous or physically inferior; he never declared that they were innately inferior mentally or incapable of intellectual development; he never described them as indolent or incapable of sustained work; he never discussed their supposed licentious nature or immorality. For an extensive sampling of statements by Republicans who did crudely express these views, see James D. Bilotta, *Race and the Rise of the Republican Party, 1848–1865* (New York: Peter Lang, 1992), esp. chap. 6. Lincoln's own views on race, on the other hand, were nearly always expressed tentatively. As Fehrenbacher points out (p. 106), "He conceded that the Negro *might not* be his equal, or he said that the Negro *was not* his equal *in certain respects.*" Even when he agreed that blacks did not have the same civil rights as whites, he nearly always added in the next

breath that they were the equal of whites in the enjoyment of the natural rights pledged in the Declaration of Independence.

221 *"beginning to end"*: Johannsen, *Lincoln-Douglas Debates*, p. 174.
221 *"petty personal matters"*: Ibid., pp. 177, 181, 184.
222 *the Republican candidate*: See the spirited account in Tufve Nilsson Hasselquist, "The Big Day: A Galesburg Swede Views the Lincoln-Douglas Debate," ed. and trans. by John E. Norton, *Knox Alumnus* (Winter 1990), pp. 16–18. (Courtesy Prof. J. Harvey Young)
222 *"their posterity forever"*: Johannsen, *Lincoln-Douglas Debates*, pp. 210, 212, 216.
222 *"Declaration of Independence"*: Ibid., p. 219.
222 " 'set him again' ": Ibid., p. 228.
223 *"the adjoining islands"*: Ibid., pp. 233–234.
223 *"a political wrong"*: Ibid., p. 254.
223 *"right or wrong"*: Ibid., p. 256.
223 *"the other counties"*: Ibid., p. 264.
223 *"side of Heaven"*: Ibid., p. 267.
223 *"to the law"*: Ibid., p. 268.
223 *"crime of slavery"*: Ibid., p. 266.
223 *"the whole earth"*: Ibid., p. 276.
223 "shall last forever": Ibid., p. 277.
223 *course on Lecompton*: Ibid., pp. 292–299.
224 *"Go it bear!"*: Ibid., p. 301. For the origins of this jest, see P. M. Zall, ed., *Abe Lincoln Laughing: Humorous Anecdotes from Original Sources by and About Abraham Lincoln* (Berkeley: University of California Press, 1982), p. 20.
224 *"and so on"*: Johannsen, *Lincoln-Douglas Debates*, p. 303.
224 *"conditions in life"*: Ibid., pp. 315–316.
224 "as a wrong": Ibid., p. 316.
224 *"right of kings"*: Ibid., p. 319.
225 *"the town together"*: Ibid., p. 42.
225 *"starved to death"*: Ibid., p. 281.
225 *"less of it"*: Ibid., p. 57.
225 *"and the same"*: CW, 2:507.
225 *on and on*: Randall, *Lincoln the President*, 1:121–122.
225 *the English bill*: Potter, *The Impending Crisis*, p. 325.
226 *"controversy with him"*: Johannsen, *Lincoln-Douglas Debates*, p. 131.
226 *"the most infamous treachery"*: Ibid., p. 100.
226 *"discussed before you?"*: Ibid., p. 176.
226 *"of ultimate extinction"*: Ibid., p. 265.
226 *"negroes in Christendom"*: Ibid., p. 326. The *Chicago Press and Tribune* reported that Douglas said "niggers in Christendom." Holzer, *Lincoln-Douglas Debates*, p. 367.
227 *were closely divided*: Bruce Collins, "The Lincoln-Douglas Contest of 1858 and Illinois' Electorate," *Journal of American Studies* 20 (Dec. 1986): 391–420, offers an informed analysis of the returns. The map in Arthur C. Cole, *The Era of the Civil War, 1848–1870* (Springfield: Illinois Centennial Commission, 1919), facing p. 178, graphically shows the distribution of votes.
227 *both men appeared*: Forest L. Whan, "Stephen A. Douglas," in William Norwood Brigance, ed., *A History and Criticism of American Public Address* (New York: McGraw-Hill Book Co., 1943), 2:823.
227 *as a whole*: Holzer, *Lincoln-Douglas Debates*, pp. 371–373.
228 *United States Senate*: Fehrenbacher, *Prelude to Greatness*, pp. 118–120, offers a clear explanation of this complicated subject.
228 *"to their numbers"*: *Rockford Register*, Nov. 13, 1858. Claiming that Republican districts had, on an average, 19,655 inhabitants and Democratic districts only 15,675, the *Illinois State Journal* argued that, under a fair apportionment, Republicans would have had a majority of seven in the House of Representatives and three in the Senate. Douglas, it concluded, "was elected for the reason that 750 voters in 'Egypt' are an offset to 1000 in Canaan [i.e., northern Illinois]." *Journal*, Nov. 10, 1858.
228 *carry key counties*: I. H. Waters to O. M. Hatch, Nov. 3, 1858, Hatch MSS, ISHL.
228 *"and other cities"*: WHH to Theodore Parker, Nov. 8, 1858, Herndon-Parker MSS, University of Iowa Library.
228 *"than all others"*: G. W. Rives to O. M. Hatch, Nov. 10, 1858, Hatch MSS, ISHL.

228 *"me except Billy"*: Henry C. Whitney to WHH, July 18, 1887, HWC.
229 *"one* hundred *defeats"*: *CW*, 3:339.

CHAPTER NINE: THE TASTE *IS* IN MY MOUTH

This chapter draws heavily on two excellent accounts of the 1860 campaign and election: William E. Baringer, *Lincoln's Rise to Power* (Boston: Little, Brown & Co., 1937), and Reinhard H. Luthin, *The First Lincoln Campaign* (Cambridge, Mass.: Harvard University Press, 1944).

For the general political background of that election, see David M. Potter, *The Impending Crisis, 1848–1861,* completed and edited by Don E. Fehrenbacher (New York: Harper & Row, 1976), and Allan Nevins, *The Emergence of Lincoln,* vol. 2, *Prologue to Civil War, 1859–1861* (New York: Charles Scribner's Sons, 1951).

For Lincoln's activities during the year before his election, Harry V. Jaffa and Robert W. Johannsen, eds., *In the Name of the People: Speeches and Writings of Lincoln and Douglas in the Ohio Campaign of 1859* (Columbus: Ohio State University Press, 1959), is indispensable.

There are several good studies of the Republican convention that nominated Lincoln: Kenneth M. Stampp, "The Republican National Convention of 1860," in his *The Imperiled Union: Essays on the Background of the Civil War* (New York: Oxford University Press, 1980), pp. 136–162; Don E. Fehrenbacher, "The Republican Decision at Chicago," in Norman A. Graebner, ed., *Politics and the Crisis of 1860* (Urbana: University of Illinois Press, 1961), pp. 32–60; and Elting Morison, "The Election of 1860," in Arthur M. Schlesinger, Jr., and Fred L. Israel, eds., *History of American Presidential Elections, 1789–1968* (New York: Chelsea House Publishers, 1971), 2:1097–1122. *Proceedings of the First Three Republican National Conventions of 1856, 1860 and 1864* (Minneapolis: Charles W. Johnson, 1893), is a rather dry record, but William B. Hesseltine, *Three Against Lincoln: Murat Halstead Reports the Caucuses of 1860* (Baton Rouge: Louisiana State University Press, 1960), recaptures the color and excitement of that gathering.

Willard L. King, *Lincoln's Manager, David Davis* (Cambridge, Mass.: Harvard University Press, 1960), is essential to an understanding of Lincoln's campaign.

The best analysis of the 1860 election returns is William E. Gienapp, "Who Voted for Lincoln?" in John L. Thomas, ed., *Abraham Lincoln and the American Political Tradition* (Amherst, Mass.: University of Massachusetts Press, 1986), pp. 50–97. For valuable essays on how immigrant groups, particularly the Germans, voted, see Frederick C. Leubke, ed., *Ethnic Voters and the Election of Lincoln* (Lincoln: University of Nebraska Press, 1971).

230 *"my private business"*: *CW*, 3:396.
230 *"even household purposes"*: *CW*, 3:337.
230 *"have already had"*: *CW*, 3:387.
231 *the Republican party*: *CW*, 3:337, 341.
231 *to remain neutral*: Don E. Fehrenbacher, *Chicago Giant: A Biography of "Long John" Wentworth* (Madison, Wis.: American History Research Center, 1957), offers a full account of this complicated feud.
231 *"languages from myself"*: *CW*, 3:380.
232 *"for that plank"*: *CW*, 3:384.
232 *"we shall disagree"*: *CW*, 3:391.
232 *"the Slave power"*: *CW*, 3:345. This phrase, which Lincoln had avoided using up through 1858, now began to appear in his speeches and letters.
232 *dangers of "Douglasism"*: *CW*, 3:379.
232 *"he absorbs them"*: *CW*, 3:367.
232 *of* Harper's Magazine: Robert W. Johannsen, "Stephen A. Douglas, 'Harper's Magazine,' and Popular Sovereignty," in *The Frontier, the Union, and Stephen A. Douglas* (Urbana: University of Illinois Press, 1989), pp. 120–145. Douglas's article is most easily available in Jaffa and Johannsen, *In the Name of the People*, pp. 58–125.
232 *"their internal polity"*: Ibid., pp. 84–85.
233 *"of the Union"*: Ibid., p. 150.
233 *"most insidious one"*: *CW*, 3:394.
233 *"the little gentleman"*: W. T. Bascom to AL, Sept. 1, 1859, Lincoln MSS, LC.
233 *"kick like thunder"*: Joseph Medill to AL, Sept. 10, 1859, Lincoln MSS, LC.
233 *"right to object"*: *CW*, 3:434, 428, 405.

233 "of public opinion": CW, 3:423.

233 "against the negro": CW, 3:431.

233 "and the reptile": CW, 3:425.

233 "country is everything": CW, 3:424.

233 "the miners and sappers": CW, 3:423.

233 "their own labor": CW, 3:446.

234 "in the world": CW, 3:477–478. For Wayland's influence on Lincoln, see Gabor S. Boritt, *Lincoln and the Economics of the American Dream* (Memphis: Memphis State University Press, 1978), pp. 122–124. Most Republican leaders shared Lincoln's belief in the labor theory of value. Heather C. Richardson, "Constructing 'the Greatest Nation of the Earth': Economic Policies of the Republican Party During the American Civil War" (unpublished Ph.D. dissertation, Harvard University, 1992), esp. chap. 1.

234 "his early condition": CW, 10:43.

234 *upward social mobility:* David R. Wrone, "Abraham Lincoln's Idea of Property," *Science and Society* 33 (Winter 1969): 54–70.

234 "or kick understandingly": CW, 3:479.

235 "free white people": CW, 2:268. Such use would presumably exclude both slaves and free blacks. Johannsen, *Lincoln, the South, and Slavery*, p. 33.

235 "to go there": CW, 10:45.

235 "President or vice": G. W. Rives to O. M. Hatch, Nov. 11, 1858, Hatch MSS, ISHL.

235 Reading *(Pennsylvania)* Journal: Baringer, *Lincoln's Rise to Power*, pp. 51–62.

235 "me as President": Henry Villard, *Memoirs of Henry Villard, Journalist and Financier, 1835–1890* (Boston: Houghton, Mifflin & Co., 1904), 1:97. Residents of Illinois were often referred to as "Suckers."

235 *archival, Judd: Chicago Democrat,* Nov. 11, 1858.

236 *movement in Ohio: CW,* 3:377, 395.

236 "habit of doing": E. A. Studley to O. M. Hatch, Sept. 7, 1859, Hatch MSS, ISHL.

237 *a best-seller:* The best account of the publishing history of this volume is David C. Mearns's introduction to *The Illinois Political Campaign of 1858: A Facsimile of the Printer's Copy of His Debates with Senator Stephen Arnold Douglas as Edited and Prepared for the Press by Abraham Lincoln* (Washington, D.C.: Library of Congress, 1958). For discussions of the various editions of the debates, see *LL,* no. 337 (Sept. 23, 1935); R. Gerald McMurtry, *The Different Editions of the "Debates of Lincoln and Douglas"* (pamphlet reprinted from *Journal of the Illinois State Historical Society,* 1934); and Jay Monaghan, *Lincoln Bibliography, 1839–1939* (Springfield: Illinois State Historical Library, 1943), 1:18–20.

237 "much of me": CW, 3:511–512.

237 *in February 1860:* Andrew A. Freeman, *Abraham Lincoln Goes to New York* (New York: Coward-McCann, 1960), gives a detailed account of Lincoln's visit.

237 *Woods & Henckle, $100: Day by Day,* 2:271.

238 *stop-Seward movement:* Randall, *Lincoln the President,* 1:135.

238 *called his "shaddow": CW,* 4:39.

238 "than his father": Francis Fisher Browne, *The Every-Day Life of Abraham Lincoln* (Chicago: Browne & Howell Co., 1913), 1:217.

238 *handsome, statesmanlike image:* This portrait is admirably reproduced in James Mellon, *The Face of Lincoln* (New York: Viking Press, 1979), p. 51. See also Charles Hamilton and Lloyd Ostendorf, *Lincoln in Photographs: An Album of Every Known Pose* (Dayton, Ohio: Morningside, 1985), pp. 36–37.

238 *at the outset:* George Haven Putnam, "The Speech that Won the East for Lincoln," *Outlook* 130 (Feb. 8, 1922); 220–222.

239 "in the federal territories": CW, 3:534.

239 "that old policy": CW, 3:537.

239 *abolitionist was "insane": CW,* 3:496, 503.

239 "refused to participate": CW, 3:541.

239 "in all events": CW, 3:543.

239 " 'be a murderer!' ": CW, 3:547.

239 "we understand it": CW, 3:550. The last sentence is in full capitals in Lincoln's *Collected Works.*

239 "since St. Paul": Baringer, *Lincoln's Rise to Power,* p. 158.

239 "I ever heard": Hiram Barney to AL, Feb. 28, 1860 (on the back of the envelope of Edward Wallace to AL, Feb. 25, 1860), Lincoln MSS, LC.

240 *"electrify as well":* Herbert Mitgang, ed., *Abraham Lincoln: A Press Portrait* (Chicago: Quadrangle Books, 1971), pp. 157–158.

240 Albany Evening Journal: Monaghan, *Lincoln Bibliography,* 1:14–15; *LL,* no. 589 (July 22, 1940).

240 *"worthy of it":* David C. Mearns, ed., *The Lincoln Papers* (Garden City, N.Y.: Doubleday & Co., Inc., 1948), 1:231.

240 *the previous September:* On this tour, see Elwin L. Page, *Abraham Lincoln in New Hampshire* (Boston: Houghton Mifflin Co., 1929).

240 *"to have one":* John S. Goff, *Robert Todd Lincoln: A Man in His Own Right* (Norman: University of Oklahoma Press, 1969), p. 32.

240 *know his father:* Marshall S. Snow, "Abraham Lincoln: A Personal Reminiscence," *Magazine of History with Notes and Queries* 11 (Feb. 1910): 64–65.

241 *"bite the children":* CW, 4:5.

241 *"we understand it":* CW, 4:29–30.

241 *for his nomination:* Jackson Grimshaw to WHH, Apr. 28, 1866, HWC.

241 *"the Illinois delegates":* CW, 3:517.

241 *"mouth a little":* CW, 4:45.

242 *he secretly owned:* CW, 3:383.

242 *"secrets from him":* CW, 10:48.

242 *"he was unequal":* "Praise for the 'Most Available Candidate,' " *JISHS* 71 (Feb. 1978): 72.

242 *"a guileless man":* David Davis to [John Wentworth], Sept. 25, 1859, Davis MSS, ISHL.

243 *ten, years younger:* CW, 4:36.

243 *for his nomination:* CW, 4:43.

243 *"chances of success":* CW, 4:33.

243 *attending the convention:* CW, 4:32.

244 *"any positive objection":* CW, 4:47.

244 *"their first love":* CW, 4:34.

244 *"a few men":* N. B. Judd to AL, Dec. 12, 1859, Lincoln MSS, LC.

244 *"be very well":* CW, 3:509.

244 *"our friends here":* CW, 3:509.

244 *more dynamic image:* This account closely follows Wayne C. Temple's excellent article, "Lincoln's Fence Rails," *JISHS* 47 (Spring 1954): 20–34.

245 *"grown to manhood":* CW, 4:48.

245 *only partially true:* Although admitting that "Lincoln was an exceptionally decent and honest politician," Gabor S. Boritt suggests that had voters known the reality rather than the myth he might have been defeated in 1860. "Was Lincoln a Vulnerable Candidate in 1860?" *Civil War History* 27 (Mar. 1981): 31–48.

245 *sent to Chicago:* Isaac N. Arnold, *The Life of Abraham Lincoln* (Chicago: Jansen, McClurg, & Co., 1885), p. 163.

246 *"unit for him":* Baringer, *Lincoln's Rise to Power,* p. 186.

246 *"stay at home":* Rufus Rockwell Wilson, ed., *Intimate Memories of Lincoln* (Elmira, N.Y.: The Primavera Press, Inc., 1945), p. 294.

246 *the Republican ticket:* Jackson Grimshaw to WHH, Apr. 28, 1866, HWC.

246 *" 'Higher Law' doctrine":* CW, 4:50.

246 *Pennsylvania and New Jersey:* Luthin, *The First Lincoln Campaign,* chap. 9, offers an excellent account of the convention proceedings.

247 *"home and abroad":* *Proceedings of the First Three Republican National Conventions,* pp. 131–133.

247 *a dark horse:* William Safire, *Safire's New Political Dictionary* (New York: Random House, 1993), pp. 166–167.

248 *of the operation:* King, *Lincoln's Manager,* pp. 135–142.

248 *to do so:* Stephen T. Logan, statement to WHH, undated, Lamon MSS, HEH.

248 *Seward backers arrived:* For a spirited account, see Baringer, *Lincoln's Rise to Power,* chap. 5.

248 *Indiana Republican parties:* William Butler to AL, May 15, 1860, Lincoln MSS, LC.

248 *"the pinch comes":* C. H. Ray to AL, May 14, 1860, Lincoln MSS, LC.

249 "devil with fire": Mark W. Delahay to AL, May 17, 1860, Lincoln MSS, LC.

249 "will bind me": CW, 4:50.

249 *his directive was unnecessary:* According to legend, Lincoln's message vastly upset his lieutenants in Chicago, and Davis overruled it, saying, "Lincoln ain't here and don't know what we have to meet!" Nevins, *The Emergence of Lincoln,* vol. 2, p. 256. But the source of the story is

Henry C. Whitney's highly unreliable *Lincoln the Citizen* (New York: Baker & Taylor Co., 1908), pp. 288–289.

249 *had no foundation:* Nevins, *The Emergence of Lincoln,* p. 256, argues that Davis did make such a pledge to Smith, but King, *Lincoln's Manager,* pp. 136–138, shows how weak the evidence for such an agreement is. For an astute analysis of the decision of the Indiana delegation, see Kenneth M. Stampp, *Indiana Politics During the Civil War* (Indianapolis: Indiana Historical Bureau, 1949), pp. 38–40.

249 *"difficult to get":* CW, 4:47.

249 *the initial ballot:* The evidence on an alleged bargain between Davis and the Cameron forces is complex and hard to evaluate. I conclude that there was no bargain, partly because Davis, Swett, and Lincoln, as quoted below, flatly denied it, partly because after the nomination Cameron and his friends pushed their claim with a nervous intensity that betrayed their uncertainty about the supposed pledge. The best conclusion may well be that of Willard L. King, who says (*Lincoln's Manager,* p. 141) that Davis made a qualified pledge of his personal support to Cameron.

249 *"to our satisfaction":* Erwin S. Bradley, *Simon Cameron, Lincoln's Secretary of War* (Philadelphia: University of Pennsylvania Press, 1966), pp. 149–151.

250 *"no mortgages executed":* Wilson, *Intimate Memories,* p. 296.

250 *"has promised nothing":* David Davis to Thomas H. Dudley, Sept. 1, 1860, Dudley MSS, HEH.

250 *"are fairly implied":* CW, 4:51. Cf. *Herndon's Lincoln,* 3:473.

250 *"and practice law":* Jesse W. Weik, *The Real Lincoln: A Portrait* (Boston: Houghton Mifflin Co., 1922), pp. 266–267.

250 *the nomination unanimous: Proceedings of the First Three Republican National Conventions,* pp. 151, 152, 155.

251 *"than I am":* Charles S. Zane, "Lincoln as I Knew Him," *Sunset Magazine* 29 (Oct. 1912): 430–438. Accounts of how Lincoln received the news of his nomination vary in detail. See Randall, *Lincoln the President,* 1:173–174.

251 *"you see me":* David Davis to AL, May 18, 1860, Lincoln MSS, LC.

251 *"in this respect":* CW, 4:75.

251 *"look up to":* C. C. Coffin, in Allen Thorndike Rice, ed., *Reminiscences of Abraham Lincoln by Distinguished Men of His Time* (New York: North American Review, 1888), pp. 168–171.

251 *"the White House":* George Ashmun, "Abraham Lincoln at Home," in *Springfield* (Mass.) *Daily Republican,* May 23, 1860.

252 *wealthy Springfield friends:* John G. Nicolay to Therena Bates, June 7, 1860, Nicolay MSS, LC; John W. Bunn to Jesse W. Weik, July 26, 1916, HWC.

252 *"truly A. Lincoln":* CW, 4:68.

252 *"deport yourself accordingly":* O. H. Browning to AL, July 4, 1860, Lincoln MSS, LC.

252 *rather than "Abram":* CW, 4:68.

252 *held his head:* Hamilton and Ostendorf, *Lincoln in Photographs,* p. 48; Mellon, *The Face of Lincoln,* pp. 10–11, 76–77.

252 *"not an objection":* Rufus Rockwell Wilson, *Lincoln in Portraiture* (New York: Press of the Pioneers, 1935), pp. 111, 93–97.

252 *"attend to them":* CW, 4:60.

253 *biographies were distributed:* Ernest J. Wessen, "Campaign Lives of Abraham Lincoln, 1860: An Annotated Bibliography," *Papers in Illinois History, 1937,* pp. 188–220, is authoritative. However, Howells's biography is important not merely because its author was to become a distinguished novelist but because Lincoln, at the request of S. C. Parks, went over a copy of the biography and corrected it. That copy has been published as W. D. Howells, *Life of Abraham Lincoln* (Springfield, Ill.: Abraham Lincoln Association, 1938). The autobiography Lincoln prepared for Scripps is in *CW,* 4:60–67. See also Grace Locke Scripps Dyche, "John Locke Scripps, Lincoln's Campaign Biographer: A Sketch Compiled from His Letters," *JISHS* 17 (Oct. 1924): 333–351.

253 *children into slavery:* CW, 4:112.

253 *"to the charge":* CW, 4:86.

253 *"fairly with all":* CW, 10:54.

253 "fairness to all": CW, 4:94.

254 *"among its' members":* CW, 4:78.

254 *"propose to forget":* CW, 4:54.

254 *"as he is":* WHH to Lyman Trumbull, June 14, 1860, Trumbull MSS, LC.

254 *"make no speeches":* CW, 4:91.

254 *"horse to town"*: WHH, interview with George M. Brinkerhoff, undated, Lamon MSS, HEH.
254 *senator's triumphant procession*: George G. Fogg to N. B. Judd, Sept. 11, 1860, Lincoln MSS, LC.
254 *dropped the idea: CW,* 4:94; George G. Fogg to AL, Aug. 18, 1860, Lincoln MSS, LC.
254 *"Wide-Awakes"*: Nicolay and Hay, 2:284–286.
254 *"dry, and irksome labor": CW,* 4:109.
255 *party campaign strategy*: See the admirable analysis in Gienapp, "Who Voted for Lincoln?" pp. 50–97. For conflicting views on the role played by foreign-born voters in this election, see Leubke, *Ethnic Voters and the Election of Lincoln.*
255 *"surpassed all expectation": CW,* 4:126–127.
255 *"upon the public": CW,* 4:135.
255 *raised their hats*: WHH to Jesse W. Weik, Nov. 14, 1885, HWC.
256 *"was upon me"*: Paul M. Angle, *"Here I Have Lived": A History of Lincoln's Springfield, 1821–1865* (New Brunswick, N.J.: Rutgers University Press, 1935), pp. 251–253; Welles, *Diary,* 1:82.
256 *the Southern states*: For election returns, see Edward Stanwood, *A History of the Presidency from 1788 to 1897* (Boston: Houghton Mifflin Co., 1926), 1:297, and Charles O. Paullin, *Atlas of the Historical Geography of the United States* (Washington, D.C.: Carnegie Institution, 1932), p. 99.
256 *"of the presidency"*: John G. Nicolay, memorandum, Oct. 25, 1860, Nicolay MSS, LC.

CHAPTER TEN: AN ACCIDENTAL INSTRUMENT

Phillip Shaw Paludan, *The Presidency of Abraham Lincoln* (Lawrence: University Press of Kansas, 1994), chaps. 2–3, offers an excellent, succinct account of Lincoln between his election and the firing on Fort Sumter.

William E. Baringer, *A House Dividing: Lincoln as President Elect* (Springfield, Ill.: Abraham Lincoln Association, 1945), is a spirited account that, like Harry J. Carman and Reinhard H. Luthin, *Lincoln and the Patronage* (New York: Columbia University Press, 1943), deals extensively with the problems of selecting a cabinet.

Lincoln's policy toward secession and the steps he took in the Sumter crisis have been repeatedly examined by careful scholars. The basic studies are David M. Potter, *Lincoln and His Party in the Secession Crisis* (New Haven, Conn.: Yale University Press, 1942 [and see also the preface to the 1962 paperback edition]); J. G. Randall, *Lincoln the President: Springfield to Gettysburg* (New York: Dodd, Mead & Co., 1945); Kenneth M. Stampp, *And the War Came: The North and the Secession Crisis, 1860–1861* (Baton Rouge: Louisiana State University Press, 1950); and Richard N. Current, *Lincoln and the First Shot* (Philadelphia: J. B. Lippincott Co., 1963). I have offered some evaluation of this controversial literature in notes at the end of the present chapter.

258 *loss for words*: Henry Villard's dispatches to the *New York Herald* give a vivid, day-by-day account of Lincoln's activities. Some of them have been collected in Henry Villard, *Lincoln on the Eve of '61: A Journalist's Story,* ed. Harold G. Villard and Oswald Garrison Villard (New York: Alfred A. Knopf, 1941).
258 *"wear standing collars"*: "True Republicans" to AL, Oct. 12, 1860, Lincoln MSS, LC.
258 *"begin it now?": CW,* 4:129–130.
258 *"puttin' on (h)airs"*: Charles Hamilton and Lloyd Ostendorf, *Lincoln in Photographs: An Album of Every Known Pose* (Dayton, Ohio: Morningside, 1985), p. 67.
259 *the youngest presidents*: James K. Polk and Franklin Pierce were slightly younger. So were John Tyler and Millard Fillmore, but they were elected Vice President.
259 *to his face: Memoirs of Henry Villard, Journalist and Financier, 1835–1900* (Boston: Houghton, Mifflin & Co., 1904), 1:143.
259 *"em a little"*: Lincoln had used this story as early as 1848. *CW,* 1:487.
259 *Kentucky or Indiana*: Lincoln made no claim that most of the stories he told were original, and many of his jokes were hundreds of years old. Reports that he told "obscene" or "smutty" stories are hard to verify. Many of these accounts came from political enemies and others from witnesses like Herndon who had no sense of humor. Lincoln's more raunchy stories rarely dealt with sexual innuendo; they usually related to bodily functions, like farting, which members of this Victorian generation considered "dirty." The ribald and Rabelaisian stories that old-timers in Menard County recounted to me some forty years ago were clearly folk-say that made little pretense to authenticity. For Herndon's views, see " 'The Coming Rude Storms' of Lincoln

Writings: William H. Herndon and the Lincoln Legend," *JISHS* 71 (Feb. 1978): 66–70. Randall, *Lincoln the President,* 3:59–82, offers a balanced statement. P. M. Zall, *Abe Lincoln Laughing: Humorous Anecdotes from Original Sources by and about Abraham Lincoln* (Berkeley: University of California Press, 1982), attempts to establish a canon of authentic Lincoln stories.

259 *"a satisfactory answer":* Segal, *Conversations,* p. 89.

260 *"of fraternal feeling":* CW, 4:142–143.

260 *"Private and confidential":* CW, 4:139–140.

260 *"the most dangerous point":* CW, 4:170.

260 *any public statement:* Thurlow Weed to AL, Nov. 7, 1860, Lincoln MSS, LC.

260 *"wolfe [sic] traps":* Joseph Medill to O. M. Hatch, Nov. 16, 1860, Hatch MSS, ISHL.

260 *"I find it":* Donn Piatt, *Memories of the Men Who Saved the Union* (Chicago: Belford, Clarke & Co., 1887), pp. 33–34.

260 *"of buckeye wood":* John G. Nicolay, memorandum, Nov. 5, 1860, Nicolay MSS, LC.

261 *"under any administration":* CW, 4:141.

261 *" 'be given them' ":* CW, 4:146. Cf. Luke 11:29: "They seek a sign, and there shall no sign be given."

261 *"may have encouraged":* CW, 4:142.

261 *in the South:* Robert W. Johannsen, *Lincoln, the South, and Slavery: The Political Dimension* (Baton Rouge: Louisiana State University Press, 1991), p. 120.

261 *M. Blair / Welles:* Undated card [Nov. 7, 1860], #6495c, Lincoln MSS, LC. Cf. the long account in Gideon Welles to Isaac N. Arnold, Nov. 27, 1871, MS in Chicago Historical Society (copy in Allan Nevins MSS, HEH), which, however, contains some errors.

262 *"was to occupy":* Harriet A. Weed, *Autobiography of Thurlow Weed* (Boston: Houghton, Mifflin & Co., 1883), p. 606.

262 *"balanced and ballasted":* Ibid., p. 610.

262 *"in the highest degree":* Day by Day, 2:298.

262 *"in the Senate":* Baringer, *A House Dividing,* p. 85.

263 *"with clean hands":* Lyman Trumbull to AL, Dec. 2, 1860, Lincoln MSS, LC.

263 *"in the case":* CW, 4:148.

263 *"much self distrust":* W. H. Seward to AL, Dec. 28, 1860, Lincoln MSS, LC.

263 *"difference between them?":* CW, 4:150.

263 *"white crows":* Weed, *Autobiography,* p. 606.

263 *Gilmer's candidacy died:* For an excellent account of this episode see Daniel W. Crofts, "A Reluctant Unionist: John A. Gilmer and Lincoln's Cabinet," *Civil War History* 24 (Sept. 1978): 225–249.

264 *"other man's hundred":* George S. Boutwell, *Reminiscences of Sixty Years in Public Affairs* (New York: McClure, Phillips & Co., 1902), 1:275.

264 *"statesman to look":* Carl Schurz, *The Reminiscences of Carl Schurz* (New York: McClure Co., 1907), 2:34.

264 *"place if offered":* J. W. Schuckers, *The Life and Public Services of Salmon Portland Chase* (New York: D. Appleton & Co., 1874), p. 201; Robert B. Warden, *An Account of the Private Life and Public Services of Salmon Portland Chase* (Cincinnati: Wilstach, Baldwin & Co., 1874), p. 365.

264 *for the navy:* The definitive biography is John Niven, *Gideon Welles: Lincoln's Secretary of the Navy* (New York: Oxford University Press, 1973).

265 *of Attorney General:* Bates, *Diary,* pp. 164–165.

265 *"go for you":* David Davis to AL, Nov. 19, 1860, Lincoln MSS, LC.

265 *"he had supposed":* Weed, *Autobiography,* p. 605.

265 *"now or never":* For an account of this choice, see Carman and Luthin, *Lincoln and the Patronage,* pp. 29–33.

265 *those of Pennsylvania:* Both Carman and Luthin, *Lincoln and the Patronage,* and Baringer, *A House Dividing,* offer very full accounts of the Cameron imbroglio, on which I have relied heavily.

265 *before the nomination:* Joseph Casey to Leonard Swett, Nov. 27, 1860, Lincoln MSS, LC.

266 *"thing nominated you":* Leonard Swett to AL, Nov. 30, 1860, Lincoln MSS, LC.

266 *"as a party":* Carman and Luthin, *Lincoln and the Patronage,* pp. 28–29.

266 *"into the cabinet":* CW, 4:169–170.

267 *"Pennsylvania, and elsewhere":* CW, 4:171.

267 *"of the place":* CW, 4:174.

268 *forced it to retreat:* For a detailed account of these developments, see Allan Nevins, *The Emer-*

gence of Lincoln, vol. 2, *Prologue to Civil War, 1859–1861* (New York: Charles Scribner's Sons, 1950), chaps. 11–12.

268 *"a constitutional right": New York Herald,* Jan. 28, 1861.
268 *not oppose it: CW,* 4:270.
268 *"suits them better": CW,* 1:438.
269 *"of physical power":* For a thorough analysis, see Thomas J. Pressly, "Bullets and Ballots: Lincoln and the 'Right of Revolution,' " *American Historical Review* 67 (Apr. 1962): 647–662.
269 *"the essence of anarchy": CW,* 4:268.
269 *"dissolution or dismemberment":* Nicolay and Hay, 3:248.
269 *"as it is": CW,* 4:154.
269 *political beliefs rested:* After the Civil War, Alexander H. Stephens wrote that Lincoln's devotion to the Union rose to the sublimity of religious mysticism, and his phrase has often been echoed by historians. See esp. Edmund Wilson's brilliant essay on Lincoln in *Patriotic Gore: Studies in the Literature of the American Civil War* (New York: Oxford University Press, 1962), pp. 99–130. But in reviewing a draft of the present book, Mark E. Neely, Jr., pointed out that Stephens's phrase was intended not as praise of Lincoln but as criticism of an unrealistic belief. There was, Neely suggests, little that was mystical in Lincoln's thinking about the Union, which he valued for realistic, tough-minded reasons.
269 *"our friends South":* Lyman Trumbull to AL, Dec. 14, 1860, Lincoln MSS, LC. See also Potter, *Lincoln and His Party in the Secession Crisis,* chap. 5.
269 *should be repealed: CW,* 4:156–157.
269 *"were hedged against": CW,* 4:183.
270 *"any time hereafter": CW,* 4:149–150.
270 *"principle in it":* Harry E. Pratt, ed., *Concerning Mr. Lincoln: In Which Abraham Lincoln Is Pictured as He Appeared to Letter Writers of His Time* (Springfield, Ill.: Abraham Lincoln Association, 1944), p. 42.
270 *"up his mind":* WHH, *Mrs. Lincoln's Denial, and What She Says,* broadside dated Jan. 12, 1874, Massachusetts Historical Society.
270 *"he is stubborn":* William Jayne to Lyman Trumbull, Jan. 21, 1861, Trumbull MSS, LC.
270 *the President-elect:* Thomas D. Jones, *Memories of Lincoln* (New York: Press of the Pioneers, 1934), pp. 7–8.
270 *"was ever delivered":* WHH to Jesse W. Weik, Jan. 1, 1886, HWC.
270 *criticism of friends:* Ida M. Tarbell, *The Life of Abraham Lincoln* (New York: Doubleday, Page & Co., 1909), 1:403–404.
270 *"an ambitious little woman":* Annie Dickson's postscript on William M. Dickson to AL, May 21, 1860, Lincoln MSS, LC.
271 *"she can be":* Pratt, *Concerning Mr. Lincoln,* p. 32.
271 *suspected social slights:* Jones, *Memories of Lincoln,* pp. 12–13.
271 *"by iron hoops":* Milton H. Shutes, *Lincoln's Emotional Life* (Philadelphia: Dorrance & Co., 1957), p. 128.
271 *deserved special treatment:* Randall, *Mary Lincoln,* pp. 191–193.
271 *"talent and experience":* Villard and Villard, *Lincoln on the Eve of '61,* p. 50.
271 *"hurt pretty bad":* Charles H. Coleman, *Abraham Lincoln and Coles County, Illinois* (New Brunswick, N.J.: Scarecrow Press, 1955), pp. 198–199.
271 *"each other again":* WHH, interview with Mrs. Thomas Lincoln, Sept. 9, 1865, HWC; A. H. Chapman to WHH, Oct. 8, 1865, ibid. For a detailed account of this visit, see Coleman, *Lincoln and Coles County,* pp. 191–210.
272 *"of the area": Day by Day,* 3:9.
272 *"to New York": New York Herald,* Feb. 16, 1861.
272 *left for Washington: Day by Day,* p. 10; Pratt, *Personal Finances,* p. 123.
272 *"had ever happened":* This repeats, almost verbatim, the account I gave in *Lincoln's Herndon,* pp. 146–147.
273 *see Lincoln off:* Victor Searcher, *Lincoln's Journey to Greatness: A Factual Account of the Twelve-Day Inaugural Trip* (Philadelphia: John C. Winston Co., 1960), is a detailed account on which the following pages rely heavily.
273 *"sufficiently to commence":* Pratt, *Concerning Mr. Lincoln,* p. 50.
273 *an affectionate farewell: CW,* 4:190.
274 *"second class city": New York Herald,* Feb. 14, 1861.
274 *"very interesting countenance": CW,* 4:206.

274 *"of the bargain"*: *CW,* 4:218.
274 *"means ill looking"*: *New York Herald,* Feb. 14, 1861; Rutherford B. Hayes to Laura Platt, Feb. 13, 1861, Hayes MSS, Hayes Presidential Center (courtesy Prof. Ari A. Hoogenboom).
274 *"of a century"*: *CW,* 4:198.
274 *"good-looking ladies"*: *CW,* 4:206.
274 *a big kiss: CW,* 4:219.
274 *"to water himself"*: *CW,* 4:204.
275 *"not want to"*: *CW,* 4:218.
275 *"short of it!"*: *CW,* 4:242.
275 *someone else:* Ruth Painter Randall, *Lincoln's Sons* (Boston: Little, Brown & Co., 1955), p. 90.
275 *harm was done:* John S. Goff, *Robert Todd Lincoln: A Man in His Own Right* (Norman: University of Oklahoma Press, 1969), pp. 36–38.
275 *"the glorious flag"*: *CW,* 4:192.
275 *"merit of mine"*: *CW,* 4:208–209.
275 *"I should say"*: *CW,* 4:193.
275 *"have a name"*: *CW,* 4:226, 204.
276 *"and growing whiskers"*: Randall, *Lincoln the President,* 1:292.
276 *"in my esteem"*: Strong, *Diary,* p. 100.
276 *"by designing politicians"*: *CW,* 4:211.
276 *"is all artificial"*: *CW,* 4:216.
276 *"time is artificial"*: *CW,* 4:238.
276 *"not deciding anything"*: *CW,* 4:195–196.
277 *"stand by it"*: *CW,* 4:220. In the source the words are in full capitals.
277 *"of this Union"*: *CW,* 4:233.
277 *"foot down firmly"*: *CW,* 4:237.
277 *passed through Baltimore:* This account of the Baltimore plot is based on the following sources: Norma B. Cuthbert, ed., *Lincoln and the Baltimore Plot, 1861* (San Marino, Calif.: Huntington Library, 1949), which publishes documents from the Pinkerton records; Benson J. Lossing, *Pictorial History of the Civil War* (Philadelphia: George W. Childs, Publishers, 1866), 1:279–281, which gives Lincoln's own version; John W. Forney, *Anecdotes of Public Men* (New York: Harper & Brothers, 1873), 1:248–256, which offers Felton's narrative; WHH, interview with Norman B. Judd, [1866], HWC; Allan Pinkerton to WHH, Aug. 23, 1866, HWC; and Ward Hill Lamon, *Recollections of Abraham Lincoln, 1847–1865,* ed. Dorothy Lamon Teillard (Washington, D.C.: 1911), pp. 40–46.
277 *"in doing so"*: Allan Pinkerton to WHH, Aug. 23, 1866, HWC.
277 *"to surrender it"*: *CW,* 4:240.
278 *"piece of cowardice"*: WHH, interview with Norman B. Judd, [1866], HWC.
278 *"out Judd's plan"*: Lamon, *Recollections,* p. 42.
278 *"at his absence"*: Cuthbert, *Lincoln and the Baltimore Plot,* p. 13.
278 *"a brainless egotistical fool"*: Ibid., p. xx.
278 *"that on me"*: Ibid., p. 82.
279 *remarkable course:* Herbert Mitgang, ed., *Abraham Lincoln: A Press Portrait* (Chicago: Quadrangle Books, 1971), p. 230.
279 *"on his Administration"*: Strong, *Diary,* p. 102.
279 *"risk was necessary"*: Cuthbert, *Lincoln and the Baltimore Plot,* p. xvi.
279 *the first day:* This account of Lincoln's schedule is based on *Lincoln Day by Day,* 3:21–22.
279 *"natural, and agreeable"*: Frederick W. Seward, *Seward at Washington . . . 1846–1861* (New York: Derby & Miller, 1891), p. 511.
279 *"peculiarly pleasant"*: Robert W. Johannsen, *Stephen A. Douglas* (New York: Oxford University Press, 1973), p. 841.
280 *"where it may"*: Baringer, *A House Dividing,* p. 307.
280 *"other the more"*: *CW,* 4:246–247.
280 *"without moral grace"*: Baringer, *A House Dividing,* p. 313.
280 *"himself laughs uproariously"*: New York *Evening Post,* Mar. 3, 1861; J. W. Schulte Nordholt, "The Civil War Letters of the Dutch Ambassador," *JISHS* 54 (Winter 1961): 361.
280 *"man Douglas is!"*: George Fort Milton, *The Eve of Conflict: Stephen A. Douglas and the Needless War* (Boston: Houghton Mifflin Co., 1934), p. 545.
281 *eleven favored Chase: CW,* 4:248.
281 *by his appearance:* My portrait of Seward is drawn from *Charles Francis Adams, 1835–1915:*

An Autobiography (Boston: Houghton Mifflin Co., 1916), pp. 57, 79; *The Education of Henry Adams: An Autobiography* (Boston: Houghton Mifflin Co., 1918), p. 104; and William Howard Russell, *My Diary North and South* (Boston: T. O. H. P. Burnham, 1863), pp. 34–35.

281 *"if he would":* Nevins, *The Emergence of Lincoln,* 2:452.

281 *"adjustment afterwards":* Frederick J. Blue, *Salmon P. Chase: A Life in Politics* (Kent, Ohio: Kent State University Press, 1987), p. 135.

282 *"he, Seward, remained":* Welles, *Diary,* 2:391.

282 *"withdraw that consent":* CW, 4:273.

282 *"the first trick":* Nicolay and Hay, 3:371.

282 *"at the top":* Ibid., 370.

282 *"the experiment successful":* Seward, *Seward at Washington,* p. 518.

282 *to the Capitol:* For a colorful description of the inauguration, see Margaret Leech, *Reveille in Washington, 1860–1865* (New York: Harper & Brothers, 1941), pp. 42–45.

283 *during the ceremony:* San Francisco *Daily Alta California,* Apr. 1, 1861. Willard L. King, *Lincoln's Manager, David Davis* (Cambridge, Mass.: Harvard University Press, 1960), p. 350, gives an even earlier source for this sometimes questioned story.

283 *"of his audience":* George W. Julian, *Political Recollections, 1840 to 1872* (Chicago: Jansen, McClurg & Co., 1884), p. 187.

283 *" 'or a sword?' ":* This first version of the inaugural speech is in *CW,* 4:249–262; the quoted passages are on pp. 254 and 261.

283 *the border states:* Browning, *Diary,* 1:455–456; Orville H. Browning to AL, Feb. 17, 1861, Lincoln MSS, LC.

284 *"and cheerful confidence":* Seward, *Seward at Washington,* pp. 512–513.

284 *"of the nation":* CW, 4:261–262.

284 *of our nature:* CW, 4:271.

284 *"of our freedom":* Mitgang, *Lincoln: A Press Portrait,* pp. 243–244.

284 *Jefferson Davis's:* Dwight L. Dumond, ed., *Southern Editorials on Secession* (Gloucester, Mass.: Peter Smith, 1964), pp. 474–475.

284 *"front against brother":* Howard Cecil Perkins, ed., *Northern Editorials on Secession* (New York: D. Appleton-Century Co., 1942), 2:618, 624, 628, 634.

284 *"obscurely stated qualifications":* Ibid., 2:645.

285 *"doing the business":* Robert L. Wilson to WHH, Feb. 10, 1866, HWC.

285 *informing Secretary Welles:* Welles, *Diary* 1:16–21.

285 *friend Elmer Ellsworth:* CW, 4:291.

285 *"all about it":* Charles Francis Adams, Diary, Mar. 10, 1861, MS, Massachusetts Historical Society.

285 *"ill-bred, ravenous crowd":* Francis Fessenden, *Life and Public Services of William Pitt Fessenden* (Boston: Houghton, Mifflin & Co., 1907), 1:127.

285 *"that hungry lot":* Villard, *Memoirs,* 1:156.

285 *"or even breathe":* John G. Nicolay to O. M. Hatch, Mar. 7, 1861, Hatch MSS, ISHL.

285 *"applications for office":* Orville H. Browning to AL, Mar. 26, 1861, Lincoln MSS, LC.

285 *"must see them":* Henry Wilson to WHH, May 30, 1867, HWC.

286 *"introductory" and "uninteresting":* Bates, *Diary,* p. 177.

286 *"to be understood":* Welles, *Diary,* 1:6. Welles added this passage to his diary later.

286 *did he need?:* CW, 4:279.

286 *"question of time":* Winfield Scott to AL, Mar. 12, 1861, Lincoln MSS, LC.

286 *got the message:* William Ernest Smith, *The Francis Preston Blair Family in Politics* (New York: Macmillan Co., 1933), 2:9–10; Francis P. Blair, Sr., to Montgomery Blair, Mar. 12, 1861, Lincoln MSS, LC.

286 *from the sea:* My account of Fox's activities in the following pages draws heavily on Ari Hoogenboom's excellent "Gustavus Fox and the Relief of Fort Sumter," *Civil War History* 9 (Dec. 1963): 383–398.

286 *"to attempt it?":* CW, 4:284.

287 *"of the Government":* The replies of all the cabinet members are in the Lincoln MSS, LC.

287 *"national destruction consummated":* CW, 4:424.

287 *"a Military* necessity": David C. Mearns, ed., *The Lincoln Papers* (Garden City, N.Y.: Doubleday & Co., 1948), 2:483–484.

287 *"be instantly withdrawn":* James Ford Rhodes, *History of the United States from the Compromise of 1850* (New York: Macmillan Co., 1906), 3:333.

287 *"the movement ruined":* San Francisco *Daily Alta California,* Apr. 1, 1861.

288 *"worth a rush"*: Kenneth M. Stampp, *And the War Came: The North and the Secession Crisis, 1860–1861* (Baton Rouge: Louisiana State University Press, 1950), p. 213.

288 *"a richous cause"*: William Butler to Lyman Trumbull, Mar. 14, 1861, Trumbull MSS, LC.

288 *"of the United States"*: Potter, *Lincoln and His Party*, p. 360.

288 *"and refused admittance"*: Stephen A. Hurlbut to AL, Mar. 27, 1861, Lincoln MSS, LC.

288 *"this Union perpetual"*: Nicolay and Hay, 3:394.

288 *"in the dumps"*: Current, *Lincoln and the First Shot*, p. 79.

289 *of General Scott:* Nicolay and Hay, 3:430–432.

289 *by April 6:* CW, 4:301. Hoogenboom, "Gustavus Fox and the Relief of Fort Sumter," p. 387, suggests that Lincoln had already approved Fox's expedition before the cabinet council of Mar. 29.

289 *"no binding engagements"*: J. G. Randall, *Lincoln the Liberal Statesman* (New York: Dodd, Mead & Co., 1947), p. 101.

289 *he "keeled over"*: Allan Nevins, *The War for the Union*, vol. 1, *The Improvised War, 1861–1862* (New York: Charles Scribner's Sons, 1959), p. 58.

290 *"nor assume responsibility"*: CW, 4:317–318.

290 *this extraordinary document:* Norman B. Ferris, "Lincoln and Seward in Civil War Diplomacy: Their Relationship at the Outset Reexamined," *Journal of the Abraham Lincoln Association* 12 (1991), 21–42, attempts a reinterpretation favorable to Seward, but, in my opinion, the comments of Richard N. Current (ibid., pp. 43–47) are more persuasive.

290 *"will come to"*: Samuel H. Allen to Christopher Prince, Mar. 31, 1861, MS in private hands.

290 *"state of things"*: Carl Schurz to AL, Apr. 5, 1861, Lincoln MSS, LC.

290 *"must do it"*: CW, 4:316–317.

290 *of this offer:* The evidence on this proposed bargain with Virginia Unionists is murky, and any conclusion has to be tentative. On this question J. G. Randall's analysis in *Lincoln the President*, 1:324–327, is persuasive. Daniel W. Crofts, *Reluctant Confederates: Upper South Unionists in the Secession Crisis* (Chapel Hill: University of North Carolina Press, 1989), is a masterful study, and his account of Lincoln's conversations with Baldwin and other Virginia Unionists (pp. 301–307) merits careful consideration. I am not, however, convinced that Lincoln gave deliberately misleading reports of his conversation with Baldwin. Shortly after Virginia seceded, Lincoln told a delegation from the western part of the state that he had promised Baldwin "to withdraw the troops from Fort Sumpter, and do all within the line of his duty to ward off collision" if the Virginia convention would "pass resolutions of adherence to the Union, then adjourn and go home." George Plumer Smith to John Hay, Jan. 9, 1863, Lincoln MSS, LC. Lincoln vouched for Smith's statement as "substantially correct." John Hay to George Plumer Smith, Jan. 10, 1863, Lincoln MSS, LC.

291 *a relief expedition:* "General M. C. Meigs on the Conduct of the Civil War," *American Historical Review* 26 (Jan. 1921): 299–302. See also Russell F. Weigley's excellent *Quartermaster General of the Union Army: A Biography of M. C. Meigs* (New York: Columbia University Press, 1959).

291 *to Fox's expedition:* Niven, *Gideon Welles*, pp. 332–336, gives a clear account of this episode.

292 *"this cruel treachery"*: Virginia Woodbury Fox, Diary, Apr. 18, 1861, Levi Woodbury MSS, LC.

292 *On April 4:* There has been a good deal of controversy about this date. The scholarly studies of J. G. Randall and David M. Potter are ranged on one side; those of Kenneth M. Stampp and Richard N. Current on the other. Stampp and Current argued that Lincoln ordered the Fort Sumter expedition to sail on Apr. 4—i.e., two days before he learned of the failure to reinforce Fort Pickens as he had directed on Mar. 11. (Meigs's relief expedition is not part of this historiographical dispute. Everybody understood that Fort Sumter would be relieved or evacuated long before Meigs could reach Florida.) If the Apr. 4 date is correct, Lincoln's report to Congress in July 1861 that he had planned a Sumter-for-Pickens swap (i.e., evacuating Anderson's garrison from Fort Sumter after reinforcing Fort Pickens) could not be correct and was, at best, a subsequent rationalization to demonstrate his peaceful purposes. Randall and Potter, on the other hand, believed that Apr. 6, the day the disappointing news from Florida reached Washington, was the key date. Though preliminary orders had been sent on Apr. 4 for the sailing of the fleet and an attempt had been made to notify Anderson (which was repeated on Apr. 6), no irrevocable step had been taken. Because Lincoln knew Fox's fleet would not actually leave New York for several days (it did not sail until Apr. 8 and 9), he still could have countermanded it had the news from Florida been good. I am persuaded by the Stampp-Current argument. See the admirable, concise summary of the evidence in Current, *Lincoln and the First Shot*, pp. 194–199.

292 *"without further notice"*: CW, 4:323.

292 *"Look to it"*: CW, 4:324.
292 *war had begun:* The historiographical controversy about Lincoln's role in the dispute over Fort
Sumter extends to the broader question of his objectives in the secession crisis. His admiring
secretary-biographers, Nicolay and Hay (*Abraham Lincoln*, 4:44–45), wrote that he expected
little from the Sumter expedition and was "reasonably certain" that it would provoke hostilities;
he wanted to make sure that if the Confederates fired on the expedition "they would not be
able to convince the world that he had begun civil war." Charles W. Ramsdell concluded
("Lincoln and Fort Sumter," *Journal of Southern History* 3 [Aug. 1937]: 259–288, esp. p. 285)
that he dispatched the Sumter expedition, which he knew would provoke war, to help solve
pressing problems in the north: "Lincoln, having decided that there was no other way than war
for the salvation of his administration, his party, and the Union, maneuvered the Confederates
into firing the first shot in order that they, rather than he, should take the blame of beginning
bloodshed." John Shipley Tilley, *Lincoln Takes Command* (Chapel Hill: University of North
Carolina Press, 1941), made much the same argument, but with more hostility toward Lincoln.
Kenneth M. Stampp ("Lincoln and the Strategy of Defense in the Crisis of 1861," *Journal of
Southern History* 11 [Aug. 1945]: 297–323) held that Lincoln, opposed both to peaceful secession and to coercion of the South, recognized "disunion as sufficiently menacing to northern
interests to justify resistance by force if necessary"; he developed a strategy of defense that
anticipated Confederate resistance at Charleston and took steps that would force the rebels to
put themselves fatally in the wrong by attacking Fort Sumter. J. G. Randall and David M. Potter,
on the other hand, stressed Lincoln's desire to avoid war and detailed the numerous steps he
took, from toning down his inaugural address to giving Governor Pickens advance notice of an
expedition to resupply, not reinforce, Sumter, in order to preserve peace. "To say that Lincoln
meant that the first shot would be fired by the other side *if a first shot was fired*," Randall
observed, "is not to say that he maneuvered to have the first shot fired." (Randall, *Lincoln the
President*, 1:350) The area of disagreement in this controversy has perhaps been exaggerated:
all authorities agree that Lincoln wished to avoid war and all agree that he was willing to run
the risk of war rather than evacuate Fort Sumter. None of these able scholars has, in my
opinion, given enough attention to Lincoln's newness to Washington, his inexperience as an
administrator, and his fatigue after his exhausting journey and inauguration. Nor has Lincoln's
essential passivity, his preference to react to events rather than to take the initiative, been
sufficiently stressed.
293 *"a military* necessity": CW, 4:424–425.
293 *"retaking the forts"*: Orville H. Browning to AL, Feb. 17, 1861, Lincoln MSS, LC.
293 *"it otherwise could"*: Browning, *Diary*, 1:477.
293 *"by the result"*: Hoogenboom, "Gustavus Fox and the Relief of Fort Sumter," p. 396.
293 *"and immediate dissolution"*: CW, 4:425.
294 *"for its preservation"*: CW, 4:426.

CHAPTER ELEVEN: A PEOPLE'S CONTEST

The fullest account of the first year of the Civil War is Allan Nevins, *The War for the Union*, vol. 1,
The Improvised War, 1861–1862 (New York: Charles Scribner's Sons, 1959). John G. Nicolay and
John Hay, *Abraham Lincoln: A History* (New York: Century Co., 1890), offers the most detailed
account of Lincoln's activities during this period. Kenneth P. Williams, *Lincoln Finds a General*
(New York: Macmillan Co., 1949), presents a reinterpretation of the battle of Bull Run and a critical
appraisal of George B. McClellan.

For Lincoln's definition of the nature of the war and his expanded view of the President's war
powers, J. G. Randall, *Constitutional Problems Under Lincoln* (rev. ed.; Urbana: University of Illinois
Press, 1951), remains authoritative. More recent scholarship on these subjects is presented in Harold
M. Hyman and William M. Wiecek, *Equal Justice Under Law: Constitutional Development, 1835–
1875* (New York: Harper & Row, 1982), esp. chap. 8. Mark E. Neely, Jr., *The Fate of Liberty: Abraham
Lincoln and Civil Liberties* (New York: Oxford University Press, 1991), is a model of scholarly
detective work and historical analysis.

My account of the Lincolns' life in the White House is taken, with a few minor changes, from my
essay " 'This Damned Old House': The Lincolns in the White House," in Frank Freidel and William
Pencak, eds., *The White House: The First Two Hundred Years* (Boston: Northeastern University Press,
1994), pp. 53–74.

The most recent overview of diplomatic relations during the Civil War is Howard Jones, *Union in Peril: The Crisis over British Intervention in the Civil War* (Chapel Hill: University of North Carolina Press, 1992). On the *Trent* affair the basic works are Ephraim D. Adams, *Great Britain and the American Civil War* (2 vols.; New York: Longmans, Green & Co., 1925); D. P. Crook, *The North, the South, and the Powers, 1861–1865* (New York: John Wiley & Sons, 1974); Norman B. Ferris, *The Trent Affair: A Diplomatic Crisis* (Knoxville: University of Tennessee Press, 1977); and Brian Jenkins, *Britain and the War for the Union* (Montreal: McGill-Queen's University Press, 1974).

Allan Nevins, *Frémont: Pathmarker of the West* (New York: Longmans, Green & Co., 1955), offers the fullest account of the Frémont imbroglio.

Stephen W. Sears, *George B. McClellan: The Young Napoleon* (New York: Ticknor & Fields, 1988), is a fine recent biography, notably anti-McClellan in tone. For the opposing view, see J. G. Randall, *Lincoln the President: Springfield to Gettysburg* (New York: Dodd, Mead & Co., 1945). T. Harry Williams, *Lincoln and His Generals* (New York: Alfred A. Knopf, 1952), is a spirited account.

On the Congresses with which Lincoln had to deal, there are two exemplary studies by Allan G. Bogue: *The Congressman's Civil War* (Cambridge: Cambridge University Press, 1989), on the House of Representatives, and *The Earnest Men: Republicans of the Civil War Senate* (Ithaca, N.Y.: Cornell University Press, 1981). For an account of the severe criticism to which the President was subjected, T. Harry Williams, *Lincoln and the Radicals* (Madison: University of Wisconsin Press, 1941), remains invaluable.

295 *"4th of July"*: Otto Eisenschiml, *Why the Civil War?* (Indianapolis: Bobbs-Merrill Co., 1958), p. 114; Wayne Andrews, ed., *The Autobiography of Carl Schurz* (New York: Charles Scribner's Sons, 1961), p. 172.

295 *"and vice versa"*: Nicolay and Hay, 4:79.

296 *"be duly executed"*: *CW,* 4:332.

296 *defend their country:* William M. Dickson to AL, Apr. 15, 1861; Richard M. Blatchford and Moses H. Grinnell to AL, Apr. 15, 1861—both in Lincoln MSS, LC; Frank Moore, ed., *The Rebellion Record: A Diary of American Events* (New York: G. P. Putnam, 1862), 1:25 (Diary).

296 *"the Federal Capital"*: Robert W. Johannsen, ed., *The Letters of Stephen A. Douglas* (Urbana: University of Illinois Press, 1961), p. 509.

296 *"preparation for war"*: Damon Wells, *Stephen Douglas: The Last Years, 1857–1861* (Austin: University of Texas Press, 1971), p. 287.

297 *"of the Government"*: William B. Hesseltine, *Lincoln and the War Governors* (New York: Alfred A. Knopf, 1948), p. 146.

297 *"and brave hearts"*: David C. Mearns, ed., *The Lincoln Papers* (Garden City, N.Y.: Doubleday & Co., 1948), 2:559.

297 *"aureole of glory"*: "Your Affectionate Son" to "Dear Mother," Fort Monroe, Va., May 25, 1861, MS used through the courtesy of Mrs. Jane Langton, Lincoln, Mass.

297 *"from North Carolina"*: Nicolay and Hay, 4:90.

297 *"inhuman and diabolical"*: Ibid.

297 *"no troops here"*: William J. Evitts, *A Matter of Allegiances: Maryland from 1850 to 1861* (Baltimore: Johns Hopkins University Press, 1974), p. 178, shows that this telegram was sent before the attack on the Sixth Massachusetts Regiment.

298 *than through, Baltimore:* Nicolay and Hay, 4:127.

298 *"and that severely"*: *CW,* 4:341–342.

298 *"don't they come!"*: Nicolay and Hay, 4:152.

299 *"only Northern realities"*: Hay, *Diary,* p. 11.

299 *"of habeas corpus"*: Neely, *The Fate of Liberty,* p. 7, gives the original text of this subsequently distorted order.

299 *"government of laws"*: Randall, *Constitutional Problems Under Lincoln,* pp. 120–121.

300 *avoided a confrontation:* E. Merton Coulter, *The Civil War and Readjustment in Kentucky* (Gloucester, Mass.: Peter Smith, 1966), remains authoritative.

300 *"not molest her"*: Segal, *Conversations,* p. 116.

300 *Internecine war resulted:* Walter B. Stevens, "Lincoln and Missouri," *Missouri Historical Review* 10 (Jan. 1916): 63–199.

301 *for West Virginia:* For a summary of the complicated process of partitioning Virginia, see J. G. Randall and David Herbert Donald, *The Civil War and Reconstruction* (Lexington, Mass.: D. C. Heath & Co., 1969), pp. 236–242.

301 *"of the government"*: Lincoln summarized these extraconstitutional actions in a message to Congress on May 26, 1862. *CW,* 5:240–242.

301 *"calm and collected"*: Nicolay and Hay, 4:108.

301 *"and assiduous coöperation"*: Frederick W. Seward, *Seward at Washington as Senator and Secretary of State, 1846–1861* (New York: Derby & Miller, 1891), p. 590.

302 *to prosecute it:* The complete message is in *CW,* 4:421–441.

303 *"as we can"*: Segal, *Conversations,* pp. 113–114. For evidence that Lincoln quite clearly understood the difference between closing the ports and declaring a blockade, see Browning, *Diary,* 1:489.

303 *"forced upon him"*: *CW,* 4:440.

303 *"competency of Congress"*: *CW,* 4:429.

303 *among legal experts:* Some of the more important controversial literature on these topics appears in Frank Freidel, ed., *Union Pamphlets of the Civil War* (2 vols.; Cambridge, Mass.: Harvard University Press, 1967). See esp. the essays by Horace Binney and Edward Ingersoll.

304 *"one be violated"*: *CW,* 4:430.

304 *of his administration:* Neely, *The Fate of Liberty,* offers a masterful examination of these problems.

304 *"own domestic foes"*: *CW,* 4:426.

304 *"race of life"*: *CW,* 4:438.

305 *and "irrepressible applause"*: *New York Times,* July 7, 1861.

305 *"ways and means"*: James Ford Rhodes, *History of the United States from the Compromise of 1850* (New York: Macmillan Co., 1906), 3:441.

305 *of Andrew Jackson: New York Weekly Tribune,* July 10, 1861; *New York World,* July 9, 1861.

305 *"of the Constitution"*: *The American Annual Cyclopaedia and Register of Important Events of the Year 1861* (New York: D. Appleton & Co., 1871), p. 234.

306 *his subsequent campaigns:* For an excellent evaluation of these plans, see Nevins, *War for the Union,* 1:150–154.

306 *"in his fall"*: *CW,* 4:385. See also Ruth Painter Randall, *Colonel Elmer Ellsworth* (Boston: Little, Brown & Co., 1960).

306 *"war by piecemeal"*: Nicolay and Hay, 4:323.

307 *bed that night:* Ibid., 4:352–355.

307 *"preserve the Union"*: Edward McPherson, *The Political History of the United States During the Great Rebellion* (3rd ed.; Washington, D.C.: Solomons & Chapman, 1876), p. 286.

308 *"you have been"*: Segal, *Conversations,* p. 126.

308 *"would do it"*: Ibid., p. 129.

309 *in the White House:* For an excellent history of the White House in Lincoln's time, with many illustrations, see William Seale, *The President's House: A History* (Washington, D.C.: White House Historical Association, 1986), chaps. 15–17.

309 *on the north side:* In describing living arrangements in the White House, I have had the inestimable good fortune of receiving privately conducted tours by four distinguished subsequent occupants: President and Mrs. John F. Kennedy in Feb. 1962, and President and Mrs. George Bush in Jan. 1990.

310 *on the arm:* For a charming account of the Lincoln children in the White House, see Ruth Painter Randall, *Lincoln's Sons* (Boston: Little, Brown & Co., 1955), and for White House pets, see Mrs. Randall's *Lincoln's Animal Friends* (Boston: Little, Brown & Co., 1958).

310 *the two windows:* William O. Stoddard, *Inside the White House in War Times* (New York: Charles L. Webster & Co., 1890), pp. 23–24. Cf. the drawing C. K. Stellwagen made of Lincoln's office in Oct. 1864, in White House Historical Association, *The White House: An Historic Guide* (Washington, D.C.: White House Historical Association, 1963), p. 128.

310 *"formality of signature"*: On Nicolay and the administration of the President's office, see Helen Nicolay, *Lincoln's Secretary: A Biography of John G. Nicolay* (New York: Longmans, Green & Co., 1949), and Edward D. Neill, *Abraham Lincoln and His Mailbag,* ed. Theodore C. Blegen (St. Paul: Minnesota Historical Society, 1964). The quotation is from the latter, on p. 12.

311 *" 'only has two' "*: Ward Hill Lamon, *Recollections of Abraham Lincoln, 1847–1865,* ed. Dorothy Lamon Teillard (Washington, D.C.: 1911), pp. 82–83.

311 *"extend seven feet"*: D. M. Jenks to AL, June 10, 1862, Lincoln MSS, LC.

311 *to describe her:* Randall, *Mary Lincoln,* offers a highly favorable portrait of Mrs. Lincoln. Baker, *Mary Todd Lincoln,* is more critical. For Mrs. Lincoln's wartime letters, which are few and not very revealing, see Turner, *Mary Todd Lincoln.*

312 *"was agreeably disappointed"*: William Howard Russell, *My Diary North and South* (Boston: T. O. H. P. Burnham, 1863), pp. 41–42.

312 *"at your feet"*: Randall, *Mary Lincoln,* pp. 259–262.

312 *a wagonload:* Stoddard, *Inside the White House,* pp. 62–63.

313 *the salary herself:* Randall, *Mary Lincoln,* pp. 254–256. Browning received a detailed account of Mrs. Lincoln's financial misconduct from W. H. Stackpole, a White House messenger. Browning, Diary, Mar. 3, 1862, MS, ISHL. His report—which, of course, is not firsthand—was considered too explosive for inclusion in his published *Diary.* It was charges like these that led David Davis many years later to charge that Mary Lincoln "was a natural born thief; that stealing was a sort of insanity with her." Browning, *Diary,* July 3, 1873, MS, ISHL. In evaluating this comment it must be remembered that it was made long after the event and that Davis heartily detested Mrs. Lincoln.

313 *his own pocket:* Benjamin Brown French, *Witness to the Young Republic,* ed. Donald B. Cole and John J. McDonough (Hanover, N.H.: University Press of New England, 1989), p. 382.

313 *"unnatural civil war"*: Jean H. Baker, *Affairs of Party: The Political Culture of Northern Democrats in the Mid-Nineteenth Century* (Ithaca, N.Y.: Cornell University Press, 1983), pp. 148–153.

313 *"majority in rebellion"*: *CW,* 5:494.

313 *cultivated War Democrats:* Christopher Dell, *Lincoln and the War Democrats: The Grand Erosion of Conservative Tradition* (Rutherford, N.J.: Fairleigh Dickinson University Press, 1975), chaps. 4–6, offers a full discussion.

314 *of public opinion:* Williams, *Lincoln and the Radicals,* pp. 33–34.

314 *"may desert myself"*: Adam Gurowski, *Diary, from March 4, 1861, to November 12, 1862* (Boston: Lee & Shepard, 1862), pp. 89–90.

315 *modify his proclamation: CW,* 4:506.

315 *"Negro into it"*: Nevins, *Frémont: Pathmarker of the West,* pp. 516–519. The last sentence is in italics in this source.

315 *of the Confiscation Act: CW,* 4:518.

316 *"is dealing with"*: *CW,* 4:513.

316 *"has another chance"*: Nevins, *War for the Union,* 1:376.

316 *"to the Union"*: Joshua F. Speed to AL, Sept. 3 and 7, 1861; Robert Anderson to AL, Sept. 13, 1861—all in Lincoln MSS, LC.

316 *"never seen surpassed"*: Coulter, *Civil War and Readjustment,* p. 112.

316 *"and the North West"*: O. H. Browning to AL, Sept. 11, 1861, Lincoln MSS, LC.

316 *in the Northwest:* Timothy Davis to W. H. Seward, Sept. 11, 1861, Seward MSS, UR.

316 *"than your order"*: L. B. Moon to AL, Sept. 16, 1861, Lincoln MSS, LC.

317 *"destroyed his country"*: Horace White to David Davis, Sept. 14, 1861, Davis MSS, ISHL.

317 *"acres of land"*: B. F. Wade to Zachariah Chandler, Sept. 23, 1861, Chandler MSS, LC.

317 *"hang a* man": Donald, *Lincoln's Herndon,* p. 150.

317 *"property by proclamation?"*: *CW,* 4:531–532.

317 *"an ordinary man"*: Browning, *Diary,* 1:516.

317 *"and unbounded confidence"*: George B. McClellan, *McClellan's Own Story* (New York: Charles L. Webster & Co., 1887), pp. 82–83.

318 *"scare-crow on horseback"*: Levi S. Gould, "Personal Recollections of Abraham Lincoln," *Magazine of History with Notes and Queries* 16 (Jan. 1913): 12.

318 *"vacil[l]ating and inefficient"*: Zachariah Chandler to Letitia Chandler, Oct. 27, 1861, Chandler MSS, LC.

318 *"French and dancing"*: B. F. Wade to Zachariah Chandler, Oct. 8, 1861, Chandler MSS, LC.

318 *taken into account:* Hay, *Diary,* pp. 31–32.

319 *"by parricidal rebellion"*: *CW,* 5:10.

319 *"do it all"*: Hay, *Diary,* p. 33.

319 *"is an idiot"*: McClellan, *Civil War Papers,* pp. 85–86.

319 *Cameron a rascal:* Ibid., pp. 106–107, 113–114.

319 *"a rare bird?"*: Williams, *Lincoln and His Generals,* p. 45.

320 *"and personal dignity"*: Hay, *Diary,* pp. 34–35.

320 *win a victory:* Nicolay and Hay, 4:469n.

320 *"ones, at variance"*: *CW,* 5:51.

320 *"Davis* at once": Zachariah Chandler to Letitia Chandler, Oct. 27, 1861, Chandler MSS, LC.

320 *"vast future also":* The full text of the message is in *CW,* 5:35–53.
321 *Secretary of State:* Clarence E. Macartney, *Lincoln and His Cabinet* (New York: Charles Scribner's Sons, 1931), p. 124.
321 *"Chicago Post Office":* Martin B. Duberman, *Charles Francis Adams, 1807–1886* (Boston: Houghton Mifflin Co., 1961), p. 257.
321 *British Foreign Office:* For a facsimile of this document, showing Lincoln's numerous corrections, see Allen Thorndike Rice, ed., *Reminiscences of Abraham Lincoln by Distinguished Men of His Time* (New York: North American Review, 1888), following the printed transcription on pp. lv–lxix.
322 *state in Washington:* I have sketched the Lincoln-Sumner relationship in *Lincoln Reconsidered: Essays on the Civil War Era* (New York: Alfred A. Knopf, 1956), chap. 6, and have drawn it in much more detail in *Charles Sumner and the Rights of Man* (New York: Alfred A. Knopf, 1970), esp. chap. 1.
322 *"justly with us":* Browning, *Diary,* 1:516.
323 *"of the nation":* Bates, *Diary,* p. 216.
323 *"at a time":* Randall, *Lincoln the President,* 2:41.
323 *"gall and wormwood":* Chase, *Diary,* p. 54.
323 *"the right one":* F. W. Seward, *Seward at Washington . . . 1861–1872,* pp. 25–26.
324 *"this great emergency":* Horace White, *The Life of Lyman Trumbull* (Boston: Houghton Mifflin Co., 1913), p. 171.
324 *through investigating committees:* The following pages draw heavily on Allan G. Bogue's original and admirable study, *The Congressman's Civil War* (Cambridge: Cambridge University Press, 1989), chap. 3.
324 *"her damnable airs":* Murat Halstead to Timothy C. Day, June 8, 1861, copy in Carl Sandburg MSS, Illinois Historical Survey, Urbana.
324 *replied "Tres poo":* John Bigelow, Diary, July 9, 1861, MS, New York Public Library.
325 *drop the investigation:* See the excellent summary in Bogue, *Congressman's Civil War,* pp. 69–71. The myth that Lincoln appeared before either this committee or the Committee on the Conduct of the War to defend Mary Lincoln has been exploded. Mark E. Neely, Jr., "Abraham Lincoln Did NOT Defend His Wife Before the Committee on the Conduct of the War," *LL,* no. 1643 (Jan. 1975).
325 *"the worst scandal":* John Henry Woodward, "A Narrative of the Family and Civil War Experiences and Events of His Life," ed. Frederick Woodward Hopkins (typescript, Library of Congress, 1919), p. 14.
325 *"advising general plans":* Nicolay, *Lincoln's Secretary,* p. 125.
325 *"as war minister":* Gustave Koerner to Lyman Trumbull, July 24, 1861, Trumbull MSS, LC.
325 *"is a thief":* John P. Cranford to AL, Aug. 10, 1861, Lincoln MSS, LC.
325 *should be removed:* O. H. Browning to AL, Aug. 19, 1861, Lincoln MSS, LC.
325 *needed to borrow:* George M. Davis to AL, Aug. 24, 1861, Lincoln MSS, LC.
325 *"settled de novo":* Schuyler Colfax to Simon Cameron, Sept. 24, 1861, Cameron MSS, LC.
325 *the Buchanan administration:* B. W. Bush to Joseph Holt, Nov. 23, 1861, Holt MSS, LC.
326 *"against the rebels":* A. Howard Meneely, *The War Department, 1861: A Study in Mobilization and Administration* (New York: Columbia University Press, 1928), p. 348.
326 *"to public trust":* Randall, *Lincoln the President,* 2:55–56, is especially good on the firing of Cameron.
326 *"in the country":* Bogue, *Congressman's Civil War,* p. 106.
326 *"least equally responsible":* *CW,* 5:241–243.
327 *played lesser roles:* T. Harry Williams, "The Committee on the Conduct of the War: An Experiment in Civilian Control," in *The Selected Essays of T. Harry Williams* (Baton Rouge: Louisiana State University Press, 1983), pp. 15–30, takes a hostile view. For other, more favorable appraisals see Brian Holden Reid, "Historians and the Joint Committee on the Conduct of the War, 1861–1865," *Civil War History* 38 (Dec. 1992): 319–341. The personnel of the committee changed slightly over the next four years, but Wade and Chandler remained firmly in control. Williams, *Lincoln and the Radicals,* p. 65.
327 *harmony was maintained:* Detroit Post and Tribune, *Zachariah Chandler: An Outline Sketch of His Life and Public Services* (Detroit: Post and Tribune Co., Publishers, 1880), pp. 217–218.
327 *"perfectly good mood":* *CW,* 5:88.
327 *"our own people":* *CW,* 5:35.

CHAPTER TWELVE: THE BOTTOM IS OUT OF THE TUB

On military affairs in 1862, and especially on Lincoln's relationship with McClellan, the standard works are Kenneth P. Williams, *Lincoln Finds a General: A Military Study of the Civil War* (New York: Macmillan Co., 1949), vols. 1–2, and T. Harry Williams, *Lincoln and His Generals* (New York: Alfred A. Knopf, 1952). I have learned much from both these historians, though I do not fully share their hostility toward McClellan. Stephen W. Sears, *George B. McClellan: The Young Napoleon* (New York: Ticknor & Fields, 1988), is the best biography. Stephen W. Sears, ed., *The Civil War Papers of George B. McClellan: Selected Correspondence, 1860–1865* (New York: Ticknor & Fields, 1989), and George B. McClellan, *McClellan's Own Story* (New York: Charles L. Webster, 1887), are invaluable.

T. Harry Williams, *Lincoln and the Radicals* (Madison: University of Wisconsin Press, 1941), is the basic work on factionalism within the Republican party. I have questioned some of Williams's conclusions—especially those concerning the solidarity of the Radical faction and the hostility of Radicals toward Lincoln—in "The Radicals and Lincoln," in *Lincoln Reconsidered: Essays on the Civil War Era* (New York: Alfred A. Knopf, 1956), and in "Devils Facing Zionwards," in Grady McWhiney, ed., *Grant, Lee, Lincoln and the Radicals: Essays on Civil War Leadership* (Evanston, Ill.: Northwestern University Press, 1964). Hans L. Trefousse, *The Radical Republicans: Lincoln's Vanguard for Racial Justice* (New York: Alfred A. Knopf, 1969), sees the Radicals as largely helping, rather than hindering, Lincoln. Allan G. Bogue, *The Earnest Men: Republicans of the Civil War Senate* (Ithaca, N.Y.: Cornell University Press, 1981), is an important, objective study that uses roll-call analysis and other statistical techniques to define membership in the Republican factions.

The best account of Lincoln's plans for what he called "gradual, and not sudden emancipation" is in J. G. Randall, *Lincoln the President: Springfield to Gettysburg* (New York: Dodd, Mead, & Co., 1945), chap. 21.

328 "power to command": Bates, *Diary,* p. 220.
328 "of boyish cheerfulness": Ralph L. Rusk, *The Life of Ralph Waldo Emerson* (New York: Charles Scribner's Sons, 1949), p. 414.
328 "submit to it": P. P. Enos to Lyman Trumbull, Jan. 7, 1862, Trumbull MSS, LC.
328 "being two nations": *Day by Day,* 3:87.
329 "to General McClellan": George W. Julian, *Political Recollections, 1840 to 1872* (Chicago: Jansen, McClurg & Co., 1884), p. 201.
329 "concert at once": *CW,* 5:87.
329 "in the South": *CW,* 5:91.
329 rather than orders: *CW,* 5:98.
329 "can be done": *CW,* 5:95.
330 "What shall I do?": "General M. C. Meigs on the Conduct of the Civil War," *American Historical Review* 26 (Jan. 1921): 292.
330 out his problems: The following paragraphs follow Irvin McDowell's diary account in William Swinton, *Campaigns of the Army of the Potomac* (New York: Charles B. Richardson, 1866), pp. 79–82.
330 adjourned the meeting: "General M. C. Meigs on the Conduct of the Civil War," pp. 292–293; Henry J. Raymond, *The Life and Public Services of Abraham Lincoln* (New York: Derby & Miller, 1865), pp. 776–777.
331 "his own hands": Virginia Woodbury Fox, Diary, Jan. 26, 1862, Levi Woodbury MSS, LC.
331 his "political education": *CW,* 4:214.
331 to veto measures: Anna Prentner, "Application of Veto Power by Abraham Lincoln," *Western Pennsylvania Historical Magazine* 6 (Jan. 1923): 51–55. Lincoln vetoed or pocket-vetoed only seven bills during his presidency, mostly unimportant measures rejected for technical reasons. The Wade-Davis bill, discussed in a subsequent chapter, was highly exceptional. For a different view of Lincoln's use of the veto, see Allan G. Bogue, *The Congressman's Civil War* (Cambridge: Cambridge University Press, 1989), pp. 52–53.
331 "look much better": Francis Fessenden, *Life and Public Services of William Pitt Fessenden* (Boston: Houghton Mifflin & Co., 1907), 1:260.
332 "mildness towards ... traitors": Hans L. Trefousse, *Benjamin Franklin Wade: Radical Republican from Ohio* (New York: Twayne Publishers, 1963), p. 186.
332 "regard to slavery": Trefousse, *The Radical Republicans,* p. 184.

332 *"feasting and dancing"*: Allan Nevins, *Frémont: Pathmarker of the West* (New York: Longmans, Green & Co., 1955), p. 552.

332 *Lincoln was President:* William Jayne to William Butler, Mar. 21, 1861, Butler MSS, Chicago Historical Society. In time, Lincoln came to have "no doubt that Judge Trumbull is not his friend." David Davis to Leonard Swett, Nov. 26, 1861, Davis MSS, ISHL.

332 *spread of liberty:* David Herbert Donald, "Abraham Lincoln and the American Pragmatic Tradition," in *Lincoln Reconsidered,* pp. 128–143.

333 *"hostile to me":* Hay, *Diary,* p. 235.

333 *mortally offended them:* John Hay to WHH, Sept. 5, 1866, HWC.

333 *whom he succeeded:* The authoritative biography is Benjamin P. Thomas and Harold M. Hyman, *Stanton: The Life and Times of Lincoln's Secretary of War* (New York: Alfred A. Knopf, 1962).

333 *"whom he fears":* Welles, *Diary,* 1:128–129.

333 *"and of loyalty":* Joseph Holt to AL, Jan. 15, 1862, Lincoln MSS, LC.

334 *"a while first":* Thomas and Hyman, *Stanton,* p. 151.

334 *"Secretary of War":* CW, 6:312.

334 *"he sometimes does":* Donald, *Lincoln Reconsidered,* p. 71.

334 *"rein on me":* CW, 5:284.

334 *"it be done":* CW, 5:206. In this case Lincoln subsequently withdrew his directive, claiming that it was "plainly no order at all." *CW,* 5:229.

334 *carrying out the order: CW,* 5:111.

334 *"the one weakened":* Browning, *Diary,* 1:523. He recommended the same strategy to General Buell. *CW,* 5:98.

335 *in eastern Kentucky:* See the excellent account of this engagement in Gerald J. Prokopowicz, "All for the Regiment: Unit Cohesion and Tactical Stalemate in the Army of the Ohio, 1861–1862" (unpublished Ph.D. dissertation, Harvard University, 1994), chap. 3.

335 *"a grievous mistake":* Helen Nicolay, *Lincoln's Secretary: A Biography of John G. Nicolay* (New York: Longmans, Green & Co., 1949), pp. 131–132.

335 *cannon to Kentucky:* Joshua F. Speed to Joseph Holt, Feb. 4, 1862, Holt MSS, LC.

336 *"ever seen here":* This description follows, with minor changes, my account in " 'This Damned Old House': The Lincolns in the White House," in Frank Freidel and William Pencak, eds., *The White House: The First Two Hundred Years* (Boston: Northeastern University Press, 1994), p. 63.

336 *probably typhoid fever:* This is the most probable diagnosis of Willie's illness, but Dr. Milton H. Shutes believed that it was "broncho-pneumonia (or pneumonitis) with damaged kidneys as a possible, determinate factor." Shutes, "Mortality of the Five Lincoln Boys," *LH* 57 (Spring–Summer 1955), p. 6.

336 *of his recovery:* John G. Nicolay, Diary, Feb. 18, 1862, Nicolay MSS, LC.

336 *"is actually gone!":* Nicolay, *Lincoln's Secretary,* pp. 132–133.

336 *"loved him so":* Ruth Painter Randall, *Lincoln's Sons* (Boston: Little, Brown & Co., 1955), p. 131.

336 *and he wept:* LeGrand B. Cannon to WHH, Oct. 7, 1888, HWC. The quotation is from *King John,* act 3, scene 4.

337 *"died—never before":* WHH, interview with Mrs. Abraham Lincoln, Sept. 5, 1866, HWC.

337 *"I cannot succeed":* CW, 4:190.

337 *"never deserted us":* CW, 4:199.

337 *"of the Universe":* CW, 4:226.

337 *"this favored land":* CW, 4:271.

337 *lived in heaven:* Edgar DeWitt Jones, *Lincoln and the Preachers* (New York: Harper & Brothers, 1948), pp. 35–38.

337 *"a process of crystallization":* Carpenter, *Six Months,* p. 189.

337 *veils and crepes:* Randall, *Mary Lincoln,* pp. 284–288.

338 *"necessary to us":* Ibid., p. 296.

338 *"not get invitations":* Baker, *Mary Todd Lincoln,* p. 215.

338 *"notions of life":* David Davis to William W. Orme, Feb. 23, 1862, Orme MSS, Illinois Historical Survey.

338 *"gambler and drunkard":* E. A. Hitchcock to "Cox," Apr. 1862, Hitchcock MSS, LC.

339 *"of our cause": CW,* 5:119–125. The quoted words are italicized in the source.

339 *"to do anything":* John G. Nicolay, Diary, Feb. 27, 1862, Nicolay MSS, LC. Nicolay discreetly recorded Lincoln's explosion as "Why in the——nation."

340 *of the engagement:* Welles, *Diary,* 1:62–65.

340 *"word of it"*: McClellan, *McClellan's Own Story*, pp. 195–196.

340 *"one we adopt"*: Williams, *Lincoln and His Generals*, p. 67.

341 *plan of campaign*: Samuel P. Heintzelman, Diary, Mar. 8, 1862, Heintzelman MSS, LC. N. P. Banks was named to command a Fifth Army Corps, to be composed of his own division and that of James Shields, which was to operate in the Shenandoah Valley. *CW*, 5:149–150.

341 *to the field*: Bates, *Diary*, p. 239.

341 *to army administration*: *CW*, 5:155.

341 *"my public duties"*: George B. McClellan to AL, Mar. 12, 1862, Lincoln MSS, LC.

342 *"been at Manasses"*: Browning, *Diary*, 1:552.

342 *"of universal liberty"*: *Congressional Globe*, 38 Cong., 2 sess., p. 441.

342 *"was never played"*: J. G. Randall, *Lincoln the Liberal Statesman* (New York: Dodd, Mead & Co., 1947), p. 72.

342 *"in the White House"*: *The Liberator*, Jan. 31, 1862.

342 *"Slave-holders rebellion"*: Joseph Medill to AL, Feb. 9, 1862, Lincoln MSS, LC.

342 *"did the President"*: Randall, *Lincoln the Liberal Statesman*, p. 67.

342 *"to think so"*: Segal, *Conversations*, p. 168.

342 *"somehow" the cause*: In his second inaugural Lincoln said that the slaves "constituted a peculiar and powerful interest" that was "somehow, the cause of the war." *CW*, 8:332.

342 *the nefarious traffic*: *CW*, 5:128–129.

343 *"remorseless revolutionary struggle"*: *CW*, 5:48–49.

343 *of ultimate extinction*: Robert W. Johannsen, ed., *The Lincoln-Douglas Debates of 1858* (New York: Oxford University Press, 1965), p. 265.

343 *"to our armies"*: Browning, *Diary*, 1:477–478.

343 *of Henry Clay*: Lincoln's ideas on colonization were actually closer to Jefferson's than to Clay's. Like Jefferson, Lincoln always advocated voluntary emigration, while Clay endorsed forcible deportation of blacks. Marvin R. Cain, "Lincoln's Views on Slavery and the Negro: A Suggestion," *The Historian* 26 (Aug. 1964): 502–520.

343 *"congenial to them"*: *CW*, 5:48.

344 *the race problem*: Of the many studies of Lincoln and colonization, I have found the following most useful: Warren A. Beck, "Lincoln and Negro Colonization in Central America," *ALQ* 6 (Sept. 1950): 162–183; Gabor S. Boritt, "The Voyage to the Colony of Linconia: The Sixteenth President, Black Colonization, and the Defense Mechanism of Avoidance," *Historian* 37 (Aug. 1975): 619–632; N. A. N. Cleven, "Some Plans for Colonizing Liberated Negro Slaves in Hispanic America," *Journal of Negro History* 11 (Jan. 1926): 35–49; Walter A. Payne, "Lincoln's Caribbean Colonization Plan," *Pacific Historian* 7 (May 1963): 65–72; Paul J. Scheips, "Lincoln and the Chiriqui Colonization Project," *Journal of Negro History* 37 (Oct. 1952): 418–453; and Michael Vorenberg, "Abraham Lincoln and the Politics of Black Colonization," *Journal of the Abraham Lincoln Association* 14 (Summer 1993): 23–45. A fascinating essay by William W. Freehling, " 'Absurd' Issues and the Causes of the Civil War: Colonization as a Test Case," in his *Reintegration of American History: Slavery and the Civil War* (New York: Oxford University Press, 1994), pp. 138–157, suggests that colonization was not an entirely impracticable scheme.

344 *to Central America*: George M. Fredrickson, *The Black Image in the White Mind: The Debate on Afro-American Character and Destiny, 1817–1914* (New York: Harper & Row, 1971), pp. 148–149.

344 *"among us" was inevitable*: Francis Preston Blair, Sr., to AL, Nov. 16, 1861, Lincoln MSS, LC.

344 *together in peace*: Montgomery Blair to AL, Nov. 21, 1861, Lincoln MSS, LC.

344 *were fully verified*: N. W. Edwards to AL, Aug. 9, 1861, Lincoln MSS, LC.

344 *"by the prospects"*: S. P. Chase to AL, Nov. 12, 1861, Lincoln MSS, LC.

345 *"has passed by"*: Edward Everett Hale, *Memories of a Hundred Years* (New York: Macmillan Co., 1904), 2:190–191.

345 *introduced as bills*: *CW*, 5:28–29; George P. Fisher, typed essay on "The Trial of John H. Surratt for the Murder of President Lincoln," Fisher MSS, LC.

345 *"with human freedom"*: Donald, *Sumner*, p. 47.

346 *"latitudes and countries"*: Frederick J. Blue, *Salmon P. Chase: A Life in Politics* (Kent, Ohio: Kent State University Press, 1987), pp. 83–84.

346 *filed away unused*: Salmon P. Chase, draft of a proposed presidential message on compensated emancipation, Mar. 6, 1862, Lincoln MSS, LC.

346 *matter of policy*: For an astute review of the relationship between the two men, see John Niven, "Lincoln and Chase, a Reappraisal," *Journal of the Abraham Lincoln Association* 12 (1991): 1–15.

346 *"of his dept."*: Hay, *Diary*, p. 145.
346 *"anything about 'money' "*: Gabor S. Boritt, *Lincoln and the Economics of the American Dream* (Memphis: Memphis State University Press, 1978), p. 203.
346 *"it in to-day"*: Donald, *Sumner*, p. 51.
347 *"may follow it"*: *CW*, 5:144–146.
347 *"the right place"*: San Francisco, *Daily Alta California*, Apr. 8, 1862.
347 *"wise a ruler"*: Herbert Mitgang, ed., *Abraham Lincoln: A Press Portrait* (Chicago: Quadrangle Books, 1971), pp. 290, 293.
347 *District of Columbia*: *CW*, 5:152–153.
347 *"and sound policy"*: Henry J. Raymond to AL, Mar. 15, 1862, Lincoln MSS, LC.
347 *"about the matter"*: John G. Nicolay, Diary, Mar. 9, 1862, Nicolay MSS, LC.
348 *"of his Country"*: Segal, *Conversations*, pp. 165–168.
348 *"office he holds"*: *The American Annual Cyclopaedia and Register of Important Events of the Year 1862* (New York: D. Appleton & Co., 1871), 2:346.
348 *"and hungry dog"*: Adam Gurowski, *Diary from March 4, 1861, to November 12, 1862* (Boston: Lee & Shepard, 1862), p. 159.
348 *by overwhelming majorities*: Though Lincoln was able to enlist the almost unanimous support of Republican congressmen for the resolution, he did not succeed in attracting bipartisan support for it. In the House of Representatives only four Democrats supported the resolution, and only one Democrat in the Senate voted for it.
348 *"greatly prefer it"*: *CW*, 5:169.
349 *"no military knowledge"*: Randall, *Lincoln the President*, 2:84–85.
349 *"he fights"*: Williams, *Lincoln and His Generals*, p. 86.
349 *"meet the crisis"*: Browning, *Diary*, 1:537–538.
349 *Washington "entirely secure"*: *CW*, 5:151.
350 *"line . . . at once"*: *CW*, 5:182.
350 *"do it himself"*: McClellan, *Civil War Papers*, p. 234.
350 *"sluggishness of action"*: Browning, *Diary*, 1:540.
350 *"you must act"*: *CW*, 5:185.
350 *"the best motives"*: George B. McClellan to Montgomery Blair, Apr. 20, 1862, Blair MSS, LC.
350 *"loss of life"*: George B. McClellan to AL, Apr. 23, 1862, Lincoln MSS, LC.
350 *scene of operations*: My account of Lincoln's Norfolk "campaign" follows Egbert L. Viele, "A Trip with Lincoln, Chase and Stanton," *Scribner's Monthly* 16 (Oct. 1878): 813–822, and William E. Baringer, "On Enemy Soil: President Lincoln's Norfolk Campaign," *ALQ* 7 (Mar. 1952): 4–26.
351 *"terror as ever"*: Chase, *Diary*, p. 85.
351 *"hurts my feelings"*: Wilson Barstow to Elizabeth Barstow, May 12, 1862, Barstow MSS, LC.
352 *all at once*: *CW*, 5:208–209.
352 *obey his orders*: *CW*, 5:219, 226–227.
352 *lost his balance*: Madeleine Vinton Dahlgren, *Memoir of John A. Dahlgren* (Boston: James R. Osgood & Co., 1882), p. 369.
352 *to approve it*: Lucius E. Chittenden, *Recollections of President Lincoln and His Administration* (New York: Harper & Brothers, 1891), pp. 307–309.
352 *"than Mr. Buchanan"*: Edward Dicey, *Six Months in the Federal States* (New York: Macmillan & Co., 1863), 1:228.

CHAPTER THIRTEEN: AN INSTRUMENT IN GOD'S HANDS

All Lincoln biographies deal extensively with the Emancipation Proclamation, and I have learned much from them. The fullest analysis is in J. G. Randall, *Lincoln the President: Springfield to Gettysburg* (New York: Dodd, Mead & Co., 1945), vol. 2, on which I have greatly relied. John Hope Franklin, *The Emancipation Proclamation* (Garden City, N.Y.: Doubleday & Co., 1963), is an excellent brief account.

354 *"different from theirs"*: *CW*, 5:278–279.
355 *"another Bull Run"*: Charles Sumner to R. H. Dana, Jr., May 31, 1862, Dana MSS, Massachusetts Historical Society.
355 *"defence of Washington"*: *CW*, 5:236.
356 *"speed you can"*: *CW*, 5:246.

356 *in two days:* T. Harry Williams, *Lincoln and His Generals* (New York: Alfred A. Knopf, 1952), pp. 100–101.

356 *"in good order":* CW, 5:255.

356 *able to move:* CW, 5:273.

356 *"Providence will permit":* CW, 5:276–277.

357 *"prolonging the war":* Stephen W. Sears, *George B. McClellan: The Young Napoleon* (New York: Ticknor & Fields, 1988), pp. 200, 203.

357 *"irresolute in action":* McClellan, *Civil War Papers,* pp. 244–245.

357 *"end of the rebellion":* Winfield Scott to AL, June 24, 1862, Lincoln MSS, LC.

357 *"attached to it":* CW, 5:284.

358 *than the unjust:* Nicolay and Hay, 5:414–415.

358 *"simply absurd":* CW, 5:301.

358 *"sacrifice this army":* McClellan, *Civil War Papers,* pp. 322–323. For Lincoln's rebuke of Marcy for speaking of capitulation, see Browning, *Diary,* 1:558–559.

358 *"browze round":* CW, 5:294; Strong, *Diary,* p. 218.

358 *" 'die sometime' ":* Browning, *Diary,* 1:559–560.

359 *"bring it out":* CW, 5:298.

359 *"satisfactory conclusion":* CW, 5:292, 296–297.

359 "break it for him": Sandburg, 1:511–512. McClellan indignantly denied the charge, saying that he protected the White House only because it was once the property of George Washington. McClellan, *Civil War Papers,* pp. 290–291.

359 *"timber at that":* Charles N. Walker and Rosemary Walker, eds., "Diary of the War of Robt. S. Robertson," *Old Fort News* 28 (Jan.–Mar. 1965): 42; McClellan, *Civil War Papers,* p. 362.

360 *"served superior":* McClellan to AL, July 7, 1862, Lincoln MSS, LC.

360 *"the whole country":* CW, 5:279.

360 *" 'I will get off' ":* Sandburg, 1:602.

360 *"the army safely?":* CW, 5:310.

360 *"magnitude of the crisis":* McClellan, *Civil War Papers,* p. 348.

361 *"General-in-Chief":* CW, 5:312–313.

361 *"General in the country":* CW, 5:284.

361 *recommended by General Scott:* Wallace J. Schutz and Walter N. Trenerry, *Abandoned by Lincoln: A Military Biography of General John Pope* (Urbana: University of Illinois Press, 1990), chap. 8.

361 *his tacit approval:* Kenneth P. Williams, *Lincoln Finds a General* (New York: Macmillan Co., 1949), 1:252–254.

362 *"no wise omit this":* CW, 5:318–319.

362 *"lived in vain!":* Francis Fisher Browne, *The Every-day Life of Abraham Lincoln* (Chicago: Browne & Howell Co., 1913), 2:423.

363 *"must be done":* Welles, *Diary,* 1:70–71.

363 *were "forever free":* CW, 5:222.

363 *"without consulting me":* CW, 5:219.

363 *"subdue the enemy":* CW, 5:222, 421.

363 *early as June 18:* For a rather too circumstantial account of this conversation, see Charles E. Hamlin, *The Life and Times of Hannibal Hamlin* (Cambridge, Mass.: Riverside Press, 1899), pp. 428–429.

364 *"slaves in the South":* David Homer Bates, *Lincoln in the Telegraph Office* (New York: Century Co., 1907), pp. 138–141. For a skeptical view of this account of the drafting of the Emancipation Proclamation, see Mark E. Neely, Jr., *The Last Best Hope of Earth: Abraham Lincoln and the Promise of America* (Cambridge, Mass.: Harvard University Press, 1993), pp. 108–109.

364 *could enforce it:* Louis M. Starr, *Bohemian Brigade: Civil War Newsmen in Action* (New York: Alfred A. Knopf, 1954), p. 125.

364 *"lose the game!":* Carpenter, *Six Months,* pp. 20–22.

364 *"the best policy":* CW, 5:329–330.

365 *"within a state":* CW, 5:329.

365 *"it may exist":* Browning, *Diary,* 1:555.

365 *a historic occasion:* Lincoln's own recollection of this meeting, as recorded by the artist Francis B. Carpenter, is in Carpenter, *Six Months,* pp. 20–22. Chase's record is in Chase, *Diary,* pp. 98–100; Stanton's memorandum, dated July 22, 1862, is in the Stanton MSS, LC. The first draft of the Emancipation Proclamation is in CW, 5:336–337.

366 *sympathy with the President:* For Smith's views, see Nelson H. Loomis, "Mr. Lincoln's Cabinet by Hon. John P. Usher . . . with a Foreword and a Sketch of the Life of the Author" [1924?], typed copy, A. J. Beveridge MSS, LC.

366 *important border states:* Benjamin P. Thomas and Harold M. Hyman, *Stanton: The Life and Times of Lincoln's Secretary of War* (New York: Alfred A. Knopf, 1962), p. 240; William Stuart to Lord Russell, Aug. 22, 1862, Stuart MSS, Public Records Office, London.

366 *"after a victory":* George Bemis, Diary, Nov. 15, 1862, Massachusetts Historical Society.

366 *"emancipating negroes":* Ida M. Tarbell, *The Life of Abraham Lincoln* (New York: Doubleday, Page & Co., 1909), 2:113–115; Leonard Swett to Laura Swett, Aug. 10, 1862, David Davis MSS, ISHL.

367 *"necessaries of life":* Private and Official Correspondence of Gen. Benjamin F. Butler During the Period of the Civil War (1917), 2:41–42.

367 *"injury than good":* Browning, *Diary*, 1:555.

367 *"join the rebellion":* Frederic Bancroft, ed., *Speeches, Correspondence and Political Papers of Carl Schurz* (New York: G. P. Putnam's Sons, 1913), 1:209.

367 *"Hamlin try it":* James G. Smart, ed., *A Radical View: The "Agate" Dispatches of Whitelaw Reid, 1861–1865* (Memphis: Memphis State University Press, 1976), 2:74–75.

367 *"good of mankind":* CW, 5:370–375.

367 *"North and South":* "The National Controversy," *Pacific Appeal*, Sept. 6, 1862.

368 *"homes in America!":* Chase, *Diary*, p. 112.

368 *"benefit of the enslaved":* Garnet, in *Pacific Appeal*, Oct. 11, 1862.

368 *"save the Union":* CW, 5:388–389.

369 *"to stand on":* Weed to Seward, Aug. 23, 1862; Ashmun to AL, Aug. 25, 1862, both in Lincoln MSS, LC.

369 *"to that music":* Howe to AL, Aug. 25, 1862, Lincoln MSS, LC.

369 *"progress of events":* Carpenter, *Six Months*, p. 22.

369 *"alone prevents it":* McClellan, *Civil War Papers*, p. 374.

369 *"without reinforcements":* Browning, *Diary*, 1:563–564.

370 *"do what I wish":* Thomas and Hyman, *Stanton*, pp. 216–217.

370 *"these people now":* Hay, *Diary*, pp. 45–46.

371 *"the contest proceeds":* CW, 5:403–404.

371 *"unknown to us":* CW, 5:478.

371 *"army with him":* Hay, *Diary*, 45–47; Welles, *Diary*, 1:113.

372 *"called me to it":* McClellan, *Civil War Papers*, p. 428.

372 *"the [War] Department":* Welles, *Diary*, 1:97–98.

372 *"disrespectful to the President":* "Opinion of Stanton, Chase, Smith & Bates of Want of Confidence in Genl. McClellan, given to the President," Sept. 2, 1862, copy, Lincoln MSS, LC.

372 *"tools we have":* Bates's note, on the document previously cited; John Niven, ed., *The Salmon P. Chase Papers,* vol. 1, *Journals—1829–1872* (Kent, Ohio: Kent State University Press, 1993), p. 369; Hay, *Diary,* p. 47. Lincoln's words in Chase's diary, "gladly resign his place," have caused some controversy among historians. J. G. Randall, in *Lincoln the President,* 2:112–113, believed the passage, which we have only in the handwriting of a copyist, should read "gladly resign his plan." I adopted that reading in my edition of Chase's diaries, *Inside Lincoln's Cabinet,* pp. 118–120, but I defer to the authoritative edition of those diaries edited by Professor John Niven and his associates.

372 *"Harrisburg and Philadelphia":* CW, 5:501.

372 *"will do anything":* Welles, *Diary*, 1:116.

373 *"side of the mountains":* CW, 5:417.

373 *"and the people":* Strong, *Diary,* p. 256; Samuel Galloway to AL, Sept. 4, 1862, Lincoln MSS, LC; Robert Laird Collier, *Moral Heroism: Its Essentialness to the Crisis. A Sermon, Preached to the Wabash Ave. M.E. Church, Chicago, Sabbath Evening, August 3, 1862,* pp. 7–8.

373 *"all the cabinet":* Garrett Davis to AL, Sept. 7, 1862, Lincoln MSS, LC.

373 *"fatal concessions":* Chase, *Diary*, p. 136.

373 *in late September:* Andrew, in Allan Nevins, *The War for the Union* (New York: Charles Scribner's Sons, 1960), 2:240. For much further detail, and some speculation, on the Altoona conference, see William Best Hesseltine, *Lincoln and the War Governors* (New York: Alfred A. Knopf, 1948), chap. 13.

374 *"as the Republicans":* Browning to AL, Sept. 10, 1862, Lincoln MSS, LC.

374 *"against the comet!":* CW, 5:420.

374 "I will do it!": Ibid.

374 *"cause of emancipation"*: Welles, *Diary,* 1:143.

374 *had sent him:* "Artemus Ward" was the pen name of Charles Farrar Browne. Lincoln read from the recently published *Artemus Ward: His Book* (1862).

375 *"other minor matter"*: Chase, *Diary,* p. 150.

375 *"feelings of . . . the people"*: Adam Gurowski, *Diary, from March 4, 1861 to November 12, 1862* (Boston: Lee & Shepard, 1862), p. 278.

375 *"forever free"*: CW, 5:433–436.

375 *"ought to take"*: Chase, *Diary,* pp. 150–151.

375 *"all my heart"*: Ibid.

376 *"weight with him"*: Welles, *Diary,* 1:144.

376 *"with difficulties"*: CW, 5:438.

CHAPTER FOURTEEN: A PUMPKIN IN EACH END OF MY BAG

Allan Nevins, *The War for the Union* (New York: Charles Scribner's Sons, 1960), vol. 2, offers the most comprehensive survey of the period between the preliminary and the final Emancipation Proclamations. I have also found especially useful William Safire's *Freedom* (Garden City, N.Y.: Doubleday & Co., 1987). Though this account is fictional, it is abundantly documented in Safire's "Underbook" of notes.

377 *"his fellow man"*: Speed to WHH, Feb. 7, 1866, HWC.

377 *"issued by man"*: Robert S. Harper, *Lincoln and the Press* (New York: McGraw-Hill Book Co., 1951), p. 177.

378 *dozen hams:* W. B. Lowry, H. Catlin, and J. F. Downing to AL, Sept. 23, 1862; McKim to AL, Sept. 27, 1862; George Cassaru to AL, Sept. 25, 1862—all in Lincoln MSS, LC.

378 *"other American man"*: Ralph L. Rusk, *The Life of Ralph Waldo Emerson* (New York: Charles Scribner's Sons, 1949), pp. 416–417.

378 *"side of the President"*: Donald, *Sumner,* p. 81.

378 *"sound policy"*: CW, 5:441.

378 *"kills no rebels"*: CW, 5:444.

378 *"Mr. Lincoln's proclamation"*: Randall, *Lincoln the President,* 2:175; Richard Nelson Current, *Lincoln's Loyalists* (Boston: Northeastern University Press, 1992), p. 50.

379 *"and of revenge"*: Ephraim D. Adams, *Great Britain and the American Civil War* (New York: Longmans, Green & Co., 1925), 2:102.

379 *"destroy the Union"*: Nevins, *War for the Union,* 2:235n.

379 *"loyal Slave States"*: Randall, *Lincoln the President,* 2:172.

379 *"no practical result"*: Virginia Jeans Laas, ed., *Wartime Washington: The Civil War Letters of Elizabeth Blair Lee* (Urbana: University of Illinois Press, 1991), p. 187.

380 *"beyond our vision"*: Harper, *Lincoln and the Press,* p. 177; *New York Evening Express,* Sept. 23, 1862.

380 *"authority of the United States"*: CW, 5:437.

380 *"less it does"*: James A. Bayard to S. L. M. Barlow, Sept. 30, 1862, Barlow MSS, HEH.

381 *not radical enough:* Carl Schurz to AL, May 19, 1862, Lincoln MSS, LC.

381 *"might be averted"*: Forney to Hannibal Hamlin, Oct. 1, 1862, Hamlin MSS, microfilm, Columbia University.

381 *"some time since"*: Chase, *Diary,* p. 151.

381 *first law partner:* Harry E. Pratt, "The Repudiation of Lincoln's War Policy in 1862—Stuart-Swett Congressional Campaign," *JISHS* 24:129–140.

382 *"plain sailing"*: DeWitt C. Clarke to W. H. Seward, Sept. 23, 1862, Seward MSS, UR.

382 *"nothing else"*: Enoch T. Carson to S. P. Chase, Sept. 25, 1862, Chase MSS.

382 *himself a dictator:* See the excellent treatment of this subject in Mark E. Neely, Jr., *The Fate of Liberty: Abraham Lincoln and Civil Liberties* (New York: Oxford University Press, 1991), pp. 51–65.

382 *"writ of 'habeas corpus' "*: Arthur C. Cole, *The Era of the Civil War, 1848–1870* (Springfield: Illinois Centennial Commission, 1919), p. 297.

382 *"red with blood"*: Seymour is quoted in John Livingston to W. H. Seward, Oct. 4, 1862, Seward MSS, UR.

382 *"overwork had wrought":* Mary A. Livermore, *My Story of the War* (Hartford: A. D. Worthington & Co., 1889), pp. 555, 560.

382 *"of holy-days":* CW, 5:452.

382 *a severe rebuff:* The best way to understand the outcome of the election is to consult the stunning maps in Kenneth C. Martis, *The Historical Atlas of Political Parties in the United States Congress, 1789–1989* (New York: Macmillan Publishing Co., 1989), pp. 115, 117.

383 *"want of confidence": New York Times,* Nov. 7, 1862.

383 *to "Africanize" Illinois:* Bruce Tap, "Race, Rhetoric, and Emancipation: The Election of 1862 in Illinois," *Civil War History* 39 (June 1993): 101–125.

383 *in Republican counties: CW,* 5:494. For refutation of the theory that more Republicans than Democrats were in the army, see Randall, *Lincoln the President,* 2:235–236.

383 *"carry on the Government":* Field to AL, Nov. 8, 1862, Lincoln MSS, LC.

383 *"made to relent":* T. J. Barnett to S. L. M. Barlow, Nov. 30, 1862, Barlow MSS, HEH.

383 *"hands of its enemy's":* Schurz to Lincoln, Nov. 8, 1862, Lincoln MSS, LC.

384 *outcome of the elections:* S. W. Oakey to AL, Nov. 5, 1862, Lincoln MSS, LC.

384 *"not surprise me":* Sandburg, 1:606–607.

385 *"intimidate the President":* Nevins, *War for the Union,* 2:231n.

385 *"to insubordination":* Ibid., 2:238.

385 *Pinkerton's long interview:* Pinkerton's report of this interview is in James D. Horan, *The Pinkertons: The Detective Dynasty That Made History* (New York: Crown Publishers, 1967), pp. 130–133.

386 *"break up that game": CW,* 5:442–443. Most historians have failed to see the importance of Key's dismissal. The best account of the affair is Safire, *Freedom,* pp. 770–775; see particularly Safire's notes, pp. 1084–1085.

387 *"wanted an example": CW,* 5:508; Chase, *Diary,* p. 219.

387 *trusted political advisers:* On Thomas M. Key's influence over McClellan, see Donn Piatt, *Memories of the Men Who Saved the Union* (New York: Belford, Clarke & Co., 1887), pp. 291–295.

387 *"into a despotism":* Bruce Catton, *Terrible Swift Sword* (Garden City, N.Y.: Doubleday & Co., 1963), pp. 464–465.

387 *opposition to the proclamations:* Montgomery Blair to McClellan, Sept. 27, 1862, McClellan MSS, LC.

387 *"manners and appearance":* Allan Nevins, ed., *A Diary of Battle: The Personal Journals of Colonel Charles S. Wainwright, 1861–1865* (New York: Harcourt, Brace & World, 1962), pp. 109–110.

387 *adjacent to McClellan's:* For a detailed chronology of the visit, see *LL,* no. 1277 (Sept. 28, 1953).

387 *"McClellan's body-guard":* Francis Fisher Browne, *The Every-day Life of Abraham Lincoln* (Chicago: Browne & Howell Co., 1913), 2:417–418.

387 *"smile of approbation":* Nevins, *Diary of Battle,* p. 110.

388 *of the Union dead:* Ward Hill Lamon, *Recollections of Abraham Lincoln, 1847–1865,* ed. Dorothy Lamon Teillard (Washington, D.C.: 1911), chap. 9; *LL,* no. 250 (Sept. 4, 1933).

388 *"general in the country":* McClellan, *Civil War Papers,* pp. 489–490.

388 *"master of the situation":* William D. Kelley, *Lincoln and Stanton* (New York: G. P. Putnam's Sons, 1885), p. 75.

388 *"indulge her baby":* Nicolay to Therena Bates, Nov. 9, 1862, Nicolay MSS, LC.

388 *"temper over it":* Nicolay to Therena Bates, Oct. 13, 1862, Nicolay MSS, LC.

389 *"the same notion":* Livermore, *My Story of the War,* pp. 556–560.

389 *"Mac's ribs":* Nicolay to John Hay, Oct. 26, 1862, Nicolay MSS, LC.

389 *"the 'Gorilla' ":* McClellan, *Civil War Papers,* p. 515.

389 *"fatigue anything?":* CW, 5:474–479.

389 *"dull to take hold":* F. P. Blair, Sr., to Montgomery Blair, Nov. 7, 1862, Blair MSS, LC.

389 *"inexpedient" to remove:* Chase to Hiram Barney, Oct. 26, 1862, Chase MSS.

390 *advance at Antietam:* For McClellan's criticism of Burnside's performance at Antietam, see William Marvel, *Burnside* (Chapel Hill: University of North Carolina Press, 1991), pp. 145–150.

390 *ground for his own:* For the high degree of Republican unanimity on measures relating to the war, see David Donald, "Devils Facing Zionwards," in Grady McWhiney, ed., *Grant, Lee, Lincoln and the Radicals* (Evanston, Ill.: Northwestern University Press, 1964), 72–91. But for clearly visible Republican factionalism, which became more evident as the war dragged on, see Allan G. Bogue, *The Earnest Men: Republicans of the Civil War Senate* (Ithaca, N.Y.: Cornell University Press, 1981), esp. chap. 3.

391 *in a single morning:* C. Van Santvoord, "A Reception by President Lincoln," *Century Magazine* 25 (Feb. 1883): 612–614.

392 *"occurrences of the day":* Turner, *Mary Todd Lincoln,* p. 187.

392 *Indians in American history:* Throughout this section I have relied heavily on David A. Nichols, *Lincoln and the Indians: Civil War Policy and Politics* (Columbia: University of Missouri Press, 1978), chaps. 6–8 and 13, and, except where otherwise indicated, all quotations are taken from this excellent monograph. *The Civil War in the American West* (New York: Alfred A. Knopf, 1991), by Alvin M. Josephy, Jr., has also been very useful in helping me to understand the Sioux rebellion.

392 *"cowardly, and shameful":* Wallace J. Schutz and Walter N. Trenerry, *Abandoned by Lincoln: A Military Biography of General John Pope* (Urbana: University of Illinois Press, 1990), p. 176.

393 *"neglected race":* CW, 5:173.

393 *"Cherokee Nation":* CW, 5:439.

393 *"our red brethren":* CW, 6:151–152. This meeting was on Mar. 27, 1863.

394 *man to his death:* CW, 5:542–543.

395 *"before the Locos":* O. J. Hollister, *Life of Schuyler Colfax* (New York: Funk & Wagnalls, 1886), p. 199.

395 *Much of the message:* The full text of the message is in *CW,* 5:518–537.

396 *"our military reach":* Madeleine Vinton Dahlgren, *Memoir of John A. Dahlgren* (Boston: James R. Osgood & Co., 1882), p. 382.

396 *"make them free":* N. Worth Brown and Randolph C. Downes, eds., "A Conference with Abraham Lincoln: From the Diary of Reverend Nathan Brown," *Northwest Ohio Quarterly* 22 (Spring 1950): 61–62.

397 *"two thirds of the States":* Chase to AL, Nov. 28, 1862, Lincoln MSS, LC.

397 *from a "hallucination":* Browning, *Diary,* 1:591.

397 *"problem is solved":* Davis to Leonard Swett, Nov. 26, 1862, Davis MSS, ISHL.

397 *"proclamation of September 22":* CW, 5:462–463.

398 *"the Apprentice System":* T. J. Barnett to S. L. M. Barlow, Nov. 30, 1861, Barlow MSS, HEH.

398 *"and extermination":* CW, 2:240–241.

398 *"hope of earth":* CW, 5:537.

399 *"bad as all that":* Henry Villard, *Memoirs* (Boston: Houghton, Mifflin & Co., 1904), 1:389–391.

399 *"disgraceful termination":* Hollister, *Colfax,* p. 203.

399 *"the traitoress Mrs. Lincoln":* H. Finch to Zachariah Chandler, Sept. 10, 1862, Chandler MSS, LC.

399 *"a new administration":* George P. Morgan to W. H. Seward, Oct. 22, 1862, Seward MSS, UR.

399 *"shape of cabinet ministers":* Grimes to Lyman Trumbull, Oct. 6, 1862, Trumbull MSS, LC.

400 *"corner with the President":* Welles, *Diary,* 1:124, 136; 2:58.

400 *their legs on:* George Bemis, Diary, Nov. 15, 1862, Massachusetts Historical Society.

400 *"as critics only":* David Davis to Leonard Swett, Nov. 26, 1862, Davis MSS, ISHL.

400 *"United States Navy":* P. M. Zall, ed., *Abe Lincoln Laughing* (Berkeley: University of California Press, 1982), p. 78.

401 *"over-borne their patriotism":* Galloway to AL, Sept. 4, 1862, Lincoln MSS, LC.

401 *"Head to the War Dept.":* Montgomery Blair to Francis P. Blair, Jr., Sept. 17, 1862, Blair Family MSS, LC.

401 *"the Silurian era":* Hollister, *Colfax,* p. 200.

401 *"Uncle Abe's nose":* Ibid.

401 *"be immediately accepted":* W. H. Seward to AL, Dec. 18, 1862, Seward MSS, UR.

401 *"What does this mean?":* Frederick W. Seward, *Seward at Washington* (New York: Derby & Miller, 1891), p. 146.

401 *extraordinary caucus:* The fullest account of this caucus meeting is in Francis Fessenden, *Life and Public Services of William Pitt Fessenden* (Boston: Houghton, Mifflin & Co., 1907), 1:231–236, but there are further details in Browning's *Diary,* 1:596–598.

402 *"on my account":* Seward, *Seward at Washington,* p. 146.

402 *outcome of the Republican caucus:* Fessenden, *Fessenden,* 1:236–238, offers a full account of these meetings, and Browning's *Diary,* 1:598-599, adds details.

402 *"conclusions reached":* Chase to Chandler, Sept. 20, 1862, Chandler MSS, LC.

403 *"a ray of hope":* Browning, *Diary,* 1:600–601.

403 *"his usual urbanity":* Again the fullest account of this conference is in Fessenden, *Fessenden,* 1:240–243.

403 *read resolutions:* A copy of these resolutions, misdated 1864, is in the Lincoln MSS (#39732-34), LC.
403 *"around the Administration":* Nevins, *War for the Union,* 2:355; Hannibal Hamlin to Ellen Hamlin, Dec. 19, 1862, Hamlin MSS, microfilm, Columbia University.
404 *"a free talk":* Bates, *Diary,* p. 269.
404 *"sufficient consultation":* The fullest accounts of this meeting are in Fessenden, *Fessenden,* 1:243–248; Bates, *Diary,* pp. 269–270; and Welles, *Diary,* 1:196–198.
405 *"this subject now":* Welles, *Diary,* 1:201–202, gives a full account of this interview.
405 *"end of my bag!":* Seward, *Seward at Washington,* p. 148.
405 *"should not do that":* Browning, *Diary,* 1:604.
405 *"He lied":* Ibid., 1:603.
405 *"and their enemies":* Frederick J. Blue, *Salmon P. Chase: A Life in Politics* (Kent, Ohio: Kent State University Press, 1987), p. 193.
405 *"confidence and esteem":* Nicolay to Therena Bates, Dec. 23, 1862, Nicolay MSS, LC.
406 *"of Almighty God": CW,* 6:23–26. For Sumner's role, see Donald, *Sumner,* p. 97.
406 *"put it through":* Hay, *Diary,* pp. 111–112.
406 *"anyone could": Herndon's Lincoln,* 3:533.

CHAPTER FIFTEEN: WHAT WILL THE COUNTRY SAY!

T. Harry Williams, *Lincoln and His Generals* (New York: Alfred A. Knopf, 1952), offers a spirited account of Lincoln's unhappy efforts to identify able commanders. In vol. 2 of *Lincoln Finds a General: A Military Study of the Civil War* (New York: Macmillan Co., 1949), Kenneth P. Williams provides an expert analysis of Hooker's campaign. On antiwar movements in the North, Wood Gray, *The Hidden Civil War: The Story of the Copperheads* (New York: Viking Press, 1942) and Frank L. Klement, *The Copperheads in the Middle West* (Chicago: University of Chicago Press, 1960), offer conflicting interpretations.

407 *the reception line:* Patricia Carley Johnson, ed., "Sensitivity and Civil War: The Selected Diaries and Papers . . . of Frances Adeline [Fanny] Seward" (unpublished Ph.D. dissertation, University of Rochester, 1963), pp. 586–587; *New York Herald,* Jan. 3, 1863.
407 *"going to be done!":* Frederick W. Seward, *Seward at Washington as Senator and Secretary of State* (New York: Derby & Miller, 1891), p. 151.
408 *"and da[u]ntless courage": CW,* 6:39.
408 *mounting* "counter-raids": *CW,* 6:108.
408 *"so, ranks you": CW,* 6:138–139.
409 *"idiotically drunk":* Murat Halstead to Salmon P. Chase, Apr. 1, 1863, Lincoln MSS, LC.
409 *"in our ranks": CW,* 6:71.
409 *"particle of responsibility":* "Extracts from the Journal of Henry J. Raymond," *Scribner's Monthly* 19 (1879–1880): 424.
409 *"not be successful": CW,* 6:15.
409 *"very disheartening" inactivity:* William Marvel, *Burnside* (Chapel Hill: University of North Carolina Press, 1991), p. 208.
409 *"letting me know": CW,* 6:22.
410 *"for that policy": CW,* 6:32.
410 *"existing conditions":* Sandburg, 1:629.
410 *"and to myself": CW,* 6:31–32.
410 *"face of the enemy": CW,* 6:13.
410 *McClellan partisans:* Samuel E. Lyon to Salmon P. Chase, Jan. 6, 1863, Chase MSS.
411 *"driving you": CW,* 6:46.
411 *"you are right":* Marvel, *Burnside,* p. 215.
411 *"sooner the better":* "Extracts from the Journal of Henry J. Raymond," *Scribner's Monthly* 19 (1879–1880): 422.
412 *"Beware of rashness": CW,* 6:78–79.
412 *"in internal commerce": CW,* 5:125–126.
412 *caused minor ripples:* Jay Monaghan, *Diplomat in Carpet Slippers: Abraham Lincoln Deals with*

Foreign Affairs (Indianapolis: Bobbs-Merrill Co., 1945), offers a spirited account of these and other personalities.

413 *captured the* Peterhoff: For a careful examination of the *Peterhoff* affair, see J. G. Randall, *Lincoln the President: Midstream* (New York: Dodd, Mead & Co., l952), pp. 334–338.

414 *"drive Lincoln into it"*: Daniel B. Carroll, *Henri Mercier and the American Civil War* (Princeton, N.J.: Princeton University Press, 1971), pp. 251–257; Hiram Barney to Salmon P. Chase, Jan. 16, 1863, Chase MSS; Donald, *Sumner,* p. 103.

414 *"urge on the war"*: *Chicago Tribune,* Feb. 18, 1863.

415 *"steadiness of purpose"*: *New York Herald,* Mar. 28, 1863.

415 *"in any country"*: *CW,* 6:63–65.

415 *"of human bondage"*: *CW,* 6:88–89.

415 *"and civilized nations"*: *CW,* 6:176.

416 *"to their rulers"*: *The American Annual Cyclopaedia and Register of Important Events of the Year 1863* (New York: D. Appleton & Co., 1871), p. 233.

416 *"all future generations"*: *New York Herald,* Jan. 9, 1863.

416 *"an informal, practical recognition"*: *American Annual Cyclopaedia . . . 1863,* pp. 265–268.

417 *"loss of blood"*: Samuel Augustus Pleasants, *Fernando Wood of New York* (New York: Columbia University Press, 1948), pp. 139–140.

417 *"anti-slavery crusade!"*: B. S. A. McClellan to Elihu B. Washburne, Jan. 13, 1863, Washburne MSS, LC.

417 *"to their level"*: Thomas Ewing, Sr., to W. H. Seward, Jan. 13, 1863, Seward MSS, UR.

418 *"blood and race"*: *CW,* 5:534–536.

418 *"cessation of hostilities"*: San Francisco *Daily Alta California,* Mar. 3, 1863.

418 *"the North itself"*: *New York Herald,* Mar. 5, 1863.

418 *"the revolted States"*: McClernand to AL, Feb. 14, 1863, Lincoln MSS, LC.

418 *without legislative authorization:* On Illinois, see Arthur Charles Cole, *The Era of the Civil War, 1848–1870* (Springfield: Illinois Centennial Commission, 1919), pp. 298–300; on Indiana, Kenneth M. Stampp, *Indiana Politics During the Civil War* (Indianapolis: Indiana Historical Bureau, 1949), chap. 8.

419 *"man I know of"*: Sandburg, 2:244.

419 *"a thousand ways"*: *CW,* 6:87.

419 *to the Republican party:* Wood Gray, *The Hidden Civil War: The Story of the Copperheads* (New York: Viking Press, 1942), gives considerable credence to these reports of conspiracies. Frank L. Klement, *The Copperheads in the Middle West* (Chicago: University of Chicago Press, 1960), argues more convincingly that they were largely political protests.

419 *"our military chances"*: Sumner to Francis Lieber, Jan. 17, 1863, Sumner MSS, Houghton Library, Harvard.

419 *"for the enemy"*: *American Annual Cyclopaedia . . . 1863,* p. 473.

420 *duration of the war: Official Records of the Union and Confederate Armies,* ser. 2, vol. 5, pp. 633–646; Frank L. Klement, *The Limits of Dissent: Clement L. Vallandigham and the Civil War* (Lexington: University Press of Kentucky, 1970), chap. 11.

420 *"kind assurance of support"*: The quotation is from Burnside to AL, May 8, 1863, Lincoln MSS, LC. Lincoln's letter has not been found.

420 *"part of Burnside"*: Welles, *Diary,* 1:306.

420 *such military tribunals:* David Davis, statement to WHH, Sept. 19, 1866, HWC.

420 *"little as possible": Official Records,* ser. 2, vol. 5, pp. 664–665. Halleck told Burnside he had just come from a conference with the President, and "No objections were made to your action in this matter. . . ."

421 *"in bloody anarchy"*: *New York Herald,* May 19, 26, June 2, 1863.

421 *than its publication:* Robert S. Harper, *Lincoln and the Press* (New York: McGraw-Hill Book Co., 1951), pp. 258–261.

421 *and military despotism:* Stewart Mitchell, *Horatio Seymour of New York* (Cambridge, Mass.: Harvard University Press, 1938), p. 293.

421 *cunning for wisdom:* Bates, *Diary,* pp. 290–291.

422 *"new organization for 1864"*: Abraham Oakey Hall to William H. Seward, Jan. 21, 1863, Seward MSS, UR.

422 *"unfortunate" and "pernicious"*: Browning, *Diary,* 1:612–613.

422 *"has ever known"*: Strong, *Diary,* p. 292.

422 *"Union and Government"*: Weed to AL, Feb. 1, 1863, Lincoln MSS, LC.

422 *joining the Democrats:* Hamlin to Ellen Hamlin, Jan. 25, 1863, Hamlin MSS, microfilm. Columbia University.

422 *"all the patriotism"*: Mitchell, *Seymour,* pp. 276–277.

422 *"their constitutional powers"*: *CW,* 6:145–146.

423 *"our next President"*: Thurlow Weed Barnes, *Memoir of Thurlow Weed* (Boston: Houghton, Mifflin & Co., 1884), p. 428; Mitchell, *Seymour,* pp. 273–274.

423 *"to destroy himself"*: Gray, *The Hidden Civil War,* p. 130.

424 *a conquered province: American Annual Cyclopaedia . . . 1863,* p. 309.

424 *National Banking Act:* For Lincoln's public and private exertions in behalf of the banking act, see G. S. Boritt, *Lincoln and the Economics of the American Dream* (Memphis: Memphis State University Press, 1978), pp. 200–202.

424 *Department of Agriculture:* For careful studies of this nonmilitary legislation, see Leonard P. Curry, *Blueprint for Modern America: Nonmilitary Legislation of the First Civil War Congress* (Nashville: Vanderbilt University Press, 1968), and Heather Cox Richardson, "Constructing 'the Greatest Nation of the Earth': Economic Policies of the Republican Party During the American Civil War" (unpublished Ph.D. dissertation, Harvard University, 1992).

424 *"if they deserve it"*: James Ford Rhodes, *History of the United States from the Compromise of 1850* (New York: Macmillan Co., 1907), 4:241n.

425 *"get along yet"*: T. Harry Williams, *Lincoln and the Radicals* (Madison: University of Wisconsin Press, 1941), pp. 280–281.

425 *"ray of hope left"*: E. B. Ward to B. F. Wade, Feb. 7, 1863, Wade MSS, LC.

425 *"of James Buchanan"*: Asa Mahan to Zachariah Chandler, Mar. 3, 1863, Chandler MSS, LC.

425 *"a traitor* out *and* out": Chandler to Letitia Chandler, Feb. 7, 1863, Chandler MSS, LC.

425 *declined to sign it:* For White's campaign against Seward, see White's unsigned memorial to AL, Jan. [12] 1863, William Butler MSS, Chicago Historical Society; White to Benjamin F. Wade, Dec. 27, 1862, Wade MSS, LC; White to Simon Cameron, Jan. 11, 1863, Cameron MSS, LC; Lyman Trumbull to William Butler, Jan. 11, 1863, Butler MSS; Donald, *Sumner,* pp. 103–105.

425 *removal of Seward: New York Tribune,* Jan. 19, 1863.

426 *"stand by the President"*: Hamlin to Ellen Hamlin, Jan. 11, 1863, Hamlin MSS, microfilm, Columbia University; Charles E. Hamlin, *The Life and Times of Hannibal Hamlin* (Cambridge, Mass.: Riverside Press, 1899), pp. 452–453.

426 *"almost dictatorial powers"*: J. F. Ankeny to E. B. Washburne, Feb. 3, 1863, Washburne MSS, LC.

426 *"be no serious opposition"*: Giddings to Salmon P. Chase, Jan. 13, 1863, Chase MSS.

426 *"and really republican"*: Salmon P. Chase to Benjamin F. Butler, Dec. 14, 1862, Chase MSS.

426 *was "growing feeble"*: Benjamin Brown French, *Witness to the Young Republic* (Hanover, N.H.: University Press of New England, 1989), pp. 416–417.

426 *"tells a joke now"*: Madeleine Vinton Dahlgren, *Memoir of John A. Dahlgren* (Boston: James R. Osgood & Co., 1882), p. 387.

426 *"as I have been"*: Moncure Daniel Conway, *Autobiography: Memories and Experiences* (Boston: Houghton, Mifflin & Co., 1904), 1:379.

427 *"of these anniversaries"*: Turner, *Mary Todd Lincoln,* p. 147.

427 *"sometimes with him"*: The evidence on Mary Lincoln and spiritualism is admirably summarized in Baker, *Mary Todd Lincoln,* pp. 217–222.

427 *her guests mechanically:* For a sympathetic account of Mrs. Lincoln during these years, see Randall, *Mary Lincoln,* esp. chap. 25.

427 *three-foot-four-inch guest:* San Francisco *Daily Alta California,* Mar. 18, 1863.

428 *"fore feet up"*: Leonard Swett to "My Dear Boy," Feb. 23, 1863, David Davis MSS, ISHL.

428 *now mostly slept:* This paragraph draws on the full, sympathetic account of Tad in Ruth Painter Randall, *Lincoln's Sons* (Boston: Little, Brown & Co., 1955), esp. pp. 137–138.

428 *"better than he had"*: Virginia Woodbury Fox, Diary, Apr. 29, 1863, Levi Woodbury MSS, LC.

429 *"was laughing at"*: Hay, *Diary,* p. 179.

429 *"a great man"*: Ibid., p. 91.

429 *"everything seem wrong"*: Conway, *Autobiography,* 1:379.

429 *use: African-Americans:* On Lincoln's decision to raise African-American troops, Dudley Taylor Cornish, *The Sable Arm: Negro Troops in the Union Army, 1861–1865* (New York: Longmans, Green & Co., 1956), is authoritative. Except where otherwise identified, all quotations in the following pages come from this book.

430 *"time has come"*: Hamlin, *Hannibal Hamlin,* pp. 431–432.
430 *"it, if practicable"*: *CW,* 6:56.
430 *"of all sorts"*: *CW,* 6:30.
430 *citizens of the United States:* For cancellation of contracts to colonize blacks, see *New York Herald,* Mar. 17, 1863, and *CW,* 6:41, 178–179.
431 *"be employed elsewhere"*: *CW,* 6:56.
431 *"rebellion at once"*: *CW,* 6:149–150.
431 *often worked creakingly:* The definitive study of Lincoln's interest in technology and of his efforts to introduce new armaments is Robert V. Bruce, *Lincoln and the Tools of War* (Indianapolis: Bobbs-Merrill Co., l956), on which I have drawn heavily in the following pages.
431 *"to Mr. Capen"*: *CW,* 6:190–191.
431 *down land patents:* William O. Stoddard, *Inside the White House in War Times* (New York: Charles L. Webster & Co., 1892), pp. 39–40.
432 *"none anywhere else"*: Dahlgren, *John A. Dahlgren,* p. 390.
433 *"as our hospitality"*: Joseph Hooker to AL, Apr. 3, 1863, Lincoln MSS, LC.
433 *"intelligent looking woman"*: Charles N. Walker and Rosemary Walker, eds., "Diary of the War of Robt. S. Robertson," *Old Fort News* 28 (Apr.–June 1965): 89–90.
433 *billowing behind him:* For Noah Brooks's spirited, detailed account of Lincoln's visit to the army, see P. J. Staudenraus, ed., *Mr. Lincoln's Washington* (New York: Thomas Yoseloff, 1967), pp. 147–164.
433 *"inspire much admiration"*: Walker and Walker, "Diary of the War of Robt. S. Robertson," p. 90.
434 *"in sp[l]endid condition"*: *New York Herald,* Apr. 11, 1863.
434 *"prepared for the worst"*: *Chicago Tribune,* June 1, 1863.
434 *"he is over-confident"*: Noah Brooks, *Washington in Lincoln's Time* (New York: Century Co., 1895), p. 52.
434 *"to the main object"*: *CW,* 6:164–165.
434 *"all of your men"*: Robert Underwood Johnson and Clarence Clough Buel, eds., *Battles and Leaders of the Civil War* (New York: Century Co., 1890), 3:155.
434 *"of intuitive sagacity"*: Welles, *Diary,* 1:265.
434 *"not a repulse"*: *New York Herald,* Apr. 19, 1863.
435 *"complaints of you"*: *CW,* 6:186.
435 *"where is Stoneman?"*: *CW,* 6:197.
435 *"to get facts"*: Welles, *Diary,* 1:291.
436 *"the country say!"*: Brooks, *Washington in Lincoln's Time,* pp. 57–58.

CHAPTER SIXTEEN: A NEW BIRTH OF FREEDOM

Garry Wills, *Lincoln at Gettysburg: The Words that Remade America* (New York: Simon & Schuster, 1992), is a brilliant study of the rhetoric and ideas of the Gettysburg Address. There is also useful information in William E. Barton, *Lincoln at Gettysburg: What He Intended to Say; What He Said; What He Was Reported to Have Said; What He Wished He Had Said* (Indianapolis: Bobbs-Merrill Co., 1930), and in Louis A. Warren, *Lincoln's Gettysburg Declaration: "A New Birth of Freedom"* (Fort Wayne, Ind.: Lincoln National Life Foundation, 1964).

437 *"smash the crockery"*: *New York Herald,* June 4, 1863.
437 *"prolong the war"*: E. M. Stanton to L. C. Turner, Sept. 19, 1863, Stanton MSS, LC.
437 *"die for it"*: *Chicago Tribune,* June 11, 1863.
438 *"act of the war"*: George Meade, *The Life and Letters of George Gordon Meade* (New York: Charles Scribner's Sons, 1913), 1:372.
438 *"with the situation"*: *Day by Day,* 3:183; *Chicago Tribune,* May 11, 1863.
438 *"cool, clear and satisfied"*: Virginia Woodbury Fox, Diary, May 7, 1863, Levi Woodbury MSS, LC.
438 *"army [was] unshaken"*: *New York Tribune,* May 9, 1863.
438 *"General Hooker twice"*: *New York Herald,* June 1, 1863.
438 *"the recent one"*: *CW,* 6:201.
438 *"kick the other"*: *CW,* 6:249.
439 *"true objective point"*: *CW,* 6:257.
439 *"as I may be"*: *CW,* 6:201, 281.

439 *"he is an expert"*: Welles, *Diary,* 1:364.
439 *"General-in-Chief"*: Ibid., 1:320.
439 *"Commanding the Army"*: *CW,* 6:628.
440 *"as regards myself"*: Welles, *Diary,* 1:333.
440 *"lose his chance"*: Ibid., 1:344.
440 *"try it again"*: Freeman Cleaves, *Meade of Gettysburg* (Norman: University of Oklahoma Press, 1960), p. 119.
440 *"to obey them"*: *CW,* 6:282.
441 *"strengthening the government"*: Browning, *Diary,* 1:631.
441 *"the government overthrown"*: Browning, *Diary,* 1:630.
441 *"and institutions rest"*: Welles, *Diary,* 1:322.
441 *"the whole world"*: Robert Garth Scott, ed., *Fallen Leaves: The Civil War Letters of Major Henry Livermore Abbott* (Kent, Ohio: Kent State University Press, 1991), p. 216.
441 *in a drawer:* Sandburg, 2:308.
442 *"and Federal Constitutions"*: *The American Annual Cyclopaedia and Register of Important Events of the Year 1863* (New York: D. Appleton & Co., 1871), 799–800.
442 *"into their notions"*: T. J. Barnett to Samuel L. M. Barlow, May 18, 1863, Barlow MSS, HEH.
442 *to the subject:* Sandburg, 2:308.
442 *"a strong paper"*: Welles, *Diary,* 1:323.
443 *"his healthful life"*: *CW,* 6:260–269.
443 *than a "Despot"*: T. J. Barnett to Samuel L. M. Barlow, June 10, 1863, Barlow MSS, HEH.
443 *"the whole land"*: John W. Forney to AL, June 14, 1863, Lincoln MSS, LC.
443 *"best state Papers"*: E. D. Morgan to AL, June 15, 1863, Lincoln MSS, LC.
443 *"than a victory"*: William A. Hall to AL, June 15, 1863, Lincoln MSS, LC.
443 *"in this state"*: Roscoe Conkling to AL, June 16, 1863, Lincoln MSS, LC.
444 *"they richly merit"*: David Tod to AL, June 14, 1863, Lincoln MSS, LC.
444 *"provided and supported"*: *CW,* 6:300–306.
445 *"a family doctor"*: Scott, *Fallen Leaves,* p. 189.
445 *"thing from Grant?"*: *CW,* 6:210, 233.
445 *"brilliant in the world"*: *CW,* 6:230.
446 *"Johnston against Grant"*: *CW,* 6:236.
446 *" 'Tad's' pistol away"*: *CW,* 6:256, 10:187.
446 *"and expressive mouth"*: Silas W. Burt, "Lincoln on His Own Story-Telling," *Century Magazine* 73 (Feb. 1907): 501.
446 *"with profoundest gratitude"*: *CW,* 6:314.
446 *"it is great!"*: Welles, *Diary,* 1:364.
446 *"whipped them myself"*: *CW,* 6:329.
447 *"go to waste"*: Nicolay and Hay, 7:278–279; *CW,* 6:318.
447 *"because of it"*: *CW,* 6:327–328.
447 *"an active pursuit"*: Meade, *Meade,* 2:132, 311–312.
447 *"a true man"*: *CW,* 6:341.
447 *"didn't sack Phil-del"*: *CW,* 10:194.
448 *"by her fall"*: *CW,* 6:314. See also Randall, *Mary Lincoln,* pp. 324–325; Katherine Helm, *The True Story of Mary, Wife of Lincoln* (New York: Harper & Brothers, 1928), p. 250.
448 *"he was not"*: Welles, *Diary,* 1:370.
448 *"can conveniently handle"*: Sandburg, 2:368.
449 *"of poor 'Nanny' "*: *CW,* 6:371–372.
449 *"I do not"*: Chase, *Diary,* p. 192.
449 *"are not mentioned"*: Bates, *Diary,* p. 302.
449 *"known to all"*: Gideon Welles to My Dear Sir, Aug. 23, 1863, Welles MSS, HEH.
449 *"end of the war"*: T. J. Barnett to Samuel L. M. Barlow, July 27, 1863, Barlow MSS, HEH.
449 *"is no cavil"*: Hay, *Diary,* p. 76.
450 *"glaringly unjust"*: *CW,* 6:370.
450 *called "a sockdolager"*: Hay, *Diary,* p. 78.
450 *a test in the courts:* *CW,* 6:369–370.
450 *"not lose time"*: *CW,* 6:391.
451 *"the utmost fidelity"*: *CW,* 6:444–449. I believe that the editors of *The Collected Works of Abraham Lincoln* erred in assigning the tentative date of September 14 to this manuscript, thinking that it was related to the proclamation of that date suspending the writ of habeas

corpus. Lincoln's argument deals less with habeas corpus than with the constitutionality and fairness of the conscription act. The date, August 15, 1863, tentatively assigned the document by Nicolay and Hay seems more plausible.

451 *problems in Missouri:* Affairs in Missouri were so complex that only a brief summary can be attempted here. For a thoughtful modern account of Missouri problems, see William E. Gienapp, "Abraham Lincoln and the Border States," *Journal of the Abraham Lincoln Association* 13 (1992): 13–46. Michael Fellman, *Inside War: The Guerrilla Conflict in Missouri During the American Civil War* (New York: Oxford University Press, 1989), is a richly detailed study.

451 *"for political influence":* CW, 6:36.

451 *"his secret sympathies":* CW, 6:20, 33–34.

452 *"by my authority":* CW, 7:86.

452 *"a great deal more":* CW, 6:516.

452 *"are set Zionwards":* Hay, *Diary,* pp. 108, 135.

452 *"so mean to do":* CW, 6:178.

453 *"to your reason":* CW, 6:218.

453 *"praised by the other":* CW, 6:234.

453 *"of a polecat":* Joseph Medill to AL, Oct. 3, 1863, Lincoln MSS, LC.

453 *"make Missouri free":* Browning, *Diary,* 1:611–612.

453 *"of immediate emancipation":* New York Herald, June 12, 1863.

453 *"vested interest therein":* Hay, *Diary,* p. 73.

453 *"pettifogging, piddling politician":* William E. Parrish, *Turbulent Partnership: Missouri and the Union, 1861–1865* (Columbia: University of Missouri Press, 1963), p. 160.

453 *"wagon or not":* Nicolay and Hay, 8:214.

454 *"what to forbear":* CW, 6:499–504.

454 "friends in Missouri": Edward Bates to AL, Oct. 22, 1863, Lincoln MSS, LC.

454 *"plowed round them":* Chicago Tribune, Oct. 30, 1863.

454 *"inspire the South":* T. J. Barnett to Samuel L. M. Barlow, Sept. 14, 1863, Barlow MSS, HEH.

454 *defeat of the Democrats:* William B. Hesseltine, *Lincoln and the War Governors* (New York: Alfred A. Knopf, 1948), pp. 319–339, offers a full account of these elections.

455 *"of President Lincoln":* S. P. Chase to Jay Cooke, Sept. 4, 1863, Chase MSS.

455 *"he was chosen":* Welles, *Diary,* 1:470.

455 *"prosecution of this war":* Nicolay and Hay, 7:378.

456 *"their old bearings":* Hay, *Diary,* p. 77.

456 *the Davis government:* For details on these abortive negotiations, see Welles, *Diary,* 1:358–363.

456 *"commenced in Illinois":* Conkling to AL, Aug. 21, 1863, Lincoln MSS, LC.

456 *"it very slowly":* CW, 6:414.

457 *"thanks to all":* CW, 6:406–410.

457 *"with the greatest enthusiasm":* James C. Conkling to AL, Sept. 4, 1863, Lincoln MSS, LC.

457 *"an historic document":* Wilson to AL, Sept. 3, 1863; Sumner to Lincoln, Sept. 7, 1863, Lincoln MSS, LC.

457 *"honest Abraham Lincoln":* New York Times, Sept. 7, 1863.

457 *"God bless Old Abe!":* Chicago Tribune, Sept. 3, 1863.

457 *"before it comes":* Hay, *Diary,* p. 92.

457 *"hit on the head":* Ibid., p. 106.

458 *"in five days":* Chase, *Diary,* pp. 201–203.

458 *"beyond all hopes":* James W. Grimes to AL, Oct. 14, 1863; James M. Scovel to AL, Oct. 11, 1863; Salmon P. Chase to AL, Oct. 14, 1863, all in Lincoln MSS, LC.

458 *"against the Democracy":* W. H. Hurlbut to Samuel L. M. Barlow, Sept. 11, 1863, Barlow MSS, HEH.

458 *"our wonderful majority":* Israel Washburn to AL, Sept. 15, 1863, Lincoln MSS, LC.

459 *"honesty, have won":* Chicago Tribune, Nov. 3, 1863.

459 *"numerous cousins":* CW, 6:537.

459 *"worthy of the occasion":* CW, 6:319–320.

460 "conditions of Peace": Greeley to John G. Nicolay, June 14, 1863, Lincoln MSS, LC.

460 *"will be crushed":* Forbes to AL, Sept. 8, 1863, Lincoln MSS, LC.

460 *"a few appropriate remarks":* David Wills to AL, Nov. 2, 1863, Lincoln MSS, LC.

460 *for this reason:* Frank L. Klement, "Ward H. Lamon and the Dedication of the Soldiers' Cemetery at Gettysburg," *Civil War History* 31 (Dec. 1985): 293–308.

460 *on November 19:* Of the many studies of the Gettysburg Address, Wills, *Lincoln at Gettysburg,*

is by far the best; it largely supersedes William E. Barton, *Lincoln at Gettysburg* (Indianapolis: Bobbs-Merrill Co., 1930). Louis A. Warren, *Lincoln's Gettysburg Declaration: "A New Birth of Freedom"* (Fort Wayne, Ind.: Lincoln National Life Foundation, 1964), contains much valuable information. Also useful is F. Lauriston Bullard, *"A Few Appropriate Remarks": Lincoln's Gettysburg Address* (Harrogate, Tenn.: Lincoln Memorial University, 1944). Philip B. Kunhardt, Jr., *A New Birth of Freedom: Lincoln at Gettysburg* (Boston: Little, Brown & Co., 1983), is an excellent pictorial history.

461 *"here be dedicated":* David C. Mearns and Lloyd A. Dunlap, eds., *Long Remembered: Facsimiles of the Five Versions of the Gettysburg Address in the Handwriting of Abraham Lincoln* (Washington, D.C.: Library of Congress, 1963), reproduces all the known copies in Lincoln's own hand. Except where otherwise identified, all quotations in the following pages are taken from what is known as the Bliss copy, which represents Lincoln's final revision of the address.

461 *half of his address:* John G. Nicolay, "Lincoln's Gettysburg Address," *Century Magazine* 47 (Feb. 1894): 597.

461 *write it all out:* There has been an immense amount of inconsequential controversy over just when and where Lincoln wrote the Gettysburg Address—at the White House, on the train going to the ceremonies, on the night before the dedication at Wills's house, on the morning of the ceremony. Compare the interminable and inconclusive discussions of this topic with the almost total neglect of significant questions like why Lincoln accepted this invitation and what he hoped to accomplish with his speech.

461 *"all the people":* Barton, *Lincoln at Gettysburg,* pp. 132, 135. Wills, *Lincoln at Gettysburg,* pp. 105–120, shows similarities between Parker and Lincoln, not just in words but in ideas— especially in ideas about the Declaration of Independence.

461 *an hourglass form:* James Hurt, "All the Living and the Dead: Lincoln's Imagery," *American Literature* 52 (Nov. 1980): 351–380, offers an insightful analysis of the form and imagery of the Gettysburg Address.

461 *Everett would say:* Noah Brooks's recollection (*Washington in Lincoln's Time* [New York: Century Co., 1895], p. 285) that Lincoln had advance proofs of Everett's speech on November 15 is unreliable. Everett's address was not set in type until the late afternoon of November 14, and it would have been impossible for the President to have a copy the next day. David C. Mearns, "Unknown at This Address," in Allan Nevins, ed., *Lincoln and the Gettysburg Address* (Urbana: University of Illinois Press, 1964), pp. 122–124.

462 *used five times:* James M. McPherson, *Abraham Lincoln and the Second American Revolution* (New York: Oxford University Press, 1990), p. viii.

462 *"obstetric analogies": New York World,* Nov. 27, 1863.

462 *power of the Declaration:* Wills, *Lincoln at Gettysburg,* has most ably made this point.

462 *272 words:* The word count of the Gettysburg Address depends on which of Lincoln's autograph versions is used, whether hyphenated words are counted as one or two, and whether the title, the date, and, in some cases, Lincoln's signature are counted. The present count is from the Bliss copy.

463 "bury the dead": James G. Smart, ed., *A Radical View: The "Agate" Dispatches of Whitelaw Reid* (Memphis: Memphis State University Press, 1976), 2:151–152. The witticism was also credited to Thaddeus Stevens.

463 *black manservant: CW,* 10:210–211.

463 *"beauty and goodness":* Allen Thorndike Rice, ed., *Reminiscences of Abraham Lincoln* (New York: North American Review, 1888), p. 511.

463 *"nothing at all": CW,* 7:17.

463 *of Lincoln's "pasquinades":* J. W. Schulte Nordholt, "The Civil War Letters of the Dutch Ambassador," *JISHS* 54 (Winter 1961): 366–367.

463 *"the human race":* George E. Baker, ed., *The Works of William H. Seward* (Boston: Houghton, Mifflin & Co., 1884), 5:490.

463 *morning of the nineteenth:* Frank L. Klement, "'These Honored Dead': David Wills and the Soldiers' Cemetery at Gettysburg," *LH* 74 (Fall 1972): 123–135, offers an excellent, detailed account of the dedication ceremonies.

464 *"was an oration":* Hay, *Diary,* p. 121.

464 *"as happens generally":* Edward Everett, Diary, Nov. 19, 1863, Everett MSS, Massachusetts Historical Society.

464 *"his masterly effort":* Benjamin Brown French, *Witness to the Young Republic,* ed. Donald B. Cole and John J. McDonough (Hanover, N.H.: University Press of New England, 1989), p. 435.

465 *interrupted by applause:* For a collection of twenty-nine diverse and contradictory firsthand accounts, see Barton, *Lincoln at Gettysburg,* chap. 21. There has been an enormous amount of pen-swinging on these subjects, none of which has the slightest historical significance.

465 *"speech won't scour!":* Ward Hill Lamon, *Recollections of Abraham Lincoln, 1847–1865,* ed. Dorothy Lamon Teillard (Washington, D.C.: 1911), p. 173. Lamon's detailed account of the Gettysburg ceremonies (pp. 169–179) is highly unreliable, but the quoted sentence does sound like Lincoln.

465 *"as was ever spoken":* For newspaper reactions, see Barton, *Lincoln at Gettysburg,* chap. 16; *LL,* no. 1284 (Nov. 16, 1953); Warren, *Lincoln's Gettysburg Declaration,* pp. 145–146.

465 *"known as the Constitution":* New York *World,* Nov. 27, 1863.

466 *" 'are created equal' ":* Herbert Mitgang, ed., *Abraham Lincoln: A Press Portrait* (Chicago: Quadrangle Books, 1971), pp. 359–361.

CHAPTER SEVENTEEN: THE GREATEST QUESTION EVER PRESENTED TO PRACTICAL STATESMANSHIP

The best account of Lincoln's reconstruction policy is Herman Belz's *Reconstructing the Union* (Ithaca, N.Y.: Cornell University Press, 1969), but there is good material in two older studies: Charles H. McCarthy's *Lincoln's Plan of Reconstruction* (New York: McClure, Phillips & Co., 1901), and William B. Hesseltine, *Lincoln's Plan of Reconstruction* (Tuscaloosa, Ala.: Confederate Publishing Co., 1960). On Lincoln's campaign for renomination, I have relied heavily on William Frank Zornow, *Lincoln and the Party Divided* (Norman: University of Oklahoma Press, 1954). Excellent, but sometimes conflicting, accounts of reconstruction in Louisiana are Peyton McCrary, *Abraham Lincoln and Reconstruction: The Louisiana Experiment* (Princeton, N.J.: Princeton University Press, 1978); LaWanda Cox, *Lincoln and Black Freedom: A Study in Presidential Leadership* (Columbia: University of South Carolina Press, 1981); and Ted Tunnell, *Crucible of Reconstruction: War, Radicalism and Race in Louisiana, 1862–1867* (Baton Rouge: Louisiana State University Press, 1984).

467 *"practical statesmanship":* Hay, *Diary,* p. 73.

468 *"vast absorbent powers":* Ibid., p. 134.

468 *"be carried out on a chip":* John G. Nicolay, Diary, Dec. 6, 1863, Nicolay MSS, LC.

468 *"not trustworthy":* Welles, *Diary,* 1:481.

469 *"government in the war":* CW, 6:555.

469 *Radicals and Conservatives:* Hay, *Diary,* pp. 123–124, 131.

470 *"whites, and freedmen":* Charles Sumner, *Works* (Boston: Lee & Shepard, 1880), 7:493–546, esp. 541.

470 *"policy of the President":* Montgomery Blair, *Speech . . . on the Revolutionary Schemes of the Ultra Abolitionists (Oct. 3, 1863).*

470 *"feel the public pulse":* T. J. Barnett to S. L. M. Barlow, Oct. 6, 1863, Barlow MSS, HEH.

470 *"Sumner's heresies":* James Dixon to Montgomery Blair, Oct. 7, 1863, Lincoln MSS, LC.

470 *"a Copperhead orator":* Thaddeus Stevens to S. P. Chase, Oct. 8, 1863, Chase MSS.

471 *"the loyal minority":* Hay, *Diary,* pp. 112–113.

471 *"a new life":* CW, 7:40.

471 *"retreated from it":* Chicago *Tribune,* Jan. 17, 1864; Christopher N. Breiseth, "Lincoln and Frederick Douglass," *JISHS* 68 (Feb. 1975): 9–26; Dorothy Wickenden, "Lincoln and Douglass: Dismantling the Peculiar Institution," *Wilson Quarterly* 14 (Autumn 1990): 102–112.

471 *"as to slaves":* CW, 7:53–56.

472 *"in any other way":* CW, 7:50–52.

472 *"revolutionary struggle":* CW, 5:49.

472 *"we are now passing":* CW, 6:411.

472 *something for everybody:* Belz, *Reconstructing the Union,* pp. 155–165, offers an able analysis of the message.

473 *"the Supreme Court":* CW, 7:54, 56.

473 *"factions of the Republican party":* New York *World,* Dec. 11, 1863.

473 *"millennium had come":* Hay, *Diary,* pp. 131–132.

473 *"his country's shame":* Jonathan T. Dorris, *Pardon and Amnesty Under Lincoln and Johnson* (Chapel Hill: University of North Carolina Press, 1953), p. 43.

474 *"of Senator Sumner"*: *New York Tribune*, Dec. 10, 1863; *New York Herald*, Dec. 11, 1863.

474 *"territorial project"*: John Hay, Diary, Dec. 10, 1863, photostat, Massachusetts Historical Society; Virginia Jeans Laas, ed., *Wartime Washington: The Civil War Letters of Elizabeth Blair Lee* (Urbana: University of Illinois Press, 1991), p. 325.

474 *"at the right time"*: E. Delafield Smith to AL, Dec. 10, 1863; Thad S. Seybold to AL, Dec. 10, 1863; R. H. McCurdy to AL, Dec. 10, 1863; William Dennison to AL, Dec. 10, 1863—all in Lincoln MSS, LC.

474 *"[Republican] convention meets"*: *Chicago Tribune*, Dec. 14, 1863; Medill to Joseph K. C. Forrest, Dec. 17, 1863, Lincoln MSS, LC.

474 *"anything about it"*: Hay, *Diary*, p. 112.

474 *"schooled to the task"*: *CW*, 8:326.

475 *"decline, if tendered"*: *CW*, 6:540.

475 *"desire—of course"*: George T. Brown to Lyman Trumbull, Nov. 12, 1863, Trumbull MSS, LC.

475 *"in the matter"*: Katherine Helm, *The True Story of Mary, Wife of Lincoln* (New York: Harper & Brothers, 1928), pp. 230–231.

475 *"I can't give him!"*: *Chicago Tribune*, Jan. 9, 1864; San Francisco *Daily Alta California*, Jan. 3, 1864; Agnes Macdonnell, "America Then and Now: Recollections of Lincoln," *Contemporary Review* 3 (1917): 567–568; William A. Croffut, "Lincoln's Washington," *Atlantic Monthly* 145 (Jan. 1930): 63.

476 *"devil of stubbornness"*: Helen Nicolay, *Lincoln's Secretary* (New York: Longmans, Green & Co., 1949), pp. 191–192.

476 *"my other friends"*: Donald, *Sumner*, pp. 167–169.

476 *"shielded the rebels"*: *Reasons Against the Re-Nomination of Abraham Lincoln. Adopted February 15, 1864, by a Republican Meeting at Davenport, Iowa*, pamphlet, HEH.

477 *"of the nation"*: Arthur C. Cole, "President Lincoln and the Illinois Radical Republicans," *Mississippi Valley Historical Review* 4 (Mar. 1918): 432.

477 *"friend to you"*: Zornow, p. 19.

478 *"reelection of Mr. Lincoln"*: Hay, *Diary*, p. 99.

478 *"affections of the masses"*: *Chicago Tribune*, Dec. 30, 1863.

478 *"should you desire it"*: Albert Smith to AL, Dec. 12, 1863, Lincoln MSS, LC.

478 *"to the Presidential chair"*: James Clay Rice to Henry Wilson, Nov. 11, 1863, Lincoln MSS, LC.

478 *"[Republican] National Convention"*: George Bergner to AL, Jan. 14, 1864, Lincoln MSS, LC.

478 *"a ratification meeting"*: Zornow, p. 46.

478 *"to its purpose"*: Hay, *Diary*, p. 152. John Niven, *Salmon P. Chase: A Biography* (New York: Oxford University Press, 1995), is a richly detailed life. Donnal V. Smith, *Chase and Civil War Politics* (Columbus, Ohio: F. J. Heer Printing Co, 1931), is indispensable.

479 *"forever of slavery"*: Welles, *Diary*, 1:410.

479 *of "colored loyalists"*: Chase to Thomas J. Durant, Nov. 19, 1863, Chase MSS; Chase to AL, Apr. 12, 1865, Lincoln MSS, LC.

480 *"head of the Treasury Department"*: Hay, *Diary*, p. 101.

480 *"spot he can find"*: Ibid., p. 110.

480 *"upon the Government"*: Leon Burr Richardson, *William E. Chandler: Republican* (New York: Dodd, Mead & Co., 1940), pp. 43–44; Harry J. Carman and Reinhard H. Luthin, *Lincoln and the Patronage* (New York: Columbia University Press, 1943), p. 235.

480 *"kept my promise"*: Erwin S. Bradley, *Simon Cameron: Lincoln's Secretary of War* (Philadelphia: University of Pennsylvania Press, 1966), pp. 237–238; Hay, *Diary*, pp. 152–153.

481 *"not a party"*: Philadelphia Union League, *Abraham Lincoln*, [1864], pamphlet, Widener Library, Harvard University.

481 *"his pre-eminent fitness"*: For this statement, and for other resolutions by Union Leagues, I am indebted to a careful memorandum prepared by Gerald Prokopowicz.

481 *urging Lincoln's reelection*: New England Loyal Publication Society, Broadside No. 158.

481 *"spirit of the age"*: For the text of this pamphlet and astute commentary on the Chase campaign, see Charles R. Wilson, "The Original Chase Organization Meeting and *The Next Presidential Election*," *Mississippi Valley Historical Review* 23 (June 1936): 61–79.

481 *"and abusive pamphlet"*: Lamon to AL, Feb. 6, 1864, Lincoln MSS, LC.

482 *"had better quit"*: Wilson, "Original Chase Organization Meeting," pp. 64–65.

482 *"other available candidate"*: S. C. Pomeroy, printed circular letter, Washington, D.C., Feb. 1864, Lincoln MSS, LC.

482 *"your entire confidence"*: *CW,* 7:200–201.
482 *the "treasury rats"*: John G. Nicolay to John Hay, Feb. 17, 1864, Nicolay MSS, LC.
482 *"inquire for more"*: *CW,* 7:212–213.
482 *"wish to bear"*: Helen Nicolay, *Lincoln's Secretary,* pp. 188–189.
483 *Indiana Republican convention:* John D. Defrees to WHH, Aug. 21, 1866, HWC.
483 *"every honorable mind"*: *Congressional Globe,* 38 Cong., 1 sess., Appendix, p. 51.
483 *"be safely landed"*: *New York Herald,* Mar. 12, 1864.
483 *"present Chase again"*: Willard L. King, *Lincoln's Manager: David Davis* (Cambridge, Mass.: Harvard University Press, 1960), pp. 215–216.
484 *"citizens of New York"*: *New York World,* Dec. 11, 1863.
484 *Kentucky, and Wisconsin:* Hesseltine, *Lincoln's Plan of Reconstruction,* p. 99.
484 *"fix the rest"*: *CW,* 7:155.
484 *"some worthy gentlemen"*: *CW,* 7:126.
485 *"right side up"*: *CW,* 5:345.
485 *"the people possible"*: *CW,* 5:505, 462.
485 *"disgusting and outrageous"*: *CW,* 5:504.
485 *"of the matter"*: *CW,* 6:364–365.
486 *"you are master"*: *CW,* 7:89–90.
486 *"the eastern States"*: Banks to AL, Dec. 6, 1863, Lincoln MSS, LC.
486 "inoperative and void": Banks to AL, Dec. 30, 1863, Lincoln MSS, LC.
486 *"or against it"*: Ibid.
487 *"has ever seen"*: Banks to AL, Feb. 25, 1864, Lincoln MSS, LC.
487 *"only [as] a suggestion"*: *CW,* 7:243.
487 *"a military officer"*: Belz, *Reconstructing the Union,* p. 192.
488 "cannot stand Radicalism": Cuthbert Bullitt to O. H. Browning, Feb. 25, 1864, Lincoln MSS, LC.
488 *"Secretary of the Treasury"*: Belz, *Reconstructing the Union,* pp. 195–196, 199.
489 *his "leg cases"*: Richard N. Current, *The Lincoln Nobody Knows* (New York: McGraw-Hill Book Co., 1958), pp. 165–166.
489 *throughout the country:* Chase, *Diary,* pp. 192–196.
489 *"on the public works"*: *CW,* 6:357.
489 *"or hang them"*: Mary Mann to E. A. Hitchcock, Nov. 18, 1863, Hitchcock MSS, LC.
489 *"act for revenge"*: J. G. Randall, *Constitutional Problems Under Lincoln* (rev. ed.; Urbana: University of Illinois Press, 1951), pp. xvi–xvii.
489 *raid against Richmond:* James Rodney Wood, Civil War Memoir, Maud Wood Park MSS, LC; Joseph George, Jr., " 'Black Flag Warfare': Lincoln and the Raids Against Richmond and Jefferson Davis," *Pennsylvania Magazine of History and Biography* 115 (July 1991): 292–318; William A. Tidwell et al., *Come Retribution: The Confederate Secret Service and the Assassination of Lincoln* (Jackson: University Press of Mississippi, 1988), pp. 242–247. For the orders allegedly found on Dahlgren's body, see Frank Moore, *The Rebellion Record* (New York: D. Van Nostrand, 1865), 8:387–388.
490 *Army of the Potomac:* Allan Nevins, ed., *A Diary of Battle: The Personal Journals of Colonel Charles S. Wainwright, 1861–1865* (New York: Harcourt, Brace & World, 1962), p. 308.
490 *"if he fails"*: *CW,* 6:518.
490 *"are pressing him"*: *CW,* 6:354.
490 *"it's objective point"*: *CW,* 6:467.
490 *"would catch him?"*: John G. Nicolay, Diary, Dec. 7, 1863, Nicolay MSS, LC.
491 *"gnawing at Grant"*: Ida M. Tarbell, *The Life of Abraham Lincoln* (New York: Doubleday, Page & Co., 1909), 2:187–189. For a thorough evaluation of Grant's position on the nomination, see John Y. Simon, ed., *The Papers of Ulysses S. Grant* (Carbondale: Southern Illinois University Press, 1982), 9:541–544.
491 *of George Washington:* Winfield Scott had held the rank of brevet lieutenant general.
491 *return to the President:* Bruce Catton, *Grant Takes Command* (Boston: Little, Brown & Co., 1969), pp. 124–126; Nicolay, *Lincoln's Secretary,* pp. 194–196; *New York Herald,* Mar. 12, 1864.
491 *"will sustain you"*: *CW,* 7:234.
492 *"for the succession"*: Dennison to AL, Mar. 12, 1864, Lincoln MSS, LC.

CHAPTER EIGHTEEN: IT WAS NOT BEST TO SWAP HORSES

William F. Zornow, *Lincoln and the Party Divided* (Norman: University of Oklahoma Press, 1954), has long been the standard account of the political campaign of 1864. David E. Long, *The Jewel of Liberty: Abraham Lincoln's Re-Election and the End of Slavery* (Mechanicsburg, Pa.: Stackpole Books, 1994), appeared too late for me to consult it in writing this chapter. T. Harry Williams, *Lincoln and His Generals* (New York: Alfred A. Knopf, 1952), is excellent on Lincoln's relations with Grant. *Why the South Lost the Civil War,* by Richard E. Beringer et al. (Athens, Ga.: University of Georgia Press, 1986), offers a fresh view of Grant's strategy. On Lincoln's growing conflict with Congress over reconstruction, Herman Belz, *Reconstructing the Union: Theory and Practice During the Civil War* (Ithaca, N.Y.: Cornell University Press, 1969), is indispensable. I have greatly profited by the opportunity to read draft chapters of Michael Vorenberg's dissertation on "The Thirteenth Amendment and the Politics of Emancipation," which is being prepared at Harvard University.

493 *"the re-election of Mr. Lincoln":* Zornow, p. 55.
493 *"foregone conclusion":* James G. Blaine to Hannibal Hamlin, Mar. 8, 1864, Hamlin MSS, microfilm, Columbia University.
493 *"people overwhelmingly":* Thompson Campbell to E. B. Washburne, Mar. 8, 1864, Washburne MSS, LC.
494 *"on the surface":* Lyman Trumbull to H. G. McPike, Feb. 6, 1864, Trumbull MSS, LC.
494 *"goes for Lincoln":* A. Denny to John Sherman, Mar. 16, 1864, Sherman MSS, LC; E. F. Drake to John Sherman, Mar. 17, 1864, Sherman MSS, LC.
494 *"to change them":* "National Convention—Postponement Requested," broadside, Mar. 25, 1864, Lincoln MSS, LC.
494 *"traits of character":* Joseph Medill to E. B. Washburne, Apr. 12, 1864, Washburne MSS, LC.
494 *"for the office":* E. D. Webster to W. H. Seward, Mar. 14, 1864, Seward MSS, UR.
494 *"Mr. C's claim":* R. M. W. Taylor to John Sherman, Mar. 18, 1864, Sherman MSS, LC.
494 *"to the Other":* J. V. Denny to John Sherman, Mar. 20, 1864, Sherman MSS, LC.
494 *meeting in Baltimore:* The best biography, Allan Nevins, *Frémont: Pathmarker of the West* (New York: Longmans, Green & Co., 1955), stresses that Frémont himself was "sincerely indifferent to any movement" to nominate him (p. 568). See also Andrew Rolle's interesting psychological portrait, *John Charles Frémont: Character as Destiny* (Norman: University of Oklahoma Press, 1991).
495 *"months after his inauguration":* Louis T. Merrill, "General Benjamin F. Butler in the Presidential Campaign of 1864," *Mississippi Valley Historical Review* 33 (Mar. 1947): 550. It cannot be shown that Lincoln authorized Cameron to approach Butler, but there is ample evidence that Cameron did so and that he reported Butler's response to the President.
495 *"tipping him out":* Benjamin F. Butler, *Butler's Book* (Boston: A. M. Thayer & Co., 1892), p. 635.
495 *Lincoln backed down:* James N. Adams, "Lincoln and Hiram Barney," *JISHS* 50 (Winter 1957): 370–373.
495 *"will be questioned":* Thurlow Weed to David Davis, Mar. 24, 1864, Davis MSS, ISHL.
495 *"to say no":* E. D. Morgan to Thurlow Weed, Mar. 27, 1864, Weed MSS, UR.
495 *"for my opinions":* Thurlow Weed to David Davis, Mar. 29, 1864, Davis MSS, ISHL.
496 *"disheartened and disappointed":* John G. Nicolay to AL, Mar. 30, 1864, Lincoln MSS, LC.
496 *"Blood and Treasure":* Glyndon G. Van Deusen, *Thurlow Weed: Wizard of the Lobby* (Boston: Little, Brown & Co., 1947), p. 307.
496 *"opposed to Lincoln":* Francis P. Blair, Jr., to Montgomery Blair, Apr. 26, 1864, Blair MSS, LC.
496 *"a compromise candidate":* *Congressional Globe,* 38 Cong., 1 sess. (Apr. 23, 1864), p. 1832.
496 *"return to the field":* CW, 7:319–320.
496 *"be set right":* Segal, *Conversations,* pp. 310–316.
497 *"men and dogs":* Albert G. Riddle, *Recollections of War Times* (New York: G. P. Putnam's Sons, 1895), p. 266.
497 *"or telegrapher":* CW, 6:350.
497 *"he has got":* Williams, *Lincoln and His Generals,* p. 272.
497 *"as he pleases":* Bruce Catton, *Grant Takes Command* (Boston: Little, Brown & Co., 1969), pp. 138–139.
498 *"rendering such assistance":* Ulysses S. Grant, *Personal Memoirs* (New York: Charles L. Webster & Co., 1886), 2:122.

498 *"restraints upon you"*: CW, 7:324.

498 *"ground of either"*: Official Records of the Union and Confederate Armies, ser. 1, vol. 34, p. 19.

498 *"lines to Richmond"*: Ibid., vol. 33, p. 394.

499 *"of East Tennessee"*: Ibid., p. 395.

499 *"superiority in numbers"*: Hay, *Diary,* p. 178.

499 *"somebody else does"*: Grant, *Memoirs,* 2:142–143.

499 *in Grant's campaign:* Ludwell H. Johnson, *Red River Campaign: Politics and Cotton in the Civil War* (Baltimore: Johns Hopkins University Press, 1958), offers a devastating account of Banks's expedition.

500 *"sickening with anxiety"*: Strong, *Diary,* p. 442.

500 *"no turning back"*: Carl Sandburg, *Abraham Lincoln: The War Years* (New York: Harcourt, Brace & Co., 1939), 3:44.

500 *"by favorable news"*: CW, 7:333.

500 *"to our Maker"*: CW, 7:334.

500 *14,000 casualties:* On numbers and casualties I have followed the figures given in Thomas L. Livermore, *Numbers & Losses in the Civil War in America, 1861–65* (Bloomington: Indiana University Press, 1957), and in Robert Underwood Johnson and Clarence C. Buel, eds., *Battles and Leaders of the Civil War* (New York: Century Co., 1884–1888), vol. 4.

500 *"ever to end!"*: Allen Thorndike Rice, ed., *Reminiscences of Abraham Lincoln* (New York: North American Review, 1888), p. 337.

500 *"care, and anxiety"*: Carpenter, *Six Months,* pp. 30–31.

501 *"takes all summer"*: John Y. Simon, ed., *The Papers of Ulysses S. Grant* (Carbondale: Southern Illinois University Press, 1982), 10:422.

501 *"Grant that wins"*: Hay, *Diary,* p. 180.

501 *"shake him off"*: Carpenter, *Six Months,* p. 283.

501 *"in our cause"*: Robert S. Harper, *Lincoln and the Press* (New York: McGraw-Hill Book Co., 1951), pp. 290–291. In addition to Harper's excellent account, see the stories and editorials in the *New York World,* May 24, 1864.

501 *"by military force"*: CW, 7:348.

502 *"head shot off!"*: Segal, *Conversations,* p. 318.

502 *"for his re election"*: Clark E. Carr to J. G. Nicolay, Mar. 14, 1864, Lincoln MSS, LC.

502 *unanimous for the President:* Harry J. Carman and Reinhard H. Luthin, *Lincoln and the Patronage* (New York: Columbia University Press, 1943), pp. 245–259, offers a good account of these and other state conventions.

502 *"conduct of the war"*: Edward McPherson, *The Political History of the United States of America During the Great Rebellion* (Washington, D.C.: Solomons & Chapman, 1876), p. 410.

503 *Frémont for President:* Full accounts of the convention proceedings appeared in the *New York World,* May 31 and June 3, 1864, and in many other newspapers.

503 *"most magnificent fizzle"*: S. Newton Pettis to AL, May 31, 1864, Lincoln MSS, LC.

503 *"controlling no votes"*: *New York Times,* June 3, 1864.

503 *"affair every way"*: Hay, *Diary,* p. 184.

503 *"four hundred men"*: Nicolay and Hay, 9:40–41. The quotation is from I Samuel 22:2.

503 *"won't swindle me"*: Hay, *Diary,* 185.

504 *"a very good man"*: Noah Brooks, "Two War-Time Conventions," *Century Magazine* 49 (Mar. 1895): 723.

504 *"pap-journalists, expectants"*: Adam Gurowski, *Diary: 1863–'64–'65* (Washington, D.C.: W. H. & O. H. Morrison, 1866), p. 249.

504 *"was at Chicago"*: John G. Nicolay to John Hay, June 6, 1864, Nicolay MSS, LC.

504 *"decent town meeting"*: James G. Smart, ed., *A Radical View: The "Agate" Dispatches of Whitelaw Reid, 1861–1865* (Memphis: Memphis State University Press, 1976), 2:164.

504 *"slavery in the United States"*: *Proceedings of the First Three Republican National Conventions of 1856, 1860 and 1864* (Minneapolis: Charles W. Johnson, 1893), p. 177. For Lincoln's role, see James A. Rawley, "Lincoln and Governor Morgan," *ALQ* 6 (Mar. 1951): 296–297.

504 *"you one foot"*: *Proceedings of the First Three Republican National Conventions,* p. 180.

504 *"and the Union"*: Ibid., p. 196.

504 *"not even interesting"*: David Davis to AL, June 2, 1864, Lincoln MSS, LC.

505 *action of the convention:* John G. Nicolay to John Hay, June 5, 1864, Lincoln MSS, LC.

505 *amendment abolishing slavery: Proceedings of the First Three Republican National Conventions,* pp. 225–226.

505 *"malignants and malcontents":* Hugh J. Hastings to F. W. Seward, June 8, 1864, Seward MSS, UR.

505 *"judge for itself":* *CW,* 7:376.

505 *"enthusiasm about it":* Smart, *A Radical View,* 2:170.

506 *balanced and inconclusive:* McClure told his story in *Abraham Lincoln and Men of War-Times* (4th ed.; Philadelphia: Times Publishing Co., 1892), pp. 115–130, and published his evidence in an appendix, "The Nicolay-McClure Controversy," pp. 457–481. The Hannibal Hamlin MSS (microfilm, Columbia University) contain a large body of material that Hamlin's grandson collected, and Nicolay defended his case in a supplement to Charles E. Hamlin, *The Life and Times of Hannibal Hamlin* (Cambridge, Mass.: Riverside Press, 1899), pp. 591–615. The charge against Sumner is skeptically reviewed in Donald, *Sumner,* pp. 169–173.

506 *endorsed his reconstruction program:* Robert L. Morris, "The Lincoln-Johnson Plan for Reconstruction and the Republican Convention of 1864," *LH* 71 (Spring 1969): 33–40.

506 *own vice presidential nominee:* This is also the conclusion of James F. Glonek, "Lincoln, Johnson, and the Baltimore Ticket," *ALQ* 6 (Mar. 1951): 255–271, the best review of the evidence. H. Draper Hunt, *Hannibal Hamlin of Maine* (Syracuse: Syracuse University Press, 1969), pp. 176–189, reaches the opposite conclusion.

506 *"called the Platform":* *CW,* 7:380.

507 *" 'when crossing streams' ":* *CW,* 7:384.

507 *word to Chase:* Chase, *Diary,* p. 224.

508 *"of open revolt":* *CW,* 7:412–413.

508 *submitted his resignation:* *CW,* 7:414.

508 *"I will go":* Hay, *Diary,* p. 199.

508 *"the public service":* *CW,* 7:419.

508 *"fitness of selection":* Chase, *Diary,* pp. 223–224.

508 *"alone this time":* Segal, *Conversations,* pp. 330–331.

508 *"than a post":* *New York Herald,* July 4, 1864.

509 *a financial crisis:* Francis Fessenden, *Life and Public Services of William Pitt Fessenden* (Boston: Houghton, Mifflin & Co., 1907), 1:315–323.

509 *"by your associates":* Ibid., 1:323.

509 *"have such wishes":* *CW,* 7:423.

509 *critical of the President:* Belz, *Reconstructing the Union,* chap. 8, offers an admirable history of the Wade-Davis bill, which I have followed closely. Quotations not otherwise identified are drawn from Belz's account.

510 *"out of place":* Henry Winter Davis to Samuel F. Du Pont, July 7 or 8, 1864, Du Pont MSS, Hagley Museum, Eleutherian Mills Historical Library, Wilmington, Del.

510 *"to prevent it":* Chase, *Diary,* pp. 232–233.

511 *"fixed within myself":* John Hay's detailed account of Lincoln's failure to sign the Wade-Davis bill is in Hay, *Diary,* pp. 205–206. The inference that Lincoln was angry is my own.

511 *decided to do so:* *CW,* 7:433–434.

512 *"I had designed":* Catton, *Grant Takes Command,* pp. 276–277.

513 *"confines of Richmond":* See the good summary of press opinion in James Ford Rhodes, *History of the United States from the Compromise of 1850* (New York: Macmillan Co., 1907), 4:465–466.

513 *"of human blood":* Horace Greeley to AL, July 7, 1864, Lincoln MSS, LC.

513 *"life is dreadful":* Isaac N. Arnold, *The Life of Abraham Lincoln* (3rd ed.; Chicago: Jansen, McClurg & Co., 1885), p. 375.

513 *"butchering business lately":* *CW,* 7:111.

514 *"all about me?":* Louis A. Warren, *Lincoln's Youth: Indiana Years, Seven to Twenty-one* (New York: Appleton-Century-Crofts, 1959), p. 225.

514 *"a technical Christian":* WHH, interview with Mary Todd Lincoln, Sept. 5, 1866, HWC.

514 *"and better man":* Joshua F. Speed, *Reminiscences of Abraham Lincoln and Notes of a Visit to California* (Louisville, Ky.: John P. Morton & Co., 1884), pp. 32–33.

514 *"given to man":* *CW,* 7:542.

514 *some Higher Power:* William J. Wolf, *The Almost Chosen People: A Study of the Religion of Abraham Lincoln* (Garden City, N.Y.: Doubleday & Co., 1959), is the best study of Lincoln's religious views. There is some good material in Edgar DeWitt Jones, *Lincoln and the Preachers* (New York: Harper & Brothers, 1948). Especially valuable is the chapter "God's Man," in *Lincoln the President: Last Full Measure* (New York: Dodd, Mead & Co., 1955), by J. G. Randall and Richard N. Current.

514 *"can claim it"*: CW, 7:281–282.
515 *"mortal could stay"*: CW, 7:535.
515 *"in the field"*: CW, 7:332, 334, 384.
515 *"seventy-five thousand men?"*: Rhodes, *History of the United States*, 4:467.
515 *"head of an army"*: Randall, *Mary Lincoln*, p. 253.
515 *"[off] right away"*: Catton, *Grant Takes Command*, p. 305.
516 *"bloodshed as possible"*: Horace Porter, *Campaigning with Grant* (New York: Century Co., 1897), pp. 216–223. Porter's unfortunate attempts to recapture African-American dialect have been silently corrected.
516 *"strengthened him mentally"*: Welles, *Diary*, 2:58.
516 *"I will go in"*: Browning, *Diary*, 1:673.
516 *"in that region"*: Bates, *Diary*, p. 378.

CHAPTER NINETEEN: I AM PRETTY SURE-FOOTED

John H. Cramer, *Lincoln Under Enemy Fire* (Baton Rouge: Louisiana State University Press, 1948), collects most of the evidence on Lincoln's activities during Early's raid. Edward C. Kirkland, *The Peacemakers of 1864* (New York: Macmillan Co., 1927), remains the most comprehensive account of the Greeley, Gilmore-Jaquess, and Raymond efforts to secure peace. Joel H. Silbey, *A Respectable Minority: The Democratic Party in the Civil War Era, 1860–1868* (New York: W. W. Norton & Co., 1977), offers a masterful interpretation of Lincoln's opponents in 1864. See also Christopher Dell, *Lincoln and the War Democrats: The Grand Erosion of Conservative Tradition* (Rutherford, N.J.: Fairleigh Dickinson University Press, 1975). T. Harry Williams, *Lincoln and the Radicals* (Madison: University of Wisconsin Press, 1941), gives a full account of Radical plans to unhorse Lincoln.

517 *"wilted down"*: E. A. Hitchcock to Mary Mann, July 14, 1864, Hitchcock MSS, LC.
518 Seeming *"almost crushed"*: Ibid.
518 *"not an order"*: CW, 7:437.
519 *"very conspicuous figure"*: Asa Townsend Abbott, Diary, Sept. 7, 1916, Abbott MSS, LC. See also Abbott's letter to "Editor Tribune," June 22 [no year], in the same collection.
519 *head knocked off*: Hay, *Diary*, p. 209.
519 *"in his hand"*: Cramer, *Lincoln Under Enemy Fire*, p. 64.
519 *"standing upon it"*: Ibid., pp. 30–31. The story that Oliver Wendell Holmes, Jr., shouted "Get down, you fool!" at the President cannot be authenticated. See Frederick C. Hicks, "Lincoln, Wright, and Holmes at Fort Stevens," JISHS 39 (Sept. 1946): 323–332.
519 *"some of them"*: Hay, *Diary*, p. 210.
519 *"all escaped"*: Browning, *Diary*, 1:676.
519 *"the past week"*: John Y. Simon, ed., *The Papers of Ulysses S. Grant* (Carbondale: Southern Illinois University Press, 1984), 11:230.
520 *"military administration"*: *Philadelphia Evening Bulletin*, quoted in Washington *National Intelligencer*, July 20, 1864.
520 *"force it"*: CW, 7:476.
520 *"about your case"*: Hagar J. Weston to AL, July 10, 1864, Lincoln MSS, LC.
520 *"blind impetuosity"*: Bates, *Diary*, p. 393.
520 *"to stab him"*: CW, 7:462–463.
521 *"be more apparant"*: CW, 7:483.
521 *"poltroons and cowards"*: Welles, *Diary*, 2:84.
521 *"to the country"*: CW, 7:439–440.
521 *"anxious for Peace"*: Lincoln had all of his and Greeley's correspondence on the Niagara peace negotiations printed, and, unless otherwise identified, all quotations in the following paragraphs are from the copy in the Lincoln MSS, LC. The originals of these letters are also in Lincoln's papers.
521 *presidential election*: See the excellent account of the Confederate mission in Larry E. Nelson, *Bullets, Ballots, and Rhetoric: Confederate Policy for the United States Presidential Contest of 1864* (University: University of Alabama Press, 1980).
522 *only Seward*: Fessenden, who interrupted a conversation between Lincoln and Seward, also knew of the negotiations.
522 *"struggled for"*: CW, 8:1–2.

523 *"we* will *have":* Edmund Kirke [James R. Gilmore], "Our Visit to Richmond," *Atlantic Monthly* 14 (Sept. 1864): 379.

523 *"coming Presidential campaign":* New York Herald, July 26, 1864.

523 *"black race":* New York World, July 22 and 24, 1864.

524 *"earnest men":* S. P. Chase to William C. Noyes, July 11, 1864, Chase MSS.

524 *"carry it out":* William Lawrence, *Life of Amos A. Lawrence* (Boston: Houghton, Mifflin & Co., 1888), p. 195.

524 *"Father Abraham":* Unidentified clipping, enclosed in Thurlow Weed to W. H. Seward, Aug. 10, 1864, Seward MSS, UR.

524 *"continuing it":* James W. Grimes to C. H. Ray, Aug. 3, 1864, Ray MSS, HEH.

524 *"make the laws":* New York Tribune, Aug. 5, 1864.

524 *"daze the President":* New York World, Aug. 9, 1864.

524 *"he was exalted":* New York Herald, Aug. 6, 1864.

524 *"befall a man":* Noah Brooks, *Washington in Lincoln's Time* (New York: Century Co., 1896), p. 170.

525 *" 'if they can' ":* Carpenter, *Six Months,* p. 145.

525 *"patriotic men":* S. P. Chase to George Opdyke, Aug. 19, 1864, Chase MSS.

525 *"the true outlines":* Charles Sumner to Francis Lieber, Aug. 19, 1864, Sumner MSS, Houghton Library, Harvard University. The expression "blue lights" dates from the War of 1812, when it was claimed that disloyal New England Federalists used blue lights to warn British ships of nearby American frigates.

525 *"unofficial governors":* Strong, *Diary,* p. 473.

525 *"if necessary":* Henry Greenleaf Pearson, *The Life of John A. Andrew* (Boston: Houghton, Mifflin & Co., 1904), 2:159.

525 *"new candidates":* Henry Winter Davis to Zachariah Chandler, Aug. 24, 1864, Chandler MSS, LC.

526 *"closed out the rebellion":* John Eaton, *Grant, Lincoln and the Freedmen* (New York: Longmans, Green & Co., 1907), pp. 186–191.

526 *"to stand upon":* CW, 7:501.

526 *"let him try me":* Ibid., 7:499–501.

526 *"both these conditions":* New York Times, Aug. 18, 1864.

527 *"come what will":* CW, 7:506–507.

527 *"serious damage":* Christopher N. Breiseth, "Lincoln and Frederick Douglass: Another Debate," *JISHS* 68 (Feb. 1975): 19–20.

527 *a broad range:* Allan G. Bogue, *The Congressman's Civil War* (Cambridge: Cambridge University Press, 1989), pp. 132–141, provides an informed view of the nature and significance of Republican factionalism.

527 *"give up the slaves":* Richard Lowitt, *A Merchant Prince of the Nineteenth Century: William E. Dodge* (New York: Columbia University Press, 1954), pp. 222–223.

528 *"a competent leader":* Browning, *Diary,* 1:676.

528 *"he is a failure":* Maurice G. Baxter, *Orville H. Browning: Lincoln's Friend and Critic* (Bloomington: Indiana University Press, 1957), p. 158.

528 *"an impossibility":* Thurlow Weed to F. W. Seward, Aug. 26, 1864, Seward MSS, UR.

528 *"Slavery be abandoned":* Thurlow Weed to W. H. Seward, Aug. 22, 1864, Lincoln MSS, LC.

528 *"probable candidate":* Abram Wakeman to AL, Aug. 12, 1864, Lincoln MSS, LC.

528 *of the Union:* Weed's editorial, "The Wade and Davis Letter," in *Albany Evening Journal,* enclosed in Ira Harris to AL, Aug. 15, 1864, Lincoln MSS, LC.

529 *"from the start":* James Kelly to W. H. Seward, Aug. 12, 1864, Lincoln MSS, LC.

529 *"Port of New York":* Charles Jones to AL, Aug. 21, 1864, Lincoln MSS, LC.

529 *"hostile hands":* Henry J. Raymond to AL, Aug. 22, 1864, Lincoln MSS, LC.

529 "badly beaten": Jessie Ames Marshall, ed., *Private and Official Correspondence of Gen. Benjamin F. Butler* (Norwood, Mass.: Plimpton Press, 1917), 5:35.

529 *"save it afterwards":* CW, 7:514.

529 *"up the Union":* CW, 8:149–150.

530 *"own conscience":* Hay, *Diary,* p. 238.

530 *"which they do":* Noah Brooks, "Two War-Time Conventions," *Century Magazine* 49 (Mar. 1896): 732.

530 *"of the States":* Edward McPherson, *The Political History of the United States of America During the Great Rebellion* (3rd ed.; Washington, D.C.: Solomons & Chapman, 1876), pp. 419–420.

530 *defeat in the election:* Joel H. Silbey, *A Respectable Minority: The Democratic Party in the Civil*

War Era, 1860–1868 (New York: W. W. Norton & Co., 1977), chap. 5, offers a thoughtful analysis of the dynamics of the Democratic convention.

530 *"wet blanket"*: Daniel Devlin to S. L. M. Barlow, Sept. 1, 1864, Barlow MSS, HEH.

530 *"universally condemned"*: William Gray to George B. McClellan, Sept. 1, 1864, McClellan MSS, LC.

530 *"their candidate"*: George T. Curtis to George B. McClellan, Sept. 1, 1864, McClellan MSS, LC.

530 *"had been in vain"*: McPherson, *Political History,* p. 421.

530 *"twaddle and humbug"*: T. J. Barnett to S. L. M. Barlow, n.d. [c. Oct. 1, 1864], Barlow MSS, HEH.

530 *"and fairly won"*: Sherman's telegram was sent on September 3 but was not received in Washington until the next day.

531 *"capture . . . of Atlanta"*: *CW,* 7:533.

531 "in the party": Donald, *Sumner,* pp. 187–189.

531 *"run Mr. Lincoln"*: Much of the correspondence leading to this meeting was published in the *New York Sun,* June 30, 1889. See also the full account of the discussions in Francis Lieber to Charles Sumner, Aug. 31, 1864, Lieber MSS, HEH.

531 *"remains the candidate"*: Pearson, *Andrew,* 2:162–163.

531 *"highest degree"*: Richard Yates to Horace Greeley et al., Sept. 6, 1864, Andrew MSS, Massachusetts Historical Society.

531 *"and re-elected"*: James T. Lewis to Horace Greeley et al., Sept. 7, 1864, Lincoln MSS, LC.

532 *"on Monday last"*: Thurlow Weed to W. H. Seward, Sept. 10, 1864, Lincoln MSS, LC.

532 *"to American history"*: Theodore Tilton to John G. Nicolay, Sept. 6, 1864, Lincoln MSS, LC.

532 *Lincoln by name:* L. E. Chittenden to AL, Oct. 6, 1864, Lincoln MSS, LC.

532 *"fruitful victory"*: Henry J. Raymond to AL, Aug. 22, 1864, Lincoln MSS, LC.

532 *"utter ruination"*: Helen Nicolay, *Lincoln's Secretary: A Biography of John G. Nicolay* (New York: Longmans, Green & Co., 1949), p. 212.

532 *"peaceful modes"*: *CW,* 7:517.

532 *"in advance"*: Nicolay and Hay, 9:221.

532 *"arduous duty"*: John G. Nicolay to Therena Bates, Sept. 4, 1864, Nicolay MSS, LC.

533 *"nothing else"*: James N. Adams, "Lincoln and Hiram Barney," *JISHS* 50 (Winter 1957): 375.

533 *"departments yesterday"*: Harry J. Carman and Reinhard H. Luthin, *Lincoln and the Patronage* (New York: Columbia University Press, 1943), p. 280.

533 *Zachariah Chandler:* The only biography is still the Detroit Post and Tribune's *Zachariah Chandler* (Detroit: Post and Tribune Co., 1880). Chandler's letters describing his mission are published in Winfred A. Harbison, ed., "Zachariah Chandler's Part in the Re-election of Abraham Lincoln," *Mississippi Valley Historical Review* 22 (Sept. 1935): 267–276.

533 *"Traitor McLelland"*: Zachariah Chandler to Letitia Chandler, Sept. 2, 1864, Chandler MSS, LC.

533 *"placed him there"*: Alphonso Taft to B. F. Wade, Sept. 8, 1864, Wade MSS, LC. See also Hans L. Trefousse, *Benjamin Franklin Wade: Radical Republican from Ohio* (New York: Twayne Publishers, 1963), pp. 227–229.

533 *"to his prospects"*: Henry Winter Davis to Samuel F. Du Pont, Sept. 28 or 29, 1864, in John D. Hayes, ed., *Samuel Francis Du Pont: A Selection from His Civil War Letters* (Ithaca, N.Y.: Cornell University Press, 1969), 3:393–394.

534 *"have his confidence"*: Harbison, "Zachariah Chandler's Part," p. 271.

534 *"take refuge anywhere"*: Hayes, *Du Pont,* 3:393.

534 *"administered the Dept."*: Francis P. Blair, Sr., to Montgomery Blair, Monday [Sept. 1864], Blair MSS, LC.

534 *"false ones"*: Ibid. For a sharply critical view of Blair, see Allan Nevins, *The War for the Union,* vol. 4, *The Organized War to Victory, 1864–1865* (New York: Charles Scribner's Sons, 1971), pp. 94–95, 104–105.

534 "but came": Harbison, "Zachariah Chandler's Part," p. 273.

535 *from the cabinet:* There has been much controversy over the alleged "bargain," in which Lincoln agreed to dismiss Blair from the cabinet if Frémont withdrew from the presidential race. Charles R. Wilson, "New Light on the Lincoln-Blair-Frémont 'Bargain' of 1864," *American Historical Review* 42 (Oct. 1936): 71–78, argues that there was no bargain, because Lincoln had already decided to drop Blair and Frémont withdrew because his campaign was foundering and his approach for an alliance with the Democrats was rejected. Allan Nevins, *Frémont: Pathmarker of the West* (New York: Longmans, Green & Co., 1955), p. 580, contends that Frémont "rejected a bargain as dishonorable." Andrew Rolle, *John Charles Frémont: Character as Destiny* (Norman: University of Oklahoma Press, 1991), p. 232, says that Frémont did not

personally demand the removal of Blair and "played no central part in this procedure." The best evidence, then, is that Lincoln did consent to a bargain, negotiated by Chandler, trading the removal of Blair for the support of Wade and Davis; that, again at Chandler's urging, he agreed to propose a bargain to Frémont; and that Frémont did not accept it but withdrew for other reasons.

535 *"be reappointed"*: Nevins, *Frémont,* pp. 579–580. These letters prove that Frémont did not feel "insulted" by the offer of a bargain and that he did not reject it out of hand.

535 *"in reputation"*: Harold A. Schofield, "The New Nation and Its Editor," *LH* 76 (Winter 1974): 206.

535 *"appear tomorrow"*: Hayes, *Du Pont,* 3:394.

535 *"financially a failure"*: McPherson, *Political History,* pp. 426–427.

535 *"support Lincoln"*: Hayes, *Du Pont,* 3:394.

535 *"pure, and dignified"*: David Davis to AL, Oct. 4, 1864, Lincoln MSS, LC.

535 *"dutifully and manfully"*: Salmon P. Chase to Charles F. Schmidt, Aug. 12, 1864, Chase MSS.

535 *"we would wish"*: Salmon P. Chase to Richard C. Parsons, Sept. 14, 1864, Chase MSS.

536 *"not know him"*: Chase, *Diary,* p. 254.

536 *"my active support"*: Salmon P. Chase to George S. Denison, Sept. 20, 1864, Chase MSS.

536 *the next Chief Justice:* David M. Silver, *Lincoln's Supreme Court* (Urbana: University of Illinois Press, 1956), chaps. 15–16, offers a full account of the controversies over naming Taney's successor. See also the careful review of all the evidence in Charles Fairman, *Reconstruction and Reunion, 1864–88* (New York: The Macmillan Co., 1971), chap. 2.

536 *"of my life"*: Edward Bates to AL, Oct. 13, 1864, Lincoln MSS, LC.

536 *"from your Cabinet"*: Francis P. Blair, Sr., to AL, Oct. 20, 1864, Blair MSS, LC.

536 *"his other recommendations"*: Nicolay and Hay, 9:391–392.

536 *"expect great things"*: Salmon P. Chase to Charles Sumner, Oct. 19, 1864, Lincoln MSS, LC.

537 *"of the nation"*: New York Herald, Aug. 23, 1864.

537 *"judgment of history?"*: Chase, *Diary,* p. 253.

537 *"the people's business"*: Emanuel Hertz, *Abraham Lincoln: A New Portrait* (New York: Horace Liveright, 1931), 2:941.

537 *"but the negro"*: Frank Freidel, ed., *Union Pamphlets of the Civil War, 1861–1865* (Cambridge, Mass.: Harvard University Press, 1967), 2:981, 988.

537 *"on the patent"*: CW, 7:508.

537 *"incompetency, and corruption"*: James Ford Rhodes, *History of the United States from the Compromise of 1850* (New York: Macmillan Co., 1907), 4:531.

537 *in St. Louis:* Turner, *Mary Todd Lincoln,* p. 180.

538 *"know was right"*: Ward Hill Lamon, *Recollections of Abraham Lincoln, 1847–1865,* ed. Dorothy Lamon Teillard (Washington, D.C.: 1911), pp. 145–149. For further comment on this matter, see Randall, *Lincoln the President,* 4:247–249.

538 *"anything to say"*: CW, 7:398.

538 *"a free Government"*: CW, 7:505.

538 *"any thing else"*: Gil Troy, *See How They Ran: The Changing Role of the Presidential Candidate* (New York: Free Press, 1991), p. 69.

538 *after the election:* For advice that Lincoln received on Pennsylvania politics, see Thomas Fitzgerald to AL, Sept. 28, 1864; Fitzgerald to John G. Nicolay, Sept. 29, 1864; William D. Kelley to AL, Sept. 30, 1864—all in Lincoln MSS, LC. Curtin's words appear in Joseph C. McKibbin to Samuel L. M. Barlow, Oct. 1, 1864, Barlow MSS.

538 *"than Mr. Conkling"*: CW, 7:498.

538 *"he thinks fit"*: CW, 7:402, 480–481.

538 *James Gordon Bennett:* In addition to the specific citations that follow, see two excellent studies: David Quentin Voigt, " 'Too Pitchy to Touch'—President Lincoln and Editor Bennett," *ALQ* 6 (Sept. 1950): 139–161, and John J. Turner, Jr., and Michael D'Innocenzo, "The President and the Press: Lincoln, James Gordon Bennett and the Election of 1864," *LH* 76 (Summer 1974): 63–69.

539 *editor with flattery:* Green Clay Smith to AL, Sept. 2, 1864, Lincoln MSS, LC.

539 *"too pitchy to touch"*: Hay, *Diary,* p. 215.

539 *"amount to much"*: CW, 7:461.

539 *"mentioning your name"*: William O. Bartlett to AL, Oct. 20, 1864, Lincoln MSS, LC.

539 *"less repulsive way"*: Turner and D'Innocenzo, "The President and the Press," p. 67.

539 *"and ruined us"*: CW, 8:100–101.

539 *September draft call:*. Stanton did grant a four-day delay, so that some state quotas and draft districts could be rearranged. Harold M. Hyman and Benjamin P. Thomas, *Stanton: The Life and Times of Lincoln's Secretary of War* (New York: Alfred A. Knopf, 1962), p. 328.

539 *"you at once":* CW, 8:11.

539 *Nevada a state:* In his *Recollections of the Civil War* (New York: D. Appleton & Co., 1898), pp. 174–177, Charles A. Dana remembered that Lincoln had actively promoted the statehood of Nevada, primarily to secure additional votes in the next session of Congress for the Thirteenth Amendment abolishing slavery and that he had liberally distributed patronage to persuade Democrats to vote for admission. But Earl S. Pomeroy, "Lincoln, the Thirteenth Amendment, and the Admission of Nevada," *Pacific Historical Review* 12 (1943), 362–368, points out numerous errors in Dana's account and shows (p. 367) "there is no reason to suppose that Nevada was a favorite project of Lincoln or that he viewed it with great warmth."

540 *"any presidential election":* CW, 8:72.

540 *"vanity, or ambition":* CW, 7:506.

540 *"to the country":* Segal, *Conversations,* p. 338.

540 *a Washington merchant:* O. H. Browning, Diary, July 3, 1873, MS, ISHL.

540 *"will know all":* Randall, *Mary Lincoln,* pp. 346–347.

540 *"all future ages":* CW, 8:96.

540 *"with their own":* CW, 8:52.

540 *"this great nation":* CW, 7:506.

541 *"fickle-minded man":* C. Peter Ripley, ed., *The Black Abolitionist Papers: The United States, 1859–1865* (Chapel Hill: University of North Carolina Press, 1992), p. 277.

541 *"Despotism and Slavery":* Ibid., p. 306. For additional statements of African-Americans' support for Lincoln, see James M. McPherson, *The Negro's Civil War* (Urbana: University of Illinois Press, 1982), chap. 21.

541 *"call you blessed":* Benjamin Quarles, *Lincoln and the Negro* (New York: Oxford University Press, 1962), p. 211.

541 *"advocated his cause":* Segal, *Conversations,* pp. 345–347.

541 *abolitionists had often:* These paragraphs draw heavily from James M. McPherson's admirable study, *The Struggle for Equality: Abolitionists and the Negro in the Civil War and Reconstruction* (Princeton, N.J.: Princeton University Press, 1964), esp. chap. 12.

542 *"to the emancipated":* *William Lloyd Garrison, 1805–1879: The Story of His Life Told by His Children* (New York: Century Co., 1889), 4:117.

542 *"us the churches":* CW, 7:350–351.

542 *"and to liberty":* CW, 7:368.

542 *"all on one side":* James H. Moorhead, *American Apocalypse: Yankee Protestants and the Civil War* (New Haven, Conn.: Yale University Press, 1978), pp. 156–157.

542 *women of letters:* For an excellent analysis of the changing views of Northern intellectuals and literary figures, see George M. Fredrickson, *The Inner Civil War: Northern Intellectuals and the Crisis of the Union* (New York: Harper & Row, 1965).

542 *"never in history":* Ralph L. Rusk, *The Life of Ralph Waldo Emerson* (New York: Charles Scribner's Sons, 1949), p. 426.

542 *"will be saved":* Samuel Longfellow, ed., *Life of Henry Wadsworth Longfellow* (Boston: Houghton, Mifflin & Co., 1886), 3:47.

542 *"in a net":* Forrest Wilson, *Crusader in Crinoline: The Life of Harriet Beecher Stowe* (Philadelphia: J. B. Lippincott Co., 1941), pp. 484–485.

542 *"who could hesitate!":* John B. Pickard, ed., *The Letters of John Greenleaf Whittier* (Cambridge, Mass.: Harvard University Press, 1975), 3:77.

543 *"and his God":* Paul Revere Frothingham, *Edward Everett: Orator and Statesman* (Boston: Houghton Mifflin Co., 1925), pp. 461–463.

543 *"a practical statesman":* James Russell Lowell, "The Next General Election," *North American Review* 99 (Oct. 1864): 570; Horace E. Scudder, *James Russell Lowell: A Biography* (Boston: Houghton, Mifflin & Co., 1901), 2:56.

543 *evening of October 11:* The following paragraphs draw on Hay's very full account in Hay, *Diary,* pp. 227–230.

543 *"give up my office":* *The Works of Charles Sumner* (Boston: Lee & Shepard, 1883), 15:66.

543 *to his column:* CW, 8:46.

544 *"if they do":* Strong, *Diary,* p. 501.

544 *"greed for spoils":* John G. Nicolay to John Hay, Oct. 19, 1864, Nicolay MSS, LC.

544 *"those votes himself"*: Zornow, p. 202.
544 *"half-filled seats"*: Henry D. Cooke to John Sherman, Nov. 8, 1864, Sherman MSS, LC.
544 *went off smoothly*: Zornow, chap. 16, offers the best analysis of the voting. There is also much excellent material in William B. Hesseltine, *Lincoln and the War Governors* (New York: Alfred A. Knopf, 1948), chap. 17, which, however, overestimates the importance of the soldier vote.
545 *"pretty sure-footed"*: Hay, *Diary*, pp. 233–234.

CHAPTER TWENTY: WITH CHARITY FOR ALL

Come Retribution: The Confederate Secret Service and the Assassination of Lincoln (Jackson: University Press of Mississippi, 1988), by William A. Tidwell, James O. Hall, and David Winfred Gaddy, offers a provocative account of attempts to kidnap and kill Lincoln. Tidwell's *April '65: Confederate Covert Action in the American Civil War* (Kent, Ohio: Kent State University Press, 1995) offers further evidence of Booth's connection with the Southern secret service. Michael Les Benedict, *A Compromise of Principle: Congressional Republicans and Reconstruction, 1863–1869* (New York: W. W. Norton & Co., 1974), and Herman Belz, *Reconstructing the Union: Theory and Policy During the Civil War* (Ithaca, N.Y.: Cornell University Press, 1969), provide illuminating accounts of the Thirteenth Amendment and of the failure of Ashley's reconstruction bill. The fullest account of the Hampton Roads peace conference is in Edward C. Kirkland, *The Peacemakers of 1864* (New York: Macmillan Co., 1927). Donald C. Pfanz, *The Petersburg Campaign: Abraham Lincoln at City Point, March 20–April 9, 1865* (Lynchburg, Va.: H. E. Howard, 1989), gives a detailed chronology of Lincoln's visit to Grant's army.

546 *"the national honor"*: Strong, *Diary*, p. 511.
546 *"in all history"*: James A. Briggs to John Sherman, Nov. 12, 1864, Sherman MSS, LC.
546 *"was a possibility"*: CW, 8:101.
546 *"limitations in politics"*: Hay, *Diary*, pp. 234, 239.
547 *"any man's bosom"*: CW, 8:101.
547 *"insatiable for our blood"*: Larry E. Nelson, *Bullets, Ballots, and Rhetoric: Confederate Policy for the United States Presidential Contest of 1864* (University: University of Alabama Press, 1980), p. 158.
547 *"despotic Caesar himself"*: Michael Davis, *The Image of Lincoln in the South* (Knoxville: University of Tennessee Press, 1971), p. 68.
547 "used *to things!*": Carpenter, *Six Months,* pp. 62–63.
548 *"of its instruments"*: Ibid., pp. 65–66.
548 *"in this city"*: Ward Hill Lamon, *Recollections of Abraham Lincoln, 1847–1865,* ed. Dorothy Lamon Teillard (Washington, D.C.: 1911), p. 275.
548 *Lincolns' private rooms:* For these increasingly careful security precautions, see George S. Bryan, *The Great American Myth* (New York: Carrick & Evans, 1940), pp. 60–66. See also "Guarding Mr. Lincoln," *Surratt Courier* 12 (Mar. 1987), pp. 1, 7.
549 *"out of the City"*: Lizzie W.S. to AL, July 1, 1864, Lincoln MSS, LC.
549 *"with your help"*: Seymour Ketchum to AL, Nov. 2, 1864, Lincoln MSS, LC.
549 *"the public good"*: Tidwell, *Come Retribution*, p. 234.
549 *"of such means"*: Ibid., p. 235.
549 *retaliation against Lincoln:* Joseph George, Jr., " 'Black Flag Warfare': Lincoln and the Raids Against Richmond and Jefferson Davis," *Pennsylvania Magazine of History and Biography* 115 (July 1991): 317–318. Jefferson Davis himself knew of Confederate plans to kidnap Lincoln, and he was the more willing to entertain the idea, because he believed there had been several Northern-inspired plots against his own life. (Davis to J. William Jones, May 10, 1876, Davis Personal Papers, Virginia State Library; J. Thomas Scharf, interview with Jefferson Davis, July 8, 1887, in *Baltimore Sunday Herald,* July 10, 1887.) The Confederate President discussed the proposed kidnapping with his young adjutant, Colonel Walter H. Taylor, who was, Davis said much later, "the only man who ever talked to me on the subject of his [Lincoln's] capture or at least the only one who I believed intended to do what he proposed." But he declined to endorse Taylor's plan "on the ground that the attempt would probably involve the killing, instead of bringing away the captive alive" (Davis to Taylor, Aug. 31, 1889, C. Seymour Bullock MSS, Southern Historical Collection, University of North Carolina). Immediately afterward Davis reported this conversation to his wife, saying that "Taylor was a brave man and of course did

not see that Mr. Lincoln could not be captured alive." After Davis explained that "the plan was impracticable for that reason if for no other," Taylor agreed to drop it, because he "would not lend himself to a plan of assassination any more than I would" (Varina Howells Davis to Henty T. Loutham, May 10, 1898, Jefferson Davis MSS, University of Alabama). For all these references on Davis, Taylor, and the kidnapping plot, I am indebted to Professor Joan E. Cashin.

549 *Thomas Nelson Conrad:* For an excellent account of Conrad's scheme, see Terry Alford, "The Silken Net: Plots to Abduct Abraham Lincoln During the Civil War" (unpublished paper, Annandale, Va., Apr. 21, 1987).

549 *"and at hand":* Anonymous to AL, Sept. 21, 1864, Lincoln MSS, LC.

550 *"plug-hat":* Lamon, *Recollections of Abraham Lincoln,* pp. 266–269, places this episode in 1862, but Tidwell, *Come Retribution,* p. 237, shows that it occurred in Aug. 1864.

550 *"humiliating failure":* Alford, "The Silken Net."

550 *"threats like these":* John W. Forney, *Anecdotes of Public Men* (New York: Harper & Brothers, 1873), 2:425.

550 *"nineteen enemies":* Carpenter, *Six Months,* p. 276. See also Harry J. Carman and Reinhard H. Luthin, *Lincoln and the Patronage* (New York: Columbia University Press, 1943), chap. 11.

550 *"more substantial service":* Wayne C. Temple and Justin G. Turner, "Lincoln's 'Castine': Noah Brooks," *LH* 73 (Fall 1971): 170.

551 *"cases—not* principles": John T. Hall to AL, Oct. 17, 1864, Lincoln MSS, LC.

552 *"otherwise certainly attain":* Segal, *Conversations,* p. 361.

552 *"opinions are known":* David M. Silver, *Lincoln's Supreme Court* (Urbana: University of Illinois Press, 1956), pp. 207–208.

552 "the rest hold back": Segal, *Conversations,* p. 361.

552 *had given him:* Kenneth A. Bernard, *Lincoln and the Music of the Civil War* (Caldwell, Idaho: Caxton Printers, 1966), pp. 278–279.

552 *"than do it."):* Virginia Woodbury Fox, Diary, Dec. 10, 1864, Levi Woodbury MSS, LC.

552 *"a reasonable objection":* Undated memorandum of a conversation with AL, Lamon MSS, HEH.

553 *"if not fearful":* CW, 8:181.

553 *"whole detached force":* CW, 8:148n.

553 *"bales of cotton":* W. T. Sherman to AL, Dec. 22, 1864, Lincoln MSS, LC.

553 *"a great light":* CW, 8:182.

553 *"any respect whatsoever":* Congressional Globe, 38 Cong., 2 sess. (Dec. 15, 1864), pp. 50–51.

553 *Era of Good Feeling:* Washington *Daily National Intelligencer,* Jan. 17, 1865.

554 *"will of the majority":* CW, 8:149.

554 *"to a close":* Segal, *Conversations,* pp. 362–364.

554 *"man in America":* Fawn Brodie, *Thaddeus Stevens: Scourge of the South* (New York: W. W. Norton & Co., 1959), p. 204.

554 *"in these matters":* Nicolay and Hay, 10:85; Donald, *Sumner,* p. 194n.

554 *influenced his change:* Allan G. Bogue, *The Earnest Men: Republicans of the Civil War Senate* (Ithaca, N.Y.: Cornell University Press, 1981), p. 253n.

554 *"all the evils":* CW, 8:254.

555 *"to be in it":* CW, 8:248.

555 *"they smelt Peace":* J. M. Ashley to WHH, Nov. 23, 1866, HWC; Arlin Turner, "Elizabeth Peabody Visits Lincoln, February, 1865," *New England Quarterly* 48 (Mar. 1975): 119–120.

555 *was an armistice:* Brooks D. Simpson, *Let Us Have Peace: Ulysses S. Grant and the Politics of War and Reconstruction, 1861–1868* (Chapel Hill: University of North Carolina Press, 1991), p. 73.

555 *ending the war:* Kirkland, *The Peacemakers of 1864,* pp. 218–222, 236n.

556 *"shall be adopted":* CW, 8:151–152.

556 *"by Constitutional Amendments":* The best account of Singleton's expedition is in Randall, *Lincoln the President,* 4:330–331.

556 *"when Savannah falls":* Blair's detailed memorandum of his visit to Richmond and his conversations with Jefferson Davis, to which the cataloguer has given the date of January 12, 1865, is in the Lincoln MSS, LC. For an excellent account of the background of Blair's mission, see Howard C. Westwood, "Lincoln and the Hampton Road Peace Conference," *LH* 81 (Winter 1979): 243–256.

557 *"one common country":* CW, 8:220–221.

557 *two separate countries: Official Records of the Union and Confederate Armies* (Washington, D.C.: Government Printing Office, 1895), ser. 1, vol. 46, pt. 3, p. 297.

557 *meet with them: CW,* 8:282.

557 *"one in authority":* Ibid.

557 *"so much husk":* Sandburg, 4:45.

557 *would be taken:* Because there was no agenda and because no notes were taken, it is not possible to re-create the exact sequence of the topics discussed. The following pages draw on Lincoln's brief report to Congress (*CW,* 8:284–285); on Stephens's account in *A Constitutional View of the Late War Between the States* (Philadelphia: National Publishing Co., 1870), 2:599–619; on Hunter's report to Jefferson Davis, in Dunbar Rowland, ed., *Jefferson Davis: Constitutionalist* (Jackson: Mississippi Department of Archives and History, 1923), 8:133–136; and on Campbell's accounts in *Reminiscences and Documents Relating to the Civil War During the Year 1865* (Baltimore: John Murphy & Co., 1887), pp. 8–19, and in *Southern Historical Society Papers,* new ser., 4 (Oct. 1917): 45–52. For a collation of these and other statements concerning the discussion, see Julian S. Carr, *The Hampton Roads Conference* (Durham, N.C.: 1917).

559 *"ended without result": CW,* 8:284–285.

559 *"in active exercise": Southern Historical Society Papers,* new ser., 4 (Oct. 1917): 48; Stephens, *Constitutional View,* 2:610–611.

559 *"of judicial tribunals":* Browning, *Diary,* 1:694.

559 *"of the Union":* Ibid., 1:699.

560 *"slavery as stated":* Stephens, *Constitutional View,* 2:617; Rowland, *Jefferson Davis: Constitutionalist,* 8:134; *Southern Historical Society Papers,* new ser., 4 (Oct. 1917): 51.

560 *was ratified: CW,* 8:260–261.

560 *"and property destroyed":* John G. Nicolay, interview with John P. Usher, Oct. 11, 1877, Nicolay MSS, LC.

561 *"[the offer was] made":* Welles, *Diary,* 2:237.

561 *"come from us":* Francis Fessenden, *Life and Public Services of William Pitt Fessenden* (Boston: Houghton, Mifflin & Co., 1907), 2:7–8.

561 *"disapproved by them": CW,* 8:260–261.

562 *the Southern states:* For an excellent account of Ashley's bill and the proposed compromise between the President and Congress, see Belz, *Reconstructing the Union,* chap. 9.

562 *"an immense political act":* Charles Sumner to Francis Lieber, [Dec. 1864], Sumner MSS, Houghton Library, Harvard University.

562 *"refuse to vote":* Hay, *Diary,* pp. 244–246.

562 *"pass this Congress":* Belz, *Reconstructing the Union,* pp. 264–265.

562 *"and not ours":* Michael Les Benedict, *A Compromise of Principle: Congressional Republicans and Reconstruction, 1863–1869* (New York: W. W. Norton & Co., 1974), p. 93.

563 *throughout the nation:* On the problems connected with the ratification of the Thirteenth Amendment, see J. G. Randall, *Constitutional Problems Under Lincoln* (Urbana: University of Illinois Press, 1951), pp. 396–401.

563 *"on all sides":* LaWanda Cox, *Lincoln and Black Freedom: A Study in Presidential Leadership* (Columbia: University of South Carolina Press, 1981), makes a powerful argument for Lincoln's quiet support of Negro suffrage. See esp. pp. 117–119, 129–130.

564 *"He is dictator":* Benedict, *A Compromise of Principle,* p. 85.

564 *"St. Paul's time":* Donald, *Sumner,* p. 203.

564 *"the proposed Senators?": CW,* 8:206–207.

564 *"and a wrong":* Donald, *Sumner,* p. 204.

564 *"centralized power":* Nicolay and Hay, 10:85.

565 *on his arm:* Donald, *Sumner,* pp. 205–207.

565 *"at home and abroad":* Herbert Mitgang, ed., *Abraham Lincoln: A Press Portrait* (Chicago: Quadrangle Books, 1971), p. 440.

565 *"end to end":* P. J. Staudenraus, ed., *Mr. Lincoln's Washington* (New York: Thomas Yoseloff, 1967), p. 419.

565 *"from her escutcheon": CW,* 8:216–217, 235.

565 *"melancholy reflections":* Adolphe de Chambrun, *Impressions of Lincoln and the Civil War* (New York: Random House, 1952), p. 37.

565 *"Johnson speak outside":* For a full account of Johnson's performance, see George Fort Milton, *The Age of Hate: Andrew Johnson and the Radicals* (New York: Coward-McCann, 1930), pp. 145–148.

565 *"over the scene":* For Lincoln's appearance at this time, see the photographs made by Henry F.

Warren on the White House balcony, March 6, 1865, in Charles A. Hamilton and Lloyd Ostendorf, *Lincoln in Photographs: An Album of Every Known Pose* (Dayton, Ohio: Morningside, 1985), p. 400.

566 *"of prosperous peace":* Salmon P. Chase to Mary Lincoln, Mar. 4, 1865, Lincoln MSS, LC. Most observers said the sun came out when Lincoln began to speak. Chase, as usual self-centered, thought it burst forth when he stepped forward to administer the oath of office.

566 *the most memorable:* The text is in *CW,* 8:332–333. The most thoughtful analysis of the second inaugural is William Lee Miller, "Lincoln's Second Inaugural: The Zenith of Statecraft," *Center Magazine* 13 (July–Aug. 1980): 53–64.

566 *"governing the world": CW,* 8:356.

567 *"of either party": CW,* 5:403–404.

567 *of exact retribution:* Ernest Lee Tuveson, *Redeemer Nation: The Idea of America's Millennial Role* (Chicago: University of Chicago Press, 1968), pp. 206–208.

567 *"the offence cometh!":* Matthew 18:7. (The Revised Standard Version offers a clearer translation of this somewhat puzzling verse: "Woe to the world for temptations to sin! For it is necessary that temptations come, but woe to the man by whom the temptation comes.") See Fred Somkin, "Scripture Notes to Lincoln's Second Inaugural," *Civil War History* 27 (June 1981): 172–173. For other biblical quotations and resonances in the second inaugural, see Herbert Joseph Edwards and John Erskine Hankins, *Lincoln the Writer* (Orono: University of Maine, 1962), pp. 104–105.

567 *" 'righteous altogether' ":* Psalms 19:9.

567 *never ending bloodshed:* For astute commentary, see Don E. Fehrenbacher, *Lincoln in Text and Context* (Stanford, Calif.: Stanford University Press, 1987), pp. 162–163.

567 *"altar of Freedom": CW,* 8:116–117. The later discovery that only two of Mrs. Bixby's sons were killed does not diminish the sincerity or eloquence of Lincoln's letter. See F. Lauriston Bullard, *Abraham Lincoln & the Widow Bixby* (New Brunswick, N.J.: Rutgers University Press, 1946). For years there has been controversy over John Hay's assertion that he, rather than the President, was the author of the Bixby letter. Most experts question Hay's claim, of which we have only indirect reports made many years later. See the pungent article in Mark E. Neely, Jr., *The Abraham Lincoln Encyclopedia* (New York: McGraw-Hill, 1982), pp. 18–19. But the question has recently been reopened by Michael Burlingame, who offers some suggestive but far from conclusive evidence pointing toward Hay's authorship in "New Light on the Bixby Letter," *Journal of the Abraham Lincoln Association* 16 (1995): 59–71.

568 *"printed in gold":* Mitgang, *Abraham Lincoln: A Press Portrait,* pp. 440, 442.

568 *away his manuscript: CW,* 8:356; Christopher N. Breiseth, "Lincoln and Frederick Douglass: Another Debate," *JISHS* 68 (Feb. 1975): 22; Carpenter, *Six Months,* p. 234.

568 *organically wrong:* It has been suggested that Lincoln's fatigue—as well as other characteristics, such as his exceptional height, his elongated fingers and large feet, and his problems with his eyes—was the result of the Marfan syndrome, a hereditary disorder of the connective tissues, manifested in skeletal, ocular, and cardiovascular disorders. The evidence for this diagnosis is slim; it is based on the occurrence of the Marfan syndrome in several twentieth-century members of the Lincoln family and on inferences from the President's physical appearance. For a fascinating exploration of the whole issue, see Gabor S. Boritt and Adam Borit, "Lincoln and the Marfan Syndrome: The Medical Diagnosis of a Historical Figure," *Civil War History* 29 (Sept. 1983): 213–229, which concludes: "The available evidence does not indicate that Lincoln suffered from the Marfan syndrome." For a lighthearted analysis of the problem, see Gabor S. Boritt, *How Big Was Lincoln's Toe? or Finding a Footnote* (Redlands, Calif.: Lincoln Memorial Shrine, 1989). See also Harold Schwartz, "Abraham Lincoln and the Marfan Syndrome," *Journal of the American Medical Association* 187 (Feb. 15, 1964): 490–495; Harvey J. Wilner and Nathaniel Finby, "Skeletal Manifestations in the Marfan Syndrome," ibid., 187 (Feb. 15, 1964): 128–133; and Harriet F. Durham, "Lincoln's Sons and the Marfan Syndrome," *LH* 79 (Summer 1977): 67–71. I have also profited from a correspondence with Dick Levinson, of the National Museum of Health and Medicine, concerning the proposal to clone Lincoln's DNA in order to determine whether the President suffered from the Marfan syndrome.

568 *that they steamed:* Joshua F. Speed, *Reminiscences of Abraham Lincoln and Notes of a Visit to California—Two Lectures* (Louisville, Ky.: John P. Morton and Co., 1884), pp. 26–28.

568 *"next four years":* Elizabeth Keckley, *Behind the Scenes* (Buffalo: Stansil & Lee, 1931), p. 155.

569 *of theatrical entertainment:* On Lincoln and the theater, see David C. Mearns, "Act Well Your Part," in his *Largely Lincoln* (New York: St. Martin's Press, 1961), pp. 114–149.

569 *enjoyed them all:* The following pages draw heavily on R. Gerald McMurtry, "Lincoln Knew Shakespeare," *Indiana Magazine of History* 31 (Dec. 1935): 265–277.

569 *understand their anxieties:* For perceptive commentary on Lincoln's interest in Shakespeare, see James A. Stevenson, "Abraham Lincoln's Affinity for *Macbeth,*" *Midwest Quarterly* 31 (Winter 1990): 270–279; Charles B. Strozier, *Lincoln's Quest for Union: Public and Private Meanings* (New York: Basic Books, 1982), pp. 228–231; and Fehrenbacher, *Lincoln in Text and Context,* pp. 157–163.

569 *"smells to heaven":* Carpenter, *Six Months,* pp. 49–50.

569 *"It is wonderful":* CW, 6:392. The reference to *Henry VIII,* which today is rarely performed or read, may seem puzzling, but the play was highly esteemed in the nineteenth century.

569 *"used to it":* CW, 6:558–559.

569 *and the opera:* The definitive treatment is Bernard, *Lincoln and the Music of the Civil War,* esp. chap. 16.

570 *"to finish it":* James Grant Wilson, "Recollections of Lincoln," *Putnam's Magazine* 5 (Feb. 1909): 528–529; and 5 (Mar. 1909): 673.

570 *"roving and travelling":* WHH, interview with Mary Lincoln, Sept. 5, 1866, HWC.

570 *comfortably provided for:* For Lincoln's savings during the presidency, see Pratt, *Personal Finances,* chap. 8.

571 *now in the army:* On Robert's enlistment and military service, see John S. Goff, *Robert Todd Lincoln: A Man in His Own Right* (Norman: University of Oklahoma Press, 1969), pp. 60–66.

571 *"and a few others":* CW, 8:367.

571 *"of the crew":* Pfanz, *The Petersburg Campaign,* p. 4. In Horace Porter, *Campaigning with Grant* (Bloomington: Indiana University Press, 1961), chaps. 26–27 offer a full account of the Lincolns' visit.

572 *"fatigued appearance":* John W. Grattan, "Under the Blue Pennant, or Notes of a Naval Officer," p. 219, Grattan MSS, LC.

572 *"him very much":* Randall, *Mary Lincoln,* p. 371.

572 *"head of affairs":* George R. Agassiz, ed., *Meade's Headquarters, 1863–1865: Letters of Colonel Theodore Lyman* (Boston: Atlantic Monthly Press, 1922), pp. 324–325.

573 *"following up the President":* For a sensational account of this episode—the only time in her years in Washington that Mary Lincoln lost control of herself—see Adam Badeau, *Grant in Peace: From Appomattox to Mount McGregor* (Hartford: S. S. Scranton & Co., 1887), pp. 358–360. For a more balanced account, see Randall, *Mary Lincoln,* pp. 372–374.

573 *"many bloody battles":* David D. Porter's statement in Segal, *Conversations,* 382–384. Cf. William T. Sherman, *Memoirs* (New York: D. Appleton & Co., 1875), 2:326–328.

573 *"conferences or conventions":* CW, 8:330–331. Though this letter is signed by Stanton, it is in Lincoln's handwriting.

574 *"lawlessness and anarchy":* Alexander K. McClure, *Recollections of Half a Century* (Salem, Mass.: Salem Press Co., 1902), p. 296.

574 *"to their homes":* Sherman's statement in Isaac N. Arnold, *The Life of Abraham Lincoln* (Chicago: Jansen, McClurg, & Co., 1885), p. 423n.

574 *"to the laws":* David D. Porter's statement in Segal, *Conversations,* p. 382.

CHAPTER TWENTY-ONE: I WILL TAKE CARE OF MYSELF

Donald C. Pfanz, *The Petersburg Campaign: Abraham Lincoln at City Point* (Lynchburg, Va.: H. E. Howard, 1989), gives a full account of Lincoln's visit to Richmond. William Hanchett, *The Lincoln Murder Conspiracies* (Urbana: University of Illinois Press, 1983), is an excellent guide to the huge literature on the conspiracy to abduct and murder Lincoln. George S. Bryan, *The Great American Myth* (New York: Carrick & Evans, 1940), remains the best account of the conspiracy. *Come Retribution: The Confederate Secret Service and the Assassination of Lincoln,* by William A. Tidwell, James O. Hall, and David Winfred Gaddy (Jackson: University Press of Mississippi, 1988), is an important study that comes close to linking the Confederate government to Booth's plot. Albert Furtwangler, *Assassin on Stage: Brutus, Hamlet, and the Death of Lincoln* (Urbana: University of Illinois Press, 1991), is a brilliant reinterpretation of the assassination in terms of the theatrical tradition of tyrannicide. Much useful information is contained in Otto Eisenschiml, *Why Was Lincoln Murdered?* (Boston: Little, Brown & Co., 1937), and in Theodore Roscoe, *The Web of Conspiracy: The Complete Story of the Men Who Murdered Abraham Lincoln* (Englewood Cliffs, N.J.: Prentice-Hall, 1959), but both are marred by attempts to link Stanton to the assassination. For a devastating critique of this discredited interpretation, see William Hanchett, "The Eisenschiml Thesis," *Civil War History* 25 (Sept. 1979): 197–217. *In Pursuit of . . . : Continuing Research in the Field of the Lincoln Assassination* (Surratt Society, 1990), provides many fascinating details on the plot and the assassins. W. Emerson Reck, *A. Lincoln: His Last 24 Hours* (Jefferson, N.C.: McFarland & Co., 1987), is a very full and complete account.

Several excellent books deal with topics related to the assassination that are outside the scope of this biography. Dorothy Meserve Kunhardt and Philip B. Kunhardt, Jr., *Twenty Days* (New York: Harper & Row, 1965), is a fascinating pictorial history mostly concerned with the aftermath of the assassination. Thomas Reed Turner, *Beware the People Weeping: Public Opinion and the Assassination of Abraham Lincoln* (Baton Rouge: Louisiana State University Press, 1982), is an excellent account by a professional historian. Roy Z. Chamlee, Jr., *Lincoln's Assassination: A Complete Account of Their Capture, Trial, and Punishment* (Jefferson, N.C.: McFarland & Co., 1990), deals largely with the fate of the conspirators.

575 *feat but failed:* Carpenter, *Six Months,* pp. 288–289.
576 *"the rebel army":* E. M. Stanton to AL, Apr. 3, 1865, Lincoln MSS, LC.
576 *"care of myself":* CW, 8:385.
576 *"to be humble":* David D. Porter, *Incidents and Anecdotes of the Civil War* (New York: D. Appleton & Co., 1885), pp. 294–295.
576 *"will hereafter enjoy":* Pfanz, *The Petersburg Campaign,* pp. 60–61.
576 *"Father Abrahams Come":* John Henry Woodward, "A Narrative of the Family and Civil War Experiences and Events of His Life" (typescript, 1919[?], LC), pp. 37–39. Woodward made an ill-conceived and demeaning attempt to recapture African-American dialect; I have substituted standard English.
577 *forces occupying Richmond:* "Lincoln's Visit to Richmond, Apr. 4, 1865," *Moorsfield Antiquarian* 1 (May 1937): 27–29; George T. Dudley, "Lincoln in Richmond," *Washington National Tribune,* Oct. 1, 1896.
577 *"me any harm":* This account of Lincoln's stay in Richmond is drawn chiefly from Pfanz, *The Petersburg Campaign,* pp. 60–69.
577 *"magnanimity and kindness":* Southern Historical Society Papers, new ser., 4 (Oct. 1917): 68.
578 *"preservation of order":* John A. Campbell, *Reminiscences and Documents Relating to the Civil War During the Year 1865* (Baltimore: John Murphy & Co., 1887), p. 39.
578 *the next morning:* Campbell's accounts of this conference, ibid., pp. 39–42, and in *Southern Historical Society Papers,* new ser., 4 (Oct. 1917): 68–70; Myers's account is reprinted in Segal, *Conversations,* pp. 388–390.
578 *confiscated Confederate property:* CW, 8:386–387.
579 *"the existing government":* Herman Belz, *Reconstructing the Union: Theory and Policy During the Civil War* (Ithaca, N.Y.: Cornell University Press, 1969), p. 297.
579 *during a transitional period:* Sherman understood the President to say "that to avoid anarchy the State governments then in existence, with their civil functionaries, would be recognized by him as the government *de facto* till Congress would provide others." William T. Sherman, *Memoirs* (New York: D. Appleton & Co., 1875), 2:327. On the basis of this understanding he made recognition of Governor Zebulon Vance's Confederate government of North Carolina part of the surrender terms that he offered Joseph E. Johnston on April 18. By this time Lincoln was dead, and Stanton and others in the government at Washington repudiated Sherman's agreement. Raoul S. Naroll, "Lincoln and the Sherman Peace Fiasco—Another Fable?" *Journal of Southern History* 20 (Nov. 1954): 459–483, convincingly argues that Sherman exceeded his instructions, yet it seems evident that Lincoln must have discussed, even if he did not endorse, recognition of Confederate state authorities at this City Point meeting.
579 *"somewhat farcical":* CW, 7:487.
579 *"the Confederate army":* Campbell, *Reminiscences,* pp. 41–42.
579 *"shortest possible time":* Nicolay and Hay, 10:222.
579 *"to the General government":* CW, 8:389.
579 *"opposition to the government":* CW, 8:388.
580 "thing *be pressed":* CW, 8:392.
580 *"hear it again":* Adolphe de Chambrun, *Impressions of Lincoln and the Civil War: A Foreigner's Account* (New York: Random House, 1952), p. 82.

580 *"touch him further"*: *Macbeth*, act 2, scene 2.

580 *"the same scene"*: Adolphe de Chambrun, "Personal Recollections of Mr. Lincoln," *Scribner's Magazine* 13 (1893): 35.

581 *left the room*: Frederick W. Seward, *Reminiscences of a War-Time Statesman and Diplomat, 1830–1915* (New York: G. P. Putnam's Sons, 1916), p. 253.

581 *"all, all jubilant"*: Welles, *Diary*, 2:278.

581 *"forth into singing"*: Turner, *Mary Todd Lincoln*, p. 216.

581 *"we fairly captured it"*: *CW*, 8:393.

582 *for "another"*: Wayne C. Temple and Justin G. Turner, "Lincoln's 'Castine': Noah Brooks," *LH* 73 (Fall 1971): 173; Noah Brooks, *Washington in Lincoln's Time* (New York: Century Co., 1895), pp. 252–255.

582 *"gladness of heart"*: Unless otherwise identified, all quotations in the following paragraphs are from *CW*, 8:399–405.

582 *"against all opposition"*: Chambrun, *Impressions of Lincoln*, p. 93.

583 *as if herding sheep*: Gideon Welles, "Lincoln and Johnson," *Galaxy* 13 (Apr. 1872): 526.

583 *" 'unbeknown' to him"*: Sherman, *Memoirs*, 2:326–327.

583 *and economic equality*: Historians who argue that Lincoln favored universal suffrage often cite a letter that he purportedly wrote to James S. Wadsworth in January 1864, announcing that he supported both universal amnesty and universal suffrage and pledging that reconstruction "must rest upon the principle of civil and political equality of both races." *CW*, 7:101–102. Ludwell H. Johnston, "Lincoln and Equal Rights: The Authenticity of the Wadsworth Letter," *Journal of Southern History* 32 (Feb. 1966): 83–87, convincingly demonstrates that this letter is spurious. Harold M. Hyman, "Lincoln and Equal Rights for Negroes: The Irrelevancy of the 'Wadsworth Letter,' " *Civil War History* 12 (Sept. 1966): 258–266, argues that, regardless of the authenticity of the Wadsworth letter, Lincoln was moving in the direction of equal rights. Ludwell H. Johnson, "Lincoln and Equal Rights: A Reply," *Civil War History* 13 (Mar. 1967): 66–73, responds that Hyman's argument is "sheer conjecture."

583 *American social fabric*: Benjamin F. Butler's reminiscence that Lincoln as late as 1865 continued to favor colonization of Negroes, especially those who had fought in the Union army, has been discredited. See Mark E. Neely, Jr., "Abraham Lincoln and Black Colonization: Benjamin Butler's Spurious Testimony," *Civil War History* 25 (Mar. 1979): 77–83.

583 *blacks and whites*: Lincoln's limited concern for the rights of African-Americans led Lerone Bennett, Jr., to label him a racist. "Was Abe Lincoln a White Supremacist?" *Ebony* 23 (Feb. 1968): 35–42. For more balanced discussions, see George M. Fredrickson, "A Man but Not a Brother: Abraham Lincoln and Racial Equality," *Journal of Southern History* 41 (Feb. 1975): 39–58, and Don E. Fehrenbacher, "Only His Stepchildren," in *Lincoln in Text and Context* (Stanford, Calif.: Stanford University Press, 1987), pp. 95–112.

584 *to other states*: Michael Les Benedict, *A Compromise of Principle: Congressional Republicans and Reconstruction, 1863–1869* (New York: W. W. Norton & Co., 1974), pp. 98–99, first suggested this conclusion to me.

584 *"strive to prevent"*: Welles, *Diary*, 2:279–280.

584 *"through the swamp"*: Paul M. Angle, ed., "The Recollections of William Pitt Kellogg," *ALQ* 3 (Sept. 1945): 333.

584 *so used again*: Donald, *Sumner*, p. 215.

584 *"rights of citizenship"*: *New York Times*, Apr. 11, 1865.

584 *"regard to complexion"*: S. P. Chase to AL, Apr. 11, 1865, Lincoln MSS, LC.

585 *John Wilkes Booth*: Francis Wilson, *John Wilkes Booth: Fact and Fiction of Lincoln's Assassination* (Boston: Houghton Mifflin Co., 1929), is still the best biography. There are insightful portraits of Booth in Robert J. Donovan, *The Assassins* (New York: Harper & Brothers, 1955), chaps. 9–10, and in Franklin L. Ford, *Political Murder: From Tyrannicide to Terrorism* (Cambridge, Mass.: Harvard University Press, 1985), chap. 15. Stanley Kimmel, *The Mad Booths of Maryland* (rev. ed.; New York: Dover Publications, 1969), offers much biographical information on John Wilkes Booth and his family, though it exaggerates the theme of madness. Eleanor Ruggles, *Prince of Players: Edwin Booth* (New York: W. W. Norton & Co., 1953), is the standard biography of John Wilkes Booth's older brother.

585 *"touch of mystery"*: Donovan, *The Assassins*, p. 231.

586 *and his joyousness*: W. J. Ferguson, *I Saw Booth Shoot Lincoln* (Boston: Houghton Mifflin Co., 1930), p. 13.

586 *"for the black man"*: Wilson, *John Wilkes Booth*, p. 51.

586 *"wait no longer":* Untitled Booth manuscript, Dec. 1860, in Robert Giroux, "The J.W.B. Manuscript, Or, The Mind of the Man Who Shot Lincoln" (unpublished paper, 1992).

586 *"are for the South":* Furtwangler, *Assassin on Stage,* p. 62.

586 *"and bought armies":* Ibid., p. 66.

586 *"for kingly succession":* Ibid., p. 67.

586 *Confederate secret service:* Tidwell, Hall, and Gaddy's *Come Retribution: The Confederate Secret Service and the Assassination of Lincoln* convincingly demonstrates that Booth was in touch with Confederate agents, both in the United States and Canada, and that his plan to kidnap Lincoln was strikingly similar to other schemes that the Confederate secret service had under consideration. It does not prove—and, indeed, it does not attempt to prove—that Booth was a Confederate agent or that his plots to kidnap, and later to kill, Lincoln were authorized by the Confederacy.

587 *team in Washington:* For sketches of all the members of the plot, see Theodore Roscoe, *The Web of Conspiracy: The Complete Story of the Men Who Murdered Abraham Lincoln* (Englewood Cliffs, N.J.: Prentice-Hall, 1959), chap. 3.

588 *"at present":* Wilson, *John Wilkes Booth,* pp. 50–54; Tidwell, *Come Retribution,* p. 405.

588 *if he wished:* Benn Pitman, *The Assassination of President Lincoln and the Trial of the Conspirators* (facsimile ed.; New York: Funk & Wagnalls, 1954), pp. 44–45.

588 *to the tyrant:* Furtwangler, *Assassin on Stage,* argues that the theatrical tradition of tyrannicide helped shape Booth's actions.

588 *"will ever make":* William Hanchett, *The Lincoln Murder Conspiracies* (Urbana: University of Illinois Press, 1983), p. 37.

589 *activities largely irrelevant:* For a defense of Campbell, see Henry G. Connor, *John Archibald Campbell: Associate Justice of the United States Supreme Court, 1853–1861* (Boston: Houghton Mifflin Co., 1920), chap. 7.

589 *"the reconstructed states":* R. F. Fuller to Sumner, Apr. 13, 1865, Sumner MSS, Houghton Library, Harvard University.

589 *"Alas!" he grieved:* Donald, *Sumner,* p. 215.

590 *"not sustain him":* Frank Abial Flower, *Edwin McMasters Stanton: The Autocrat of Rebellion, Emancipation, and Reconstruction* (New York: Western W. Wilson, 1905), pp. 271–272.

590 *"governments as legal":* Welles, "Lincoln and Johnson," *Galaxy* 13 (Apr. 1872): 524.

590 *"government of Virginia":* Charles H. Ambler, *Francis H. Pierpont: Union War Governor of Virginia and Father of West Virginia* (Chapel Hill: University of North Carolina Press, 1937), p. 256.

590 *"if he had":* Welles, *Diary,* 2:280.

590 *of his orders:* One authority asserts flatly: "Thus Lincoln broke faith with the Virginians." William M. Robinson, Jr., *Justice in Grey: A History of the Judicial System of the Confederate States of America* (Cambridge, Mass.: Harvard University Press, 1941), p. 593. For a more balanced view, which faults Lincoln for not initially making his intentions clear, see Randall, *Lincoln the President,* 4:355–359.

590 *"to their homes":* CW, 8:406–407.

590 *in better spirits:* Chase, *Diary,* p. 268.

591 *"ever seen him":* Moorfield Storey, "Dickens, Stanton, Sumner, and Storey," *Atlantic Monthly* 145 (Apr. 1930): 464.

591 *"of the inhabitants":* Seward, *Reminiscences of a War-Time Statesman,* pp. 256–257.

591 *"before the war":* CW, 8:410.

591 *"for early reconstruction":* Chase, *Diary,* p. 268.

591 *"do it badly":* Seward, *Reminiscences of a War-Time Statesman,* p. 256.

591 *bear further study:* Welles, "Lincoln and Johnson," p. 526.

591 *"any future Cabinet":* Ibid., pp. 526–527.

592 *"could not participate":* Ibid., p. 526.

592 *"an indefinite shore":* Welles added the last four words of this sentence to his diary later. Welles, *Diary,* 2:282.

592 *"most of yours":* Ibid., p. 283.

593 *signed more papers:* For a careful, detailed chronicle of the President's activities, see Reck, *A. Lincoln: His Last 24 Hours.*

593 *"correspondingly exhilarating":* Katherine Helm, *The True Story of Mary, Wife of Lincoln* (New York: Harper & Brothers, 1928), p. 253.

593 *"been very miserable"*: Turner, *Mary Todd Lincoln,* pp. 283–285; WHH, interview with Mary Lincoln, Sept. 5, 1866, HWC.

593 *"in the morning"*: Isaac N. Arnold, *The Life of Abraham Lincoln* (Chicago: Jansen, McClurg & Co., 1885), p. 431.

594 *"can toward it"*: Benjamin P. Thomas and Harold M. Hyman, *Stanton: The Life and Times of Lincoln's Secretary of War* (New York: Alfred A. Knopf, 1962), p. 395; Bryan, *Great American Myth,* p. 137.

594 *"great an exposure"*: Storey, "Dickens, Stanton, Sumner, and Storey," p. 464.

594 *"you with us"*: David Homer Bates, *Lincoln in the Telegraph Office* (New York: Century Co., 1907), pp. 366–367.

595 *$2.50 each:* C. H. Martin, "Reminiscences of a Columbia Boy of the Assassination of President Lincoln," *Papers Read Before the Lancaster County Historical Society* 31 (June 3, 1927): 72.

595 *"never-to-be-forgotten smiles"*: E. R. Shaw, "The Assassination of Lincoln," *McClure's Magazine* 32 (Dec. 1908): 181–184.

595 *above the stage:* For Alfred Waud's contemporary sketch and precise measurements, see Robert H. Fowler, *The Assassination of Abraham Lincoln* (Conshohocken, Pa.: Eastern Acorn Press, 1984), p. 15.

595 *"order of the President!"*: Furtwangler, *Assassin on Stage,* p. 104.

595 *"witnessing his enjoyment"*: Bryan, *Great American Myth,* p. 176.

595 *"thing about it"*: Randall, *Mary Lincoln,* p. 382.

596 *"must be done"*: William Hanchett, "Booth's Diary," *JISHS* 72 (Feb. 1979): 40.

596 *elections in the North:* John C. Brennan, "Why the Attempt to Assassinate Secretary of State William H. Seward?" *Surratt Courier* 12 (Jan. 1987).

596 *"taken at R[ichmon]d"*: Bryan, *Great American Myth,* p. 119.

596 *"not to kill"*: Wilson, *John Wilkes Booth,* p. 97.

596 *a superior officer:* Brennan, "Why the Attempt to Assassinate . . . Seward?" p. 4.

597 *"will justify me"*: Wilson, *John Wilkes Booth,* p. 107.

597 *"for this end"*: Hanchett, "Booth's Diary," pp. 40–41.

597 *"I had ever seen"*: Shaw, "The Assassination of Lincoln," p. 185.

597 *John Parker:* The whereabouts of Parker has been a subject of considerable controversy. The clearest statement of the evidence is in Champ Clark, *The Assassination: The Death of the President* (New York: Time-Life Books, 1987), pp. 82–83.

597 *10:13 P.M.:* This is the time that Otto Eisenschiml arrived at after much research and calculation. Eisenschiml, *The Case of A. L., Aged 56* (Chicago: Abraham Lincoln Book Shop, 1943), p. 13.

597 *"him very weak"*: *Surratt Courier* 12 (Nov. 1987): 2.

597 "Sic semper tyrannis": Since events moved so quickly, there was understandable controversy about what Booth said and when he said it. In his diary he claimed, "I shouted Sic semper *before* I fired." Hanchett, "Booth's Diary," p. 40. Most witnesses agreed that he gave his shout after jumping to the stage. Some claimed that he also shouted, "The South is avenged." James S. Knox to his father, Apr. 15, 1865, Lincoln MSS, LC.

597 *"a bull frog"*: Reck, *A. Lincoln: His Last 24 Hours,* p. 107.

597 *"shot the President!"*: Annie F. F. Wright, "The Assassination of Abraham Lincoln," *Magazine of History* 9 (Feb. 1909): 113–114.

597 *President was dead:* Most of the details on Lincoln's medical history in the following pages are taken from Dr. John K. Lattimer's highly professional study *Kennedy and Lincoln: Medical and Ballistic Comparisons of Their Assassinations* (New York: Harcourt Brace Jovanovich, 1980). Esp. valuable is Dr. Leale's report, pp. 28–32.

598 *"tendered their services"*: Ibid., p. 34.

598 *chance of recovery:* Most present-day medical experts agree with that judgment, but Dr. Richard A. R. Fraser, of New York Hospital–Cornell Medical Center, has recently suggested that the bullet wound was not necessarily fatal and that it was the probing performed by Dr. Leale and Dr. Stone that did irreparable damage. UPI dispatch, Jan. 25, 1995, on the Internet.

598 *"any man could"*: Reck, *A. Lincoln: His Last 24 Hours,* p. 137.

598 *her husband's side:* Mrs. Dixon's letter, dated May 1, 1865, in *Surratt Society News* 7 (Mar. 1982): 3.

598 *"let her in again"*: Lattimer, *Kennedy and Lincoln,* p. 32.

599 *and barely alive:* For a graphic account of the attack on Seward, see Patricia Carley Johnson, ed., "Sensitivity and the Civil War: The Selected Diaries and Papers, 1858–1866, of Frances

Adeline [Fanny] Seward" (unpublished Ph.D. dissertation, University of Rochester, 1963), pp. 875–892.

599 *"is no more!"*: Mrs. Dixon's letter, in *Surratt Society News* 7 (Mar. 1982): 4.

599 *manner removed it:* I have here closely followed A. F. Rockwell, "At the Death-bed of President Lincoln," *Century Magazine* 40 (June 1890): 3'1.

599 *"to the ages":* There has been controversy over just what Stanton said. Some witnesses reported "He belongs to the ages now," "He now belongs to the Ages," and "He is a man for the ages." Bryan, *Great American Myth,* p. 189; Eisenschiml, *Why Was Lincoln Murdered?* pp. 482–485.

Index